Conservation and Management of Marine Mammals

CONSERVATION AND MANAGEMENT OF MARINE MAMMALS

EDITED BY JOHN R. TWISS JR.
AND RANDALL R. REEVES

TECHNICAL EDITOR, SUZANNE MONTGOMERY

SMITHSONIAN INSTITUTION PRESS
Washington and London

Copy editor: Eileen D'Araujo
Production editor: Duke Johns
Designer: Janice Wheeler

Library of Congress Cataloging-in-Publication Data
Conservation and management of marine mammals / edited by
John R. Twiss, Jr. and Randall R. Reeves.
p. cm.
Includes bibliographical references and index.
ISBN 1-56098-778-2 (alk. paper)
1. Marine mammals. 2. Endangered species. 3. Wildlife conservation. I. Twiss, John R. II. Reeves, Randall R.
QL713.2.C65 1999
333.95'95—dc21 98-39366

British Library Cataloguing-in-Publication Data available

Manufactured in the United States of America
06 05 04 03 02 01 00 99 5 4 3 2 1

♾ The paper used in this publication meets the minimum requirements of the American National Standard for Information Sciences—Permanence of Paper for Printed Library Materials ANSI Z39.48-1984.

This book is dedicated to the memory of

MICHAEL A. BIGG
W. NIGEL BONNER
DAVID K. CALDWELL
MELBA C. CALDWELL
DOUGLAS G. CHAPMAN
RICHARD A. COOLEY
FRANCIS H. FAY
DAVID E. GASKIN
MATTHEW IYA
MURRAY L. JOHNSON
BARBARA LAWRENCE
J. STEPHEN LEATHERWOOD
A. STARKER LEOPOLD
KENNETH S. NORRIS
MARGARET WENTWORTH OWINGS
JOHN H. PRESCOTT
WILLIAM E. SCHEVILL
JESSE R. WHITE
HOWARD E. WINN
FORREST G. WOOD

Contents

Preface

In 1992, when John Reynolds first broached the subject of our doing a text on marine mammal science and policy, the need was so obvious that I wondered why we had not talked about it before. For years, John and others had been teaching marine mammal science without benefit of a formal text; they pieced their courses together by drawing from their own writings and experience, from reprints of others' works, and from parts of different biology texts. Believing that marine mammal science taught in a policy vacuum gave students only part of the picture, John and others also had been coming to me for copies of the Marine Mammal Commission's annual reports, letters, and policy papers to use as teaching materials.

By 1992 John and I had both been involved with marine mammals for almost 20 years, and we felt comfortable asking our colleagues to share their knowledge with those now entering the field. Although we knew that the text could not be exhaustive, we believed that we could introduce students to marine mammal science and policy in a way that would afford a person with a passing interest a good basic knowledge while also providing carefully referenced departure points for those interested in further study. With these ideas in mind, we approached the Smithsonian Institution Press with an outline and were encouraged to move forward.

My interest in marine mammals had begun with casual observations of pinnipeds and cetaceans in the Antarctic, both from sea ice and on research cruises, and in the Canadian Arctic during the 1960s. While at the National Science Foundation in the 1970s, I became interested in the Marine Mammal Protection Act and the Marine Mammal Commission because I felt both could have a profound influence on marine mammal conservation and wildlife management in general.

The Marine Mammal Protection Act of 1972 was unique in that it mandated an ecosystem approach to wildlife conservation. The Act focused on marine mammal species and stocks, but it did so within the context of maintaining the health and stability of their ecosystems. To promote management practices that take into account the interdependence of species—rather than continuing to rely on traditional, single-species, maximum sustainable yield concepts—would be, I felt, a significant advance.

The practical impact of this approach soon became apparent. In 1978 agencies of the United States government were arguing among themselves to develop a national negotiating position for a convention to govern exploitation of Antarctic marine living resources. All involved agencies except the Marine Mammal Commission and the Council on Environmental Quality proposed basing the convention on traditional maximum sustainable yield management. Even though the principal target, Antarctic krill, was the primary component of the diet of many species of whales, seals, and penguins, the significance of that fact seemed lost on those who advocated a harvesting regime concerned only about yields of the target species. Eventually, the group was persuaded that single-species management did not make sense and that it was important to consider the impacts of taking on dependent and related species as well. To advocate such an approach was almost heresy then, and the primary reason the United States adopted an ecosystems-based negotiating position was because our words could be backed by law, the Marine Mammal Protection Act.

The Act's emphasis on the role of science in developing policy was important to me as well. Provisions to ensure that decision making be based on sound science were incorporated throughout the legislation, and scientific advice was afforded an almost unprecedented force in law. Closely linked to dependence on good science in developing policy was the Act's precautionary approach to exploitation. For the first time, the burden of proof that exploitation could be undertaken without unacceptable impacts on a species or population was placed on those wishing to exploit rather than on those charged with protecting wildlife.

Conservation and Management of Marine Mammals is focused on policy and issues. After providing the reader some understanding of the societal and legal contexts within which marine mammals are viewed, particularly in North America, the text goes on to discussions of selected issues, critical problems related to specific marine mammal species, and broader conservation activities and policies, including principles for the conservation of wild living resources. Although the chapters are structured to give the reader a factual appreciation of the subject, the more important purpose is to provide insight into how people have thought about issues—issues that are often a complex mixture of scientific, social, economic, and political considerations. As the authors make clear, the resolution of marine mammal issues and problems often requires making judgments based on uncertainties, assumptions, and incomplete information, and success in these efforts almost always depends on the cooperative involvement of people from many disciplines, organizations, and backgrounds. These discussions of past and ongoing efforts will, we hope, help those trying to deal with similar problems in the future.

I thank Peter Cannell of the Smithsonian Institution Press for having encouraged us in this undertaking and for his patience.

Randy Reeves as coeditor has been critical to the success of this volume; he has shown extraordinary dedication and made major contributions in all areas. One could not have asked for a more competent technical editor than Suzanne Montgomery. Graciously and patiently, she worked with authors through numerous rewrites, edited both this volume and its companion (*Biology of Marine Mammals,* edited by John Reynolds and Sentiel Rommel, 1999), and managed the daunting flow of paper.

When embarking on this project, I spent considerable time choosing authors and coauthors whose backgrounds would complement each other and lead to comprehensive chapters through differing perspectives. I am deeply indebted to them not only for their willingness to share their many years of experience with those now entering the field, but also for the way in which they accepted comments of reviewers and revised their texts. Every chapter was rigorously reviewed, and most authors had at least six sets of reviewers' comments to deal with. Some chapters even went through two rounds of peer review. The process was demanding, but the results, I believe, make the efforts worthwhile. The volume should serve as a valuable reference, unlike any other, for students, scientists, conservationists, and policy makers.

Thanks are due to several people at the Marine Mammal Commission. Bob Hofman coauthored two chapters and reviewed many others. Mike Gosliner wrote one chapter and coauthored a second. David Laist took the lead in one coauthored chapter and reviewed others. Jan Sechrist organized and helped manage some aspects of the review process. In addition, Alison Kirk Long, Melissa Boness, Lisa Jackson, and Sherry Novak all contributed to completion of the project.

For photographs, we are indebted to the many people identified in the captions. Particular thanks, however, are due Bill Curtsinger, the late Steve Leatherwood, and Douglas Faulkner.

As noted earlier, this volume was intensively peer-reviewed, and its strength derives in no small measure from the work of the many reviewers. I thank Alex Aguilar, Thomas F. Albert, Dayton L. Alverson, Brad Andrews, Raymond V. Arnaudo, Donald C. Baur, John L. Bengtson, Daryl J. Boness, Gregory D. Bossart, Ian L. Boyd, Barbara Britten, Robert L. Brownell Jr., Phillip J. Clapham, Kevin Collins, Paul K. Dayton, Douglas P. DeMaster, Daryl P. Domning, Greg Early, James M. Farley, Charles W. Fowler, William W. Fox Jr., Kathryn J. Frost, Steven R. Galster, Joseph R. Geraci, William G. Gilmartin, Michael L. Gosliner, John Grandy IV, James T. Harvey, Burr Heneman, Robert J. Hofman, Aleta A. Hohn, Sidney J. Holt, Suzanne Iudicello, Charles H. Johnson, James Joseph, Kristin Karmon, Robert D. Kenney, Lee A. Kimball, Stephen J. Kohl, Scott D. Kraus, David W. Laist, David M. Lavigne, Gerald B. Leape, the late J. Stephen Leatherwood, Burney J. Le Boeuf, Jack W. Lentfer, Thomas R. Loughlin, Lloyd F. Lowry, Marc Mangel, George J. Mannina, Bruce R. Mate, Robert M. May, James G. Mead, William Medway, Donald C. Mitchell, Ronald S. Naveen, the late Kenneth S. Norris, Daniel K. Odell, Thomas J. O'Shea, P. Michael Payne, William F. Perrin, the late John H. Prescott, George B. Rabb, Katherine S. Ralls, Galen B. Rathbun, G. Carleton Ray, Stephen B. Reilly, John E. Reynolds III, Sam H. Ridgway, Patrick M. Rose, Dale F. Schwindaman, Jan M. Sechrist, Peter D. Shaughnessy, Kenneth S. Sherman, Gregory K. Silber, Donald B. Siniff, Tim D. Smith, Lee M. Talbot, Raymond J. Tarpley, Craig van Note, Richard L. Wallace, Michael L. Weber, the late Howard E. Winn, and Michael Young.

I had no idea how much time this book would take. Throughout the process, my wife and children have been patient, supportive, and forgiving of time lost. I thank them.

John R. Twiss Jr.

Conservation and Management of Marine Mammals

1

JOHN R. TWISS JR. AND RANDALL R. REEVES

Introduction

The literature on marine mammals ranges from travel accounts by whalers and sealers to arcane treatises on anatomy and physiology by biologists. It also encompasses a wide range of "gray literature"—government reports, contract studies, graduate-student theses, and other documents not published in peer-reviewed books or journals. Surprisingly few titles are available, however, that focus on conservation issues and the interplay of science and management that leads to formulation and achievement of conservation goals.

The purpose of this book is to help fill that niche. Our compilation is by no means comprehensive. Rather, the topics and authors have been selected to help readers appreciate the diversity of conservation issues and the thought processes involved in identifying and addressing them. The book is written primarily for students interested in marine mammal careers, but we trust that it will also serve as a useful reference for practicing scientists, managers, legislators, and conservationists.

Below, we provide comments about each of the chapters.

Chapter 2: The Evolution of North American Attitudes toward Marine Mammals, by David M. Lavigne, Victor B. Scheffer, and Stephen R. Kellert

This chapter examines how attitudes toward marine mammals have evolved in North America in recent decades. Those of us who have been working in the field of marine mammal science and conservation for many years tend to make our own assumptions about how attitudes have changed or not changed. Rarely before, however, has anyone tried to characterize and quantify the changes, as the authors of this chapter do. They state their working hypotheses and subject them to critical scrutiny, using the data at hand.

The chapter is organized around three main ways that humans "use" marine mammals: killing them for meat, oil, and skins (consumptive use); watching them for enjoyment or learning (nonconsumptive use); and displaying or studying them in captivity (low-consumptive use). From the 1960s to the 1980s the numbers of cetaceans and pinnipeds killed for commercial use declined. During the same period, more and more people took whale-watching trips and visited zoos and oceanariums. In the 1990s some of these trends slowed or even reversed. Large-scale commercial sealing resumed in Canada, and Norway expanded its commercial hunt for minke whales. Japan continued its "scientific whaling" in the Antarctic and North Pacific and sought international approval for reopening a commercial hunt. Several conservation and animal welfare groups began campaigning to return captive whales and dolphins to the wild, while opposing further live captures.

Over this period, public awareness about marine mammals has increased enormously. Concern about the survival of species and the welfare of individual animals has created a dedicated community of advocates. These advocates, working individually and collectively through nongovernmental organizations, have influenced legislation, regulations, and international negotiations. At the same time, the utilitarian view of marine mammals still prevails throughout much of the world, and the attitudes that contributed to the depletion and endangerment of so many species in the past remain firmly entrenched. It would be a mistake to conclude from the plethora of books, movies, conferences, and symposia, and from the body of legislation and regulation in the United States and some other countries designed to protect and conserve marine mammals, that these animals and their ecosystems are secure. In fact, as the authors suggest in their discussion, the "wise use movement," with its emphasis on short-term economic gain and its tendency to downplay biological and ecological concerns, seeks to undo much of what has been achieved through enlightened, risk-averse conservation measures.

Chapter 3: The Laws Governing Marine Mammal Conservation in the United States, by Donald C. Baur, Michael J. Bean, and Michael L. Gosliner

The Marine Mammal Protection Act of 1972 has, in one way or another, mandated, catalyzed, shaped, or influenced virtually every topic addressed in this book. Anyone in the United States who intends to study marine mammals, work in the marine environment (e.g., in scientific experimentation, fishing, hunting, aquaculture, seismic exploration, shipping, and even military operations), launch a whale- or seal-watching tour, build an oceanarium, or lobby to change the way oceanariums are regulated, needs to be aware of the Act's provisions and implications.

The Marine Mammal Protection Act and the Endangered Species Act of 1973 form the legal bedrock of marine mammal conservation in the United States. Familiarity with the legislative history, the record of judicial interpretation, and the agency actions taken to implement the provisions of these acts is necessary for a full understanding of how marine mammal conservation is practiced in this country.

In addition to describing the history and development of marine mammal legislation, the authors of this chapter explain how law and science can converge in the process of establishing a conservation regime. The Marine Mammal Protection Act replaced what the authors describe as the previous "patchwork of inconsistent state laws" with a uniform federal standard of protection. It also recognized particular issues, such as the importance of ensuring that Native people in Alaska are able to continue their hunting of marine mammals for subsistence and the need to limit the unintentional killing of marine mammals in commercial fisheries. The Act provides a framework for addressing these and other problems. Among the examples used by the authors to explore the Act's strengths and weaknesses are California sea otter and Alaska polar bear conservation, the issuance of public display and incidental take permits, and the negotiation of international agreements.

The Marine Mammal Protection Act was certainly ambitious. It articulated some conservation goals that proved unattainable in the short term but that remain laudable long-term objectives. The concept of ecosystem protection, for example, was visionary for its time. Its dominant presence in the 1972 Act was the result of the extraordinary deference shown to scientists by those who drafted the text. The influence of science remains evident as the Act evolves, and the views of scientists continue to affect events, just as the drafters of the Act intended for them to do.

Chapter 4: Ecosystems: Patterns, Processes, and Paradigms, by Marc Mangel and Robert J. Hofman

This chapter addresses one of the major scientific tenets of the Marine Mammal Protection Act—that the conservation and management of marine mammal populations should be pursued from the perspective of their role in a given ecosystem. Although the chapter may strike some readers, as it did some of the reviewers, as all science and no policy, its inclusion in this book was deliberate. The authors provide policy-oriented readers, as well as readers who are being trained as scientists, with a tutorial on how to think with ecosystems in mind. After finishing this chapter, the student should understand the need to think about marine mammals and other organisms as components of ecosystems rather than as populations in isolation. The challenge is to look for linkages and consequences that are not obvious when one sees a whale blowing in the distance, a school of dolphins churning the sea surface, or a group of seals hauled out on a beach.

Truisms always deserve to be questioned. An example discussed in this chapter is that marine mammals are good indicators of ecosystem health. We often hear or read that marine mammals are equivalent to the caged canaries that coal miners took underground with them to test air quality. As the authors point out, this appealing metaphor is only partially appropriate. With their long life spans and low reproductive rates, marine mammals can be relatively resilient to short-term environmental change. Thus, the apparent stability of a fur seal population, for example, might mask a rapid decline in one of the seals' prey species. Similarly, the persistence of a dolphin population in a heavily contaminated area might be mistakenly interpreted as a sign that all is well with the local environment.

Ecosystem protection found its first legislative expression in the Marine Mammal Protection Act. Over the years since 1972, the ecosystem approach has become a watchword for conserving natural resources. Programs have been restructured and conservation strategies reformulated around this concept. Yet the many practical implications of shifting emphasis away from species concerns and toward system-level management are only gradually becoming apparent and appreciated. The goal of conserving and managing marine mammal populations as "functioning elements" of ecosystems remains an ideal that is easier to conceptualize than to attain.

Conflicts between Marine Mammals and Fisheries

Whenever marine mammals and fisheries occur in the same area, they are likely to interact in some way. The following three chapters focus on a variety of these interactions and the ways in which people have sought to address them.

Chapter 5: Marine Mammal Interactions with Fisheries, by Simon P. Northridge and Robert J. Hofman

Interactions between marine mammals and fisheries can have adverse effects on the fisheries, the marine mammals, or both. They fall into two broad categories: operational interactions and biological interactions. Operational interactions include accidental entanglement of marine mammals in gillnets and other types of fishing gear; instances when marine mammals take bait and damage or destroy fish caught on hooks or in nets; and the shooting of marine mammals by fishermen to protect their gear or catch, or to use parts of the animals as bait. Biological interactions are indirect, and their consequences are often difficult to define, measure, and track through time and space. They include competition for resources between marine mammals and fisheries and the transmission of parasites between marine mammals and fish.

Historically, efforts to manage conflicts between marine mammals and fisheries were aimed primarily at reducing the impacts on fisheries, whether real or perceived. During the past few decades, there has been a growing awareness that certain populations of marine mammals, and possibly the structure and dynamics of the ecosystems, are being harmed by interactions with fisheries.

This chapter begins by describing the general nature and scale of impacts, both biological-ecological and socioeconomic, resulting from interactions between marine mammals and fisheries. It reviews some of the national, regional, and international mechanisms that have been developed to reduce impacts and resolve conflicts. It then offers four case studies to illustrate the range of issues and how they have been addressed: krill fishing in the Antarctic, the culling of seals to protect fisheries, large-scale pelagic driftnet fishing in the North Pacific Ocean and the Southern Ocean, and the bycatch of harbor porpoises in the Gulf of Maine and elsewhere. Although much of this book covers matters of particular interest to people in North America, the selection of case studies reflects the authors' international perspectives.

Chapter 6: The Tuna-Dolphin Controversy, by Michael L. Gosliner

The tuna-porpoise, or tuna-dolphin, issue is one of the most complex problems of fishery–marine mammal interactions to have been addressed under the Marine Mammal Protection Act. No issue has engendered more litigation, and none has been as demanding in terms of legislative review, regulatory action, and public participation.

The problem arose because schools of yellowfin tuna and schools of dolphins (or porpoises, as some people call them) associate with one another in the eastern tropical Pacific Ocean. During the 1950s American tuna fishermen began exploiting the bond between dolphins and tuna, using purse seine nets to encircle dolphins and catch the tuna with them. This technique produced more tuna with less effort and expense than was possible with the old hook-and-line method. Although it was a breakthrough in fishing technology, "fishing on porpoise" was disastrous for the marine mammals. All too frequently, the dolphins died before they could be released from the nets.

The problem provides a fascinating case study for assessing the successes and failures of the Marine Mammal Protection Act. In its original form, the Act explicitly addressed the problem but left ample latitude for subsequent judicial and scientific debate. It charged the National Marine Fisheries Service with what many would consider conflicting goals—to protect marine mammals and preserve the tuna industry. The requirement that the dolphin kill be reduced to "insignificant levels approaching zero" seemed unrealistic initially—hundreds of thousands of dolphins were killed each year. As Gosliner notes, Judge Charles Richey's landmark decision in May 1976 "gave the needed teeth to the Marine Mammal Protection Act." Richey interpreted the law literally, finding that the Act gave the well-being of marine mammal populations precedence over the interests of the fishing industry.

The tuna-dolphin controversy shows how the combination of clear legislative guidelines, coupled with sound science, a motivated industry, a regulatory agency subject to statutorily required independent oversight provided in this instance by the Marine Mammal Commission, and pressure from nongovernmental organizations can achieve dramatic results. The author's reconstruction of the legislative, judicial, and regulatory history offers several useful lessons. First, a law is only as good as the implementing and enforcement agencies make it. A reluctant or compromised agency cannot bring about the desired changes. Second, solving a problem of this magnitude often becomes an adaptive, or iterative, process. Framework legislation initiates the process, but then an open review mechanism is necessary to shape and amend that legislation as experience dictates. Third, good science is essential. Legislators and judges need to understand the role of uncertainty, just as scientists need to be frank and open about the limits of their knowledge. Finally, the roles of nongovernmental organizations and of committed individual citizens are indispensable.

Chapter 7: Seals, Sea Lions, and Salmon in the Pacific Northwest, by Mark A. Fraker and Bruce R. Mate

Interactions between pinnipeds and salmon have caused controversy in the northwestern United States and western Canada, where growing numbers of California sea lions and harbor seals have been blamed for reduced fish populations. There is no question that marine mammals eat fish and may contribute to dwindling fish stocks— both as adult fish return to freshwater spawning streams and as the smolts and fry move down rivers and into the sea—but it is unlikely that pinniped predation is a principal cause of the situation in the first place.

Scientists, noting that the increases in pinniped populations may represent recovery from past depletion, point out that the severe recent declines in salmonid stocks are due to a suite of factors, many of them less conspicuous but with greater impact than predation by pinnipeds. Spawning and rearing habitat has been lost or degraded as a result of flawed forestry practices, wetland drainage, and agriculture; dams, locks, and other artificial barriers impede the migratory movements of fish; and, of course, many stocks have simply been overfished.

The authors of this chapter focus on the situation at Ballard Locks in Seattle, Washington. As they explain, the "Herschel Problem," named after a sea lion that specialized in eating endangered steelhead trout in the vicinity of the locks, is far more complex than it has been portrayed in the popular media. For a variety of reasons, the steelhead population fell from about 3,000 to less than 100 between the early 1980s and mid-1990s, and sea lions seen eating the few remaining fish focused attention on pinnipeds as culprits. Scientists and managers tried numerous approaches to removing or deterring the sea lions, but with only limited and usually short-lived success. Eventually the Ballard Locks situation was brought under control by permanently removing only four sea lions and deploying underwater acoustic devices.

To a certain extent, Ballard Locks is a microcosm of a much broader issue. The crisis of lost and disappearing runs of salmonids in the Pacific Northwest bespeaks society's failure to understand and address the ecosystem-level consequences of our activities. From a holistic perspective, Herschel and his fellow sea lions may be little more than scapegoats, held to account for problems of our own making.

International Institutions and Approaches

In the following two chapters, marine mammal conservation is considered in an international context. Management of commercial whaling has been a defining issue for the worldwide conservation movement since the early 1970s. The International Whaling Commission, as the international authority responsible for conserving the great whales, epitomizes both the potential and the shortcomings of intergovernmental approaches. Development of the Antarctic Treaty System has proceeded on many fronts, with less rancor and controversy than the whaling regime. The two examples provide interesting subjects for comparative examination.

Chapter 8: The International Whaling Commission and the Contemporary Whaling Debate, by Ray Gambell

In its early years, the International Whaling Commission, established under the 1946 International Convention for the Regulation of Whaling, became infamous for its failure to protect the world's stocks of large whales from severe depletion. During the 1960s and 1970s things began to change, thanks in no small measure to scientific analyses by three scientists—Douglas Chapman, Sidney Holt, and K. R. Allen (later joined by John Gulland)—and the organized campaigning of many activists. By the 1980s the commission had been transformed into a body that most environmentalists viewed as worth fighting for, rather than against.

The author, Secretary of the International Whaling Commission, is uniquely qualified to give an international civil servant's perspective on operations of the commission. The purpose of the chapter is not to advocate one side in the debate but rather to describe how the commission functions.

The International Whaling Commission's significance to

marine mammal conservation cannot be overstated. Enormous amounts of scientific, economic, and political resources have been invested in its activities over the years, showing how important the great whales are to people in many nations. The revised management procedure, a risk-averse method for managing the exploitation of whale populations under uncertainty, was recently developed by the commission's Scientific Committee. This procedure has been hailed for its potential application to other fishery and wildlife-use contexts.

The commission's survival is increasingly threatened by the schism between proponents and opponents of whaling. To remain effective, it may need to redefine its role to reflect changing values and new scientific knowledge, without losing its recently gained commitment to conservation and its long-standing commitment to international cooperation.

Chapter 9: The Antarctic Treaty System, by Lee A. Kimball

Antarctica's geographical position and its environment have precluded large-scale human settlement, but nations' competing claims have posed challenges for conserving its rich marine resources. Considering what has been at stake, this chapter reveals a truly remarkable legacy of international cooperation and good sense.

The Antarctic has been a testing ground for scientists and policy makers to explore cooperative approaches to managing a well-defined, highly productive commons both equitably and sustainably. The history of commercial whaling and sealing in the Antarctic provided object lessons in how not to manage the commons. In contrast, the development and implementation of the Convention for the Conservation of Antarctic Seals (1972) demonstrated the willingness of treaty nations to act responsibly to prevent the repetition of past conservation failures. In subsequent negotiations, particularly those relating to the Convention on the Conservation of Antarctic Marine Living Resources and the Environmental Protocol, these same nations advanced such important concepts as consensus decision making, a precautionary approach to exploitation, "transparency" to ensure public access to the reasoning and trade-offs behind policy decisions, and shifting the burden of proof to the proponents of resource use.

This chapter merits careful study not only because of its detailed explanation of the Antarctic Treaty System, but also because of the possibilities that it implies for conservation strategies elsewhere. In many respects, the Antarctic example provides a model of how a system of treaties, conventions, protocols, agreements, and recommendations can be woven together to protect a unique and fragile ecosystem. The lessons learned in Antarctica are waiting to be applied elsewhere.

Case Studies of Endangered Species

Endangered species are the focus of the next six chapters. All too frequently, conservationists are faced with the need to manage human activities so that an endangered species or population can recover to "safe" levels of abundance and productivity. It is instructive to compare the strategies used to promote recovery of several different species. The examples presented below offer a broad range of possibilities, from dramatic cooperation and progress (e.g., Florida manatees and North Atlantic right whales) to utter failure (e.g., the baiji or Yangtze River dolphin). Certain common factors seem to be essential for assisting the recovery of an endangered species. Among them are a commitment to the task on the part of all, or nearly all, parties who can affect its welfare, cooperation at national and international levels, public education, and a sound scientific understanding of the species' biology and behavior.

Chapters 10 and 11: The Hawaiian Monk Seal: Biology of an Endangered Species, by Timothy J. Ragen and David M. Lavigne, and The Hawaiian Monk Seal: Management of an Endangered Species, by David M. Lavigne

The three species of monk seals in the genus *Monachus* constitute one of the most vulnerable groups of extant marine mammals. The Caribbean or West Indian monk seal is considered extinct. Many of the tropical beaches on which it once hauled out and nursed its young have been turned into fishing villages and resort hotels. The Mediterranean monk seal clings to a marginal existence, competing for space and other resources with the people of southern Europe and northern Africa. A catastrophic die-off of seals in the only remaining large colony—on the Saharan coast of northwestern Africa—occurred in 1997.

The third species, the Hawaiian monk seal, is experiencing substantial declines in portions of its limited range. Because this seal is endemic to the Hawaiian Islands, the United States has a special responsibility to ensure its survival. We considered it appropriate to devote two chapters to this endangered species—one covering the scientific aspects of recovery efforts and one the management aspects.

From a policy perspective, the welfare of the Hawaiian monk seal recovery program has been closely linked to the attitudes of those in leadership positions within the National Marine Fisheries Service. During the 1970s, having described the monk seal as a relict species with no prospect of recovery, they decided to do nothing. It was only when U.S. Senator Daniel K. Inouye focused attention on the issue and made money available that sustained research and management activities became possible. Fortunately, the Service's attitude toward the monk seal has changed, and there is now a commitment at all levels to work toward the species' recovery.

In comparison with the Mediterranean monk seal, the Hawaiian monk seal's study and protection should be straightforward. The Hawaiian species lives entirely in waters of the United States and is subject only to U.S. law and regulatory policies. Nevertheless, similar problems have afflicted both species, including jurisdictional conflicts, epidemics, poisoning by naturally occurring toxins, bycatch in fisheries, and loss of critical pupping and pup-rearing habitat. A basic lesson is that small populations, meaning a few hundred or even just a few thousand animals, are simply not sufficient. Only by maintaining sufficiently large, productive populations of wild species can we hope to avoid the chronic demands, and frustrations, of crisis management.

Chapter 12: Efforts to Conserve the Manatees, by John E. Reynolds III

The Florida manatee is a test of our resolve to preserve natural diversity while attempting to maintain our affluent lifestyles. The manatee has a completely inoffensive nature, thrives on aquatic plants for which people have no evident need, and seems to tolerate most human activities. What it requires from us, apart from being left in peace, is a supply of clean, fresh water; ample plant life on which to feed; and access to warm water during winter cold snaps, a need met artificially through warm-water discharge from power plants. Clayton Ray and Daryl Domning, writing in the journal *Marine Mammal Science* in 1986 (vol. 2, no. 1, p. 77), summed up the situation this way: "The misfortune of the meek and mild manatee is to meet us at the intensely active land-water interface. The crucial issues are whether we want to leave enough of that waterfront property undeveloped, whether we are willing to slow down our overpowered boats, whether we will limit other desires (and especially our desires to reproduce and retire in Florida) sufficiently to maintain room for manatees in a highly utilized environment."

As the author of this chapter reminds us, other manatee populations face a more familiar array of threats. In Latin America and West Africa, manatees are hunted and trapped for food. Like their relative, Steller's sea cow, which was hunted to extinction in the Bering Sea during the eighteenth century, they are viewed by some people in nonaffluent societies as good meat. In some areas, they are even regarded as nuisances that damage rice fields and remove fish from nets.

The manatee is an excellent example of how conservation strategies must be tailored to the context and how some situations require action on many fronts by various concerned parties. Progress made in protecting manatees and their habitat in Florida would not have been possible without the dedicated efforts of concerned individuals, the Save the Manatee Club, other conservation organizations, manatee scientists, and representatives of state and federal government agencies. Although the Florida manatee's future is far from secure, renewed work in some areas and more intense effort in others, particularly in protecting habitat, may help ensure that manatees continue to grace Florida's waterways for many generations to come.

Chapter 13: Selected Examples of Small Cetaceans at Risk, by William F. Perrin

In this chapter on small cetaceans at risk, the author offers personal insights, many from first-hand experience, about what is needed to achieve conservation goals. His examples are a study in contrasts. On one hand, the vaquita and baiji, both endemic to waters heavily used by fishermen and, in the case of the baiji at least, by vessel traffic associated with a rapidly industrializing society, are disappearing. Their prospects for survival are grim.

On the other hand, eastern spinner dolphins, a uniquely adapted population of a pantropical species, are recovering from the depletion caused by more than two decades of massive killing in the eastern Pacific tuna fishery. Their improved circumstances are the result of a protracted campaign that cost many tens of millions of dollars and involved enormous amounts of scientific, technical, legal, legislative, and administrative attention.

The ongoing hunt for small cetaceans in Japan represents yet another type of conservation challenge. Fishermen in this affluent maritime nation seem intent on continuing to hunt striped dolphins despite strong international opposition. Japanese fishery managers have disregarded warnings that the recent failure of fishermen to catch even their reduced quotas of this species signifies severe depletion. The author suggests that this situation proves the need for small cetaceans to be subject to an international conservation agreement—if not the International Convention for the Regulation of Whaling then an equivalent legal instrument that can bring about meaningful, well-reasoned conservation measures.

Although the tone of this chapter is often pessimistic, the author's own demonstrated commitment to science-based conservation should serve as an inspiration. The many and varied threats to small cetaceans will probably never disappear entirely, but many of them can at least be managed to allow population recovery and head off more extinction crises. The author's "lessons learned along the way" should not be taken as final pronouncements but rather as useful advice for those who decide to apply their energies and abilities to the challenges of conserving small cetaceans.

Chapter 14: Efforts to Conserve the North Atlantic Right Whale, by Steven K. Katona and Scott D. Kraus

In the early 1970s right whales were occasionally sighted in the Gulf of Maine, but only a handful of scientists took notice. Among them were William E. Schevill and William A. Watkins at the Woods Hole Oceanographic Institution in Massachusetts, who had begun their ground-breaking studies of right whale acoustics and feeding behavior. Yet the right whale's struggle to recover from near-extinction due to commercial whaling was not on the national conservation agenda.

In the late 1970s and early 1980s, Scott Kraus, one of the authors of this chapter, joined John Prescott and others at the New England Aquarium in Boston, the University of Rhode Island, and the Center for Coastal Studies in Provincetown, Massachusetts, to form the right whale consortium. Consortium members recognized how little was known about this endangered species, yet they found it impossible to raise needed research funding in conventional ways. Undaunted, they launched a successful fund-raising appeal directly to Congress. Their subsequent studies have revealed a population of about 300 individuals experiencing an alarming level of mortality from ship strikes and encounters with fishing gear. In response to these findings, the U.S. government has taken steps to identify and protect the species' critical habitat, and a formal recovery plan is in place to guide management on many fronts.

In this chapter, the authors outline the biology and behavior of the North Atlantic right whale, insofar as these are known. They also summarize the history of protective measures and the processes by which new threats have been identified and addressed. Although the nature and scale of human activities in the North Atlantic have changed enormously since the days when Basque whalers sailed to Labrador to hunt right whales, our actions continue to impede the recovery of this whale population. Governments, intergovernmental organizations such as the International Whaling Commission and the International Maritime Organization, the naval forces of various countries, the international shipping industry, fishermen, private boaters, and even the U.S. Army Corps of Engineers must all remain involved, or become involved, in protecting right whales and their habitat.

Chapter 15: Endangered Species: The Common Denominator, by Daryl P. Domning

As a paleontologist, the author of this chapter brings a unique point of view to the subject of endangered species. The time horizon for most of us extends only a few centuries into the past, but paleontologists think in terms of epochs. Their awareness not only of the organisms currently sharing the planet with us, but also of a much richer vanished world, full of evolutionary cul-de-sacs, detours, and flowerings, gives the idea of extinction a special poignancy.

The author was asked to put the foregoing studies of endangered species into a wider context. In doing so, he provides a philosophical basis for many of the hands-on conservation activities discussed in those chapters. He also offers a perspective that, although heavily informed by science, is shaped primarily by moral and ethical considerations.

Chapter 16: Marine Debris Pollution, by David W. Laist, James M. Coe, and Kathryn J. O'Hara

In the early 1980s Charles Fowler, a staff scientist with the U.S. National Marine Fisheries Service, provided convincing evidence that an observed decline in the population of northern fur seals had been caused, in part, by entanglement in debris at sea. In doing so, he brought to light what was, for most marine mammalogists, a new and sinister threat. The debris-related mortality and debilitation of fur seals in the North Pacific apparently was caused mainly by trawl-net fragments, but a wide array of other materials was also implicated, from plastic six-pack holders to gaskets and headlight rings. In the South Atlantic Ocean, polypropylene straps used as packaging bands frequently end up as "neck collars" on Antarctic fur seals. In all areas where the problem of entanglement in marine debris has been investigated, the main fault has been found to lie with cast-off materials from the fishing industry.

Fowler's important work initially went unheeded. In fact, the response from one senior U.S. government official was a classic: "This is not really a problem. Even if debris is the cause of the decline, cleaning up the debris in the ocean would be too big a problem to solve."

Against that unhelpful background of denial and noninvolvement, a number of individuals and groups, including some representatives of the fishing industry, took the matter to heart. They worked to get the issue recognized and fought for funding to support needed research. Eventually, after much pushing and prodding, they convinced domestic agencies and intergovernmental organizations to focus on marine debris pollution and acknowledge its significance.

Several of the points emphasized in this chapter apply to many conservation issues. First, defining the problem is a critical first step. In the case of marine debris, it was easy to demonstrate that marine organisms of many kinds were being killed or maimed by entanglement, but it was not obvious that the scale was large enough to affect populations or species. Thus the importance of Fowler's analyses. Second, problem definition must be followed by tenacious action to evoke an appropriate policy response. Once the scientific documentation was in place, it fell to managers and activists to join scientists in placing the issue of marine debris on national and global policy agendas—and to keep it there long enough to build lasting institutional commitments. Third, well-informed public involvement is vital. Making the link between the actions of individual fishermen, beachgoers, and boaters and the problem of marine debris pollution led to the next step—mobilizing fishermen and private citizens to participate in solutions. Finally, there is no substitute for committed people in government and industry who are willing to expand their agency's, or their company's, horizons and accept new responsibilities. In the case of marine debris, the efforts made by the U.S. Navy and U.S. Coast Guard to comply with the provisions of Annex V of the MARPOL Convention are exemplary and stand in marked contrast to the initially unhelpful response by the leadership of the National Marine Fisheries Service in the early 1980s.

Chapter 17: Marine Mammal Die-Offs: Causes, Investigations, and Issues, by Joseph R. Geraci, John Harwood, and Valerie J. Lounsbury

When the frequency of strandings in a particular area suddenly increases above background levels, scientists and managers begin to suspect that a die-off could be under way. Although die-offs were virtually unheard of 20 to 25 years ago, they now feature prominently in the thinking of marine mammalogists, marine resource managers, and scientists in related fields. The mass die-offs of harbor seals in the North Sea in 1988, bottlenose dolphins off the eastern United States in 1987–1988, Florida manatees in 1996, and Mediterranean monk seals in northwestern Africa in 1997 are four of more than 20 such events that have been documented since 1970. The detection, investigation, and management of die-offs have become a central concern of management agencies and research laboratories.

As the authors of this chapter emphasize, the timely appearance of a "response team" is not something that can be taken for granted. Die-offs simply begin, with no prior notice. They take officials by surprise. Yet the public expects an immediate, structured response. There is almost always some anxiety about the implications for human health. Can people catch the disease that is killing the dolphins? Will the red-tide organisms that are killing manatees affect other species, including humans? Does the sudden death of hundreds of seals mean that some threshold of marine pollution has been reached? Scientists and managers come under intense pressure to speak quickly and authoritatively about the causes and implications of die-offs. However, not only is it difficult to confirm that a die-off is under way, but the ensuing challenges are also formidable: marshaling and mobilizing the appropriate experts to investigate causes, locating and recovering dead or dying animals, performing necropsies, disposing of the carcasses, and managing public relations.

Nothing about the study and management of marine mammal die-offs is simple. However, much has been learned about the die-off phenomenon in the past decade, thanks in no small measure to the rigorous efforts of the authors of this chapter and their associates.

Chapter 18: Marine Mammal Stranding Networks, by Dean Wilkinson and Graham A. J. Worthy

The sight of an entire school of dolphins, pilot whales, or sperm whales swimming into the surf and becoming stranded prompts many questions—some of them scientific, others philosophical or ethical. Why do they do it? Can we, or should we, try to get them back into the water? If there is no hope for them to survive, how can we minimize their suffering? From another perspective, what should a fisherman, a lifeguard, or a family picnicking on the beach do when a dead seal or whale washes ashore? How does a person responsible for public sanitation cope with a rotting 50-ton sperm whale sloshing around at the water's edge?

James G. Mead, curator of marine mammals at the Smithsonian Institution's National Museum of Natural History, inaugurated North America's first national stranding network in 1972. As this chapter shows, the small team of enthusiasts who initially accompanied him on all-night drives to fetch porpoises, dolphins, and whales from far-flung East Coast beaches is now a throng of trained volunteers, following a well-orchestrated response protocol and operating out of strategically located regional nodes.

Strandings of marine mammals pose intriguing scientific questions, offer valuable research opportunities, and challenge public officials in many ways. A well-organized, efficient stranding network can make major contributions to scientific inquiry, while at the same time satisfying the public's insistence that animals be treated humanely and responsibly. The individuals involved can feel, with justification, that their efforts have led to something meaningful. By providing opportunities for nonspecialists, many of whom are motivated mainly by compassion for the animals, to participate in stranding response efforts, scientists and managers can further the important goals of public education and awareness.

Chapter 19: Marine Mammals in Captivity, by Randall R. Reeves and James G. Mead

As William Perrin points out in his chapter on the conservation of small cetaceans, the engagement between people and wild animals in captivity can benefit conservation. From close encounters with living dolphins, seals, and manatees, people make connections with the animals as fellow living creatures. As a result, they are more likely to act in support of protective measures. Proponents of captivity also emphasize the value of having a few captive subjects to provide researchers with opportunities to study behavior, physiology, sensory abilities, and other aspects of marine mammal biology. These proponents, however, represent only one side of a heated debate.

Opponents of maintaining animals in captivity challenge the very concept of zoos and zoolike displays. Cetaceans, in particular, provide a lightning rod for the captivity issue. Some people decry the morality of confining whales and dolphins in pools or tanks, whatever the potential benefits might be. They believe that public display is no longer justifiable, because opportunities to see animals in the wild are more accessible today than in the past. The harm done to the individual mammals, they claim, outweighs any possible good done by raising the awareness or heightening the sensitivities of oceanarium visitors.

In this chapter, the authors seek to elucidate the history as well as the issues behind the controversy. Their avowed goal is to address the subject objectively, airing the extreme views on both sides and setting forth the main lines of argument, for and against. Unquestionably, the captivity issue is something on which people of good will and clear conscience can simply disagree. Although science can provide guidance on some questions, it cannot do much to reconcile philosophical disagreements that arise from beliefs about the rights of animals and about humanity's responsibilities toward fellow beings.

Chapter 20: Marine Mammal Conservation: Guiding Principles and Their Implementation, by Gary K. Meffe, William F. Perrin, and Paul K. Dayton

The final chapter describes a set of principles for the conservation of wild living resources and offers suggestions as to how these might be implemented. In the mid-1990s, the Marine Mammal Commission initiated a series of consultations and workshops intended to refine and update an earlier set of principles. The earlier principles were articulated in an article by Sidney Holt and Lee Talbot published in 1978. Although they reflected the best thinking of their time, those principles were no longer adequate to guide and stimulate conservation action in the 1990s and beyond. The new principles, published in a journal article by Marc Mangel and a host of collaborators in 1996, emphasize the importance of approaching conservation from an ecosystem perspective, drawing on expertise from all relevant disciplines, involving in conservation planning all parties who have a serious stake in the outcome, and taking a precautionary approach to decision making.

The authors of Chapter 20, whose own research and conservation efforts have embodied many of the principles in question, discuss three simple but fundamental tenets that should underlie everything done in the name of conservation. These are (1) to acknowledge and accept that human knowledge will always be imperfect, and therefore that we need to incorporate uncertainty into all of our decision making; (2) to proceed cautiously in the face of that uncertainty and to err in a direction that will benefit conservation, and (3) to make sure that any ecological change caused by humans is reversible. It will be difficult to live up to these ideals in all circumstances, but unless we try, the game is certain to be lost.

Chapter 20 summarizes and reinforces many of the ideas that are implicit in the other chapters of this book. If nothing else, we hope our readers will gain a greater appreciation for the need to think and act in many dimensions to advance conservation goals. Durable progress will only be achieved if it is rooted in a solid understanding of ecological relationships, openness to differing points of view, a broad and inclusive vision, and a willingness to stand firm when essential values are at risk.

2

DAVID M. LAVIGNE, VICTOR B. SCHEFFER, AND STEPHEN R. KELLERT

The Evolution of North American Attitudes toward Marine Mammals

Attitudes toward animals and their natural habitats have been evolving for centuries (Nash 1989, Worster 1994). Traditionally, both were viewed mainly from a utilitarian perspective. Over the past 150 years or so, however, a conflicting vision has emerged: that individual animals, like people, have intrinsic rights, and that animals and their habitats have other values beyond the purely utilitarian or economic. When John Muir spoke in the United States in 1867 of "the rights of all the rest of creation," he was echoing the sentiments of a philosophical movement that had begun earlier in the United Kingdom (Nash 1989:39). By 1915 Albert Schweitzer was writing about "reverence for life" (Nash 1989:6, 60). In the late 1940s Aldo Leopold, in his classic *Sand County Almanac* (1949), advocated a "land ethic," a philosophy that would change "the role of *Homo sapiens* from conqueror of the land-community to plain member and citizen of it" (Leopold 1966:240). It was not until the 1960s and 1970s, however, that societal attitudes began to broaden from those of the utilitarian "progressive conservation" tradition, pioneered by Gifford Pinchot (1947) early in the twentieth century, to include Leopold's more ecological consciousness (Nash 1989, Worster 1994). In recent decades there have been calls for the "liberation" of nature (Marcuse 1972, cited in Nash 1989:6) and the "liberation" of animals (Singer 1975). Nowadays, virtually any discussion about our relationship with nature includes mention of animal rights.

The evolution of societal attitudes toward animals and the natural world has obviously included marine mammals. For centuries, whales (order Cetacea), seals (order Carnivora, families Otariidae, Odobenidae, Phocidae), sea otters (order Carnivora, family Mustelidae), polar bears (order Carnivora, family Ursidae), and sirenians (order Sirenia) were viewed largely as commodities or resources—sources of food, clothing, and other products to be exploited by humans. Today, however, there are a number of organizations concerned with the protection of marine mammals, a global moratorium on commercial whaling, and a growing tourist industry associated with whale watching. It is not entirely clear, however, what these observations tell us precisely about changes in attitudes toward marine mammals because no one, to our knowledge, has undertaken the necessary analysis.

Here, we begin such an examination by attempting to track changes in North American (specifically American and Canadian) attitudes toward marine mammals, particularly over the past 40 years. Our major objective is to document, as quantitatively as possible, *how* attitudes have changed in recent years. To place our review in a broader context, we attempt to draw some comparisons between North American attitudes and those in other countries. But before going further, a few words on the subject of attitudes, and on our approach in this chapter, are warranted.

Our Approach

In this chapter, we define "attitudes" simply as learned predispositions "to respond in a consistently favorable or unfavorable manner" (Fishbein and Ajzen 1975:6). In much of the wildlife and environmental literature, the terms *attitudes* and *values* are often used as synonyms. Hunters, for example, may be said to exhibit a utilitarian attitude (Kellert 1980) or to view wildlife in terms of its utilitarian value (Rolston 1989, Kellert 1996).

Various schemes have been proposed to describe the range of attitudes (or values) that society exhibits toward animals and the natural world (Kellert 1980, Rolston 1989, Fox 1990). The one developed by Kellert during a national survey of U.S. attitudes toward wildlife conveniently characterizes the diversity of attitudes held by individuals and society at large (Table 2-1; for recent discussions, see Kellert 1993, 1996).

Ideally, a study of attitudinal change would be based on a series of studies documenting societal attitudes over the time period under consideration. Unfortunately, in the case of marine mammals, no such longitudinal studies have been conducted. In their absence, we attempted to glean some insights from the limited attitudinal data that are available. To gain additional insights, we also attempted to use a number of indicators of attitudinal change. These indicators—selected because they relate specifically to one or more of the attitudes described in Table 2-1—include patterns in consumptive exploitation of marine mammals and the appearance of nongovernmental organizations that promote consumptive use; changes in the number of people participating in marine mammal watching (a form of recreation or tourism); changes in attitudes toward keeping marine mammals in captivity; the appearance of nongovernmental organizations concerned with the well-being of marine mammals; the coverage of marine mammals by popular media; the evolution of legislation related to marine mammals and their habitats (arguably the ultimate measure of changing societal attitudes); and society's willingness to invest in marine mammal research, the numbers of marine mammal researchers, and their publication output.

For each indicator, we describe briefly what has happened in recent decades. Readers are encouraged to draw their own conclusions about what the assembled information says about the evolution of North American attitudes toward marine mammals. Our interpretations and conclusions follow in the Discussion.

Attitudinal Surveys

Data from attitudinal surveys document one recent attitudinal change in the United States pertaining exclusively to whales. A 1978 study revealed that three-fourths of Americans endorsed the hunting of nonendangered whales if it resulted in a useful product (Kellert 1980). In 1993 only 26% of Americans approved of whaling under any circumstance (Freeman and Kellert 1994). And, according to a 1997 poll, conducted by Penn, Schoen and Berland Associates for the International Fund for Animal Welfare, only 14% of Americans now support (strongly or somewhat) "whaling or the killing of whales for their meat, blubber, or other purposes."

The decline in the utilitarian attitude of Americans toward whales over the past two decades is consistent with the general decline in the utilitarian attitude toward all wildlife species witnessed in the United States since the end of

Table 2-1. Attitudes toward Animals

Term	Definition
Naturalistic	Affection for wildlife and the outdoors; satisfaction from direct experience / contact with nature
Humanistic	Affection for individual animals; emotional attachment, "love" for nature
Aesthetic	Interest in the physical appeal and beauty of nature
Symbolic	Interest in the use of nature for metaphorical expression, language, expressive thought
Moralistic	Concern about the treatment of animals, with strong opposition to exploitation or cruelty toward animals; strong affinity, spiritual reverence, ethical concern for nature
Scientistic	Interest in the physical attributes and biological functioning of animals
Ecologistic	Concern for the environment as a system, for interrelationships between wildlife species and natural habitats
Utilitarian	The practical and material exploitation of natural resources including animals or their habitats
Dominionistic	The mastery and control of animals and their habitats
Negativistic	Fear, aversion, and alienation from nature
Neutralistic	Passive avoidance of animals because of indifference or lack of interest

Source: Adapted from Kellert (1980, 1993).

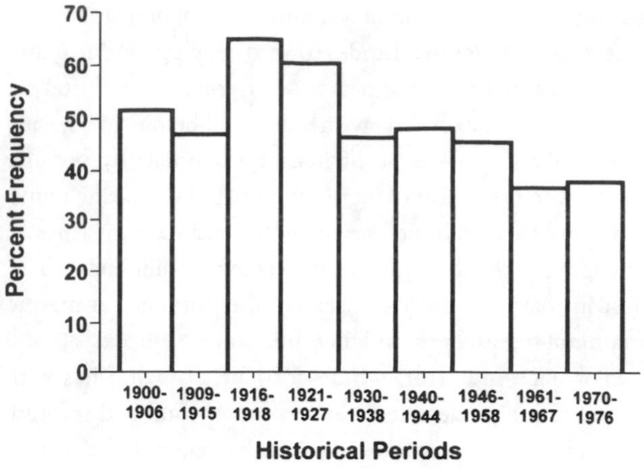

Figure 2-1. Changes in utilitarian attitudes in the United States. (Redrawn from Kellert and Westervelt 1982)

World War I (Fig. 2-1) (see Kellert and Westervelt 1982). Despite this trend, the utilitarian view was still held by some 39% of Americans as recently as 1970–1976 (Fig. 2-1). A range of attitudes toward marine mammals continues to be expressed among segments of North American society and elsewhere. Consider, for example, the results of a 1991 study of Canadian attitudes toward marine mammals (Kellert 1991, Kellert et al. 1995). That study included random samples of commercial sealers, fishermen, and the Canadian public, distinguished by age, sex, education, income, province, and location (urban versus rural) of residence.

Canadian attitudes endorsing people's right to exploit marine mammals occurred to a significantly greater extent among rural dwellers, the elderly, fishermen, and residents of Newfoundland especially and, to a lesser degree, New Brunswick and Nova Scotia. In contrast, college-educated and younger Canadians expressed far more affection and ethical concern for marine mammals, even when it involved sacrificing various economic activities. Only small proportions of college-educated, younger, and urban Canadians, in contrast to a majority of sealers, fishermen, and Newfoundland residents, supported the economic exploitation of whales or commercial fishing when it injured or killed marine mammals. A sample of some attitudinal scale results is presented in Figures 2-2 and 2-3.

Generally, one of the most important demographic factors determining attitudes about animals in North American society is sex (Kellert and Berry 1987). Females are more likely to value wild animals as objects of affection and to express concern regarding the consumptive exploitation of wildlife. Males, on the other hand, tend to be more knowledgeable and less fearful of wildlife and more likely to value animals for practical and recreational reasons (Kellert and Berry 1987; also see Jackson et al. 1989).

Surveys conducted in other countries during the 1990s

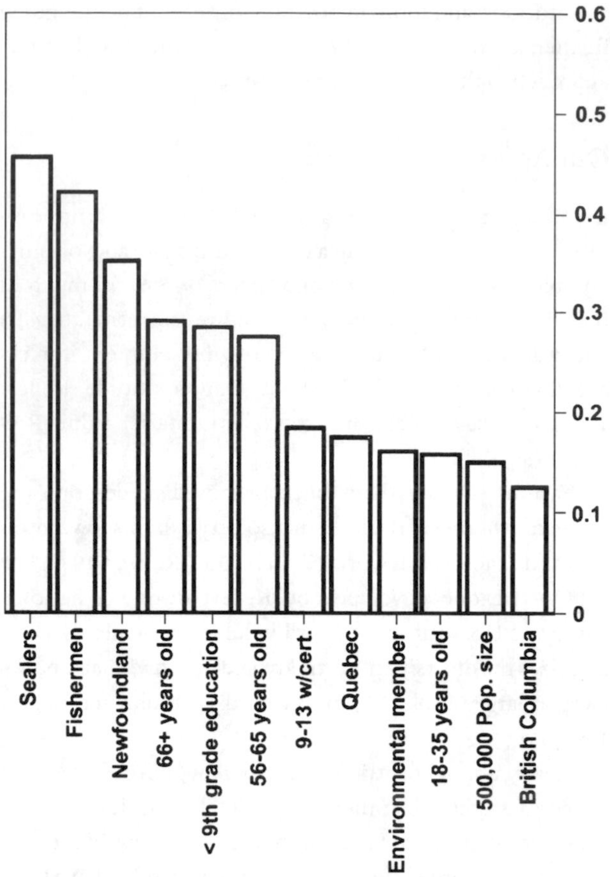

Figure 2-2. Utilitarian attitudes toward marine mammals. The *y* axis represents an attitude scale constructed from survey results (see Kellert 1991 for details).

indicate that a majority of people in England, Germany, Australia, and Canada also oppose whaling under almost all circumstances, with the exception of hunting by aboriginal peoples (Kellert 1991, Freeman and Kellert 1994). Elsewhere, the utilitarian view remains dominant. In 1992, for example, the majority of Japanese and Norwegians were not opposed to the hunting of whales (Freeman and Kellert 1994). They, like Canadian sealers, commercial fishermen, and Newfoundland residents, continue to support whaling so long as it is "properly regulated," the species is not endangered, and the practice yields significant economic and cultural benefits.

Consumptive Exploitation

At the turn of the nineteenth century, both the United States and Canada were whaling and sealing nations (Barchard 1978, Tønnessen and Johnsen 1982, Busch 1985, Ellis 1991). Both countries ceased commercial whaling in 1972, well before 1986 when the International Whaling Commission implemented an indefinite moratorium on commercial

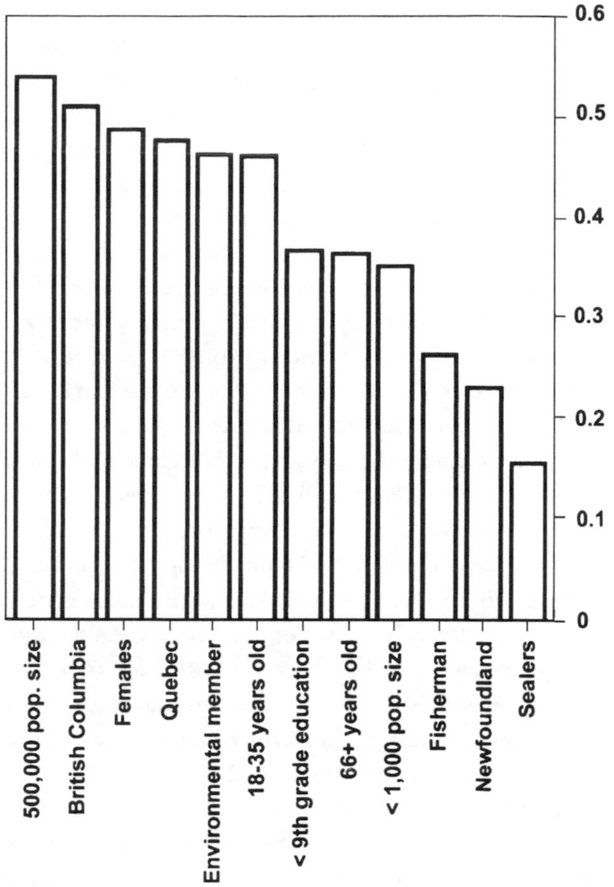

Figure 2-3. Moralistic attitudes toward marine mammals. The *y* axis represents an attitude scale constructed from survey results (see Kellert 1991 for details).

whaling (Papastavrou 1996). Today, whaling in North America is restricted to Native communities, as is the exploitation of sea otters (*Enhydra lutris*). Hunting of polar bears (*Ursus maritimus*) in the United States (Alaska) is conducted only by Native peoples; in Canada, nonnatives can also participate, but only under permits issued to indigenous peoples. The sealing situation is more complicated.

Whaling off the east coast of the United States ended on 26 August 1924 when the last of the "Yankee whalers," sailing out of New Bedford, Massachusetts, broke up on the rocks at Cuttyhunk Island (Ellis 1991). Whalers from Long Island, New York, are credited with the final kill, striking their last right whale (*Eubalaena glacialis*) with a bomb lance in February of the same year (Reeves and Mitchell 1986).

Shore-based whaling continued on a small scale on the west coast of the United States until the last whaling station closed in Richmond, California, in 1972 (Ellis 1991). The United States remains a member of the International Whaling Commission, but the only whaling today is conducted by Alaska Natives for bowhead (*Balaena mysticetus*) and beluga (*Delphinapterus leucas*) whales (Marine Mammal Commission 1996). (In August 1995 two North Pacific gray whales (*Eschrichtius robustus*) were also taken by Native hunters on Little Diomede Island, Alaska. Because the United States had not had a quota for gray whales from the International Whaling Commission since 1988, these takes were considered an infraction and punished by a fine [International Whaling Commission n.d.].)

In 1996 the United States submitted a proposal to the International Whaling Commission to authorize the Makah Indians of Washington State—members of the Nuu-Chah-Nulth people of the Pacific Northwest—to take five gray whales annually for subsistence use. After a heated—and largely negative—debate, the United States withdrew the proposal (Marine Mammal Commission 1997). The Makah have now formed their own "Whaling Commission,"[1] and the proposal was resubmitted for consideration at the 1997 meeting of the International Whaling Commission (Marine Mammal Commission 1997). Faced with more "fierce opposition" (Reuters 1997), the United States paired its proposal with another one submitted on behalf of Chukotka Indians by the Russian Federation. The joint proposal (as amended), to permit the taking of gray whales by "aborigines or a Contracting Party on behalf of aborigines . . . whose traditional subsistence and cultural needs have been recognized," was eventually adopted by consensus (International Whaling Commission 1997). Nonetheless, a number of delegations who recognized the traditional subsistence and cultural needs of the Chukotka did not accept that the Makah had demonstrated such needs.

Confusion arose, therefore, over the interpretation of the adopted schedule amendment. The U.S. delegation issued a press release claiming that "The International Whaling Commission today adopted a quota that allows a five-year aboriginal subsistence hunt of an average of four non-endangered gray whales a year for the Makah Indian Tribe, combined with an average annual harvest of 120 gray whales by Russian natives of the Chukotka region" (Anonymous 1997a). Others disagreed with this interpretation. The Australian delegation, for example, explicitly rejected the U.S. claim, arguing that "after a lapse of some 71 years of whaling activity . . . and the consequent absence of whale meat and other whale products from their subsistence or other diet," the Makah have failed to establish "traditional aboriginal subsistence and cultural needs" (Anonymous 1997b). Because of the ambiguity of the amendment, plans by the Makah to resume whaling in October 1998 were challenged in the U.S. courts (Associated Press 1997, Swardson 1997). A 1998 court decision determined that whaling could proceed if conducted in a manner consistent with the International Whaling Commission's schedule.[2]

The long history of commercial whaling off Canada's

east coast (Mowat 1984) also ended in 1972 when the Minister of Fisheries declared a moratorium "not only for economic reasons but also to preserve stocks" (Tønnessen and Johnsen 1982:648). The end came gradually, catches having declined from a postwar high of >10,000 in 1956 to 685 in 1972 (Reeves and Mitchell 1987). As in the United States, the only whaling in Canada today is conducted by Native people who hunt beluga, narwhal (*Monodon monoceros*), and bowhead whales. The recent resumption of bowhead whaling is controversial because Canada is no longer a member of the International Whaling Commission, having withdrawn in 1982 on the grounds that it no longer had a direct interest in whaling (International Whaling Commission 1996). At its 1996 meeting the Commission passed a resolution sponsored by France, the Netherlands, the United Kingdom, and the United States that encouraged "the Government of Canada to rejoin the IWC if it continues to have a direct interest in whaling" (International Whaling Commission 1996).

In contrast, commercial sealing in North America continued through the 1970s. Some changes in the pattern of exploitation began to emerge, however, during the 1980s. In the United States, the hunt for northern fur seals (*Callorhinus ursinus*) on Alaska's Pribilof Islands was conducted into the early 1980s under the terms of the international Interim Convention on North Pacific Fur Seals (Fig. 2-4) (see Lyster 1985). The Convention lapsed in 1984, however, and management of northern fur seals in U.S. waters reverted to domestic authority under the Fur Seal Act of 1966 and the Marine Mammal Protection Act of 1972 (Marine Mammal Commission 1996). The commercial hunt was stopped, and the only subsequent exploitation has been a smaller subsistence hunt by Aleuts in the Pribilof Islands (Fig. 2-4). Despite reduced hunting, the fur seal population, which had been declining through the 1970s for reasons still not completely understood, has yet to show signs of recovery. In 1988 it was designated as "depleted" under the Marine Mammal Protection Act (Marine Mammal Commission 1996).

On Canada's east coast, the hunt for harp seals (*Phoca groenlandica*) and hooded seals (*Cystophora cristata*) also continued, albeit in the face of increasing public protests and controversy (Lust 1967; Davies 1970, 1991; Lavigne 1978; Coish 1979; Henke 1985; Malouf 1986; Lavigne and Kovacs 1988). Quota management was introduced for the harp seal hunt in 1971 and for the hooded seal hunt in 1974 (Lavigne and Kovacs 1988). Harp seal catches generally increased during the late 1970s to 1981, when more than 200,000 animals were landed (Fig. 2-5). Although hooded seal catches fluctuated from year to year, there was no obvious trend from 1970 to 1982 (Fig. 2-6). For both species, the situation changed rapidly after the defeat of a 1983 proposal to list a number of northern phocid seals—including harps and hoods—on Appendix II of the Convention on International Trade in Endangered Species of Wild Fauna and Flora (Herscovici 1985, Lavigne 1985). Later that year, the European Community (now the European Union) imposed an import ban on products derived from whitecoat harp seal pups and blueback hooded seal pups, which together had constituted most of the historical catch (Lavigne and Kovacs 1988). Catches plummeted to a low in 1986 of 25,934 harp and 33 hooded seals. Between 1983 and 1995 catches of harp and hooded seals averaged only about 54,700 and 1,000, respec-

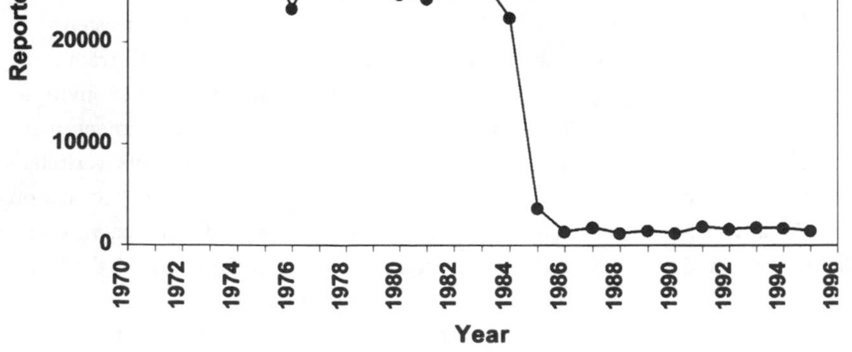

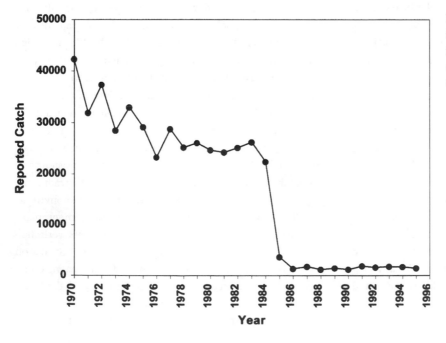

Figure 2-4. Reported catches of northern fur seals on the Pribilof Islands. (Compiled from various U.S. government sources obtained from the U.S. Marine Mammal Commission)

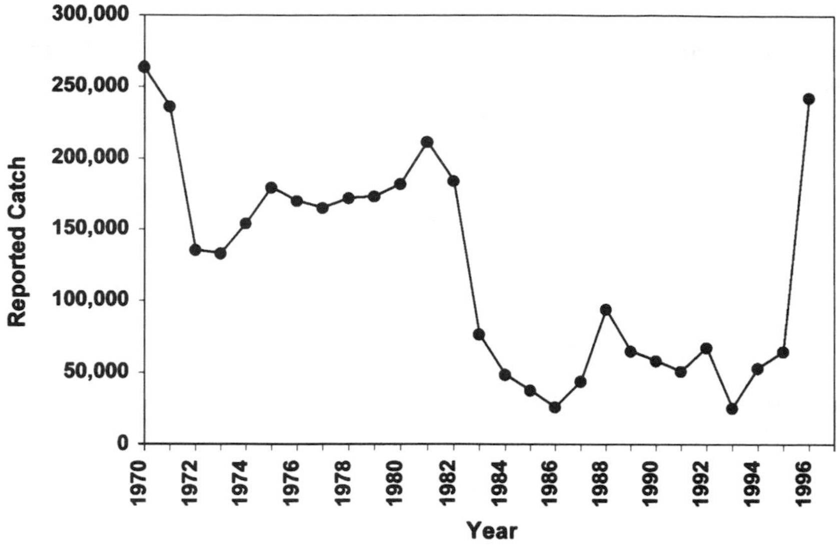

Figure 2-5. Reported catches of harp seals in the northwestern Atlantic off eastern Canada. (Compiled from various Canadian Department of Fisheries and Oceans sources)

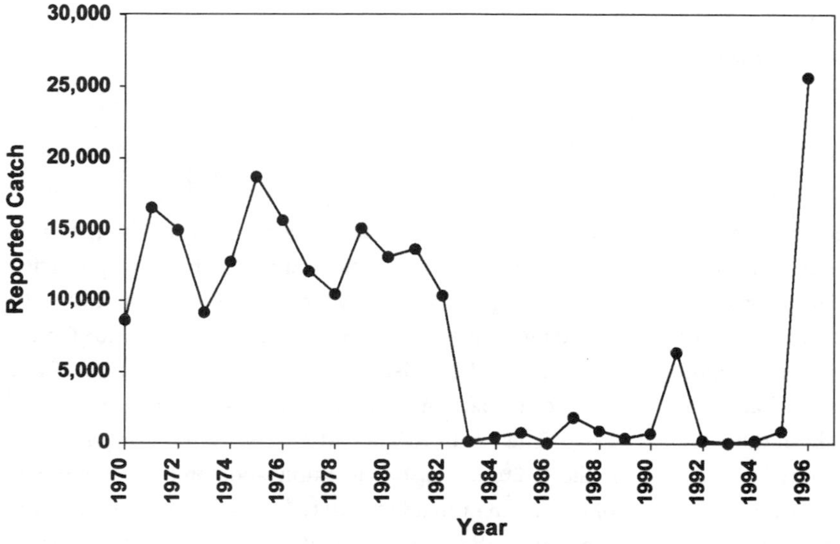

Figure 2-6. Reported catches of hooded seals in the northwestern Atlantic off eastern Canada. (Compiled from various Canadian Department of Fisheries and Oceans sources)

tively, far below the annual total allowable catch of 186,000 harp seals and between 2,340 and 15,000 (depending on the year) hooded seals (Anonymous 1995a).

In December 1995, however, Canada increased the total allowable catch for harp seals to 250,000 and, for the second year in a row, provided subsidies to encourage sealing, ostensibly to benefit depleted cod (*Gadus morhua*) stocks (Anonymous 1995a, Lavigne 1995, Hutchings et al. 1997). During the hunt the following spring, more than 242,000 harp seals and 25,000 hooded seals (more than three times the 1996 total allowable catch of 8,000) were reported killed in the largest seal hunt since 1970 (Figs. 2-5 and 2-6). Then, in December 1996 Canada's fisheries minister increased the total allowable catch for the 1997 harp seal hunt to 275,000; the hooded seal quota remained at 8,000 (Fisheries and Oceans Canada 1996a). A total of 261,036 harp seals and 7,058 hooded seals was reported landed in the 1997 hunt.[3]

As far as other North American marine mammals are concerned, the West Indian manatee (*Trichechus manatus*) is classified as an endangered species and is fully protected against exploitation in the United States under the Marine Mammal Protection Act and the Endangered Species Act (Reynolds and Odell 1991). Aside from the aforementioned seals, no North American marine mammal species is now commercially exploited, although polar bears are still hunted by Native peoples and, in Canada, also by sport hunters under permits issued to Native peoples. In addition, sea otters in Alaska and walruses (*Odobenus rosmarus*) and several species of northern phocids in both the United States and Canada continue to be hunted by Native peoples (Strong 1989; Anonymous 1991a, 1992a,b, 1993a, 1994a, 1995b; Marine Mammal Commission 1996). A number of seal and polar bear pelts and walrus and narwhal tusks enter into commerce even though the hunting of these animals is usually defined as a "subsistence" activity.

Elsewhere in the world, Norway and Japan continue to

Table 2-2. Catches of Minke Whales following the International Whaling Commission's Indefinite Moratorium on Commercial Whaling, Which Was Implemented in 1986–1987[a]

	Japanese Scientific Whaling		Norwegian Whaling		
Season	Antarctic	North Pacific	Commercial	Scientific	Total
1987–1988	273			29[b]	302
1988–1989	241		0	17	258
1989–1990	330		0	5	335
1990–1991	327		0	0	327
1991–1992	288		0	95	383
1992–1993	330		157	69	556
1993–1994	330	21	202	77	630
1994–1995	330	100	218	0	648
1995–1996	440	77	388	0	965
1996–1997	440	100	503		
1997–1998	438	100	624		

Source: Compiled from the Chairman's reports of the International Whaling Commission (1989–1998).

[a]Iceland also continued whaling after the moratorium, taking 80 fin whales and 20 sei whales in 1987, 68 f ins and 19 seis in 1988, and 68 fins in 1989. Iceland left the IWC in 1992.

[b]Northern Hemisphere operations are counted in the latter year (i.e., Norwegian whaling in 1995–1996 means that the hunt actually occurred in 1996).

hunt minke whales (*Balaenoptera acutorostrata*) in the northeastern Atlantic Ocean, Southern Ocean, and North Pacific Ocean despite the moratorium on commercial whaling that has been in effect since 1986–1987 (Table 2-2). Total catches are now increasing annually and recent press reports indicate that Norwegian whalers want their minke whale quotas increased to 1,700–1,800—the levels caught in the early 1980s.[4] Both Norway and Japan recently submitted proposals to downlist a number of minke whale, Bryde's whale (*Balaenoptera edeni*), and gray whale populations from Appendix I (protected from commercial trade) to Appendix II (commercial hunting permitted, but with specific requirements documenting trade in products) of the Convention on International Trade in Endangered Species of Wild Fauna and Flora to the 1997 Conference of the Parties in Zimbabwe. One of the proposals was subsequently withdrawn and none of the others received sufficient support from the voting delegates to be adopted. Nonetheless, some of the proposals, especially the Norwegian proposal to downlist northeastern and central Atlantic minke whale stocks from Appendix I to Appendix II, received considerable support. Although the latter failed to receive the necessary two-thirds majority, it did achieve a simple majority of 57 for, 51 against. Another Japanese proposal, which if adopted would have weakened the link between the Convention on International Trade in Endangered Species and the International Whaling Convention, was also defeated.

Apparent dissatisfaction with the functioning of the International Whaling Commission led to the formation in 1992 of the North Atlantic Marine Mammal Commission (North Atlantic Marine Mammal Commission 1994). Its founding members consisted of Norway, Iceland, Greenland, and the Faroe Islands. Canada, Russia, Denmark, and Japan often participate in its meetings as "observers" (Hoel 1993). The North Atlantic Marine Mammal Commission is dedicated to the sustainable utilization and "development" of marine mammal "resources," including both baleen and toothed whales, as well as seals. Unlike "legitimate" (or appropriate) "regional organizations"—in the context of the United Nations Convention on the Law of the Sea, and Agenda 21 (see Holt 1993)—the North Atlantic Marine Mammal Commission, although open to jurisdictions like Greenland and the Faroe Islands that are not sovereign states, does not automatically grant membership to all sovereign range states in the North Atlantic. Rather, membership seems to be limited to jurisdictions whose governments support and promote the exploitation of whales and seals. At an October 1995 meeting of North Atlantic fisheries ministers, hosted by Canada, officials from each of the North Atlantic Marine Mammal Commission jurisdictions, together with representatives of Canada and Russia, reaffirmed that seals were a "marine resource" and declared that "the abundance of seals in the Northwest Atlantic continues to be a conservation problem" (Anonymous 1995c). Contrary to available scientific advice (Lavigne 1995, Hutchings et al. 1997), the implication was that seal numbers must be controlled to protect commercially important fisheries. The European Union was the only participant in the meeting that did not sign the statement.

More recently, the North Atlantic Marine Mammal Commission arranged an international conference and exhibition on "Sealing—The Future," in cooperation with the Inuit Circumpolar Conference, the Nordic Council of Ministers, the Nordic Atlantic Cooperation, Indigenous Survival International, and the High North Alliance (see below), and hosted by the Government of Newfoundland and Labrador (North Atlantic Marine Mammal Commission 1997a,b). In April 1997 the Canadian House of Commons Standing Committee on Foreign Affairs and International Trade recommended that the "Government should move to become a full member of the North Atlantic Marine Mammal Commission, if such a move is supported in formal consultations with northern indigenous groups" (Graham 1997:221).

Other recent developments include the appearance of a number of nongovernmental organizations that promote the exploitation of marine mammals. Such organizations are part of a larger, global initiative, now known as the "sustainable use" or "wise use" movement. In Japan, the Institute for Cetacean Research, the successor of the Whales Research Institute, was founded in 1987 "to contribute to the proper conservation, management and rational utilization of marine resources" (Institute for Cetacean Research 1997). In Norway, the High North Alliance, based in Reine, the Lofoten Islands, was founded in 1991. Its objective is to protect "the rights of whalers, sealers and fishermen to harvest renewable resources in accordance with the principles of sustainable management." It currently represents member organizations from Canada, the Faroe Islands, Greenland, Iceland, and Norway (High North Alliance 1997). In early 1997 an organization billed as the World Council of Whalers opened an office on Nuu-Chah-Nulth territory in Port Alberni, British Columbia, Canada. An international organization with representatives from 10 countries (including Norway and Japan), the Council was formed "to promote the sustainable and equitable use of marine living resources, to protect the cultural, social, economic and dietary rights of whaling people and to address their concerns" (Anonymous 1997c, Stabler 1997).

Marine Mammal "Watching"

The decline in consumptive exploitation, particularly of whales in recent decades, coincided with a dramatic increase in the viewing of marine mammals in their natural habitats. Such changes in human activities related to marine mammals have paralleled those involving terrestrial wildlife. Recreational hunting, for example, has decreased in the United States over the past several decades, both in absolute and relative terms, whereas interest in other recreational pursuits—such as bird watching and wildlife tourism—has soared (Kellert 1996, 1997).

Commercial whale watching began in the United States in 1955 (Hoyt 1992), focusing on the migration of gray whales along the southern California coast (De Bell 1973, Kaza 1982, Payne 1995). By 1975 the market for short whale-watching trips was well established. A market for longer trips of several days' duration to Baja California, Mexico, also developed in the 1970s (De Bell 1973, Kaza 1982). The popularity of whale watching soon spread to other regions of the United States, including New England (Kelly 1983, Lewis 1988, Beach and Weinrich 1989), Hawaii, and Alaska, as well as to other countries, including Canada (Hoyt 1992, 1995).

Efforts have been made to assign dollar values to whale watching and other non- (or low-) consumptive uses (Duffus and Dearden 1990) of marine mammals. At the 1976 Scientific Consultation on the Biology and Management of Marine Mammals in Bergen, Norway, a small group of attendees compiled a crude inventory of the dollar returns from all low-consumptive uses of marine mammals (Payne 1976, Food and Agriculture Organization 1978). Based chiefly on North American data, the inventory showed "a gross annual value of 225 million dollars." Although it was more an intellectual exercise than a definitive economic analysis, the results surprised even its authors. Among other things, it highlighted the wide range of goods and services generated by live marine mammals.

The popularity of whale watching, in particular, has grown phenomenally in recent years (Hoyt 1992, 1995) (see Table 2-3). Hoyt's (1995) study indicates the following: some

Table 2-3. Estimated Monetary Value of Whale Watching around the World

		Whale-Watching Revenue (Millions of Dollars)	
Year	No. of Whale Watchers	Direct[a]	Total
1981		4.1	14
1988		11–16	38.5–56.0
1992	4.0 million	75.6[b]	317.9
1994	5.4 million	122.4	504.3

Source: Hoyt (1992, 1995).

[a]Here, direct revenues are tour costs only. Total revenues are tour costs plus peripheral costs, such as transportation to and from the point of departure, food, accommodations, film, special clothing, books, and souvenirs.

[b]From Hoyt (1992); Hoyt (1995) gave a figure of 77 million.

50 independent countries and 14 overseas territories or dependencies (plus Antarctica) now have some level of commercial whale watching; 27 of the 40 member countries of the International Whaling Commission, and 24 nonmembers, now have at least some whale-watching activity (among the latter, Canada, with 462,000 whale watchers in 1994, is the leader); about 66% of all whale watching occurs in the United States, where growth has begun to level off; a number of small communities around the world have been transformed by the economic (and, in some cases, educational and scientific) returns from whale watching; for many countries, whale watching provides a valuable source of foreign currency; about 85% of all whale watching involves large whales, whereas 15% involves small cetaceans such as dolphins and killer whales (*Orcinus orca*); yet, most of the approximately 80 species of cetaceans—excepting beaked whales—are included in whale-watching programs; between 1992 and 1994, 17 countries and overseas territories initiated commercial whale watching and eight more were expected to start in 1995–1996.

The rapid growth of the whale-watching industry, often in the absence of any restrictions, has given rise to concerns about its impacts on wild populations. As a consequence, a workshop was held in 1995 to discuss the scientific aspects of managing whale watching, to provide a framework to guide the process of defining new rules and modifying existing ones, and to provide recommendations for further research, including monitoring to determine any impacts of whale-watching activities (Anonymous 1996a).

Marine mammal viewing is not, however, restricted solely to whales. The idea that a tourist industry could be established in the Gulf of St. Lawrence to view harp seals on their whelping grounds was first advanced in 1969 by Brian Davies, founder of the International Fund for Animal Welfare. An intermittent activity throughout the 1970s, seal watching became an annual event in the Gulf in 1986 (Lavigne and Kovacs 1988). Some 500–700 tourists now visit the whelping ice each year (Campbell 1992). Ninety percent are non-Canadian, mostly from the United States, Europe, and Japan. Four or five operators carry tourists to the ice by helicopter from either Prince Edward Island or the Magdalen Islands, Quebec. The entire season, beginning in late February, lasts only about three weeks. For the 1992 season, the economic benefits to Canada were "conservatively" estimated to be at least Can$1,270,000 (Campbell 1992). The only study of the impact of seal tourism conducted to date was sponsored by the International Fund for Animal Welfare. Evidently, the behavior of the seals (mainly nursing mothers with pups) is altered in the presence of tourists, but the impact is short-lived; behavior returns to normal within an hour after the tourists depart (Kovacs and Innes 1990).

Manatees are the principal marine mammal tourist attraction in Florida. It is difficult to estimate how much money is generated by manatee tourism and spin-offs such as the sale of T-shirts, "manatee" wine, and other souvenirs. Every year, for example, some 65,000 tourists swim with manatees in the Crystal River (Bergman 1991). Over the three-year period 1990–1992, the state sold nearly 200,000 special "Save the Manatee" automobile license plates (Florida Department of Environmental Protection communication, 18 October 1993). And, according to a recent economic study, Floridians place a total "asset value" of $2.6 billion (or $14.78 per household per year) on the protection of their manatee population (Bendle and Bell 1995).

Polar bears are an important tourist attraction in Churchill, Manitoba. The bears now draw some 4,000 visitors in October–November, and the industry is operating at full capacity (S. Elliot, Travel Manitoba, pers. comm.; also see Weaver et al. 1995).

Sea otters—together with seals and sea lions—play a role in tourism in California. In 1985 Scheffer noted that tourism in Monterey and Santa Cruz Counties—the heartland of California sea otters—was worth half a billion dollars annually. What percentage can be attributed to the otters is not known, but their contribution to the marine mammal mystique of the region will be appreciated by almost anyone who has spent time along the central California coast.

Captive Display

Although interest in viewing marine mammals in the wild has grown substantially, a far more common opportunity to see these animals occurs in zoos and aquariums. More Americans visit zoos and aquariums yearly than attend all professional baseball, basketball, and football games combined (Kellert 1996). On a global scale, Conway (1994:15) noted that "with over 800 million visitors annually, the world's 1,100 zoos and aquariums are among our society's greatest and longest-running recreational attractions." Figures provided by the American Zoo and Aquarium Association suggest that the North American aquarium industry has grown dramatically this century (Fig. 2-7). Johnson (1990) estimated that in the United States alone the captive marine mammal industry provided some 9,000 jobs and an estimated $300 million in annual revenues.

Since 1989 the American Zoo and Aquarium Association has maintained separate attendance figures for its member aquariums in the United States and Canada. The number of members has ranged from 17 in 1989 to 27 in 1995, and attendance figures have ranged from 23 to 35 million (Table 2-4). Such data provide an order of magnitude indication of the current popularity of North American commercial

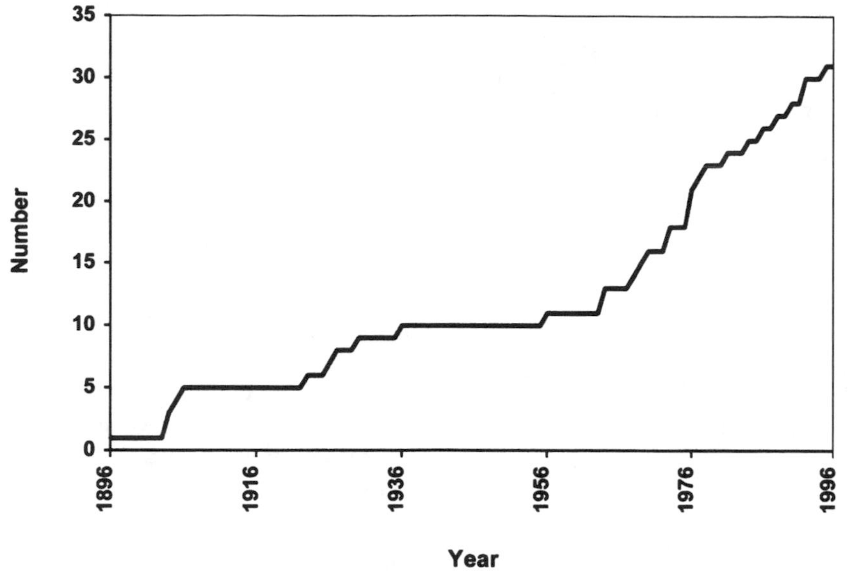

Figure 2-7. Cumulative number of American Zoo and Aquarium Association member aquariums in North America. (Data provided by the American Zoo and Aquarium Association)

Table 2-4. Attendance Figures for Members of the American Zoo and Aquarium Association

Year	No. of AZAA Members	Attendance
1989	17	23,042,616
1990	20	24,520,550
1991	21	24,750,410
1992	23	30,734,641
1993	26	35,485,101
1994	26	34,289,580
1995	27	34,770,315

Source: A. Wainwright (pers. comm.).

aquariums, many of which house marine mammals. Data supplied by the Vancouver Aquarium—a Canadian member of the American Zoo and Aquarium Association that holds marine mammals—provide a basis for examining trends at one institution (Fig. 2-8). On average, attendance has increased at more than 5% per year since the late 1950s, considerably faster than the growth rate of the Canadian (1.3%), U.S. (1.1%), and world (1.8%) populations over the same period (http://www.census.gov on the World Wide Web).

Since 1976 the number of marine mammals held in captivity has also increased, but not at the same pace as the appearance of new facilities or the increase in attendance (Figs. 2-7, 2-8, and 2-9). The disparity indicates either that a number of new aquariums are not featuring marine mammals or that the number of animals per facility is dropping. In the most recent published survey (Asper et al. 1990), 1,550 marine mammals (not including polar bears), representing more than 30 species, were displayed in such facilities. Two-thirds were pinnipeds, 28% were cetaceans (76% of which were bottlenose dolphins, *Tursiops truncatus*), and the rest were sea otters and manatees. These figures, however, do not provide an absolute measure of the total number of individual marine mammals held in U.S. aquariums over the entire time period. Animals die in the interval from one census to the next and may be replaced by newly captured animals or by individuals born in captivity. To study the implications of this turnover, the reader is referred to the U.S. Marine Mammal Inventory Report, a recent edition of which tracks marine mammals in captivity from 1973 to 1994 (National Marine Fisheries Service 1994).

In Canada the government's Advisory Committee on Marine Mammals recently reported that there were five facilities holding cetaceans for live display, one of which was in the process of closing down (Anonymous 1992c). The committee expected that by 1993, there would be two aquariums in Canada with killer whales, one with belugas, three with bottlenose dolphins, and one with Pacific white-sided dolphins (*Lagenorhynchus obliquidens*).

As the popularity of commercial aquariums has been increasing, controversy has also been developing around the morality of keeping marine mammals, especially cetaceans, in captivity, particularly for entertainment, but also for education and research (Reeves and Mead, this volume; see also Bellerive Foundation 1990, Anonymous 1992c, Hoyt 1992, Humane Society of the United States 1995). For example, in 1990 delegates from 32 animal welfare organizations in nine countries formally recorded their opposition "to the confinement of all whales, dolphins and porpoises" (Bellerive Foundation 1990:78). More recently, the Humane Society of the United States (one of the largest animal welfare organizations in the world) argued ". . . that the reality of the entire captive experience for wild-caught marine mammals is so sterile and contrary to even the most basic elements of compassion and humaneness that it should be rejected"

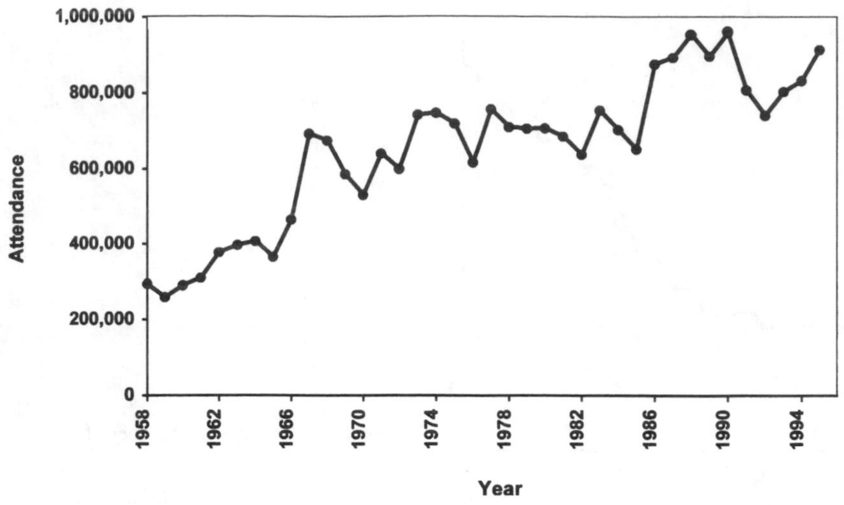

Figure 2-8. Annual attendance figures from the Vancouver Aquarium. (Data provided by the Vancouver Aquarium)

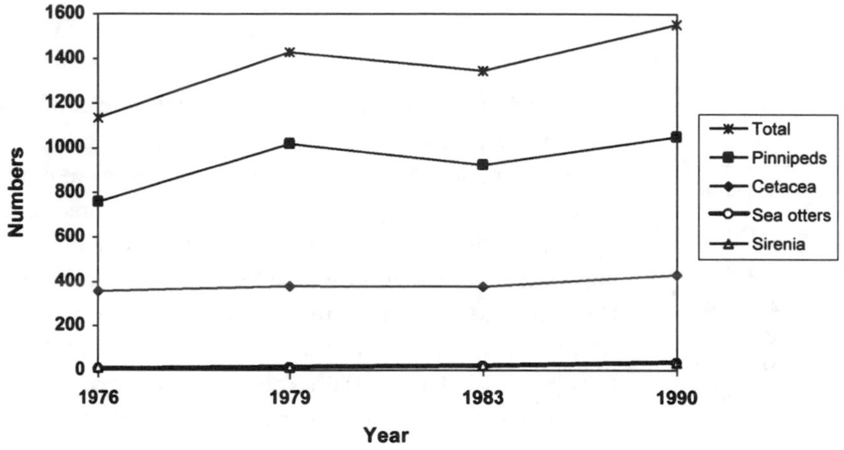

Figure 2-9. Numbers of marine mammals reportedly on captive display in the United States (Asper et al. 1990).

(Humane Society of the United States 1995:35). Indeed, it was public opposition to the live capture of killer whales in the waters of Washington State (Griffin 1966, Scheffer 1970) that years ago convinced state lawmakers to pass a resolution against capturing additional animals for display (Washington State Legislature 1979). At the time, Washington's secretary of state noted that 55 live killer whales had been captured in the Pacific Northwest, of which only 17 were still alive (Munro 1982).

As a consequence of public opposition and controversy, some facilities have chosen not to display captive cetaceans. The Monterey Bay Aquarium in California, which now attracts more than two million visitors a year, decided before its opening day in 1984 not to do so. In Canada, some 80% of the public has expressed opposition to maintaining marine mammals in zoos and aquariums unless significant educational and scientific benefits result (Kellert 1991). Because of such opposition, the Vancouver Aquarium no longer has its resident marine mammals perform in traditional "shows." Australia's state of Victoria banned the capture of dolphins in 1985. In the United Kingdom, no cetaceans remain captive in marine parks and aquariums (Anonymous 1993b).

Controversy over keeping marine mammals in captivity has resulted in a number of court cases. In 1970 an animal trainer released a dolphin held on Bimini Island, Bahamas. He was arrested and fined $5 for trespassing (O'Barry 1988). In another widely reported instance, two men in 1977 freed dolphins from a research laboratory at the University of Hawaii. They were arrested and charged with grand theft. In the court case that followed, the judge ruled—to the dismay of many animal rights supporters and over the objection of the defendants—that the only pertinent moral issue was the theft of property worth more than $200 (Daws 1983). "Although society does not yet appear to be prepared to extend human rights to animals," observed *Science* reporter Constance Holden (1978:37), "the [Hawaii] dolphin liberation case feeds into increasing sensitivity about the treatment of animals in captivity."

Actions against the holding of marine mammals in captivity have been countered with responses from the aquarium industry. In 1987 the Alliance of Marine Mammal Parks and Aquariums was established to promote the public display of marine mammals. Representing 37 marine life parks, aquariums, zoos, scientific research facilities, and professional organizations, this group is "dedicated to the protection of marine mammals through public display, education, conservation and research programs (Alliance of Marine Mammal Parks and Aquariums n.d.). In 1991 the directors of the New England Aquarium challenged activists who had charged them with violating the U.S. Marine Mammal Protection Act. On 17 November, they filed SLAPP suits (Strategic Lawsuits Against Public Participation) against the Progressive Animal Welfare Society (PAWS), the Citizens to End Animal Suffering from Exploitation, and the Animal League Defense Fund, seeking more than $5 million in damages (Adler 1991, New England Aquarium 1991). In a precedent-setting decision, a U.S. district court judge ruled that the Marine Mammal Protection Act may not be used by activist groups to bring suits against organizations such as aquariums (Goldfarb 1993).

In another legal development, the federal Animal Enterprise Protection Act of 1992[5] placed stiff penalties on "animal enterprise terrorism." The Act offers protection to animals used in agriculture, research, education, and entertainment, including zoos and aquariums.

As with consumptive exploitation, the issue of maintaining marine mammals in captivity is one where diverse attitudes lead to conflicting societal objectives and, inevitably, conflict (Norton et al. 1995; see Reeves and Mead, this volume). Those who support captivity argue that the confined animals act as ambassadors, which inspire aquarium visitors to help preserve their wild counterparts. They also argue that the educational effect of display animals on children is especially valuable because young minds are more impressionable than are those of adults. Moreover, captive marine mammals in commercial aquariums and, more important, in scientific institutions, facilitate research. Data on daily energy requirements, reproduction, sleep, vision, hearing, and the ability to learn can often be obtained only from captive animals. "My guess," wrote whale biologist Kenneth Norris (1991:19), "is that on balance three-quarters of what we really know about . . . the dolphin has come from captive partners in experimentation." And captive animals, it is noted, serve as banks to save the genetic lines of endangered species. Those who oppose holding marine mammals captive for purposes of public display believe these arguments are unfounded.

Animal Welfare Organizations

A clear indication of changing North American attitudes toward marine mammals is the emergence of a movement having a strong interest in protecting these animals and their habitats. From the late 1960s to the late 1980s, animal welfare organizations proliferated throughout North America (Table 2-5). Several emphasize the well-being of marine mammals as a special concern. These include the American Cetacean Society (founded in 1967), Friends of the Sea Otter (1968), the International Fund for Animal Welfare (1969), the Center for Marine Conservation (1972), the Connecticut Cetacean Society (1974), which later became the Cetacean Society International (1986), the Marine Mammal Center (1975), the Sea Shepherd Conservation Society (1977), the Pacific Whale Foundation (1980), and the Save the Manatee Club (1981). In addition, other organizations—including the Sierra Club (founded by John Muir in 1892), the Animal Welfare Institute (1951), the Humane Society of the United States (1954), Fund for Animals (1967), Friends of the Earth (1969), Greenpeace (1970), the Cousteau Society (1973), and Earth Island Institute (1982)—have sponsored action programs for the benefit of marine mammals.

Table 2-5. Establishment of Private "National Organizations (Human, Animal Welfare / Protection)" in the United States from 1952 to 1991

Five-Year Period	No. Founded
1952–1956	1
1957–1961	4
1962–1966	0
1967–1971	9
1972–1976	6
1977–1981	16
1982–1986	24
1987–1991	8

Source: From Reece (1992).

On occasion, organizations have joined forces to exchange information and to cooperate on specific missions. Witness the Monitor Consortium, which was formed in Washington, D.C., in 1972, and the Marine Mammal Protection Coalition, comprising 24 organizations representing more than two million members worldwide. The latter gave testimony to the lawmakers who were drafting the Marine Mammal Protection Act Amendments of 1994 (Hodges 1993, Rose 1994). In Canada 29 national and international nongovernmental organizations attending a 1992 meeting on Canadian marine issues endorsed a Blueprint for Change. This document called upon the Canadian government to prohibit the capture of marine mammals for display anywhere, to improve the standards for holding those marine mammals already in captivity, to investigate opportunities for returning captives to the wild, to protect and enhance marine mammal habitats, and to ensure that marine mammal mortalities caused by Canadians—in Canadian waters and elsewhere—be minimized (Anonymous 1992d).

In an attempt to gauge American public support for animal welfare organizations, we examined data from U.S. Internal Revenue Service Form 990 filings for the years 1989–1995 (Clifton and Larson 1991a,b; Anonymous 1992e, 1993c, 1994b, 1995d, 1996b). In 1989, 42 of "the most visible national animal protection groups" reported combined annual budgets of about $215 million. Forty of these groups reported combined total assets of almost $274 million (Clifton and Larson 1991a,b). These dollar figures are impressive, but should be considered in relation to all charitable contributions. According to the 1992–1993 Nonprofit Almanac (Hodgkinson et al. 1992), only 0.5% ($614 million) of the U.S. charity dollar goes to animal-related causes, and this is divided among the 2,604 groups filing Form 990 returns. Another 0.7% ($842 million) goes to environmental organizations.

To get some idea of funding trends, we examined the annual budgets of selected animal welfare organizations involved in marine mammal issues during 1989–1995. We found complete data for 10. Annual budgets (presumably reflecting donor contributions, membership dues, etc.) increased over the period, even when standardized to 1989 dollars (Fig. 2-10). There is clearly no decline in support for these animal welfare groups. To fully appreciate the growth of the animal welfare movement, it must be remembered that many of the organizations noted above did not even exist 30 years ago.

The growth of interest in the welfare of marine mammals has been accompanied by the rise and spread of national conferences and symposia devoted entirely to such animals, especially cetaceans. We offer a brief review of four such meetings.

A National Whale Symposium was convened at Indiana University in 1974 (Anonymous 1975, Indiana University Libraries 1993). Its program included music by humans and whales, whales in folklore, modern whaling, cetaceans in captivity, fossil whales, children's drawings of whales, whale intelligence, Jonah as interpreted in psychology, and "the mathematics of conservation."

In 1979 delegates from eight animal interest groups convened in Washington, D.C., at a meeting announced as Whales and Ethics: A National Symposium Relative to World Policy (Anonymous 1979). The symposium featured a screening of the National Geographic Society's 1977 award-winning film, *The Great Whales;* a recording of a 1976 Walter Cronkite broadcast, "Dolphins and Ethics"; and supportive remarks from two members of Congress.

A meeting on Cetacean Behaviour and Intelligence and the Ethics of Killing Cetaceans was held in Washington, D.C., in 1980. Sponsored by the International Whaling Commission, the Institute for Delphinid Research, the Animal Welfare Institute, and the governments of Australia and the United States (Ovington 1980), the meeting's participants affirmed that "whaling" should be redefined to include enjoying live whales as well as killing them for the market.

Boston's New England Aquarium hosted another meeting: Whales Alive: Global Conference on the Non-Consumptive Utilization of Cetacean Resources (Anonymous 1983). There, Russell E. Train of the World Wildlife Fund proposed that we should be more "polite" to whales; that doing so would be a mark of our civilization. Relevant to our earlier discussion, it was also here that Sir Peter Scott

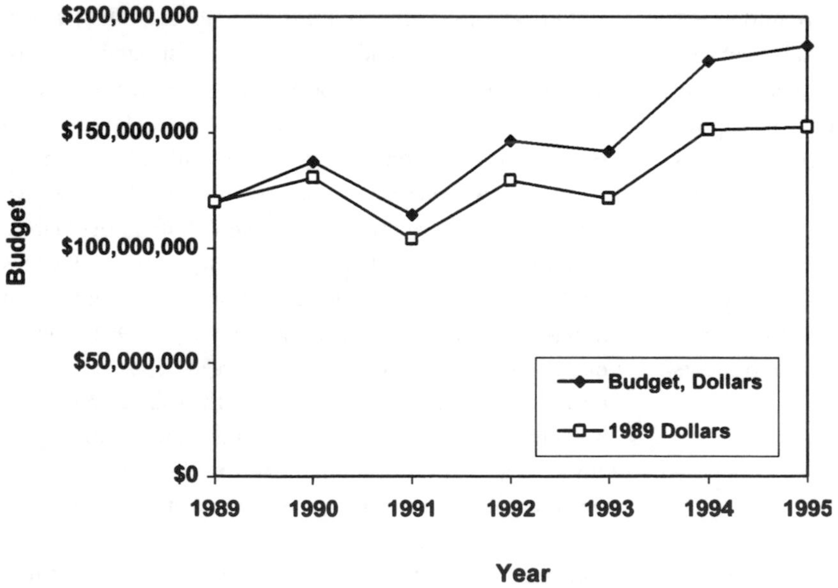

Figure 2-10. Total annual budget of 10 U.S. "animal welfare organizations" (Animal Protection Institute, Defenders of Wildlife, Friends of Animals, Fund for Animals, Humane Society of the United States, International Fund for Animal Welfare, People for the Ethical Treatment of Animals, Sierra Club, Sierra Club Legal Defense Fund, World Wildlife Fund) for which complete data were available for the years 1989–1995. (Calculated from U.S. Internal Revenue Service Form 990 filings, sources given in the text)

of the Wildfowl Trust expressed the view that dolphinariums will be acceptable to society for only a few more years, when they will give way to "happening places where people and cetaceans can meet" (Scheffer 1983).

Popularization in the Media

Books and magazines, television, sound recordings, and motion pictures have in recent decades brought marine mammals to the attention of millions of people. To what extent these media efforts have simply reflected public interest or actually influenced public attitudes is difficult to say. According to Justice Rosalie Abella of the Ontario (Canada) Court of Appeal, in a speech entitled "The Media and the Courts" (1997:A25), "There can be little doubt that as the chief informer to the public, the media also play a role as chief *former* of that public's opinions. Because the media decide what the public will know, the media act as the gatekeeper of public policy, agendas and ideas. They decide what to bring to light and how to light it." Certainly, there are instances where attitudes toward marine mammals have been influenced by media coverage.

Any attempt to review the media's treatment of marine mammals is, inevitably, somewhat arbitrary. Nonetheless, we examined a few, readily available databases to gauge trends in public interest and, where possible, to glean insights into changing attitudes.

Books

We searched listings of marine mammal publications for 1898 to 1996 provided by the U.S. Library of Congress on the World Wide Web (http://www.loc.gov) using the key words whales, dolphins, porpoises, pinnipeds, fur seals, sea lions, walruses, seals, sea otters, polar bears, and manatees. We then deleted duplicate listings (but not multiple book editions) to produce a decade-by-decade summary of publications dealing with each marine mammal group. For the twentieth century, we found a total of 983 marine mammal listings, including 668 (68%) dealing with cetaceans, 226 (23%) with pinnipeds, and 27 (3%), 24 (3%), and 38 (4%) dealing with sea otters, polar bears, and manatees, respectively. To examine trends in the appearance of publications, we plotted the average number of listings per year (lumped by decade) for each group. Listings for all marine mammal groups showed a similar trend, namely, an exponential increase in the appearance of new listings, beginning in the 1960s and continuing steadily through the 1990s (Fig. 2-11). Marine mammal books not only surged in numbers in the latter half of the twentieth century, but they also changed in tone. Many authors began to treat marine mammals with greater compassion than in the past.

Scott McVay, then an administrator at Princeton University, was among the first writers to alert the public to the imperiled status of the great whales. His milestone article, "The Last of the Great Whales," published in *Scientific American* in 1966, was followed by others in popular magazines and in the *New York Times.* He later received the Albert Schweitzer Memorial Prize. Shortly thereafter, John Lilly argued in *The Mind of the Dolphin* (1967) that the dolphin's brain is in several respects superior to that of humans (Nash 1989), and he provoked heated discussion of the notion that dolphins can be taught to "talk." Peter Lust's *The Last Seal Pup: The Story of Canada's Seal Hunt* (1967) chronicled the early days of the antisealing movement; Scheffer's *The Year of the Whale* (1969) was selected as a Book of the Month

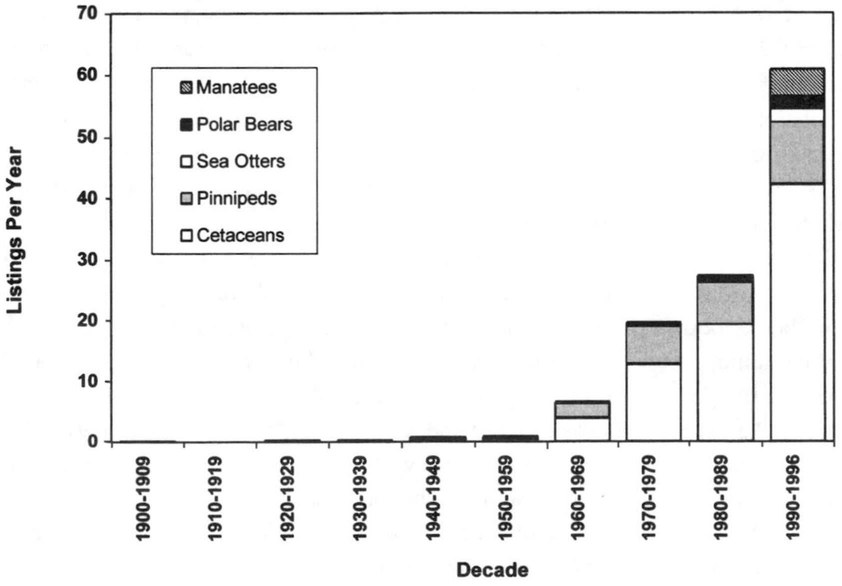

Figure 2-11. Average number of marine mammal publications per year per decade in the U.S. Library of Congress (see text for details).

Club alternate and abstracted in *Reader's Digest;* Karl Kenyon's *The Sea Otter in the Eastern Pacific Ocean* (1969, republished 1975) became a widely consulted reference. Brian Davies' *Savage Luxury: The Slaughter of the Baby Seals* (1970) gave an impassioned account of the Northwest Atlantic harp seal hunt; and George Small's *The Blue Whale* (1971), a history of the whaling industry, won a National Book Award.

Canadian Farley Mowat's controversial *A Whale for the Killing* (1972) told of a fin whale (*Balaenoptera physalus*) trapped by the tides in a salt-water lagoon and subsequently used as a rifle target by Newfoundland villagers. Joan McIntyre, president of Project Jonah—a save-the-whales organization founded at the 1972 Stockholm conference (see below)—compiled an influential work entitled *Mind in the Waters* (1974). It expressed the opinions of authors coming from widely diverse fields—from poetry and painting to neurology and wildlife management. Teacher Tamar Griggs' children's book, *There's a Sound in the Sea,* included paintings and poems produced by her young pupils. There, Margaret Rakas, age 10, wrote: "The men kill the great whale / They do not waste the great whale / Except its beauty" (Griggs 1975:73). Greg Gatenby edited *Whales: A Celebration* (1983), a collection of historical and contemporary works by artists who "found inspiration in the great whales and dolphins." A poet, Gatenby had become interested in whales and dolphins when he studied linguistics in university and, like others before him, began to investigate the possibilities of dialogue between humans and cetaceans.

Moreover, books about marine mammals in earlier times were revived. George Allen England's (1924) classic firsthand account of the Newfoundland seal hunt, originally entitled *Vikings of the Ice,* was reprinted in 1969 as *The Greatest Hunt in the World.* In 1972 Newfoundlanders Cassie Brown and Harold Horwood wrote *Death on the Ice,* the story of the great Newfoundland sealing disaster of 1914. In 1984 Mowat chronicled the historical exploitation of the Northwest Atlantic, including seals and whales, in *Sea of Slaughter.* Historian Briton Cooper Busch (1985) wrote *The War Against the Seals: A History of the North American Seal Fishery.* In 1988 Jeremy Cherfas published *The Hunting of the Whale: A Tragedy That Must End.*

It is perhaps significant that marine mammal books, both nonfiction and fiction, for children and young adults increased along with those for older readers. Among the children's books was Rosalie Fry's *The Secret of the Ron Mor Skerry* (1985, subsequently released as a movie in 1994 and republished in 1995, both under the title *The Secret of Roan Inish*), and several by the late Jacques Cousteau (1992a,b, 1993). Among the fiction books were novels for adults that wove marine mammals into their story lines (e.g., Allan Dean Foster's [1980] *Cachalot* and Paul Quarrington's [1989] *Whale Music,* which was also made into a feature film and resulted in two compact disks released under the same title).

Magazines

To gain insight into marine mammal coverage by magazines, we selected *National Geographic* magazine because of its prominence (e.g., Fig. 2-12) and the availability of a useful database on the National Geographic Society's home page on the World Wide Web (http://cliff.nationalgeographic.com). Our search turned up 44 articles, which, by their titles, deal specifically with marine mammals. Of these, 24 (55%) are about cetaceans, 17 (39%) are about pinnipeds (including 5 on walruses alone), and 1 (2%) each on sea otters, polar bears, and manatees. Again, if publication rate tells us anything about popular interest in marine mammals, then clearly that interest increased dramatically in the 1970s and 1980s (Fig. 2-13).

National Geographic's titles provide further insights into the changing interests of its editors, if not of the magazine's readership. Some of the earlier features focused on commercial exploitation: for example, Dobbs (1911), Smith (1911), Bartlett (1928), and Backer (1948). More recent articles focus on the biological mysteries of marine mammals: for example, Scheffer (1976), Payne (1979), Whitehead (1984), and Darling (1988); or on endangered species: for example, Larsen (1971), Graves (1976), Hall (1984), and Ackerman (1992).

Television

The natural history of marine mammals also captured the attention of television producers. At first, they aimed simply to entertain. Later, they began to educate viewers about wildlife biology and conservation. The antics of *Flipper* (actually five different female bottlenose dolphins) were telecast serially until 1967 (O'Barry 1988). Flipper displayed to millions of people an endearing species that few would ever see in the wild.

The harp seal controversy, which began in 1964 and continues today, is a textbook example of the power of television to change the popular image of an animal species and, consequently, to affect the management of its wild populations (Lavigne 1978, McCloskey 1979, Henke 1985, Malouf 1986, Lavigne and Kovacs 1988, Tilt and Spotila 1991). The controversy began with a 1964 film produced by Artek Studios of Montreal showing a seal pup being skinned alive on the ice off eastern Canada. The film, which was broadcast on television into living rooms around the world, touched

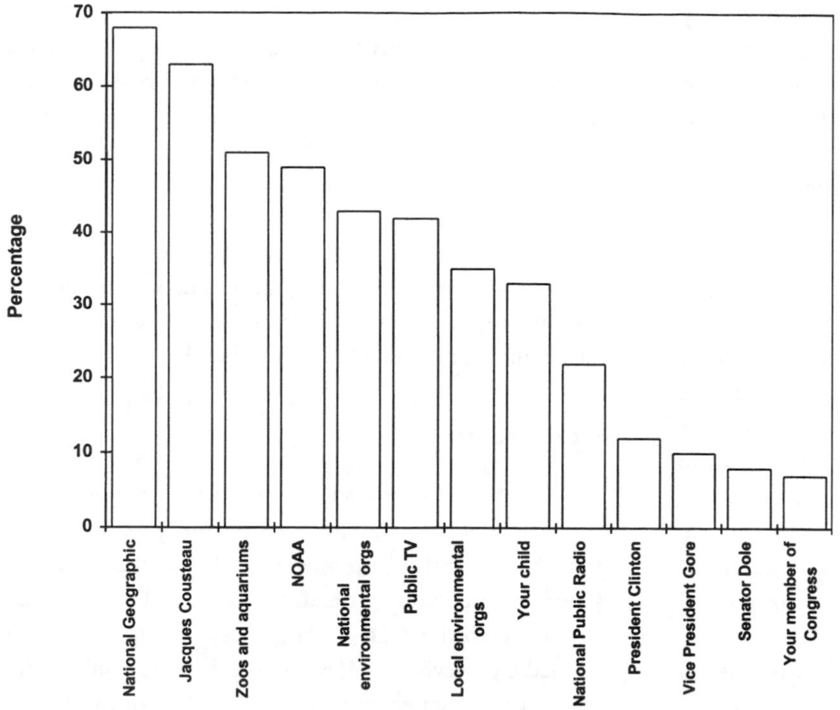

Figure 2-12. Percentage of Americans who "trust a great deal" what various groups and individuals have to say about ocean protection (The Mellman Group 1996).

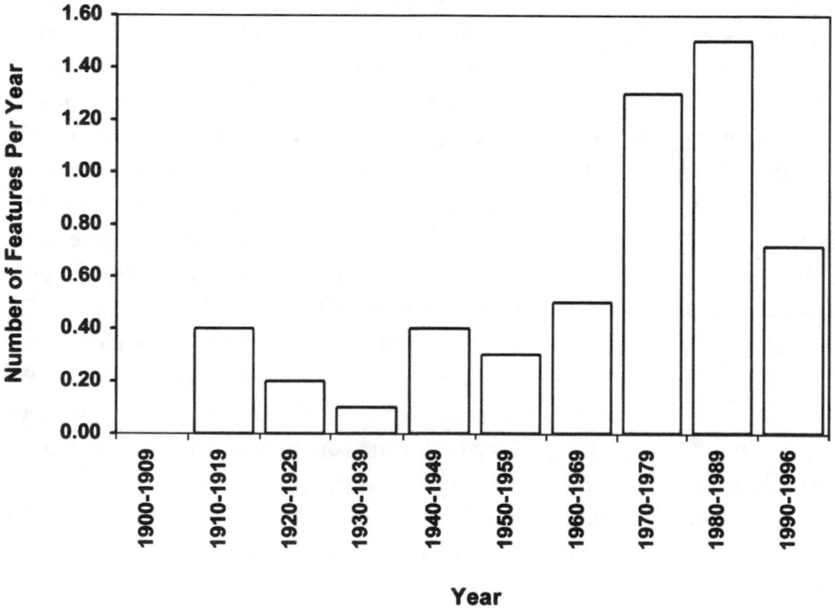

Figure 2-13. Average number of articles on marine mammals published per year per decade by *National Geographic* magazine (see text for details).

off an explosion of protest, especially against the clubbing of "baby seals," the whitecoat pups of the harp seal. Thus was born the "anti-sealing movement" (Lavigne and Kovacs 1988).

In 1972 the United States banned the import of whitecoat pelts, and in 1983 the European Community followed suit (Lavigne and Kovacs 1988). The world market for harp seal products virtually collapsed during the 1980s. By 1986 a Royal Commission on Seals and the Sealing Industry in Canada concluded that "There is very strong public opposition to the clubbing of harp seal pups (whitecoats) and hooded seal pups (bluebacks). This hunt is widely viewed as abhorrent both in Canada and abroad" (Malouf 1986, 1:38). The Commission recommended that the commercial hunting of harp and hooded seal pups be ended (Malouf 1986), and in late 1987 the Canadian government banned the commercial killing of whitecoats and bluebacks (Lavigne and Kovacs 1988).

Anyone who has taught budding marine mammalogists in their freshman year at university over the past 20 years is aware of Jacques Cousteau's influence in generating interest and shaping attitudes toward marine mammals. Through his various books, films, and television series—particularly *The Undersea World of Jacques Cousteau* (1968–1976)—he brought his vision of the oceans and of marine mammals to millions of people worldwide. To appreciate his impact, readers should remember that when Americans were recently asked "whether you trust what this group or person has to say about ocean protection a great deal, some, not too much or not at all," Cousteau ranked a close second to *National Geographic* (trusted a great deal by 63 and 68% of respondents, respectively [Fig. 2-12]).

It was also through television that Sam LaBudde (1988), a self-described "itinerant biologist," contributed to public and Congressional understanding of the tuna-dolphin issue (Gosliner, this volume). For five months in 1987–1988, he worked as a seaman and cook—although covertly as a spy for Earth Island Institute—on a Panamanian tuna boat. He videotaped hundreds of dolphins being killed or injured in the fishing operations. His tapes—not for the weak of stomach—were aired nationally on CBS, ABC, and CNN, and in 1991 they won him the $60,000 Goldman Environmental Prize.

The power of television was perhaps never more evident than in the autumn of 1988 when headlines began to describe the plight of three young gray whales trapped in ice off northern Alaska (Fraker 1989). For a few days, even the American presidential election took second place in the news. A Soviet icebreaker finally cut a path to the whales (one of which had disappeared), and the survivors swam to freedom. The cost of the rescue was estimated at $1.3 million. The incident spawned a book, by journalist Tom Rose (1989), with the provocative title, *Freeing the Whales—How the Media Created the World's Greatest Non-Event.*

Music

One of the more influential factors in creating a new image of marine mammals was the discovery in the late 1960s that humpback whales (*Megaptera novaeangliae*) produce sounds equivalent to songs. That discovery gained wide publicity, first through a sound recording for general audiences (*Songs of the Humpback Whale,* New York Zoological Society and Communications Research/Machines, Los Angeles, 1970), then through written accounts (Payne 1970, Payne and McVay 1971, Payne 1995). Soon, humpback calls began to reverberate in music composed by Judy Collins (*Whales and Nightingales,* Electra 76-7638501, 1970), Alan Hovhaness (*And God Created Great Whales,* Columbia Stereo M30390, 1970), and George Crumb (*Vox Balaenae: Voice of the Whale,* Columbia Records, M-32739, 1974). In 1980 the Paul Winter Consort recorded another album mingling marine mammal vocalizations with instrumental music (*Callings,* Living Music Records, 1980; see Payne 1995). Marine mammals were rapidly gaining support from show-business personalities. And perhaps others. For, when the United States launched the *Voyager 1* and *Voyager 2* spacecraft toward other possible sentient life in our galaxy in 1977, included in them were recordings of classical and rock music, greetings in more than 50 human languages, and, yes, the song of the humpback whale (Beilenson 1989). "The whole concept of sending a spacecraft carrying words, music, and whale sounds," Roger Payne (1995:353) wrote years later, "conveys a message about what we are like and what we believe in."

Motion Pictures

Since the 1960s the motion picture industry has been producing, at an increasing rate, films featuring marine mammals. The original *Flipper* movie (1963) told the story of a fisherman's son, who befriends a dolphin and is persuaded to return it to the wild (Anonymous 1997d). The movie spawned the television series earlier mentioned and several sequels, the most recent in 1996. The plots of the *Flipper* movies seem remarkably contemporary in the attitudes they portrayed, but some of the other earlier films were quite different. In *Whale of a Tale* (1976), for example, "a young boy trains a killer whale to appear in the big show in the main tank at Marineland" (Anonymous 1997d:816). *Orca* (1977) portrayed a fictitious killer whale chasing a bounty hunter named Derek Harris to avenge the murder of its pregnant mate. The whale eventually "chomps Derek's leg off," leading one reviewer to rate the film as "great for gore lovers" (Anonymous 1997d:560).

Contrast these 1970s movies with more recent ones. *Star Trek 4: The Voyage Home* (1986), which has the good ship *Enterprise* going back in time (to the 1980s) to save a humpback whale cow and calf from commercial whalers, was seen by some people as unabashed antiwhaling propaganda. And then there is *Free Willy.* As most readers know, this film tells the fictional story of a troubled boy who develops a friendship with a killer whale held captive in a theme park. ("Willy" was both a real killer whale in a Mexican aquarium and, in about half the scenes, a robot.) Rather than training the whale to perform in an aquarium—remember *Whale of a Tale* mentioned earlier—the boy helps it to escape and rejoin its pod in the open sea.

While *Free Willy* was showing in San Diego in July 1993, an animal welfare organization—In Defense of Animals—handed out more than 100,000 leaflets in front of theaters calling on patrons who had seen the film to take action toward freeing killer whales wherever they were being held captive (Anonymous 1993d). Such action soon began, but not before a second movie, *Free Willy 2: The Adventure Home,* was released in 1995. In this sequel, the real "Willy" (originally known as Keiko) does not appear (Anonymous 1997d), and a different issue—the threat posed to marine mammals by oil spills—is addressed. As a result of efforts spearheaded by the Earth Island Institute and the Free Willy–Keiko Foundation, approximately $8 million was eventually raised to move the real Keiko from his small Mexican pool to a more suitable facility. On 7 January 1996 Keiko was airlifted—by United Parcel Service—to a special pool at the Oregon Coast Aquarium in Newport. In December 1996 "Keiko's Story" was featured in an hour-long documentary shown on the Discovery Channel (U.S. Cable TV), and *Free Willy 3: The Rescue* appeared in North American theaters in August 1997. By late 1997 Keiko was at the center of more controversy—another attitudinal conflict—which the press described as a "political war between animal rights activists who want him freed and marine park owners who fear freeing one whale will lead to pressure to free all whales" (Canadian Press 1997:2A).

When the directors of the Vancouver Aquarium previewed the original *Free Willy,* they voted to emphasize its positive values. They announced: "The personal relationship between Willy [and the boy] illustrates the impact living animals can have *on changing people's perceptions and attitudes*" (emphasis added) (Vancouver Aquarium 1993). The aquarium had already replaced its killer whale shows, aimed at entertainment, with sessions, narrated by staff naturalists, aimed at public education.

Two recent movies about pinnipeds are also worthy of note. *Andre* (1994) told the true story of an orphaned harbor seal in Maine (featured in a 1968 *National Geographic* article). However, as one critic observed (Anonymous 1997d:50), "For those who are sticklers for accuracy, Andre is actually portrayed [in the movie] by a sea lion and not a seal." Nonetheless, this movie, like *Free Willy,* raised questions about whether Andre should be returned to the wild. The second movie, *The Secret of Roan Inish* (1994), mentioned earlier, brought a children's book, and the ancient Celtic myth of the selkies,[6] to the big screen. And another dolphin movie, *Zeus and Roxanne,* opened in movie theaters throughout North America in late 1996.

The Evolution of Marine Mammal Legislation

When certain attitudes or values become widely held in democratic societies, they eventually influence public policy and, ultimately, legislation. "Legislation," as Henry Salt (1894, cited in Nash 1989:30) reminded us, "is the record, the register, of the moral sense of the community." More simply put, laws "implement the ideals of the community" (Nash 1989:5). As societal attitudes evolve over time, so do wildlife laws (Bean 1977, 1983). Here, we review important laws pertaining to marine mammals and their habitats in relation to the five eras that have been identified in the history of U.S. wildlife management (Table 2-6). Since protective legislation for marine mammals is broadly dealt with elsewhere in this book (Baur et al., this volume), we will simply examine the chronological emergence of laws in the United States (Table 2-7) (also see Montague 1993) as an indicator of changing public attitudes.

Table 2-6. Eras of Wildlife Conservation and Management

1600–1849	Era of Abundance
1850–1899	Era of Over-exploitation
1900–1929	Era of Protection
1930–1965	Era of Game Management
1966–1984	Era of Environmental Management
1985–?	Era of ?

Source: Modified from Shaw (1985). Shaw's chronology ended in 1984, just before the publication of his book. By the mid to late 1980s, we had arguably entered a new era. It remains to be seen what this era will be called (see Discussion).

What is first evident from Table 2-7 is that the vast majority of U.S. legislation affecting marine mammals, their populations, and their habitats has emerged since 1966, beginning with Shaw's Era of Environmental Management and continuing into the currently unnamed, post-1985 era. The first legislation dealing with marine mammals was aimed at reducing the impacts of excessive consumptive exploitation, which characterized the last half of the nineteenth century, both on land and at sea (Shaw 1985, Lavigne et al. 1996). Indeed, the first national wildlife refuge in the United States was established by presidential proclamation to protect, among other species, seals, walruses, and sea otters on Alaska's Afognak Island (Nash 1989:171). Specifically, the island was reserved "in order that salmon fisheries in the waters of the Island, and salmon and other fish and sea animals, and other animals and birds . . . may be protected and preserved unimpaired" (cited in Bean 1977:26). Similarly, the North Pacific Fur Seal Act of 1910 was designed to halt the decline of the North Pacific fur seal population in the Pribilof Islands of Alaska following decades of poorly regulated exploitation (Busch 1985). The Act's origins were rooted simply in the principles of sound livestock management, at least so far as they were understood at the time. The Act banned the killing of "any female seal or any seal less than one year old."

The Era of Protection came with the recognition that the most obvious cause of the precipitous decline of North American wildlife in the late nineteenth century was direct overexploitation (Shaw 1985), usually for commercial purposes (Lavigne et al. 1996). It was fitting, therefore, that the

Table 2-7. Important Events in U.S. Marine Mammal Management

Era of Over-exploitation (1850–1899)	
1892	First wildlife refuge established on Alaska's Afognak Island to protect seals, walruses, and sea otters, as well as salmon and marine birds (Nash 1989; also see Bean 1977, 1983)
Era of Protection (1900–1929)	
1900	Lacey Act
1910	North Pacific Fur Seal Act
Era of Game Management (1930–1965)	
1948	62 Stat. 1096
1949	63 Stat. 89
1953	Outer Continental Shelf Lands Act (OCSLA)
1954	North Pacific Fisheries Act
Era of Environmental Management (1966–1984)	
1966	Laboratory Animal Welfare Act
1966	Endangered Species Preservation Act
1966	National Wildlife Refuge System Administration Act
1966	Fur Seal Act
1969	Endangered Species Conservation Act
1969	National Environmental Policy Act
1970	Laboratory Animal Welfare Act renamed the Animal Welfare Act
1970	Pelly Amendment to the Fishermen's Protective Act of 1967
1971	Airborne Hunting Act
1972	Marine Mammal Protection Act (MMPA)
1972	Marine Protection, Research, and Sanctuaries Act
1972	Coastal Zone Management Act
1973	Endangered Species Act (ESA)
1976	Whale Conservation and Protection Study Act
1976	Magnuson-Stevens Fishery Conservation and Management Act
1976	Amendments to the Animal Welfare Act
1978	Amendments to ESA
1978	Amendment to OCSLA for management and protection of outer continental shelf
1981	The Lacey Act Amendments of 1981
1981	Packwood Amendment to the Magnuson-Stevens Fishery Conservation and Management Act
1982	Amendments to ESA specifying the determination of critical habitat
1982	The Fishery Amendments to the Commercial Fisheries Research and Development Act of 1964
1984	Amendments to MMPA
Era of ? (1985–?)	
1985	Amendments to the Animal Welfare Act
1986	Amendments to MMPA and ESA allow incidental take of depleted species
1987	Driftnet Impact Monitoring, Assessment, and Control Act
1990	Dolphin Protection Consumer Information Act
1990	Amendments to the Animal Welfare Act
1992	International Dolphin Conservation Act
1992	High Seas Driftnet Fisheries Enforcement Act
1992	Hawaiian Islands National Marine Sanctuary Act
1992	Marine Mammal Health and Stranding Response Act
1994	Amendments to MMPA
1997	International Dolphin Conservation Program Act

Source: After Shaw (1985); Bean (1977, 1983), Montague (1993), Gosliner (this volume).

era dawned in the United States with the passage of the Lacey Act of 1900. The Lacey Act helped to curb market hunting by making the interstate transportation of illegally killed wildlife a federal offense (Shaw 1985). Additional laws enacted in 1948 and 1949 (62 Stat. 1096 and 63 Stat. 89) called for "transportation of wild birds and animals [*sic*] under humane and healthful conditions." Even stronger regulations were mandated by the Lacey Act Amendments of 1981. The latter, however, met with resistance and did not become effective until 1992.

The introduction of new laws notwithstanding, wild animals in the United States continued to be regarded largely as commodities up to the middle of the twentieth century. Although this view still persists in some quarters, attention began to shift in the late 1960s to endangered species or populations, which came to be regarded as unique gene pools to be saved from extinction (e.g., endangered species legislation; see Table 2-7). Over the years, there also has been an increasing tendency to view wild animals as individual beings deserving of "humane treatment."

For example, the purpose of 1976 and 1985 amendments to the 1966 Laboratory Animal Welfare Act (renamed in 1970 the Animal Welfare Act) was to make it progressively more effective in reducing injury and distress to individual animals, including marine mammals, maintained in laboratories, aquariums, and carnivals.

Similarly, the Airborne Hunting Act of 1971 ended the pursuit of Alaskan polar bears using aircraft. This Act was significant because, between 1961 and 1972, the average annual kill of polar bears in Alaska was 250, 87% of which were taken using aircraft (Gaines and Schmidt 1978).

In 1972 the U.S. Marine Mammal Protection Act was passed. Among other things, it forbade "harassment" and other forms of "taking"[7] of marine mammals, as well as the importation of any marine mammal or its products, if the animal was pregnant or nursing or was less than eight months old. The Act also specified that the taking of any marine mammal must involve "the least possible degree of pain and suffering practicable." Perhaps most significant, it defined the objective of marine mammal management, not in terms of a yield or harvest to be removed from the population annually, but in terms of the size of the population left in the wild. This new objective—the optimum sustainable population (OSP)—required that populations be maintained somewhere between the size required to produce the maximum net productivity (i.e., the number of animals required to produce the maximum sustainable yield [MSY]) and the maximum equilibrium population size (i.e., the carrying capacity). Populations reduced below OSP are deemed "depleted" and given increased protection.

The Marine Mammal Protection Act attempted to accommodate both the protectors and utilizers of marine mammals. This, of course, is not surprising, given the varied and often contradictory attitudes of society toward marine mammals, and the diverse and mutually exclusive objectives that various segments of society have for them (see Lavigne, this volume, Table 11-1). From the beginning, the Act recognized other aspects of prevailing public opinion and specifically exempted Alaska Native peoples using marine mammals for subsistence and for creating handicrafts from its take prohibition and humaneness clauses.

From the outset, the Marine Mammal Protection Act also tried to accommodate the interests of commercial fishermen, allowing permits to be issued authorizing the incidental take of marine mammals, provided the affected stocks were not depleted. Significantly, the Act was amended in 1988 to include, on an interim basis, a blanket authorization for the incidental taking of marine mammals, other than California sea otters, from any species or stock, including depleted stocks. The intentional lethal taking of species damaging catches or gear was also permitted, with the exception of Steller sea lions, any cetacean, or any marine mammals designated as depleted. A more permanent incidental taking regime was enacted in 1994. Although intentional lethal taking incidental to commercial fishing was no longer permitted, the 1994 amendments allowed "the nonlethal deterrence of marine mammals that damage the gear or catch of commercial or recreational fishermen, damage private or public property, or endanger personal safety." Under certain specified circumstances, the 1994 amendments also opened the possibility of the intentional *lethal* removal of individually identifiable nuisance pinnipeds, which habitually exhibit "dangerous or damaging" behavior by depredating threatened salmonid stocks, that cannot be deterred by any other means (see e.g., Anonymous 1994c, 1995e, 1996c; Fraker 1994; Fraker and Mate, this volume). The amendments also reopened the door for the importation by U.S. citizens of polar bear hides legally acquired in Canadian sport hunts, so long as the affected population is maintained at a sustainable level and the practice does not contribute to illegal trade in bear parts.[8]

Consistent with the shift in concern from populations to ecosystems, which is evident in Shaw's eras of wildlife conservation and management (Table 2-6), it was concern more for the state of the oceans, rather than of marine mammal populations in particular, that led to the enactment of the Marine Protection, Research, and Sanctuaries Act of 1972, which was designed mainly to prevent the dumping of harmful materials. In addition, it provided for the creation of sanctuaries along the continental shelf, to preserve "conservation, recreational, ecological, or aesthetic values." Marine mammals would presumably be among the beneficiaries of any new sanctuaries.

Five laws were also introduced to reduce the injury and killing of dolphins in commercial fisheries in the eastern tropical Pacific: the 1984 and 1988 amendments to the Marine Mammal Protection Act, the 1990 Dolphin Protection Consumer Information Act, the International Dolphin Conservation Act of 1992, and the International Dolphin Conservation Program Act of 1997. From 1971 through 1984, the estimated average annual kill of dolphins by the U.S. fleet had been 99,271, whereas from 1985 through 1992, it was only 11,596 (Hofman 1989, Marine Mammal Commission 1993; see Gosliner, this volume).

Large-scale driftnet fishing in the North Pacific had begun to arouse public indignation as early as the 1970s, largely because of its deadly impact on nontargeted species. By the mid-1980s, North Pacific fishermen were deploying up to 40,000 km of monofilament nets nightly (Marine Mammal Commission 1993). "In 1990, just 10 percent of Japan's driftnet fleet killed 1,758 whales and dolphins, 253,288 tuna, 81,956 blue sharks, 30,464 sea birds and more than 3 million non target fish" (Anonymous 1991b). Congress responded by passing the Fishery Amendments of 1982; the Driftnet Impact Monitoring, Assessment, and Control Act of 1987; and the 1992 High Seas Driftnet Fisheries Enforcement Act (see Northridge and Hofman, this volume). Congress also passed in 1992 the Hawaiian Islands National Marine Sanctuary Act to prevent the harassment of humpback whales and the 1992 Marine Mammal Health and Stranding Response Act (Wilkinson 1996).

Over the latter half of the twentieth century, the U.S. Congress has thus established that the humane treatment of wild animals (including marine mammals) is a national, as well as a state, a community, and a personal responsibility. In two specific instances, the United States also passed laws intended to influence other sovereign nations deemed not to be respecting international fishery or conservation agreements. The Pelly Amendment to the Fishermen's Protective Act of 1967,[9] enacted in 1971 and amended in 1978 and 1992, requires that the U.S. Secretary of Commerce or, in some cases, the Secretary of the Interior, notify the President whenever a foreign state acts to diminish the effectiveness of an international fishery conservation program or a program designed to protect threatened or endangered species to which the United States is party. Given an affirmative determination, the President may prohibit importation into the United States of any products from the offending country to the extent that such prohibition is permitted under the General Agreement on Tariffs and Trade (Table 2-8). More specifically, the 1979 Packwood-Magnuson Amendment (also known as the Packwood Amendment) to the Magnuson-Stevens Fishery Conservation and Management Act of 1976 imposes an automatic reduction in any fishery allocations in U.S. waters to nations certified to be diminishing the effectiveness of the International Convention for the Regulation of Whaling (Table 2-8). Although once a significant deterrent, the threat has lessened considerably as U.S. fisheries have become "Americanized" and foreign allocations have disappeared.

Trade provisions have also been used to strengthen U.S. initiatives regarding tuna purse seining operations in the eastern tropical Pacific. Section 101(a)(2) of the Marine Mammal Protection Act, as amended, includes specific comparability requirements that must be met by foreign nations seeking to import tuna into the United States. Under this provision, tuna embargoes have been imposed.

In Canada the evolution of wildlife management has generally paralleled developments in the United States, with

Table 2-8. Important International Treaties and Conventions Related to Marine Mammal Management

Era of Over-exploitation (1850–1899)	
Era of Protection (1900–1929)	
1911	Treaty for the Preservation and Protection of Fur Seals (terminated 1941)
Era of Game Management (1930–1965)	
1931	Convention for the Regulation of Whaling (came into force 1935)
1946	International Convention for the Regulation of Whaling (came into force 1948)
1946	General Agreement on Tariffs and Trade (GATT)
1957	Interim Convention on the Conservation of North Pacific Fur Seals (lapsed 1984)
Era of Environmental Management (1966–1984)	
1972	United Nations Conference on the Human Environment (Stockholm Conference)
1973	Convention on International Trade in Endangered Species of Wild Fauna and Flora
1973	Agreement on the Conservation of Polar Bears
1979	Convention on the Conservation of Migratory Species of Wild Animals
1980	Convention on the Conservation of Antarctic Marine Living Resources
1983	European Directive banning importation of products derived from whitecoated harp seals and bluebacked hooded seals
1983	United Nations Convention on the Law of the Sea
Era of ? (1985–?)	
1992	United Nations Conference on Environment and Development (Rio Conference)
1992	Agenda 21
1992	Convention on Biodiversity
1994	World Trade Agreement establishes the World Trade Organization, including GATT

certain exceptions: Canada has no marine mammal act and no federal endangered species act. Although a draft Endangered Species Protection Act, Bill C-65, passed through first reading in the House of Commons on 31 October 1996, it died on the order paper when a federal election was called in April 1997. Under Canadian law, pinnipeds and cetaceans are a federal responsibility. They are also classified as fish. The principal Canadian legislation governing the management of seals and whales is, therefore, the Fisheries Act, which has appeared in several forms since first enacted in 1868 (Table 2-9). Under the Act, a number of marine mammal protection regulations were promulgated between 1966 and 1982 (Table 2-9). These regulations actually had more to do with regulating the exploitation of various pinnipeds and cetaceans than with providing increased protection for species or their habitats. In 1993 these regulations were consolidated into a single set of regulations under the name Marine Mammal Regulations.

Ninety-two years after the United States passed its Lacey Act, Canada enacted a law regulating international and interprovincial trade in wildlife—the Wild Animal and Plant Protection and Regulation of International and Interprovincial Trade Act (Table 2-9). In 1996 Canada passed an Oceans Act. This act "mandates the Minister of Fisheries and Oceans to promote the sustainable management of our oceans and their resources" (Fisheries and Oceans Canada 1996b), reinforcing the view that under Canadian law, marine mammals are still viewed largely as resources. The Oceans Act does, however, provide for the designation of marine protected areas, which, among other things, "can be established for the purposes of conserving and protecting commercial and non-commercial fishery resources, including marine mammals, and their habitats" (Fisheries and Oceans Canada 1996b).

The recognition of "existing Aboriginal and treaty rights" in the Constitution Act, 1982 set the stage for some profound changes in marine mammal management in Canada (Anonymous 1996d:18). Although the federal Minister of Fisheries still retains ultimate authority for the conservation of fishery resources, including pinnipeds and cetaceans, the settlement of Native land claims is beginning to formalize the "cooperative management" of marine resources, giving specific management responsibilities to aboriginal peoples (Clarke 1993). Three formal cooperative management committees currently exist for Arctic marine fisheries (Clarke 1993). Under these (and other) agreements, the government has relinquished considerable control to Native resource users who, in turn, are required to take responsibility for their decisions. Native management boards are now involved in setting quotas and monitoring catches, developing regulations, carrying out stock assessments, and identifying research needs (Clarke 1993).

Such changes in Canada's relationships with Native peoples have significant ramifications for marine mammal management in the Canadian Arctic. The acknowledgment of aboriginal land claims and the signing of cooperative

Table 2-9. Important Events in Canadian Marine Mammal Management

Era of Over-exploitation (1850–1899)	
1867	British North America Act 1867 (later renamed Constitution Act 1867)
1868	Fisheries Act
Era of Protection (1900–1929)	
Era of Game Management (1930–1965)	
1954	Fisheries Act
1957	Pacific Fur Seals Convention Act
Era of Environmental Management (1966–1984)	
1966	Seal Protection Regulations (revoked 1993)
1978	Narwhal Protection Regulations (revoked 1993)
1970	An Act to amend the Fisheries Act
1977	An Act to amend the Fisheries Act and to amend the Criminal Code in consequence thereof
1980	Walrus Protection Regulations (revoked 1993)
1980	Beluga Protection Regulations (revoked 1993)
1982	Constitution Act, 1982
1982	Cetacean Protection Regulations (revoked 1993)
1985	Fisheries Act
Era of ? (1985–?)	
1992	Wild Animal and Plant Protection and Regulation of International and Interprovincial Trade Act
1993	Marine Mammal Regulations
1996	Oceans Act

Source: After Shaw (1985).

management agreements have essentially created a third tier of government (in addition to the federal and territorial governments) involved in Arctic marine mammal management (VanderZwaag and Duncan 1992). On a variety of marine mammal issues, therefore, the Canadian government is now constrained from acting alone (i.e., without the agreement of Native leaders), either within the country or in international arenas, unless there are overriding conservation concerns.

No country, especially these days, exists in isolation, so we also reviewed a number of international events that are relevant to this chapter (Table 2-8). The international pattern is similar essentially to that observed in the United States: a proliferation of treaties and conventions since 1966 that provide increasing protection for marine mammals. Most of the early developments, including the multilateral treaties and agreements involving the United States and Canada, were aimed at regulating exploitation (e.g., the Fur Seal Treaty of 1911 and the 1957 Interim Convention on the Conservation of North Pacific Fur Seals paralleled earlier-mentioned national legislation). Being whaling nations, both the United States and Canada were signatories to the 1946 International Convention for the Regulation of Whaling. Canada, as noted previously, eventually withdrew from the International Whaling Commission, despite the fact that Inuit in that country are once again hunting bowhead whales under permits unilaterally provided by the Canadian government. The renewed hunting of bowheads has been interpreted by some as a violation of the spirit, if not the intent, of the United Nations Convention on the Law of the Sea, which Canada signed but has yet to ratify, and Agenda 21, arising out of the 1992 United Nations conference in Rio de Janeiro (which it also signed). The latter specifically recognizes "the responsibility of the International Whaling Commission for the conservation and management of whale stocks and the regulation of whaling" (United Nations Conference on Environment and Development 1992). Consistent with this interpretation, U.S. President Bill Clinton considered imposing trade sanctions on Canada in early 1997. In a letter to Congress dated 10 February 1997, the President confirmed that Canada had been "certified" under section 8 of the Fishermen's Protective Act of 1967, as amended (the Pelly Amendment),[10] "for conducting whaling activities that diminish the effectiveness of the International Whaling Commission." Canada's certification, specifically, was based on "the issuance of whaling licenses by the Government of Canada in 1996 and the subsequent killing of two bowhead whales under those licenses." President Clinton instructed the State Department "to oppose Canadian efforts to address takings of marine mammals within the newly formed Arctic Council . . . [and] to oppose Canadian efforts to address trade in marine mammal products within the Arctic Council." Further, he "instructed the Department of Commerce," in implementing the Marine Mammal Protection Act, "to withhold consideration of any Canadian requests for waivers to the existing moratorium on the importation of seals and/or seal products into the United States." Noting that the International Whaling Commission had passed a resolution at its 1996 meeting encouraging Canada to refrain from issuing whaling licenses and to rejoin the Commission (International Whaling Commission 1996), President Clinton also urged Canada "to reconsider its unilateral decision to authorize whaling on endangered stocks and to authorize whaling outside the [International Whaling Commission]."

The International Whaling Commission has been much maligned over the years. Although there are some good reasons for this, we must also make the following observation (also see Gambell, this volume). Although it has often proceeded at a painfully slow pace, it has nonetheless proceeded in a consistent manner, attempting to offer increased protection for exploited whale populations at every step. Unregulated whaling was first replaced by the "blue whale unit." In retrospect, the blue whale unit virtually assured the continued overexploitation of the larger baleen whales and, as David Gaskin (1982:364) remarked, "doomed the blue whale population as surely as if no kind of quota system was in use at all." But when its failure could no longer be doubted, the blue whale unit was replaced with the new management procedure (NMP), based on the principle of maximum sustainable yield that, significantly, placed a lower bound on how far a population could be reduced before it was totally protected from further exploitation (Gaskin 1982, Holt and Young 1990). When the NMP failed to achieve both biological and economic objectives, it too was scrapped and eventually replaced in 1982 by an indefinite moratorium on commercial whaling, which came into effect in 1986–1987. In accepting that it did not know how to manage exploitation sustainably, the International Whaling Commission made an admission that few other international (or national) management authorities have been willing to acknowledge (see Lavigne, this volume). Now, the Scientific Committee of the International Whaling Commission has developed a revised management procedure (RMP) (Young 1993), which was accepted by the International Whaling Commission in 1994 (Cooke 1995). This procedure is even more precautionary than previous approaches to management. The intent is that, should the current moratorium on commercial whaling be lifted, any future whaling would be biologically sustainable.

In the interim, the International Whaling Commission

also declared the Indian Ocean a sanctuary in 1979, in part to reflect the wishes of the Indian Ocean coastal states, most of whom were not members of the Commission and had no intention of whaling. In 1994, recognizing the impossibility of ever policing whaling in the Southern Ocean, it also declared this remote area a sanctuary for an indefinite period. Several populations of whales in the Southern Ocean have been reduced to very low numbers and the sanctuary is intended to allow for their recovery.

Not all member nations agree with the direction taken by the International Whaling Commission. As noted earlier, for example, Norway and Japan have continued to hunt whales (Table 2-2) and Iceland withdrew from the Commission in 1992.

The idea for a moratorium on commercial whaling itself has a long history. It was at the 1972 United Nations Conference on the Human Environment (the Stockholm Conference) that a resolution was first passed calling for a 10-year moratorium on commercial whaling (Table 2-8). (As indicated above, it took 10 years for the International Whaling Commission to adopt the idea, and even longer before a moratorium was implemented.) Following Stockholm, the Convention on International Trade in Endangered Species of Wild Fauna and Flora was signed in Washington, D.C., in 1973 (Lyster 1985). It is intended to offer increased protection to species, including a number of marine mammals, that are threatened, or may become threatened, by legal or illegal international trade. In the same year, an international agreement was signed by five range nations—Canada, Denmark (including Greenland), Norway, the United States, and the Union of Soviet Socialist Republics—to promote the conservation of polar bears (Table 2-8) (see Lyster 1985).

A number of other international agreements provide protection for marine mammals (Table 2-8). These include the Convention for the Conservation of Antarctic Seals (1972), which will regulate future sealing in the Antarctic—this was the first international conservation agreement to be concluded prior to any significant commercial exploitation of the resource it was intended to protect (Lyster 1985); the Convention on the Conservation of Migratory Species of Wild Animals (the Bonn Convention of 1979), which recognized whales (but not seals) as highly migratory species; the Convention on the Conservation of Antarctic Marine Living Resources (1980); the United Nations Convention on the Law of the Sea (1983), which singled out marine mammal conservation for special treatment; and Agenda 21 (1992), which was mentioned above.

Moved by both scientific and ethical concerns, the European Union, as noted previously, also imposed a temporary ban on the importation of whitecoat harp and blueback hooded seal pelts in 1983. The ban was renewed in 1985 and made permanent in 1989 (Lavigne and Kovacs 1988).

Concern about the on-going loss of biodiversity (e.g., International Union for the Conservation of Nature and Natural Resources 1996) resulted in the signing of the Convention on Biodiversity at the 1992 United Nations conference in Rio de Janeiro. Canada was one of its signatories, but it has yet to implement endangered species legislation as required by the Convention. On the other hand, the United States, which arguably has the most advanced endangered species legislation of any country, did not sign the Biodiversity Convention.

Finally, if one is looking for glimpses of where things may be heading in the future, it is worthwhile to remember that the 1972 United Nations conference in Stockholm was about the "human environment" and that its 1992 conference in Rio was about "environment *and development*" (emphasis added).

Scientific Research

Increasing concern for the well-being of marine mammals as individuals and as species, together with the appearance of radically new federal laws calling for data on marine mammals, would be expected to stimulate scientific research. Indeed, such a relationship is evidenced by the growing number of researchers and research projects, and the corresponding number of publications concerned with marine mammals.

In 1949 the journal *Ecology* began to publish guides to life history studies of important animal groups. A 1952 guide included a bibliography of 146 books and articles in the field of marine mammalogy (Scheffer 1952). Among their authors were about 70 scientists who were engaged in marine mammal research in various parts of the world. Contrast that number with the 885 men and women in 50 different countries who, in 1988, identified themselves as "marine mammal scientists" (Pearson 1988). Although the above comparison is not rigorous, data from the U.S. National Marine Fisheries Service and the National Biological Service (Waring 1996) confirm the upward trend. From 1976 to 1995 the number of people assigned to marine mammal administration and research in the United States more than doubled from 100 to 213 (Fig. 2-14). Similarly, the number of federally funded research projects reported to the Marine Mammal Commission increased from 113 in 1974 to 213 in 1995 (Fig. 2-15).

In tandem with the number of marine mammal administrators and researchers, and their funded projects, one might assume that dollar funding would also have increased. The raw data seem to show this relationship, but

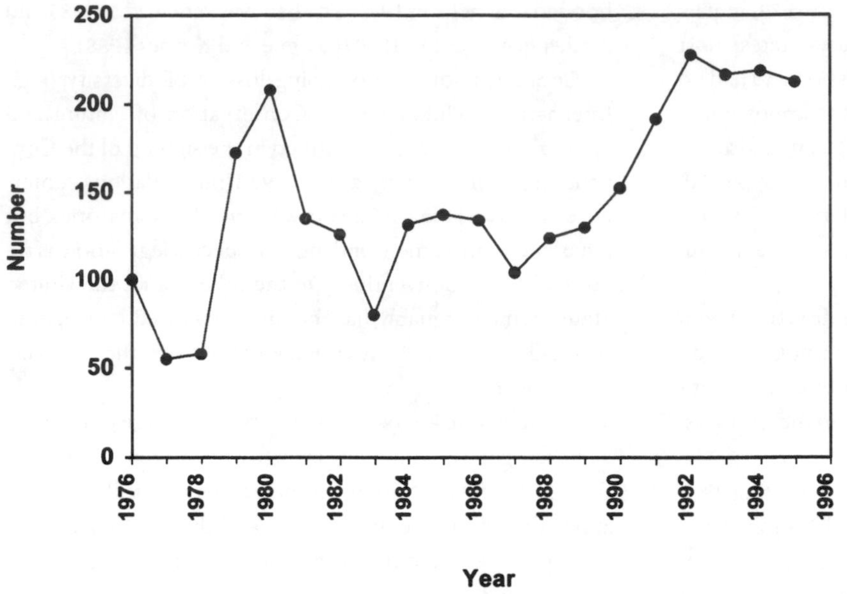

Figure 2-14. Number of people employed in marine mammal research and administration in the United States (Waring 1996).

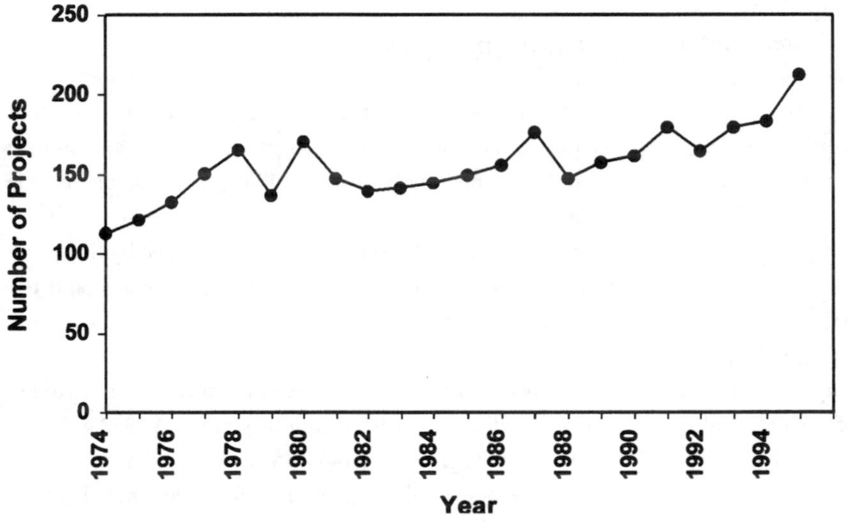

Figure 2-15. Number of marine mammal projects funded by the U.S. government (Waring 1996).

when they are corrected by the consumer price index, U.S. support for marine mammal research (expressed in 1978 dollars) has actually remained virtually unchanged (Fig. 2-16). Essentially the same picture emerges when marine mammal research dollars are expressed as a percentage of total science funding—both standardized to 1978 dollars using the same price index (Fig. 2-17).

How were research funds partitioned among various government agencies and among marine mammal taxa? During the 16 fiscal years 1976–1991, the U.S. government spent $242 million on marine mammal research (Waring 1992). That sum was spent by 24 agencies, the greater proportion (92.4%) by only five: the Departments of the Interior, Commerce, Defense, Health and Human Services, and the National Science Foundation. By taxon, the subjects of research were cetaceans, 63%; pinnipeds, 19%; polar bears and sea otters, together, 14%; and sirenians, 4%.

To analyze trends in the number of scientific publications arising from marine mammal research, we searched two databases: the Aquatic Sciences and Fisheries Abstracts (ASFA) produced by Cambridge Scientific Abstracts and released as two SilverPlatter CD-ROMs dated 1978–1987 and 1988–1996, which produced "hits" (using all the obvious key words for marine mammal taxa) spanning the years 1974–1996, and Wildlife Review and Fisheries Review (WRFR), 1971–September 1996, produced by the National Information Service Corporation and released as NISC CD-ROMs, which provided "hits" from 1932 to 1996. The results for the years 1950–1995 are summarized in Figure 2-18. Both databases show a far greater increase in publication

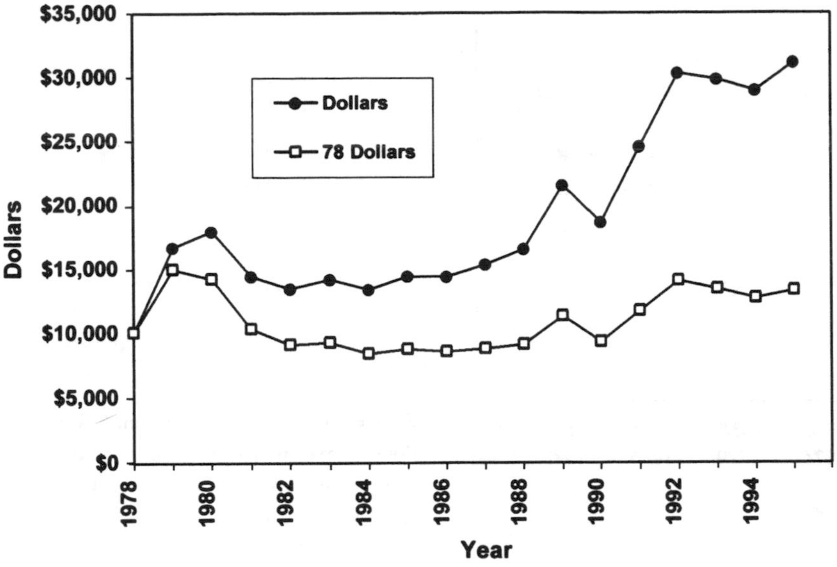

Figure 2-16. Research dollars (in absolute terms and corrected to constant 1978 dollars using the consumer price index) invested in marine mammal research by the U.S. government (Waring 1996).

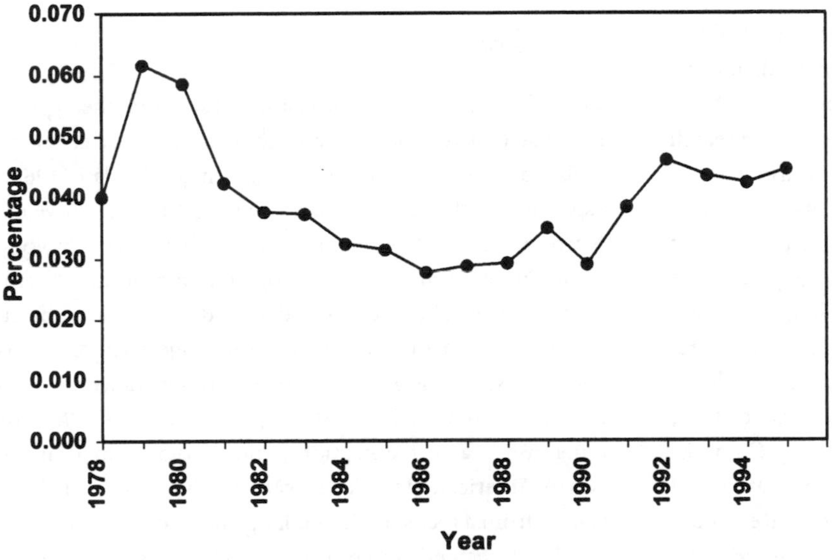

Figure 2-17. Marine mammal research dollars, expressed as a percentage of total science funding by the U.S. government (Waring 1996).

rate from 1975 to the present than would be expected from trends in numbers of scientists, numbers of projects, and (perhaps most important) research funding.

In pace with the growth of marine mammal research, new laboratories and societies designed to further it came into being. Among the new societies was the International Association of Aquatic Animal Medicine, founded in 1969 in part to improve the husbandry of captive marine mammals. The association holds an annual conference and now has about 650 members in the United States, Canada, and Mexico, as well as in Argentina, Israel, South Africa, China, Japan, and Australia (International Association for Aquatic Animal Medicine 1996). Among the new laboratories was the Biological Sonar Laboratory (affiliated with Stanford Research Institute from 1964 to 1970 and later independent), a brainchild of physicist Thomas C. Poulter. In 1964 Poulter organized the first Conference on Biological Sonar and Diving Mammals. After the tenth and last conference in 1973, the laboratory closed. In 1974 its files went to Kenneth S. Norris at the University of California, Santa Cruz. Marine mammalogists nonetheless continued to hold meetings, and in 1981 Norris and others founded the Society for Marine Mammalogy. The Society now publishes a journal, *Marine Mammal Science,* and holds biennial meetings. Its 1995 meeting in Orlando, Florida, drew nearly 1,600 participants.

Moreover, universities became increasingly involved in marine mammal research. Since the 1960s laboratories have been established, for example, at the University of California at Santa Cruz and at Texas A&M University at Galveston. In Canada, laboratories opened at the University of

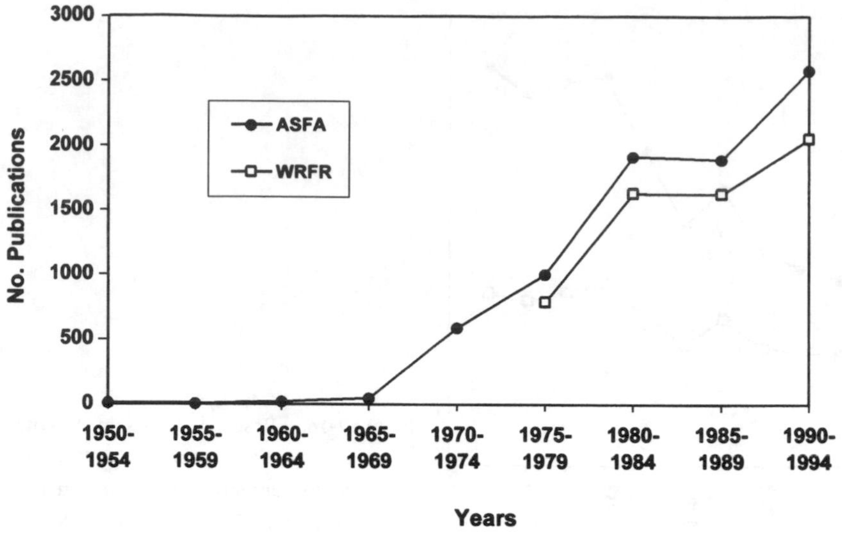

Figure 2-18. Number of scientific publications on marine mammals (per decade) recorded in two bibliographic databases (see text for details).

Guelph (now closed); Dalhousie University in Halifax; Memorial University in St. John's, Newfoundland; and the University of British Columbia in Vancouver.

Changes in the quantity of marine mammal research have been accompanied by *qualitative* changes (also see Hofman 1995). Research is becoming more concerned with marine mammals as individuals, as well as stocks. Throughout its history, marine mammal science has largely been the study of dead animals, as in commercial whaling and sealing (Watson 1981). Although such "invasive" or "lethal" research is still conducted, it is being increasingly replaced by "noninvasive" or "benign" methods (e.g., Scheffer 1980, Payne 1995). In 1988 the International Whaling Commission held a workshop on the use of photo identification and other remote sensing techniques to estimate cetacean population parameters (Hammond et al. 1990). In 1995 the World Wide Fund for Nature, the International Fund for Animal Welfare, and Greenpeace sponsored a workshop on nonlethal whale research in the Southern Ocean sanctuary, the report of which was later submitted to the International Whaling Commission (Anonymous 1995f). Such nonlethal approaches as sighting surveys, acoustics, photo identification and photogrammetry, tagging and instrumentation, biological sampling of live animals, observer programs, and behavioral observations now provide high-quality scientific information to address a number of important questions. Indeed, the revised management procedure of the International Whaling Commission requires as input data only recent abundance estimates and historical catch data to set catch limits (Cooke 1995). No additional animals need be killed for the purpose of carrying out the estimation procedures.

Discussion

Virtually every indicator we examined supports the hypothesis that North American attitudes toward marine mammals have shifted and broadened since the late 1960s, especially in the United States. During the past 30 years, North Americans have gained new insights into the biology of marine mammals and developed admiration for them. Such changes in awareness and attitudes have brought increased concern for threatened and endangered populations and ecosystems, as well as an increased reluctance to harm individual animals for reasons perceived as needless or cruel. With a few exceptions, most notably in Canada, North American attitudes toward marine mammals have shifted from a focus on their killing and material utilization to a more aesthetic interest in observing these creatures in the wild, in captivity, and in various media forms.

Not all marine mammals, however, have been equal beneficiaries of attitudinal change. Pinnipeds, for example, are more likely to be hunted, culled, or placed on public display than are cetaceans. Cetacean watching is more popular and widespread than is seal watching. Whales are more often featured in books and magazine articles, on television programs, and in music and motion pictures, than are seals and other marine mammals (Table 2-10). Whales are more often singled out in international agreements than are seals and other marine mammals. That the Florida manatee gets proportionately more attention than might be expected for a single species undoubtedly reflects the special concern that Americans have for "native" endangered species.

The change in attitudes toward whales, in particular, has led some people to conclude that they now occupy a unique

Table 2-10. Relative Representation of Marine Mammal Taxa in Various Indices Considered in This Chapter

Taxon	No. of Species	% Species	% of Captive Marine Mammals	% *National Geographic* Articles	% Books	% Movies	% Funding
Cetaceans	49	74	28	55	68	71	63
Pinnipeds	14	21	68	39	23	25	19
Sea otters	1	2	2	2	3	0	
Polar bears	1	2	N/A[a]	2	3	4	
(Sea otters/ Polar bears)	(2)[b]	(4)	(N/A)	(4)	(6)	(4)	(14)
Manatees	1	1	2	2	4	0	4

[a]Data for polar bears not included (Asper et al. 1990).

[b]Parentheses indicate data for sea otters and polar bears combined.

place in the hearts and minds of North Americans. "The whale," said Gilbert Grosvenor (1976:721), then president of the National Geographic Society, "has become a symbol for a way of thinking about our planet and its creatures." And Roger Payne (1995:15) believes that whales "are the only animals that can impress us enough to persuade us to change our minds about the importance of the wild world." Yet when Americans were asked in the late 1970s to rank 33 animals in terms of "species preference," "whale" and "walrus" (a pinniped) ranked only sixteenth and seventeenth, behind such animals as "dog, horse, swan, robin, butterfly, eagle, elephant, raccoon, and moose" (Kellert 1980). And when Americans were asked in a 1997 poll how concerned they were with the welfare and treatment of seven animal groups, whales tied for second with elephants (68% were extremely or very concerned about both groups), behind dogs and cats (78%), only one percentage point ahead of "African wildlife in general," and seven points higher than primates (Penn, Schoen and Berland Associates 1997). Obviously, some people may be persuaded by whales to change their minds about "the importance of the wild world." But for others the most powerful symbols are other animals—like the giant panda (*Ailuropoda melanoleuca*), elephants (*Loxodonta africana* and *Elephas maximus*), harp seal pups, or wolves (*Canis lupus*)—or even old-growth or tropical rain forests.

It is also apparent that North American attitudes toward whales, and marine mammals generally, are tempered by concerns for Native peoples and their cultures. Where these concerns come into conflict, public opinion, policy, and law have tended to favor the interests of Native peoples. Obviously, this interpretation is from the perspective of North American society as currently constituted. Many Native groups would argue that so long as they are denied "first nation" status and the right to self-determination, their interests will always be subjugated by those of the majority.

North American society is, nonetheless, much more likely to support exploitation of marine mammals by aboriginal peoples, particularly for subsistence and cultural reasons, than they are to support their commercial exploitation by nonnatives. Here, subsistence means using wildlife locally for food, clothing, and shelter, and for making tools, rather than putting wildlife products into trade. Native groups have argued, however, that such definitions deny the right of their cultures, including the concept of "subsistence" hunting, to evolve. Canada addressed this issue at the 1985 meeting of the Convention on International Trade in Endangered Species in Buenos Aires. There, it redefined "subsistence" hunting as anything that turns an animal into "hard cash." The argument is that if a Native person sells wildlife products into trade, the money earned can be used to buy the necessities of life. Using this definition, commercial exploitation qualifies as "subsistence" hunting (Wenzel 1991, Caulfield 1994). Semantics aside, the fact remains that, in both the United States and Canada, aboriginal peoples have been granted special status to hunt marine mammals, including endangered species such as the bowhead whale. Today, graphic media reports about the killing of bowhead whales by Native people in the Canadian Arctic, no matter how gruesome or wasteful (La Semaine Verte 1997), elicit little response from within the country, and the government largely ignores international reactions, such as those voiced by the International Whaling Commission and President Clinton, mentioned previously.

The overall change in North American attitudes toward marine mammals has in many respects paralleled the evolution of attitudes toward the environment, endangered species, and wilderness. Increasing awareness of the state of the environment is often dated from the publication of Rachel Carson's *Silent Spring* (1962). Awareness of endangered species was enhanced with the publication of the International Union for the Conservation of Nature and Natural Resources' first Red Data Book of threatened and endangered species in 1966 (Simon 1966). Renewed interest in and concern for wilderness followed the publication of Nash's (1967) classic book, *Wilderness and the American Mind.* Such concerns were strengthened by warnings about the exponential growth of the human population (Ehrlich 1968), the 1972 United Nations Conference on the Human Environment in Stockholm, and the growing acceptance that nonhuman organisms have intrinsic (Singer 1975) and legal (Stone 1972) "rights." A detailed discussion of these broader events is beyond the scope of this chapter, but Donald Worster's history of ecology (1977, 1994), Nash's (1989) history of environmental ethics, and Kellert's (1996) *The Value of Life* provide starting points for students who wish to learn more about the larger context in which attitudes toward marine mammals have evolved.

In the specific case of marine mammals, changes in North American attitudes arose through a widening of understanding and a shifting of ethical values and thus reflect the influences of both reason and sentiment. Such changes in attitudes, like the environmental movement itself (Nash 1989), were promoted during the 1960s by a young, well-educated, upwardly mobile, and disproportionately large "baby boomer" generation, which sustained the movement for the next 30 years.

Changing attitudes were also facilitated undoubtedly by a rapid and continuing population shift from rural to urban environments (The Canadian World Almanac 1987, U.S. Census Bureau 1995), the rise of the women's movement (e.g., Jackson et al. 1989), and the emergence of new environmental philosophies, including "deep ecology" and ecofeminism (Zimmerman et al. 1993).

In addition, the influence of a rapidly growing communications field, from the increasing accessibility of television that started in the 1950s to the emergence of the World Wide Web in the 1990s, cannot be underestimated. Increased knowledge about and familiarity with marine mammals through the development of new research techniques, the emergence of novel scientific findings, and increased media attention further embellish the image of marine mammals in the public eye.

A number of other factors have helped to shape human attitudes and actions toward marine mammals during the twentieth century. For example, the increasing availability of petroleum hydrocarbons offered an economical alternative to many oil products derived from whales and seals (Ellis 1991). Declining economic prospects, exacerbated by an increasing scarcity of large whales due to overexploitation, contributed to the demise of commercial whaling enterprises (Ellis 1991). It was public opinion in Europe—where most of the traditional markets for seal pelts resided—rather than in Canada or the United States that led originally to the 1983 European import ban on seal pup products (Lavigne and Kovacs 1988), the decline in the seal hunt throughout the 1980s and early 1990s (Figs. 2-5 and 2-6), and ultimately, to the Canadian government's ban on the commercial hunt for whitecoats and bluebacks.

The evolution of attitudes toward marine mammals in North America and elsewhere has not gone unnoticed or unchallenged by those who still want to exploit them consumptively for commercial purposes. Countries such as Japan and Norway continue certain of their whaling activities in opposition to the spirit and intent of the global moratorium on commercial whaling. They also continue to promote commercial whaling in a variety of international forums, reflecting public attitudes in those countries. Norway, together with Iceland, the Faroe Islands, and Greenland, also promotes sealing and whaling through the North Atlantic Marine Mammal Commission (North Atlantic Marine Mammal Commission 1994). And "sustainable use" or "wise use" groups like the High North Alliance (High North Alliance 1997) and the World Council of Whalers (World Council of Whalers 1997), among others, have appeared on the scene to counter the activities and successes of pro-animal conservation groups, including those that oppose both whaling and sealing (Rowell 1996).

The "wise use movement" deserves some comment. It differs considerably from the traditional conservation movement, which originated in North America in the early years of the twentieth century (Pinchot 1947, Leopold 1966, Nash 1989, Worster 1994) and, arguably, built the most successful system of wildlife management anywhere in the world (Geist 1993, 1994; Lavigne et al. 1996). The conservation movement, from its early days, was not an antiuse movement but one which was predicated on the idea of "wise use" (Pinchot 1947). It promoted the idea that if natural resources were to be used, then such use should be sustainable (Pinchot 1947, International Union for the Conservation of Nature and Natural Resources / United Nations Environment Programme / World Wildlife Fund 1980). In those days, "sustainable use" meant that populations should not be reduced to levels from which they could not easily recover (International Union for the Conservation of Nature and Natural Resources / United Nations Environment Programme / World Wildlife Fund 1980). The emerging conservation movement also required that resources not be wasted (Pinchot 1947) and that management decisions should be based on the best available scientific information. As this movement evolved, largely through trial and error, it became more and more precautionary in its approach, for example, banning market hunting and trade in many wildlife species and placing limits on the size to which natural populations could be reduced, while still attempting to maximize the yield removed from them (Lavigne et al. 1996).

The "wise use movement" of the latter twentieth century is something quite different (Lavigne et al. 1996). In the United States, it dates from 1988 (Gottlieb 1989), and today it comprises a largely informal amalgamation of individuals and groups from around the world. In their own words, they "fight for private property, individual liberties and free enterprise against environmentalist oppression" (Center for the Defense of Free Enterprise 1994:3). When it comes to marine mammals (and wildlife, generally) the movement advocates and promotes the "consumptive" use of resources under the mantra of "sustainable utilization." They do not distinguish between consumptive use and "nonconsumptive use" (e.g., Southern Africa Sustainable Use Specialist Group 1996), regardless of whether the latter, as usually defined, might on occasion be equally or more profitable, and more likely sustainable, than the former. In essence, they argue that, to be conserved, animals must have value in the marketplace, a perspective that has come to be known as "the use it or lose it" philosophy (Child and Child 1990, Baskin 1994).

One apparent strategy of the "wise use movement" is to exploit the ambivalent views of society toward wildlife and aboriginal peoples. In Arctic regions, marine mammals are the target animals; in Africa, it is terrestrial species, especially elephants (Adams and McShane 1992, Bonner 1993, Freeman and Kreuter 1994). Viewed from this perspective, the opening of an office by the World Council of Whalers on an Indian reservation in British Columbia may not be coincidental. Rather, one might postulate, it is putting into practice a strategy first suggested in 1985 by the Canadian Department of External Affairs in a paper entitled, "In Defense of the Fur Trade." To counteract the threat posed by the "antifur movement" (Doncaster 1988) to the future of the fur industry, the paper noted that "dramatic counter action" may be required. "Such action," the paper continued, "could be based on contradictory emotional themes to the same target publics, e.g., preservation of indigenous cultures." In other words, by aligning itself with Native groups, the fur industry—or in this instance, whalers—might hope to counteract public opposition to the exploitation of wildlife by capitalizing on society's concern for Native peoples. The strategy is now frequently extended in an attempt to create the image that all whalers, including Norwegians, Japanese, Faroese, and Icelanders, are at least "semiaboriginal" (Stroud 1996:60). In its opening statement to the 1996 meeting of the International Whaling Commission, Norway, for example, stated, "The Norwegian traditional small type minke whaling is not unlike some of the aboriginal whaling today." By adopting such a strategy, any attacks on whaling activities—including commercial whaling, whether it is portrayed as above as "traditional" or not—can always be countered with charges of "ethnocentrism,"[11] "cultural arrogance," "cultural imperialism" (Kalland 1993, Stroud 1996), or "cultural racism."[12]

In the last decade, proponents of "wise use" have become prominent participants in such international forums as the International Union for the Conservation of Nature and Natural Resources (now the World Conservation Union), the International Whaling Commission, and the Convention on International Trade in Endangered Species. They were also active at the 1992 United Nations Conference on Environment and Development. In such forums, they promote the consumptive exploitation and free trade of wildlife, its parts, and derivatives, all in the name of "conservation." Their objective, it seems, is to roll back the gains, including national and international legislation, that have been made in past decades by more traditional conservationists, which have provided increased protection for wildlife (including marine mammals) against unsustainable and inhumane practices.

The "wise use movement" has been quite successful in appropriating the language of the traditional conservation movement, co-opting (and redefining) such terms and concepts as "wise use," "sustainable use," "sustainable development," and the "precautionary principle." Such terms have long been used by the traditional conservationists, dating back in some cases to the early years of the twentieth century (Pinchot 1947). But now, they are taking on new meanings. For example, a publication produced by the Southern Africa Sustainable Use Specialist Group of IUCN's Species Survival Commission (1996:16) argued that "The precautionary principle should be applied in this sense: it is risky not to use resources—therefore we should use them." It also said "there is no arbitrary population size threshold below which use should be prohibited . . ." (p. 15). Further, the document claimed that "use can be regarded as sustainable . . . provided a species population is not reduced to the level that extinction is a real threat . . ." (p. 15). Such statements, which "are not necessarily those of the . . . [Species Survival Commission] or IUCN," are obviously aimed at currently accepted definitions—which emerged out of the traditional conservation movement—of what constitutes both a sustainable yield and a sustainable population. Consider, for example, the definitions of "optimum sustainable population" and "depleted population" under the U.S. Marine Mammal Protection Act. Also consider what the United Nations Convention on the Law of the Sea had to say about the management of whale stocks and the fact that the International Whaling Commission has long deemed that populations reduced to about half of their original size require protection from further exploitation.

The "wise use movement" may be seen as an integral part of the shift in Western societies toward the conservative right, which has also been promoting, with some success, free trade and the globalization of the economy (Rowell 1996). On its side, it has the World Trade Organization, which tends to view any legislation that offers increased protection to animals or their environments as an impediment to free trade. Now, countries can challenge such protective legislation as being in violation of World Trade Organization rules. Mexico, for example, has challenged the U.S. ban on tuna caught in ways in which dolphins were incidentally killed in the eastern tropical Pacific (Housman and Zaelke 1992). The High North Alliance has circulated a legal opinion that the U.S. Marine Mammal Protection Act may be in violation of the General Agreement on Tariffs and Trade under which the World Trade Organization operates (McDorman 1995, but see Jenkins 1996). Similar suggestions have been made regarding the European Union import ban on seal pup products. A resolution, submitted by a number of "wise use" nongovernmental organizations, requesting that the European Union rescind its directive (Anonymous 1997e) was defeated at the 1996 meeting of the International Union for Conservation of Nature and Natural Resources in Montreal. Nonetheless, only weeks after the 1997 Conference of the Parties to the Convention on International Trade in Endangered Species in Zimbabwe, a headline in the *New York Times* read: "Whalers say the wind is turning in their favor" (Gibbs 1997:A4).

It is too early to say whether the "wise use movement" will leave the sort of lasting mark on marine mammal conservation implied by the *New York Times* headline or whether any apparent gains it has made thus far will be seen in retrospect only as short-term setbacks to the conservation advances made earlier this century. It is clear, nonetheless, that as we approach the end of the second millennium, we are at a crossroads. Following the period of 1960–1987 in which attitudes toward marine mammals clearly became more benevolent, we are now witnessing a reversal in some quarters. Some have called it "the war against the greens" (Helvarg 1994); others characterize it as the "green backlash" (Rowell 1996) or "brownlash" (Ehrlich and Ehrlich 1996). Viewed dispassionately, what currently confronts society is a classic conflict among three different worldviews: that of the environmental and pro-animal movements, which is characterized largely by moralistic and humanistic attitudes toward animals and their habitats; that of the traditional conservation movement, which is characterized largely by scientistic and ecologistic attitudes; and that of the "wise use movement," which is characterized by the utilitarian and dominionistic attitudes that, in past centuries, composed the dominant worldview. To the extent that such conflicts are ever resolved, the outcome will ultimately be determined, in democratic countries at least, by the weight of public opinion, expressed either in the marketplace or through the ballot box (Lavigne 1985).

How the current conflict of attitudes and objectives eventually works out will determine the name of the current era of wildlife management in North America (Table 2-6). If the trends established between 1966 and 1984 are any indication, it may well end up being remembered as the era of conservation biology, after the emerging field of environmental research of the same name, with its several journals (e.g., *Conservation Biology, Biological Conservation*) and textbooks bearing similar titles (e.g., Meffe and Carroll 1994). The other possibility is that the current period will be remembered as the era of "wise use," a time when the conservation gains of the twentieth century began to erode, ostensibly to facilitate economic growth and development through the consumptive use of wildlife and international trade in wildlife products. If this were to occur, the twentieth century would be viewed, in retrospect, as an anomaly, a time when people tried, for a while at least, to reduce their impacts on wild populations and their habitats, and, to their own detriment, ultimately failed.

Acknowledgments

We thank John Twiss for inviting us to participate in the writing of this chapter. At various stages of its evolution, the manuscript benefitted from five anonymous reviews. In addition, Randy Reeves, John Twiss, Mike Gosliner, Stuart Innes, David Johnston, Peter Meisenheimer, Suzanne Montgomery, and Vassili Papastavrou provided constructive comments on the manuscript, in whole or in part. Numerous people also generously assisted in procuring data. These include Anne Veronica Chesworth, Merritt Clifton, Janice Hannah, Stuart Innes, Suzanne Montgomery, David Johnston, Vassili Papastavrou, Barb Stewart, Randy Reeves, and John Reynolds III. Original research included in the chapter was funded by the International Marine Mammal Association.

Notes

1. Letter signed by Hubert Markshtum, Makah Tribal Council, and Ben Johnson, Makah Whaling Commission, on the letterhead of the Makah Tribal Council, dated 9 June 1997, provided to the authors by the Sea Shepherd Conservation Society.
2. *Metcalf* v. *Daley*, no. C98-5289FDB (W.D. Wash. 21 Sept. 1998) (order granting summary judgment).
3. After completion of this chapter, the Canadian government revised its catch statistics for the 1997 seal hunt. The figure for harp seals increased to 264,204 (see Lavigne [in press]).

4. A number of examples are documented in an unpublished 1996 report by Greenpeace, entitled "What Do Norway's Whalers Really Want?"
5. Public Law 102-346, 106 Stat. 928.
6. There are many descriptions of the selkie myth but none more endearing than that found on the insert of the audiocassette *Seal Song* by Ossian (Iona Records 1981). "Seals have been a subject of Scottish myth and superstition since time immemorial. Caithness fishermen believed they were fallen angels, Shetlanders believed that 'certain persons came over from Norway in the guise of seals' and that these 'sea-trows' could cast off their skins and walk on land like ordinary humans. The females were reputed to be of great beauty and it was said that if their discarded seal-skins were seized, they would be unable to return to the sea. The McCodrum family of North Uist were believed to be descended from a sealwoman who fled back to the sea when one of her sons unwittingly gave her back the seal-skin which his father had hidden in the family chest."
7. The term *take* is statutorily defined in the United States to mean "to harass, hunt, capture, or kill, or attempt to hunt, capture, or kill, any marine mammal."
8. 16 U.S.C. §1374(a)(5), 50 C.F.R. §18.30.
9. 85 Stat. 786.
10. 22 U.S.C. §1978.
11. See note 1 above.
12. Ibid.

Literature Cited

Abella, R. S. 1997. Judges should make law—and always have. Toronto Star, 24 April, p. A25.

Ackerman, D. 1992. Last refuge of the monk seal. National Geographic 181 (1): 128–144.

Adams, J. S., and T. O. McShane. 1992. The Myth of Wild Africa: Conservation without Illusion. W. W. Norton and Company, New York, NY.

Alder, S. J. 1991. Boston aquarium countersues activists. Wall Street Journal, 18 September, p. B6.

Alliance of Marine Mammal Parks and Aquariums. N.d. Alliance of Marine Mammal Parks and Aquariums, Alexandria, VA. 1 p.

Anonymous. 1975. In praise of whales. Animal Welfare Institute Quarterly 24 (4): 6.

Anonymous. 1979. Whales and ethics. A national symposium relative to world policy. Sponsored by American Cetacean Society, Connecticut Cetacean Society, Center for Action on Endangered Species, Center for Oceans Law and Policy, The Humane Society of the United States, National Audubon Society, Ocean Education Project, and the Oceanic Society. 11 April 1979, Washington, DC.

Anonymous. 1983. Whales Alive: Report of Global Conference on the Non-Consumptive Utilisation of Cetacean Resources. 7–11 June 1983, Boston, MA. IWC/35/19. Connecticut Cetacean Society, Wethersfield, CT; Animal Welfare Institute, Washington, DC.

Anonymous. 1991a. Annual summary of fish and marine mammal harvest data for the Northwest Territories. 1988–1989. Vol. 1. Fisheries and Oceans, Canada, Ottawa.

Anonymous. 1991b. U.S. to ban imported fish caught in drift nets. The Seattle Times, 19 September, p. A12.

Anonymous. 1992a. Annual summary of fish and marine mammal harvest data for the Northwest Territories. 1989–1990. Vol. 2. Fisheries and Oceans, Canada, Ottawa.

Anonymous. 1992b. Annual summary of fish and marine mammal harvest data for the Northwest Territories. 1990–1991. Vol. 3. Fisheries and Oceans, Canada, Ottawa.

Anonymous. 1992c. Capture and maintenance of cetaceans in Canada. A report prepared by the Advisory Committee on Marine Mammals for the Minister of Fisheries and Oceans. Ottawa, Canada. 52 pp.

Anonymous. 1992d. Marine mammal protection in Canada. Blueprint for change. Petition to the Government of Canada signed by 29 nongovernmental organizations. 4 pp.

Anonymous. 1992e. Who gets the money? Budgets, expenses, and assets. Animal People (December): 12–14.

Anonymous. 1993a. Annual summary of fish and marine mammal harvest data for the Northwest Territories. 1991–1992. Vol. 4. Fisheries and Oceans, Canada, Ottawa.

Anonymous. 1993b. Flamingo Land dolphins fly out. The Yorkshire (U.K.) Evening Press, 9 March, p. 1.

Anonymous. 1993c. Who gets the money? Budgets, expenses, and assets. Animal People (December): 11–14.

Anonymous. 1993d. Foes of marine-mammal parks try to capitalize on "Free Willy." Bellevue (WA) Journal American, 23 July, p. A2.

Anonymous. 1994a. Annual summary of fish and marine mammal harvest data for the Northwest Territories. 1992–1993. Vol. 5. Fisheries and Oceans, Canada, Ottawa.

Anonymous. 1994b. Who gets the money? Budgets, assets, fundraising, and overhead. Animal People (December): 11–14.

Anonymous. 1994c. Report and recommendations of the Ballard Locks Pinniped-Fishery Interaction Task Force. 22 November (corrected version).

Anonymous. 1995a. Tobin announces 1996 Atlantic seal management plan. Government of Canada News Release NR-HQ-95-142E, 18 December. 2 pp.

Anonymous. 1995b. Annual summary of fish and marine mammal harvest data for the Northwest Territories. 1993–1994. Vol. 6. Fisheries and Oceans, Canada, Ottawa.

Anonymous. 1995c. Joint statement. The Ministers of Fisheries for Canada, the Faroe Islands, Iceland, Norway, Russia, and the Representative of Greenland. 19 October. Office of the Minister of Fisheries and Oceans, Canada, Ottawa.

Anonymous. 1995d. Who gets the money? Budgets, assets, fundraising, and overhead. Animal People [no month]: 1–4.

Anonymous. 1995e. Report and recommendations of the Ballard Locks Pinniped-Fishery Interaction Task Force. Evaluation of effectiveness of 1995 actions and additional recommendations for the 1995/96 activities. 8 November.

Anonymous. 1995f. Report of a workshop to outline a programme of non-lethal whale research in the Southern Ocean Sanctuary. 2–5 May 1995, Galway, Ireland. IWC/SC/47/019.

Anonymous. 1996a. Report on the Workshop on the Scientific Aspects of Managing Whale-Watching. 30 March–4 April 1995, Montecastello di Vibio, Italy. International Fund for Animal Welfare, Crowborough, U.K.

Anonymous. 1996b. Who gets the money? Animal People (December): 11–14.

Anonymous. 1996c. Report and recommendations of the Ballard Locks Pinniped-Fishery Interaction Task Force. Evaluation of effectiveness of 1995/96 actions and additional recommendations for 1996/97 activities. 25 October.

Anonymous. 1996d. People to people, nation to nation. Highlights from the Report of the Royal Commission on Aboriginal Peoples. Minister of Supply and Services, Canada, Ottawa.

Anonymous. 1997a. Whaling Commission approves combined Russian-Makah gray whale quota. United States Delegation News Release. 23 October. Forty-ninth Meeting of the International Whaling Commission, Monaco.

Anonymous. 1997b. Statement on aboriginal subsistence whaling. Australian Delegation. 23 October. Forty-ninth Meeting of the International Whaling Commission, Monaco.

Anonymous. 1997c. Whalers open secretariat with Nuu-chah-nulth. Alberni Valley Times (Port Alberni, B.C., Canada), 27 February, p. A1.

Anonymous. 1997d. Videohound's Golden Movie Retriever. Visible Ink Press, Detroit, MI.

Anonymous. 1997e. Conservation of harp seals. Resolution CGR1.79 submitted to the IUCN World Conservation Congress. 14–23 October 1996, Montreal, Canada.

Asper, E. D., D. A. Duffield, N. Dimeo-Ediger, and E. D. Shell. 1990. Marine mammals in zoos, aquaria and marine zoological parks in North America: 1990 census report. International Zoo Yearbook 29:179–187.

Associated Press. 1997. Makah prepare to hunt whales. Vancouver Province, 27 October, p. A22.

Backer, O. F. 1948. Seal hunting off Jan Mayen. The National Geographic Magazine 48 (1): 57–72.

Barchard, W. W. 1978. Estimates of historical stock size for Northwest Atlantic harp seals, *Pagophilus groenlandicus*. M.Sc. thesis, University of Guelph, Guelph, Ontario, Canada.

Bartlett, R. A. 1928. The sealing saga of Newfoundland. The National Geographic Magazine 56 (1): 91–130.

Baskin, Y. 1994. There's a new wildlife policy in Kenya: Use it or lose it. Science 265:733–734.

Baur, D. C., M. J. Bean, and M. L. Gosliner. 1999. The laws governing marine mammal conservation in the United States. (This volume)

Beach, D. W., and M. T. Weinrich. 1989. Watching the whales: Is an educational adventure for humans turning out to be another threat for endangered species? Oceanus 32 (1): 84–88.

Bean, M. 1977. The evolution of National Wildlife Law. Prepared for the Council on Environmental Quality by the Environmental Law Institute. Superintendent of Documents, U.S. Government Printing Office, Washington, DC.

Bean, M. J. 1983. The Evolution of National Wildlife Law. Praeger, New York, NY.

Beilenson, N. 1989. Celebrating Whales. Peter Pauper Press, White Plains, NY.

Bellerive Foundation. 1990. Chairman's conclusions. Pages 78–82 *in* Proceedings, Symposium on Whales and Dolphins in Captivity. 9–10 July, Geneva, Switzerland.

Bendle, B. J., and F. W. Bell. 1995. An estimation of the total willingness to pay by Floridians to protect the endangered West Indian manatee through donations. Florida Department of Environmental Protection and Florida State University, Tallahassee, FL.

Bergman, C. 1991. Manatees and the metaphors of desire. Orion 10 (3): 20–27.

Bonner, R. 1993. At the Hand of Man. Peril and Hope for Africa's Wildlife. Alfred A. Knopf, New York, NY.

Brown, C., with H. Horwood. 1972. Death on the Ice: The Great Newfoundland Sealing Disaster of 1914. Doubleday Canada Limited, Toronto.

Busch, B. C. 1985. The War against the Seals: A History of the North American Seal Fishery. McGill-Queen's University Press, Kingston and Montreal, Canada.

Campbell, D. R. 1992. Commercial benefits of seal tourism in Canada: A study prepared for the International Fund for Animal Welfare, Yarmouth Port, MA.

Canadian Department of External Affairs. 1985. In defence of the fur trade. A Discussion Paper prepared by the Department of External Affairs, Ottawa, Canada.

Canadian Press. 1997. CBC-TV reports on the business of whaling. Cape Breton (Nova Scotia) Post, 8 November, p. 2A.

Canadian World Almanac & Book of Facts 1988, The. 1987. Global Press, Toronto.

Carson, R. 1962. Silent Spring. Fawcett Publications, Greenwich, CT.

Caulfield, R. A. 1994. Aboriginal subsistance whaling in West Greenland. Pages 263–292 *in* M. M. R. Freeman and U. P. Kreuter (eds.), Elephants and Whales: Resources for Whom? Gordon and Breach Publishers, Basel, Switzerland.

Center for the Defense of Free Enterprise. 1994. The Wise Use Address Book. One Thousand Names, Addresses of Activists for Property Rights, Jobs, Communities, and Access to Federal Lands. A report by the Center for the Defense of Free Enterprise, Bellevue, WA.

Cherfas, J. 1988. The Hunting of the Whale: A Tragedy That Must End. Penguin Books, London.

Child, G., and B. Child. 1990. An historical perspective of sustainable wildlife utilisation. Paper prepared for Workshop No. 7. 18th IUCN General Assembly, Perth, Australia.

Clark, R. McV. 1993. An overview of Canada's Arctic marine fisheries and their management with emphasis on the Northwest Territories. Pages 211–241 *in* L. S. Parsons and W. H. Lear (eds.), Perspectives on Canadian Marine Fisheries Management. National Research Council of Canada and Department of Fisheries and Oceans, Ottawa.

Clifton, M., and D. Larson. 1991a. Who gets the money? The Animals' Agenda (March): 33–35.

Clifton, M., and D. Larson. 1991b. Who gets the money? Part II. The Animals' Agenda (July/August): 34–35.

Coish, E. C. 1979. Season of the Seal. Breakwater Books Ltd., St. John's, Newfoundland, Canada.

Conway, W. 1994. Preface. Pages 13–15 *in* L. Koebner (ed.), Zoo Book: The Evolution of Wildlife Conservation Centers. Tom Doherty Associates, New York, NY.

Cooke, J. 1995. The International Whaling Commission's revised management procedure as an example of a new approach to fishery management. Pages 647–657 *in* A. S. Blix, L. Walløe, and Ø. Ulltang (eds.), Whales, Seals, Fish and Man. Proceedings of the International Symposium on the Biology of Marine Mammals in the North East Atlantic. 29 November–1 December 1994, Tromsø, Norway. Elsevier, Amsterdam.

Cousteau, J. 1992a. Dolphins. Simon & Schuster, New York, NY.

Cousteau, J. 1992b. Seals. Simon & Schuster, New York, NY.

Cousteau, J. 1993. Whales. Simon & Schuster, New York, NY.

Darling, J. D. 1988. Whales: An era of discovery. National Geographic 174 (6): 872–909.

Davies, B. 1970. Savage Luxury: The Slaughter of the Baby Seals. The Ryerson Press, Toronto.

Davies, B. 1991. Red Ice. Magna Print Books, Long Preston, North Yorkshire, England.

Daws, G. 1983. "Animal liberation" as crime: The Hawaii dolphin case. Pages 361–371 *in* H. B. Miller and W. H. Williams (eds.), Ethics and Animals. Humana Press, Clifton, NJ.

De Bell, G. 1973. Where the whales are. Saturday Review of the Sciences 1 (2): 19–20.

Dobbs, B. D. 1911. Hunting the walrus. The National Geographic Magazine 22 (3): 285–290.

Doncaster, A. (ed.). 1988. Skinned. Activists condemn the horrors of the fur trade. International Wildlife Coalition, North Falmouth, MA.

Duffus, D. A., and P. Dearden. 1990. Non-consumptive wildlife-oriented recreation: A conceptual framework. Biological Conservation 53:213–231.

Ehrlich, P. 1968. The Population Bomb. Ballantyne Books, New York, NY.

Ehrlich, P. R., and A. H. Ehrlich. 1996. Betrayal of Science and Reason: How Anti-Environmental Rhetoric Threatens Our Future. Island Press/Shearwater Books, Washington, DC/Covelo, CA.

Ellis, R. 1991. Men and Whales. Alfred A. Knopf, New York, NY.

England, G. A. 1924. Vikings of the Ice: Being the Log of a Tenderfoot on the Great Newfoundland Seal Hunt. Doubleday, New York, NY.

England, G. A. 1969. The Greatest Hunt in the World. Tundra Books, Montreal.

Fishbein, M., and I. Ajzen. 1975. Belief, Attitude, Intention and Behavior: An Introduction to Theory and Research. Addison-Wesley Publishing Company, Reading, MA.

Fisheries and Oceans Canada. 1996a. Mifflin announces 1997 Atlantic seal management measures. News Release KNOWER-HQ-96-101E, 23 December. 1 p.

Fisheries and Oceans Canada. 1996b. Minister Mifflin welcomes passage of the Oceans Act. News Release NR-HQ-96-100E, 19 December. 2 pp.

Food and Agriculture Organization. 1978. Mammals in the Seas. Vol. 1. Report of the FAO Advisory Committee on Marine Resources Research. Working Party on Marine Mammals. FAO Fisheries Series No. 5.

Foster, A. D. 1980. Cachalot. Ballantyne Books, New York, NY.

Fox, W. 1990. Toward a Transpersonal Ecology: Developing New Foundations for Environmentalism. Shambhala, Boston, MA.

Fraker, M. A. 1989. A rescue that moved the world. Oceanus 32 (1): 96–102.

Fraker, M. A. 1994. California sea lions and steelhead trout at the Chittenden Locks, Seattle, Washington. Marine Mammal Commission, Washington, DC.

Fraker, M. A., and B. R. Mate. 1999. Seals, sea lions, and salmon in the Pacific Northwest. (This volume)

Freeman, M., and S. R. Kellert. 1994. International attitudes to whales, whaling and the use of whale products: A six-country survey. Pages 293–315 *in* M. M. R. Freeman and U. Kreuter (eds.), Elephants and Whales: Resources for Whom? Gordon and Breach Publishers, Basel, Switzerland.

Freeman, M. M. R., and U. P. Kreuter (eds.). 1994. Elephants and Whales: Resources for Whom? Gordon and Breach Publishers, Basel, Switzerland.

Fry, R. K. 1995. The Secret of Roan Inish (originally published as The Secret of the Ron Mor Skerry, 1985). Hyperion Paperbacks for Children, New York, NY.

Gaines, S. E., and D. Schmidt. 1978. Laws and treaties of the United States relevant to marine mammal protection policy. (Available from National Technical Information Service, Springfield, VA. PB 281 024.)

Gambell, R. 1999. The International Whaling Commission and the contemporary whaling debate. (This volume)

Gaskin, D. E. 1982. The Ecology of Whales and Dolphins. Heinemann, London.

Gatenby, G. (ed.). 1983. Whales: A Celebration. Prentice-Hall Canada/Lester and Orpen Dennys, Toronto.

Geist, V. 1993. Great achievements, great expectations: Successes of North American wildlife management. Pages 47–72 *in* A. W. L. Hawley (ed.), Commercialization and Wildlife Management: Dancing with the Devil. Krieger Publishing Company, Malabar, FL.

Geist, V. 1994. Wildlife conservation as wealth. Nature 368:491–492.

Gibbs, W. 1997. Whalers say the wind is turning in their favor. New York Times, 23 July, p. A4.

Goldfarb, S. 1993. Federal judge rules animal right groups have no legal standing in dolphin transfer suit against aquarium. Decision sets precedent in Massachusetts courts. New England Aquarium News Release, 28 October.

Gosliner, M. L. 1999. The tuna-dolphin controversy. (This volume)

Gottlieb, A. M. (ed.). 1989. The Wise Use Agenda: The Citizen's Policy Guide to Environmental Resource Issues. A Task Force Report to the Bush Administration by the Wise Use Movement. The Free Enterprise Press, Bellevue, WA.

Graham, B. 1997. Canada and the circumpolar world: Meeting the challenges of cooperation into the twenty-first century. Report of the House of Commons Standing Committee on Foreign Affairs and International Trade, Ottawa, Canada.

Graves, W. 1976. The imperiled giants. National Geographic 150 (6): 722–751.

Griffin, E. L. 1966. Making friends with a killer whale. National Geographic 129 (3): 418–446.

Griggs, T. (compiler). 1975. There's a Sound in the Sea: A Child's Eye View of the Whale. Scrimshaw Press, San Francisco, CA.

Grosvenor, G. M. 1976. Editorial. National Geographic 150 (6): 721.

Hall, A. J. 1984. Man and Manatee: Can we live together? National Geographic 166 (3): 400–418.

Hammond, P., S. A. Mizroch, and G. P. Donovan (eds.). 1990. Individual recognition of cetaceans: Use of photo-identification and other techniques to estimate population parameters. Reports of the International Whaling Commission (Special Issue 12).

Helvarg, D. 1994. The War against the Greens: The "Wise-Use" Movement, the New Right and Anti-Environmental Violence. Sierra Club Books, San Francisco, CA.

Henke, J. S. 1985. Seal Wars! An American Point of View. Breakwater Books Ltd., St. John's, Newfoundland, Canada.

Herscovici, A. 1985. Second Nature: The Animal-Rights Controversy. CBC Enterprises, Toronto.

High North Alliance. 1997. About the High North Alliance (available on the World Wide Web at http://www.highnorth.no/hnatext.htm).

Hodges, J. A. 1993. Statement on behalf of the Marine Mammal Coalition [at a House hearing on H.R. 2760 to amend the Marine Mammal Protection Act]. 103d Cong., lst sess., 4 August. Serial No. 103-57:117–126.

Hodgkinson, V. A., M. S. Weitzman, C. M. Toppe, and S. M. Noga. 1992. Nonprofit Almanac, 1992–1993. Dimensions of the Independent Sector. Jossey-Bass Publishers, San Francisco, CA.

Hoel, A. H. 1993. Regionalization of international whale management: The case of the North Atlantic Marine Mammals [*sic*] Commission. Arctic 46:116–123.

Hofman, R. J. 1989. The Marine Mammal Protection Act: A first of its kind anywhere. Oceanus 32 (1): 21–25.

Hofman, R. J. 1995. The changing focus of marine mammal conservation. Tree 10 (11): 462–465.

Holden, C. 1978. Assertion of dolphin rights fails in court. Science 199:37.

Holt, S. J. 1993. The regulation of commercial whaling. Consideration of the commercial moratorium and Norway's resumption of minke whaling in the Northeast Atlantic. Paper presented at Symposium on Arctic Wildlife and Whaling: Conflicts in Management, convened within the 5th World Wilderness Congress. 24 September–1 October 1993, Tromsø, Norway.

Holt, S. J., and N. M. Young. 1990. Guide to Review of the Management of Whaling. Center for Marine Conservation, Washington, DC.

Housman, R. F., and D. J. Zaelke. 1992. The collision of the environment and trade: The GATT tuna / dolphin decision. Environmental Law Reporter 22:10268–10278.

Hoyt, E. 1992. Whale watching around the world: A report on its value, extent and prospects. International Whale Bulletin: Journal of the Whale Conservation Society 7:1–8.

Hoyt, E. 1995. Whalewatching takes off. Whalewatcher 29 (2): 3–7.

Humane Society of the United States. 1995. The Case against Marine Mammals in Captivity. Washington, DC.

Hutchings, J. A., C. Walters, and R. L. Haedrich. 1997. Is scientific inquiry incompatible with government information control? Canadian Journal of Fisheries and Aquatic Sciences 54:1198–1210.

Indiana University Libraries. 1993. Selected items copied from the Indiana Daily Student and the student yearbook, Arbutus (1975–1976: 54–55), relating to the National Whale Symposium of 1975. Bloomingdale, IN.

Institute for Cetacean Research. 1997. About ICR (available on the World Wide Web at http: / / www.whalesci.org / abouticr.html).

International Association for Aquatic Animal Medicine. 1996. About the IAAAM (available on the World Wide Web at http: / / members.aol.com / iaaamweb / about.html).

International Union for the Conservation of Nature and Natural Resources. 1996. Re 1996 IUCN Red List of Threatened Animals. IUCN, Gland, Switzerland.

International Union for the Conservation of Nature and Natural Resources / United Nations Environment Programme / World Wildlife Fund. 1980. World Conservation Strategy. Living Resource Conservation for Sustainable Development. Gland, Switzerland.

International Whaling Commission. 1996. Chairman's report of the forty-eighth annual meeting of the International Whaling Commission. Resolution on Canadian whaling. IWC Resolution 1996-9, p. 54.

International Whaling Commission. 1997. Proposal by the Russian Federation and the United States of America. IWC / 49 / 27 (amended). Forty-ninth Annual Meeting of the International Whaling Commission, Monaco.

International Whaling Commission. N.d. Report on infractions of the International Convention for the Regulation of Whaling, 1946. Aboriginal Subsistence Whaling. The International Whaling Commission, Histon, Cambridge, U.K.

Jackson, R. M., S. L. McCarty, and D. Rusch. 1989. Developing wildlife education strategies for women. Transactions of the North American Wildlife and Natural Resources Conference 54:445–454.

Jenkins, L. 1996. Analysis of MMPA seal provisions under GATT. The Harrison Institute for Public Law, Georgetown University Law Center, Washington, DC.

Johnson, W. 1990. The Rose-Tinted Menagerie. Heretic Books, London.

Kalland, A. 1993. Management by totemization: Whale symbolism and the anti-whaling campaign. Arctic 46:124–133.

Kaza, S. 1982. Recreational whalewatching in California: A profile. Whalewatcher 16 (1): 6–8.

Kellert, S. R. 1980. Activities of the American public relating to animals. Phase II. Results of a U.S. Fish and Wildlife Service funded study of American attitudes, knowledge and behaviors toward wildlife and natural habitats. Superintendent of Documents, U.S. Government Printing Office, Washington, DC.

Kellert, S. R. 1991. Canadian perceptions of marine mammal conservation and management in the Northwest Atlantic. International Marine Mammal Association Inc. Technical Report No. 91-04. 86 pp.

Kellert, S. R. 1993. The biological basis for human values of nature. Pages 42–69 *in* S. R. Kellert and E. O. Wilson (eds.), The Biophilia Hypothesis. Island Press, Washington, DC.

Kellert, S. R. 1996. The Value of Life: Biological Diversity and Human Society. Island Press / Shearwater Books, Washington, DC.

Kellert, S. R. 1997. Kinship to Mastery: Biophilia in Human Evolution and Development. Island Press / Shearwater Books, Washington, DC.

Kellert, S. R., and J. K. Berry. 1987. Attitudes, knowledge, and behaviors toward wildlife as affected by gender. Wildlife Society Bulletin 15:363–371.

Kellert, S. R., and M. O. Westervelt. 1982. Historical trends in American animal use and perception. Transactions of the North American Wildlife and Natural Resources Conference 47:649–664.

Kellert, S. R., J. Gibbs, and T. Wohlgenant. 1995. Canadian perceptions of commercial fisheries and marine mammal management. Anthrozoös 8:20–30.

Kelly, J. E. 1983. The value of whale-watching. Global Conference on the Non-Consumptive Utilisation of Cetacean Resources. 7–11 June 1983, Boston, MA. Transcript of talk. 11 pp.

Kenyon, K. W. 1969 (republished 1975). The Sea Otter in the Eastern Pacific Ocean. Dover Publications, New York, NY.

Kovacs, K. M., and S. Innes. 1990. The impact of tourism on harp seals (*Phoca groenlandica*) in the Gulf of St. Lawrence, Canada. Applied Animal Behaviour Science 26:15–26.

LaBudde, S. 1988. Net-death, net loss. Earth Island Journal (spring): 27–30.

Larsen, T. 1971. Polar bear: Lonely nomad of the north. National Geographic 139 (4): 574–590.

La Semaine Verte. 1997. Radio Canada, Sainte-Foy, Quebec. 9 February. 55 min.

Lavigne, D. M. 1978. The harp seal controversy reconsidered. Queen's Quarterly 85:377–388.

Lavigne, D. M. 1985. Seals, science, and politics: Reflections on Canada's sealing controversy. Brief submitted to The Royal Commission on Seals and the Sealing Industry in Canada. La Vie Wildlife Research Associates Ltd., Rockwood, Ontario, Canada.

Lavigne, D. M. 1995. Seals and fisheries, science and politics. Invited paper *in* Symposium II, The Role of Science in Conservation and Management. Eleventh Biennial Conference on the Biology of Marine Mammals. 14–18 December 1995, Orlando, FL (available on the World Wide Web at http: / / www.imma.org).

Lavigne, D. M. In press. Estimating total kill of Northwest Atlantic harp seals, 1994–1998. Marine Mammal Science.

Lavigne, D. M. 1999. The Hawaiian monk seal: Management of an endangered species. (This volume)

Lavigne, D. M., and K. M. Kovacs. 1988. Harps & Hoods: Ice-Breeding Seals of the Northwest Atlantic. University of Waterloo Press, Waterloo, Canada.

Lavigne, D. M., C. J. Callaghan, and R. J. Smith. 1996. Sustainable utilization: The lessons of history. Pages 250–265 *in* V. J. Taylor and N. Dunstone (eds.), The Exploitation of Mammal Populations. Chapman and Hall, London.

Leopold, A. 1949. A Sand County Almanac and Sketches Here and There. Oxford University Press, New York, NY.

Leopold, A. 1966. A Sand County Almanac with Essays on Conservation from Round River. A Sierra Club/Ballantine Book, New York, NY.

Lewis, K. T. 1988. Survey of attitudes and knowledge of New England whalewatchers. Yale School of Forestry and Environmental Studies, New Haven, CT.

Lilly, J. C. 1967. The Mind of the Dolphin: A Nonhuman Intelligence. Doubleday, Garden City, NY.

Lust, P. 1967. The Last Seal Pup: The Story of Canada's Seal Hunt. Harvest House, Montreal.

Lyster, S. 1985. International Wildlife Law. An Analysis of International Treaties Concerned with the Conservation of Wildlife. Grotius Publications Ltd., Cambridge.

Malouf, A. 1986. Seals and sealing in Canada. Report of The Royal Commission on Seals and the Sealing Industry in Canada. 3 vols. Supply and Services Canada, Ottawa.

Marine Mammal Commission. 1993. Annual report to Congress for 1992. (Available from National Technical Information Service, Springfield, VA. PB95-154995.)

Marine Mammal Commission. 1996. Annual report to Congress for 1995. (Available from National Technical Information Service, Springfield, VA. PB96-157482.)

Marine Mammal Commission. 1997. Annual report to Congress for 1996. (Available from National Technical Information Service, Springfield, VA. PB97-142889.)

McCloskey, W. 1979. Bitter fight still rages over the seal killing in Canada. Smithsonian 10 (8): 54–63.

McDorman, T. L. 1995. The GATT consistency of the U.S. import embargo on harp-seal fur coats from Greenland. Report contracted by The High North Alliance, Reine i Lofoten, Norway.

McIntyre, J. (ed.). 1974. Mind in the Waters: A Book to Celebrate the Consciousness of Whales and Dolphins. Scribner's and Sierra Club, New York, NY, and San Francisco, CA.

McVay, S. 1966. The last of the great whales. Scientific American 215 (2): 13–21.

Meffe, G. K., and C. R. Carroll. 1994. Principles of Conservation Biology. Sinauer Associates, Sunderland, MA.

Mellman Group, The. 1996. Presentation of findings from a nationwide survey and focus groups. SeaWeb, Washington, DC.

Montague, J. J. 1993. Introduction. Pages 1–21 *in* J. J. Burns, J. J. Montague, and C. J. Cowles (eds.), The Bowhead Whale. Society for Marine Mammalogy, Special Publication No. 2.

Mowat, F. 1972. A Whale for the Killing. McClelland and Stewart Limited, Toronto.

Mowat, F. 1984. Sea of Slaughter. McClelland and Stewart Limited, Toronto.

Munro, R. 1982. Communication to Canadian Minister of Fisheries, 11 August. Secretary of State, Olympia, WA.

Nash, R. 1967. Wilderness and the American Mind. Yale University Press, New Haven, CT.

Nash, R. F. 1989. The Rights of Nature: A History of Environmental Ethics. The University of Wisconsin Press, Madison, WI.

National Marine Fisheries Service. 1994. Marine Mammal Inventory Report. Washington, DC.

New England Aquarium. 1991. New England Aquarium countersues animal extremists for $5 million for defamation and abuse of [due] process. News Release, 17 September, Boston, MA.

Norris, K. 1991. The importance to research of captive cetaceans. Whalewatcher 25 (1): 19.

North Atlantic Marine Mammal Commission. 1994. Agreement on Cooperation in Research, Conservation and Management of Marine Mammals in the North Atlantic. Nuuk, 1992. *In* Marine Mammal Commission, The Marine Mammal Commission Compendium of Selected Treaties, International Agreements, and Other Relevant Documents on Marine Resources, Wildlife, and the Environment, R. L. Wallace, compiler. 3 vols. Marine Mammal Commission, Washington, DC.

North Atlantic Marine Mammal Commission. 1997a. Sealing—The Future. International Conference & Exhibition. 25–27 November 1997, St. John's, Newfoundland. First Announcement. North Atlantic Marine Mammal Commission, c/o University of Tromsø, Norway.

North Atlantic Marine Mammal Commission. 1997b. Sealing—The Future. International Conference and Exhibition. 25–27 November 1997, Delta St. John's Hotel and Conference Centre, St. John's, Newfoundland, Canada.

Northridge, S. P., and R. J. Hofman. 1999. Marine mammal interactions with fisheries. (This volume)

Norton, B. G., M. Hutchins, E. F. Stevens, and T. L. Maple (eds.). 1995. Ethics on the Ark: Zoos, Animal Welfare, and Wildlife Conservation. Smithsonian Institution Press, Washington, DC.

O'Barry, R. 1988. Behind the Dolphin Smile. Algonquin Books, Chapel Hill, NC.

Ovington, J. D. 1980. Report on Meeting on Cetacean Behaviour and Intelligence and the Ethics of Killing Cetaceans. International Whaling Commission, Institute for Delphinid Research, Animal Welfare Institute, and the Governments of Australia and the United States. 28 April–1 May 1980, Washington, DC. Document IWC/32/15.

Papastavrou, V. 1996. Sustainable use of whales: Whaling or whale watching? Pages 102–113 *in* V. J. Taylor and N. Dunstone (eds.), The Exploitation of Mammal Populations. Chapman and Hall, London.

Payne, R. S. 1970. Songs of the Humpback Whale. Book of 40 pages and 40-minute stereo phonograph record. New York Zoological Society and Communications Research/Machines, Inc., Los Angeles, CA.

Payne, R. S. 1976. Low-consumptive uses of marine mammals. Scientific Consultation on Marine Mammals. 31 August–9 September 1976, Bergen, Norway. United Nations Food and Agricultural Organization. Draft report. ACMRR/MM/SC/WG 24 (unpublished).

Payne, R. 1979. Humpbacks: Their mysterious songs. National Geographic 155 (1): 18–25.

Payne, R. 1995. Among Whales. Charles Scribner's Sons, New York, NY.

Payne, R. S., and S. McVay. 1971. Songs of humpback whales. Science 173:585–597.

Pearson, S. (compiler). 1988. International marine mammal scientists directory. National Marine Mammal Laboratory, Seattle, WA. Draft, 79 pp.

Penn, Schoen and Berland Associates, Inc. 1997. Poll taken for the International Fund for Animal Welfare. May 1997.

Pinchot, G. 1947. Breaking New Ground. Island Press, Washington, DC, and Covelo, CA.

Quarrington, P. 1989. Whale Music. Vintage Canada, n.p.

Reece, K. A. 1992. Animal Organization and Services Directory, 1992–1993, 5th ed. Animal Stories, Manhattan Beach, CA.

Reeves, R. R., and J. G. Mead. 1999. Marine mammals in captivity. (This volume)

Reeves, R. R., and E. D. Mitchell. 1986. The Long Island, New York, right whale fishery: 1650–1924. Reports of the International Whaling Commission (Special Issue 10): 201–220.

Reeves, R. R., and E. D. Mitchell. 1987. Cetaceans of Canada. Underwater World. Communications Directorate, Department of Fisheries and Oceans, Canada, Ottawa.

Reuters. 1997. U.S. whale hunt request triggers outcry. Kelowna Courier (Kelowna, B.C., Canada), 23 October, p. A7.

Reynolds, J. E., III, and D. K. Odell. 1991. Manatees and dugongs. Facts on File, Inc., New York, NY.

Rolston, H. R., III. 1989. Philosophy Gone Wild: Environmental Ethics. Prometheus Books, Buffalo, NY.

Rose, N. A. 1994. Amendments to MMPA needed. HSUS News (Humane Society of the United States) 39 (1): 8–9.

Rose, T. 1989. Freeing the Whales—How the Media Created the World's Greatest Non-Event. Carol Publishing Group, New York, NY.

Rowell, A. 1996. Green Backlash: Global Subversion of the Environment Movement. Routledge, London and New York, NY.

Scheffer, V. B. 1952. Outline for ecological life history studies of marine mammals. Ecology 33:287–296.

Scheffer, V. B. 1969. The Year of the Whale. Charles Scribner's, Sons, New York, NY.

Scheffer, V. B. 1970. The cliche of the killer. Natural History 79 (8): 26, 28–29, 76–78.

Scheffer, V. B. 1976. Whales of the world. National Geographic 150 (6): 752–767.

Scheffer, V. B. 1980. Benign uses of wildlife. International Journal for the Study of Animal Problems 1 (1): 19–32.

Scheffer, V. B. 1983. Address to the Global Conference on the Non-Consumptive Utilisation of Cetacean Resources. 7–11 June 1983, Boston, MA (unpublished).

Scheffer, V. B. 1985. Sea otters or shellfish: A choice. Marine Mammal Science 1:261–262.

Shaw, J. H. 1985. Introduction to Wildlife Management. McGraw-Hill Book Company, New York, NY.

Simon, N. 1966. Red Data Book, Vol. 1. International Union for the Conservation of Nature and Natural Resources, Morges, Switzerland.

Singer, P. 1975. Animal Liberation: A New Ethics for Our Treatment of Animals. Avon Books, New York, NY.

Small, G. L. 1971. The Blue Whale. Columbia University Press, New York, NY.

Smith, H. M. 1911. Making the fur seal abundant. The National Geographic Magazine 22 (12): 1139–1165.

Southern Africa Sustainable Use Specialist Group. 1996. Sustainable Use Issues and Principles. Southern Africa Sustainable Use Specialist Group, IUCN Species Survival Commission, [Gland, Switzerland].

Stabler, J. M. 1997. Letter to the editor. BBC Wildlife Magazine, 28 April.

Stone, C. D. 1972. Should Trees Have Standing? Toward Legal Rights for Natural Objects. Avon Books, New York, NY.

Strong, J. T. 1989. Reported harvest of narwhal, beluga and walrus in the Northwest Territories, 1948–1987. Canadian Data Report of Fisheries and Aquatic Sciences, No. 734.

Stroud, C. 1996. The ethics and politics of whaling. Pages 55–87 *in* M. P. Simmonds and J. D. Hutchinson (eds.), The Conservation of Whales and Dolphins: Science and Practice. John Wiley and Sons, Chichester, U.K.

Swardson, A. 1997. Whales dwarfted by larger forces: Lobbyists and politics. Washington Post, 24 October, p. A36.

Tilt, W., and J. Spotila. 1991. Wildlife management or animal rights: Lessons from the harp seals. Pages 409–422 *in* Transactions, 56th North American Wildlife and Natural Resources Conference, 17–22 March 1991.

Tønnessen, J. N., and A. O. Johnsen. 1982. The History of Modern Whaling. University of California Press, Berkeley and Los Angeles, CA.

United Nations Conference on Environment and Development. 1992. Agenda 21: Programme of action for sustainable development. United Nations Publications, New York, NY.

U.S. Census Bureau. 1995. Table 1. Urban and Rural Population: 1900–1990 (available on the World Wide Web at http://www.census.gov/population/censusdata/urpop0090.txt).

Vancouver Aquarium. 1993. Aquarium director gives Free Willy "two flukes up." News Release, 15 July, Vancouver, B.C., Canada.

VanderZwaag, D., and L. Duncan. 1992. Canada and environmental protection: Confident political faces, uncertain legal hands. Pages 3–23 *in* R. Boardman (ed.), Canadian Environmental Policy: Ecosystems, Politics and Process. Oxford University Press, Toronto.

Waring, G. H. 1992. Survey of Federally-Funded Marine Mammal Research and Studies, FY 74–FY 91. Marine Mammal Commission, Washington, DC.

Waring, G. H. 1996. Survey of Federally-Funded Marine Mammal Research and Studies, FY74–FY95. Marine Mammal Commission, Washington, DC.

Washington State Legislature. 1979. Senate Resolution No. 1976-222. Journal of the Senate, 64th day, 9 March, pp. 736–738.

Watson, L. 1981. Sea Guide to Whales of the World: A Complete Guide to the World's Living Whales, Dolphins & Porpoises. Hutchinson, London.

Weaver, D. B., C. L. Glenn, and R. C. Rounds. 1995. The Rural Development Institute, Brandon University, Brandon, Manitoba. RDI Series 1995-5.

Wenzel, G. 1991. Animal Rights, Human Rights: Ecology, Economy and Ideology in the Canadian Arctic. University of Toronto Press, Toronto.

Whitehead, H. 1984. Realm of the elusive sperm whale. National Geographic 166 (6): 774–789.

Wilkinson, D. M. 1996. National Contingency Plan for Response to Unusual Marine Mammal Mortality Events. U.S. Department of Commerce, NOAA Technical Memorandum NMFS-OPR-9.

World Council of Whalers. 1997. World Council of Whalers opens Secretariat in Port Alberni, B.C., Canada. News Release. 2 pp.

Worster, D. 1977. Nature's Economy: The Roots of Ecology. Sierra Club Books, San Francisco, CA.
Worster, D. 1994. Nature's Economy: A History of Ecological Ideas, 2d ed. Cambridge University Press, Cambridge, U.K.
Young, N. M. (ed.). 1993. Examining the components of a revised management scheme. Center for Marine Conservation, Washington, DC.
Zimmerman, M. E., J. B. Callicott, G. Sessions, K. J. Warren, and J. Clark. 1993. Environmental Philosophy: From Animal Rights to Radical Ecology. Prentice Hall, Upper Saddle River, NJ.

3

DONALD C. BAUR, MICHAEL J. BEAN,
AND MICHAEL L. GOSLINER

The Laws Governing Marine Mammal Conservation in the United States

"Once destroyed, biological capital cannot be recreated." With these words, Congressman John Dingell opened the floor on 9 September 1971 to public debate over the first attempt by the U.S. Congress to design a comprehensive program to conserve a broad array of wildlife species. The topic under consideration was how to fashion a law to protect marine mammals, a law that would govern human conduct so as to allow the marine ecosystem of which such mammals are a part to remain healthy and function according to the "laws of nature." The ambitious nature of this effort is evident in Chairman Dingell's opening remarks, in which he recognized (1) the groups of animals to be covered—"whales, seals, walruses, sea otters, polar bears, and the sea cows"; (2) that these animals "are found on the high seas, in territorial waters, and on U.S. lands"; (3) that Congress would have to address problems of overlapping jurisdiction and the lack of consistency in the degree of protection afforded each species; and (4) that the legislation would have to be developed in spite of the fact that "hard evidence" was too often lacking (U.S. House 1971a).

During the course of the hearings, lawmakers were to hear from witnesses representing a wide spectrum of interest groups and affected parties: members of Congress, federal and state officials, environmental groups, animal welfare groups, the commercial fishing industry, businesses and trade associations, Alaska Native organizations, zoological parks and aquariums, and many concerned individuals. In crafting the law, Congress also relied extensively on the advice of biologists and other experts from the field of conservation.

The members of Congress harbored no illusions that sufficient information existed about marine mammals to guide the law-making process. As the House Merchant Marine and Fisheries Committee declared in its report on the proposed 1971 marine mammal bills:

> In the teeth of this lack of knowledge of specific causes, and of the certain knowledge that these animals are almost all threatened in some way, it seems elementary common sense to the Committee that legislation should be adopted to require that we act conservatively—that no steps should be taken regarding these animals that might prove to be adverse or even irreversible in their effects until more is known. As far as could be done, we have endeavored to build such a conservative bias into the legislation here presented (U.S. House 1971b).

This dearth of information and understanding about marine mammals gave rise to an enduring legacy: the important role of science in the decision-making process. Perhaps more than any other federal environmental law, the statute that resulted from Congress' deliberations in 1971—the Marine Mammal Protection Act—calls for active and continued reliance on scientific experts. Scientists played a preeminent role in drafting the Act in 1971 and in the crafting of subsequent amendments (1977, 1978, 1981, 1984, 1986, 1988, 1990, 1992, 1994). Scientists play a day-to-day role in the implementation of the Act as they help provide the basis for marine mammal conservation decisions by federal agencies; advise those agencies on and, in many cases, themselves make decisions; participate in international diplomatic efforts to protect marine ecosystems and species; assist, advise, and represent private and nonprofit-sector entities seeking authorization to undertake activities that involve or affect marine mammals; represent environmental, animal welfare, fisheries, sport hunting, Native American, and other interests involved in marine mammal issues; and, of course, conduct research for the fundamental purpose of enhancing the store of information and understanding of these animals and their habitats.

Just as marine mammal scientists and others have played an important role in crafting and implementing the Marine Mammal Protection Act, the statute in turn has had a profound influence in shaping the direction and conduct of marine mammal research. For example, research to address the recovery of right whales, Hawaiian monk seals, and manatees and the incidental take of dolphins in the eastern tropical Pacific tuna fishery has been supported through specific funding under the Marine Mammal Protection Act. Likewise, research carried out under the Act to determine the status of marine mammal stocks and to differentiate among them has led to improved survey techniques (both ship and aircraft) and to advances in radio tagging and remote sensing. In addition, most of the work done on nonlethal research methodology has been precipitated by requirements under the Act, and studies of the effects of sounds on marine mammals and research on bycatch in fisheries can be directly related to the Act.

Attaining the goals of the Act remains as challenging today as it was in 1971. Although more is now known about marine mammals and their habitat, the task of developing solutions to the threats to the species is in many cases more complex and intractable now than it was when the law was enacted. And, despite all the advances that have occurred in marine mammal biology, much remains to be learned. Whether the Act's goals will be achieved will be determined, in no small measure, by the ability of marine biologists, working within the framework of existing environmental policy and law, to apply scientific findings successfully to resolve problems.

In this chapter we discuss the laws governing marine mammal conservation and management in the United States. Because the Marine Mammal Protection Act is the primary legal authority in this area, the bulk of this chapter is devoted to it. Other laws, such as the Endangered Species Act, the Animal Welfare Act, the National Environmental Policy Act, the Magnuson-Stevens Fishery Conservation and Management Act, and protected area laws, as well as several international treaties, such as the International Convention for the Regulation of Whaling, the Agreement on the Conservation of Polar Bears, and regional seas agreements, are of great importance as well.

Taken together, these authorities provide the legal framework for conservation and protection of marine mammals and their habitats. To date, some of these legal authorities have been underutilized, and some have been applied incorrectly or inadequately. Others have been used with great success. The history of the application of these laws should be understood by marine biologists and others who wish either to use them as they stand to affect the course of marine mammal conservation or to improve them to better serve their intended purposes and meet the challenges of new problems. This chapter is intended to give some insight into how law and science can interact to advance environmental policy, in general, and the protection and conservation of marine mammals and their habitats, in particular.

Pre-Act Authorities Governing Marine Mammals

One of the principal reasons that Congress saw a need to enact the Marine Mammal Protection Act was the lack of consistency or adequate protection under the hodgepodge of laws that previously applied to marine mammals and their habitat. The laws that did exist were often inconsistent and were limited to a few species; many marine mammal species were afforded no protection at all.

For example, the North Pacific Fur Seal Act of 1966 covered only the northern fur seal (*Callorhinus ursinus*) and the sea otter (*Enhydra lutris*). Its prohibition against taking was limited to the high seas, which meant the Act did not address the most significant threats to the species—those occurring in nearshore waters. It also failed to establish any kind of comprehensive research or conservation program. Even the federal Endangered Species Conservation Act of 1969 (later replaced by the much-strengthened Endangered Species Act of 1973) failed to provide meaningful protection to those marine mammals at greatest risk. The law contained no prohibition on taking, had no meaningful protection for habitat, and did nothing to address threats to individual populations that were threatened or endangered.

Similar problems existed at the state level. Many states with jurisdiction over waters within 3 nautical miles (5.5 km) of the coast had no laws covering marine mammals. Such laws that did exist often varied from state to state, meaning that animals from a single stock could be subjected to different levels of protection (or exploitation), depending on which state's waters they happened to be in. The laws sometimes provided inadequate protection. For example, polar bear biologists generally agreed that sport hunting was a significant threat to the species, and Congress concurred (Baur 1996). Yet, despite the strong management program established by the state of Alaska, there was concern that the polar bear population was declining due to overharvesting. Conversely, other state programs, rather than being designed to protect marine mammals, encouraged taking, such as bounty programs for seals thought to be competing with fishermen.

Finally, on the international front, little was being done to provide coherent and adequate protection for marine mammals. The International Convention for the Regulation of Whaling had proven to be ineffective at maintaining whale populations at healthy levels. The Interim Convention on the Conservation of North Pacific Fur Seals, although held up by some as a model of successful marine mammal management at the time the Act was first being considered, came under increasing attack because of its provision allowing an annual harvest of seals on the Pribilof Islands as the population began to decline in the 1970s. And, although the involved countries concurred on the need to protect polar bears, no such treaty or agreement had been completed. Likewise, little had been done to establish multinational agreements to protect habitats or the marine environment. Indeed, the focus of most previous international efforts involving marine resources was on maximizing economic gain from continued exploitation, not on conservation as an end in itself.

Marine mammals never received the benefit of comprehensive protection until enactment of the Marine Mammal Protection Act. By preempting the patchwork of inconsistent state laws, establishing a uniform code of federal requirements, and emphasizing the need for coordinated international conservation efforts consistent with U.S. goals, Congress put all marine mammals on the same protected plane. This uniformity of regulation has been one of the most significant features of the Marine Mammal Protection Act. The remainder of this chapter discusses the key elements of the program established under the Marine Mammal Protection Act and other laws.

Enactment of the Marine Mammal Protection Act

In the late 1960s and early 1970s Congress engaged in deliberations that would produce many environmental laws, including the Wild and Scenic Rivers Act (1968), the National Environmental Policy Act (1969), the Clean Air Act (1970), the Clean Water Act (1972), the Coastal Zone Management Act (1972), and the Endangered Species Act (1973). The public sentiment that led to this remarkable spurt of legislative activity on the environment also provided fertile ground for developing a law to protect sea mammals (Gaines and Schmidt 1976).

The Framework of Marine Mammal Protection

In examining the need for marine mammal protection, four themes emerged on the congressional and public agendas. First was concern over the fate of individual species. Second was the call for broader protection of marine ecosystems. Third was the recognition that little information existed about marine mammals and their status and that a major investment in scientific research was needed. Finally, all participants in the debate saw the need for greater international cooperation.

Species of Special Concern

Coinciding with congressional efforts in the early 1970s to protect the environment were a number of high-profile ecological disputes and catastrophes involving marine mammals. One of these was the commercial harvest of seals, and drawing the strongest outcry was the annual harvest of newborn harp seals (*Phoca groenlandica*) and hooded seals (*Cystophora cristata*) off Canada's east coast. Each spring, tens of thousands of seals less than one week old were killed for the fur trade, and effective antisealing campaigns by several animal protection groups had provoked a groundswell of protest.

At the same time, there was strong concern over the decline of most whale stocks. Whaling was still a commercial enterprise for many nations, including the United States, and the International Whaling Commission, charged with conserving the stocks, had been ineffective at this task. Indeed, in 1970 eight species of great whales were listed under the then-existing Endangered Species Act as endangered or threatened with extinction, heightening the call for better protection.

Meanwhile, in the eastern tropical Pacific Ocean, the U.S. tuna fleet was exploiting an unusual bond between yellowfin tuna (*Thunnus albacares*) and dolphins (see Gosliner, this volume) by drawing large purse seine nets around schools of dolphins, thereby trapping the fish swimming below the dolphins. The disastrous result was that by 1971 an estimated five million dolphins had perished in the tuna purse seine fishery. At the time of the 1971 congressional hearings, it was estimated that more than 400,000 dolphins were being killed every year (U.S. House 1971b:13). The public outcry over this fishing practice grew throughout the consideration of the legislation, and it had become a major issue by the time the Marine Mammal Protection Act was enacted in 1972.

Other marine mammal species received considerable attention. These included, for example, polar bears (*Ursus maritimus*), thought by some to be threatened as a result of overhunting; West Indian manatees (*Trichechus manatus*), which had previously been overhunted and which at the time were being killed by motorboats and losing important feeding habitat; and the California population of sea otters, driven once before to the brink of extinction and now threatened by malicious taking, oil spill risks, and habitat loss.

All these species received special consideration. But as Congress was then aware, and as research conducted in subsequent years has borne out, an even wider array of marine mammals was at risk. As the House Merchant Marine and Fisheries Committee summed up in its 1971 report on the Act:

> Recent history indicates that man's impact upon marine mammals has ranged from what might be termed malign neglect to virtual genocide. These animals, including whales, porpoises, seals, sea otters, polar bears, manatees and others, have only rarely benefitted from our interest; they have been shot, blown up, clubbed to death, run down by boats, poisoned, and exposed to a multitude of other indignities, all in the interest of profit or recreation, with little or no consideration of the potential impact of these activities on the animal populations involved (U.S. House 1971b:11–12).

The result was a law that Congress intended would ensure that "future generations will be able to enjoy a world populated by all species of marine mammals" (U.S. Senate 1972a).

To advance this goal, Congress developed two innovative legal features to govern decisions under the Marine Mammal Protection Act—features that would be incorporated into subsequent wildlife legislation. These had to do with (1) building in a conservative bias in favor of the species and (2) assigning the burden of proof to the party seeking to take or import the species.

The first feature was a mandate for a risk-adverse approach: in cases of doubt or ambiguity, decisions would favor marine mammals. The House Merchant Marine and Fisheries Committee made clear its intent to "build such a conservative bias into the legislation here presented" (U.S. House 1971b:24). The Senate expressed a similar view. "Scientists generally will state that our level of knowledge of marine mammals is very low. . . . Barring better and more information, it would therefore appear to be wise to adopt a cautious attitude toward the exploitation of marine mammals" (U.S. Senate 1971).

In keeping with this principle, the courts generally have given the interests of marine mammals priority over the interests of other parties, such as commercial fisheries and tour boat operators, who seek to use these animals for economic gain. In *Committee for Humane Legislation, Inc.* v. *Richardson,* one of the first court decisions to interpret the Act, Judge Charles Richey held that the Act should be interpreted "for the benefit of the protected species rather than for the benefit of commercial exploitation."[1] Similarly, in *Kokechik Fishermen's Ass'n* v. *Secretary of Commerce,* the District of Columbia Circuit Court of Appeals declared that, when balancing commercial and conservation interests under the Act, "the interest in maintaining healthy populations of marine mammals comes first."[2]

The second legal precept inherent to the Act as first enacted applies in conjunction with the first. It is that any party wishing to exploit marine mammals should have the burden of proof that such activity will be consistent with the Act's overall goals and not disadvantage the species or stock involved. As stated in the House Merchant Marine and Fisheries Committee report: "If that burden is not carried—and it is by no means a light burden—the permit may not be issued. The effect of this set of requirements is to insist that the management of the animal populations be carried out with the interests of the animals as the prime consideration" (U.S. House 1971b:18). The presumption is in favor of protection. Activities that take marine mammals will be authorized only if the requesting party proves that its activities will not disadvantage the species, harm the marine ecosystem, or result in needless pain to the animal. As stated by Judge Richey in *Committee for Humane Legislation* v. *Richardson,* the Act's mandate is "to proceed knowledgeably and cautiously." As discussed later in this chapter, Congress has since shied away from this precept in enacting a new regime for managing the incidental take of marine mammals in commercial fisheries.

Ecosystem Protection

Interspersed throughout the testimony of witnesses and statements by members of Congress during the original consideration of the Act were expressions of concern over the health of the marine environment and the ecosystems of which marine mammals are a part. The result was a strong and unified expression of the need for action to protect marine ecosystems. The Act, however, did not contain explicit provisions to accomplish this goal.

In the section-by-section analysis of the 1972 report on the original Senate bill, the Commerce Committee noted that the Act's finding regarding the importance of marine mammals as functioning parts of their ecosystems was meant to emphasize "the need to protect those geographic areas of significance for each species of marine mammals from adverse activities." The Committee observed that "[a]ll of these animals are a part of the ocean biomass and are important in maintaining an ecological balance" (U.S. Senate 1972a:10–11).

Witnesses representing the scientific community also referred to the need for a comprehensive, ecosystem-based program. As Dr. Kenneth Norris of the Marine Mammal Council testified before the Senate subcommittee: "The management [of marine mammals] should be based not only upon the biological health of the individual species, but upon the health of the ecosystem of which it is a part. . . . Such management must be based upon continuing reappraisal of the health of both animal and ecosystem. . . . Enlightened management today is no longer species management, it is instead ecosystem management" (U.S. Senate 1972b).

Stating the theme that would become one of the underlying principles of the Act, Dr. Lee Talbot of the Council on Environmental Quality drew a careful distinction between management for human versus ecological purposes. As he explained:

> [I]t is possible to manage a wild species for a maximum sustained yield under conditions which may alter or make less stable other parts of the environment. Therefore, the maximum sustained yield in some cases may not be necessarily the yield level at which the optimum environmental balance . . . may be maintained. . . . [T]he objective of management, as we see it, should not be purely economic gain . . . but environmental balance and economic gain consistent with that (U.S. Senate 1972b:146–147).

From this consideration emerged the species-specific conservation goal of the Act, that all marine mammals should be brought to and maintained at their optimum sustainable population (OSP) level, provided that efforts to do so are consistent with maintaining the overall health and stability of the marine environment.

Reflecting these concerns, the report accompanying the 1971 House bills noted the habitat-related threats to marine mammals from ocean dumping, pesticides, heavy metals, and reduced availability of food. The report summarized: "[m]an's taking alone, without these factors, might be tolerated by animal species or populations, but in conjunction with them, it could well prove to be the proverbial straw added to the camel's back" (U.S. House 1971b:15).

Research

Congress was clear about its intent to make research a key element of the Act. For all of the high-minded goals, principles, and concepts reflected in the Marine Mammal Protection Act, the law would be ineffective without more information about the species and their habitats. Congress recognized the need for studies on nutrition and diseases, effects of contaminants, life history, and population dynamics. Unfortunately, the modest level of funding that was authorized did not ensure that such studies could be undertaken. Congress acknowledged the role of the scientist to be immense and declared a goal of the Act to be nothing short of making it possible for "science [to] make an adequate interpretation of the entire marine environment to predict what will happen to marine mammals under different management programs and increasing utilization of marine resources by society and industry" (U.S. Senate 1972a:10).

International Cooperation

Members of Congress, federal officials, and others involved in drafting the Act agreed that, for many species, the application of stringent laws to U.S. waters and U.S. citizens would not be enough. Because of the migratory nature of many marine mammals, and the fact that the activities of foreign citizens posed some of the most severe threats, cooperative international efforts would be needed. Among the species especially in need of international protection were most whales, many species of dolphins, harp seals, fur seals, polar bears, manatees, and dugongs (*Dugong dugon*).

In addressing this need, Congress directed the State Department and other federal agencies to pursue protective treaties and agreements. To reduce the incentive for killing marine mammals in foreign countries, Congress adopted a moratorium on imports of marine mammals and their products. Congress also saw the need to give the United States some leverage against foreign nations that were undermining international conservation efforts. This was to be achieved through the economic pressure of trade sanctions, authorized by the Act and another measure, the Pelly Amendment to the Fishermen's Protective Act (discussed below).

Requirements to Implement the Principles of Protection

With these goals in mind, Congress fashioned the provisions that became the Marine Mammal Protection Act of 1972. The final product was a compromise between two opposing points of view as reflected in more than 40 bills. On the one hand were the members of Congress and others who favored total protection and a complete ban on the killing and harassing of marine mammals. This group supported the Harris-Pryor bill (H.R. 6554). On the other hand were those who favored a more management-oriented approach that would afford protection while leaving room for utilization of species when consistent with their protection. The views of this group were reflected in the Anderson-Pelly bill (H.R. 10420) (Bean 1983).

The legislative compromise resulted in the expression of broad and somewhat ambiguous policy goals. It was protectionist in tone, but stopped short of a full ban on taking marine mammals. In retrospect, Congress appeared to exhibit a certain naïveté in its belief that broad mandates would lead to solving a broad array of problems. As experience gained from more than 25 years of implementation of the Marine Mammal Protection Act has demonstrated, the specific provisions developed by Congress have not always been adequate to accomplish the desired goals. In the remainder of this section we discuss the key provisions of the Act and how they have been interpreted by the courts and amended by Congress over the years.

Policies of the Act

In section 2 of the Marine Mammal Protection Act,[3] Congress set forth six "findings" that have endured throughout the Act's history and that serve as the basis for the law's substantive requirements.

First, Congress recognized that certain species and populations were or may be in danger of extinction as a result of human activities [section 2(1)].

Second, species and stocks "should not be permitted to diminish beyond the point at which they cease to be a significant functioning element in the ecosystem of which they are a part, and, consistent with this major objective, they should not be permitted to diminish below their optimum sustainable population level" [section 2(2)]. Immediate action, Congress directed, should be taken to encourage recovery of stocks that have fallen below this level, and particular efforts are to be made to protect essential habitats.

Third, Congress found that there is inadequate information on the ecology and biology of marine mammals [section 2(3)]. Although much has certainly been learned, this need for more information about these species remains as critical as when the law was enacted.

Fourth, Congress issued a finding calling for international efforts to encourage research on, and conservation of, all marine mammals [section 2(4)].

Fifth, Congress recognized the economic importance of marine mammals by noting that they either "move in interstate commerce" or "affect the balance of marine ecosystems in a manner which is important to other animals and animal products which move in interstate commerce" [section 2(5)]. The focus, however, may have had more to do with exercising jurisdiction over marine mammal issues than on an actual concern about interstate commerce.

Congress listed last what is actually designated as the foremost goal of the Marine Mammal Protection Act. As set forth in section 2(6):

> [M]arine mammals have proven themselves to be resources of great international significance, esthetic and recreational as well as economic, and it is the sense of the Congress that they should be protected and encouraged to develop to the greatest extent feasible commensurate with sound policies of resource management and that the primary objective of their management should be to maintain the health and stability of the marine ecosystem. Whenever consistent with this primary objective, it should be the goal to obtain an optimum sustainable population keeping in mind the carrying capacity of the habitat.

Thus, Congress declared that the foremost goal of the Act is maintaining the health and stability of the marine ecosystem.

These findings and goals serve as the policy basis for the requirements of the Act. In construing the meaning of the Act's requirements, agencies and the courts have consistently harkened back to these six statements of congressional purpose. The result has been to cast, through judicial decision and agency precedent, a strong patina favoring marine mammal protection over all of the Act's requirements.

Requirements of the Act

As its name implies, the Act provides protection to all marine mammals. The Act applies to "any mammal which (A) is morphologically adapted to the marine environment (including sea otters and members of the orders Sirenia, Pinnipedia and Cetacea), or (B) primarily inhabits the marine environment (such as the polar bear)" [section 3(6)]. The Act also covers "any part of any such marine mammal, including its raw, dressed, or dyed fur or skin."

In section 3(12), jurisdiction over marine mammals is divided between two federal agencies. The Secretary of Commerce, through the National Marine Fisheries Service, has responsibility for cetaceans and all pinnipeds except the walrus, and the Secretary of the Interior has responsibility for all other marine mammals (i.e., sea otters, marine otters, manatees, dugongs, walruses, and polar bears). Within the Department of the Interior, marine mammal research is undertaken by the U.S. Geological Service and regulatory and management actions are taken by the U.S. Fish and Wildlife Service.

Title II of the Act establishes the independent Marine Mammal Commission, a commission of three members appointed by the President, with the advice and consent of the Senate. The President must make his selection from a list of names unanimously agreed to by the Chairman of the Council on Environmental Quality, the Secretary of the Smithsonian Institution, the Director of the National Science Foundation, and the Chairman of the National Academy of Sciences. Commissioners must be knowledgeable in marine ecology and resource management.

The Marine Mammal Commission has numerous statutory duties, including reviewing the condition of marine mammal stocks, methods for their protection and conservation, humane methods of take, and research programs conducted or proposed under the Act; undertaking, or causing to be undertaken, studies for marine mammal protection and conservation; making recommendations regarding species to be listed as endangered or threatened under the Endangered Species Act; making recommendations on international marine mammal policies; and making recommendations regarding the protection of Alaska Natives, whose livelihood may be adversely affected by actions taken under the Act. Federal agencies are required by the Act to respond to all Commission recommendations. Detailed written explanations must be provided to the Commission by an agency that declines to follow its recommendations.

In carrying out its duties, the Commission is required to consult with its nine-member Committee of Scientific Advisors on Marine Mammals. The members of the Committee must be "knowledgeable in marine ecology and marine mammal affairs." They are appointed by the Chairman of the Commission, in consultation with the other commissioners and after consultation with the Chairman of the Council on Environmental Quality, the Secretary of the Smithsonian Institution, the Director of the National Science Foundation, and the Chairman of the National Academy of Sciences. Committee recommendations not adopted by the Commission must be forwarded to the appropriate federal agency along with a detailed explanation of the reasons why they were rejected.

FEDERAL PREEMPTION. As noted above, one concern of the drafters of the Marine Mammal Protection Act was the number of federal and state government entities and conflicting laws involved in marine mammal management. To bring some order, Congress consolidated the marine mammal program in the hands of the federal government. Using its "constitutional power . . . to regulate traffic in these animals and their products, deeply involved as they are in interstate and foreign commerce," Congress provided through section 109 that "[n]o State may enforce or attempt to enforce, any State law or regulation relating to the taking of any species . . . of marine mammal within the States." Federal preemption also applies to the importation of marine mammals (*Fouke Company* v. *Mandel*).[4] This sweeping step of replacing all state regulation with federal control was controversial and strongly opposed by state fish and wildlife agencies. Nevertheless, Congress felt that such action was necessary because marine mammal protection varied so greatly from state to state, resulting in inadequate measures to achieve the desired conservation goals. Ironically, section 109 also has the effect of preempting state laws (except in cases where special cooperative agreements are in place or the state has obtained return of management) that would be more protective of marine mammals than the Act.

This differs from the Endangered Species Act, which permits states to enact laws or adopt regulations with respect to the taking of listed species that are more restrictive than those applicable under federal law. In the case of marine mammals listed as endangered or threatened under the Endangered Species Act, federal authorities have resolved the conflicting provisions of the two laws by permitting states to be more restrictive. For example, despite the Marine Mammal Protection Act's preemption, the Commonwealth of Massachusetts has adopted regulations prohibiting approaches to endangered right whales in state waters to no closer than 500 yards (457 m).

Congress also set in place provisions that would allow return of management to the states. Under this authority, in the mid-1970s Alaska sought the return of management for 10 marine mammal species. A transfer was granted for Pacific walrus (*Odobenus rosmarus*) (Fig. 3-1),[5] but the state's authority was enjoined as a result of a lawsuit filed by Alaska Natives, who challenged the Secretary's determination that the Act's Native take exemption terminated upon the transfer. In *People of Togiak* v. *United States*,[6] the court determined that the Native take exemption survived the return of management. As a result, Alaska elected not to pursue a return of management for any marine mammal species or stock, and the state's request was withdrawn.[7]

In response to this decision, Congress amended section 109 in 1981 to clarify the process for returning management

Figure 3-1. Walruses huddled on an ice floe in the Chukchi Sea approximately 100 miles (160 km) off the northwestern coast of Alaska in 1977. (Photograph © Bill Curtsinger)

to the states. These new procedures, which remain in effect, require the Secretary to determine whether the state involved has a program that is consistent with the Act and includes a process for determining the population status of the affected stocks and whether and to what extent taking may be allowed. If this finding is made, the Secretary may transfer management authority to the state, but no taking may be allowed until the state conducts adjudicatory hearings to determine if the species or stock involved is within its optimum sustainable population range and how many animals may be taken without reducing the species or stock below that level. To date, no state has sought a transfer of management under the section 109 procedures as revised in 1981 although Alaska has expressed interest at various times since then.

OPTIMUM SUSTAINABLE POPULATION. Section 2(6) of the Act provides that, whenever consistent with the primary objective of maintaining the health and stability of the marine ecosystem, "it should be the goal to obtain an optimum sustainable population keeping in mind the carrying capacity of the environment." This is the species or stock conservation goal of the Act. Optimum sustainable population (OSP) is defined in section 3(9) to mean "with respect to any population stock, the number of animals which will result in the maximum productivity of the population of the species keeping in mind the carrying capacity of the habitat and the health of the ecosystem of which they form a constituent element."

The Fish and Wildlife Service and the National Marine Fisheries Service share a common regulatory definition of the term, which recognizes OSP as a population size that falls "within a range from the population level of a given species or stock which is the largest supportable within the ecosystem to the population level that results in maximum net productivity."[8] Because the maximum net productivity level is the lower end of the OSP range, it has been the focal point, or target, of conservation efforts under the Act. Maximum net productivity is defined to mean "the greatest net annual increment in population numbers or biomass resulting from additions to the population due to reproduction and/or growth less losses due to natural mortality."[9] As applied in numerous Commerce Department rulemaking proceedings on pinniped stocks, the term has been generally interpreted for some species to mean a population size that represents 60% of the species' or stock's carrying capacity.[10] Any species or stock that is below its OSP is considered "depleted" under section 3(1) of the Act.

The OSP standard has considerable regulatory significance under the Marine Mammal Protection Act. In addition to serving as the conservation objective of the Act, OSP establishes a threshold for determining when certain activities are to be prohibited or restricted. The Act has been interpreted to mean, for example, that a waiver of the moratorium cannot be granted for species or stocks below their OSP levels (depleted). Public display permits may not be issued for depleted marine mammals, and additional requirements are applicable to scientific research involving depleted marine mammals. Regulations limiting hunting areas and seasons used by Alaska Natives to take marine mammals for subsistence or handicraft purposes, or even prohibiting taking altogether, may be established for species that are below their OSP levels. However, such regulations are to be rescinded once the need for their imposition has disappeared. After a transfer of management, no take may be authorized by a state for a species or stock below its OSP level.

As a result of amendments enacted in 1988 and 1994, however, OSP plays a less important role than under the original Act. Before these amendments, commercial fisheries could not obtain authorization to take marine mammals unless the affected species or stock was above its maximum net productivity level and the take would not cause it to decline below that level.[11] Under an interim exemption adopted in 1988 and a long-term provision enacted in 1994, OSP and maximum net productivity standards are not directly involved. Under the 1994 amendments, fisheries receive general authorization to take marine mammals not listed under the Endangered Species Act. Incidental take reduction plans must be developed for those species or stocks for which incidental take exceeds the potential biological removal level, effectively replacing OSP as the benchmark for marine mammal management in the context of incidental take in commercial fishing activities. Section 3(20) of the Marine Mammal Protection Act defines the potential biological removal level as "the maximum number of animals, not including natural mortalities, that may be removed from a marine mammal stock while allowing that stock to reach or maintain its optimum sustainable population." It differs from the OSP standard in that it is designed to ensure that stocks within or at OSP remain so and stocks below OSP increase to OSP within a reasonable period of time. When human-caused take exceeds the potential biological removal level, measures must be developed under the plan to reduce take below that amount. These levels are calculated by multiplying the minimum population estimate by one-half the net productivity rate and a recovery factor of between 0.1 and 1.0.[12]

THE MORATORIUM ON TAKING AND ITS EXCEPTIONS. The centerpiece of the Act is its moratorium on taking in section 101(a). The moratorium establishes a general ban on the taking of marine mammals throughout areas subject to U.S. jurisdiction and by any person, vessel, or conveyance subject to the jurisdiction of the United States on the high seas.

"Take" is defined under section 3(13) of the Act to mean "to harass, hunt, capture, or kill, or attempt to harass, hunt, capture, or kill any marine mammal." The prohibited act of taking is defined by regulation by the Fish and Wildlife Service as follows:

> Take means to harass, hunt, capture, collect, or kill, or attempt to harass, hunt, capture, collect, or kill any marine mammals, including, without limitation, any of the following: the collection of dead animals or parts thereof; the restraint or detention of a marine mammal, no matter how temporary; tagging a marine mammal; or the negligent or intentional operation of an aircraft or vessel, or the doing of any other negligent or intentional act which results in the disturbing or molesting of a marine mammal.[13]

The National Marine Fisheries Service uses the same definition, except for the prohibition added in 1991 against "feeding or attempting to feed a marine mammal in the wild."[14] This expansion of the definition of taking was designed primarily to prohibit commercial tour boat operators and their passengers from feeding wild dolphins for the purpose of luring them nearer to vessels for viewing. This definition was challenged by tour boat operators on the grounds that the Act's take prohibition does not extend to actions that do not reduce an animal to possession or disturb it sufficiently to cause it to flee. The challenge was rejected by the Fifth Circuit Court of Appeals in *Strong* v. *United States,* which determined that such a prohibition is consistent with the Act's definition of take (i.e., feeding constitutes a form of harassment) and is within the agency's discretion.[15]

Neither the original Act nor its regulations defined the term *harass,* and the meaning of the prohibition on this type of taking has come under judicial review in several cases. In the first case, *United States* v. *Hayashi,* the Ninth Circuit held that, to be prohibited, such action must involve "direct and significant intrusions upon the normal, life-sustaining activities of a marine mammal."[16] In advancing that interpretation, which is at odds with the Fifth Circuit decision in *Strong* v. *United States,* the Ninth Circuit overturned a criminal conviction of a fisherman who shot in the direction of four small cetaceans ("porpoises") to deter them from interacting with his gear and catch. The court concluded that shooting at the animals did not have the significance or sustained effect necessary to constitute a take by harassment. This rationale was subsequently repeated in a case involving photographers who pursued, swam with, and touched wild pilot whales (*Globicephala* sp.) without a permit. Even though one of the people involved apparently disturbed the whale to the point of being bitten and dragged underwater to a depth of 12 m (40 feet), the District Court for the Northern District of California ruled in *Tepley* v. *National Oceanic and Atmospheric Administration* that the U.S. government had not met its burden of demonstrating that harassment had occurred.[17]

These cases were seemingly at odds with previous interpretations of the Act and its goals. Even though the *Hayashi* decision was subsequently modified by the Ninth Circuit, Congress took up this issue in 1994 by amending section 2 of the Act to clarify the meaning of the "harassment" by defining it as "any act of pursuit, torment, or annoyance which (i) has the potential to injure a marine mammal or marine mammal stock in the wild; or (ii) has the potential to disturb a marine mammal or marine mammal stock in the wild by causing disruption of behavioral patterns, including, but not limited to, migration, breathing, nursing, breeding, feeding, or sheltering." Harassment that has the potential to injure a marine mammal is considered Level A harassment; other forms of harassment are classified as Level B. This new definition provides greater specificity and should effectively prohibit the types of activities at issue in the *Hayashi* and *Tepley* cases.

Under sections 101(a) and (b) of the Act, the taking of marine mammals is allowed in a few limited situations. These are taking for (1) scientific research, (2) public display, (3) photography for educational or commercial purposes, (4) enhancing the survival or recovery of a species or stock, (5) the incidental take of marine mammals in commercial fishing operations (for endangered and threatened marine mammals), (6) the incidental, but not intentional, take of small numbers of marine mammals over a period of five consecutive years by citizens of the United States engaged in a specified activity other than commercial fishing within a specified geographical area, or, if by harassment only, over a one-year period, (7) take by any Indian, Aleut, or Eskimo who resides in Alaska and who dwells on the coast of the North Pacific Ocean or the Arctic Ocean if such taking is for subsistence or handicraft purposes and is not accomplished in a wasteful manner, (8) take by nonlethal means to protect personal safety, private property, or fishing gear or catch, and (9) for purposes of self-defense or to save the life of a person in immediate danger.

A variety of determinations must be made before these exceptions may be invoked. Taking for scientific research, public display, photography, and species enhancement generally requires a permit issued under section 104 of the Act after notice and opportunity for comment. Formerly, authorization to take marine mammals incidental to commercial fishing operations required a permit pursuant to an on-the-record rulemaking proceeding. After the 1994 amendments, however, virtually all domestic and foreign fisheries subject to U.S. jurisdiction, with the exception of the eastern tropical Pacific tuna fishery, are now subject to section 118, added to the Act by the 1994 amendments. Section 118 does not require a permit although fishermen are required to register to engage lawfully in some fisheries. The eastern tropical Pacific tuna fishery remains subject to special permitting requirements. After amendments enacted in 1997 enter into force, each U.S. vessel participating in the fishery will be required to obtain an annual permit that, among other things, will set a vessel-specific dolphin mortality limit. The commercial fishing small-take exemption for species listed under the Endangered Species Act requires notice and opportunity for comment under section 101(a)(E)(i), and the small-take exception for other than commercial fishing operations requires rulemaking, unless only harassment is involved, in which case notice and comment, but not rulemaking, is required [section 101(a)(5)].

Nonwasteful Native take of nondepleted marine mammals for subsistence and handicraft purposes is not subject to regulation [section 101(b)]. Special statutory requirements govern the take of dolphins incidental to tuna purse seine fishing operations [section 104(h)] (see Northridge and Hofman, this volume), and the incidental take of California sea otters.[18]

Section 104(b)(2)(B) of the Act specifies that any take authorized by permit must be "humane." Humane is defined under section 3(4) as that "method of taking which involves the least possible degree of pain and suffering practicable to the mammal involved." The take must also be consistent with the purposes of the Act as indicated in section 104(d)(3).

In addition to these exceptions, section 101(a)(3)(A) of the Act allows the moratorium to be waived. A waiver can be obtained only after notice and opportunity for on-the-record rulemaking. The waiver must be "compatible" with the purposes of the Act and in accord with "sound principles of resource protection and conservation." More specifically, a waiver may not be granted for any depleted species or stock. Any waiver must accord "due regard to the distribution, abundance, breeding habits, and times and lines of migratory movements of such marine mammals."

The complexity, expense, and evidentiary burden of the waiver process has caused parties to avoid using it. Indeed, only two waivers have been formally requested: one, to import fur seal (*Arctocephalus pusillus*) pelts from South Africa (1975) and the second, to return management to the state of Alaska (1975). Although both were initially granted, neither waiver ultimately succeeded. The fur seal import waiver was invalidated because the harvest exceeded the permissible quota and because some skins came from animals that were less than eight months old or that were still nursing in contravention of the Act's import provisions.[19] As discussed previously, the Secretary of the Interior's determination that the Native take exemption did not survive a transfer of management was invalidated in court, and Alaska therefore decided not to pursue the waiver further (*People of Togiak*, supra).

Finally, under section 109(h) a federal, state, or local government official, or person formally designated under the Act for such purpose may take a marine mammal "in the course of his or her duties" as an official or designee, if such taking is for the protection of the animal, the protection of the public health or welfare, or the nonlethal removal of nuisance animals.

Violations of the Act are subject to potentially severe penalties. Under section 1054, civil penalties can result in fines of up to $10,000. Any person who knowingly violates the Act is subject to a fine of up to $100,000 for each violation and as much as one year imprisonment. Section 106 provides that vessels involved in unlawful taking are subject to seizure and forfeiture of cargo, a fine of up to $25,000, and imposition of a lien against the vessel.

One of the most significant problems of marine mammal conservation is incidental take in commercial fishing operations (see Northridge and Hofman, this volume, and Gosliner, this volume). Indeed, the incidental take of small cetaceans in the purse seine tuna fishery was one of the principal factors leading to enactment of the Marine Mammal Protection Act. Numerous other fishery-related takes have had major impacts on marine mammal populations. The take of sea otters in California set net fisheries; northern right whale dolphins (*Lissodelphis borealis*), Dall's porpoises (*Phocoenoides dalli*), and other marine mammals in high-seas driftnet fisheries; vaquitas (*Phocoena sinus*) in Gulf of California gillnet fisheries; harbor porpoises (*Phocoena phocoena*) in salmon gillnet, cod trap, herring weir, and demersal sink gillnet fisheries; and many other marine mammals in other fisheries have presented serious challenges for the Act.

As first enacted, the Act provided only one means of regulating the take of marine mammals incidental to commercial fishing operations, that provided under section 101(a)(2). To obtain a permit, the applicant had to satisfy the requirements of section 103, which involved an adjudicatory process including an on-the-record hearing with sworn testimony before a federal administrative law judge. In practice, however, these rigorous requirements were applied fully to only two fisheries, the eastern tropical Pacific yellowfin tuna fishery and the Japanese high-seas fisheries for salmon in the North Pacific, which occurred partially in U.S. waters.

The permit decision, to be implemented through regulations, was to be based on the "best scientific evidence available," and any authorized take could not be to "the disadvantage" of the affected species or stock. The take also had to be consistent with the purposes and policies of the Act. Hence, under section 104 the take of depleted species could not be allowed. The economic and technological feasibility of implementing the permit were factors to be considered, but they were secondary to the interests of the marine mammals. And, as specified in section 101(a)(2), an "immediate goal" of the taking authorization was to reduce the incidental kill and serious injury rate "to insignificant levels approaching a zero mortality and serious injury rate."

This permitting procedure became one of the hallmarks of the Act. During the 1970s the U.S. tuna fleet sought a series of permits under section 101(a)(2). These permit proceedings, described in greater detail in Gosliner (this volume), brought together many of the Act's key provisions and principles. The tuna fleet carried the burden of proof to demonstrate that its take would meet the disadvantage test, including not reducing dolphin stocks to depleted status. The permit applicant also had to show that it was making progress toward meeting the zero mortality rate goal. This burden of proof had to be satisfied in a contested proceeding before an independent administrative law judge, who would weigh the evidence presented by the applicant against that presented by the other parties to the proceeding, including the National Marine Fisheries Service, the Marine Mammal Commission, and the environmental community. Scientific experts played a major role, offering their views and being subject to cross-examination under oath by counsel to the parties. And, through all of this process, the evidence was tested according to the conservative bias inherent in the Act.

These contested proceedings proved to be the essence of what the drafters of the Act had in mind to force a protective regime into place. Adjudicatory proceedings before an administrative law judge occurred in 1974, 1975, 1976–1977, and 1980 for the tuna fleet's incidental take permit. They also took place in 1981 and 1986 for the Japanese high-seas salmon driftnet permit.

The results were generally favorable to marine mammals. That is, they established quotas on allowable takes and gradually forced reductions in the numbers of marine mammals taken. In each case, general permits were issued to associations representing the fisheries (the American Tunaboat Association and the Federation of Japan Salmon Fisheries Cooperative Association, respectively), and quotas were set that pushed the allowed take levels lower and lower. Improved gear was required; new research was ordered; observers were placed on fishing vessels; and the permit holders were required to return to the same proceeding within a few years to obtain a new permit and once again meet their burden of proof and satisfy the Act's requirements.

Under this rigorous process, take levels declined dramatically. In 1972 it is estimated that 368,600 dolphins died in the U.S. tuna purse seine fishery. By 1976 the estimated kill level had dropped to 108,740. In 1977 it fell to 25,542; by 1980 the estimate was 15,305, although the number killed increased somewhat in subsequent years. Thus, the rigorous rule-making process had achieved its goal of dramatically reducing take, but not without some impact on the tuna fishery. Regulation, combined with the availability of cheaper labor in other countries, prompted many U.S. vessels to register under other flags or relocate to the western Pacific (see Gosliner, this volume).

A similar pattern emerged in the effort to reduce the incidental take of Dall's porpoises and other marine mammals in the Japanese high seas salmon driftnet fishery. Under international treaty, the Japanese were permitted to fish at certain times for salmon inside the U.S. 200–nautical mile (370.4-km) exclusive economic zone. In a general permit issued under the Marine Mammal Protection Act in 1981, the Japanese fleet received an annual quota of 5,500 Dall's porpoises, 450 northern fur seals, and 25 Steller sea lions (*Eumetopias jubatus*) for the portion of the fishery within the U.S. exclusive economic zone. The take of Dall's porpoises before the permit was issued is not known, but it is estimated to have been about 5,900 in 1980 (Jones 1984). Under the 1981 general permit, the estimated take for the 1981, 1982, and 1983 fishing seasons covered by the permit was 1,850, 4,187, and 2,906, respectively. (The 1981 level was low because of reduced fishing effort.)

The tuna-dolphin proceedings led to a spate of lawsuits filed by environmental groups and industry, including two of the most important court cases interpreting the Act. The first of these was *Committee for Humane Legislation, Inc.* v. *Richardson,* in which animal welfare and environmental groups challenged the first permit issued by the National Marine Fisheries Service to the American Tunaboat Association. In his 1976 decision, Judge Richey construed the Act to have "one basic purpose": protecting marine mammals.[20] He gave judicial recognition to the conservative bias of the Act in favor of marine mammals. His decision gave form to the disadvantage test by declaring that if the Secretary could not find that it would be met (i.e., by ruling out the possibility that the stock "would be reduced to a less-than-optimal level"), then he could not issue a permit. Judge Richey's construction, which put a strong protectionist slant on the Act, was further strengthened when the D.C. Circuit Court of Appeals affirmed the environmentalists' victory.[21]

The second key case arose in 1981 when the tuna industry challenged the authority of the Secretary to place observers on fishing vessels to monitor compliance with the American Tunaboat Association's incidental take permit. In *Balelo* v. *Baldrige,* the Ninth Circuit Court of Appeals initially ruled in favor of the industry, thereby jeopardizing the key element of the Act's enforcement program.[22] Ultimately, the Ninth Circuit reheard the case *en banc* and reversed its earlier ruling, recognizing the Secretary's broad rule-making power under the Act and the authority to require observers.[23]

By 1981 it had become apparent that many fisheries involved incidental takes of marine mammals but in such small numbers that the expensive, time-consuming, contentious adjudicatory process could not be justified (U.S. House 1981). Thus, Congress created a new, streamlined process governing small takes of marine mammals incidental to commercial fishing. This provision allowed for the authorization of the incidental, but not intentional, taking of small numbers of nondepleted marine mammals by any U.S. fishery. No permit or regulations were required if the Secretary, after providing public notice and opportunity for public comment, made a finding that such taking would have a negligible impact on the species or stock. This provision rarely was invoked, and eventually it was replaced by a new incidental take regime established by amendments enacted in 1988 in response to the *Kokechik* decision (see below).

In 1982 Congress took another step away from strict application of the Act's incidental permit regime. With the Japanese salmon fishery's incidental take permit set to expire in 1983, Congress stepped in to "legislate" the permit through 1987 under amendments to the North Pacific Fisheries Act. Thus, the 1981 general permit quotas remained in place although the amendments required the Japanese to conduct research on new fishing gear and techniques to reduce incidental take and to participate in and fund an observer program.[24]

A further retreat from the adjudicatory process occurred in the 1984 amendments to the Act. The U.S. tuna fleet's general permit was up for renewal, and the industry sought to avoid another contentious and costly proceeding (see Gosliner, this volume). In addition, at least two stocks of dolphins were thought to be depleted and hence taking could not be authorized under the existing law.

To address these concerns, the tuna fleet in essence negotiated a new permit with environmental groups, and Congress amended the Marine Mammal Protection Act to reflect that agreement. In doing so, Congress took a dramatic step away from the concepts underlying the Act as first enacted. No longer did the permit applicant have to meet a burden of proof to obtain authorization to take; neither did the agencies have the discretion to fashion permit terms based on the best available science. Instead, Congress in effect assumed the role of the National Marine Fisheries Service and passed judgment on what should be required of the fishery.

One of the most significant steps taken by Congress was to extend the existing quota, thereby setting an indefinite quota of 20,500 dolphins per year and reducing the impetus for further reductions of take. Nevertheless, section 104(h)(2)(B) of the statute provided authority for reducing the quota, or changing the permit terms and conditions in certain circumstances. These amendments were consistent with an earlier amendment, enacted in 1981, which defined the zero mortality rate goal for the tuna fleet as "a continuation of the application of the best marine mammal safety techniques and equipment that are economically and technologically practicable" [section 101(a)(2)].

The 1984 amendments applied only to the eastern tropical Pacific tuna fishery, however. Therefore, the Japanese high-seas salmon fleet needed to apply for a new permit under section 101(a)(2) in 1986. For the last time, the section 103 adjudicatory process for authorizing incidental take was activated. After a lengthy, contested proceeding, including a week-long hearing, the administrative law judge issued findings of fact in March 1987. He determined that no progress had been made toward the zero mortality rate goal during the years of the "legislated" permit when estimated take levels were 2,443 in 1984, 2,760 in 1985, 1,456 in 1986, and 741 in 1987 (due to low fishing effort).

Based on the judge's findings and recommendations, the Under Secretary of Commerce for Oceans and Atmosphere issued a final decision granting a three-year permit. To ensure progress toward the zero mortality rate goal, he set an aggregate quota for all three years of 789 porpoises from the Bering Sea stock and 2,494 porpoises from the North Pacific Ocean stock. He denied the request to take northern fur seals and Steller sea lions on the grounds that the Japanese Federation and the National Marine Fisheries Service (as the proponent of its proposed regulations) had failed to meet the burden of proof that these species were within their optimum sustainable population range and would not be disadvantaged. In this regard, the Under Secretary observed that one stock of fur seals involved had been designated as depleted.

Alaska Native organizations and environmental groups immediately challenged the permit. One of the grounds for challenge was the fact that the permit authorized the take only of Dall's porpoises, even though all parties conceded that small numbers of other marine mammals also would be taken. One of these species was the northern fur seal, a species for which no permit could be issued because it had been designated as depleted. The D.C. District Court and Court of Appeals agreed with the plaintiffs that, under these circumstances, no permit could be issued for the take of any species. As a result of this decision in *Kokechik Fishermen's Ass'n* v. *Secretary of Commerce*, the Japanese fleet could no longer fish for salmon in U.S. waters.

The *Kokechik* decision also raised concerns, expressed by the National Marine Fisheries Service and fisheries groups, that permits could not be issued for many other commercial fisheries because it was sufficiently certain that they would take marine mammals that either were depleted, and therefore outside the scope of section 103, or were not known to be above their maximum net productivity level, rendering it impossible to make the required no-disadvantage finding (U.S. Senate 1985). Rather than run the risk that many commercial fisheries would be shut down as a result of their inability to obtain an incidental take permit, Congress amended the Act in 1988 to establish a five-year exemption from the moratorium for the incidental take of marine mammals for most commercial fisheries [section 113(a)]. During this interim exemption period, the Secretary of Commerce, through the National Marine Fisheries Service, and based on recommended guidelines developed by the Marine Mammal Commission, was to develop a long-term program to govern incidental take once the interim exemption expired. This program was to be submitted to Congress in the form of recommended amendments to the Act to address the *Kokechik* problem.

The proposal subsequently developed by the Secretary was not entirely acceptable to the affected interest groups. Commercial fishing and environmental groups developed their own joint proposal after extensive negotiations. That proposal borrowed on some of the key concepts of the National Marine Fisheries Service program and became the basis for congressional action in 1994 to develop a new approach to regulate incidental take in commercial fisheries under new sections 117 and 118 instead of section 101(a)(2).

Under the 1994 amendments, participants in a fishery no longer need to obtain an incidental take permit and no longer have the burden of demonstrating that a marine mammal stock is at its OSP and would not be disadvantaged by any authorized take. Instead, participants in commercial fisheries are allowed to take marine mammals incidental to their operations simply by registering their vessels and abiding by certain statutory and regulatory requirements. Although monitoring and reporting requirements are applicable across broad categories of fisheries, the Secretary is authorized to establish fishery-specific limits on incidental mortality and serious injury or to impose time, area, gear, or other restrictions on a fishery where necessary to reduce such taking to less than the potential biological removal level calculated for the stock. Thus, one of the most notable features of the Act during its first 20 years—the fact-intensive, potentially contested proceeding before an administrative law judge in which the party seeking to exploit the marine mammal stock must prove it is entitled to do so—has been replaced with a more business-as-usual approach. It is now a numbers-driven exercise in which a take reduction plan is developed and implementing regulations are required only if necessary to reduce the level of take below a stock's potential biological removal level.

The new program governing incidental take in commercial fisheries is quite detailed, comprising 10 pages of text in the United States Code Annotated. This level of detail, too, amounted to a dramatic shift from the approach under the original Marine Mammal Protection Act. Before the Japanese salmon fishery permit was extended by legislation in 1982, the tuna-dolphin legislative fix of 1984, and the *Kokechik*-inspired amendments of 1988 and 1994, the Act set forth only a general framework for regulation. The Secretary, responding to permit applications, would be called on to develop the detailed regulatory approach that would govern the relevant fishery. Hence, after the tuna-dolphin hearings, the National Marine Fisheries Service promulgated complex regulations to govern take levels, gear requirements, and other aspects of the fishery. As discussed above, Congress greatly reduced the Secretary's discretionary role, in the case of the tuna-dolphin controversy, in 1984 by simply "legislating the permit." It did so largely in response to pressure from the tuna industry to avoid the cost and controversy of another contested hearing process. Some of the environmental groups that had participated in the rulemaking also agreed that a revised process was needed (Scheele and Wilkinson 1988). In the 1994 amendments, Congress continued this trend by legislating the details of the regulatory process for all domestic fisheries with incidental takes of marine mammals, and by replacing the requirement to determine that stocks are within OSP with a directive that human-caused taking be reduced to less than a stock's potential biological removal level.

The first phase of the commercial fishery incidental take program under the 1994 amendments called for the Secretaries of Commerce and the Intèrior to prepare stock assessments under section 117 of the Act for each marine mammal stock that occurs in U.S. waters. These stock assessments, which are updated periodically, serve as the basis for regulation.

In 1994, pursuant to section 117(a), the Secretary of Commerce established three regional scientific review groups under section to assist in the preparation of the stock assessments. These groups were for Alaska, the Pacific coast (including Hawaii), and the Atlantic coast (including the Gulf of Mexico). Final assessments were issued in 1995 by the National Marine Fisheries Service and the Fish and Wildlife Service for species under their respective jurisdictions. In addition to providing information on the status of a stock, each assessment includes (1) descriptions of the commercial fisheries that interact with it, (2) estimates of the number of vessels in each fishery, (3) fishery-specific estimates of mortality and serious injury levels and rates, (4) a description of seasonal or area differences in incidental mortality and serious injury, (5) an analysis of whether incidental take levels are approaching a zero mortality and serious injury rate, (6) an estimate of the potential biological removal level for the stock, along with an explanation of how it was calculated, and (7) an evaluation of whether the level of human-caused mortality and serious injury exceeds the potential biological removal calculated for this stock. Stocks that are listed as endangered or threatened under the Endangered Species Act, designated as depleted under the Marine Mammal Protection Act, or for which estimated human-caused mortality and serious injury equals or exceeds the potential biological removal are categorized as strategic stocks.

The section 118 regulatory regime follows from information developed in the section 117 stock assessments. Actions required to implement the new incidental take regime are the responsibility of the Secretary of Commerce. The amendments require, however, that the Secretary of Commerce consult with the Secretary of the Interior before taking any action or making any determination that affects or relates to marine mammal stocks under the jurisdiction of the Department of the Interior.

The new regime established under section 118 retains the Act's original goal of reducing the mortality and serious injury of marine mammals incidental to commercial fisheries, as set forth in section 101(a)(2), to insignificant levels approaching a zero rate. This goal is to be achieved by 30 April 2001. The Secretary is required to conduct an interim review of progress made by each fishery toward achieving the zero mortality and serious injury goal and report the findings to Congress by 30 April 1998. If sufficient progress has not been made by a fishery, the Secretary is to promulgate regulations to advance the goal.

To determine what level of regulation is appropriate, the Secretary had to categorize fisheries according to whether they frequently (category I), occasionally (category II), or rarely (category III) kill or injure marine mammals. Vessels participating in category I or category II fisheries are required to register to obtain authorization to take marine mammals. It is a violation of the Marine Mammal Protection Act to engage in a category I or category II fishery without the required authorization. In addition, the Secretary may suspend or revoke an authorization to take marine mammals if the vessel owner fails to register, does not comply with reporting requirements, refuses to carry an observer when required to do so, or fails to comply with applicable take reduction plans or emergency regulations.

The 1994 amendments also direct the Secretary to establish a program to monitor marine mammal mortality and serious injury incidental to commercial fisheries. The Secretary may require vessels participating in category I and category II fisheries to carry observers, but may place observers on vessels in category III fisheries only with the consent of the vessel owner. The National Marine Fisheries Service published final regulations implementing these requirements of section 118 on 30 August 1995.[25]

The 1994 amendments also required the Secretary to develop and implement an incidental take reduction plan for each strategic stock that interacts with a category I or category II fishery. Under section 118, the Secretary may also develop take reduction plans for other marine mammal stocks that interact with a category I fishery if it is determined, after public notice and comment, that the fishery is responsible for high levels of mortality and serious injury for a number of marine mammal stocks.

Take reduction plans are to include, among other things, recommended regulatory or voluntary measures designed to reduce incidental mortality and serious injury, and to recommend dates for achieving objectives of the plan. The plans are to be developed by take reduction teams composed of interested parties, which were to have been established by 21 September 1995.

The immediate goal of a take reduction plan for a strategic stock is to reduce within six months incidental mortality or serious injury to levels less than the potential biological removal level. The long-term goal of the plan is to reduce incidental mortality and serious injury to insignificant levels approaching a zero rate within five years, taking into account the economics of the fishery, existing technology, and applicable state or regional fishery management plans. Plans are submitted within six or eleven months from the date of the establishment of the take reduction team, depending on the level of protection required for the stock. If these deadlines are not met, the Secretary is to develop proposed plans independently.

As of the end of May 1997 five take reduction teams had been established and four draft take reduction plans had been developed. However, more than three years after enactment of the 1994 amendments, none of these plans had yet been implemented.

Finally, if the Secretary determines that incidental mortality and serious injury of marine mammals resulting from commercial fisheries is having, or is likely to have, an immediate and significant adverse effect on a species or stock, emergency regulations are to be promulgated to reduce the level of take. Emergency regulations are to expire at the end of the applicable fishing season or at the end of 180 days, whichever is earlier. Under section 118, they may, however, be extended for an additional 90-day period if needed to address a continuing threat.

The section 118 incidental take regime does not apply to marine mammals that are listed as endangered or threatened under the Endangered Species Act. A new section 101(a)(5)(E), added to the Marine Mammal Protection Act in 1994, enables the Secretary to allow under certain circumstances the taking of marine mammals listed as threatened or endangered under the Endangered Species Act incidental to commercial fishing. Such authorizations are limited to a three-year period and apply only to vessels of the United States or foreign vessels permitted to fish under section 204(b) of the Magnuson-Stevens Fishery Conservation and Management Act. Section 118 specifies that the taking of California sea otters may not be authorized under this provision.

Before issuing an authorization under section 101(a)(5)(E), the Secretary must determine, after notice and opportunity for public comment, that (1) the mortality and serious injury of the species incidental to commercial fisheries will have a negligible impact on the species or stocks (a "negligibility finding"); (2) a recovery plan has been, or is being, developed for the species or stock under the Endangered Species Act; and (3) where required under the new incidental take regime for commercial fisheries (section 118), a monitoring program has been established, the vessels are registered, and a take reduction plan has been, or is being, developed. If the required determinations are made, the Secretary is to publish a list of the fisheries to which the authorization applies and, for vessels required to register under section 118, issue appropriate permits. Vessels participating in fisheries included in the list, but which are not required to register, are covered by the authorization provided that they report any such incidental mortality or serious injury.

On 31 August 1995 the National Marine Fisheries Service announced negligibility findings for three stocks of marine mammals listed under the Endangered Species Act: the central North Pacific stock of humpback whales and eastern and western stocks of Steller sea lions. Consequently, an interim permit authorizing take from these stocks was issued to 22 commercial fisheries. The Service announced that it could not make negligibility findings for seven other stocks of listed marine mammals that were interacting with fishery operations. Hence, all take of these species was prohibited.[26]

"Small takes" of marine mammals incidental to all activities other than commercial fishing are addressed under section 101(a)(5). Like the original small-take provision for commercial fisheries, Congress added this provision in 1981 to establish a more streamlined procedure than the waiver requirement when only small numbers of marine mammals will be affected and the likely impact will be negligible. This form of take authorization has been used most frequently in connection with oil and gas activities that have the potential to cause incidental take of marine mammals. It has also been used to authorize taking incidental to such activities as space shuttle launches and ship shock tests conducted by the U.S. Navy. This provision originally allowed incidental taking to be authorized only from marine mammal species that were not depleted. In 1986 the provision was amended to allow incidental taking of depleted as well as nondepleted species. Congress believed that such a change was needed to parallel the incidental take provisions of the Endangered Species Act more closely.

A take may be authorized only when requested by a citizen of the United States. Before authorization, the Secretary must find that the proposed take will have a negligible impact on the species or stock and will not have an unmitigable adverse impact on the use of the species for subsistence purposes by Alaska Natives, as specified in section 101(a)(5)(A). The Secretary also must publish regulations setting forth the permissible methods of taking and other requirements pertaining to habitat protection, reporting, and monitoring. Such an authorization is valid for not more than five consecutive years.

In 1994 Congress established an even less complex mechanism for authorizing the take of small numbers of marine mammals incidental to activities other than commercial fishing when only harassment is involved. Such authorizations are to be issued for periods of up to one year if the Secretary determines, after notice and opportunity for public comment, that such taking will have a negligible impact on the marine mammal species or stock and will not have unmitigable adverse impacts on the availability of the marine mammals for subsistence use by Alaska Natives. The authorization of incidental taking other than by harassment remains subject to rulemaking under section 101(a)(5)(D)(i).

This procedure has been used to authorize the incidental take of marine mammals for a large variety of activities, including harassment of harbor seals (*Phoca vitulina*) incidental to the demolition and reconstruction of a dock in Puget Sound by the Washington Department of Corrections; harassment of harbor seals incidental to launches of space vehicles from Vandenberg Air Force Base in California; harassment of several species of cetaceans incidental to seismic surveys in the Santa Barbara Channel; and harassment of walruses and polar bears incidental to oil and gas activities in the Chukchi Sea.

THE MORATORIUM ON IMPORTATION AND ITS EXCEPTIONS. The moratorium under section 101(a) of the Marine Mammal Protection Act also applies to the importation of marine mammals and marine mammal products into the United States. As with the moratorium on taking, the moratorium on importing marine mammals may be waived, provided that certain determinations are made in the course of a formal rulemaking. In addition, permits authorizing imports for purposes of scientific research, public display, and enhancement of the species can be issued under the same conditions as for taking. Also, under the 1994 amendments, exceptions were created for the importation of marine mammal products that are (1) legally possessed and exported by a U.S. citizen for purposes of foreign travel if reimported by the same person; (2) acquired outside the United States as part of a cultural exchange by an Alaska Native; or (3) owned by a Native inhabitant of Russia, Canada, or Greenland and imported for noncommercial purposes in conjunction with travel inside the United States or as part of a cultural exchange with an Alaska Native.

Except for purposes of scientific research or species enhancement, section 102(b) of the Act specifies that no exception may be granted for the importation of a marine mammal that was pregnant or nursing at the time of taking or less than eight months old, taken from a depleted species or stock, or taken in an inhumane manner. An exception to these general prohibitions allows importation if necessary for the protection or welfare of the animal. No marine mammal taken in violation of the Act or the law of a foreign nation may be imported for any reason. Both the taking and importation prohibitions do not apply to animals taken or imported before enactment of the Act. Marine mammals also may be imported by the Secretary or a designee "if . . . necessary to render medical treatment that is otherwise not available."

In a significant change from the Act's original provisions, the 1994 amendments established an exception under section 104(c)(5)(A) to allow the issuance of permits for the importation of certain polar bear trophies legally taken in sport hunts in Canada. Although the existing waiver authority of the Act was available for this purpose, Congress responded to lobbying from U.S. trophy hunters to relax the previous importation restrictions.

This permit authority has been controversial. The proposed regulations, published by the Fish and Wildlife Service in January 1995, were attacked by animal welfare groups opposed to such importation. Sport hunting groups supported the authorization but opposed certain aspects of the proposal as too stringent and expensive. In February 1997 the Service issued final regulations authorizing the issuance of permits for 5 of the 12 management units used by Canada to manage its polar bears. Sport hunting groups and several members of Congress were particularly critical of the regulations, as were animal protection groups who believed the restrictions did not go far enough. Proponents of the amendments believed that the Service had thwarted the intent of Congress by limiting imports of trophies taken before the 1994 amendments to those from the five approved management units. Although the Service agreed that allowing trophy imports from polar bears that were already dead would have no impact on polar bear conservation, it believed that its regulations reflected the "plain language" of the statute. Although the Service was reluctant to amend its regulations in response to congressional criticism, for fear of inviting costly, and likely adverse, litigation, it was willing to support a statutory amendment to allow import permits to be issued for all polar bear trophies legally taken in Canada before the date of enactment of the 1994 amendment, regardless of the status of the population or the adequacy of Canada's management program. Such an amendment was signed into law in June 1997.

Finally, the 1994 amendments for the first time added an export prohibition to the Act. Section 102(a)(4) was amended to prohibit the unauthorized export or attempted export of a marine mammal or marine mammal product. This section was further amended to make the prohibition on transporting, purchasing, selling, exporting, or attempting to engage in such activities applicable if the marine mammal or marine mammal product was taken in violation of the Act or if such activities are for any purpose other than public display, scientific research, or enhancing the survival of a species or stock authorized under section 104(c).

This amendment was enacted as part of a large-scale overhaul of the Act's permit provisions, particularly as they relate to public display of marine mammals, and it is not clear that legislators recognized the possible applicability of the new export prohibition to other endeavors, such as the making and selling of handicrafts by Alaska Natives. It is likely that this provision will be revisited during the next reauthorization of the Act and other exceptions to the export prohibition considered.

HABITAT PROTECTION. In its findings and declaration of policy, the Marine Mammal Protection Act emphasizes habitat and ecosystem protection. The habitat and ecosystem goals set forth in section 2 of the Act include:

(1) management of marine mammals to ensure they do not cease to be a significant functioning element of the ecosystem of which they are a part;
(2) protection of essential habitats, including rookeries, mating grounds, and areas of similar significance "from the adverse effect of man's actions";
(3) recognition that marine mammals "affect the balance of marine ecosystems in a manner that is important to other animals and animal products" and that marine mammals should therefore be protected and conserved; and
(4) the primary objective of maintaining "the health and stability of the marine ecosystem."

The Act also refers to habitat in the definition of *conservation* and *management*. Those terms are defined to include "habitat acquisition and improvement."

Without referring specifically to habitat protection or other measures, section 112 authorizes the Secretary to "prescribe such regulations as are necessary and appropriate to carry out the purposes of the Marine Mammal Protection Act." This authority, although general, arguably can be used to promulgate regulations to protect habitat areas. In the legislative history of the 1994 amendments, Congress made it clear that section 112 includes such authority. As stated by the House Merchant Marine and Fisheries Committee, it added the phrase "essential habitats" to section 2(2) to underscore that "[t]he Committee believes that the Secretary currently has the authority to protect marine mammals and their habitats under the general rulemaking authority of section 112 of the Act" (U.S. House 1994). The Committee noted, for example, that this authority would allow the Secretary "to protect polar bear denning, feeding, and migration routes in order to fully comply with the United States obligations under Article II of the Agreement on the Conservation of Polar Bears."

To date, neither the Fish and Wildlife Service nor the National Marine Fisheries Service has relied exclusively on this authority to protect marine mammal habitat. Before the 1994 amendments, both agencies were concerned that section 112 of the Act alone did not provide sufficient authority to protect habitat. Section 112 has been used in conjunction with the Endangered Species Act, however, to protect marine mammal habitat. For example, the Fish and Wildlife Service, in cooperation with the state of Florida, designated motorboat speed zones in the Crystal River area to protect manatees.[27] Also, the Marine Mammal Protection Act, the Endangered Species Act, and the National Park Service Organic Act were jointly used as authority to designate zones in Glacier Bay National Park to protect humpback whales from disturbance by cruise ships and other vessels.[28]

RESEARCH. As discussed previously, the Marine Mammal Protection Act places a high priority on research. In section 2(3), Congress set forth the finding and declaration of policy that "there is inadequate knowledge of the ecology and population dynamics of such marine mammals and of the factors which bear upon their ability to reproduce themselves successfully." Congress also declared that "negotiations should be undertaken immediately to encourage the development of international arrangements for research on, and conservation of, all marine mammals." In defining the terms *conservation* and *management,* section 3 of the Act includes "the entire scope of activities that constitute a modern scientific resource program, including, but not limited to, research, census" and other activities.

In section 110, the Act provides for grants or other forms of financial assistance to qualified entities or persons "to undertake research in subjects which are relevant to the protection and conservation of marine mammals." Waivers of the moratorium and permits authorizing the taking of marine mammals also must be based on "the best scientific evidence available."

Finally, the importance placed by Congress on scientific research was confirmed by the establishment of the Marine Mammal Commission and its Committee of Scientific Advisors on Marine Mammals. The Commission is charged with a number of scientific research responsibilities, and its studies and recommendations must be made in consultation with the Committee of Scientific Advisors. The Commission itself is to consist of three members who are "knowledgeable in the fields of marine ecology and resource management," and the nine members of the Committee are to be "scientists knowledgeable in marine ecology and marine mammal affairs."

Although the Marine Mammal Protection Act recognizes the importance of research on marine mammals and related ecosystem components, the authorized funding levels, particularly in recent years, have been too low to enable the responsible agencies to undertake comprehensive research programs. This problem has been exacerbated by the addition of new research-intensive responsibilities, such as the preparation of stock assessments, without any appreciable increase in funding. Nevertheless, some research projects have received specific congressional attention and have resulted in supplemental funding. For example, amendments enacted in 1984 specifically authorized $4 million to be appropriated for a program to monitor the indices of abundance and trends of dolphin stocks affected by the eastern tropical Pacific tuna fishery. Amendments enacted in August 1997 authorized appropriations of $12 million over a four-year period to conduct abundance surveys and stress studies to assess the status of dolphin stocks and examine the effects on dolphins of chase and encirclement by tuna seiners.

INTERNATIONAL COOPERATION. The Act's international program is set forth in section 108. It requires the Secretary of Commerce or the Secretary of the Interior, working through the Secretary of State, to "initiate negotiations as soon as possible for the development of bilateral or multinational agreements with other nations for the protection and conservation of all marine mammals." It also directs the federal government to encourage other agreements to protect specific ocean and land regions "which are of special significance to the health and stability of marine mammals" and to amend any existing treaty to make it consistent with the purposes and policies of the Act.

In 1994 Congress took specific note of concerns that had been raised over the effectiveness of the Agreement on the Conservation of Polar Bears by amending section 113 of the Act to require two reviews of the treaty (Fig. 3-2). First, the Secretary of the Interior, in consultation with the Secretary of State and the Marine Mammal Commission, was directed to review the effectiveness of U.S. implementation, particularly with respect to the Agreement's habitat protection mandates. A report of that review was to have been submitted to Congress by 30 April 1995, but as of September 1997, it was still undergoing review within the Department of the Interior. Second, the Secretary of the Interior, in consultation with the other parties to the Agreement, was to initiate a review of its effectiveness and establish a process for conducting similar reviews in the future. Although overtures have been made to the other parties concerning the need for an international review of the Agreement, no such review has been undertaken.

In addition, under section 113 the Secretary of the Interior, acting through the Secretary of State and in consultation with the Marine Mammal Commission and the state of Alaska, is to consult with appropriate officials of the Russian Federation on the development of enhanced cooperative research and management programs for the conservation of polar bears in Russia and Alaska. Reports on this consultation and follow-up research and management programs are to be submitted to Congress. Recent efforts in this regard are discussed later in this chapter.

INTERNATIONAL ENFORCEMENT. Congress also foresaw the need to use more aggressive measures to en-

Figure 3-2. This polar bear, on the pack ice of the Chukchi Sea off northern Alaska in 1977, has successfully stalked and killed a young walrus by biting it in the back of the head. While feeding on the carcass, the bear has turned the walrus's skin inside out. (Photograph © Bill Curtsinger)

force international commitments or to project U.S. standards internationally. The Act encouraged the use of a carrot, but also provided federal agencies a stick to wield when necessary.

As initially enacted, section 101 of the Act required the Secretary of the Treasury to "ban the importation of commercial fish or products from fish which have been caught with commercial fishing technology which results in the incidental kill or incidental serious injury of ocean mammals in excess of United States standards." In the tuna-dolphin context, this provision was construed in National Marine Fisheries Service regulations published in 1974 to allow the importation of yellowfin tuna only if the harvesting vessel from the foreign country used certain fishing technology and practices required of the U.S. fleet.[29] As discussed further in Gosliner (this volume), provisions specific to the eastern tropical Pacific purse seine tuna fishery have resulted in embargoes of yellowfin tuna from virtually all of the countries participating in that fishery.

This requirement was otherwise ignored by the National Marine Fisheries Service throughout the early history of the Act. More recently, however, the National Marine Fisheries Service used the threat of an import ban under section 101(a)(2) to prompt Chile into taking steps to prevent its fishermen from killing and using dolphins as crab bait. Nevertheless, the lackluster record of implementing the foreign enforcement tools represents one of the low points of the Act's history. It is mirrored, in many respects, by the failure of the United States to apply the Pelly Amendment effectively (see below).

SPECIES-SPECIFIC AMENDMENTS. From time to time, Congress has seen the need to enact legislation to address specific marine mammal problems. These instances are exceptions to the general rule of the Act, which is that Congress should avoid becoming embroiled in species-specific problems and instead make general prescriptions providing a framework for agency action. The theory behind this general principle is that species-specific amendments lead down a slippery slope, forcing Congress to become the arbiter of complex factual and policy disputes that congressional committees are ill-equipped to handle and lack the time to address.

One of the most notable species-specific acts of Congress is the 1986 law creating the southern sea otter translocation program.[30] The Fish and Wildlife Service in 1977 listed the southern sea otter (the California population) as a threatened species under the Endangered Species Act. This population is extremely vulnerable to the effects of oil spills because the insulating properties of sea otter fur are severely compromised by oil, causing the animal to die of hypothermia. This physical characteristic, combined with the proximity of the population's limited range to shipping and vessel transit lanes, are the principal reasons the Service listed the southern sea otter under the Endangered Species Act.

In enacting the 1986 law, Congress responded to two key administrative findings. The first, reached by the sea otter recovery team established under the Endangered Species Act, was that a second population, sufficiently removed from the parent population, was needed to provide adequate protection for the small population in central California from the risk of an oil spill.[31] The second was the 1980 recommendation of the Marine Mammal Commission, later adopted by the Fish and Wildlife Service, that "zonal management" was needed to establish areas along the California coast where otters were excluded to protect commercial and recreational shellfish stocks from otter predation.

A new law was needed to facilitate the translocation of sea otters because in 1986 the Act did not authorize any taking of depleted species (and the southern sea otter was automatically considered depleted because of its listing under the Endangered Species Act) for recovery or management purposes. (Congress would add a general provision in 1988 authorizing permits to be issued for species enhancement activities.) Thus, Congress crafted a special law to authorize the Fish and Wildlife Service to move a portion of the parent population to another location. The new population was to reside within a "translocation zone" where full Marine Mammal Protection Act and Endangered Species Act protections would apply. Around this translocation zone would be a "management zone," with only limited protection. Sea otters that strayed into this management zone were to be removed by nonlethal means.

After a lengthy decision-making process under this law, and an unsuccessful lawsuit by certain California shellfish groups seeking to block translocation, the Fish and Wildlife Service began moving otters to San Nicolas Island in the Channel Islands in 1987. By 1990, 139 animals had been translocated. Many of these animals returned to the mainland population, contrary to expectation. Others simply disappeared. Counts in 1994 and 1995 indicated that the translocated population was stable at about 15 animals, with six pups born at San Nicolas in 1995. Although the population size is much smaller than expected, it appears that a reproducing population has successfully established itself at the island. In the meantime, the parent population has grown slowly but steadily from about 1,350 animals in 1982 to about 2,300 animals in 1996 (Marine Mammal Commission 1997). Recently, however, the population has again begun to decline for unknown reasons.

Although the southern sea otter translocation law is a free-standing act of Congress and not a part of the Marine Mammal Protection Act, several sections of the Act address species-specific marine mammal problems. As noted above, in 1984 Congress amended section 104 to authorize the take of dolphins in the U.S. tuna fishery. Congress revisited the tuna-dolphin controversy in 1990 through the dolphin-safe labeling requirements, in 1992 added a new title to the Act in an effort to establish a global moratorium on setting on dolphins, and, in 1997, implemented an international dolphin conservation program (see Gosliner, this volume).

In 1994 Congress amended the Act to address interactions between pinnipeds and fisheries (section 120). The amendments, among other things, established a special procedure to address the problem of sea lion predation of salmon stocks off the northwestern coast of the United States (see Fraker and Mate, this volume). Specifically, this amendment would allow the National Marine Fisheries Service to authorize the killing of problem sea lions after studying the situation and making certain findings. Once again, Congress created a new avenue for authorizing takes rather than relying on the procedure originally envisioned to address such a problem, the waiver process of section 101(a)(3). In this instance, an amendment was necessary because National Marine Fisheries Service scientists had stated that the California sea lion population, although believed to be at historically high levels, was growing at its maximum rate, suggesting that the stock was depleted. Thus, the Service did not believe it could issue a waiver to authorize a take from this population. Although the National Marine Fisheries Service established a pinniped-fishery interaction task force in 1994 to review the situation at Ballard Locks in Seattle, Washington, and subsequently authorized lethal removal of "predatory" sea lions, to date, no lethal taking has occurred. Rather, problem sea lions have been removed for temporary or permanent maintenance in captivity.

Large numbers of bottlenose dolphin (*Tursiops truncatus*)

Figure 3-3. The bottlenose dolphin is a familiar sight along the southern coasts of the United States. It frequently approaches boats to ride the bow waves and swim and breach in the wake. (Photograph by Steve Leatherwood)

(Fig. 3-3) strandings and mortalities in 1987–1988 led to enactment of special provisions for addressing such events. Although these legal provisions, as set forth in title IV of the Act, are of a general nature, they were derived in response to a species-specific phenomenon. They provide for creation of an interagency stranding working group, development of contingency plans to guide response actions, establishment of a fund to pay for response actions, development of objective criteria for releasing animals back into the wild, and other actions (see Geraci et al., this volume; Wilkinson and Worthy, this volume).

Finally, two laws have been enacted to implement international treaties involving marine mammals: the Fur Seal Act of 1966[32] to implement the Interim Convention on the Conservation of North Pacific Fur Seals, and the North Pacific Fisheries Act[33] to implement the International Convention for the High Seas Fisheries of the North Pacific Ocean and authorize the incidental take of Dall's porpoises. The parts of these laws that implemented the treaties have become obsolete as a result of (1) the failure of the United States to ratify a protocol to extend the Fur Seal Convention beyond 1984, thus ending the commercial fur seal harvest on the Pribilof Islands, and (2) the voiding of the Marine Mammal Protection Act permit to the Japanese high seas salmon fleet under the *Kokechik* decision.

Other Legal Authorities Applicable to Marine Mammal Protection

The Marine Mammal Protection Act is the principal legal authority governing marine mammal conservation. Several other laws, as well as international agreements, also serve this purpose. These other authorities are discussed briefly in this section.

The Endangered Species Act

The year after enactment of the Marine Mammal Protection Act, Congress passed the Endangered Species Act of 1973.[34] This law superseded the Endangered Species Preservation Act of 1966 and the Endangered Species Conservation Act of 1969. The Endangered Species Act sought to establish a comprehensive federal program to conserve (with the goal of ensuring the survival and recovery of listed species) plant and animal species facing extinction. The Endangered Species Act reflected a mixture of ethical and utilitarian concerns about humanity's responsibility for other life forms and our ultimate dependence on many of them for future advances in medicine, agriculture, science, industry, and other spheres of endeavor. The relentless exploitation of the great whales, which had galvanized the attention of much of the fledgling environmental movement in the late 1960s and early 1970s, and which had been a major factor in enactment of the Act, contributed to the perceived need for the Endangered Species Act (Bean 1983:329–331).

The authors of the Endangered Species Act recognized, however, that commercial exploitation of wild creatures was not the only threat to their survival; it was not necessarily even the most important one. The larger array of threats was captured in the Act's very first sentence: "The Congress finds and declares that . . . various species of fish, wildlife, and plants in the United States have been rendered extinct as a consequence of economic growth and development untempered by adequate concern and conservation."

The idea that economic growth and development would be responsible for anything negative ran counter to the pro-growth, pro-development mindset that had characterized American thinking virtually throughout the nation's history, and especially in the post–World War II era. Economic growth and development had made U.S. society one of the wealthiest in the world, thus making possible the leisure time and personal security that fostered an appreciation of the environment. That economic prosperity could also be a source of environmental problems and that the society's long-standing goals now needed to be "tempered" were unfamiliar and unsettling notions. However easy it might have been to state such propositions in the abstract, it would prove difficult to put them into practice.

Reflecting its ambitious purpose, the Endangered Species Act contains novel and far-reaching powers. Like the Marine Mammal Protection Act, it prohibits the "taking" of endangered species and defines that prohibition in broad terms. The Endangered Species Act goes beyond the Marine Mammal Protection Act by adding activities that "harm" listed species to its definition of taking. This term has been construed by regulation—and upheld by the U.S. Supreme Court—to include habitat modification that actually kills or injures wildlife.[35] Unlike the Marine Mammal Protection Act, the Endangered Species Act in section 5 specifically authorizes the federal government to acquire habitat for conservation purposes and in sections 3 and 4 to designate and specially protect areas as "critical habitat" for endangered and threatened species.

Even more novel is the Endangered Species Act's recognition that the actions of the federal government itself can often contribute to the endangerment of our most imperiled species. For that reason, section 7 of the Act requires that each federal agency "insure that any action authorized, funded, or carried out by [it] is not likely to jeopardize the continued existence of any endangered species or result in the destruction or adverse modification of critical habitat." This obligation is to be met in consultation with either the Fish and Wildlife Service or the National Marine Fisheries Service (depending on the species involved), thus giving them some degree of influence over the programs and actions of other federal agencies. The ultimate decision, however, remains that of the action agency.

Marine mammals protected by the Endangered Species Act include nine species of whales; the Steller sea lion; the Hawaiian, Mediterranean, and Caribbean monk seals (*Monachus schauinslandi, M. monachus,* and *M. tropicalis,* respectively); the Guadalupe fur seal (*Arctocephalus townsendi*); the ringed seal (*Phoca hispida*) of Lake Saimaa, Finland; the marine otter (*Lutra felina*) of South America; the southern sea otter; the West Indian, West African, and Amazonian manatees (*Trichechus manatus, T. senegalensis,* and *T. inunguis,* respectively); the dugong; two species of river dolphins (the baiji [*Lipotes vexillifer*] and the Indus River dolphin [*Platanista minor*]); and the vaquita or Gulf of California harbor porpoise. Of the species found in U.S. waters, the Fish and Wildlife Service has primary responsibility for the manatee and sea otter; the others are the primary responsibility of the National Marine Fisheries Service.

In recognition of the interplay between the Endangered Species Act and the Marine Mammal Protection Act for these species, Congress opted for the maximum protection, and section 17 of the Endangered Species Act provides that, in the case of conflict between these two laws, the more stringent measure shall apply. Also, unlike the Marine Mammal Protection Act, which preempts state regulatory authority, the Endangered Species Act in section 6 specifically allows states to adopt measures that are more restrictive than federal law.

The impact of the Endangered Species Act on marine mammal conservation can be illustrated with the Florida manatee, a mammal that frequents many of Florida s rivers, lakes, and canals (see Reynolds, this volume). In southern Florida, an extensive network of canals, levees, flood control gates, and pumping stations has been established to reduce flooding of developed and agricultural areas. The U.S. Army Corps of Engineers, a federal agency, constructed much of this network and shares in its maintenance and operation. The operation of some of the facilities in this network, particularly the closing of some of the giant floodgates, has been responsible for numerous manatee deaths over the years (Odell and Reynolds 1979). Using its consultation authority under section 7 of the Endangered Species Act and its authority to enforce the prohibition against "taking" endangered species, the Fish and Wildlife Service has worked with the Corps and others to modify flood control structures and operations to reduce the inadvertent killing of manatees.

Another example of the Endangered Species Act's beneficial influence involves the control of boat speeds in certain parts of Florida. State and local government authorities often view the exercise of federal control as an unwelcome intrusion into local matters, and fear of federal involvement often prompts state or local action to preempt the need for federal action. Collisions with boats constitute the largest single source of nonnatural mortality to manatees (Ackerman et al. 1995). After a period of years in which boat collisions had caused an alarming number of manatee deaths, pressure grew either to close certain areas altogether to boat traffic or to reduce boat speeds in those areas. The Endangered Species Act's prohibition against "taking" endangered species and the fact that unregulated boat traffic undeniably was responsible for taking large numbers of manatees meant that the federal government could have taken steps to regulate boating directly. This possibility was among the considerations that prompted state and local governments in Florida to initiate their own efforts to identify key waterways where manatees were at risk from vessel collisions and to limit boats to safe speeds in those areas.

The Magnuson-Stevens Fishery Conservation and Management Act

Perhaps the most widespread and intensive constant human activity in ecosystems occupied by marine mammals is fishing. Fishing can affect marine mammals in a variety of ways (see Northridge and Hofman, this volume). For example, nets and other fishing gear intended to capture fish often inadvertently capture marine mammals; fishing practices can damage marine mammal habitat; the presence of boats and fishing activities near pinniped rookeries can disturb the animals engaged in vital activities (molting, resting, nursing, etc.); humans and marine mammals sometimes pursue the same fish species, perhaps limiting the availability of marine mammal prey and occasionally causing those engaged in fishing to view the mammals as competitors to be dispersed or dispensed with by whatever means is necessary; and, finally, lost or discarded fishing gear can drift with the ocean currents, entangling and killing marine mammals and other creatures in a phenomenon sometimes known as "ghost fishing" (see Laist et al., this volume).

In the United States, fishing within the "exclusive economic zone" that extends from 3 to 200 nautical miles (5.5 to 370.4 km) from the coast is regulated by the federal government under the Magnuson-Stevens Fishery Conservation and Management Act of 1976[36] (see Sobeck and Gosliner 1991). Fisheries in the zone are to be managed in accordance with fishery management plans prepared by regional fishery management councils. The fishery management councils are unique institutions, composed of federal and state agency representatives and others appointed by the Secretary of Commerce from lists of people recommended by the governors of the states within the jurisdiction of the councils. The councils have the initial responsibility for drafting fishery management plans; the Secretary of Commerce has the ultimate authority to approve, amend, or disapprove them.

All fishery management plans must comply with 10 national standards set forth in the Magnuson-Stevens Act. The first and most important of these is that plans must prevent overfishing and assure an "optimum" yield from each fishery. The Act defines the term *optimum yield* to mean the amount of fish that "will provide the greatest overall benefit to the Nation, particularly with respect to food production and recreational opportunities, and taking into account the protection of marine ecosystems . . ." (U.S. House 1994). Although broadly enough defined to encompass considerations of the impact of fish harvest on marine mammals, in practice the focus of optimum yield determinations has been almost exclusively upon the targeted fish stocks and other fish stocks that may be affected as "bycatch." Since 1990 the Act has contained provisions requiring that bycatch of immature fish be considered in developing management plans, but nothing in the statute specifically addresses the problem of incidental catches of marine mammals, seabirds, and other species. The detailed provisions of the Marine Mammal Protection Act and the more general provisions of the Endangered Species Act provide the principal mechanisms for addressing the incidental catch of marine mammals in commercial fisheries. The Sustainable Fisheries Act, enacted in 1996, reauthorized and amended the Magnuson-Stevens Act. The amendments generally do not address issues involving marine mammals, but a directive to identify and protect "essential fish habitats" is likely to have indirect benefit for other marine species that inhabit such areas.

The National Environmental Policy Act

The National Environmental Policy Act[37] is often regarded as the centerpiece of the environmental legal framework enacted by Congress in the late 1960s and early 1970s. The Act has ambitious goals, such as to (1) create and maintain conditions under which humans and nature can exist in productive harmony; (2) fulfill the responsibilities of each generation as trustee of the environment for succeeding generations; (3) maintain, wherever possible, an environment that supports diversity; and (4) enhance the quality of renewable resources.

Inspiring as these goals may be, they have had little practical application. The procedural requirements of the Act have proven to be its greatest contribution to environmental protection generally and to wildlife conservation in particular.

The focal point of the Act's implementation has been the requirement to prepare detailed environmental impact statements on "major Federal actions significantly affecting the quality of the human environment." These statements must be prepared through an open process that includes consulting with other agencies, obtaining public comments through a "scoping" process and preparing a draft statement, analyzing those comments and preparing a final statement, and relying on that final statement to inform the agency's decision makers on how the proposed action will affect the environment. As the courts have demonstrated since the first significant case, *Wilderness Society* v. *Hickel*,[38] in which the construction of the Trans-Alaska pipeline was enjoined because of an inadequate impact statement, the National Environmental Policy Act can be a powerful mechanism for making agencies give adequate consideration to environmental impacts and for exposing agency decision-making practices to public scrutiny. Indeed, the Act has become the most litigated of all environmental laws; literally thousands of cases have raised claims under this statute.

Because the statute itself provides no detail about what should go into an environmental impact statement or how it should be prepared, the federal agency created by the Act—the President's Council on Environmental Quality—has developed regulations to flesh out the law's procedural requirements.[39] These regulations prescribe in detail what an agency must do to satisfy the Act's requirements. They also dictate the contents of an environmental impact statement: a detailed description of the proposed action; alternatives to it (including no action); a discussion of direct, indirect, and cumulative effects of the proposal and its alternatives; and identification of any irreversible and irretrievable commitment of resources.

The regulations also provide for the preparation of environmental assessments. These documents are short versions of environmental impact statements used either to determine whether a full statement is required or to document that the action is likely to have no significant environmental impact.

The statute's scope has been interpreted sufficiently broadly to include discussion of the impact of a proposed action on wildlife. As the reviewing court stated in *Natural Resources Defense Council* v. *Grant,* a case decided in 1972, any action that substantially affects, beneficially or detrimentally, the depth or course of streams, plant life, wildlife habitats, fish and wildlife, or the soil or air "significantly affects the quality of the human environment."[40] This proposition has become widely accepted, and environmental impact statements now routinely consider the likely impacts of federal actions on marine mammals and other wildlife.

Under the Act, a wide array of federal activities has been subject to environmental impact statements that consider impacts on marine mammals. A typical example is the 1995 impact statement prepared by the Department of the Interior's Minerals Management Service on the proposed sale of oil and gas leases in the Gulf of Mexico. The statement analyzes the potential impacts of degradation of water quality, helicopter traffic, vessel activity, and potential spills on a number of cetaceans, and it describes several measures intended to minimize the risks to these species.

Another example is the proposed construction and operation of a space launch complex by the U.S. Air Force at Vandenberg Air Force Base in California. The statement considers the potential impacts on pinnipeds (primarily California sea lions [*Zalophus californianus*]), southern sea otters, and gray whales (*Eschrichtius robustus*) from launch noise, sonic booms, construction activities, and at-sea vessel supply routes.

Although often raised in conjunction with substantive claims under the Marine Mammal Protection Act or other statutes, challenges to federal actions involving marine mammals based on procedural deficiencies under the National Environmental Policy Act have proven to be an effective tool in the hands of environmental organizations and animal welfare groups opposed to those actions. For example, National Environmental Policy Act claims have been used successfully by these groups to (1) invalidate a permit issued by the National Marine Fisheries Service authorizing the collection of killer whales (*Orcinus orca*) by a public display facility in Alaskan waters,[41] (2) stop a researcher from taking biopsy samples from killer whales in Puget Sound,[42] and (3) prevent the Navy from posting bottlenose dolphins, a warm-water species, as sentries at a base in Bangor, Washington.[43]

Marine Mammal and Marine Mammal Habitat Protection through Protected Area Classifications

Marine mammals and their habitats also can be protected through special land and water area designations, such as parks, refuges, and marine sanctuaries. Habitat areas in these classifications are protected from all or selected types of adverse modification. These designations are especially important for marine mammals because, although the Marine Mammal Protection Act provides authority to set aside or otherwise protect such areas under section 112 regulations, federal agencies have been reluctant to use this authority (Baur 1991).

Wildlife Refuges

One set of protective habitat classifications is represented by the National Wildlife Refuge System. There are more than 500 refuges encompassing nearly 40 million ha (100 million acres). Of this total, more than 32 million ha (80 million acres) are in Alaska. Important marine mammal habitat is found in numerous refuges, including the Arctic National Wildlife Refuge (polar bears, seals, and whales); the Alaska Maritime National Wildlife Refuge (walruses, seals, sea lions, sea otters, cetaceans); Hawaiian Islands (monk seals, cetaceans); Seal Beach, California (seals); and Crystal River, Florida (manatees). A number of the refuges in Alaska were established by Congress expressly for the purpose of protecting marine mammals and their habitat.

The units of the refuge system are administered by the Fish and Wildlife Service and governed under the National Wildlife Refuge System Administration Act,[44] which authorizes the Secretary of the Interior by regulation to "permit the use of any area within the System for any purpose, including but not limited to hunting, fishing, public recreation and accommodations, and access wherever he determines that such uses are compatible with the major purposes for which such areas were established." This authority has been construed by one court as imposing a duty to manage the refuge "by regulating human access in order to conserve the entire spectrum of wildlife found therein."[45]

Under the compatibility test of the Refuge Administration Act, the Fish and Wildlife Service has generally given primacy to protecting and enhancing wildlife and wildlife habitat. In refuges in coastal areas, this generally includes protecting the resident marine mammals and their habitat. Where "compatible" with these protection goals, the Fish and Wildlife Service has considerable discretion to define what "secondary uses" are permissible. These secondary uses, such as recreational activities and commercial uses including timber harvest and oil and gas production, are the source of controversy and frequent litigation. Indeed, in 1989 the General Accounting Office issued a report concluding that secondary uses harmful to wildlife occur on 59% of the units of the refuge system. Since then, the extent of these conflicts has been reduced somewhat, but the dispute over compatibility remains a major controversy in the administration of the Refuge System.

Because the National Wildlife Refuge System has long been hampered by the absence of any unifying set of guiding principles, in 1996 President Clinton issued Executive Order No. 12996, Management and General Public Use of the National Wildlife Refuge System.[46] In this order, the President defined the central mission of the system to be to preserve and conserve wildlife and plant habitats.

National Parks

Since Congress set aside protected lands in the Yosemite Valley in California in 1864, the National Park System (formally established in 1916) has been the principal protective federal land classification. As of 1995 the National Park System consisted of 368 units covering more than 33 million ha (83 million acres). Among the areas that provide protection for marine mammals and their habitat are Alaska units including the Cape Krusenstern National Monument and Bering Land Bridge National Preserve (polar bears, seals, walruses, cetaceans) and Glacier Bay National Park (seals, cetaceans). Other areas include Olympic National Park, Washington (sea otters, seals, sea lions); Channel Islands National Park, California (cetaceans, sea otters, seals, sea lions); Point Reyes National Seashore (seals and sea lions); Everglades National Park (manatees, dolphins); and Acadia National Park, Maine (seals, porpoises).

The centerpiece of the legal framework governing the National Park System is the National Park Service Organic Act.[47] The Act's central mandate is that the National Park Service is to manage the park system so as to: "conserve the scenery and the natural and historic objects and the wildlife therein and to provide for the enjoyment of the same in such manner and by such means as will leave them unimpaired for the enjoyment of future generations."

In formulating the Organic Act's section 1 mandate, Congress in 1916 explained that, unlike national forests, which are established to promote multiple use values, units of the park system are intended to address "the question of the preservation of nature as it exists. . . ." (U.S. Senate 1916).

This principle was addressed in detail in a report to the Secretary of the Interior, prepared by an independent advisory board (Advisory Board on Wildlife Management 1963). The national parks, according to the advisory board, "should represent a vignette of primitive America." The Department of the Interior adopted this goal, and it has been central to many aspects of National Park Service management strategy ever since. The strong protectionist philosophy in the report has ensured that wildlife in areas under National Park Service jurisdiction, including marine mammals, receives full protection.

Park system statutory requirements are supplemented by regulations promulgated under the authority of section 3 of the Organic Act. Using its rulemaking authority, the National Park Service has prohibited all taking of wildlife except where authorized by Congress.[48] In addition, the Park Service has promulgated regulations specifically to protect humpback whales in Glacier Bay National Park, Alaska. Based on concern that these whales, which have consistently used the bay as an essential habitat area, were being adversely affected by disturbances caused by a proliferation of cruise ships and other vessels, the Service established vessel entry limitations by regulation in 1985.[49] In response to an Endangered Species Act biological opinion from the National Marine Fisheries Service, the Park Service limited vessel entries to 1982 levels. These regulations were amended in 1987 to raise the vessel limitations in response to apparent increases in humpback whale presence and again modified in 1996 to further increase the permissible level of vessel traffic, subject to a detailed monitoring program.[50]

Marine Sanctuaries

In the Marine Protection, Research, and Sanctuaries Act of 1972,[51] Congress recognized the need to protect unique areas in the marine environment. Marine sanctuaries can be designated in U.S. coastal and oceanic waters and in the Great Lakes and their connecting waters. The goal is to provide enhanced protection for these areas through comprehensive and coordinated conservation and management.

The National Oceanic and Atmospheric Administration is responsible for administering the marine sanctuaries program. Currently, 11 sanctuaries have been designated. These sanctuaries range in size from less than 1 square nautical mile (3.4 km^2) (the Fagatele Bay Sanctuary in American Samoa) to approximately 2,600 square nautical miles (8,920 km^2) (the Florida Keys National Marine Sanctuary).

To further the purposes of the Marine Sanctuaries Act, the Secretary of Commerce may designate areas with "special national significance" because of the area's resource or human use values. When making a designation, the Secretary is to consider the area's natural resource and ecological qualities; its historical, cultural, educational, and archeological significance; and its current and potential uses for commercial and recreational purposes.

Designation can occur only after a lengthy decision-making process that includes public review and extensive consultation with congressional committees, other federal agencies, fishery management councils, and affected states. This process includes the development of a management plan and protective regulations.[52] If the proposed sanctuary is located partially or entirely within the seaward boundary of any state, the governor of that state can veto the designation as to such portions.

Similar to other protected areas discussed in this chapter, marine sanctuaries are individually regulated to provide specific protection for the resources found within their boundaries. For example, the Point Reyes/Farallon Islands Sanctuary, designated to preserve marine mammal and seabird habitat, is subject to special regulations devised to protect the ecosystem and the habitat of those species. The Secretary of Commerce has considerable discretion in promulgating marine sanctuaries regulations, and the degree of protection provided by each designation is determined by how restrictive these implementing regulations are.

A recent court case tested the Secretary's authority to develop protective regulations under the Marine Sanctuaries Act. The case involved 1992 regulations restricting the use of so-called "personal watercraft" (e.g., jet skis) in the Monterey Bay National Marine Sanctuary in California. The National Oceanic and Atmospheric Administration promulgated the regulations because, in the words of the Circuit Court that heard the case, jet skis and other thrill craft had become "a headache" because they "interfered with the public's recreational safety and enjoyment of the Sanctuary and posed a serious threat to the Sanctuary's flora and fauna."[53]

Noting that the Sanctuary was home to 31 species of marine mammals, including sea otters, the court rejected a challenge to the regulations brought by the Personal Watercraft Industry Association. Upholding the regulations, the court noted that such action was appropriate inasmuch as "[t]he concept of a 'sanctuary' entails elements of serenity, peace and tranquility." This case confirms that strong regulations can be promulgated under the Marine Sanctuaries Act to protect marine mammals and their habitat from human activities.

Protection for Individual Marine Mammals under the Marine Mammal Protection Act and the Animal Welfare Act

The Marine Mammal Protection Act does not limit its protection to species, population stocks, and habitat. The law also provides protection to individual animals. Most notably, the prohibitions set forth in section 102(a) of the Act make the unauthorized taking of "*any* marine mammal" by anyone subject to U.S. jurisdiction unlawful (emphasis added).

Although many of the policy goals set forth in the Act focus on species and population stocks, extension of the Act's protective provisions to individual animals, including those held in captivity, furthers the congressional goal of section 2(6) that all marine mammals "should be protected . . . to the greatest extent feasible. . . ."

The Act includes a number of provisions that address the well-being of individual marine mammals. Foremost among these is the requirement under section 104 that all permitted taking be conducted in a "humane" manner, that is, as defined in section 3, that method of taking "which involves the least possible degree of pain and suffering practicable to the mammal involved." In addition, the Act seeks to protect individual animals subject to take in foreign countries by prohibiting the importation of any marine mammal or marine mammal product if the animal was pregnant or nursing at the time of taking or less than eight months old. Noting the practical difficulty of determining when a marine mammal may be pregnant, regulations implementing this provision have defined pregnant to mean "pregnant near term."[54]

Protection for individual marine mammals also occurs through the permit issuance process of sections 101(a)(1) and 104. Such permits, which are available for taking of marine mammals for scientific research, public display, photography, and species enhancement, are subject to terms and conditions designed to protect the animals.

Historically, requirements under the Act included in permits, especially those involving scientific research and public display, have been quite detailed and stringent. This is the result of the requirement in the Act that such permits shall specify "the methods of capture, supervision, care, and transportation" that must be observed "pursuant to such taking and importation." For example, a typical research permit will impose limits on the numbers of animals to be taken; specify the manner in which take can occur; require periodic reports so that the federal agencies can monitor the progress of the project; and mandate final reports to assess compliance with the permit, gauge impacts on the species and animals, and further understanding about the research. As discussed below, amendments enacted in 1994 all but eliminated the ability of the National Marine Fisheries Service and the Fish and Wildlife Service to condition public display permits with respect to how captive animals are maintained or what may be done with them.

The manner in which research permits were processed and issued drew criticism from certain members of the scientific community during the 1994 reauthorization of the Act. In particular, these scientists complained that it took too long to obtain such permits and that they frequently were subject to stringent terms and conditions that hindered research intended to benefit marine mammals. Congress responded by amending section 104 of the Act to provide a streamlined process for scientific research involving only low-level (Level B) harassment to the animal (U.S. House 1994).

When marine mammals are maintained in captivity, another federal law, the Animal Welfare Act, comes into play. The Animal Welfare Act establishes the regulatory framework for how animals are housed, transported, and cared for when held in captivity. It covers a wide range of uses of animals, including laboratory research, public display and shows, and sale as pets. First enacted in 1966 to prevent the theft of household pets for use in research and other purposes, the Animal Welfare Act was expanded in the 1970s to require the Secretary of Agriculture to establish standards to govern the humane handling, care, treatment, and transportation of warm-blooded animals, including marine mammals, by dealers and exhibitors. Amendments enacted in 1985 significantly expanded the coverage of the Act with respect to animals maintained by research facilities.

The Animal Welfare Act is administered by the Animal and Plant Health Inspection Service in the U.S. Department of Agriculture. Much of the Service's work is handled by veterinarians who have numerous responsibilities under nearly two dozen animal health programs, including facility licensing, inspections, and enforcement.

The Animal Welfare Act is particularly important to the protection of marine mammals as a result of its regulatory standards for the maintenance and care of animals in captivity. The Act itself includes among its goals ensuring that animals intended for use in research facilities or for exhibition are provided humane care and treatment, and ensuring humane treatment of animals during transport. This is done by requiring that licenses be issued to exhibitors, research facilities be registered, and regulatory standards for the humane handling, care, treatment, and transportation of certain animals be promulgated.

The Service has promulgated regulations covering animals ranging from rodents to marine mammals. Based on the fairly broad mandate to establish minimum standards for the care and maintenance of certain animals, the Animal and Plant Health Inspection Service in 1979 promulgated specific regulations for captive marine mammals.[55] These include requirements pertaining to facility construction, space requirements, pool temperature, feeding, water quality, sanitation, training of employees, veterinary care, care in transit, and numerous other marine mammal health care and maintenance issues.

Over the years, dispute has centered on two areas of concern regarding the Animal Welfare Act as it applies to marine mammals. First, as a general problem under the Act, the Animal and Plant Health Inspection Service has often been criticized for failing to enforce the law adequately. Indeed, the agency's record, especially during the early years of the Animal Welfare Act's implementation, was far from adequate. From 1968 to 1980, for example, only three criminal prosecutions were brought against Animal Welfare Act violators, and only 122 administrative prosecutions were completed. Criticisms were raised in a 1985 General Accounting Office study over the inadequacy of staff training and the infrequency and insufficiency of facility inspections. The General Accounting Office concluded that in most cases these problems were the result of a heavy agency workload and inadequate funding.

The second area of controversy concerned claims that the Animal and Plant Health Inspection Service had not developed standards sufficient to protect captive marine mammals. It was this concern that frequently led the Marine Mammal Commission to recommend, and the National Marine Fisheries Service and the Fish and Wildlife Service to impose, additional permit terms and conditions.

Some of the Animal and Plant Health Inspection Service's difficulties in both areas had been addressed under the Marine Mammal Protection Act, which allowed the National Marine Fisheries Service and the Fish and Wildlife Service to condition permits to provide additional care and maintenance requirements and to bring the expertise of the staffs of their agencies and of the Marine Mammal Commission to bear. Historically, this approach had been particularly helpful because it brought into play the extensive experience of these agencies on marine mammals in an area of veterinary science where it was particularly difficult for the Animal and Plant Health Inspection Service to become deeply involved, because of funding limitations and the extensive training required to become expert in the field.

This approach of shared responsibility brought criticism from the public display industry, however. Some parks and aquariums expressed concern that applying the Marine Mammal Protection Act to the care and maintenance of marine mammals in captivity added unnecessary red tape and unpredictability to permit issuance and enforcement. They also objected to the ability of the marine mammal agencies to develop their own standards of care and maintenance that were more stringent than those of the Department of Agriculture. These concerns caused some members of the industry to argue that the Marine Mammal Protection Act was not intended to cover individual animal care and maintenance issues. They maintained, contrary to numerous provisions in the marine mammal law itself, that the Act covered only marine mammals in the wild. Once removed from the wild, they argued, marine mammals lost protection under the Marine Mammal Protection Act and fell solely under the Animal Welfare Act.

This dispute spilled over into litigation in 1992 when Mirage Resorts challenged the authority of the National Marine Fisheries Service to withhold approval of a swim-with-the-dolphin program during which members of the public would be allowed to enter the water and interact with captive bottlenose dolphins. In a holding based on a superficial and highly questionable reading of the statute, the Federal District Court for Nevada ruled in 1993 that the Marine Mammal Protection Act only applied to "marine mammals in the wild."[56] Ignoring the express requirement of the Act that National Marine Fisheries Service permits were to cover "methods of capture, supervision, care and transportation pursuant to *and after* [emphasis added] taking," the court held that jurisdiction over marine mammals in captivity rests exclusively with the Animal and Plant Health Inspection Service. Because of the limited applicability of this ruling—it technically applied only in Nevada, which had a single marine mammal facility—the U.S. government chose not to appeal the ruling. The issue presented in this case became moot in 1994 when Congress amended the Marine Mammal Protection Act to remove the National Marine Fisheries Service's and the Fish and Wildlife Service's authority to regulate swim-with-the-dolphin programs and other aspects of captive maintenance.

Responding to concerns of the public display industry, Congress in 1994 also amended the permit requirements of section 104 of the Act to limit the permit authority to the import of animals or their removal from the wild. In other words, after the 1994 amendments, the National Marine Fisheries Service and the Fish and Wildlife Service may impose requirements over animal care at the point of capture but may no longer impose such conditions on the maintenance of captive animals once the taking (or importation) has occurred. With respect to public display, Congress further limited the scope of the Marine Mammal Protection Act to ensuring that the permit holder was engaged in legitimate education or conservation programs, met the Animal Welfare Act standards, and held its facilities open to the public. In this manner, Congress imposed limits on the ability of agencies to use the Marine Mammal Protection Act to impose standards that go beyond those set forth under the Animal Welfare Act. The Marine Mammal Protection Act still is important in this area, but the Animal and Plant Health Inspection Service now clearly has the lead for administering this program, and the two regulatory agencies (the National Marine Fisheries Service and the Fish and Wildlife Service) have been forced to play an advisory role.

International Legal Authorities

To the extent that marine mammals are migratory, or live primarily on the high seas, and are thus not subject to a single nation's jurisdiction, their conservation should be of concern to all range nations and require international cooperation. As a result, a number of international treaties and agreements have been developed over many years to protect marine mammals and marine mammal habitat. Some of the most important of these authorities are discussed briefly in this section.

The International Convention for the Regulation of Whaling

Concern about overexploitation of whales by commercial whaling prompted the first whaling treaty in 1931 under the auspices of the League of Nations.[57] Unfortunately, not only were the measures far too weak to effect significant change in whaling practices, but the agreement was also doomed to obsolescence, as it had no mechanism for amending initially adopted regulations. Furthermore, and typically devastating to any international agreement, the nonaccession of several of the nations most directly affected by and responsible for the declining status of whales rendered futile any attempt by the compliant parties to realize the goals of the treaty.

By 1946 a new international agreement, the International Convention for the Regulation of Whaling, had been negotiated.[58] In addition to revising previous approaches to the regulation of an enormous international industry that once employed more than 70,000 people in the United States alone (Scarff 1977:345), the Convention established in Article III(1) the International Whaling Commission (IWC) (see Gambell, this volume). The membership of the IWC consists of one voting representative of each party to the Convention, who, along with experts and advisors, meet annually to consider research findings and, if necessary, amend the Schedule to the Convention. The IWC evolved from a body dominated by the interests of whaling companies to one that came to recognize the need for the conservation of whales by imposing a global moratorium on commercial whaling. This is summarized by Birnie (1985) and Gambell (this volume).

Under its research mandate, the IWC—independently or in collaboration with other public or private organizations—is to gather, analyze, and disseminate information on the current conditions and trends of whale stocks, the effects of whaling, and "methods of maintaining and increasing the populations of whale stocks." Based on its research findings, the IWC may make recommendations to the member governments. Not included in the authority of the IWC are the allocation of catch quotas among the parties and restriction of the number or nationality of factory ships or land stations involved in whaling.

The goals of the Convention and the IWC as originally conceived were not protectionist, but rather aimed at "the orderly development of the whaling industry." All amendments to the regulations, contained in the Schedule to the Convention, are to be based on scientific findings and "take into consideration the interests of the consumers of whale products and the whaling industry."

The continued decline of many whale stocks throughout the decades following the entry into force of the Convention made it clear that the IWC's regulations were insufficient and largely ineffective from a conservation standpoint (Birnie 1985).

One of the impediments to effective implementation of the Convention is the ease by which member nations can effectively nullify an action by filing an objection. Another problem is inherent in the very nature of international agreements. Accession to or withdrawal from such agreements is at will (and in the case of the Whaling Convention requires only written notification). Not all nations that, based on their involvement in whaling, would be expected to be party to the Whaling Convention find sufficient incentive to submit to the restrictions imposed by the agreement. Regulations adopted by the parties are not binding on nonparty whaling nations. As a more drastic measure, and as Iceland chose to do following years of disapproval of IWC policies, a nation can withdraw its accession to the Convention under a simple notification process.

For all practical purposes, then, enforcement becomes a matter of political and economic pressure levied by individual governments against noncompliant nations (see discussion of the Pelly Amendment, below). National governments of competent jurisdiction are directed by the Convention to "take appropriate measures" to apply its provisions and punish any infractions. Prosecutions by IWC members, however, have been minimal. Enforcement is further complicated by the fact that whaling has sometimes been conducted under flags of convenience, that is, by citizens or vessels of party nations, which are limited by the Convention, while under the protective flag of a nonparty nation against which the terms of the Convention would be unenforceable.

Heavy reliance on the ability and willingness of member governments to carry out enforcement measures reveals the intrinsic weakness of the Commission. The IWC has developed numerous research programs, yet its research scientists are employed by individual governments. Implementation of an international observer program required mutual voluntary agreements. Scientific research permits, although subject to review by the IWC's Scientific Committee, are granted by governments with or without IWC approval. All that is required by parties issuing permits is to notify the IWC of all authorizations and subsequently to report the results of the research conducted.

Fortunately, where the limitations of international law have detracted from the IWC's effectiveness, national laws (notably the Pelly Amendment in the United States, which authorizes sanctions against countries that undermine the effectiveness of an international fishery conservation program) have compensated to some extent. This system of national enforcement with only international oversight will be tested again, however, if commercial whaling resumes. Significant limitations of the Convention—as to definitions of species to be managed; no formal recognition of the IWC's competence to regulate the taking of small cetaceans; and lack of a clear focus on the importance of habitat protec-tion, ecosystem balance, and nonconsumptive values of whales—will have to be addressed if effective international conservation of cetaceans by the IWC is to be achieved.

Agreement on the Conservation of Polar Bears

While debating marine mammal protection legislation in 1971, members of Congress and witnesses in hearings considered the polar bear to be at considerable risk of endangerment as a result of overhunting and threats to habitat (U.S. Senate 1972a). Recognizing the polar bear's vulnerability to human activities in the five circumpolar range states (Canada, Denmark [Greenland], Norway, the Soviet Union, and the United States), House and Senate committees concurred that the State Department should take action to develop an international agreement on polar bear conservation (U.S. House 1971b, U.S. Senate 1972a).

In fact, discussions about the need for such a treaty had been under way among a scientific specialist group representing the five nations since 1965 (Baur 1996:13). Spurred on by the rising tide of concern about marine mammals throughout the world and the mandate in the Marine Mammal Protection Act to pursue international cooperation, the five nations agreed in 1973 to the terms of the Agreement for the Conservation of Polar Bears (Baur 1996:26–27).

The Agreement resembles the Marine Mammal Protection Act in certain respects. Like the Act, the Agreement in Article I broadly prohibits the taking of polar bears, defined as "hunting, killing and capturing." It does not, however, prohibit taking by harassment. Article III sets forth exceptions to the take prohibition. It allows taking for research, for conservation purposes, by local people using traditional methods in the exercise of their traditional rights, and wherever polar bears have or might have been subject to taking by traditional means by that party's nationals. The intent of these provisions was to make offshore areas a polar bear sanctuary where only limited forms of take could occur (Baur 1996:32–35). The parties to the Agreement also adopted a nonbinding resolution that prohibits the hunting of female polar bears with cubs and the cubs themselves and the hunting of bears in denning areas. This resolution is more protective than the Marine Mammal Protection Act, which does not limit the allowable take by Alaska Natives to male bears and female bears without cubs.

Other key provisions of the Agreement include requirements to manage polar bears based on "sound conservation practices" and the best available scientific data, and to protect the ecosystems of which polar bears are a part, with special attention to denning, feeding, and migration areas; a prohibition on trade in bears taken in violation of the Agreement; a directive to encourage cooperative research and information sharing; and a directive that the parties continue to consult with one another on polar bear management and research.

Under the 1994 amendments to the Marine Mammal Protection Act, Congress directed the Fish and Wildlife Service to take a number of actions to ensure adequate protection of polar bears and to foster U.S. compliance with the Agreement. In section 113, the amendments require the agency to (1) in consultation with the other parties, review the effectiveness of the Agreement; (2) report to Congress on the effectiveness of U.S. implementation of the Agreement; and (3) pursue discussions with the Russian Federation on the development of an agreement to enhance cooperative research on and management of polar bears. Pursuant to the last of these directives, the Fish and Wildlife Service has held a series of informal discussions with the Russian Federation and with Alaska Natives and Russian Natives. The goal is to develop a new bilateral agreement to protect and facilitate research on polar bears in the Bering and Chukchi Seas, which belong to a stock shared by the two countries. Formal negotiation of an agreement is expected to begin in 1997. A separate, parallel agreement is being sought between Alaska Natives and Russian Natives governing their activities involving polar bears.

Overall, the 1973 Agreement has been effective in reducing the hunting pressure on polar bear stocks. Hunting is no longer a widespread problem. Although some Native take occurs in the United States that is arguably inconsistent with the Agreement because cubs and females with cubs are taken, this level does not appear to be affecting the stocks involved, and efforts are being made by Alaska Natives (as well as Natives in Canada and Russia) to control such activities through self-regulation. Currently, the most significant threats to polar bears are from impacts resulting from habitat degradation and illegal taking in Russia. To date, the parties to the Agreement have taken few significant steps to address these problems, and much more attention needs to be focused on these areas.

Driftnets

Large-scale pelagic driftnet fishing, often in waters outside the jurisdiction of individual nations, has aroused tremendous international concern. This fishing method causes the deaths of immeasurable numbers of seabirds, marine mammals, and other nontarget living resources (see Northridge and Hofman, this volume).

These highly effective plastic gillnets, often many tens of kilometers long, are set in the evening and left overnight, during which time they catch large amounts of the target species and lethally entangle countless others. Compounding the problems created by this immediate bycatch is the continued incidental mortality of marine mammals, seabirds, and other marine species in nets that have been abandoned or lost at sea yet which continue to catch both target and nontarget organisms. These "ghost fishing" nets and their kill are seldom retrieved, making their take levels, which are likely substantial, speculative.

Attempts were made to improve mortality data and to curb the expansion of this fishing practice through unilateral legislative initiatives, regional agreements, and international resolutions. Unilateral efforts, discussed earlier, included the 1981 extension of the incidental take permit for the Japanese high-seas salmon driftnet fishery, which established certain reporting and monitoring requirements. A more sweeping measure emerged in the Driftnet Impact Monitoring, Assessment, and Control Act of 1987.[59] The Driftnet Act applies to all nets at least 2.4 km (1.5 miles) in length. Because most nets used by vessels under U.S. ownership are not this long, they are not subject to the Driftnet Act and are regulated under other laws, such as the Magnuson-Stevens Fishery Conservation and Management Act. An explicit prohibition on all "large-scale driftnet fishing" in U.S. waters and by U.S. vessels in waters beyond the exclusive economic zone of any nation was enacted in the Fishery Conservation Amendments of 1990,[60] which amended the Magnuson-Stevens Act.

Acting under the directives of the Driftnet Act, in 1989 the United States entered into monitoring and enforcement agreements with each of the three countries with North Pacific driftnet fishing fleets—Japan (with Canada joining as a party), Taiwan, and South Korea. The Pelly Amendment, discussed below, provided a mechanism for inducing governments to enter into these agreements. These were to include detailed arrangements for the deployment of observers on foreign driftnet fishing vessels and the collection and release of information. These agreements were renegotiated each year until 1992, when a global moratorium on large-scale high-seas driftnet fishing declared by United Nations General Assembly Resolution 44/225, later revised and reaffirmed by Resolution 46/215, came into effect.

In spite of initial resistance by driftnet fishing nations, most notably Japan, during earlier discussions of a proposed moratorium, there has been a surprising level of international compliance. In those cases in the North Pacific in which illegal driftnet fishing has been detected, the respective governments have taken appropriate measures to penalize the violators. In fact, the governments of Japan, South Korea, and Taiwan have established mechanisms designed to prevent pelagic driftnet fishing by their nationals. These include refusal to issue licenses for driftnet fishing, compensation of driftnet fishermen for loss of income and equipment, provision of funds to scrap or refit driftnet vessels, a vessel buyback program, deployment of patrol vessels, and other plans to detect illegal driftnet fishing.

Together with these measures, the United States has developed its own procedures for enforcing the United Nations moratorium, including the use of Navy and Coast Guard surveillance. China, too, has agreed to certain bilateral boarding and inspection arrangements with the United States and has taken responsibility for prosecuting its citizens who have violated the United Nations resolution.

Although the international moratorium on large-scale pelagic driftnet fishing neglects to address (a) fishing with large-scale gear within a nation's exclusive economic zone, and (b) the use of small driftnets on the high seas, individual nations have shown strong interest in enforcing the terms of the existing resolution. Equally encouraging is the fact that good-faith efforts have been made to enforce the many regional agreements involving the North Pacific, South Pacific, and North Atlantic Oceans, the Mediterranean Sea, waters surrounding Antarctica, and virtually every other high seas body of water.

Convention on International Trade in Endangered Species of Wild Fauna and Flora

Negotiated in 1973, the Convention on International Trade in Endangered Species of Wild Fauna and Flora (CITES)[61] has as its goal securing cooperation among the nations of the world to regulate trade that might threaten the survival of wild plant and animal species. The Convention is implemented through a system of graduated trade controls that are most stringent for species most in peril of extinction and less stringent for those that are less imperiled (Wijnstekers 1990).

The degree of trade control applicable to a species depends on whether it is listed on Appendix I, II, or III of the Convention. Species that are currently in danger of extinction and affected by trade are listed on Appendix I. No international commercial trade in Appendix I species is allowed unless a CITES member nation enters a "reservation" at the time of the listing. Species are added to or removed from the appendices by a two-thirds vote of the member nations present at biennial conferences of the parties. The power to enter reservations allows nations to opt out of listings with which they disagree—similar to the reservation provision in the International Convention for the Regulation of Whaling, noted above.

Appendix II consists of species not currently in danger of extinction, but likely to become so in the foreseeable future. International commercial trade in these is not prohibited, but it is subject to a system of monitoring and control. Specifically, an Appendix II species cannot be imported or exported unless it is accompanied by an export permit from its country of origin. Such export permits may only be issued upon a finding by the exporting country that the export will not be detrimental to the survival of the species. In this manner, the purpose of an Appendix II listing is not to prohibit trade in such species but rather to ensure that such trade is documented and kept at a level that is not detrimental.

Appendix III functions much like Appendix II, except that a range nation may unilaterally place a species within its jurisdiction on Appendix III as a way of seeking international cooperation to control trade. The desired effect of an Appendix III listing is to have an importing nation require a valid export permit before allowing the listed species to be imported.

All cetaceans, marine otters, and sirenians, as well as 14 pinniped species, are currently listed on the CITES appendices.

Regional Conservation Agreements

Marine mammal protection also is advanced under a variety of international agreements entered into to protect the quality of a particular region's marine environment. There are numerous international agreements that fall into this category, too many to describe here. As a general rule, these agreements identify specified coastal and oceanic regions shared by a number of countries and define measures that will protect the resources of those areas from specified threats, such as pollution or destruction of habitats. In many cases, such agreements have as a goal the protection of wildlife and living marine resources, including wildlife.

The United Nations Environment Programme (UNEP) Regional Seas Programme has helped develop several such agreements, including the Caribbean Convention, the Convention for the Protection of the Marine Environment and Coastal Area of the South-East Pacific, and the Barcelona Convention (for the Mediterranean Sea), to name a few.

The Caribbean Convention is a typical regional seas agreement. It establishes an underlying cooperative mechanism to protect the Caribbean Sea from pollution and other threats. This general framework is then supplemented with protocols that address specific issues.

For example, the Caribbean Convention includes a Specially Protected Area and Wildlife Protocol, which obligates each party to "regulate and, where necessary, prohibit activities having adverse effects on [designated] areas and species." Measures specifically designed to protect wildlife include the regulation or prohibition of dumping or discharging wastes and other substances that may endanger protected areas; fishing, hunting, or harvesting of endangered or threatened species; activities that result in the destruction of endangered or threatened species (total prohibition) or are likely to harm or disturb such species, their habitats, or associated ecosystems; trade in threatened or endangered species or parts, products, or eggs thereof; and tourist or recreational activities that might endanger the ecosystems of protected areas or the survival of threatened or endangered species. The Protocol also establishes an affirmative duty to undertake measures aimed at conserving, protecting, or restoring natural processes, ecosystems, or populations for which the protected areas were established.

As under other international agreements, successful achievement of these ambitious goals depends on the effectiveness of the implementation measures taken by the parties. To date, favorable progress has been made to follow up on some of these measures by some of the signatories to the Convention, but more aggressive measures are needed to achieve full implementation.

In addition to the UNEP Regional Seas Programme, there are many other agreements applicable to the marine environment and marine wildlife. Some of these deal specifically with marine mammals (e.g., the Convention on the Conservation of Antarctic Seals and the Convention on the Conservation of Antarctic Marine Living Resources [see Kimball, this volume]; the Agreement on the Conservation of Small Cetaceans of the Baltic and North Seas [1994], and the Agreement on the Conservation of Cetaceans of the Mediterranean and Black Seas [about to be signed in 1997 at the time of this writing], both under the auspices of the Convention on the Conservation of Migratory Species of Wild Animals [the Bonn Convention]).

Other agreements cover pollution problems. Examples of these agreements include the International Convention for the Prevention of Pollution from Ships (known as the MARPOL Convention), in particular Annex V, which prohibits the disposal of plastic into the sea (see Laist et al., this volume) and the Convention on the Prevention of Marine Pollution by Dumping of Wastes and Other Matter, which prohibits the deliberate dumping of wastes at sea. Together, these two conventions help control the disposal of many items that cause the entanglement of marine mammals and other species and adversely impact habitat. Still others, such as the Convention for the Establishment of an Inter-American Tropical Tuna Commission, govern the exploitation of resources that affect marine mammals, in this case, dolphins (see Gosliner, this volume).

To be effective, international agreements must be implemented and enforced by the parties. Typically, the parties to an agreement enact implementing laws that apply to their citizens. For example, Annex V of MARPOL is implemented in the United States by the Marine Plastic Pollution Research and Control Act of 1987,[62] which amended the Act to Prevent Pollution from Ships. The Marine Plastic Pollution Research and Control Act applies Annex V's prohibitions to all U.S. ships wherever located, as well as to foreign ships in U.S. waters. It also requires adequate reception facilities at ports and terminals (Baur and Iudicello 1990).

Many individual members of MARPOL that have ratified Annex V, especially smaller countries, have yet to achieve effective implementation because of lack of technical ability, finances, or political will. To address these problems, diplomacy, financial assistance, and technical guidance provided by other members are essential. One way that these problems have been addressed under MARPOL is through the Marine Environment Protection Committee of the International Maritime Organization (IMO), an international organization consisting of more than 100 nations with an interest in marine shipping. The Committee assists in implementing the agreements entered into by IMO members by taking actions such as the development of guidelines on how port officials can establish adequate facilities to handle wastes subject to the Annex V prohibition on disposal. To be effective, most international agreements concerning the marine environment need a centralized clearinghouse and technical assistance entity of this nature.

Finally, the ultimate test of the effectiveness of an international agreement is the existence of effective enforcement mechanisms. Most international agreements lack any enforcement body that can apply sanctions against offending members. As a result, many treaties depend primarily upon the goodwill and cooperative spirit of their members to be effective. Unfortunately, as in the case of whaling, this is often not enough. One possible solution is discussed in the next section.

The Pelly Amendment

The Pelly Amendment to the Fishermen's Protective Act of 1967[63] has played a significant role in marine mammal conservation efforts. Ironically, when the Pelly Amendment was originally enacted, it had nothing to do with marine mammal conservation. Rather, it arose out of a salmon dispute among the United States, Denmark, Germany, and Norway. The three European nations had refused to abide by certain salmon fishing regulations promulgated under the authority of the International Convention for the Northwest Atlantic Fisheries. As originally created, the Pelly Amendment authorized the President of the United States to restrict importation of fish products if the Secretary of Commerce certifies that the nationals of the country are "conducting fishing operations in a manner or under circumstances which diminish the effectiveness of an international fishery conservation program." In addition to protecting international fishery conservation programs, the Pelly Amendment authorized the President to restrict importation of wildlife products from a nation that directly or indirectly engaged in trade or taking that diminished the effectiveness of any international program for endangered or threatened species. In 1992 Congress amended the Pelly Amendment to allow the imposition of trade sanctions against any products imported from the offending nation. The International Whaling Commission's conservation program fits under either prong of the Pelly Amendment. Not only is the program designed to protect endangered and threatened species, but it is considered to be an international fishery conservation program. This broadly worded authority would eventually become a key tool in the effort of the United States to pressure other nations into complying with whale conservation measures agreed to by the International Whaling Commission.

Before establishment of the commercial whaling moratorium, the United States effectively used the threat of Pelly Amendment trade sanctions to foster compliance with IWC decisions. Certification of Japan and the Soviet Union in 1974 for exceeding minke whale quotas prompted those countries to adopt new conservation measures. Threatened certifications during the late 1970s and early 1980s resulted in Chile, Peru, and South Korea taking steps to join the IWC, in Spain taking steps to limit its take of fin whales, and in Taiwan banning whaling altogether. The success of actual or threatened certification in bringing about compliance with the moratorium on commercial whaling adopted by the IWC in 1982 was more mixed. Ultimately, Japan withdrew its objection to the moratorium, and the Soviet Union agreed to abide by the moratorium. Despite certification, Norway maintains its objection to the moratorium.

The potential impact of certification became stronger in 1979 when Congress enacted the Packwood-Magnuson Amendment to the Magnuson-Stevens Fishery Conservation and Management Act. This amendment provides for the imposition of automatic restrictions on fishery allocations to foreign countries whose actions diminish the effectiveness of the International Convention for the Regulation of Whaling. The amendment was partly a reaction to the protracted process and wide discretion afforded to the Secretary of Commerce and the President in imposing trade restrictions under the Pelly Amendment. Under the Packwood-Magnuson Amendment, upon certification, the Secretary of State, in consultation with the Secretary of Commerce, must reduce by a minimum of 50% the offending country's fishing allocation that it maintains in the waters of the United States. Although such a sanction may have been significant during the early 1980s, as U.S. fisheries became "Americanized" and fishery allocations to foreign countries dwindled, the threat of sanctions under the Packwood-Magnuson Amendment became less important. Today, these sanctions are of no consequence.

Trade sanctions to compel compliance with international agreements are a two-edged sword. The United States is not simply an importer of foreign goods; it is also an exporter of products and goods to foreign markets. If the United States were to follow through on its threats and actually impose import restrictions against a major trading partner, such as Japan, it would run the risk that the trading partner would retaliate by imposing trade restrictions of its own. Given the importance that the United States attaches to the principle of free trade, the risk of precipitating an ever-escalating trade war over a marine mammal conservation dispute is a consideration that cautions against using the sanctions that the Pelly Amendment authorizes. Moreover, trade is but one part of the United States' political relationship with other nations. The potential for trade sanctions to strain cooperation on military and diplomatic initiatives with allied nations such as Japan and Norway undoubtedly led many in the higher councils of government to caution against them. Very likely for reasons such as these, the threat of trade sanctions under the Pelly Amendment to achieve marine mammal conservation has often been made but has yet to be carried out.

The risk of making frequent threats that are never carried out is that the threats will cease to be taken seriously. That appears to be the case with respect to the dispute over "research whaling" that arose with Japan and Norway after the moratorium against commercial whaling took effect. Taking advantage of a provision of the International Convention for the Regulation of Whaling that allows whales to be harvested for scientific research purposes, Japan and Norway continued whaling, although at much-reduced levels, after adoption of the commercial whaling moratorium. In an almost annual ritual, the United States would threaten Pelly Amendment trade sanctions over the research whaling, but eventually decline to impose them on the basis of vague assurances with respect to future negotiations. As a result, the Pelly Amendment, which once had a major influence on the actions of other nations with respect to whaling matters, has become something of a paper tiger.

The effectiveness of the Pelly Amendment has been further compromised by the emergence of the General Agreement on Tariffs and Trade[64] (GATT) and its role in regulating international trade. Although the Pelly Amendment grants the President broad discretion to impose sanctions against any products from a certified nation, it limits that power by specifying that any such import ban is permissible only "to the extent that such prohibition is sanctioned by the General Agreement on Tariffs and Trade." Recent GATT rulings suggest that an embargo of unrelated products (i.e., anything other than whale products, which already are banned from import into the United States) would not be found GATT-consistent. With their growing awareness of trade protections provided under the GATT, whaling countries are less likely to respond to the threat of trade sanctions and are more likely to challenge any sanction that may be imposed.

Alaska Native Authorities

Recognizing the important role marine mammals have played in the lives of Alaska Natives, Congress established an exemption from the taking moratorium established under section 101 of the Marine Mammal Protection Act for "any Indian, Aleut, or Eskimo who resides in Alaska and dwells on the coast of the North Pacific Ocean or the Arctic Ocean" if such taking is for subsistence or for creating and selling "authentic native articles of handicrafts and clothing." With the exception of stocks that are designated as depleted, the only statutory limitation on such taking is that it shall not be accomplished in a wasteful manner. There also may be limits imposed by U.S. treaty obligations. For example, the U.S. government has taken the position that Alaska Natives cannot take bowhead whales unless authorized by the International Whaling Commission.

The intent behind this provision was to allow Alaska Natives to continue their traditional use of marine mammals for personal sustenance and handicraft economies without creating the risk of the emergence of significant new markets for marine mammal products. The latter goal was to be ensured by the limitations that the authentic marine mammal handicraft items had to be worked from their natural condition and produced through traditional methods, such as "weaving, carving, stitching, sewing, lacing, beading, and painting." As the courts have held, Alaska Natives are not limited as to what items they can produce so long as these established methods of production are used.[65]

From time to time, the Fish and Wildlife Service has chafed under its limited ability to impose restrictions on take by Alaska Natives. During the 1988 and 1994 reauthorizations of the Marine Mammal Protection Act, for example, the Fish and Wildlife Service's Alaska Regional Office proposed amendments that would allow for regulation of Native take without making a depletion finding. These initiatives to amend the Act were rejected at the policy level of the Department of the Interior and were not advanced. By proposing them, however, the Fish and Wildlife Service generated significant distrust within the Native community.

At the same time that the Alaska Regional Office was advancing the view that increased federal regulatory authority was needed, Native organizations were headed in the opposite direction, making significant progress in achieving self-regulation of marine mammal and other wildlife harvesting and seeking greater recognition of autonomous government bodies patterned after federally recognized tribes in the contiguous United States. Under both trends, Alaska Natives were sending the strong signal that they intended to control their own resource utilization practices and take appropriate steps to conserve marine mammals. They also expected to be dealt with on a government-to-government basis.

In the area of self-regulation of marine mammals, numerous Alaska Native organizations have been established to address conservation and management issues for the species involved. The first such organization to be established was the Alaska Eskimo Whaling Commission. The Commission was created in the 1970s during a time of great controversy over the Native hunt of bowhead whales and the authority of the International Whaling Commission to regulate such take. It sets village-by-village quotas and other controls governing the take of this endangered whale. It also imposes its own sanctions against whalers who do not comply. In 1981 the Commission entered into a memorandum of understanding with the National Oceanic and Atmospheric Administration, recognizing the Eskimos' lead role in regulating the harvest. This approach has been quite successful, with the Eskimo Commission playing an important role in improving whaling practices so fewer whales are struck and lost and proving that self-regulation can go hand in hand with federal control.

A number of other Alaska Native self-regulation organizations have been patterned after the Alaska Eskimo Whaling Commission, including the Eskimo Walrus Commission, the Alaska Nanuuq Commission (for polar bears), the Alaska Sea Otter Commission, the Fur Seal Commission, and the Bering Sea Coalition (Bering Sea ecosystem protection).

These relatively new entities are beginning to develop an impressive body of yet another form of authority to protect marine mammals—self-imposed, self-enforced Native take standards. For example, the North Slope Borough Fish and Game Management Committee and the Inuvialuit Game Council of Canadian Northwest Territories in 1988 entered into a cooperative agreement to govern the management of the Beaufort Sea polar bear population, which is shared by both countries. This Native-to-Native agreement sets quotas, protects cubs and female bears, establishes hunting seasons, prohibits the use of aircraft to hunt bears, and imposes additional measures. None of these restrictions could be imposed under the Marine Mammal Protection Act because of the prohibition on regulating Native take of nondepleted species, and hence the agreement has advanced marine mammal conservation without interfering with the rights of indigenous peoples. A similar agreement is now being developed for the Bering/Chukchi Seas polar bear stock between Russian Natives and Alaska Natives in western Alaska.

The lesson learned from the emerging pattern of self-regulation has not been lost on the federal agencies or Congress. Since the Fish and Wildlife Service's Alaska Region last attempted to amend the Act to allow federal regulation of Native take, a greater effort has been made by the federal agencies to work with Alaska Native organizations to achieve shared research, management, and conservation goals. Congress set the tone for these efforts in 1994 when it amended the Act to add a new section 119 to authorize the Fish and Wildlife Service and National Marine Fisheries Service to enter into cooperative agreements to provide for "co-management of subsistence use" by Alaska Natives. These agreements are to address data gathering, monitoring of harvests, participation in federal research, developing co-management structures, and funding Alaska Native efforts.

In addition, Congress established a special program under section 110 for a long-term research project to address the problems presented by the decline of numerous marine species in the Bering Sea. This program is to actively involve Alaska Natives.

Finally, Congress in 1994 sent a clear message that the federal agencies should not interfere with self-regulation absent exceptional circumstances. Although regulation of Native take from a depleted stock has always been subject to formal, on-the-record rulemaking, Congress imposed the additional requirement in section 101 that the underlying depletion also be subject to adjudication.

The Successes and Failures of the Legal Authorities Protecting Marine Mammals

As the Act reaches its twenty-fifth anniversary, we should assess how well the law has achieved its goals and what remains to be done. In many ways, this book provides such a review as the expert authors describe what they see as right and wrong about marine mammal conservation programs and the laws on which they are based. One thing is clear: whatever the successes of the past quarter century, the challenges that lie ahead are imposing.

The Marine Mammal Protection Act and other marine mammal conservation laws have functioned well in improving the lot of many species and populations. The moratorium on taking may have seemed draconian at the time, but it was the needed prescription to curb excessive exploitation and give certain species and populations a chance to begin to recover.

In 1972, for example, U.S. and foreign tuna fleets accounted for an estimated incidental kill of more than 400,000 dolphins, a number that now has been reduced to less than 5,000 (Marine Mammal Commission 1996). Bycatch of marine mammals and other organisms in high-seas salmon driftnet fisheries has been drastically reduced, as have the takes of polar bears in Alaska by commercial and sport hunters. Although the incidental take of California sea otters in the early 1980s was threatening the survival of the species, the level has been significantly reduced, and the population has grown from about 1,300 in the early 1980s to a current population of about 2,300 animals, although it may now be declining again.

Commercial whale and seal harvests, both commonplace in the United States in 1972, were halted, as was the bounty hunting of seals. The eastern North Pacific gray whale population, numbering but a few thousand in the early 1900s, is now estimated to exceed 23,000 animals, and it has been removed from the List of Endangered and Threatened Wildlife. The population of bowhead whales on which Alaska Natives depend has increased and is now thought to number about 8,200 animals.

Equally important, several species, such as the manatee and the Hawaiian monk seal, on the verge of extinction at the time of the Marine Mammal Protection Act's passage, are now substantially better off. Although numbers are relatively static, protective steps to prevent adverse impacts have been and are being taken, thanks to the legislation.

Internationally, the conservation program of the International Whaling Commission has been improved dramatically in its effectiveness, the Agreement on the Conservation of Polar Bears entered into force with beneficial results, great progress has been made with high-seas driftnet fisheries, and the Intergovernmental Maritime Organization is successfully focusing efforts to address boats and ships as sources of marine pollution.

It is also worth noting that the legislative emphasis on research in marine mammal–related fields has proven helpful in furthering the purposes and policies of the Act. Investment in federally funded marine mammal research has increased from $5,013,300 in 1974 to $28,782,400 in 1996, and the knowledge gained has much improved our ability to conserve marine mammals worldwide.

Some of the Endangered Species Act's and the Marine Mammal Protection Act's apparent successes, however, can also be viewed as failures. For example, it can be argued that, although the steps that have been taken to conserve manatees and monk seals have at least allowed maintenance of the status quo, they have not led to the recovery of these species. The picture is bleaker for some other species like the northern fur seal, the Steller sea lion, and the Alaskan stocks of harbor seals, all of which have actually seen their status worsen since 1972.

One area in which a great deal of effort is still needed is in achieving the statute's foremost goal of promoting the long-term "health and stability" of the marine environment. By setting an agenda focused primarily on species-by-species conservation and containing no specific provisions to protect habitat, the Act lacks cohesive management tools that would assist in the effort to conserve and enhance the marine ecosystem as an integrated whole. Marine mammals, fish, seabirds, habitat areas, and water quality are governed by separate laws and regulatory regimes that focus on constituent elements of the ecosystem rather than their interactions. As a result, in areas such as the Bering Sea, where 16 species of marine mammals, seabirds, and fish are in decline, and Georges Banks, where a host of commercially valuable fish species have become seriously depleted, entire ecosystems are showing signs of collapse. A basic question is whether the various legislative authorities can be amended in ways that might reverse these declines and establish an effective approach for ecosystem-based management of marine resources.

In the coming years, questions that should be considered as Congress reviews laws governing marine mammals include the following:

What changes might be made to strengthen statutory directives addressing habitat protection—probably the single most important issue facing marine mammals?

Should regulatory action designed to protect habitat, even if no direct take of marine mammals is involved, be limited to areas under federal jurisdiction or should such protection be extended, if needed, to areas subject to state or private control?

Are legislative directives indicated to better address contaminant and pollutant issues?

Are there legislative needs indicated with respect to furthering the precautionary principle in wildlife management, for example, by retaining or strengthening the burden on parties engaged in the taking of marine mammals to show that their activities will not adversely affect marine mammal populations and the ecosystems on which they depend?

Does the potential biological removal formula provide sufficient assurance that stocks will either remain within or increase toward their optimum sustainable population range, or are statutory changes indicated, particularly for the Steller sea lion and harbor seal stocks in Alaska that are declining for unknown reasons?

Will the potential biological removal–based approach bring species to recovery and maintain them there? If so, should it be expanded to cover taking other than that incidental to commercial fishing?

Should the Marine Mammal Protection Act or related laws be amended to establish clearer mechanisms for ensuring that indirect predator-prey relationships and direct bycatch interactions in commercial fisheries are factored into fishery management policies?

Does it make sense to preempt more protective state laws? Should the desire for a unified national program cancel out the potential for conservation gains that might be realized if more flexibility were available?

Considering the difficulties in using trade sanctions to police international behavior, are other mechanisms available for this purpose that have less potential to run afoul of free trade principles? If so, should these be statutorily described?

Has the program for protecting marine mammals in captivity suffered as a result of concentrating regulatory power in an agency concerned with the welfare of a broad range of captive animals rather than sharing authority with agencies having a specific mandate to protect marine mammals and, if it has, should the applicable legislation be strengthened?

Should the Marine Mammal Protection Act be amended to clarify policies regarding interactions between humans and marine mammals in the wild?

Should Congress continue to draft highly detailed provisions that constrain agency discretion or would more flexibility be desirable to allow the National Marine Fisheries Service and the Fish and Wildlife Service to respond more efficiently and effectively to problems as they arise?

Should Congress continue to draft species-specific amendments, such as the polar bear trophy import amendments enacted in 1994 and 1997? If so, when are such provisions appropriate?

Just as was true in 1971, so too today the answers to many of the most difficult questions about marine mammal conservation must come from the scientific community. Members of Congress, agency officials, concerned citizens and, yes, lawyers, cannot assess and improve the effectiveness of the Act and the other laws discussed in this chapter without the guidance and good counsel of marine biologists, ecologists, veterinarians, and scientists from other disciplines.

In 1969 one of the leading scientists responsible for the movement that resulted in passage of the Marine Mammal Protection Act, Victor B. Scheffer, published his book *The Year of the Whale.* In addition to helping generate public support for whale conservation efforts, Scheffer's book captured the unique relationship between these marvelous creatures and the scientists who study them. In doing so, he predicted with foresight that the bond between animal and scientist would grow stronger and more important over the course of the Act's history. As he wrote about the sperm whale and the biologists who study them:

> The whale biologist does the best he can. He scrapes a film of alga scum from the back of a harpooned animal towed to a whaling station and surmises that the animal had recently lived in colder waters, where this kind of alga is known to flourish. He slices the ovaries of a whale, counts the scars of pregnancy, and reconstructs in imagination the reproductive history and age of the beast. Or he counts the ripple marks on the roots of the teeth, or in the whalebone plates, or on the earwax plug, as a forester counts rings on the butt of a tree, and arrives at another estimate of age. He reads that a sperm whale has tangled in a telephone cable on the sea floor at a depth of over three thousand feet, and he gets new insight into the astounding diving ability of the whale. He finds a mother whale, dead in giving birth, white-blanketed with gulls, at final rest on a sandy beach. The head of the baby protrudes from her body. After a twinge of pity he notes in his record book: "Sperm whale, cephalic presentation."
>
> It is difficult to think about whales without thinking about men; the devoted men who study whales and whaling over the world and who write about them in a dozen languages. . . . The sympathetic thing about them is their pervading interest in conserving whales, not merely their particular skills and interests in zoology. As I write about one particular whale, I try to show, too, how men feel about whales and what they do to whales, and what whales do to men (Scheffer 1969).

Whatever the future may hold in store for the laws governing marine mammals, scientists will play a major role in forging the path taken. Ideally, sound science and a strong conservation ethic will continue to determine the shape of marine mammal law.

Notes

1. 540 F.2d 1141, 1148 (D.C. Cir. 1976).
2. 839 F.2d 795, 802 (D.C. Cir. 1988), *cert. denied, sub nom., Verity* v. *Center for Envtl. Educ.,* 488 U.S. 1004 (1989).
3. 16 U.S.C. §1361.
4. 386 F. Supp. 1341 (D. Md. 1974).
5. 40 *Fed. Reg.* 54,959 (1975).
6. 470 F. Supp. 423, 428 (D.D.C. 1979).
7. 44 *Fed. Reg.* 45,565 (1979).
8. 50 C.F.R. §216.3 (NMFS); 44 *Fed. Reg.* 2540, 2541–2542 (1979) (FWS).
9. 50 C.F.R. §216.3.

10. 42 *Fed. Reg.* 64,548 (1977); 45 *Fed. Reg.* 72,178 (1980).
11. 839 F.2d 795, 802 (D.C. Cir. 1988), *cert. denied, sub nom., Verity* v. *Center for Envtl. Educ.*, 488 U.S. 1004 (1989).
12. See H.R. Rept. No. 439, 103d Cong., 2d sess. 20, 24 (1994).
13. 50 C.F.R. §18.3.
14. 50 C.F.R. §216.4.
15. *Strong* v. *United States*, 5 F.3d 905 (5th Cir. 1993).
16. *United States* v. *Hayashi*, 22 F.3d 859 (9th Cir. 1993).
17. *Tepley* v. *National Oceanic and Atmospheric Administration*, 908 F. Supp. 708 (N.D. Cal. 1995).
18. Public Law 99-625, 99 Stat. 163 (1986).
19. *Animal Welfare Institute* v. *Kreps*, 561 F.2d 1002 (D.C. Cir. 1977).
20. 414 F. Supp. at 306.
21. *Committee for Humane Legislation, Inc.* v. *Richardson*, 540 F.2d 1141 (D.C. Cir. 1976).
22. 13 Envtl. L. Rept. 20203 (9th Cir. 5 Jan. 1983).
23. *Baldrige*, 724 F.2d 753 (9th Cir. 1984).
24. Public Law 97-389, §201, 96 Stat. 1949 (amending 16 U.S.C. §1034).
25. 60 *Fed. Reg.* 45,086–45,106 (1995).
26. 60 *Fed. Reg.* 45,399–45,401 (1995).
27. 50 C.F.R. §17.100–17.108.
28. 36 C.F.R. §13.65(b).
29. 39 *Fed. Reg.* 2482 (1974).
30. Public Law 99-625, 100 Stat. 3500.
31. 132 *Cong. Rec.*, S17322 (daily ed. 18 Oct. 1986) (statement of Sen. Cranston).
32. 16 U.S.C. §1151 *et seq.*
33. 16 U.S.C. 1034.
34. Public Law 93-205, 87 Stat. 884 (1973).
35. *Babbitt* v. *Sweet Home*, 515 U.S. 687 (1995).
36. Public Law 94-265, 90 Stat. 331 (1976), 16 U.S.C. §1801 *et seq.*
37. 42 U.S.C. §4321 *et seq.*
38. 325 F. Supp. 422 (D.D.C. 1970).
39. 40 C.F.R. Part 1500.
40. 341 F. Supp. 356, 367 (E.D.N.C. 1972).
41. *Jones* v. *Gordon*, 792 F.2d 821 (9th Cir. 1986).
42. *Greenpeace* v. *Evans*, 688 F. Supp. 579 (W.D. Wash. 1987).
43. *Progressive Animal Welfare Society* v. *Department of the Navy*, 725 F. Supp. 475 (W.D. Wash. 1989).
44. 16 U.S.C. §§668dd–668ee.
45. *Trustees for Alaska* v. *Watt*, 524 F. Supp. 1303, 1309 (D. Alas. 1981), *aff'd*, 690 F.2d 1279 (9th Cir. 1982).
46. 61 *Fed. Reg.* 13,647 (1996).
47. 16 U.S.C. §1 *et seq.*
48. 36 C.F.R. §2.2(a)(1).
49. 36 C.F.R. §13.65(b).
50. 61 *Fed. Reg.* 27,008–27,019 (1996).
51. 16 U.S.C. §§1431–1445.
52. 15 C.F.R. §§922.31–922.34.
53. *Personal Watercraft Industry Ass'n* v. *Dep't of Commerce*, 48 F.3d 540, 545 (D.C. Cir. 1995).
54. 50 C.F.R. §18.3; §216.3.
55. 9 C.F.R. §3.100 *et seq.*
56. *Mirage Resorts* v. *Franklin*, No. CV-S-92-759-PMP, slip op. at 14 (D. Nev. 24 Nov. 1993).
57. 49 Stat. 3079, T.S. No. 880.
58. 161 U.N.T.S. 72; T.I.A.S. No. 1849.
59. Public Law 100-220, 101 Stat. 1477.
60. Public Law 101-627.
61. 27 U.S.T. 1087, T.I.A.S. No. 8249.
62. Public Law 100-220, tit. II, 101 Stat. 1460 (1987) (codified in scattered sections of 33 U.S.C.).
63. 22 U.S.C. §1978.
64. Ibid.
65. *Katelnikoff-Beck* v. *U.S. Department of the Interior*, 657 F. Supp. 659 (D. Alas. 1986), *aff'd sub nom., Beck* v. *United States Dep't of Interior*, 982 F.2d 1332 (9th Cir. 1992).

Literature Cited

Ackerman, B. B., S. D. Wright, R. K. Bonde, D. K. Odell, and D. J. Banowetz. 1995. Trends and patterns in mortality of manatees in Florida, 1974–1992. Pages 223–258 *in* T. J. O'Shea, B. B. Ackerman, and H. F. Percival (eds.), Population Biology of the Florida Manatee. U.S. Department of the Interior, National Biological Service, Information and Technology Report 1.

Advisory Board on Wildlife Management. 1963. Wildlife management in units of the National Park System. Reprinted as pages 103–104 *in* National Park Service Administrative Policies. (1970).

Baur, D. C. 1991. Federally protected areas. Pages 222–268 *in* Natural Resources Law Handbook. Government Institutes, Inc., Rockville, MD.

Baur, D. C. 1996. Reconciling polar bear protection under United States laws and the International Agreement for the Conservation of Polar Bears. Animal Law 2:9–99.

Baur, D. C., and S. Iudicello. 1990. Stemming the tide of marine debris pollution. Ecology Law Quarterly 17:71–142.

Bean, M. J. 1983. The Evolution of National Wildlife Law. Praeger, New York, NY.

Birnie, P. (ed.). 1985. International Regulation of Whaling: From Conservation of Whaling to Conservation of Whales and Regulation of Whale-Watching. 2 vols. Oceana Publications, New York, NY. 1,053 pp.

Fraker, M. A., and B. R. Mate. 1999. Seals, sea lions, and salmon in the Pacific Northwest. (This volume)

Gaines, S. E., and D. R. Schmidt. 1976. Wildlife population management under the Marine Mammal Protection Act of 1972. Environmental Law Reporter 6:50096–50114.

Gambell, R. 1999. The International Whaling Commission and the contemporary whaling debate. (This volume)

Geraci, J. R., J. Harwood, and V. J. Lounsbury. 1999. Marine mammal die-offs: Causes, investigations, and issues. (This volume)

Gosliner, M. L. 1999. The tuna-dolphin controversy. (This volume)

Jones, L. L. 1984. Incidental take of the Dall's porpoise and the harbor porpoise by Japanese salmon driftnet fisheries in the western North Pacific. Reports of the International Whaling Commission 34:531–541.

Kimball, L. A. 1999. The Antarctic Treaty system. (This volume)

Laist, D. W., J. M. Coe, and K. J. O'Hara. 1999. Marine debris pollution. (This volume)

Marine Mammal Commission. 1996. Annual report to Congress for 1995. (Available from National Technical Information Service, Springfield, VA. PB96-157482.) 235 pp.

Marine Mammal Commission. 1997. Annual report to Congress for 1996. (Available from National Technical Information Service, Springfield, VA. PB97-142889.) 247 pp.

Northridge, S. P., and R. J. Hofman. 1999. Marine mammal interactions with fisheries. (This volume)

Odell, D. K., and J. E. Reynolds III. 1979. Observations on manatee mortality in South Florida. Journal of Wildlife Management 43 (2): 572–577.

Reynolds, J. E., III. 1999. Efforts to conserve the manatees. (This volume)

Scarff, J. E. 1977. The international management of whales, dolphins, and porpoises: An interdisciplinary assessment. Ecology Law Quarterly 6:323–638.

Scheele, L., and D. Wilkinson. 1988. Background paper on the eastern tropical Pacific tuna / dolphin issue. Pages 62–126 *in* To Authorize Appropriations to Carry out the Marine Mammal Protection Act of 1972 for Fiscal Years 1989 through 1993: Hearings on H.R. 4189 before the Subcommittee on Fisheries and Wildlife Conservation of the House Committee on Merchant Marine and Fisheries, 100th Cong., 2d sess.

Scheffer, V. B. 1969. The Year of the Whale. Charles Scribner's Sons, New York, NY. 213 pp.

Sobeck, E., and M. L. Gosliner. 1991. Wildlife and fisheries laws. Pages 269–306 *in* Natural Resources Law Handbook. Government Institutes, Inc., Rockville, MD.

U.S. House. 1971a. Marine mammals: Hearings before the Subcommittee on Fisheries and Wildlife Conservation of the House Committee on Merchant Marine and Fisheries, 92nd Cong., 1st sess. 1–3 (1971) (statement of Rep. Dingell).

U.S. House. 1971b. H.R. Rept. No. 707, 92d Cong., 1st sess.

U.S. House. 1981. H.R. Rept. No. 228, 97th Cong., 1st sess.

U.S. House. 1994. H.R. Rept. No. 439, 103d Cong., 2d sess.

U.S. Senate. 1916. S. Rept. No. 700, 64th Cong., 1st sess.

U.S. Senate. 1971. 118 *Cong. Rec.* S15680 (daily ed. 4 Oct. 1971) (statement of Sen. Packwood).

U.S. Senate. 1972a. S. Rept. No. 863, 92d Cong., 2d sess.

U.S. Senate. 1972b. Ocean mammal protection. Hearing on S. 685 et al. Subcommittee on Oceans and Atmosphere, Senate Commerce Committee, 92d Cong., 2d sess.

U.S. Senate. 1985. S. Rept. No. 592, 100th Cong., 2d sess.

Wijnstekers, W. 1990. The evolution of CITES. A reference to the Convention on International Trade in Endangered Species of Wild Fauna and Flora, 2d rev. ed. Secretariat of the Convention on International Trade in Endangered Species of Wild Fauna and Flora, Lausanne, Switzerland. 284 pp.

Wilkinson, D., and G. A. J. Worthy. 1999. Marine mammal stranding networks. (This volume)

4

MARC MANGEL AND ROBERT J. HOFMAN

Ecosystems

Patterns, Processes, and Paradigms

As part of the celebration of its seventy-fifth anniversary, the British Ecological Society conducted a survey of members in which individuals were asked to list the 10 most important ideas in ecology (Cherrett 1989). At the top of the ranked list was "The Ecosystem," and nearly 70% of the respondents included it somewhere on their lists. This is indeed appropriate because the ecosystem is at the foundation of ecology (e.g., McIntosh 1985, Anderson and Kikkawa 1986, Waring 1989, Real and Brown 1991, Toft and Mangel 1991, Hagen 1992, Likens 1992, Golly 1993).

Our goal in this chapter is to consider how one can think about ecosystems and the marine mammals that are part of them. We focus discussion on different ways of thinking about ecosystems, in terms of patterns, processes, and paradigms. We accomplish the task by considering a number of factors exemplified by real ecosystems described in the literature. Various characteristics of ecosystems emerge to form concepts of crucial practical importance. We consider elements of variability in time and space, and the complexity and intensity of interactions among species that also differ in time and space. The concepts we describe are often interrelated and apply to all ecosystems. We begin with what ecosystems are, consider the various concepts, and end with discussion and examples of practical application.

Defining the Ecosystem

The ecosystem is the community of organisms, the physical environment, and the interactions between and among organisms and abiotic environments. This definition avoids a description of the physical boundaries of the ecosystem. For the practical questions regarding marine mammals, the boundaries will perforce be vague and determined to some extent by the kinds of questions being asked. This definition leads to two crucial questions: what is a community and what is the nature of the interactions?

There is still disagreement about the meaning of a community of organisms (e.g., Price et al. 1984, Diamond and Case 1986). Here we adopt Fager's (1963:415) concept that communities are "recurrent organized systems of organisms with similar structure in terms of species presence and abundances." In other words, communities consist of mixtures of organisms. A given mixture can vary over time and space, but there is consistent pattern to the mixture, even if it can only be described in terms of probabilities (Fager 1957, 1963; Hubalek 1982).

There are alternative definitions. For example, Stenseth (1985:61) defined a community on the basis of systemic integrity or stability as "being such that neither a mutant strategy of an existing species nor any new species can invade." This is a fundamentally static viewpoint, whereas Fager's concept is fundamentally dynamic.

It is difficult to study communities at any large scale in a fully experimental manner (Hairston 1981). We must rely on good thinking, clever experiments (when possible), use of opportunities provided by natural perturbations ("natural experiments"), and thoughtful interpretation of data to discern relationships. Because we are far from having a science that is as sophisticated as ecosystem organization, we need to alternate our thinking between the particular and the general. Thus, it is important to know a few systems thoroughly, but to think broadly. We must adopt a pluralistic approach to understanding communities and ecosystems, which means "using a diversity of methodologies to obtain data, and a diversity of models to interpret data" (Diamond and Case 1986).

Large Marine Ecosystems, Fisheries Resources, and Marine Mammals

Many marine mammals are found in large marine ecosystems (LMEs) (Sherman 1990, 1991) that are located around the margins of the ocean basins and are characterized by distinct physical and biological features. About 95% of the annual production in the world's oceans is found in such areas (Bardach 1990). We use recent reviews of LMEs (Sherman and Alexander 1986; Sherman et al. 1990, 1991; Sherman 1994) to help identify some of the main concepts for thinking about ecosystems, particularly coastal upwelling areas.

Coastal upwellings are caused by winds blowing warm surface waters offshore so that cold bottom water containing nutrients rises to the surface. The five major coastal upwelling areas in the world are the California, Peru, Canary, Benguela, and Somalia Currents. These upwelling areas support a mix of species and generally contain the world's most productive fisheries. Other important upwelling areas are off the coasts of India, Java, and Costa Rica. Although upwelling areas constitute only 0.1% of the ocean surface, they produce half of the world's commercial fish harvest (Frye 1983; also see Sherman 1991:6–10). They are important areas for marine mammals as well.

The small geographic extent but large production of these upwelling areas (Table 4-1) leads to the first concept in the study of ecosystems:

Table 4-1. Productivity in Different Ocean Regimes

Ocean Regime	Standing Stock of Finfish Biomass (tons/km^2)
Open continental shelf with upwelling circulation	
Tropics	24–45
Medium latitudes	40–60
Higher latitudes	30–40
Open continental shelf without upwelling circulation	
Tropics	15–30
Medium latitudes	25–45
Higher latitudes	20–35
Wide marginal seas	25–45
Semienclosed seas	12–288
Open ocean	
Low latitudes	3–6
High latitudes	5–12

Source: Bax and Laevastu (1990).

Concept 1: Patchiness and Variability in Space and Time Are Characteristics of Most Ecosystems

The study of marine ecosystems requires methods for investigating patchiness and variability. For example, the emerging technologies of earth-orbiting satellites, geographic information systems, and spatial statistics have the potential to be of great importance for the study of ecosystems.

Natural subdivisions of the ocean are delineated by the presence, size, and depth of the continental shelf, current systems and their boundaries, and regimes of temperatures (Bax and Laevastu 1990:190). Because of this complexity, understanding ecosystems holistically requires us to consider numerous cause-and-effect relationships, rather than focusing on a single cause or effect. In this sense, ecosystem science is similar to evolutionary biology because "explanations of all but the simplest biological phenomena usually consist of sets of causes" (Mayr 1976:370). For example, the walleye pollock (*Theragra chalcogramma*) supports a large fishery in the Bering Sea and the sources of mortality are varied. In addition to diseases and parasites, large predators cause substantial mortality (Table 4-2). Take by apex predators is estimated from abundance estimates, some food-habit data, and assumptions about consumption rates. Apex predators (marine mammals and birds) are believed to be responsible for about the same amount of predation as fishing, but neither is the main cause of mortality of walleye pollock. Thus, determining the cause of a change in walleye pollock population size must consider a variety of possibilities in addition to fishing mortality. Likewise, determining the cause of food-related declines in predator populations must consider more than fishing mortality.

Table 4-2. Sources of Mortality of Walleye Pollock in the Bering Sea

Source	Contribution (%)
Other pollock (cannibalism)	61
Catch	9
Apex predators	9
Squid	3
Other fish	18

Source: Bax and Laevastu (1990).

We now turn to some specific LMEs chosen because they have implications for marine mammals and exemplify the concepts for thinking about ecosystems. Further details about particular LMEs can be found in publications by Sherman (1986, 1994) and Sherman et al. (1990, 1991).

The Weddell Sea (Hempel 1990) is a polar sea that has seasonal or permanent ice cover, year-round low temperatures, and intense seasonality in solar radiance. It contains a deep (approximately 100 m) surface mixed layer that is not a good environment for phytoplankton development. Annual primary production is poor and highly seasonal. The zooplankton are mainly a species of krill, *Euphausia superba,* and copepods. Many fish species depend upon the benthos for food. The top predators are mainly Weddell seals (*Leptonychotes weddellii*) and crabeater seals (*Lobodon carcinophagus*), emperor penguins (*Aptenodytes forsteri*), Adélie penguins (*Pygoscelis adeliae*), and southern minke whales (*Balaenoptera bonarensis*) and killer whales (*Orcinus orca*). Eight major land-based breeding sites are shared by emperor penguins and Weddell seals (150,000 adult penguins and 20,000 adult seals). Weddell seals feed on silverfish (*Pleuragramma antarcticum*) in summer and icefish in winter. Emperor penguins feed on krill, squid, and silverfish. Thus, the prey species are subject to a variety of sources of mortality.

Variability in sources of mortality is a common feature of ecosystems (Incze and Schumacher 1986; also see Fig. 4-1). Variability in top predators, combined with other biotic elements and variability in time and space, leads to:

Concept 2: Ecosystems are Characterized by Multiple Cause-Effect Relationships among Biotic and Abiotic Ecosystem Components

During at least one warming period, catches of Atlantic cod (*Gadus morhua*) in waters off western Greenland rose significantly (Hovgard and Buch 1990). This was followed (around 1970) by a cooling period in which cod catches decreased abruptly. During a second very strong cooling (1982–1983), catches of cod declined to almost zero. This nearly total collapse can be traced to a combination of recruitment failure, surface transport of larvae, and changes in fishing technology and effort (Hovgard and Buch 1990:38).

The Caribbean Sea (Richards and Bohnsack 1990) is the second-largest semienclosed sea in the world. It contains many islands, most of which are small, nonindustrialized countries. Between 1976 and 1985, 38 Caribbean countries reported catches of fish, crustaceans, and mollusks. The fishery resources included spiny lobsters (*Panulirus argus*), coral reef fishes, turtles, conches, and sea urchins.

Several epizootics occurred recently in this ecosystem. A massive fish kill occurred in the reefs in 1980, the cause of which is still unknown (Richards and Bohnsack 1990). In 1983 there was a mass mortality of sea urchins (*Diadema* spp.); in many areas 98% of the population died (Lessios 1988). In areas where the urchins have recovered, the size distribution of the population has changed considerably even though the total biomass has not (Levitan 1988). Because urchins eat algae, and the urchins temporarily disappeared, the reefs are now carpeted by macroalgae that are smothering the corals. From these examples, we derive:

Concept 3: The Consequences of Events at One Trophic Level Often Will Be Manifested across Many Other Trophic Levels

Fish and invertebrate resources of the Caribbean are transboundary resources (i.e., they are shared by two or more countries), but they are not treated as such, often with devastating consequences. Richards and Bohnsack (1990:51) noted that "many of the countries are poor and suffer overpopulation problems, but because of natural beauty and mild climate they are actively pursuing growth through tourism expansion. . . . the real crisis lies in the lack of coordinated support among the 38 nations to monitor the system." From this, we derive:

Concept 4: Organisms Do Not Recognize Political Boundaries and Management Should Be Structured Accordingly

The sea urchin recovery in the Caribbean also reminds us that organisms adapt to new conditions through changes in behavior, development, and life history, as well as genetics. Early views of the ecosystem tended to focus on energy flows (Toft and Mangel 1991), but in a seminal paper Fowler and MacMahon (1982) argued that the structure and functioning of ecosystems can be explained effectively by the processes of selective extinction and speciation. Their ideas can be summarized as follows: new species are produced

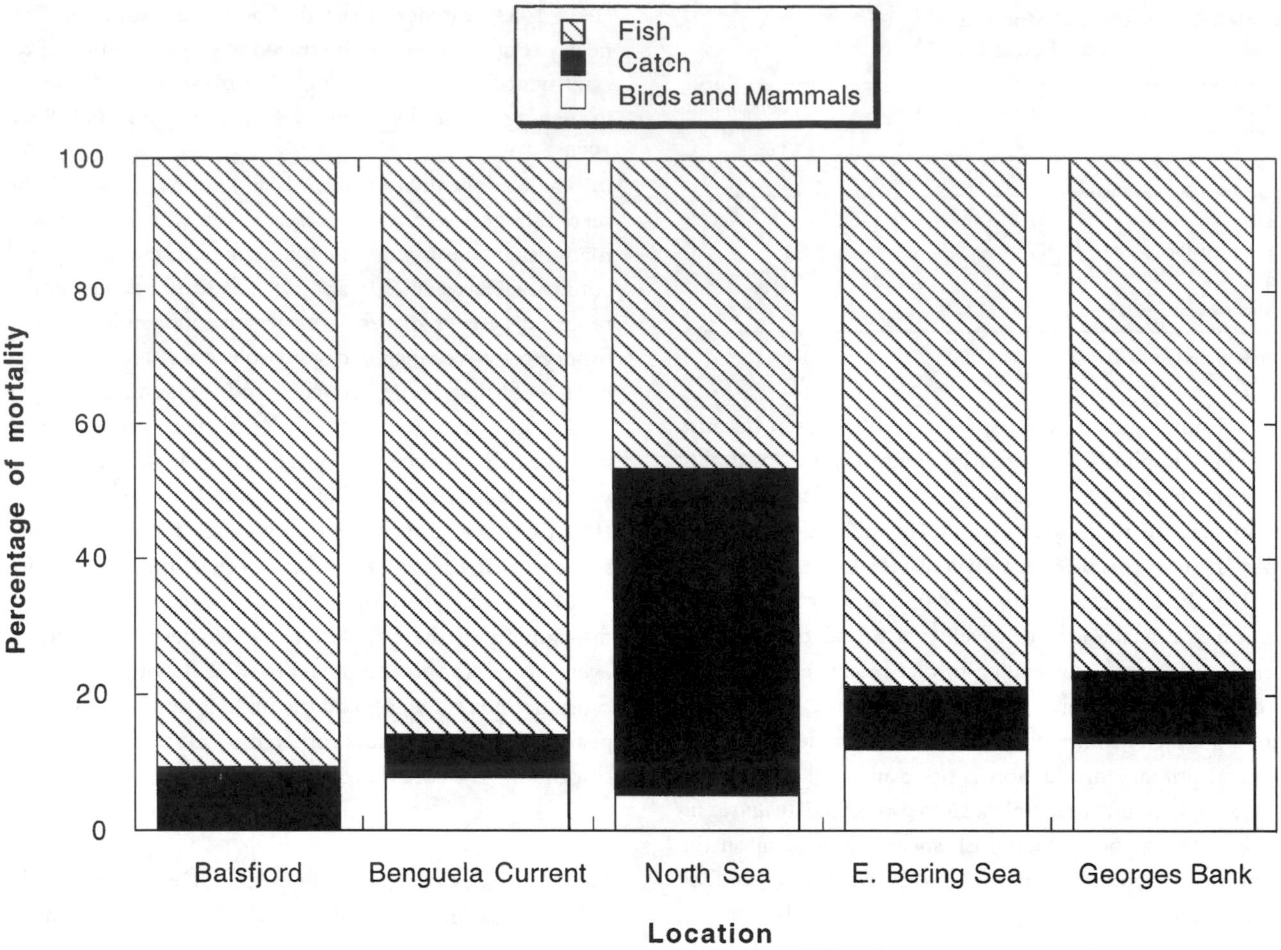

Figure 4-1. Sources of major mortality of fish in five different ecosystems, illustrating the variability of the sources. (From Bax and Laevastu 1990)

through natural selection and are subject to selective extinction and differential speciation. This means that the presence of species and their roles in ecosystems are not random but are the results of natural selection (especially at the species level). Thus, the current structure of living resource systems is shaped by evolutionary history (Fowler and MacMahon 1982, Crozier 1992), and resource managers must act within the constraints imposed by that history. This understanding can be summarized as:

Concept 5: Ecosystems Should Be Viewed as the Current State of an Ongoing Process of Selective Extinction and Differential Speciation

Furthermore, it is important to recognize that the ongoing processes of selective extinction and differential speciation involve considerable amounts of chance. Even if starting conditions are the same, we should not expect the same outcome. Instead, we should expect a distribution of potential ecosystem configurations from the same starting conditions. This concept, along with those covered earlier (over time and space) lead us to:

Concept 6: Change Is the Rule, Not the Exception, in Ecosystems

For example, the sources of variability and the strengths of various biotic interactions in marine mammal populations and other components of marine ecosystems may themselves vary over time and among ecosystems. Sherman (1990:215) offered the following hypotheses concerning changes in fish populations.

- In the Oyashio, Kuroshio, California, Humboldt, and Benguela Currents, and Iberian coastal ecosystems, increases in clupeid populations were due to natural environmental perturbations.
- In the Yellow Sea, the northeastern United States continental shelf, and Gulf of Thailand ecosystems, declines

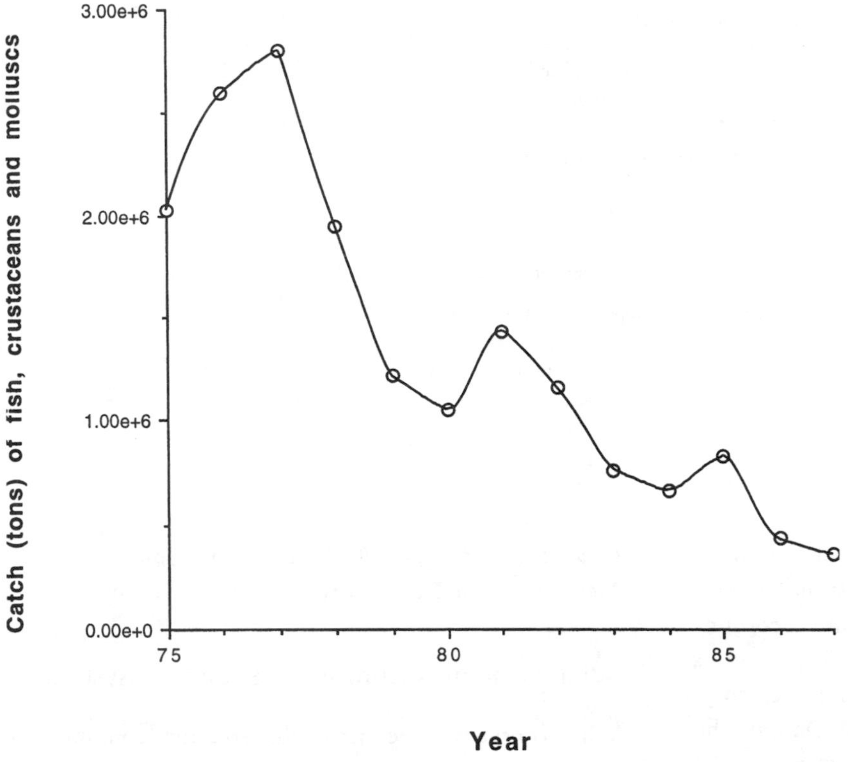

Figure 4-2. Collapse of the Barents Sea fishery. (Data from Borisov 1991)

of fish stocks were caused by a combination of excessive fishing mortality and predation.

- In the Great Barrier Reef ecosystem, predation on corals by the crown-of-thorns starfish (*Acanthaster planci*) interrupted the existing food chain between primary production and the fish components of the reef ecosystem.
- In the East Greenland shelf, Barents Sea, and Norwegian shelf ecosystems, natural environmental perturbations, such as large-scale changes in water movement and temperature, caused major shifts in the biomass of different fish stocks.
- In the Baltic Sea ecosystem, human-induced perturbations (mainly nitrate enrichment from agricultural runoff) increased primary production levels and ultimately increased the abundance of some fish stocks.
- In the Antarctic marine ecosystem, changes in krill abundance are caused by a combination of predation and environmental factors that may include changes in the ice edge, water movement and temperature, and ozone depletion.

The Barents Sea (Borisov 1991, Rosenberg et al. 1991) was traditionally one of the most productive areas of the ocean, with fish productivity (the main commercial species were capelin, herring, cod, haddock, redfish, and halibut) nearly three times that of the mean ocean fish production (720 kg/km^2 versus 225 kg/km^2). This is no longer true (Fig. 4-2). A retrospective analysis points to two main reasons for the recent collapse in the productivity of the Barents Sea: (1) a natural cyclic decrease in the inflow of warm Atlantic water in the 1980s and (2) the additional heavy stress of excessive fishing mortality, which impeded replacement. Overfishing occurred because fishery regulation was inadequate.

A further example of this kind of variability is seen in the California Current (MacCall 1990, Mullin 1991). This current sweeps southward along the west coast of North America. Coastal upwelling occurs along the more exposed sections of the coastline, creating a nutrient-rich environment that is highly productive. Natural variability is evidenced by changes in the deposition rates of sardine and anchovy scales found in bottom cores (Smith and Moser 1988).

During the 1800s, many marine mammal species in the ecosystem were seriously overexploited and driven to near extinction (both economic and biological). These include the northern fur seal (*Callorhinus ursinus*), the Guadalupe fur seal (*Arctocephalus townsendii*), the California sea otter (*Enhydra lutris*), the northern elephant seal (*Mirounga angustirostris*), the gray whale (*Eschrichtius robustus*), and the California sea lion (*Zalophus californianus*). We can only speculate how these reductions affected other ecosystem components. Under protection, some of these species are now recovering. We need methods to predict how the recovered stocks will influence ecosystem structure and productivity.

Table 4-3. Biological Interactions across Different Trophic Levels

Trophic Level	Main Biotic Interaction Limiting Abundance
A. The view proposed by Hairston et al. (1960) in which competition is the main factor limiting populations	
Piscivores	Competition
Planktivores	Predation
Producers	Competition
B. An alternative view proposed by Schoener (1989) in which predation and competition play more balanced roles	
Medium or large piscivores	Competition
Small piscivores or large planktivores	Predation
Small planktivores	Competition
Producers	Predation

MacCall (1990) showed that anchovy population size affects pelican production but not vice versa (because pelicans, when compared with all other predators, consume a relatively small number of anchovies). This is an example of a "one-way effect": components of the ecosystem affect a focal stock but not vice versa. On the other hand, California sea lions and northern elephant seals may consume 1.5 million mt of fish (Riedman 1990). Such consumption is likely to have a direct effect on fish population dynamics (that is, a two-way effect, discussed in more detail below). Likewise, sea otters consume large quantities of abalones, clams, and sea urchins and, as they reoccupy their former range in California, are having impacts on fisheries that developed in their absence. Consumption of sea urchins that eat macroalgae may be enhancing growth of kelp and kelp communities, including kelp-associated fish species valued by recreational and commercial fisheries (Estes and VanBlaricom 1985, Wendell et al. 1986). We thus conclude:

Concept 7: Interactions between Components of Ecosystems May Be Both One Way and Two Way

Interactions among biotic components of ecosystems are often portrayed by food webs (Schoener 1989, Collie 1991, Dagg et al. 1991, Yoder 1991). Brown et al. (1991) quantified the prey consumption requirements of several species in the Gulf of Mexico. They considered one cetacean (the bottlenose dolphin, *Tursiops truncatus*) and 33 species of fish, including 12 oceanic pelagics, 13 coastal pelagics, 5 reef fish, and 3 estuary-related species. Their work shows the complexity of linkages between predators and prey in food webs. Moreover, food webs are snapshots—the interactions between species often depend on the life history stage: fish that are prey as larvae or juveniles may be predators as adults. We summarize this by:

Concept 8: Marine Food Chains Are Complex, and in Many Species the Trophic Level Varies with Life Stage

What Structures Communities and Ecosystems?

When considering the factors that structure communities within ecosystems, Price (1984) stressed the importance of alternative paradigms and suggested a focus on resources, the response of individuals, and the response of populations to those resources. For more than 30 years, the dominant model was that of Hairston et al. (1960; also see Hairston and Hairston 1993). This model focused on three trophic levels, with competition as the major factor limiting populations (Table 4-3, A). That is, top predators are limited by competition among them for prey, the midtrophic-level planktivores are limited by predation from above, and the producers are once again limited by competition for resources, usually abiotic ones.

Schoener (1989) proposed an alternative model with four trophic levels, obtained by separating the larger predators from the smaller ones (Table 4-3, B). Schoener's model stressed the equal importance of competition and predation in the interactions. Thus:

Concept 9: Competition and Predation Both Contribute to the Structuring of Food Webs, But Their Relative Importance Varies

Predicting the effects of competition and predation is fraught with difficulty. For example, in approximately 20% of published studies, predator removal resulted in decline (rather than increase) in the prey population (Pimm 1991); these results should caution us about assuming that culling of marine mammal stocks will improve fisheries.

Next we consider how stocks interact with their physical environment. For example, how do physical processes, such as oceanic transport, affect food chain dynamics? The most common view is based on the assumptions of stationarity and one-way linkage. To understand these, assume that in a particular environment, E, we observe a stock level, S, and recruitment level, R. Now assume that the environment is perturbed to E′, the stock to S′, and recruitment to R′. The assumption of stationarity is that when the environment returns to E after the perturbation is removed, the stock will return to S, and the recruitment to R (Walters 1987a,b; Walters and Collie 1988). This assumption allows one to draw a "stock-recruitment" curve without regard to how the stock got to where it is.

An alternative hypothesis is that the history of the stock matters in determining current recruitment. In other words, when the environment returns to E, the stock may not return to S or, even if it does, recruitment may not return to R (recall the sea urchins). The assumption of one-way linkage is that the environment affects the stock, but not vice versa. An alternative possibility is that the stock has itself changed the ecosystem, so that even when the perturbation is removed, the environment may equilibrate to a completely different state, E″, even if the stock returns to S. Herring stocks show the characteristics of two-way linkages (Walters 1987a). The assumption of two-way, nonstationary linkages is that the stock affects the ecosystem, which in turn affects the stock, which in turn affects the ecosystem. These linkages mean that the ecosystem may exist in more than one configuration and that, after relaxation of a perturbation, the system need not return to its preperturbation state. We should thus expect alternative population, community, and ecosystem states, none of which may persist for long periods of time.

The linkages just discussed are implicitly temporal phenomena. Ecosystems also contain many spatial scales. For example, in the California Current, the communities of zooplankton and their predators involve characteristic spatial scales of 50 m for fish schools, 300 m for plankton aggregations, 1,000 m for gaps between plankton aggregations, and 10,000 m for gaps between fish school groups (Smith et al. 1989). Assessment of the possible pros and cons of alternative approaches to fishery and marine mammal management must consider both the temporal and spatial variability in food webs and linkages between components of the web.

Marine Mammals as the "Canary in the Cage"

The notion of a "healthy ecosystem" has different meanings to different people. For example, from the perspective of some fishermen, the healthiest ecosystem might be one that is entirely devoid of marine mammals. Most scientists and conservationists do not share this perspective. However, one thing that can be agreed upon is that virtually all ecosystems have suffered some kind of human impact in recent times. For marine ecosystems, pollution and poor fishery practices, particularly those resulting in large bycatch, are major sources of stress, but they are not always acknowledged as affecting the ecosystem. For example, although there has been recent discussion of the relative costs and benefits of high-seas driftnet fisheries (Burke et al. 1994), there has been little study of the potential ecosystem effects of these fisheries (Dayton et al. 1995; Northridge 1995; Northridge and Hofman, this volume).

Can top-level predators, such as marine mammals, be used as "canaries in the cage" to assess the health of ecosystems in the same way canaries were used by miners to test quality of the air in a mine shaft? Levels of contaminants in certain marine mammals that die and wash ashore might provide a useful indicator of certain pollutants in coastal marine ecosystems, particularly pollutants that are lipophilic and are bio-magnified in marine food webs. However, robust or declining marine mammal stocks are not necessarily a reliable indicator of healthy or unhealthy ecosystems. The following example illustrates why the health of a component population may not be an indicator of the health of the ecosystem.

Suppose that a stock grows according to the logistic equation:

$$N(t+1) = N(t) + rN(t)\left(1 - \frac{N(t)}{K(t)}\right) \tag{1}$$

where $N(t)$ is the number of individuals at the start of year t, r is the maximum per capita reproduction rate, and K is the carrying capacity. If r is not too large (to avoid deterministic chaos) and carrying capacity is fixed, then if the population starts below K, it will increase toward K; if it starts above K, it will decrease toward K.

Now assume that habitat degradation results in an annual decrease of carrying capacity. Thus, we append dynamics for the carrying capacity

$$K(t+1) = fK(t) \tag{2}$$

where $f < 1$. In each year, carrying capacity decreases, and thus population size decreases. However, the decrease in population lags considerably behind the decrease in carrying capacity (Fig. 4-3), so that the marine mammal stock gives an overly optimistic view of what is happening in the environment. Things are worse than they appear, using the marine mammal populations as the "canary in the cage."

The converse is also true when carrying capacity increases: the ecosystem, with "health" indexed by the

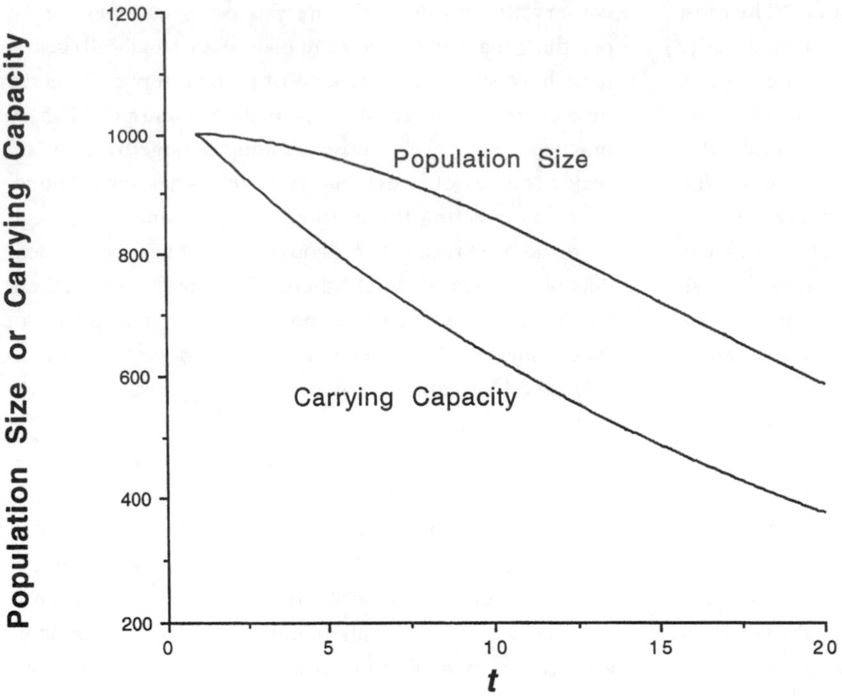

Figure 4-3. When a logistically growing population starts at carrying capacity, but the carrying capacity declines, the population declines but at a slower rate over time (t) than the carrying capacity. Parameters for this computation are $r = 0.07$ (a reasonable value for marine mammals), $K = 1{,}000$, and $f = 0.95$. Thus, the population does not provide an accurate picture of the decrease in habitat.

carrying capacity of the target species, is better off than indicated by the population trend. Thus we are led to:

Concept 10: Top Predators Such as Marine Mammals May Have Population Dynamics That Prohibit Using Their Abundance and Productivity as Effective Indicators of the Current Health of Ecosystems, Although They May Be Good Indicators of the Long-Term Effects of Certain Pollutants

In fact, it is unlikely that we can determine the health of ecosystems by monitoring any single species. A human metaphor may help: a healthy liver does not imply a healthy heart, or a healthy person for that matter. However, just as a diseased liver indicates an unhealthy person, a problem with one particular species could indicate an ecosystem-level problem. Unfortunately, finding a problem with a species often does not identify the cause or scale of the problem, particularly when the problem is not the product of direct human-caused mortality.

To assess ecosystem health, we must consider a variety of indicators. For example, Mullin (1991) described ways of measuring secondary production in the California Current ecosystem: indirect methods include extrapolation from primary production, metabolic mass balance, productivity/biomass ratio, biochemical measures, and egg production; direct measures involve counts at "sampling stations."

Another form of indirect observation involves using harvest data. There is a long history in fisheries science of using measures of catch and fishing effort to estimate and monitor relative abundance (Hilborn and Walters 1992, Smith 1994). These methods are complicated by the generally nonlinear and unknown relationship between the abundance of the stock and catch. In the Southern Ocean, for example, the most accurate index of krill abundance in the areas commonly fished is derived from the catch per fishing effort per search time (Mangel 1989, 1990). The catch per fishing effort provides an index of the density of krill once the fishing vessel is in a patch of krill, and the reciprocal of search time provides an index of the density of such patches of krill. However, changes in characteristics of certain krill predators, such as egg production and hatching and fledging success of Adélie penguins, may provide a more accurate and sensitive index of regional krill abundance.

Management of Ecosystems and Conservation

Conservation is concerned with how we sustain renewable resources in ecosystems so that future options are maintained (Collie 1991, Sherman 1991). There are many causes for the loss of resources in ecosystems, ranging from blooms of noxious phytoplankton (Smayda 1991) to marine pollution caused by humans (Marine Mammal Commission 1993). Ludwig et al. (1993) stressed that human social factors must be given greater prominence than they have been in the assessment and management of resource systems. In his classic work, Clark (1976, 1990) demonstrated that we cannot think of biology or economics alone when considering the use of renewable natural resources. He derived what might be called the "golden rule of bioeconomics," which relates the optimal size of the harvested stock to the growth rate of that stock and the interest rate that money can earn. This rule helps to explain some of the disastrous depletions of whale and fish stocks caused by commercial exploitation. Simply put, if the sole owner of a resource can earn more money in his or her lifetime (say, 8% per year) by killing and selling all of his or her slowly growing (say 3% per year) animals, then the economically "optimal" action for that individual is to drive the stock to extinction. Other factors common to the oceans, such as uncertainty concerning the future of the resource (Roughgarden and Smith 1996) and competition between harvesters, only exacerbate the situation. The implications of Clark's work are extremely important because they show that in many situations, the economically optimal action is to drive a stock or species to extinction. This means that we must perforce think of management and conservation with criteria broader than purely economic ones. A new kind of economics, based on ecological science, is required (Roughgarden and Smith 1996). It also means that biological-ecological considerations, not market demand, must set the limits on harvest levels.

Principles for Ecosystem Conservation

It is common now to speak of "ecosystem management." It would be better to speak of "ecosystem approaches" to management and to recognize from the outset that what is managed is almost always human intervention in ecosystems. Even those cases in which humans are removed completely from ecosystems involve managing human actions. Mangel et al. (1996) recently articulated a set of basic principles for the conservation of wild living resources.

An Example: Krill Fisheries in the Southern Ocean

In cases in which marine mammals are predators of the same fish or shellfish that humans harvest (Alverson 1992), how should we account for this competition? A particularly interesting example is the fishery for krill in the Southern Ocean, where nearly all fish, birds, and mammals are no more than one or two steps in the food chain away from krill (Everson 1992, Hunt et al. 1992, Nicol and de la Mare 1993 and references therein). Thus, a fishery for krill will potentially have effects on at least three trophic levels (concept 3). The fishery for krill has developed in the past 20-odd years and reached a peak catch of more than 500,000 mt of krill. There is inter-annual consistency and predictability in the fishing locations, suggesting that there is some constancy to the spatial and temporal patterns in the abundance of krill (concept 1).

It is clear that the standing biomass of krill is enormous. Indeed, estimates of annual production range from 75 million to more than 1,500 million mt. The issue regarding krill harvest is how much of that can be taken from highly localized areas near the breeding colonies of marine mammals and birds (Butterworth et al. 1991, 1992; Nicol and de la Mare 1993) without affecting those colonies in unacceptable ways. In the early 1980s the Convention for the Conservation of Antarctic Marine Living Resources was concluded for dealing with this and other issues.

A motivation for the fishery for krill was the presumption that overharvesting and decline of the krill-eating whale stocks left a vast "surplus" of krill "unaccounted for" or "going to waste" each year that could be harvested (Mackintosh 1970). The argument presumed that the standing stock of krill could be partitioned, with a fraction going to the whales and other marine mammals, a fraction to the fish, a fraction to the birds, and so forth, and that when the whales were depleted, there was no response by the other predators to the increased availability of prey. Such a presumption violates the concepts about the complexity of food chains (concept 8), expecting multiple effects (concept 2), adaptability of organisms (concept 5), and change (concept 6). Furthermore, consistent with our concept of multiple causes, in at least one case it has been proposed that the observed increase in the abundance of at least some krill predators has nothing to do with the krill "surplus." Fraser et al. (1992) argued that the increase in penguin populations was due to a slow decrease in the frequency of cold years.

Article II of the Convention for the Conservation of Antarctic Marine Living Resources calls for harvesting and associated activities in the convention area to be carried out to (1) prevent any harvested population from being reduced below its maximum net productivity level, (2) maintain the ecological relationships between harvested, dependent, and related populations, (3) restore populations that have been depleted as a direct or indirect consequence of harvesting, and (4) prevent or minimize the risk of ecosystem changes that are not potentially reversible within two or three decades (see Hofman 1993 for a discussion of these and other features of the Convention).

In response to the developing fishery for krill, the commission established by the convention adopted "precautionary" krill catch limits in 1991 and refined them in 1992. In the first action, a cap of 1.5 million mt was placed on the annual catch in one of the most important fishing areas. It was further specified that if catch in that area exceeded the previously highest commercial take of 620,000 mt, then subarea quotas would be established. In the second action, a precautionary limit of 390,000 mt was established for the South Indian Ocean where there is currently exploratory fishing for krill. These catch limits were based on the work of Butterworth et al. (1991, 1992) and are described in a less technical fashion in Nicol and de la Mare (1993). The models of Butterworth and colleagues are implicitly based on one-way linkages between krill and their predators, in which the predators have no effect on krill mortality. They also use a management goal of keeping the krill population size above an assumed critical level. The assumption of one-way linkages need not be true (concept 7), especially in cases in which interest is not in the entire Antarctic krill population but in those stocks that pass close to the land-based breeding colonies of predators. The Commission for the Conservation of Antarctic Marine Living Resources maintains a program of ecosystem monitoring to provide data that can be used to assess the status of the krill and their predators. As of now, however, available information is insufficient to ascertain the functional and numerical aspects of the linkages.

Conclusions

In this chapter we describe a set of general concepts to stimulate and guide further thinking about marine ecosystems and the marine mammals in them. These concepts reflect the view that ecosystems are dynamic and are the results of ongoing processes of speciation and extinction. Ecosystems are patchy in time and space and are characterized by multiple cause-effect relationships in which consequences at one trophic level are often experienced throughout the ecosystem. Interactions in ecosystems are sometimes one way and sometimes two ways. Marine food webs are expected to be complex, and both predation and competition play important roles in their structure and operations. Finally, ecosystems often cross international boundaries, which are human constructs not recognized by marine mammals or other biota.

Acknowledgments

M. M. thanks P. Daltrop and K. Jones for hospitality during the preparation of early drafts of the chapter. The original work on krill fisheries was supported by the Commission for the Conservation of Antarctic Marine Living Resources and by the National Marine Fisheries Service. For comments on early versions of the manuscript, we thank Charles W. Fowler, Randall R. Reeves, Cathy Toft, and 11 anonymous referees.

Literature Cited

Alverson, D. L. 1992. A review of commercial fisheries and the Steller sea lion (*Eumetopias jubatus*): The conflict arena. Reviews in Aquatic Sciences 6:203–256.

Anderson, D. J., and J. Kikkawa. 1986. Development of concepts. Pages 3–16 *in* J. Kikkawa and D. J. Anderson (eds.), Community Ecology: Pattern and Process. Chapman and Hall, New York, NY.

Bardach, J. 1990. Sustainable development of fisheries. Proceedings Globe 1990 Conference, Vancouver, B.C., Canada.

Bax, N. J., and T. Laevastu. 1990. Biomass potential of large marine ecosystems. A systems approach. Pages 188–205 *in* K. Sherman, L. M. Alexander, and B. D. Gold (eds.), Large Marine Ecosystems: Patterns, Processes and Yields. AAAS Press, Washington, DC.

Borisov, V. M. 1991. The state of the main commercial species of fish in the changeable Barents Sea Ecosystem. Pages 193–203 *in* K. Sherman, L. M. Alexander, and B. D. Gold (eds.), Food Chains, Yields, Models, and Management of Large Marine Ecosystems. Westview Press, Boulder, CO.

Brown, B. E., J. A. Browder, J. Powers, and C. D. Goodyear. 1991. Biomass, yield models, and management strategies for the Gulf of Mexico Ecosystem. Pages 125–163 *in* K. Sherman, L. M. Alexander, and B. D. Gold (eds.), Food Chains, Yields, Models, and Management of Large Marine Ecosystems. Westview Press, Boulder, CO.

Burke, W. T., M. Freeberg, and E. L. Miles. 1994. The United Resolutions on driftnet fishing: An unsustainable precedent for high seas coastal fisheries management. Ocean Development and International Law 25:127–186.

Butterworth, D. S., A. E. Punt, and M. Basson. 1991. A simple approach for calculating the potential yield from biomass survey results. CCAMLR Document, Working Group Krill, 91/23. Commission for the Conservation of Antarctic Marine Living Resources, Hobart, Tasmania, Australia.

Butterworth, D. S., G. R. Gluckman, and S. Chalis. 1992. Further computations of the consequences of setting the annual krill catch limit to a fixed fraction of the estimate of krill biomass from a survey. Preprint, Working Group Krill, 92/4. Commission for the Conservation of Antarctic Marine Living Resources, Hobart, Tasmania, Australia.

Cherrett, J. M. 1989. Key concepts: The results of a survey of our members' opinions. Pages 1–16 *in* J. M. Cherrett (ed.), Ecological Concepts. Blackwell Scientific Publications, Oxford, U.K.

Clark, C. W. 1976. Mathematical Bioeconomics. John Wiley and Sons, New York, NY.

Clark, C. W. 1990. Mathematical Bioeconomics, 2d ed. John Wiley and Sons, New York, NY.

Collie, J. S. 1991. Adaptive strategies for management of fisheries resources in large marine ecosystems. Pages 225–242 *in* K. Sherman, L. M. Alexander, and B. D. Gold (eds.), Food Chains, Yields, Models, and Management of Large Marine Ecosystems. Westview Press, Boulder, CO.

Crozier, R. H. 1992. Genetic diversity and the agony of choice. Biological Conservation 61:11–15.

Dagg, M., C. Grimes, S. Lohrenz, B. McKee, R. Twilley, and W. Wiseman. 1991. Continental shelf food chains of the northern Gulf of Mexico. Pages 67–99 *in* K. Sherman, L. M. Alexander, and B. D. Gold (eds.), Food Chains, Yields, Models, and Management of Large Marine Ecosystems. Westview Press, Boulder, CO.

Dayton, P. K., S. F. Thrush, M. T. Agardy, and R. J. Hofman. 1995. Viewpoint: Environmental effects of marine fishing. Aquatic Conservation: Marine and Freshwater Ecosystems 5:205–232.

Diamond, J., and T. J. Case. 1986. Community Ecology. Harper and Row, New York, NY.

Estes, J. A., and G. R. VanBlaricom. 1985. Sea-otters and shellfisheries. Pages 187–235 *in* J. R. Beddington, R. J. H. Beverton, and

D. M. Lavigne (eds.), Marine Mammals and Fisheries. George Allen and Unwin, London.

Everson, I. 1992. Managing southern ocean krill and fish stocks in a changing environment. Philosophical Transactions of the Royal Society B 338:311–317.

Fager, E. W. 1957. Determination and analysis of recurrent groups. Ecology 38:586–595.

Fager, E. W. 1963. Communities of organisms. Pages 415–437 *in* M. N. Hill (ed.), The Sea, Vol. 2. Interscience, New York, NY.

Fowler, C. W., and J. A. MacMahon. 1982. Selective extinction and speciation: Their influence on the structure and functioning of communities and ecosystems. American Naturalist 119:480–498.

Fraser, W. R., W. Z. Trivelpiece, D. G. Ainley, and S. G. Trivelpiece. 1992. Increases in Antarctic penguin populations: Reduced competition with whales or a loss of sea ice due to environmental warming? Polar Biology 11:525–531.

Frye, R. 1983. Climatic change and fisheries management. Natural Resources Journal 23:77–96.

Golly, F. B. 1993. A History of the Ecosystem Concept in Ecology. Yale University Press, New Haven, CT. 354 pp.

Hagen, J. B. 1992. An Entangled Bank: The Origins of Ecosystem Ecology. Rutgers University Press, New Brunswick, NJ. 320 pp.

Hairston, N. G. 1981. Ecological Experiments. Cambridge University Press, New York, NY.

Hairston, N. G., G. F. E. Smith, and L. B. Slobodkin. 1960. Community structure, population control and competition. American Naturalist 94:421–425.

Hairston, N. G., Jr., and N. G. Hairston, Sr. 1993. Cause-effect relationships in energy flow, trophic structure, and interspecific interactions. American Naturalist 142:379–411.

Hempel, G. 1990. The Weddell Sea: A High Polar Ecosystem. Pages 5–18 *in* K. Sherman, L. M. Alexander, and B. D. Gold (eds.), Large Marine Ecosystems: Patterns, Processes and Yields. AAAS Press, Washington, DC.

Hilborn, R., and C. J. Walters. 1992. Quantitative Fisheries Stock Assessment. Chapman and Hall, New York, NY.

Hofman, R. J. 1993. Convention for the Conservation of Antarctic Marine Living Resources. Marine Policy 17 (6): 534–536.

Hovgard, H., and E. Buch. 1990. Fluctuation in the cod biomass of the West Greenland sea ecosystem in relation to climate. Pages 36–43 *in* K. Sherman, L. M. Alexander, and B. D. Gold (eds.), Large Marine Ecosystems: Patterns, Processes and Yields. AAAS Press, Washington, DC.

Hubalek, Z. 1982. Coefficients of association and similarity, based on binary (presence-absence) data: An evaluation. Biological Reviews 57:669–689.

Hunt, G. L., D. Heinemann, and I. Everson. 1992. Distributions and predator-prey interactions of macaroni penguins, Antarctic fur seals, and Antarctic krill near Bird Island, South Georgia. Marine Ecology Progress Series 86:15–30.

Incze, L., and J. D. Schumacher. 1986. Variability of the environment and selected fisheries resources of the Eastern Bering Sea Ecosystem. Pages 109–143 *in* K. Sherman and L. M. Alexander (eds.), Variability and Management of Large Marine Ecosystems. AAAS Selected Symposium 99. Westview Press, Boulder, CO.

Lessios, H. 1988. Mass mortality of *Diadema antillarum* in the Caribbean: What have we learned? Annual Review of Ecology and Systematics 19:371–393.

Levitan, D. R. 1988. Algal-urchin biomass responses following mass mortality of *Diadema antillarum* Philipp at Saint John, U.S. Virgin Islands. Journal of Experimental Marine Biology and Ecology 119:167–178.

Likens, G. E. 1992. Ecosystem Approach: Its Use and Abuse. The Ecology Institute, Olendorf/Luhe, Germany. 166 pp.

Ludwig, D., R. Hilborn, and C. Walters. 1993. Uncertainty, resource exploitation, and conservation: Lessons from history. Science 260:17–36.

MacCall, A. D. 1990. Dynamic Geographic of Marine Fish Populations. University of Washington Press, Seattle, WA.

Mackintosh, N. A. 1970. Whales and krill in the twentieth century. Pages 195–212 *in* M. W. Holdgate (ed.), Antarctic Ecology, Vol. 1. Academic Press, New York, NY.

Mangel, M. 1989. Analysis and modeling of the Soviet southern ocean krill fleet, Part 1. Pages 127–235 *in* Selected Scientific Papers of the Scientific Committee for the Conservation of Antarctic Marine Living Resources 1988. Commission for the Conservation of Antarctic Marine Living Resources, Hobart, Tasmania, Australia.

Mangel, M. 1990. Analysis and modeling of the Soviet southern ocean krill fleet, Part 2, Estimating the number of concentrations. Pages 283–322 *in* Selected Scientific Papers of the Scientific Committee for the Conservation of Antarctic Marine Living Resources 1989. Commission for the Conservation of Antarctic Marine Living Resources, Hobart, Tasmania, Australia.

Mangel, M., L. M. Talbot, G. K. Meffe, M. T. Agardy, D. L. Alverson, J. Barlow, D. B. Botkin, G. Budowski, T. Clark, J. Cooke, R. H. Crozier, P. K. Dayton, D. L. Elder, C. W. Fowler, S. Funtowicz, J. Giske, R. J. Hofman, S. J. Holt, S. R. Kellert, L. A. Kimball, D. Ludwig, K. Magnusson, B. S. Malayang III, C. Mann, E. A. Norse, S. P. Northridge, W. F. Perrin, C. Perrings, R. M. Peterman, G. B. Rabb, H. A. Regier, J. E. Reynolds III, K. Sherman, M. P. Sissenwine, T. D. Smith, A. Starfield, R. J. Taylor, M. F. Tillman, C. Toft, J. R. Twiss Jr., J. Wilen, and T. P. Young. 1996. Principles for the conservation of wild living resources. Ecological Applications 6:338–362.

Marine Mammal Commission. 1993. Annual report to Congress for 1992. (Available from National Technical Information Service, Springfield, VA. PB95-154995.) 241 pp.

Mayr, E. 1976. Evolution and the Diversity of Life: Selected Essays. Belknap Press, Harvard University, Cambridge, MA.

McIntosh, R. P. 1985. The Background of Ecology: Concepts and Theory. Cambridge University Press, New York, NY.

Mullin, M. M. 1991. Spatial-temporal scales and secondary production estimates in the California Current ecosystem. Pages 165–191 *in* K. Sherman, L. M. Alexander, and B. D. Gold (eds.), Food Chains, Yields, Models, and Management of Large Marine Ecosystems. Westview Press, Boulder, CO.

Nicol, S., and W. de la Mare. 1993. Ecosystem management and the Antarctic krill. American Scientist 81:36–47.

Northridge, S. 1995. Environmental mismanagement on the high seas; a retrospective analysis of the squid and tuna driftnet fisheries of the North Pacific. Report to the U.S. Marine Mammal Commission. (Available from National Technical Information Service, Springfield, VA. PB95-238945.) 76 pp.

Northridge, S. P., and R. J. Hofman. 1999. Marine mammal interactions with fisheries. (This volume)

Pimm, S. L. 1991. The Balance of Nature? Ecological Issues in the Conservation of Species and Communities. University of Chicago Press, Chicago, IL.

Price, P. 1984. Alternative paradigms in community ecology. Pages

353–383 *in* P. W. Price, C. N. Slobodchikoff, and W. S. Gaud (eds.), A New Ecology: Novel Approaches to Interactive Systems. John Wiley and Sons, New York, NY.

Price, P. W., C. N. Slobodchikoff, and W. S. Gaud (eds.). 1984. A New Ecology: Novel Approaches to Interactive Systems. John Wiley and Sons, New York, NY.

Real, L. A., and J. H. Brown. 1991. Foundations of Ecology. University of Chicago Press, Chicago, IL.

Richards, W. J., and J. A. Bohnsack. 1990. The Caribbean Sea: A large marine ecosystem in crisis. Pages 44–53 *in* K. Sherman, L. M. Alexander, and B. D. Gold (eds.), Large Marine Ecosystems: Patterns, Processes and Yields. AAAS Press, Washington, DC.

Riedman, M. 1990. The Pinnipeds: Seals, Sea Lions and Walruses. University of California Press, Berkeley, CA. 439 pp.

Rosenberg, A. A., M. Basson, and J. R. Beddington. 1991. Predictive yield models and food chain theory. Pages 205–224 *in* K. Sherman, L. M. Alexander, and B. D. Gold (eds.), Food Chains, Yields, Models, and Management of Large Marine Ecosystems. Westview Press, Boulder, CO.

Roughgarden, J., and F. Smith. 1996. Why fisheries collapse and what to do about it. Proceedings of the National Academy of Sciences 93:5078–5083.

Schoener, T. W. 1989. Food webs from the small to the large. Ecology 70:1559–1589.

Sherman, K. 1986. Measurement strategies for monitoring and forecasting variability in large marine ecosystems. Pages 203–236 *in* K. Sherman and L. M. Alexander (eds.), Variability and Management of Large Marine Ecosystems. AAAS Selected Symposium 99. Westview Press, Boulder, CO.

Sherman, K. 1990. Productivity, perturbations, and options for biomass yields in large marine ecosystems. Pages 206–219 *in* K. Sherman, L. M. Alexander, and B. D. Gold (eds.), Large Marine Ecosystems: Patterns, Processes and Yields. AAAS Press, Washington, DC.

Sherman, K. 1991. Sustainability of resources in large marine ecosystems. Pages 1–34 *in* K. Sherman, L. M. Alexander, and B. D. Gold (eds.), Food Chains, Yields, Models, and Management of Large Marine Ecosystems. Westview Press, Boulder, CO.

Sherman, K. 1994. Sustainability, biomass yields, and health of coastal ecosystems: An ecological perspective. Marine Ecology Progress Series 112:277–301.

Sherman, K., and L. M. Alexander (eds.). 1986. Variability and Management of Large Marine Ecosystems. AAAS Selected Symposium 99. Westview Press, Boulder, CO.

Sherman, K., L. M. Alexander, and B. D. Gold (eds.). 1990. Large Marine Ecosystems: Patterns, Processes and Yields. AAAS Press, Washington, DC.

Sherman, K., L. M. Alexander, and B. D. Gold (eds.). 1991. Food Chains, Yields, Models, and Management of Large Marine Ecosystems. Westview Press, Boulder, CO.

Smayda, T. 1991. Global epidemic of noxious phytoplankton blooms and food chain consequences in large ecosystems. Pages 275–307 *in* K. Sherman, L. M. Alexander, and B. D. Gold (eds.), Food Chains, Yields, Models, and Management of Large Marine Ecosystems. Westview Press, Boulder, CO.

Smith, P. E., and H. G. Moser. 1988. CalCOFI time series: An overview of fishes. California Cooperative Fisheries Investigations Report 29:66–77.

Smith, P. E., M. D. Ohman, and L. E. Eber. 1989. Analysis of the patterns of distribution of zooplankton aggregations from an acoustic Doppler current profiler. California Cooperative Fisheries Investigations Report 30:89–103.

Smith, T. D. 1994. Scaling Fisheries. Cambridge University Press, New York, NY.

Stenseth, N. 1985. Darwinian evolution in ecosystems: The Red Queen view. Pages 55–72 *in* P. J. Greenwood, P. H. Harvey, and M. Slatkin (eds.), Evolution: Essays in Honour of John Maynard Smith. Cambridge University Press, New York, NY.

Toft, C. A., and M. Mangel. 1991. From individuals to ecosystems; the papers of Skellam, Hutchinson and Lindeman. Bulletin of Mathematical Biology 53:121–134.

Walters, C. J. 1987a. Nonstationarity of production relationships in exploited fish populations. Canadian Journal of Fisheries and Aquatic Sciences 44 (Supplement II): 156–165.

Walters, C. J. 1987b. Adaptive Management of Renewable Resources. Macmillan, New York, NY.

Walters, C. J., and J. S. Collie. 1988. Is research on environmental factors useful to fisheries management? Canadian Journal of Fisheries and Aquatic Sciences 45:1848–1854.

Waring, R. H. 1989. Ecosystems: Fluxes of matter and energy. Pages 17–41 *in* J. M. Cherrett (ed.), Ecological Concepts. Blackwell Scientific Publications, Oxford, U.K.

Wendell, F. E., R. A. Hardy, J. A. Ames, and R. T. Burge. 1986. Temporal and spatial patterns in sea otter, *Enhydra lutris,* range expansion and the loss of Pismo clam fisheries. California Fish and Game 72 (4): 197–212.

Yoder, J. A. 1991. Warm-temperature food chains of the southeast shelf ecosystem. Pages 49–66 *in* K. Sherman, L. M. Alexander, and B. D. Gold (eds.), Food Chains, Yields, Models, and Management of Large Marine Ecosystems. Westview Press, Boulder, CO.

5

SIMON P. NORTHRIDGE AND ROBERT J. HOFMAN

Marine Mammal Interactions with Fisheries

Most species of marine mammals interact in some way with fisheries. Individuals of almost all species (hundreds of thousands of individuals, in some cases) are known to have been killed in fishing operations, and many marine mammal species prey on organisms that are fished commercially (Northridge 1984, 1991a). Almost all kinds of fishing operations have at least some impact on marine mammals (see Table 5-1). Interactions between marine mammals and fisheries represent some of the most significant threats to marine mammal populations at a global level (see, for example, Reijnders et al. 1993, Reeves and Leatherwood 1994).

In this chapter, we describe the variety of interactions between marine mammals and fisheries and examine ways in which these can be managed. In most cases, this means addressing how fishery managers seek to regulate fishing activities to reduce or eliminate conflicts between fisheries and marine mammals. The measures taken to manage such conflicts have undergone a considerable evolution in the past few decades, not just in the United States with the passage in 1972 of the Marine Mammal Protection Act, but globally with the gradual introduction of new concepts into fishery management regimes. Increasing awareness of the functional relationships among marine living resources, and concerns for the conservation of marine mammal populations, have led to radical changes in the philosophy underpinning the management of the ocean's living resources. These changes are reflected in both national legislation and international agreements and, ultimately, in the ways that interactions between fisheries and marine mammals are viewed and managed.

We begin by describing and classifying the types of interactions that occur between marine mammals and fisheries, using examples from around the world. We then consider the legislative frameworks within which management measures have been formulated to address some of these interactions. Following from this, we consider the types of measures that have been adopted and the processes by which these have been shaped by current legislative frameworks and fishery management axioms. To illustrate these processes, we then consider four case studies:

(1) The Convention for the Conservation of Antarctic Marine Living Resources, under which conservation measures and a monitoring program have been devised to ensure that krill fishing has minimal adverse impacts on marine mammals, birds, or other species that depend upon krill as their principal food;
(2) Seal culling, which has been proposed and practiced in many areas with the expectation that it will increase fishery yields by reducing seal predation on fish stocks;

Table 5-1. Examples of Interacting Fisheries and Marine Mammals

Gear Type	Area	Marine Mammals	Information Sources[a]
Gillnet	Gulf of California	Vaquita	1
	Mediterranean	Striped dolphin, common dolphin, bottlenose dolphin, pilot whale, Risso's dolphin	1, 2
	Indian Ocean	Bottlenose dolphin, hump-backed dolphin, striped dolphin, common dolphin	1, 2
	Peru/Chile	South American sea lion, Burmeister's porpoise, common dolphin	1
	North Atlantic	Harbor seal, gray seal, harbor porpoise, pilot whale, common dolphin, bottlenose dolphin, Risso's dolphin, minke whale, hump-back whale, right whale	1, 3, 4
	Central North Pacific	Steller sea lion, North Pacific harbor seal, fur seal, Dall's porpoise, northern right whale dolphin, common dolphin, Pacific white-sided dolphin	1, 2, 3, 5
	West Coast, United States	California sea lion, elephant seal, harbor seal, white-sided dolphin, common dolphin, harbor porpoise, sea otter	1, 6, 7, 8
Trawl	South Africa	Cape fur seal	9
	Bering Sea/Gulf of Alaska	Northern fur seal, spotted seal, ringed seal, ribbon seal, bearded seal, elephant seal, Steller sea lion, walrus, sea otter, Dall's porpoise, Pacific white-sided dolphin, minke whale	3,6
	Northwestern Atlantic	Harp seal, hooded seal, pilot whale, common dolphin, Risso's dolphin, bottlenose dolphin, pilot whale, false killer whale	3, 10
	Oregon, California, Alaska	Steller sea lion, California sea lion, northern fur seal, harbor seal	3
Purse seine	Pacific	Spotted dolphin, spinner dolphin, common dolphin	11
Longline	Alaska	Steller sea lion, killer whale, Pacific white-sided dolphin	3
Pot, ring net, and trap	Alaska	Sea otter, harbor seal, Steller sea lion, minke whale, gray whale	3
	North Atlantic	Right whale, hump-back whale, minke whale, pilot whale	4
Mariculture pens	Tasmania	Australian fur seal	12
	Puget Sound	Steller sea lion, California sea lion, harbor seal	3
	North Atlantic	Harbor seal, gray seal	3, 13

[a]1, Perrin et al. (1994); 2, Northridge (1984); 3, 58 *Fed. Reg.* (112): 32905–32913 (1993); 4, Lien (1994); 5, Loughlin et al. (1983); 6, Barlow et al. (1994); 7, Hanan and Diamond (1989); 8, Hanan et al. (1993); 9, Shaughnessy (1985); 10, Pemberton et al. (1994); 11, Gosliner (this volume); 12, Pemberton and Shaughnessy (1993); 13, Anonymous (1996).

(3) Large-scale high-seas driftnet fishing, which, particularly in the 1980s, was responsible for the indiscriminate killing of large numbers of marine mammals and many other nontarget organisms; and
(4) Harbor porpoises (*Phocoena phocoena*), which are killed accidentally in large numbers in fishing operations in the Gulf of Maine.

Types of Interactions

A primary distinction is that between "operational" interactions and "biological" interactions (IUCN 1981, Beverton 1985). In the former, animals interact directly with the actual fishing operation, for example, by removing fish from nets or becoming entangled in nets. Biological interactions are less direct. They include competition between marine mammals and fisheries for the same prey species and transmission of parasites between marine mammals and commercial fishery resources. Such interactions can be regarded as population-level, rather than individual, interactions.

The distinction between operational and biological interactions is important partly because the two types of interaction require different approaches for management. For example, where marine mammals are seen to cause problems by damaging fishing operations, fishermen often assume that the mammals are also competing with them for the same fishery resources (see, for example, Lister-Kaye 1978) (Fig. 5-1). Establishing the distinction between operational and biological interactions helps to maintain clarity when assessing potential conflicts and avoids the blurring of one sort of problem into another.

Operational Interactions

Operational interactions can be negative or positive to either the marine mammal or the fishery. Most can be assigned to one of four categories, as follows:

Mutually Beneficial

There are several situations around the world in which wild marine mammals assist fishermen in catching fish. In some areas, dolphins signal the presence of fish, or herd fish toward fishermen, either coincidentally or deliberately (Bus-

Figure 5-1. A bottlenose dolphin, one of about 130 that inhabit Moray Firth, Scotland, is shown attempting to eat a large salmon. This kind of demonstrative feeding on valuable fish understandably irritates fishermen. (Photograph courtesy of Aberdeen University / Sea Mammal Research Unit, St. Andrews, Scotland)

nel 1973, Pryor et al. 1990). Fishermen may reward this behavior by throwing some of the fish that they catch to the mammals or the mammals may find it easier to catch fish as they drive them into the fishermen's nets. In such cases, both the fishermen and the dolphins benefit from the interaction.

Negative Effects on Fisheries

Marine mammals are often observed to forage around fishing vessels, for example, taking fish as they escape through the cod-end of a trawl (Corkeron et al. 1990, Fertl and Leatherwood 1995) or, more significantly, taking fish from nets or hooks—fish that would otherwise have been brought on board (Sivasubramanian 1964, Yano and Dahlheim 1995, Ashford et al. 1996). Their efforts to remove fish from hooks and nets often damage fishing gear, causing considerable expense to fishermen. This is especially important in situations where fish stocks are under pressure from excessive fishing effort, profits are down, and any additional fish losses or damage to gear have come to be perceived as highly significant. In some areas, marine mammal depredation may be so severe that fishing is effectively made impossible. Such interactions are at least superficially beneficial to the marine mammal, but are generally detrimental to the fishery.

Negative Effects on Marine Mammals

In some cases, marine mammals may be attracted to fish caught in nets or on hooks and are caught themselves when they attempt to take the fish (Fig. 5-2). Marine mammals may also simply swim into and become caught in nets because they fail to detect or recognize the danger posed by a net. Such accidental capture has been recognized as an important, and for some populations a critical, source of mortality (Perrin et al. 1994, Reeves and Leatherwood 1994). Clearly, operational interactions of this kind are detrimental to the mammals involved. They are also often detrimental to the fishermen. Gear may be damaged or destroyed as entangled marine mammals attempt to free themselves, and fishermen may be injured or even killed in trying to release marine mammals, whether dead or alive.

Beneficial to Fishermen

In a few cases, the incidental capture of marine mammals in fishing gear can be beneficial to fishermen. In some countries, fishermen are able to use or sell marine mammals caught in their gillnets and other gear (Leatherwood and Reeves 1989, and see below). In some tuna fisheries, fishermen use the presence of dolphins to indicate the presence of tuna schools and so set their nets deliberately around the dolphins to catch the tuna (Perrin 1969; Gosliner, this volume; and see below).

Two types of operational interactions are problematic: when marine mammals cause significant economic loss to a fishery, and when a fishery causes significant mortality to a marine mammal population. In this regard, it is important to recognize that fishermen, fishery managers, marine mammalogists, and animal welfare advocates are likely to have differing views as to what constitutes a significant economic loss and a significant impact on a marine mammal population.

There are numerous examples of situations in which marine mammals damage fishing gear or catch (Northridge 1984, 1991a). The species involved include both large and small cetaceans, pinnipeds, sea otters, and sirenians, and the affected fishing operations include both stationary gear such as gillnets and fish traps and mobile gear such as trawls and

Figure 5-2. This forlorn gray seal was hauled ashore by fishermen in Berwick-on-Tweed, Scotland, using a salmon seine net (sweep net). The seal would not have been caught if it had not been trying to take salmon out of the net. (Photograph courtesy of Sea Mammal Research Unit, St. Andrews, Scotland)

purse seines (Table 5-1). Humpback whales (*Megaptera novaeangliae*), for example, that collided with fish traps along the coast of Newfoundland caused several hundred thousand dollars worth of damage annually during the 1970s (Lien and Merdsoy 1979). During the 1980s killer whales (*Orcinus orca*) removed hooked sablefish (*Anoplopoma fimbria*) and other target species from a substantial percentage of the longlines set in the Bering Sea, causing the fishery to lose at least tens of thousands of dollars (Yano and Dahlheim 1995).

Around Sardinia, bottlenose dolphins (*Tursiops truncatus*) forage near trawlers, and fishermen complain of reduced catches (Consiglio et al. 1992). In this instance, the possible economic loss to the fishery, if any, has not been estimated. Along much of the west coast of the United States, from Alaska to California, Steller (northern) sea lions (*Eumetopias jubatus*), California sea lions (*Zalophus californianus*), and harbor seals (*Phoca vitulina*) cause hundreds of thousands of dollars worth of damage annually through damaged and lost fish, especially salmon, and damage to gear (Matkin and Fay 1980; Beach et al. 1981; Miller et al. 1983; DeMaster et al. 1985; Fraker and Mate, this volume). Throughout much of their North Atlantic range, gray seals (*Halichoerus grypus*) and harbor seals are reported to damage or remove fish from gillnets. McCarthy (1985), for example, found that harbor seals removed up to 45% of salmon in gillnet fisheries in some instances in parts of Ireland. In South Africa, Cape fur seals (*Arctocephalus pusillus*) cause considerable damage to purse seine fisheries for small pelagic fish, with sometimes hundreds of fur seals mobbing purse seines and removing fish that would otherwise be brought on board (Shaughnessy 1985). Estimates of total cost to the industry worldwide range from 1.6% to 4.1% of the landed value of the catch (Wickens 1995).

Deaths of marine mammals caused by fishery operations also involve a wide range of mammal species and types of fisheries (Table 5-1). In several cases, such mortalities threaten species or populations with extinction. Examples include the vaquita and the baiji.

The vaquita (*Phocoena sinus*), a porpoise endemic to the Gulf of California, is in danger of extinction largely because of mortalities in gillnet fisheries. The total vaquita population is almost certainly less than 1,000 animals and could be in the low hundreds (Villa-R. 1993, Barlow et al. 1997). It has been estimated that 30 to 40 individuals are killed every year in gillnets (Boyer and Silber 1990, Vidal 1991). Barlow et al. (1997) estimated that the population may have declined at a rate of around 20% per year between 1986 and 1993.

The baiji, or Yangtze River dolphin (*Lipotes vexillifer*), is also in danger of extinction, in part because of incidental mortalities in fisheries (Zhou and Zhang 1991). Historically, this species occurred throughout much of the length of the Yangtze River and in some of its tributaries. Construction of dams and other development along the river has severely reduced its range. In the past 15 years, the baiji is reported to have declined from about 400 to 150 or fewer animals (Ellis et al. 1994). Much of this decline seems due to entanglement in longlines set to snag bottom-feeding fish. The lines have sharp hooks every few centimeters, and when dolphins come near snagged fish, they too may become snagged. Some baiji are also caught in gillnets and fish traps (Perrin and Brownell 1989).

It is important to realize that not all marine mammal mortalities due to interactions with fishing gear are immediate. Injuries to the animal, or gear fragments that remain attached to the animal, may make the animal more susceptible to death at a later time from infection, starvation, or some other cause. In some species, injuries received from interactions with fishing gear may therefore represent a significant source of "cryptic" mortality, which is very difficult to assess.

Other species and populations of marine mammals that may be threatened by mortality and injury incidental to fisheries include the Mediterranean and Hawaiian monk seals (*Monachus monachus* and *M. schauinslandi*, respectively) (Ragen and Lavigne, this volume), the North Atlantic right whale (*Eubalaena glacialis*) (Katona and Kraus, this volume), and some populations of harbor porpoises (Bjorge and Donovan 1995).

Although in most such cases marine mammal mortalities and injuries are accidental, and detrimental to the fishery in terms of lost time and damaged gear, in a few cases the marine mammals may be deliberately targeted or at least treated as a valuable bycatch. In the eastern tropical Pacific, for example, some tuna vessels seek out schools of pelagic dolphins that are easily visible from the surface. Large yellowfin tuna (*Thunnus albacares*) school beneath the dolphins and setting a purse seine around a dolphin school can mean that a large catch of tuna is made. Once the net is set, and the two schools are surrounded, the net is pursed at the bottom to trap the tuna. The dolphins may then be released, although in the past hundreds of thousands of dolphins perished in such operations (see Gosliner, this volume, for a full description of this issue). In this example, marine mammal mortality has been a consequence of deliberate actions by fishermen to improve their tuna catch.

In some countries, notably Peru, Sri Lanka, and the Philippines, small cetaceans caught accidentally in gillnet fisheries have been landed and sold. As a consequence, a market for these species has been stimulated, so that what was initially an incidental catch (i.e., incidental to the main fishing activity) has become an important bycatch (i.e., a catch of some value beside the main target) (Read et al. 1988, Leatherwood and Reeves 1989, Dolar 1994, van Waerebeek and Reyes 1994). At this point, an "operational interaction" may become a targeted "fishery" for marine mammals.

In most cases, the accidental capture of marine mammals occurs below the surface, where it is difficult to observe. In such cases, it is generally not known exactly when, why, or how the animals get caught. In the case of gillnets, marine mammals may not be aware of the potential danger. Although both dolphins and porpoises are apparently capable of detecting the nets by means of their acoustic sense (Dawson 1991, Au 1993), they become caught when they hit the nets and become entangled. If they are unable to extricate themselves either by breaking the netting or by disentangling themselves, they suffocate. Seals and sea lions are also taken in gillnets, but they are more often able to break free, presumably with the aid of their claws in tearing the meshes. Larger animals, such as whales, may be able to break through a net made of fine twine or one that is firmly anchored. Even large cetaceans like sperm whales, however, can be killed if the meshes are strong enough or the net is not anchored securely.

Catches in towed gear may also impose substantial mortalities on some marine mammal populations. Animals may be caught because they are foraging in front of net openings or as a consequence of a net's size and towing speed. Some pelagic trawls stretch over many hundreds of meters and are towed at speeds of 8 knots (14.4 km/hour) or more. Animals in the path of such a trawl, especially if they are confused with regard to the geometry of the net, may find it very difficult to get out of the way.

Biological Interactions

Biological interactions are more complex and less easily studied and understood than operational interactions. At the simplest level, fisheries and marine mammals can be seen as competing for the same food. This means that marine mammals, especially those with large populations, could be depriving fishermen of what they might otherwise catch or, alternatively, that fisheries could be depriving marine mammals of fish, mollusks, crustaceans, or other organisms that they otherwise would eat.

This description of the situation, however, belies the complexity of the ecological linkages involved. Most marine mammals forage on a variety of organisms, many of which may be predators of one another at different stages in their life histories. The nature and implications of such relationships are only beginning to be understood and appreciated.

As noted earlier, biological interactions may also include the special case of parasite transmission. Most fish are subject to infestation by parasites such as nematodes. In some stocks this infestation can become a problem either from a marketing perspective, because consumers do not like to purchase fish infested with worms, or from a human health perspective (Margolis 1977). Some of the nematodes that parasitize fish are the juvenile stage of a parasite that completes its life cycle in marine mammal predators of the fish. In these cases, marine mammal culls have been used, or proposed, to try to reduce the parasite load in the affected fish stock. Culling has been pursued even though epidemiological modeling has suggested that a more effective strategy, at least in some circumstances, would be to increase fishing pressure on affected fish stocks, thereby removing older fish that harbor more parasites. We will not consider this issue further here; the interested reader is referred to Bowen (1990) and des Clers and Wooton (1990).

As with operational interactions, biological interactions may be beneficial or detrimental to either marine mammals or fisheries. Usually, however, the detrimental aspects are stressed. Increasing marine mammal numbers are often held to be responsible for declining fishery yields (examples below), and declining marine mammal numbers may be blamed on increased fishing. In almost all cases, there is such a poor understanding of the ecological complexities of the marine environment that demonstrating cause and effect proves difficult or impossible. This problem is generic to marine ecological studies. Rarely is it possible to manipulate the marine environment to test a hypothesis. Moreover, many of the important parameters, such as fish stock size, are subject to considerable variability resulting from environmental factors. The following are some examples of situations in which possible detrimental interactions have been noted.

In the Bering Sea and Gulf of Alaska, there have been substantial declines since the 1970s in the numbers of Steller sea lions, harbor seals, and northern fur seals (*Callorhinus ursinus*), as well as several species of fish-eating birds. With the possible exception of the fur seal decline, which has stopped, all of these appear to have been due to decreased food availability (Anonymous 1993). Walleye pollock (*Theragra chalcogramma*) is a key component in the diet of each of the declining species, and the declines parallel the development of the pollock fishery (Swartzman and Hofman 1991). It is curious, however, that despite the fishery, pollock abundance has been relatively high over much of this period. Moreover, although the fishery has targeted large fish, the mammals and birds tend to consume smaller fish. Also, during the same time there have been dramatic changes in the oceanographic conditions of the eastern North Pacific that could have affected the distribution and availability of food species. To make matters more complicated, pollock are cannibalistic, with larger ones feeding on smaller ones, so that the effects of the fishery on the food supply of the mammals are uncertain (Wooster 1993).

Several converse examples are available, in which fishery yields have declined as marine mammal numbers increased. In such cases, a causal connection often has been assumed. The annual Canadian hunt for harp seals (*Phoca groenlandica*) has been justified, for example, as a means of reducing seal predation on fish stocks (Malouf 1986) and, in recent years, to assist the recovery of collapsed cod (*Gadus morhua*) stocks (MacKenzie 1996). Culling has been called for by fishing interests in several other countries, including Italy, the United Kingdom, Ireland, Japan, and South Africa (reviewed by United Nations Environment Programme 1994, Earle 1996), based on the supposition that reducing marine mammal numbers will increase fishery yields. In none of these instances has any evidence been adduced to show a causal relationship between marine mammal numbers and fishery yields. Nevertheless, such "interactions" clearly are perceived in many areas to represent significant conflicts.

Predation by sea otters (*Enhydra lutris*) on shellfish provides another example. Sea otters were extirpated from most of their range along the rim of the North Pacific Ocean by hunting in the eighteenth and nineteenth centuries. As they recolonized their former range in California during the twentieth century, there have been corresponding declines in commercial and recreational catches of abalone, clams, and other invertebrates commonly eaten by sea otters. Although some of the declines have been caused by overharvesting, there is no doubt that some have been due to sea otter predation. This has led to conflicts between commercial and recreational fishermen and sea otter advocates (Estes and VanBlaricom 1985). The conflicts have been heightened by the fact that entanglement of sea otters in coastal set net fisheries effectively stopped growth of the California sea otter population from the mid-1970s through the mid-1980s (Wendell et al. 1985). The conflict is complicated by the fact that several of the principal sea otter prey species eat kelp, so that growth of kelp beds, which are commercially valuable and important habitat for a number of finfish, is enhanced by the presence of sea otters (Estes and Palmisano 1974).

Biological interactions between marine mammals and fisheries need not always be detrimental to one or the other. There are several examples in which fisheries are held to have altered the structure of fish populations in such a way as to benefit marine mammals, although once again it is difficult to substantiate such hypotheses. Heavy fishing of herring (*Clupea harengus*) and mackerel (*Scomber scombrus*) in the North Sea during the 1960s and 1970s, for example, may have led to the observed increase in the abundance of smaller species such as the sand lances (*Ammodytes* spp. [called sand eels in Europe]) and the sprat (*Sprattus sprattus*) (Hempel 1978). Over the same period, gray seals, which feed predominantly on sand lances in the North Sea, increased in number at around 7% per year (Harwood and Prime 1978). It is quite possible that this increase was related to a fishery-induced increase in sand lance abundance.

Similar changes in the fish community in the northwestern Atlantic, including increases in sand lance biomass, have been correlated with decreases in herring biomass during the 1970s (Sherman et al. 1981). The increased biomass of planktivorous sand lance has been linked to a local decrease in planktivorous right whales in the northwestern Atlantic by Payne et al. (1990).

The examples above, although by no means comprehensive, indicate the range of possible interactions. Some are more serious than others because, for example, they result in high levels of marine mammal mortality or in substantial financial losses to a fishery.

In past decades, significant problems were generally defined as those about which fishermen complained most loudly. As we discuss below, few attempts were made to reduce marine mammal mortality in fishing operations until the 1970s. Nor were efforts made to safeguard the food supplies of marine mammals from fishing pressures until even more recently. Indeed, until the past few decades, management measures to address conflicts between marine mammals and fisheries usually took the form of culls or bounty schemes for reducing marine mammal populations (Bonner 1982, Earle 1996). This reflected the fact that the resolution of conflicts between marine mammals and fisheries was generally the responsibility of national fishery agencies, which were (and in many instances still are) most responsive to the wishes and perceptions of the fishing industry.

More recently, attitudes have changed. As a result of the precipitous declines in populations of many marine mammal species due to whaling and sealing during the nineteenth and early to mid-twentieth centuries, it became clear that marine mammal populations were highly vulnerable to depletion (see, for example, Food and Agriculture Organization 1978). Such concerns have had far-reaching effects, not only on the way that fishery interactions with marine mammals are addressed at a management level, but also less directly, as we point out below, in the way that fishery management regimes are formulated. Increasingly, management measures directed at interactions between marine mammals and fisheries are driven not simply by the concerns of the fishing industry, but by national and international legislation that reflects growing scientific knowledge and widespread public concerns about the effects of human activities on the health and welfare of marine mammals and marine ecosystems.

In the next section, we examine the ways that fishery management and national laws and international agreements governing fisheries management have been influenced by increased knowledge and concern for the welfare of marine mammals, fishery resources, and the world's oceans in general. This in turn provides us with a context in which to examine the management measures now being used to address problematic interactions between fisheries and marine mammals.

The Legislative Framework

It is clear from the wording of relevant international treaties that, before the 1960s, little thought was given by the international community to the effects of fishing upon the marine environment in general or marine mammals in particular. The text of the 1958 Convention on Fishing and Conservation of the Living Resources of the High Seas, for example, defined conservation as "the aggregate of measures rendering possible the optimum sustainable yield from those resources so as to secure a maximum supply of food and other marine products" and specified that "[c]onservation programs should be formulated with a view to securing in the first place a supply of food for human consumption." By the time the United Nations Convention on the Law of the Sea (UNCLoS) was being drafted in the 1970s, this completely utilitarian view of fishery management had begun to be recognized as inadequate. Article 61.3 of UNCLoS, for example, states that conservation and management measures are to be "designed to maintain or restore populations of harvested species at levels which can produce the maximum sustainable yield, *as qualified by relevant environmental and economic factors*" (emphasis added).

Several things that occurred in the 1960s and 1970s were responsible for this change in philosophy. During the 1960s it became clear that, despite the increasing efforts of the International Whaling Commission and its Scientific Committee, whale populations had declined precipitously and were continuing to do so. The 1960s and 1970s also saw the collapse of several key fish stocks, including several North Atlantic herring stocks and the Peruvian anchovy stock (Gulland 1983). During the early 1970s, the nature and scale of dolphin mortality in the eastern tropical Pacific purse seine fishery for tuna also became apparent (see Gosliner, this volume). At the same time, the general public, at least in the industrialized nations, became much more familiar with a whole range of conservation issues and, particularly through the medium of television, became more familiar with the marine environment (Holt and Talbot 1978). Finally, the 1960s and 1970s saw a proliferation of highly vocal and influential pressure groups and nonprofit organizations devoted to environmental protection (see Lavigne et al., this volume). These developments led to a critical reappraisal of fishery management measures that continues to the present.

Although concern for marine mammals was not exclusively responsible for the changes to the legislative framework for marine conservation, it was clearly a key issue. Article 65 of UNCLoS, for example, states that "Nothing in this Part restricts the right of a coastal state or the competence of an international organization, as appropriate, to prohibit, limit, or regulate the exploitation of marine mammals more strictly than provided for in this Part." Marine mammals were thereby afforded a unique status internationally under this legal framework. Subsequent national legislation and international agreements have reinforced this status (e.g., see chapter 17.47 in the Report on Agenda 21 from the United Nations Conference on Environment and Development [UNCED] [1992], 3–14 June 1992, Rio de Janeiro, Brazil).

UNCLoS was the first of several significant United Nations agreements that have redefined the nature and goals of marine living resource management. Among these, Agenda 21, the Convention on Biological Diversity, the United Nations Agreement on Highly Migratory Fish Stocks and Straddling Fish Stocks, and the Food and Agriculture Organization's Code of Conduct on Responsible Fishing have codified several key concepts in international law.

Agenda 21, the Convention on Biological Diversity, and the U.N. Agreement on Highly Migratory Fish Stocks and Straddling Fish Stocks all affirmed the importance of the "precautionary principle" (see O'Riordan and Cameron 1994 and Food and Agriculture Organization 1995 for further details). Agenda 21 and the U.N. Agreement on Highly Migratory Fish Stocks and Straddling Fish Stocks also affirmed the importance of the "ecosystem" approach to management, by which conservation measures are to be adopted to protect nontarget as well as target species that might be affected by a fishery. Both the U.N. Agreement on Highly Migratory Fish Stocks and Straddling Fish Stocks and the Food and Agriculture Organization's Code of Conduct on Responsible Fishing stress the importance of developing and using selective gear types that minimize "impacts on associated or dependent species, in particular endangered species." UNCLoS, Agenda 21, and the Biodiversity Convention all stress the importance of sustainable use of natural living resources.

These United Nations agreements reflect principles previously established in a number of national laws and regional agreements, several of which date from the 1970s. Two examples are the U.S. Marine Mammal Protection Act enacted in 1972 and the Convention on the Conservation of Antarctic Marine Living Resources (CCAMLR) concluded in 1980. The primary objective of the Marine Mammal Protection Act of 1972, for example, is to maintain the health and stability of the marine ecosystem and, when consistent with this objective, to restore and maintain marine mammal populations at optimum sustainable levels. The objectives of CCAMLR are to prevent the depletion of harvested populations and to maintain the ecological relationships among harvested, dependent, and related populations of Antarctic marine living resources. Article 1 of CCAMLR defines "Antarctic marine living resources" as "the populations of finfish, mollusks, crustaceans and all other species of living organisms, including birds [and marine mammals] found south of the Antarctic Convergence."

Legislative changes have, in some cases, followed changes in fishery management practice. In others, legislation has forced fishery managers to reexamine the ways in which they operate. In relation to marine mammals, one of the most immediate effects has been a reassessment of what constitutes a significant interaction with fisheries. Whereas in previous decades only effects on fisheries generally were viewed as problems, far more attention is now given to effects on marine mammals and other ecosystem components. Likewise, culls and bounty schemes historically were the primary response to complaints about marine mammals from the fishing industry (see Bonner 1982 and Earle 1996 for examples), but a more rational approach to culling is now the norm (for exceptions, see below).

As a result of increasing knowledge and awareness of the interrelationships among ecosystem components and changes in public opinions and perceptions regarding marine mammals, most national governments are now obliged by domestic legislation or international agreements to conserve marine mammal populations. Although these statutory obligations are helpful in promoting the conservation of marine mammal populations, they do not, by themselves, ensure that appropriate measures are adopted. What really matters are the actions taken by the responsible agencies to ensure that the legislative intent is achieved. In the next section, we review the types of measures available to managers, before considering some specific case studies.

Potential Management Measures

Identifying a Problem

From a natural resource manager's perspective, a requirement is to determine whether a particular interaction between a fishery and marine mammals constitutes a "significant" problem and, therefore, whether it needs to be addressed by any management action. In those instances when marine mammals cause damage to gear or to fish already caught, the significance can be measured in terms of the estimated economic loss in relation to the total value of the fishery (e.g., a $10,000 loss to a fishery with a total catch valued at $100,000 would be much more significant than a $10,000 loss to a fishery with a catch worth $1,000,000 or more). Also, managers have to weigh the estimated loss to the fishery against the expected costs of mitigative measures. Other factors, such as fleet overcapitalization, may also contribute to the significance of economic impact. Further, costs and benefits may be more than simply economic. There may well be political repercussions from any management action or inaction as groups with special interests in the affected fisheries or marine mammals respond to management decisions.

The same is true with respect to marine mammal mortality in fishing operations. Managers need to assess the significance of the mortality with respect to its impacts on the size and productivity of the affected marine mammal population and its relationships with other ecosystem components. In some countries, there may be a legal basis for determining levels of mortality that are acceptable. In the United States, for example, the Marine Mammal Protection Act requires takes to be reduced "to insignificant levels approaching a zero mortality and serious injury rate." In other countries, where there is no such legal requirement, international agreements such as the Convention on Biological Diversity and Agenda 21 may provide a rationale for determining whether the level of fishery-related mortality is acceptable.

"Sustainability" is a criterion often used to evaluate the significance and acceptability of mortality and injury. However, it is not the only criterion. For example, some people and marine mammal interest groups oppose the killing or injury of marine mammals, particularly cetaceans, for any reason (see, for example, the discussion of the tuna-dolphin controversy by Gosliner in this volume).

Deciding when ecological interactions are significant is much more difficult. As we discuss further below, most marine mammals feed on a variety of species, some or all of which may interact with one another. It is therefore very difficult to estimate the impact of marine mammal predation on fishery catches. Likewise, it is equally difficult to judge the extent to which fishery catches affect availability of food to marine mammals. In one or two particular cases, such as that of the sea otters discussed above, some measure of the scale of the interaction may be possible, but this is unusual. Once again, national legislation and international agreements can sometimes help to determine whether action is required. As noted earlier, for example, the U.S. Marine Mammal Protection Act requires that marine mammal populations under U.S. jurisdiction be maintained at optimum sustainable population levels, keeping in mind the health and stability of the ecosystem of which they are a part. Similarly, at the international level, UNCLoS requires nations to manage their fishery resources to maintain or restore associated or dependent species above levels at which their reproduction may become seriously threatened. The Convention on Biological Diversity requires nations to "anticipate, prevent and attack the causes of significant reduction or loss of biological diversity at source." These international instruments do not refer to ecosystem relationships or the "functional role" of marine mammal populations, however, and "seriously threatened" and "significant reduction" are left to subjective interpretation. Regional agreements such as CCAMLR (discussed below) go further and specify precise targets or triggers for management action. They seek to minimize the risk of long-term environmental change.

Potential Solutions to Damaged Catch and Gear

There are numerous examples of attempts to reduce marine mammal damage to gear through technological solutions (Wickens 1995). One is the use of small explosive devices to try to scare animals away from fishing gear. This approach has been taken in several countries and in several different types of fisheries, but it does not appear to have been very effective anywhere (Mate 1980, Mate and Harvey 1987).

More elaborate means of trying to keep pinnipeds and cetaceans away from fishing gear have included playback of killer whale sounds and deployment of dummy killer whales (Wickens 1995). Although some of these means have worked for a while (see, for example, Fish and Vania 1971), most have not worked in the long term, because the animals concerned either have become habituated to the devices or have discovered ways of avoiding them to continue depredation.

One well-studied example of how difficult it is to deter marine mammals from interacting with a fishery is seen in Prince William Sound, Alaska, where killer whales began in 1985 to remove sablefish from longlines. One pod of about 35 animals seems to have been responsible for most of the damage, which includes gear loss and damage as well as lost fish (Matkin 1986). These animals have learned that food is readily available when longlines are being hauled, and they apparently are able to determine from acoustic cues when this procedure is under way. They are reported to station themselves near buoys marking where longlines were set and wait for retrieval to begin (Yano and Dahlheim 1995). In 1985, at least eight members of the pod had visible gunshot wounds, presumably inflicted by fishermen trying to prevent depredation (Matkin and Saulitis 1994). Despite numerous attempts to scare these animals away or to confuse them, the only measures that appeared to reduce depredation were to switch target species or to fish with pots rather than longlines.

Recently, the use of high-powered acoustic harassment devices (AHDs) has been heralded as an effective means of reducing fish loss and damage caused by marine mammals, especially seal depredation of salmon being raised in net pens. AHDs are intended to generate noises loud enough to cause pain in mammals that come close to the nets of penned fish. Although industry trials suggest that they have this effect, other studies suggest that they may also have detrimental effects on nontargeted marine mammals in the area. P. Olesiuk (pers. comm.) found that in British

Columbia such devices had the effect of excluding harbor porpoises from an area of up to 3 km in radius from the site of deployment. Where AHDs are used in large numbers, this may have the effect of excluding porpoises from a substantial part of their range.

In the extreme, fishery authorities may try to remove the animals causing the problem. This was the case in Iceland in the 1950s when killer whale depredation of longlines prompted fishery authorities to approach the United States Navy for help in destroying the animals. The results of subsequent naval bombardments were poorly recorded (Earle 1996). There are several other examples in which bounties and culls have been used to reduce marine mammal depredation (see United Nations Environment Programme 1994, Earle 1996). Analyses of the effects of these initiatives are generally lacking, however, so it is not clear whether they have ever been effective.

Reeves et al. (1996) provided an assessment of the effectiveness and secondary effects of efforts to date to use acoustic devices to reduce harmful interactions between marine mammals and fisheries. In most instances, the most effective way of reducing marine mammal damage to fishing operations has been to change aspects of the fishery. Changing gear may be one option, and switching area may be another. Ultimately, a fishery may be forced to close if damage is severe enough. The task of reducing marine mammal damage to fishing operations has often been left to the fishermen themselves, who either attempt to eliminate the depredating marine mammals or change their fishing gear or methods to avoid or minimize interactions.

Reducing Marine Mammal Mortality in Operational Interactions

Whereas there is a strong incentive for fishermen to devise means of limiting marine mammal damage to their gear or catch, there is usually far less motivation for them to devise means of limiting incidental mortality and injury of marine mammals.

Although the capture or entanglement of a marine mammal may cause a loss in time spent fishing or damage to the fishing gear, it may be inconsequential to the individual fisherman if it occurs only rarely. This could be true even though the aggregate effect of all such incidents across an entire fishing fleet might be highly significant for the affected marine mammal population. Indeed, in some countries where marine mammals have a market value, fishermen may benefit from bycatches, making it even less likely that bycatch will be curtailed by fishermen's initiatives alone.

Control of marine mammal mortality, wherever it is deemed a conservation problem, usually requires external intervention or pressure. Mortality and injury of marine mammals in fishing operations, especially of cetaceans, have been addressed by national laws in some countries. Also a number of international agreements provide for the reduction of marine mammal, particularly cetacean, bycatch. These include the La Jolla Agreement, negotiated under the auspices of the Inter-American Tropical Tuna Commission (see Gosliner, this volume), the Agreement on Small Cetaceans of the Baltic and North Seas and the forthcoming Agreement on Cetaceans in the Mediterranean and Black Seas. The United Nations Environment Programme has also concluded 16 Regional Seas Agreements, several of which have protocols aimed specifically at protecting marine mammals, especially from excessive incidental mortality in fishing operations.

Various technical measures and changes in fishing technique have been adopted to limit mortality and injury of marine mammals. Perhaps the most widely known relates to the tuna purse seine fishery in the eastern tropical Pacific. A full history of the approaches taken to reduce dolphin mortality in this fishery is provided by Gosliner in this volume. The technological innovation and change in fishing technique that helped to reduce dolphin mortality in this fishery, from hundreds of thousands per year during the 1960s to less than 5,000 per year in recent years, were the Medina panel and the backdown procedure, respectively.

Named after the skipper who developed it, the Medina panel is a section of small-mesh netting set into the body of the purse seine net. When the set has been made and both tuna and dolphins are encircled, the vessel is put into reverse (backdown), forcing a part of the floatline to sink below the surface, creating a passage for dolphins to escape. On its own, the backdown procedure was inadequate for preventing many dolphins from becoming entangled as they moved through the escape passage. The small-mesh Medina panel helped by reducing entanglement at the point of escape.

Another promising technical measure is the electronic pinger. Pingers are small, battery-operated electronic devices that intermittently emit a high-pitched noise (a "ping") underwater. They are attached to gillnets to scare porpoises and other small cetaceans away from potentially hazardous fishing gear, without affecting fish, and initial experiments showed that they can be highly effective (Reeves et al. 1996, Kraus et al. 1997). We discuss an application of these devices further below.

Technical measures, or technical measures together with changes in fishing practices, such as those implemented in the tuna purse seine fishery, can be effective in reducing incidental mortalities of marine mammals, but only if use of the measures can be ensured. The situation in the tuna purse seine fishery is unusual because the fishery is subject to a very high level of observer coverage (100% in recent years), so that monitoring the implementation of backdown procedures and the use of a Medina panel is possible. In most other fisheries, such as coastal gillnet fisheries, ensuring that the entire fleet complies with regulations is difficult. It may not be practical to achieve a high level of observer coverage or a required change in fishing practice, such as the conversion from one gear type to another.

Another effective management strategy is to prohibit fishing at times when and in places where incidental mortalities are known to be high. Season and area closures have been implemented in gillnet fisheries in the Gulf of Maine (see below) and New Zealand (Dawson and Slooten 1993). In other instances, the more drastic solution of closing an entire fishery has been adopted (see below). Usually such an approach would only be adopted under extreme circumstances.

Approaches to Managing Competitive Interactions

In contrast to the situation with operational interactions, the available range of management options to control ecological interactions is limited. The measure most often proposed is to cull marine mammals in the hope of boosting fishery yields. The objective of a cull is to reduce marine mammal numbers and thereby reduce predation on fishery resources. There has been considerable debate and analysis of the rationale for culling operations, discussed below. In brief, for most situations there is little reason to believe that culls have had or will have the desired effect of boosting fishery yields.

Culling is not, of course, the only option for reducing population size of marine mammals. "Shooing" has been tried in South Africa to reduce numbers of breeding females at fur seal breeding sites, evidently with little success because calls for culls persist (United Nations Environment Programme 1994). Treatment of gray seals with contraceptives has been proposed in Canada and the United Kingdom. Although trials have been done in Canada (Brown et al. 1996), the effect on population growth has not yet been assessed. At a local level, groups of animals have been translocated from sensitive areas, but again without any marked success, because such animals tend to return (see Fraker and Mate, this volume).

Most concerns regarding marine mammal predation on fish stocks arise where there is a declining fish catch or an increasing marine mammal population, or both. Calls for culls derive either from a perception that a fish stock is declining or from increasing sightings of marine mammals in areas where fish catches are declining. In many if not most cases, the declining fish catches are caused by overfishing, not marine mammal predation. Thus, better fishery management to prevent and reverse declines in fish stocks would generally be a more effective management strategy.

Increasing populations of marine mammals might also be viewed as the result of fishery-induced changes to the ecosystem, as discussed above. This leads to the possibility that population sizes might be stabilized if and when stocks of larger, predatory fish recover.

Few attempts have yet been made to ensure adequate food supplies for marine mammals. In theory, by monitoring marine mammal feeding or breeding success, one should be able to control fishing effort in response to changes detected in these characteristics of the mammal population. This is the approach taken by the Commission for the Conservation of Antarctic Marine Living Resources, which we discuss further below.

Another possible means of addressing at least some concerns regarding the possible ecosystem-level impacts of fisheries would be to establish marine sanctuaries or reserves. The past two decades have witnessed the proliferation of marine protected areas to conserve fish stocks and marine biodiversity (see, for example, Shackell and Willison 1995, Gubbay 1996). Some of these areas have been aimed specifically at protecting marine mammals (IUCN 1979, Rogan and Berrow 1995, Phillips 1996), but few attempts have been made to use such designations to limit fishing activity and protect site-specific sources of food for marine mammals. To be practical in this respect, a protected area would probably need to cover a critical feeding zone for marine mammals. There are few situations where a critical feeding zone can be associated with an area of seabed, because most marine mammal food is mobile. Exceptions may involve marine mammal species such as sea otters and walruses that feed primarily on sedentary invertebrates, or areas that are subject to regular fish aggregations, such as spawning banks, which are a significant localized source of food for a marine mammal population.

Case Studies

Below we briefly consider four case studies that illustrate the range of issues. First, we discuss the management of fisheries to ensure stability of marine mammal populations, using the CCAMLR example. We then examine culling as a potential management measure and the United Nations moratorium on large-scale high-seas driftnet fishing as an example of preventing operational interactions. Finally, we examine a species-specific interaction, namely the incidental take of harbor porpoises in the Gulf of Maine sink-gillnet fishery.

Managing Fishery Impacts on Marine Mammal Food

Although several international agreements and national laws aim to ensure that fisheries are managed to promote the stability of populations of nontarget or "associated species," few attempts have been made to develop management tools for addressing this objective. An important exception is the CCAMLR Ecosystem Monitoring Program (CEMP). CEMP is possibly the most important attempt yet made to manage fisheries from an ecosystem perspective, putting into practice the objectives of CCAMLR.

CEMP was established by the Scientific Committee of CCAMLR in 1984 to help meet Article 2 of the Convention. Among other things, Article 2 requires that any harvesting in Antarctic waters be conducted in a manner that maintains the "ecological relationships between harvested, dependent and related populations of Antarctic marine living resources. . . ." CEMP was established with the aim of detecting any significant changes in key components of the Southern Ocean ecosystem, while distinguishing between changes due to commercial harvesting and those due to natural causes (CCAMLR 1991a).

The principal impetus for CCAMLR was concern that the developing fishery for a species of Antarctic krill (*Euphausia superba*) would adversely affect the many bird, mammal, and fish species in the Southern Ocean whose diet is mainly krill. As initially conceived, CEMP was designed to detect changes in populations of "representative" krill predators likely to have been caused by the developing krill fishery. The program had three main elements: (1) comprehensive studies of krill and related environmental conditions in three integrated study areas; (2) monitoring of selected krill predators (as possible indicator species) at a series of land-based sites throughout Antarctica and adjacent islands; and (3) studies of crabeater seals in the pack ice (CCAMLR 1991b). Monitoring of krill is done by reference to fishery data and through the use of regular fishery-independent surveys. Studies of predators focus on their reproductive success, growth and condition, feeding ecology and behavior, abundance, and distribution.

Ultimately, data from CEMP are to be passed to the Scientific Committee of CCAMLR, whose mandate is to provide management advice to the Commission, the decision-making body established by the Convention. The Commission, acting on the advice provided by the Scientific Committee, is to limit krill fishing to levels consistent with the previously noted objectives of the Convention.

Because of marketing problems, a large-scale krill fishery has not yet developed. This has made the planning and implementation of a monitoring program much easier than would otherwise have been possible. Few other areas in the world have had slowly developing fisheries along with sufficient multinational interest to support programs to detect changes in ecosystem parameters. Thus, CEMP provides a pioneering example of a possible strategy for detecting fishery impacts on the wider ecosystem by monitoring selected reproductive, behavioral, and growth parameters of key indicator species.

It is clear that if the objectives of UNCLoS, Agenda 21, the Biodiversity Convention, and numerous regional agreements and national laws are to be met, it will be necessary for approaches similar to CEMP to be developed in other areas.

Culling Marine Mammals as a Means of Improving Fishery Yields

In Canada and some other North Atlantic nations culling is still viewed as a viable management option for addressing perceived conflicts between seals and fisheries. The annual Canadian commercial hunt for harp seals (*Phoca groenlandica*) and hooded seals (*Cystophora cristata*) in Newfoundland and the Gulf of St. Lawrence is justified, in part, as a predator-control exercise to boost recovery of overfished cod stocks in the region (MacKenzie 1996). Similar arguments are still being advanced to justify culling of seals in Norway, Iceland, the United Kingdom, and elsewhere. Culls such as these, which are intended to reduce the overall mammal population size and so boost fish stocks, should not be confused with more limited removals of individual animals from specific areas to reduce operational interactions.

The justification for culling is seemingly simple. Populations of species such as harp, hooded, and gray seals in the North Atlantic number in the hundreds of thousands or millions. Total fish consumption by these seals may be similar in magnitude to commercial fish catches of the same stocks. Reducing overall seal numbers will prevent large amounts of fish from being eaten, and this, it is assumed, will boost fish stocks and catches.

The ecological complexity of the marine environment, however, suggests that this is a greatly oversimplified rationale. In reality, predation by marine mammals represents only one of many sources of mortality for most fish stocks, and the consequences of reducing that one source are difficult to predict or measure. The issue has received considerable scientific attention.

Both Beverton (1985) and DeMaster and Sisson (1992) provided theoretical critiques of the rationale for culling. DeMaster and Sisson (1992) examined the uncertainties surrounding the cause-effect relationships between pinniped population control and commercial fish-stock enhancement. They cited four generally accepted ecological tenets that belie the idea that fisheries can be enhanced by culling pinnipeds: (1) prey species almost always have more than one predator; (2) pinnipeds are rarely dependent on a single prey species; (3) recruitment rates of most fish stocks are highly variable and are therefore the most important factor in determining stock size; and (4) other fish are generally much more significant predators of fish than are mammals or birds. Consequently, there is usually little chance of predicting how a decrease in total marine mammal numbers would influence the abundance and catches of target fishery species. Most marine mammals eat a fairly broad range of prey species. Very few marine mammal species can be considered the major predator of an individual fish population. In most cases, predation by mammals is only a small part of the total predation by all other predators (DeMaster and Sisson 1992). Reducing predation by a small amount has little or no discernible effect on the prey population. Furthermore, because the number of different prey species eaten by most marine mammals is large, there are potential secondary interactions to consider as well (i.e., changes in predation on one species may influence predation on others). There are numerous other complexities, such as differences in seasonal and spatial feeding patterns among the mammals concerned and differences in feeding habits of different age and size classes of mammals.

The benefits that might or might not be expected from a specific marine mammal cull were discussed in detail at a workshop in South Africa (Anonymous 1991). Participants attempted to develop a general protocol for quantifying the effects of pinniped predation on the yields to fisheries. Using the South African fur seal's interactions with local fisheries as their prime example, they explored the data requirements for making informed management decisions about the benefits of a cull. These include an understanding of the size and dynamics of the seal (or other mammal) population and an understanding of the feeding habits of the population as a whole. The workshop produced agreement that it would also be necessary to examine the predatory interactions of the prey species consumed by the seal (mammal) population. Recognizing that large and complex models of food webs are unlikely to produce easily interpreted results, it was suggested at the workshop that decoupled portions of the whole system be examined, with a limited number of parameters used to explore some of the more important predatory interactions.

The importance of considering the predatory interactions in this way was simply illustrated at the workshop. South African fur seals prey on both anchovies and squid, and a simple understanding of this situation suggests that reducing fur seal numbers should increase the amount of anchovies available to fisheries. Understanding that squid also consume anchovies makes it clear that a reduction in seal numbers could lead to an overall increase in anchovy predation, if a larger squid population resulted. It was pointed out at the South African workshop that minor increases in the complexity of the model employed could lead to a wide range of possible conclusions.

Taking a more general approach, the United Nations Environment Programme convened a workshop in 1994 (United Nations Environment Programme 1994) to examine procedures for the specification and evaluation of cull proposals. It was concluded at the workshop that the evaluation of any proposed cull should address the following issues: the objectives of the cull; a definition of the performance measure of the objectives, such as the fishery yield over the decade after the cull; an evaluation of the quality of available data; sensitivity of the predicted cull benefits to the assumptions and uncertainties; and identification in advance of indices by which the efficacy of the cull in relation to its objectives could be measured. A more detailed protocol for evaluating cull proposals is now under development (United Nations Environment Programme 1997).

If culling is proposed as a means of addressing a perceived conflict between a marine mammal population and a fishery, it is important to ensure that it be rigorously planned, implemented, and evaluated. The United Nations Environment Programme protocol would provide nations that are considering a cull with a mechanism or procedure for considering the issue in a rational manner, rather than accepting the oversimplified argument outlined at the start of this section.

Despite numerous studies into the relationship between marine mammal predation and the abundance of their prey populations, Beverton (1985) could find no clear evidence that marine mammals had caused the depletion of any commercial fish stock. Furthermore, there does not appear to be any clear evidence that culling marine mammals has benefitted commercial fisheries (see, for example, Merriam 1901, Bonnot 1929, IUCN 1981, Bowen 1985). Nevertheless, culling is being continued in several countries. If rational approaches to the management of living marine resources are to be pursued at a global level, then the results of the South African and United Nations Environment Programme workshops and analyses like that by DeMaster and Sisson (1992) need to be more widely disseminated and applied.

The Large-Scale High-Seas Driftnet Fisheries

Our third case study involves one particular fishing method—large-scale driftnet fishing—that was a serious threat to marine mammal populations on the high seas. This problem was resolved, at least temporarily, after global concerns over the issue had been vociferously and persistently expressed.

Large-scale high-seas driftnet fisheries gained notoriety during the 1980s, in large part because they killed large numbers of marine mammals, birds, turtles, sharks, and other nontarget species. They were suspended in 1992 after the United Nations General Assembly passed a resolution calling for a moratorium on the use of large-scale driftnets. This was a significant event because it demonstrated the General Assembly's willingness to address the objectives of UNCLoS (maintaining populations of associated species) and its acceptance of the concepts of sustainability and precaution espoused in Agenda 21, the Convention on Biological Diversity, and other instruments.

The principal characteristics of the high-seas driftnet fisheries were that they operated outside national exclusive economic zones, and that each vessel deployed very long, drifting gillnets, ranging in length from about 15 km in salmon fisheries to perhaps 50 km in squid fisheries (Northridge 1991b). These fisheries appear to have developed in response to three things: (1) development of durable, inexpensive, lightweight plastic netting; (2) loss of, or reduced access to, traditional fishing grounds as coastal nations began to exercise 200-mile (370.4-km) exclusive fishery conservation zones; and (3) overexploitation and depletion of fishery resources in more accessible national and international waters.

Japanese vessels had been using long driftnets for catching salmon on the high seas since the 1940s. The North Pacific high-seas salmon driftnet fishery peaked in the mid-1950s and was progressively phased out thereafter, initially through international agreements designed to protect North American–origin salmon. This resulted in a number of salmon driftnet vessels relocating to the South Pacific in 1987, after a series of successful research cruises by the Japanese fisheries research agency during the early 1980s targeting albacore (*Thunnus alalunga*). The albacore fishery was centered in the Tasman Sea and grew rapidly from 29 vessels (Japanese, Taiwanese, and South Korean) in 1987 to more than 120 the following year. This rapid growth alarmed the coastal nations of the South Pacific, fearful that the new driftnet fishery would affect the productivity of local tuna fisheries and concerned by reports of high catch levels of nontarget species.

The high-seas driftnet fishery for neon flying squid (*Ommastrephes bartrami*) in the North Pacific was initiated by Japanese vessels in 1978. This fishery grew steadily during the 1980s and expanded eastward, prompting fears that it would affect U.S.-origin salmon. By the mid-1980s, more than 800 vessels from Japan, Taiwan, and South Korea were participating in the squid, tuna, and salmon driftnet fisheries in the North Pacific. Together they deployed as much as 40,000 km of net every night. Observer programs confirmed that relatively large numbers of marine mammals, birds, and fish were being taken (summarized by Northridge 1991b). In 1990, for example, observers on 75 of 457 Japanese vessels participating in the squid fishery reported catches of 7,939,252 neon flying squid (the target species), 2,917 other cephalopods, 9,747 salmon of different species, 81,956 blue sharks, 7,612 other sharks and rays, 162,631 skipjack tuna, 90,011 albacore tuna, 347 other tunas, 499 billfish, 3,224,055 Pacific pomfret, 410,573 other fishes, 30,464 seabirds, 2,325 marine mammals, and 35 sea turtles (Table 24 in International North Pacific Fisheries Commission 1991).

During the late 1970s and the 1980s, the Canadian Department of Fisheries and Oceans also conducted an experimental driftnet fishery for neon flying squid. High takes of marine mammals were observed in the 1986 and 1987 trials, and as a consequence the fishery was terminated (Jamieson and Heritage 1988).

By the time that the Japanese albacore driftnet fishery started in the Tasman Sea, there was therefore already considerable evidence that large-scale driftnet fisheries had high catch rates of nontarget species, including marine mammals (Fig. 5-3). Although the initial concern among the nations of the South Pacific, and in New Zealand in particular, was that the expanding albacore driftnet fishery would result in a depleted albacore stock, with serious consequences for local fisheries, the issues of mortalities of nontarget species and of poor species selectivity were also raised. As a consequence of regional concerns, the States and Territories of the South Pacific agreed upon a convention, in November 1989, to ban the use of any driftnets more than 2.5 km long in their own exclusive economic zones, to prohibit importation or transportation of driftnet-caught fish, and to deny port facilities to vessels engaged in driftnet fishing (Hewison 1993). This is known as the Wellington Convention.

The diplomatic actions of the South Pacific nations, coupled with the campaign efforts of several nongovernmental organizations, appear to have had the effect of stimulating nations in other areas to take further actions. The Organization of Eastern Caribbean States, for example, signed the Castries Declaration in November 1989, calling for the establishment of a regime to manage pelagic resources of the region that would outlaw driftnet fishing (Food and Agriculture Organization 1990). Heads of government of the Commonwealth of Nations[1] signed the Langkawi Declaration in October 1989, which among other things pledged the Commonwealth nations to ban pelagic driftnetting (Food and Agriculture Organization 1990).

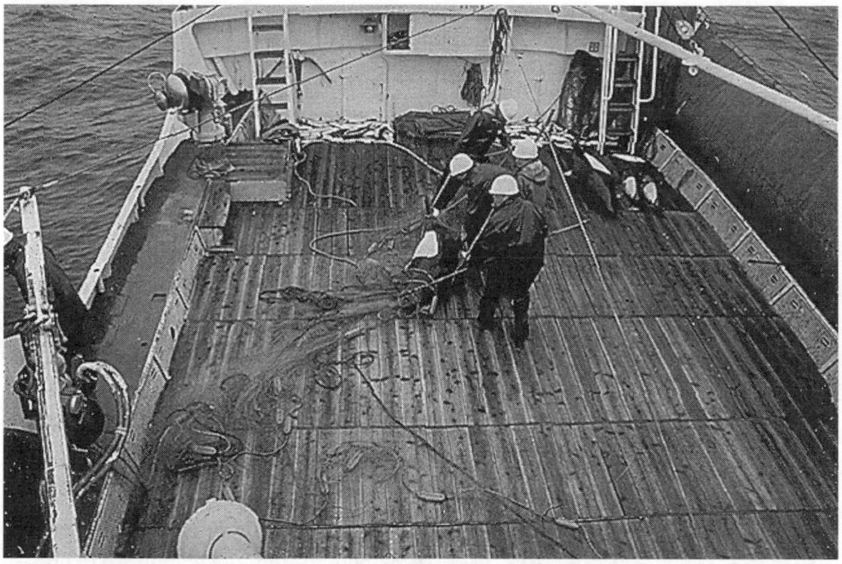

Figure 5-3. Japanese salmon fishermen and their bycatch of Dall's porpoises (*Phocoenoides dalli*) aboard a catcher boat in the North Pacific. The large-scale high-seas driftnet fishery killed tens of thousands of Dall's porpoises and other nontargeted species before it was suspended by the United Nations in 1992. (Photograph by Steven Swartz)

The first United Nations General Assembly resolution (44/225) on driftnet fishing was passed unanimously in December 1989. The General Assembly considered that this fishing method "threaten[ed] the effective conservation of living marine resources, such as highly migratory and anadromous species of fish, birds and marine mammals." Recognizing the particular concerns of the South Pacific nations, the General Assembly also called for a progressive reduction in driftnet fishing in the South Pacific, with a complete cessation by July 1991. The Japanese, Taiwanese, and South Korean authorities accepted the concerns of the South Pacific nations and the U.N. General Assembly, and the South Pacific driftnet fishery was terminated in 1991.

Resolution 44/225 went on to call for the enhanced collection and sharing of statistically sound scientific data on the effects of driftnet fishing, and for a review of "the best available scientific data on the impact of large-scale pelagic driftnet fishing" by 30 June 1991. In the absence of "effective conservation and management measures . . . based upon statistically sound analysis to be jointly made by concerned parties of the international community with an interest in the fishery resources of the region," a moratorium on all other driftnet fisheries was called for from June 1992. Further expansion of high-seas driftnet fishing was to cease immediately, with no further high-seas driftnet fishing outside the North Pacific.

The review of the best available scientific data on the North Pacific driftnet fisheries took place in Sidney, British Columbia, in June 1991. An estimate that 11,000 northern right whale dolphins (*Lissodelphis borealis*) were being killed per year in the squid and tuna driftnet fisheries was presented (Hobbs and Jones 1993). The meeting participants concluded that the dolphin mortality caused by the driftnet fisheries was unsustainable and that it was therefore having a significant impact on at least this species.

The results of the Sidney meeting were conveyed to the Secretary General of the United Nations, and in 1991 the General Assembly passed resolution 46/215, noting that "grounds for concerns expressed in resolutions 44/225 and 45/197 about the unacceptable impact of large-scale pelagic driftnet fishing have been confirmed and that evidence has not demonstrated that the impact can be fully prevented." The resolution called upon all members of the international community to ensure a global moratorium on large-scale pelagic driftnet fishing on the high seas by the end of 1992. Japan, South Korea, and Taiwan agreed to abide by this resolution. Consequently, more than a thousand vessels were withdrawn from driftnet fishing on the high seas.

An important reason that the driftnet fisheries aroused such fierce opposition was that no international mechanism was in place to manage them. Whereas UNCLoS had established the rights of coastal nations to manage and control fisheries within their 200-mile (370.4-km) exclusive economic zones, no single national, regional, or global authority was empowered by UNCLoS to control fishing activities outside the exclusive economic zones. Further, none of the nations whose vessels participated in these fisheries took action, individually or collectively, to determine and limit catches of target and nontarget species to sustainable levels. Had a management body existed or had the fishery nations acted to ensure long-term rather than short-term interests, technical measures or changes in fishing practice might have been developed to make the fishing sustainable and less destructive. Japanese scientists experimented with the use of nets set below the surface, but this modification did not have the desired result (Hayase and Yatsu 1993). In any event, without a management and enforcement authority to ensure compliance, a technical solution alone would not have solved the problem.

Closure of the high-seas driftnet fisheries was an important milestone in marine conservation. It was the first time that a U.N. General Assembly resolution forced the adoption of a fishery management measure. Also, the wording of Resolution 46/215 makes clear that the international community accepts the precautionary principle for the management of living resources, reflecting the provisions of both the United Nations Conference on Environment and Development and the Convention on Biological Diversity.

Harbor Porpoise Mortality in the Gulf of Maine Sink-Gillnet Fishery

Our final case study involves the interaction between one species of small cetacean and a fishery. The bycatch of harbor porpoises in fisheries along the northeastern United States and southeastern Canada has been the subject of much controversy and considerable research. This example demonstrates some of the practical problems inherent in resolving such an issue.

The U.S. Marine Mammal Protection Act, as amended in 1994, requires the National Marine Fisheries Service and the Fish and Wildlife Service to prepare and periodically update assessments of the status of marine mammal stocks in U.S. waters (see Baur et al., this volume). Furthermore, the amendments require that mortality and serious injury of marine mammals in commercial fishing operations be reduced to insignificant levels approaching zero by the year 2001. In the interim, take-reduction plans are to be developed for fisheries that frequently take animals from "strategic stocks"—stocks listed as endangered, threatened, or depleted or for which the bycatch in fisheries is at or above the calculated potential biological removal level described below.

Take-reduction plans are to be designed by take-reduction teams consisting of knowledgeable scientists and representatives of the fishing and conservation communities (stakeholders). The immediate objective is to reduce incidental mortality to less than the potential biological removal level. The potential biological removal level is defined in the Marine Mammal Protection Act as "the maximum number of animals, not including natural mortalities, that may be removed from a marine mammal stock while allowing that stock to reach or maintain its optimum sustainable population." The optimum sustainable population, in turn, is defined as "the number of animals which will result in the maximum productivity of the population of the species keeping in mind the carrying capacity of the habitat and the health of the ecosystem of which they form a constituent element."

One of the largest incidental takes of marine mammals in any U.S. fishery occurs in the Gulf of Maine. Harbor porpoises are vulnerable to entanglement in fishing gear, especially in gillnets, throughout their range (Bjorge and Donovan 1995). In the Gulf of Maine and lower Bay of Fundy, they are caught primarily in bottom-set gillnets (sink gillnets); they are also caught frequently during summer in herring weirs in the Bay of Fundy.

The National Marine Fisheries Service has provided an assessment of the status of the porpoise population, including its potential biological removal level (Blaylock et al. 1995). Shipboard sighting surveys in the northern Gulf of Maine and Bay of Fundy during the summer resulted in population estimates of 37,500 in 1991 and 67,500 in 1992 (95% confidence intervals 26,700–86,400 and 32,900–104,600, respectively). The reasons for this difference are not clear, but interannual changes in porpoise distribution may at least partly explain it. The National Marine Fisheries Service adopted an estimate for the population of 47,200 (confidence interval 39,500–70,600) (Smith et al. 1993).

The Marine Mammal Protection Act specifies that the potential biological removal level is to be calculated by multiplying the minimum population size estimate by one-half of the maximum theoretical net productivity rate for the population concerned and a recovery factor between 0.1 and 1 to account for additional uncertainties other than the precision of the abundance estimate. The National Marine Fisheries Service has adopted guidelines for determining what constitutes a stock, estimating minimum population size, and determining the appropriate recovery factor to use for stocks according to their status (endangered, unknown, threatened, etc.) (Wade and Angliss 1997). In the case of the Gulf of Maine population of harbor porpoises, the potential biological removal level was calculated to be 403 animals (Blaylock et al. 1995).

Estimates of the numbers of animals killed in the Gulf of Maine sink-gillnet fishery have been made annually since 1990 based on an intensive on-board observer program. The National Marine Fisheries Service estimated an annual average of 1,876 porpoises taken in the U.S. sink-gillnet fishery (Blaylock et al. 1995), and there is clearly additional mortality in other fisheries.

The immediate task of the take-reduction team, in this instance, was to recommend measures to reduce porpoise takes from around 1,900 to around 400 per year. Both technical solutions and changes in fishing pattern have been pursued as management measures to solve the problem, and the fishing industry has taken a lead role in developing solutions.

In 1992 a group of fishermen, concerned about the implications to their fishery of continued high mortality of harbor porpoises, set up their own trial fishery using acoustic pinger devices, designed by Jon Lien of Memorial University in Newfoundland, Canada, to deter porpoises from their nets. These devices emit a high-pitched noise every few seconds, intended to scare porpoises away from the nets. The initial trials in 1992 and 1993 seemed promising, but the results were inconclusive and a more rigorous experiment was called for. In the autumn of 1994 a full-scale experiment was run on Jeffreys Ledge, off the coast of New Hampshire, in an area where and at a time of year when high porpoise mortality had been observed in most years. The results of the experiment were very encouraging, with only two porpoises taken in 421 strings of gillnets set with active pingers and 25 porpoises taken in 423 strings with inactive pingers (Kraus et al. 1997).

Meanwhile, the National Marine Fisheries Service devised a computer simulation model, based on a geographical information system, that enabled managers to plan closed seasons and areas for the gillnet fishery with some idea of the likely effect in terms of reduced fish catch and reduced porpoise mortality (Smith et al. 1993). Using this model, the take-reduction team proposed a series of closed seasons and areas. One problem with this approach is that, if the times and areas of highest catch rate are not consistent between years, the effectiveness will be undermined.

In late 1995 and early 1996, four experimental fisheries were conducted. Fishermen were allowed to fish in the closed areas provided that they carried observers and used active pingers on their nets. Although the pingers resulted in low catch rates in two of these areas, catches of porpoises remained high in the other two. The reasons why the pingers apparently work so well in some areas and at some times and not so well in others are not known (Potter et al. 1996). The experimental fisheries, however, highlighted one of the problems of technical solutions—they may not always work. An intensive observer program may be required to ensure that such measures work and continue to work in the future.

To meet the requirements of the Marine Mammal Protection Act, the National Marine Fisheries Service implemented a take-reduction plan in 1997, based on the recommendations of the take-reduction team, involving a combination of revised time-area closures, along with designations of areas and seasons in which pinger use is mandatory. This strategy should, in theory, reduce takes to less than the potential biological removal level (A. Read, pers. comm.). Its success will depend, of course, on the pingers continuing to work and on porpoise take rates remaining low in the unclosed times and areas. Continued monitoring by observers will be necessary, possibly indefinitely.

Compared with many situations in other parts of the world, the conservation objective for porpoises in the Gulf of Maine is very well defined. That is, the level of incidental take must be reduced immediately to the potential biological removal level and to insignificant levels approaching zero by 2001. Such precision has been useful in focusing the attention of fishermen, managers, and scientists, but it has also revealed how difficult (and expensive) it is to achieve this kind of objective. There is considerable uncertainty, for example, concerning the population estimate. There is also no clear confirmation of the assumption that the porpoises caught throughout the region and surveyed in the summer at the northern end of the Gulf of Maine all belong to the same population. Estimates of total catches in the gillnet fishery are also subject to some uncertainty, but more significantly, there are mortalities in other fisheries, in Canadian waters, and in other gillnet fisheries off the U.S. "mid-Atlantic" states in winter (Palka 1994, Trippel et al. 1996). Most of the latter remain undocumented. Further, if a substantial part of the population turns out to be subject to Canadian catches, then meeting the objectives of the Marine Mammal Protection Act would require a bilateral agreement with Canada.

Determining the minimum time frames and spatial scales for fishery closures that will deliver the required reduction in porpoise mortality is necessarily a process of trial and error. Several years of changing time and area closures may be necessary to find the optimal pattern, always assuming that changes in porpoise distribution do not confound the attempt altogether. Technical solutions have proved elusive, and not just because the pingers appear to reduce entanglement only sporadically. There is no clear understanding of how they actually function, so no conceptual model is readily at hand with which to address their failure. Furthermore, there are concerns that the widespread use of pingers might have unforeseen, and undesirable, effects on other species by increasing ambient noise in the Gulf of Maine (see, for example, Reeves et al. 1996). At any rate, if a technical measure of some kind is to be used to keep mortality below the potential biological removal level, there must be an adequate observer and enforcement program, both to monitor the measure's effectiveness and to ensure compliance.

The detailed nature of the amended Marine Mammal Protection Act has forced scientists and managers to make a comprehensive evaluation of available conservation tools and, where necessary, to develop new ones. They have had to explore problems that they otherwise might have ignored as intractable. As an illustration of the problems involved in reconciling public aspirations with the realities of a complex interaction between fisheries and marine mammals, this example is sure to prove instructive for addressing similar problems in other areas of the world.

Summary

Until relatively recently, most marine mammal interactions with fisheries were either ignored or addressed by culling. The past few decades have witnessed fundamental changes in the way that fishery conflicts, and incidental catches in particular, are viewed and addressed around the world. First, it has become evident that incidental catches in certain fisheries are a serious threat to some marine mammal populations. Second, a paradigm shift is occurring as human society learns to view the marine environment and the ways in which fisheries are managed in a new light. Third, national, regional, and global statutes and agreements enacted over the past 20 to 30 years articulate new responsibilities for national governments and regional fishery management bodies. Increasing knowledge of the codependence of species and changes in public awareness have driven all three processes.

The U.S. Marine Mammal Protection Act is probably the most detailed of such national laws and the most comprehensive legislative attempt to address marine mammal fishery interactions anywhere in the world. By placing a high priority on the conservation of marine mammals, the Marine Mammal Protection Act has shifted the focus of managerial attention away from maximizing economic benefits and has encouraged technological innovations and changes in fishery practice as ways to address harmful operational interactions with fisheries. In at least two major controversies, namely the tuna-dolphin interaction in the eastern tropical Pacific and the harbor porpoise–gillnet interaction in the Gulf of Maine, pressure resulting from the Marine Mammal Protection Act has led fishermen themselves to seek solutions.

The CCAMLR Ecosystem Monitoring Program represents perhaps the best attempt to address ecological interactions. Clearly there is considerable scope elsewhere in the world for refinement and elaboration of the techniques pioneered by CEMP.

At regional and global levels, numerous treaties and agreements have placed issues concerning the incidental mortality and injury of marine mammals in fishing operations high on the agenda of marine policy makers. The extent to which this will lead to practical resolution of these urgent problems remains to be seen. In some of the poorer and less-developed nations of the world, meeting the aspirations of the texts of international agreements may present considerable problems if the resources to address the issues are not available and a restriction of fishing activities is politically and socially impossible.

Acknowledgments

This chapter was greatly improved thanks to comments on an early draft by Michael Weber, Randy Reeves, and several anonymous reviewers.

Note

1. The Commonwealth of Nations is a 53-nation association (including the United Kingdom and many former British colonies), originally serving as a trading block. It now focuses on cultural, sporting, and similar links.

Literature Cited

Anonymous. 1991. Report on the Benguela Ecology Program Workshop on Seal-Fishery Biological Interactions. Report on the Benguela Ecology Program, South Africa 22. 65 pp.

Anonymous. 1993. Is It Food? Addressing Marine Mammal and Seabird Declines: Workshop Summary. Alaska Sea Grant Publication 93-01.

Anonymous. 1996. Report of Gulf of Maine aquaculture–pinniped interaction task force. Report to the National Marine Fisheries Service, Office of Protected Resources, Silver Spring, MD. 70 pp.

Ashford, J. R., P. S. Rubilar, and A. R. Martin. 1996. Interactions between cetaceans and longline fishery operations around South Georgia. Marine Mammal Science 12:452–457.

Au, W. W. L. 1993. The Sonar of Dolphins. Springer-Verlag, New York, NY. 277 pp.

Barlow, J., R. W. Baird, J. E. Heyning, K. Wynne, A. M. Manville, L. F. Lowry, D. Hanan, J. Sease, and V. N. Burkanov. 1994. A review of cetacean and pinniped mortality in coastal fisheries along the west coast of the USA and Canada and the east coast of the Russian Federation. Reports of the International Whaling Commission (Special Issue 15): 405–426.

Barlow, J., T. Gerrodette, and G. Silber. 1997. First estimates of vaquita abundance. Marine Mammal Science 13:44–58.

Baur, D. C., M. J. Bean, and M. L. Gosliner. 1999. The laws governing marine mammal conservation in the United States. (This volume)

Beach, R. J., A. C. Geiger, S. J. Jeffries, and S. D. Treacy. 1981. Marine mammal–fishery interactions on the Columbia River and adjacent waters, 1981. Second Annual Report to the NMFS/Northwest and Alaska Fishery Center, Grant No. 80-ABD-0012. 184 pp.

Beverton, R. J. H. 1985. Analysis of marine mammal fishery interactions. Pages 3–33 *in* J. R. Beddington, R. J. H. Beverton, and D. M. Lavigne (eds.), Marine Mammals and Fisheries. George Allen and Unwin, London.

Bjorge, A., and G. P. Donovan (eds.). 1995. Biology of the phocoenids. Reports of the International Whaling Commission (Special Issue 16). 552 pp.

Blaylock, R. A., J. W. Hain, L. J. Hansen, D. L. Palka, and G. T. Waring. 1995. U.S. Atlantic and Gulf of Mexico Marine Mammal Stock Assessments. U.S. Department of Commerce, NOAA Technical Memorandum NMFS-SWFC-363. 211 pp.

Bonner, W. N. 1982. Seals and Man: A study of Interactions. Washington Sea Grant, University of Washington Press, Seattle and London. 170 pp.

Bonnot, P. 1929. Report on the seals and sea lions of California. State of California Fishery Bulletin No. 14. 62 pp.

Bowen, W. D. 1985. Harp seal feeding and interactions with commercial fisheries in the North West Atlantic. Pages 135–152 *in* J. R. Beddington, R. J. H. Beverton, and D. M. Lavigne (eds.), Marine Mammals and Fisheries. George Allen and Unwin, London.

Bowen, W. D. (ed.). 1990. Population biology of sealworm *Pseudoterranova decipiens* in relation to its intermediate and seal hosts. Canadian Department of Fisheries and Oceans, Ottawa, No. 222. 314 pp.

Boyer, P., and G. Silber. 1990. An estimate of the mortality of the vaquita, *Phocoena sinus,* in commercial fisheries. International Whaling Commission Conference on Mortality of Cetaceans in Passive Fishing Nets and Traps. October 1990, La Jolla, CA (abstract).

Brown, R. G., W. C. Kimmins, M. Mezei, J. Parsons, B. Pohajdak, and W. D. Bowen. 1996. Birth control for grey seals. Nature 379:30–31.

Busnel, R. G. 1973. Symbiotic relationship between man and dolphins. Annals of the New York Academy of Sciences 35 (2): 112–131.

CCAMLR. 1991a. CCAMLR Ecosystem Monitoring Program. Commission for the Conservation of Antarctic Marine Living Resources, Hobart, Tasmania, Australia.

CCAMLR. 1991b. CCAMLR Ecosystem Monitoring Program (CEMP). Standard methods for CEMP monitoring studies. Commission for the Conservation of Antarctic Marine Living Resources, Hobart, Tasmania, Australia.

Consiglio, C., A. Arcangella, B. Cristo, L. Mariani, L. Marini, and A. Torchio. 1992. Interactions between bottle-nosed dolphins, *Tursiops truncatus,* and fisheries along north-eastern coasts of Sardinia, Italy. Pages 35–36 *in* P. Evans (ed.), European Research on Cetaceans: Proceedings of the Sixth Annual Conference of the European Cetacean Society. 20–22 February 1992, San Remo, Italy.

Corkeron, P. J., M. M. Bryden, and K. E. Hedstrom. 1990. Feeding by bottlenose dolphins in association with traveling operations in Moreton Bay, Australia. Pages 329–336 *in* S. Leatherwood and R. R. Reeves (eds.), The Bottlenose Dolphin. Academic Press, San Diego, CA.

Dawson, S. M. 1991. Modifying gillnets to reduce entanglement of cetaceans. Marine Mammal Science 7:274–282.

Dawson, S., and E. Slooten. 1993. Conservation of Hectors dolphin: The case and process which led to establishment of the Banks Peninsula Marine Mammal Sanctuary. Aquatic Conservation: Marine and Freshwater Ecosystems 3:207–221.

DeMaster, D. P., and J. E. Sisson. 1992. Pros and cons of pinniped management along the North American coast to abet fish stocks. Pages 321–329 *in* D. R. McCullough and R. H. Barrett (eds.), Wildlife 2001: Populations. Elsevier Applied Science, London.

DeMaster, D., D. Miller, J. R. Henderson, and J. M. Coe. 1985. Conflicts between marine mammals and fisheries off the coast of California. Pages 111–118 *in* J. R. Beddington, R. J. H. Beverton, and D. M. Lavigne (eds.), Marine Mammals and Fisheries. George Allen and Unwin, London.

des Clers, S., and R. Wooton. 1990. Modelling the population dynamics of the sealworm *Pseudoterranova decipiens.* Netherlands Journal of Sea Research 25 (1–2): 291–299.

Dolar, M. L. L. 1994. Incidental takes of small cetaceans in fisheries in Palawan, central Visayas and northern Mindanao in the Philippines. Reports of the International Whaling Commission (Special Issue 15): 355–363.

Earle, M. 1996. Ecological interactions between cetaceans and fisheries. Pages 167–204 *in* M. P. Simmonds and J. D. Hutchinson (eds.), The Conservation of Whales and Dolphins: Science and Practice. John Wiley and Sons, Chichester, U.K.

Ellis, S., K. Zhou, S. Leatherwood, M. Bruford, and U. Seal (eds.). 1994. Baiji (*Lipotes vexillifer*) population and habitat viability assessment, 1–4 June 1993, Nanjing, China. Mammalogical Society of China, IUCN/SSC Cetacean Specialist Group, IUCN/SSC Captive Breeding Specialist Group.

Estes, J. A., and J. F. Palmisano. 1974. Sea otters: Their role in structuring nearshore communities. Science 185:1058–1060.

Estes, J. A., and G. R. VanBlaricom. 1985. Sea-otters and shellfisheries. Pages 187–235 *in* J. R. Beddington, R. J. H. Beverton, and D. M. Lavigne (eds.), Marine Mammals and Fisheries. George Allen and Unwin, London.

Fertl, D., and S. Leatherwood. 1995. Cetacean interactions with trawls: A preliminary review. NAFO Scientific Council Research Document 1995, No. 95/82. 34 pp.

Fish, J. F., and J. S. Vania. 1971. Killer whale, *Orcinus orca,* sounds repel white whales, *Delphinapterus leucas.* Fishery Bulletin 69:531–535.

Food and Agriculture Organization. 1978. Mammals in the Seas. Vol. 1. Report of the FAO Advisory Committee on Marine Resources Research. Working Party on Marine Mammals. FAO Fisheries Series No. 5.

Food and Agriculture Organization. 1990. Report of the expert consultation on large-scale pelagic driftnet fishing. 2–6 April 1990, Rome, Italy. FAO Fisheries Report No. 434.

Food and Agriculture Organization. 1995. Precautionary approach to fisheries. Part 1: Guidelines on the precautionary approach to capture fisheries and species introductions. Elaborated by the Technical Consultation on the Precautionary Approach to Capture Fisheries (Including Species Introductions). 6–13 June 1995, Lysekil, Sweden. FAO Fisheries Technical Paper 350.1. 52 pp.

Fraker, M. A., and B. R. Mate. 1999. Seals, sea lions, and salmon in the Pacific Northwest. (This volume)

Gosliner, M. L. 1999. The tuna-dolphin controversy. (This volume)

Gubbay, S. (ed.). 1996. Marine Protected Areas: Principles and Techniques for Management. Chapman and Hall, London. 232 pp.

Gulland, J. A. 1983. World resources of fisheries and their management. Pages 839–1061 *in* O. Kinne (ed.), Marine Ecology: A Comprehensive Integrated Treatise on Life in Oceans and Coastal Waters. Vol. 5. Ocean Management, Part 2, Ecosystems and Organic Resources. N.p.

Hanan, D. A., and S. L. Diamond. 1989. Estimates of sea lion, harbor seal, and harbor porpoise mortalities in California set net fisheries for the 1986–87 fishing year. Report to the National Marine Fisheries Service, Southwest Region, Terminal Island, CA. 10 pp.

Hanan, D. A., D. B. Holts, and A. L. Coan. 1993. The California drift gillnet fishery for sharks and swordfish, 1981–82 and 1990–91. California Department of Fish and Game Fish Bulletin 175:1–95.

Harwood, J., and J. Prime. 1978. Some factors affecting the size of British grey seal populations. Journal of Applied Ecology 15:401–411.

Hayase, S., and A. Yatsu. 1993. Preliminary report of a squid subsurface driftnet experiment in the North Pacific during 1991. Pages 557–576 *in* J. Ito, W. Shaw, and R. L. Burgner (eds.), Symposium on Biology, Distribution and Stock Assessment of Species Caught in the High Seas Driftnet Fisheries in the North Pacific Ocean. INPFC Bulletin No. 53 (3).

Hempel, G. 1978. North Sea fisheries and fish stocks—a review of recent changes. Rapports et Procès-Verbaux des Réunions. Conseil International pour l'Exploration de la Mer 173:145–167.

Hewison, G. J. 1993. High seas driftnet fishing in the South Pacific and the Law of the Sea. Georgetown International Environmental Law Review 5 (2): 239–514.

Hobbs, R. C., and L. L. Jones. 1993. Impacts of high seas driftnet fisheries on marine mammal populations in the North Pacific. Pages 409–434 *in* J. Ito, W. Shaw, and R. L. Burgner (eds.), Symposium on Biology, Distribution and Stock Assessment of Species Caught in the High Seas Driftnet Fisheries in the North Pacific Ocean. INPFC Bulletin No. 53 (3).

Holt, S. J., and L. M. Talbot. 1978. New principles for the conservation of wild living resources. Wildlife Monographs No. 59.

International North Pacific Fisheries Commission. 1991. Final report of 1990 observations of the Japanese high seas driftnet fisheries in the North Pacific Ocean. Joint report by the National Sections of Canada, Japan, and the United States. 198 pp.

IUCN. 1979. Proceedings of the Workshop on Cetacean Sanctuaries. Tijuana and Guerrero Negro, B. C., Mexico, 4–9 February 1979. International Union for the Conservation of Nature and Natural Resources, Gland, Switzerland. 37 pp.

IUCN. 1981. Report of the IUCN workshop on marine mammal/fishery interactions, La Jolla, California, 30 March–2 April 1981. International Union for the Conservation of Nature and Natural Resources, Gland, Switzerland.

Jamieson, G. S., and G. D. Heritage. 1988. Experimental flying squid fishery off British Columbia, 1987. Canadian Industry Report of Fisheries and Aquatic Sciences No. 186.

Katona, S. K., and S. D. Kraus. 1999. Efforts to conserve the North Atlantic right whale. (This volume)

Kraus, S. D., A. J. Read, A. Solow, K. Baldwin, T. Spradlin, E. Anderson, and J. Williamson. 1997. Acoustic alarms reduce porpoise mortality. Nature 388:525.

Lavigne, D. M., V. B. Scheffer, and S. R. Kellert. 1999. The evolution of North American attitudes toward marine mammals. (This volume)

Leatherwood, S., and R. R. Reeves. 1989. Marine mammal research and conservation in Sri Lanka 1985–1986. United Nations Environment Programme, Oceans and Coastal Areas, Marine Mammal Technical Report 1:1–138.

Lien, J. 1994. Entrapments of large cetaceans in passive inshore fishing gear in Newfoundland and Labrador (1979–1990). Reports of the International Whaling Commission (Special Report 15): 149–163.

Lien, J., and B. Merdsoy. 1979. The humpback whale is not over the hump. Natural History 88 (6): 46–49.

Lister-Kaye, J. 1978. Seal Cull. The Grey Seal Controversy. Penguin Books, Harmondsworth, Middlesex, England. 174 pp.

Loughlin, T. R., L. Consiglieri, R. L. DeLong, and A. T. Actor. 1983. Incidental catch of marine mammals by foreign fishing vessels, 1978–1981. Marine Fisheries Review 45 (7-8-9): 44–49.

MacKenzie, D. 1996. Seals to the slaughter. New Scientist (16 March): 36–39.

Malouf, A. 1986. Seals and Sealing in Canada. Report of The Royal Commission on Seals and the Sealing Industry in Canada. 3 vols. Supply and Services Canada, Ottawa.

Margolis, L. 1977. Public health aspects of "cod-worm" infection: A review. Journal of the Fisheries Research Board of Canada 34:887–898.

Mate, B. R. 1980. Report of a December 1977 workshop on marine mammal-fisheries interactions in the northeastern Pacific. Report to the Marine Mammal Commission, Contract MM8AC003. (Available from National Technical Information Service, Springfield, VA. PB80-175144.) 48 pp.

Mate, B. R., and J. T. Harvey (eds.). 1987. Acoustical deterrents in marine mammal conflicts with fisheries. Oregon Sea Grant Publication ORESU-W-86-001. Sea Grant Communications, Oregon State University, Corvallis, OR. 116 pp.

Matkin, C. O. 1986. Killer whale interactions with the sablefish longline fishery in Prince William Sound, Alaska 1985 with comments on the Bering Sea. Report to the National Marine Fisheries Service, Juneau, AK, under contract no. 010686. 10 pp.

Matkin, C. O., and F. H. Fay. 1980. Marine mammal–fishery interactions on the Copper River and in Prince William Sound, Alaska. 1978. Report to the Marine Mammal Commission. (Available from National Technical Information Service, Springfield, VA. PB80-159536.) 71 pp.

Matkin, C. O., and E. L. Saulitis. 1994. Killer whale (*Orcinus orca*) biology and management in Alaska. Report to the Marine Mammal Commission. (Available from National Technical Information Service, Springfield, VA. PB95-166203.) 46 pp.

McCarthy, D. T. 1985. Interactions between seals and salmon drift net fisheries in the West of Ireland. Fishery Leaflet No. 126. An Roinn Iascaigh agus Foraoiseachta.

Merriam, C. H. 1901. Food of sea lions. Science (ns) 38:777–779.

Miller, D. J., M. G. Herder, and J. P. Scholl. 1983. California marine mammal–fishery interactions study. 1979–1981. NMFS/Southwest Fisheries Center Administrative Report 1983 (H).

Northridge, S. P. 1984. World review of interactions between marine mammals and fisheries. Food and Agriculture Organization Fisheries Technical Paper 251.

Northridge, S. P. 1991a. An updated world review of interactions between marine mammals and fisheries. Food and Agriculture Organization Fisheries Technical Paper 251, Suppl. 1.

Northridge, S. P. 1991b. Driftnet fisheries and their impact on non-target species: A worldwide review. Food and Agriculture Organization Fisheries Technical Paper 320.

O'Riordan, T., and J. Cameron (eds.). 1994. Interpreting the Precautionary Principle. Earthscan Publications, London. 315 pp.

Palka, D. 1994. Results of a scientific workshop to evaluate the status of harbor porpoise (*Phocoena phocoena*) in the western North Atlantic. Northeast Fisheries Science Center Reference Document 94-09.

Payne, M. P., S. Pittman, P. J. Clapham, and J. W. Jossi. 1990. Recent fluctuations in the abundance of baleen whales in the southern Gulf of Maine in relation to changes in selected prey. Fishery Bulletin 88:687–696.

Pemberton, D., and P. D. Shaughnessy. 1993. Interaction between seals and marine fish-farms in Tasmania, and management of the problem. Aquatic Conservation: Marine and Freshwater Systems 3:149–158.

Pemberton, D., B. Merdsoy, R. Gales, and D. Renouf. 1994. The interaction between offshore cod trawlers and harp *Phoca groenlandica* and hooded *Crystophora cristata* seals off Newfoundland, Canada. Biological Conservation 68:123–128.

Perrin, W. F. 1969. Using porpoises to catch tuna. World Fishing 18:42–45.

Perrin, W. F., and R. L. Brownell Jr. (eds.). 1989. Report of the Workshop. Pages 1–22 *in* W. F. Perrin, R. L. Brownell Jr., K. Zhou, and

J. Liu (eds.), Biology and Conservation of the River Dolphins. Occasional Papers of the IUCN Species Survival Commission No. 3.

Perrin, W. F., G. P. Donovan, and J. Barlow (eds.). 1994. Gillnets and Cetaceans. Reports of the International Whaling Commission (Special Issue 15). 629 pp.

Phillips, C. 1996. Conservation in practice: Agreements, regulations, sanctuaries and action plans. Pages 447–466 *in* M. P. Simmonds and J. D. Hutchinson (eds.), The Conservation of Whales and Dolphins: Science and Practice. John Wiley and Sons, Chichester, U.K.

Potter, D., T. Smith, D. Palka, and F. Serchuk. 1996. Further results from experimental fisheries using acoustic devices to reduce harbor porpoise bycatch. Working Paper 19 presented to the Small Cetacean Sub-committee of the International Whaling Commission. June 1996, Aberdeen.

Pryor, K., J. Lindbergh, S. Lindbergh, and R. Milano. 1990. A dolphin-human fishing cooperative in Brazil. Marine Mammal Science 6:77–82.

Ragen, T. J., and D. M. Lavigne. 1999. The Hawaiian monk seal: Biology of an endangered species. (This volume)

Read, A. J., K. van Waerebeek, J. C. Reyes, J. S. McKinnon, and L. C. Lehman. 1988. The exploitation of small cetaceans in coastal Peru. Biological Conservation 46:53–70.

Reeves, R. R., and S. Leatherwood. 1994. Dolphins, porpoises and whales. 1994–1998 Action Plan for the Conservation of Cetaceans. IUCN/SSC Cetacean Specialist Group. IUCN, Gland, Switzerland. 91 pp.

Reeves, R. R., R. J. Hofman, G. K. Silber, and D. Wilkinson. 1996. Acoustic Deterrence of Harmful Marine Mammal–Fishery Interactions. Proceedings of a Workshop Held in Seattle, Washington, 20–22 March 1996. U.S. Department of Commerce, NOAA Technical Memorandum NMFS-OPR-10.

Reijnders, P., S. Brasseur, J. van der Toorn, P. van der Wolf, I. Boyd, J. Harwood, D. Lavigne, and L. Lowry. 1993. Seals, Fur Seals, Sea Lions and Walrus. Status Survey and Conservation Action Plan. IUCN/SSC Seal Specialist Group. IUCN, Gland, Switzerland. 87 pp.

Rogan, E., and S. D. Berrow. 1995. The management of Irish waters as a whale and dolphin sanctuary. Pages 671–681 *in* A. S. Blix, L. Walløe, and Ø. Ulltang (eds.), Whales, Seals, Fish and Man. Elsevier Science B.V., Amsterdam.

Shackell, N. L., and J. H. M. Willison. 1995. Marine protected areas and sustainable fisheries. Proceedings of the Symposium on Marine Protected Areas and Sustainable Fisheries conducted at the Second International Conference on Science and the Management of Protected Areas, held at Dalhousie University, Halifax, Nova Scotia, Canada, 16–20 May 1994. Science and Management of Protected Areas Association, Wolfville, Nova Scotia, Canada. 300 pp.

Shaughnessy, P. D. 1985. Interactions between fisheries and Cape fur seals in Southern Africa. Pages 119–134 *in* J. R. Beddington, R. J. H. Beverton, and D. M. Lavigne (eds.), Marine Mammals and Fisheries. George Allen and Unwin, London.

Sherman, K., C. Jones, L. Sullivan, W. Smith, P. Berrien, and L. Ejsymont. 1981. Congruent shifts in sand eel abundance in western and eastern North Atlantic ecosystems. Nature 291:486–489.

Sivasubramanian, K. 1964. Predation of tuna longline catches in the Indian Ocean by killer whales. Bulletin of the Fisheries Research Station Colombo (17): 221–236.

Smith, T., K. Bisack, N. Garret–Logan, M. Kander, R. Mayo, S. North-ridge, D. Palka, D. Sheehan, and J. Walden. 1993. Estimating the effects of season-area controls on fishing on by-catch and landings. Abstract from the Tenth Biennial Conference on the Biology of Marine Mammals. 11–15 November 1993, Galveston, TX.

Swartzman, G. L., and R. J. Hofman. 1991. Uncertainties and research needs regarding the Bering Sea and Antarctic marine ecosystems. Final Contract Report to the Marine Mammal Commission. (Available from National Technical Information Service, Springfield, VA. PB91-201731.) 111 pp.

Trippel, E. A., J. Y. Wang, M. B. Strong, L. S. Carter, and J. D. Conway. 1996. Incidental mortality of harbour porpoise (*Phocoena phocoena*) by the gillnet fishery in the lower Bay of Fundy. Canadian Journal of Fishery and Aquatic Science 53:1294–1300.

United Nations Conference on Environment and Development. 1992. Agenda 21: Programme of action for sustainable development. United Nations Publications, New York, NY.

United Nations Environment Programme. 1994. Report of the Third Meeting of the Scientific Advisory Committee of the Marine Mammal Action Plan on Marine Mammal/Fishery Interactions: analysis of cull proposals. 24–27 August 1994, Crowborough, U.K.

United Nations Environment Programme. 1997. Eighth Meeting of the Planning and Coordinating Committee (PCC) of the Marine Mammal Action Plan. 6–8 May 1996, Gland, Switzerland. Report of the Meeting.

van Waerebeek, K., and J. C. Reyes. 1994. Interactions between small cetaceans and Peruvian fisheries in 1988/89 and analysis of trends. Reports of the International Whaling Commission (Special Issue 15): 495–502.

Vidal, O. 1991. The vaquita: Extinction is forever. Baja Explorer (December): 10–11.

Villa-R., B. 1993. Recovery plan for the vaquita, *Phocoena sinus.* Final Contract Report to the Marine Mammal Commission. (Available from National Technical Information Service, Springfield, VA. PB93-169415.) 40 pp.

Wade, P. R., and R. P. Angliss. 1997. Guidelines for Assessing Marine Mammal Stocks: Reports of the GAMMS Workshop, 3–5 April 1996, Seattle, WA. U.S. Department of Commerce, NOAA Technical Memorandum NMFS-OPR-12. 93 pp.

Wendell, F. E., R. A. Hardy, and J. A. Ames. 1985. Assessment of the accidental take of sea otters, *Enhydra lutris,* in gill and trammel nets. Marine Resources Branch, California Department of Fish and Game, Morro Bay, CA. 32 pp. + 10 tables and 2 figures (unpublished).

Wickens, P. 1995. A review of operational interactions between pinnipeds and fisheries. Food and Agriculture Organization Fisheries Technical Paper 346. 86 pp.

Wooster, W. S. 1993. Is it food? An overview. Pages 1–3 *in* Is It Food? Addressing Marine Mammal and Seabird Declines: Workshop Summary. Alaska Sea Grant Publication 93-01.

Yano, K., and M. E. Dahlheim. 1995. Killer whale, *Orcinus orca,* depredation on longline catches of bottomfish in the southeastern Bering Sea and adjacent waters. Fishery Bulletin 93:355–372.

Zhou, K., and X. Zhang. 1991. Baiji: The Yangtze River Dolphin and Other Endangered Animals of China. The Stonewall Press, Washington, DC. 132 pp.

6

MICHAEL L. GOSLINER

The Tuna-Dolphin Controversy

Perhaps no issue better exemplifies the successes and failures of the Marine Mammal Protection Act than the tuna-dolphin problem. In 1971 and 1972, during congressional consideration of the plight of marine mammals, the death of dolphins in the eastern tropical Pacific tuna fishery emerged as one of the key concerns that led to enactment of the Marine Mammal Protection Act. Although the focus of the controversy has shifted considerably over the past 25 years, the issue continues to spark substantial debate today. No marine mammal issue has received more attention from legislators, led to more amendments of the Marine Mammal Protection Act, consumed a larger share of research funding under the Act, or spawned more litigation than has the incidental taking of dolphins in this fishery. For roughly half of the 25-year history of the Marine Mammal Protection Act, lawsuits challenging various aspects of the U.S. tuna-dolphin program have been pending.

The tuna-dolphin issue also provides a good illustration of the interplay between law and science and the difficulties that can arise when, as is often the case, regulatory decisions must be based on incomplete scientific information. The difficulties were particularly acute during the period following enactment of the Marine Mammal Protection Act as regulators and scientists grappled with defining the new management concept of optimum sustainable population (OSP) and developing the information needed to authorize incidental taking.

As the United States slowly brought dolphin mortality by its fishermen under control, the number of dolphins being killed again skyrocketed in the mid- to late 1980s as a shrinking U.S. fleet was replaced by ones from Mexico, Venezuela, and other nations (DeMaster et al. 1992). Through the use of trade sanctions, and ultimately international cooperation, dolphin mortality has recently been reduced to levels generally believed to be biologically insignificant. Nevertheless, the use of dolphins to locate and catch tuna will remain controversial as long as any of these charismatic cetaceans are killed or injured in the process.

The Eastern Tropical Pacific Purse Seine Tuna Fishery

The eastern tropical Pacific Ocean, an area of more than seven million square miles (18.1 million km^2) stretching from southern California to Chile, has been an important tuna fishing area for several decades. The roots of the current fishery can be traced to the 1910s, when a fleet of small purse seine vessels based in southern California began targeting bluefin tuna (*Thunnus thynnus*) (Green et al. 1971). As improved refrigeration methods were developed, it became practical to build larger vessels that could venture farther out to sea. And as these vessels entered warmer waters to the south, fishermen began to target yellowfin tuna (*Thunnus albacares*) and skipjack (*Katsuwonus pelamis*), rather than the bluefin tuna and albacore (*Thunnus alalunga*) found in more temperate waters. Fishermen soon learned that the cotton purse seines then in use deteriorated rapidly in these tropical waters and found that they could operate more profitably using pole and line gear. Pole and line fishing, using live bait (thus known as baitboats), soon dominated the fishery (Green et al. 1971).

The number of boats using pole and line gear in the fishery began to decline early in the 1950s as foreign-caught tuna entered the U.S. market and competition from alternative sources of low-cost protein drove prices down. Faced with economic difficulties, the U.S. fleet began to explore more efficient fishing methods (McNeely 1961). Two technical developments, nylon nets and the power block, proved to be the salvation of the fishery. These innovations made the use of large purse seine nets to catch tuna in the warm waters of the tropical Pacific practical for the first time. The net, which is up to a mile (1.6 km) long and 600 feet (183 m) deep, is deployed to encircle an entire school of fish. It is then "pursed" by drawing the bottom of the net together to form a large sack, preventing the catch from escaping.

Conversion of the fleet to purse seine technology was swift. Of the 140 baitboats operating in the fishery in 1959, more than half had been converted to purse seiners by 1961 (Green et al. 1971). Throughout the 1960s the U.S. purse seine fleet continued to grow as new and larger vessels were added. Between 1961 and 1970 the capacity of the fleet more than doubled, and by 1975 it had more than doubled again (Inter-American Tropical Tuna Commission 1995).

As had the baitboat operators, the purse seiners made use of the long-known association between tuna and dolphins in the eastern tropical Pacific to locate schools of tuna. The dolphins, being air breathers, are visible on the surface and can be detected at a considerable distance by searching the horizon for surface splashing by the dolphins and for foraging seabirds that often gather over them (Au and Pitman 1986). Originally, purse seiners exercised care to avoid capturing the dolphins as they set their nets (McNeely 1961). Tuna fishermen, however, soon learned that the bond between the tuna and the dolphins is very tight and, unless a large portion of the dolphin school is encircled along with the tuna, the set is usually unsuccessful (Perrin 1968). If even a few dolphins escape encirclement, the tuna can follow and be lost. The fishermen refined their fishing technique, using speedboats to herd the dolphins and the associated tuna into a cluster around which the net could be set (Fig. 6-1). As noted by Green et al. (1971:191), "[m]aking a good set on porpoise[1] is a fine art, and good 'fishing skippers' are in high demand. . . ." By 1966 more than half of the yellowfin tuna caught by purse seiners in the eastern tropical Pacific came from sets on dolphins (Perrin 1968).

Initially, fishermen did not know how to release dolphins once the purse seine had been closed, so the entire contents were hauled on board, the tuna sorted out, and the dolphins thrown overboard. Not only did this process result in substantial dolphin mortality and injury, it took considerable time and effort (Perrin 1968). After much experimentation, fishermen developed a "backdown" procedure for releasing many of the dolphins from the net. This procedure entails putting the vessel into reverse after about half of the net has been hauled aboard. This forms the net into a long, narrow channel and causes the corkline at the apex of the net to sink. Dolphins are herded toward the apex, where they can escape over the submerged rim of the net (Fig. 6-2).

Although adoption of the backdown procedure no doubt saved many dolphins, these small cetaceans continued to be killed in large numbers in the fishery. Perrin (1969:45) noted that "[s]ome porpoise die in every set, the number depending on the skill of the captain in backing down and the conditions of the set." No reliable data from on-board observers were collected before enactment of the Marine Mammal Protection Act. Thus, although some estimates of annual dolphin mortality between 1959 and 1972 are as high as 350,000 to 650,000, all that can be said with much assurance is that mortality was very high (National Research Council 1992, Wade 1995). Estimates of mortality since 1959 are presented in Table 6-1.

Enactment of the Marine Mammal Protection Act

Legislative Background

Fueled by a growing awareness of environmental problems and a concern that many ocean mammals were becoming endangered as a result of human activities, U.S. legislators introduced more than 30 different bills designed to protect these marine species during the 1971 session of Congress. The proposed legislation, designed to address a wide range of marine mammal issues, can be placed into four broad categories (U.S. House 1971:216). The first group of bills would have imposed a total ban on the taking of marine mammals, subject to a few narrowly drawn exceptions (e.g., taking for scientific research and replacement of zoo animals). A second group of bills was concerned with the use of humane methods in taking marine mammals. Their focus was on the elimination of clubbing as a means of harvesting seals. The third category of bills was directed primarily at promoting

A

B

Figure 6-1. (*A*) When a school of dolphins believed to be associated with tuna is sighted, speedboats are dispatched to herd them toward the purse seine vessel. There is some concern that the high-speed chase of dolphins before encirclement stresses the animals sufficiently to cause physical impairment of the animals or reduced production of the populations. (Photograph courtesy of National Marine Fisheries Service) (*B*) In this aerial view of a purse seine set, speedboats can be seen maneuvering just outside the open portion of the net to prevent the escape of dolphins and tuna until encirclement is complete. (Photograph courtesy of Inter-American Tropical Tuna Commission–Wayne Perryman)

further research into marine mammal issues, apparently in the belief that too little was known to craft appropriate and comprehensive protective legislation. The fourth group was an amalgam of the others. H.R. 10420, the bill originally passed by the House of Representatives, would have established a general prohibition on taking marine mammals, but would have given the Secretary of the Interior broad authority to authorize taking, provided the affected population was not threatened with extinction and was managed on a sustained-yield basis. H.R. 10420 also called for increased research on marine mammals and included a provision for the creation of an independent Marine Mammal Commission to oversee such research.

The Subcommittee on Fisheries and Wildlife Conservation of the House Committee on Merchant Marine and Fisheries held four days of hearings on the proposed marine mammal legislation in September 1971. Although legislators focused considerable attention on the plight of the great whales and whitecoat harp seals, there also was a growing appreciation of the need to address the issue of dolphin mortality in the eastern tropical Pacific tuna fishery. As the witness representing Friends of Animals noted on the first day of the hearings, ". . . 200,000 porpoise deaths is extremely high to be called 'accidental' and . . . it is unconscionable that our Government permits the use of these [purse seine] nets . . ." (U.S. House 1971:89). What emerged from the hearings was a general recognition that large numbers of dolphins were being killed in the tuna fishery, but estimates of the extent of the take were based on scant information. Further, witnesses recognized that there was virtually no in-

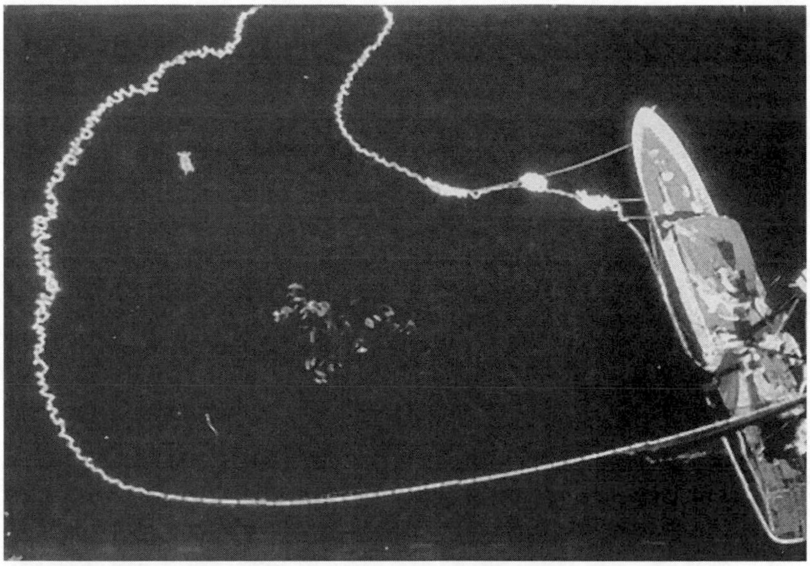

A

B

Figure 6-2. (*A*) Adoption of the backdown procedure has been credited with saving millions of dolphins from dying in tuna nets. Here dolphins congregate in the center of the net while it is being pursed. A rubber raft used to assist in rescuing dolphins can be seen near the apex of the net. (Photograph courtesy of Inter-American Tropical Tuna Commission–Wayne Perryman) (*B*) Dolphins successfully released from the net during backdown swim away from the net. Note the reconfiguration of the net into a narrow channel to facilitate the dolphins' escape during backdown. (Photograph courtesy of Inter-American Tropical Tuna Commission–Wayne Perryman)

Table 6-1. Estimated Incidental Kill of Dolphins in the Tuna Purse Seine Fishery in the Eastern Tropical Pacific Ocean, 1959–1997

Year	U.S. Vessels	Non-U.S. Vessels	Year	U.S. Vessels	Non-U.S. Vessels
1959	23,485		1979	17,938	3,488
1960	503,879		1980	15,305	16,665
1961	558,572		1981	18,780	17,199
1962	226,396		1982	23,267	5,837
1963	252,607		1983[a]	8,513	4,980
1964	410,195		1984	17,732	22,980
1965	482,331		1985	19,205	39,642
1966	392,441		1986	20,692	112,482
1967	262,947		1987	13,992	85,185
1968	239,051		1988	19,712	61,881
1969	457,903		1989	12,643	84,403
1970	433,201		1990	5,083	47,448
1971	249,373		1991	1,002	26,290
1972	368,600	55,078	1992	439	15,111
1973	206,697	58,276	1993	115	3,601
1974	147,437	27,245	1994	106	4,095
1975	166,645	27,812	1995	0	3,274
1976	108,740	19,482	1996	0	2,766
1977	25,452	25,901	1997	0	3,005
1978	19,366	11,147			

Source: Based on Wade (1995) and data provided by the Inter-American Tropical Tuna Commission and the National Marine Fisheries Service.

[a]The anomalous mortality figures for 1983 resulted in large part from the displacement of much of the tuna fleet to other fishing areas (e.g., the western Pacific) in response to a shift in tuna distribution during the 1983 El Niño event.

formation on the sizes of the affected dolphin stocks and that, absent such information, it was difficult, if not impossible, to assess the effects of the estimated take.

A note of promise also emerged from the hearings. Joe Medina, a tunaboat skipper, presented testimony on the effectiveness of a dolphin-saving innovation he and his cousin had developed. They had found that the insertion of a strip of small-mesh netting, known as a "Medina panel" or "dolphin safety panel," into the area of the purse seine where dolphins are released during backdown greatly reduced the risk of entanglement. Citing early successes with the new net, Medina concluded: "We have the problem licked" (U.S. House 1971:348). Nevertheless, another tuna industry representative believed that continued taking was inevitable and recognized that, without some exclusion from the proposed take prohibition, the U.S. tuna fleet would be unable to operate (U.S. House 1971:355).

Committee Action

H.R. 10420 emerged from committee strengthened in certain respects.[2] The sustained-yield concept of the original bill had been expanded such that taking could only be authorized after it was determined that the taking would "not be to the disadvantage of those species or population stocks and . . . [would] be consistent with the purposes and policies . . . of this Act." Among the stated purposes and policies was obtaining an "optimum sustained yield" of marine mammal populations. The reported bill also contained a provision designed to put foreign tuna fleets on an even footing with the soon-to-be-regulated U.S. fleet by prohibiting the importation into the United States of fish caught in a manner determined to be injurious to marine mammals. As noted in the Committee report, "[i]f foreign fleets elect to continue to catch tuna fish by these methods, this section will close the United States market to the tuna. . . ."[3]

The Senate, in its marine mammal bill, took a slightly different tack.[4] This bill, too, would have created a general moratorium on the taking of marine mammals, but it included more circumscribed exceptions and more demanding criteria for waiving the moratorium. Rather than tie marine mammal management to sustained yield, the Senate bill used the novel concept of maintaining marine mammal stocks at optimum sustainable population levels. It also established as an "immediate goal" that any permitted "incidental kill or incidental serious injury of marine mammals . . . be reduced to insignificant levels approaching a zero mortality and serious injury rate."

Although the Senate bill included more rigorous criteria for authorizing the taking of marine mammals incidental to fishing operations, it recognized the difficulty in implementing the new requirements and thus provided for an initial two-year exemption. During the first 24 months following enactment, such incidental taking would be permitted subject to interim regulations that would ensure the use of fishing techniques and gear designed to produce the lowest feasible number of marine mammal fatalities.

When the House and Senate bills were reconciled, the Senate provisions with respect to optimum sustainable population and incidental taking in commercial fisheries were adopted. The final bill also contained a somewhat stricter provision concerning fish imports from other countries. It directed the Secretary of the Treasury to ban the importation of fish that "have been caught with commercial fishing technology which results in the incidental kill or incidental serious injury of ocean mammals in excess of United States standards."

Conflicting Directives

The Marine Mammal Protection Act was signed into law on 21 October 1972. It presented conflicting messages with respect to the fate of the purse seine tuna fishery. On one hand, there was an underlying sentiment that the U.S. tuna fleet should be able to continue to set on dolphins, albeit subject to certain requirements designed to minimize incidental mortality. In this regard, the Senate report explained:

> The Secretary, for example, in regulating the operations of the tuna industry with respect to the incidental catching of porpoises must consider the technical capability of these fishermen to avoid injury to porpoises. It is not the intention of the Committee to shut down or significantly to curtail the activities of the tuna fleet so long as the Secretary is satisfied that the tuna fishermen are using economically and technologically practicable measures to assure minimal hazards to marine mammal populations.[5]

Nevertheless, the legislation started a two-year clock for the Secretary of Commerce[6] to collect sufficient information on which to make a rather rigorous determination that the taking would not disadvantage the affected dolphin stocks (i.e., would maintain the affected stocks at optimum sustainable population levels). To meet the statutory prerequisites for authorizing the taking, the Secretary, in conjunction with the Marine Mammal Commission and the tuna industry, would presumably need to (1) determine the species composition and stock structure of eastern tropical Pacific dolphins, (2) obtain reliable estimates of the numbers being taken, (3) determine what constitutes optimum sustainable populations, both generally and for each affected stock, and (4) demonstrate that the stocks would not be disadvantaged by specific levels of take. At the same time, the government agencies and the tuna industry were expected to undertake research to develop improved fishing methods to reduce or eliminate incidental mortality. If the required findings could not be made at the end of the two-year period, an incidental take permit could not be issued and, faced with the prospect of substantial penalties, the U.S. fleet would, as a practical matter, be forced to cease setting on dolphin schools.

The seemingly conflicting expectations regarding the Marine Mammal Protection Act's effect on the tuna fishery might be attributed to the scientific naïveté of the legislators. That is, perhaps they did not understand how formidable a task they had placed on the regulatory agency and the fleet. This view, however, is belied by other statements in the legislative history of the Act. As the House recognized in its deliberations on H.R. 10420, "with respect to almost every species and stock of animals today, there is little evidence to indicate what should be done one way or the other, and that development of this evidence will take time—in most cases more than two years."[7] Further, in declining to incorporate an unconditional two-year moratorium on taking marine mammals into the House bill, the oversight committee acknowledged that, under its existing proposal "[a]s a practical matter, with regard to practically all of the species and stocks involved, there will exist a de facto moratorium for at least two years, and very probably longer."[8]

Perhaps Congress was convinced that technical innovations such as the Medina panel and those that might be developed during the Act's first two years would significantly reduce, if not eliminate, the dolphin kill. As the mortality estimates for the fishery amply demonstrate, this optimism proved unwarranted. It would be some 20 years before mortality was reduced to what are generally considered to be biologically insignificant levels. Moreover, we have come to recognize that, as long as dolphins are encircled to catch tuna, there is bound to be some incidental mortality.

Perhaps Congress did not care that it had taken action seemingly in conflict with its stated goal of preserving the U.S. purse seine fleet. For the time being, the tuna industry was satisfied with the initial two-year exemption and with the assurances that its operations would not be substantially curtailed under the Act. The environmental community was pleased that research would be directed at understanding and perhaps solving the tuna-dolphin problem and with the guarantee that more exacting standards would soon be applicable.

Actions to Implement the Marine Mammal Protection Act

Interim Regulations

As directed by the Act, the National Marine Fisheries Service issued interim regulations early in 1974 to govern the eastern tropical Pacific tuna fishery.[9] These regulations required that (1) each U.S. vessel install a "porpoise safety panel" of specified minimum dimensions, (2) vessel owners certify that the panels had been installed, (3) the Service inspect and approve the nets, and (4) backdown or other dolphin-release procedures be followed for any sets in which marine mammals were captured "until all live animals have been released from the net."[10] Another key feature of the 1974 interim regulations was the requirement that vessels accommodate, on a space-available basis, Service personnel conducting research on or observing fishing operations.

The regulations also gave effect to the prohibition on importing fish caught in ways inconsistent with U.S. standards. Yellowfin tuna caught by foreign vessels could be imported only if the vessel had installed a safety panel in its net and met the backdown requirements applicable to U.S. vessels.

The 1974 Rulemaking

In anticipation of the expiration of the two-year "grace period" for commercial fisheries, the National Marine Fisheries Service on 13 March 1974 published a notice of its intent to prescribe regulations to govern the taking of marine mammals incidental to commercial fishing operations, including the eastern tropical Pacific tuna fishery.[11] That notice, among other things, was to set forth the information required by section 103(d) of the Act, including:

(1) a statement of the estimated existing levels of the species and population stocks of the marine mammal concerned;
(2) a statement of the expected impact of the proposed regulations on the optimum sustainable population of such species or population stock;
(3) a statement describing the evidence before the Secretary upon which he proposes to base such regulations; and
(4) any studies made by or for the Secretary or any recommendations made by or for the Secretary or the Marine Mammal Commission which relate to the establishment of such regulations.

Despite some glaring informational gaps concerning the effects of the tuna fishery on eastern tropical Pacific dolphins, the Service moved inexorably toward satisfying its rulemaking timeline. As to the required estimates of population size for eastern tropical Pacific dolphin species, the Service merely indicated that they were "unknown." With respect to the expected impact of the proposed regulations on OSP levels, the Service stated that it was "not known due to lack of knowledge of the sizes of porpoise populations and other population dynamic factors. . . ."[12]

Proposed regulations were published on 5 April 1974.[13] Unlike the interim regulations, these regulations were subject to formal rulemaking, an adjudicatory process before an administrative law judge in which the interested parties are able to present testimony in support of or against the proposed regulations and to cross-examine the witnesses of the other parties. Based on the record developed at the hearing and a recommended decision by the administrative law judge, the Administrator of the National Oceanic and Atmospheric Administration issues final regulations. The regulations provide the basis for issuing incidental take permits to the fishermen. In the case of the eastern tropical Pacific yellowfin tuna fishery, a single permit was issued to the representative of the fishermen, the American Tunaboat Association, and individual operators were issued certificates of inclusion under the permit. Congress required that the more-demanding formal rulemaking process be followed in authorizing taking incidental to commercial fishing to guarantee adequate public participation and to enhance the scrutiny of agency decisions.

After a two-day hearing on the proposed regulations, the administrative law judge issued his recommended decision in July 1974. Although the proposed regulations were to apply to all commercial fisheries incidentally taking marine mammals, the decision underscored the central importance of the tuna fishery in the proceeding: "[t]hough cast in general terms, the statutory provisions . . . are aimed at one fishery . . . the yellowfin tuna fishery in the eastern tropical Pacific" (McAlpin 1974:4). "With respect to all forms of gear other than tuna purse seines," the judge wrote, "the requirements under the regulations are that a holder of a certificate of inclusion should return to the water without further injury any animals taken accidentally. . . ." (McAlpin 1974:7). When one examines the legislative history of the Marine Mammal Protection Act, this focus on the tuna fishery was no doubt warranted. Not only was the tuna fishery taking several orders of magnitude more marine mammals than any other fishery, it was the only fishery that intentionally captured marine mammals as part of its operations.[14]

The most crucial aspect of the administrative law judge's recommendation was his resolution of the conflicting goals of the Act to protect marine mammals and preserve the tuna fishery. The judge concluded that "The legislative history of the Act shows it to be the intent of the Congress that marine mammal mortalities be reduced significantly—and as fast as possible—but there must be an appropriate balancing of the equities between the two extremes of a zero mortality rate and elimination of a commercial fishing industry" (McAlpin 1974:9). Consistent with this view, the administrative law judge recommended that a permit be issued even though certain crucial pieces of information were lacking. The judge seemed unconcerned that neither the National Marine Fisheries Service nor the applicant (the American Tunaboat Association) had met its burden of demonstrating that dolphin stocks would not be disadvantaged by continued take, as the statute ostensibly required. It is also curious that the judge felt compelled to specify a recommended term of validity for the American Tunaboat Association permit "as expressly required by the Act in Section 104(b)(2)(C)," but ignored the equally explicit requirement of section 104(b)(2)(A) that requires such permits to specify the number and kind of animals authorized to be taken.

Final regulations were published by the Service in September 1974, in time to become effective before the 21 October expiration of the two-year grace period. Changes from the interim regulations were relatively modest. Except for a new requirement that vessel operators maintain and submit to the Service log books of fishing operations specifying the numbers and species of dolphins encircled and killed, no substantial new burdens were placed on the fishery.

Regulations Challenged

It is not surprising that environmental groups promptly filed a lawsuit challenging the Service's issuance of regulations and intention to issue a general permit. The Committee for Humane Legislation asserted that the agency had violated section 103(d) of the Marine Mammal Protection Act by not providing the required information concerning the affected marine mammal populations and the expected impact of permit issuance on those populations. The plaintiffs also contended that the Service had improperly issued regulations without first determining that the authorized take would not disadvantage any of the dolphin stocks and was in accord with sound principles of resource protection and conservation. Plaintiffs further argued that the Act's zero mortality rate goal had been violated inasmuch as the Service had failed to show that the regulations would reduce dolphin mortality and serious injury to insignificant levels.

On another front, shortly after the regulations went into effect, the Service decided to hold a public hearing to consider possible revisions. This initiative was based, in part, on a preliminary finding by the Service's Southwest Fisheries Center that the population of spotted dolphins (*Stenella attenuata*) was dangerously low. Kenneth S. Norris, participating in the hearing on behalf of the Marine Mammal Commission, summed up the current state of affairs when he noted that ". . . even the most conservative estimate of porpoise mortality in the Eastern Tropical Pacific Tuna Fishery . . . represents an unacceptably high level of mortality, both in terms of the specific charge of the Marine Mammal Protection Act to reduce the rate of such mortality and serious injury to insignificant levels approaching zero and in terms of the overall protection and conservation policy objectives of the Act . . ." (Norris 1974). After the hearing, the Service added a requirement that during and after backdown at least two crew members be stationed at the corkline to extricate and assist in the release of entangled dolphins (Fig. 6-3). The Service declined to adopt other proposed changes, including limiting the number of dolphin sets that could be made or the number of dolphins that could be taken. It did, however, establish a "goal for 1975" to reduce dolphin mortality by 50% from the estimated level of 1.1 dolphins killed per ton of yellowfin tuna caught. The Service was careful to note that this was not a quota, but rather "an attainable objective contingent upon full cooperation of the U.S. tuna fleet. . . ."[15]

Throughout the first part of 1975, the U.S. fleet continued to fish under the American Tunaboat Association's general permit pending action by the U.S. district court on the challenge of the Service's regulations filed by environmental organizations.

Research and Related Actions to Reduce Dolphin Kill

Research aimed at reducing dolphin mortality in the purse seine fishery had begun before enactment of the Marine Mammal Protection Act. During the late 1960s and early 1970s fishermen, on their own initiative, had developed both the backdown procedure for releasing encircled dolphins and the Medina panel to minimize dolphin entanglement in the apex of the net where dolphins are released. Federal efforts to understand the nature and magnitude of the tuna-dolphin problem and to consider ways to reduce incidental mortality began at about that same time (Coe et al. 1984). Early in 1972 the National Marine Fisheries Service formed a committee to prepare an action plan for investigating the problem. The committee recommended that highest priority be given to research into possible modification of the existing purse seine fishing methods and gear to reduce dolphin mortality to the lowest possible levels. Secondarily, the Service was to give consideration to new fishing systems that would enable large yellowfin tuna to be caught without encircling dolphins (Coe et al. 1984).

Between 1972 and 1975 the Service's research program

A

B

Figure 6-3. (*A*) Dolphins that remain in the net after backdown are released over the corkline by hand. Sometimes fishermen will enter the water to facilitate release, putting themselves at risk to save dolphins. (Photograph courtesy of National Marine Fisheries Service) (*B*) Despite the use of the backdown procedure and hand-release of dolphins, thousands of dolphins continued to die in the fishery each year. Here, dolphins killed in a purse seine are being retrieved with the net. (Photograph courtesy of National Marine Fisheries Service)

examined several aspects of the tuna-dolphin problem. Using purse seine vessels as research platforms, agency scientists observed the behavior of encircled dolphins, examined the effectiveness of the Medina panel in eliminating dolphin entanglement, explored the causes of net collapses and other events that led to high dolphin mortality, and tested modified fishing practices and gear refinements (Ralston 1977).

The Service's research into the effectiveness of dolphin-saving gear and fishing techniques quickly yielded valuable results. The use of speedboats stationed at three points around the purse seine proved to be an effective means of preventing net collapse (Ralston 1977). Research also showed that, despite widespread use of the Medina panel by the U.S. fleet, entanglement in nets continued to be a major cause of dolphin mortality. During 93 observed sets, more than 370 dolphins became entangled in the panel itself, suggesting that a mesh size smaller than the required 2 inches (5.08 cm) was needed (Southwest Fisheries Center 1975). Another development that resulted from the Service's research program was the "porpoise apron," a trapezoidal piece of small-mesh webbing added to the net above the Medina panel (Coe et al. 1984). The apron serves to prevent the formation of canopies that can trap dolphins during backdown and also reduces the depth at the apex of the net, helping to facilitate the release of dolphins.

By 1975 about 95% of the dolphins encircled by purse seines were being released successfully during backdown

(Southwest Fisheries Center 1975). Others escaped from the net by jumping over the corkline or were released from the net by the fishermen (Southwest Fisheries Center 1975). About 2% of encircled dolphins were being killed (Southwest Fisheries Center 1975). A large proportion of this mortality (52%) involved those dolphins left in the net after the completion of backdown (Ralston 1977). Thus, it was believed that dolphin mortality could be reduced further by improving backdown effectiveness and enhancing post-backdown rescue efforts. Placement of a small rubber raft inside the net proved effective. It provided a platform from which the relative positions of fish and dolphins in the net could be observed and enabled operators to control backdown speed accordingly. The raft also provided a platform from which fishermen could hand-release dolphins left in the net after the completion of backdown (Ralston 1977).

In September 1975 the National Marine Fisheries Service undertook a research cruise aboard a tuna seiner, the *Bold Contender,* to test the combination of modified fishing practices. By using speedboats to hold open the net as a preventive, rather than a remedial, measure, an oversized safety panel of 1.25-inch (3.18-cm) mesh, a porpoise apron, and a rubber raft to help detect and free dolphins, and by continuing backdown until all live dolphins were released from the net, researchers were able to reduce dolphin mortality to 3.9 dolphins per set, a more than 75% reduction from the fleet-wide average (Ralston 1977).

Investigations into the status of dolphins were also being undertaken by the National Marine Fisheries Service. In 1974 the Service conducted a pilot aerial survey to estimate the abundance and assess the distribution of dolphins in the eastern tropical Pacific (Smith 1974). Although intended primarily as a feasibility study, the survey provided an independent source of information to augment data collected from fishing vessels. Reliable estimates of population sizes were needed to determine the status of dolphin populations. These estimates, in conjunction with data on fishing effort and kill rates and estimates of mortality and reproduction rates, were used to backcalculate estimates of pre-exploitation population sizes, which were compared with then-current population estimates to assess the relative health of the stocks (Southwest Fisheries Center 1976, Smith 1983).

The National Marine Fisheries Service was not alone in efforts to address the tuna-dolphin issue. Some vessel owners, enticed at least in part by a special yellowfin tuna quota earmarked for research efforts that allowed them to fish in areas that would otherwise be closed, provided space for researchers and cooperated in testing modifications to gear and fishing practices. In addition, the tuna industry voluntarily participated in an observer program begun by the National Marine Fisheries Service in 1971 (Coe et al. 1984). Also, beginning in 1972 the American Tunaboat Association conducted workshops for skippers and other vessel personnel to exchange information on the latest developments in dolphin-saving fishing techniques (Ralston 1977). Another important initiative was the establishment of the Porpoise Rescue Foundation, an industry-sponsored group formed in 1975 to promote and support educational and research activities related to the reduction of dolphin mortality.

The Marine Mammal Commission also played a key role in efforts to reduce dolphin mortality. In 1975 the Commission entered into a cooperative agreement with the National Marine Fisheries Service and the Porpoise Rescue Foundation to facilitate the exchange and evaluation of data being collected under the various research programs and to coordinate current and future research and development projects to make the best use of available funds (Ralston 1977).

Although the Commission sponsored some directed research into gear modifications on its own (Gonsalves 1977), its primary contribution came through its efforts to secure funding for needed research and the planning and carrying out of cooperative research efforts. The Commission, believing that innovative research might suggest new approaches to the problem of dolphin mortality, convened a workshop late in 1975 (Hofman 1979). Workshop participants believed that the fishing gear and practices used on the *Bold Contender* cruise were encouraging, but concluded that even their fleet-wide use was unlikely to eliminate dolphin kill entirely. They believed it would be desirable to develop fishing techniques that would facilitate the release of dolphins before backdown. The participants recommended that the association between tuna and dolphins be investigated to determine if there might be a way to separate them, either before encirclement or in the net. Among other things, it was suggested that more emphasis be placed on making behavioral observations and that research be undertaken to determine the roles of visual, olfactory, and acoustic stimuli in forming and maintaining the tuna-dolphin association in an effort to identify ways in which the association might be broken.

In response to the workshop, behavioral experiments directed at understanding the association between tuna and dolphin, as well as further gear-related research, were conducted in 1976 during a cruise aboard the *Elizabeth C. J.* Observations of dolphins on that cruise indicated that dolphins could be herded within the net, suggesting that research efforts, then directed primarily at improving backdown operations, should be expanded to consider ways in which dolphins might be released before backdown (Norris et al.

1978). Investigators also noticed that dolphins exhibited behavior indicative of learning from prior exposure to tuna vessels (Pryor and Norris 1978). Some dolphin schools tried to "hide" from an approaching seiner by diving under water and remaining motionless. Others schools managed to avoid encirclement by cutting across the bow of the seiner or diving beneath the vessel's wake. Once encircled, dolphins also exhibited familiarity with the situation. They seemed to congregate away from the vessel and the wall of the net until pursing of the net had been completed, moving to the apex of the net before backdown began (Pryor and Norris 1978). Dolphins were also observed engaging in "sleeping" behavior, in which they lay passively on the submerged net, apparently as a result of stress associated with chase and encirclement (Pryor and Norris 1978).

The 1975 Rulemaking

In anticipation that the American Tunaboat Association would seek to renew its general permit later that year, the Service published a progress report on tuna-dolphin research in August 1975 (Southwest Fisheries Center 1975). In addition to assessing progress made toward reducing dolphin mortality, that report provided the first assessments of the status of the offshore spotted dolphin and the eastern spinner dolphin (*Stenella longirostris orientalis*). The Service tentatively concluded that, if the populations were changing as a result of the incidental take, they were doing so at a slow rate. These assessments, however, did not attempt to estimate the status of either stock relative to its OSP.

Perhaps the most significant finding in the Service's progress report was that dolphin mortality in 1975 would probably fall between 93,000 and 214,000, likely exceeding the then-estimated 1974 kill of 113,000 dolphins. The main reasons given for the projected increase were an increased number of sets on dolphins and a higher percentage of sets being made on mixed-species schools of dolphins, for which mortality rates were markedly higher. For whatever reason, it was clear that the goal of reducing mortality by 50% in 1975 would not be achieved.

In August 1975 the American Tunaboat Association, as expected, applied for a renewal of its general permit, due to expire at the end of the year. The Association, perhaps sensing the difficulty with the approach taken by the Service in 1974, stated in its application that "[a]pproximately 85,060 dolphin mortalities are projected and an unknown number will be injured."[16]

One month later, the Service published proposed regulations for the 1976 fishing season, indicating its intention to establish a quota of between 50,000 and 110,000 dolphin mortalities.[17] Population estimates were provided for offshore spotted and eastern spinner dolphins, the two stocks most often taken in the fishery. However, the Service noted that "[o]ptimum sustainable population levels have not been determined; therefore no statement can be made as to the effect of the proposed action on optimum sustainable populations."[18] Based on available information, however, the Service was able to conclude that "At these [proposed] levels of incidental fishing mortality, the present population stocks are either stable or increasing or decreasing slightly. There is no evidence that the porpoise populations would substantially increase or decrease as a result of the regulations and reissuance of the general permit."[19] Apparently the Service believed that a population would not be disadvantaged as long as it was kept at or near existing levels. Or, more likely, the Service was merely balancing its responsibility to reduce dolphin mortality with a perceived responsibility not to shut down or significantly curtail the operations of the U.S. tuna fleet.

Whatever the reason, the Service was not alone in its willingness to accommodate the powerful tuna industry. Even the environmental organizations that participated in the rulemaking hearings, although pushing for the establishment of annual quotas, an expanded research program, and placement of observers on board all tuna vessels, generally did not suggest that a permit be withheld because the explicit requirements of the Marine Mammal Protection Act had not been met. Their willingness to seek ways to work with the tuna industry to improve the situation rather than pushing to bring the full force of the Marine Mammal Protection Act to bear in an effort to shut down the fishery was driven, to a considerable extent, by the fear that vessels would simply transfer to foreign registry, thereby making it unlikely that the tuna-dolphin problem would be satisfactorily addressed.

The National Marine Fisheries Service published final regulations for the 1976 season on 5 December 1975.[20] The regulations backed away from the earlier proposal to establish an overall quota. Instead, a quota was deferred until part way through the fishing year, to be imposed only if the estimated kill was projected to exceed 70% of the final estimated kill for 1975. The Service also backed away from a proposal to place observers on board 100% of the trips during 1976, in part because the Marine Mammal Commission did not think that full coverage was necessary, feasible, or worth the expenditure of time, effort, or money (National Marine Fisheries Service 1975). The Commission, which later became a proponent of full observer coverage, believed that reliable data on mortality levels could be obtained with something less than a 100% observer program, provided that a substantial portion of the fleet carried observers during the course of the season. The Service's regulations, however, required placement of observers on only 10% of the trips.

Judicial Response to Rulemakings

The Richey Decision

The house of cards that the National Marine Fisheries Service had built by regulating on the basis of the best available, and in many cases nonexistent, scientific information came crashing down on 11 May 1976, the day Judge Charles Richey issued his ruling in *Committee for Humane Legislation* v. *Richardson*.[21] As a threshold matter, Judge Richey determined that the Congress had enacted the Marine Mammal Protection Act for one basic purpose, "to provide marine mammals, especially porpoise, with necessary and extensive protection against man's activities."[22] After reviewing the legislative history of the Act, he concluded that "[t]he interests of the marine mammals come first under the statutory scheme, and the interests of the industry, important as they are, must be served only after protection of the animals is assured."[23] There was to be no balancing of these interests as the National Marine Fisheries Service and others had assumed.

The court then turned its eye to whether the agency had met its specific responsibilities under the Act with respect to the incidental take regulations. Again, Judge Richey found the legislative intent clear. He took to heart this statement made by Congressman Dingell, one of the primary architects of the Act, on the House floor during debate on the bill: "Before issuing any permit for the taking of a marine mammal the Secretary must first have it proven to his satisfaction that any taking is consistent with the purposes and policies of the act—that is to say, that taking will not be to the disadvantage of the animals concerned. If he cannot make that finding, he cannot issue a permit. It is that simple."[24] Reconciling the specific provisions of the Act with its more general declaration of policy, the judge equated the disadvantage test with the goal of maintaining marine mammal stocks at OSP: ". . . only by knowing whether the population level would be reduced to less-than-optimum level as a result of the taking could the agency determine whether such taking would be to the 'disadvantage' of the animals involved."[25] Henceforth, the Service would not be able to regulate incidental take on the basis of available, yet insufficient, information or even on a demonstration that existing stock levels would be unaffected by the take. Judge Richey proclaimed that an assessment of the effect of the authorized take relative to a stock's OSP level was the only standard permissible under the Act.

The judge then turned his attention to the specific mandate of the Act that each permit specify the number and kind of marine mammals authorized to be taken. Although the American Tunaboat Association had estimated a total dolphin mortality level for 1976, albeit without any discussion of whether that level would be to the disadvantage of the stocks, the Service had declined to impose any restriction on the numbers or species that could be taken. Again, it was clear to the court that the Service had breached its responsibility. The general permits needed to impose numerical limits on the marine mammals that could be taken, and those limits had to be stock-specific.

Judge Richey declared the incidental take regulations, the American Tunaboat Association's general permit, and the certificates of inclusion that had been issued to individual vessels under the permit to be void. He further enjoined the National Marine Fisheries Service from authorizing any such incidental taking until it complied with the Marine Mammal Protection Act's requirements as he had interpreted them.

It was the Richey decision that gave the needed teeth to the Marine Mammal Protection Act, making it an effective vehicle for conserving marine mammals. It was just this objective assessment of the statutory language and its intent that was needed to get implementation of the Act on track. The responsible regulatory agency apparently did not have the willingness or wherewithal to implement the statutory scheme on its own. Until the Richey decision, most of the other participants in the process also seemed content to work toward reducing incidental mortality without having first determined whether any mortality could be authorized.

Congress, too, seemed content to let matters proceed as they had. The responsible congressional committees knew full well that the Service had issued incidental take permits without knowing the OSP levels of the affected dolphin stocks or the effect of the take on those stocks. Yet, during oversight hearings in 1975 there had been no objections. By 1973 Congressman Dingell, who had spoken so forcefully about the statutory requirements just a year before, was saying that a "rule of reason" should be followed with respect to the incidental taking of dolphins such that fishing would not be brought to a halt (U.S. House 1974).

Even some environmental groups were willing to work toward improving the situation, rather than pushing for strict adherence to the law. The Environmental Defense Fund, a plaintiff-intervenor in the Committee for Humane Legislation lawsuit, proposed that the court adopt a middle ground, whereby a quota based on one-half of the estimated mortality for 1975 would be imposed in 1976, to be cut by half each succeeding year. The court praised the group's spirit of conciliation but rejected the proposal because it, too, lacked any assessment of the effect of the proposed take on the dolphin stocks.[26] The court also was unswayed by the argument that invalidating the permit would only worsen the situation by driving U.S. vessels to foreign flags. It was not in the court's purview to question the reasonableness of the law, merely to interpret what had been enacted. If, in fact, there were unintended consequences of the law, it was up to Congress to remedy the situation.

Appellate Review

The National Marine Fisheries Service and the tuna industry promptly appealed Judge Richey's decision and sought a stay of the effect of his ruling pending review by the appellate court. In support of its request for a stay, the Service indicated its intent to impose a quota of 78,000 dolphins for the 1976 season. In light of the potentially disastrous effect of the district court ruling on the tuna industry, the assurance that some limit on mortality would be in place, and the belief that the Service would quickly be able to obtain the necessary information for making OSP determinations, the court of appeals granted the stay. Regulations establishing the 78,000-dolphin quota and increasing the number of observers to be placed aboard tuna vessels were published on 11 June 1976.[27]

On 6 August 1976 the appellate court issued its ruling upholding Judge Richey's decision.[28] The court expressed concern that the Service was now indicating that it would take three to seven years to obtain scientifically valid estimates of OSP levels. The court could not countenance such a delay in achieving compliance with the Act, but it was willing to stay the effect of the ruling until the end of the year to cushion the impact on the tuna industry.

Despite the stay of the district court order, the Service estimated that the tuna fleet would reach the dolphin quota by 19 October and prohibited setting on dolphins for the remainder of 1976.[29] That prohibition was immediately challenged by a group of tunaboat owners.[30] The reviewing court granted a stay of the prohibition pending its review of the case and, after upholding the Service's action, granted another stay to provide time for an appeal of its ruling. The appellate court upheld the ruling and the prohibition went into effect.[31] During the three weeks that it had taken to resolve the matter, however, approximately 30,000 more dolphins had been killed.

Congressional Response

Congressional reaction to the Richey decision was also swift. Less than two weeks after the ruling, legislation had been introduced to overturn it, and hearings had been held. The leading bill, H.R. 13865, would have permitted fishing to continue under the existing permit through year's end. Thereafter, a bifurcated permitting process would have been implemented. For marine mammal stocks at or above OSP, the preexisting rulemaking procedures and standards would remain applicable. Incongruously, less rigorous, informal rulemaking would be used to authorize taking from depleted stocks and those of unknown status. Taking from a stock of unknown status could be authorized if it would not significantly diminish existing population levels. For those stocks determined to be below their OSPs, taking could be authorized if it would not prevent a depleted population from reaching its OSP. Such taking would be subject to regulations requiring the use of the best practical technology available. Although reported out by the House subcommittee, no further action to pass the bill was taken.

Rulemaking under the Richey Decision

The 1976–1977 Rulemaking

In the midst of this flurry of legal and legislative activity, the National Marine Fisheries Service was scrambling to compile the information it would need to promulgate incidental take regulations consistent with Judge Richey's order. Toward this end, the Service convened a workshop of 12 experts to review the status of dolphin stocks and grapple with the problem of applying the statutory definition of OSP to those stocks (Southwest Fisheries Center 1976). The participants identified 21 population stocks comprising 11 species of small cetaceans involved in the eastern tropical Pacific yellowfin tuna fishery and provided population estimates for each. More important, they developed a working definition of OSP that established the lower bound as the population level at which maximum net productivity is achieved. The participants concluded that the maximum net productivity (MNP) level for dolphins is likely to be somewhere between 50% and 70% of carrying capacity and that 60% would be a prudent approximation when information is not otherwise available to determine a stock's MNP level. Using estimates of annual kill, and what, at that time, was known about reproductive and natural mortality rates, the participants backcalculated to estimate the initial, "preexploitation" size of each population. OSP determinations were then made by comparing preexploitation and current population estimates. Using this methodology, the workshop participants estimated that eastern spinner, offshore spotted, and white-belly spinner (*Stenella longirostris*) dolphin stocks had been reduced, respectively, to 54, 64, and 76% of their preexploitation sizes. Other stocks were determined to have been affected by the tuna fishery to a lesser degree.

Relying heavily on the stock assessment workshop report, the National Marine Fisheries Service proposed regulations to govern incidental taking during 1977.[32] The Service proposed, among other things, the establishment of an allowable take limit for each species or stock, with an aggregate quota of 29,920, which for the first time took account of dolphin mortality incidental to foreign fleet operations. Inasmuch as foreign fleets were not subject to U.S. jurisdiction, any mortality attributable to their operations needed to be subtracted from the quota that could otherwise be issued to the U.S. fleet. Based on the workshop's determination that the eastern spinner dolphin was below its OSP, the Service proposed that no taking of this stock be allowed.

Although an adjudicatory hearing had been held on the proposed regulations, the administrative law judge had not issued a recommended decision by the end of 1976. When it became apparent that final regulations and a general permit might not be forthcoming for some time, tunaboat owners filed suit seeking to stay enforcement of the Marine Mammal Protection Act. Four days after the administrative law judge's decision had been issued, but before the National Marine Fisheries Service had taken final action, the district court granted the fishermen's request.[33] The court permitted fishing to resume subject to the gear and dolphin rescue requirements of the 1976 regulations and under an interim quota of 10,000 dolphins to be counted against the 1977 quota, when and if issued. The relief given the tuna fleet was short-lived, however, because the district court order was overturned on appeal the following month.[34]

Meanwhile, in response to the government's failure to promulgate timely regulations and to protest what many operators anticipated would be overly restrictive regulations, much of the U.S. fleet refused to go to sea. Their "strike" idled some 5,000 fishermen and cannery workers in the San Diego area and put considerable pressure on Congress to amend the Marine Mammal Protection Act.

The National Marine Fisheries Service published final regulations for 1977 on 1 March.[35] In several crucial respects, the Service deviated from the administrative law judge's recommendations. It rejected a recommendation that the lower bound of OSP be established at 50% of a stock's preexploitation size, opting instead for 60%. As a result, the Service found the eastern spinner dolphin to be depleted. Despite a determination that up to 6,600 eastern spinners could be taken while still providing a "virtual certainty" that the stock would increase, the Service determined that the depletion finding precluded authorization of any level of take. In an effort to tailor the available science to the rulemaking process, the Service used a sliding scale of confidence intervals in setting quotas, depending on the status of the stock. For the offshore spotted dolphin, which was considered to be at 64% of its preexploitation level, the Service opted to establish a take level midway between that which would provide "reasonable confidence" (97.5% confidence) and "virtual certainty" (99.9% confidence) that the stock would not be disadvantaged. As a result, the 64,393 quota recommended by the administrative law judge for this most commonly taken species, which was derived using midpoint estimates, was reduced to 43,090. Using the higher value for the MNP level and a statistically based approach for establishing quotas, the aggregate quota established in the final regulations was 59,050, as opposed to the 96,100 total recommended by the administrative law judge.

The 1977 regulations also imposed new gear requirements designed to reduce dolphin mortality, including the requirement that purse seiners carry and use a rubber raft from which dolphins submerged in a net could be observed. This requirement stemmed, in part, from the research conducted aboard the *Elizabeth C. J.*, during which encircled dolphins were observed engaging in "sleeping" behavior. If the net is retrieved before these dolphins rise for air, they become entangled and suffocate. However, by stationing observers equipped with face masks in a raft to spot these dolphins, the backdown configuration can be maintained until the dolphins surface and can be released. Another noteworthy feature of the 1977 regulations was the establishment of an expert skipper's panel, which replaced the informal workshops held by the American Tunaboat Association. The skipper's panel was tasked with identifying poor performers in the fleet and recommending corrective actions that should be taken to reduce excessive dolphin mortality.

Judicial Review

After issuance of the regulations, the Committee for Humane Legislation filed suit, alleging that they were defective in several ways. Among other things, the plaintiffs asserted that the Service had violated the law by establishing a quota only for dolphin mortality and not for other forms of taking,[36] such as chase and encirclement. The matter once again came before Judge Richey, who this time upheld the validity of both the regulations and the permit.[37] A lawsuit was also filed by the American Tunaboat Association and other members of the tuna industry challenging the regulations as overly restrictive. That case, however, was dismissed when the American Tunaboat Association failed to pursue the matter.

Congressional Reaction

A number of bills were introduced in Congress in April and May 1977 to provide relief to the tuna industry. One of these, H.R. 6970, would have increased the total dolphin quota to 78,000, including an eastern spinner dolphin quota of 6,500.

A counterpart bill in the Senate would have increased the overall quota to 69,000, but with the additional requirement that dolphin mortality be reduced by 50% by 1980 and by an additional 50% every two years thereafter. That bill also would have restricted transfers of U.S. tuna vessels to foreign flags.

An amended version of H.R. 6970, which would have established a quota of 68,910, restricted transfers of U.S. vessels, and mandated a 100% observer program, was passed by the House of Representatives on 1 June. By that time, however, the issue was no longer perceived as a crisis. Most tuna vessels had returned to sea. More important, the National Marine Fisheries Service had adopted an enforcement policy under which it would not prosecute any "accidental" take of eastern spinner dolphins as a violation of the Act.[38] In light of the changed circumstances, the Senate took no action to amend the Act and H.R. 6970 died a quiet death.

In part because vessels had remained in port during the first part of the year, dolphin mortality for 1977 dropped dramatically to less than 26,000. This heralded a turning point for the U.S. fleet, which never again approached the massive dolphin mortalities that characterized the fishery in previous years. Although the significant reduction in incidental mortality resulted from several factors (e.g., widespread use of and increasing familiarity with dolphin-saving fishing techniques, development of gear modifications, a decrease in the number of U.S. vessels, etc.), the specter of the Richey decision no doubt motivated fishermen to take dolphin conservation more seriously.

The 1977 Rulemaking

In what must have seemed to the involved parties as a never-ending treadmill of rulemaking and litigation, the Service began gearing up for the next round with the publication of proposed regulations in July 1977 for the forthcoming fishing season.[39] Unlike its previous endeavors, the Service proposed quotas to cover the next three years. After convening the required hearing before an administrative law judge, the Service issued final regulations establishing quotas of 51,945 for 1978, 41,610 for 1979, and 31,150 for 1980.[40] The Service determined that it would be contrary to the Act's zero mortality and serious injury rate goal to establish constant annual quotas if lower quotas were economically and technologically achievable. Also, for the first time, specific quotas were established for total take and encirclement. The only significant change to the gear provisions was the requirement that the "super-apron" system, developed under the Service's gear research program, be installed in purse seine nets.

As it had the previous year, the Service determined the eastern spinner dolphin to be depleted. It again eased the impact of the problem by continuing to follow its accidental-take policy. This time, however, the Service considered employing statistical methodology for making depletion determinations. The Service calculated the probability that the population was depleted from the range of the estimated initial population size and the range of possible lower bounds of OSP. Using this technique, the Service determined that, more likely than not, the population was within its OSP. Even using the more traditional approach, it appeared that the stock was inching toward its MNP level. The Service projected that by 1980 the eastern spinner dolphin stock would be at 58% of its preexploitation size.

Operation under the Three-Year Permit

In comparison with earlier years, the tuna fleet operated rather serenely under the new regulations, achieving record low incidental dolphin mortality each of the three years. Nevertheless, an exodus of U.S. vessels to other fleets that had begun in 1976 continued (Fig. 6-4). During 1978–1980, 13 U.S. purse seiners reregistered under foreign flags. Although a desire to avoid regulation under U.S. law may have been a contributing factor in some of these transfers, it appears that economic factors were the primary impetus for the shift in U.S. fishing vessels and canning operations overseas (Sakagawa 1991).

Research was also progressing on several fronts. Most important, the tuna industry made available to scientists a vessel dedicated completely to research efforts, and the National Marine Fisheries Service endeavored to refine its estimates of the status of dolphin stocks.

The Dedicated Vessel Program

The Marine Mammal Commission and the National Marine Fisheries Service cosponsored a workshop early in 1977 to review results from the previous year's research program, including preliminary results from work done aboard the *Elizabeth C. J.*, and to chart the direction of future research (Ralston 1977).

For some time, the Commission and the Service, along with the environmental community, had been advocating that the tuna industry provide a dedicated research vessel. Although tuna seiners had provided valuable platforms for conducting research, in most instances, research efforts were secondary to catching tuna (DeBeer 1980). Moreover, many research projects simply could not be accomplished without seriously interfering with normal fishing operations. Therefore, workshop participants were directed to assume that a dedicated vessel would be available as they mapped out a research strategy (Ralston 1977).

The United States Tuna Foundation agreed to charter a

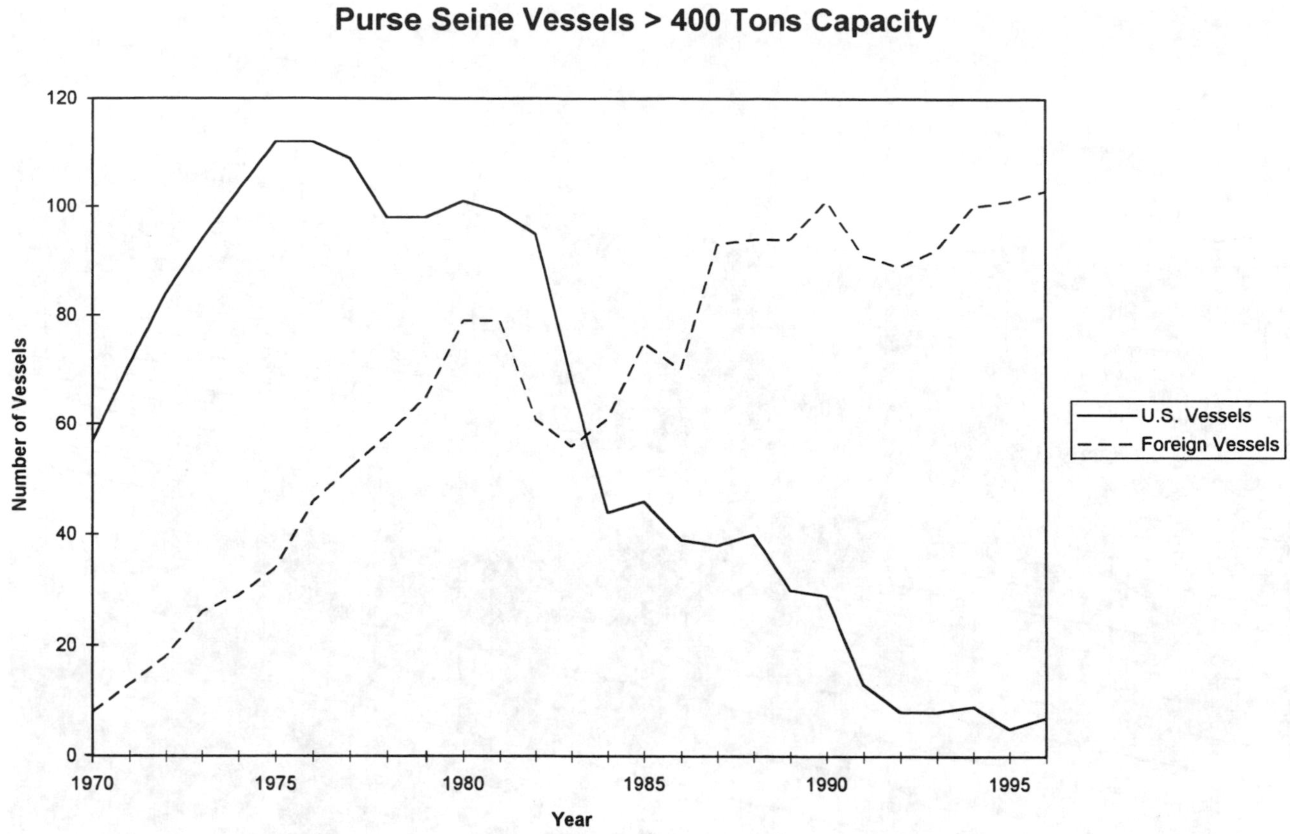

Figure 6-4. At its peak in the mid-1970s, the U.S. fleet dominated the eastern tropical Pacific purse seine fishery. As U.S. vessels transferred to foreign flags and moved to the western Pacific, the U.S. role in the fishery steadily declined. The exodus of the U.S. fleet has largely been offset by an increase in the number of foreign vessels. It is possible, however, that under the 1997 amendments to the Marine Mammal Protection Act some U.S. vessels may return to the fishery. (Data provided by the Inter-American Tropical Tuna Commission)

purse seine vessel, the M/V *Queen Mary,* for calendar year 1978 to be dedicated to research activities (Fig. 6-5). The Tuna Foundation, the Marine Mammal Commission, and the National Marine Fisheries Service signed a cooperative research agreement on 30 December 1977 to formalize responsibilities and to set forth the conditions under which the research program would be conducted. Five research cruises were made aboard the dedicated vessel involving 32 scientists from 10 organizations. Each cruise focused on a different aspect of the tuna-dolphin problem (e.g., mortality reduction, alternative fishing methods, stock assessment, and the tuna-dolphin bond). Although the program did not produce any short-term breakthroughs in reducing dolphin mortality, participants believed that they had achieved significant results that could have long-term importance (DeBeer 1980).

Status of Stocks

In 1977 the National Marine Fisheries Service conducted a second, more extensive aerial survey of the eastern tropical Pacific to obtain better information on dolphin distribution and abundance than it had been able to collect in 1974 (Holt and Powers 1982). However, the use of different aircraft to conduct the two surveys made comparisons of the estimates of stock sizes problematic. The Service therefore conducted a third aerial survey in 1979 to try to resolve this problem (Holt and Powers 1982). After completion of that survey, the Service convened a second status-of-stocks workshop in preparation for the rulemaking for the 1981 and subsequent fishing seasons. The workshop findings were potentially disastrous for the U.S. tuna industry (Holt and Powers 1982). The estimated abundances of the affected dolphin stocks were substantially lower than those estimated in 1976. The workshop report cautioned, however, that the reductions should not be construed as indicating large decreases in stock size since 1976 (Smith 1979). Rather, they were almost certainly the result of improved estimation procedures and better data.

The most significant conclusion was that the northern offshore spotted dolphin was at only 34 to 55% of its pre-exploitation population size, and therefore depleted (Smith 1979). Thus, no incidental take of this stock could be

Figure 6-5. These eastern spinner dolphins were caught during one of the cruises of the dedicated research vessel, the M/V *Queen Mary.* Studies of specimens such as these provided valuable life history information that was used by the National Marine Fisheries Service in its assessments of the status of eastern tropical Pacific dolphin stocks. (Photograph courtesy of National Marine Fisheries Service)

authorized despite the fact that approximately 70 to 80% of the yellowfin tuna caught by setting "on porpoise" in the eastern tropical Pacific had historically been taken in sets on this stock (Inter-American Tropical Tuna Commission 1989).

The workshop participants also reexamined the estimate of the MNP level for small cetaceans. They concluded that earlier estimates had relied too heavily on data from small mammals and that, for larger mammals like dolphins, the MNP level was probably between 60 to 85% of carrying capacity. The participants recommended that the midpoint of this estimate, 72.5%, be used as the lower bound of OSP for dolphins (Smith 1979).

The 1980 Rulemaking

Consistent with the workshop findings, the Service published proposed regulations on 15 February 1980 that would have determined the northern offshore spotted and eastern spinner dolphins to be depleted and prohibited any taking from these stocks.[41] Under the proposed rule, the incidental-take policy would remain in force for eastern spinner dolphins but would not be extended to northern offshore spotted dolphins. Any taking from this stock would be considered intentional because northern offshore spotted dolphins occur only in pure or mixed schools in which they are the primary component. They do not occur as occasional individuals mixed with schools of other species. The Service also proposed to prohibit "sundown sets" (those that cannot be completed before darkness falls), in which higher than average mortality occurs. The Service proposed that the new regulations be applicable for the remainder of 1980 and for 1981. The decision not to propose regulations for a longer period was based on the assumption that, if sets on northern offshore spotted dolphins were prohibited, most of the effort would likely shift to sets on dolphin stocks that had not been fished on extensively in the past. It was feared that such a shift would have unforeseen but possibly serious consequences if dolphins with little exposure to encirclement and backdown procedures were more prone to panic and entanglement than were "experienced" dolphins.

Lengthy hearings were held on the proposed regulations. By far the most contentious issue was the status of the northern offshore spotted dolphin. The administrative law judge presiding at those hearings issued a recommended decision in mid-July. Although the decision addressed the methodology and information base that should be used to make status-of-stocks determinations, it made no specific recommendation as to the status of the northern offshore spotted dolphin. The administrative law judge did, however, take issue with many of the findings of the 1979 workshop, chastising the National Marine Fisheries Service for its "rush to judgment" on the underlying science. In particular, the administrative law judge believed that the methodology for making status determinations simply was not appropriate in the context of formal rulemaking if it "can only be comprehended by a small band of [the Service's] population dynamicists . . ." (Dolan 1980:95).

The recommended decision also concluded that the proposal to use 60 to 85% of a stock's preexploitation size as the MNP level was not adequately supported. In deferring to the 50 to 70% level used in earlier rulemakings, the administrative law judge seemed to afford it the status of legal precedent, noting that any changes should be based on empirical data rather than on revised theories of population dynamics. It did not seem to matter to the administrative law judge that the earlier estimates had no more, and perhaps less, scientific basis.

The administrative law judge's recommended decision also addressed the possible implications of a depletion finding for northern offshore spotted dolphins. He found the Service's proposal "economically disastrous" to the U.S. tuna industry and speculated that dolphin mortality would increase as other dolphin stocks were targeted and foreign vessels entered the fishery. The administrative law judge went so far as to recommend that the Department of Commerce sponsor legislation to remedy the situation if a determination were made that the stock was depleted. One can only speculate as to the extent to which the administrative law judge's views regarding the underlying science were influenced by a desire to avoid the anticipated adverse effects of the Service's proposal.

The administrative law judge, having dodged the key question of the status of the northern offshore spotted dolphin, left the Administrator of the National Oceanic and Atmospheric Administration, the agency decision maker, with plenty of room to maneuver—and maneuver he did. Although the Administrator agreed with the theoretical approach for establishing MNP levels adopted at the 1979 workshop, he opted for the 60% figure, as recommended by the administrative law judge, noting that the International Whaling Commission used 60% of carrying capacity as a threshold value in its management of large whale exploitation.[42] Further, the Administrator agreed with arguments made by the American Tunaboat Association that, in allocating the historic kill, the workshop participants had not accounted for the gradual westward movement of the fleet's operations since the early 1960s. Thus, the Administrator concluded, workshop participants had overestimated the historic take of northern offshore spotted dolphins by some 1.3 million and underestimated the historic take of coastal spotted dolphins by 670,000. Based on this reapportionment, the Administrator determined that the northern offshore spotted dolphin stock was at 63% of its preexploitation level and therefore not depleted. The reapportionment, however, resulted in a determination that the coastal spotted dolphin was at 27% of its initial population level and therefore depleted. Consequently, taking from this stock, as well as the depleted eastern spinner dolphin stock, was prohibited. Nevertheless, the potentially catastrophic consequences to the tuna industry of a prohibition on encirclement of northern offshore spotted dolphins were averted.

The Administrator applied the incidental take rate for the most recent three-year period to the highest annual tuna catch during that period and concluded that it was economically and technologically feasible for the tuna industry to operate within a quota of 22,320 dolphin mortalities per year. This figure was further reduced in proportion to the percentage of operations involving sundown sets, which were prohibited under the final regulations,[43] to arrive at an overall quota of 20,500 per year for 1981 through 1985. However, had the Administrator taken into account that the mortality rate for sundown sets is higher than for daytime sets, the adjustment in the quota would have been larger. Unlike the previous rulemaking, there was no ratcheting down of the quota over the five-year period for which the regulations were valid.

Ensuing Litigation

Two lawsuits promptly followed issuance of the regulations. Friends of Animals and the Committee for Humane Legislation challenged the decisions not to designate the northern offshore spotted dolphin as depleted and not to establish a declining quota, which they contended was required by the Act's zero mortality rate goal. The reviewing court upheld the regulations, noting that particular deference must be given to the agency's decisions regarding technical and scientific matters.[44]

The American Tunaboat Association challenged the regulations as being too restrictive. It argued that the Administrator had improperly rejected the administrative law judge's recommendations concerning mean school size, density, and the range of dolphin stocks, the parameters that had been used to estimate dolphin abundance. In particular, the plaintiffs argued that the Administrator had arbitrarily declined to use data collected by industry and government observers on board fishing vessels. He had discounted these data as being biased by the tendency of fishing vessels to target large dolphin schools and the inability of untrained industry observers to estimate school size accurately. The judge in this case did not give the same deference to the agency's scientific expertise as had the judge in *Friends of Animals* and directed the Service to submit recalculations of the density, size, and ranges of dolphin schools and revised status determinations based on those new figures.[45] The lower court's decision was upheld on appeal.[46] However, these decisions merely required the Service to submit recalculations based on revised assumptions. They did not mandate that the quotas established in 1980 be revised. Nevertheless, the ruling added another arrow to the tuna industry's quiver as it prepared for the 1985 rulemaking.

A third lawsuit, filed by the tuna industry just before issuance of the final regulations, challenged the statutory and Constitutional authority of the National Marine Fisheries Service to use information gathered by observers for purposes of enforcing the quotas and other provisions of the applicable regulations.[47] The district court agreed with the tuna industry. It ruled that observers could be placed on board tuna vessels to gather scientific information but that, absent explicit statutory authority, the use of observer data for enforcement purposes violated the Fourth Amendment. The reviewing appellate court went even further, finding that the mandatory placement of observers on board tuna vessels for any purpose was impermissible unless specifically authorized by Congress.[48] Obviously, both the regulatory and scientific integrity of the tuna-dolphin program would be put in jeopardy if the on-board observer program were abolished. The federal government therefore petitioned the court of appeals to have the matter reconsidered by an en banc panel.[49] Although such petitions are rarely granted, the court decided to convene a panel in this instance. The panel determined that the Marine Mammal Protection Act conferred broad rulemaking authority to the agency, implicitly authorizing the observer program.[50] Inasmuch as the program was reasonably related to the Act's purpose of protecting and conserving marine mammals and was the only practical way to enforce the established take limits, the panel reversed the earlier rulings and allowed the government to place observers on board tuna vessels for both scientific and enforcement purposes.

1981 Amendments to the Marine Mammal Protection Act

Among several amendments to the Marine Mammal Protection Act enacted in 1981, two were geared specifically to the eastern tropical Pacific tuna fishery. Despite its success in reducing dolphin mortality and in securing an incidental take permit in the 1980 rulemaking, the tuna industry remained concerned that its operations might be vulnerable to challenge as running afoul of the Act's zero mortality rate goal. In response, Congress amended section 101(a)(2) of the Act to specify that the goal of reducing fishery-related mortality and serious injury of marine mammals to levels approaching zero "shall be satisfied in the case of the incidental taking of marine mammals in the course of purse seine fishing for yellowfin tuna by a continuation of the application of the best marine mammal safety techniques and equipment that are economically and technologically practicable."

The second amendment added specific language directing the Secretary of Commerce to undertake or to fund research into new methods of locating and catching yellowfin tuna not involving the incidental taking of dolphins. Among other things, Congress believed that research into fish-aggregating devices should be pursued.[51]

Shortly before enactment of these amendments, the Marine Mammal Commission, in cooperation with the Inter-American Tropical Tuna Commission and the National Marine Fisheries Service, had convened a workshop to consider research into alternative means of catching tuna that did not rely on setting on dolphins (Hofman 1981). Workshop participants noted that widespread use of dolphin-saving fishing techniques within the U.S. fleet had brought the kill rate down to about 3.8 dolphins per set. They believed that "little if any further improvement in existing fishing gear and practices may be technically or economically feasible" and suggested that any further reduction in incidental kill or injury may require development of an alternative to the practice of encircling dolphins. Three different lines of possible research were suggested: (1) developing a means for separating tuna from dolphins before encirclement, (2) developing technology capable of detecting and catching large yellowfin tuna when they are not associated with dolphins, and (3) using fishing gear other than purse seines. Although workshop participants believed that all of these areas of research merited attention, they recognized that several years of intensive effort would likely be needed to determine whether any might produce a useful alternative.

Despite the directive of the 1981 amendments and the identification of several possible lines of investigation, little research into alternative fishing methods was undertaken. First, in the wake of the 1980 rulemaking, the National Marine Fisheries Service had set as its top research priority improving the quality of survey data and refining the methodology used to determine the status of stocks. Second, the 1980 presidential election had resulted in a shift away from research into gear modifications and alternative fishing methods not requiring the encirclement of dolphins. Shortly after the Reagan Administration assumed the reins of government, it moved to dismantle the gear research program altogether.

1984 Amendments to the Marine Mammal Protection Act

In 1983 the National Marine Fisheries Service prepared to consider extension of the American Tunaboat Association's incidental take permit. Its preliminary analyses indicated that the northern offshore spotted dolphin was substantially below its MNP level. Thus, the Service intended, once again, to propose that no taking from this stock be authorized. Also posing a problem was the fact that estimates of incidental take resulting from the operations of the growing foreign purse seine fleet were highly uncertain. Although the Inter-American Tropical Tuna Commission had agreed in 1977 to establish an international tuna-dolphin research and observer program, only extremely low levels of coverage were achieved until 1986 (Joseph 1994, Hall 1998).

During oversight hearings in 1984 Congress explored the difficulties with the existing system for authorizing the incidental take of dolphins (U.S. House 1984). The Committee on Merchant Marine and Fisheries concluded that the process remained as lengthy and as complex as when the level of take was many times greater. The Committee recognized that the method for determining the status of stocks might work well if precise estimates of historic and current population sizes were available. However, because of the paucity of historic data and the technical difficulties in accurately estimating stock levels over a vast area of ocean, better estimates would be difficult or impossible to obtain. All parties concerned were coming to the realization that they had crafted a system based on exacting legal standards that were unrealistic, given the imprecision of the available scientific information.

Concern was voiced about the growing impact of foreign purse seine operations in the eastern tropical Pacific. At its height in the mid-1970s, the U.S. fleet had consisted of 112 large purse seine vessels and accounted for about 75% of the fishery capacity (unpublished data, Inter-American Tropical Tuna Commission). By 1984 the U.S. fleet operating in the eastern tropical Pacific contained only 44 large seiners, and the U.S. share of the fishery capacity had fallen to 42% (Inter-American Tropical Tuna Commission 1994) (see Fig. 6-4). With this shift in the fishery, it was likely that the gains made by the United States in reducing dolphin mortality were being offset by high incidental mortality among non-U.S. vessels (Fig. 6-6).

In response to these concerns, Congress amended the Marine Mammal Protection Act in three fundamental ways.[52] First, the amendments extended the American Tunaboat Association's 1980 general permit for an indefinite period, obviating the need for periodic rulemakings. The overall quota of 20,500 was retained, and quotas of 2,750 for eastern spinner dolphins and 250 for coastal spotted dolphins were added. Second, Congress tightened the comparability requirements applicable to countries that export yellowfin tuna to the United States. Evidence now had to be submitted showing that the government had adopted a regulatory program comparable with that of the United States and that the average rate of incidental take for the nation's fleet was comparable to that achieved by U.S. vessels. Third, the amendments directed a shift away from a research program designed to estimate absolute numbers of dolphins and make status determinations to one that would monitor "indices of abundance and trends" in the dolphin populations. The monitoring program was to last a minimum of five years. It would provide the basis for amending the incidental mortality quotas if it were determined that the level of take was having "a significant adverse effect" on any population.

Although the 1984 amendments had obviated the need for periodic, contentious status determinations and rulemakings, life under the amendments was not tranquil. Incidental take estimates for the first quarter of 1986 suggested that the overall quota for dolphin mortality and serious injury would be reached before the end of the year. By 29 June, the National Marine Fisheries Service estimated, dolphin mortality for the year had already reached 17,729. Among the factors possibly contributing to the high mortality were an increased number of sets on dolphins and a record high tuna catch rate of about 25 tons of tuna per set (Fig. 6-7). Large schools of tuna may tend to associate with large schools of dolphins and, therefore, more dolphins may have been encircled than in previous years. Whatever the reason, there was an unusually large number of sets with high dolphin mortality.

The Service responded to the high mortality rate by increasing observer coverage and by assessing mortality on a weekly, rather than biweekly, basis. The increased observer coverage resulted in more accurate tracking of dolphin mortality, but also had the anomalous effect of lowering the year-to-date estimated kill. On 20 July the Service estimated

Sets on Dolphins

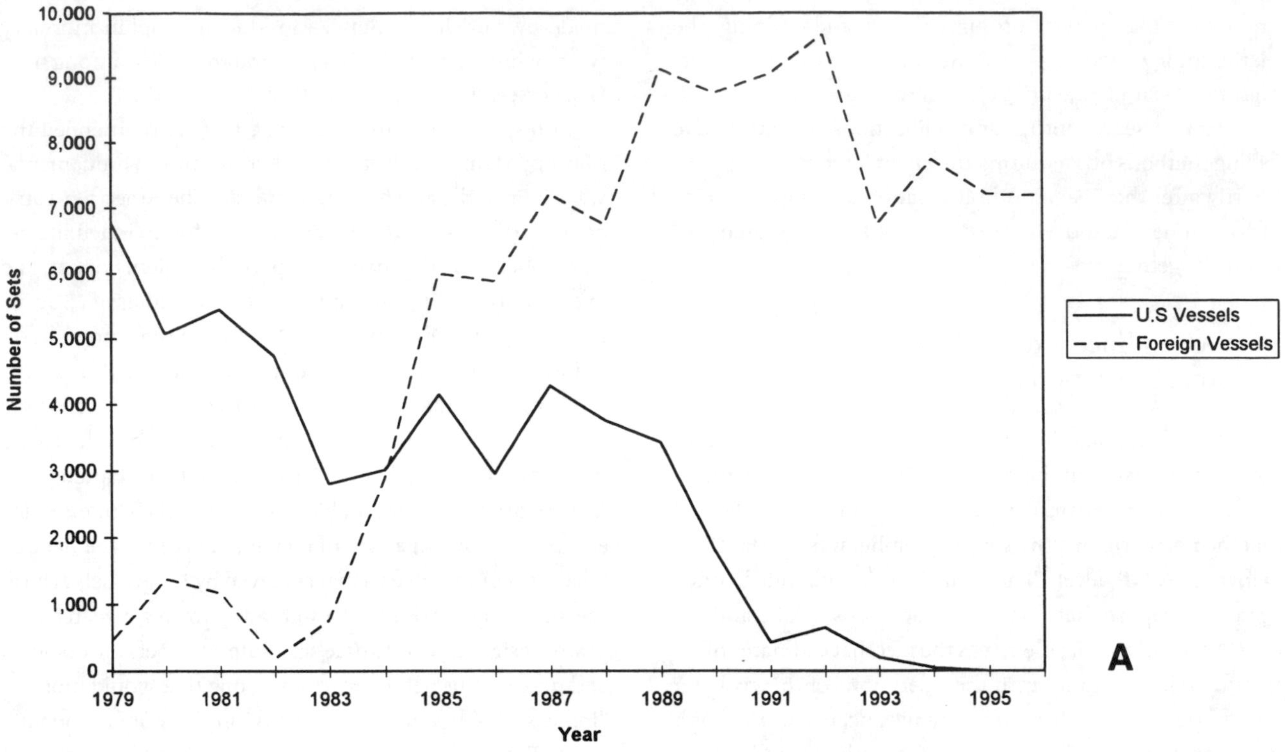

Dolphin Mortality Rates

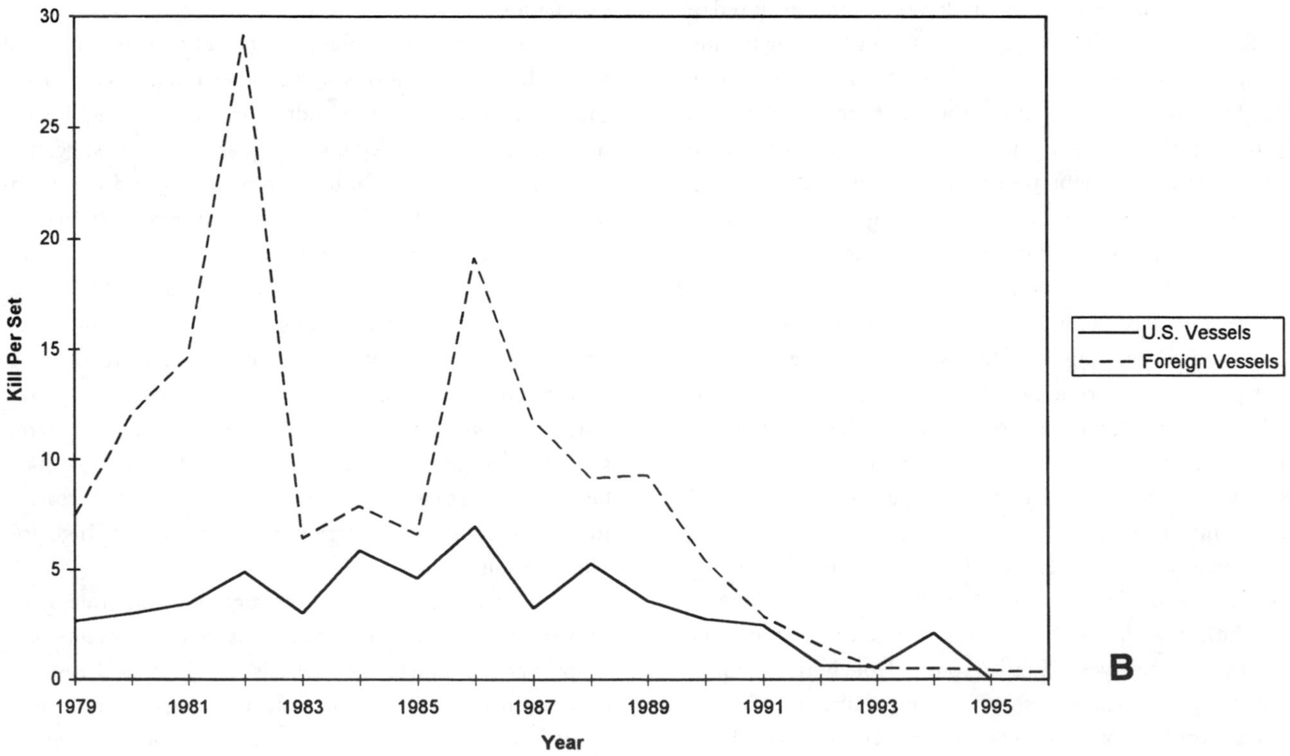

Figure 6-7. This dead spotted dolphin, brought on board with the catch, is being separated from a small portion of the roughly 20 tons of large yellowfin tuna typically caught in a set on dolphins. Large tuna catches have been associated with higher dolphin mortality. (Photograph courtesy of National Marine Fisheries Service)

dolphin mortality for the year to be only 16,438, nearly 1,300 fewer dolphins than its estimate three weeks earlier. As it continued to monitor dolphin mortality, the Service projected that the quota of 20,500 dolphins would be reached on 21 October 1986 and, as of that date, closed the fishery for the remainder of the year. An exception was made for any U.S. vessel voluntarily carrying an observer to verify that no further sets on dolphins were made.

Neither the environmental community nor the tuna industry was pleased with the closure. As Greenpeace observed, the "resurrection of the dolphins" that had occurred after the increase in observer coverage "had the convenient result of forestalling the closure by four months" (Scheele and Wilkinson 1988). In contrast, the tuna industry believed that the methodology used by the Service to track incidental mortality tended to overestimate the number of dolphins taken and argued that the fishery had been closed prematurely.

Tuna fishermen advocated that a new method of estimating mortality be adopted and that the Service increase observer coverage to 100%. Environmental groups, who long had theorized that fishermen behave differently when an observer is present and, therefore, that observer data underestimate the fleet-wide dolphin mortality rate, also supported an increase in observer coverage. The Service responded by agreeing to review its methodology for estimating dolphin mortality and establishing a target of 100% observer coverage throughout the 1987 fishing season.

Some tuna industry representatives asserted that, if the dolphin quota had been exceeded in 1986, it was because a small number of vessels in the fleet had exceptionally high kill rates. They believed that the operators of those vessels lacked either the skill or the motivation to achieve low dolphin mortality and requested that the Service establish performance standards to keep poor operators from penalizing the remainder of the fleet. When draft performance standards were circulated early in 1987, however, the American Tunaboat Association voiced strong opposition, stating that "there is no significant, widespread skipper performance problem in the fleet that supports the complicated and financially burdensome regulatory process" envisioned by the Service. Instead, it recommended that the existing expert skipper's panel be used to address the problems of high mortality sets and underperforming operators.

Overall dolphin mortality attributable to the U.S. fleet dropped sharply in 1987. The take of eastern spinner dolphins, however, was unusually high and the fleet risked closure of all or a part of the fishery as it flirted with exceeding the quota for that stock. Mortality of eastern spinner dolphins was again high in 1988. Although the fleet exceeded the stock-specific quota in 1988, it did not do so until the final reporting period for the year. Thus, no closure occurred.

Figure 6-6. (*facing*) (*A*) It is not surprising, given the shifts in the fishery, that the number of dolphin sets by the U.S. fleet has declined over the past 15 years, while the number of dolphin sets by foreign vessels has increased. What is surprising is the fact that the number of dolphin sets by the foreign fleet has remained relatively stable at about 7,000 to 9,000 per year, despite the promotion by the United States of dolphin-safe fishing methods. (Based on data provided by the Inter-American Tropical Tuna Commission and the National Marine Fisheries Service) (*B*) The significant decline in dolphin mortality over the past decade has been attributable largely to improved performance by the fleet, rather than a reduction in fishing effort. Dolphin mortality per set declined by more than 95% over that period. (Based on data provided by the Inter-American Tropical Tuna Commission and the National Marine Fisheries Service)

Following enactment of the 1984 amendments, dolphin mortality resulting from foreign fleet operations soared, climbing to over 100,000 in 1986 (Table 6-1). Despite the strengthened comparability requirements applicable to foreign-caught tuna, however, no new embargoes were imposed. In fact, an embargo against Mexican tuna imposed in 1981, when Mexico failed to provide updated information for making a comparability finding, was lifted by the National Marine Fisheries Service in 1986 based on pre-1984 regulatory criteria.

1988 Amendments to the Marine Mammal Protection Act

Legislative Background

In 1988, during hearings on reauthorization of the Marine Mammal Protection Act, considerable criticism was leveled at the 1984 amendments and at the lack of progress by the National Marine Fisheries Service in implementing them. Greenpeace contended that the indefinite extension of the 1981 quota was contrary to the zero mortality rate goal of the Act (Scheele and Wilkinson 1988). Further, Greenpeace argued that it was unjustified to allow the U.S. fleet, which they said numbered 34 vessels in 1986, to operate under a quota promulgated when the fleet comprised more than 90 vessels. Environmental groups were also critical of steps taken by the Service to downgrade certain gear requirements to nonenforceable guidelines. Further, it was becoming apparent that the Service's monitoring program was capable of detecting only very large changes in dolphin abundance. To determine with acceptable certainty (i.e., at the 90% probability level) that dolphins were being adversely affected by incidental mortality, an annual decrease of about 10% would have had to occur for at least five years (Holt et al. 1987).

The heaviest criticism, however, was aimed at the failure to address adequately the problem of dolphin kill by foreign fleets. The National Marine Fisheries Service had acted slowly to implement the comparability requirements of the 1984 amendments. When it ultimately published interim final regulations, nearly four years after the amendments had been enacted and just weeks before the first scheduled reauthorization hearing, the measures of comparability were lenient and complex.[53] For example, estimates of kill rates would depend on the area fished and the number of observed trips for each fleet. Moreover, the Service decided not to base tuna import bans on kill rate comparisons until 1991, provided a nation's kill rate maintained a negative trend.

More important, the extent of the problem with respect to foreign-caused mortality was finally coming to light. For the first time, enough observers were being placed on board foreign purse seiners to provide statistically reliable estimates, and the figures released by the Inter-American Tropical Tuna Commission caused alarm (Inter-American Tropical Tuna Commission 1988). The Tuna Commission estimated that 112,482 dolphins were killed by the foreign fleet in 1986 and 85,185 in 1987. The nature of the kill was vividly brought home in video footage taken by Sam LaBudde, an environmental activist working undercover, who had signed on aboard a Panamanian purse seiner in 1987 (Brower 1989). The video, which was aired on national television, graphically depicted numerous, inhumane dolphin deaths.

Domestic Requirements

In enacting amendments in 1988, Congress effectively crossed over from its role as legislator to that of regulator. Rather than defer to the expertise of the Executive Branch agency (the National Marine Fisheries Service) to work out the nuts and bolts of implementation as it had in the past, Congress set forth explicit and exacting standards to be met by U.S. tuna fishermen and those foreign fishermen seeking access to the U.S. market. Sundown sets were prohibited except for skippers who could demonstrate a history of low dolphin mortality in such sets. Beginning with the 1989 season, 100% observer coverage was required on board the U.S. fleet. The use of explosives other than seal bombs[54] to herd dolphins was prohibited, and the use of seal bombs was to be discontinued unless a study to be conducted by the National Marine Fisheries Service demonstrated that these devices were not harmful to dolphins. The Service was to establish performance standards to identify skippers whose dolphin mortality rates were consistently and substantially higher than average. Problem skippers would be given supplemental training, but if high mortality rates persisted, their certificates of inclusion would be suspended or revoked. Congress, recognizing that little had been done to investigate alternative means of catching large yellowfin tuna, directed the Service to contract with the National Academy of Sciences for an independent review of alternative fishing techniques that did not involve the incidental taking of marine mammals (See National Research Council 1992).

Foreign Comparability

The amendments also prescribed the elements that must be part of a comparable foreign program. Congress specified that a foreign fleet's incidental mortality rate would be considered comparable only if it did not exceed twice that of the

U.S. fleet during 1989 and was not more than 1.25 times the U.S. rate in subsequent years. Limits on the take of eastern spinner and coastal spotted dolphins were also established.[55] As a way of preventing "tuna laundering," the amendments restricted imports from third-party countries that imported yellowfin tuna from countries subject to direct U.S. tuna embargoes. The amendments also directed that a comparable foreign program achieve observer coverage equal to that for the U.S. fleet (i.e., 100%) unless the National Marine Fisheries Service determined that lesser coverage would "provide sufficiently reliable documentary evidence of the [nation's] average rate of incidental taking." The National Marine Fisheries Service exercised its discretion under this provision to specify that 33% coverage would be sufficient during 1989.[56] For 1990 acceptable coverage for large fleets remained at 33%, but coverage for fleets of fewer than 10 vessels needed to be increased to 50%.[57] In part, because of institutional difficulties in expanding the international observer program, observer coverage throughout the international fleet did not approach 100% until 1992.

Reluctant Implementation

Despite explicit direction from Congress, the National Marine Fisheries Service continued to seek ways around the Act's requirements, at times seeming to go out of its way to avoid embargoing tuna from other nations. The opening salvo of protracted litigation to force compliance was prompted by the Service's announcement that it lacked sufficient funding to place observers aboard all U.S. vessels during 1989. Earth Island Institute sought and obtained a temporary restraining order mandating that no certificated U.S. tuna vessel could depart on a fishing trip or set on dolphins without an observer unless the court had determined that, for reasons beyond the control of the Secretary of Commerce, an observer was not available.[58]

Subsequently, Earth Island Institute challenged comparability findings then in effect for several nations. The plaintiffs contended that, as of 1 January 1990, the Service was required to embargo tuna from any country that had not demonstrated that its dolphin kill rate was no more than twice that of the U.S. fleet. The National Marine Fisheries Service countered that the comparability findings had to be based on data from the entire 1989 season and could not be made until after the end of July, when complete data were available and had been analyzed. The court found that the statute did not afford such latitude and ordered tuna embargoes to be imposed against all yellowfin tuna caught by foreign fleets in the eastern tropical Pacific pending the required findings.[59] The court noted, however, that, although findings with respect to the taking of eastern spinner and coastal spotted dolphins must be based on data from a full calendar year, the mortality rate comparability findings did not.

The court-ordered embargo of all tuna caught by foreign purse seiners in the eastern tropical Pacific went into effect on 6 September 1990. The following day, however, the Service completed its review of 1989 dolphin mortality data submitted by three countries and, based on those data, lifted the embargoes applicable to Venezuela and Vanuatu.[60] Mexico presented a stickier problem. Data from 1989 showed a mortality rate 2.39 times that of the United States and an impermissibly high take of eastern spinner dolphins. Anticipating that a comparability finding could not be made based on its 1989 performance, Mexico also submitted data for the first eight months of 1990, seeking reconsideration based on its more recent performance. Despite its earlier argument that making comparability findings required considerable time, the Service, just 10 days after the court's decision, was able to issue an affirmative comparability determination for Mexico based on this new information.[61] The court-ordered embargo of Mexican tuna had remained in effect for less than a single day.

Earth Island Institute promptly challenged the lifting of the embargo of Mexican tuna. The environmental organization claimed that the stricter 1.25 multiplier must be applied to a comparability finding based on 1990 data. Further, plaintiffs contended that failure to meet the eastern spinner quota in 1989 could only be corrected by meeting the standard for the entirety of 1990. The district court found that the 2.0 multiplier remained in place until the end of 1990 but reiterated its earlier ruling that a finding under the stock-specific quotas must be based on a full season's data.[62] The embargo of Mexican tuna was reimposed.

The Service promptly appealed and obtained a stay of the district court ruling pending review by the appellate court.[63] The appellate court affirmed the lower court ruling that the findings with respect to eastern spinner and coastal spotted dolphins required data from an entire calendar year.[64] The court rejected the Service's policy-based argument that the reconsideration provision offered countries an incentive to hasten their efforts to comply with the Marine Mammal Protection Act. Instead, it found that the reconsideration provisions merely allowed nations to continually exceed the Act's limits for part of each year, yet never face an import ban. The court noted, for example, that Mexico had exceeded the Act's standards for the entirety of 1990, yet had been subject to an embargo for just one day during the year. Further, the court found the Service's contention that it sought only to provide additional incentives to further dolphin protection to be inconsistent with the Service's record of lax enforcement that had necessitated enactment of the 1988 amendments in the first place.

Pursuit of the Zero Mortality Goal

Buoyed by their legislative success in 1988, several environmental organizations, led by Earth Island Institute, set their sights on eliminating, rather than merely reducing, dolphin mortality. These groups began to organize a consumer boycott of eastern tropical Pacific tuna caught by encircling dolphins and to push legislation that would require tuna to be labeled according to the method by which it was caught. The three largest U.S. tuna canners seized on that initiative, and on 12 April 1990 announced that they would no longer purchase tuna caught in association with dolphins. Shortly thereafter, the Dolphin Protection Consumer Information Act[65] was enacted, providing for labeling certain tuna as "dolphin safe." To qualify as dolphin-safe, tuna caught in the eastern tropical Pacific must have been caught by a vessel too small to deploy its nets on dolphins[66] (i.e., with a carrying capacity of less than 400 short tons [362.8 mt]) or must be accompanied by an observer's certification that no sets on dolphins were made during the entire trip on which the tuna was caught.

Further Litigation

At the beginning of 1991 the National Marine Fisheries Service was faced with assessing foreign dolphin mortality using the more stringent 1.25 kill-rate comparability factor. In preparation, it issued an interim rule to give foreign nations until 15 March to submit the 1990 data and to extend existing comparability findings until 31 May 1991. If it could not avoid the inevitable imposition of additional tuna embargoes, the Service intended to do its best to delay their effect. The Service quickly found itself back in court and again on the losing side of a challenge by Earth Island Institute.[67] Nevertheless, by flouting the court's earlier ruling on the timing of the comparability findings, the Service had bought Venezuela and Vanuatu an additional three months of access to the U.S. market.

Earth Island Institute next took aim at the third-party embargoes in an effort to increase the pressure on foreign nations to reduce dolphin mortality. Again, the reviewing court sided with the plaintiffs, ruling that the Marine Mammal Protection Act required every intermediary nation to provide certification and reasonable proof that it has acted to prohibit the import of the same products that are banned from direct imports in the United States.[68] In the court's view, it was insufficient for an intermediary nation merely to demonstrate that it had discontinued the importation of tuna subject to a primary embargo. The nation must act affirmatively to prohibit importation of the offending tuna and tuna products. Further, the court ruled that the required embargo of tuna from an intermediary nation was broader than that from a harvesting nation, covering all yellowfin tuna, not just that caught in the eastern tropical Pacific.

General Agreements on Tariffs and Trade

Concurrent with this domestic legal activity, the tuna embargoes under the Marine Mammal Protection Act were being reviewed by an international tribunal for consistency with United States obligations under the General Agreements on Tariffs and Trade (GATT). The GATT is an international agreement that limits the use of trade restrictions. Mexico had challenged the tuna embargoes as unwarranted and impermissible restrictions on international trade. Arguments were heard before a three-person dispute resolution panel, which issued a ruling on 3 September 1991 (GATT 1991). The panel found the U.S. tuna embargoes to be inconsistent with the provisions of the GATT. The United States had argued that the embargoes were permissible because foreign-caught tuna was being treated no less favorably than tuna caught by U.S. fishermen. The panel rejected that argument because the U.S. embargoes did not apply to the tuna itself, as a product, but rather to the method by which it was caught. The panel also found that the U.S. embargo provisions did not fit within exceptions allowing GATT parties to adopt trade measures "necessary to protect human, animal or plant life or health" or "relating to the conservation of exhaustible natural resources. . . ." The panel ruled that these exceptions did not apply to measures taken to protect animals or other resources beyond the jurisdiction of the country applying those measures. To interpret the exceptions more broadly, the panel concluded, would enable a party to dictate unilaterally the environmental policies from which other countries could not deviate without jeopardizing their rights under the General Agreements. However, the panel decision held out the prospect that a similar embargo provision designed to enforce an international conservation regime might pass GATT muster.

Under then-existing rules of the General Agreements,[69] a panel decision would not become effective unless it was adopted unanimously by the GATT Council of Representatives. Thus, one nation could block adoption of a panel decision. Although an adverse ruling adopted by the GATT parties would not have forced the United States to change its domestic law to conform to the requirements of the General Agreements, failure to do so could have subjected the United States to retaliatory trade sanctions (Housman and

Zaelke 1992). The panel decision concerning U.S. tuna embargoes has never been adopted as a formal GATT ruling.

The 1992 Amendments to the Marine Mammal Protection Act

It was against the backdrop of the adverse GATT ruling that the United States and Mexico sought to work out an accommodation that would allow Mexico and other embargoed nations access to the U.S. tuna market, while satisfying the U.S. goal of reducing dolphin mortality in the eastern tropical Pacific. The State Department believed that it had worked out an agreement with Mexico to solve the GATT impasse and forwarded a legislative proposal to Congress in 1992. That proposal, enacted on 26 October 1992 as part of the International Dolphin Conservation Act of 1992[70] amended the Marine Mammal Protection Act to provide a mechanism for lifting the tuna embargoes. Any nation that formally committed to abide by a five-year, international moratorium on setting on dolphins to catch tuna in the eastern tropical Pacific, beginning on 1 March 1994, would not be subject to tuna embargoes in the interim, provided that the nation's tuna fleet reduced incidental dolphin mortality by a statistically significant amount each year until the moratorium took effect. In essence, the amendment offered the nations a year and a half of continued access to the U.S. market in exchange for agreeing to cease setting on dolphins for the subsequent five-year period. Despite assurances from the State Department that this approach was acceptable to other countries, no eastern tropical Pacific fishing nation committed to the moratorium.

Although a moratorium on setting on dolphins was never implemented, other provisions of the International Dolphin Conservation Act significantly affected tuna fishing operations in the eastern tropical Pacific. Recognizing that the U.S. fleet had declined dramatically since the dolphin quota of 20,500 was established, the Act amended the American Tunaboat Association's general permit to reduce the 1992 quota to 1,000 dolphins. A quota of 800 dolphin mortalities was set for the period from 1 January 1993 to 1 March 1994, the date on which the proposed moratorium was to begin. If no major tuna fishing nation committed to the moratorium, the American Tunaboat Association general permit was to continue in force until the end of 1999, but under a quota to be reduced by a statistically significant amount each year. The amendments also rescinded the quotas for eastern spinner and coastal spotted dolphins adopted in 1984. Intentional sets on individuals from these stocks would no longer be allowed. Other key features of the 1992 amendments were (1) the imposition, effective 1 June 1994, of a prohibition on selling, purchasing, offering for sale, transporting, or shipping any tuna in the United States that is not dolphin-safe, and (2) the authorization of $1 million in each of fiscal years 1992 and 1993 for research to develop dolphin-safe methods of locating and catching large yellowfin tuna.

The La Jolla Agreement: An Alternative to the Moratorium

While the 1992 amendments were pending before Congress, efforts to conclude a new international initiative were being pursued under the auspices of the Inter-American Tropical Tuna Commission. The member countries and other nations that fish for yellowfin tuna in the eastern tropical Pacific negotiated an agreement at the Tuna Commission's 1992 meeting in La Jolla (Inter-American Tropical Tuna Commission 1993). The "La Jolla Agreement" was to have profound effects on reducing incidental dolphin mortality. The Agreement established, for the first time, annual, international dolphin quotas. Under these quotas, dolphin mortality was to decline incrementally from 19,500 in 1993 to less than 5,000 by 1999. The crucial feature of the Agreement, however, was the establishment of a system for allocating the allowable mortality among the vessels participating in the fishery. Each vessel could request to receive a "dolphin mortality limit" under which it would fish each year. After a vessel reached its share of the overall dolphin quota, it was required to cease setting on dolphins for the remainder of the year. In this way, the fate of each vessel was in its own hands. If it performed well, it could continue to set on dolphins to catch tuna throughout the year. If it performed poorly, it would be precluded from setting on dolphins once the vessel-specific allocation had been reached.

The La Jolla Agreement proved to be a remarkable success. Previous measures (i.e., the comparability requirements of the Marine Mammal Protection Act and the increased efforts by the Inter-American Tropical Tuna Commission to provide training to skippers throughout the international fleet) had resulted in significant reductions in dolphin mortality. However, with a vessel owner's fate tied to the vessel's own performance, dolphin mortality plummeted. As shown in Figure 6-6, the decline in dolphin mortality has come largely from a decline in dolphin mortality per set, rather than decreasing fishing effort on dolphins. In the first year of the new program, total dolphin mortality dropped to 3,601, well below the target established for 1999. During 1994, total mortality increased slightly but was still below the 5,000 quota set for 1999. Dolphin mortality has continued to drop, with record lows being achieved in both

1995 and 1996. Dolphin mortality increased somewhat in 1997 to 3,005.

Depletion Determinations

Another initiative launched by environmental organizations was also progressing along a path that was to affect first the U.S. fleet and then the international fleet. In 1991 these groups petitioned the National Marine Fisheries Service to designate eastern spinner and northern offshore spotted dolphins as depleted under the Marine Mammal Protection Act. The Service, after determining that the eastern spinner dolphin was at approximately 44% of its preexploitation size (Wade 1993a), published a depletion finding in August 1993.[71]

After reassessing the stock structure of spotted dolphins in the eastern tropical Pacific, the Service found that the northeastern offshore stock[72] was at 19 to 28% of its historic level (Wade 1993b) and also depleted.[73] Apparently, the northeastern offshore stock of spotted dolphins had been reduced to less than its MNP level by 1972, when the Marine Mammal Protection Act was enacted, and, despite contrary determinations in the permit proceedings between 1976 and 1980, likely has remained below that level ever since.

By 1993 the U.S. fleet operating in the eastern tropical Pacific had been reduced to a shell of its former self. Only six large U.S. purse seiners remained in the fishery, and only three of these continued to set on dolphins. Armed with the depletion finding for northeastern offshore spotted dolphins, Earth Island Institute dealt a knockout blow to the practice of setting on dolphins by the U.S. fleet.

In its ongoing challenge to the National Marine Fisheries Service's implementation of the U.S. tuna-dolphin program, Earth Island Institute argued that the depletion finding necessitated a zero quota for the stock under the American Tunaboat Association's general permit. Moreover, plaintiffs argued that, because some individuals of this stock would inevitably be encircled and killed unless sets on the western/southern stock of offshore spotted dolphins were also prohibited, sets on all stocks of offshore spotted dolphins needed to be prohibited. The Service countered that, inasmuch as the 1980 general permit and its quotas had been legislatively extended in 1984, there was no requirement that it prohibit sets on either stock.

A 27 January 1994 court ruling in the matter found that the general permit remained subject to its original conditions, including the implied condition that taking from depleted stocks could not be authorized.[74] The presiding judge initially was attracted to the argument that the taking of the western/southern stock must also be prohibited if individuals from the depleted northeastern stock would invariably be taken. Upon hearing additional arguments on the underlying science, however, he backed away from that view. Experts for the American Tunaboat Association had explained that the stock delineation was not based on absolute differences between individuals, but on average differences between the populations. As such, morphological differences could not be used reliably to identify individual dolphins as belonging to one stock or the other. The judge reasoned that it would be "conceptually incoherent" to regard any dolphin taken outside the area used to define the stock as belonging to that stock. Therefore, it was not necessary to prohibit encirclement of spotted dolphins south of 5°N latitude, the dividing line between the two putative stocks of offshore spotted dolphins. The resulting prohibition against setting on northeastern offshore spotted dolphins, coupled with the prohibition on selling tuna in the United States after 1 June 1994 that was not certified as dolphin-safe, was nevertheless sufficient to end the practice of setting on dolphins by the vestigial U.S. fleet. No dolphin sets were made by the U.S. fleet during 1995 or subsequent years.

Under the comparability provisions of the Marine Mammal Protection Act, any foreign nation that did not adopt a parallel ban on setting on northeastern offshore spotted dolphins could not sell any of its yellowfin tuna caught in the eastern tropical Pacific—even its dolphin-safe tuna—in the United States. And with the United States achieving zero dolphin mortality in 1995 and subsequent years, there was no prospect that any foreign fleet continuing to set on dolphins would ever meet the Act's comparability requirements.

Recent Efforts to Address U.S. Tuna Embargoes

The exclusion from the U.S. market of most tuna caught by foreign nations in the eastern tropical Pacific has become a growing source of strain. From the perspective of the fishing nations, they have made a good-faith effort to participate in the International Dolphin Conservation Program established under the La Jolla Agreement. In fact, they have succeeded in reducing dolphin mortality dramatically. Yet there has been little tangible benefit to offset the resources and effort that have been expended. From the perspective of the U.S. government, the tuna embargoes have been a nagging concern with respect to GATT compliance and a continuing source of friction with important trading partners, particularly Mexico.

Environmental Effects of Dolphin-Safe Policy

The possible consequences of switching to dolphin-safe fishing methods have been studied over the past few years. The

Inter-American Tropical Tuna Commission and the National Marine Fisheries Service compared the bycatch resulting from sets on dolphins with the bycatch related to the primary dolphin-safe alternatives—sets on schools of tuna not associated with dolphins (school sets) and sets on logs and other floating objects under which tuna often congregate (log sets) (U.S. House 1996a:315, 321). Although dolphin mortality almost never occurs in school sets and rarely occurs in log sets, the bycatch of other marine organisms, such as sharks, billfish, and sea turtles, is significantly higher in these set types (U.S. House 1996b:198, Hall 1998).

Dolphin-safe fishing methods also result in much higher bycatch of small tunas (Hall 1998). Whereas the tunas caught in association with dolphins are almost exclusively large, mature yellowfin averaging about 20 kg (45 pounds), log and school fishing yields a mixture of smaller yellowfin and skipjack tunas averaging about 4.5 to 6.8 kg (10 to 15 pounds). On average, about 90 kg (200 pounds) of tuna are discarded per dolphin set. For school sets, the average discard is about one ton of tuna per set. The tuna discard rate jumps to approximately 10 tons for each log set. That is, each school set generates about 10 times the tuna bycatch and each log set generates about 100 times the tuna bycatch of each dolphin set. Although the breakdown of fishing effort among the three set types varies somewhat from year to year, generally about 50% of the effort in the eastern tropical Pacific tuna fishery consists of dolphin sets. School sets and log sets each account for about 25% of the fishing effort.

Proponents of continuing the practice of setting on dolphins contend that, if a substantial portion of the effort involving dolphin sets were redirected to the other set types, bycatch of other species and of small tunas would increase to a level where it could have significant adverse effects on these species and on tuna recruitment. The Inter-American Tropical Tuna Commission asserts that such a shift would prove damaging to the fishery. It estimates that without sets on dolphins, the average size of tuna being caught would be reduced by more than 50%. Further, the Tuna Commission predicts that, over time, the catch of yellowfin tuna would be reduced by between 25 and 60% (U.S. House 1996a:326).

Congressional Hearings

In light of the broader bycatch problems associated with school and log sets, several tuna fishing nations, as well as the Inter-American Tropical Tuna Commission, have expressed the belief that continued fishing on dolphins will result in better tuna management and utilization. In their view, setting on dolphins is the most environmentally benign purse seine method of catching yellowfin tuna when the overall health of the eastern tropical Pacific ecosystem is considered. Consistent with this view, six tuna fishing nations issued a joint statement in June 1995 urging the United States to lift the tuna embargoes for those countries operating in accordance with the La Jolla Agreement. They also called on the United States to amend the definition of dolphin-safe tuna to include all tuna caught in compliance with the International Dolphin Conservation Program. The statement suggested that failure by the United States to accommodate these concerns would prompt some nations to abandon, or at least reconsider, their participation in the International Dolphin Conservation Program.

Shortly thereafter, the House Resources Committee held a hearing on possible amendments to the Marine Mammal Protection Act (U.S. House 1996b). Representatives of the State Department, the Inter-American Tropical Tuna Commission, and the U.S. tuna industry all supported amending the Act to allow imports of tuna harvested by those nations participating in the International Dolphin Conservation Program. The tuna industry and the State Department also advocated amendments that would allow U.S. fishermen to reenter the eastern tropical Pacific tuna fishery on an equal footing with other fishermen—that is, they would be able to set on dolphins and import tuna into the United States, provided they obtained a dolphin mortality quota under the International Dolphin Conservation Program. Noting the importance of cooperative efforts with Latin American countries in conserving other fishery resources and fearing retaliatory trade sanctions being applied to U.S. seafood products, other segments of the U.S. fishing industry also supported easing the Act's tuna import restrictions.

Environmental groups showed a less united front. In fact, they have become highly polarized over this issue. Some groups believed that the United States should continue to push for the elimination of all incidental dolphin mortality by retaining the prohibition against importing tuna caught in association with dolphins (U.S. House 1996b:105–124). They pointed to the experience of the handful of U.S. vessels that have remained in the eastern tropical Pacific and have been using dolphin-safe fishing methods as evidence that a commercially viable fishery can be maintained without setting on dolphins. These groups further asserted that, even if no dolphins die directly in a set, repeated chase and encirclement of dolphins by tuna fishermen likely causes severe stress that could manifest itself in physical impairment (Cowan and Walker 1979) or death of dolphins or in reduced fecundity (Southwest Fisheries Center 1977:118–121). They were also fearful of the United States ceding primary authority for dolphin conservation programs to the Inter-American Tropical Tuna Commission, which they believed would place its historic mission of ensuring sustainable tuna production above its concern for dolphin conservation.

Other environmental groups believed that the Marine Mammal Protection Act's tuna-dolphin provisions needed to be reexamined (U.S. House 1996b:60–71). In particular, they concluded that some aspects of the 1992 amendments, which had been premised on establishing an international moratorium on the practice of setting on dolphins, did not make sense in the absence of such a moratorium. Although they expressed concern over the potentially adverse effects of the bycatch of sharks, billfish, and sea turtles in log and school sets, these groups noted that available data were too preliminary to draw any definitive conclusions. They therefore recommended that an independent, international review of the issue be undertaken. They also recommended a multilateral approach to resolving the issues stemming from the U.S. tuna embargoes through negotiation of a binding international agreement to replace the nonbinding La Jolla Agreement.

The tuna fishing nations were heartened somewhat by what had transpired at the congressional oversight hearing. Nevertheless, in a subsequent joint declaration, the nations stated that lifting the tuna embargoes without also amending the definition of dolphin-safe tuna would not sufficiently address their concerns. They reiterated their position that continued adherence to the La Jolla Agreement was in jeopardy unless the United States promptly enacted legislation lifting the tuna embargoes, codifying the terms of the Agreement, and redefining dolphin-safe tuna to include all tuna harvested in accordance with the International Dolphin Conservation Program.

Declaration of Panama

Concerned that an opportunity to consolidate the gains that had been made under the La Jolla Agreement was ebbing away, a coalition of five environmental groups seized the initiative by entering into secret discussions with representatives of Mexico to develop the framework for a new international agreement. The compromise that was forged proved acceptable to U.S. officials and to the other tuna fishing nations. It formed the basis for the Declaration of Panama, signed by 12 nations, including the United States, on 4 October 1995 (Inter-American Tropical Tuna Commission 1997:315). Signatories to the Declaration reaffirmed their commitment to reducing dolphin mortality in the eastern tropical Pacific tuna fishery to levels approaching zero and declared their intention to formalize the La Jolla Agreement as binding under international law, contingent on certain changes in U.S. law. The envisioned changes included lifting the primary and secondary embargoes for tuna caught in compliance with the La Jolla Agreement, as it would be modified under the Declaration of Panama, allowing access to the U.S. market for all such tuna, whether dolphin-safe or not, and redefining the term dolphin-safe to include any tuna caught in the eastern tropical Pacific by a purse seine vessel in a set in which no observed dolphin mortality occurred.

When these changes to U.S. law had been enacted, the signatory nations would conclude a binding agreement that, among other things, would set an annual limit on overall dolphin mortality of 5,000 and establish stock-specific quotas. An annual quota of between 0.1 and 0.2% of the minimum population estimate[75] would be set for each stock until the year 2000. Thereafter, the annual per-stock quota would be set at 0.1% of a stock's minimum population size. After a stock-specific quota had been reached, all sets on that stock and any mixed schools containing that stock would cease for the remainder of the year. Other provisions to be included in the agreement would address the bycatch of juvenile tuna and other nontarget species, require parties to enact implementing legislation, and provide incentives to vessel owners to reduce dolphin mortality further.

Congressional Response to the Declaration of Panama

Bills were promptly introduced in both the Senate and the House of Representatives to amend the Marine Mammal Protection Act as called for by the Declaration of Panama. Counterproposals soon followed and a legislative debate was under way. The tuna-dolphin issue, which for so long had been dominated by scientific and technological considerations, had become focused into a debate over ethics and economics.

Dolphin mortality in the eastern tropical Pacific had finally dropped to a level that the scientific community generally believed to be biologically insignificant to the survival and recovery of the affected stocks (Norris et al. 1996; U.S. House 1996a:317, 334; Hall 1998). Supporters of the Declaration of Panama considered it a fair trade for tuna fishing nations to provide assurances that annual dolphin mortality in the eastern tropical Pacific would never again exceed 5,000 in exchange for the United States granting access to its lucrative market. Opponents of the Declaration, in essence, viewed any mortality resulting from sets on dolphins as unnecessary and morally unacceptable, although they also voiced concern over the possible biological significance of "cryptic kill." The purported cryptic kill involves those dolphins that may die but go undetected by an observer or those that may die later because of fishery-related injuries or stress resulting from chase and encirclement.

The two sides also disagreed on the likelihood that tuna fishing nations would abandon the La Jolla Agreement and revert to the high kill rates of the 1980s if the Declaration of Panama were not implemented. Proponents of legislation to implement the Declaration believed that Mexico and other tuna fishing nations had or could readily develop alternative markets for their tuna; thus they took the threats of the fishing nations seriously. Opponents of the amendments believed that fishing nations, denied access to the U.S. market, had been forced to stockpile large quantities of canned tuna that other markets could not absorb. They therefore considered renewed access to the U.S. market, even for only a portion of the tuna caught in the eastern tropical Pacific, to be a powerful bargaining chip. Their alternative legislative proposal would have lifted the embargo, but only for dolphin-safe tuna. If enacted, this proposal would have allowed approximately one-third of the yellowfin tuna from the eastern tropical Pacific (that caught by vessels with a carrying capacity of less than 400 short tons [362.8 mt] or on trips during which no dolphins were intentionally encircled) to be imported (Inter-American Tropical Tuna Commission 1997). Such a change also would be expected to encourage other fishermen to consider switching to dolphin-safe fishing methods. Although not discounting completely the broader bycatch concerns regarding log and school sets, supporters of this approach believed that these problems should be addressed through research and imposition of gear or other restrictions aimed at reducing the bycatch, not by sanctioning the encirclement of dolphins.

The most contentious issue, however, was the proposed revision of the definition of dolphin-safe tuna. It is that labeling standard that gives consumers the power to influence what methods are used to catch tuna. All participants in the debate fully recognized that access to the U.S. market would be of little consequence to fishing nations if consumers were not willing to buy their product.

Originally, the exporting nations had sought a redefinition to allow all tuna caught in accordance with the International Dolphin Conservation Program to be labeled dolphin-safe. During the negotiations between environmental groups and Mexico that led to the Declaration of Panama, the fishing nations accepted a middle ground that would allow such tuna to be labeled dolphin-safe only if no dolphins were killed in the set in which the tuna was caught. Critics of the Declaration assailed that proposed redefinition as tantamount to consumer fraud. How, they argued, could the use of a fishing method that inevitably resulted in dolphin mortality be countenanced even in those instances when no mortality occurred? Further, the critics contended that it would be inappropriate to characterize tuna caught by encircling dolphins as dolphin-safe even when none are killed in light of the possible detrimental effects of chase and encirclement. They also questioned the ability of a single observer to detect all dolphin mortality that might occur in a large purse seine net and the ability of the government to track tuna from a specific set through the canning process. They believed that these uncertainties would make it impossible to devise any reliable means for certifying particular tuna as dolphin-safe.

Action in the 104th Congress

When H.R. 2823, one of the bills introduced during the 1995–1996 session of Congress to conform U.S. law to the terms of the Declaration of Panama, reached the floor of the House of Representatives, the debate between the two factions had boiled down to the sanctity of the dolphin-safe labeling standard. Opponents of the bill had abandoned their efforts to exclude tuna caught in compliance with the International Dolphin Conservation Program, but which is not dolphin-safe, from the U.S. market. The sole amendment they offered would have defined dolphin-safe tuna as that caught without killing, chasing, harassing, injuring, or encircling dolphins. In the end, H.R. 2823 was passed by the House without amendment by a comfortable 316 to 108 vote margin.[76]

The road faced by the legislation in the Senate was somewhat rockier. Senators Barbara Boxer of California and Joseph Biden of Delaware, who fiercely opposed amending the dolphin-safe definition, threatened a filibuster to prevent consideration of the matter. In the closing days of the 1996 session of Congress, these two senators successfully blocked an attempt to pass the legislation by unanimous consent.

Key congressional supporters of the Declaration of Panama immediately pledged to pursue similar legislation during 1997. This sentiment was echoed by President Clinton, who, in a 7 October 1996 letter to Mexican President Zedillo, indicated his intention to have implementing legislation considered at the earliest opportunity by the 105th Congress.

Despite these commitments, the parties to the La Jolla Agreement expressed considerable displeasure with the failure of the United States to enact the legislation called for by the Declaration of Panama. Mexico went so far as to suspend its active participation in the International Dolphin Conservation Program and announced at the October 1996 meeting of the parties that its vessels would no longer seek dolphin mortality limits or be bound by the quotas established under the La Jolla Agreement. Mexico indicated, however, that, at least for the time being, its vessels would continue to carry observers as called for under the Agreement. Heartened somewhat by subsequent efforts by the

United States to enact legislation to implement the Declaration of Panama, Mexico announced in June 1997 that it intended once again to participate fully in the International Dolphin Conservation Program.

The 1997 Amendments

When the new Congress convened in January 1997, two bills, H.R. 408 and S. 39, were promptly introduced to amend U.S. law as called for under the Declaration of Panama. The House bill was virtually identical to the bill passed during the previous session. Opponents in the House again introduced alternative legislation. Their bill, in certain respects, was even more restrictive than the bill introduced in 1995. For example, access to the U.S. tuna market would not have been tied to adherence to the annual dolphin mortality quota of 5,000 set forth in the Declaration of Panama. Rather, the bill would have required that dolphin mortalities not exceed the observed 1996 mortality level of 2,766. The number of dolphin mortalities in subsequent years would have had to continue to decline for tuna fishing nations to retain access to the U.S. market.

In response to criticism that the existing definition of dolphin-safe tuna inappropriately focused on fishing methods rather than the effectiveness of those methods in eliminating dolphin mortalities, the bill also would have redefined dolphin-safe tuna from the eastern tropical Pacific as that (1) caught by a vessel "of a type or size that . . . is not capable of chasing, netting, killing, or seriously injuring dolphins" and that cannot accommodate an observer on board, or (2) caught during a voyage on which no dolphins were chased and netted, killed, or seriously injured, as certified by an approved observer. Under this definition, not only would all tuna from a trip on which any dolphin set was made fail to meet the dolphin-safe criteria, but any tuna caught by fishermen exclusively making log or school sets who were unlucky enough to kill or seriously injure a single dolphin on a fishing trip would similarly not qualify for the dolphin-safe label. The bill also would have directed the Secretary of State to take actions to ensure that the Inter-American Tropical Tuna Commission adopt a bycatch reduction program for nontarget species.

Despite strong lobbying by environmental groups opposed to implementing the Declaration of Panama, members of the House Committee on Resources were reluctant to embrace any amendments that would deviate from the terms of the Declaration. Only slight modifications were made to H.R. 408 before it was sent to the full House for consideration. Although some support for the legislation had eroded, the measure was passed by the House in May 1997 by a 262 to 166 vote.

Meanwhile, the Senate continued to seek a middle ground that would be acceptable to all interest groups. Such a solution proved elusive, but just before a showdown to determine if there were sufficient votes to sustain a filibuster, a compromise was reached. Under the compromise, a change in the definition of dolphin-safe tuna was made contingent on the results of a study to be conducted by the National Marine Fisheries Service on the effects of chase and encirclement on dolphin populations. The compromise bill was embraced by Congress, passing by a 99-0 vote in the Senate and by unanimous consent in the House, and signed into law by the President on 15 August 1997.[77]

The new law, the International Dolphin Conservation Program Act, made several changes to the U.S. tuna-dolphin program. Revised section 304 of the Marine Mammal Protection Act directs the Secretary of Commerce, in consultation with the Marine Mammal Commission and the Inter-American Tropical Tuna Commission, to conduct a study of the effects of chase and encirclement on dolphins and dolphin stocks taken in the course of purse seine fishing for yellowfin tuna in the eastern tropical Pacific. The study is to consist of two parts: abundance surveys to be conducted during a three-year period beginning in 1998 and stress studies designed to determine whether chase and encirclement are having a significant adverse impact on any depleted dolphin stock. The stress studies are to include (1) a literature review of stress-related research and an assessment of necropsy samples from dolphins taken by tuna vessels, (2) a one-year review of historical demographic and biological data related to depleted dolphins, and (3) an experiment involving the repeated chase and capture of dolphins to determine the effects of intentional encirclement. Appropriations totaling $12 million were authorized to carry out the studies.

Based on the preliminary results of the research program and any other relevant information, the Secretary is to make an initial finding by March 1999 as to the effects of intentional encirclement on depleted dolphin stocks. The Secretary is to make and report a final finding to Congress by the end of 2002. If the Secretary finds that chase and encirclement are having a significant adverse impact, the definition of dolphin-safe tuna will remain as before. If no such determination is made, tuna will be considered dolphin-safe if no dolphins were killed or seriously injured during the sets in which the tuna were caught.

However, the amendments do not become effective until (1) the international program called for under the Declaration of Panama has been formally established under a binding resolution of the Inter-American Tropical Tuna Commission or some other legally binding international instrument and (2) the Secretary of Commerce certifies that sufficient funding is available to complete the first year of the abundance surveys and stress studies.

Although it will remain subject to the dolphin-safe labeling requirements, all tuna caught in the eastern tropical Pacific after the effective date of the amendments may be imported into the United States, provided it was caught in accordance with the requirements of the International Dolphin Conservation Program. The amendments further require that the total dolphin mortality limits and the per-stock limits for nations importing tuna to the United States progressively decline from 1997 levels. After the amendments become effective, the zero quota and stock-specific restrictions that have prevented U.S. fishermen from setting on dolphins will be lifted. They will be able to apply for a permit allowing them to take dolphins in accordance with the provisions of the International Dolphin Conservation Program. Unlike the multiyear, general permits issued to the American Tunaboat Association in the past, annual permits would be issued to individual vessels.

Although the impasse over whether U.S. law should be changed to conform to the Declaration of Panama has been broken, the controversy that has surrounded the tuna-dolphin issue is unlikely to vanish. The future of the dolphin-safe label has not been definitively resolved. Rather, it has been tied to the results of a research program that is unlikely to produce unequivocal results within the specified time frames. Thus, it appears likely that the battle over the definition has merely been deferred to another time and another venue. In any event, the research program to be conducted should provide the two sides in the debate with more and better data on which to base their cases.

It should be noted that the 1997 amendments are written so as to favor a change in the definition of dolphin-safe tuna. The burden is placed on the Secretary of Commerce to demonstrate that chase and encirclement are having significant adverse effects on depleted dolphin stocks. Absent such a finding, the definition will change. If this occurs by default because of a lack of information, or a lack of diligence by the responsible officials in designing and carrying out an adequate research program, environmental groups opposed to the redefinition are likely once again to pursue the issue in court or to brandish the weapon they have threatened to use before, a consumer boycott of tuna products.

Conclusion

Although it took some 20 years, the assessment by Joe Medina at the 1971 hearings that the problem of dolphin mortality in the eastern tropical Pacific tuna fishery has been "licked" has largely come to pass. There have been many twists and turns along the way, but dolphin mortality is no longer considered by most marine mammal scientists to be biologically significant. There also have been many casualties along the way. Since enactment of the Marine Mammal Protection Act in 1972, more than 2 million dolphins have been killed in tuna nets. Northeastern offshore spotted and eastern spinner dolphins, although likely not threatened with extinction, are depleted and are likely to remain so for many years to come. The once-dominant U.S. fleet is all but gone, having registered under other flags or moved to fishing grounds in the western Pacific. Jobs in the once-burgeoning U.S. tuna canning industry also have largely migrated overseas.

In light of all that has transpired over the past quarter century concerning the tuna-dolphin issue, it is ironic that Joe Medina may have been closer to the mark than we have given him credit for. There has been no "magic bullet" developed to drastically reduce dolphin mortality. Although there have been some incremental technical innovations and certain refinements of fishing procedures, the mainstays of reducing dolphin mortality have remained the use of the backdown procedure and installation of the Medina panel.

What seems to have changed over the years is the pressure that has been placed on fishermen and their desire to use the available techniques effectively. Dolphin mortality resulting from U.S. operations dropped markedly after the Richey decision and the imposition of specific quotas. Faced with the alternative of early closure of their fishery, it is not surprising that fishermen began taking dolphin rescue more seriously.

The success of the foreign fleet in reducing dolphin mortality provides an even more remarkable example of this phenomenon. The imposition of tuna embargoes by the United States under the 1988 amendments to the Marine Mammal Protection Act resulted in almost immediate reductions in dolphin mortality. These were followed by even greater reductions under the La Jolla Agreement after each vessel's fate was tied to its individual performance.

Some portion of the reduction in dolphin mortality is no doubt attributable to increased familiarity with dolphin-saving techniques, due in part to the training efforts of the Inter-American Tropical Tuna Commission. However, the underlying desire of the fishermen to minimize dolphin mortality is likely the most critical factor. There has been some drop-off in the number of sets being made on dolphins over the past few years, but the reduction in overall dolphin mortality has resulted largely from improved performance. The number of dolphins killed per set by foreign fleets in 1995 was one-twentieth what it was just six years before (Fig. 6-6).

Although this has been said prematurely before, it may be that we are finally approaching the point at which further reductions in dolphin mortality using traditional fishing methods are unlikely. Currently, about 88% of sets on dolphins result in no incidental mortality (Inter-American Tropical Tuna Commission 1997, Hall 1998). Further reductions may be achievable only through new technical advances or a shift toward dolphin-safe fishing methods, raising other bycatch concerns. The question of whether any level of dolphin mortality incidental to tuna fishing is acceptable will no doubt continue to stir controversy, but under the 1997 amendments to the Marine Mammal Protection Act, the debate, for the time being, will likely be confined to the assessment of the effects of chase and encirclement. It is unlikely, however, that the planned study will resolve the scientific issues to the satisfaction of all interested parties. Thus, although the battle in the political arena has subsided, the controversy is likely to be aired further in U.S. courts and, more important, in the court of public opinion.

Acknowledgments

I am grateful to several individuals who assisted in preparation of this chapter by providing information or reviewing early drafts. They include Martín Hall, Liz Edwards, Doug DeMaster, Bill Perrin, Jim Coe, Martin Hochman, Eileen Sobeck, Bob Hofman, Randy Reeves, and Suzanne Montgomery.

Notes

1. For much of its history, this issue has been referred to as "tuna-porpoise" and the technique of encircling dolphins as fishing "on porpoise." However, the cetaceans taken in the fishery technically are delphinids (dolphins) rather than phocoenids (true porpoises). Thus, the use of the term *tuna-dolphin* to refer to this issue has now gained general acceptance.
2. H.R. Rept. No. 707, 92d Cong., 1st sess. (1971).
3. Ibid., 24.
4. S. Rept. No. 863, 92d Cong., 2d sess. (1972).
5. Ibid., 16.
6. The Marine Mammal Protection Act divides jurisdiction over marine mammals between the Secretary of Commerce and the Secretary of the Interior. The Secretary of Commerce has responsibilities for all cetaceans and all pinnipeds except the walrus. Most responsibilities under the Act have been delegated by the Secretary of Commerce to the National Oceanic and Atmospheric Administration and its subagency, the National Marine Fisheries Service.
7. H.R. Rept. No. 707, 92d Cong., 1st sess. 20 (1971).
8. Ibid.
9. 39 *Fed. Reg.* 2481 (1974).
10. Ibid., 2482.
11. 39 *Fed. Reg.* 9685 (1974).
12. Ibid.
13. 39 *Fed. Reg.* 12356 (1974).
14. Nevertheless, one cannot help but wonder whether greater attention to the letter of the law with respect to other fisheries at the outset might not have obviated the crisis created by the decision in *Kokechik Fishermen's Association* v. *Secretary of Commerce,* 839 F.2d 795 (D.C. Cir. 1988), and the need to enact an interim exemption in 1988 to accommodate other fisheries. (See Chapter 2.)
15. 40 *Fed. Reg.* 765 (1975).
16. *Committee for Humane Legislation* v. *Richardson,* 414 F. Supp. 297, 305 (D.D.C. 1976).
17. 40 *Fed. Reg.* 41536 (1975).
18. Ibid.
19. Ibid.
20. 40 *Fed. Reg.* 56889 (1975).
21. 414 F. Supp. 297 (D.D.C. 1976).
22. Ibid., 306.
23. Ibid., 309.
24. 118 *Cong. Rec.*, 7686 (1972).
25. *Committee for Humane Legislation* v. *Richardson,* 414 F. Supp. 297, 310, n. 30 (D.D.C. 1976).
26. Ibid., 314.
27. 41 *Fed. Reg.* 23680 (1976).
28. *Committee for Humane Legislation* v. *Richardson,* 540 F.2d 1141 (D.C. Cir. 1976).
29. 41 *Fed. Reg.* 45569 (1976).
30. *Motor Vessel Theresa Ann* v. *Richardson,* 7 Envtl. L. Rept. 20065 (S.D. Cal. 2 Nov. 1976).
31. *American Tunaboat Association* v. *Richardson,* No. 76-3309 (9th Cir. 11 Nov. 1976).
32. 41 *Fed. Reg.* 45015 (1976).
33. *Motor Vessel Theresa Ann* v. *Richardson,* 7 Envtl. L. Rept. 20588 (S.D. Cal. 21 Jan. 1977).
34. *Motor Vessel Theresa Ann* v. *Kreps,* 548 F.2d 1382 (9th Cir. 1977).
35. 42 *Fed. Reg.* 12010 (1977).
36. The Marine Mammal Protection Act defines take to mean "to harass, hunt, capture, or kill, or attempt to harass, hunt capture, or kill any marine mammal."
37. *Committee for Humane Legislation* v. *Kreps,* No. 77-0564 (D.D.C. 30 June 1977).
38. 42 *Fed. Reg.* 22575 (1977). It should be noted that such an accidental take policy was rejected for other fisheries in *Kokechik Fishermen's Association* v. *Secretary of Commerce.* The court in that case ruled that the Secretary could not authorize the incidental taking of one species of marine mammal if it were inevitable that other species, for which a permit could not be issued, would also be taken.
39. 42 *Fed. Reg.* 37217 (1977).
40. 42 *Fed. Reg.* 64548 (1977).
41. 45 *Fed. Reg.* 10552 (1980).
42. 45 *Fed. Reg.* 72178 (1980).
43. Although the rules promulgated in 1980 prohibited sundown sets, the prohibition was suspended eight days after it went into effect until an in-depth comparison of daytime versus nighttime mortality could be conducted.
44. *Friends of Animals* v. *Roe,* No. 80-2870 (D.D.C. 31 July 1981).
45. *American Tunaboat Association* v. *Baldrige,* No. 80-1952-G (S.D. Cal. 10 Mar. 1982).
46. *American Tunaboat Association* v. *Baldrige,* 738 F.2d 1013 (9th Cir. 1984).
47. *Balelo* v. *Klutznick,* 519 F. Supp. 573 (S.D. Cal. 1981).
48. *Balelo* v. *Baldrige,* 13 Envtl. L. Rept. 20203 (9th Cir. 5 Jan. 1983).
49. Routinely, U.S. courts of appeal hear matters before a panel of three judges. In exceptional situations, an en banc panel consisting of a greater number of judges is convened. In the Ninth

Circuit Court of Appeals, which decided the *Balelo* case, such a panel consists of 11 judges.

50. *Balelo* v. *Baldrige*, 724 F.2d 753 (9th Cir. 1984).
51. H.R. Rept. No. 228, 92th Cong., 1st sess. (1981).
52. Public Law 98-364, 98 Stat. 440 (1984).
53. 53 *Fed. Reg.* 8910 (1988).
54. Seal bombs are small explosive devices about the size and power of an M-80 firecracker. Use of all but Class C devices (those with 40 grains or less of explosive material) to chase and encircle dolphins was banned outright by the 1988 amendments. The study of Class C devices determined that they would likely cause injury if detonated within about half a meter of a dolphin and their use in the tuna fishery was prohibited in 1990 (Myrick et al. 1990).
55. These limits were necessarily based on percentages of a country's dolphin mortality rather than absolute numbers because no numerical cap on a foreign nation's total kill had been established. Some have argued that this put foreign fishermen in an unfair position because U.S. fishermen could exceed these percentages without penalty, as long as they did not exceed the numerical quotas established for these stocks. Others have contended that these stock-specific limits were quite generous. The percentages established (2% for coastal spotted dolphins and 15% for eastern spinner dolphins) exceeded those that would be applicable to U.S. fishermen if they took the entire annual quota of 20,500 dolphins. Moreover, foreign fishermen could "cleanse" an overly high take of coastal spotted or eastern spinner dolphins by concentrating their effort on other stocks.
56. 54 *Fed. Reg.* 20171 (1989).
57. 54 *Fed. Reg.* 51918 (1989).
58. *Earth Island Institute* v. *Verity*, No. C88-1380 (N.D. Cal. 18 Jan. 1989).
59. *Earth Island Institute* v. *Mosbacher*, 746 F. Supp. 964 (N.D. Cal. 1990).
60. 55 *Fed. Reg.* 37730 (1990).
61. Ibid.
62. *Earth Island Institute* v. *Mosbacher*, No. C88-1380 (N.D. Cal. 4 Oct. 1990).
63. *Earth Island Institute* v. *Mosbacher*, No. 90-16581 (9th Cir. 14 Nov. 1990).
64. *Earth Island Institute* v. *Mosbacher*, 929 F.2d 1449 (9th Cir. 1991).
65. Public Law 101-627, §901, 104 Stat. 4465.
66. Regulations promulgated by the National Marine Fisheries Service determined that vessels with a carrying capacity of less than 400 short tons (362.8 mt) were too small to set on dolphins (50 C.F.R. §216.91). However, information considered by the parties to the International Dolphin Conservation Program at a February 1997 meeting indicated that smaller vessels are capable of setting on dolphins. During 1994–1996, 18 sets on dolphins were made by vessels with a carrying capacity of less than 400 short tons (362.8 mt).
67. *Earth Island Institute* v. *Mosbacher*, No. C88-1380 (N.D. Cal. 26 Mar. 1991).
68. *Earth Island Institute* v. *Mosbacher*, 785 F. Supp. 826 (N.D. Cal. 1992).
69. Under the rules of the World Trade Organization, established in 1995 under revisions to the General Agreements, panel decisions are now adopted automatically.
70. Public Law 102-523, 106 Stat. 3425.
71. 58 *Fed. Reg.* 45066 (1993).
72. Taxonomic studies by Service scientists had determined that the offshore spotted dolphin should be reclassified into northeastern and western/southern stocks (Dizon et al. 1994).
73. 58 *Fed. Reg.* 58285 (1993).
74. *Earth Island Institute* v. *Brown*, 865 F. Supp. 1364 (N.D. Cal. 1994).
75. The Declaration of Panama specifies that minimum population estimates are to be calculated either by the National Marine Fisheries Service or by using an equivalent calculation standard. The methodology to be used presumably is that presented in Barlow et al. (1995).
76. 142 *Cong. Rec.*, H9449 (daily ed. 31 July 1996).
77. Public Law 105-42, 111 Stat. 112 (1997).

Literature Cited

Au, D. W. K., and R. L. Pitman. 1986. Seabird interactions with dolphins and tuna in the eastern tropical Pacific. Condor 88:304–317.

Barlow, J., S. L. Swartz, T. C. Eagle, and P. R. Wade. 1995. U.S. Marine Mammal Stock Assessments: Guidelines for Preparation, Background, and a Summary of the 1995 Assessments. U.S. Department of Commerce, NOAA Technical Memorandum NMFS-OPR-6.

Brower, K. 1989. The destruction of dolphins. The Atlantic Monthly (July): 35–58.

Coe, J. M., D. B. Holts, and R. W. Butler. 1984. The "tuna-porpoise" problem: NMFS dolphin mortality reduction research, 1970–81. Marine Fisheries Review 46 (3): 18–33.

Cowan, D. F., and W. A. Walker. 1979. Disease factors in *Stenella attenuata* and *Stenella longirostris* taken in the eastern tropical Pacific yellowfin tuna purse seine fishery. Southwest Fisheries Center Administrative Report No. LJ-79-32C.

DeBeer, J. 1980. Cooperative dedicated vessel research program on the tuna-porpoise problem: Overview and final report. Final Contract Report for the Marine Mammal Commission. (Available from National Technical Information Service, Springfield, VA. PB80-150097.)

DeMaster, D. P., J. Sisson, L. Stevensen, and S. Montgomery. 1992. Report of the third and final meeting to review progress in reducing dolphin mortality in the ETP purse seine fishery for tunas. NOAA Administrative Report.

Dizon, A. E., W. F. Perrin, and P. A. Akin. 1994. Stocks of dolphins (*Stenella* spp. and *Delphinus delphis*) in the eastern tropical Pacific: A phylogeographic classification. NOAA Technical Report NMFS 119.

Dolan, H. J. 1980. Recommended decision: In the matter of: Proposed regulations to govern the taking of marine mammals incidental to commercial fishing operations. (Docket no. MMPAH 1980-1.)

GATT. 1991. United States—Restrictions on imports of tuna (adopted 3 Sept. 1991) (Panel Report No. DS21/R).

Gonsalves, J. T. 1977. Improved method and device to prevent porpoise mortality; Application of polyvinyl panels to purse seine nets. Final Contract Report for the Marine Mammal Commission. (Available from National Technical Information Service, Springfield, VA. PB-274 088.)

Green, R. E., W. F. Perrin, and B. P. Petrich. 1971. The American tuna purse seine fishery. Pages 182–194 *in* H. Kristjonsson (ed.), Modern Fishing Gear of the World 3. Fish Finding, Purse Seining, Aimed Trawling. Fishing News (Books), London.

Hall, M. A. 1998. An ecological view of the tuna-dolphin problem: Impacts and trade-offs. Reviews in Fish Biology and Fisheries 8 (1): 1–34.

Hofman, R. J. 1979. A workshop to identify new research that might contribute to the solution of the tuna-porpoise problem. Marine Mammal Commission Report. (Available from National Technical Information Service, Springfield, VA. PB-290 158.)

Hofman, R. J. 1981. Identification and assessment of possible alternative methods for catching yellowfin tuna. Marine Mammal Commission Report. (Available from National Technical Information Service, Springfield, VA. PB83-138933.)

Holt, R. S., and J. E. Powers. 1982. Abundance Estimation of Dolphin Stocks Involved in the Eastern Tropical Pacific Yellowfin Tuna Fishery Determined From Aerial and Ship Surveys to 1979. U.S. Department of Commerce, NOAA Technical Memorandum NMFS-SWFC-23.

Holt, R. S., T. Gerrodette, and J. B. Cologne. 1987. Research vessel survey design for monitoring dolphin abundance in the eastern tropical Pacific. Fishery Bulletin 85:435–446.

Housman, R. F., and D. J. Zaelke. 1992. The collision of the environment and trade: The GATT tuna / dolphin decision. Environmental Law Reporter 22:10268–10278.

Inter-American Tropical Tuna Commission. 1988. Annual Report of the Inter-American Tropical Tuna Commission, 1987.

Inter-American Tropical Tuna Commission. 1989. Incidental mortality of dolphins in the eastern tropical Pacific tuna fishery, 1979–1988, a decade of the Inter-American Tropical Tuna Commission's Scientific Technician Program. Working Document 2 from the Tuna-Dolphin Workshop. 14–16 March 1989, San José, Costa Rica.

Inter-American Tropical Tuna Commission. 1993. Annual report of the Inter-American Tropical Tuna Commission, 1992. Appendix 2, pp. 298–303.

Inter-American Tropical Tuna Commission. 1994. Data report no. 8, Statistics of the eastern Pacific Ocean tuna fishery, 1979 to 1992.

Inter-American Tropical Tuna Commission. 1995. Annual report of the Inter-American Tropical Tuna Commission, 1994.

Inter-American Tropical Tuna Commission. 1997. Annual report of the Inter-American Tropical Tuna Commission, 1995.

Joseph, J. 1994. The tuna-dolphin controversy in the eastern Pacific Ocean: Biological, economic, and political impacts. Ocean Development and International Law 25:1–30.

McAlpin, H. S. 1974. Recommended decision: In re: Proposed regulation to govern the incidental taking of marine mammals in the course of commercial fishing operations (50 C.F.R. §216.24).

McNeely, R. L. 1961. The purse seine revolution in tuna fishing. Pacific Fisherman 59 (7): 27–58.

Myrick, A. C., Jr., E. R. Cassano, and C. W. Oliver. 1990. Potential for physical injury, other than hearing damage, to dolphins from seal bombs used in the yellowfin tuna purse-seine fishery: Results from open-water tests. Southwest Fisheries Center Administrative Report No. LJ-90-07.

National Marine Fisheries Service. 1975. Final environmental impact statement on promulgation of rules and proposed issuance of permits to commercial fishermen allowing the taking of marine mammals in the course of normal commercial fishing operations.

National Research Council. 1992. Dolphins and the Tuna Industry. National Academy Press, Washington, DC.

Norris, K. S. 1974. Testimony at National Marine Fisheries Service hearing, 10–11 December 1974. *In Committee for Humane Legislation* v. *Richardson,* 414 F. Supp. 297, 304 (D.D.C. 1976).

Norris, K. S., J. H. Prescott, L. F. Lowry, W. E. Evans, D. Challinor, J. L. Dunn, D. P. Costa, D. L. Alverson, T. Samansky, E. S. Skoch, B. Fenwick, W. Blanshard, S. Lister, K. J. Frost, G. Worthy, G. Woodwell, D. St. Aubin, J. Boehm, W. Y. Brown, S. Paynter, G. Griffith, C. Gaspar, and S. Nachbar. 1996. Letter from concerned scientists on the tuna dolphin problem. 142 *Cong. Rec.,* H9430 (daily ed. 31 July 1996).

Norris, K. S., W. E. Stuntz, and W. Rogers. 1978. The behavior of porpoises and tuna in the eastern tropical Pacific yellowfin tuna fishery—Preliminary studies. Final Contract Report for the Marine Mammal Commission. (Available from National Technical Information Service, Springfield, VA. PB-283 970.)

Perrin, W. F. 1968. The porpoise and the tuna. Sea Frontiers 14:166–174.

Perrin, W. F. 1969. Using porpoises to catch tuna. World Fishing 18:42–45.

Pryor, K., and K. S. Norris. 1978. The tuna / porpoise problem: Behavioral aspects. Oceanus 21 (2): 31–37.

Ralston, F. 1977. A workshop to assess research related to the porpoise / tuna problem, 28 February, 1–2 March. Southwest Fisheries Center Administrative Report No. LJ-77-15.

Sakagawa, G. T. 1991. Are U.S. regulations on tuna-dolphin fishing driving U.S. seiners to foreign-flag registry? North American Journal of Fisheries Management 11:241–252.

Scheele, L., and D. Wilkinson. 1988. Background paper on the eastern tropical Pacific tuna / dolphin issue. Pages 62–126 *in* To authorize appropriations to carry out the Marine Mammal Protection Act of 1972 for fiscal years 1989 through 1993: Hearings on H.R. 4189 before the Subcommittee on Fisheries and Wildlife Conservation of the House Committee on Merchant Marine and Fisheries, 100th Cong., 2d sess.

Smith, T. D. 1974. Estimates of porpoise population sizes in the eastern tropical Pacific, based on an aerial survey done in early 1974. Southwest Fisheries Center Administrative Report LJ-74-38.

Smith, T. D. (ed.). 1979. Report of the Status of Porpoise Stocks Workshop. 27–31 August 1979, La Jolla, CA. Southwest Fisheries Center Administrative Report No. LJ-79-41.

Smith, T. D. 1983. Changes in size of three dolphin (*Stenella* spp.) populations in the eastern tropical Pacific. Fishery Bulletin 81:1–13.

Southwest Fisheries Center. 1975. Progress of research on porpoise mortality incidental to tuna purse-seine fishing for fiscal year 1975. Southwest Fisheries Center Administrative Report No. LJ-75-68.

Southwest Fisheries Center. 1976. Report of the Workshop on Stock Assessment of Porpoises Involved in the Eastern Pacific Yellowfin Tuna Fishery. Southwest Fisheries Center Administrative Report No. LJ-76-29.

Southwest Fisheries Center. 1977. Prepared testimony submitted by SWFC staff at hearing to consider amendment of regulations governing incidental taking of marine mammals in the course of commercial fishing operations, 22–29 August 1997, in San Diego. Southwest Fisheries Center Administrative Report No. LJ-77-27.

U.S. House. 1971. Legislation for the preservation and protection of marine mammals: Hearings on H.R. 690 etc. before the Subcommittee on Fisheries and Wildlife Conservation of the House Committee on Merchant Marine and Fisheries, 92d Cong., 1st sess.

U.S. House. 1974. Legislation for the preservation and protection of marine mammals: Hearings on oversight of the Marine Mammal

Protection Act of 1972 before the Subcommittee on Fisheries and Wildlife Conservation of the House Committee on Merchant Marine and Fisheries, 93d Cong., 2d sess., p. 22.

U.S. House. 1984. A Bill to authorize appropriations to carry out the Marine Mammal Protection Act of 1972 for fiscal years 1985, 1986, and 1987: Hearings on H.R. 4997 before the Subcommittee on Fisheries and Wildlife Conservation of the House Committee on Merchant Marine and Fisheries, 98th Cong., 2d sess.

U.S. House. 1996a. A bill to amend the Marine Mammal Protection Act of 1972 to support the International Dolphin Conservation Program in the eastern tropical Pacific Ocean, and for other purposes: Hearings on H.R. 2823 before the Subcommittee on Fisheries, Wildlife and Oceans of the House Committee on Resources, 104th Cong., 2d sess., ser. 104-58.

U.S. House. 1996b. The provisions of the International Dolphin Conservation Act, how it is affecting dolphin mortality, and what measures can be effected to keep the mortality to a minimum: Hearings before the Subcommittee on Fisheries, Wildlife and Oceans of the House Committee on Resources, 104th Cong., 1st sess., ser. 104-58.

Wade, P. R. 1993a. Estimation of historical population size of the eastern stock of spinner dolphin (*Stenella longirostris orientalis*). Fishery Bulletin 91:775–787.

Wade, P. R. 1993b. Assessment of the northeastern stock of offshore spotted dolphin (*Stenella attenuata*). Southwest Fisheries Center Administrative Report LJ-93-18.

Wade, P. R. 1995. Revised estimates of incidental kill of dolphins (Delphinidae) by the purse-seine tuna fishery in the eastern tropical Pacific, 1959–1972. Fishery Bulletin 93:345–354.

7

MARK A. FRAKER AND BRUCE R. MATE

Seals, Sea Lions, and Salmon in the Pacific Northwest

In 1983 people watched with some amusement when a large male California sea lion (*Zalophus californianus*), nicknamed "Herschel," situated himself near the Ballard ship locks in Seattle and caught steelhead trout (*Oncorhynchus mykiss*), a species of Pacific salmon, as they returned to Lake Washington and their spawning streams (Fig. 7-1). During the next few years, Herschel was joined by others. By the mid-1980s up to 60 male sea lions were present around the locks and nearby parts of Puget Sound.

The number of individual sea lions that were preying on steelhead is unknown, but those that were involved were consuming more than half of the returning steelhead each year. Fishery managers realized that the problem had become serious, and if the steelhead were to survive, something would have to be done to greatly reduce predation. Thus was born the "Herschel problem," which became a high-profile issue in the Seattle area and ultimately led the U.S. Congress to amend the Marine Mammal Protection Act. Cartoons show the lighter side of the issue, while at the same time giving a sense of its prominence (Fig. 7-2).

Despite the actions taken from the mid-1980s to the early 1990s to counter sea lion predation, the number of returning steelhead that managed to migrate upstream past the locks fell from about 2,400 per year before heavy sea lion predation to fewer than 200 in 1993. To most people concerned about the steelhead, the solution was obvious: get rid of the sea lions. But the situation was more complex than that, both politically and biologically.

The Herschel problem is of more than just local significance in the Seattle area. Steelhead and other salmon populations are in trouble throughout the Pacific Northwest. Nehlsen et al. (1991) identified 214 native runs at risk in California, Oregon, Idaho, and Washington. Some have been listed or are proposed for listing under the Endangered Species Act (Federal Register 1996). But while many salmon runs have been declining, harbor seal (*Phoca vitulina*) and California sea lion populations have been growing rapidly and steadily. Although it is agreed that human activities are the root cause of nearly all salmon declines, many fishermen and business people who depend on commercial and sport fisheries are concerned that expanding populations of seals and sea lions may be causing further decline (or impeding the recovery) of various salmon runs in the Pacific Northwest (Contos 1982, General Accounting Office 1993).

In this chapter, we briefly outline the reasons for the decline of salmon stocks, the population trends of pinnipeds, and some of the situations that raise concern about the interaction between these groups of animals. Although these species have coevolved and coexisted in many locations, there are apparently new situations in which pinnipeds

Figure 7-1. "Herschel" eating a steelhead at the Ballard Locks. California sea lions consumed about 60% of returning Lake Washington steelhead in some years. One sea lion was observed to eat 12 steelhead in one eight-hour period. (Photograph courtesy of *Seattle Post-Intelligencer*)

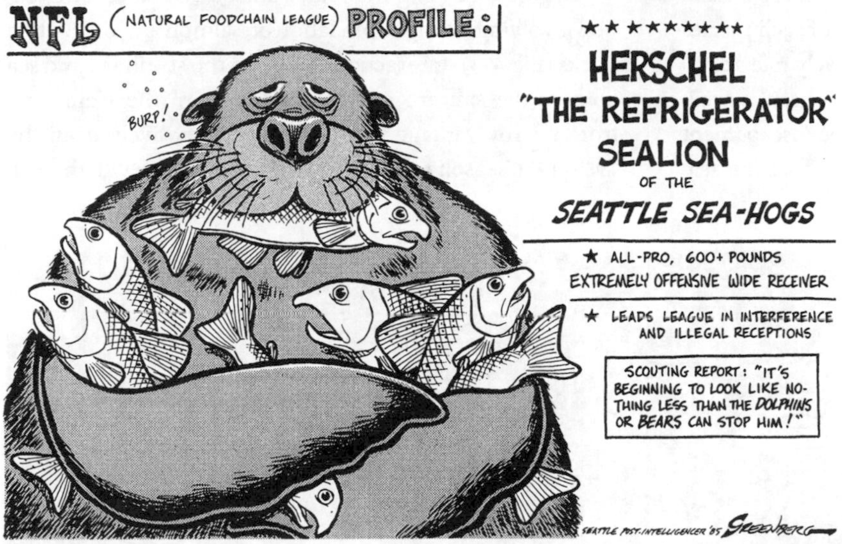

Figure 7-2. Cartoons reflect the high profile of the "Herschel problem" in the Seattle area. (Courtesy of *Seattle Post-Intelligencer*)

could greatly influence the future of specific depressed fish populations. How important is pinniped predation to the future prospects of salmon populations? Is the Ballard Locks situation a microcosm of what is happening more generally in the Pacific Northwest? Or is it artificial and unique? And, where pinnipeds are believed to be having a significant impact on salmon runs, what actions might be taken?

Pacific Salmon Life History

Pacific salmon (*Oncorhynchus*) spawn in freshwater, where their eggs hatch and the young spend from a few months to two years before migrating to the sea, where they achieve most of their growth. Those that remain in freshwater for an extended period grow to about 20 cm and become "smolts" before migrating to salt water. After one to three years at sea, the salmon return as adults to their natal streams, where they spawn and die. The fish of each species that return to a particular stream are collectively referred to as a "run." The number of fish needed to fully use the available spawning habitat is set by managers as the "escapement goal." The terms *winter-run* or *summer-run* denote the season of the spawning migration. Steelhead are exceptional among salmon in that some spawners, about 10% in a given year, go back to the sea and return to spawn the next year.

When salmon leave or return to freshwater, they become concentrated in streams and estuaries. They tend to linger near the mouths of rivers as they make physiological adjustments to the change between salt water and freshwater; adults may take additional time to reach a particular stage of maturation before proceeding upstream to spawn. When they are concentrated and physiologically stressed, salmon are easier prey for pinnipeds, especially if man-made structures like dams or locks impede their movement. Such structures can alter water flow, limit access to fish ladders, or result in the clearing of normal debris (especially logs and limbs) that creates places where salmon can gain protection from predators.

The most thoroughly studied and best understood situation involving pinniped predation on salmon is at the Ballard Locks (Fig. 7-3). Interactions between the steelhead and sea lions at the site are easily surveyed from the water and from nearby vantage points. Studied intensively from the 1985–1986 season to the time of this writing (1998), the Bal-

Figure 7-3. Aerial view of the Ballard Locks and adjacent ship canal, looking east. The locks provide a rare instance of a marine mammal presence in the inner city. (Photograph courtesy of U.S. Army Corps of Engineers, Seattle District)

lard Locks situation has been especially instructive because many types of interventions have been tried and evaluated there. The area is also unique in the degree to which it has permitted investigators to document predation and the effectiveness of predation countermeasures.

Throughout the Pacific Northwest, the complex circumstances facing other salmon stocks, including the role of pinnipeds as predators and, perhaps most important, ecological and economic uncertainties, can create a climate in which conflicting claims can seem equally valid. The great importance of salmon and their habitats in the economies and cultures of this region ensures that people with vested interests will champion the interpretation of the evidence that best suits those interests. Policy makers seeking to balance competing interests must take into account an almost intractable array of factors: incomplete scientific knowledge, treaty commitments, legal requirements (e.g., the Endangered Species Act and the Marine Mammal Protection Act), cultural and political views of various interest groups, and so on.

Clearly, seals and sea lions do eat salmon, but we are not aware of any situations where pinnipeds have put a robust salmon population in jeopardy. The primary causes of depleted runs are almost invariably human activities (i.e., direct removal by fisheries or actions resulting in habitat loss or deterioration [Cone and Ridlington 1996, National Research Council 1996]).

The Plight of Salmon in the Pacific Northwest

Salmon were a major resource of Native Americans (Indians) and consequently played a major role in their domestic economies and cultures. In some cases, treaties define Indian rights to salmon. The precontact population of Native Americans appears to have been stable at about 50,000 in the Columbia River basin and may have consumed more than 8,000 mt (18 million pounds) of salmon annually (Hunn 1991). By the 1840s disease had reduced the Native American population to about 10,000, and an equal number of Europeans had settled in the region.

Salmon have been an important factor in the non–Native American economy of the Pacific Northwest for more than a century. Substantial harvests of salmon did not occur until after canneries began large harvests in the 1860s (Smith 1979). By 1883 there were 55 canneries on the Columbia, and they processed a catch of 19.5 million kg (43 million pounds) of chinook in that year. Although chinook declined from 1886, the catch of all salmonids peaked in 1911 and declined steadily after 1925 (Robbins 1996).

Salmon in the Pacific Northwest are now in serious trouble. The Committee on Protection and Management of Pacific Northwest Anadromous Salmonids (National Research Council 1996) reported that salmon have disappeared from about 40% of their historical spawning range in Washington, Oregon, Idaho, and California; of the remaining runs, many are severely depressed (Nehlsen et al. 1991). For example, the annual return of salmon to the Columbia River system has declined by 80% or more over the past 100 years (from 12 to 16 million in the 1880s to about 2.5 million in the 1980s [Northwest Power Planning Council 1986]), despite a large hatchery program.

This immense loss is mainly a direct result of human activities (Table 7-1), although identifying the specific causes in any particular case can be difficult or impossible. Multiple causes are typical, and different combinations of factors have operated to different degrees in various cases. Furthermore, these declines have occurred over many decades, so that determining the relative contributions of the various causes is usually impossible. Nearly always there has been significant environmental degradation from human activities. Unregulated high seas fisheries and inadequately managed domestic fisheries have resulted in too few adult salmon reaching their spawning grounds. Mixed-stock fisheries often result in the removal of too many fish from one run, even when overall average fishing rates appear to be sustainable.

The loss of salmon from a stream cannot be remedied by simply restoring habitat and releasing salmon of the species and seasonal-run types that were formerly present. The well-known ability of salmon to return to their natal streams with a high degree of accuracy has a critically important biological function: it maintains the specific adaptations that allow these fish to cope with the environmental conditions peculiar to each stream. Salmon from different areas differ in size and morphology, behavior (e.g., migration timing, agonistic behavior), response to temperature, disease resistance, and life history (Taylor 1991). Such differences exist on both local and regional levels and between seasonal ecotypes in the same stream. These adaptations are the expression of the "genetic diversity" that enables salmon to respond to the varying environmental conditions that affect spawning and rearing success (e.g., floods, droughts, and El Niños). The loss of a run can mean the loss of adaptive genetic diversity and ecological function.

Knowing what to do to restore salmon runs depends on understanding more than just what caused the declines in the first place. In some cases, reversing the changes that caused the decline will not be enough and may, in fact, be impossible or impractical (e.g., removing dams). Perhaps there are factors, such as predation by seals and sea lions, that were not important when the runs were healthy, but that are currently slowing or preventing the recovery of extremely depressed runs.

Table 7-1. Factors Causing Declines in Salmon in the Pacific Northwest

Factors	Effects
Dams	Blockage of returning adult salmon, inundation of spawning grounds; mortality and injury of out-migrating juvenile salmon passing through turbines; increased predation by birds and fish on injured juveniles; habitat change from river to lake with temperature, chemical, and biological changes; nitrogen supersaturation of water below dams (Long et al. 1975, Collins 1976, Northwest Power Planning Council 1986, National Research Council 1996)
Forestry practices	Increased water run-off; stream blockage with logging debris; siltation; increased peak stream flows, decreased low flows; increased summer water temperatures, nutrient concentrations, and algal growth; river channel damage from log transport practices (Kimmins 1987, National Research Council 1996)
Agriculture / grazing	Siltation; fertilizer / pesticide inputs; livestock reduce vegetation and compact soils (increasing surface run-off and erosion) and walk in streams and spawning areas (Platts 1991, Armour et al. 1994)
Flood control / irrigation	Juvenile fish stranded in channels or damaged or killed at intakes; unnatural fluctuations in water flows and levels; stream straightening resulting in reduced quality and quantity of habitat; water returned to streams with increased temperature, fertilizer nutrients, pesticides, silt, parasitic nematodes (Northwest Power Planning Council 1986)
Urbanization / industrialization	Reduced forest cover; increased impermeable surfaces (e.g., roads, buildings, parking lots); changes in water chemistry; other changes similar to those from flood control, logging, and agriculture (Booth 1991; Edmondson 1991a,b; Lucchetti and Fuerstenberg 1993)
Mining	Hydraulic and stream bed dredging; stream diversions and blockage; siltation (Northwest Power Planning Council 1986)
Fishing	Overfishing; mixed-stock fisheries (National Research Council 1996)
Wetland drainage	Loss of water flow regulation; decreased water quality; loss of spawning and rearing habitat (Dahl 1990, National Research Council 1996)
Forest fire protection	Catastrophic fires caused or exacerbated by increased forest fuel (branches, needles, leaves) and understory development result in increased erosion, nutrient loss, etc. (as with forestry practices, above)
Salmon hatcheries	Reduced genetic diversity; competition with wild salmon; complication of mixed-stock fishery management (Hilborn 1992, Meffe 1992, Winton and Hilborn 1994)
Fewer beavers	Beaver impoundments formerly were significant regulators of water flows and quality (National Research Council 1996)
Natural events	Floods, droughts, El Niños, etc.

In a nutshell, then, the restoration of salmon stocks is a biological problem (stock size, population genetics, biodiversity, habitat, predation, food supply), with dimensions related to the physical environment (floods, large-scale oceanographic changes), politics (interests of natural resource industries, conservationists, animal rights activists), culture (Native American and other interests), and law (Indian treaty rights, Endangered Species Act, Marine Mammal Protection Act). Doing what is meaningful and possible within each of these realms is a daunting task. Knowing what to do to promote the recovery of depressed salmon populations requires a broad understanding that extends well beyond the technical.

California Sea Lions and Lake Washington Steelhead: "The Herschel Problem"

Lake Washington steelhead spawn in streams that flow into Lake Washington, a large lake (30 km long, 3 km wide) situated in the center of the greater Seattle area (Fraker 1994) (Fig. 7-4). They use these streams despite major alterations of their habitat. Originally, Lake Washington drained to the south into a now nonexistent river that flowed into Puget Sound. But in 1917 the U.S. Army Corps of Engineers dug the Lake Washington Ship Canal, with the Ballard (Chittenden) Locks at its western end. The dam and locks serve to maintain Lake Washington and the ship canal within a nar-

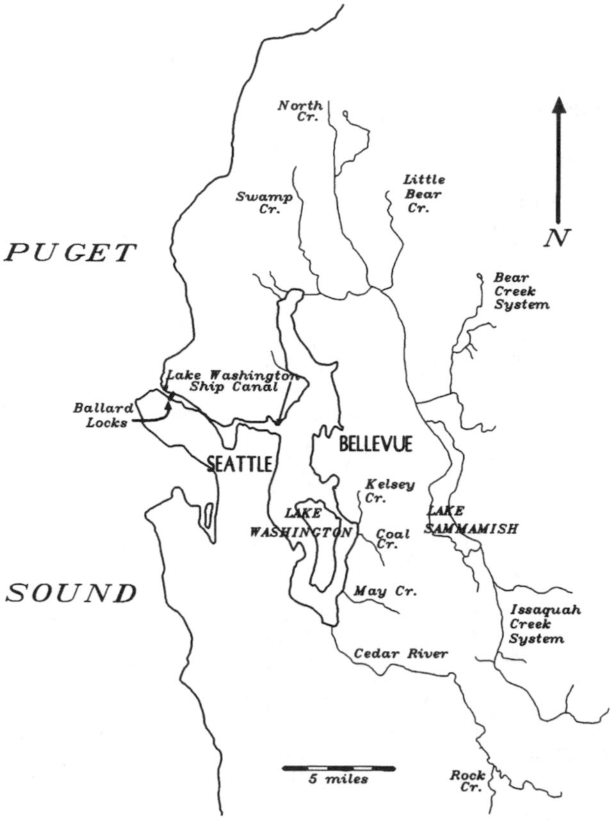

Figure 7-4. Lake Washington watershed showing principal spawning streams used by winter-run steelhead. Currently, significant numbers of fish are using only the Cedar River and some of its tributaries. The Washington Department of Fish and Wildlife intends to reestablish steelhead in formerly used streams in an effort to restore the run. (After Fraker 1994)

row range of water levels, and to permit vessels to move between the lake system and tidewater, which is always at a lower level.

In the immediate vicinity of the locks is an urban mix of businesses, light industries, and residences. The locks operate 24 hours a day, seven days a week. About 80,000 vessels pass through the locks each year, including pleasure craft, barges, commercial fishing vessels, and government research vessels (U.S. Army Corps of Engineers 1993). The locks receive about a million visitors per year, and the migrating fish and sea lions are a large part of the attraction. A guide to Puget Sound marine mammals even recommends visiting the locks to view California sea lions (Osborne et al. 1988).

To move past the dam and locks, the steelhead travel up the fish ladder around the dam and locks (or through the locks), through the ship canal, into Lake Washington, and on to their spawning grounds. This run maintained itself for nearly 70 years, despite environmental degradation from industrial development, agriculture, logging, fishing, and Seattle's urban sprawl. Although the steelhead population must have suffered from these changes (no detailed studies were conducted until recently), it survived sufficiently well to support a small harvest by sport and Treaty Indian fishermen.

Many of the streams in the Lake Washington watershed were spawning grounds for steelhead. Currently, however, the fish are restricted to the main stem of the Cedar River and a few of its tributaries. The Cedar, managed by the City of Seattle as a source of drinking water, contains high-quality steelhead habitat.

The steelhead and the sea lions that interact near the Ballard Locks have been studied during the steelhead winter-run since 1984–1985. Together, the National Marine Fisheries Service, responsible for the conservation and management of pinnipeds in U.S. waters, and the Washington Department of Fish and Wildlife have had investigators present at the locks from December through March or April in most years.

The number of Lake Washington steelhead returning from the sea each year has declined from a mean of about 2,400 in the mid-1980s to a low of 76 in 1993–1994 (Fig. 7-5). Some of these escaped to the spawning grounds, some were eaten by sea lions, and others were caught in Indian and sport fisheries. (The timing of the return of the steelhead is such that the fish are generally not intercepted by commercial fishermen.) Fishing was significant only until 1987–1988. For five of seven winters (1984–1985 to 1990–1991), sea lion predation accounted for about 60% of the returning fish. Predation control measures described below were effective for 1985–1986 and 1986–1987.

The Marine Mammal Protection Act mandates cooperation between the states and the federal government. In the Pacific Northwest, there has been a long history of state-federal cooperation and good relations among biologists and managers. This relationship is evident in the cooperative studies by biologists of the Washington Department of Fish and Wildlife and the National Marine Fisheries Service over more than a decade. Even though management authority for marine mammals rests with the federal government, all states on the Pacific coast have marine mammal biologists on their staffs who engage in cooperative research with Service biologists.

The studies at the Ballard Locks have been aimed at determining (1) how the fish interact with their environment, (2) how the sea lions hunt, (3) the number of fish killed, and (4) the effectiveness of various predation management measures. Most of the effort has focused on predation at the locks, where observations have been made from dawn to dusk. All-night observations of the well-lit locks have

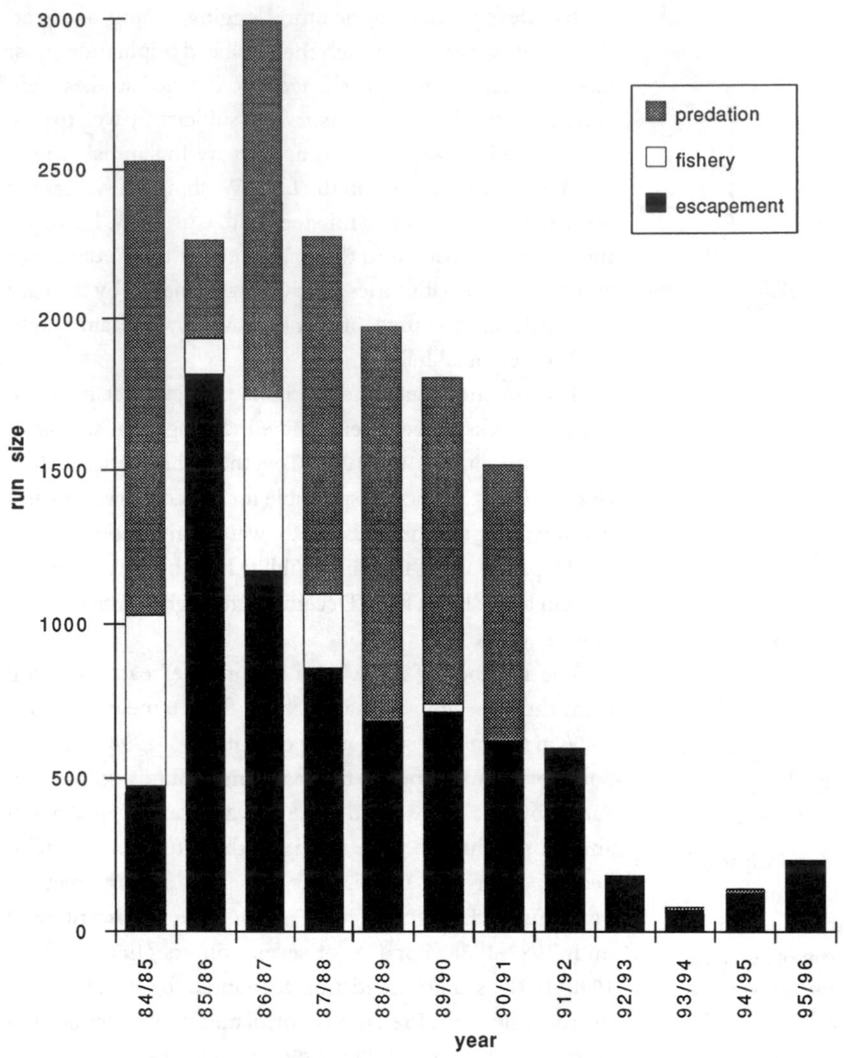

Figure 7-5. Estimated run size, escapement, harvest, and predation of Lake Washington steelhead. (See Table 7-2 for data)

established that little predation occurs at night. The highest predation rates occur between 0900 and 1500 hours. The number of steelhead escaping to the spawning grounds has been estimated from the counts of spawning nests (redds) during stream surveys. Additional effort has been directed at understanding the functioning of the lock facilities (i.e., dam, fish ladder, internal plumbing, and lock operations) and identifying modifications that might improve fish passage or reduce predation by sea lions.

Actions to Reduce Predation, 1985–1994

In 1985, when the first attempts were made to manage sea lion predation, the Marine Mammal Protection Act limited the actions of federal, state, and local government officials to taking marine mammals in a humane manner (including euthanasia) for (1) the protection or welfare of the mammal, (2) the protection of public health and welfare, or (3) the nonlethal removal of nuisance animals.

The National Marine Fisheries Service and the Washington Department of Fish and Wildlife applied a great deal of effort and ingenuity toward trying to solve the problem within the bounds of "nonlethal removal." In the winter of 1985–1986, they tried seal bombs and electronic acoustic deterrent devices. These were placed on the bottom just below the locks and produced intense sounds in the 12- and 17-kHz range (Greenlaw 1987). Concern about the possibly adverse effects of the devices on fish had been addressed for earlier models by Mate and Harvey (1987) and Mate et al. (1987). Seal bombs (large, weighted firecrackers that produce a flash of bright light in addition to an explosion) were thrown near sea lions from walkways around the locks and from small boats. The goals of using these deterrents were to startle and annoy pinnipeds while having little or no effect on fish. Sea lions were also harassed and chased by boats from the area around the locks.

The first year's (1985–1986) efforts were encouraging (Gearin et al. 1986). During the control periods (when the deterrents were not used), the sea lions consumed an average of 18.55 steelhead per day, but this dropped to 0.61 per day when the deterrents were applied, a 97% reduction. The 1985–1986 escapement goal of 1,600 was met (Table 7-2; Fig. 7-5). As many as five sea lions were present at any one time, but because only two were individually recognizable, the total number involved was unknown.

The same approach was tried in 1986–1987, but with less success (Gearin et al. 1988). The estimated consumption rate dropped from 15.3 steelhead per day during the control period to 5.0 per day during the deterrent period, a 67% reduction. In this season, sea lions were present near the locks during 111 of 115 days (96%) when deterrents were applied, compared with 60 of 80 days (75%) the previous year. It was clear that the animals had become more tolerant of the various countermeasures. In this season, up to seven sea lions were present at times. The pattern of initial success followed by a decline in effectiveness is typical of harassment methods used routinely to exclude pinnipeds from specific areas (Mate and Harvey 1987).

A physical barrier was tried in 1987–1988 (Pfeifer et al. 1989). A 40-cm mesh, heavy-duty nylon net was placed below the locks to exclude the sea lions from areas near the dam and fish ladder where most of the sea lions caught steelhead. Tests in the fish ladder around the locks suggested that migrating salmon passed through the net freely, and it was hoped that the barrier would create an area of refuge where the steelhead would be safe before entering the fish ladder.

The barrier did not work; predation losses were similar whether or not the net was present, even though the sea lions were largely excluded from areas where the highest rates of feeding had occurred previously. The sea lions were able to catch the steelhead outside the barrier, perhaps because the steelhead did not move freely through the net as supposed. Seven sea lions managed to get behind the barrier (some by going through the locks and coming over the dam!); two others were caught in the net and drowned. The barrier also presented a number of practical problems. Logs, plywood, plastic garbage bags, and other debris accumulated against the net, despite weekly cleaning, and eventually it collapsed under the water's force. Seal bombs and harassment were also used that year, but with little success.

One novel attempt at deterrence was the insertion of lithium chloride (LiCl), an emetic, into dead steelhead (Gearin et al. 1988). It was hoped that sea lions that ate steelhead containing LiCl would get sick and develop an aversion to steelhead. Four or five sea lions accepted the tethered dead steelhead laced with LiCl. They moved downstream where they appeared to vomit. But within two hours they reoccupied their usual feeding territories and resumed catching steelhead although they declined further offers of dead steelhead.

In 1988–1989 and 1989–1990 the agencies tried to solve the problem by catching sea lions in traps on a large mooring buoy and then releasing them a long distance away (Jeffries et al. 1989, Pfeifer 1991). In the winter of 1989, 39 sea lions were captured and 37 were marked and transported to the southwestern coast of Washington; two died from the immobilizing drugs. Twenty-nine returned to the vicinity of the locks in 4 to 45 days. Nine animals were

Table 7-2. Total Estimated Run Size, Escapement, Harvest, and Predation of Lake Washington Steelhead

Run Year	Estimated Run Size	Steelhead Escapement	Escapement Goal	% of Goal	Fishery Harvest	Sea Lion Predation	Predation as % of Run
1984/1985	[2,527]	474	1,600	30	554	[1,500][a]	[60][a]
1985/1986	2,261	1,816	1,600	114	116	329	15
1986/1987	2,997	1,172	1,600	73	571	1,254	42
1987/1988	2,274	858	1,600	54	238	1,178	52
1988/1989	1,973	686	1,600	43	0	1,287	65
1989/1990	1,806	714	1,600	45	27	1,065	59
1990/1991	1,520	621	1,600	39	0	899	59
1991/1992	?	599	1,600	37	0	No data	No data
1992/1993	?	184	1,600	12	0	No data	No data
1993/1994	76	70	1,600	4	0	8	11
1994/1995	137	126	1,600	8	0	11	8
1995/1996	234	234	1,600	15	0	0	0

Sources: Fraker (1994); S. Foley (pers. comm.).

Escapement estimated from the number of spawning nests found during stream surveys. Total run size is the sum of escapement, harvest, and predation.

[a]Total run size based on a sea lion predation rate of 60%, the approximate mean rate observed in 1987–1988 through 1990–1991 when run size was >1,500 and no effective deterrents were employed.

translocated twice; one, three times; and two, four times. Cynical observers viewed this as a very expensive way to exercise sea lions. In any case, the effort did not solve the problem, even temporarily.

In 1990 six sea lions were taken to the Channel Islands off southern California; unusually cold weather in Puget Sound prevented capturing a larger number. Three returned to Puget Sound in 30 to 45 days, and another was radio-tracked as far as the mouth of the Columbia River before it turned southward. Capturing, holding, and transporting male California sea lions (200 to 450 kg) long distances was not only expensive and dangerous; it did not work.

Harassing sea lions away from the locks with a small radio-controlled boat (Gearin et al. 1988) and with a crossbow shooting blunt rubber-tipped bolts (Pfeifer 1991) was also tried and found ineffective.

Amendments to Allow Lethal Takes

By the winter of 1993–1994 all efforts to control sea lion predation had failed and the steelhead run was dwindling. The U.S. Congress considered ways to deal with the sea lions at Ballard Locks and with other situations in which pinnipeds were preying on salmon. Interest groups on all sides lobbied intensively. As a result, the Marine Mammal Protection Act was amended to permit lethal removals of seals and sea lions under very limited conditions: "A State may apply to the Secretary to authorize the intentional lethal taking of individually identifiable pinnipeds which are having a significant negative impact on the decline or recovery of salmonid fishery stocks which, (1) have been listed as threatened or endangered species under the Endangered Species Act of 1973 (16 USC. 1531 et seq.); (2) the Secretary finds are approaching threatened or endangered species status (as those terms are defined in that Act); or (3) migrate through the Ballard Locks at Seattle, Washington."

The third point was added because no attempts had been made to list the Lake Washington steelhead under the Endangered Species Act. However, most observers agreed that the situation at the Ballard Locks did meet the two initial criteria for authorizing lethal takes: (1) individual pinnipeds could be identified as preying on salmon, and (2) they were having a significant negative effect on the fish stock. In a decade, probably $3 million had been spent on studies at Ballard Locks. In June 1994 the Washington Department of Fish and Wildlife applied to the Secretary of Commerce for permission to kill individual California sea lions identified as predators on steelhead at Ballard Locks.

In response to the application, and as required by the Act's amendments, the Secretary established a pinniped-fishery interaction task force, charged with recommending to the Secretary whether to approve or deny the application for an intentional lethal take of pinnipeds. Along with its recommendation, the task force was to provide a description of the specific pinnipeds to be taken; the proposed location, time, and method of such taking; criteria for evaluating the success of the action; and the duration of the intentional lethal taking authority. Under the Act, the task force was also directed to suggest nonlethal alternatives, "if available and practicable," including a recommended course of action.

The task force consisted of representatives from the National Marine Fisheries Service, the Washington Department of Fish and Wildlife, the U.S. Army Corps of Engineers, several universities, two Treaty Indian tribes (the Suquamish and Muckleshoot), the Northwest Indian Fishery Commission, Greenpeace, the Center for Wildlife Conservation, the Progressive Animal Welfare Society, the Marine Mammal Protection Coalition, the Washington Environmental Council, the King County Outdoor Sports Council, and Trout Unlimited.

The Act's requirement that the group consider nonlethal alternatives caused great debate. Because of the previous lack of success, a majority of the task force members felt that further exploration of the "available and practicable" nonlethal alternatives was precluding the lethal-take options as the fish continued to decline.

The task force deliberated during the fall of 1994. It considered the physical aspects of the locks, dam, and associated facilities, as well as the biology and behavior of the steelhead and sea lions. The majority of the members concluded that, although sea lions were clearly responsible for a heavy mortality to the returning steelhead, the physical modifications to the environment caused by the locks contributed to the situation. The nonlethal alternatives considered by the task force included new harassment techniques, reducing the number of resting sites used by sea lions, temporary captive holding, the construction of artificial fish refuges, and modifications of structures (dam, locks, fish ladders) or their operation. Five major actions were taken:

One, more powerful acoustic deterrent devices were deployed in the winter of 1993–1994 (Norberg and Bain 1994, Reeves et al. 1996). When these were in use, sea lions did not appear to enter the ensonified zone as often, and if they did, they appeared to stay for shorter periods. Unfortunately, deployment of the new devices coincided with a greatly diminished run size (i.e., 76 in 1993–1994 compared with 1,500 to 3,000 per year from 1985 through 1991). Thus, it was impossible to know whether the reduced presence of sea lions was a consequence of the new devices, the lack of sufficient steelhead to attract them, or both. Seal bombs were also used whenever a sea lion stayed within the ensonified zone for more than five minutes, and sometimes the sea lions were harassed with small boats. The 1994–1996 estimated predation rates were only 0–11% (Table 7-2; Fig. 7-5).

Two, sea lion exclusion devices (SLEDs) were placed on navigation buoys near the locks to deprive sea lions of convenient haul-out (resting) sites and to enhance the capture rate at the sea lion trap on the mooring buoy.

Three, lock operations were modified. Although major changes to the physical structure of the locks would have cost millions of dollars, the following modifications to the water management improved the environment for steelhead, especially for the out-migrating smolts.

(a) The water conduits used to fill the locks from upstream are large (approximately 2.4 by 3.0 m and rectangular in cross section) with 90-degree bends and outflow into small locking chambers (0.3 by 0.6 m). Because barnacle encrustations on the conduit walls create rough surfaces that injure or kill smolts, and injured smolts are probably more vulnerable to predation by pinnipeds and birds such as gulls and cormorants, the locks are now filled slowly during daylight hours when smolts are most actively migrating. This lowers the velocity of water in the plumbing. Increasing the proportion of ships passing through the locks at night would also reduce the number of smolts that pass through the plumbing.

(b) Changes in the way water levels are managed in Lake Washington and the ship canal have also benefitted steelhead smolt when they encounter the dam. Although the Army Corps of Engineers is required to maintain the water level in Lake Washington and the ship canal within certain limits, the allowance of higher levels during smolt outmigration permits more water flow to be directed through the fish ladder or over the dam, which are safer routes for the smolts to follow. Six water control gates at the dam can be raised or lowered to alter water flow, and currently one gate is fitted with a sloping device that allows the smolts to pass over the dam less violently. Additional "smolt slides" might further improve smolt passage.

Four, the main spawning stream in the Lake Washington watershed currently is the Cedar River, which is managed by the Seattle Water Department as the city's water supply. The city is cooperating with the Washington Department of Fish and Wildlife to maintain adequate water flows in the Cedar to ensure that the steelhead redds (spawning nests) do not become dry before the fry have emerged from the gravel (S. Foley, pers. comm.).

As the fifth and final change, hatchery fish are no longer released into Lake Washington. For many years, the Washington Department of Fish and Wildlife released hatchery-reared steelhead smolts into Lake Washington to provide increased fishing opportunities. These were from a stock that originated in a stream in southern Puget Sound and returned from the sea earlier in the season. These fish may have helped to attract and hold sea lions in the vicinity of the locks so that they were present when the wild fish arrived. The stocking program ceased in 1994.

Carrying Capacity, Maximum Net Productivity, and Optimum Sustainable Population

Populations of both harbor seals and California sea lions in the Pacific Northwest have increased over the past 25 years, while the population of Steller (or northern) sea lions has remained more or less constant in size. How much of the increase in pinniped populations can be attributed to the protection afforded by the Marine Mammal Protection Act in the United States and to protective regulations in Canada? Earlier, widespread shooting of pinnipeds was actively encouraged in some jurisdictions, and such activities kept the populations relatively stable at "reduced" levels. Much of the recent population growth could be considered the "recovery" of these populations from exploitation. However, something more than recovery may be occurring in the waters off the coast of the Pacific Northwest.

Bringing every marine mammal population to its optimum sustainable population (OSP) level is the primary goal of the Marine Mammal Protection Act. The OSP level, a source of considerable confusion and debate, is defined by the Act to mean: "with respect to any population the number of animals which will result in the maximum productivity of the population, keeping in mind the carrying capacity of the habitat and the health of the ecosystem of which they form a constituent element." Two aspects of the definition that pose difficulties in practice are "carrying capacity" and "health of the ecosystem."

The carrying capacity of an environment is the largest average number of individuals of a species that can be supported over a long period. The concept assumes that the mechanisms that regulate populations are density-dependent; that is, as populations grow, some aspect of the habitat, often food or space, will slow and ultimately stop growth. Thus, as populations approach the carrying capacity of their environment, reproduction rates decrease and mortality rates increase, resulting in reduced or zero growth. Populations can also be affected by factors that act independent of density (e.g., severe weather).

For many terrestrial animals, carrying capacity can be defined operationally and related to measurable attributes of the environment, such as the abundance of certain kinds of plants, the distribution of water holes, or the number of nest sites. The ecology of many game animals is well enough understood that wildlife managers can modify the habitat to provide for a larger or smaller number of individuals (Burger 1979, Taber and Raedeke 1979). Marine mammal biologists do not have the same ability as terrestrial mammal biologists to assess the carrying capacity of the marine environment.

With respect to "health of the ecosystem," animals always have some effect on their environment. For example, they affect the populations of prey or the plant communities on which they forage. Even at population levels where animals and their habitats appear "healthy," there are subtle effects. The composition of plant communities may be changed by deer long before overuse becomes obvious. Even if it may be intuitively easy to recognize habitats that have been overgrazed by deer, it is difficult to determine objectively the population size at which the carrying capacity has been reached and the "health of the ecosystem" compromised.

It is generally assumed that aboriginal people had no significant effect on the California sea lion population and that it was at carrying capacity before European presence along the west coast of North America. That may not have been the case, but there are no data. The Marine Mammal Protection Act also assumes (implicitly, at least) that the carrying capacity of the environment is stable or constant over long periods of time. However, marine environments are not constant, and carrying capacities fluctuate (DeLong et al. 1991, 1993). These variations can be natural or human-caused (e.g., by overfishing or pollution).

Sometimes the environment, and consequently carrying capacity, varies in obvious ways. For example, during El Niño events, abnormally warm water intrudes farther north than usual in the North Pacific, and this affects marine organisms on which sea lions and other marine mammals feed. The result can be large reductions in reproduction and survival of pinnipeds (DeLong et al. 1991). Often it is assumed that the sorts of changes resulting from El Niño events are short-term and reversible, so that a long-term average carrying capacity can still be recognized. In the short term, carrying capacity is always changing to some degree. The expansion of California sea lions into formerly unoccupied areas suggests a recent increase in carrying capacity. What has caused or allowed this expansion?

To think about population growth and optimum sustainable populations, consider the growth of a population that starts with a few individuals introduced into an unpopulated environment. Typically, there is a period of slow growth. Next, growth accelerates to a relatively rapid and constant rate that is determined largely by number of young born, how fast the animals reach maturity and reproduce, how frequently they reproduce, and how long they continue to reproduce. During the period of rapid population growth, the animals are in good physical condition, and both reproduction and survival are high. The point of maximum growth rate (= maximum net productivity [MNP]) comes when a relatively large population size, high reproduction rate, and high survival rate combine so that the largest possible number of animals are added to the population per capita.

After the population increases beyond its MNP level, it continues to grow, but at a progressively slower rate. Several changes may occur, assuming that food becomes more and more scarce: body condition declines, growth of individuals is slower, the age at first reproduction increases, pregnancy rates decrease, and survival rates decline. These changes result in a slowing of population growth until deaths equal births and population size and age and sex composition stabilize. The population is now "the largest supportable within the ecosystem." It has reached its carrying capacity.

Another pattern is also possible. Sometimes a rapidly growing population "overshoots" the long-term carrying capacity of its environment. When this happens, the carrying capacity of the environment may be temporarily reduced (e.g., as with overgrazing), and the population "crashes," falling below the long-term carrying capacity level. This population crash may be followed by a period of ups and downs as the population oscillates around its true carrying capacity. Kenyon (1969) suggested this kind of sequence of events for sea otters, and Fay et al. (1989) for walruses in the North Pacific. In extreme cases, a population may damage its environment to such an extent that the long-term carrying capacity is reduced.

In the context of the Marine Mammal Protection Act, a population is at the OSP level if it is above the point where the growth rate has slowed (i.e., above the level of MNP). Populations below MNP are considered depleted even though the animals may be abundant. The Act does not explicitly consider populations that are above their carrying capacities. Although the Act qualifies its goal of OSP with concern about the "health of the ecosystem," there is no guidance on defining ecosystem health or whether human use (e.g., sport and commercial fishing, alternate uses of habitats) ought to be considered.

Status of Pinniped Stocks in the Pacific Northwest

Only in the past 50 years have there been reliable estimates of pinniped distribution and abundance in the Pacific Northwest, and even these are often limited in geographic coverage and do not reflect an understanding of seasonal movement patterns. For many years preceding those estimates, people had harassed and killed pinnipeds. Before the arrival and settlement of non-Natives in the Pacific Northwest, we assume that all species of pinnipeds were plentiful, and salmon runs were enormous. As commercial salmon-canning industries developed on the Columbia River and smaller rivers like the Rogue, seals and sea lions came to be viewed as important competitors. Both state and private bounty programs were established to reduce their populations. Sea lions were also commercially harvested from the 1840s through the early 1940s in southern California (National Marine Fisheries Service 1997a). Even into the 1960s members of some civic groups and the military considered killing and harassing local pinniped populations as a means of enhancing salmon runs. The killing and the lack of early quantitative information on population sizes make it difficult to know just how large the populations were even as recently as a century ago. Thus, it is impossible to tell whether recent population growth is "recovery" of depleted stocks to their former abundance or to unprecedented levels in response to increased carrying capacity. For example, during the first half of the twentieth century, the Steller sea lion population, for unknown reasons, declined and has now completely disappeared from the Channel Islands off southern California (Bartholomew 1967). If the cause was environmental change, this may have, in turn, increased the carrying capacity for California sea lions.

With reduced harassment and less frequent shooting after implementation of the Marine Mammal Protection Act in 1972, the numbers of harbor seals and California sea lions in rivers and estuaries have increased as their populations have reoccupied their historic ranges. Sightings of pinnipeds in rivers had become so uncommon for several human generations that people now view them as abnormal. Many coastal residents now believe that seal and sea lion populations have increased to unnaturally high levels and are adversely affecting populations of salmon and other species.

Harbor Seals (*Phoca vitulina*)

In the U.S. Pacific Northwest, three stocks of harbor seals are recognized: the California stock, the Oregon and Washington coastal waters stock (inhabiting the waters of Oregon and the outer coast of Washington), and the Washington inland waters stock (inhabiting Puget Sound and the Strait of Juan de Fuca).

Population estimates are a product of raw counts and extrapolation factors. There are problems in interpreting raw counts of harbor seals. The number of seals hauled out at any specific time is affected by tide, time of day, weather, season, and human disturbance. The peak in abundance of harbor seals on shore usually occurs during the early summer molt. Improvements in census techniques (e.g., visual estimates versus more precise counting from photographs), the discovery of additional haul-out areas over time, and replicate counts within a season, which allow researchers to select the highest counts, all tend to make recent censuses more nearly complete. Barlow et al. (1997) reviewed the harbor seal counts from California (Hanan 1996), which showed an increasing trend from 1979 to 1995 (Fig. 7-6). The change from roughly 6,000 animals in 1979 to 17,000 in 1982, however, suggests an impossible 283% increase in three years (44% per year). So what has been the actual rate of increase?

Because the 1979 count is obviously too low, it is prudent to consider the 1982 count of 17,000 as the first in the series. By 1991 the annual total count had risen to about 23,000 seals. This would require an average annual rate of increase of 3.5%. The rate of increase was not constant throughout

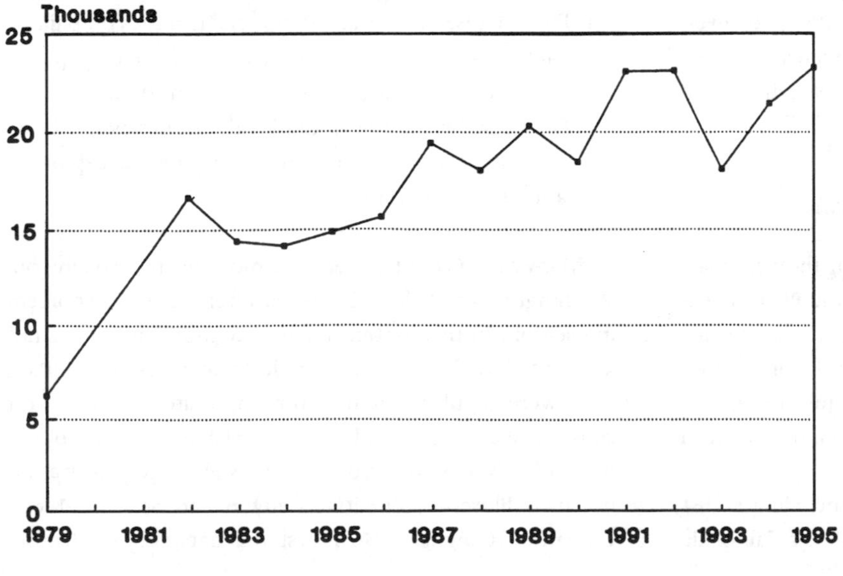

Figure 7-6. Counts of harbor seals on haul-out sites in California, 1979 to 1995. (Data from Hanan [1996] in Barlow et al. [1997] as shown in National Marine Fisheries Service–Pacific States Marine Fisheries Commission 1997)

this period, however (Fig. 7-6). Some of the fluctuations can be explained by changes in ocean productivity, which declined during significant El Niño events in 1982–1983 and 1993. The effects of lowered ocean productivity can sometimes be documented over several years. During an El Niño event, most adult seals survive, but the birth rate is lowered and pup survival is poor. Adult females can be in such poor physiological condition that they do not ovulate or carry a pregnancy to term even during the following year. Figure 7-6 suggests that it took four years after the 1982–1983 El Niño for the harbor seal population to recover to the 1982 level.

Hanan (1996) determined the proportion of seals usually at sea and derived a correction factor of 1.3 times the number hauled out to estimate the total population. Thus, his 1995 California count of 23,302 seals represents a total population of 30,293 (Barlow et al. 1997, National Marine Fisheries Service 1997b). The relatively low rate of increase from 1987 (and especially since 1991) suggests that harbor seals are approaching their carrying capacity or at least that they are above MNP.

The combined haul-out count of the Oregon and Washington coastal and Washington inland waters stocks, whose ranges include the lower reaches of the Columbia River, was 22,310 in 1993. Huber (1995) used radio tags to derive a specific correction factor of 1.53, which was applied to this region to calculate a total abundance of 34,140. From 1978 to 1993 these stocks increased at an estimated annual rate of 7.7%.

As has been the case farther south, harbor seal abundance in British Columbia has increased over the past 25 years, following efforts to reduce numbers to protect fisheries earlier in the century. From the early 1970s to the late 1980s, overall population growth was estimated at 12.5% per year (Olesiuk et al. 1990), a rate that approximates the maximum intrinsic rate of increase. Since 1992, however, the population size has been stable or increasing only slowly; in 1996 the harbor seal population in British Columbia was about 124,000 (P. F. Olesiuk, pers. comm.).

California Sea Lions (*Zalophus californianus*)

Two stocks of California sea lions occur along the west coast of North America from southern British Columbia to central Mexico: the Gulf of California stock and the west coast of Baja California/U.S. stock. The U.S. population is often discussed as a separate stock, but there is no justification for believing it to be reproductively isolated from the Mexican Pacific population.

In July 1975, 65,862 California sea lions, including 11,761 pups, were counted along the Pacific coast of Baja California and California (Mate 1977). From 1975 to 1995 pup counts in southern California increased at a rate of 6% per year, approximately tripling in 20 years (Lowry et al. 1992). Based on pup counts, the number of California sea lions in the United States was estimated in 1995 at between 167,000 and 188,000, with a minimum of at least 111,339 individuals (Barlow et al. 1997). Further summer counts along central and northern California showed an increase from 11,209 in 1982 (Bonnell et al. 1983) to 14,300 in 1995 (Sydeman, cited in National Marine Fisheries Service 1997a). El Niño events in 1983 and 1992 dramatically decreased the number of births and pup survival (DeLong et al. 1991, 1993). Recent surveys showing lower numbers of sea lions at selected haul-out sites along the west coast of Baja California, Mexico, suggest that some of the increase seen in southern California may have been the result of immigration as well as reproduction (B. Mate, unpublished data).

There has been a historic northward shift in the northern limit of the range of the California sea lion and in the southern limit of the range of the Steller sea lion. The latter species was predominant throughout the California Channel Islands at the turn of the century (Bartholomew 1967), but no longer occurs there. It is possible that the current northward extension of the ranges of breeding and nonbreeding California sea lions is a continuation of a long-term trend. There are several possibilities.

(1) During El Niño years, the distribution of several species of fish, sea turtles, and cetaceans (bottlenose dolphins [*Tursiops truncatus*] and short-finned pilot whales [*Globicephala macrorhynchus*]) shifted north. There is evidence that some of the dolphins stayed farther to the north after the event (Wells et al. 1990). Over time, this may result in a "ratcheting" northward of breeding and nonbreeding ranges.
(2) The collapse of several commercial fisheries off Baja California due to overfishing also may have helped motivate California sea lions to move northward.
(3) The growth in southern California could possibly be a recovery of the population from commercial exploitation earlier in this century.

Many male California sea lions move north into Oregon, Washington, and British Columbia after the summer breeding season. In the winter, males now move into areas not known to have been occupied in historic times. In the 1950s they were regular, but uncommon, visitors to the west coasts of Washington and Vancouver Island, British Columbia, and only a few adult males were sighted regularly as far north as Florence, Oregon (Kenyon and Scheffer 1962). Cowan and Guiguet (1956:350) stated that a very small number of ". . . California sea lions occur almost every winter in the Barkley Sound area on [the southwestern coast of] Vancouver Island." From 1968 to 1972 Mate (1975) documented the substantial fall migration of male California sea lions through waters off Oregon and counted as many as 5,000 animals in individual aerial-photo surveys.

There is no mention in the literature of California sea lions in Puget Sound, Washington, or the Gulf of Georgia, British Columbia, until the late 1970s. In about 1960 small numbers began wintering on Race Rocks in the Strait of Juan de Fuca, southwest of Victoria, British Columbia (Guiguet 1971). The maximum number of sea lions on Race Rocks increased from about 10 to 20 in winter 1965–1966 to nearly 300 in winter 1979–1980 (Bigg 1985). Bigg (1988) reported an increase in both numbers and distribution in the Strait of Juan de Fuca and Gulf of Georgia during late-winter surveys from 1972 to 1984, when the count of sea lions observed increased from 45 on 25 February 1972 to 1,702 on 15–16 February 1984, and the number of sites occupied increased from two to six.

The expansion of California sea lions into Puget Sound is consistent with the pattern seen in Canadian waters. Everitt et al. (1979) reported 108 California sea lions near Everett in 1979, the first published record for Puget Sound. They were first seen at the Ballard Locks in 1980 (Fraker 1994). Surveys of Puget Sound were flown in April 1987 and 1988, with 650 and 477 sea lions counted, respectively. Numbers counted near Everett were 376 in 1987 and 467 in 1988.

Whether California sea lions are now occupying new territory is perhaps just a matter of the time scale being used. Lyman (1988) pointed out that there was large-scale commercial exploitation of marine mammals in the northeastern Pacific during the eighteenth and nineteenth centuries although detailed records of the numbers, species, and locations of this exploitation are lacking. He believes that the presence of remains of California sea lions of all ages and both sexes at two sites along the Oregon coast indicates that this species bred there at some time roughly 100 to 400 years ago. Remains have also been reported from the west coasts of northern Washington (Huelsbeck 1983) and Vancouver Island (Calvert 1980, Dewhirst 1980, Loy 1983). Although the archeological record shows that California sea lions have been present on the northwest coast of North America for a long period of time, it is impossible to judge how abundant they were or how consistent their occurrence in any particular area might have been.

Steller Sea Lions (*Eumetopias jubatus*)

In contrast with the harbor seal and California sea lion, the population of Steller sea lions along the Pacific coast south of Alaska has not grown in recent years and the southern limit of its breeding range has shifted north (Hill et al. 1996). The numbers off Oregon and California have been relatively stable, going from about 10,300 in the 1960s to about 9,300 in 1994. The population in British Columbia was reduced from about 14,000 to 3,800 between 1900 and 1970 (Bigg 1988). Bigg attributed much of this decline to deliberate culls as a means of predator control and the targeting of haul-out areas during military exercises. However, the population in Canada has been growing at about 4% per year since the mid-1970s and currently (1996) numbers about 9,500 (P. F. Olesiuk, pers. comm.). Farther north, the population in the Aleutians west of 144°W decreased by about 70% between 1960 and 1989 (U.S. Department of Commerce 1992, Fritz et al. 1995, York et al. 1996). From 1990 to 1994 it declined another 21%. Some researchers have attributed the decline to fishery-induced changes in the abundance of prey species (York et al. 1996). Unlike California sea lions, Steller sea lions rarely enter rivers and estuaries.

Predation by Seals and Sea Lions

Can predation by pinnipeds have a significant impact on salmon populations? An examination of how scientific methods have been applied to specific examples helps answer this complicated question. Both direct and indirect methods can be applied to assess the impact of pinnipeds on fish runs. Direct methods include observations of pinnipeds feeding and identification of food remains in feces (scats), vomitus (spewings), or stomach contents. Scars on fish from encounters with pinnipeds and seasonal movements of pinnipeds in relation to salmon migrations may also be used to make inferences about levels of predation. Such indirect evidence is, however, difficult to interpret.

Nocturnal Feeding

In 1993 L. Milette first observed nocturnal predation by harbor seals on out-migrating (i.e., swimming downstream to the sea) chum salmon fry and coho salmon smolts in the Puntledge River on Vancouver Island, British Columbia. In 1995 P. F. Olesiuk (pers. comm.) and his coworkers made systematic observations to describe the nature of this predation and to estimate its significance. During March through June, seals move into the river starting about an hour before dusk and remain there until about an hour after dawn. They situate themselves on the bottom, in the shadows of two bridges where they look upward and remain more or less stationary. The bridge lights allow the seals to easily detect and catch fry and smolts. At any one time, up to 26 seals have been observed spaced at about 3-m intervals across the river. Because the investigators could recognize individual seals, it was clear that there was flux in the "feeding population" over the course of the night, with some individuals arriving well after dusk and others leaving well before dawn.

The estimated number of chum fry eaten by harbor seals was 3.1×10^6 (95% confidance interval $\pm 1.3 \times 10^6$), between 7 and 31% of the total 1995 fry production, depending on egg survival rates. Coho predation was estimated at 1.38×10^5 (95% confidence interval $\pm 0.79 \times 10^5$), which was about 15% of total 1995 coho smolt production (P. F. Olesiuk, pers. comm.).

A. Trites (pers. comm.) and coworkers conducted additional work in 1996. They found that turning off the bridge lights had no effect on the rate of predation although predation was no longer confined primarily to the bridge areas. The seals were apparently able to detect fry and smolts by using the incidental light from the town of Courtney, through which the Puntledge River flows. Thus, it appears that the seals did not require the relatively intense light from the bridges. Harbor seals, with their large eyes, may be well adapted for foraging in low light, indicating that the ability to function under low light conditions has played an important role in seal feeding at depth or by moon and starlight over evolutionary time. Therefore, nocturnal predation might be an important natural factor in many salmon streams with sufficient clarity, but its distribution, magnitude, and importance are unknown. The observation of night feeding by harbor seals is in contrast to the almost exclusive daytime feeding by sea lions at the Ballard Locks. However, California sea lions on Shell Island at Cape Arago, Oregon, typically left the area at dusk and returned in the early morning with fresh hake (*Merluccius productus*) as stomach contents, suggesting nocturnal feeding in the open ocean (Mate 1975).

Food Habits Studies

Examining food remains contained in the scat and vomitus left at haul-out sites is the most common approach to studying the diets of seals and sea lions. In 1985–1986 and 1986–1987 Gearin et al. (1986, 1988) collected scats and spewings (vomitus) to determine the California sea lion's diet in Puget Sound outside the Ballard Locks area. Samples came from sites in Shilshole Bay (near the Ballard Locks) and near Everett, about 40 km to the north. Squid beaks and fish otoliths were used to identify prey species. Otoliths are the ear bones of fish; they can be used to identify the species, size, and age of the fish.

Samples from both areas contained remains of a variety of fish species (Table 7-3). Hake, herring (*Clupea harengus*), and spiny dogfish (a small shark) (*Squalus acanthius*) occurred with the greatest frequency; salmon (including steelhead) were more common in samples from the Shilshole area than from the Everett area. Remains of squid were not recorded during studies in the mid-1980s, although late in 1993 large numbers of squid came into Shilshole Bay and as far as the locks, where sea lions were observed feeding on them (R. Pfeifer, pers. comm.). These results illustrate an important limitation of food habit studies. Because of individual variability and limited sample sizes, it is not valid to extrapolate a localized food-habit study to an entire population.

Methodology can also bias the results of a food habit study. For example, Roffe and Mate (1984) compared visual observations of fish brought to the surface by sea lions feeding in the Rogue River with fish found in the stomachs of sea lions collected from the same river. The two techniques gave different results. The observations of surface feeding emphasized lamprey and large salmon. Sea lions killed the latter by tearing out their belly during violent thrashing at the surface. This behavior was apparent even to casual spectators. The prolonged activity of the predating sea lions and the large size of salmon made them easier than smaller fish to identify as prey. Casual observers often suspected that the remainder of the fish was wasted. However, sea lions usually consumed the rest of the fish underwater. Commonly, they did not eat the head, so otoliths of large salmon were underrepresented both in stomach contents and scats. Small fish showed up in the stomach contents but were not apparent from surface observations. Sea lions probably ingest most small fish underwater.

Such sources of bias make it difficult to describe the food habits of pinniped populations, but the average diet of the population is not necessarily very helpful. The most relevant question may be how to determine the diets of the few individual seals or sea lions involved in significant predation on depressed salmon runs.

At Ballard Locks in the winter of 1988–1989, 40% of all steelhead eaten by known sea lions were taken by an animal identified as number 38; animals number 19 and 25 took another 40%. At the Puntledge River, on eastern Vancouver Island, 10 of 32 known harbor seals accounted for about 60% of the consumption of coho smolts and another 10 known seals accounted for an additional 20–30%.

Predation Rates

In calculating a predation rate on salmon by harbor seals, Bigg et al. (1990) assumed that it was, on average, constant during daylight hours and half that rate at night. They also assumed that they were able to detect all predation events during their sample periods. Under these assumptions, har-

Table 7-3. Percentage Frequency of Occurrence of Prey Remains Found in Scats and Vomitus of California Sea Lions Collected at Puget Sound Haul-Out Sites in 1985–1986 and 1986–1987

Prey Category	1985–1986 Port Gardner and Elliot Bay (*n* = 100)	1986–1987 Shilshole Bay (*n* = 71)	1986–1987 Everett (*n* = 48)
Hake *Merrluccius productus*	88.0%	71.8%	91.6%
Pacific herring *Clupea harengus*	26.0%	36.6%	50.0%
Spiny dogfish *Squalus acanthius*	8.0%	28.1%	14.5%
Miscellaneous codfishes Gadidae	6.0%	11.2%	8.3%
Salmonids Salmonidae	5.0%	25.3%	6.2%
Walleye pollock *Theragra chalcogramma*	5.0%	5.6%	2.0%
Pacific cod *Gadus macrocephalus*	2.0%	5.6%	0.0%
Octopus *Octopus* sp.	1.0%	0.0%	0.0%
Pacific lamprey *Lampetra tridentatus*	1.0%	0.0%	0.0%
Shiner perch *Cymatogaster aggregata*	0.0%	1.4%	0.0%
Eelpout Zoarcidae	0.0%	0.0%	2.0%
Fish bone	0.0%	100.0%	100.0%

Source: After Gearin et al. (1988).

Sample size, *n*, is the number of individual scat and vomitus deposits collected.

bor seals appeared to exert a relatively low (<10%) rate of predation on the abundant hatchery-based runs of pink, chum, and coho salmon. However, the chinook run in the Puntledge River, which had been reduced to 1,300 fish by overfishing and habitat degradation, suffered a disproportionately high rate of predation (46%). Does the relatively slow-moving Puntledge River provide a better foraging environment for the seals than faster-moving salmon rivers? We do not know.

Roffe and Mate (1984) estimated that pinnipeds consumed <1% of the adult spring chinook returning to spawn, 5 to 6% of the immature steelhead moving downriver to the ocean, and <1% of the mature steelhead migrating up the river to spawn. These levels were relatively insignificant from a biological standpoint, and fish counts upriver continued to grow over the next several years. Only harbor seals ate upriver summer steelhead. Sea lions took 3 to 6 times as many chinook and 2.5 to 5 times as many downriver immature steelhead as did seals. Because sea lions also "stole" hooked fish from sportfishing gear, their presence reduced the sportfishing reputation of the Rogue River and had a detrimental effect on the local tourism-based economy.

Lampreys are common prey for pinnipeds (Jameson and Kenyon 1977, Bowlby 1981, Roffe and Mate 1984, Beach et al. 1985, Riemer and Brown 1996). They are slow-moving and easy to catch. They are also rich in energy and available for much of the year in most coastal rivers. Lampreys are parasitic and can cause death for a wide variety of fish. They attach themselves with grasping mouthparts and leave characteristic scars when they are dislodged. It is not known how many juvenile and adult fish a lamprey kills or seriously injures in its lifetime, but salmon are among the many species that lampreys parasitize. In some river systems, lamprey scars are found on more than half of the returning adult salmon, suggesting a significant impact. On the Fraser River, 65% of returning salmon are scarred by lamprey (Mills 1971). In some rivers, lampreys are the most important pinniped prey species. Because this predation takes place during the lamprey's upstream spawning migration, fewer lampreys are produced. Each female lamprey spawns 30,000 to 120,000 eggs. Of 28 California sea lions and 13 seals collected by Roffe and Mate (1984) on the Rogue River from 1976 to 1978, lampreys were the principal food species by weight (69.1%) and frequency (92.9%).

Perhaps pinniped predation on lampreys saves the lives of more salmon than the pinnipeds consume. The increased number of pinnipeds in coastal rivers may be responsible for the recent decline in lamprey populations along the northeastern Pacific coast (H. Li, pers. comm.). Will the lower numbers of lampreys increase the likelihood of pinnipeds feeding on salmon?

Is Scarring an Indication of Predation Pressure?

Pinnipeds are not always successful in their capture attempts. In the Columbia River system, significant numbers of pinniped-injured salmon were first noted about 1990 (Harmon et al. 1994, Fryer 1998). This probably was not a new situation, but had not been previously documented. From 1990 to 1993 Harmon et al. (1994) examined spring-summer chinook and steelhead returning to the Lower Granite Dam on the Snake River, 700 km upstream from the mouth of the Columbia River. They identified three types of pinniped-caused injuries: (1) scratches on the flanks of the salmon, presumably made during an attempt to grasp the fish with the front flippers, resulting in scale loss; (2) arch-shaped scratches, apparently from canine teeth, also resulting in scale loss; and (3) open wounds that were attributed to teeth penetrating the skin. Harmon et al. (1994) found that the proportion of spring-summer chinook with abrasions ranged from 18.3 to 19.2% and the proportion with open wounds ranged from 5.1 to 6.6%. The figures for steelhead were 5.4 to 14.2% with abrasions and 1.3 to 4.2% with open wounds. No trend was observed over the four years.

Fryer (1998) recorded the occurrence of damage apparently caused by pinnipeds to sockeye and spring-summer chinook salmon returning to the Bonneville Dam, 243 km up the Columbia River, from 1991 to 1995. The proportion of chinook with abrasions and other wounds increased from 10.5% in 1991 to 31.8% in 1994, falling to 22.2% in 1995. Injuries to sockeye increased steadily from 2.8% in 1991 to 10.9% in 1995. The proportion of injuries judged to be severe enough that the fish might not be able to spawn was low, ranging from 0 to 2.6% for chinook and 0 to 1.8% for sockeye.

No significant difference between the injury rates of hatchery-origin (identified by a clipped adipose fin) and wild-origin chinook was found (Fryer 1998). However, it was not always possible to discriminate between the types because some hatchery-produced fish were not fin-clipped. Determining whether wild and hatchery-produced fish differ in their vulnerability to pinniped predation is significant because of the importance of hatcheries in maintaining many runs.

The data on abrasions and wounds are difficult to interpret and lead to more questions than answers. Why did both Harmon et al. (1994) and Fryer (1998) find higher injury rates in chinook than in other species? Are the larger chinook slower and easier to scar or catch so that seals and sea lions target them, or are they harder to catch, resulting in fewer fish caught but more fish injured? Most important, how does the number of injured fish relate to the total number killed (i.e., the number eaten by pinnipeds and the number of wounded fish that died before they reached the study sites)? Is the ratio of injuries to mortality the same for both the large chinook and the smaller steelhead and sockeye? Is there a relationship between the predation rate and the presence of alternative prey (including lampreys and other runs of salmon), water flow rates, and distance upstream? We simply do not know at this time.

Movements

Insights into the relationship between pinnipeds and their prey may be gained by examining the overlap of their seasonal movements. For instance, the fall northward migration of California sea lions parallels the ocean migration of hake, their primary winter prey in offshore waters of the Pacific Northwest (Mate 1975) and in the Everett area of Puget Sound (Table 7-3). It is apparent that some seals and sea lions also learn where and when salmon and steelhead are easiest to catch. They then regularly visit these places at the appropriate time of year.

As their name implies, harbor seals are frequently found in estuaries. Although they are considered nonmigratory, seals often have regional home ranges that include several estuaries (Brown 1981, Brown and Mate 1983, Harvey 1987). In 1989 and 1990 Bigg et al. (1990) estimated that 200 harbor seals used Comox Harbour and the Puntledge River estuary area during salmon nonspawning periods (most of the year). This was equivalent to about 5% of the total number of seals inhabiting the area between southern Vancouver Island and the mainland. However, from August through November, pink, chum, coho, and chinook salmon spawn, and the number of harbor seals in this area grows to about 700 (17% of the regional population) (Fig. 7-7). In Oregon, Brown and Mate (1983) found that radio-tagged harbor seals moved 65 km south from Tillamook Bay to Netarts Bay, a movement coinciding with the onset of the Netarts chum salmon run. Pregnant seals radio-tagged in the Columbia River moved to Grays Harbor, Willapa Bay, and Tillamook Bay during the pupping season (spring) after the late winter spawning run of eulachon (*Thaleichthys pacificus*) (Jeffries 1984).

Although it is clear that seals and sea lions travel to areas where fish are abundant, we do not know what influences their diet, apart from availability. Is it ease of capture, caloric benefit:cost ratio, behavior learned from their mothers, dietary needs, or merely "taste" preference? We suspect that learning plays a large role in determining the diet of individual seals and sea lions. Each probably learns the behavior and habitat of particular prey species, thereby becoming specialized and more efficient predators. Obviously, they have a wide range of acceptable prey species and sizes. Do pinnipeds move specifically to areas with preferred species or high prey densities? We do not know.

Effects of Hatcheries on Predation

For decades, hatchery-produced fry and smolts have been released into streams and rivers to compensate for the loss of upriver spawning habitats caused by dams and human activities. Unfortunately, this policy often did not recognize the importance of (nor did it protect) the natural genetic diversity of wild stocks. One expression of this diversity is the duration of the period over which a given salmon run returns to spawn. The protracted runs of wild fish probably evolved as a means of buffering against extremes of drought or high temperature that might adversely affect the hatching success or the out-migration timing of fry or smolts. We do not know whether the pinniped predation success is correlated with prey density. If it is, large releases of hatchery fish may attract pinnipeds.

Conclusions

Concern about the effects of pinniped predation on salmon runs is likely to become more acute. Many salmon runs are either declining or failing to recover, and many freshwater habitats that have been degraded are not being restored. In some cases, damaging activities (e.g., operation of dams, overfishing, pollution, and livestock grazing) continue. Large-scale changes also may be occurring in the marine environment. The determination that some runs should be classified as threatened or endangered under the Endangered Species Act will result in further restriction of important economic activities, such as logging, commercial fishing, and sportfishing. Inevitably, those who are affected will seek solutions that minimize the impact on themselves.

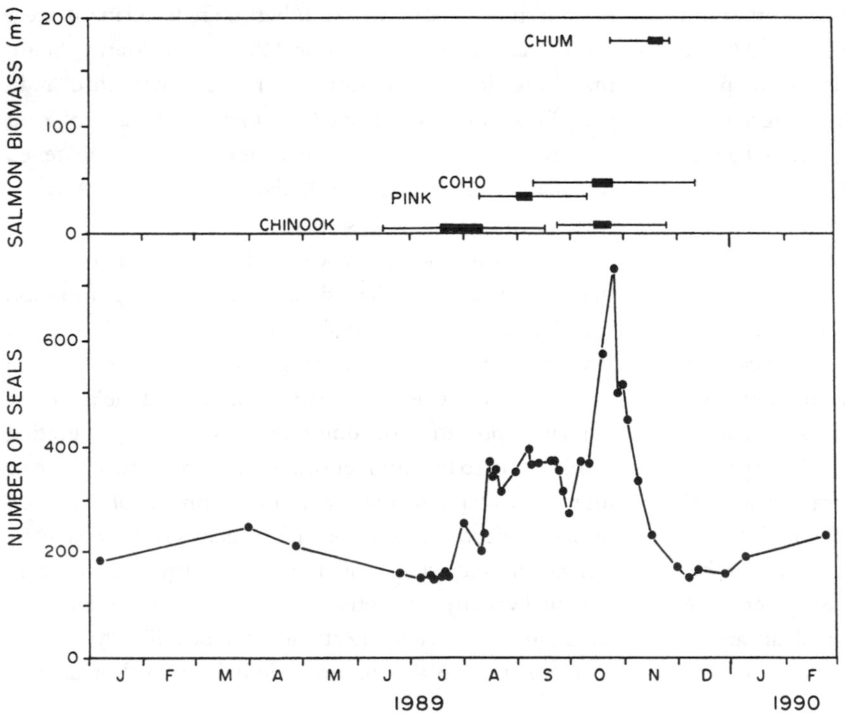

Figure 7-7. Seasonal changes in the number of harbor seals counted in Comox Harbour and in the biomass of salmon returning to the Puntledge River, British Columbia. Upper panel uses lines to depict the timing of runs, with the peak of the run shown as a black bar. (From Bigg et al. [1990], courtesy of Pacific Biological Station, Canada Department of Fisheries and Oceans)

Furthermore, with populations of harbor seals and California sea lions already at high levels and continuing to grow, these animals are being and will continue to be blamed, rightly or wrongly, for part of the plight of salmon in the Pacific Northwest. The following elements are important:

Information Gaps

Gaining an understanding of the effects of pinnipeds on salmon runs is extremely difficult. Even in the case of the Herschel problem, in which access and observation conditions were nearly ideal, it took millions of dollars and nearly a decade to gather sufficient data to document the interaction between California sea lions and steelhead trout and to prove that "nonlethal" means were inadequate to reduce predation to a nonthreatening level. We still have a lot to learn about fundamental aspects of pinniped behavior and ecology: witness the recent discovery of nocturnal feeding on salmon smolts and fry in the Puntledge River. Pinnipeds are intelligent predators, often able to adapt to and exploit new situations. Our understanding of circumstances will change over time, but so also might the situations we study. What was true yesterday may not be true tomorrow. In most cases, it will be difficult or impossible to conduct studies that are adequate to determine whether pinnipeds are significantly affecting salmon.

Even late in the twentieth century, there is much that we still do not understand about marine ecosystems and how seals and sea lions function within them. "Carrying capacity" and "health of the ecosystem," which relate to optimum sustainable population, the fundamental goal of the Marine Mammal Protection Act, are difficult to define in an operational sense. Marine mammal biologists, unlike terrestrial mammalogists, may not be able to recognize a habitat whose carrying capacity has been exceeded.

Seals and Sea Lions Are Individuals

Even where seals or sea lions are significantly affecting salmon populations, only a few individuals in the local populations are likely to be involved. Indiscriminate culling will not be successful at controlling predation unless virtually all of the local population is killed. A preferable approach would be to remove only identified "problem individuals," as is presently specified under the Marine Mammal Protection Act. Lethal removals can be effective when the number of experienced animals is greatly reduced. Such removals may also reduce the rate at which new individuals are recruited into the pool of problem animals.

Certain Conditions Are Necessary for Pinniped Predation to Be a Significant Factor in Reducing Salmon Populations

Perhaps we know enough now that we can identify the general conditions under which significant interactions can occur:

(1) the salmon population or run is already depleted (depressed) from human activities (overfishing, habitat deterioration);
(2) the salmon are concentrated, encounter natural or man-made impediments to migration (rapids, dams, and fish ladders), or gather near hatcheries;
(3) the fish are physiologically stressed while making the transition between salt water and freshwater in estuaries; and
(4) the fish find themselves in simplified habitats that have been cleared of natural debris and other environmental complexity that might have provided them with escape habitat.

There may be interventions, instead of or in addition to removing problem pinnipeds, that can mitigate the situation in favor of the fish. These will be highly site-specific, as they were at the Ballard Locks.

Legal Constraints

If seals or sea lions are believed to be seriously affecting a salmon run, how can their numbers be reduced in the area? A state can apply under section 120(a) of the Marine Mammal Protection Act for authority to lethally remove "individually identifiable pinnipeds that are having a significant negative impact . . ." on salmon runs that (a) are threatened or endangered (under the Endangered Species Act), or (b) are approaching such status.

As we have discussed above, it is difficult to document that pinnipeds are in fact significantly affecting a salmon run. Experience at the Ballard Locks and the Puntledge River suggests that few situations will lend themselves to gathering the needed information. Because of the difficulty in relating predation of adult spawners or of out-migrating smolts or fry to the number of adult fish that return three or four years later, any assessment of the impact of predation or of the effectiveness of control measures will probably be limited and subject to more than one interpretation. There are usually many factors that will be changing through time, so assigning cause and effect will often be difficult.

In addition to the option of lethal removal, it may be

possible to develop nonlethal experimental management strategies in some regions. These might provide both insight into the nature of the problem and some measure of relief. Sometimes using more than one technique (that is only partially effective on its own) can have significant results.

Polarized Views

Fishermen, Native peoples, loggers, farmers, sportsmen, conservationists, environmentalists, animal rights activists, and others all claim a stake in the process of protecting and restoring Pacific salmon stocks. To many of these people, the maintenance of the salmon stocks is more important than the lives of individual pinnipeds whose populations are not endangered.

Captive Holding, Physical Barriers, and So Forth

The capture and temporary holding of problem marine mammals is not a practical long-term solution. For example, building a suitable facility (at a cost of up to $1 million) to hold 40 animals seasonally may address ethical concerns about killing, but this creates a whole new set of continuing problems and costs (e.g., providing food, sewage disposal, and veterinary care). Animals held in captivity may become accustomed to humans, resulting in other problems after release (e.g., acting without caution near humans, remaining dependent on humans, or being overtly aggressive).

Few of the questions posed in the introduction to this chapter can currently be answered. We do not know in what ways and to what extent pinniped predation affects salmon runs. The Ballard Locks case, like any particular situation, is unique, but some elements of it are probably common to many pinniped-salmon interactions. For example, only a small proportion of the local pinniped population is involved, the salmon run is depressed, the habitat is simplified, the interaction occurs at the interface between freshwater and salt water, and interest groups are highly polarized.

The issues surrounding seals, sea lions, and salmon involve colliding values and interests. Economic issues involve dams, agriculture, forestry, commercial fishing, industry, and urban development, and all of these affect salmon conservation. Environmental issues involve endangered species, biological diversity, the dynamic equilibrium of predator and prey populations, and ecosystem restoration. Cultural issues related to Native Americans and national differences in fishery management policies among the United States, Mexico, and Canada also come into play.

It would be imprudent, if not largely ineffective, to eliminate or reduce pinnipeds wherever they "compete" with humans, when just a small percentage of the population may consume salmon. This is not merely an issue between animal rights activists and fish harvesters. We need to understand the fundamental ecological relationships between pinnipeds and human-harvested fish species if we are going to successfully manage both. The recovery of salmon will require attention to all aspects of the problem: access to high-quality spawning and rearing habitat, maintaining water flows, properly managing harvests, and possibly limiting predation by pinnipeds on severely depleted salmon runs. To be effective in reducing the predation pressure of pinnipeds on salmonids, any pinniped removal (lethal or nonlethal) must be targeted on appropriate individuals. Using pinnipeds in simplistic models as scapegoats to justify large-scale culling is not socially acceptable or scientifically defensible.

Acknowledgments

In considering the nature and importance of interactions between seals, sea lions, and salmon, we consulted many colleagues who shared freely of their information and insights. We thank Robert DeLong, Robert Everitt, Steve Foley, Patrick Gearin, Robert Hofman, Steve Jeffries, Karl Kenyon, Steve Leider, Brent Norberg, Peter Olesiuk, Bob Pfeifer, Karen Pryor, Sandy Ridlington, Victor Scheffer, Joe Scordino, Court Smith, and Andrew Trites. We also thank Sallie Beavers and Sara Heimlich-Boran for their editorial assistance.

Literature Cited

Armour, C., D. Duff, and W. Elmore. 1994. The effects of livestock grazing on western riparian and stream ecosystem. Fisheries 19:9–12.

Barlow, J., K. A. Forney, P. S. Hill, R. L. Brownell Jr., J. V Carretta, D. P. DeMaster, F. Julian, M. S. Lowry, T. Ragen, and R. R. Reeves. 1997. U.S. Pacific Marine Mammal Stock Assessments: 1996. U.S. Department of Commerce, NOAA Technical Memorandum, NMFS-SWFSC-248, Southwest Fisheries Science Center, National Marine Fisheries Service, La Jolla, CA. 223 pp.

Bartholomew, G. A. 1967. Seal and sea lion populations of the California islands. Pages 229–244 *in* R. N. Philbrick (ed.), Proceedings of the Symposium on the Biology of the Channel Islands, Santa Barbara (CA) Botanic Garden, 1965. University of California at Santa Barbara, CA.

Beach, R. J., A. C. Geiger, S. J. Jeffries, S. D. Treacy, and B. L. Troutman. 1985. Marine mammals and their interactions with fisheries of the Columbia River and adjacent waters, 1980–1982. Northwest and Alaska Fisheries Center Processed Report 85-04. 316 pp.

Bigg, M. A. 1985. Status of the Steller sea lion (*Eumetopias jubatus*) and California sea lion (*Zalophus californianus*)in British Columbia. Canadian Special Publication of Fisheries and Aquatic Sciences 77. 20 pp.

Bigg, M. A. 1988. Status of the California sea lion, *Zalophus californianus,* in Canada. Canadian Field-Naturalist 102:307–314.

Bigg, M. A., G. M. Ellis, P. Cottrell, and L. Milette. 1990. Predation by harbour seals and sea lions on adult salmon in Comox Harbour and Cowichan Bay, British Columbia. Canadian Technical Report of Fisheries and Aquatic Sciences. 31 pp.

Bonnell, M. L., O. Pierson, and G. D. Farrens. 1983. Pinnipeds and sea otters of central and northern California, 1980–1983: Status, abundance and distribution. Report to the Pacific OCS Region, Minerals Management Service, Department of the Interior. (Available from the Alaska Fisheries Science Center, National Marine Fisheries Service, Seattle, WA.) 220 pp.

Booth, D. B. 1991. Urbanization and the natural drainage system—impacts, solutions, and prognoses. Northwest Environmental Journal 7:93–118.

Bowlby, C. E. 1981. Feeding behavior of pinnipeds in the Klamath River, northern California. M.S. thesis, Humboldt State University, Arcata, CA. 74 pp.

Brown, R. 1981. Abundance, movements and feeding habits of the harbor seal, *Phoca vitulina,* at Netarts Bay, Oregon. M.S. thesis, Oregon State University, Corvallis, OR.

Brown, R., and B. Mate. 1983. Abundance, movements and feeding habits of harbor seals, *Phoca vitulina,* at Netarts and Tillamook Bays, Oregon. Fishery Bulletin (U.S.) 81:291–301.

Burger, G. V. 1979. Principles of wildlife management. Pages 89–97 *in* R. D. Teague and E. Decker (eds.), Wildlife Conservation—Principles and Practices. The Wildlife Society, Bethesda, MD.

Calvert, S. G. 1980. A cultural analysis of faunal remains from three archeological sites in Hesquiat Harbour, BC. Ph.D. dissertation, University of British Columbia, Vancouver, B.C., Canada. 336 pp.

Collins, G. B. 1976. Effects of dams on Pacific salmon and steelhead trout. Marine Fisheries Review 38 (11): 39–46.

Cone, J., and S. Ridlington (eds.). 1996. The Northwest Salmon Crisis: A Documentary History. Oregon State University Press, Corvallis, OR. 374 pp.

Contos, S. M. 1982. Workshop on marine mammal–fisheries interactions. Final report to the Marine Mammal Commission. (Available from National Technical Information Service, Springfield, VA.)

Cowan, I. McT., and C. J. Guiguet. 1956. The Mammals of British Columbia. British Columbia Provincial Museum Handbook 11. 413 pp.

Dahl, T. E. 1990. Wetland losses in the United States: 1780s to 1980s. U.S. Fish and Wildlife Service, Washington, DC. 13 pp.

DeLong, R. L., G. A. Antonelis, C. W. Oliver, B. S. Stewart, M. C. Lowry, and P. K. Yochem. 1991. Effects of the 1982–83 El Niño on several population parameters and diet of California sea lions on the California Channel Islands. Pages 166–172 *in* F. Trillmich and K. A. Ono (eds.), Pinnipeds and El Niño. Ecological Studies 88. Springer-Verlag, New York, NY.

DeLong, R. L., S. R. Melin, and G. A. Antonelis. 1993. Comparison of 1983 and 1992 El Niño impacts on California sea lion and northern fur seal populations in California. Abstract, Tenth Biennial Conference on the Biology of Marine Mammals. 11–15 November 1993, Galveston, TX.

Dewhirst, J. 1980. An archeological pattern of faunal resource utilization of Yuquot, a Nootkan outside village: 1000 BC–1966. Paper presented at the meetings of the Society for American Archeology, Vancouver, B.C., Canada, 1979.

Edmondson, W. T. 1991a. The Uses of Ecology: Lake Washington and Beyond. University of Washington Press, Seattle, WA. 329 pp.

Edmondson, W. T. 1991b. Responsiveness of Lake Washington to human activity in the watershed. Pages 629–638 *in* Proceedings, Puget Sound Research '91. Puget Sound Water Quality Authority, Olympia, WA.

Everitt, R. D., C. H. Fiscus, and R. L. DeLong. 1979. Marine Mammals of Northern Puget Sound and the Strait of Juan de Fuca: A Report on Investigations November 1, 1977 to October 31, 1978. NOAA Technical Memorandum ERL MESA-41. Environmental Research Laboratory, Boulder, CO. 191 pp.

Fay, F. H., B. P. Kelly, and J. L. Sease. 1989. Managing the exploitation of Pacific walruses: A tragedy of delayed response and poor communication. Marine Mammal Science 5:1–16.

Federal Register. 1996. Endangered and threatened species: Proposed endangered status for five ESUs of steelhead and proposed threatened status for five ESUs of steelhead in Washington, Oregon, Idaho, and California. Federal Register 61 (155): 41541–41561.

Fraker, M. A. 1994. California sea lions and steelhead trout at the Chittenden Locks, Seattle, WA. Unpublished report to the Marine Mammal Commission, Washington, DC. vii + 42 pp. + appendices.

Fritz, L. W., R. C. Fererro, and R. J. Berg. 1995. The threatened status of Steller sea lions, *Eumetopias jubatus,* under the Endangered Species Act: Effects of Alaska groundfish fisheries management. Marine Fisheries Review 57 (2): 14–27.

Fryer, J. K. 1998. Frequency of pinniped-caused scars and wounds on adult spring-summer chinook and sockeye salmon returning to the Columbia River. North American Journal of Fisheries Management 18:46–51.

Gearin, P., B. Pfeifer, and S. Jeffries. 1986. Control of California sea lion predation of winter-run steelhead at the Hiram M. Chittenden Locks, Seattle, December 1985–April 1986. Fishery Management Report 86-20, Washington Department of Wildlife, Mill Creek, WA. xi + 108 pp.

Gearin, P. J., R. Pfeifer, S. J. Jeffries, R. L. DeLong, and M. A. Johnson. 1988. Results of the 1986–87 California sea lion–steelhead trout predation control program at the Hiram M. Chittenden Locks. Northwest and Alaska Fisheries Center Processed Report 88-30. ix + 111 pp.

General Accounting Office. 1993. Protected species, marine mammals' predation of varieties of fish. GAO/RCED-93-204. 12 pp.

Greenlaw, C. F. 1987. Psychoacoustics and pinnipeds. Pages 11–15 *in* B. R. Mate and J. T. Harvey (eds.), Acoustical deterrents in marine mammal conflicts with fisheries. Oregon Sea Grant Publication ORESU-W-86-001. Sea Grant Communications, Oregon State University, Corvallis, OR.

Guiguet, C. J. 1971. An apparent increase in California sea lion, *Zalophus californianus* (Lesson), and elephant seal, *Mirounga angustirostris* (Gill), on the coast of British Columbia. Syesis 4:263–264.

Hanan, D. A. 1996. Dynamics of abundance and distribution for Pacific harbor seals, *Phoca vitulina richardsi,* on the coast of California. Ph.D. dissertation, University of California at Los Angeles, CA. 158 pp.

Harmon, J. R., K. L. Thomas, K. W. McIntyre, and N. N. Paasch. 1994. Prevalence of marine mammal tooth and claw abrasions on adult anadromous salmonids returning to the Snake River. North American Journal of Fisheries Management 14:661–663.

Harvey, J. T. 1987. Population dynamics, annual food consumption, movements, and dive behavior of harbor seals, *Phoca vitulina,* in Oregon. Ph.D. dissertation, Oregon State University, Corvallis, OR. 177 pp.

Hilborn, R. 1992. Hatcheries and the future of salmon in the Northwest. Fisheries 17:5–8.

Hill, P. S., D. P. DeMaster, and R. J. Small. 1996. Draft Alaska marine mammal stock assessments 1996. Unpublished report of National Marine Mammal Laboratory, National Marine Fisheries Service, Seattle, WA. 129 pp.

Huber, H. 1995. The abundance of harbor seals (*Phoca vitulina richardsi*) in Washington, 1991–1993. M.S. thesis, University of Washington, Seattle, WA. 56 pp.

Huelsbeck, D. R. 1983. Mammals and fish in the subsistence economy of the Ozette. Ph.D. dissertation, Department of Anthropology, Washington State University, Pullman, WA.

Hunn, E. S. 1991. Nch'I-wana "The Big River": Mid-Columbia Indians and Their Land. University of Washington Press, Seattle, WA.

Jameson, R. J., and K. W. Kenyon. 1977. Prey of sea lions in the Rogue River, Oregon. Journal of Mammalogy 58:672.

Jeffries, S. J. 1984. Seasonal movement patterns and population trends for harbor seals (*Phoca vitulina richardsi*) in the Columbia River and adjacent waters. Final report to Marine Mammal Commission, Washington, DC.

Jeffries, S. J., R. L. DeLong, P. J. Gearin, H. Kajimura, and S. R. Melin. 1989. California sea lion capture and translocation: A solution to fishery interaction. Paper presented at the Eighth Biennial Conference on the Biology of Marine Mammals. 7–11 December 1989, Pacific Grove, CA.

Kenyon, K. W. 1969. The Sea Otter in the Eastern Pacific Ocean. North American Fauna, No. 68. Bureau of Sport Fisheries and Wildlife, Washington, DC. xiii + 352 pp. Reprinted (1975) by Dover Publications, New York, NY.

Kenyon, K. W., and V. B. Scheffer. 1962. Wildlife surveys along the northwest coast of Washington. Murrelet 42:29–37.

Kimmins, J. P. 1987. Forest Ecology. Macmillan, New York, NY. 531 pp.

Long, C. W., F. J. Ossiander, T. E. Ruehle, and G. M. Matthews. 1975. Final report on survival of coho salmon fingerlings passing through turbines. Unpublished report to U.S. Army Corps of Engineers, Seattle, WA, by National Marine Fisheries Service, Northwest Fisheries Center. 16 pp.

Lowry, M. S., P. Boveng, R. J. DeLong, C. W. Oliver, B. S. Stewart, H. DeAnda, and J. Barlow. 1992. Status of the California sea lion (*Zalophus californianus*) population in 1992. NMFS Administrative Report LJ-92-32. 24 pp. + tables and figures.

Loy, T. H. 1983. Prehistoric blood residues: Detection on tool surfaces and identification of species of origin. Science 220:1269–1271.

Lucchetti, G., and R. Fuerstenberg. 1993. Urbanization, habitat conditions and fish communities in small streams of western King County, Washington, USA, with implications for management of wild coho salmon. Proceedings of American Fisheries Society Coho Workshop. May 1992, Nanaimo, B.C., Canada.

Lyman, R. L. 1988. Zoogeography of Oregon coast marine mammals: The last 3,000 years. Marine Mammal Science 4:247–264.

Mate, B. R. 1975. Annual migration of the sea lions *Eumetopias jubatus* and *Zalophus californianus* along the Oregon USA coast. Rapports et Procès-Verbaux des Réunions. Conseil International pour l'Exploration de la Mer 169:455–461.

Mate, B. R. 1977. Aerial censusing of pinnipeds in the eastern Pacific for assessment of population numbers, migratory distributions, rookery stability, breeding effort, and recruitment. Report No. MMC-75/01. Marine Mammal Commission, Washington, DC. 67 pp.

Mate, B. R., and J. T. Harvey (eds.). 1987. Acoustical deterrents in marine mammal conflicts with fisheries. Oregon Sea Grant Publication ORESU-W-86-001. Sea Grant Communications, Oregon State University, Corvallis, OR. 116 pp.

Mate, B. R., R. F. Brown, C. F. Greenlaw, J. T. Harvey, and J. Tempte. 1987. An acoustic harassment technique to reduce seal predation on salmon. Pages 23–36 *in* B. R. Mate and J. T. Harvey (eds.), Acoustical deterrents in marine mammal conflicts with fisheries. Oregon Sea Grant Publication ORESU-W-86-001. Sea Grant Communications, Oregon State University, Corvallis, OR.

Meffe, G. K. 1992. Techno-arrogance and halfway technologies: Salmon hatcheries on the Pacific coast of North America. Conservation Biology 6:350–354.

Mills, D. 1971. Salmon and Trout: A Resource, Its Ecology and Management. Oliver and Boyd, Edinburgh, Scotland. 351 pp.

National Marine Fisheries Service. 1997a. Investigation of scientific information on the impacts of California sea lions and Pacific harbor seals on salmonids and on the coast ecosystems of Washington, Oregon and California. (Available from National Technical Information Service, Springfield, VA.) 86 pp. + appendices.

National Marine Fisheries Service. 1997b. Report to Congress on Washington State marine mammals. iii + 39 pp. + 3 attachments.

National Marine Fisheries Service–Pacific States Marine Fisheries Commission. 1997. Draft report to Congress: Results of discussions regarding recommendations for addressing the impacts of California sea lions and Pacific harbor seals on salmonids and west coast ecosystems. 17 pp.

National Research Council. 1996. Upstream: Salmon and society in the Pacific Northwest. Committee on Protection and Management of Pacific Northwest Anadromous Salmonids, Board on Environmental Studies and Toxicology, National Research Council, Washington, DC. 452 pp.

Nehlsen, W., J. E. Williams, and J. A. Lichatowich. 1991. Pacific salmon at the crossroads: Stocks at risk from California, Oregon, Idaho, and Washington. Fisheries 16:4–21.

Norberg, B., and D. E. Bain. 1994. Implementation and assessment of the acoustic barrier at the Hiram M. Chittenden Locks using calibrated measurements of the sound field. Unpublished report to the National Marine Fisheries Service, Seattle, WA. 67 pp. + appendices.

Northwest Power Planning Council. 1986. Compilation of information on salmon and steelhead losses in the Columbia River Basin. Appendix D of the 1987 Columbia Basin Fish and Wildlife Program, Portland, OR. 252 pp.

Olesiuk, P. F., M. A. Bigg, and G. M. Ellis. 1990. Recent trends in the abundance of harbour seals, *Phoca vitulina,* in British Columbia. Canadian Journal of Fisheries and Aquatic Sciences 47:992–1003.

Osborne, R., J. Calambokidis, and E. M. Dorsey. 1988. A Guide to Marine Mammals of Greater Puget Sound. Island Publishers, Anacortes, WA. 191 pp.

Pfeifer, B. 1991. Monitoring of 1989–90 California sea lion control program in the Lake Washington estuary. Fishery Management Report 90-17, Washington Department of Wildlife, Mill Creek, WA. ix + 94 pp.

Pfeifer, B., P. J. Gearin, S. J. Jeffries, M. Johnson, and R. L. DeLong. 1989. Evaluation of the 1987–88 California sea lion control program in the Lake Washington estuary. Fishery Management Report 89-9, Washington Department of Wildlife, Mill Creek, WA.

Platts, W. S. 1991. Livestock grazing. Pages 389–424 *in* W. R. Meeham (ed.), Influences of Forest and Rangeland Management on

Salmonid Fishes and Their Habitats. American Fisheries Society Special Publication 19.

Reeves, R. R., R. J. Hofman, G. K. Silber, and D. Wilkinson. 1996. Acoustic Deterrence of Harmful Marine Mammal–Fishery Interactions. Proceedings of a Workshop held in Seattle, WA, 20–22 March 1996. NOAA Technical Memorandum NMFS-OPR-10. 70 pp.

Riemer, S. D., and R. F. Brown. 1996. Marine mammal (pinniped) food habits in Oregon. Unpublished report to Pacific States Marine Fisheries Commission, Portland, OR, from the Oregon Department of Fish and Wildlife, Newport, OR. 26 pp.

Robbins, W. G. 1996. The world of Columbia River salmon: Nature, culture and the great river of the west. Pages 2–24 *in* J. Cone and S. Ridlington (eds.), The Northwest Salmon Crisis: A Documentary History. Oregon State University Press, Corvallis, OR. 374 pp.

Roffe, T. J., and B. R. Mate. 1984. Abundances and feeding habits of pinnipeds in the Rogue River, Oregon. Journal of Wildlife Management 48 (4): 1262–1274.

Smith, C. L. 1979. Salmon Fishes of the Columbia. Oregon State University Press, Corvallis, OR.

Taber, R. D., and K. J. Raedeke. 1979. Population dynamics. Pages 98–106 *in* R. D. Teague and E. Decker (eds.), Wildlife Conservation—Principles and Practices. The Wildlife Society, Bethesda, MD.

Taylor, E. B. 1991. A review of local adaptation in Salmonidae, with particular reference to Pacific and Atlantic salmon. Aquaculture 98:185–207.

U.S. Army Corps of Engineers. 1993. Lake Washington Ship Canal and Hiram M. Chittenden Locks. Brochure prepared by the Seattle District, U.S. Army Corps of Engineers, Seattle, WA.

U.S. Department of Commerce. 1992. Final recovery plan for Steller sea lion, *Eumetopias jubatus*. 92 pp. (Available from National Marine Mammal Laboratory, Seattle, WA.)

Wells, R. S., L. J. Hansen, A. Baldridge, T. Dohl, K. L. Kelly, and R. H. Defran. 1990. Northward extension of the range of bottlenose dolphins along the California coast. Pages 421–431 *in* S. Leatherwood and R. R. Reeves (eds.), The Bottlenose Dolphin. Academic Press, New York, NY.

Winton, J., and R. Hilborn. 1994. Lessons from supplementation of chinook salmon in British Columbia. North American Journal of Fisheries Management 14:1–13.

York, A. E., R. Merrick, and T. Loughlin. 1996. An analysis of the Steller sea lion metapopulation in Alaska. Pages 259–292 *in* D. R. McCulloch (ed.), Metapopulations and Wildlife Conservation. Island Press, Anacortes, WA.

8

RAY GAMBELL

The International Whaling Commission and the Contemporary Whaling Debate

Whaling can be traced back at least to the Stone Age. Archaeological excavations and early historical records clearly indicate that whales were taken for subsistence use (Slijper 1962, Matthews 1975, Kalland 1995). Commercial whaling began as early as the ninth century in the North Sea and English Channel (De Smet 1981) and the twelfth century in the Bay of Biscay (Ellis 1991). As the European stocks of northern right whales (*Eubalaena glacialis*) were reduced, whalers were forced to search farther afield, and they reached the coast of North America in the sixteenth century (Proulx 1993). The Greenland right whale, or bowhead (*Balaena mysticetus*), was taken in the so-called northern whale fishery in the northern North Atlantic and the adjacent Arctic Ocean from 1611 until early in the 1900s (Jackson 1978). The primary products were oil, used for lighting, heating, and soap and paint manufacturing, and baleen, which provided pliable stiffening for such articles as umbrella ribs, corset stays, and carriage springs.

Hunting of sperm whales (*Physeter macrocephalus*) began off the New England coast of North America in 1712 and soon extended into a worldwide hunt that also included humpback whales (*Megaptera novaeangliae*). The result was depletion of many stocks by the early 1900s (Mackintosh 1965). The subsequent decline in the sperm whale hunt was accelerated by the discovery of petroleum, which replaced sperm oil in a variety of manufacturing processes (Kugler 1981). Whalers from New England dominated this phase of whaling, with the British and other nationalities involved in the expansion from the Atlantic into the Pacific and Indian Oceans (Berzin 1972, McNab 1975), including the establishment of shore-based whaling stations in Australia, New Zealand, and southern Africa (Dakin 1977, Best and Ross 1986). Southern and northern right whales (*E. australis* and *E. glacialis,* respectively) and bowhead whales were all seriously reduced by the beginning of the twentieth century, as was the gray whale (*Eschrichtius robustus*), which migrated close to the Pacific coasts of North America and Asia.

Until late in the nineteenth century, hunting had been targeted on the relatively slow-swimming species that usually float when dead. Whalers hunted in open boats powered by sail or oars, initially using hand-held harpoons and lances. These weapons were largely replaced by darting guns and bomb lances during the second half of the nineteenth century (Mitchell et al. 1986). Parallel with the European whaling, a separate Japanese coastal fishery existed, possibly dating before the tenth century for right whales and to the sixteenth century for gray whales, using hand-held harpoons (Omura 1986). Beginning in 1675 a netting technique allowed Japanese whalers to catch mainly humpback, right, and gray whales (Omura 1984).

Modern Whaling

The advent of modern whaling can be dated from 1864 when the Norwegian Svend Foyn successfully used explosive grenade harpoons fired from a cannon mounted on a powered catcher boat. This technology brought even the fastest-swimming and largest whale species, such as the blue, fin, and sei whales (*Balaenoptera musculus, B. physalus,* and *B. borealis,* respectively), within reach of shore-based whalers (Tønnessen and Johnsen 1982). Foyn's invention spread widely in the whaling operations in the North Atlantic. The stocks of many of the whales that could be exploited from coastal stations were soon depleted, the carcasses having been cut up and the raw materials processed into oil, meal for animal feed, fertilizers, and other products. Norwegian-type whaling was first attempted in eastern Asia in 1889 off the coast of Korea (Risting 1931) and then in Japan in 1900.

The hunt spread farther afield and eventually extended into the rich and productive waters of the Antarctic. The first land station opened on South Georgia in 1904, and rapid expansion followed. In addition to land stations, floating factory ships were moored in sheltered harbors where the carcasses could be flensed alongside the vessel and the blubber and flesh hoisted aboard. The limited amount of space on shore and the limited number of suitable anchorages, together with restrictive governmental controls, initially kept catches in check. In 1925, however, the development of floating factory ships with stern slipways made it possible to haul whales on deck for processing. These vessels and their attendant catcher fleets were able to operate on the high seas wherever whales could be found (Bonner 1980). Within five years there were six shore stations, 41 British and Norwegian factory ships, and 232 whale catchers working in the Antarctic (Jahn 1937). Such intensive exploitation led inevitably to a decline in the industry after the 1930s (Fig. 8-1). The war provided a brief respite during 1939–1945, but the reduction of many of the major whale stocks continued in all the oceans. Finally, a worldwide pause in commercial whaling was introduced for the member nations of the International Whaling Commission, with effect from the 1986 coastal and the 1985–1986 pelagic whaling seasons.

Figure 8-1. British Antarctic whaling was based in South Georgia, a sub-Antarctic island in the South Atlantic Ocean, from the early 1900s to the 1960s. This scene of Grytviken as it appeared in the 1980s is mute testimony to the utter decline in this once-profitable industry. (Photograph by Steve Leatherwood)

Table 8-1 lists total reported catches of the major whale species (blue, fin, humpback, sei, Bryde's [*Balaenoptera edeni*], sperm, gray, bowhead, and right whales) from 1874 to 1995. Table 8-2 demonstrates clearly how the catches of minke whales (*Balaenoptera acutorostrata*) increased from the early 1970s when this small species became a primary target of Antarctic whaling.

The exploitation of whales has therefore spread from coastal to offshore waters and from pole to pole, causing the successive depletion of one species and stock after another and culminating in the decline of the whaling industry itself (Jahn 1933, Mackintosh 1965, Allen 1980, Evans 1987).

Regulation

During the 1930–1931 Antarctic whaling season, more whale oil was produced than the world market could absorb. As a result, the whaling companies competing in the Antarctic agreed to limit their output (Jackson 1978). Because the industry was concerned primarily with production rather than the number of whales taken, it devised a plan to regulate catches by the amount of oil produced. Thus, the blue whale unit (BWU) was conceived as a means of appraising whales based on average oil yields; that is, one blue whale was equivalent to two fin whales, two and one-half humpbacks, or six sei whales. Annual quotas were thus expressed in BWUs rather than in whales. During the following decade, several intergovernmental agreements to regulate the industry were reached (Gambell 1993). The first of these was the Convention for the Regulation of Whaling, signed in Geneva in 1931. This was followed by a further agreement in 1937 and protocols adopted in 1938, 1944, and 1945. Finally, in 1946 the whaling nations adopted the International Convention for the Regulation of Whaling, which established the International Whaling Commission (IWC).

The International Whaling Commission

The International Convention for the Regulation of Whaling was signed in Washington, D.C., on 2 December 1946. It consists of two parts: the convention proper and a schedule of the precise regulations governing whaling operations (Marine Mammal Commission 1994). The schedule, an integral part of the convention, can be amended by a three-fourths majority of the contracting governments present and voting. This is usually done at an annual meeting. The purpose of the convention, as set out in its preamble, is to provide for the proper conservation of whale stocks and thus make possible the orderly development of the whaling industry (IWC 1950).

Table 8-1. Officially Reported Catches of "Great Whales" (Excluding Minke Whales) by Modern Whaling as Recorded in the International Whaling Statistics

Year[a]	Total Catch	Year	Total Catch	Year	Total Catch
1874	51	1915	18,320	1958	64,075
1875	39	1916	17,542	1959	64,373
1876	45	1918	9,468	1960	63,489
1877	36	1919	10,242	1961	65,641
1878	116	1920	11,369	1962	66,090
1879	130	1921	12,174	1963	63,579
1880	163	1922	13,940	1964	63,001
1881	283	1923	18,120	1965	64,680
1882	351	1924	16,839	1966	57,891
1883	569	1925	23,253	1967	52,238
1884	485	1926	28,240	1968	46,645
1885	1,423	1927	24,215	1969	42,126
1886	986	1928	23,593	1970	42,480
1887	925	1929	28,115	1971	38,771
1888	709	1930	38,300	1972	32,133
1889	585	1931	43,130	1973	32,605
1890	799	1932	12,992	1974	31,905
1891	910	1933	28,915	1975	29,961
1892	1,330	1934	32,586	1976	22,049
1893	1,607	1935	39,311	1977	16,309
1894	1,528	1936	44,896	1978	13,638
1895	1,526	1937	51,586	1979	10,668
1896	1,925	1938	54,902	1980	3,542
1897	1,791	1939	45,783	1981	2,928
1898	1,993	1940	37,709	1982	2,050
1899	1,541	1942	8,072	1983	1,683
1900	1,635	1943	8,346	1984	1,743
1901	2,204	1944	6,197	1985	1,202
1902	3,065	1945	5,906	1986	843
1903	3,867	1946	19,384	1987	817
1904	4,931	1947	34,820	1988	266
1905	4,592	1948	43,382	1989	287
1906	3,519	1949	44,002	1990	225
1907	4,490	1950	45,093	1991	233
1908	5,509	1951	55,812	1992	275
1909	8,490	1952	49,816	1993	67
1910	12,301	1953	44,988	1994	108
1911	20,408	1954	53,615	1995	157
1912	24,838	1955	55,041	1996	104
1913	25,673	1956	58,062	1997	158
1914	22,980	1957	58,990		

Source: International Whaling Statistics. Records for 1946–1972 in particular are liable to adjustment upward because of revision of the Union of Soviet Socialist Republics catch reports.

Note: Catches for some years after World War II were actually greater than reported (Yablokov 1994, Zemsky et al. 1995). Also substantial catches were made by the old-style industry in the nineteenth and early twentieth centuries (e.g., Best 1987).

[a]1910 = 1909–1910 + 1910 season, etc.

Table 8-2. World Catches of Minke Whales

Year[a]	Total Catch	Year	Total Catch	Year	Total Catch
1930	33	1953	2,939	1976	10,592
1931	194	1954	3,974	1977	12,211
1932	369	1955	4,848	1978	9,467
1933	545	1956	4,394	1979	9,900
1934	731	1957	4,483	1980	11,667
1935	905	1958	5,762	1981	10,559
1936	1,075	1959	3,942	1982	11,547
1937	1,283	1960	4,179	1983	10,417
1938	1,415	1961	3,950	1984	8,653
1939	989	1962	3,884	1985	7,169
1940	727	1963	4,095	1986	6,473
1941	2,365	1964	3,877	1987	5,736
1942	2,460	1965	3,418	1988	421
1943	1,911	1966	3,277	1989	333
1944	1,610	1967	3,580	1990	430
1945	1,875	1968	4,840	1991	437
1946	2,012	1969	4,073	1992	497
1947	2,732	1970	2,513	1993	672
1948	3,897	1971	4,582	1994	743
1949	4,188	1972	8,304	1995	921
1950	2,279	1973	10,454	1996	1,085
1951	3,204	1974	11,621	1997	1,203
1952	3,912	1975	10,969		

Source: International Whaling Statistics.

[a]1955 = 1954–1955 + 1955 season, etc.

The main duty of the IWC is to review and revise as necessary the measures in the schedule that govern the conduct of whaling in all waters where whaling is prosecuted from factory ships, land stations, and whale catcher boats under the jurisdiction of the contracting governments. These measures, among other things, accord complete protection to certain species, designate specified areas as whale sanctuaries, set limits on the numbers and size of whales that may be taken, prescribe open and closed seasons and areas for whaling, and prohibit the capture of sucklings and female whales accompanied by calves. The compilation of catch reports and other statistical and biological records is also required. In addition, the IWC encourages, coordinates, and funds whale research, publishes the results of this and other scientific research, and promotes studies of related matters, such as the humaneness of the killing operations.

Membership

Membership in the IWC is open to any nation that formally adheres to the 1946 Convention. Originally there were 15 signatories, but membership increased considerably during the late 1970s and early 1980s because of the upsurge in interest among governments (Porter and Brown 1991). The current membership of 40 is shown in Table 8-3. Each member country is represented by a commissioner, who is assisted by experts and advisers. The chairman and vice chairman are elected from among the commissioners and usually serve for three years.

Since 1976 the IWC has had a full-time secretariat headquartered in Cambridge, England. The personnel include the secretary, executive officer, scientific editor, computing manager, and supporting staff. The task of collecting and publishing the world whaling catch records was transferred to the IWC Secretariat in 1984 from the Bureau of International Whaling Statistics in Sandefjord, Norway, which had initiated and carried out this work since 1930.

Meetings and Procedures

Annual meetings of the commission are held, usually in May or June, either in a member nation, by its invitation, or in the United Kingdom, where the secretariat is based.

The Commission has three main committees: Scientific, Technical, and Finance and Administration. Standing subcommittees deal with issues related to aboriginal subsistence whaling and infractions. Other ad hoc working groups are formed to deal with a wide range of issues as these arise. Commissioners may opt for their countries to be represented in any or all of these activities.

The Scientific Committee meets during the two weeks before the Commission meeting; it may also hold special meetings during the year to consider particular topics. The information and advice it provides on the status of the whale stocks form the basis on which the Commission develops whaling regulations. The Technical Committee is effectively a meeting of the entire Commission during which major items can go through a first round of discussion and, if necessary, be recommended to the Commission by simple majority.

Any changes in the regulations adopted by the Commission as amendments to the schedule become effective 90 days after unless a member nation lodges an objection. This may occur when a government considers that its national interest or sovereignty is unacceptably affected by the decision. In such a situation, the amended regulation is not binding on that country, and there is a further period of 90 days during which other governments may lodge objections. After the second 90-day period, the change takes effect for all the nonobjecting members. The regulations adopted internationally by the Commission are implemented through national legislation by member nations, which appoint inspectors to oversee their whaling operations. Inter-

Table 8-3. List of IWC Member Nations (as of 1998)

Antigua and Barbuda	India	* Russian Federation (former USSR)
* Argentina	Ireland	Saint Kitts–Nevis
* Australia	Italy	Saint Lucia
Austria	Japan	Saint Vincent and the Grenadines
* Brazil	Kenya	Senegal
* Chile	South Korea	Solomon Islands
People's Republic of China	Mexico	* South Africa
Costa Rica	Monaco	Spain
* Denmark	* Netherlands	Sweden
Dominica	* New Zealand	Switzerland
Finland	* Norway	* United Kingdom
* France	Oman	* United States
Germany	* Peru	Venezuela
Grenada		

*Original signatory of the 1946 Convention.

national observers may also be appointed by the IWC to whaling operations.

The creation of the Commission was an achievement of considerable statesmanship, bringing together as it did all the major whaling nations (Ruud 1956). It is now obvious, however, that the measures taken in the IWC's early years, heavily influenced as it was by the whaling industry, were not adequate to prevent serious reductions of many of the major whale resources (Scarff 1977). The Commission itself has little power; it is in effect a forum for discussion among the interested parties. Decisions reached are by agreement of the nations concerned, which themselves must implement, enforce, and monitor the activities of the whaling operations under their control. The Commission can exercise persuasion, but in the end, the individual contracting governments are responsible for the practical application of any decisions bearing on the level of catches and other conservation measures (Mackintosh 1965). The restrictions imposed on catches in the Antarctic, although insufficient, have slowed the rate of decline of the stocks and allow greater overall yields than would otherwise have been possible. Despite this, it must be said that the IWC failed in its primary task of conserving the stocks and maintaining the industry (Gulland 1966).

Noting the difficulty in enforcing international agreements such as the Whaling Convention, the United States enacted domestic legislation through which it can encourage other nations to follow internationally adopted policies with respect to whaling and other conservation issues. The 1971 Pelly Amendment to the 1965 Fishermen's Protective Act[1] requires that the U.S. Secretary of Commerce assess whether a foreign nation is acting to diminish the effectiveness of an international fishery conservation program or a program to protect threatened or endangered species to which the United States is a party. This includes the International Convention for the Regulation of Whaling. In the case of an affirmative determination, the government in question is certified under the U.S. law, with the result that an embargo can be placed on the importation of fish products from that nation into the United States. In 1992 this was expanded to include the importation of any products, not just fishery products, from a certified country (the High Seas Driftnet Fisheries Enforcement Act).[2] Under the 1979 Packwood-Magnuson Amendment to the Fishery Conservation and Management Act of 1976, an automatic reduction in any fishery allocations in U.S. waters is imposed on nations certified to be diminishing the effectiveness of the International Convention for the Regulation of Whaling (Wilkinson 1989).

These legislative measures have been used, or, more often, their use has been threatened, to persuade nonmember whaling nations to join the IWC and therefore be bound by IWC decisions (or at least abide by IWC decisions even if they do not join). The measures have also been used to encourage compliance with formal IWC decisions as well as with recommendations and resolutions that are essentially nonbinding (Martin and Brennan 1989).

IWC Management Actions

Although whaling was a worldwide industry before 1939, by far the richest whaling grounds were those in the Antarctic. The peak prewar catch was made in the 1937–1938 Antarctic season and the 1938 season in the rest of the world. That year 35 shore stations and 35 floating factories with 356 catcher vessels took 54,902 whales worldwide. Of this total, two shore stations, 31 floating factories, and 256 catchers in the Antarctic took 46,039 of these whales, 84% of the total.

The United Kingdom took 35% of the catch in the Antarctic; Norway, 32.5%; Japan, 12%; Germany, 11%; Panama and the United States, 3% each, and Argentina, 2%. The Antarctic whale oil production of 3,340,330 barrels made up 92% of the total world whale oil production of 3,640,248 barrels (International Whaling Statistics 1942).

With the resumption of whaling after World War II, the Antarctic was once again the major area of interest, and its proportion of equipment, catches, and oil production soon approached prewar levels. The whaling industry continued to dominate the IWC, which led to continuing overexploitation of the whale stocks in the Antarctic as well as in the rest of the world (Caldwell 1990). By the 1959–1960 season, the worldwide commercial whale catch was as follows: Japan, 30%; the Soviet Union, 18%; Norway, 18%; the United Kingdom, 8%; South Africa, 6%; and Australia, Chile, and the Netherlands, each approximately 3%. (Note that these values were based on official Soviet data, which underreported the total catches; the real share of the catch by the Soviet Union is therefore greater than indicated here.)

Eventually, the accumulating evidence of the damage being done to Antarctic stocks led the IWC to borrow from the field of fishery science the developing techniques of stock assessment and management. As a first step, in 1961 the IWC appointed a special committee comprising three experts in the field of population dynamics and drawn from countries not engaged in pelagic whaling in the Antarctic. They were charged with carrying out an independent analysis of the blue, fin, sei, and humpback whale stocks being hunted in the Antarctic and with making recommendations to the Commission. The so-called Committee of Three was made up of Douglas G. Chapman of the United States, K. R. Allen, then of New Zealand, and Sidney J. Holt, representing the United Nations Food and Agriculture Organization in Rome. The committee was later expanded to four members with the addition of John Gulland of the United Kingdom. With the cooperation of the IWC Scientific Committee, the committee subjected catch data and available biological information to detailed analyses to estimate the sizes of the stocks and the levels of yield that they could sustain (Chapman et al. 1964, 1965).

In response to the specific recommendations of the special committee, complete protection was afforded humpback whales in the Antarctic in 1963; similar protection was extended to Antarctic blue whale stocks in 1964. The Commission also expressed its intent to bring the Antarctic catch limit into line with the scientific findings by 1964, while taking into account the interests of the consumers of the whale products and the whaling industry itself. Inevitably the whaling countries argued that they could not accept such a drastic reduction of the 1963–1964 catch limit as the scientific evidence indicated was needed, and the nonwhaling countries could not support any limit substantially higher than warranted by this evidence (IWC 1966a). The situation was eventually resolved when the member governments agreed that the catch limit would be reduced over a three-year period to below the sustainable yield of the stocks, estimated according to the best scientific evidence available (IWC 1966b). Unfortunately, there was a further delay in achieving this target because the scientists revised their calculations of the sustainable yields as a result of a new interpretation of age determination in the whales and their life spans. In 1972 Antarctic catch limits were finally set by individual species rather than by blue whale units.

Changing Membership and Attitudes in the IWC

Because the whale stocks continued to decline, pressure increased for a blanket ban on commercial whaling. A resolution was adopted at the United Nations Conference on the Human Environment, held in Stockholm in 1972, calling for a 10-year moratorium on whaling. This was coupled with a strengthening of the IWC (and a full-time secretariat was established in 1976 as a result) and an increase in international research on whales (IWC 1974). In the following years the membership of the IWC increased nearly threefold. Most of the new member nations had little or no direct association with whaling, but they were concerned about the effects of overhunting and the ethics of whaling (Porter and Brown 1991). The proposal for a ten-year moratorium on commercial whaling, or a total ban on such whaling, was put forward at successive meetings of the IWC but failed to gain the necessary three-fourths majority to amend the schedule. However, reductions in catches were progressively implemented as the character and balance of the membership changed. In 1972, 8 of the 14 members carried out commercial whaling; by 1980 the Commission comprised 10 whaling and 30 nonwhaling members.

The majority group at that time could generally be characterized as like-minded antiwhaling nations (Asgrimsson 1989). Chief among these were Australia, France, the Seychelles, the United Kingdom, and the United States. They were widely supported by an increasing number of nongovernmental organizations whose representatives attend IWC annual meetings as observers. Slowly but surely, through the 1970s and 1980s the numbers of whales and the areas in which they could be taken by the commercial industry were reduced.

The New Management Procedure

On the advice of its Scientific Committee, the IWC responded to the Stockholm Conference resolution by embarking on a period of intensified research known as the International Decade of Cetacean Research. Subsequently the IWC adopted a management regime, often and confusingly called the "new management procedure." This was designed to set catch limits at levels no greater than the stocks could sustain, to bring all the stocks to their most productive levels, and to regulate the catches from each stock individually rather than by a blanket action (IWC 1976).

The procedure was based on the concept of the maximum sustainable yield (MSY). The theory is that, through the interplay of the natural responses for a stock to increase when its numbers are reduced, at each particular size of stock there is a certain surplus of recruitment over natural mortality. This surplus is low when the stock is at or close to its initial, unexploited level and also at very low stock levels, and it increases to a maximum at some intermediate point somewhere around 50 to 60% of the original abundance. This yield represents a harvest that can be taken for an indefinite time without depleting the stock (Chapman et al. 1964). Although there is some dispute over the precise details and interactions, the biological mechanisms involved in the enhanced rate of recruitment probably include a reduction in age at sexual maturity and an increase in pregnancy and survival rates. These are possibly brought about by improved feeding conditions for the survivors in populations reduced by hunting. Such improvement, among other things, results in increased growth rates and ovulation frequencies (Gambell 1973, Lockyer 1978, Horwood 1987).

Under the IWC's new management procedure, stocks were to be classified on the advice of the Scientific Committee into one of three categories according to their abundance relative to the level providing the MSY. A *Sustained Management Stock* was one between 10% below and 20% above the MSY level. Catches were to be set at not more than 90% (to give some margin of safety) of the MSY for these stocks, with a progressive reduction for any stocks estimated to be between the MSY level and 10% below that level. A similar level of catch of 90% of the MSY, with a provision that no more than 5% of the estimated initial stock could be taken in certain circumstances, was prescribed for a stock more than 20% above the MSY stock level, which was termed an *Initial Management Stock*. A stock more than 10% below the MSY stock level was designated a *Protection Stock*, and no commercial whaling was permitted on such a stock to allow the maximum rate of recovery toward the MSY level (IWC 1977a).

The procedure looked attractive in principle because it seemed to offer an essentially mechanical process for classification and setting the appropriate catch limit for each stock. Unfortunately, the IWC Scientific Committee found full implementation difficult to achieve. The amount of information needed on current and original levels of abundance and on reproductive and mortality rates to calculate the sustainable yields and catch limits was more than could be obtained. In addition, estimating the MSY and the stock level at which the MSY could be taken turned out to be more difficult than anticipated. Even when estimates were made for a particular stock, the changes in estimates as they were updated annually often led to wide fluctuations in catch limits, especially for stocks thought to be close to the MSY level. Such year-to-year variability was disliked by the whaling industry, which preferred a smoother transition if any adjustment was necessary.

The range calculated for population estimates and sustainable yields, using the best estimates and their upper and lower bounds, meant that by the early 1980s the Scientific Committee found it almost impossible to reach agreement on any recommendations for the classification or catch limits of stocks subject to commercial whaling except in the case of most protection stocks.

Comprehensive Assessment

The difficulties in the management process and the uncertainty over the status of stocks were important factors leading to the Commission's 1982 decision to introduce a pause in commercial whaling. This was implemented by setting catch limits at zero for commercial whaling on all stocks, effective with the 1986 coastal and 1985–1986 pelagic whaling seasons (IWC 1983a). It may be noted that in 1981 the Scientific Committee had been informed that the moratorium proposals then being put forward did not contain material requiring review by the Scientific Committee (IWC 1982). In the following year, a variety of views was expressed about the scientific aspects of the proposed moratorium, with no clear conclusion (IWC 1983b,c).

At its 1982 meeting the Commission also agreed that by 1990, at the latest, it would undertake a comprehensive assessment of the effects of the moratorium on whale stocks and would consider modification of the decision and the establishment of other catch limits. Thus, the Scientific Committee embarked on what has come to be known as the "comprehensive assessment" of whale stocks. In the absence of any direction from the Commission, this was defined by the Scientific Committee as an in-depth evaluation of the status and trends of all whale stocks in the light of management objectives and procedures (Donovan 1989). Priority stocks were identified as those currently being exploited or likely to be exploited and for which data were available (IWC 1987). To date, detailed assessments have been conducted for gray whales in the North Pacific (IWC 1993c); bowhead whales off Alaska (IWC 1992b); minke whales in the Southern

Hemisphere (IWC 1991b, Haw 1993), North Atlantic (IWC 1990, 1991c, 1993b, 1997), and western North Pacific (IWC 1992c); and fin whales in the North Atlantic (IWC 1992e, 1993b). Included in this process is the estimation of current numbers of whales in the different stocks. The Scientific Committee has also accepted some other analyses, notably for humpback whales (IWC 1989) and long-finned pilot whales (*Globicephala melas*) (IWC 1993b) in the North Atlantic. Table 8-4 shows the numbers that the IWC is prepared to give as the best estimates available.

Revised Management Procedure

Another part of the comprehensive assessment process was the development of a revised management procedure. Five different procedures were developed by groups of Scientific Committee members and tested by a series of computer simulation trials (Kirkwood 1992). It soon became clear that no new management procedure could be ready by the original deadline of 1990. However, by comparing the results of the individual workers, the Scientific Committee was able at its 1991 annual meeting to recommend that the Commission adopt the procedure developed by British scientist Justin Cooke as suitable for replacing the 1975 procedure (IWC 1992a).

The Commission formally adopted this procedure, with some modifications, for calculating catch limits for baleen whales in a revised management procedure (IWC 1995a). The aim of the revised management procedure (RMP) is to provide an acceptable balance between conservation and

Table 8-4. Whale Population Estimates (Rounded to the Third Significant Figure)

Type / Area	Year	Population Size	95% Confidence Interval
Minke whales			
Southern Hemisphere	1982–1983—1988–1989	761,000	510,000–1,140,000
North Atlantic[a] (excluding Canadian east coast area)	1987–1995	149,000	120,000–182,000
North Pacific (Northwest Pacific and Okhotsk Sea)	1989–1990	25,000	12,800–48,600
Fin whales			
North Atlantic	1969–1989	47,300	27,700–82,000
Sei whales			
Central North Atlantic	1989	10,300	6,100–17,700
Gray whales			
Eastern North Pacific[b]	1987–1988	21,000	19,800–22,500
Bowhead whales			
Bering-Chukchi-Beaufort Seas[c]	1988	7,500	6,400–9,200
Humpback whales			
Western North Atlantic[d]	1979–1986	5,500	8,120–2,890
Pilot whales			
Central and Eastern North Atlantic	1989	780,000	440,000–1,370,000
Blue whales			
Southern Hemisphere	1985–1986—1990–1991	460	210–1,000

Notes: Because of the considerable scientific uncertainty over the numbers of whales of different species and in different geographical stocks, the International Whaling Commission decided in 1989 that it would be better not to give population figures except for those species or stocks that have been assessed in detail and for which there is statistical certainty with respect to the numbers.

[a]Subject to possible slight adjustment.

[b]Assuming a constant rate of increase, the population was increasing at a rate of 3.2% (95% confidence interval 2.4–4.3%) over the period 1967–1968 to 1987–1988 with an average annual catch of 174 whales.

[c]The net rate of increase of this population has been estimated as 2.3% per year (75% confidence interval 0.9–3.4%).

[d]A rate of population increase of 10.3% (95% confidence interval 2–23%) was obtained from the Gulf of Maine.

exploitation of baleen whales and to provide a simple and convenient method for setting catch limits with minimal requirements for data. The procedure seeks to ensure that depleted stocks are rehabilitated and that no whaling is permitted on stocks that are below 54% of their initial abundance. The aim is to obtain the highest possible continuing yield, with stable catch limits, to bring all exploited stocks to the target level of 72% of their initial level.

The procedure is based on a current population estimate and the known catch history. The notional unexploited stock size is estimated using a simplified production model that includes no biological parameters. Initially, a fixed MSY rate is assumed, but as more data accumulate, the procedure tends gradually toward one based on the best estimate of the MSY rate obtained by fitting the production model (IWC 1991d). The procedure has been tested in simulation trials over 100 years and is robust to a range of factors, including underestimation of historic catches by up to 50%, variations over time in carrying capacity and recruitment, environmental degradation, and a wide range of uncertainties, including the definition of stock units and differing assumptions about population dynamics (IWC 1995b). The procedure is precautionary in the sense that the allowed level of take is lower when data are sparse, and a key feature is its flexibility with regard to the amount of survey data required. The approach used to develop the RMP has potentially wider applicability in fishery management (Cooke 1995).

Revised Management Scheme

Although the Commission has accepted the mathematical and scientific elements of the RMP, it has also noted that additional steps are required before catch limits for baleen whales can be considered. These include agreement on minimum data standards, guidelines for conducting surveys and analyzing the results, a fully effective inspection and observation scheme, arrangements to ensure that total catches over time are within the limits set under the RMP, and the incorporation of the elements of this revised management scheme (RMS) into the schedule (IWC 1993a). Additional concerns have been raised, notably the question of progress on humane killing emphasized by the United Kingdom, and the issues of unauthorized ("pirate") whaling, illicit trade in whale products, underreporting of catch data, and the effects of environmental degradation, which have been raised particularly by the United States (IWC 1995a). A satisfactory resolution of all these matters is considered as a prerequisite by the majority of contracting governments before there can be any relaxation of the current moratorium on commercial whaling.

Aboriginal Subsistence Whaling

Aboriginal subsistence whaling is not formally defined within the 1946 Convention or its associated schedule of regulations although provisions of the schedule speak of establishing "catch limits for aboriginal whaling to satisfy aboriginal subsistence need" (paragraph 13[a]). An ad hoc Technical Committee Working Group on Development of Management Principles and Guidelines for Subsistence Catches of Whales by Indigenous (Aboriginal) Peoples, which met immediately before the IWC's 1981 annual meeting, agreed to the following definitions:

Aboriginal subsistence whaling means whaling for purposes of local aboriginal consumption carried out by or on behalf of aboriginal, indigenous, or native peoples who share strong community, familial, social, and cultural ties related to a continuing traditional dependence on whaling and on the use of whales.

Local aboriginal consumption means the traditional uses of whale products by local aboriginal, indigenous, or native communities in meeting their nutritional, subsistence, and cultural requirements. The term includes trade in items that are by-products of subsistence catches.

Subsistence catches are catches of whales by aboriginal subsistence whaling operations (Donovan 1982).

The special status of aboriginal subsistence catches thus continued the conceptual approach found in the 1931 Convention, which included as Article 3 an exemption for coast-dwelling aborigines, provided that they used canoes, pirogues, or other exclusively native craft propelled by oars or sail; they did not carry firearms; and the products were for their own use (Birnie 1985). The first schedule to the 1946 Convention carried this concept forward by a specific exception to the general prohibition on the commercial catching of gray and right whales when the meat and products are to be used exclusively for local consumption by aborigines (IWC 1950).

Aboriginal subsistence whaling has therefore been recognized for at least 60 years as having a distinctive character that separates it from larger-scale, commercial whaling operations. As just noted, both the 1931 and 1946 agreements included specific exemptions for aboriginal subsistence whaling (Gambell 1993).

However, the adoption by the IWC in 1975 of its new management procedure for commercial whaling led to the recognition of the need for a specific management regime for aboriginal subsistence whaling. This occurred during a period of very contentious discussions on the size of the bowhead whale stock hunted off Alaska and the numbers of whales being harvested by Alaska Natives (Doubleday 1989). Eventually, after consideration of the many biological, nutritional, and social aspects involved, at the 1982 annual meeting of the IWC a resolution was adopted agreeing to implement an aboriginal subsistence whaling regime. This recognized that the full participation and cooperation of the affected aboriginal peoples are essential for effective whale management. For stocks above the MSY level, aboriginal subsistence catches are permitted up to 90% of MSY; for stocks below the MSY level, catch levels are set so as to permit the stocks to rebuild to the MSY level, and the Scientific Committee was asked to advise on both a rate of increase toward the MSY level and a minimum stock level below which whales should not be taken from each stock. A standing Aboriginal Subsistence Whaling Subcommittee of the Commission was established to consider documentation on nutritional, subsistence, and cultural needs relating to aboriginal subsistence whaling and the uses of whales taken for such purposes, and to provide advice to the Technical Committee for its consideration and determination of appropriate management measures (IWC 1983a). The IWC has now asked its Scientific Committee to begin a review of possible alternative management regimes for aboriginal subsistence whaling (IWC 1995a).

Four whale-hunting operations are currently regulated by the IWC as aboriginal subsistence whaling activities, and catch limits are set for each of them.

Alaskan Bowhead Whaling

The village communities on the north coast of Alaska have a long history and culture based upon the hunting of bowhead whales (Fig. 8-2). The stock was severely depleted by commercial whaling that began in 1848. When this commercial fishery ended about 1910 because of changes in the market and the declining number of whales, the Alaska Natives continued their traditional hunt using their old methods and skills augmented by nineteenth-century technology acquired through contact with commercial whalers (Stoker and Krupnick 1993).

An average of 12 whales was landed each year from 1910 until 1969. From 1970 to 1977 there was a substantial increase in the catch, and an average of 32 animals was landed per year (Marquette and Bockstoce 1980), along with a greatly increased number of whales struck but lost. This gave rise to serious concerns for what was thought at the time to be the most endangered whale species and caused the IWC to ban all hunting in 1977 (IWC 1978). However, the Alaska Native community persuaded the U.S. government to press for a modest take of bowhead whales to satisfy their subsistence and cultural needs, and the government also committed itself to a major research effort to learn more about the status of the bowhead whale stock. These actions in turn led to the development of the IWC's aboriginal subsistence whaling management policy (Gambell 1983).

In practice, the way that the current aboriginal subsistence whaling regime is implemented for the Alaskan bowhead hunt is for the U.S. government to calculate subsistence need as the historic harvest per capita of the human population involved, multiplied by the current human population. The IWC took this figure as a basis for setting the catch limit as 204 bowheads to be landed in the four years 1995–1998, reflecting the estimated annual Alaska Native population growth rate of 4.7% for the 10 whaling villages concerned between 1990 and 1992. This catch limit is less than the estimated current annual replacement yield from the stock of 199 animals (95% confidence interval 97–300).

The catch limit was increased for the five seasons 1998 to

Figure 8-2. The scene after butchering a bowhead whale at Point Hope, Alaska, May 1975, showing the large chunks of skin and blubber in the foreground, whale meat in the center, and the upper jaw and baleen in the upper left. (Photograph by Bill Marquette, courtesy of National Marine Fisheries Service)

2002 to a total of 280 with an annual limit of 67 strikes to accommodate a request from the Russian Federation for a harvest of five bowhead whales for its Chukotka people (IWC 1998a).

Greenland Whaling

The subsistence lifestyle of the Native people inhabiting Greenland has always included the hunting of whales, seals, and land animals. Whaling was carried on for centuries using traditional weapons and techniques, but Europeans introduced firearms in the eighteenth and nineteenth centuries. More recently, humpback, fin, and minke whales have been taken regularly as part of a multispecies exploitation of the local resources by dual-purpose fishing/whaling vessels using modern whaling technology (Kapel and Petersen 1982) (Fig. 8-3).

Hunting of humpback whales was a traditional activity that was continued by the Danish authorities from 1924 until 1955 by the provision of a catcher boat. This vessel also caught a small number (20 to 25 per year) of fin whales. The general protection of humpback whales from 1955 carried an exception until 1985 for Greenlanders using small vessels. The local minke whale fishery began in 1948 in West Greenland. The quota of 19 fin whales landed and 175 minke whales struck in each of the years 1998–2002 in West Greenland is equivalent to more than 420 mt of meat and products, but this does not match the accepted need for 670 mt (IWC 1995a, 1998a). There is an annual catch limit of 12 minke whales for the people of East Greenland. There is thus little apparent consistency in the way the aboriginal subsistence management scheme is implemented or applied to the Alaska Natives and the Greenlanders.

Siberian Gray Whaling

Evidence of aboriginal whaling for both bowhead and gray whales in the northwestern Pacific goes back at least 2,000 years to prehistoric times (Rice and Wolman 1971). The gray whale was hunted along the Chukotka Peninsula using traditional methods until U.S. commercial whalers introduced more advanced technology. Whaling by the aboriginal hunters from small boats stopped in the 1960s and was replaced by a modern catcher-vessel operation taking enough whales to meet the needs of the 10 villages to which the whales were towed for processing (Krupnick 1984). The limit of 140 gray whales for each of the years 1998–2002, with an overall total of 620 whales in the five seasons, corresponds to the catch requested by the government of the Russian Federation (IWC 1995a). Included within these figures is now an annual quota of five gray whales requested by the United States to satisfy a revival of the cultural tradition of the Makah Indian tribe (IWC 1998a). This can be compared with the estimated annual replacement yield of 611 whales with 95% confidence limits of 452–786 (IWC 1995b).

Caribbean Humpback Whaling

One or two humpback whales may be taken each year in a small-scale open-boat hunt from the Caribbean island of Bequia in Saint Vincent and the Grenadines (Price 1985).

Small-Type Whaling

Small-type whaling was defined by the IWC in 1976 to mean operations using powered vessels with mounted harpoon

Figure 8-3. A deck-mounted harpoon gun on the bow of a Greenlandic multipurpose fishing/whaling vessel, West Greenland, 1988. (Photograph by Steve Leatherwood)

guns to take minke, bottlenose (*Hyperoodon* spp.), pilot, or killer whales (*Orcinus orca*) (IWC 1977b). This definition was adopted on the recommendation of the Scientific Committee, which recognized the need for systematic collection of data from all whaling, including land stations and pelagic operations such as the North Atlantic minke whale hunt, and not only the factory ship operations described in the then-current schedule (IWC 1977c).

Since the 1982 moratorium on commercial whaling took effect, the government of Japan, in particular, has made strenuous efforts to gain recognition of, and to alleviate, the distress caused in its coastal communities that formerly relied heavily on small-type whaling. It has presented much documentation, based on social, scientific, and anthropological research, to support the contention that Japanese small-type coastal whaling has a character distinct from other forms of industrial whaling and that it shares some features with aboriginal subsistence whaling (Kalland and Moeran 1990). The small-type coastal whaling in Japan is a small-scale, limited-access fishery involving four coastal communities that take minke whales within 30 miles (48 km) of the shore. The whale meat obtained from these catches is claimed to play an important role in the cultural and social cohesion of the communities (IWC 1991a, 1993a).

Norway has also presented evidence that, although modern minke whaling was introduced in the 1920s, small cetaceans have been hunted in Norway for millennia. The whalers are also fishermen whose operations are generally based on household units of ownership and crew. These activities are claimed to give strong support to the traditions and way of life of the remote northern communities concerned. Considerable resentment has been expressed within those communities against the prohibition on whaling imposed by the IWC (IWC 1993a).

The governments of Japan and Norway have argued that the moratorium on small-type whaling operations from their communities, based as it is on the supposition by the IWC that they constitute commercial whaling, is unjustified. It is causing problems in the communities because of their dependence on the social and cultural activities associated with whaling and on the distribution and consumption of whale products. In these respects, small-type whaling is similar to aboriginal subsistence whaling. The latter, however, is not prohibited by the IWC because of the recognition of its special socioeconomic and cultural roles in the lives of the communities concerned.

The difficulty for some governments in agreeing to allow small-type whaling lies mainly in the commercial aspects of these operations, even though catches would be regulated and controlled through application of the RMP developed for commercial whaling. Requests by Japan for an interim relief allocation of 50 minke whales and a plan to resume Norwegian coastal whaling where a cultural and subsistence need is demonstrated have not been accepted by the IWC. However, the Commission did adopt a resolution at its 1993 annual meeting recognizing the socioeconomic and cultural needs of the four small coastal communities in Japan and the distress to these communities caused by the cessation of minke whaling. The Commission resolved to work expeditiously to alleviate this distress at its 1994 annual meeting. Nonetheless, at subsequent annual meetings, the Commission again rejected proposals from Japan for an interim relief allocation of 50 minke whales even though the products were to be distributed and used under a specifically noncommercial regime within the coastal communities (IWC 1995a, 1998a).

The government of Norway lodged formal objections in 1982 to the moratorium on commercial whaling that became effective from 1986, and in 1985 to the classification of the northeastern Atlantic stock of minke whales as a protection stock. Thus, when Norway resumed commercial whaling on this stock under its own regulations in 1993, it did so legally.

Iceland and Norway have stated that, because the IWC seems reluctant to allow the resumption of commercial whaling, they might find it necessary to turn to alternative forums where the issues of catch limits can be discussed in good faith (IWC 1991a). Iceland, in fact, withdrew from the IWC in 1992. In this context, the newly established North Atlantic Marine Mammal Commission, comprising government representatives from the Faroe Islands, Greenland, Iceland, and Norway, is relevant (Hoel 1993). The stated objective of the Commission is to contribute through regional consultation and cooperation to the conservation, rational management, and study of marine mammals in the North Atlantic.

The United Nations Convention on the Law of the Sea (the internationally accepted and recognized text on customary practice in this area) does not specify which international body, or even if there is to be only one body, is the appropriate organization through which coastal nations are to cooperate with respect to the management and conservation of the whale resources (Burke 1994). The idea of regional bodies to oversee the whaling activities of coastal nations in particular parts of the world is not without precedent. The governments of Chile, Ecuador, and Peru formed the Permanent Commission of the Conference on the Use and Conservation of the Marine Resources of the South Pacific in 1952. They established catch regulations for whaling broadly similar to those in force for the IWC at that time (Birnie 1985). Those three governments have subsequently joined the IWC—Chile and Peru in 1979 and Ecuador in 1991, although the latter withdrew in 1994.

Scientific Research Catches

Article VIII of the 1946 Convention allows any contracting government to grant a special permit for the taking of whales for scientific research purposes. In response to proposals to issue permits since the moratorium decision, the IWC has established detailed guidelines for its Scientific Committee to review and comment on such proposals. These concern the objectives of the research and whether they relate to the Commission's needs; the methodology to be employed, the whales to be taken, and the feasibility of using nonlethal techniques to obtain equivalent information; the expected effects of the proposed catch on the stock; and the arrangements for participation by scientists from other countries (IWC 1989). The IWC may also make recommendations to the governments concerned although it has no power to forbid or rescind the issuance of a permit (IWC 1996).

From 1988 to 1995 Norway carried out a research program that included the taking of 289 minke whales. Its stated purpose was to study and monitor the species in the northeastern Atlantic, including investigations on feeding ecology, age determination, and energetics. The study was part of a broader ecological program designed to provide information for future multispecies management in the Barents Sea. The IWC has adopted resolutions each year inviting Norway to reconsider the proposed lethal takes.

Following two years of feasibility studies starting in the 1987–1988 season to resolve the problems of collecting representative samples, Japan embarked on a 16-year research program in the Antarctic that included an annual catch of 300 (and since 1995–1996, 400) ± 10% minke whales. The main objectives were to estimate the biological parameters that could be used for management, in particular natural mortality, to refine understanding of stock identity, and to elucidate the role of whales in the Antarctic ecosystem. Again the IWC has adopted a resolution each year inviting Japan to reconsider its research program, to which the Japanese authorities have consistently given serious consideration and a reasoned response.

Japan also put forward a proposal to clarify the stock structure and mixing rates of minke whales around Japan, based on problems encountered by the Scientific Committee in trying to assess the northwestern Pacific stocks. A first-year feasibility study in 1994 included the take of 100 animals, which has continued in the following years, and the IWC again asked Japan to reconsider this program (IWC 1995a, 1998a).

A number of countries have issued scientific permits over the years to allow limited catches of whales that would otherwise not have been sampled in normal commercial operations, such as lactating females, undersized animals, or protected species. The catches made under such permits are listed in Table 8-5.

One aspect of the recent research catches that has created some concern is the requirement of the 1946 Convention that the whales taken must be processed so far as practicable. Because commercial whaling is currently prohibited, the suspicion has been that these catches are a way of circumventing the moratorium or of maintaining a low level of whaling operations until such time as full-scale whaling resumes. Whatever the truth is, it must be said that useful results from these research activities have been presented to the Scientific Committee although the objectives of some of the research have fallen outside the guidelines adopted by the IWC (IWC 1998b).

Whale Sanctuaries

As well as management measures governing catch and size limits, species, and seasons, the IWC can also designate open and closed areas for whaling.

Antarctic

A sanctuary in the Antarctic was established in 1938 south of 40°S latitude and between 70°W and 160°W longitude. The original reason was that commercial whaling had not been prosecuted in this sector, and it was thought highly desirable that the protection of whales in the area should be maintained. The sanctuary was continued by the IWC from its inception until 1955, when the area was opened initially for three years and then permanently, as a means of reducing the pressure of catches on the rest of the Antarctic whaling grounds (IWC 1958).

Indian Ocean

After a short debate, the Indian Ocean Sanctuary was established by the IWC in 1979, extending south to 55°S latitude, as an area where commercial whaling is prohibited. This provision was an initiative of the newly joined government of Seychelles to provide freedom from disturbance for species or groups of whales in an ecologically coherent area. Seychelles confirmed that such a proposal was supported by the coastal nations bordering the Indian Ocean, both members and nonmembers of the IWC (IWC 1980). The Indian Ocean Sanctuary was initially established for 10 years, and it has since been extended twice. It will be reviewed again by

Table 8-5. Special Permit Catches

Country	Year	Species and Number
Australia	1955	2 humpback + 2 calves
	1963	55 sperm, 1 pygmy blue
Canada	1953	10 gray
	1967	4 fin, 1 sei, 5 sperm
	1969	6 humpback
	1970	15 humpback
	1971	20 humpback
Iceland	1986	76 fin, 40 sei
	1987	80 fin, 20 sei
	1988	68 fin, 10 sei
	1989	68 fin
Japan	1956	1 right
	1961	3 right
	1962	3 right
	1963	3 right
	1964	1 fin
	1965	20 sperm
	1966–1967	3 fin + calves, 3 pygmy blue, 51 sperm
	1968	1 sei + calf, 2 right
	1969–1970	2 pygmy blue
	1971	200 sperm
	1971–1972	2 fin
	1976	80 sperm, 1 minke
	1976–1977	225 Bryde's
	1977–1978	114 Bryde's
	1978–1979	120 Bryde's
	1987–1988	273 minke
	1988–1989	241 minke
	1989–1990	330 minke
	1990–1991	327 minke
	1991–1992	288 minke
	1992–1993	330 minke
	1993–1994	330 minke
	1994	21 minke
	1994–1995	330 minke
	1995	100 minke
	1995–1996	440 minke
	1996	77 minke
	1996–1997	440 minke
	1997	100 minke
	1997–1998	438 minke
South Korea	1986	69 minke
New Zealand	1963–1964	77 sperm, 1 fin
Norway	1966	1 blue, 1 humpback
	1970	19 fin
	1988	29 minke
	1989	17 minke
	1990	5 minke
	1992	95 minke
	1993	69 minke
	1994	74 minke

Table 8-5 continued

Country	Year	Species and Number
Union of Soviet Socialist Republics	1961–1962	1 right
	1970–1971	5 pygmy blue, 4 Bryde's, 3 pygmy right
	1971–1972	3 pygmy blue, 1 Bryde's, 8 sei, 3 humpback
	1972	13 Bryde's, 11 sperm
	1972–1973	3 blue, 4 pygmy blue, 5 humpback
	1977–1978	5 Bryde's
United Kingdom	1954	6 humpback
United States	1959	2 gray
	1962	4 gray
	1964	20 gray
	1966	52 gray, 22 sperm
	1967	99 gray, 50 sperm
	1968	119 gray
	1969	74 gray, 34 sperm
	1970	30 sperm

the commission at its annual meeting in the year 2002 (IWC 1993a).

Southern Ocean

At the IWC's 1992 meeting the government of France submitted a proposal to establish a whale sanctuary in the Southern Hemisphere south of 40°S latitude. The stated purpose of the proposed sanctuary was to help rehabilitate the Antarctic marine ecosystem and protect all Southern Hemisphere species and populations of baleen whales and the sperm whale on their feeding grounds. This would also link up with the Indian Ocean Sanctuary to provide a large area within which whales would be free from commercial catching (IWC 1993a).

Consideration of the proposal was deferred to the 1993 annual meeting, at which time a working group examined the matter. It became apparent that a number of problems had to be resolved, including legal, political, ecological, geographical, management, financial, and global environmental issues. The Commission therefore endorsed the concept of establishing a sanctuary in the Southern Ocean and accepted an offer from the government of Australia to host an intersessional working group of member nations to address these issues and formulate recommendations. The goal was to enable the Commission to make a decision on the sanctuary proposal at its 1994 annual meeting (IWC 1994a).

The working group met on Norfolk Island in February

1994. At its 1994 annual meeting the Commission adopted the Southern Ocean Sanctuary, designating it as an area in which commercial whaling is prohibited. The northern boundary of the sanctuary follows the 40°S parallel of latitude except in the Indian Ocean sector, where it joins the southern boundary of that sanctuary at 55°S, and around South America and into the South Pacific, where the boundary is at 60°S. This sanctuary will be reviewed 10 years after its initial adoption and at succeeding 10-year intervals, at which times it can be revised by the Commission (IWC 1995a).

Japan lodged an objection to the establishment of the Southern Ocean Sanctuary to the extent that it applies to Antarctic minke whale stocks, partly on the grounds that it was not justified by scientific advice. Japan is also continuing its long-term research program, which includes catches under special permit (see above).

The Indian Ocean Sanctuary has so far failed to act as a significant stimulus to cetacean research (for a review of the limited work, see Leatherwood and Donovan 1991). There is some hope, however, that designation of the Southern Ocean Sanctuary will encourage a greater degree of enthusiasm for investigations into the whale stocks, their role in the Antarctic ecosystem, and environmental aspects (IWC 1995a).

Whale Killing Methods

The IWC has considered the killing methods used in whaling operations over many years and has encouraged the development of more humane techniques (Donovan 1986, Mitchell et al. 1986). The issue of humane killing is, however, a subject of great controversy. Apart from any pain caused when an individual whale is killed, there is concern that the pursuit, and in some cases the selection of one individual from a group of whales, results in stress and possibly fear and panic both in the target whale and in other whales nearby. These aspects need to be considered to ensure the fullest possible interpretation of the humaneness of the whaling operations. It is a complex and specialized subject that has not been explored to any great extent. Thus, most consideration of humane killing has been confined to the immediate question of whether a whale is struck in such a way as to induce rapid unconsciousness and death.

As a working definition, the IWC has accepted that humane killing means causing death without pain, stress, or distress perceptible to the animal. That is the ideal. Any humane killing technique aims first to render the animal insensitive to pain as swiftly as is technically possible. In practice, this cannot be instantaneous in the strictly scientific sense.[3]

Achieving a rapid, painless death would also increase the efficiency of whaling operations and improve the quality of the meat obtained by reducing the stress to the animal. Thus, the whaling industry is interested in attaining the same objectives for commercial as well as humanitarian reasons.

Commercial Whaling

Modern whaling for large whales has generally involved use of the explosive harpoon invented in the 1860s (see above). Since the 1950s the original pointed head has been replaced by a flat head that is less prone to ricochet off the whale or to be deflected on entering the body. The gunner aims to hit the whale just behind the flipper about the horizontal midline while the whale is swimming away from the vessel. Such a hit should cause the harpoon to pierce the heart.

Factory ship and small-type whaling for minke whales initially employed cold (i.e., nonexplosive) grenades because the explosive grenade used for larger whale species destroys too much meat. The gunner again aimed just behind the flipper along the horizontal midline, although in this case the shock waves rather than hemorrhaging were expected to kill or render the animal unconscious. If the whale was not killed instantaneously in the Japanese operations, an electric lance was employed. Electrodes are inserted on either side of the heart, and an electric shock is applied. The effectiveness of this technique in causing rapid insensibility and death has been under debate (IWC 1996).

In 1979 legislation was introduced in Norway requiring each small-type whaling vessel to carry and use a large-caliber rifle to kill a whale that had been hit but not killed by a harpoon. This method has proved successful in those instances when it has been used, and Japan has now said that it too will use the rifle as the main secondary killing technique rather than the electric lance (IWC 1998a).

Also beginning in 1979, a replacement for the traditional black powder was developed. This new explosive material, penthrite, is a physical mixture of sulphur, saltpeter, and charcoal. Penthrite detonates at supersonic speed and produces great quantities of carbon dioxide gas. Coupled with improved triggering devices to ensure that the grenade explodes within the body of the whale, and with safety provisions for the crew handling the harpoons at sea, the penthrite grenade has greatly improved results (IWC 1984, 1985).

As a result of these technical improvements, the IWC was able to prohibit the use of cold grenade harpoons in all whaling operations after 1983.

Aboriginal Whaling

Alaska Native bowhead whaling involves capture techniques adapted from late nineteenth-century American whaling. In earlier years, a bomb-lance was fired at the whale to kill or disable it sufficiently to allow whalers to approach close enough to harpoon the animal. If the whale was not killed or disabled, it could escape before it was harpooned. Recent practice requires that all whales are first harpooned to avoid their loss because at least some of the escaped animals suffer serious wounds. A penthrite grenade has now been developed to improve the efficiency of the hand-harpoon technique, based to a large extent on the Norwegian expertise gained during development of the newest commercial whaling technology (Øen 1995).

Small Cetaceans

One topic over which there is a major division of views among the member governments of the IWC is the question of the legal competence of the Commission to make management decisions with respect to small cetaceans. The problem revolves around two main issues: the scope of the 1946 Convention and the question of national sovereignty within the 200–nautical mile (370-km) exclusive economic zones.

The 1946 International Convention for the Regulation of Whaling does not define the term *whale.* Some governments, including those of Brazil, Chile, Denmark, Japan, Mexico, Norway, and Saint Vincent and the Grenadines, consider the species listed in the Annex of Nomenclature to the Final Act of the 1946 Convention to be the ones of interest to the contracting governments at that time. This list comprises all the baleen whales, the sperm whale, and the bottlenose whales (International Whaling Statistics 1948). Although the 1946 Annex of Nomenclature is not part of the Convention, it is interpreted by these governments to reflect the intentions of the drafters of the Convention. These countries do not believe that the IWC has legal competence with respect to small cetaceans. However, there are many species and stocks of cetaceans outside this list, and these governments do recognize that the IWC Scientific Committee deals with the smaller species under the terms of a resolution drawn up in 1980 (IWC 1981).

Other governments, including those of Australia, Germany, Ireland, the Netherlands, New Zealand, Oman, Switzerland, the United Kingdom, and the United States, believe that nothing in the 1946 Convention explicitly limits jurisdiction to the larger cetaceans and that the Annex of Nomenclature has no legal or other basis to restrict the competence of the IWC. Indeed, the Commission has established catch regulations for the unlisted killer whales taken in pelagic operations (IWC 1981).

Many of the smaller species of cetaceans occur within 200 nautical miles (370 km) of shore, and some governments maintain that national or regional regulation is most appropriate, especially because only 38 of the world's 140 coastal nations are members of the IWC. Other governments, which argue that the 1946 Whaling Convention does cover all cetaceans, insist that the IWC should be the responsible international authority. The great need for proper management of the exploitation of these smaller cetaceans is undeniable. Many stocks have been shown by the IWC Scientific Committee to be under considerable threat from both directed and incidental catches (IWC 1992d, 1994b).

In this situation the Commission has no way of adopting or enforcing regulations, but all the member governments are committed to overcoming the differences of view on this subject because of the obvious need for action to conserve small cetaceans (IWC 1994a). Many coastal nations are ready for—indeed are in need of—the expertise that the IWC can offer, but there is great sensitivity to possible infringement of national interests. The appropriate legal language needs to be devised.

In addition to the questions of national sovereignty and jurisdiction, account must also be taken of the other intergovernmental organizations that have some responsibility for or expertise on small cetaceans. These include the United Nations Environment Programme (particularly through its Regional Seas Programme), the Convention on International Trade in Endangered Species of Wild Fauna and Flora, the Bonn Convention on the Conservation of Migratory Species of Wild Animals, and some regional fisheries bodies such as the Inter-American Tropical Tuna Commission. The partially overlapping roles of these treaties or agencies also need to be seen against the general background of the rights and responsibilities of coastal nations under the newly established United Nations Convention on the Law of the Sea. These include cooperating with other coastal nations with a view to ensuring conservation and promoting the objective of optimum utilization of species that migrate both within and beyond a nation's exclusive economic zones, either directly or through the appropriate international organizations. There is also a duty for nations to work through the appropriate international organizations for the conservation, management, and study of cetaceans (United Nations 1983).

Conclusions

Commercial whaling has a long history of overexploitation of species and stocks of whales as they were discovered or as the technology advanced to permit their capture. Regulations have not prevented this from happening in the past in the face of persistent economic demands from the industry. With a pause in commercial whaling now in place, the current emphasis is on ensuring that any future catches will not harm the stocks and that there will be no opportunity to conceal illicit catches.

It has recently been reported that the official catch statistics submitted by the Soviet Union on its whaling operations in the Southern Hemisphere dating from 1949–1950 were considerably falsified (Yablokov 1994, IWC 1995b, Zemsky et al. 1995). Such evidence of the unreliability of these past data underlines the importance of having totally credible inspection and international observation of any future whaling activities. The IWC implemented an International Observer Scheme in 1972 after 12 years of discussions and negotiations. This enabled observers appointed by the Commission, and reporting directly to it, to be stationed at the whaling operations of the member nations to confirm their compliance with the agreed whaling regulations (IWC 1974). The quality of the official Soviet records improved after this scheme came into force when compared with the original records collected on the whaling vessels. Such problems and evidence reinforce the view of those people and nations who are reluctant to see a resumption of commercial whaling unless there are very strict controls under international supervision, as well as a large sanctuary to provide a pool of whales that are sure to be safe from hunting.

On the other hand, it is argued, with some justification, that some stocks undoubtedly could sustain carefully regulated and controlled catches. In addition, certain coastal communities that are currently prevented from whaling have societal structures and traditions similar to those communities that are allowed to continue hunting whales for subsistence purposes.

Recent thinking now enshrined in the United Nations Convention on the Law of the Sea and the 1992 Earth Summit in Rio de Janeiro, particularly in the areas of coastal nation sovereignty and the developing trend toward the precautionary principle of management (Cicin-Sain and Knecht 1993), has caused profound changes in the interpretation and application of the 1946 Whaling Convention, and the consequent management policies by which it is implemented. Tensions between the objectives of the conservation of the whale resources and the orderly development of the whaling industry continue today. Some governments, such as those of Iceland, Japan, and Norway, argue for a resumption of commercial whaling as an example of sustainable development of the resource now that the scientific aspects of a revised management procedure have been agreed upon.

However, the majority of IWC member countries still resist any such move. For example, the United Kingdom has stated that it will not even contemplate the lifting of the current moratorium on commercial whaling until it is fully satisfied that whale stocks are proved to be at "healthy levels," methods used to take whales are humane, and effective procedures for the management of whale stocks are in place and enforceable.[4] In addition, the United States announced in 1993 that, in response to public opinion and the views of the U.S. Congress, it opposes the resumption of commercial whaling even if these requisite conditions are satisfied.[5]

Whales are increasingly being recognized as only one component, albeit very important top predators, in the marine ecosystem. There is a need to view the role of these animals in relation to all the other elements in the energy flow of these systems and to appreciate the impact of environmental change on the whales (Food and Agriculture Organization 1978). This latter issue has therefore been examined at two levels in the IWC. First, in the context of the revised management procedure, the Scientific Committee has concluded from its testing procedures that the RMP adequately addresses the possibility that whale stocks are affected by environmental change. However, it also noted that the species most vulnerable to such effects might well be those reduced to levels at which the RMP, even if applied, would result in zero catches. Second, the Scientific Committee has held two workshops, one in March 1995 in Bergen, Norway, on the effects of chemical pollutants and another in March 1996 in Hawaii on the effects of climate change (global warming and ozone depletion). The IWC has reaffirmed its view of the importance of these issues (IWC 1995b).

The emphasis on sustainable use of resources does not necessarily imply that whales are to be regarded just as providers of food and other products. But in a world where the human population is expected to double in the next century, pressure to harvest these animals again for their protein and oil will not disappear. Nonconsumptive utilization can also be economically attractive because of the revenues generated by whale watching and allied activities around the world, which allow the same animals to be seen repeatedly without removing them from their habitat (Hoyt 1984).

Whale watching is a major new development in the IWC's consideration of the sustainable use of cetacean resources. In 1993 the IWC invited contracting governments to undertake a preliminary assessment of the extent, and economic and scientific value, of whale-watching activities. These national reports give some insight into the value and potential of whale watching. Further progress resulted from discussions at a workshop sponsored by a number of nongovernmental organizations held in Italy in 1995 and other workshops on particular aspects held subsequently. All this has led the IWC to reaffirm its interest in the subject, encourage some scientific work, and establish a working group to develop appropriate guidelines for preventing harmful impacts of whale watching on the whales (IWC 1996).

Finally, there is a growing sense, particularly in the more affluent Western world, that whales are special animals that should not be considered as just so many steaks for human consumption but as the focus of whale-watching and educational programs because of their perceived esthetic and sentient values. Here the different cultural viewpoints and traditions of the people and nations making up the IWC come into conflict.

The 1946 International Convention for the Regulation of Whaling was drawn up as an agreement to control the catching operations of a particular fishery that, throughout its long history, has overexploited the resource. It is now being interpreted as a conservation instrument more in tune with the current environmental ethic, but one that is not universally agreed upon or accepted by some of the communities most affected.

Notes

1. 22 U.S.C. §1978.
2. Public Law 102-582 §201(a)(1).
3. International Whaling Commission, Report of the Workshop on Humane Killing Techniques for Whales, 10–14 November 1980, Cambridge. (Available from the Office of the Commission.)
4. Hansard, 25 February 1993.
5. United States opening statement to the Forty-fifth Annual Meeting of the International Whaling Commission, Kyoto, Japan, 1993. (Available from the Office of the Commission.)

Literature Cited

Allen, K. R. 1980. Conservation and Management of Whales. University of Washington Press, Seattle, WA.

Asgrimsson, H. 1989. Developments leading to the 1982 decision of the International Whaling Commission for a zero catch quota 1986–90. Pages 221–231 *in* S. Andressen and W. Østreng (eds.), International Resource Management: The Role of Science and Politics. Belhaven Press, London and New York, NY.

Berzin, A. A. 1972. The Sperm Whale. Israel Program for Scientific Translations, Jerusalem. (Translation of Kashalot, Pishchevaya Promyshlennost, Moskva, 1971.)

Best, P. B. 1987. Estimates of landed catch of right (and other whalebone) whales in the American fishery, 1805–1909. Fishery Bulletin 85:405–418.

Best, P. B., and G. J. B. Ross. 1986. Catches of right whales from shore-based establishments in southern Africa. Reports of the International Whaling Commission (Special Issue 10): 275–289.

Birnie, P. 1985. International Regulation of Whaling: From Conservation of Whaling to Conservation of Whales and Regulation of Whale-Watching. 2 vols. Oceana Publications, New York, NY.

Bonner, W. N. 1980. Whales. Blandford Press, Poole, Dorset, U.K.

Burke, W. 1994. The New International Law of Fisheries. Oxford University Press, Oxford, U.K.

Caldwell, L. K. 1990. International Environmental Policy—Emergence and Dimensions. Duke University Press, Durham, NC.

Chapman, D. G., K. R. Allen, and S. J. Holt. 1964. Report of the Committee of Three Scientists on the special scientific investigation of the Antarctic whale stocks. Reports of the International Whaling Commission 14:32–106.

Chapman, D. G., K. R. Allen, S. J. Holt, and J. A. Gulland. 1965. Report of the Committee of Four Scientists. Reports of the International Whaling Commission 15:47–63.

Cicin-Sain, B., and R. W. Knecht. 1993. Implications of the Earth Summit for Ocean and Coastal Governance. Ocean Development and International Law 24:323–353.

Cooke, J. G. 1995. The International Whaling Commission's revised management procedure as an example of a new approach to fishery management. Pages 647–657 *in* A. S. Blix, L. Walløe, and Ø. Ulltang (eds.), Whales, Seals, Fish and Man. Elsevier, Amsterdam.

Dakin, W. J. 1977. Whalemen Adventurers in Southern Waters. Angus and Robertson, Sydney.

De Smet, W. M. A. 1981. Evidence of whaling in the North Sea and English Channel during the Middle Ages. FAO Fisheries Series No. 5. Vol. 3: 301–309.

Donovan, G. P. 1982. The International Whaling Commission and aboriginal/subsistence whaling: April 1979 to July 1981. Reports of the International Whaling Commission (Special Issue 4): 79–86.

Donovan, G. P. 1986. The International Whaling Commission and the humane killing of whales, 1982–1986. Reports of the International Whaling Commission (Special Issue 7): 141–153.

Donovan, G. P. 1989. Preface. The comprehensive assessment of whale stocks: The early years. Reports of the International Whaling Commission (Special Issue 11).

Doubleday, N. C. 1989. Aboriginal subsistence whaling: The right of Inuit to hunt whales and implications for international environmental law. Denver Journal of International Law and Policy 17:373–393.

Ellis, R. 1991. Men and Whales. Alfred A. Knopf, New York, NY.

Evans, P. G. H. 1987. The Natural History of Whales and Dolphins. Christopher Helm, London.

Food and Agriculture Organization. 1978. Mammals in the Seas. Vol. 1. Report of the FAO Advisory Committee on Marine Resources Research. Working Party on Marine Mammals. FAO Fisheries Series No. 5.

Gambell, R. 1973. Some effects of exploitation on reproduction in whales. Journal of Reproduction and Fertility, Supplement 19:531–551.

Gambell, R. 1983. Bowhead whales and Alaskan Eskimos: A problem of survival. Polar Record 21:467–473.

Gambell, R. 1993. International management of whales and whaling: An historical review of the regulation of commercial and aboriginal subsistence whaling. Arctic 46:97–107.

Gulland, J. A. 1966. The effect of regulation on Antarctic whale catches. Journal du Conseil Permanent International pour l'Exploration de la Mer 30:308–315.

Haw, M. D. 1993. Corrections to estimates of abundance of Southern Hemisphere minke whales obtained from IWC/IDCR data. Reports of the International Whaling Commission 43:114.

Hoel, A. H. 1993. Regionalization of international whale manage-

ment: The case of the North Atlantic Marine Mammals Commission. Arctic 46:116–123.
Horwood, J. W. 1987. The Sei Whale: Population Biology, Ecology and Management. Croom Helm, Ltd., Beckenham, Kent, U.K.
Hoyt, E. 1984. The Whale Watcher's Handbook. Doubleday and Company, Garden City, NY.
International Whaling Commission. 1950. International Convention for the Regulation of Whaling. Reports of the International Whaling Commission 1:9–14.
International Whaling Commission. 1958. Ninth report of the Commission. Reports of the International Whaling Commission 9:3–6.
International Whaling Commission. 1966a. Sixteenth report of the Commission. Reports of the International Whaling Commission 16:3–10.
International Whaling Commission. 1966b. Chairman's report of the sixteenth meeting. Reports of the International Whaling Commission 16:15–22.
International Whaling Commission. 1974. Chairman's report of the twenty-fourth meeting. Reports of the International Whaling Commission 24:20–36.
International Whaling Commission. 1976. Chairman's report of the twenty-sixth meeting. Reports of the International Whaling Commission 26:24–33.
International Whaling Commission. 1977a. Chairman's report of the twenty-seventh meeting. Reports of the International Whaling Commission 27:6–15.
International Whaling Commission. 1977b. Chairman's report of the twenty-eighth meeting. Reports of the International Whaling Commission 27:22–35.
International Whaling Commission. 1977c. Report of the Scientific Committee. Reports of the International Whaling Commission 27:36–60.
International Whaling Commission. 1978. Chairman's report of the twenty-ninth meeting. Reports of the International Whaling Commission 28:18–37.
International Whaling Commission. 1980. Chairman's report of the thirty-first annual meeting. Reports of the International Whaling Commission 30:25–41.
International Whaling Commission. 1981. Chairman's report of the thirty-second annual meeting. Reports of the International Whaling Commission 31:17–40.
International Whaling Commission. 1982. Report of the Scientific Committee. Reports of the International Whaling Commission 32:43–67.
International Whaling Commission. 1983a. Chairman's report of the thirty-fourth annual meeting. Reports of the International Whaling Commission 33:20–42.
International Whaling Commission. 1983b. Report of the Scientific Committee. Reports of the International Whaling Commission 33:43–73.
International Whaling Commission 1983c. Comments on moratorium proposals (agenda item 8.1). Reports of the International Whaling Commission 33:183–184.
International Whaling Commission. 1984. Chairman's report of the thirty-fifth annual meeting. Reports of the International Whaling Commission 34:13–34.
International Whaling Commission. 1985. Chairman's report of the thirty-sixth annual meeting. Reports of the International Whaling Commission 35:9–30.
International Whaling Commission. 1987. Report of the special meeting of the Scientific Committee on planning for a comprehensive assessment of whale stocks. Reports of the International Whaling Commission 37:147–157.
International Whaling Commission. 1989. Report of the Scientific Committee. Reports of the International Whaling Commission 39:33–157.
International Whaling Commission. 1990. Report of the Scientific Committee. Reports of the International Whaling Commission 40:39–86.
International Whaling Commission. 1991a. Chairman's report of the forty-second annual meeting. Reports of the International Whaling Commission 41:11–50.
International Whaling Commission. 1991b. Report of the Sub-Committee on Southern Hemisphere Minke Whales. Reports of the International Whaling Commission 41:113–131.
International Whaling Commission. 1991c. Report of the Sub-Committee on North Atlantic Minke Whales. Reports of the International Whaling Commission 41:132–171.
International Whaling Commission. 1991d. Comprehensive assessment of whale stocks progress report on development of revised management procedures. Reports of the International Whaling Commission 41:213–218.
International Whaling Commission. 1992a. Report of the Scientific Committee. Reports of the International Whaling Commission 42:51–86.
International Whaling Commission. 1992b. Report of the bowhead whale assessment meeting. Reports of the International Whaling Commission 42:137–155.
International Whaling Commission. 1992c. Report of the Sub-Committee on North Pacific Minke Whales. Reports of the International Whaling Commission 42:156–177.
International Whaling Commission. 1992d. Report of the Sub-Committee on Small Cetaceans. Reports of the International Whaling Commission 42:178–234.
International Whaling Commission. 1992e. Report of the comprehensive assessment special meeting on North Atlantic fin whales. Reports of the International Whaling Commission 42:595–644.
International Whaling Commission. 1993a. Chairman's report of the forty-fourth annual meeting. Reports of the International Whaling Commission 43:11–53.
International Whaling Commission. 1993b. Report of the Scientific Committee. Reports of the International Whaling Commission 43:55–92.
International Whaling Commission. 1993c. Report of the special meeting of the Scientific Committee on the assessment of gray whales. Reports of the International Whaling Commission 43:241–259.
International Whaling Commission. 1994a. Chairman's report of the forty-fifth annual meeting. Reports of the International Whaling Commission 44:11–39.
International Whaling Commission. 1994b. Report of the Workshop on Mortality of Cetaceans in Passive Fishing Nets and Traps. Reports of the International Whaling Commission (Special Issue 15): 6–57.
International Whaling Commission. 1995a. Chairman's report of the forty-sixth annual meeting. Reports of the International Whaling Commission 45:15–52.
International Whaling Commission. 1995b. Report of the Scientific

Committee. Reports of the International Whaling Commission 45:53–103.

International Whaling Commission. 1996. Chairman's report of the forty-seventh annual meeting. Reports of the International Whaling Commission 46:15–48.

International Whaling Commission. 1997. Report of the Scientific Committee. Reports of the International Whaling Commission 47:59–121.

International Whaling Commission. 1998a. Chairman's report of the forty-ninth annual meeting. Reports of the International Whaling Commission 48: (in press).

International Whaling Commission. 1998b. List of scientific papers arising our of JARPA. Reports of the International Whaling Commission 48: (in press).

International Whaling Statistics. 1942. XVI. Oslo, Norway.

International Whaling Statistics. 1948. XVIII. Oslo, Norway.

Jackson, G. 1978. The British Whaling Trade. A. & C. Black, London.

Jahn, G. 1933. Review of the results of International Whaling Statistics. International Whaling Statistics IV:3–38.

Jahn, G. 1937. Whaling in the Antarctic 1935–36. International Whaling Statistics VIII:3–16.

Kalland, A. 1995. Marine mammals in the culture of Norwegian coastal communities. Pages 689–697 *in* A. S. Blix, L. Walløe, and Ø. Ulltang (eds.), Whales, Seals, Fish and Man. Elsevier, Amsterdam.

Kalland, A., and B. Moeran. 1990. Endangered Culture: Japanese Whaling in Cultural Perspective. Nordic Institute of Asian Studies, Copenhagen, Denmark.

Kapel, F. O., and R. Petersen. 1982. Subsistence hunting—the Greenland case. Reports of the International Whaling Commission (Special Issue 4): 51–74.

Kirkwood, G. P. 1992. Background to the development of revised management procedures. Reports of the International Whaling Commission 42:236–243.

Krupnick, I. I. 1984. Gray whales and the Aborigines of the Pacific Northwest: The history of aboriginal whaling. Pages 103–120 *in* M. L. Jones, S. L. Swartz, and S. Leatherwood (eds.), The Gray Whale *Eschrichtius robustus.* Academic Press, Orlando, FL.

Kugler, R. C. 1981. Historical records of American sperm whaling. FAO Fisheries Series No. 5. Vol. 3: 321–326.

Leatherwood, S., and G. P. Donovan (eds.). 1991. Cetaceans and cetacean research in the Indian Ocean Sanctuary. UNEP Marine Mammal Technical Report 3. Nairobi, Kenya.

Lockyer, C. 1978. A theoretical approach to the balance between growth and food consumption in fin and sei whales, with special reference to the female reproductive cycle. Reports of the International Whaling Commission 28:243–249.

Mackintosh, N. A. 1965. The Stocks of Whales. Fishing News (Books), London.

Marine Mammal Commission. 1994. The Marine Mammal Commission Compendium of Selected Treaties, International Agreements, and Other Relevant Documents on Marine Resources, Wildlife, and the Environment, R. L. Wallace, compiler. Marine Mammal Commission, Washington, DC. Vol. 2: 1400–1580.

Marquette, W. M., and J. R. Bockstoce. 1980. Historical shore-based catch of bowhead whales in the Bering, Chukchi, and Beaufort Seas. Marine Fisheries Review 42 (9–10): 5–19.

Martin, G. S., and J. W. Brennan. 1989. Enforcing the International Convention for the Regulation of Whaling: The Pelly and Packwood-Magnuson amendments. Denver Journal of International Law and Policy 17:293–315.

Matthews, L. H. (ed.). 1975. The Whale. Crescent Books, New York, NY.

McNab, R. 1975. The Old Whaling Days. Golden Press, Auckland.

Mitchell, E. D., R. R. Reeves, and A. Evely. 1986. Whale killing methods: An annotated bibliography. Reports of the International Whaling Commission (Special Issue 7): 1–12.

Øen, E. O. 1995. Killing Methods for Minke and Bowhead Whales. Norwegian College of Veterinary Medicine, Oslo, Norway.

Omura, H. 1984. History of gray whales in Japan. Pages 57–77 *in* M. L. Jones, S. L. Swartz, and S. Leatherwood (eds.), The Gray Whale *Eschrichtius robustus.* Academic Press, Orlando, FL.

Omura, H. 1986. History of right whale catches in the waters around Japan. Reports of the International Whaling Commission (Special Issue 10): 35–41.

Porter, G., and J. W. Brown. 1991. Global Environmental Politics. Westfield Press, Boulder, CO.

Price, W. S. 1985. Whaling in the Caribbean: Historical perspective and update. Reports of the International Whaling Commission 35:413–419.

Proulx, J.-P. 1993. Basque whaling in Labrador in the 16th century. Studies in Archaeology, Architecture and History. Environment Canada, Ottawa.

Rice, D. W., and A. A. Wolman. 1971. The life history and ecology of the gray whale (*Eschrichtius robustus*). American Society of Mammalogists, Special Publication No. 3: 1–142.

Risting, S. 1931. The development of modern whaling. International Whaling Statistics II:4–15.

Ruud, J. T. 1956. International regulation of whaling. A critical survey. Norsk Hvalfangst-tidende 45:374–387.

Scarff, J. E. 1977. The international management of whales, dolphins and porpoises: An interdisciplinary assessment. Ecology Law Quarterly 6:323–638.

Slijper, E. J. 1962. Whales. Hutchinson and Company, London.

Stoker, S. W., and I. I. Krupnick. 1993. Subsistence whaling. Pages 579–629 *in* J. J. Burns, J. J. Montague, and C. J. Cowles (eds.), The Bowhead Whale. Society for Marine Mammalogy, Special Publication No. 2.

Tønnessen, J. N., and A. O. Johnsen. 1982. The History of Modern Whaling (a shortened translation of Den Moderne Hvalfangsts Historie: Opprinnelse og Utvikling, vols. 1–4, 1959–1970). C. Hurst and Company, London.

United Nations. 1983. The Law of the Sea. New York, NY.

Wilkinson, D. M. 1989. The use of domestic measures to enforce international whaling agreements: A critical perspective. Denver Journal of International Law and Policy 17:271–291.

Yablokov, A. V. 1994. Validity of whaling data. Nature 367:108.

Zemsky, V. A., A. A. Berzin, Y. A. Mikhalyev, and D. D. Tormosov. 1995. Materials on whaling by Soviet Antarctic whaling fleets (1947–1972). Center for Russian Environmental Policy, Moscow.

9

LEE A. KIMBALL

The Antarctic Treaty System

The seventh continent is unique in many ways. From the perspective of international law, Antarctica is the only continent where humans are a nonindigenous species and where no national territory is recognized. Reinforced by the harsh environment, the remote location, and the sense of camaraderie that these inspire, international cooperation is woven throughout the history of human penetration south. As long as the early adventurers stayed at sea, the international law of the high seas governed; that is, each country was responsible for its own nationals. As they took to land, some countries sought to extend the high seas rules, others to stake national claims. In the end, the necessity of cooperation forged a path-breaking regime of international law. Studying the evolution of Antarctic legal agreements illustrates the opportunities and constraints of building effective conservation arrangements. It indicates how Antarctic achievements have drawn on and influenced developments in international environmental law.

The effects of the Antarctic agreements (see Appendix) on marine mammals are both direct and indirect. The 1959 Antarctic Treaty governs activities on the continent and its massive ice cover. For seals, whose breeding colonies are located on land, it provides protection from harvest and human disturbance. Measures to curtail pollution of the marine environment from activities on the continent indirectly benefit seals and the marine species on which they feed. The killing or capturing of seals in the ocean is governed by the 1972 Convention for the Conservation of Antarctic Seals. There has been no commercial sealing in the waters surrounding Antarctica since the Convention was concluded in 1972.

The 1980 Convention on the Conservation of Antarctic Marine Living Resources (referred to in this chapter as CCAMLR) provides for the conservation of all marine species and the ecosystems of which they are a part. Relevant measures adopted pursuant to the Antarctic Treaty must be observed by the countries that are contracting parties to CCAMLR. The Convention leaves to the earlier, specialized conventions—the Antarctic Seals Convention and the 1946 International Convention for the Regulation of Whaling (see Gambell, this volume)—the regulation of sealing and whaling, respectively, but it takes into account these activities in addressing the marine ecosystem as a whole and calls for cooperation with these and other international forums. In this respect, the Southern Ocean whale sanctuary adopted by the International Whaling Commission in 1994 is perfectly consistent with CCAMLR. The mandate of CCAMLR is to ensure that the harvest of other marine species in the region does not adversely affect either the target species or nontarget species that feed on them, such as whales and seals (Fig. 9-1).

Because there are few current developments under the Antarctic agreements that directly address marine mammal issues, this chapter concentrates on the evolution of international law in Antarctica from the broader perspective of protecting their terrestrial and marine habitat. For the most part, the events affecting marine mammals in Antarctica precede the Antarctic agreements (Table 9-1). The discovery and exploitation of seals in the region took place from the late eighteenth through the early twentieth centuries. By the 1830s commercial exploitation for fur and oil had reduced the populations of Antarctic fur seals (*Arctocephalus gazella*) and southern elephant seals (*Mirounga leonina*) to the point where harvesting was no longer profitable. The whaling industry moved into the Southern Ocean early in the 1900s, but, as with the seals earlier, the stocks were quickly overexploited.

Figure 9-1. The crabeater seal is the most abundant marine mammal in the Antarctic. The one shown here in the company of Adélie penguins is at Cape Crozier, Antarctica, 1971. (Photograph © Bill Curtsinger)

The value of the whale stocks, however, influenced the United Kingdom to claim several sub-Antarctic islands in 1908. This claim included the first territorial claim in Antarctica. After World War I, the British sponsored scientific expeditions to gain understanding of the conditions affecting whaling. Subsequent scientific and political developments in the region led, ultimately, to the Antarctic Treaty.

Antarctica does not suffer human intruders lightly. Interior temperatures average from –30°C to –65°C and wind speeds can exceed 450 km/hour. On a normal summer day at the coast, the temperature may rise above freezing but averages slightly below. The shortest distance from the Antarctic Peninsula to the tip of South America crosses 990 km of the "roaring forties" (40°S latitudes), "furious fifties" (50°S latitudes), and "screaming sixties" (60°S latitudes). New Zealand, Australia, and South Africa are 2,000, 2,500, and 3,800 km distant, respectively. During the winter months, frozen sea ice expands in area by a factor of six to form a solid defensive moat of 20 million km^2 around the continent, further discouraging visits. Ships are locked out, and aircraft may venture in only in emergencies. As in the high Arctic, 24-hour darkness persists throughout austral midwinter. Without its winter moat, Antarctica at 14 million km^2 is larger than either Australia or Europe. Its coastline measures 30,000 km. Year-round, more than 98% of the continent is covered with ice, which averages 2,450 m in thickness. The ice mass is bisected by a mountain range 4,000 km long with many peaks more than 4,000 m high (Central Intelligence Agency 1978, Hill 1983, Fifield 1987).

Although life at the extreme has not been conducive to human presence, the teeming populations of native marine mammals and birds proved too attractive to keep people away. Sir Francis Drake reported thousands of geese near Tierra del Fuego in the 1500s, and Dampier noted millions of seals in the Juan Fernández Islands in the late 1600s. The improved navigation techniques of the mid-eighteenth century permitted ships to sail farther and farther south, precipitating voyages not only of discovery but of exploitation. When Captain James Cook circumnavigated Antarctica in 1774–1776, he too noted vast fur seal populations on the sub-Antarctic islands north of the continent (Central Intelligence Agency 1978, Hatherton 1986, Berkman 1992). Within 20 years the slaughter of fur seals had progressed, island by island, around Antarctica, eliminating whole populations. By the 1830s they were virtually extinct. The other Antarctic seals—crabeater (*Lobodon carcinophagus*), leopard (*Hydrurga leptonyx*), Ross (*Ommatophoca rossii*), and Weddell (*Leptonychotes weddellii*)—were less commercially desirable, and the pack ice around Antarctica protected them to some extent from the ships (Central Intelligence Agency 1978, Berkman 1992).

Table 9-1. A Brief Historical Outline

Year	Event
1700s	Southern Ocean exploration begins
1820–1821	Discovery of the Antarctic continent
1870–1910	Exploitation of seals on sub-Antarctic islands
1897–1900	First overwintering offshore and onshore Antarctica
1908	United Kingdom makes an Antarctic claim
1911–1912	Amundsen and Scott expeditions to the South Pole
1904–1986	Exploitation of whales in the Southern Ocean
1923	New Zealand makes an Antarctic claim
1924	France makes an Antarctic claim
1933	Australia makes an Antarctic claim
1939	Norway makes an Antarctic claim
1940	Chile makes an Antarctic claim
1943	Argentina makes an Antarctic claim
1957	Establishment by the International Council of Scientific Unions of what is to become the Scientific Committee on Antarctic Research (SCAR)
1957–1958	International Geophysical Year, which includes major scientific investigations in Antarctica and the establishment of some 40 research stations in the region
1959	Adoption of Antarctic Treaty. Entry into force 1961
1964	Adoption of Agreed Measures for the Conservation of Antarctic Fauna and Flora (including seals) pursuant to the Antarctic Treaty
1972	Adoption of Convention for the Conservation of Antarctic Seals. Entry into force 1978
1980	Adoption of the Convention on the Conservation of Antarctic Marine Living Resources (CCAMLR). Entry into force 1982
1988	Adoption of Convention on the Regulation of Antarctic Mineral Resources Activities
1991	Adoption of the Protocol on Environmental Protection to the Antarctic Treaty. Entry into force 1998
1994	International Whaling Commission establishes a Southern Ocean Whale Sanctuary

The extraction of oil from whale blubber led to the next assault on Antarctic marine mammals. The "modern" whaling era was launched in the 1860s with the introduction of the harpoon gun and steam-driven vessels. It reached Antarctica when the first whaling stations were established on sub-Antarctic islands in 1904. Within three years these whaling stations and factory ships moored in sheltered harbors were producing more oil than the rest of the world combined (Hatherton 1986).

Enter International Law

International law is shaped by many factors: concern for national security, aspirations for territorial and economic gain, technological innovations and scientific discoveries, and increasing human impacts on resources and environments. Its application in Antarctica has been influenced by developments within and outside the region.

In 1609 Dutch jurist Hugo Grotius supported the Queen of England when he advocated that the seas should be open to the innocent use and mutual benefit of all, whether for navigation or fisheries. This view prevailed over the Papal Bull of 1493, which had reinforced exclusive claims by Spain and Portugal over most of the Atlantic and Pacific Oceans. It prevailed not least because the English, Dutch, and others were as anxious as the Spanish and the Portuguese to claim riches across and under the seas. By the early 1700s the concept that each nation could claim sovereignty over a narrow belt of coastal waters to protect itself from attack by sea had emerged to complement the freedom of the high seas rule. A Dutch judge, Cornelius van Bynkershoek, defined the "territorial sea" more precisely in 1702 as the range of a cannon shot: one league, or 3 nautical miles (5.5 km) (Morrell 1992).

Two centuries later, this cannon-shot rule became the basis for the early regulation of whaling. The first sub-Antarctic whaling station of 1904 was a Norwegian-operated Argentine station on the island of South Georgia (Fig. 9-2). It was followed by Norwegian floating factories in the South Shetland Islands. In 1908 the British government claimed South Georgia, the South Shetlands, and other Falkland Islands dependencies as well as a pie-shaped wedge of the continent, south to the Pole. It did so in part to be able to regulate the whaling industry (Central Intelligence Agency 1978). In accordance with international law, the government could control any activities out to the limit of the 3-mile (5.5-km) territorial sea. This allowed it to restrain whaling not only on the land stations but also on the factory ships anchored immediately offshore—but not for long. To avoid having to obtain licenses and abide by the catch quotas set by the British, the industry developed mobile factory ships capable of processing the catch outside the territorial sea limit. By 1925 it could once again elude the arm of the

Figure 9-2. Elephant seals, penguins, and reindeer (introduced in 1910) coexist peaceably on the shores of South Georgia, a sub-Antarctic island in the South Atlantic Ocean, February 1990. (Photograph by Steve Leatherwood)

law. This made it increasingly apparent that action by individual nations was insufficient to regulate an activity pursued on a worldwide commons. (For discussion of international agreements to control high seas whaling, see Gambell, this volume, and Katona and Kraus, this volume.)

The foundations for international conservation law in the Antarctic were also laid early. James Weddell, for whom the Weddell seal is named, lamented early in the 1800s that if the sealers in the South Shetlands had been prohibited from killing mother fur seals until the young could take to the water and until the mothers appeared to be old, and if they had been encouraged to harvest a proportionate number of males, an annual harvest of furs might have been preserved for years to come. He drew an analogy with limits set by law on the mesh size of fishing nets to avoid harvesting the young (Hatherton 1986, Anonymous 1990).

Thus, during the nineteenth century no attempt was made to establish legal authority to control Antarctic sealing. By the early twentieth century the British territorial claims allowed the government to regulate sealing and whaling on land. The British took advantage of the international legal right to a territorial sea to curtail the offshore whaling industry, albeit with brief effect. The global whaling conventions constituted the next step. Where Weddell sought to protect the sealing industry from extinction by stabilizing harvests, the British sought to protect the whaling industry by restricting the catch to stabilize prices. Whatever the motive, the objective of sustainable use had been articulated.

As worldwide exploration progressed during the nineteenth century, the search for trade routes and territory was complemented increasingly by scientific studies and expeditions. Antarctica was no exception. But it was only after World War I that direct links between scientific research and sustainable use were established. Beginning in the 1920s the British invested revenues from their whaling licenses in efforts to gather scientific information on conditions affecting Antarctic whaling, particularly the abundance of a species of krill (*Euphausia superba*), a small shrimp on which several whale species feed. These so-called Discovery Investigations, carried out over a span of 15 years, ultimately produced results of much broader relevance for understanding the physical, chemical, and biological components of the Southern Ocean (Hatherton 1986, Rutford 1986).

The final impetus to international law in the Antarctic came as a result of territorial disputes and the onset of the Cold War. Following the United Kingdom, six other countries claimed parts of Antarctica and the sub-Antarctic islands between 1908 and 1943. These were Argentina, Australia, Chile, France, New Zealand, and Norway. The overlapping claims of Argentina, Chile, and the United Kingdom caused periodic flare-ups, and as recently as 1952 the United Kingdom and Argentina exchanged gunfire on the Antarctic Peninsula. Naval activities during World War II gave rise to fears that a power-hungry nation might attempt to control the Drake Passage off the tip of South America and thus dominate the route between the Atlantic and Pacific Oceans. The level of postwar Soviet interest in Antarctica reinforced concerns about national and international security, as did the disputed claims. The United States and the Soviet Union were among the countries that firmly rejected other nations' territorial claims in Antarctica, but they maintained their own right to make a claim. Fifteen percent of Antarctica remains unclaimed to this day. A creative solution was needed to defuse growing tensions in the region (Central Intelligence Agency 1978, Quigg 1983, Orrego-Vicuna 1986).

The cornerstone for the Antarctica Treaty was laid with the 1957–1958 International Geophysical Year (IGY). The world's scientists were eager to pursue research in the polar regions to better understand global phenomena. After World War II they began to consider how to build on the investigations of the first and second international polar years (1882–1883 and 1932–1933). They formed a committee, the Scientific Committee on Antarctic Research, under the auspices of the nongovernmental International Council of Scientific Unions, to plan and coordinate an international research program of unprecedented scope. As a result, 12 nations established some 40 research stations in Antarctica during the 18-month period known as the International Geophysical Year (Rutford 1986). When it was over, the diplomats seized on the idea to perpetuate peaceful activity in the region. At the invitation of the United States, the 12 countries active in the effort met in Washington, D.C., and on 1 December 1959 *adopted* (see Glossary for terms in italics) the Antarctic Treaty (Table 9-2). It establishes Antarctica as a continent for "freedom of scientific investigations . . . and cooperation toward that end, as applied during the IGY" (Article II). The treaty affirms that Antarctica shall be used for peaceful purposes only and prohibits any measure of a military nature (Article I). As for the disputed claims, "No acts or activities taking place while the present Treaty is in force shall constitute a basis for asserting, supporting or denying a claim to territorial sovereignty in Antarctica or create any rights of sovereignty in Antarctica" (Article IV).

The Antarctic Treaty Evolves

The external factors affecting Antarctic legal regimes are the same as those that shape international law elsewhere: economics, science and technology, international politics, national security, and, increasingly, the growth of human activities and impacts in the region. When the Antarctic Treaty was concluded in 1959, its primary purpose was to prevent conflict. From that basis a strong program of international scientific research has been built, conservation regimes for seals and other marine living resources have been established, and environmental protection has been elevated from a means to preserve the continent as a pristine laboratory for research to an end in its own right: the 1991 Protocol on Environmental Protection designates Antarctica as "a natural reserve, devoted to peace and science."

Three aspects internal to the treaty have also been influential in its evolution. These attributes, and the intentions they reflect, form guiding principles of many other international legal arrangements.

First, the 1959 treaty is the original "framework" regime. Although the treaty itself is not detailed, it provides for regular meetings among the *contracting parties* to exchange information and consult about shared concerns. The drafters expressly contemplated that these meetings would be used to formulate additional measures to further the principles and objectives of the treaty, including cooperation in scientific research and "preservation and conservation of living resources in Antarctica" (Article IX.1[f]). The network of binding requirements and nonbinding guidelines adopted by the parties has grown substantially since 1959, building on the framework. With the 1991 Protocol, five detailed annexes have already been adopted and future technical measures may become binding on the parties without recourse to a lengthy ratification process. These features expedite further development of the framework.

Second, the treaty's consensus decision-making system precludes either majority or minority rule. The disputed territorial status of Antarctica makes it essential to avoid any threat to the position of either those nations with claims (claimant nations) or those nations that refuse to recognize any claims (nonclaimant nations). The position of the United States and the former Soviet Union is also reflected in the treaty. Both have maintained that they have a basis for making a claim in Antarctica although they have never acted on it. It is impossible to understand the Antarctic agreements without understanding that in every one of them, these positions are and must be preserved. The Antarctic Treaty does not dispense with or ignore the claims; it freezes for safekeeping each government's position on claims. The consensus decision-making system reassures each

Table 9-2. The Contracting Parties to the Conventions

Nation	1959 Antarctic Treaty	1991 Protocol	1972 CCAS	1980 CCAMLR
Argentina	CP*	1993	1978	CM/1982
Austria	NCP/1987			
Australia	CP*	1994	1987	CM/1981
Belgium	CP*	1996	1978	CM/1984
Brazil	CP/1975/1983	1995	1991	CM/1986
Bulgaria	CP/1978/1998			NCM/1992
Canada	NCP/1988		1990	NCM/1981
Chile	CP*	1995	1980	CM/1981
China	CP/1983/1985	1994		
Colombia	NCP/1989			
Cuba	NCP/1984			
Czech Republic	NCP/1962			
Denmark	NCP/1965			
Ecuador	CP/1987/1990	1993		
Finland	CP/1984/1989	1996		NCM/1989
France	CP*	1993	1975	CM/1982
Germany	CP/1979/1981	1994	1980	CM/1982
Greece	NCP/1987			NCM/1987
Guatemala	NCP/1991			
Hungary	NCP/1984			
India	CP/1983/1983	1996		CM/1985
Italy	CP/1981/1987	1995	1992	CM/1989
Japan	CP*	1997	1980	CM/1981
North Korea	NCP/1987			
South Korea	CP/1986/1989	1996		CM/1985
Netherlands	CP/1967/1990	1994		NCM/1990
New Zealand	CP*	1994		CM/1982
Norway	CP*	1993	1973	CM/1983
Papua New Guinea	NCP/1981			
Peru	CP/1981/1989	1993		NCM/1989
Poland	CP/1961/1977	1995	1980	CM/1984
Romania	NCP/1971			
Russian Federation	CP*	1997	1978	CM/1981
Slovak Republic	NCP/1962			
South Africa	CP*	1995	1972	CM/1981
Spain	CP/1982/1988	1992		CM/1984
Sweden	CP/1984/1988	1994		CM/1984
Switzerland	NCP/1990			
Turkey	NCP/1996			
Ukraine	NCP/1992			CM/1994
United Kingdom	CP*	1995	1974	CM/1981
United States	CP*	1997	1977	CM/1982
Uruguay	CP/1980/1985	1995		NCM/1985
European Community				CM/1982

CP, consultative party (decision-making rights); NCP, nonconsultative party (no decision-making rights); CM, Commission member (decision-making rights); NCM, non-Commission member (no decision-making rights); date/date, date of accession/date attained CP status.

*Original signatory.

government that it will be able to protect its fundamental legal position.

Third, governments recognized that regular discussions pursuant to the treaty might not be sufficient to relax tensions over national aspirations in the region. To promote confidence in each other's forbearance, they agreed to exchange information on planned activities and to permit each other to verify ongoing compliance with treaty provisions. Each government is required to give advance notice of any Antarctic expedition or the establishment of stations and to permit other parties to inspect its facilities in Antarctica without prior notice. The right to make unannounced on-site inspections set an important precedent in international law that to this day has rarely been emulated. To further international scientific cooperation, governments agreed to exchange information on planned research programs and to ensure that the results were exchanged and made freely available (Articles III and VII). Thus, among the decision-making parties active in Antarctica, transparency and accountability were built into the Treaty from the outset. During the 1980s substantial progress was made in extending the information flow to all the contracting parties to the treaty (that is, to include the nonconsultative parties), to the international community as a whole through the United Nations, and to interested nongovernmental organizations, such as the World Conservation Union (IUCN).

The Original "Framework" Regime

Today the term "framework convention" brings to mind the global conventions on climate change and biodiversity concluded in 1992 or the 1985 Vienna Convention and its 1987 Montreal Protocol dealing with ozone depletion. But the Antarctic Treaty serves as a model for the gradual extension of a comprehensive system of regional governance. The relative isolation of Antarctica from the rest of the world, the few countries originally active there, the limited nature of their activities, and the unique, quasi-international status of Antarctica make it a microcosm of international cooperation.

Strengthening and Expanding the Scope of Antarctic Measures

The Antarctic Treaty provides that representatives of the *consultative parties* shall "recommend" to their governments the various measures adopted at their meetings. The intent behind the term was to tread lightly on sensitivities about national claims and the question of who is in charge of ensuring that the measures are, in fact, applied. Were Antarctica national territory, it would clearly be the responsibility of the sovereign nation to apply and enforce the measures vis-à-vis its own citizens and visitors from other countries. A nonclaimant nation like the United States takes a different view: that each country has jurisdiction over its own citizens in Antarctica and that no country may exercise sovereignty on the basis of a territorial claim. Hence, tread lightly to keep the peace.

Today, Antarctic Treaty recommendations and measures are considered binding once approved by all the consultative parties, but there was little insistence on compliance with the recommendations during the 1960s and 1970s. From the claimant's perspective, raising questions of compliance verged on international interference in domestic affairs. More to the point, the recommendations themselves are "soft" in that governments are "encouraged," "insofar as feasible and practicable" to "make every effort" to implement them. Thus, there are few unqualified directives with which a government must comply. As to the inspection provision (Article VII), the United States was the only government to regularly exercise this right until well into the 1980s. Its primary purpose in doing so was to verify that no military activities were taking place.

As long as science dominated the Antarctic agenda and a mere handful of research stations dotted an area larger than North America, little controversy arose among governments active in the region. The impetus to collaborate with respect to transportation, telecommunications, and emergency response was far greater than the urge to assert opposing national views on sovereignty. The only competition was between researchers and native birds and mammals over the limited number of relatively accessible, ice-free coastal areas. Governments took steps early on to minimize human activities that disturbed native species or disrupted their breeding and to avoid contamination from wastes and other matter. Their objective was as much to preserve the pristine nature of the continent and its species for scientific research as to conserve and protect the wild populations. In any event, these concerns with environmental protection began to expand the scope of their deliberations. And as they settled into a noncontentious consultative pattern, governments became less wary of tackling each other's compliance. Over time, a changing appreciation of the unique ecology of the interior dry valleys of Antarctica, its inland lakes, and the extensive zones of pack ice around the continent focused new attention on protecting the Antarctic environment. So did awareness that the frozen continent retains the imprint of human presence—whether in the form of discarded equipment, food waste, or cigarette butts—until it is frozen into the ice and, centuries hence, calves into the sea embedded in glacial chunks.

The Agreed Measures on Antarctic Fauna and Flora

In 1964 the consultative parties adopted the Agreed Measures on the Conservation of Antarctic Fauna and Flora (Recommendation III-8). These direct governments to prohibit the killing, wounding, or capturing of any native mammal or bird; to minimize harmful interference with native species; and to grant special protection to designated areas. Limited exemptions from these rules require a permit. Several protected areas include important seal habitat, and fur seals and Ross seals are accorded a higher level of protection than other native mammals. The Agreed Measures also prescribe precautionary measures to prevent the accidental introduction of parasites and diseases into the treaty area (i.e., they require that imported sled dogs be inoculated and prohibit the entry of live poultry). The major die-off in 1988 of harbor seals in parts of the North Atlantic Ocean, caused by a distemper virus, led the Antarctic Treaty governments to strengthen these protections in *Annex* II of the 1991 *Protocol* (Table 9-2).

The Agreed Measures represent the first step from the "softer" treaty recommendations toward more binding measures. Annexes II and V of the 1991 Protocol (on conservation and protected areas, respectively) advance that process. Thus, the Agreed Measures strengthen the requirement that national governments report annually on what they have done to implement the requirements, and they specify that records and statistics on species killed and the state of native mammal and bird populations must be exchanged. They call for a common form, which simplifies reporting by governments and facilitates the synthesis and analysis of the information. Under the Protocol, information exchange and reporting requirements have been further expanded, as have the means for reviewing that information to identify emerging issues and foster compliance. These issues are considered in "The Feedback Factor," below.

The progression from recommendatory to binding measures in Antarctica has taken place not only with respect to the issues addressed in the Agreed Measures, but also regarding waste disposal, environmental impact assessment, protected areas, and oil contamination from ships. It illustrates the use of "soft law" in international agreements. This term refers to nonbinding measures that guide and inform the practice of nations. Although soft law does not require compliance, it can provide the basis, if not the impetus, for the development of binding legal instruments. It may serve as a step toward mandatory international commitments or as a model for enforceable national laws.

Environmental Impact Assessment

The evolution toward binding commitments is clearly demonstrated by procedures for environmental impact assessment in Antarctica. In 1975 the consultative parties first adopted guidelines for the planning of major operations in the Antarctic Treaty area (Recommendation VIII-11). These state that an evaluation of the environmental impacts of the proposed activity should be carried out, which describes the proposed action and its potential benefits and impacts and considers alternatives. The evaluation is to be circulated to nations active in Antarctica for information purposes. As a result of a process that began in 1983, a much-revised recommendation on environmental impact assessment was adopted in 1987. The 1991 Protocol subsequently improved on that recommendation and strengthened its binding nature.

Continuing pressure from nongovernmental groups and the general thrust toward stronger environmental protection worldwide certainly stimulated these developments. The Scientific Committee on Antarctic Research also played a major role when it submitted a report and recommendations on the subject as requested (Benninghoff and Bonner 1985). But a major breakthrough came as the United Nations Environment Programme considered nonbinding goals and principles on environmental impact assessment (Kimball 1994). These principles were adopted by the program's Governing Council in 1987 just as some of the same governments were opposing the revised measures on environmental assessment in the Antarctic Treaty forum. When participants in the Antarctic meeting brought this to the attention of the hesitant governments, they found it difficult to maintain their opposition. Thus, the early soft law developed within the context of the Antarctic Treaty, together with the soft law formulated under the auspices of the United Nations Environment Programme, influenced the development of binding Antarctic measures on environmental impact assessment.

Extending the Reach of Antarctic Measures

During the period that the scope of Antarctic Treaty recommendations was expanding, the consultative parties also considered questions about the impacts of activities within the treaty area caused by countries that were not contracting parties and the impacts of activities carried out in Antarctica outside the treaty area.

The Agreed Measures and Marine Pollution

The Agreed Measures were the first to attempt to reach beyond the consultative parties to the treaty. They indicate that when the parties' Antarctic expeditions use ships sailing under the flags of other nations, they "shall, as far as feasible, arrange with the owners of such ships that the crews of these ships observe the Agreed Measures" (Agreed Measures, Article XI). Although recognizing that the flag nation, under international law, is responsible for ships flying its flag, this places the onus on the consultative parties to employ ships that they can rely on to respect the Agreed Measures. The 1991 Protocol strengthens the idea of applying treaty measures to ships operating in the treaty area even when the flag nation is not a treaty party, particularly regarding safeguards against marine pollution when these ships are supporting the Antarctic operations of consultative parties (Protocol, Article 13 and Annex IV, Article 2).

During the late 1970s the consultative parties considered briefly the possibility that ships supplying Antarctic facilities might contaminate the marine environment with oil. They concluded that despite the particularly hazardous nature of Antarctic ship operations, the existing international conventions governing oil pollution from ships were adequate (Recommendations IX-6, X-7) (Anonymous 1990). The drawback to this approach was that not all governments operating in the Southern Ocean were parties to the existing conventions, concluded under the auspices of the International Maritime Organization.

When the *Bahia Paraiso* went aground on 28 January 1989 on an underwater reef near the Antarctic Peninsula, it raised anew questions about the adequacy of existing international legal arrangements for ship-source pollution in the Antarctic region. The *Bahia Paraiso* was an Argentine ship en route to supply Argentine research stations with fuel. In addition, it carried a small contingent of tourists. By February, between 125,000 and 150,000 gallons (473,175 to 567,810 liters) of petroleum products were estimated to have leaked into the marine environment (Marine Mammal Commission 1990). The oil spill damaged local bird and plant colonies, but its worst effects may have been to compromise long-term research programs ongoing in the area of the spill.

On the positive side, the consultative parties began to fashion more stringent international restraints on marine pollution from ships. At their fifteenth meeting later in 1989, they recommended that the treaty area be designated a "special area" pursuant to Annexes I and V of the International Convention for the Prevention of Pollution from Ships (MARPOL 73/78; see Laist et al., this volume). This was accomplished by a decision of the International Maritime Organization and the designations went into effect in March 1992 (Wonham 1992). The MARPOL 73/78 annexes address in detail the discharge of oil and garbage from ships. "Special area" status invokes more stringent discharge restrictions than apply elsewhere in the ocean. The result is that all the contracting parties to the MARPOL 73/78 annexes must follow these rules when operating in the Antarctic Treaty area; that is, the action reaches beyond the parties to the Antarctic Treaty. The decision was then reinforced by Annex IV to the 1991 Antarctic Treaty Protocol. The latter reiterates the provisions for special areas in MARPOL 73/78. With the *entry into force* of the Protocol in 1998, the requirements will bind contracting parties to the Protocol even if they are not parties to MARPOL 73/78.

Thus, by utilizing existing international agreements, it was possible to achieve more stringent protection for the Antarctic marine environment and extend their application beyond the Antarctic Treaty parties. By reiterating those protections within the Antarctic agreements, it was possible to cast the net over all of the Antarctic Treaty parties to ensure that those not party to MARPOL 73/78 would nevertheless be bound by the same requirements. This illustrates how linkages between international treaties can strengthen environmental protection.

Sealing

The possible resurgence of Antarctic sealing in the 1960s provided another stimulus to an agreement that could involve a larger group of countries than those traditionally active in Antarctica. Fishing, which includes sealing, is a freedom of the high seas under international law. The Antarctic Treaty area extends north to 60°S latitude. It applies to Antarctica, including all ice shelves (that is, the freshwater glaciers that project into the surrounding seas from the continent), but it is without prejudice to high seas rights and freedoms. The restrictions on sealing in the Agreed Measures therefore apply only on the continent and ice shelves. During the early 1960s interest was expressed in pelagic, or open water, sealing in the region. Canadian scientists had recommended that Canadian and Norwegian long-distance sealing fleets turn their attention to the Antarctic to reduce pressure on depleted harp seal (*Phoca groenlandica*) stocks in the western North Atlantic, and Norway conducted an exploratory sealing expedition in 1964 (Sergeant 1971, Marine Mammal Commission 1988, Anonymous 1990).

This high seas activity was clearly outside the scope of the Agreed Measures. Moreover, there might be countries interested in sealing in the Southern Ocean that were not party to the Antarctic Treaty. For these reasons, the consultative parties decided that a convention should be drawn up outside the framework of the Antarctic Treaty (Anonymous 1990). In 1970 they commenced special, informal meetings based on previous discussions in their regular meetings. These led to the adoption of the Convention for the Conservation of Antarctic Seals in 1972 (Table 9-2). No commercial sealing has taken place in Antarctica since then. The Soviet Union undertook an experimental sealing expedition in 1986–1987, concluding that it was unlikely that commercial sealing would begin in the Antarctic within the next 5 to 10 years (Anonymous 1990).

Hazardous Substances

The concern that activities in Antarctica might have repercussions in adjacent regions was first expressed in relation to radioactive wastes. Despite the treaty's prohibition on disposal in Antarctica, the growth in nuclear power facilities during the early 1970s and the need to isolate nuclear wastes from the biosphere for periods up to 250,000 years led to public speculation that the Antarctic ice sheet might offer a suitable home. This prompted the consultative parties at their eighth meeting in 1975 to reaffirm opposition to waste disposal in the treaty area. In the words of Ambassador Keith G. Brennan, the representative of Australia, with which several other representatives associated themselves: "Australia is concerned that the Antarctic environment and the surrounding oceans and atmosphere should not become contaminated by radioactive waste. . . . In light of . . . the conclusions reached by the group of scientific experts [convened by the Scientific Committee on Antarctic Research in 1974, that the safe disposal and storage of radioactive waste in the Antarctic ice sheet could not be guaranteed on the basis of existing knowledge] . . . , Australia would firmly oppose any move to permit the disposal or storage of radioactive waste in the Antarctic ice sheet" (Anonymous 1990:2212).

As the world confronts difficult choices over where to dispose of other hazardous substances, new fears have arisen about possible Antarctic disposal. Moreover, the countries that are not party to the Antarctic Treaty are not bound by its restrictions. This has produced another link between the Antarctic Treaty and a global agreement. The Basel Convention on the Control of Transboundary Movements of Hazardous Wastes and Their Disposal, concluded in 1989, prohibits the export of hazardous material to the Antarctic Treaty area for disposal (Basel Convention, Article 4.6).

New Resource Management Questions: Fish and Minerals

During the mid-1970s the consultative parties took up the two issues that, to date, have posed the greatest challenge to their ability to avoid disputes between nations with Antarctic claims and nations that do not recognize the claims. These are the harvesting of marine living resources and the possible exploitation of nonliving natural resources such as oil and gas or ore deposits. (The parties used the term "mineral resources" as a shorthand to include all nonliving natural nonrenewable resources, even though oil and gas are not technically minerals. The term is so used in this chapter.) Simultaneous developments in the 15 years of negotiations over the 1982 United Nations Convention on the Law of the Sea made it clear by 1976 that coastal nations would gain sovereign rights to exploit and manage living and nonliving resources in the 200–nautical mile (370.4-km) zones (exclusive economic zones) adjacent to their coasts. They could control nonliving resources development even farther offshore if the natural prolongation of the continental land mass extended beyond 200 nautical miles (370.4 km). For nations claiming sovereignty in Antarctica, it became more difficult to refrain from asserting resource rights in Antarctic claims and associated offshore areas—and enjoying the exclusive benefit of any revenues that might accrue—than it had been to refrain from asserting their perceived right to control scientific research. Of course, the reverse was also true. For the nonclaimant nations, any concession to the claimants granting them special rights to regulate, tax, or enforce the rules governing resource activities would amount to a recognition of claims and prejudice the legal position of the nonclaimants. It might also deprive their own treasuries of potential tax revenues.

The consultative parties took these issues up gingerly. They decided it would be easier to deal first with marine living resources. Because these resources are renewable, it would be in every nation's interest to agree on conservation rules that would ensure long-term, sustainable use. Moreover, because the Southern Ocean includes extensive areas beyond 200 nautical miles (370.4 km) of Antarctica, they could base the new convention on high seas fishing rights without sparking claimant/nonclaimant tensions. That is, the area to which the convention applied would cover vast areas clearly beyond national jurisdiction as well as areas that the claimants would consider subject to national jurisdiction under the new law of the sea regime. As with the Antarctic Seals Convention, it would be appropriate for other interested nations, in addition to the consultative parties, to participate in the agreement. (The issue of national control over offshore marine areas did not cause difficulties when the Seals Convention was negotiated because there was no international agreement in the early 1970s that recognized coastal nation rights in extensive offshore zones.) Another reason to proceed first with living resources was that fishing for krill had intensified during the 1960s and 1970s and there were plans for significant expansion.

The successful conclusion of CCAMLR in 1980 inspired confidence among the governments concerned that it would be possible to deal with the more sensitive political questions involved in negotiating a minerals treaty. Unlike CCAMLR, the minerals treaty negotiations were prompted not by knowledge of commercially valuable deposits in the region, but by the possibility that they might one day be found. The minerals treaty was viewed as a means to avoid conflicts that might arise if minerals of commercial value were discovered and to avoid adverse environmental consequences from any development that occurred. The problem was that deposits would be located in areas that in other regions would clearly be subject to national (coastal nation) control; that is, ore deposits would be under the ice on the continent, and oil and gas deposits were thought most likely to be in the offshore continental shelf.

Three events triggered further discussion of a legal regime for Antarctic minerals development: expressions of interest in prospecting for oil by private companies in 1969–1970; circumstantial evidence of potential oil and gas in the Ross Sea continental shelf, from the results of drilling by the *Glomar Challenger* in 1973 as part of an international research venture; and the oil embargo imposed by the Organization of Petroleum Exporting Countries in 1972–1973, which caused a jump in the price of oil (Kimball 1988a, Office of Technology Assessment 1989). To date, no substantial resource deposits have been located, many of the technologies required to exploit them safely in Antarctic conditions are only beginning to emerge, and the economics of recovery and transportation to remote markets remain prohibitive. The consultative parties decided to proceed with negotiating a regime because they feared that if they waited until exploitable deposits were found and the technology became available, the potential stakes would make agreement a far more difficult and contentious process. The treaty was negotiated in a series of meetings from 1982 to 1988.

After the adoption and *signature* of the Antarctic Minerals Convention in 1988, several countries, led by Australia and France, changed their minds about its desirability. As an alternative, they proposed in 1989 a comprehensive convention on Antarctic environmental protection that would ban minerals activities in Antarctica. Because the concurrence of these claimant nations was necessary for the minerals convention to enter into force, the consultative parties decided to set the Antarctic Minerals Convention aside and ban mineral resource activities in Antarctica for the foreseeable future. The prohibition in Article 7 of the 1991 Protocol may be altered by consensus of the consultative parties. After 50 years, it may be amended or modified as provided in Article 25, which does not require consensus.

The negotiation of the Antarctic Minerals Convention paralleled consideration in the regular Antarctic Treaty meetings of several of the same environmental issues: environmental impact assessment, waste management, strengthening the system of Antarctic protected areas, the need for a well-integrated environmental monitoring and data management system for Antarctic scientific and environmental data, and determining how to ensure that the growing range of activities in Antarctica—from scientific research, logistics, and fisheries to tourism and potential mineral resources activities—was carried out in a mutually compatible manner. In most cases, the individuals representing their governments were the same, as were those representing nongovernmental organizations. Discussions often carried over from one forum to the other. When more forward-looking provisions on environmental impact assessment were accepted in the Minerals Convention, these influenced developments in the Antarctic Treaty forum and, ultimately, the 1991 Protocol. The ecosystem standard in CCAMLR (discussed below) laid the groundwork for the principles to be used in judging the acceptability of minerals activities in the Minerals Convention. These in turn form the basis for the environmental principles in the 1991 Protocol. Conversely, governments sometimes resisted proposals in one forum if they were concerned that they might arise in another. For example, provision for an international system of inspection, ultimately accepted in the Minerals Convention and later in the 1991 Protocol, was resisted initially in CCAMLR to avoid prejudicing the minerals treaty negotiations.

The Antarctic Marine Ecosystem

Both resource questions—but in particular the possibility of mineral resources development—stimulated concerns about impacts in adjacent regions. The nations nearest to Antarctica, Chile and Argentina, were particularly worried about the possible effects of pollution on harvests of marine living resources. The consultative parties collectively expressed this concern in 1975. They noted that mineral resources exploration and exploitation could adversely affect not only the unique Antarctic environment but also other ecosystems dependent on it, and they called for further study of these questions, as considered below (Recommendation VIII-14). The final agreement provides for protection of the Antarctic environment and dependent and associated ecosystems (Convention on the Regulation of Antarctic Mineral Resources Activities, Articles 2 and 4 [Kimball 1988a, Mangel et al. 1996]).

The concept of an Antarctic marine ecosystem found its detailed expression in the Convention on the Conservation of Antarctic Marine Living Resources (CCAMLR) (Table 9-2). CCAMLR was negotiated during a period when fisheries management concepts were in a state of flux. It was becoming apparent that emphasis on single-species management was misplaced and that important predator/prey relationships and environmental factors affecting marine species should be taken into account. The failure of maximum sustainable yield models to consider species other than those harvested led to serious reevaluation of the concept and the testing and application of new multispecies models. The Smithsonian Institution collaborated with several other organizations in sponsoring two workshops on this subject in 1975. These produced new principles for the conservation of wild living resources that addressed the need to maintain the ecosystem in a desirable state and anticipated the precautionary principle (Holt and Talbot 1978, Brown 1983; also see Mangel et al. 1996).

A related initiative on marine ecosystems focused specifically on the Antarctic. The concern in the Southern Ocean was that too little was known about the marine ecosystem and in particular about krill, which plays a central role in the food web (Fig. 9-3). If significant fisheries developed for krill or other species, it would not be possible to determine potential impacts on harvested or dependent and associated species, including seals and whales (Brown 1983, Hofman 1987). To improve understanding of the structure and dynamics of Antarctic marine ecosystems as a basis for managing the resources, the Scientific Committee on Antarctic Research and another organ of the International Council of Scientific Unions, the Scientific Committee on Oceanic Research, spearheaded the development of a 10-year research program in 1976 known as the Biological Investigation of Marine Antarctic Systems and Stocks, or BIOMASS (Hofman 1987).

The discussion of new approaches to fisheries management coincided with the development of the fisheries provisions of the 1982 Law of the Sea Convention. Effectively concluded in 1977, these articles refer in an inchoate manner to the need to take into account the interdependence of stocks and the effects of harvests on associated or dependent species. They call for maximum sustainable yield to be qualified by relevant environmental and economic factors. The CCAMLR negotiations, which took place between 1977 and 1980, raised multispecies ecosystem management to a new level. CCAMLR requires that any harvesting and associated activities be conducted in accordance with the following principles of conservation (Article II.3):

(a) prevention of decrease in the size of any harvested population to levels below those which ensure its stable recruitment. For this purpose its size should not be allowed to fall below a level close to that which ensures the greatest net annual increment;

(b) maintenance of the ecological relationships between harvested, dependent and related populations of Antarctic marine living resources and the restoration of depleted populations to the levels defined in sub-paragraph (a) above; and

(c) prevention of changes or minimization of the risk of changes in the marine ecosystem which are not potentially reversible over two or three decades, taking into account the state

A

B

Figure 9-3. (*A*) The *Chiyo Maru* No. 2 fished for krill in CCAMLR statistical area 58 (Wilkesland region, Indian Ocean) in February–March 1995. (*B*) Krill being dumped from the trawl net into the vessel's hold. (Photographs by Wes Armstrong)

of available knowledge of the direct and indirect impact of harvesting, the effect of the introduction of alien species, the effects of associated activities on the marine ecosystem and of the effects of environmental changes, with the aim of making possible the sustained conservation of Antarctic marine living resources.

CCAMLR encompasses ecosystem management geographically as well: it extends the boundaries of the regime north of the Antarctic Treaty area (60°S latitude) to conform with the natural boundary of the ecosystem. The "Antarctic convergence" is defined as the transition zone where colder Antarctic waters mix with and sink below warmer sub-Antarctic waters from the north. It is considered the northern limit of most Antarctic populations.

Marine Protected Areas

By 1983 the system of protected areas in Antarctica had grown to include "specially protected areas" (Agreed Measures, Recommendation III-8, 1964), "sites of special scientific interest" (Recommendation VIII-3, 1975), the various historic sites and monuments designated from 1961 on, and the seal reserves and sealing zones designated under the Antarctic Seals Convention (Anonymous 1990) (Fig. 9-4). There had been efforts since the mid-1970s to designate marine sites as protected areas to safeguard ongoing research, but nations fearing that marine designations might be used to restrict high seas navigation freedoms or to subtly affirm claims prevented agreement until 1987 (Recommendation XIV-6, 1987).

In the meantime, the Scientific Committee on Antarctic Research was requested in 1983 to carry out a comprehensive study of the several protected area classifications in Antarctica and make recommendations for improvement (Scientific Committee on Antarctic Research 1985, 1987; Anonymous 1990). These proposals formed the basis for extending and elaborating the Antarctic protected areas system to include marine designations as well as "specially reserved areas" (Recommendation XV-10, 1989) and "multiple-use planning areas" (Recommendation XV-11, 1989). Annex V of the 1991 Protocol merges and rationalizes this system into two categories: "specially protected areas" to protect outstanding environmental, scientific, historic, esthetic, or wilderness values, or ongoing or planned scientific research, and "specially managed areas," whose purposes are to assist in the planning and coordination of activities in congested areas, where the intensity of use may cause conflicts, and to minimize environmental impacts. Marine areas may be included in either category, but no marine areas may be designated without the prior approval of the CCAMLR commission (1991 Protocol, Annex V, Article 6.2). In some cases, the Antarctic Treaty designations are used to protect long-term research under CCAMLR's ecosystem monitoring program, which includes study of krill predators such as seals at a network of land-based sites (Anonymous 1990). The more systematic approach to protected areas in Annex V is likely to improve environmental management in Antarctica and help integrate marine and terrestrial concerns.

Incidental Mortality and Marine Debris

By the late 1980s the surge in international environmental negotiations and the fact that the individuals involved—representatives of governments as well as the nongovernmental organizations—often took part in several of these negotiations meant that ideas were transposed from one forum to another. These influences can be illustrated by an example relevant to marine mammals. As the impacts on

Figure 9-4. The field camp at Seal Island in the South Shetland Islands is a site of special scientific interest as defined under the Antarctic Treaty System. Here, Antarctic fur seals and chinstrap penguins appear to be undisturbed by the camp activities. (Photograph by Wes Armstrong)

marine species of entanglement in lost or discarded fishing gear or other debris began to be recognized in the Northern Hemisphere, this issue was taken up by the CCAMLR commission (also see Laist et al., this volume). In 1984 the commission called for studies and surveys to gain a better understanding of the dimensions of the problem in the Southern Ocean. The early surveys indicated that although not yet significant, the incidence of entanglement and marine debris was growing. In 1986 the commission agreed that members should ratify Annex V of MARPOL 73/78, which governs the discharge of garbage from ships, and the 1972 Convention on the Prevention of Marine Pollution by Dumping of Wastes and other Matter (Commission on the Conservation of Antarctic Marine Living Resources 1984, 1986). By the 1990s the survey results were mixed. They indicated significant entanglement of seabirds, declines in fur seal entanglement, a reduction in some types of debris, and an increase in others. The commission has adopted additional protective measures and continues to review surveys and reports. Noting that marine debris problems in the CCAMLR area are related to fisheries outside, the commission has supported more extensive cooperation and information exchange with other international fisheries bodies as well as international forums dealing with garbage from ships. Beach surveys are an important component in the CCAMLR program, further linking marine and terrestrial management (Commission on the Conservation of Antarctic Marine Living Resources 1991, 1992, 1993, 1994, 1995; Marine Mammal Commission 1992, 1993, 1994a, 1995, 1996).

Consensus Decision Making

Consensus decision making in international agreements has been much maligned as an excuse for protracting decisions and for producing "lowest common denominator" results. Some have termed it a veto for the powerful few. Yet the alternative, a simple or qualified majority, tends to override the views of the minority. In this regard, it should be recalled that majority votes rarely make international law for the minority. If a country's national interests are overridden, it may withdraw from the agreement or simply refuse to apply the offending measure. In such situations, consensus becomes a proactive means to obtain widespread agreement instead of risking only partial support. In the words of the Fijian ambassador during the law of the sea negotiations (Kimball 1980:55), "The consensus procedure . . . is based upon a philosophy . . . deeply rooted in many cultures in the Third World. . . . [P]eople are encouraged to take account of one another's views and interests and to accommodate one another's needs. In fact, in Fiji and in the South Pacific we call it the 'Pacific Way,' which, coincidentally, is the same as the 'peaceful way.'"

Accelerated Technical Amendment

At the same time, the international community has designed creative means to expedite decisions and encourage acceptance of stringent obligations. In Antarctica, several procedures are used to approve detailed or technical *implementing measures* that flesh out fundamental treaty obligations. The objection or "opt out" procedure was pioneered by the early international fishing agreements and the "tacit acceptance" procedure in treaties governing ship safety and pollution control (Kimball 1989). Like the use of nonbinding targets and timetables in more recent agreements on climate change and marine pollution control, these procedures permit a timely response to new scientific understanding, innovative technologies, or deteriorating environmental conditions. By separating formal treaty provisions from more technical annexes, it becomes easier to adopt different amendment procedures for the technical annexes that allow them to be updated more expeditiously. At the national level, the technical updates may be made effective by a simple administrative stroke of the pen, which does not require approval by a parliament or legislature.

Under the Seals Convention, amendments to the annex containing conservation measures enter into force for all contracting parties 180 days after they are circulated. This occurs only if no objections are received within 120 days of circulation and if two-thirds of the parties have notified the *depositary* in writing of their approval. If an objection is received, additional consultations ensue and the amendment enters into force only for the parties that have accepted it, provided at least two-thirds have done so (Article 9).

Under CCAMLR, a similar procedure allows accelerated entry into force of conservation measures adopted at commission meetings, subject to an objection procedure. There is no presumption, however, that positive approval by two-thirds, in the absence of an objection, binds the others. After the commission approves a conservation measure by consensus, any member has 90 days to object, excepting itself from the application of the measure. For other members, the measure enters into force in 180 days (Article IX.6). This represents a tacit acceptance procedure because nations need take no positive action for the measure to enter into force.

Similarly, under the annexes to the 1991 Protocol, amendments or modifications may become effective in an accelerated manner in accordance with a tacit acceptance procedure. That is, they become effective for all consultative parties within one year of consensus adoption unless a consultative party notifies the *depositary* that it wishes an extension or is unable to approve the changes. Unlike CCAMLR, if a nation objects, the amendment does not become effective for the other nations that did not object.

These opt-out and tacit-acceptance procedures take advantage of peer pressure or moral persuasion to forestall disagreements. Used imaginatively, they create a double bind, putting pressure on a nation to agree to a measure in the first place with the assurance that it has the safety valve of opting out later. After the measure is adopted and if others do not object, a nation may be reluctant to call attention to itself by raising an objection. To date, there has been no objection to any CCAMLR conservation measure. The tacit acceptance procedures in the annexes to the Protocol have not yet been tested.

The Place of Scientific Research

The Antarctic Treaty was founded on the premise of freedom of scientific investigation and cooperation toward that end. As the treaty system has evolved, science has taken on new dimensions. The concern that scientists not foul their own laboratory today encompasses the need to avoid disrupting Antarctica's role in global environmental systems and respect for Antarctica's wilderness and esthetic values (Protocol, Article 3). Sound management of intensifying human activities in Antarctica requires adequate scientific and technical information. This raises questions about how to improve the generation and presentation of scientific and technical advice for Antarctic decision making, the role of environmental and other information in determining the effectiveness of legal regimes and compliance with them, and responsibility to the international community as a whole for environmentally sound activities in Antarctica.

In the United States and other countries, Antarctic scientists are worried that, as the Protocol is implemented, stringent requirements to minimize adverse environmental impacts may impede the conduct of research. They fear that funds available to support basic research will be reduced in favor of directed research or environmental monitoring. This has caused friction between scientists and environmentalists—groups that in principle share the goal of protecting the integrity of the Antarctic environment. The challenge is to reduce adverse impacts from the conduct of science to a minimum while ensuring that the science carried out is of high quality and truly benefits humankind (National Research Council 1993). The Protocol accords priority to the value of Antarctica for the conduct of scientific research, in particular research essential to understanding the global environment.

Precautionary Measures and the Burden of Proof

With the onset of the resource regimes and new concerns regarding the impacts of scientific and related logistics activities, data collection and environmental monitoring took on added significance. Without sufficient understanding of the workings of Antarctic ecosystems, there would be no basis for judging the possible impacts of proposed activities. From the outset of the CCAMLR discussions, governments expressed concern over the inadequacy of information on stocks of Antarctic marine living resources and the need to develop a sound scientific foundation for appropriate conservation measures. The responsibilities of CCAMLR's commission and scientific committee emphasize research and data collection related to the ecosystem as a whole, as well as collecting statistics on fishing catch and effort. As the CCAMLR research program developed, a special working group was set up to design and coordinate a multinational research program for assessing and monitoring key components of the Antarctic marine ecosystem, building on BIOMASS.

CCAMLR conservation measures must be based on the "best scientific evidence available," the standard applied in the 1982 Law of the Sea Convention's fisheries provisions. In the Antarctic minerals treaty, the potential for more significant environmental damage from minerals development resulted in yet higher standards. The Minerals Convention's "information sufficiency" standard effectively blocks any prospecting, exploration, or exploitation unless sufficient information is available to enable informed judgments to be made about possible impacts. Principles regarding unacceptable impacts are outlined in the Convention. Moreover, the burden for acquiring the information necessary to prove the activity acceptable is placed on those who would carry out the activity. This is counter to the normal presumption that the activity may proceed unless the regulator can produce reliable evidence of potential damage (see Mangel et al. 1996 for related discussions). The Minerals Convention also provides that no activities may take place unless technology and procedures are available to ensure that operations will be carried out in conformity with the principles. In addition, the capacity must exist to monitor key environmental parameters and ecosystem components to identify any adverse effects and to respond effectively to accidents. These are not "best available" standards, subject to what is on the market today. Rather, they prevent the activity unless it can be demonstrated that a fairly high, qualitative, technical threshold actually exists. Under the 1991 Protocol, the principles for judging potentially adverse effects are similar to those in the Antarctic Minerals Convention, including the requirement for sufficient information to allow prior assessment and informed judgments. The requirements for technologies and other capabilities do not deter the activity so much as promote the use of what is appropriate. This helps balance the ongoing conduct of science with available and environmentally sound procedures.

During the 1990s the information sufficiency requirements in the Antarctic Minerals Convention and the Protocol have influenced measures adopted under CCAMLR that take a precautionary approach to fishing activities. In 1990 the United States issued a permit for exploratory crabfishing in the CCAMLR area, in keeping with the Convention. As discussions of this venture ensued in the commission, it was agreed that new fisheries should be structured to help develop the necessary information base in step with the fishery so that harvesting could be conducted consistent with CCAMLR's ecosystem principle. In 1993 this approach was applied not just to new fisheries but to ongoing fisheries when there is insufficient information to estimate potential sustainable yield and the impacts of fishing on other system components. To implement the approach, the scientific committee must prepare and annually update a plan identifying data needs and how to collect them. The plan may specify the location, gear, effort, or other restrictions on the fishery, which are calculated to produce the necessary information. In addition, a precautionary limit on harvests is set at a level slightly above the take expected from the directed fishery. Each government engaged in the fishery is then responsible for indicating how its proposed fishing activities will comply with the committee's plan. This information is reviewed by the scientific committee and the commission (Commission on the Conservation of Antarctic Marine Living Resources 1991, 1992, 1993; Marine Mammal Commission 1991, 1992, 1993, 1994a). This novel approach allows controlled fishing to occur while ensuring that those operating the fishery provide the information needed to make informed decisions in pace with the fishing activity. Its example is being explored by other fisheries bodies.

Scientific and Technical Advisory Mechanisms

The increase in international environmental conventions during the 1980s and 1990s has focused new attention on the best means of obtaining reliable and credible scientific and technical advice. The costs of research continue to grow and compete with other demands on national budgets. Sophisticated monitoring programs are required to determine how ecosystems work, whether in the Antarctic or elsewhere. Relevant data collections and research results may be housed in many different national and international institutions. This leads to questions. How does a given program, such as CCAMLR, become aware of and use these resources cost-effectively? What procedures best ensure that scientific and technical advice is not distorted to suit narrow national or policy interests?

During the CCAMLR negotiations, and as the Antarctic Treaty has expanded in scope, the governments involved have sought to establish good working relationships with a variety of international institutions. Strong informal ties were developed early with the Scientific Committee on Antarctic Research as a result of its role in the 1957–1958 geophysical year. This nongovernmental body continues to help define and coordinate international Antarctic research programs. Scientists involved in the Scientific Committee on Antarctic Research have participated on national delegations to Antarctic Treaty meetings from the beginning, and numerous recommendations adopted under the treaty request that the committee provide advice to the parties on logistics and organizational arrangements for Antarctic research (Anonymous 1990). Under the Seals Convention, in a unique international treaty arrangement, the nongovernmental Scientific Committee on Antarctic Research serves as the interim (to date, effectively permanent) scientific advisory body.

When the minerals question was posed in the 1970s, the committee was asked to evaluate potential environmental impacts (Scientific Committee on Antarctic Research 1977, 1986). Its advisory role on environmental matters expanded during the 1980s on such questions as environmental impact assessment (Benninghoff and Bonner 1985), the protected areas system (Scientific Committee on Antarctic Research 1987), and waste disposal practices. But this growing involvement in advising governments on Antarctic policies did not come without controversy. Although most believed it beneficial that a body of independent scientific experts contribute to policy debates, many governments preferred that treaty advisory bodies be composed of experts nominated by governments, with members of the Scientific Committee on Antarctic Research providing input and peer review. For some governments, the groups's nongovernmental standing was an impediment to financing the studies requested. As resources management became an issue, membership on the committee was less representative of management experience or disciplines such as population dynamics. Both within and outside governments, there was concern that the group's scientific community was too narrowly focused on its own research agenda. Members of the committee themselves were of mixed mind. Some wished to define a role for the body in Antarctic conservation (Scientific Committee on Antarctic Research 1990), while others expressed reservations about taking too active a role in providing policy advice in view of the group's constitution (see Scientific Committee on Antarctic Research 1989). In the end, the committee continues to provide advice and review as requested by the different Antarctic forums, but specific advisory bodies, composed of government representatives, are established by CCAMLR and the 1991 Protocol.

When CCAMLR was concluded, it was clear that, in addition to the Scientific Committee on Antarctic Research, it would be useful to collaborate with the United Nations Food and Agriculture Organization in fisheries statistics, research, and management. It was also essential to coordinate with the International Whaling Commission (IWC), with regulatory authority over whaling worldwide. Oceanographic research sponsored by the Intergovernmental Oceanographic Commission of the United Nations Educational, Scientific and Cultural Organization was equally relevant, and the Oceanographic Commission had a longstanding relationship with the Scientific Committee on Oceanographic Research. CCAMLR thus calls for cooperation with these bodies and has granted these and other intergovernmental and nongovernmental organizations observer status at its meetings.

It was more difficult to achieve collaboration with outside organizations in the Antarctic Treaty forum. The claimant nations were concerned that the involvement of United Nations agencies would further "internationalize" the consultative meetings, undermining their legal position. Other parties were nervous that global politics might intrude into the Antarctic Treaty system. (See below.) But the expanding scope of Antarctic policy discussions made it difficult to justify excluding organizations that could contribute scientific, technical, and environmental expertise. Since 1987 a growing number of representatives of intergovernmental and nongovernmental organizations have been invited to participate as experts in Antarctic Treaty meetings and negotiations. This outsider/insider balance is one means of ensuring independent review of scientific and technical advice provided by governments. Combined with public availability of documents and reports, expert participation in meetings helps ensure wider peer review and offers opportunities to question assumptions and analyses and provide supplementary evidence.

A related issue is how to define the relationship between the advisory body and the decision-making body. This relationship in the IWC has led to comments that scientific advice is influenced by political considerations (Birnie 1989, Caron 1995, Weber and Spivy-Weber 1995). The Antarctic Treaty system has attempted to avoid this problem in the advisory procedures established under CCAMLR. These require that a summary of the scientific committee's deliberations, conclusions, and recommendations be transmitted to the decision-making commission, including the rationale for all findings and recommendations, all views expressed, and any minority reports (Commission on the Conservation of Antarctic Marine Living Resources 1988). Attempts by the fishing nations to require agreed advice and recommendations in the committee's rules of procedures did not succeed.

What lies at the heart of the debate over procedures for scientific advice is how to ensure that the findings are based on the best scientific evidence available, that they are intelligible to decision makers, and that they reduce the potential for political influence and personal bias. If the advisors are required to present only agreed conclusions, when there are differing views concerning risks, uncertainties, and the sufficiency of available information, the decision makers will be forced to make decisions without a full understanding of their implications. Moreover, they are less accountable for their decisions because they can shift responsibility to the conclusions drawn by the scientists. Opportunities for widespread peer review may bring new information to light and enhance the credibility of the analyses. These concerns must be taken into account as the procedures are developed for the advisory committee established by the Protocol.

The Feedback Factor: Reviewing Progress

In 1959 the consultative parties were sensitive about the right to monitor each other's Antarctic activities in view of claimant/nonclaimant tensions and the Cold War. But they were determined to verify that military activities, prohibited by the treaty, were not taking place. Treaty provisions on information exchange and inspection were intended first and foremost to achieve this goal. At their first meeting in 1961 the consultative parties structured a loose annual exchange of information and requested follow-up reports to revise information submitted in advance of planned activities. Nevertheless, they were reluctant to question one another about Antarctic operations. Gradually, they expanded the information exchange to cover facilities for emergency assistance, species killed or captured in accordance with the Agreed Measures, and notice of tourist or nongovernmental expeditions. During the late 1980s reduced political tensions and greater environmental awareness allowed them to add a substantial volume of new information to the exchange, including final environmental impact assessments and national waste management plans. The consultative meetings themselves increasingly became a forum for sharing information and documentation on national practices in Antarctica.

It is obviously difficult to evaluate and improve measures to protect the Antarctic environment or native species of fauna and flora without information on current practices and impacts. Although the consultative parties began to consider improvements in waste management in 1983, it took six years simply to compile information on existing national practices. Beginning in 1984 a few governments and representatives of nongovernmental organizations urged that a more systematic approach be developed to Antarctic reporting and information and that Antarctic inspections be used to evaluate national implementation of the treaty's environmental measures. In 1987 the consultative meeting acknowledged that inspections could bring to light emerging environmental problems and help identify useful practices to avoid or mitigate them. The meeting also encouraged follow-up visits to protected sites to determine whether objectives were being met. (Reports on these visits, as well as recommendations adopted under the Antarctic Treaty, background information, excerpts from the reports of treaty meetings, and other documents relevant to the development of the Antarctic Treaty System, are included in the *Handbook of the Antarctic Treaty System* [Anonymous 1990], published and updated regularly by the Scott Polar Research Institute, Cambridge, United Kingdom.) Finally, after several years of discussion, checklists for inspecting Antarctic stations, abandoned facilities, waste disposal sites, and vessels in the treaty area were approved in 1995 (Resolution 5, 1995).

The high-seas setting for CCAMLR made it easier to agree on detailed reporting requirements than under the Antarctic Treaty and to review them collectively in commission meetings. Finely tuned requirements for each government to report on catch and effort were developed during CCAMLR's first years of operation. These ensure that when catch limits are reached, the fishery stops immediately. Between 1987 and 1989 the commission elaborated an observer and inspection system for fishing vessels that includes a checklist and an agreed format for reporting the results. The commission is specifically charged with reviewing these reports, after the nation in question has had a chance to comment on and respond to them.

The 1991 Protocol consolidates and improves upon the information and review provisions developed under the Antarctic Treaty, drawing on the experience of CCAMLR and the Minerals Convention negotiations. Inspection provisions amplify those of the Antarctic Treaty, reiterate the procedure followed under CCAMLR of allowing the inspected nation to comment on the report before it is circulated to other parties, and require that reports be submitted to the committee for environmental protection and be made publicly available. Annual reports are required of each party and are likewise submitted to the committee and made publicly available. In addition, when proposed activities may have more than a minor or transitory impact, the national environmental assessment must be reviewed by the committee before the country proposing the activity makes a final decision. The committee is also supposed to receive information called for pursuant to the Protocol's annexes on Antarctic fauna and flora, waste management, and the protected areas system. Now that the Protocol is in force, collective review has finally been formalized under the Antarctic Treaty and an environmental evaluation institutionalized.

To effectively meet its responsibilities, the committee will require administrative support. Since the early 1980s the consultative parties have considered establishing a secretariat to facilitate communications and information exchange among the growing number of countries active in Antarctica. In 1992 they agreed that a small secretariat should be established. Because of differences between two claimant states, Argentina and the United Kingdom, there is not yet agreement on where the secretariat should be located.

The Antarctic Treaty system feedback mechanisms—the exchange of information on national activities and best practices and technologies, collective review of national submissions, environmental monitoring, and public availability of information—all contribute to the implementation of commitments to conserve Antarctic species and protect terrestrial and marine environments in the region. They all help identify when existing measures are inadequate or when governments do not meet their commitments. Their evolution demonstrates the constructive interplay between confidence-building measures and verification procedures in arms control agreements and subsequent developments under international environmental law. The emphasis on reporting and review provisions in other international environmental conventions reflects progress made in the Antarctic agreements and vice versa.

International Responsibility and Accountability

Antarctica's vital contributions to global environmental stability, and its value as a relatively pristine area for monitoring the global impacts of human activities, have not gone unnoticed outside the Antarctic Treaty system. After the 1972 Stockholm Conference on the Human Environment, the newly established United Nations Environment Programme took an interest in the region (Anonymous 1990). This prompted the consultative parties, wary of United Nations involvement and potential internationalization, to assert their prime responsibility for protecting the Antarctic environment (Recommendation VIII-13, 1975). After this initial foray, the United Nations stayed out of Antarctic matters for nearly 10 years. With the initiation of the Minerals Convention negotiations in 1982, however, interest in potential revenues from minerals development provoked discussions in the United Nations General Assembly, beginning in 1983. Many developing nations sought to apply the common heritage of mankind concept to Antarctica and its resources, as was done with the seabed beyond national jurisdiction in the 1982 Law of the Sea Convention. They urged that any minerals regime for Antarctica be negotiated under United Nations auspices and with the full participation of the international community. The contracting parties affirmed their support for the Antarctic Treaty as the appropriate forum for these discussions, noting that all nations may join. They refused to take part in voting on the annual United Nations resolutions.

As the debate continued, scientific investigations revealed the Antarctic ozone hole in 1985 and underscored the crucial role played by cold Antarctic waters in global oceanic circulation and worldwide heat balances. Speculation that significant and sustained global warming might reduce the Antarctic ice sheet to meltwater and raise sea level worldwide by some 60 m drew further attention to Antarctica's pivotal, if not yet fully understood, role in global welfare. By 1990 a striking turnabout had occurred in the United Nations. The annual United Nations resolutions supported a ban on minerals activities in Antarctica and advocated that a comprehensive environmental protection regime be formulated under United Nations auspices. After the Protocol was concluded, the United Nations General Assembly was finally able to adopt a consensus resolution in 1994 for the first time since 1985, which was supported by the contracting parties to the Antarctic Treaty. The several sources of their earlier opposition had all been adequately resolved. The product of one part politics and one part stronger environmental ethic, Antarctica's role in global political and environmental systems has been acknowledged (United Nations Association 1983–1995).

Several steps were taken by the governments active in Antarctica to respond to growing international interest. The term *transparency,* used in reference to intergovernmental forums, was coined in the course of their debates over opening up the Antarctic Treaty system. Influenced by practice in the United Nations and other treaty forums, the consultative parties adopted new measures inviting the nonconsultative parties (Recommendation XIII-15, 1985) and experts from intergovernmental and nongovernmental organizations (Recommendation XIII-2, 1985 [Anonymous 1990]) to participate in treaty meetings. They agreed to make most treaty documents available to the public (Recommendations XIII-1, 1985; XIV-1, 1987), and they adopted a more forthcoming attitude to wider international involvement in research activities and stations by drawing attention to environmentally sound practices and technologies appropriate for Antarctic conditions (Convention on the Regulation of Antarctic Mineral Resources Activities, Article 26.6; Recommendation XV-15; 1991 Protocol, Article 6). These Antarctic developments were intertwined with a new "partnership" approach in other international conventions to provide technical and financial assistance to developing nations to help them meet environmental goals and objectives (e.g., the Montreal Protocol on Substances that Deplete the Ozone Layer and the Framework Convention on Climate Change).

U.S. Policy Development and the Role of Nongovernmental Organizations

Within the United States, it is the Senate's responsibility to give advice and consent to an international treaty before it is signed by the President and *enters into force.* Through this process of consultation with the Congress and presidential signature, the treaty is *ratified.* The United States ratified the Antarctic Treaty in 1960, the Antarctic Seals Convention in 1976, and CCAMLR in 1982. The Senate gave its advice and consent to the 1991 Protocol on 7 October 1992, but the United States did not submit its instrument of ratification to the *depositary* until April 1997. It awaited approval of the implementing legislation (the Antarctic Science, Tourism, and Conservation Act of 1996) and certain regulations called for in the legislation so that full authority for the government to implement the Protocol would be in place. Other major laws affecting Antarctica are the Antarctic Conservation Act of 1978, which implements the Agreed Measures; the 1984 Antarctic Marine Living Resources Convention Act, which implements CCAMLR; and the 1990 Antarctic Protection Act, which imposed an interim prohibition on mineral resource activities pending entry into force of an international agreement for the United States establishing an indefinite prohibition. The 1996 law amends and updates the 1978 Antarctic Conservation Act, the 1990 Antarctic Protection Act, and the Act to Prevent Pollution from Ships, which governs ongoing implementation of MARPOL 73/78.

In view of the national security aspects that initially dominated U.S. Antarctic policies, the government agencies traditionally involved in the formulation and implementation of Antarctic law and policy were the Departments of State and Defense and the National Science Foundation. As natural resources issues emerged during the 1970s, other agencies have played a larger role. These include the Departments of Commerce (National Oceanic and

Atmospheric Administration), the Interior, and Energy, the Marine Mammal Commission, and the Environmental Protection Agency. The State Department retains lead responsibility for international policies pursued by the United States at treaty meetings. It convenes regular consultations among the relevant government agencies to determine these policies. The National Science Foundation manages the Antarctic Research Program, and the National Oceanic and Atmospheric Administration, consistent with the CCAMLR implementing legislation, takes the lead in the development and annual updating of a directed research plan and oversees any fishing conducted by U.S. nationals in the Southern Ocean.

Within its mandate, the Marine Mammal Commission has played a leading role in the formulation and evolution of Antarctic law and policy since it was established by the Marine Mammal Protection Act of 1972. Engaged initially in 1974 as the U.S. government considered ratification of the Antarctic Seals Convention, and based on its statutory mandate, the Marine Mammal Commission became deeply involved in promoting the ecosystem approach in CCAMLR. It was concerned that growing international interest in harvesting krill, the linchpin of the Southern Ocean food chain, could have profound impacts on whale and seal populations (Marine Mammal Commission 1976, 1979). Later, a representative of the commission was the first U.S. delegate to the CCAMLR scientific committee. The CCAMLR decisions in 1992–1993 on new and developing fisheries can be traced to early comments by the Marine Mammal Commission on the development of the CCAMLR regime: "[The] greatest weakness [of the proposal for a possible regime] is the assumption that existing knowledge is adequate to implement a meaningful conservation regime allowing for substantial exploitation. . . . In light of the uncertainties and associated risks, the discussion here and elsewhere should be expanded to consider the desirability of a regime designed to provide the information needed for conservation of the resources while permitting effectively controlled, experimental harvesting in conjunction with the mandatory collection of needed data" (Marine Mammal Commission 1979).

The Marine Mammal Commission's interest in Antarctic policy continued throughout the development of the Antarctic Minerals Convention and the 1991 Protocol. Its goal has been to avoid activities that might adversely affect whales and seals or other components of the Southern Ocean ecosystem on which they depend. It has consistently promoted the development of a comprehensive biological/ecological research and monitoring program in the Antarctic capable of supporting CCAMLR, any mineral resources regime that emerged, and, more recently, implementation of the Protocol.

Nongovernmental Organizations

Antarctic resources issues drew another set of interested players into the development of Antarctic policies—the more activist nongovernmental organizations. Beginning in the early 1970s the International Institute for Environment and Development in London and Washington, D.C., the Sierra Club, and the Center for Law and Social Policy in Washington, D.C., began to study and raise questions about policies related to Antarctic resources and the operation of the treaty system. The United States, well in advance of other nations and in keeping with long-standing practice, invited representatives of these groups to participate on its delegations to Antarctic Treaty meetings and to the negotiations that produced CCAMLR, the Minerals Convention, and the 1991 Protocol. A representative of the Center for Law and Social Policy, in collaboration with Australian environmental organizations, developed a worldwide coalition of nongovernmental organizations to further Antarctic conservation. The Antarctic and Southern Ocean Coalition was launched in 1978 (Kimball 1988b).

In April 1985 the Scientific Committee on Antarctic Research and the International Union for the Conservation of Nature and Natural Resources (now IUCN, the World Conservation Union), jointly sponsored a meeting in Bonn, Germany, on Scientific Requirements for Antarctic Conservation. These two organizations collaborated on a long-term conservation plan for Antarctica, issued in 1986 (International Union for the Conservation of Nature and Natural Resources [IUCN]/Scientific Committee of Antarctic Research [SCAR] 1986), and in 1991 IUCN completed its own Antarctic Conservation Strategy (International Union for the Conservation of Nature and Natural Resources 1991). In 1980 IUCN became the first of the activist organizations to be invited to attend an Antarctic meeting as an observer—the final diplomatic conference for the adoption and signing of CCAMLR. Since then, IUCN and the Antarctic and Southern Ocean Coalition have represented this perspective in Antarctic meetings (Kimball 1988b).

Without the pressure mounted by the nongovernmental groups from the 1970s onward, it is doubtful whether conservation and environmental protection in Antarctica would have advanced as far or as fast as they have. The worldwide network of the environmental groups enabled them to coordinate lobbying efforts in many of the Antarctic Treaty countries and to exchange information on evolving national positions more quickly than governments. The responsibilities of a government official tend to be circumscribed to a limited range of issues and contacts in the areas for which he or she is responsible, but the environmental organizations could draw on relatively small staffs active in a wide range of international treaty negotiations to exchange information about developments. At the national level, frequent consultations among like-minded individuals in government agencies, parliaments, and nongovernmental groups played a major role in the evolution of Antarctic policies. At the time, this was less common than it is today (Kimball 1988b).

Antarctica turned out to be one of the premier testing grounds for the role of nongovernmental groups in the formulation of international environmental policy and law. Their in-depth involvement in policy development at the national level in some countries, the international network they established to communicate rapidly worldwide, and the development of position papers and information documents to inform delegates at international meetings, tailored to the agenda at hand, are now routine. Conversely, efforts to promote transparency through participation in formal and informal meetings and greater availability of documents drew on developments in other international forums.

Conclusion: the Challenges Ahead

The Antarctic Treaty System demonstrates how a skeletal, framework agreement may develop into a fairly comprehensive system of international governance. It illustrates how the unique (disputed) legal status of Antarctica allowed international environmental commitments to encroach on perceived sovereign rights, building from the concern with arms control. Soft law has taken on an increasingly binding character, and international inspections of national environmental practices are now routine. The gradual elaboration of more detailed information and reporting requirements serves both the analysis of environmental conditions and trends and the success (or failure) of implementing measures and national practice.

CCAMLR has had a pioneering role in the development and application of an ecosystem approach to marine living resources management and in devising practical means for taking precautionary action. Its arrangements for scientific and technical advice may be further refined as the Protocol enters into force and serve as a model for other intergovernmental forums. The formation of an extensive global coalition of environmental nongovernmental organizations was also pioneered in the Antarctic context, and its role continues today in other forums where an even greater degree of openness has been reached.

With respect to marine mammals, the protection afforded seals on land is maintained under the Antarctic Treaty, and CCAMLR is poised to ensure that harvesting of other marine species does not adversely affect the marine mammal populations that feed on them. The Antarctic Treaty mandate has been substantially strengthened by the 1991 Protocol to ensure adequate protection of marine and terrestrial environments as well as native species on the continent.

The next challenges in the evolution of Antarctic legal regimes are primarily those of implementation. It will be important to strengthen the relationships between Antarctic agreements and other international conventions on resources management and environmental protection so that they increasingly reinforce one another. A large component of that interaction will consist of improving the way that scientific and technical information is gathered and exchanged. Understanding ecosystem dynamics in Antarctica and its role in global environmental systems depends on information and knowledge generated worldwide, whether in relation to glaciology, climate, or whales. External influences like marine debris or ozone depletion are controlled through other international legal arrangements, as are pollution and wastes from ships, but measures adopted in these forums can reduce adverse impacts in Antarctica. If global warming causes significant melting of the Antarctic icecap, activities outside the region would radically alter Antarctica and impact coastal areas around the world. Conversely, the conservation measures adopted for Antarctica, and the information developed pursuant to Antarctic agreements, provide reassurances that activities in Antarctica will not undermine regional and global natural systems and amplify understanding of them. All agreements help stimulate scientific and technical developments that can reduce adverse impacts from human activities, wherever located, and it is vital that this information be widely exchanged. The integration of Antarctica into global ecological and political systems creates greater interdependence between the Antarctic Treaty and other international legal arrangements.

Uniquely in Antarctica, the consensus decision-making procedure assumes the burden of protecting the contracting parties' differing positions on territorial claims. It could be argued that consensus decision making broke down over the minerals issue although it was restored with adoption of the 1991 Protocol and its ban on minerals activities. The possibility of modifying or amending the ban after 50 years is not, strictly speaking, a consensus procedure. The question is whether majority decision making in the twenty-first century will favor stronger environmental protection or the pursuit of Antarctica's mineral resources potential. For the resources regimes in place, the Seals Convention and CCAMLR, alteration in either direction will be channeled by well-established institutional processes. Further tests may come, however, if the nations with claims seek preferential offshore fishing rights or if the number of nations competing for marine living resources increases substantially. If interest in minerals development reemerges and commercially attractive deposits are discovered, the outlook is less predictable.

In comparison with the possibility of growing resource interests in Antarctica, the challenges posed by scientific research activities appear far less daunting. Nevertheless, demands to apply stringent environmental measures that are out of touch with the practical reality of on-the-ground implementation in Antarctic conditions could lead to disputes between the scientists and environmental nongovernmental organizations. The level of scientific use deemed compatible with conservation and protection goals, or vice versa, may yet become contentious under the 1991 Protocol.

Growing tourism in Antarctica impacts both scientific research and the environment. The number of visitors now exceeds scientists and support personnel in Antarctica (Marine Mammal Commission 1996). This includes tourist visits by ship as well as adventure expeditions for skiing or other purposes. A number of measures already govern these activities, and, drawing on past experience, the procedures for reporting have kept pace. Nevertheless, significant growth could raise new issues.

Further study of the governance arrangements for Antarctica is vital for marine mammal conservation in the region as well as conservation initiatives elsewhere.

Glossary

adoption, signature, ratification, or accession Before an international treaty becomes binding on a nation (*enters into force*), it must be adopted in accordance with the decision-making rules in the forum where it was negotiated; it must be signed by each government, indicating the government's intention to become bound by it; and it must then be ratified by the government in accordance with national procedures. In most cases, if a country did not take part in adopting or signing a convention, it may still accede to it later and thus become bound by it. In the United States, the Senate of the Congress must give its advice and consent to international treaties before they are signed by the President, completing ratification procedures. An instrument of ratification must then be transmitted to the *depositary* before the agreement becomes binding. No agreement becomes binding until it has been ratified by the minimum number of countries stipulated in the agreement for it to *enter into force*.

consultative and nonconsultative parties Of the countries that are "contracting parties" to the Antarctic Treaty, the consultative parties have the right to take part in decisions, whereas the nonconsultative parties may attend meetings and participate in discussions but they do not formally take part in decisions.

contracting parties Those governments that have formally ratified or acceded to an international convention (treaty) and are legally bound by its provisions. Governments that have not ratified or acceded to an international convention are not legally bound.

depositary The country or organization, such as the United Nations, which archives the original, authenticated copy of the signed treaty and related legal paperwork and bears responsibility for related communications among the contracting parties.

entry into force Each convention specifies how many, and in some cases which, nations must ratify or accede to it in order for it to enter into force (become binding). Once the convention is adopted, it is opened for signature for a specified period of time. After countries sign it, as noted above, they must then ratify it.

implementing measures Most conventions provide that the contracting parties, or some executive unit of contracting parties, may adopt decisions, resolutions, recommendations, guidelines, or other measures that provide more specific indications of steps for implementing the convention. The rules and procedures for making those decisions are agreed by the contracting parties, as is their legally binding nature.

protocols and annexes Many international conventions include more detailed, technical, or subject-specific documents. These may address dispute settlement, a specific topic such as controlling marine pollution, or decisions and commitments as they are adopted and updated. These form an integral part of the convention and are just as legally binding.

Literature Cited

Anonymous. 1990. Handbook of the Antarctic Treaty System. Polar Publications. Scott Polar Research Institute, Cambridge, U.K.

Benninghoff, W. S., and W. N. Bonner. 1985. Man's impact on the Antarctic environment: A procedure for evaluating impacts from scientific and logistic activities. Scientific Committee on Antarctic Research. Scott Polar Research Institute, Cambridge, U.K.

Berkman, P. A. 1992. The Antarctic marine ecosystem and humankind. Reviews in Aquatic Sciences 6:295–333.

Birnie, P. W. 1989. International legal issues in the management and protection of the whale: A review of four decades of experience. Natural Resources Journal 29:903–934.

Brown, W. Y. 1983. The conservation of Antarctic marine living resources. Environmental Conservation 10:187–196.

Caron, D. A. 1995. The International Whaling Commission and the North Atlantic Marine Mammal Commission: The institutional risks of coercion in consensual structures. American Journal of International Law 89:159–163.

Central Intelligence Agency. 1978. Polar Regions Atlas. Washington, DC.

Commission on the Conservation of Antarctic Marine Living Resources. 1984. Report of the 3rd meeting of the Commission. CCAMLR Secretariat, Hobart, Tasmania, Australia.

Commission on the Conservation of Antarctic Marine Living Resources. 1986. Report of the 5th meeting of the Commission. CCAMLR Secretariat, Hobart, Tasmania, Australia.

Commission on the Conservation of Antarctic Marine Living Resources. 1988. Scientific Committee rules of procedure in basic documents. CCAMLR Secretariat, Hobart, Tasmania, Australia.

Commission on the Conservation of Antarctic Marine Living Resources. 1991. Report of the 10th meeting of the Commission. CCAMLR Secretariat, Hobart, Tasmania, Australia.

Commission on the Conservation of Antarctic Marine Living Resources. 1992. Report of the 11th meeting of the Commission. CCAMLR Secretariat, Hobart, Tasmania, Australia.

Commission on the Conservation of Antarctic Marine Living Resources. 1993. Report of the 12th meeting of the Commission. CCAMLR Secretariat, Hobart, Tasmania, Australia.

Commission on the Conservation of Antarctic Marine Living Resources. 1994. Report of the 13th meeting of the Commission. CCAMLR Secretariat, Hobart, Tasmania, Australia.

Commission on the Conservation of Antarctic Marine Living Resources. 1995. Report of the 14th meeting of the Commission. CCAMLR Secretariat, Hobart, Tasmania, Australia.

Fifield, R. 1987. International Research in the Antarctic. Oxford University Press, Oxford, U.K.

Gambell, R. 1999. The International Whaling Commission and the contemporary whaling debate. (This volume)

Hatherton, T. 1986. Antarctica prior to the Antarctic Treaty—A historical perspective. Pages 15–32 *in* Antarctic Treaty System: An Assessment. Proceedings of a Workshop Held at Beardmore South Field Camp, Antarctica, January 7–13, 1985. National Academy Press, Washington, DC.

Hill, J. 1983. New Zealand and Antarctica. Commission for the Environment, Wellington, New Zealand.

Hofman, R. J. 1987. Conservation of marine living resources in Antarctica. Pages 216–229 *in* The Polar Regions. Report of the 11th annual seminar, 26–28 March 1987. Center for Oceans Law and Policy. University of Virginia, Charlottesville, VA.

Holt, S. J., and L. M. Talbot. 1978. New principles for the conservation of wild living resources. Wildlife Monographs No. 59.

International Union for the Conservation of Nature and Natural Resources (IUCN). 1991. A Strategy for Antarctic Conservation. IUCN, Gland, Switzerland.

International Union for the Conservation of Nature and Natural Resources (IUCN)/Scientific Committee of Antarctic Research (SCAR). 1986. Conservation in the Antarctic. Report of the Joint IUCN/SCAR Working Group on Long-Term Conservation in the Antarctic. IUCN and SCAR.

Katona, S. K., and S. D. Kraus. 1999. Efforts to conserve the North Atlantic right whale. (This volume)

Kimball, L. A. 1980. Implications of the arrangements made for deep sea mining for other joint exploitations. Columbia Journal of World Business 15:52–61.

Kimball, L. A. 1988a. Special Report on the Antarctic Minerals Convention. International Institute for Environment and Development—North America and World Resources Institute, Washington, DC. Republished (1990) *in* J. F. Splettstoesser and G. A. N. Dreschhoff (eds.), Mineral Resources Potential of Antarctica. Antarctic Research Series 51:273–310. American Geophysical Union, Washington, DC.

Kimball, L. A. 1988b. The role of NGOs in Antarctic Affairs. Pages 33–63 *in* C. C. Joyner and S. K. Chopra (eds.), The Antarctic Legal Regime. Martinus Nijhoff Publishers, Dordrecht, the Netherlands.

Kimball, L. A. 1989. International law and institutions: The oceans and beyond. Ocean Development and International Law 20:147–165.

Kimball, L. A. 1994. Environmental law and policy in Antarctica. Pages 122–139 *in* Philippe Sands (ed.), Greening International Law. The New Press, New York.

Laist, D. W., J. M. Coe, and K. J. O'Hara. 1999. Marine debris pollution. (This volume)

Mangel, M., L. M. Talbot, G. K. Meffe, M. T. Agardy, D. L. Alverson, J. Barlow, D. B. Botkin, G. Budowski, T. Clark, J. Cooke, R. H. Crozier, P. K. Dayton, D. L. Elder, C. W. Fowler, S. Funtowicz, J. Giske, R. J. Hofman, S. J. Holt, S. R. Kellert, L. A. Kimball, D. Ludwig, K. Magnusson, B. S. Malayang III, C. Mann, E. A. Norse, S. P. Northridge, W. F. Perrin, C. Perrings, R. M. Peterman, G. B. Rabb, H. A. Regier, J. E. Reynolds III, K. Sherman, M. P. Sissenwine, T. D. Smith, A. Starfield, R. J. Taylor, M. F. Tillman, C. Toft, J. R. Twiss Jr., J. Wilen, and T. P. Young. 1996. Principles for the conservation of wild living resources. Ecological Applications 6:338–362.

Marine Mammal Commission. 1976. Annual report to Congress for 1975. (Available from National Technical Information Service, Springfield, VA. PB 269-711.) 50 pp.

Marine Mammal Commission. 1979. Annual report to Congress for 1978. (Available from National Technical Information Service, Springfield, VA. PB80-106784.) 108 pp.

Marine Mammal Commission. 1988. Annual report to Congress for 1987. (Available from National Technical Information Service, Springfield, VA. PB88-168984.) 209 pp.

Marine Mammal Commission. 1990. Annual report to Congress for 1989. (Available from National Technical Information Service, Springfield, VA. PB90-196361.) 239 pp.

Marine Mammal Commission. 1991. Annual report to Congress for 1990. (Available from National Technical Information Service, Springfield, VA. PB91-164236.) 280 pp.

Marine Mammal Commission. 1992. Annual report to Congress for 1991. (Available from National Technical Information Service, Springfield, VA. PB92-139930.) 228 pp.

Marine Mammal Commission. 1993. Annual report to Congress for 1992. (Available from National Technical Information Service, Springfield, VA. PB95-154995.) 241 pp.

Marine Mammal Commission. 1994a. Annual report to Congress for 1993. (Available from National Technical Information Service, Springfield, VA. PB95-154530.) 260 pp.

Marine Mammal Commission. 1994b. The Marine Mammal Commission Compendium of Selected Treaties, International Agreements, and Other Relevant Documents on Marine Resources, Wildlife, and the Environment, R. L. Wallace, compiler. Marine Mammal Commission, Washington, DC. 3,547 pp.

Marine Mammal Commission. 1995. Annual report to Congress for 1994. (Available from National Technical Information Service, Springfield, VA. PB95-173233.) 270 pp.

Marine Mammal Commission. 1996. Annual report to Congress for 1995. (Available from National Technical Information Service, Springfield, VA. PB96-157482.) 236 pp.

Morrell, J. B. 1992. The Law of the Sea: The 1982 Treaty and Its Rejection by the United States. McFarland and Company, Jefferson, NC.

National Research Council. 1993. Science and Stewardship in the Antarctic. National Academy Press, Washington, DC.

Office of Technology Assessment. 1989. Polar Prospects: A Minerals Treaty for Antarctica. OTA-O-428. Congress of the United States. U.S. Government Printing Office, Washington, DC.

Orrego-Vicuna, F. 1986. Antarctic conflict and international cooperation. Pages 55–64 *in* Antarctic Treaty System: An Assessment. Proceedings of a Workshop Held at Beardmore South Field Camp, Antarctica, January 7–13, 1985. National Academy Press, Washington, DC.

Quigg, P. W. 1983. A Pole Apart. McGraw-Hill Book Company, New York, NY.

Rutford, R. H. 1986. Summary of science in Antarctica prior to and including the International Geophysical Year. Pages 87–101 *in* Antarctic Treaty System: An Assessment. Proceedings of a Workshop Held at Beardmore South Field Camp, Antarctica, January 7–13, 1985. National Academy Press, Washington, DC.

Scientific Committee on Antarctic Research. 1977. A Preliminary Assessment of the Environmental Impact of Mineral Exploration/Exploitation in Antarctica. Scott Polar Research Institute, Cambridge, U.K.

Scientific Committee on Antarctic Research. 1985. Conservation Areas in the Antarctic. Scott Polar Research Institute, Cambridge, U.K.

Scientific Committee on Antarctic Research. 1986. Antarctic Environmental Implications of Possible Mineral Exploration and Exploitation. Scott Polar Research Institute, Cambridge, U.K.

Scientific Committee on Antarctic Research. 1987. The Protected Area System in the Antarctic. Scott Polar Research Institute, Cambridge, U.K.

Scientific Committee on Antarctic Research. 1989. Manual. Scott Polar Research Institute, Cambridge, U.K.

Scientific Committee on Antarctic Research. 1990. SCAR Group of Specialists on Environmental Affairs and Conservation. Scott Polar Research Institute, Cambridge, U.K.

Sergeant, D. L. 1971. Calculation of production of harp seals in the western North Atlantic. International Commission on Northwest Atlantic Fisheries. Redbook [1971], Part 3:157–184.

United Nations Association. 1983–1995. Section on Antarctica in the annual Issues Before the 38th–46th General Assembly of the United Nations. United Nations Association, New York, NY.

Weber, M. L., and F. Spivy-Weber. 1995. Proposed Elements for International Regimes to Conserve Living Marine Resources. (Available from National Technical Information Service, Springfield, VA. PB96-119078.)

Wonham, J. 1992. Sensitive areas and particularly sensitive areas. Pages 364–370 *in* P. Fabbri (ed.), Ocean Management and Global Change. Elsevier Applied Science, London.

Appendix

The Antarctic Treaty System

Four treaties constitute what is commonly referred to as the Antarctic Treaty System. They all apply to the area south of 60°S. The 1959 Treaty governs activities on the continent and its ice shelves but does not prejudice high seas rights recognized under international law (e.g., navigation, fishing). The conventions governing marine activities (sealing, conservation of marine living resources) are separate instruments, coordinated with the Antarctic Treaty. The fourth convention governing mineral resource activities has not entered into force and is no longer widely supported. Also included in the treaty system are all of the implementing measures adopted pursuant to each treaty, including subsidiary legal instruments such as *protocols and annexes* (see Glossary).

The 1959 Antarctic Treaty

The Antarctic Treaty entered into force on 23 June 1961. The United States is the depositary. The treaty aims to preserve Antarctica for peaceful uses only and to promote freedom of scientific investigation and international cooperation to that end. Decisions are taken by consensus. It restricts decision making to the 12 countries that originally signed the treaty in 1959 and to additional countries that have since accepted the treaty and its obligations during such time as they are conducting substantial research in Antarctica. These decision-making or "consultative parties" today number 27. Countries that have accepted the treaty but do not undertake substantial research are commonly referred to as the "nonconsultative parties." Since 1983 the nonconsultative parties have been invited to treaty meetings as observers. They may take part fully in the proceedings, but they do not participate in decision making. In 1991 the consultative parties decided to meet annually instead of biennially.

In recognition of the fundamental importance of scientific research under the treaty and the role of the international scientific community in its establishment, the nongovernmental Scientific Committee on Antarctic Research (SCAR), an organ of the International Council of Scientific Unions, plays a special role in responding to requests for scientific and technical advice. When the consultative parties decide at their meetings to seek advice from the committee, the request is transmitted through each country's national SCAR committee.

More than 200 *Recommendations* have been adopted at the Antarctic Treaty consultative meetings. These provide governments with more detailed guidance on how to implement the Treaty. They must be adopted by consensus of the consultative parties. They subsequently *enter into force* (become binding) after each consultative party at the time of adoption completes its national procedures for signifying approval. The Agreed Measures for the Conservation of Antarctic Fauna and Flora are found in the eighth Recommendation adopted by the third meeting of the consultative parties in 1964 (Recommendation III-8). At their nineteenth meeting in 1995, the consultative parties adopted a new system to clarify and distinguish the actions taken at meetings. *Measures* are those considered legally binding after subsequent approval by each consultative party in accordance with national procedures. *Decisions* govern internal matters and are operative at the time of adoption or as specified. *Resolutions* are nonbinding expressions of intent. All three must be adopted by consultative party consensus.

On 4 October 1991 the Protocol on Environmental Protection to the Antarctic Treaty was adopted and opened for signature, together with four annexes. These entered into force in January 1998 after the 26 consultative parties adopting them completed national approval procedures. A fifth annex was adopted at the sixteenth Antarctic Treaty meeting on 17 October 1991. It will enter into force after approval by all 26 consultative parties, provided that the Protocol has already entered into force. The Protocol establishes a committee for environmental protection to provide advice and formulate recommendations for the parties. The five annexes to the Protocol are as follows:

Annex I, Environmental Impact Assessment
Annex II, Conservation of Antarctic Fauna and Flora
Annex III, Waste Disposal and Waste Management
Annex IV, Prevention of Marine Pollution
Annex V, Area Protection and Management

The 1972 Convention for the Conservation of Antarctic Seals

The Seals Convention entered into force on 11 March 1978. The United Kingdom is the depositary. The purposes of the Convention are to regulate seal harvesting to avoid exceeding optimum sustainable yield and to improve related scientific knowledge. Certain decisions require the concurrence of all original signatories to the Convention; others may be approved by a two-thirds majority. Specific conservation measures are included in an annex. No commercial sealing has taken place since the Convention entered into force. The Convention must be reviewed at least every five years, and minor amendments to the Annex were adopted at the 1988 review.

The Seals Convention provides complete protection for three species of Antarctic seals (Ross, elephant, and fur) and sets quotas for harvests of the remaining three (crabeater, leopard, and Weddell). It prohibits killing or capturing seals during six months of the year and in specified zones during a portion of the remaining six months. In addition, no killing or capturing is permitted in three reserves set aside for breeding or long-term scientific studies. The Scientific Committee on Antarctic Research serves in an advisory capacity to the contracting parties. It is charged with assessing the information the parties are required to submit, encouraging scientific research and the exchange of results, and alerting the contracting parties to any harmful impacts of seal harvests.

The 1980 Convention on the Conservation of Antarctic Marine Living Resources (CCAMLR)

The Convention entered into force on 7 April 1982. The government of Australia is the depositary. The Convention's objective is to conserve living resources in the Southern Ocean. The contracting parties meet annually to review the operation of the agreement and to adopt additional implementing measures. Like the Antarctic Treaty, decisions are taken by consensus, and there is a distinction between the members of the decision-making commission, which have full voting rights, and other contracting parties. Commission members include governments taking part in the adoption of CCAMLR and other nations during such time as they are engaged in harvesting activities or related research. The contracting parties that are not commission members may be invited to meetings as observers. The Convention establishes a scientific committee to promote research and analysis and prepare reports and recommendations for the commission. Its annual meetings coincide with those of the commission.

The 1988 Convention on the Regulation of Antarctic Mineral Resource Activities

The Antarctic Minerals Convention was concluded to deal with the possibility that resources development might take place. It sets in place a means of assessing possible impacts, determining whether minerals development is acceptable, and governing any approved activities. The government of New Zealand serves as depositary. The Convention is unlikely to enter into force. Instead, the 1991 Protocol to the Antarctic Treaty bans mineral resource activities and establishes requirements and procedures for lifting the ban.

10

TIMOTHY J. RAGEN AND DAVID M. LAVIGNE

The Hawaiian Monk Seal

Biology of an Endangered Species

Among the species listed in the first IUCN *Red Data Book* of endangered mammals were nine pinnipeds, including the three modern monk seals (order Carnivora, family Phocidae, genus *Monachus*): the Hawaiian monk seal, *M. schauinslandi;* the Caribbean monk seal, *M. tropicalis;* and the Mediterranean monk seal, *M. monachus* (Simon 1966). The Hawaiian monk seal was listed as "vulnerable," the Mediterranean and Caribbean species as "endangered."

By the early 1990s the Caribbean monk seal, which has not been observed and positively identified since the 1950s, was presumed extinct (Scheffer 1958, Kenyon 1977, Le Boeuf et al. 1986); the other two monk seals were classified as endangered (Reijnders et al. 1993). At the end of 1995 the Hawaiian monk seal numbered about 1,400 animals and was declining; perhaps as few as 400–600 Mediterranean monk seals remained (Israëls 1992, Reijnders et al. 1993), making it one of the most endangered of all extant mammals. Accordingly, the 1996 IUCN Red List, which introduced new categories and criteria for describing threatened animals, declared the Caribbean monk seal "extinct," the Hawaiian monk seal "endangered," and the Mediterranean monk seal "critically endangered" (Baillie and Groombridge 1996).

The decline of monk seals raises a number of questions. After persisting for millions of years (Repenning and Ray 1977), are they simply approaching the end of a natural evolutionary process? Are they no longer able to adapt to naturally changing environmental conditions? Or, alternatively, are humans to blame? Have we so disturbed them or disrupted their habitats that they are simply unable to cope? These are the sorts of questions that scientists and managers who work with endangered species must routinely confront, and, in the following pages, we attempt to address them for the Hawaiian monk seal.

Understanding the current status of any species requires some knowledge of its evolutionary history (e.g., Sarich 1969a). We begin, therefore, by reviewing briefly the origins of pinnipeds and the subsequent arrival of monk seals in Hawaii. We then examine the natural history and current status of the species, information that is fundamental to the development of a conservation[1] strategy. Ultimately, we hope that this synthesis will promote a broader awareness of the current endangered status of the Hawaiian monk seal and encourage a more informed discussion of the steps required to promote its recovery.

Origins

Modern pinnipeds are divided into three families: the Otariidae (fur seals and sea lions), the Odobenidae (walrus), and the Phocidae (including two subfamilies: the Phocinae, the so-called northern true seals; and the Monachinae, including the monk seals, elephant seals, and the Antarctic phocids). The origins of these families are a controversial subject. Today, the best available evidence from comparative anatomy (e.g., Wyss 1987, 1988, 1989; Flynn 1988; Berta and Ray 1990) and, most convincing, from a variety of biochemical and molecular techniques (e.g., Sarich 1969a,b, 1975, 1976; De Jong 1982; Árnason and Widegren 1986; Árnason et al. 1995) indicates that all three families are monophyletic (i.e., they are descended from a common ancestor [for a discussion of the older, diphyletic hypothesis, which is rejected by the above data, see McLaren 1960, Tedford 1976]). Consistently, the oldest known fossil pinniped, *Enaliarctos mealsi,* is now considered the sister taxon of all pinnipeds, including the phocid seals (Berta et al. 1989; for a contrary view, see Mitchell and Tedford 1973, Repenning 1990). *Enaliarctos* lived in the northern Pacific, along the coast of present-day California, some 23 million years ago (mya) (Berta et al. 1989).

From this early beginning, it is not clear precisely how and when monk seals reached the Hawaiian Islands (Fig. 10-1). Nor is it known whether the ancestors of Hawaiian monk seals originated in the Pacific Ocean or in the Atlantic basin, possibly in the Caribbean, as proposed by Repenning et al. (1979; for another view, see Muizon 1982). What is known is that the Hawaiian monk seal is a "living fossil" possessing some anatomical features that are less derived than those observed in the earliest known fossil monachines, dated some 14–16 mya and found in Maryland and Virginia on the east coast of the United States (Ray 1976, Repenning et al. 1979, Barnes et al. 1985). This observation suggests that monk seals actually may have made their way to Hawaii as early as 14–16 mya (Repenning et al. 1979; also see Árnason et al. 1995).

Whenever they arrived, they almost certainly found an archipelago quite different from the one that exists today. Geologically, the Northwestern Hawaiian Islands—where the monk seal now survives—range in age from about 30 my in the west (Kure Atoll) to 11.3 and 7.5 my in the east at Necker and Nihoa Islands, respectively (Fig. 10-1) (Macdonald et al. 1983). These islands are considerably older than the main Hawaiian Islands, which range in age, from west to east, from less than 6 my (Kauai) to less than 0.5 my (Mauna Loa, Hawaii) (Macdonald et al. 1983).

The gradual development of the archipelago obviously produced a succession of new opportunities for dispersing Hawaiian monk seals. One result undoubtedly was the establishment over time of a number of local or island-based subpopulations, collectively composing, in current terminology, a metapopulation (Hanski and Gilpin 1991). But whether this metapopulation eventually extended throughout the entire Hawaiian Archipelago remains unknown. If it did, the island chain still would have provided monk seals with limited shoreline for hauling out, resting, pupping, and nursing. In addition, the surviving Hawaiian monk seals, like Mediterranean monk seals (and Caribbean monk seals in the past), are unique among modern phocid seals in that they exclusively occupy subtropical waters (Hansen et al. 1995) characterized by relatively warm temperatures and, generally, low levels of secondary productivity (Davies 1958, Lavigne et al. 1989). Space, food availability, and, possibly, ambient air temperatures (see Hansen et al. 1995) may thus be limiting factors for seals in Hawaii. As a consequence, the species was probably never very abundant, presumably numbering, at the most, in the thousands (as opposed to hundreds of thousands).

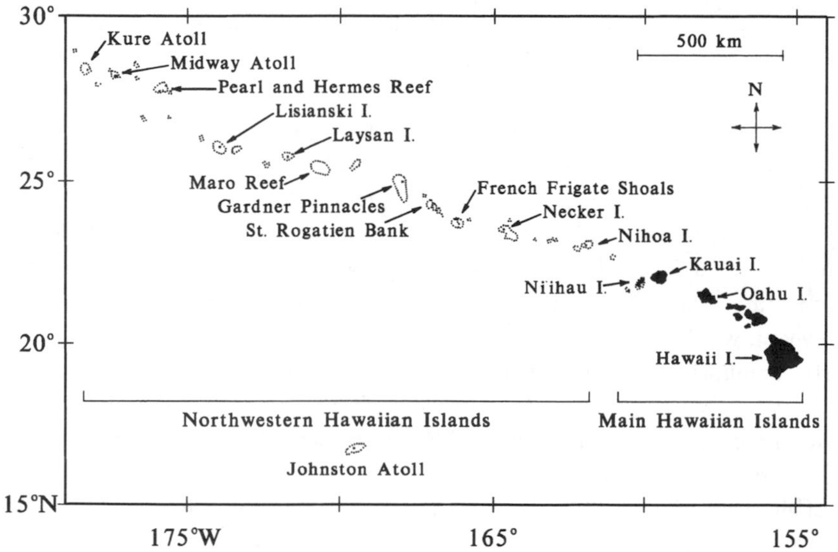

Figure 10-1. The Hawaiian Archipelago, including the main hauling sites of the endangered Hawaiian monk seal. The dotted lines around atolls and islands in the Northwestern Hawaiian Islands indicate the 100-fathom (183-m) isobath.

Recorded History

In contrast to the Mediterranean monk seal, for which recorded history dates back more than 2,500 years, nothing is known of the Hawaiian monk seal in antiquity. Written reports began with the Russian explorer Lisianski (1814), who in 1805 observed seals on the island that now bears his name. Records from voyages of the *Aiona* in 1824 (Bryan 1915) and the *Gambia* in 1859 suggest that the species' distribution and abundance were reduced by unregulated seal hunts in the early to mid-1800s (Busch 1985). The *Gambia,* for example, reportedly returned to Honolulu with 1,500 skins (although the authenticity of this report has been questioned; see Kenyon and Rice 1959). The seals were killed not only for pelts and oil; they were also killed for food by ship-wrecked sailors and by guano and feather hunters (Dill and Bryan 1912, Wetmore 1925, Clapp and Woodward 1972).

The effect of such killing on the distribution and abundance of Hawaiian monk seals was never documented, but presumably it was severe. By the late 1800s sightings were rare (Bailey 1952). No seals were observed, for example, at Midway Atoll (Fig. 10-1) over a period of 14 months in 1888–1889, and only one was seen on Laysan Island during three months of observation in the winter of 1912–1913 (Bailey 1952).

If the Hawaiian monk seal was hunted to low levels by the late 1800s, then the species must have partially recovered during the first half of the twentieth century and recolonized at least some of the sites from which it had previously disappeared. Any recovery, however, was also poorly documented (Svihla 1959, Rice 1964, Busch 1985, Hiruki and Ragen 1992).

Current Distribution

The current distribution of the Hawaiian monk seal is restricted almost entirely to the remote islands, atolls, and waters of the Northwestern Hawaiian Islands, which extend more than 2,000 km to the northwest of the main Hawaiian Islands (Fig. 10-1). The total land area today is only about 13.5 km^2 (Armstrong 1983); the beach area suitable for hauling out amounts to only a fraction of this. If monk seals did indeed inhabit the main Hawaiian Islands at one time, then the current distribution is only a fraction of what it was in the past. This raises the possibility that the arrival of humans somewhere between A.D. 800 and 1000 (Armstrong 1983, Stannard 1989) may have reduced the species' range and contributed to its current endangered status.

In the past decade, approximately 95% of all recorded births have occurred at French Frigate Shoals, Laysan Island, Lisianski Island, Pearl and Hermes Reef, and Kure Atoll. Historical records (Rice 1960) indicate that Midway Atoll was also an important reproductive site, but seals virtually disappeared from there in the late 1960s. For the most part, the few seals currently at this site are immigrants from Pearl and Hermes Reef or Kure Atoll (Eberhardt and Eberhardt 1994).

Monk seals also haul out at Necker and Nihoa Islands, but these islands lack the beaches and shallow nearshore areas that females prefer for pupping and nursing. A small number of seals (perhaps three dozen) reside in the main Hawaiian Islands and, on rare occasions, seals have been seen at Johnston Atoll (Schreiber and Kridler 1969), almost 1,000 km south of the Northwestern Hawaiian Islands (Fig. 10-1); at Palmyra Atoll, more than 1,800 km south of Nihoa Island (National Marine Fisheries Service, unpublished data); and at Wake Island, 2,000 km southeast of the Northwestern Hawaiian Islands (National Marine Fisheries Service, unpublished data).

Relationships among the monk seals inhabiting different islands cannot be fully characterized (Dizon et al. 1992) because our current understanding of their natural history is based almost entirely on their activities on land; little is known about their behavior and movements at sea. Nonetheless, the species' distribution is still best characterized as that of a restricted metapopulation. For our purposes, we will designate the animals living at each of the major islands or atolls as subpopulations, which interact via individuals moving intermittently from one island to another.

Although the majority of Hawaiian monk seals exhibit a high degree of fidelity to their place of birth, sightings on land confirm that some individuals move between islands or atolls. As might be expected, such movements are more frequent between nearby sites than between widely separated ones (Johnson and Kridler 1983). Seals commonly move among Kure Atoll, Midway Atoll, and Pearl and Hermes Reef (Eberhardt and Eberhardt 1994), which are within 250 km of each other, but no movements have been documented between Kure and French Frigate Shoals, a distance of 1,200 km. Similarly, many of the seals at Necker and Nihoa Islands were tagged as weaned pups at French Frigate Shoals, approximately 140 and 400 km, respectively, to the west (Finn and Rice 1994, Ragen and Finn 1996). For young seals, movement rates among the different subpopulations appear to be low, but relatively constant with respect to age. By age 10, approximately 10% are found at locations other than their natal island (National Marine Fisheries Service, unpublished data).

Phenotypic variation among the different subpopulations has not been investigated systematically. At present, the only observed physical difference is the small size of young seals at French Frigate Shoals (National Marine Fisheries Service, unpublished data). This difference, however, probably has more to do with food availability (discussed below) than any inherent differences among subpopulations.

An initial study (Kretzmann et al. 1997) suggested that the species is characterized by low genetic variability, some genetic differentiation among subpopulations, and perhaps some local inbreeding. The potential for genetic drift should have increased when seal numbers were reduced in the nineteenth century, but any tendency for genetic divergence among subpopulations probably has been offset by the interisland movements of seals.

Population Parameters

The status (i.e., size and trend) of any population is ultimately determined by four primary parameters. Animals are added to a population through *births* and *immigration* and are lost through *deaths* and *emigration*. Trends in abundance are determined by the difference (positive or negative) between additions to and losses from the population over time.

We have already noted that some movement (immigration and emigration) occurs among Hawaiian monk seal subpopulations. Next we summarize what is known about reproduction and mortality.

Reproduction and Growth

The following description of the annual cycle of adult female Hawaiian monk seals is based primarily on data from Laysan Island, where reproductive events have been studied most thoroughly (Fig. 10-2) (Johanos et al. 1994).

Births have been documented in virtually all months of the year (National Marine Fisheries Service, unpublished data), but are most common between February and August, with a peak in late March and early April (Johnson and Johnson 1980, Johanos et al. 1994). Pregnant females select a suitable site for parturition (Westlake and Gilmartin 1990) and give birth to a single offspring. Newborn pups of both sexes are covered with black lanugo (fetal hair) and weigh approximately 14–17 kg (Kenyon and Rice 1959, Wirtz 1968). On average, pups nurse for five to six weeks (Kenyon and Rice 1959; Johnson and Johnson 1978, 1984; Boness 1990; Johanos et al. 1994) and weigh 60 to 75 kg at weaning (Kenyon and Rice 1959; M. Craig, pers. comm.).

As with many phocids (Kovacs and Lavigne 1986), female monk seals usually fast and remain with their pups throughout the nursing period. Nursing mothers are generally intolerant of other seals, including other mother-pup pairs, and may have trouble identifying their own pups (Kenyon and Rice 1959). This can lead to the switching of pups, especially when pairs occur close together (Johnson and Johnson 1978, Boness 1990). Also, a mother may foster another pup if her own becomes lost or dies (Alcorn and Henderson 1984, Gerrodette et al. 1992). Switching or fostering of pups appears to have minimal effect on first-year survival (Boness 1990), but larger sample sizes are needed to verify this conclusion.

Weaning occurs when the mother abandons her pup and returns to the sea to resume feeding. Over the next few months, she will regain the considerable amount of mass lost during lactation. About three to four weeks after weaning her pup, she will mate, and, five to six weeks later, she will haul out again for 10 to 14 days or more to molt (Johanos et al. 1994). For all Hawaiian monk seals except pups, molting involves the shedding of the hair and the outer layers of skin (Kenyon and Rice 1959), as in elephant seals (*Mirounga* sp.). In contrast, a pup will begin its molt late in the nursing period and will simply shed and replace its lanugo over a period of several weeks (Kenyon and Rice 1959).

For the pup, weaning marks an abrupt and critical transition to independence, and, in the ensuing months, it must learn to feed and fend for itself. In the process, it will lose a considerable amount of the mass gained during nursing. At French Frigate Shoals, for example, pups in the 1990 to 1992

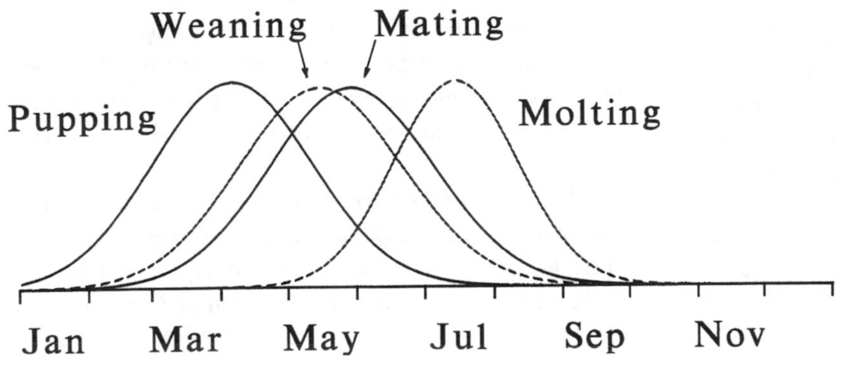

Figure 10-2. Major events in the annual cycle of adult female Hawaiian monk seals, based on data from the Laysan Island subpopulation (Johanos et al. 1994). The timing of molting is estimated from observations of injuries assumed to be related to mating (Hiruki, Gilmartin et al. 1993).

cohorts had a mean mass at weaning of 62.7 kg (± 15.9 kg SD, $n = 167$), a mean length of 125.9 cm (± 7.7 cm, $n = 266$), and a mean axillary girth of 102.7 cm (± 10.5 cm, $n = 267$). By the end of the first year, these same pups had gained 10 cm in length, but had lost 10 kg and 10 cm in mass and axillary girth, respectively (M. Craig, unpublished data). Such a growth pattern during the first year is not unusual among seals (McLaren and Smith 1985).

Few adults have been weighed or measured, so a complete growth curve is not available. Rice (1964) suggested that adult females weigh approximately 205 kg and are about 2.3 m long, whereas the average adult male is smaller, at about 170 kg and 2.1 m. Sexual dimorphism, with females larger than males, is the norm among monachine seals, with the exception of the elephant seals (Kovacs and Lavigne 1986).

Females give birth for the first time between the ages of five and nine years. Data on age-specific birth rates are becoming available as tagged animals mature; results from studies through 1995 suggest that reproductive parameters vary substantially among subpopulations in a manner that may reflect density-dependent effects or local environmental conditions (e.g., prey availability). At French Frigate Shoals, for example, maturation occurs approximately one to two years later than at Laysan Island (Fig. 10-3). Because the onset of sexual maturity in pinnipeds usually coincides with the attainment of some percentage of final body size (Laws 1956), this delay is consistent with (and probably related to) the slower growth rate of juvenile seals at French Frigate Shoals noted above.

Age of sexual maturity for males is unknown, but their size and behavior suggest that they reach maturity at approximately the same age as females. Little is known about male reproductive success because mating occurs at sea and is rarely observed. A small number of observations indicate that the male mounts the female's back by grasping her sides with his foreflippers and biting her back (e.g., Johanos et al. 1990). When mating is not observed, bite marks or injuries on the dorsum of the female provide the only evidence that it might have occurred.

The reproductive behavior of male seals has become a serious concern in recent years because of a phenomenon called "mobbing." Mobbing occurs when a number of males gather and repeatedly attempt to mount and mate with a single seal (e.g., Johanos et al. 1990). The mobbed seal, which may be an adult female or an immature animal of either sex, is often severely injured or killed (Hiruki, Gilmartin et al. 1993; Hiruki, Stirling et al. 1993) (Fig. 10-4). The significance of this behavior will be considered further when the dynamics of individual subpopulations are discussed.

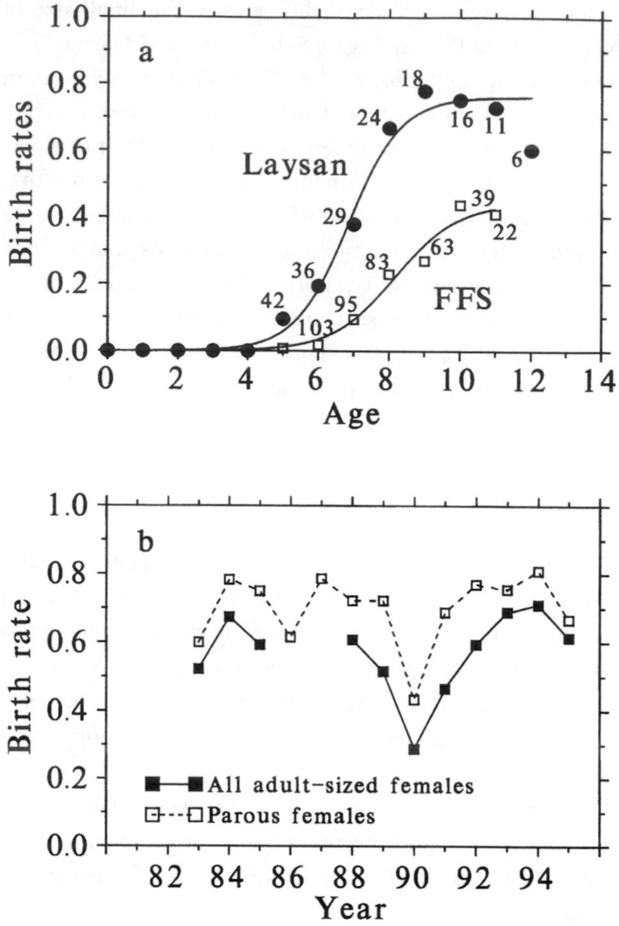

Figure 10-3. Age-specific birth rates observed at Laysan Island and French Frigate Shoals (*top*) and observed birth rates for all adult-sized and known parous females at Laysan Island (*bottom*).

Mortality

In addition to mobbing, other sources of natural mortality include starvation (primarily affecting young seals) (Banish and Gilmartin 1992), predation by sharks (particularly the tiger shark, *Galeocerdo cuvier*) (Balazs and Whittow 1979; Alcorn and Kam 1986; Hiruki, Gilmartin et al. 1993), and disease and trauma (Banish and Gilmartin 1992; Hiruki, Gilmartin et al. 1993). Although virtually all wild seals carry internal parasites (Golvan 1959, Rausch 1969, Whittow et al. 1980, Dailey et al. 1988), their importance as a source of mortality is not known. Biotoxins, such as ciguatoxin, are also suspected causes of mortality (Gilmartin et al. 1980).

Anthropogenic sources of mortality include disturbance (Kenyon 1972), entanglement and entrapment in marine debris (Fig. 10-5) (Henderson 1985, 1990), fishery interactions (Nitta and Henderson 1993), research and rehabilitation, and illegal killing (*United States* v. *Kaneholani*).[2] As is often the

Figure 10-4. An adult female Hawaiian monk seal with a severe mobbing wound. (Photograph courtesy of National Marine Fisheries Service)

Figure 10-5. A young male Hawaiian monk seal with a fishing line tightly wrapped around its neck, Kure Atoll, 1989. (Photograph by John Henderson)

case in wildlife management, anthropogenic sources of mortality are difficult to quantify. Intentional illegal killing, for example, has only been confirmed on one occasion.

Data on age-specific survival rates are available only for seals tagged as pups over the past 10 to 12 years. Gilmartin et al. (1993) estimated that, for the period 1982–1987, survival rate from weaning through the first year of life was approximately 0.80 to 0.90, ranging from 0.77 to 0.99 yr^{-1}. They also indicated that survival for this age class varied with island, year, and sex (females generally experienced better survival than males). Estimates for juveniles ranged from 0.85 to 0.98 yr^{-1}.

A full analysis of survival rates has not been completed for animals older than juveniles, but preliminary analyses again suggest marked variability with island, year, sex, and age. Such variation is particularly apparent at French Frigate Shoals, where observed annual survival rates have dropped dramatically in recent years, apparently because of starvation (also see discussion of the French Frigate Shoals subpopulation, below).

Food and Feeding Behavior

Our understanding of Hawaiian monk seal foraging ecology and feeding behavior is based on scats, spews, and the stomach contents of dead animals, and several preliminary studies of diving patterns (DeLong et al. 1984, Schlexer 1984; National Marine Fisheries Service, unpublished data). From such limited and biased sources, we know that these seals prey on octopus (order Octopoda), squid (order Teuthoidea), lobster (infraorder Palinura), and a variety of reef and benthic fishes. We do not know, however, the relative importance of different prey types in the diet; neither can we describe with any certainty where the seals feed. As with other seal species, prey types and foraging habitat may vary for animals of different sizes or sex classes (e.g., Lowry et al. 1980, Lowry et al. 1982, Antonelis et al. 1994, Stewart and DeLong 1995), with season, year, or subpopulation (e.g., Frost and Lowry 1980, Antonelis et al. 1984, Perez and Bigg 1986), and with abundance of prey species.

Studies using archival or satellite-linked time-depth recorders attached primarily to subadult and adult males (DeLong et al. 1984, Schlexer 1984; National Marine Fisheries Service, unpublished data) suggest that Hawaiian monk seals typically are not deep divers. The vast majority of recorded dives are less than 100 m, although one subadult male from French Frigate Shoals repeatedly dived to at least 500 m (the limit of the depth recorder).

Diving locations are also being studied, but the results are confounded by measurement error. Locations are estimated on the basis of signals received by satellites from seal-borne transmitters, but the estimation algorithm varies in reliability depending on, among other things, the number of signals received. In some cases, the error is similar in magnitude to estimated movement patterns. Nevertheless, of six subadult or adult males instrumented at French Frigate Shoals in 1992 or 1993, five appeared to concentrate their foraging efforts near the northern edge of the atoll's fringing reef. The sixth seal deviated markedly from this pattern, feeding in two- to three-week bouts approximately 60 to 100 km to the east-northeast of French Frigate Shoals. Additional studies are under way to characterize the error associated with these observations and to describe more completely the foraging distribution of the Hawaiian monk seal.

Recent Trends in Abundance

The first range-wide surveys of Hawaiian monk seals were conducted in the late 1950s (Kenyon and Rice 1959, Rice 1960), and additional counts were conducted at Midway Atoll in 1956–1958 (Rice 1960) and at Kure Atoll in 1963–1965 (Wirtz 1968). Surveys were repeated throughout the 1960s and 1970s, but the methods were not standardized. Although the results are difficult to compare, they suggest that the species declined by about 50% between the late 1950s and the mid-1970s (Kenyon 1973, Johnson et al. 1982).

In recent years, three annual indices have been used to assess the status of the species: the total number of pups, the total of the mean beach counts at the main reproductive sites (the numbers reported below do not include data from Midway because of the lack of consistent effort at that site), and the composition of the pooled beach counts. In the past decade, the total number of pups (Fig. 10-6, top panel) has been variable, increasing from 164 in 1983 to 224 in 1988, then declining sharply to 140 in 1990, and recovering from 1991 through 1993. In 1995, 175 pups were counted at the main reproductive sites. The most abrupt change, the decline from 1988 to 1990, reflects a range-wide drop in production, but the overall variability was driven primarily by a decrease in the number of pups born at French Frigate Shoals (Fig. 10-6).

The recent trend in the total of mean beach counts also reflects the general decline in the number of monk seals at French Frigate Shoals (Fig. 10-6, middle panel) (National Marine Fisheries Service, unpublished data). A log-linear regression suggests that from 1985 to 1993 beach counts

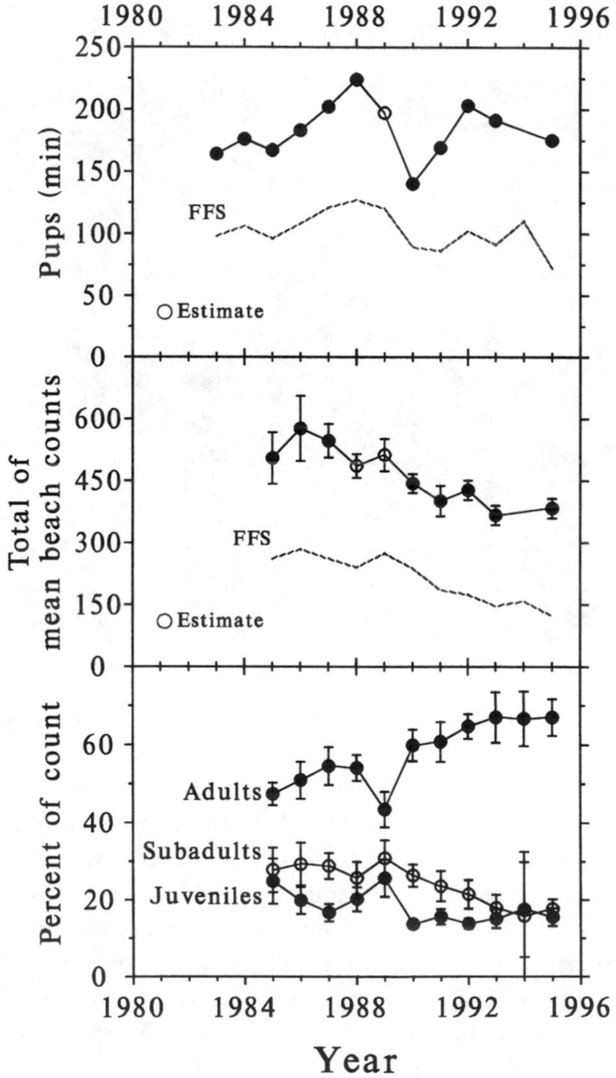

Figure 10-6. Recent trends in demographic indices of the Hawaiian monk seal, based on data combined from the main reproductive populations. The trends at French Frigate Shoals (FFS [dashed lines in the top and middle panels]) have a strong influence on observed trends.

declined at the rate of approximately 5% yr^{-1} ($R^2 = 0.78$, $P < 0.01$). Although some proportion of the decline may have been due to changes in haul-out patterns (e.g., seals may be spending more time at sea foraging and less time hauled out on the beaches), the beach counts clearly indicate a decrease in total abundance.

In addition, the composition of the beach counts has shifted since 1989, with a relative reduction in the number of juvenile and subadult seals (Fig. 10-6, bottom panel). The loss of younger seals portends a decrease in future reproductive recruitment and productivity, and a continued decline in the species.

As an index of abundance, beach counts are particularly important because they have been conducted in most years since the late 1950s (Fig. 10-7). Although the counts in the 1950s do not necessarily reflect the carrying capacity (i.e., several subpopulations were depleted at that time), they clearly suggest that the total abundance of the species was much larger only four decades ago. The overall decline is best understood by a separate evaluation of the individual subpopulations. When dealing with endangered metapopulations, such detailed information is also an essential prerequisite for the development of appropriate conservation policies and management plans.

Necker and Nihoa Islands

Necker and Nihoa Islands are not considered important reproductive sites. The potential for growth at both locations is limited by the lack of suitable terrestrial habitat (Westlake and Gilmartin 1990). Their shorelines are rocky, inaccessible, and surrounded by turbulent nearshore waters. Where the seals can come ashore, they are found in relatively high density, which is not conducive to successful pupping and nursing.

Nonetheless, counts of seals at both islands have increased over the past two decades (Fig. 10-7). In 1993 beach counts were, on average, about 22 and 18 seals (excluding

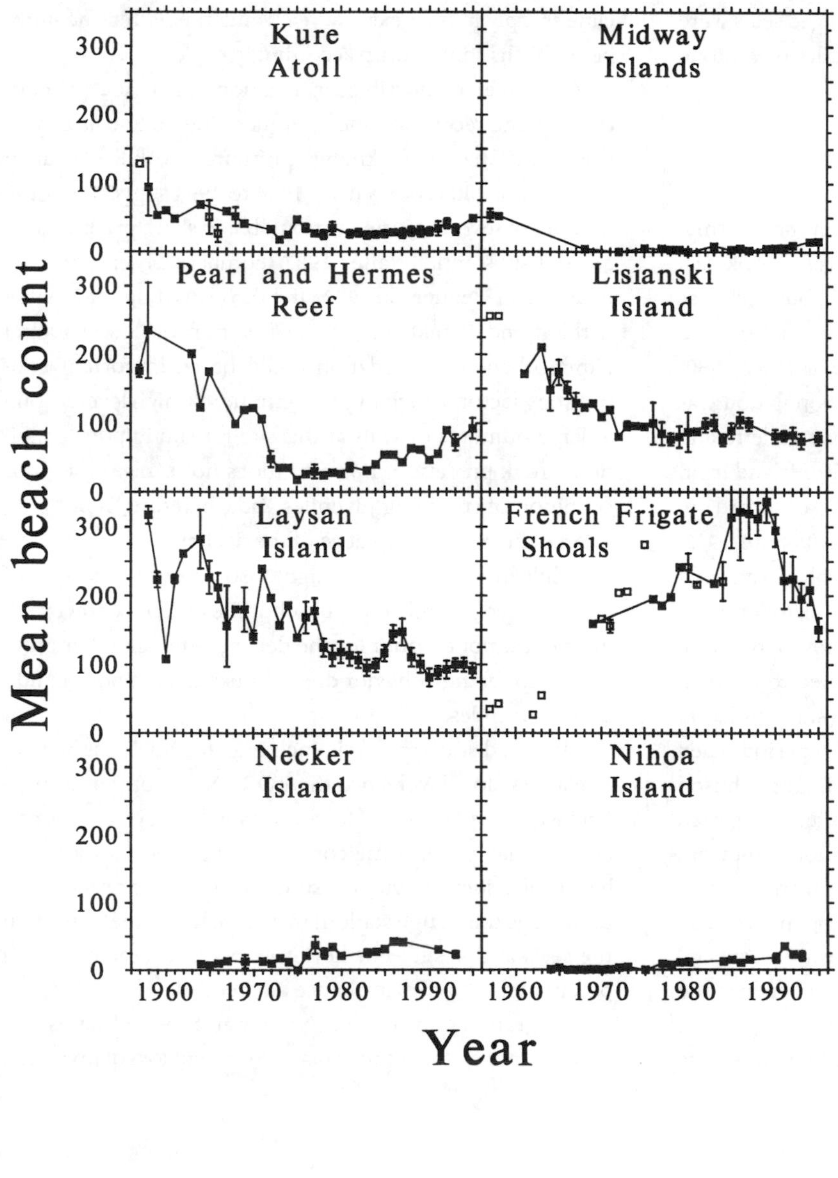

Figure 10-7. Long-term trends in beach counts for the various subpopulations of the Hawaiian monk seal. Counts include pups. Closed boxes indicate land-based surveys; open boxes indicate surveys by boat or aircraft.

pups) at Necker and Nihoa Islands, respectively (Finn and Rice 1994, Ragen and Finn 1996), indicating total numbers on the order of 55 to 65 seals at each site (assuming beach counts represent about one-third of the local abundance; see, for example, Becker et al. 1996). Opportunities for scientists to visit these islands are infrequent and brief, so pup production is rarely assessed. The number of pups observed on Necker Island has ranged from three in 1983 and 1984 to none in both 1986 and 1987 (National Marine Fisheries Service, unpublished data). The number of pups observed on Nihoa Island has ranged from one in both 1986 and 1987 to nine in 1991 (National Marine Fisheries Service, unpublished data).

The increased counts at Necker and Nihoa Islands are apparently due to immigration from French Frigate Shoals. During a seven-day period at Necker Island in 1993, 14 tagged seals were sighted, all of which had been marked as weaned pups at French Frigate Shoals (Finn and Rice 1994). During the same period, 12 tagged seals were sighted at Nihoa Island, 10 of which were from French Frigate Shoals (Ragen and Finn 1996). Virtually all of the tagged seals were subadults (large immature animals) or adults (see Stone 1984 for size classifications).

French Frigate Shoals

French Frigate Shoals is an atoll consisting of nine permanent and several ephemeral islets. The largest monk seal subpopulation is currently found at this atoll, but such was not always the case. Atoll-wide beach counts in 1957 and 1958 totaled only 35 (Fiscus et al. 1978) and 43 (Rice 1960) animals, respectively. It is likely that the subpopulation was depressed because of human disturbance (Gerrodette and Gilmartin 1990). The U.S. Navy occupied Tern Island from 1942 to 1948 and, more important, the U.S. Coast Guard operated a LORAN station at East Island from 1944 to 1952, when it was moved to Tern Island. Presumably, East Island had been the main pupping area in the atoll (Gerrodette and Gilmartin 1990), and, after the station was moved, pup production and survival rates apparently returned to normal.

Thereafter, the French Frigate Shoals subpopulation grew rapidly until the late 1970s (Fig. 10-7), a period when the more western subpopulations were declining. Johnson and Kridler (1983) reviewed tagging records and suggested that the growth at French Frigate Shoals did not result from immigration. In the mid-1980s beach counts increased to a new level; in 1986 the mean count (excluding pups) was 284 (National Marine Fisheries Service, unpublished data), approximately six to eight times higher than it had been in the late 1950s (Fig. 10-7).

More recently, however, the recovery at French Frigate Shoals has sharply reversed. Since 1989 beach counts have declined by approximately 55%, and total abundance in 1995 was estimated at approximately 450 seals (M. Craig, pers. comm.) (Table 10-1). The annual number of births dropped from a high of 127 in 1988 to 72 in 1995 (Fig. 10-8) (Craig et al. 1993, National Marine Fisheries Service, unpublished data).

The most severe demographic changes at this site have involved survival rates of immature animals. The natural logarithm of the number of seals in each of the last 10 cohorts is plotted in Figure 10-9 (see also Gilmartin et al. 1993); each line represents a separate cohort and the slope of any particular line indicates survival rate (steeper slopes indicate poorer survival). First-year survival has declined severely in recent years, and these cohorts have continued to experience poor survival beyond their first year. As a result, the age distribution of the subpopulation is now inverted, with the cohorts of eight- and nine-year-olds being larger than the two- to five-year-old cohorts (Fig. 10-10). Consequently, the number of females reaching maturity is expected to decline sharply in the next few years and, thereafter, the number of births should drop accordingly.

A number of possible explanations as to the primary cause of the recent decline at French Frigate Shoals can be ruled out. Sharks are known to injure and kill Hawaiian monk seals, and reports from 1984 to 1994 suggest that the number of severe injuries attributable to shark predation increased substantially after 1987 (compare observations in Eliason and Henderson 1992 with those in Craig et al. 1994). If this trend is real (i.e., not a function of observational effort), then such predation could be an important contributing factor, which might continue at a high level as long as large numbers of seals at this site remain in poor condition. Shark predation, however, does not explain the poor condition of surviving juveniles and, therefore, is not considered the underlying cause of the decline.

Adult male aggression might also account for some of the observed juvenile mortality, but the number of recorded injuries cannot account for the decline. And, like shark predation, mobbing behavior does not explain the poor condition of juveniles.

Human disturbance at French Frigate Shoals has been at a relatively low level since the LORAN station on Tern Island was closed in 1979. However, even low levels of human activity may cause some corresponding amount of disturbance, and such activity (to study seals or other species, or to manage the refuge station) may have had some impact on the seals at this site. Further attempts to characterize this potential source of disturbance are needed.

Emigration to places like Necker and Nihoa Islands (see above) is not sufficient to explain the recent loss of juveniles.

Table 10-1. Status of Hawaiian Monk Seals in 1995 (see text for additional details)

	Type	Approximate Abundance[a]	Adult Sex Ratio	Major Problem	Trend in Abundance	Comments
Nihoa	Immigrants	55[b]	Unknown	None reported	Increasing	Limited by terrestrial habitat
Necker	Immigrants	65[b]	Unknown	Fisheries competition?	Increasing	Limited by terrestrial habitat
French Frigate Shoals	Breeding	450[c]	Unknown	Decreased prey availability	Declining severely	Largest subpopulation
Laysan	Breeding	250[d]	0.97:1.0	Mobbing	Declining slowly	Sex ratio recently "normalized" by intervention
Lisianski	Breeding	220[d]	1.58:1.0	Mobbing and entanglement	Declining slowly	No remedial action
Pearl and Hermes Reef	Breeding	225[d]	1.0:1.0	None reported	Increasing	Growing naturally
Midway	Potential breeding	45[d]	0.64:1.0	Human disturbance	Unknown	Primarily immigrants
Kure	Breeding	100[d]	0.69:1.0	Previous human disturbance	Increasing	Growing after intense management
Main islands	Potential breeding	40[e]	Unknown	Human disturbance?	Unknown	Status unknown

[a]Abundance estimates reflect counts during the reproductive season, and include all pups born.

[b]Numbers very approximate: based on beach counts in 1993 and the assumption that approximately one-third of the animals were hauled out during the counts.

[c]Number based on the number of identified animals in the subpopulation (411) and a subjective estimate that approximately 40 to 50 animals were not identified (M. Craig, pers. comm.).

[d]Numbers based on long-term identification studies allowing enumeration of virtually all animals in each subpopulation.

[e]An "educated" guess.

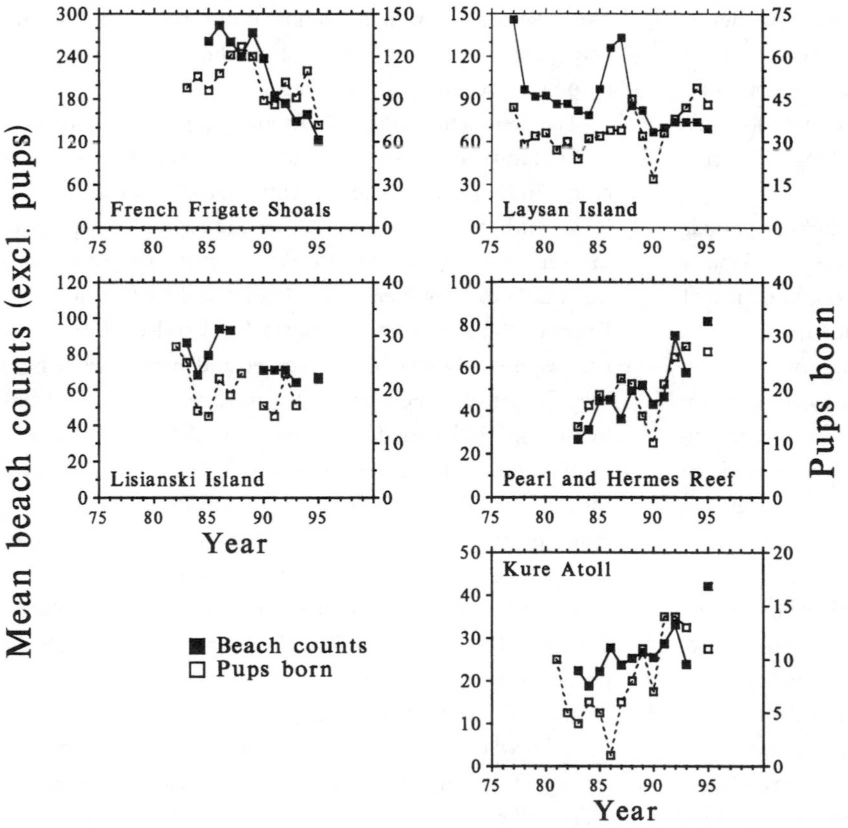

Figure 10-8. Annual mean beach counts (excluding pups; left *y* axis) and number of pups (right *y* axis) at the main reproductive sites (excluding Midway Atoll). Note that the scales of the *y* axes vary for the different subpopulations.

Changes in haul-out patterns might explain lower beach counts and would be consistent with the observed poor condition of juveniles. However, in view of the extensive resighting effort at this atoll, changes in haul-out patterns probably would not account for the low number of seals resighted at least once during a season. In effect, changes in haul-out patterns are more likely to be a consequence, rather than a cause, of any underlying problem.

Preliminary studies conducted in April–May and September 1992 (National Marine Fisheries Service, unpublished data) found various levels of parasitic infestation but no obvious signs of disease. The roles of disease and para-

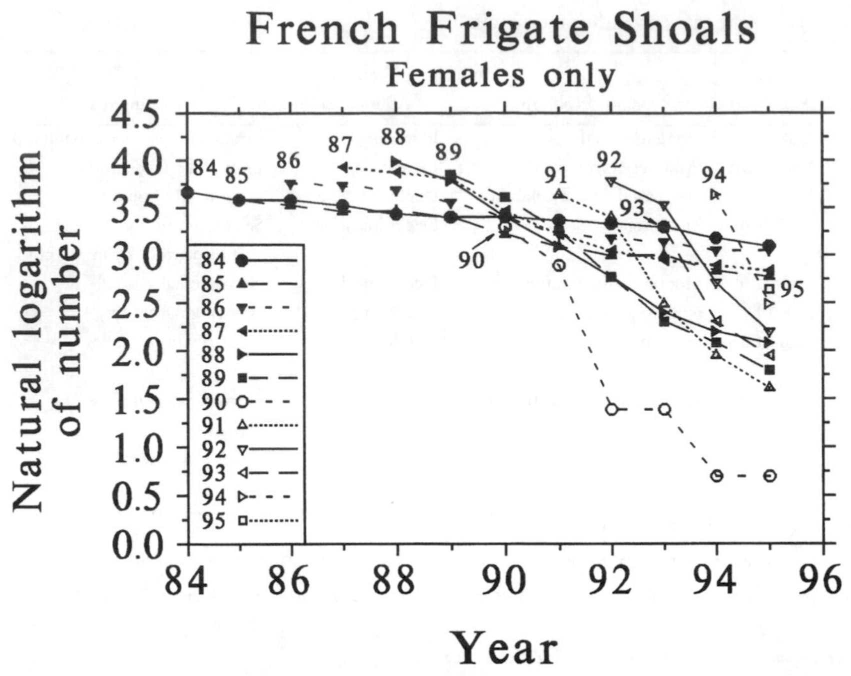

Figure 10-9. Trends in survival of recent cohorts at French Frigate Shoals. The ordinate is the natural logarithm of the number of females in each cohort (tagged as weaned pups and not removed for rehabilitation). With approximately constant survival, the slope for any particular cohort should be correspondingly linear. Steeper slopes indicate lower survival rates, which have clearly worsened for recent cohorts.

sitism in this decline are not clear, but warrant further investigation. Ciguatoxin is an unlikely cause because the expected signs of such poisoning—a range of debilitating gastrointestinal, neurological, and cardiovascular disorders that occur over a period of days to weeks or longer (Withers 1982)—have not been observed.

Finally, the observed decline of the French Frigate Shoals subpopulation could be due to decreased prey availability. Although the reasons for prey scarcity are not known with certainty, this hypothesis is consistent with the observed changes in reproduction, survival, and condition of surviving seals. Growth over the previous three decades, for example, may have brought this subpopulation to carrying capacity. If these seals feed primarily in reef or shallow-water benthic habitats, then abundance of potential prey may be limited and easily overexploited.

The observed changes in seal population parameters and fishery yields are also consistent with another possible explanation for the decline in prey availability: a shift in environmental conditions resulting in lower productivity throughout the Northwestern Hawaiian Islands. Polovina et al. (1994) indicated that from the late 1970s to the late 1980s, wind-driven surface mixing in the central North Pacific increased, thereby increasing the depth of the mixed layer and stimulating productivity. Decreased productivity observed in the late 1980s and early 1990s, including changes in abundance of coral reef fishes at French Frigate Shoals (DeMartini et al. 1993), may simply reflect a long-term oscillation in oceanographic conditions. To the extent that these oceanographic events affected monk seals in the Northwestern Hawaiian Islands, the impact was presumably greater at French Frigate Shoals because the subpopulation was closer to carrying capacity.

The abundance of certain monk seal prey (e.g., lobsters and octopus) has also been reduced in recent years by a commercial fishery. The Northwestern Hawaiian Islands lobster fishery began in the 1970s and expanded rapidly in the early 1980s (Polovina 1993). The primary fishing sites from 1983 to 1994 were Maro Reef, Gardner Pinnacles, St. Rogatien Bank, and Necker Island (Wetherall et al. 1995), all sites where seals have been observed and presumably where they forage. Between 1982 and 1991, catch-per-unit-effort by the fishery declined by almost 80% (Polovina 1993), and in 1993 the lobster fishery was closed. The extent to which the reduction in the lobster stock has affected monk seals remains uncertain because the importance of lobsters in their diet and the availability of alternate prey are not known.

Regardless of the reasons for decreased prey availability, the lack of food for monk seals at French Frigate Shoals poses a serious threat to the persistence of the Hawaiian monk seal. Even if these changes reflect natural processes, the relatively high mortality of juveniles due to starvation represents an important loss of reproductive potential that will significantly impede recovery of this subpopulation and of the entire species.

Laysan Island

The abundance of Hawaiian monk seals at Laysan Island declined significantly after the late 1950s. Although numbers

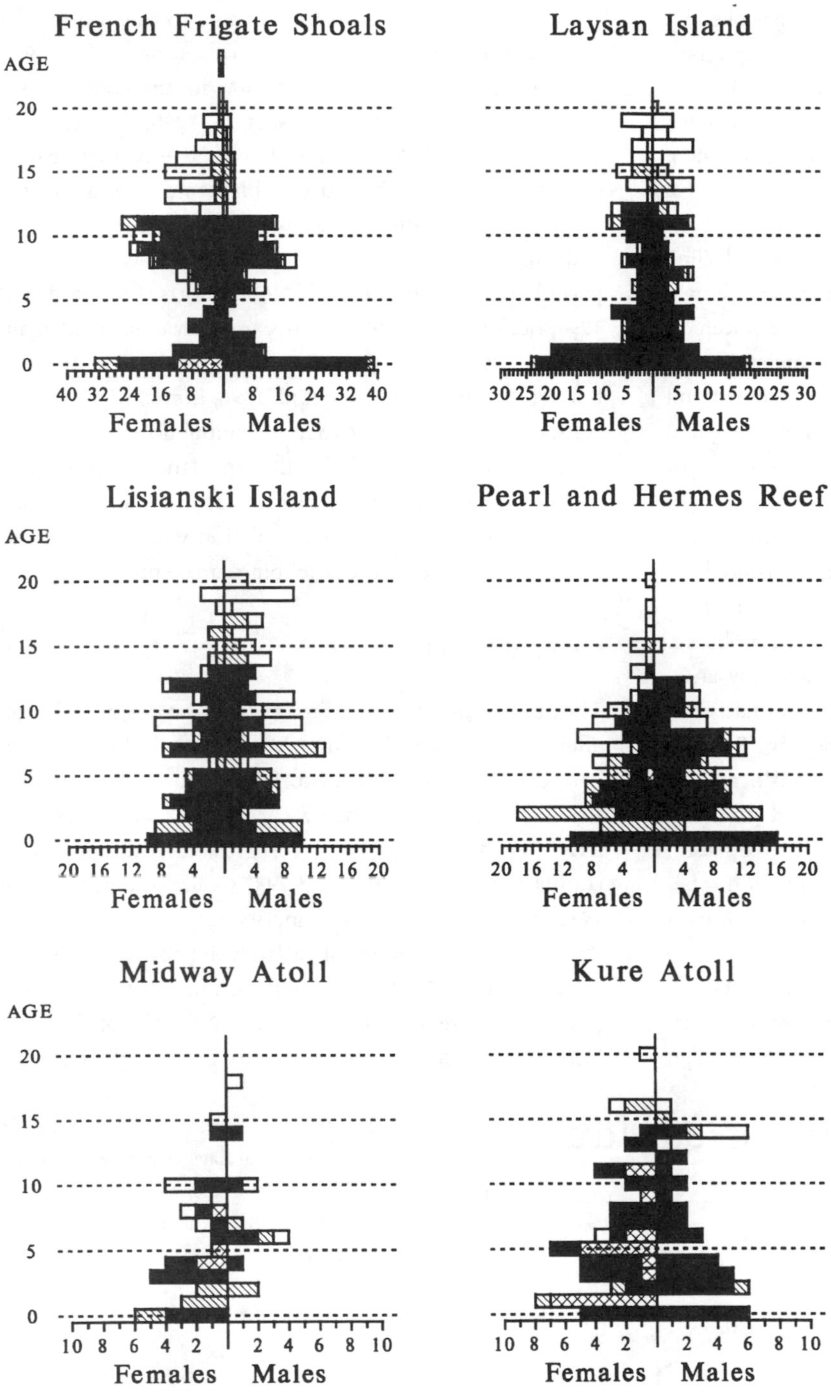

Figure 10-10. The 1995 age distributions of the main reproductive populations. Solid bars indicate animals of known age (i.e., tagged as weaned pups), striped bars indicate animals of either estimated sex (pups only) or age (i.e., the animals were tagged when immature and age was estimated on the basis of size), cross-hatched bars indicate animals that were captured as weaned pups for rehabilitation, and open bars indicate animals of minimum age (i.e., animals first identified as adults, assumed to be at least six years old at that time, and then distributed randomly among older age classes according to an approximate survival schedule). The number of adults older than age 11 is unknown at French Frigate Shoals and is based on a "best guess" only. The apparent imbalance in the sex ratio at French Frigate Shoals probably reflects greater effort to identify adult females. Note that the scales of the *x* axes vary among the graphs, and comparisons between sites must be made with that in mind.

may have stabilized in the past few years, this subpopulation still shows no signs of recovery (Fig. 10-7). The nature of the decline before the late 1970s has not been determined; beach counts varied widely, but much of the apparent variability may be attributed to poorly standardized counting methods. A mass mortality involving at least 50 seals occurred at Laysan in 1978 (Johnson and Johnson 1981a). The cause was never determined, although Gilmartin et al. (1980) suggested that it may have been related to ciguatera. Similar mass mortalities were not observed before 1978 (although observation effort was low) and have not been observed subsequently at this or any other site.

Mean beach counts have remained low since 1978 (log-linear regression, $R^2 = 0.21$, $P = 0.07$) (Fig. 10-8), despite the fact that the numbers are well below historical levels (Fig. 10-7). For some undetermined reason, beach counts increased significantly in 1986 and 1987 (Alcorn and Westlake 1993, Becker et al. 1994), but then dropped again in 1988 (Johanos et al. 1990) (Fig. 10-8). Abundance in 1995 was estimated at about 250 seals (B. L. Becker, pers. comm.) (Table 10-1).

The sex ratio of adult seals at Laysan Island has been biased toward males (Fig. 10-11). In 1983 and 1984 (and perhaps in preceding years; see Johnson and Johnson 1981b), the subpopulation included at least two adult males for each adult female (Johanos et al. 1987, Alcorn and Buelna 1989). Since 1983 the ratio has declined, and in 1994 there were 1.2 males per female (Becker et al. 1996).

The above factors are thought to be related; the decline in abundance appears to be the result of increased female mortality from mobbing, which occurs more often at locations where the sex ratio is skewed toward males. In 1989 at least seven adult females died after they were mobbed, and at least one other female was mobbed and never seen again; these eight animals represent 13% of the total number of adult females at Laysan Island that year (Becker et al. 1994). From 1982 to 1994, 63 deaths of seals older than pups were confirmed; of those, 45 (71%) died as a result of mobbing (B. Becker, pers. comm.). Twenty-six of the 63 were adult females, and 23 (88%) of those animals died from mobbing.

In 1994, 22 adult males were removed from the Laysan Island subpopulation to reduce the adult male-female ratio and thereby decrease the probability of mobbing. Twenty-one survived the capture period and were translocated to the main Hawaiian Islands; none were resighted at Laysan Island during the 1995 spring-summer reproductive season (B. Becker, pers. comm.). The Laysan subpopulation is being monitored closely to assess the effect of the removal on the rate of mobbing-related injuries and deaths.

Another impediment to recovery appeared in 1989–1990 when the number of immature seals fell because of a combination of low birth rates and poor juvenile survival (Fig. 10-10). Survival of pups from weaning to the end of their first year declined from a previous range of 80–90% (Gilmartin et al. 1993) to 65% and 56% for the 1988 and 1989 cohorts, respectively (Johanos et al. 1990, Becker et al. 1994). In 1990 only 30% of the adult-sized females gave birth (approximately half the expected birth rate) (Lombard et al. 1994). The birth rate returned to expected values after 1990, and survival from weaning to age one was within the expected range for the 1990 and 1991 cohorts (Lombard et al. 1994, Becker et al. 1995). First-year survival declined again, however, to 66%, 41%, and 64% for the 1992 to 1994 cohorts, respectively (Becker et al. 1996, Lombard et al. 1996; National Marine Fisheries Service, unpublished data).

The paucity of females at Laysan Island, whether from mobbing-related mortality or low birth rate and poor survival, suggests that this subpopulation will be slow to recover even if the effects of mobbing can be mitigated.

Lisianski Island

The number of seals at Lisianski Island also declined sharply after the late 1950s (Fig. 10-7). Most of the decline occurred before the mid-1970s. By historical standards, the subpopulation at this site is well below carrying capacity and should have considerable potential for growth. Although beach counts increased in 1986 and 1987 (Johanos and Withrow 1988, Westlake and Siepmann 1988), the same years that they increased at Laysan Island, they did not continue to do so, and since 1972 the subpopulation has failed to recover (log-linear regression, $R^2 = 0.11$, $P = 0.14$; National Marine Fisheries Service, unpublished data). Estimated abundance

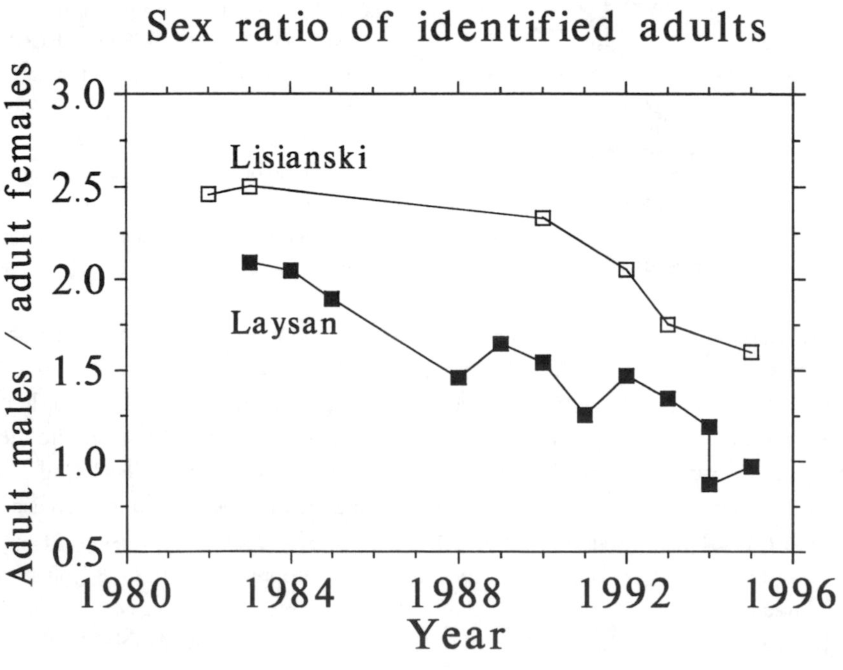

Figure 10-11. The observed adult sex ratio (males/females) at Laysan and Lisianski Islands. The drop in the ratio at Laysan Island in 1994 reflects the removal of 22 adult males.

in 1995 was about 220 seals (H. Johnston, pers. comm.) (Table 10-1).

Since 1982 the number of pups born has been variable but low (Fig. 10-8), as has the number of immature seals (Fig. 10-10). The observed variability in beach counts appears, however, to reflect fluctuations in the number of adults. In spite of this variability, the adult sex ratio has remained persistently and strongly in favor of males (Fig. 10-11). Recently, the ratio has declined, and in 1995 the subpopulation included 1.6 adult males per adult female (H. Johnston, pers. comm.). Mobbing has been observed at Lisianski (e.g., Johanos and Kam 1986), but its incidence has not been quantified because of insufficient monitoring. Nonetheless, mobbing is considered the most likely explanation for the failure of this subpopulation to increase.

Entanglement in marine debris from fisheries and other sources also may have contributed to the lack of growth at this site (see Laist et al., this volume). Henderson (1990) reviewed records for all locations from 1982 to 1988 and found the highest rate of entanglement at Lisianski Island. Although only four deaths due to entanglement have been confirmed (Henderson 1990), the full extent of mortality related to marine debris remains unknown.

Pearl and Hermes Reef

The number of Hawaiian monk seals at Pearl and Hermes Reef declined severely (by as much as 90%) after the late 1950s (Fig. 10-7). Here, too, the nature of the decline remains undetermined, but it may have been related to human disturbances associated with military excursions from Midway Atoll in the 1950s and 1960s (Woodside and Kramer 1961, Kramer 1963). Contrary to trends observed at Laysan and Lisianski Islands, this subpopulation reversed its decline and has been increasing at approximately 6% per year since the mid-1970s (log-linear regression, $R^2 = 0.71$, $P < 0.01$) (Fig. 10-8). Beach counts indicate that all age groups (including the number of pups born annually) are currently increasing (Fig. 10-8), and the age composition appears to be more consistent with that of a stable, growing population (Fig. 10-10) (Gilmartin and Eberhardt 1995). Estimated abundance in 1995 was about 225 seals (J. Henderson, pers. comm.) (Table 10-1).

This subpopulation provides an important reference for management of the Hawaiian monk seal. First, the observed growth rate is assumed to be the best estimate of r_{max} (i.e., the maximum growth rate for a population with a stable age distribution) for the species. Second, mobbing is not known to occur at Pearl and Hermes Reef, thereby providing an important contrast to those sites where mobbing does occur. Data collected in 1995 indicate a slight bias toward males (about 1.1 to 1.0) for seals aged five and older, but a balanced sex ratio (ca. 1:1) for younger animals (J. Henderson, pers. comm.). The seals at this site appear to be in good condition, and prospects for local recovery are encouraging.

Midway Atoll

Historical records suggest that this subpopulation was depleted by the late 1800s, but recovered, at least partially, in the first half of this century. The highest recorded counts were made in 1957–1958 (nine counts with a mean ± SD of 55.7 ± 9.1 seals) (Kenyon 1972), with virtually all observed seals limited to three small islets between Sand and Eastern Islands, the two main islands at Midway. Thus, the Midway subpopulation was probably well below carrying capacity in the 1950s. Within a decade, this subpopulation had essentially disappeared (Fig. 10-7); a single seal was observed during an aerial survey in March 1968 (Kenyon 1972). Most of the small number of seals now observed at this site are immigrants from Pearl and Hermes Reef and Kure Atoll (Eberhardt and Eberhardt 1994) (see Fig. 10-10).

The decline of the Midway subpopulation has been attributed to human disturbance and its effects on reproduction and juvenile survival (Kenyon and Rice 1959, Rice 1964, Kenyon 1972). Permanent human habitation of the atoll began in 1902 with the establishment of a cable station for trans-Pacific telegraph service. A runway was built in 1935 by Pan American Airways, and the atoll was exposed to severe disturbance during World War II (Bryan 1956). The number of human inhabitants declined in the late 1940s but increased again in the 1950s to a maximum of nearly 3,000. Human access to Eastern Island was restricted in the late 1950s, and the small islets between Eastern and Sand Islands were rarely visited (Kenyon 1972). By 1968, however, access to these areas was no longer restricted, and visitors again became more frequent. In 1978 the human population, which had decreased to about 1,600, was further reduced to approximately 250 and has subsequently remained at this level. The Midway Naval Air Facility was closed in 1993, and the U.S. Navy has recently transferred jurisdiction of Midway Atoll to the U.S. Fish and Wildlife Service.

A recent attempt was made to supplement the number of monk seals at Midway using animals translocated from French Frigate Shoals. The attempt failed (see Lavigne, this volume), but further translocations have been proposed following an analysis of the initial effort.

Kure Atoll

The number of seals at Kure Atoll is currently increasing. Abundance declined abruptly in the late 1950s and early

1960s after the construction and occupation of a U.S. Coast Guard LORAN station on Green Island, the largest island in the atoll (Fig. 10-7) (Kenyon 1972, Gerrodette and Gilmartin 1990). Kenyon (1972) attributed this decline to human disturbance, which caused adult females to abandon prime pupping habitat. Pup survival fell first (Wirtz 1968), followed by a decline in recruitment of breeding females and the development of an age structure skewed toward older animals (Johnson et al. 1982). The sex ratio of adults also became heavily biased toward males (Reddy and Griffith 1988), and seals were observed with mobbing wounds. Births declined steadily from the late 1970s to the mid-1980s, and only a single pup was born in 1986 (Reddy 1989, Gerrodette and Gilmartin 1990). Thereafter, the number of births increased steadily (with the exception of 1990 when births were low at all locations) to between 11 and 14 in 1991–1993 and 1995 (Fig. 10-8) (Finn and Swensen 1995, Henderson et al. 1996; National Marine Fisheries Service, unpublished data). Beach counts have also increased since 1986 at about 5% yr^{-1} (log-linear regression, $R^2 = 0.70$, $P = 0.05$). Abundance in 1995 was estimated at about 100 seals (L. Keith, pers. comm.) (Table 10-1).

The recent increase in this subpopulation has been attributed to two factors. First, human disturbance at prime pupping areas was reduced by changes in Coast Guard regulation of beach activities and by the presence of National Marine Fisheries Service biologists who encouraged compliance with those regulations (Gilmartin et al. 1986). Second, between 1985 and 1995, 54 immature female seals originally from French Frigate Shoals were released at Kure. A number of these females have reached reproductive maturity and are now producing offspring (National Marine Fisheries Service, unpublished data). In addition, the adult sex ratio has returned to a presumably normal level near 1:1 (Fig. 10-10) (Van Toorenburg et al. 1993). In July 1992 the Coast Guard closed the LORAN station on Green Island; by September 1993 the atoll had been vacated, and air transportation to Kure was discontinued. Barring unforeseen events, there are reasons for optimism about the future of monk seals at Kure.

Discussion

The overall status of the Hawaiian monk seal is extremely grave. Only four decades ago, beach counts at five of the six main reproductive sites totaled 969 seals (Rice 1960). In 1995 the comparable count totaled 383 seals, a decline of about 60%. Increasing trends at Kure Atoll and Pearl and Hermes Reef notwithstanding, a continuing decline in total population size over the next few years seems inevitable because of the status and trends of the subpopulations at French Frigate Shoals and at Laysan and Lisianski Islands. And, if the species continues to decline at the current rate, it will become as endangered as its Mediterranean counterpart in only 15 to 20 years.

According to Ehrenfeld (1970:130) the hypothetical "most endangered animal" is a large predator that reproduces in aggregates, has a long gestation period, and produces few young per litter. It exhibits a narrow habitat tolerance and has a restricted distribution, but travels across international boundaries. It is hunted for a natural product or for sport, but is not subject to efficient game management. It is intolerant of humans and exhibits nonadaptive behavioral idiosyncrasies. Ehrenfeld considered the existence of such an animal unlikely but suggested that, with one or two exceptions, his model nearly described the polar bear, *Ursus maritimus*.

He might just as well have chosen the monk seal (Table 10-2). Hawaiian monk seals are large marine predators that, by virtue of their metapopulation structure, are aggregated in six main reproductive subpopulations (including Midway); they have a long gestation period (about 11 months) (Johanos et al. 1994) and produce a single young per litter. With rare exceptions, the species is found only in the Northwestern Hawaiian Islands and, therefore, it also has a very restricted distribution.

As we have seen, Hawaiian monk seals were also subjected to unregulated hunting in the past century, but this has not been an issue in recent decades. By all accounts, however, the effects of other types of human disturbance have been severe (Kenyon 1972, Gerrodette and Gilmartin 1990). The most extreme disturbance must have occurred at Midway Atoll during World War II and probably led to the decline in monk seals there, well before the first counts were made in the 1950s. Other military operations were conducted throughout the Northwestern Hawaiian Islands during the 1960s (Woodside and Kramer 1961, Kramer and Beardsley 1962, Marshall 1962, Kramer 1963) and perhaps at other times. As recently as 1976, correspondence in the files of the Marine Mammal Commission refers to the "bombing, strafing, [and] depth charge detonating in the area along the migratory routes of the Hawaiian monk seal that occur while the seals may be transiting the area."[3] The extent of such activities and their effects on seals and other wildlife are not well documented, however, and may never be described in detail. Nonetheless, these activities almost certainly played a role in the decline of Hawaiian monk seals.

More subtle forms of disturbance also appear to have precipitated major changes in the demography of this species. Seemingly benign activities such as beachcombing, particularly with pet dogs, have caused adult females to abandon prime pupping habitat, leading to poor juvenile

Table 10-2. Characteristics of the Hypothetical Most Endangered Animal (Ehrenfeld 1970) Compared with Those of the Hawaiian Monk Seal

Hypothetical Most Endangered Animal	Hawaiian Monk Seal
Individuals of large size	Yes; a relatively large mammal; large relative to many true seals
Narrow habitat tolerance	?; critical habitat requirements not known
Valuable fur, hide, oil, etc.	Yes; hunted for pelts and oil in nineteenth century
Hunted for the market or hunted for sport where there is no effective game management	Yes; hunted for markets and subsistence in the absence of any game management in the nineteenth century
Restricted distribution: island, etc.	Yes; distribution restricted to the Hawaiian Island chain for possibly 15 million years
Lives largely in international waters or migrates across international boundaries	No; lives exclusively under U.S. jurisdiction
Intolerant of the presence of humans	Yes; considerable evidence that monk seals are intolerant of human activities
Species reproduction in one or two vast aggregates	?; reproductive subpopulations determined by limited hauling beaches in Northwestern Hawaiian Islands
Long gestation period	Yes; approximately 11 months
One or two young per litter or maternal care	Yes; nursing lasts five to six weeks
Has behavioral idiosyncrasies that are nonadaptive today	Yes; male mobbing behavior; also gets caught in/on fishing gear, eats commercially important species, depends on haul-out sites used by humans for other purposes (e.g., military operations)

survival and, eventually, to decreased reproductive recruitment. Such effects have been well described for monk seals at French Frigate Shoals and at Midway and Kure Atolls (Kenyon 1972, Gerrodette and Gilmartin 1990).

In addition, military and Coast Guard operations have physically reshaped several islands (e.g., Tern Island at French Frigate Shoals, and Sand and Eastern Islands at Midway) and nearshore areas and have left undetermined amounts of debris and potentially harmful substances either buried on the islands or in nearshore waters.

Other disturbances may also have occurred at sea where the Hawaiian monk seal spends two-thirds of its life (Johanos and Kam 1986). These include a range of human activities and products associated with the development of commercial fisheries. As noted above (see the section on Lisianski Island), entanglement in marine debris, especially lost or abandoned fishing gear, is a serious threat to the seals, but is also notoriously difficult to quantify because seals may become entangled at sea and never be observed.

In addition to entanglements, most of the known or suspected direct interactions between monk seals and fisheries occurred in the late 1980s and early 1990s, with the expansion of the pelagic longline fishery (Reddy and Griffith 1988, Craig et al. 1993). The recent establishment of a protected species zone[4] seems to have reduced the number of longline interactions.

Monk seals also interact directly with the Northwestern Hawaiian Islands bottomfish fishery, primarily by consuming discarded kahala (*Seriola dumerii*). The kahala are discarded because they may contain high levels of ciguatoxins and, therefore, may pose a threat to the seals (Nitta and Henderson 1993).

Indirect interactions, such as competition for prey, are more difficult to evaluate. As noted in the section on French Frigate Shoals, one potential conflict is between monk seals and the lobster fishery. To date, little progress has been made in evaluating such interactions.

Finally, the mobbing behavior exhibited by male Hawaiian monk seals seems to qualify as an example of what Ehrenfeld (1970) termed a nonadaptive behavioral idiosyncrasy. The aggression exhibited by males probably reflects normal reproductive drive, but such aggression becomes nonadaptive (at least from a population point of view) where sex ratios are severely skewed and mobbing occurs. Island geography and monk seal haul-out behavior probably exacerbate the problem by creating localized, extreme imbalances in the ratio of males to females. Mobbing may be particularly threatening to this species, especially if it results in a positive (runaway) feedback loop where mortality from mobbing further distorts the sex ratio, thereby increasing the likelihood that additional mobbing will occur.

In addition to sharing many characteristics of Ehrenfeld's "hypothetical most endangered animal," the Hawaiian monk seal's small and fragmented subpopulations make it inherently vulnerable to extinction through demographic stochasticity, environmental stochasticity, and catastrophes, and through the loss of genetic variability (Shaffer 1981, Caughley 1994, Burkey 1995). Demographic stochasticity results from random factors that affect individuals independently, and its consequences can be particularly severe in small populations. Starfield et al. (1995), for example, demonstrated that the sex ratio of adult monk seals is more likely to become skewed toward males as population size becomes smaller simply because of demographic variation in both the sex ratio at birth and the survival of males and females. Such variation provides one possible explanation for the skewed adult sex ratios at Laysan and Lisianski Islands.

In contrast, all individuals are affected by environmental stochasticity. Mean values for population parameters such as birth rate and survival are, therefore, altered. The large drop in birth rate at all breeding sites in 1990 appears to provide a recent example of environmental stochasticity affecting Hawaiian monk seals.

Another possible example is the catastrophic mass mortality experienced in mid-1997 by the largest surviving population of Mediterranean monk seals, which lives on the Cabo Blanco Peninsula of the Western Sahara. Early indications are that this event was associated with a toxic algal bloom, although the involvement of a virus has yet to be ruled out. Goodman (1987) suggested that a catastrophe such as this is best viewed as an extreme environmental event (also see Caughley 1994). Shaffer (1981), however, separated natural catastrophes from environmental stochasticity. For the Hawaiian monk seal, where human activity can lead to catastrophe as surely as natural factors, the frequency of observed catastrophes suggests that they are best considered separately from extreme environmental variation.

In the past five decades, a number of catastrophic "events" have been documented for Hawaiian monk seals: the occupation of Midway Atoll by the Navy and the virtual extinction of that subpopulation in the 1960s, the occupation of Kure Atoll by the Coast Guard and the subsequent decline at that site, the severe decline (about 90%) at Pearl and Hermes Reef, similar declines at Laysan and Lisianski Islands, the die-off at Laysan in 1978, and the recent and severe decline of the French Frigate Shoals subpopulation.

Inbreeding depression may also be playing a role in the decline of Hawaiian monk seals, perhaps through a reduction in juvenile survival or adult female reproduction (Kretzmann et al. 1997). Currently, we know little about the role of genetics in the decline of the Hawaiian monk seal.

To complicate matters, the above sources of variability interact. Catastrophes, for example, reduce the size of a subpopulation and thereby increase its vulnerability to the effects of demographic stochasticity and loss of genetic variability. Such interactions can be important components of an extinction vortex (Gilpin and Soulé 1986).

The fragmented nature of Hawaiian monk seal habitat in an isolated archipelago may contribute further to the species' tenuous existence. Burkey (1995) suggested that species are more likely to go extinct on sets of small islands before they go extinct on a single large island. Movements of monk seals among islands might ameliorate this effect, but not without the attendant risks of increased mortality associated with dispersal and the possibility of disease transmission among subpopulations (Burkey 1995). Alternatively, the fragmented metapopulation structure of the species may provide some buffer against localized environmental perturbation. Although the net effect of fragmentation is not yet evident, the maintenance of as many viable subpopulations as possible is critical to the future of this species.

We are now in a position to return to the questions posed at the beginning of this chapter. There are two distinct lines of thought about the current status of modern monk seals. One view, clearly expressed by Charles Repenning (1980:24) shortly after the Hawaiian monk seal was declared endangered, is that "In modern times the Caribbean monk seal has shown, and the Mediterranean and Hawaiian monk seals are showing, that inability to adapt [to changing environments] leads to extinction." This is a convenient view for humans; it lets us off the hook. As Repenning was quick to suggest, "Mankind need not feel responsible for something that began 8 million years ago. . . ."

The problem with such views is, first and foremost, that they are not amenable to scientific testing. Perhaps Repenning and those who share such views are correct; perhaps they are not. It does seem a remarkable coincidence, however, that all three species of modern monk seals should converge on the brink of extinction at virtually the same instant in geological time. After all, one of the three species may have been around for upwards of 15 million years, whereas the other two species have rather shorter histories; the three species also live in widely disparate parts of the globe under rather different circumstances. There is also overwhelming evidence that humans have had considerable impacts on all three species over various lengths of recorded history. In other words, regardless of the monk seals' abilities to adapt to changing environmental conditions, which we cannot yet measure or quantify, it seems self-evident that humans have contributed substantially to their decline. If we decide that we want to preserve monk seals, one option available to us is to minimize our current and future impacts on these animals and their habitats.

Conclusions

Although Ehrenfeld's (1970) hypothetical "most endangered animal" provides a framework for discussing the Hawaiian monk seal, the endangered status of this species is anything but hypothetical. The loss of the Caribbean monk seal is a simple but blunt reminder of the reality of extinction. And the struggle to save the Mediterranean monk seal clearly illustrates how much more difficult the situation may become.

Is the Hawaiian monk seal doomed to extinction? Yes.

But all species are so doomed. The pertinent question is whether such extinction must be at the hands of our species. Clearly, further scientific study of this (and other) endangered species is required to identify and understand those factors that are essential to its conservation. But how we act to save this species, with or without full knowledge and understanding, is not just a matter of science. It is also a matter of management—both of the species itself and of human activities that threaten its existence. And when we move from the realm of science to the realm of management, our orientation changes from the search for truth to the implementation of societal values (see Lavigne et al., this volume). Our discovery of the truth depends on the rigor of our scientific investigations, but the values deemed most important to modern society depend on many other factors (e.g., Kellert 1996). So, perhaps, the most important question is not "Can we save this species?" but rather "Will we?" What are our values?

Acknowledgments

Any opinions expressed in this chapter represent the personal views of one or both of the authors. Under no circumstances should they be construed as necessarily representing the views or opinions of their respective employers or any funding organizations.

We thank the editors for the invitation to contribute this chapter to the book. John Twiss generously provided access to background material from the Marine Mammal Commission, which provided a unique perspective of the subject matter. He was also very understanding when we repeatedly missed deadlines and, without his continuous optimism and encouragement, it is safe to say that the manuscript would never have been completed. Suzanne Montgomery, also of the Marine Mammal Commission, was particularly helpful during the editing process.

Maria Kretzmann kindly gave us a preprint of her paper on Hawaiian monk seal genetics, and Ward Chesworth provided background references on the history of the Hawaiian Islands. We thank Bud Antonelis, Brenda Becker, Mitchell Craig, Bill Gilmartin, Thea Johanos, Bill Johnson, David Johnston, Maria Kretzmann, David Laist, Peter Meisenheimer, Randy Reeves, Rick Smith, John Twiss, and several anonymous reviewers for comments and suggestions on early drafts of the chapter. We also thank Daniel Goodman for discussions about the metapopulation structure of the species and, particularly, for pointing out that human settlement of the Hawaiian Archipelago may have affected significantly not only the species' distribution but also its metapopulation dynamics.

Much of the information presented in this chapter is the result of extensive research conducted by the Honolulu Laboratory of the National Marine Fisheries Service. Many persons, both employees and volunteers, have contributed substantially to this research effort. Brenda Becker, Mitchell Craig, Bill Gilmartin, John Henderson, Thea Johanos, Amy Sloan, and other members of the Hawaiian monk seal program, past and present, deserve special thanks for their generosity in sharing the information presented in this chapter.

T.J.R.'s research on the Hawaiian monk seal was conducted as an employee of the National Marine Fisheries Service. D.M.L.'s research on pinnipeds has been funded largely by the Natural Sciences and Engineering Research Council of Canada, the International Fund for Animal Welfare, and the International Marine Mammal Association Inc.

Notes

1. "Conservation," wrote Olver et al. (1995:1584), "like beauty, is clearly in the eye of the beholder." To avoid any misunderstanding of our meaning here, we follow Johnson and Lavigne (1995) and define conservation simply to mean the "preservation from destructive influences . . . protection from undesirable changes" (Oxford English Distionary, 2d ed., s.v. "conservation").
2. 945 F.2d 254 (9th Cir. 1991).
3. Letter from A. F. Fugaro, Rear Admiral, U.S. Coast Guard, Chief, Office of Marine Environment and Systems, to J. R. Twiss, Executive Director, Marine Mammal Commission, Washington, DC, 23 July 1976.
4. 56 *Fed. Reg.* 15,842 (18 April 1991); 56 *Fed. Reg.* 52,214 (18 October 1991).

Literature Cited

Alcorn, D. J., and E. K. Buelna. 1989. The Hawaiian Monk Seal on Laysan Island, 1983. U.S. Department of Commerce, NOAA Technical Memorandum NMFS-SWFSC-124. 46 pp.

Alcorn, D. J., and J. R. Henderson. 1984. Resumption of nursing in "weaned" Hawaiian monk seal pups. 'Elepaio 45:11–12.

Alcorn, D. J., and A. K. H. Kam. 1986. Fatal shark attack on a Hawaiian monk seal (*Monachus schauinslandi*). Marine Mammal Science 3:313–315.

Alcorn, D. J., and R. L. Westlake. 1993. The Hawaiian Monk Seal on Laysan Island, 1986. U.S. Department of Commerce, NOAA Technical Memorandum NMFS-SWFSC-191. 25 pp.

Antonelis, G. A., Jr., C. H. Fiscus, and R. L. DeLong. 1984. Spring and summer prey of California sea lions, *Zalophus californianus,* at San Miguel Island, California, 1978–79. Fishery Bulletin 82:67–76.

Antonelis, G. A., M. S. Lowry, C. H. Fiscus, B. S. Stewart, and R. L. DeLong. 1994. Diet of the northern elephant seal. Pages 211–223 *in* B. J. Le Boeuf and R. M. Laws (eds.), Elephant Seals: Population Ecology, Behavior, and Physiology. University of California Press, Berkeley, CA.

Armstrong, R. W. 1983. Atlas of Hawaii, 2d ed. University of Hawaii Press, Honolulu, HI. 238 pp.

Árnason, Ú., and B. Widegren. 1986. Pinniped phylogeny enlightened by molecular hybridizations using highly repetitive DNA. Molecular Biology and Evolution 3:356–365.

Árnason, Ú., K. Bodin, A. Gullberg, C. Ledje, and S. Mouchaty. 1995. A molecular view of pinniped relationships with particular emphasis on the true seals. Journal of Molecular Evolution 40:78–85.

Bailey, A. M. 1952. The Hawaiian monk seal. Museum Pictorial, Denver Museum of Natural History 7:1–32.

Baillie, J., and B. Groombridge (eds.). 1996. 1996 IUCN Red List of Threatened Animals. International Union for Conservation of Nature and Natural Resouces, Gland, Switzerland. 368 pp. + 2 annexes.

Balazs, G. H., and G. C. Whittow. 1979. First record of a tiger shark observed feeding on a Hawaiian monk seal. 'Elepaio 39:107–109.

Banish, L. D., and W. G. Gilmartin. 1992. Pathological findings in the Hawaiian monk seal. Journal of Wildlife Diseases 28:428–434.

Barnes, L. G., D. P. Domning, and C. E. Ray. 1985. Status of studies on fossil marine mammals. Marine Mammal Science 1:15–53.

Becker, B. L., P. A. Ching, L. M. Hiruki, and S. A. Zur. 1994. The Hawaiian Monk Seal on Laysan Island, 1987 and 1989. U.S. Department of Commerce, NOAA Technical Memorandum NMFS-SWFSC-213. 20 pp.

Becker, B. L., J. R. Klavitter, L. P. Laniawe, W. A. Machado, T. J. Ragen, and M. B. Tarleton. 1995. The Hawaiian monk seal on Laysan Island, 1992. Pages 23–36 *in* T. C. Johanos, L. M. Hiruki, and T. J. Ragen (eds.), The Hawaiian Monk Seal in the Northwestern Hawaiian Islands, 1992. U.S. Department of Commerce, NOAA Technical Memorandum NMFS-SWFSC-216. 128 pp.

Becker, B. L., H. L. Johnston, L. W. Keith, and C. A. Vanderlip. 1996. The Hawaiian monk seal on Laysan Island, 1994. Pages 23–41 *in* T. C. Johanos and T. J. Ragen (eds.), The Hawaiian Monk Seal in the Northwestern Hawaiian Islands, 1994. U.S. Department of Commerce, NOAA Technical Memorandum NMFS-SWFSC-229. 111 pp.

Berta, A., and C. E. Ray. 1990. Skeletal morphology and locomotor capabilities of the archaic pinniped *Enaliarctos mealsi*. Journal of Vertebrate Paleontology 10:141–157.

Berta, A., C. E. Ray, and A. Wyss. 1989. Skeleton of the oldest known pinniped, *Enaliarctos mealsi*. Science 244:60–62.

Boness, D. J. 1990. Fostering behavior in Hawaiian monk seals: Is there a reproductive cost? Behavioral Ecology and Sociobiology 27:113–122.

Bryan, E. H., Jr. 1956. History of Laysan and Midway Islands. Pages 8–13 *in* A. M. Bailey (ed.), Birds of Midway and Laysan Islands. Museum Pictorial, Denver Museum of Natural History 12:1–30.

Bryan, W. A. 1915. The whaling industry. Pages 303–304 *in* Natural History of Hawaii. The Hawaiian Gazette Company, Ltd., Honolulu, HI.

Burkey, T. V. 1995. Extinction rates in archipelagoes: Implications for populations in fragmented habitats. Conservation Biology 9:527–541.

Busch, B. C. 1985. The War against the Seals: A History of the North American Seal Fishery. McGill-Queen's University Press, Kingston and Montreal, Canada. 374 pp.

Caughley, G. 1994. Directions in conservation biology. Journal of Animal Ecology 63:215–244.

Clapp, R. B., and P. W. Woodward. 1972. The natural history of Kure Atoll, Northwestern Hawaiian Islands. Atoll Research Bulletin 164:303–304.

Craig, M. P., D. J. Alcorn, R. G. Forsyth, T. Gerrodette, M. A. Brown, B. K. Choy, L. Dean, L. M. Dennlinger, L. E. Gill, S. S. Keefer, M. M. Lee, J. S. Lennox, C. R. Lorence, G. L. Nakai, and K. R. Neithammer. 1993. The Hawaiian Monk Seal at French Frigate Shoals, 1988–89. U.S. Department of Commerce, NOAA Technical Memorandum NMFS-SWFSC-178. 83 pp.

Craig, M. P., J. L. Megyesi, C. S. Hall, J. L. Glueck, L. P. Laniawe, E. A. Delaney, S. S. Keefer, M. A. McDermond, M. Schulz, G. L. Nakai, B. L. Becker, L. M. Hiruki, and R. J. Morrow. 1994. The Hawaiian Monk Seal at French Frigate Shoals, 1990–91. U.S. Department of Commerce, NOAA Technical Memorandum NMFS-SWFSC-210. 70 pp.

Dailey, M. D., R. V. Santangelo, and W. G. Gilmartin. 1988. A coprological survey of helminth parasites of the Hawaiian monk seal from the Northwestern Hawaiian Islands. Marine Mammal Science 4:125–131.

Davies, J. L. 1958. Pleistocene geography and the distribution of modern pinnipeds. Ecology 39:97–113.

De Jong, W. W. 1982. Eye lens proteins and vertebrate phylogeny. Pages 75–114 *in* M. Goodman (ed.), Macromolecular Sequences in Systematics and Evolutionary Biology. Plenum Press, London.

DeLong, R. L., G. L. Kooyman, W. G. Gilmartin, and T. R. Loughlin. 1984. Hawaiian monk seal diving behavior. Acta Zoologica Fennica 172:129–131.

DeMartini, E. E., F. A. Parrish, and J. D. Parrish. 1993. Temporal changes in reef fish prey populations at French Frigate Shoals, Northwestern Hawaiian Islands: Implications for juvenile monk seal (*Monachus schauinslandi*) predators. Honolulu Laboratory, Southwest Fisheries Science Center, National Marine Fisheries Service, NOAA, Honolulu, HI. Southwest Fisheries Science Center Administrative Report H-93-06. 49 pp.

Dill, H. R., and W. A. Bryan. 1912. Report on an expedition to Laysan Island in 1911. U.S. Department of Agriculture Biological Survey Bulletin 42:1–30.

Dizon, A. E., C. Lockyer, W. F. Perrin, D. P. DeMaster, and J. Sisson. 1992. Rethinking the stock concept: A phylogeographic approach. Conservation Biology 6:24–36.

Eberhardt, L. L., and K. V. Eberhardt. 1994. The Hawaiian monk seal on Midway Atoll, 1994. Honolulu Laboratory, Southwest Fisheries Science Center, National Marine Fisheries Service, NOAA, Honolulu, HI. Southwest Fisheries Science Center Administrative Report H-94-08. 14 pp.

Ehrenfeld, D. W. 1970. Biological Conservation. Holt, Rinehart and Winston of Canada Ltd., Toronto. 226 pp.

Eliason, J. J., and J. R. Henderson. 1992. Hawaiian Monk Seal Observations at French Frigate Shoals, 1984. U.S. Department of Commerce, NOAA Technical Memorandum NMFS-SWFSC-177. 61 pp.

Finn, M. A., and M. A. Rice. 1994. Hawaiian monk seal observations at Necker Island, 1993. `Elepaio 55:7–10.

Finn, M. A., and H. J. Swensen. 1995. The Hawaiian monk seal at Kure Atoll, 1992. Pages 77–90 *in* T. C. Johanos, L. M. Hiruki, and T. J. Ragen (eds.), The Hawaiian Monk Seal in the Northwestern Hawaiian Islands, 1992. U.S. Department of Commerce, NOAA Technical Memorandum NMFS-SWFSC-216. 128 pp.

Fiscus, C. H., A. M. Johnson, and K. W. Kenyon. 1978. Hawaiian monk seal (*Monachus schauinslandi*) survey of the Northwestern (Leeward) Hawaiian Islands, July 1978. Processed report (Available from National Marine Mammal Laboratory, National Marine Fisheries Service, Seattle, WA.) 27 pp.

Flynn, J. J. 1988. Ancestry of sea mammals. Nature 334:383–384.

Frost, K. J., and L. F. Lowry. 1980. Feeding of ribbon seals (*Phoca fasciata*) in the Bering Sea in spring. Canadian Journal of Zoology 58:1601–1607.

Gerrodette, T., and W. G. Gilmartin. 1990. Demographic consequences of changed pupping and hauling sites of the Hawaiian monk seal. Conservation Biology 4:423–430.

Gerrodette, T. M., M. P. Craig, and T. C. Johanos. 1992. Human-assisted fostering of Hawaiian monk seal pups. `Elepaio 52:43–46.

Gilmartin, W. G., and L. L. Eberhardt. 1995. Status of the Hawaiian monk seal (*Monachus schauinslandi*) population. Canadian Journal of Zoology 73:1185–1190.

Gilmartin, W. G., R. L. DeLong, A. W. Smith, L. A. Griner, and M. D. Dailey. 1980. An investigation into unusual mortality in the Hawaiian monk seal, *Monachus schauinslandi*. Pages 32–41 *in* R. W. Grigg and R. T. Pfund (eds.), Proceedings of the Symposium on Status of Resource Investigation in the Northwestern Hawaiian Islands, University of Hawaii, Honolulu, HI. UNIHI-SEAGRANT-MR-80-04.

Gilmartin, W. G., R. J. Morrow, and A. M. Houtman. 1986. Hawaiian Monk Seal Observations and Captive Maintenance Project at Kure Atoll, 1981. U.S. Department of Commerce, NOAA Technical Memorandum NMFS-SWFSC-59. 9 pp.

Gilmartin, W. G., T. C. Johanos-Kam, and L. L. Eberhardt. 1993. Survival rates for the Hawaiian monk seal (*Monachus schauinslandi*). Marine Mammal Science 9:407–420.

Gilpin, M. E., and M. E. Soulé. 1986. Minimum viable populations: Processes of species extinction. Pages 19–34 *in* M. E. Soulé (ed.), Conservation Biology: The Science of Scarcity and Diversity. Sinauer Associates, Inc., Sunderland, MA.

Golvan, Y. J. 1959. Acanthocéphales du genre *Corynosoma* Lühe 1904. Parasites de mammifères d'Alaska et de Midway. Annales Parasitologie Humaine et Compare 34:288–321.

Goodman, D. 1987. Consideration of stochastic demography in the design and management of biological reserves. Natural Resource Modeling 1:205–234.

Hansen, S., D. M. Lavigne, and S. Innes. 1995. Energy metabolism and thermoregulation in juvenile harbor seals (*Phoca vitulina*) in air. Physiological Zoology 68:290–315.

Hanski, I., and M. Gilpin. 1991. Metapopulation dynamics: Brief history and conceptual domain. Pages 3–16 *in* M. Gilpin and I. Hanski (eds.), Metapopulation Dynamics: Empirical and Theoretical Investigations. Academic Press, Harcourt Brace Jovanovich, Publishers, New York, NY.

Henderson, J. R. 1985. A review of Hawaiian monk seal entanglements in marine debris. Pages 326–335 *in* R. S. Shomura and H. O. Yoshida (eds.), Proceedings of the Workshop on the Fate and Impact of Marine Debris. U.S. Department of Commerce, NOAA Technical Memorandum NMFS-SWFSC-54.

Henderson, J. R. 1990. Recent entanglements of Hawaiian monk seals in marine debris. Pages 540–553 *in* R. S. Shomura and M. L. Godfrey (eds.), Proceedings of the Second International Conference on Marine Debris. 2–7 April 1989, Honolulu, HI. U.S. Department of Commerce, NOAA Technical Memorandum NMFS-SWFSC-154.

Henderson, J. R., R. M. Visnak, and J. P. Tavares. 1996. The Hawaiian monk seal at Kure Atoll, 1993. Pages 75–88 *in* T. C. Johanos and T. J. Ragen (eds.), The Hawaiian Monk Seal in the Northwestern Hawaiian Islands, 1993. U.S. Department of Commerce, NOAA Technical Memorandum NMFS-SWFSC-227. 141 pp.

Hiruki, L. M., and T. J. Ragen. 1992. A Compilation of Hawaiian Monk Seal (*Monachus schauinslandi*) counts. U.S. Department of Commerce, NOAA Technical Memorandum NMFS-SWFSC-172. 185 pp.

Hiruki, L. M., W. G. Gilmartin, B. L. Becker, and I. Stirling. 1993. Wounding in Hawaiian monk seals (*Monachus schauinslandi*). Canadian Journal of Zoology 71:458–468.

Hiruki, L. M., I. Stirling, W. G. Gilmartin, T. C. Johanos, and B. L. Becker. 1993. Significance of wounding to female reproductive success in Hawaiian monk seals (*Monachus schauinslandi*) at Laysan Island. Canadian Journal of Zoology 71:469–474.

Israëls, L. D. E. 1992. Thirty years of Mediterranean monk seal protection, a review. Nederlandsche Commissie Voor Internationale Natuurbescherming. Mededelingen No. 28. 65 pp.

Johanos, T. C., and A. K. H. Kam. 1986. The Hawaiian Monk Seal on Lisianski Island: 1983. U.S. Department of Commerce, NOAA Technical Memorandum NMFS-SWFSC-58. 37 pp.

Johanos, T. C., and R. P. Withrow. 1988. Hawaiian Monk Seal and Green Turtle Research on Lisianski Island, 1987. U.S. Department of Commerce, NOAA Technical Memorandum NMFS-SWFSC-121. 18 pp.

Johanos, T. C., A. K. H. Kam, and R. G. Forsyth. 1987. The Hawaiian Monk Seal on Laysan Island: 1984. U.S. Department of Commerce, NOAA Technical Memorandum NMFS-SWFSC-70. 38 pp.

Johanos, T. C., B. L. Becker, M. A. Brown, B. K. Choy, L. M. Hiruki, R. E. Brainard, and R. L. Westlake. 1990. The Hawaiian Monk Seal on Laysan Island, 1988. U.S. Department of Commerce, NOAA Technical Memorandum NMFS-SWFSC-151. 44 pp.

Johanos, T. C., B. L. Becker, and T. J. Ragen. 1994. Annual reproductive cycle of the female Hawaiian monk seal (*Monachus schauinslandi*). Marine Mammal Science 10:13–30.

Johnson, A. M., and E. Kridler. 1983. Interisland movement of Hawaiian monk seals. `Elepaio 44:43–45.

Johnson, A. M., R. L. DeLong, C. H. Fiscus, and K. Kenyon. 1982. Population status of the Hawaiian monk seal (*Monachus schauinslandi*), 1978. Journal of Mammalogy 63:415–421.

Johnson, B. W., and P. A. Johnson. 1978. The Hawaiian monk seal on Laysan Island: 1977. Report No. MMC-77/05. Marine Mammal Commission. (Available from National Technical Information Service, Springfield, VA. PB-285-428.) 38 pp.

Johnson, B. W., and P. A. Johnson. 1981a. The Hawaiian monk seal on Laysan Island: 1978. Report No. MMC-78/15. Marine Mammal Commission. (Available from National Technical Information Service, Springfield, VA. PB-82-109661.) 17 pp.

Johnson, B. W., and P. A. Johnson. 1981b. Estimating the Hawaiian monk seal population on Laysan Island. Report No. MMC-80/06. Marine Mammal Commission. (Available from National Technical Information Service, Springfield, VA. PB-82-106113.) 29 pp.

Johnson, B. W., and P. A. Johnson. 1984. Observations of the Hawaiian Monk Seal on Laysan Island from 1977 through 1980. U.S. Department of Commerce, NOAA Technical Memorandum NMFS-SWFSC-49. 65 pp.

Johnson, P. A., and B. W. Johnson. 1980. Hawaiian Monk Seal Observations on French Frigate Shoals, 1980. U.S. Department of Commerce, NOAA Technical Memorandum NMFS-SWFSC-50. 47 pp.

Johnson, W. M., and D. M. Lavigne. 1995. The Mediterranean Monk Seal: Conservation Guidelines. International Marine Mammal Association Inc., Guelph, Canada. 52 pp.

Kellert, S. R. 1996. The Value of Life: Biological Diversity and Human Society. Island Press, Washington, DC. 263 pp.

Kenyon, K. W. 1972. Man versus the monk seal. Journal of Mammalogy 53:687–696.

Kenyon, K. W. 1973. The Hawaiian Monk Seal. International Union for the Conservation of Nature and Natural Resources, Publications, New Series, Supplemental Paper No. 39: 88–97.

Kenyon, K. W. 1977. Caribbean monk seal extinct. Journal of Mammalogy 58:97–98.

Kenyon, K. W., and D. W. Rice. 1959. Life history of the Hawaiian monk seal. Pacific Science 31:215–252.

Kovacs, K. M., and D. M. Lavigne. 1986. Maternal investment and neonatal growth in phocid seals. Journal of Animal Ecology 55:1035–1051.

Kramer, R. J. 1963. A report on a survey trip to the Hawaiian Islands National Wildlife Refuge, February 1963. Unpublished report, Hawaii State Division of Fish and Game, 10 pp. + appendix. (Available from Protected Species Investigation, National Marine Fisheries Service, Honolulu, HI.)

Kramer, R. J., and J. W. Beardsley. 1962. A report on a survey trip to the Hawaiian Islands National Wildlife Refuge, June 1962. Unpublished report, Hawaii State Division of Fish and Game, 15 pp. (Available from Protected Species Investigation, National Marine Fisheries Service, Honolulu, HI.)

Kretzmann, M. B., W. G. Gilmartin, A. Meyer, G. P. Zegers, S. R. Fain, B. F. Taylor, and D. P. Costa. 1997. Low genetic variability in the Hawaiian monk seal. Conservation Biology 11:482–490.

Laist, D. W., J. M. Coe, and K. J. O'Hara. 1999. Marine debris pollution. (This volume)

Lavigne, D. M. 1999. The Hawaiian monk seal: Management of an endangered species. (This volume)

Lavigne, D. M., R. J. Brooks, D. A. Rosen, and D. A. Galbraith. 1989. Cold, energetics and populations. Pages 403-432 *in* L. C. H. Wang (ed.), Advances in Comparative and Environmental Physiology. Vol. 4. Animal Adaptation to Cold. Springer-Verlag, Berlin.

Lavigne, D. M., V. B. Scheffer, and S. R. Kellert. 1999. The evolution of North American attitudes toward marine mammals. (This volume)

Laws, R. M. 1956. Growth and sexual maturity in aquatic mammals. Nature 178:193–194.

Le Boeuf, B., K. W. Kenyon, and B. Villa-Ramirez. 1986. The Caribbean monk seal is extinct. Marine Mammal Science 2:70–72.

Lisianski, U. 1814. A Voyage round the World in the Years 1803–1806 in the Ship *Neva*. John Booth, London.

Lombard, K. B., B. L. Becker, M. P. Craig, G. C. Spencer, and K. Hague-Bechard. 1994. The Hawaiian Monk Seal on Laysan Island, 1990. U.S. Department of Commerce, NOAA Technical Memorandum NMFS-SWFSC-206. 16 pp.

Lombard, K. B., B. L. Becker, J. R. Klavitter, and P. S. Armstrong. 1996. The Hawaiian monk seal on Laysan Island, 1993. Pages 23–36 *in* T. C. Johanos and T. J. Ragen (eds.), The Hawaiian Monk Seal in the Northwestern Hawaiian Islands, 1993. U.S. Department of Commerce, NOAA Technical Memorandum NMFS-SWFSC-227. 141 pp.

Lowry, L. F., K. J. Frost, and J. J. Burns. 1980. Feeding of bearded seals in the Bering and Chukchi Seas and trophic interaction with Pacific walrus. Arctic 33:330–342.

Lowry, L. F., K. J. Frost, D. G. Calkins, G. L. Swartzmann, and S. Hills. 1982. Feeding habits, food requirements, and status of Bering Sea marine mammals. North Pacific Fisheries Management Council, Anchorage, AK, Document 19. 292 pp.

Macdonald, G. A., A. T. Abbott, and F. L. Peterson. 1983. Volcanoes in the Sea: The Geology of Hawaii, 2d ed. University of Hawaii Press, Honolulu, HI. 517 pp.

Marshall, D. B. 1962. Report of Hawaiian Islands National Wildlife Refuge inspection trip, June 6 through 26, 1962. Unpublished report. (Available from Protected Species Investigation, National Marine Fisheries Service, Honolulu, HI.) 8 pp.

McLaren, I. A. 1960. Are the pinnipedia biphyletic? Systematic Zoology 9:18–28.

McLaren, I. A., and T. G. Smith. 1985. Population ecology of seals: Retrospective and prospective views. Marine Mammal Science 1:54–83.

Mitchell, E. D., and R. H. Tedford. 1973. The Enaliarctinae, a new group of extinct aquatic carnivores and a consideration of the origin of the Otariidae. Bulletin of the American Museum of Natural History 151:201–284.

Muizon, Ch. de. 1982. Phocid phylogeny and dispersal. Annals of the South African Museum 89 (2): 175–213.

Nitta, E. T., and J. R. Henderson. 1993. A review of interactions between Hawaii's fisheries and protected species. Marine Fisheries Review 55:83–92.

Olver, C. H., B. J. Shuter, and C. K. Minns. 1995. Toward a definition of conservation principles for fisheries management. Canadian Journal of Fisheries and Aquatic Sciences 52:1584–1594.

Perez, M. A., and M. A. Bigg. 1986. Diet of northern fur seals, *Callorhinus ursinus,* off western North America. Fishery Bulletin 84:957–971.

Polovina, J. J. 1993. The lobster and shrimp fisheries in Hawaii. Marine Fisheries Review 55 (2): 28–33.

Polovina, J. J., G. T. Mitchum, N. E. Graham, M. P. Craig, E. E. DeMartini, and E. N. Flint. 1994. Physical and biological consequences of a climate event in the central North Pacific. Fisheries Oceanography 3:15–21.

Ragen, T. J., and M. A. Finn. 1996. The Hawaiian monk seal on Necker and Nihoa Islands, 1993. Pages 89–104 *in* T. C. Johanos and T. J. Ragen (eds.), The Hawaiian Monk Seal in the Northwestern Hawaiian Islands, 1993. U.S. Department of Commerce, NOAA Technical Memorandum NMFS-SWFSC-227. 141 pp.

Rausch, R. L. 1969. Diphyllobothriid cestodes from the Hawaiian monk seal, *Monachus schauinslandi* Matschie, from Midway Atoll. Journal of the Fisheries Research Board of Canada 26:947–956.

Ray, C. E. 1976. Geography of phocid evolution. Systematic Zoology 25:391–406.

Reddy, M. L. 1989. Population Monitoring of the Hawaiian Monk Seal, *Monachus schauinslandi,* and Captive Maintenance Project for Female Pups at Kure Atoll, 1987. U.S. Department of Commerce, NOAA Technical Memorandum NMFS-SWFSC-123. 38 pp.

Reddy, M. L., and C. A. Griffith. 1988. Hawaiian Monk Seal Population Monitoring, Pup Captive Maintenance Program, and Incidental Observations of the Green Turtle at Kure Atoll, 1985. U.S. Department of Commerce, NOAA Technical Memorandum NMFS-SWFSC-101. 35 pp.

Reijnders, P., S. Brasseur, J. van der Toorn, P. van der Wolf, I. Boyd, J. Harwood, D. Lavigne, and L. Lowry. 1993. Seals, Fur Seals, Sea Lions, and Walrus. Status Survey and Conservation Action Plan. IUCN/SSC Seal Specialist Group, International Union for Conservation of Nature and Natural Resources, Gland, Switzerland. 88 pp.

Repenning, C. A. 1980. Warm-blooded life in cold ocean currents. Following the evolution of the seal. Oceans 13 (3): 18–24.

Repenning, C. A. 1990. Oldest pinniped. Science 248:499–500.

Repenning, C. A., and C. E. Ray. 1977. The origin of the Hawaiian monk seal. Proceedings of the Biological Society of Washington 89:667–688.

Repenning, C. A., C. E. Ray, and D. Grigorescu. 1979. Pinniped biogeography. Pages 357–369 *in* J. Gray and A. J. Boucet (eds.), Historical Biogeography, Plate Tectonics and the Changing Environment. Oregon State University Press, Corvallis, OR.

Rice, D. W. 1960. Population dynamics of the Hawaiian monk seal. Journal of Mammalogy 41:376–385.

Rice, D. W. 1964. The Hawaiian monk seal: Rare mammal survives in Leeward Islands. Natural History 73 (2): 48–55.

Sarich, V. M. 1969a. Pinniped origins and the rate of evolution of the carnivore albumins. Systematic Zoology 18:286–295.

Sarich, V. M. 1969b. Pinniped phylogeny. Systematic Zoology 18:418–425.

Sarich, V. M. 1975. Pinniped systematics: Immunological comparisons of their albumens and transferrins. American Zoologist 15 (3): 826.

Sarich, V. M. 1976. Transferrin. Transactions of the Zoological Society of London 33:165–171.

Scheffer, V. B. 1958. Seals, Sea Lions, and Walruses: A Review of the Pinnipedia. Stanford University Press, Stanford, CA. 179 pp.

Schlexer, F. V. 1984. Diving Patterns of the Hawaiian Monk Seal, Lisianski Island, 1982. U.S. Department of Commerce, NOAA Technical Memorandum NMFS-SWFSC-41. 4 pp.

Schreiber, F. W., and E. Kridler. 1969. Occurrence of an Hawaiian monk seal (*Monachus schauinslandi*) on Johnston Atoll, Pacific Ocean. Journal of Mammalogy 50:841–842.

Shaffer, M. L. 1981. Minimum population sizes for species conservation. BioScience 31:131–134.

Simon, N. 1966. Red Data Book, Vol. 1. International Union for the Conservation of Nature and Natural Resources, Morges, Switzerland.

Stannard, D. E. 1989. Before the Horror: The Population of Hawai`i on the Eve of Western Contact. University of Hawaii Press, Honolulu, HI.

Starfield, A. M., J. D. Roth, and K. Ralls. 1995. "Mobbing" in Hawaiian monk seals (*Monachus schauinslandi*): The value of simulation modeling in the absence of apparently crucial data. Conservation Biology 9:166–174.

Stewart, B. S., and R. L. DeLong. 1995. Double migration of the northern elephant seal. Journal of Mammalogy 76:196–205.

Stone, H. S. 1984. Hawaiian Monk Seal Population Research, Lisianski Island, 1982. U.S. Department of Commerce, NOAA Technical Memorandum NMFS-SWFSC-47. 33 pp.

Svihla, A. 1959. Notes on the Hawaiian monk seal. Journal of Mammalogy 40:226–229.

Tedford, R. H. 1976. Relationship of pinnipeds to other carnivores (Mammalia). Systematic Zoology 25:363–374.

Van Toorenburg, R. A., W. G. Gilmartin, and J. R. Henderson. 1993. Composition of the Hawaiian monk seal population at Kure Atoll, 1990. Pacific Science 47:211–214.

Westlake, R. L., and W. G. Gilmartin. 1990. Hawaiian monk seal pupping locations in the Northwestern Hawaiian Islands. Pacific Science 44:366–383.

Westlake, R. L., and P. J. Siepmann. 1988. Hawaiian Monk Seal and Green Turtle Research on Lisianski Island, 1986. U.S. Department of Commerce, NOAA Technical Memorandum NMFS-SWFSC-119. 18 pp.

Wetherall, J. A., W. R. Haight, and G. T. DiNardo. 1995. Computation of the preliminary 1995 catch quota for the Northwestern Hawaiian Islands lobster fishery. Honolulu Laboratory, Southwest Fisheries Science Center, National Marine Fisheries Service, NOAA, Honolulu, HI. Southwest Fisheries Science Center Administrative Report H-95-04. 35 pp.

Wetmore, A. 1925. Bird life among lava rock and coral sand. The National Geographic Magazine 48 (1): 77–108.

Whittow, G. C., G. H. Balazs, and G. D. Schmidt. 1980. Parasitic ulceration of the stomach in a Hawaiian monk seal (*Monachus schauinslandi*). `Elepaio 39:83–84.

Wirtz, W. O., II. 1968. Reproduction, growth and development, and juvenile mortality in the Hawaiian monk seal. Journal of Mammalogy 49:229–238.

Withers, N. W. 1982. Ciguatera fish poisoning. Annual Review of Medicine 33:97–111.

Woodside, D. H., and R. J. Kramer. 1961. A report on a survey trip to the Hawaiian Islands National Wildlife Refuge, March 1961. Unpublished report, Hawaii State Division of Fish and Game. (Available from Protected Species Investigation, National Marine Fisheries Service, Honolulu, HI.) 30 pp.

Wyss, A. R. 1987. The walrus auditory region and the monophyly of pinnipeds. American Museum of Natural History Novitates 2871:1–31.

Wyss, A. R. 1988. Evidence from flipper structure for a single origin of pinnipeds. Nature 334:427–428.

Wyss, A. R. 1989. Flippers and pinniped phylogeny: Has the problem of convergence been overrated? Marine Mammal Science 5:343–375.

11

DAVID M. LAVIGNE

The Hawaiian Monk Seal

Management of an Endangered Species

In 1976 the National Marine Fisheries Service designated the Hawaiian monk seal (*Monachus schauinslandi*) as depleted under the Marine Mammal Protection Act.[1] At the recommendation of the Marine Mammal Commission, the species was also declared endangered under the Endangered Species Act.[2]

Since that time, the Hawaiian monk seal has been the focus of intensive research and management activities. Considerable progress has been made in understanding its life history, assessing trends and dynamics of individual island subpopulations, enhancing the subpopulation at Kure Atoll, balancing the adult sex ratio at Laysan Island, and addressing direct interactions with the pelagic longline fishery (Ragen and Lavigne, this volume). Nevertheless, vital information is still lacking on the species' marine ecology and foraging patterns, the full extent of interactions with fisheries (e.g., entanglement or competition for prey), the overall health and condition of animals in the different island subpopulations, their susceptibility to biotoxins, and so on. Total abundance of the species continues to decline (Ragen and Lavigne, this volume), and, clearly, management cannot be deemed a success unless the decline is reversed and the species recovers—using today's criteria—to something approaching the optimum sustainable population level as defined under the Marine Mammal Protection Act (see Baur et al., this volume).

In today's world, wildlife management aimed at achieving such a conservation objective requires not only an understanding of the biology of the target species, but also an understanding of the human environment in which management decisions are made. That human environment is determined, at least in part, by social, economic, ethical, and political values that may conflict with and, ultimately, compromise conservation efforts (Reeves et al. 1992). I begin this chapter, therefore, with an examination of the bureaucratic framework within which the management of Hawaiian monk seals occurs. I then review and assess the management actions that have taken place over the past 20 years to stop the species' decline and promote its recovery, examine impediments to the management process, and discuss what else might be attempted to save the species from extinction.

The Management Bureaucracy

Management of the Hawaiian monk seal is undoubtedly simplified because the species lives exclusively within the jurisdiction of one sovereign country, the United States. Management remains complicated, nonetheless, by the involvement of several government agencies at the federal and state levels, as well as a number of commissions, committees, and nongovernmental organizations, each of which has different responsibilities and different and potentially conflicting institutional objectives. The main participants are described briefly:

National Marine Fisheries Service, U.S. Department of Commerce

In addition to its mandate for fishery management, the National Marine Fisheries Service is the lead agency responsible for the conservation and management of the Hawaiian monk seal. Since the early 1980s it has conducted most of the research on the species. Within the Fisheries Service, responsibilities are distributed among an array of offices and divisions (Fig. 11-1).

Hawaiian Monk Seal Recovery Team

The director of the Service's Southwest Region appoints the Hawaiian Monk Seal Recovery Team, as required under the Endangered Species Act of 1973. The original recovery team was appointed in 1980 to prepare a recovery plan and to identify critical habitat. The plan was completed in 1983, and the team, as then constituted, held its last meeting in 1984. A second team was appointed but never met. In 1989 the team was reconstituted and reconvened, and it has met annually since then. Its primary function has been to review management and research activities aimed at species recovery and to make recommendations to the director.

U.S. Marine Mammal Commission

The Marine Mammal Commission regularly reviews the status and management of marine mammal stocks and makes recommendations to promote their protection and conservation. With respect to the Hawaiian monk seal, the Commission identifies important management and research activities, makes recommendations to the National Marine Fisheries Service and various other agencies, and facilitates interactions among all involved parties. Since 1979 the Commission also has been instrumental in identifying and advising Congress on funding needs for monk seal research and management.

Fish and Wildlife Service, U.S. Department of the Interior

The Fish and Wildlife Service manages the Hawaiian Islands National Wildlife Refuge and the Midway Atoll National Wildlife Refuge, which together include the

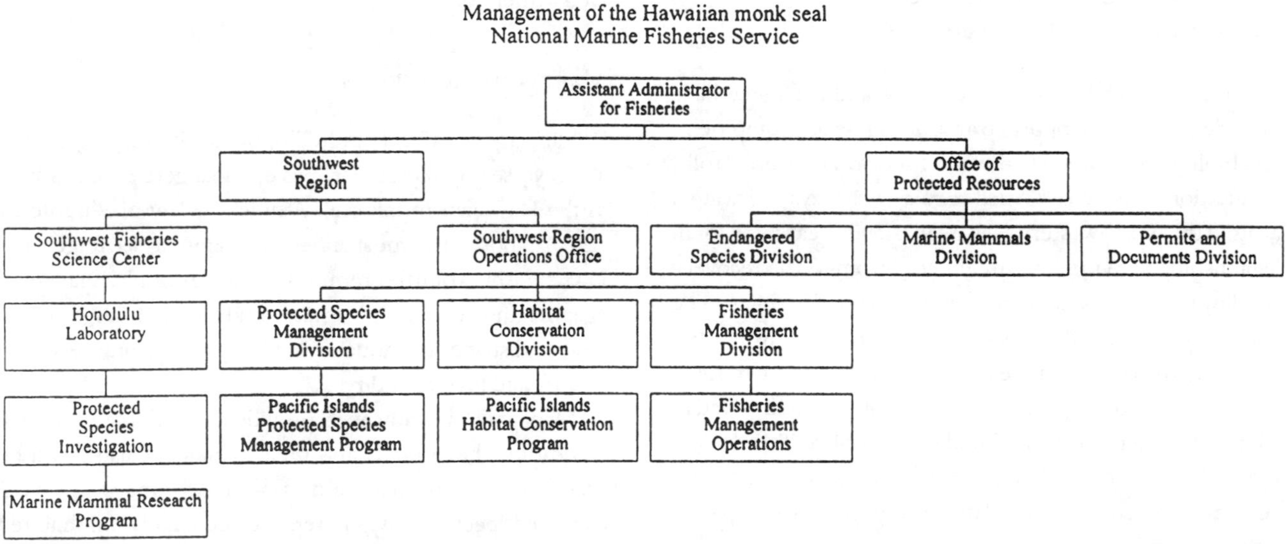

Figure 11-1. Organizational structure of the National Marine Fisheries Service as it pertains to the study and management of the Hawaiian monk seal. Virtually all research and management that directly affects the seals is conducted by the Marine Mammal Research Program (lower left), under the direction of the Honolulu Laboratory Director and, in turn, the Director of the Southwest Fisheries Science Center. The Pacific Islands Protected Species Management Program, Pacific Islands Habitat Conservation Program, and Fisheries Management Operations manage human activities that affect monk seals. Three divisions within the Office of Protected Resources oversee research and management of the species. The Endangered Species Division and the Marine Mammals Division review budgets for monk seal research and management, prepare biological opinions on issues such as the potential impact of fisheries, and interact with outside agencies on issues that may affect monk seals. The Permits and Documents Division authorizes all proposed research and management activities that directly involve or affect the seals.

majority of islands and atolls currently used by monk seals. Its primary goal is to maintain the ecosystems of the Northwestern Hawaiian Islands. Generally, the Fish and Wildlife Service and the National Marine Fisheries Service cooperate on logistical operations throughout the Hawaiian Archipelago.

Western Pacific Regional Fishery Management Council

Fisheries in the exclusive economic zone (from 3 to 200 nautical miles [5.55 to 370 km] offshore) around the Hawaiian Islands are managed by the National Marine Fisheries Service based on the advice of the Western Pacific Regional Fishery Management Council. The Council, established by the Magnuson-Stevens Fishery Conservation and Management Act of 1976, consists of members from territorial, state, and federal governments with fisheries authority and representatives of the fishing community. Its stated goal is to conserve fishery resources while allowing fishing at sustainable levels. The Council participates in the management of the Hawaiian monk seal through the development of management plans that regulate fishing activity in regions where interactions with monk seals may occur.

U.S. Coast Guard, Navy, Air Force, and Army Corps of Engineers

Recently, the U.S. Coast Guard, Navy, and Air Force have provided logistic support, transporting seals, equipment, and biologists between Oahu and Midway and Kure Atolls. In addition, the Coast Guard regularly surveys the waters around the Northwestern Hawaiian Islands, searching for illegal fishing activities that might compromise the recovery of Hawaiian monk seals or other protected species. The Navy is completing the process of cleaning up Midway Atoll following the closure of the Naval Air Facility there in 1993. The Army Corps of Engineers has recently been involved in a long-delayed project to rebuild the seawall at Tern Island, French Frigate Shoals. This project, which is essential to prevent erosion of the island and its runway, must be completed if the Fish and Wildlife Service is to maintain its refuge station at this important site.

State of Hawaii

The state of Hawaii owns and manages Kure Atoll and issues permits for field activities, including those of the National Marine Fisheries Service, at the atoll. A state biologist serves as a member of the Hawaiian Monk Seal Recovery Team.

Sea Life Park, Inc.

Since 1989 Sea Life Park, Inc., in Hawaii has provided facilities, supplies, personnel, and expertise to rehabilitate undersized monk seal pups as part of an effort to reduce mortality in the wild (see below). In addition, the park permanently houses a number of adult seals (currently five). These animals have served as research subjects, and several have been placed on public display.

Waikiki Aquarium, University of Hawaii

Seals have also been held in captivity at the University of Hawaii's Waikiki Aquarium. Although the aquarium participated in rehabilitation efforts in the 1980s, its current efforts are directed toward research and public education.

Captive Care Committee

The director of the National Marine Fisheries Service's Honolulu Laboratory appoints a Captive Care Committee to provide recommendations and guidelines for the care and study of Hawaiian monk seals in captivity. The guidelines are to ensure that all activities are in compliance with the U.S. Animal Welfare Act; they supplement those issued by the Animal and Plant Health Inspection Service of the U.S. Department of Agriculture.

Management Actions

Wildlife agencies have limited options when trying to stop and reverse population declines of endangered species such as the Hawaiian monk seal. A quick review of Ehrenfeld's (1970) hypothetical most endangered animal (see Ragen and Lavigne, this volume) reminds us, for example, that managers cannot change the monk seal's large body size, restricted distribution, aquatic mating strategy, long gestation period, and low fecundity.

Managers can, however, provide and enforce legal protection for the animals and their habitats. This should be easier for the Hawaiian monk seal than for many other endangered species: it lives in remote and largely uninhabited areas under the jurisdiction of one country, which has a marine mammal protection act and, arguably, the most enlightened endangered species legislation anywhere. Compare this situation, for example, with that of the Mediterranean monk seal, which not only lives in several countries and disputed territories but also moves back and forth across international boundaries.

Managers can also facilitate scientific research and monitoring to learn more about the problems facing the endangered species and to provide a basis for implementing remedial management actions. Often managers can undertake a variety of steps to enhance additions to the population (reproduction) and to reduce losses (mortality). They can also attempt to regulate or prohibit human activities that may potentially harm the endangered species. In the case of Hawaiian monk seals, such activities include military operations, commercial fishing, recreational pursuits (e.g., tourism), and the disposal or loss of marine debris (see Laist et al. this volume).

Against this framework, I now review management actions that have been taken to date.

Legal Protection

In marked contrast to many jurisdictions, the United States requires that certain federal agencies undertake specific actions on behalf of species designated as endangered. Required actions in the case of monk seals include research and monitoring, the appointment of a recovery team, the designation of critical habitat, and consultation with the National Marine Fisheries Service whenever actions taken by another federal agency might affect monk seals or their habitat. Further protection is provided by federal regulations applicable to the Hawaiian Islands National Wildlife Refuge, the Midway Atoll National Wildlife Refuge, and fisheries in the vicinity of the Northwestern Hawaiian Islands (see the section on habitat protection below).

Development of a Recovery Plan

The first Hawaiian Monk Seal Recovery Team met in 1980 to develop a Hawaiian monk seal recovery plan (Gilmartin 1983). The plan emphasized (1) the identification and mitigation of factors causing decreased survival and productivity; (2) the characterization of habitat, including foraging areas; (3) the assessment and monitoring of population trends; (4) the documentation and mitigation of negative effects from human activities; (5) the implementation of conservation-oriented management actions; and (6) the development of educational programs.

Two subsequent three-year work plans have been developed (Gilmartin 1990, 1993). These emphasized the importance of (1) mitigating the effects of mobbing behavior at Laysan and Lisianski Islands; (2) monitoring of the main reproductive subpopulations, (3) facilitating the recovery of monk seals at Pearl and Hermes Reef and Midway and Kure Atolls, (4) implementing a research and management plan for French Frigate Shoals (Gilmartin 1993), and (5) analysis and publication of data.

Habitat Protection

Designation of "critical habitat" for the Hawaiian monk seal was first recommended by the Marine Mammal Commission in 1975. In 1980 the National Marine Fisheries Service completed a draft environmental impact statement that proposed that critical habitat extend out to the 10-fathom (18.3-m) isobath adjacent to pupping and haul-out islands.

The following year, 1981, the Service reviewed and submitted a biological opinion on a combined fishery management plan, environmental impact statement, and regulatory analysis for the spiny lobster fisheries of the western Pacific region. The lobster fishery began in the Northwestern Hawaiian Islands during the late 1970s (Ragen and Lavigne, this volume) and created a potential source of direct and indirect fishery interactions with protected species such as the Hawaiian monk seal and the green turtle (*Chelonia mydas*). To minimize such interactions, the management plan (1) prohibited fishing in waters less than 10 fathoms (18.3 m) deep in the fishery conservation zone[3] of the Northwestern Hawaiian Islands and within 20 nautical miles (37 km) of Laysan Island, (2) required permits for fishing and the reporting of catch and effort data, and (3) provided a mechanism for evaluating and responding to interactions involving monk seal mortality.

A supplemental environmental impact statement to designate critical habitat for the Hawaiian monk seal was prepared by the Fisheries Service in 1984. It also proposed to include the major haul-out and pupping islands and surrounding waters out to the 10-fathom (18.3-m) isobath.

In 1986 a master plan/environmental impact statement of the Hawaiian Islands National Wildlife Refuge was completed by the Fish and Wildlife Service. This plan provided essential protection of the majority of islands and atolls inhabited by the Hawaiian monk seal.

In the same year, the National Marine Fisheries Service prepared a biological opinion on a combined draft fishery management plan, environmental assessment, and regulatory impact review for the bottomfish and seamount groundfish fisheries in the western Pacific Ocean. Among other actions, this plan prohibited the use of bottom trawls, bottom-set gillnets, explosives, and poisons in the fishery conservation zone, and established a permit requirement for fishing for bottomfish in the fishery conservation zone of the Northwestern Hawaiian Islands, including an allowance for experimental fishery permits.

As with the lobster fishery, the bottomfish and seamount fisheries created a potential source of direct and indirect interactions with monk seals. Accordingly, the Marine Mammal Commission recommended that the plan be amended to provide for monitoring and verification of interaction rates with Hawaiian monk seals and other protected species. Amendment 4 of this plan established a protected species zone extending out 50 nautical miles (92.5 km) from the Northwestern Hawaiian Islands and gave the National Marine Fisheries Service authority to place observers on vessels planning to fish within the zone.[4]

The Fisheries Service also submitted a biological opinion on a fishery management plan for the pelagic fisheries of the western Pacific region in 1986. This plan prohibited foreign longline vessels from fishing within 100 nautical miles (185 km) of the Northwestern Hawaiian Islands. Foreign longliners wishing to fish in the remaining open areas of the fishery conservation zone were required to submit effort plans, obtain permits, carry observers when requested, and report data on catch, effort, and interactions with marine mammals and sea turtles. The plan prohibited all drift gillnetting in the fishery conservation zone, except for fishing by domestic vessels with an experimental fishery permit; these vessels were also required to collect and submit data on catch, effort, and interactions with sea turtles and marine mammals.

Critical habitat for Hawaiian monk seals was finally designated in 1986. It included all beach areas, lagoon waters, and ocean waters out to a depth of 10 fathoms (18.3 m) around Kure Atoll, Midway Atoll (except Sand Island), Pearl and Hermes Reef, Lisianski Island, Laysan Island, Gardner Pinnacles, French Frigate Shoals (Fig. 11-2), Necker Island, and Nihoa Island;[5] for locations, see Ragen and Lavigne (this volume, Fig. 10-1). Because of concerns raised by the Marine Mammal Commission and the Hawaiian Monk Seal Recovery Team, and the threat of legal action by Greenpeace International and the Sierra Club Legal Defense Fund, the National Marine Fisheries Service reopened the comment period on critical habitat. In 1988 the definition of critical habitat was extended to include Maro Reef and waters around existing habitat out to the 20-fathom (36.6-m) isobath.[6]

New threats to the habitat of the Hawaiian monk seal have required attention in recent years. First, the pelagic longline fishery in Hawaiian waters grew from approximately 37 vessels in 1987 to approximately 140 in 1990 (Ito 1992). The rapid growth of the fishery raised concern that monk seal interactions with longline operations would increase. In May 1990 unconfirmed reports suggested that such interactions were indeed occurring.

In August 1990 the Western Pacific Regional Fishery

Figure 11-2. A monk seal in an underwater coral reef cave at French Frigate Shoals, 1991. (Photograph © Bill Curtsinger)

Management Council recommended an emergency action under its bottomfish and pelagic fisheries management plans. In November 1990 the National Marine Fisheries Service published an emergency rule[7] requiring that (1) longline vessels obtain permits from the Fisheries Service (permits were already required for vessels fishing for bottomfish), (2) both longline and bottomfish vessels provide daily logs with information on their interactions with monk seals and other protected species, (3) these vessels notify the Fisheries Service before fishing within 50 nautical miles (92.5 km) of the Northwestern Hawaiian Islands and accept an observer on board if so requested by the Fisheries Service, and (4) longline operators attend an orientation meeting to learn about procedures for protecting endangered and threatened species.

By January 1991 seals at French Frigate Shoals were observed with injuries, including embedded longline hooks and head injuries suggesting the possibility of clubbing, providing evidence of further interactions. The Western Pacific Regional Fishery Management Council recommended a moratorium on pelagic longline fishing within a protected species zone extending 50 nautical miles (92.5 km) around the Northwestern Hawaiian Islands and corridors between the islands. In April 1991 the National Marine Fisheries Service published emergency rules establishing such a protected species zone, and in October 1991 the rules were made permanent.[8]

Two unresolved but important issues involving habitat protection include the reconstruction of the seawall at Tern Island (the only inhabited island at French Frigate Shoals) and the management of Midway Atoll.

During World War II, the U.S. Navy dredged the area around Tern Island to enlarge the island and build a runway. The enlarged island and runway were secured by a seawall built around the island, but the seawall has deteriorated, creating an entrapment hazard for wildlife and threatening the loss of the runway and, eventually, the Fish and Wildlife Service's Refuge Station on the island. Among other things, this runway and station have facilitated monk seal research and the recovery activities at French Frigate Shoals and provided an emergency air evacuation site for injured fishermen. Because of the declining status of the local monk seal subpopulation, the repair or reconstruction of the seawall and the maintenance of the runway and the refuge station are generally considered vital to further research and management activities at the site. To date, however, little progress has been made.

Midway Atoll, at one time the site of a monk seal breeding colony (Ragen and Lavigne, this volume), is located between the only two currently growing subpopulations (Kure Atoll and Pearl and Hermes Reef). The proximity of the sites and the movement of seals among islands suggest that disruptive human activities at Midway could have a detrimental effect on neighboring subpopulations. The control and management of Midway is, therefore, vital to Hawaiian monk seal conservation. The Navy recently closed its facility at Midway and in 1997 gave control of the atoll to the Fish and Wildlife Service. The National Marine Fisheries Service maintains a refuge station at the site, in cooperation with a privately owned company that supports the station, in part, through tourism. I will return to the latter development in the final section of the chapter.

Research and Monitoring

Scientific investigations, which began in the 1950s, verified that the species had recovered (to some unknown degree) from the low point at the turn of the century (Kenyon and Rice 1959; Rice 1960, 1964; Wirtz 1968) and provided an important baseline for measuring its subsequent decline. More intensive investigation of the natural history of the species and its decline began shortly after the species was declared endangered.

In the mid- to late 1970s, most research on Hawaiian monk seals was supported by the Marine Mammal Commission, and in 1978 the Commission sponsored a workshop to identify research needs. The workshop resulted in a five-year work plan to address a list of important research questions (Kenyon 1978), which were revisited in the subsequent development of the recovery plan (Gilmartin 1983).

Field studies were conducted at Laysan Island from 1977 to 1980 under contracts from the Marine Mammal Commission (Johnson and Johnson 1978, 1981a,b, 1984), and additional research, sponsored by the Fish and Wildlife Service, was conducted at Kure Atoll in 1977 and 1978 (Johnson et al. 1982). These studies began to provide essential information on the life history, behavior, and status of monk seals at those sites.

The Commission sponsored a second workshop in 1978 to review and plan management and research priorities. This was followed by a third workshop in 1980 to review the 1978 die-off at Laysan Island (Johnson and Johnson 1981a, 1984; Ragen and Lavigne, this volume) and to develop a contingency plan for responding to future mass mortalities (Gilmartin 1987).

In addition to investigating the 1978 die-off (Gilmartin et al. 1980), a number of other research projects were undertaken, including studies of hematology and serum chemistry of 12 weaned pups (Banish and Gilmartin 1988) and parasitology (Golvan 1959, Rausch 1969, Furman and

Dailey 1980, Whittow et al. 1980, Dailey et al. 1988). However, with two exceptions—a survey of parasites in fecal samples (Dailey et al. 1988) and the examination of 19 juvenile seals at French Frigate Shoals in 1992 (T. Ragen, pers. comm.)—no systematic health surveys of Hawaiian monk seals have been conducted.

In 1980 the National Marine Fisheries Service began annual studies at Lisianski Island, and similar investigations were initiated at Laysan Island and Kure Atoll in 1981 and at French Frigate Shoals and Pearl and Hermes Reef in 1982. These studies have been based largely on the identification of individual animals, using flipper tags and natural markings (e.g., scars). One study, initiated in 1982, indicated that flipper tagging did not have significant effects on weaned pups (Henderson and Johanos 1988). Thereafter, most weaned pups at the main reproductive sites have been tagged (Fig. 11-3).

The research conducted each year at these sites was designed (1) to provide demographic and natural history information such as population size and composition, reproduction, survival, growth, foraging patterns, and behavior, and (2) to detect problems impeding recovery, such as entanglement in debris, fishery interactions, and other causes of mortality (e.g., mobbing).

Extensive research has been directed at the mobbing problem (see the section on attempts to reduce mortality, below). Related field studies have focused on the reproductive behavior of adult seals and mobbing-related injuries (Hiruki, Gilmartin et al. 1993; Hiruki, Stirling et al. 1993). In addition, several captive studies have examined questions related to reproductive physiology (e.g., Atkinson and Gilmartin 1992, Atkinson et al. 1993).

Attempts to Enhance Survival and Reproduction

The rehabilitation and translocation of undersized or otherwise unfit juvenile seals has been one of the few options available for managers to intervene directly to promote Hawaiian monk seal recovery. In 1981 the National Marine Fisheries Service initiated a "captive maintenance project" designed to restore the then-depleted subpopulation at Kure Atoll (Gilmartin et al. 1986). The project became known as the "headstart program," and its objective was to enhance the survival of young females and thereby increase their subsequent recruitment into the adult female population.

From 1981 to 1991, 32 weaned female pups at Kure Atoll were captured and temporarily held (from weeks to several months) in a shoreline enclosure, where they were protected from sharks, aggressive adult males, and human disturbance that would force them into waters where such threats existed. During their temporary captivity, weanlings were able to develop independent feeding skills in relative safety. After release, 26 (81%) of these females survived to the end of their first year. Based on these data alone, the headstart program appears to have been an unqualified success. However, of 33 males weaned during the same period but not held in the enclosure, 27 (82%) survived to the end of their first year, suggesting that placement in the enclosure did not enhance survival. Rather, new Coast Guard regulations, and educational and enforcement efforts by the National Marine Fisheries Service, reduced disturbance and apparently increased survival of both females and males.

The Fisheries Service supplemented its headstart program with another program involving the rescue, rehabilitation, and translocation of undersized female monk seals

Figure 11-3. A newly weaned monk seal pup being tagged at French Frigate Shoals while an adult seal (its mother?) looks on, 1991. (Photograph © Bill Curtsinger)

from French Frigate Shoals. Of 54 immature females taken from French Frigate Shoals and released at Kure Atoll between 1985 and 1995 (see Ragen and Lavigne, this volume), 49 were initially rehabilitated in some manner whereas 5 were transferred directly from French Frigate Shoals to Kure Atoll. First-year survival for these females (pooled into a single group) was at least 66% (31 / 47; survival of seven released in 1995 had not been determined at the time of this writing). Collectively, the above restoration efforts augmented immature size classes on Kure (Ragen and Lavigne, this volume), enhanced reproductive recruitment, and returned the adult sex ratio to a presumably normal level of ca. 1:1 (Van Toorenburg et al. 1993).

The females introduced to the Kure subpopulation were taken from French Frigate Shoals because this subpopulation appeared to be food-limited and the survival of undersized, weaned females (i.e., those selected for rehabilitation and translocation) was thought to be sufficiently low to justify intervention. In the 1990s, however, survival of all immature seals at French Frigate Shoals plummeted, resulting in a severe loss of reproductive potential in that subpopulation (Ragen and Lavigne, this volume). In an attempt to reduce this loss, rehabilitation efforts were increased. Because the Kure subpopulation apparently was growing, the release site for rehabilitated seals was shifted to Midway Atoll. Twenty-four immature females were collected in 1991 and 1992. These seals were in poor condition and were judged likely to perish without intervention. After capture, they were held in captivity and force-fed to increase or at least maintain their mass. All of them underwent some form of rehabilitation, either on Midway or on Oahu, or both. Eighteen of the animals survived captivity and were released at Midway between May 1992 and January 1993. For reasons not yet determined, 16 of the 18 either died or disappeared. Translocations in 1993 through 1995 were, therefore, directed back to Kure.

In 1995 12 weaned female pups were taken from French Frigate Shoals to a rehabilitation facility on Oahu. Nine of the 12 seals developed an eye ailment with potentially serious complications, including temporary but severe visual impairment. Two of the animals died early in 1997 and eight of the remaining ten have developed cataracts and are considered functionally blind (T. Ragen, pers. comm.). The cause of the eye ailment and its presence in nature have not been determined, and it seems unlikely that these seals can ever be returned to the wild.

Attempts to Reduce Mortality

Management has also directed considerable effort toward reduction of mortality due to mobbing by adult males. Mobbing was first observed in 1978 (Johnson and Johnson 1981a), but injuries consistent with such behavior were noted earlier (Walker 1964, Kridler 1966, Wirtz 1968, Olsen 1969, DeLong et al. 1976, Johnson and Johnson 1978).

Mobbing was listed as a limiting factor and a threat to the species in the 1983 recovery plan (Gilmartin 1983). In the fall of 1984, 10 adult males were removed from Laysan Island to assess the feasibility of one possible management solution to the mobbing problem: the physical removal of males from affected subpopulations. One of the males died before release, and the remaining nine were released at Johnston Atoll. However, all nine subsequently disappeared; the last confirmed sighting was in March 1986 (T. C. Johanos, pers. comm.).

Throughout the 1980s and early 1990s field research was conducted on adult reproductive behavior to examine if, and to what extent, male breeding is influenced by a dominance hierarchy, and to determine if the behavior patterns of individual males (other than their participation in mobbings) could be used to separate them into behavioral types that are more or less inclined to be involved in mobbing (i.e., mobbers versus nonmobbers).

In 1987 a workshop was held to develop a plan for managing the mobbing problem (Gilmartin and Alcorn 1987). That same year, five more males were captured at Laysan Island and transported to Oahu, where they were kept in permanent captivity. These males had been observed participating in mobbing and were collected to provide subjects for studies of mobbing behavior and mitigation. The seasonal pattern of testosterone levels in the blood (Atkinson and Gilmartin 1992) and the reduction of testosterone levels following drug treatment (Atkinson et al. 1993) were investigated.

Large-scale removals of adult males from Laysan Island were considered in 1992 and 1993, but were not possible because of lack of funding. Computer modeling studies (Ralls and Starfield 1995, Starfield et al. 1995) supported the option of male removal, and in 1993 a workshop was held to review methods of selecting males for removal. In 1994, 22 adult males were captured at Laysan Island and translocated to the main Hawaiian Islands (Ragen and Lavigne, this volume). The effects of this removal on the incidence of mobbing are still being assessed.

Mobbing is also considered a major impediment to recovery of the Lisianski subpopulation. As of mid-1997, however, the extent of mobbing at this site had not been fully assessed—again, because of funding constraints—and no remedial action had been undertaken.

Other actions designed to reduce monk seal mortality have been the opportunistic freeing of seals entangled in fishing gear and the clearing of potentially entangling debris from island beaches (Henderson 1985, 1990). The importance of such actions cannot be underestimated, because entanglement may be as serious a problem as mobbing at Lisianski Island as well as being a problem elsewhere in the Northwestern Hawaiian Islands (Laist et al., this volume). The mere presence of biologists in the field also deters disturbance of the seals on inhabited islands and on uninhabited islands that are occasionally visited by humans.

Impediments to Management Success

The above review of management actions aimed at recovery of the Hawaiian monk seal reveals a number of accomplishments. Extensive information has been collected on the natural history of the species and on the demographic trends of its main subpopulations (Ragen and Lavigne, this volume). (Compare this situation, for example, with the lack of specific information currently available for Mediterranean monk seals; for a recent review, see Israëls 1992.) Cooperative efforts with the U.S. Coast Guard and Sea Life Park seem to have stopped the decline at Kure Atoll and stimulated an increase in the number of seals at that site. The establishment of the protected species zone around the Northwestern Hawaiian Islands has reduced the potential for direct fishery interactions. And the adult sex ratio at Laysan Island was recently brought close to 1:1 with the aim of reducing mobbing-related mortality.

The fact remains, however, that the species continues to decline. In 1958 969 seals (excluding pups) were tallied in beach counts at Kure Atoll, Pearl and Hermes Reef, Lisianski and Laysan Islands, and French Frigate Shoals (Rice 1960). In 1985 the mean beach counts at these locations totaled 509 animals. By 1995 the number was 383. Viewed on an ecological timescale and from the perspective of the entire species, these numbers suggest that the Hawaiian monk seal is rapidly disappearing. If this perspective is meaningful, then it is both instructive and important to consider the obstacles to management efforts to promote species recovery. Demographic trends and the problems of individual subpopulations have been considered in the previous chapter (see Ragen and Lavigne, this volume). Here I focus on the obstacles to management itself, beginning with some general comments on wildlife management as a human endeavor. Such comments provide a backdrop against which to evaluate resource management decisions generally and the recent history of Hawaiian monk seal management in particular.

The "Wildlife Management" Framework

When I first typed this subtitle, I could almost hear the echo of Sidney Holt's opening remarks to the United Nations Food and Agriculture Organization's Consultation on the Biology and Management of Marine Mammals, held in Bergen, Norway, in 1976: "Although we might wish to *manage* wild marine animals or their environment, as yet we don't know how. What perhaps we humans can *manage* are our own activities which affect the marine mammals, to our own ultimate benefit or harm" (Holt 1978:263). Holt's remark encapsulates, I suggest, a universal impediment to marine mammal management: the deeply entrenched myth—some have called it arrogance—that we humans actually know how to manage wild populations or ecosystems (Lavigne 1996). There is a wealth of evidence to the contrary, and a dose of humility might go a long way to improving management institutions and the management process itself.

Implicit in Holt's comment is another truism. Management of endangered species, like wildlife management generally, is not a precise science. In the words of Aldo Leopold (1933), it is "an Art." Management does not occur in the controlled environment of a scientific laboratory but in the stochastic and often unpredictable "worlds" of nature and human society. Different elements of society—including various bureaucracies involved directly in the management process—frequently have inherently different and conflicting objectives regarding the management of marine mammals, including endangered species such as the Hawaiian monk seal (Table 11-1). Management decisions are influenced, therefore, not only by scientific concerns, but also by sociocultural, economic, ethical, legal, and political considerations (Fig. 11-4) (also see Reeves et al. 1992). And ultimately management decisions are made by politicians, not scientists. It is for reasons such as these that management decisions regarding Hawaiian monk seals have not always seemed to correspond with the principal objective of saving the species from extinction. On many occasions, conflicting objectives have taken precedence, as we shall see below.

The Nature of Bureaucracies

Two other general problems involve the structure and function of bureaucracies (e.g., government agencies) that have a mandate to "manage" wildlife, including endangered species. Having read the earlier section on the management bureaucracy, one anonymous reviewer was moved to comment specifically on the "ponderous Byzantine, complicated bureaucracy that oversees actions relating to the Hawaiian monk seal. . . . This specter," the reviewer continued, "left me with the feeling that there was no hope for saving the monk seal from extinction . . . [a] conclusion [that] should be obvious to all readers." Presumably, the reviewer was referring to the array of agencies and organizations, each with its own particular values and objectives, currently involved in Hawaiian monk seal management.

But this is only part of the story. The other part has to do with the "culture" of organizational systems, such as those involved in Hawaiian monk seal management. This is a subject that is usually not dealt with in textbooks on fisheries and wildlife management. To gain some important insights, every student should read Reeves et al.'s (1992) "Ethical questions for resource managers," published—to its credit—by the U.S. Department of Agriculture.

By their very nature, bureaucratic systems are not designed to evaluate critically their actions and to take appropriate steps to rectify any problems that might be identified. Rather such systems are designed to avoid controversy and value-based conflicts (Lichatowich 1992). In other words, there is considerable pressure on individuals within a bureaucratic system to conform.

Within such a system, the role of scientists is simply to provide scientific advice to managers. Most young scientists entering such a system are understandably concerned primarily with "career consolidation" (Erickson 1950); they are anxious for promotion; they are usually willing to accept all aspects of the system and, consequently, they tend to follow the rules (Vaillant 1977; also see Kennedy 1984). Older, established scientists, who may become uncomfortable with such conformity (Kennedy 1984), can be prevented from voicing dissenting views in a number of ways. Peer pressure within the bureaucracy is often sufficient to keep most individuals in line. Failing that, institutional policies—including gag orders, the threat of a reprimand, or worse— usually ensure that scientists and others in the system toe the party line (for recent Canadian examples, see Cook 1997, Enman 1997, Hutchings et al. 1997).

Such a system is maintained by, among other things, a number of "management myths" (Lichatowich 1992). One example is the myth that "protecting a resource

Table 11–1. Objectives of Marine Mammal Management

Socioeconomically oriented objectives

1. Providing commodity yields (including food, industrial products, luxury items, etc.)
   (a) from marine mammals
   (b) from competitors of marine mammals (e.g., upper trophic level fishes)
   (c) from prey species of marine mammals (fish, invertebrates)
2. Providing recreation and tourism
   (a) oriented toward hunting and fishing for sport
   (b) oriented toward nature observation, ecotourism (e.g., whale watching)
3. Providing employment and cash income
4. Maintaining cultural diversity (e.g., survival of traditional and subsistence economies)
5. Providing for distribution of benefits to all levels of society
   (a) locally
   (b) regionally
   (c) nationally
   (d) internationally
6. Providing for scientific uses and increased knowledge
7. Providing educational benefits
8. Providing for human health
9. Providing for domestication (e.g., as sources of food and other commodities, for captive breeding programs)

Ecologically oriented objectives

10. Maintaining ecosystem diversity (biodiversity)
11. Maintaining ecosystem stability
12. Maintaining gene pools and genetic diversity
13. Maintaining the ability of populations to survive fluctuating environmental conditions

Ethically oriented objectives

14. Minimizing human impacts on marine mammal populations
15. Avoiding inhumane or cruel practices involving marine mammals
16. Enhancing survival chances of marine mammals, especially threatened and endangered species
17. Not killing animals at all
18. Maintaining options for future human generations

There are no clear boundaries between the three main headings; various objectives clearly overlap and, in some cases, objectives are either in conflict or mutually exclusive with others under the same or different heading. All objectives must be considered in relation to both long-term sustainable benefits and intermediate or short-term benefits (modified after Food and Agriculture Organization 1978). For completeness, a fourth category, politically oriented objectives, could be included in this list. Because it was not in the original, I have not added it here.

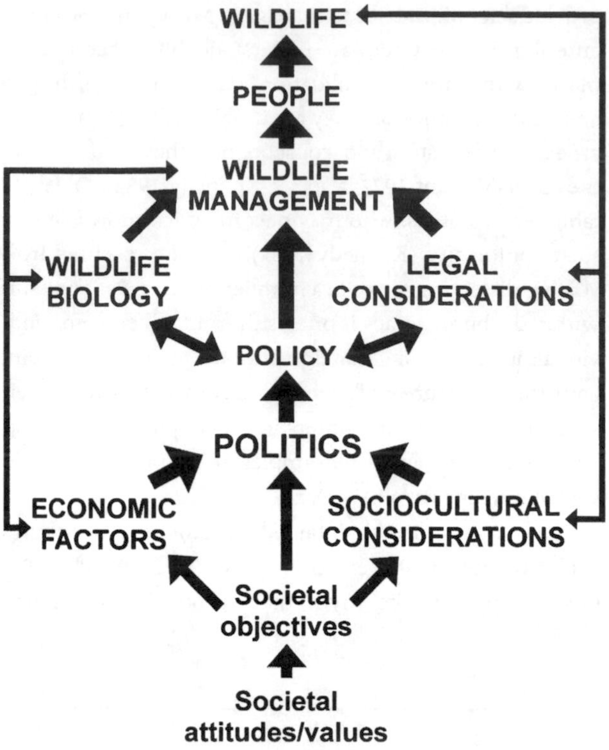

Figure 11-4. Wildlife management: A framework. Societal attitudes (or values) determine societal objectives that influence politicians, either through the ballot box, or through economic and sociocultural (including ethical) considerations. Politicians develop policy and pass legislation, which governs wildlife management decisions and actions. Wildlife biology (science), which is influenced by a variety of societal factors, may affect policy formation, but its major role is providing scientific advice to wildlife managers. Wildlife managers essentially attempt to manage human activities in ways that affect so-called managed wildlife populations. Their decisions, which are ultimately political decisions, are obviously based on a variety of inputs, of which science is only one consideration.

management agency by compromising the resource actually protects the resource"; another is that "government biologists agree with every decision their administrators make" (Lichatowich 1992:14). The latter myth results in the evolution of "team-players" who believe that an agency decision not only directs what work they do but overrides their need to think independently (Lichatowich 1992). Individuals who do not conform are branded "trouble-makers" (Bella 1992:23) and marginalized within the system or encouraged to leave it (Enman 1997). As a consequence, those scientific assessments that promote the policies of the bureaucracy (or those of their political masters) and, therefore, do not disrupt the system "have survival value; contrary assessments tend to be systematically filtered out" (Bella 1992:19). In the process, scientific information is often manipulated, misrepresented, or suppressed (e.g., Lavigne 1985a, Cook 1997, Hutchings et al. 1997).

Of course, such an environment is not conducive to doing scientific research, which by its very nature depends on the free and open exchange of ideas and information and the freedom to reject pet hypotheses in the face of new evidence. Yet government scientists often find themselves unable to comment on management policies or decisions, and certainly they are well advised not to criticize government decisions, even when such decisions are contrary to the best available scientific advice (e.g., Lavigne 1995, Hutchings et al. 1997). Of course, there are rather similar pressures on scientists in academia and in the private sector who depend on governments for research grants and contract funding (Lavigne 1985b). When pressed, many scientists defend their silence by resorting to yet another myth—one that is widely held only in the scientific community, by the way—that science and, therefore, scientists are unbiased and objective, and that commenting on policy issues or becoming involved in public controversies is somehow inappropriate.

Such "filtering" results in systematic distortion within an organizational system and probably explains why bureaucracies frequently exhibit an emergent property that the late historian Barbara Tuchman (1984) termed "wooden-headedness." Wooden-headedness consists of "assessing a situation in terms of preconceived fixed notions while ignoring or rejecting any contrary signs. It is acting according to wish while not allowing oneself to be deflected by the facts" (Tuchman 1984:7). Such is the world in which we live and work.

Conflicting Values and Objectives

Shortly after the Hawaiian monk seal was declared an endangered species, Karl Kenyon (1980:54), at the time the foremost authority on the three species of modern monk seals, wrote: "We can only hope that enlightened programs to control human activities within the monk seals' habitat will help the seals to survive." Yet, in the intervening years, we have failed even to characterize fully, let alone protect, essential monk seal habitat, especially in the marine environment. For students of wildlife management and endangered species conservation, the reasons for this failure are instructive.

Some agencies involved in the management of the Hawaiian monk seal (e.g., the Western Pacific Regional Fishery Management Council, the state of Hawaii, the Navy, and the Coast Guard) have objectives that may conflict with the objective of protecting monk seals. Other agencies (e.g., the Marine Mammal Commission and the Hawaiian Monk Seal Recovery Team) are primarily concerned with monk seal conservation. And at least one agency, the National Marine Fisheries Service, is mandated to serve both fisheries and seals, which can lead to a conflict of interest because objectives for fisheries and for seals cannot always be achieved simultaneously. Such conflicts are commonplace in fisheries and wildlife management, and my interpretation here is from the sole perspective of attaining monk seal recovery. Obviously, fishing interests would have a different interpretation.

The designation of critical habitat for the Hawaiian monk seal is an example of one such conflict. Problems emerged soon after the species was listed as endangered, and they were exacerbated by uncertainty surrounding the at-sea distribution, behavior, and prey preferences of monk seals, and by uncertainty regarding the link between critical habitat designation and fisheries regulations.

In the late 1970s the Marine Mammal Commission was strongly urging the National Marine Fisheries Service to designate critical habitat for the Hawaiian monk seal. In December 1978 the chairman of the Western Pacific Regional Fishery Management Council wrote to the Southwest regional director of the Fisheries Service: "the Council has been much concerned over the possible effects that a critical habitat declaration for the monk seal might have on its management planning for the fisheries of the NWHI [Northwestern Hawaiian Islands], and by extension on the prospects for the development and expansion of fisheries in that area."[9]

Five months later, the governor of the state of Hawaii wrote to the assistant administrator of fisheries (the top administrator of the National Marine Fisheries Service) to explain the state's position on critical habitat: "you must understand that our *primary* (emphasis added) concern is the *indirect* (emphasis Ariyoshi's) repercussions that such a designation will have on fisheries development in the NWHI."[10]

The question for fishery advocates was whether the designation of pelagic areas as critical habitat for monk seals would impede or prevent fisheries development. Advocates of monk seal conservation, on the other hand, were concerned about whether the development of fisheries would threaten the persistence of the monk seal.

The dilemma for the Fisheries Service was clearly expressed in its fishery management plan for the lobster fishery (National Marine Fisheries Service 1981:107): "Each of the measures designed to reduce the risk of adverse impacts on monk seals will likely reduce the potential for a profitable fishery."

The debate, as noted above, eventually focused on the seaward limit of critical habitat: Should it extend from the islands to the 10-fathom (18.3-m) isobath, the 20-fathom (36.6-m) isobath, or a distance of 3 nautical miles (5.55 km) offshore? Because of the lack of information about monk seal foraging patterns and the concern that designation would be accompanied by fishery restrictions, the state of Hawaii, the Western Pacific Regional Fishery Management Council, and the local fishing community argued that designation of critical habitat was either unnecessary or premature. In contrast, the Marine Mammal Commission and the Hawaiian Monk Seal Recovery Team argued that the available information was sufficient to demonstrate that seals used habitat well beyond the 10-fathom (18.3-m) isobath and, on that basis, they recommended that the limit be set at the 20-fathom (36.6-m) isobath.

The Fisheries Service eventually designated critical habitat as extending to the 10-fathom (18.3-m) isobath.[11] The agency argued that

> the habitat which may be in need of special management considerations or protection is that habitat utilized by monk seals for pupping and nursing, where weaned pups learn to swim and forage, and major hauling out areas where growth has been substantial and pupping is imminent. A precise boundary to the area in need of special management considerations or protection is difficult to draw, but designating critical habitat out to 10 fathoms will include all such areas. The depth-of-dive studies and other available information do not indicate that any portion of the foraging habitat is more important than other portions, and no need for special management measures to protect any of the foraging habitat has been identified.

Thus, the Fisheries Service concluded that, for animals older than recently weaned pups, foraging areas did not merit special management consideration because none had been identified as exceptionally important. The statement failed to acknowledge, however, that although the depth-of-dive studies and other information available at that time were adequate to show that the seals ventured beyond the 10-fathom (18.3-m) isobath, presumably to forage, they were simply not adequate to describe foraging patterns of Hawaiian monk seals. The decision was based, therefore, on an "absence of evidence" argument.

The approach taken by the National Marine Fisheries Service to define critical habitat conveyed two important messages. First, in the face of uncertainty, the Fisheries Service did not take a precautionary approach and err on the side of caution to enhance protection of a species as severely endangered as the Hawaiian monk seal. Second, in those instances that pitted the protection of an endangered species (the Hawaiian monk seal) against fisheries development, the Fisheries Service took the traditional management position that the burden of proof falls on advocates of protection. In short, the Fisheries Service, as the lead agency responsible for the conservation of the Hawaiian monk seal, resolved its conflict-of-interest position in the usual way (Lichatowich 1992) by placing the utilitarian economic interests of fisheries above the conservation interests of an endangered species.

The Marine Mammal Commission objected to the 10-fathom (18.3-m) isobath ruling. Consequently, the National Marine Fisheries Service reopened the debate, and in 1988 extended the designation to the 20-fathom (36.6-m) isobath. The extension of the boundary was not, however, accompanied by any changes in fisheries regulations pertinent to the enclosed areas.

Since the designation was expanded in 1988, poor understanding of the monk seal's marine habitat has continued to impede management and conservation efforts. The potential for interactions with pelagic longline fisheries, for example, was not recognized until after interactions had begun. The recent severe decline of monk seals at French Frigate Shoals appears to be due to a lack of prey (Ragen and Lavigne, this volume), but only now is a serious effort being initiated to understand the foraging ecology of seals at this site. And although competitive interactions with the lobster fishery potentially pose a serious threat to the seals, evidence for or against such interactions remains largely hypothetical or, at most, circumstantial.

More recently, however, the National Marine Fisheries Service has begun to shift its position with respect to the conflict between conservation of protected species and enhancement of fisheries. Pilot studies of foraging ecology have been initiated and, most recently, the Office of Protected Resources has allocated funds specifically for study of the foraging ecology of Hawaiian monk seals. The National Marine Fisheries Service has formally recognized the conflict between fisheries and protected species in goal 4 of its strategic plan (National Marine Fisheries Service 1991:14) to integrate conservation of protected species and fisheries management. Here, the plan states: "It is also possible that continued growth of protected marine mammal populations may reduce fishery production, or that development of fisheries on forage species may jeopardize recovery of endangered marine mammal populations. Legislative action may be required to solve conflicts."

To achieve goal 4, the Fisheries Service has identified five objectives. These are to (1) identify and resolve conflicts between the Marine Mammal Protection Act, the Endangered Species Act, and fisheries; (2) determine the status of protected species; (3) monitor marine mammal "take" by fisheries and assess its significance; (4) implement endangered species recovery plans; and (5) reduce fishery and passive viewing impacts on protected species.

Whether the Fisheries Service will be able to achieve these objectives and integrate conservation of the monk seal with fisheries management, particularly in today's sociopolitical climate, remains to be seen. The persistence of this species and, ultimately, an entire genus of marine mammals may depend on it.

Process Versus Outcome

Finally, in evaluating progress toward the recovery of the Hawaiian monk seal, it is important to distinguish between process and outcome. An enormous amount of management energy and resources is devoted to tasks such as developing management plans, completing reports, holding meetings (e.g., reviews, workshops, and recovery team meetings), and completing the extensive bureaucratic business of wildlife management. These activities are, however, *processes* that do not directly affect the desired outcome: the recovery of the species. Rather, they affect recovery only if they are somehow linked to the implementation of some direct recovery action.

Similarly, research and monitoring are processes that, in and of themselves, cannot directly achieve recovery and conservation. Unless they are coupled with recovery activities, they simply provide documentation for the historical record. Such was the case, for example, with much of the monitoring of Hawaiian monk seals from the late 1950s to the mid-1970s.

It is fundamentally important, therefore, not to confuse these processes with the desired outcome by using them as measures of management success. However necessary such processes may be, they do not provide a basis for achieving success. That can only be measured by progress toward the ultimate goal: recovery of the species.

Discussion

With the clarity of 20/20 hindsight it is easy to criticize past attempts to conserve endangered species, especially when those attempts have failed to achieve the objective of population recovery. What is important now is to reflect on the current situation, learn from the past, and move forward in a positive and constructive manner.

So what can or should be done to promote the survival of the Hawaiian monk seal? This question has been asked since before the species was first listed as endangered in 1976. In the mid-1970s, some National Marine Fisheries Service personnel argued that the monk seal was a relict species that was doomed to extinction. This view, similar to that of Charles Repenning (1980) discussed in the previous chapter (Ragen and Lavigne, this volume), suggests that intervention would be a waste of time and resources (e.g., Ackerman

1995). This opinion was not shared, however, by the Marine Mammal Commission, which held that the Hawaiian monk seal was an ideal candidate for recovery work, a view shared by many members of the scientific and conservation communities.

Such fundamental differences of opinion are common in wildlife management. Ultimately, they are usually resolved by the "decision makers" (i.e., politicians) in response to contemporary societal attitudes. In the case of the Hawaiian monk seal, the Marine Mammal Commission's views largely prevailed because they were based on reasoned interpretations of the available scientific evidence and reflected widely held societal attitudes, embodied in the legislation of the day, the Marine Mammal Protection Act and the Endangered Species Act (Norton 1987).

Whether that same decision will be made in the future remains to be seen. With the recent swing to the political right, society's views toward environmental issues, including endangered species, are again changing (Lavigne et al., this volume). A U.S. Secretary of the Interior recently asked, for example, "Do we have to save every subspecies?" (Olive 1992:92). This is a revealing question from the person charged with implementing the Endangered Species Act. And although many countries endorsed a biodiversity treaty at the 1992 Earth Summit in Rio de Janeiro, the United States under President George Bush did not. Neither has the United States signed the convention under the Clinton Administration. So it remains to be seen whether the United States will continue its global leadership in attempting to preserve endangered species.

The fact is, however, that if an endangered species like the Hawaiian monk seal, living in a largely uninhabited part of the world, exclusively under the jurisdiction of the United States with its highly developed endangered species legislation, cannot be saved, what hope is there for other endangered species, like the Mediterranean monk seal, which often occurs close to human settlements and in areas subject to several jurisdictions, few of which seem able to provide any real legal protection? And the conclusion that the Hawaiian monk seal is not necessarily doomed to imminent extinction continues to be supported by the weight of available evidence. Human influences have almost certainly played a large role in driving it to near-extinction. Were this not the case, it would be an unusual case study indeed. For, as far as Soulé (1983:112) could determine, "no biologist has documented the extinction of [any] continental species of a plant or animal caused solely by non-human agencies. . . ." Even more tellingly for our purposes, Caughley (1994:240) recently wrote, "I cannot recollect hearing of a non-anthropogenic extinction of an island species (as against an island population) occurring within the last 8000 years."

The main anthropogenic influences that have contributed to the two declines of the Hawaiian monk seal are exploitation during the nineteenth century (Ragen and Lavigne, this volume) and habitat degradation and loss in the twentieth century. Habitat degradation and loss, as we have seen, involve a variety of human disturbances, including habitation of atolls in the Northwestern Hawaiian Islands, occupation of beaches, military exercises, entanglement in marine debris, and, to some undetermined degree, fishing the species' food base (e.g., lobsters).

Given the above conclusions and assuming that preservation of endangered species remains a priority in the United States, the question remains: Where should we go from here in our attempts to minimize further human impacts on Hawaiian monk seals and to stop and reverse the decline of the species throughout its current range?

Where Should We Go from Here?

Probably no one has all the answers, and I certainly do not. Preserving endangered species is a complex business (e.g., Schaller 1993), and there are no "magic bullets" (Fuller 1995) that guarantee success. Yet, it is also obvious that managers have not yet exhausted all reasonable options to protect Hawaiian monk seals and to promote their recovery. The same conclusion applies to the Mediterranean monk seal, and I draw on a set of "conservation guidelines" recently compiled for that species (Johnson and Lavigne 1995) to structure my recommendations. These guidelines stress that management actions should proceed in a logical, stepwise, or sequential manner, guided at each step by the precautionary approach: in the face of uncertainty, management should always err on the side of caution (e.g., Food and Agriculture Organization 1995). "Absence of evidence" arguments should no longer be used to ignore potentially damaging activities or to justify management inaction.

In Situ Protection

It is generally agreed that the first priority for the conservation of endangered species, including monk seals, is to secure legal in situ protection for the animals and their habitats (Johnson and Lavigne 1995). Yet, 20 years after its listing as an endangered species, and despite the requirements of the Marine Mammal Protection Act and the Endangered Species Act, full and permanent protection of the Hawaiian monk seal and its habitats has yet to be secured.

For Hawaiian monk seals, the identification of important terrestrial habitat is straightforward and includes areas where the seals haul out to rest, give birth, nurse their young, interact during the mating season, and molt. From

Nihoa Island to Kure Atoll, essentially all beach areas have been used for these purposes. The majority of the islands and atolls are protected within the Hawaiian Islands National Wildlife Refuge and the Midway Atoll National Wildlife Refuge, which are managed by the Fish and Wildlife Service. The closure of the naval air facility at Midway and the LORAN station at Kure (Ragen and Lavigne, this volume) should reduce disturbance in these areas considerably. But the subsequent development of Midway as a tourist destination raises new questions.

In 1975 Kenyon wrote that "unless fishing and/or tourist activities can be excluded from the Hawaiian breeding grounds, then the remnant populations of these rare and unique seals may . . . follow the Caribbean monk seal into extinction" (1975:499). Now, more than 20 years later, the only breeding subpopulations that currently are increasing are ones where human impacts are unknown (Pearl and Hermes Reef) or where they have been mitigated and reduced to a minimum (Kure Atoll). So, does it really make sense—if the objective of management is to provide the remaining Hawaiian monk seals with maximum protection—that Midway Atoll, a former breeding site, is now a tourist destination? Currently, tourists are housed at the abandoned air facility on Sand Island. They can wander along beaches where they may actually encounter (disturb?) a sleeping monk seal and go SCUBA diving—yes, there is a dive concession on Midway—or sportfishing in monk seal habitat, both in nearby lagoons and in waters offshore (Brower 1997). Since 1997 they can enjoy meals at a new restaurant built on one of the beaches.

One magazine advertisement includes a picture of a Hawaiian monk seal and describes the island as "one of the most remote spots on earth, where wildlife thrive . . ." (Islands, June 1997). Yet, the Hawaiian monk seal is clearly not thriving, and it is difficult to see how tourism will benefit its recovery. Such development will of course yield benefits to the management bureaucracy, providing continued support for the Fish and Wildlife Service station on the island. It will also ease the logistical problems for scientists who wish to study the animals on the islands, and it will provide an opportunity for public education. But the conservation benefits of tourism for monk seals at Midway will not be measured by the numbers of visitors or their vacation experience, only by its effects on the seals. Although these remain to be determined, one can only wonder what would happen if humans simply vacated Midway entirely.

Poor understanding of the monk seal's pelagic ecology has also been a significant obstacle to the identification and protection of its critical marine habitat and to the prevention of detrimental fisheries interactions. It has also impeded the identification and assessment of monk seal prey, the explanation of population trends, and the assessment of relationships among the different subpopulations (Ragen and Lavigne, this volume). Because of the tenuous status of the Hawaiian monk seal, such lack of understanding can no longer be used as an excuse for doing nothing. Instead of having prolonged debates about whether critical marine habitat should be bounded by the 10-fathom (18.3-m) or 20-fathom (36.6-m) isobath, managers now faced with incomplete knowledge or uncertainty must surely invoke the precautionary approach (e.g., Food and Agriculture Organization 1995), adopt the most conservative of available management options, and squarely address the identified gaps in knowledge with directed scientific studies. Regarding the latter point, the burden of proof must be shifted from the advocates of monk seal protection to the proponents of potentially harmful developments, including the expansion of commercial fisheries and, indeed, tourism. Before proceeding with new initiatives, the proponents should be required to demonstrate beyond reasonable doubt that their proposed activities will not have detrimental effects on monk seals. Such a requirement would represent a major change in policy; until now, conservation actions have usually been taken only after detrimental impacts have been observed (i.e., the approach has been reactive rather than proactive).

The Management Bureaucracy

Fundamental changes in management philosophy, such as those proposed above, may require changes in the existing management bureaucracy. In an ideal world, competing interests, including federal and state governments, the military, commercial fisheries, tourist operators, and advocates of monk seal protection, would adopt the common objective of ensuring that the monk seal and its habitat have the legal in situ protection necessary to minimize human impacts. Such a common objective would require increased cooperation and coordination among participating interests and better integration of their activities.

One might also argue that the management bureaucracy currently involved in the monk seal management process could be streamlined considerably, thereby reducing interagency conflicts and freeing administrative funds for vital research and management actions. Borrowing from a recommendation of the Royal Commission on Seals and Sealing in Canada (Malouf 1986), consideration should be given to separating management responsibility for endangered Hawaiian monk seals (and other marine mammals) from those in the National Marine Fisheries Service responsible for serving the interests of fisheries. This would resolve the Service's conflict of interest and would place the interests of monk seal conservation on a more equal footing with the conflicting objectives of commercial fishing interests.

To reduce bureaucratic interference even further, one might also recommend that scientific research conducted for government agencies be publicly funded by a politically independent institution, as has been suggested recently for Canada's Department of Fisheries and Oceans (Hutchings et al. 1997, Lavigne 1997). In other words, place government science at arms' length from the political process. Give science and scientists the same freedoms enjoyed by the judiciary in democratic societies (Hutchings et al. 1997, Lavigne 1997). In this way, science and the work of scientists would not be compromised when decisions are made that go against the best scientific advice (Lavigne 1997).

Management Actions

Regardless of the management structure, there are some obvious management actions that would increase protection of the Hawaiian monk seal. The recent transfer of Midway Atoll to the Fish and Wildlife Service's National Wildlife Refuge System would have been a first step, had the military presence not been replaced by tourist activities. Second, commercial fisheries that have the potential to compete with monk seals should almost certainly be excluded from the protected species zone. New technologies have vastly improved our ability to investigate the seals' pelagic ecology and, with persistence, it should soon be possible to describe better their marine habitats, including movement corridors and feeding areas, rather than simply guessing about them. Such research is essential before any fisheries are reopened or new fisheries developed.

Because entanglement in marine debris may be an important source of mortality for monk seals, it would be prudent also to mount dedicated clean-up efforts on beaches and reefs and to increase efforts to locate and free entangled seals. Laist (1996:118) noted "the predominance of fishing-related debris in entanglement incidents" and made a number of additional recommendations to avoid the loss and promote the recovery of such items. These include requiring fishermen to report when, where, and under what circumstances fishing gear is lost; investigating the feasibility of cleaning up lost fishing gear in areas where such debris is likely to be concentrated; and requiring that fishermen retain all plastic or entangling gear caught incidentally during fishing operations for later disposal on land.

RESEARCH NEEDS. Of course, there is still a need for continued scientific research to learn more about the problems facing Hawaiian monk seals, to monitor trends in abundance, and to evaluate management actions. Following the example outlined in the Mediterranean monk seal conservation guidelines, research activities should be conducted with minimal disturbance to individuals and subpopulations (Johnson and Lavigne 1995). Priority should be given to research programs with demonstrable practical value, aimed at enhancing the survival of individuals and the protection, recovery, and conservation of the species.

Research might also be initiated to ascertain whether the fishing industry operating in the Northwestern Hawaiian Islands might actually benefit from the conservation of Hawaiian monk seals and thereby be encouraged to protect the seals and their habitats. This suggestion may not be as naive as it might at first seem: marine protected areas designed to protect monk seals would also provide sanctuary for other species in the marine community, including commercially important fish and their habitats, and other endangered species (in this case, the green turtle). They also can result in the creation of a reservoir that supplies adjacent, nonprotected areas with a renewable supply of preferred resource species (Ballantine 1991, Olver et al. 1995, Roberts 1997). Whether such a win-win situation is possible in the Northwestern Hawaiian Islands remains to be seen.

CONTINGENCY PLANNING. The increasing frequency of mass mortality events involving marine mammals (see Geraci et al., this volume) should also serve as a warning to those involved in Hawaiian monk seal conservation. The catastrophic loss in mid-1997 of more than half of the largest surviving Mediterranean monk seal population, possibly due to toxic algae, emphasizes the point that maintaining as many viable reproductive colonies (or subpopulations) as possible increases the likelihood that species will persist. In the case of the Hawaiian monk seal, we are reminded again that reestablishing a breeding colony at Midway is a much higher priority (to monk seal conservation) than promoting the islands as a tourist destination.

The Mediterranean monk seal die-off and a 1996 event in Florida involving the endangered West Indian manatee (*Trichechus manatus*) (Marine Mammal Commission 1997; also see Reynolds, this volume) also emphasize the importance of having a detailed contingency plan in place in case a similar event were to occur in Hawaii. Following the 1980 workshop (discussed above), a Hawaiian monk seal die-off response plan was eventually produced as an administrative report marked "not for publication" (Gilmartin 1987). Much has been learned since 1980, however, about mass mortality events affecting marine mammals. It would be timely, therefore, to revise and make widely available a contingency plan for the Hawaiian monk seal. Lessons learned from the manatee die-off—conveniently summarized in communications between John R. Twiss Jr., executive director of the Marine Mammal Commission, and the U.S. Fish and Wildlife Service,[12] and "A contingency plan for catastrophic manatee rescue and mortality events" prepared by the Manatee Recovery Program (Anonymous 1997)—could have been used to good advantage during the early stages of the Mediterranean monk seal die-off. Additional lessons were learned during that event as well. Collectively, and with the general coverage provided in Wilkinson (1996), the basis for drafting a workable document for Hawaiian monk seals appears readily at hand.

RESCUE, REHABILITATION, AND TRANSLOCATION. Direct management intervention, including rescue, rehabilitation, and release of wounded, sick, or undersized animals, has been implemented in the past and is likely to be deemed necessary in the future. The objectives of such efforts are to salvage the reproductive potential that would otherwise be lost if management did not intervene and to enhance depleted subpopulations through the addition of rehabilitated female seals. Generally, experience indicates that the chances of successful translocation of threatened or endangered species are low, especially for carnivores (like monk seals) that are characterized by delayed maturity, a low reproductive rate, and, hence, a low intrinsic rate of increase (Griffith et al. 1989). Nonetheless, such intervention—the primary management approach to counteract the catastrophic loss of immature monk seals at French Frigate Shoals since the late 1980s—has enhanced the Kure Atoll subpopulation (Ragen and Lavigne, this volume). Recent failures, such as the loss of the 16 juvenile females translocated to Midway Atoll in 1992–1993, indicate, however, that future efforts must be more carefully planned and executed than in the past.

Translocations pose a variety of potential problems (Griffith et al. 1989), especially in the Northwestern Hawaiian Islands where seals have had little contact with mammals other than humans (or mammals introduced by humans, such as dogs at French Frigate Shoals and Kure Atoll, rabbits at Laysan Island, and rats at Midway and Kure; the dogs have now been removed and the rabbits eradicated). Currently, the greatest threat of exposure to other mammals and disease vectors occurs during rehabilitation on Oahu, and the return of such exposed animals to the wild is not without risks. Although the seals are screened for diseases before release, the screening process may miss important evidence of disease. When results are positive, the affected animals may not be treated if the disease is not considered life-threatening and if it also occurs in the wild. Without more extensive surveys, however, assumptions about the prevalence or importance of certain diseases or conditions in the wild are fraught with uncertainty. The seals captured in 1995 for rehabilitation and translocation, and now mostly blind, provide an example (see above).

When seals are moved directly from one subpopulation to another, there is a similar risk that the recipient subpopulation could be exposed to diseases originally found only in the donor subpopulation. The natural movements of Hawaiian monk seals between the islands suggests that contagious diseases are unlikely to be localized in specific subpopulations. But again, our poor understanding of disease processes in monk seals and the recent appearance of a variety of novel morbilliviruses in marine mammal populations (e.g., Visser 1993; Geraci et al., this volume) reminds us that direct translocations may be risky. Indeed, the low genetic variability in the Hawaiian monk seal (Kretzmann et al. 1997) may render it particularly susceptible to catastrophes related to introduced diseases.

In addition to disease problems, other fundamental questions about rehabilitation and translocation remain: What criteria should be used to select animals for rehabilitation? Should they be rehabilitated on site or returned to Honolulu? What are the best methods of care during the captive period? What criteria should be used to determine when animals are ready for release? When and where should they be released? How should potential release sites be evaluated? Should the animals be held at the release site to allow time to acclimate before release? How should the long-term success of such programs be evaluated?

These and other questions require extensive study, but such studies are essential if translocation efforts are to be continued in the future. To ensure that these questions are addressed, that translocations are used judiciously, and that translocation success is maximized, previous efforts must be evaluated to identify key areas for improvement. Improved protocols need to be developed to guide all aspects of capture, care, transport, and release. The lessons to be learned have important implications for the management of this species, as well as for the management and conservation of the Mediterranean monk seal, for which translocations have recently been discussed (ICONA 1994a,b).

Another issue that may require intervention is the problem of mobbing in those subpopulations where the sex ratio remains skewed toward males. If the recent removal of males from Laysan Island has the desired effect of reducing mobbing mortalities, similar management actions at Lisianski Island might be considered.

CAPTIVE BREEDING. For some individuals and organizations, the final component in a conservation action plan (or recovery plan) for endangered species like the Hawaiian monk seal is the initiation of a captive breeding program.

Such an option has not, to my knowledge, been formally suggested for the Hawaiian monk seal. But because it has been suggested repeatedly for Mediterranean monk seals (reviewed in Johnson and Lavigne 1994), I address it briefly here (also see Reeves and Mead, this volume).

Like other management options, captive breeding of endangered species is a potentially useful recovery tool. It provides the eventual possibility of supplementing depleted wild populations with captive-born seals.

Captive breeding, however, is not without attendant costs and risks, which must be compared with the expected benefits in the context of the entire recovery program. Such costs and risks include the removal of animals from the wild and the associated loss of reproductive potential in the donor population, the exposure of the captive animals and their offspring to the risks associated with captivity (e.g., diseases and disease vectors in the captive environment), the possible introduction of such diseases into the recipient population if captive animals are released, the uncertain ability of released animals to acclimatize successfully, and the costs of conducting a captive breeding program, which may divert limited, vital resources from more pressing conservation objectives.

To ensure that these costs and risks are minimized and do not outweigh the expected benefits, any proposal for captive breeding of the Hawaiian monk seal should be rigorously evaluated by the scientific and conservation communities, as has been suggested for its Mediterranean counterpart (Johnson and Lavigne 1995).

Concluding Remarks

We are now approaching the 200th anniversary of recorded human impacts on Hawaiian monk seals. The first serious efforts to understand and assess the species began in the 1950s, but it was not until the 1970s that dedicated, long-term efforts were made to study and protect it. Clearly, much remains to be done. The extinction of the Caribbean monk seal and the recent catastrophic loss of Mediterranean monk seals in Northwest Africa remind us that the stakes are high. Although it is impossible to predict what future societal objectives may conflict with conservation of Hawaiian monk seals, there is, for the moment, a way forward. If we proceed thoughtfully in a logical, stepwise, and precautionary manner, and take actions in such a way that they can be readily evaluated to see if objectives have been realized, to test hypotheses, and to answer pressing questions, we will not only increase our knowledge but also provide a firmer basis for modifying and adapting subsequent management activities in an appropriate manner. Such an approach can never guarantee success, but it will almost certainly increase the likelihood that the ultimate objective of Hawaiian monk seal conservation may be realized.

Acknowledgments

This chapter emerged from my collaboration with Tim Ragen on the biology of the Hawaiian monk seal (see Ragen and Lavigne, this volume). All those who contributed to our joint effort in that chapter also deserve mention here. I especially thank the anonymous reviewer whose observations about the management bureaucracy seemed so pertinent that I took the unconventional step of incorporating them into the chapter. I also thank those individuals who, in some cases unintentionally, contributed further to my understanding of the politics of marine mammal science and management. And again, I must specifically acknowledge the various efforts of John Twiss, Suzanne Montgomery, Randy Reeves, and David Laist. But most of all, I thank Tim Ragen. Tim generously shared his insights, his encyclopedic knowledge of Hawaiian monk seal biology, management, and conservation, and provided Figure 11-1. Above all else, he maintained his sense of perspective in the face of adversity, never for a moment losing track of what is truly important, both in monk seal conservation and in life. At the end of this odyssey, however, I must include the conventional disclaimers: all opinions expressed in this chapter are entirely my responsibility; any remaining errors are also mine.

Notes

1. 41 *Fed. Reg.* 30,120 (1976).
2. 41 *Fed. Reg.* 51,611 (1976).
3. Under the Magnuson-Stevens Fishery Conservation and Management Act of 1976, the United States assumed complete management jurisdiction over a fisheries conservation zone, which extends 200 miles (370.4 km) seaward of U.S. shorelines.
4. 56 *Fed. Reg.* 51,849 and 52,214 (1991).
5. 51 *Fed. Reg.* 16,047 (1986).
6. 53 *Fed. Reg.* 18,988 (1988).
7. 55 *Fed. Reg.* 49,285 (1990).
8. 56 *Fed. Reg.* 51,849 and 52,214 (1991), respectively.
9. Letter from W. Y. H. Yee, chairman of the Western Pacific Regional Fishery Management Council, to G. V. Howard, director, Southwest Region, National Marine Fisheries Service, 14 December 1978.
10. Letter from G. R. Ariyoshi, governor of the state of Hawaii, to T. L. Leitzell, assistant administrator for fisheries, 29 March 1979.
11. 51 *Fed. Reg.* 16,047 (1986).
12. Letters from J. R. Twiss Jr., executive director, Marine Mammal Commission, to The Honorable M. H. Beattie, director, U.S. Fish and Wildlife Service, 10 May 1996, and to The Honorable J. G. Rogers, acting director, U.S. Fish and Wildlife Service, 31 December 1996.

Literature Cited

Ackerman, D. 1995. The Rarest of the Rare: Vanishing Animals, Timeless Worlds. Random House, New York, NY. 84 pp.

Anonymous. 1997. A contingency plan for catastrophic manatee rescue and mortality events. Prepared by Manatee Recovery Program, Jacksonville, Florida Field Office, Southeast Region, U.S. Fish and Wildlife Service, Atlanta, GA. 1 April 1997. 37 pp.

Atkinson, S., and W. G. Gilmartin. 1992. Seasonal testosterone pattern in Hawaiian monk seals. Journal of Reproduction and Fertility 96:35–39.

Atkinson, S., W. G. Gilmartin, and B. L. Lasley. 1993. Testosterone response to a gonadotrophin-releasing hormone agonist in Hawaiian monk seals (*Monachus schauinslandi*). Journal of Reproduction and Fertility 97:35–38.

Ballantine, W. J. 1991. Marine reserves for New Zealand. University of Auckland, Leigh Laboratory Bulletin No. 25. 200 pp.

Banish, L. D., and W. G. Gilmartin. 1988. Hematology and serum chemistry of the young Hawaiian monk seal (*Monachus schauinslandi*). Journal of Wildlife Diseases 24:225–230.

Baur, D. C., M. J. Bean, and M. L. Gosliner. 1999. The laws governing marine mammal conservation in the United States. (This volume)

Bella, D. A. 1992. Ethics and the credibility of applied science. Pages 19–32 *in* G. H. Reeves, D. L. Bottom, and M. H. Brookes (eds.), Ethical questions for resource managers. U.S. Department of Agriculture, Forest Service, Pacific Northwest Research Station. General Technical Report PNW-GTR-288. 39 pp.

Brower, K. 1997. Midway. Islands 17 (3): 106–121.

Caughley, G. 1994. Directions in conservation biology. Journal of Animal Ecology 63:215–244.

Cook, D. G. 1997. Editorial. Canadian Journal of Fisheries and Aquatic Sciences 54:iii–v.

Dailey, M. D., R. V. Santangelo, and W. G. Gilmartin. 1988. A coprological survey of helminth parasites of the Hawaiian monk seal from the Northwestern Hawaiian Islands. Marine Mammal Science 4:125–131.

DeLong, R. L., C. H. Fiscus, and K. W. Kenyon. 1976. Survey of monk seal (*Monachus schauinslandi*) populations of the Northwestern (Leeward) Hawaiian Islands. Processed report (available from National Marine Mammal Laboratory, National Marine Fisheries Service, Seattle, WA.). 36 pp.

Ehrenfeld, D. W. 1970. Biological Conservation. Holt, Rinehart and Winston of Canada Ltd., Toronto. 226 pp.

Enman, C. 1997. Science silenced to hide 'disasters.' Ottawa Citizen, 27 June. p. A1.

Erickson, E. 1950. Childhood and Society. Norton, New York, NY. 448 pp.

Food and Agriculture Organization. 1978. Mammals in the Seas. Vol. 1. Report of the FAO Advisory Committee on Marine Resources Research. Working Party on Marine Mammals. FAO Fisheries Series No. 5.

Food and Agriculture Organization. 1995. Draft guidelines on the precautionary approach to capture fisheries (including species introductions). Technical Consultation on the Precautionary Approach to Capture Fisheries (Including Species Introductions). 6–13 June 1995, Lysekil, Sweden. 63 pp.

Fuller, S. 1995. Death to all magic bullets. New Scientist (5 May): 53–54.

Furman, D. P., and M. D. Dailey. 1980. The genus *Halarachne* (Acari: Halarachnidae), with the description of a new species from the Hawaiian monk seal. Journal of Medical Entomology 17:352–359.

Geraci, J. R., J. Harwood, and V. J. Lounsbury. 1999. Marine mammal die-offs: Causes, investigations, and issues. (This volume)

Gilmartin, W. G. 1983. Recovery plan for the Hawaiian monk seal, *Monachus schauinslandi*. (In cooperation with the Hawaiian Monk Seal Recovery Team.) U.S. Department of Commerce, NOAA, National Marine Fisheries Service, Southwest Region, Terminal Island, CA. 29 pp. + tables and appendices.

Gilmartin, W. G. 1987. Hawaiian monk seal die-off response plan, a workshop report. Honolulu Laboratory, Southwest Fisheries Science Center, National Marine Fisheries Service, NOAA, Honolulu, HI. Southwest Fisheries Science Center Administrative Report H-87-17. 7 pp.

Gilmartin, W. G. 1990. Hawaiian monk seal work plan, fiscal years 1991–93. Honolulu Laboratory, Southwest Fisheries Science Center, National Marine Fisheries Service, NOAA, Honolulu, HI. Southwest Fisheries Science Center Administrative Report H-90-14. 43 pp.

Gilmartin, W. G. 1993. Research and management plan for the Hawaiian monk seal at French Frigate Shoals, 1993–1996. Honolulu Laboratory, Southwest Fisheries Center, National Marine Fisheries Service, NOAA, Honolulu, HI. Southwest Fisheries Science Center Administrative Report H-93-16. 83 pp.

Gilmartin, W. G., and D. J. Alcorn. 1987. A plan to address the Hawaiian monk seal adult male "mobbing" problem. Honolulu Laboratory, Southwest Fisheries Science Center, National Marine Fisheries Service, NOAA, Honolulu, HI. Southwest Fisheries Science Center Administrative Report H-87-12. 24 pp.

Gilmartin, W. G., R. L. DeLong, A. W. Smith, L. A. Griner, and M. D. Dailey. 1980. An investigation into unusual mortality in the Hawaiian monk seal, *Monachus schauinslandi*. Pages 32–41 *in* R. W. Grigg and R. T. Pfund (eds.), Proceedings of the Symposium on Status of Resource Investigation in the Northwestern Hawaiian Islands, University of Hawaii, Honolulu. UNIHI-SEAGRANT-MR-80-04.

Gilmartin, W. G., R. J. Morrow, and A. M. Houtman. 1986. Hawaiian Monk Seal Observations and Captive Maintenance Project at Kure Atoll, 1981. U.S. Department of Commerce, NOAA Technical Memorandum, NMFS-SWFSC-59. 9 pp.

Golvan, Y. J. 1959. Acanthocéphales du genre *Corynosoma* Lühe 1904. Parasites de mammifères d'Alaska et de Midway. Annales Parasitologie Humaine et Compare 34:288–321.

Griffith, B., J. M. Scott, J. W. Carpenter, and C. Reed. 1989. Translocation as a species conservation tool: Status and strategy. Science 245:477–480.

Henderson, J. R. 1985. A review of Hawaiian monk seal entanglements in marine debris. Pages 326–335 *in* R. S. Shomura and H. O. Yoshida (eds.), Proceedings of the Workshop on the Fate and Impact of Marine Debris. U.S. Department of Commerce, NOAA Technical Memorandum, NMFS-SWFSC-54.

Henderson, J. R. 1990. Recent entanglements of Hawaiian monk seals in marine debris. Pages 540–553 *in* R. S. Shomura and M. L. Godfrey (eds.), Proceedings of the Second International Conference on Marine Debris. 2–7 April 1989, Honolulu, HI. U.S. Department of Commerce, NOAA Technical Memorandum NMFS-SWFSC-154.

Henderson, J. R., and T. C. Johanos. 1988. Effects of tagging on weaned Hawaiian monk seal pups. Wildlife Society Bulletin 16:312–317.

Hiruki, L. M., W. G. Gilmartin, B. L. Becker, and I. Stirling. 1993. Wounding in Hawaiian monk seals (*Monachus schauinslandi*). Canadian Journal of Zoology 71:458–468.

Hiruki, L. M., I. Stirling, W. G. Gilmartin, T. C. Johanos, and B. L. Becker. 1993. Significance of wounding to female reproductive success in Hawaiian monk seals (*Monachus schauinslandi*) at Laysan Island. Canadian Journal of Zoology 71:469–474.

Holt, S. J. 1978. Opening plenary meeting. Mammals in the Seas. Vol. 1. Report of the FAO Advisory Committee on Marine Resources Research. Working Party on Marine Mammals. FAO Fisheries Series No. 5, Vol. 1, Appendix 5: 262–264.

Hutchings, J. A., C. Walters, and R. L. Haedrich. 1997. Is scientific inquiry incompatible with government information control? Canadian Journal of Fisheries and Aquatic Sciences 54:1198–1210.

ICONA. 1994a. Feasibility action for the estabilization [*sic*] of the Atlantic monk seal population. Instituto Nacional para la Conservación de la Naturaleza (ICONA). Consejería de Polica Territorial del Gobierno Canario, Madrid, Spain. 7 pp.

ICONA. 1994b. Résumé de la Proposition. Reintroduction du Phoque Moine de l'Atlantique dans l'ile de Lobos: Experiment pilote. LIFE 94/A.2.2.2. 1 p.

Israëls, L. D. E. 1992. Thirty years of Mediterranean monk seal protection, a review. Nederlandsche Commissie Voor Internationale Natuurbescherming. Mededelingen No. 28. 65 pp.

Ito, R. Y. 1992. Western Pacific pelagic fisheries in 1991. Honolulu Laboratory, Southwest Fisheries Science Center, National Marine Fisheries Service, NOAA, Honolulu, HI. Southwest Fisheries Science Center Administrative Report H-92-15. 38 pp.

Johnson, A. M., R. L. DeLong, C. H. Fiscus, and K. Kenyon. 1982. Population status of the Hawaiian monk seal (*Monachus schauinslandi*), 1978. Journal of Mammalogy 63:415–421.

Johnson, B. W., and P. A. Johnson. 1978. The Hawaiian monk seal on Laysan Island: 1977. Report No. MMC-77/05. Marine Mammal Commission. (Available from National Technical Information Service, Springfield, VA. PB-285-428.) 38 pp.

Johnson, B. W., and P. A. Johnson. 1981a. The Hawaiian monk seal on Laysan Island: 1978. Report No. MMC-78/15. Marine Mammal Commission. (Available from National Technical Information Service, Springfield, VA. PB-82-109661.) 17 pp.

Johnson, B. W., and P. A. Johnson. 1981b. Estimating the Hawaiian monk seal population on Laysan Island. Report No. MMC-80/06. Marine Mammal Commission. (Available from National Technical Information Service, Springfield, VA. PB-82-106113.) 29 pp.

Johnson, B. W., and P. A. Johnson. 1984. Observations of the Hawaiian Monk Seal on Laysan Island from 1977 through 1980. U.S. Department of Commerce, NOAA Technical Memorandum, NMFS-SWFSC-49. 65 pp.

Johnson, W. M., and D. M. Lavigne. 1994. Captive breeding and the Mediterranean monk seal—a focus on Antibes Marineland. International Marine Mammal Association Inc., Guelph, Canada. 44 pp.

Johnson, W. M., and D. M. Lavigne. 1995. The Mediterranean Monk Seal: Conservation Guidelines. International Marine Mammal Association Inc., Guelph, Canada. 52 pp.

Kennedy, J. J. 1984. Understanding professional career evolution—An example of Aldo Leopold. Wildlife Society Bulletin 12:215–226.

Kenyon, K. W. 1975. The monk seal's cloistered life. Its refuge in Leeward Islands is off limits to visitors. Defenders of Wildlife 50:497–499.

Kenyon, K. W. 1978. A five-year research plan for the Hawaiian monk seal: Results of an 18–19 October 1978 Research Planning Meeting. Unpublished report to the U.S. Marine Mammal Commission. (Available from Protected Species Investigation, National Marine Fisheries Center, Honolulu, HI.) 32 pp.

Kenyon, K. W. 1980. No man is benign: The endangered monk seal. Oceans 13 (3): 48–54.

Kenyon, K. W., and D. W. Rice. 1959. Life history of the Hawaiian monk seal. Pacific Science 31:215–252.

Kretzmann, M. A., W. G. Gilmartin, A. Meyer, G. P. Zegers, S. R. Fain, B. F. Taylor, and D. P. Costa. 1997. Low genetic variability in the Hawaiian monk seal. Conservation Biology 11:482–490.

Kridler, E. 1966. Hawaiian Islands National Wildlife Refuge, trip report, March 17–April 16, 1966. Unpublished report, Bureau of Sport Fisheries and Wildlife, U.S. Fish and Wildlife Service. (Available from Protected Species Investigation, National Marine Fisheries Service, Honolulu, HI.) 24 pp.

Laist, D. W. 1996. Impacts of marine debris: Entanglement of marine life in marine debris including a comprehensive list of species with entanglement and ingestion records. Pages 99–139 *in* J. M. Coe and D. R. Rogers (eds.), Marine Debris: Sources, Impacts, and Solutions. Springer-Verlag, New York, NY.

Laist, D. W., J. M. Coe, and K. J. O'Hara. 1999. Marine debris pollution. (This volume)

Lavigne, D. M. 1985a. Seals, science, and politics: Reflections on Canada's sealing controversy. Brief submitted to The Royal Commission on Seals and the Sealing Industry in Canada. La Vie Wildlife Research Associates, Ltd., Rockwood, Ontario, Canada.

Lavigne, D. M. 1985b. Canada's sealing controversy: The issues and the interest groups. Brief submitted to The Royal Commission on Seals and the Sealing Industry in Canada. La Vie Wildlife Research Associates, Ltd., Rockwood, Ontario, Canada.

Lavigne, D. M. 1995. Seals and fisheries, science and politics. Invited paper *in* Symposium II, The Role of Science in Conservation and Management. Eleventh Biennial Conference on the Biology of Marine Mammals, 14–18 December 1995, Orlando, FL (available on the World Wide Web at http://www.imma.org).

Lavigne, D. M. 1996. Ecological interactions between marine mammals, commercial fisheries, and their prey: Unravelling the tangled web. Pages 59–71 *in* W. A. Montevecchi (ed.), Studies of high-latitude seabirds. 4. Trophic relationships and energetics of endotherms in cold ocean systems. Canadian Wildlife Service Occasional Paper 91.

Lavigne, D. M. 1997. The role of science in fisheries management. Advisory Committee on Protection of the Sea. Conference on Oceans and Security. Panel on Oceans and Seas of the Americas. U.S. House of Representatives. 19–21 May 1997, Washington, DC. 7 pp.

Lavigne, D. M., V. B. Scheffer, and S. R. Kellert. 1999. The evolution of North American attitudes toward marine mammals. (This volume)

Leopold, A. 1933. Game Management. Charles Scribner's Sons. Reprinted 1986, The University of Wisconsin Press, Madison, WI. 481 pp.

Lichatowich, J. 1992. Managing for sustainable fisheries: Some social, economic, and ethical considerations. Pages 11–17 *in* G. H. Reeves, D. L. Bottom, and M. H. Brookes. 1992. Ethical questions for resource managers. U.S. Department of Agriculture, Forest Service, Pacific Northwest Research Station. General Technical Report PNW-GTR-288. 39 pp.

Malouf, A. 1986. Seals and sealing in Canada. Report of The Royal Commission on Seals and the Sealing Industry in Canada. 3 vols. Supply and Services Canada, Ottawa.

Marine Mammal Commission. 1997. Annual report to Congress for 1996. (Available from National Technical Information Service, Springfield, VA. PB97-142889.) 247 pp.

National Marine Fisheries Service. 1981. Final combined fishery management plan, environmental impact statement, regulatory analysis and draft regulations for the spiny lobster fisheries of the western Pacific region. National Marine Fisheries Service, Honolulu, HI.

National Marine Fisheries Service. 1991. Strategic plan of the National Marine Fisheries Service: Goals and objectives. (Available from Protected Species Investigation, National Marine Fisheries Service, Honolulu, HI.)

Norton, B. G. 1987. Why Preserve Natural Variety. Princeton University Press, Princeton, NJ. 281 pp.

Olive, D. 1992. Political Babble: The 1,000 Dumbest Things Ever Said by Politicians. John Wiley and Sons, Inc., New York, NY. 246 pp.

Olsen, D. L. 1969. Expedition report, Midway, Lisianski, and Laysan Islands, 9–13 November 1969. Unpublished report, Bureau of Sport Fisheries and Wildlife, U.S. Fish and Wildlife Service. (Available from Protected Species Investigation, National Marine Fisheries Service, Honolulu, HI.) 17 pp., including 13 plates.

Olver, C. H., B. J. Shuter, and C. K. Minns. 1995. Toward a definition of conservation principles for fisheries management. Canadian Journal of Fisheries and Aquatic Sciences 52:1584–1594.

Ragen, T. J., and D. M. Lavigne. 1999. The Hawaiian monk seal: Biology of an endangered species. (This volume)

Ralls, K., and A. M. Starfield. 1995. Choosing a management strategy: Two structured decision-making methods for evaluating the predictions of stochastic simulation models. Conservation Biology 9:175–181.

Rausch, R. L. 1969. Diphyllobothriid cestodes from the Hawaiian monk seal, *Monachus schauinslandi* Matschie, from Midway Atoll. Journal of the Fisheries Research Board of Canada 26:947–956.

Reeves, G. H., D. L. Bottom, and M. H. Brookes. 1992. Ethical questions for resource managers. U.S. Department of Agriculture, Forest Service, Pacific Northwest Research Station. General Technical Report PNW-GTR-288. 39 pp.

Reeves, R. R., and J. G. Mead. 1999. Marine mammals in captivity. (This volume)

Repenning, C. A. 1980. Warm-blooded life in cold ocean currents. Following the evolution of the seal. Oceans 13 (3): 18–24.

Reynolds, J. E., III. 1999. Efforts to conserve the manatees. (This volume)

Rice, D. W. 1960. Population dynamics of the Hawaiian monk seal. Journal of Mammalogy 41:376–385.

Rice, D. W. 1964. The Hawaiian monk seal: Rare mammal survives in Leeward Islands. Natural History 73 (2): 48–55.

Roberts, C. M. 1997. Ecological advice for the global fisheries crisis. Trends in Ecology and Evolution 12:35–38.

Schaller, G. 1993. The Last Panda. University of Chicago Press, Chicago and London. 291 pp.

Soulé, M. E. 1983. What do we really know about extinctions? Pages 111–124 *in* C. M. Schoenewald-Cox, S. M. Chambers, B. MacBryde, and W. L. Thomas (eds.), Genetics and Conservation: A Reference for Managing Wild Animal and Plant Populations. Benjamin/Cummings Publishing Company, Menlo Park, CA.

Starfield, A. M., J. D. Roth, and K. Ralls. 1995. "Mobbing" in Hawaiian monk seals (*Monachus schauinslandi*): The value of simulation modeling in the absence of apparently crucial data. Conservation Biology 9:166–174.

Tuchman, B. 1984. The March of Folly: From Troy to Viet Nam. Alfred A. Knopf, New York, NY. 447 pp.

Vaillant, G. E. 1977. Adaptations to Life. Little, Brown and Company, Boston, MA. 396 pp.

Van Toorenburg, R. A., W. G. Gilmartin, and J. R. Henderson. 1993. Composition of the Hawaiian monk seal population at Kure Atoll, 1990. Pacific Science 47:211–214.

Visser, I. K. G. 1993. Morbillivirus infections in seals, dolphins and porpoises. Universiteit Utrecht, Utrecht, the Netherlands. 167 pp.

Walker, R. L. 1964. Leeward Hawaiian Islands expedition, field notes, 5–22 March 1964. Unpublished report, State of Hawaii, Department of Land and Natural Resources, Division of Fish and Game. (Available from Protected Species Investigation, National Marine Fisheries Service, Honolulu, HI. 35 pp.

Whittow, G. C., G. H. Balazs, and G. D. Schmidt. 1980. Parasitic ulceration of the stomach in a Hawaiian monk seal (*Monachus schauinslandi*). `Elepaio 39:83–84.

Wilkinson, D. M. 1996. National Contingency Plan for Response to Unusual Marine Mammal Mortality Events. U.S. Department of Commerce, NOAA Technical Memorandum NMFS-OPR-9. 118 pp.

Wirtz, W. O., II. 1968. Reproduction, growth and development, and juvenile mortality in the Hawaiian monk seal. Journal of Mammalogy 49:229–238.

12

JOHN E. REYNOLDS III

Efforts to Conserve the Manatees

The Florida manatee (*Trichechus manatus latirostris*) occupied the news media across the United States a great deal during the first few months of 1996. In February scientists conducting a statewide aerial survey counted 2,639 manatees, exceeding the previous high count by nearly 800 animals. Immediately the public, speaking through the popular press, wanted to know: What does such a high count mean? Are manatees still endangered? Does the high count indicate that regulations and laws enacted to protect manatees are working well? Can such regulations be relaxed? Is the manatee population growing or did the scientists simply see more manatees?

A month later, a terrible manatee die-off caused by red tide began (Marine Mammal Commission 1996, Bossart et al. 1998). In southwestern Florida 158 manatee carcasses were recovered between 5 March and the end of April, when the die-off abruptly ended. During the first four months of 1996, more than 250 dead manatees were reported in Florida, compared with 1990's previous record high number of 206 for the entire year (Ackerman et al. 1995). Ultimately, 415 dead manatees were recovered in 1996, about 16% of the animals counted in the record February survey. Again the press raised questions: Why did so many manatees die? Will the die-off spread? Will the die-off happen again? Will manatees go extinct? Did people influence the magnitude of the die-off in some way? What are scientists and managers going to do? How can people protect manatees better?

The mixed messages and uncertainty arising in 1996 reflect the larger situation with manatees and their conservation. Good news and apparent progress (in terms of better scientific data, enactment of laws and regulations to protect manatees and their habitat, creation of protected areas for this purpose, and increased agency cooperation and public support) have been offset by factors that cause concern. These include habitat loss, high and rising levels of manatee mortality, and politically powerful opposition to the basic idea of protecting manatees and, indeed, endangered species in general. Overall, causes of concern have tended to outweigh reasons for hope, and the survival of the three extant species of manatees remains uncertain.

The precarious status of manatees is due to their biological traits (e.g., low reproductive potential), directed and incidental take by humans, and degradation or elimination of habitat. The loss of suitable habitat constitutes the greatest threat to the survival of most manatee populations both now and in the future, thanks to a growing human population and our escalating use of natural resources.

The question, of course, is whether manatees and the habitats on which they depend can be conserved. Because manatee biology can change only within the limits imposed by genotype, conservation requires changes in human institutions, activities, and values. Norris (1978) called the term *wildlife management* a misnomer and a measure of human arrogance. What is usually being sought is the management of human enterprises and activities in such a way that people can satisfy their desires or needs while attempting to maintain wild populations, communities, and ecosystems. Norris' assessment may oversimplify the situation, but with the development of the field of conservation biology, it becomes increasingly clear that management of people is necessary to conserve wildlife.

This chapter is divided into three sections. The first addresses the biology and status of manatees and discusses human impacts on manatee populations. The second provides a history of manatee conservation activities. The third identifies keys to success in manatee conservation, offers suggestions for enhancing conservation efforts, and illustrates some of the dilemmas faced by conservationists. My objectives in the final section are (1) to document a process that has achieved some success and that could provide a useful model for conservation of other species, and (2) to suggest ways to augment or modify existing efforts and thereby increase the chance that manatees will survive.

Biology and Status of Manatees

There are three living manatee species: the Amazonian manatee (*Trichechus inunguis*), the West African manatee (*T. senegalensis*), and the West Indian manatee (*T. manatus*). The latter species comprises two recognized subspecies, the Antillean manatee (*T. m. manatus*) and the Florida manatee (*T. m. latirostris*). Both the Amazonian and West Indian manatees are designated as endangered under the U.S. Endangered Species Act, and the West African manatee is listed as threatened. All species and subspecies of manatees are classified as vulnerable by the World Conservation Union-IUCN (Table 12-1).

In 1967 Daniel S. Hartman initiated a comprehensive study of Florida manatee behavior and ecology; his insights into the species' biology (Hartman 1979) suggested the vulnerability of manatees to extinction and laid the groundwork for manatee conservation efforts begun in the 1970s. Like other K-selected species (see Ricklefs 1990), manatees are iteroparous (breed repeatedly during their lifetimes), have small litter sizes (typically one), take years to reach sexual maturity, and have long life spans (see summary of population traits [Lefebvre and O'Shea 1995]; see also Table 12-2). Their low reproductive potential makes manatee populations easy to overexploit and slow to recover from overexploitation. In addition, Hartman (1979) suggested that manatee populations are small and possibly fragmented, conditions that can jeopardize long-term survival because of demographic factors, environmental variability, and the loss of genetic variation (Norse 1993, Talbot 1996). Finally, manatees share habitats and resources with humans, exposing them to the injurious effects of many of our activities (Hartman 1979).

The Florida Manatee

The Florida manatee is the largest trichechid and, in fact, the largest extant sirenian, with exceptional individuals weighing nearly 1,500 kg (1.65 tons) and measuring almost 4 m long. Females tend to be somewhat larger than males although body size cannot be used to determine the sex of an individual (Boyd et al. 1999).

The biology and population status of the Florida manatee are more thoroughly documented than is the case for the other manatees (see, for example, Odell 1982, Lefebvre et al. 1989, Reynolds and Odell 1991, O'Shea et al. 1995; various chapters in Reynolds and Rommel 1999). Some biological attributes of the Florida subspecies may apply to other manatees as well; thus, for conservation purposes, certain data (e.g., gestation times, food requirements, longevity, sensory

Table 12-1. Species of Manatees and Their Status

Scientific Name	Common Name	CITES[a]	WCU-IUCN[b]	U.S. ESA[c]
Trichechus inunguis	Amazonian manatee	Appendix I	Vulnerable	Endangered
Trichechus manatus[d]	West Indian manatee	Appendix I	Vulnerable	Endangered
Trichechus senegalensis	West African manatee	Appendix II	Vulnerable	Threatened

[a]Convention on International Trade in Endangered Species of Wild Fauna and Flora. Appendix I, Species threatened with extinction; Appendix II, Species not necessarily threatened with extinction currently.

[b]World Conservation Union-International Union for the Conservation of Nature and Natural Resources. Vulnerable is a category one level less critical than endangered.

[c]United States Endangered Species Act. Threatened corresponds to vulnerable in the WCU-IUCN scheme.

[d]Domning and Hayek (1986) documented that there are two subspecies of *Trichechus manatus: Trichechus manatus manatus* (Antillean manatee) and Trichechus manatus latirostris (Florida manatee).

Table 12-2. Estimated Population Traits of the Florida Manatee Based on Long-Term Life History Research

Trait	Estimated Age or Duration
Maximum life expectancy	60 years
Gestation period	11–13 months
Litter size	1
Percentage of twins	1.79% Blue Spring 1.40% Crystal River
Sex ratio at birth	1:1
Calf survival to 1 year	0.60 Blue Spring 0.67 Crystal River
Annual adult survival	90% Atlantic coast 96% Blue Spring 96% Crystal River
Earliest age of first reproduction of female	3–4 years
Mean age of first reproduction of female	5 years
Earliest onset of spermatogenesis	2–3 years
Proportion of adult females pregnant	0.33 salvaged carcasses 0.41 Blue Spring
Proportion of nursing first-year calves during winter season	0.36 (mean) 0.36 Crystal River 0.30 Blue Spring 0.38 Atlantic coast
Mean period of calf dependency	1.2 years
Mean interbirth interval	2.5 years
Highest number of births	May–September
Highest frequency in mating herds	February–July
Cumulative number of salvaged carcasses	2,613 (1974–1995)
Cumulative number documented in ID catalog	1,033 (1975–May 1996)
Highest count (aerial surveys)	2,639 in February 1996

Source: Data are from the National Biological Service and the Florida Department of Environmental Protection. The table is modified from Lefebvre and O'Shea (1995). C. Beck (National Biological Service) provided updated figures.

capabilities) regarding Florida manatees may be applied, albeit with caution, to other manatees until adequate data for those species or subspecies are available.

Florida manatees occupy coastal and riverine waters of Florida and southern Georgia, with individuals wandering (on rare occasion) as far north as Rhode Island or as far west as Texas during the summer (Fig. 12-1). A physiological inability to withstand prolonged or intensive cold limits the distribution of all living sirenians. In fact, manatees in Florida respond to cold weather by forming large aggregations at a few widely separated natural warm-water springs (e.g., those at Crystal River and Blue Spring) and artificial warm-water discharges (notably power plants at Riviera Beach, Cape Canaveral, Port Everglades, Fort Myers, and Apollo Beach in Tampa Bay (Figs. 12-2*A* and 12-2*B*). Water temperatures below about 20°C induce manatees to seek warm water although individual animals vary in their response to cold weather.

In warm weather, the manatees disperse widely. Their distribution, however, is neither random nor uniform. Certain individuals show great fidelity to their thermal refugia in winter and to the general areas where they spend their summers (National Biological Service, Sirenia Project 1993).

Particular locations contain preferred habitat. In summer these include certain waters in Brevard County, Everglades National Park, waters of the "Big Bend" along Florida's northwestern coast, and Tampa and Biscayne Bays (Fig. 12-2*B*). The habitat features most important to manatees are abundant sea grasses or other food, access to fresh water for drinking (probably not a physiological necessity but an apparent preference), and the absence of human waterborne activities, such as boating. The locations in Florida where manatee use has increased dramatically in the past few decades (e.g., around Cape Canaveral, at Crystal River, and around the Tampa Electric Company [TECO] plant at Apollo Beach in Tampa Bay) (Fig. 12-2*A*) share common characteristics: they possess resources sought by manatees (e.g., food and fresh or warm water), but, more important, they also provide areas where all human activities are prohibited. This suggests that manatees take advantage, at least to some extent, of the best and safest habitat by congregating in areas with particular characteristics.

The record high count of 2,639 manatees in 1996 was due, in part, to near-perfect survey conditions, including prolonged cold weather (which causes the animals to aggregate in areas with warm water), low winds (which make it easier for observers to detect animals), and sunny skies (which encourage manatees to bask at the surface) (B. Ackerman, Florida Department of Environmental Protection, pers. comm.). Because some individuals may have been counted more than once and others not at all, the count cannot be considered 100% accurate. The difficulty in sampling manatees using aerial and other survey methods makes it inappropriate for scientists to say exactly how many manatees exist. However, understanding population trends may be more useful than knowing the precise number of animals. A provisional model created using several long-term databases suggests that the numbers of manatees in certain parts of Florida are increasing, but that changes in adult survival could be especially critical in maintaining particular populations. The manatee population on the east coast of Florida might be especially vulnerable (Eberhardt and O'Shea 1995).

Other trend analyses have been done using specific databases. Aerial survey data suggest that the manatee population on Florida's east coast may have increased between 1982 and 1991 (Garrott et al. 1995). Other authors using essentially the same data but applying different statistical tests have suggested that the population in this area increased

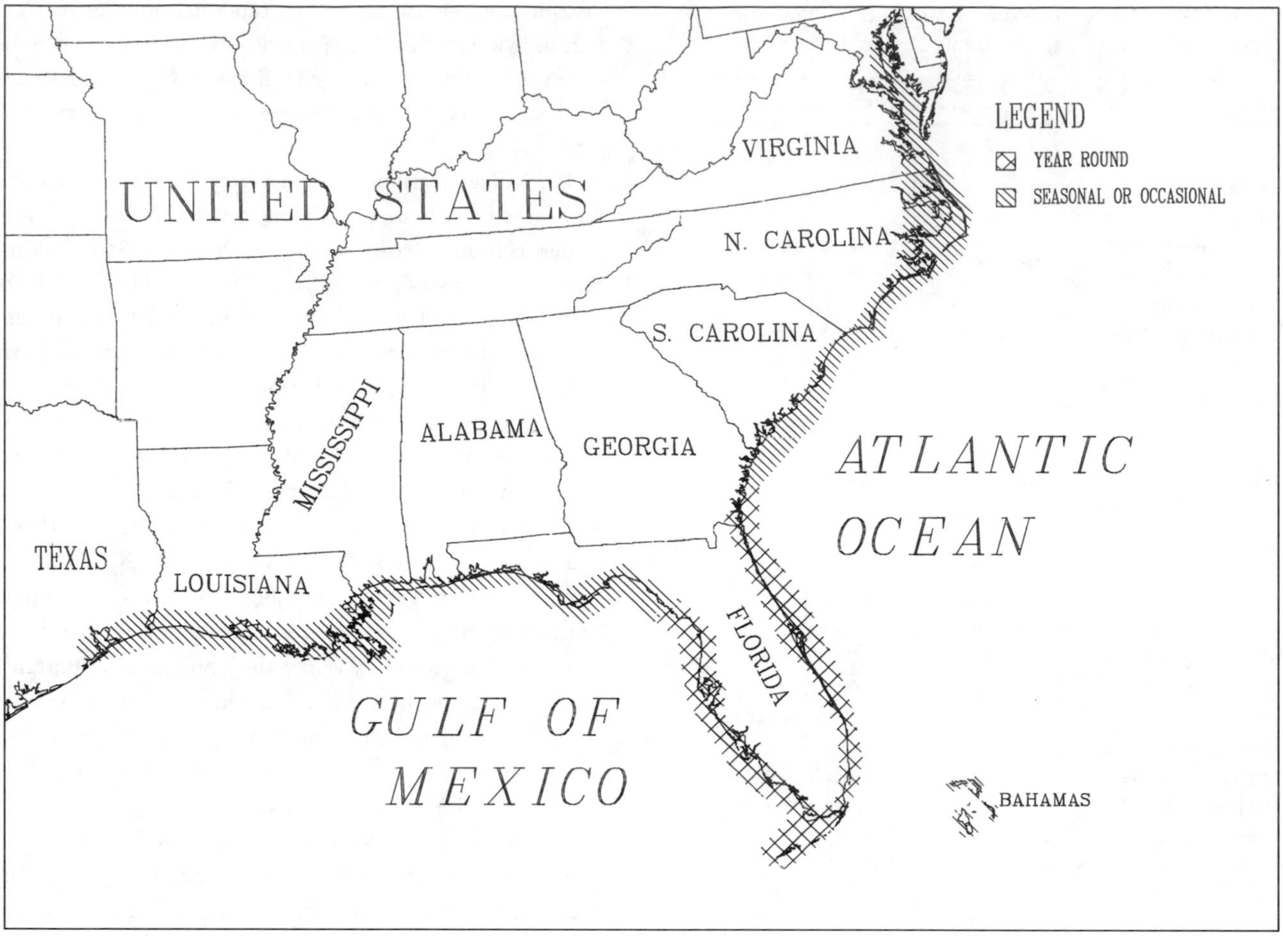

Figure 12-1. Distribution of Florida manatees. Note that occasional individuals (e.g., "Chessie") travel as far north as Rhode Island during the summer. (Map by L. Ward-Geiger, Florida Marine Research Institute)

through the 1980s but was stable or decreased slightly in the early 1990s (Craig et al. 1997). O'Shea and Langtimm (1995) assessed adult survival using photo-identification data and suggested that abundance along the east coast may be declining slightly.

Marmontel et al. (1997) did a population viability analysis for Florida manatees and thereby reinforced how vital adult survival is. Based on certain assumptions, those authors concluded that manatee numbers in Florida may be declining slightly at present and that the probability of persistence of the subspecies is only 0.44 over 1,000 years (i.e., there is a 44% chance of survival for 1,000 years). In their analysis, a 10% decrease in adult mortality would allow population growth, whereas a 10% increase in adult mortality would drive it to extinction. Models such as this one underscore the importance of adult survival in the manatee's population dynamics. Unusual mortality events such as the March–April 1996 die-off, in which more adults died than juveniles or calves (Bolen 1997), can have devastating consequences.

Female Florida manatees can reach sexual maturity as early as three years of age (Marmontel 1995), and some males exhibit spermatogenesis when only two years old (Hernandez et al. 1995). Most manatees more than 2.7 m long are probably sexually mature, although there is considerable individual variation in both age and size at sexual maturity (see review by Boyd et al. 1999).

Marmontel (1993) examined growth layers in ear bones and demonstrated that manatees can live at least 50 years. Bolen (1997) found that no female manatees and virtually no males that died in the 1996 epizootic were more than 20 years old. Two captive manatees, Romeo and Juliet, held at the Miami Seaquarium since 1957 and 1958, respectively (Salisbury and Beck 1992), are presumably at least in their mid-40s and are still breeding (Zeiller 1992). Another sirenian, the dugong (*Dugong dugon*), lives at least 60 years (Mitchell 1976).

Gestation time in Florida manatees is unknown, but most estimates range between 11 and 13 months (Boyd et al. 1999). Newborn manatees, which can appear in any season

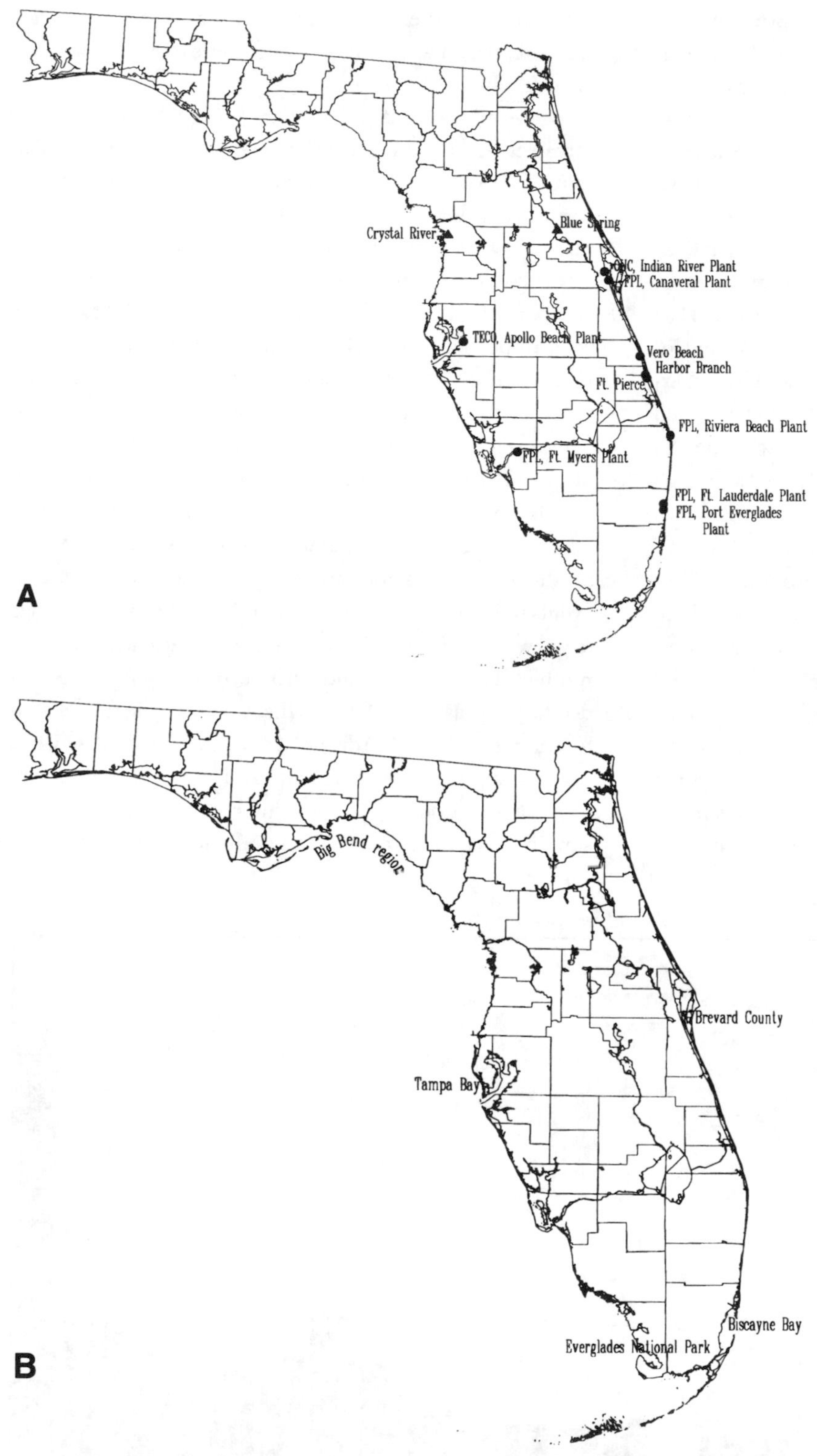

Figure 12-2. Locations in Florida where manatees are common: (*A*) during winter (power plants and springs); and (*B*) during warmer months (Brevard County, Everglades National Park, the Big Bend region, and Tampa and Biscayne Bays). (Maps by L. Ward-Geiger, Florida Marine Research Institute)

although infrequently in winter, measure about 120 cm long and weigh about 30 kg. About 1.4% of births are twins (Rathbun et al. 1995). Calves remain with their mothers for one to two years, during which time they apparently learn where to find abundant food and fresh water year-round and warm water in winter (Rathbun et al. 1995).

Most female manatees give birth approximately every 2.5 years (Rathbun et al. 1995) and may reproduce successfully over several decades. Thus, a 50-year-old female that reached sexual maturity at age 3 and produced a calf every three years would theoretically have a lifetime reproductive potential of 16 offspring. Of course, some females reach sexual maturity at an older age, and not all offspring survive; as noted later in this chapter, perinatal mortality (i.e., death for no discernible reason of manatees that are assumed, based primarily on body length, to be close to newborn) is the fastest-rising category of manatee mortality. O'Shea and Hartley (1995) suggested that Florida manatees have reached their maximum level of reproductive output.

Scientists do not know the proportion of adult manatees that live out their natural life spans or the proportion of calves that reach sexual maturity. However, a great deal has been learned over the past two decades about causes and locations of manatee mortality (recently reviewed by Ackerman et al. 1995 and Wright et al. 1995). In 1974 D. K. Odell of the University of Miami and other scientists with the Department of the Interior's Sirenia Project initiated a carcass-salvage program in an attempt to understand what kills manatees. That program has been maintained since 1985 by scientists at the Florida Department of Environmental Protection. The availability of fresh carcasses has provided opportunities for scientists to assess causes of death and to conduct research on topics such as gross, microscopic, and ultrastructural anatomy of various organs or tissues (e.g., pituitary, brain, gastrointestinal tract, hemopoietic tissues, kidneys, heart, reproductive organs), stomach content analyses, and assessments of parasites. Although examination of deceased marine mammals may lack the glamour of field studies of their behavior, fresh marine mammal carcasses represent a wealth of opportunities for basic and applied research.

Between 1976 and the present, the number of manatee carcasses recovered annually has risen steadily. Until the disastrous die-off of 1996, the maximum number recovered in a single year was 206 in 1990; as noted earlier, in 1996, 415 carcasses were recovered in Florida (Fig. 12-3).

Between 1976 and 1996 the number of watercraft-related and perinatal deaths rose at rates of 7.5% and 11.6% per year, respectively (B. Ackerman, pers. comm.) (Fig. 12-4). Human-related causes accounted for at least 31% of all documented manatee mortality in Florida over that same time period (Fig. 12-5; note that the 1996 die-off places a huge number of carcasses in the undetermined category, thereby skewing what one sees in a "typical" year). Perinatal mortality (Fig. 12-4) includes unfit newborn animals but may also include calves that are orphaned because of natural events (e.g., hurricanes) or the impacts of human activities (e.g., watercraft collisions, excessive disturbance) on the mother. Between 1990 and 1993 both the total number of deaths per year (Fig. 12-3) and the number of deaths related to watercraft (Fig. 12-4) dropped. It has been speculated, but not well supported by data, that the drops occurred for any or a combination of the following reasons: (1) there were simply fewer manatees in the population; (2) boating and

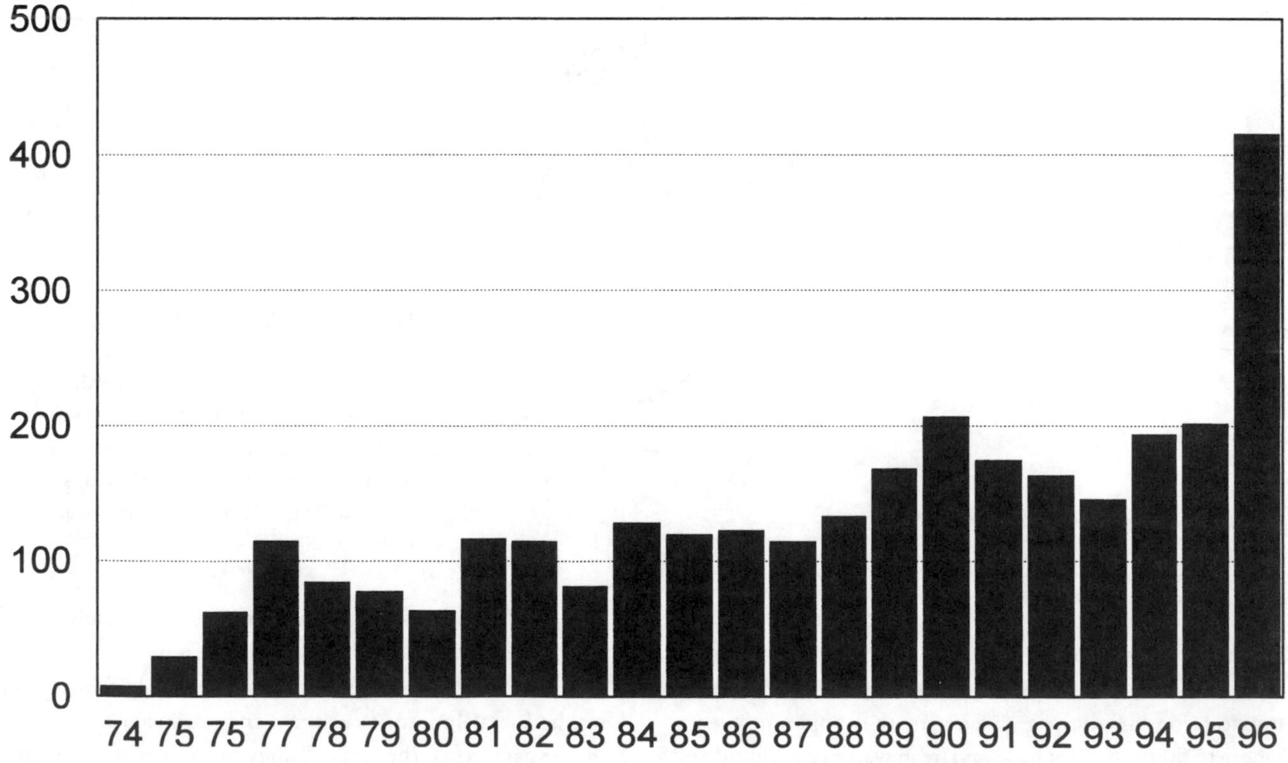

Figure 12-3. Mortality of Florida manatees between 1974 and 1996. (Graph by S. Wright, Florida Marine Research Institute)

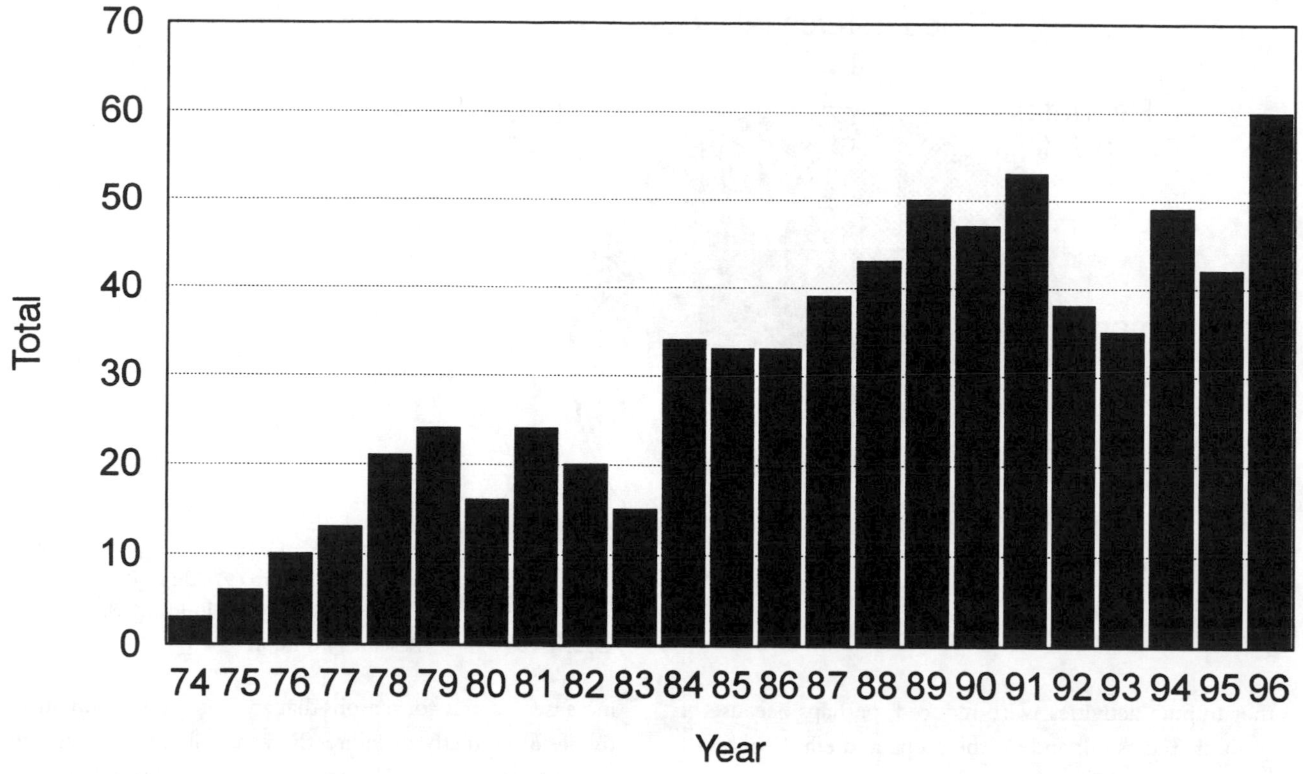

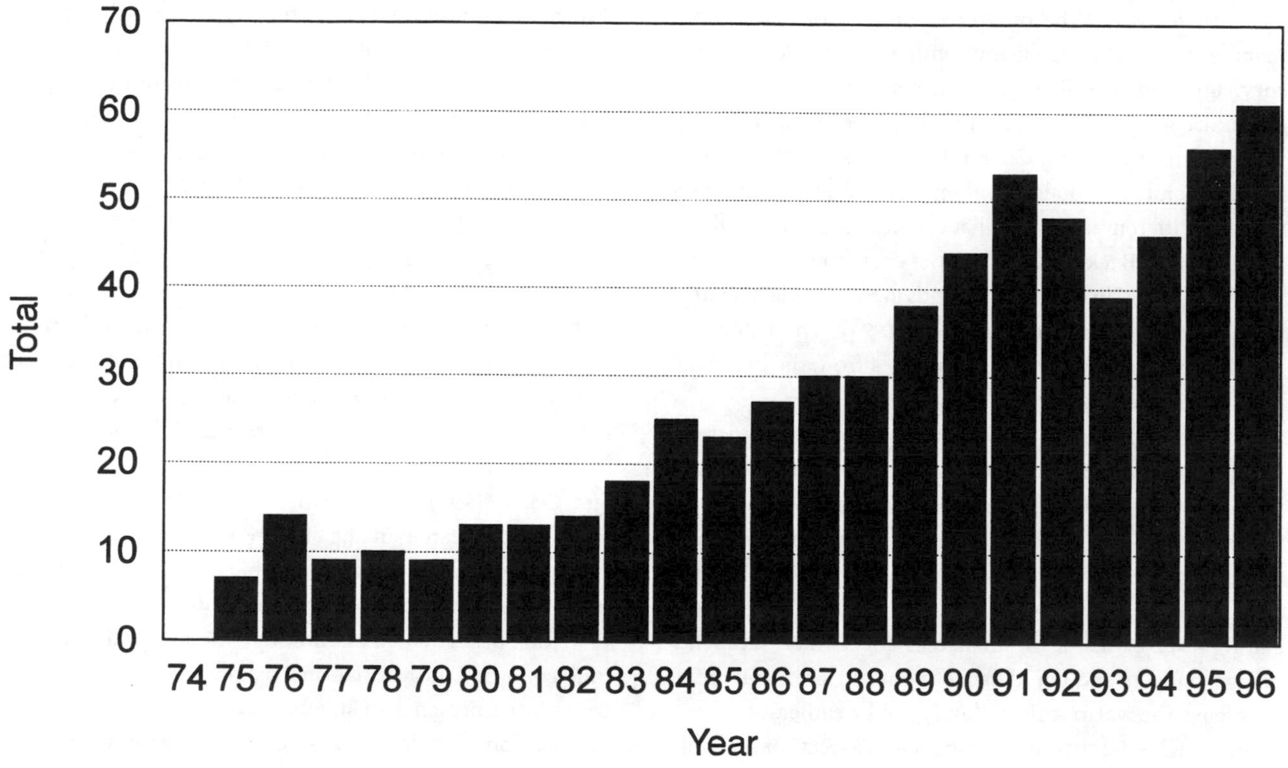

Figure 12-4. Watercraft-related (*top*) and perinatal (*bottom*) mortality of Florida manatees. (Graphs by S. Wright, Florida Marine Research Institute)

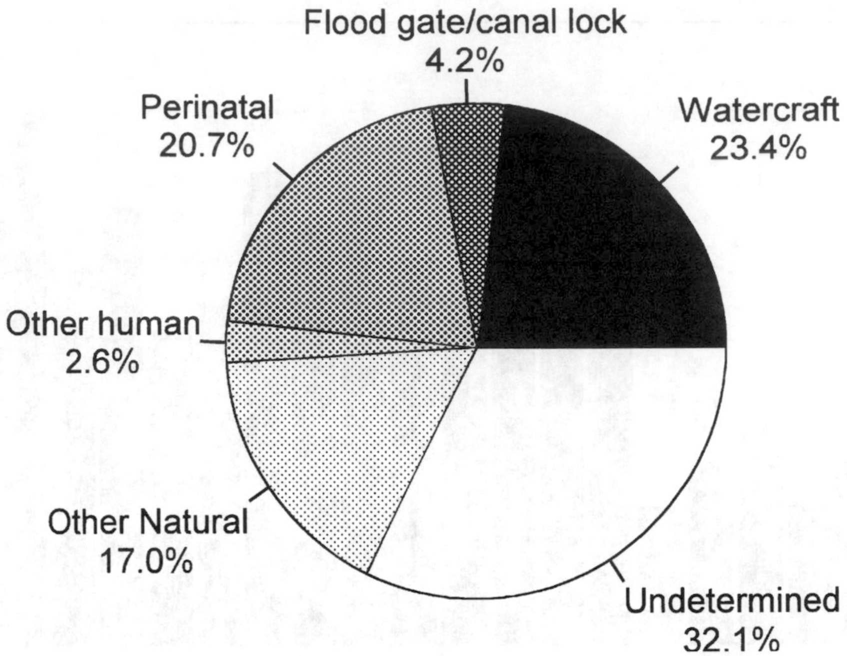

Figure 12-5. Categories of Florida manatee mortality from 1974 through 1996. (Graph by S. Wright, Florida Marine Research Institute)

other human activities were reduced, perhaps because of economic recession; and (3) the scope and effectiveness of conservation and education programs increased.

Mortality is not the only direct impact of humans on manatees (Fig. 12-6). Collisions with watercraft leave some surviving manatees disabled. Scars resulting from such collisions are graphic reminders that high-speed boats can severely injure manatees. Currently, scientists at the Sirenia Project maintain a catalog containing photographs of more than 900 different manatees that can be recognized by their scar patterns (Beck and Reid 1995); data from this catalog have been useful in suggesting trends in the Florida manatee population (O'Shea and Langtimm 1995). The extent to which serious injury removes manatees from the breeding population is unknown.

Human activities on the water may also cause manatees to expend more energy than they normally would and cause them to leave optimal habitats. For example, when manatees aggregate at Crystal River and nearby areas in winter, thousands of divers come for the experience of being in the water with the animals. O'Shea (1995) suggested that the resulting disturbance of the manatees affects their time and energy budgets and could cause them to sicken and die if they leave the warm springs during cold weather.

Although scientists understand some aspects of the biology of Florida manatees, questions remain. Both the number of manatees that exist and population trends are still uncertain; however, several conclusions can be stated with some assurance: rather small increases in mortality (especially of adults) can dramatically reduce persistence of the species; the number of carcasses recovered, especially those of calves, increases steadily for reasons that are not known; human activities are directly or indirectly responsible for about one-third of all documented manatee deaths; cold weather limits distribution; the subspecies is strongly K-selected, with limited reproductive potential; and favored habitat coincides with areas used extensively by a burgeoning human population. Both the uncertainties and the certainties argue for conservative decision making to maintain future options to the greatest extent possible (Mangel et al. 1996).

The Antillean Manatee

Although it is morphologically similar to the Florida manatee, the Antillean subspecies is found throughout the wider Caribbean and Gulf of Mexico (including Mexico and perhaps Texas) and the northeastern (i.e., Atlantic) coast of South America (Fig. 12-7). Lefebvre et al. (1989), Reynolds and Odell (1991), and Marmontel (1994) provided overviews of Antillean manatee biology and status.

Relatively little research has been done on Antillean manatees, and population size and trends are far less known than for Florida manatees. Although the subspecies is found in 19 countries, its distribution is patchy and probably relates to both the presence of suitable habitat and the history of exploitation. Antillean manatees have been extirpated or severely depleted in many areas by directed hunting and trapping and by incidental capture in fishing gear. Cold weather is not a factor influencing Antillean manatee ecology, but anecdotal accounts suggest that rainy and dry seasons influence manatee distribution in particular areas. Belize and Quintana Roo (Mexico) may share the largest

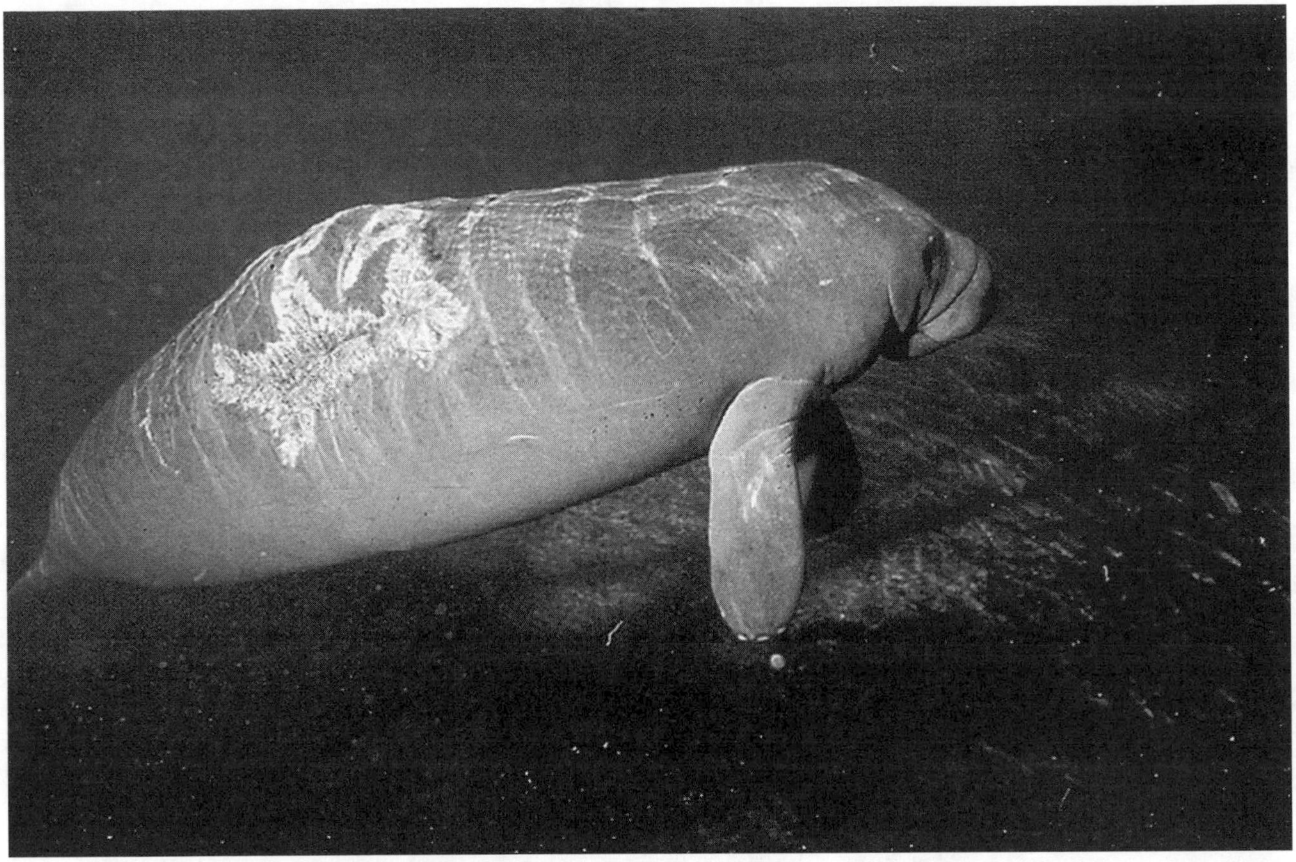

Figure 12-6. A Florida manatee. Note the presence of scars, caused by a boat propeller, on the animal's back. (Photograph courtesy of Sirenia Project, National Biological Service)

population of Antillean manatees (well over 100), and Belize has been described as "a last stronghold for manatees in the Caribbean" (O'Shea and Salisbury 1991:156).

Anecdotal reports (see Reynolds and Odell 1991) suggest that sharks prey on Antillean manatees, but the primary predators are humans. There is a long history of manatee hunting in the Caribbean, and manatees figure prominently in folklore (reviewed by Marmontel 1994). In the early 1990s an unfortunate situation arose in the coastal Miskito Indian village of Haulover in Nicaragua (Carr 1994). Among the Miskito Indians, young men traditionally underwent a ritual of manhood, which included killing a manatee. That practice ceased during the 1960s but was revived in a single village in 1992. By early 1994 young men had killed 22 manatees, likely a significant percentage of Nicaragua's manatees (T. Carr, pers. comm.). As of mid-1994 the situation remained unresolved, but it illustrates both the extent to which activities of a small group of people can suddenly and dramatically influence the survival of local groups of manatees, and how cultural beliefs and values can affect local resource use. Although intensive hunting of Antillean manatees appears to be rare, the impact of manatee hunting in certain countries may have influenced the behavior of some animals that have become nocturnal and/or crepuscular in Honduras (Rathbun et al. 1983), Costa Rica (Reynolds et al. 1995), and elsewhere (Reynolds and Odell 1991).

Human activities other than deliberate killing have an impact on Antillean manatees. For example, although precise data are lacking, incidental take of manatees in fishing nets may well be the most serious single threat to certain populations. Other potential problems include effects of runoff containing agricultural pesticides and herbicides, ingestion of plastic bags used on banana plantations (Reynolds et al. 1995), and tourism (e.g., in Southern Lagoon, Belize [see Horwich et al. 1993]). "Ecotourism," in fact, is often viewed simplistically as a solution that provides for the economic needs of local people while maintaining natural resources. In practice, ecotourism, or nature tourism, like all forms of economic development, requires careful planning to minimize undesirable and unforeseen impacts (see, for example, Lindberg and Hawkins 1993).

Small but multifaceted research programs are under way in Quintana Roo (Mexico), Belize, Puerto Rico, Jamaica, Cuba, Guatemala, and Brazil (see reviews by Reynolds and Odell 1991, Marmontel 1994). By means of aerial surveys, interviews with local residents, including fishermen and

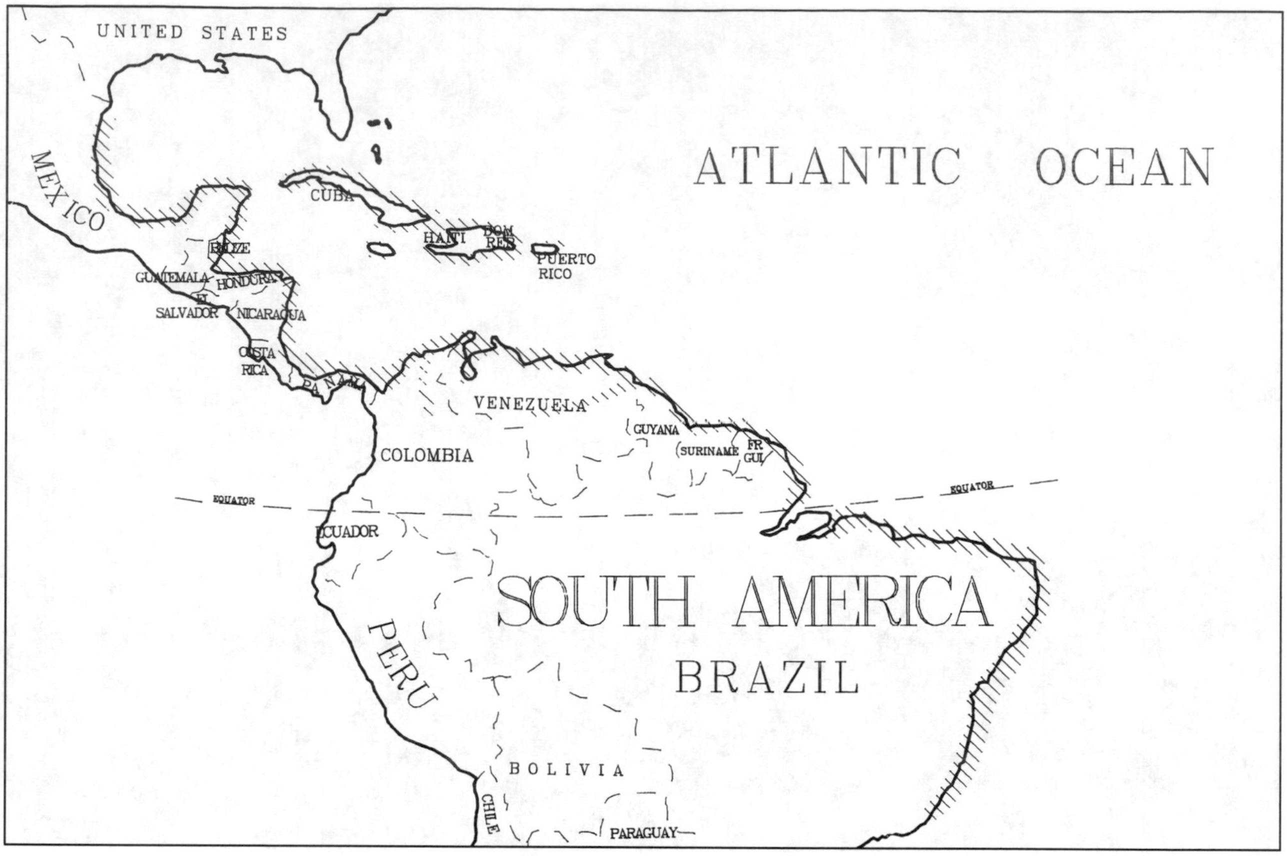

Figure 12-7. Distribution of Antillean manatees. Note that the map is based, in some cases, on dated or anecdotal information. As additional research is conducted, a more definitive picture of the distribution of Antillean manatees should emerge. (Map by L. Ward-Geiger, Florida Marine Research Institute)

hunters, and, in some cases, telemetry, scientists have begun to identify high-use areas for manatees in some countries. Currently, knowledge is expanding, but life history information regarding Florida manatees is often used to fill gaps. R. K. Bonde (Sirenia Project, pers. comm.) noted that this approach is not without some danger because, behaviorally at least, Antillean and Florida manatees differ. For example, Antillean manatees do not form dense, seasonal aggregations (as Florida manatees do) and tend to avoid humans as much as possible (something Florida manatees often cannot do). Thus, behavioral differences alone suggest that different approaches to conservation may be necessary to conserve manatees in Central and South America. If one adds differences in socioeconomic and political conditions (i.e., the "people management" noted at the outset of this chapter), it is clear that solutions to manatee conservation problems in Florida do not necessarily work well elsewhere.

The West African Manatee

The West African manatee is even less studied than the Antillean manatee (Reynolds and Odell 1991). The range of West African manatees extends from Senegal to at least as far south as the Kwanza River in Angola (Fig. 12-8). The general appearance and habitat preferences of this species are similar to those of the Florida manatee. For example, West African manatees are not found in waters colder than 18°C, close to the temperature that induces manatee migrations and aggregations in Florida. However, as has been suggested for Antillean manatees, West African manatees appear to respond to the rainy season by migrating up rivers and to dry seasons by migrating to the coasts (Reynolds and Odell 1991).

As with other manatee species, little is known about population sizes, habitat use, and population trends of West African manatees. Humans, and possibly sharks and crocodiles, kill and eat West African manatees. One hunter in Sierra Leone claimed to have killed more than 200 manatees, and interviews with hunters among the Mende of the Pujehun District of that country suggested an average annual catch of 20 manatees (Reeves et al. 1988). As with Antillean manatees, manatee hunting in Africa has a long history and is rooted in tradition and folklore. In some cases, the killing of manatees is not done primarily to obtain meat

Figure 12-8. Distribution of West African manatees. As noted for Figure 12-7, the map is based, at least to some extent, on dated or anecdotal information and may not depict the actual current distribution of *T. senegalensis*. (Map by L. Ward-Geiger, Florida Marine Research Institute)

or other products. For instance, the Mende in Sierra Leone hunt manatees, at least in part, to reduce manatee numbers and thereby to prevent the animals from tearing fishing nets, destroying fish in nets, and plundering rice fields (Reeves et al. 1988).

On the other hand, local myths and traditions may protect manatees. Villagers in the Korup region of Cameroon consider manatees to be fierce, dangerous animals; this perception, coupled with a distaste for manatee meat, means that people in that area rarely hunt manatees (Grigione 1996).

James A. Powell Jr. worked in the 1980s for Wildlife Conservation International in a number of West African countries to learn about local manatee populations and to help establish manatee conservation and research programs. The longevity and scope of the programs he helped to create are unknown, but lack of stable funding makes long-term studies, so valuable to scientists and conservationists involved with Florida manatees, virtually impossible.

The Amazonian Manatee

The final species to be considered, the Amazonian manatee, is morphologically and ecologically quite different from its congeners (Reynolds and Odell 1991). The Amazonian manatee is confined to freshwater habitats (Fig. 12-9), where it reaches a maximum length of 2.8 m and a weight of about 480 kg (making it the smallest extant species of manatee). Rosas (1994) provided an excellent overview of the biology, conservation, and status of the species.

Although studies of Amazonian manatees have occurred in several countries (see Timm et al. 1986, Reeves et al. 1996), the best known program is in Brazil. The Brazilian government's Instituto Nacional de Pesquisas da Amazonia (INPA) began Projeto Peixe Boi (the Manatee Project) in 1975, and Brazilian and foreign scientists have studied Amazonian manatees, using facilities in Manaus and Tefé as headquarters. Scientists have learned that the species apparently prefers areas characterized by abundant vegetation and water temperatures between 25° and 30°C. The day-to-day existence of manatees in the Amazon basin is closely regulated by seasonal availability of water. During the dry season (November and December in Brazil), when water levels fall as much as 10–15 m, Amazonian manatees may go without food for periods of perhaps 200 days, although much shorter periods of fasting are more likely (Best 1983). At such times, manatees may become concentrated in the

Figure 12-9. Distribution of Amazonian manatees. A recent description of the distribution of *T. inunguis* in Peru appears in Reeves et al. (1996). As noted for Figures 12-7 and 12-8, the distribution of Amazonian manatees is not well documented. See Rosas (1994) for a recent review. (Map by L. Ward-Geiger, Florida Marine Research Institute)

few remaining deep pools, where they may be vulnerable to natural predators (e.g., jaguars, caimans) or human hunters. People killed hundreds of manatees in Brazilian lakes during the extremely dry season of 1963 (Thornback and Jenkins 1982).

Amazonian manatee hunting has been done for both subsistence and profit. Domning (1982) documented that tens of thousands of manatee skins (used to make durable leather products, including machine belts) were exported from the Brazilian Amazon between 1935 and 1954, and that the production of manatee meat for export peaked in the late 1950s.

Catch records are not kept in areas where Amazonian manatees are hunted and trapped, so little is known about the scale of killing. However, it is clear that deliberate hunting and incidental capture of Amazonian manatees still occur throughout the species' range despite legal protection at the national level and sometimes at the local level. For example, Timm et al. (1986) noted that in Ecuador and Peru, manatee hunters were employed in the 1980s to provide meat to military personnel patrolling the borders. More recently, Reeves et al. (1996) noted that Peruvians continue to kill manatees for meat, which finds a ready market in towns and villages; the annual take in the Samiria River system alone may number in the "few tens." Reeves et al. (1996) are pessimistic about the survival of manatees in Peru unless a major change occurs in the way human activities are managed.

Amazonian manatees might be able to sustain continued low-level harvesting if that were the only impact of humans. However, deforestation and pollution related to mining and agricultural development may eliminate critical manatee habitat, thereby hastening the species' demise. Burgess (1995) provided a good overview of the extent to which tropical deforestation has affected both biodiversity and economics. She noted that in the 1980s Latin American countries eliminated 7.4 million ha of tropical forests per year; Brazil sustained the greatest annual loss with 3.2 million ha per year. However, Myers (1988) stated that, where remote sensing data exist, the documented deforestation is greater than had been estimated using other methods. Even though it is impossible to be accurate, Wilson (1987, cited by Myers 1988) suggested that 10,000 tropical forest species go extinct each year. Although scientists have not assessed the extent to which deforestation and mining directly or indirectly affect the carrying capacity of manatee habitat, clearly the disruption of energy flows, loss of species, introduction of toxicants, and other consequences of mining and deforestation will do nothing to promote survival of manatees. In his review of threats to Amazonian manatees, Rosas (1994) suggested that construction of hydroelectric dams could limit interchange of genes among manatees in the Amazon River, thereby limiting genetic variability of isolated groups of manatees; this, too, could impair species survival.

This discussion began with the premise that scientific research on manatee biology provides information that facilitates species conservation. For example, once scientists identify locations of high manatee use, those areas can be protected. However, it should be clear that scientific knowledge alone is not sufficient to conserve species. Human activities influence the persistence of species, regardless of the extent to which scientific data exist. When economic interests lead to habitat destruction, species dependent on that habitat are jeopardized. The following sections describe what people have done or should do to conserve manatees.

History of Manatee Conservation Efforts

Efforts to study and conserve manatees and dugongs have been stepped up in the past decade, and important partnerships have developed (Marsh and Lefebvre 1994). To date, the conservation efforts for Florida manatees have been most productive.

Conservation Efforts in the United States

In Florida an infrastructure of federal and state agencies, businesses, academic institutions, and conservation organizations was created in the mid- or late 1970s to promote the use of scientific knowledge for manatee conservation (see reviews by Reynolds and Gluckman 1988, Reynolds 1995). Together these groups work to obtain and interpret biological data, promulgate and enforce laws and other regulations, identify and prevent loss of critical habitat for manatees, develop plans to accommodate human population growth and its effects, and educate the public. A great deal of communication and coordination is needed to prevent unnecessary duplication of effort, assure that finite human and financial resources are used optimally, and set priorities for management and conservation tasks.

An important entity in the coordination process is the Florida Manatee Recovery Team, established in 1980. The team, which has included representatives of 13 agencies and organizations, has developed recovery plans (e.g., U.S. Fish and Wildlife Service 1989, 1996) that include carefully conceived implementation schedules with assigned tasks. In fact, a properly constructed recovery plan, with broad agency and private representation, is a key to effective conservation of endangered species, and the Florida Manatee Recovery Plan has been hailed as an extraordinarily useful planning document, worthy of imitation (Wallace 1994). The manatee coordinator for the Fish and Wildlife Service in Jacksonville, Florida, is head of the recovery team.

Federal Agency Responsibilities

On the federal side, three agencies—the Marine Mammal Commission, the Fish and Wildlife Service, and the National Biological Service (now the Biological Resources Division of the U.S. Geological Survey)—have played particularly important roles in manatee conservation. The Marine Mammal Commission, created under Title II of the Marine Mammal Protection Act of 1972, is an independent agency with oversight for conservation of and research on marine mammals in the United States. In the 1970s the Commission recognized the precarious status of the Florida manatee population and the magnitude of human impacts on the species, as well as the lack of an organized interinstitutional approach to manatee conservation, and it became a catalyst for research and conservation activities (Table 12-3, Table 12-4). Possibly the Commission's most important achievement was to persuade the Fish and Wildlife Service and the Florida Department of Natural Resources to appoint a single knowledgeable person (Patrick M. Rose) to take charge of the manatee program. The agencies agreed that the manatee coordinator would work under contract to the Fish and Wildlife Service for the first three years and thereafter be supported by the Florida Department of Natural Resources.

Among the other actions prompted by the Commission are the creation of the Manatee Technical Advisory Council to serve as an independent advisory group to the executive director of the Florida Department of Natural Resources; development of the original Florida Manatee Recovery Plan in 1980 and subsequent revisions of the plan (U.S. Fish and Wildlife Service 1989, 1996); comprehensive overviews of research and management activities by the state of Florida and the Fish and Wildlife Service; support of training programs in manatee biology and the enforcement of state and

Table 12-3. Summary of Recent and Ongoing Research or Research-Related Activities Conducted by the Federal Government and the State of Florida Concerning West Indian Manatees

Agency	Recent and Current Research	Primary Locations
U.S. Fish and Wildlife Service[a]	Life history studies	Crystal River/Blue Spring
	Carcass salvage	Southeastern United States
	Radio and satellite telemetry	Florida, east and west coasts; Cumberland Island, Georgia
	Behavioral studies	Crystal River/Blue Spring
	Ecosystem studies	Hobe Sound/Crystal River/Blue Spring
	Aerial surveys	Crystal River/Florida east coast
	Scar catalog	State of Florida
	Advice	Worldwide
	Age determination	State of Florida
Cooperative Fish and Wildlife Research Unit	Human recreational activities	Crystal River
	Research and management plans	Crystal River
	Aerial surveys	Caloosahatchee and Crystal Rivers
	Aerial surveys/human activities	Northeastern Florida
	Radio tracking	Cumberland Sound
	Description of habitat types and manatee distribution	Crystal River
Florida Department of Environmental Protection	Carcass salvage	State of Florida
	Aerial surveys	State of Florida
	Geographic information systems	State of Florida
	Radio and satellite telemetry	Central, west Florida
	Ecosystem studies	Hobe Sound
	Human activities (boat use patterns)	Manatee County
U.S. Army Corps of Engineers	Overview of manatee status	State of Florida
	Aerial surveys	Florida east coast
	Radio tracking	State of Florida
National Aeronautics and Space Administration	Aerial surveys	Banana River
	Ecosystem studies	Banana River
Marine Mammal Commission	Constituting/convening the Manatee Technical Advisory Council	State of Florida
	Protection and research	State of Florida
	Research and management plans	Crystal River
	Food sources and feeding habits	Hobe Sound
National Marine Fisheries Service	Ecosystems studies	Hobe Sound
National Park Service	Aerial surveys	Cumberland Island, Georgia; Everglades National Park
	Radio telemetry	Cumberland Sound
U.S. Navy	Radio telemetry	Cumberland Sound
Chassahowitzka National Wildlife Refuge	Aerial surveys	Citrus County

Source: Updated from Reynolds and Gluckman (1988) and Reynolds (1995).

[a]For much of its history, the Sirenia Project was administered through the U.S. Fish and Wildlife Service. Although the project was briefly associated with the National Biological Survey and the National Biological Service in the early to mid-1990s, most recently (October 1996) authority was turned over to the U.S. Geological Survey. All of these agencies are or were part of the Department of the Interior.

federal laws for officers of the Florida Marine Patrol and the Game and Freshwater Fish Commission; a workshop in 1989 (Reynolds and Haddad 1990) to determine the utility of geographic information systems as a tool to study and manage manatees and manatee habitat; studies to assess local manatee populations (Packard 1981) and survey methods by which population trends might be assessed (Packard et al. 1986) and quality of habitat (Packard and Wetterquist 1986); studies to develop techniques to determine the age of manatees and investigate population viability (Marmontel 1993); assessment of management needs in general (Marine Mammal Commission 1986, 1989); and enhancement of annual operating budgets for the Fish and Wildlife Service. The Commission's activities are described in its annual reports to Congress (e.g., Marine Mammal Commission 1994, 1996).

The Department of the Interior has responsibility for research and management activities involving manatees, but

Table 12-4. List of Agencies Involved in Management of Manatees or Manatee Habitat, and Brief Listing of Agency Duties in Terms of Management

Agency	Duties
Florida Department of Community Affairs	Local management plan approval; considers and approves developments of regional impact
Florida Department of Environmental Protection	Development of local management plans; enforcement; use of state-owned lands; regulatory activities; review of permit applications
Florida Game and Freshwater Fish Commission	Enforcement
Marine Mammal Commission	Oversight for all marine mammal activities in the United States
U.S. Army Corps of Engineers	Permitting of various human activities; initiates section 7 consultations
U.S. Fish and Wildlife Service	Section 7 consultations and jeopardy opinions; enforcement; review of permit applications; development and updating of Species Recovery Plan

Source: Modified from Reynolds (1995).

Note: These agencies specifically deal with planning, permitting, regulatory, and enforcement activities. For fuller descriptions of agency involvement, see Reynolds and Gluckman (1988).

these are handled by different agencies (Table 12-3, Table 12-4). The Fish and Wildlife Service has direct responsibility for manatee conservation in the United States and for enforcement of federal laws that include manatees (i.e., the Marine Mammal Protection Act of 1972 and the Endangered Species Act of 1973). Since October 1996 the U.S. Geological Survey has been the federal agency responsible for research on manatees, although such activities were conducted initially in 1974 and for two decades thereafter as Fish and Wildlife Service initiatives.

Through its office in Jacksonville, Florida, the Fish and Wildlife Service serves an important function by reviewing human activities that could prove detrimental to local manatee populations. As stipulated by section 7 of the Endangered Species Act of 1973, the Service reviews actions by other federal agencies to judge whether a particular activity "authorized, funded or carried out by such agency . . . is not likely to jeopardize the continued existence" of manatees or cause destruction of critical habitat. To date, more jeopardy opinions have been issued for manatees than for all other endangered species combined in the United States (Reynolds 1995). As noted earlier, the Fish and Wildlife Service coordinates implementation of the Florida Manatee Recovery Plan, the document that sets priorities and guides manatee research and conservation activities by involved parties, including federal and state agencies and other organizations.

The U.S. Geological Survey's Biological Resources Division (formerly the National Biological Service) is the biological research agency of the Department of the Interior (Table 12-3). Survey scientists are part of the Sirenia Project, located in Gainesville, Florida. Since 1974 these scientists have initiated many of the long-term studies that continue today (see Reynolds 1995). In addition, the Sirenia Project has been the primary source of assistance and advice for individuals in foreign countries who wish to study or conserve manatees.

Other federal agencies involved with manatees and manatee habitat include the U.S. Army Corps of Engineers, the U.S. Coast Guard, the National Aeronautics and Space Administration, and the U.S. Navy (Table 12-3). In addition, some of the habitat and other research carried out by National Marine Fisheries Service scientists relates to status of manatee habitat.

There are many notable instances of federal agencies working together to protect the Florida manatee. For example, in the late 1970s, in response to concerns raised by the Marine Mammal Commission, the National Aeronautics and Space Administration altered the design of certain ships, used to recover solid rocket boosters, to use waterjet propulsion, rather than propellers, when traversing waterways between Cape Canaveral and the ocean. This change has proved enormously effective in protecting manatees in those narrow waterways. Similarly, the Navy installed propeller shrouds on tugs and other port vessels at the Kings Bay (Georgia) submarine base, used large fenders to prevent the crushing of manatees by ships at the Mayport Naval Base (Florida), developed manatee public education and awareness programs at most of its installations in Georgia and Florida, and established manatee reserves in the waters of two Navy facilities.

State Responsibilities

Several branches of the Florida state government are also engaged in manatee conservation efforts (Table 12-3, Table 12-4). Until 1992 the primary agency was the Department of Natural Resources. In 1993 that department merged with the Department of Environmental Regulation to form a single entity, the Department of Environmental Protection, which is involved with both research and management of manatees.

The research arm of the department is the Florida Marine Research Institute located in St. Petersburg. The involvement of institute scientists in manatee studies is relatively recent although the department currently devotes more personnel and funding to manatee research than all other agencies combined. The source of funds for departmental programs is the Save the Manatee Trust Fund, which is supported by revenue from sources such as voluntary donations from Florida citizens, boat registration fees, and the sale of save-the-manatee license plates (Florida Department of Environmental Protection 1995). Institute scientists maintain the long-term program of manatee carcass recovery and analysis, conduct aerial surveys, interact with other scientists to develop manatee population models, and conduct telemetric research and assess habitat use by manatees. Scientists at the institute have also taken the lead in applying geographic information systems to marine research and management. Use of this technology has permitted easy integration of geographically referenced data to facilitate manatee research and conservation (Reynolds and Haddad 1990, Ward and Weigle 1993). In addition to its research activities, the institute is involved in education and awareness programs for manatees and other coastal and estuarine resources.

The management arm of the Department of Environmental Protection is the Office of Protected Species Management located in Tallahassee. The office develops recommendations for regulations to govern human activities (e.g., boat speed and access, locations of docks and marinas) that have an impact on manatees. The rulemaking process is long, complex, and controversial, and it requires extensive interaction with citizens of counties in which manatees are abundant or in which manatee mortality is high, as well as state legislators and the governor and cabinet. The office relies heavily on up-to-date scientific information from the Florida Marine Research Institute, the Sirenia Project, and others to make its decisions. In addition, the use of geographic information systems provides a valuable tool by which management staff can communicate scientific information on manatees, habitat, and human activities to legislators.

The Office of Protected Species Management has focused on creating regulations for 13 key counties where manatee mortality is high or manatees are numerous. Eventually, all coastal counties in Florida must conform to the Local Government Comprehensive Planning and Land Regulation Act of 1985 (informally called the Growth Management Act) by developing and implementing plans for human population growth that are compatible with protection of manatees and other natural resources. In a state whose population stands at approximately 13 million and grows by some 4,600 new residents a week (Florida Conservation Foundation 1993), such plans can scarcely be implemented too soon.

The third arm of the Department of Environmental Protection involved in manatee protection is the enforcement branch, the Florida Marine Patrol. Like the Office of Protected Species Management, the Florida Marine Patrol relies on briefings from scientists at the Marine Research Institute to understand manatees and their needs. The Marine Patrol, for example, frequently assists in rescuing injured, diseased, or orphaned calves; this activity requires some knowledge regarding when a manatee is truly in need of help.

A primary duty of the Florida Marine Patrol is to enforce the provisions of the Florida Manatee Sanctuary Act of 1978; however, the Marine Patrol is also responsible for enforcing other important laws (e.g., those involving interdiction of drug smugglers) and for protecting boaters and swimmers. Marine Patrol officers are cross-deputized with federal enforcement agents so that they can enforce federal laws. However, the size of its staff limits the Marine Patrol's ability to cover all areas of the state adequately (Reynolds 1995).

Other Florida state agencies involved in activities that affect manatees include the Department of Community Affairs and the Game and Freshwater Fish Commission (Table 12-4).

Although Florida is the state that provides the most resources for manatee research and conservation, the Georgia Department of Natural Resources is also involved in these activities. For example, the most recent Florida Manatee Recovery Plan (U.S. Fish and Wildlife Service 1996) identified the Georgia Department of Natural Resources as one of the primary agencies responsible for a number of tasks, including but not limited to carcass salvage, various types of research (e.g., on causes and trends in mortality, life history, habitat utilization), maintenance of a photo-identification catalog, habitat acquisition and protection, enforcement of laws, and public education and awareness.

Contributions by Private Groups

In addition to the extensive involvement by federal and state agencies, a number of nongovernmental entities contribute substantially to efforts to manage and conserve manatees (Table 12-5). Zoos and aquariums such as Homosassa Springs Nature World, Lowry Park Zoological Garden, Miami Seaquarium, and Sea World of Florida have played an important role by caring for diseased, injured, or orphaned manatees and providing facilities for certain types of research that is difficult to accomplish in the field. Some of the

Table 12-5. Summary of Research Activities Conducted or Sponsored by Private Organizations or Individual Scientists

Organization/Individual	Recent or Ongoing Research Activity	Primary Location
Florida Power & Light Company	Aerial surveys	East and southwest Florida coasts
	Scar catalog	Statewide
	Radio/satellite telemetry	Florida, east and west coasts
	Water temperatures	Caloosahatchee River
Save the Manatee Club	Aerial surveys	Tampa Bay
	Immunogenetics	N/A
	Photo-identification	State of Florida
	Various other projects	Belize, Ivory Coast, Costa Rica, Guatemala, state of Florida
D. Odell and colleagues (Sea World)	Clinical parameters	South and central Florida
	Carcass salvage	South Florida
	Morphometrics	N/A
	Parasites	N/A
	Aerial surveys	Everglades
	Behavior and ecology	South Florida
G. Bossart (Miami Seaquarium)	Clinical parameters	South Florida
	Immunology	
J. Reynolds and colleagues (Eckerd College)	Carcass salvage	South Florida
	Aerial surveys	State of Florida
	Functional anatomy	N/A
	Behavior and ecology	South Florida
	Immunogenetics	N/A
D. Domning (Howard University)	Anatomy	N/A
	Paleontology and systematics	N/A
	Feeding ecology	Hobe Sound
	Bibliography and index	N/A
J. Koelsch and colleagues (Mote Marine Laboratory)	Aerial surveys	Florida west coast
	Photo-identification	Florida west coast
	Acoustics	Marine zoological parks
J. Morris (Florida Institute of Technology)	Ecology and behavior	Florida, central east coast, Homosassa Springs
	Analysis of vocalizations	Homosassa Springs
	Nutrition	Homosassa Springs
E. Gerstein (Florida Atlantic University)	Acoustics	Marine zoological parks
J. and M. Provancha (Bionetics Corp.)	Aerial surveys	Brevard County
	Habitat assessment	

Source: Updated from Reynolds and Gluckman (1988) and Reynolds (1995).

research provides data useful to conservation of manatees in the wild (e.g., studies of manatee reproduction, osmoregulatory capabilities, and sensory abilities). The private institutions have also provided an opportunity for the public to observe manatees (Table 12-5). At Sea World alone, more than 14 million people had an opportunity to observe and learn about manatees between the mid-1970s and 1994 (J. Stofan, Sea World Education Department, pers. comm.). Educating people about manatee conservation as they watch recuperating animals in a zoo setting can make a strong impression that may do more to encourage actual conservation than reading an article or watching a documentary about manatees.

Other groups (Table 12-6) that have played prominent roles in educating the public about manatees are the Save the Manatee Club, Florida Power & Light Company, and Tampa Electric Company. The Save the Manatee Club, created by executive order of then-Governor Bob Graham in 1981, currently distributes its newsletter to more than 35,000 members worldwide. As of early 1994 the club estimated that it had distributed more than 87,000 educational publications of various types and reached more than two

Table 12-6. List of Organizations Involved in Manatee Education and Awareness Programs in Florida

Organization	Program
Colleges and universities	Classes; public lectures
Florida Department of Environmental Protection	Brochures, bumper stickers, posters, public lectures, etc.
Florida Power & Light Company	Booklets, bumper stickers, Educator's Guide, company film, public workshops
Marine Mammal Commission	Funding support for development of educational materials and for *Sirenews;* distribution of annual reports and other literature
Zoos and aquariums	Tours, efforts focused on children and teachers, educational displays
Port Everglades Authority	Bumper stickers, brochures, public tours and lectures
Save the Manatee Club	Newsletter, public service announcements, signs, press releases, in-service programs for teachers, brochure
Tampa Electric Company	Manatee viewing platform, lectures
U.S. Fish and Wildlife Service	Interpretive/Education Center literature distribution

Source: From Reynolds (1995).

Note: For more complete information regarding education and awareness, see Reynolds and Gluckman (1988).

million people (J. Vallee, pers. comm.). The club has supported a variety of research projects in the United States and elsewhere. Perhaps its greatest asset is its grass-roots approach to conservation, which involves extensive lobbying of legislators. This is an extremely valuable component of a comprehensive conservation effort and is a task that other groups cannot or will not do.

Florida Power & Light Company has supported numerous manatee education and awareness activities. Through mid-1994 the company had distributed more than 14 million booklets, bumper stickers, and other materials, and conducted manatee awareness workshops attended by more than 12,000 people (J. R. Wilcox, pers. comm.). Like Florida Power & Light Company, Tampa Electric Company is interested in educating the public about manatees in general and specifically about those found at power plants in winter. Both power companies have built manatee viewing areas near the warm-water discharge of a selected power plant; the viewing areas are patrolled to prevent inadvertent harm to the manatees, and educational information is provided.

More traditional educational activities occur within parks and wildlife refuges, schools, colleges, and universities (Table 12-5). At Eckerd College, for example, two different courses deal to at least some extent with manatee biology and management.

Conservation Efforts Elsewhere

The infrastructure that exists to deal with other species of manatees is minimal compared with that for the Florida subspecies. However, some efforts are being taken to extend protection to other manatee species.

The Antillean Manatee

For the Antillean manatee, communication and coordination are building at three levels: within some countries, between and among adjacent countries, and Caribbean-wide. All 19 Caribbean range nations with manatees have protective legislation in place (Marmontel 1994). That is not to say that the legislation is or can be strictly enforced. Nonetheless, the legal authority to protect manatees exists, and this is an important first step. In addition, teams of scientists have begun to study manatees within certain Caribbean countries, including Mexico, Belize, Honduras, Jamaica, Puerto Rico, and Venezuela, as well as in Brazil. In some cases (e.g., in Belize, Jamaica, Puerto Rico, and Mexico), education and awareness programs have been initiated by agencies or private concerns (e.g., the Belize Zoo, El Colegio de la Frontera Sur-Unidad Chetumal [ECOSUR] in Mexico, and the Red Caribena de Varamientos [Caribbean Stranding Network] in Puerto Rico). In Panama, Guyana, Puerto Rico, Belize, Nicaragua, Costa Rica, Mexico, and Jamaica, manatee experts from the United States have provided information or assistance.

Because Antillean manatees cross national borders, efforts to conserve them must be multinational. In September 1992 a meeting was held in Chetumal, Quintana Roo, Mexico, to attempt to formalize an approach to manatee conservation and research between Belize and Quintana Roo. Scientists representing the Marine Mammal Commission and the National Biological Service (now the Biological Resources Division of the U.S. Geological Survey) attended to advise scientists and administrators representing the Centro de Investigaciones de Quintana Roo (now called ECOSUR) and the Government of Belize. To date, the joint Belize-Mexico manatee program has made good progress by doing aerial surveys and telemetry, publishing educational materials, providing public awareness information via radio, and, perhaps most important, creating an excellent model for other countries with shared manatee populations.

At the regional level, activities have been initiated to protect manatees in the wider Caribbean Sea area as part of an initiative by the United Nations Environment Programme. The Protocol Concerning Specially Protected Areas and Wildlife (SPAW Protocol) was adopted in January 1990. In part, the protocol calls for "the establishment, publication and dissemination of general guidelines and criteria for the management and recovery of endangered and threatened species of regional concern, in the form of regional management plans" (Marmontel 1994). In March 1994 government representatives of several Caribbean range nations, United Nations Environment Programme officials, representatives of nongovernmental organizations, and scientists working with manatees in the United States, Mexico, Belize, Honduras, Puerto Rico, Jamaica, Venezuela, Trinidad and Tobago, and Suriname, met in Kingston, Jamaica. Those present agreed to (1) approve a regional management plan (Marmontel 1994); (2) allocate funds for expansion of education programs dealing with manatees throughout the Caribbean; (3) approve funding to continue the joint education and research efforts between Belize and Mexico, and to expand those efforts to involve scientists and administrators in Honduras; and (4) provide some funds for a regional manatee coordinator to help particular countries develop national manatee recovery plans. The U.S. Department of State provided financial support for these activities.

The stage is therefore set for significant progress to occur in both research and management involving the Antillean manatee.

The West African Manatee

The same cannot be said for the West African manatee. Although the species is totally protected under Class A of the African Convention for the Conservation of Nature and Natural Resources, which was signed by 38 countries in 1969 (see Reynolds and Odell 1991), enforcement is difficult and minimal. The same probably holds true for national laws protecting manatees in specific countries. As noted earlier, there have been some isolated studies of West African manatees, but such work remains piecemeal. Moreover, there is no evidence that linkages have been established between research findings and policies.

The Amazonian Manatee

The Amazonian manatee fortunately occupies areas under the jurisdiction of only four countries: Brazil, Ecuador, Peru, and Colombia. Although manatee research programs have been developed in a number of locations, Projeto Peixe Boi, located in Manaus, Brazil, has served as the center for Amazonian manatee research and conservation for a number of years. Despite minimal funding, project scientists accomplished a great deal between 1975 and 1986, when the leader of Projeto Peixe Boi, Robin Best, died. With his loss, work slowed. It is encouraging that support of activities there started to increase in the early 1990s. In addition, a new manatee research program, Projeto Mamiruá in Tefé, initiated extensive field research on manatees in the Brazilian Amazon (Marsh and Lefebvre 1994). Scientists now have a reasonable knowledge of the biology of the species; Rosas (1994) summarized available data regarding species morphology, behavior, reproduction, growth, husbandry, and habitat utilization. Rosas (1994) considered historical large-scale commercial exploitation, followed by more recent habitat destruction, to be the primary reasons for presumed reductions in the size of Amazonian manatee populations.

Summary of Efforts

In review, a large and effective infrastructure exists to support conservation and management of Florida manatees. The stage is set for expansion of national and multinational efforts to conserve Antillean manatees in much of their range. A long-term program is in place in Brazil to consider Amazonian manatee research and conservation, but that program is not well linked to development and other human activities that threaten the species with extinction. Little, if any, infrastructure exists to promote the conservation of the West African manatee.

How well do manatee conservation programs measure up? Even the most comprehensive program, that of the Florida manatee, falls short. Although efforts have been made to mitigate the effects of human population growth and to involve as many stakeholders as possible in decision making, much more needs to be done in all areas.

Habitat Conservation Programs

Conservation efforts focused solely on manatees are doomed to fail if the habitat required by the animals is lost. Soileau et al. (1985:471) indicated that "loss of habitat now is the most critical fish and wildlife problem in the United States, and the lessening or replacement of these losses is an absolute necessity." Habitat loss for manatees is a problem not only in the United States; it is a major impediment to species survival and recovery worldwide. Identification and conservation of critical habitat is, therefore, an essential element to any manatee conservation program.

U.S. Programs

In the United States, manatee habitat has been conserved in a number of ways (Reynolds and Gluckman 1988), the two most important being habitat acquisition and the promulgation and enforcement of rules and regulations governing human activities in critical locations (Fig. 12-10). Although considerable progress has occurred in both of these areas, more work is needed to maintain adequate habitat for Florida manatees. Hefner (1986), for example, documented the extent to which Florida's wetlands have been diminished (e.g., an average loss through the mid-1970s of 29,000 ha a year out of 500,000 ha of wetlands presumed to have existed statewide before development).

The Fish and Wildlife Service maintains a system of national wildlife refuges; the National Park Service and state and local governments protect species within park boundaries; the state of Florida prevents certain activities on state submerged lands; and both the federal and state governments, as well as private groups such as The Nature Conservancy, acquire key property and set it aside. For habitat that is accessible to the public, rules and regulations may be promulgated to minimize impacts. For example, powerboats cannot operate over certain Florida sea grass beds. As noted earlier, the largest and most active agency involved in regulating human activities in public waterways is the state Office of Protected Species Management.

In addition, the state's Ecosystem Management Implementation Strategy Committee and the Department of Environmental Protection recently developed an action plan for ecosystem management (Barnett et al. 1995). Using the central theme of stewardship, the action plan advocates four general approaches: (1) place-based (local) management; (2) common-sense regulation, which encourages incentives for compliance with regulations as a supplement to traditional enforcement of regulatory programs; (3) cultural change to promote voluntary partnerships between governmental and nongovernmental groups; and (4) use of "foundations" such as technology, science, environmental education, and program audits. The program's goals include development of a strong conservation ethic and better protection of environmental resources (Barnett et al. 1995).

The Marine Mammal Commission has also been an important and long-term advocate of developing strategies to protect marine mammal habitat in general (e.g., Ray et al.'s 1978 study, which was funded by the Commission) and

Figure 12-10. The warm, spring-fed waters at Crystal River, Florida, attract both manatees and human divers. Making sure that human recreational activities are compatible with the manatee's habitat needs represents a never-ending challenge for conservationists. (Photograph © Douglas Faulkner)

manatee habitat specifically (Marine Mammal Commission 1986, 1989).

Superficially at least, it appears that adequate provisions exist to protect manatee habitat in Florida. However, three factors might argue against this conclusion: (1) lack of knowledge regarding manatee feeding preferences and details of manatee ecology may limit our ability to protect some of the most important feeding areas; (2) despite existing habitat protection measures, coastal and estuarine habitat has been decimated in certain parts of the state (Reynolds and Gluckman 1988); and (3) the human population of the state continues to grow at a high rate. Although the individual and cumulative effects of that growth are not fully documented (and, indeed, would be difficult to document even with unlimited funds!), it is clear that human population growth has not been well managed. More high-use manatee habitat needs to be acquired and protected, and safe corridors connecting those high-use habitats need to be created.

Efforts Elsewhere

Outside the United States, a number of areas used by manatees fall within parks or other officially protected areas. In such locations, living resources in general receive legal protection. In addition, some areas in the Caribbean are designated specifically to protect manatees (see review by Marmontel 1994). In 1979 Guatemala created the first reserve for manatees outside of Florida, the Biotopo para la Conservación del Manatí Chocón-Machacas. The Southern Lagoon of Belize is an extremely important area for manatees; a Manatee Special Development Area, declared under the Land Utilization Act, currently includes both the Southern and Northern Lagoons and the Southern Lagoon has been designated as a manatee sanctuary (Marmontel 1994; J. A. Powell, pers. comm.). In Mexico, Bahía de Chetumal has recently been declared a manatee refuge (B. Morales-Vela, pers. comm.).

In contrast to the situation for West Indian manatees, there are no areas specifically designated as manatee protection areas for West African manatees. However, Amazonian manatees exist in protected areas such as 2,080,000-ha Pacaya-Samiria National Reserve in Peru (Reeves et al. 1996) and the 1,124,000-ha Estaçao Ecológica do Lago Mamiruá in western Brazilian Amazonia (Marsh and Lefebvre 1994). Rosas (1994) strongly advocated creation of protected areas in locations where Amazonian manatees are currently abundant.

A Blueprint for Manatee Conservation

Through experience gained with the Florida manatee, lessons have been learned that should make future efforts to conserve manatees worldwide more effective. The following elements may be useful in developing a model for manatee conservation:

(1) The presence of committed and informed individuals. This may seem trite, but courageous people who are truly interested in conservation of manatees and their habitat can accomplish a great deal. Students often may wonder what they, as individuals, can accomplish. One need only consider the impact of Marjory Stoneman Douglas' *The Everglades: River of Grass* (1947) on conservation of the Florida Everglades (Davis and Ogden 1994) to understand that committed individuals can make an enormous difference.

The general infrastructure that exists for Florida manatee conservation has remained virtually unchanged for some time. However, the effectiveness of the system has varied, depending on the motivation, background, and temperament of specific individuals holding key positions.

(2) Communication and coordination of activities, ideally through a well-conceived recovery plan. All rational entities with a vested interest must be involved, including groups whose activities threaten, or have the potential to threaten, a species or habitat. For example, the fact that a representative of the Marine Industries Association (a business group involved in manufacture and sales of boats and other equipment and in promoting use of Florida waterways) signed the Florida Manatee Recovery Plan enhanced the utility of the plan by demonstrating that entities whose objectives appear to run counter to manatee protection were willing to work toward mutually acceptable solutions. Excluding certain rational groups simply because they have a different point of view works against the goals of recovery planning.

Although people involved in manatee research and management communicate reasonably well, wildlife scientists in general should be more active in shaping policy (Franklin 1995, Meffe and Viederman 1995). The need for environmental "stakeholders" to communicate effectively is being recognized among social and natural scientists and is even giving rise to its own jargon: O'Hara (1996) for example, described the role that "discursive ethics" could play in ecosystems valuation and environmental policy.

A corollary of effective communication is to take advantage of all the information and tools that are available. Natural and social scientists must publish or otherwise provide their data in a form accessible to managers, legislators, and educators, all of whom must use scientific, sociological, economic, political, and other information responsibly. Different people have different strengths; an effective recovery team, like a sports team, uses people in ways that maximize individual strengths and compensate for weaknesses.

(3) Deal with people honestly and sincerely and attempt to understand that all points of view may have merit. Tolerance for the beliefs of others, be they of the same or different cultures or socioeconomic backgrounds, is essential.

(4) Avoid seduction by technology. Technological innovations (e.g., telemetry, geographic information systems, polymerase chain reaction) are remarkable tools that permit scientists to ask and answer new questions and to address old questions with greater resolution. Technology is quite useful in that regard. But too often people assume that technology can provide answers when it simply cannot. Similarly, people sometimes assume that if we wait long enough, we will be able to solve any problem using technological innovations. This belief permits people to avoid confronting real problems.

Another danger lies in a premature rush toward technology. For instance, the Sirenia Specialist Group of the World Conservation Union–IUCN's Species Survival Commission has noted that scientists initiating sirenian research programs in less-developed countries often want to begin their programs by using satellite telemetry and geographic information systems (Marsh and Lefebvre 1994). Although such technology can produce important data, it can also consume a disproportionate share of scarce research funds. The Sirenia Specialist Group has recommended strongly that more fundamental, cost-effective research be done before starting a more high-technology approach.

(5) Create a value system that considers more than just economics. Domning (1991) provided an articulate response to the question, why save the manatee? In his response, he suggested more than a half dozen "values" of manatees. Even if economics remains as a primary value of wildlife (and there is no reason to expect that economics will soon be displaced), it is important to find other ways to reach economic goals. Well-planned tourism activities, for example, may provide equal money in the short term and far more in the long term when a harvested resource would be gone.

It is also important to recognize that the total economic value of a resource equals the "sum of expected consumer surplus and the existence value" (Pearce and Perrings 1995), where existence value (also called intrinsic value) of a resource is independent of its use by people. Typically, the value that a species possesses simply because of its existence continues to be overlooked.

(6) Acknowledge "wildlife management" as a process that requires management of human affairs. Until and unless people admit that the primary problem facing wildlife populations today is too many people consuming too many resources relative to the carrying capacity of the planet and then take steps to control that human population and its effects, efforts to slow environmental degradation and prevent species extinction will have minimal impact (Norse 1993).

Among the strategies suggested for conserving biodiversity are expanding education of women and the roles played by women; establishing an international debt management authority, a system of debt-for-nature swaps, or other means of reducing the economic need for debt-ridden countries to overharvest resources; and increasing incentives for local stewardship (World Resources Institute et al. 1992).

(7) Be conservative and far-sighted in decision making. As K-selectors living in close proximity to people, manatees represent precisely the sort of species that can be irreparably damaged over a short period of time by a combination of natural mortality, excessive harvest, and habitat alteration or destruction. As Mangel et al. (1996) suggested, make decisions that maximize future options.

(8) Place the burden of proof on individuals who stand to benefit from use of resources that influence the survival of manatees (see, for example, Mangel et al. 1996). For example, if a developer wishes to build a marina in a coastal area frequented by manatees, it should be up to the developer (the entity that may benefit financially) to demonstrate conclusively that the activity would not unduly harm manatees, rather than up to scientists or agencies to demonstrate that the activity would have unacceptable consequences. This principle is one of the most powerful features of the Marine Mammal Protection Act of 1972 (Hofman 1989).

(9) Be open to creative new ideas and approaches. The precarious status of many species and ecosystems suggests that traditional approaches to resource use and conservation have been unsatisfactory (see Mangel et al. 1996). New tools and interdisciplinary, team-oriented approaches may lead to better results.

For example, Barnett et al. (1995) suggested supplementing traditional regulation and enforcement approaches with incentives that encourage Floridians to exercise greater stewardship over natural resources. The use of incentives to maintain biodiversity is developed more fully by World Resources Institute et al. (1992).

An area in which changes in incentives would be extremely useful involves communication by scientists to the public and to policy makers. Traditionally, scientists have been assessed professionally by their productivity in terms of peer-reviewed publications. Communication through nontechnical publications has generally not been rewarded or encouraged. If academic and other institutions were to weigh other accomplishments besides peer-reviewed publications as criteria for tenure and promotions, communication among scientists, policy makers, economists, and others would be enhanced.

New models are being developed that apply to decision making and wildlife conservation. For example, Ralls and Starfield (1995) applied a two-structured decision-making approach to facilitate management decisions involving endangered Hawaiian monk seals (*Monachus schauinslandi*). Use of such techniques may lead to better outcomes for both humans and natural resources.

(10) Have patience. Existing human institutions were not created overnight; neither are effective solutions to problems created by those institutions. Rulemaking and passage of new legislation and the development of grass-roots support may require considerable time. Inertia is difficult, but not impossible, to overcome. On the other hand, excessive patience in dealing with manatee conservation will probably not be viewed by history as a virtue.

Typical Dilemmas for Decision Makers

The following two examples illustrate the complexity of causes and effects and the diversity of interests involved in manatee conservation. They portray the difficulties facing decision makers who must find the proper balance between often-competing demands for the same limited resources.

Winter Aggregations

Manatees in Florida move seasonally into warm-water refugia to avoid effects of cold weather (Fig. 12-11). Some of the locations where the largest aggregations occur are the warm-water discharges of power plants (Reynolds and Wilcox 1994). Manatees have learned to use the discharge zones and now rely on them. For example, in 1985 the Fort Myers plant, which regularly attracts 200–300 manatees during cold weather, was off-line for economic reasons. During an intensely cold period, manatees came to the plant anticipating warm water; when that water did not appear, the animals remained in the neighborhood of the plant. Eventually, the plant began operating in response to human demands for electricity, and a potential disaster for manatees was avoided. The power company involved, Florida Power & Light, subsequently installed deep wells at that plant to pump warm artesian water into manatee aggregation areas in winter in case a similar circumstance were to arise in the future (Reynolds and Wilcox 1986).

Power plants currently operating in Florida save millions of dollars by being allowed to discharge warm water directly into the environment even though the discharge can cause certain environmental damage (e.g., see reviews of effects of warm-water discharges on seagrasses in Thayer et al. 1975, Zieman 1982). The magnitude of the savings is enormous: capital cost to install mechanical cooling towers at each power plant is approximately \$100–\$150 million, and the annual operating cost for such towers is \$2 to \$4 million each (J. R. Wilcox, pers. comm.). Warm-water discharges are permitted, in part, because they help large numbers of endangered manatees avoid the consequences of exposure to cold winter weather. This has expanded manatee winter range and may have allowed the manatee population to grow earlier in this century (see Eberhardt and O'Shea 1995). Superficially, warm-water discharges from power plants appear to benefit the species. On closer inspection, however, there are potential problems associated with such manatee aggregations.

For example, animals in aggregations can easily transmit diseases among themselves; alternatively, when manatees are tightly aggregated, a change in the local environment can affect a large percentage of the manatee population. In fact, the magnitude of the 1996 manatee die-off (caused by an intensely strong red tide in southwestern Florida) was almost certainly influenced by the fact that cold weather caused record numbers of manatees to gather at a power plant discharge in southwestern Florida. Recall that the die-off affected approximately three times the number of manatees that die each year from collisions with watercraft (the most publicized cause of manatee mortality).

In addition, power plants have an operating life of 40 to 50 years. What happens when a power plant is retired and manatees continue to seek warm water there (note that on Florida's east coast, at least, some manatees move from one plant to another during the winter; on the west coast, the degree of movement is unknown but may be small)? Similarly, what happens if a plant shutdown occurs because of mechanical problems or economic decisions when

Figure 12-11. Manatees aggregated at the Riviera Plant during very cold winter weather. (Photograph by J. Reynolds and Florida Power & Light Company)

manatees are aggregated there for warmth? The artesian wells at the Fort Myers plant have been useful in warming manatees at that location, but are additional wells at other plants good options in light of groundwater depletion in many parts of Florida (Florida Conservation Foundation 1993)? Should a plant that might otherwise be closed down continue to operate at a cost of $2,000 to $10,000 per hour because wells or other backups are not available? Deregulation of the power industry may bring all these questions to the fore in the near future.

As noted earlier, the presence of manatees in the warm-water discharges has saved power companies a great deal of money. Commendably, some power companies have responded by maintaining warm-water flow during the winter at plants that routinely attract manatees to be certain that the animals will find the sought-after thermal refuge. In addition, Florida Power & Light Company (and to a lesser extent Tampa Electric Company) have invested money in manatee research and public education and awareness projects.

In summary, power plant discharges save individual manatees from death or illness due to exposure to cold weather; aggregated manatees are more susceptible to certain diseases, pollutants, and other stresses than are nonaggregated manatees, and an epizootic (i.e., a disease attacking large numbers of animals simultaneously) could kill tens or hundreds of manatees in a short time; local seagrass beds on which manatees depend for food may be affected by warm-water discharges; manatees that have learned to seek warmth at a particular location may die in large numbers if the source of that warmth disappears; and economic decisions associated with deregulation may cause plants to cease operations.

How should scientists and conservationists address this situation? What are the roles and responsibilities of those who created the warm-water refugia for manatees?

Boats and Manatees

Among the ways that the Florida Department of Environmental Protection seeks to conserve manatees is by identifying sites where the regulation of boat speeds could substantially decrease the number and severity of collisions with manatees, thereby reducing serious injury and death of the animals. At hearings before the governor and cabinet, proposed rules to regulate boating generate intense, but divergent opinions. Primary points of contention involve economics, philosophy, and the law (O'Shea 1995).

An important consideration in regulating the boating industry is the economic impact. In Florida the direct economic benefit of boating is suggested by the $330 billion in gross sales claimed for 1994 (presentation by B. J. Bendle, cited by Florida Center for Public Management 1995); boating also enhances the Florida economy by creating jobs related to the boating industry.

The number of registered recreational vessels in Florida approached 687,000 in 1994; in addition, there were more than 33,000 registered commercial vessels (Florida Center for Public Management 1995). Many opponents to the regulation of boat speeds or boat access claim economic hardship. They point out that commercial and recreational interests in Florida would suffer if boats were not permitted in certain areas or if boat speeds were slowed "excessively." Although the dollar amounts are difficult to document, it is certainly possible that businesses would be affected by enactment of proposed rules. For example, commercial fishermen who would have to traverse extensive slow-speed zones claim that the lost time in transit would reduce their earnings considerably. A survey of Broward County boaters (Baker et al. 1992) suggested that a proposed seasonal county-line-to-county-line slow speed zone could have an economic impact well in excess of $20 million. Marine-related industries suggested an economic impact approaching a quarter of a billion dollars. As noted later in this chapter, such figures appear to be at odds with other results of the same survey indicating that most registered boaters in Broward County actually favored the restrictions.

Loss of business opportunities associated with boating has broader impacts. The state of Florida does not levy a personal income tax, and the state economy is "largely based on tourism" (Florida Center for Public Management 1995). O'Shea (1995) noted that 40 million people visit Florida each year, and many visitors enter the state by boat. Boating regulations that discourage tourists and thereby reduce spending of tourist dollars could possibly affect Florida's economic stability (Florida Center for Public Management 1995).

On the conservation side of the economic argument, Bendle and Bell (1995) assessed the willingness of citizens of Florida to pay to protect manatees; those authors found that Floridians place an enormous economic value (i.e, they are willing to pay $1,500,000 per animal for manatee protection) on each manatee in Florida. Such intrinsic economic valuation generally is not, but should be, considered by national, state, and local financial accounting. In addition, a survey by Parker and Wang (1996) indicated that 90% of survey respondents who own a boat registered in Florida support boat speed reductions to conserve manatees.

Some people who object to proposed regulations do so on philosophical grounds. At least some recreational boaters have voiced the opinion that waterways belong to human users and that it simply is up to other organisms to learn to get out of the way. The philosophical argument has another side as well. Without denying that humans have rights, conservationists argue that humans have responsibilities to maintain the integrity of natural resources and thus to ensure the preservation of biodiversity. The issue of stewardship, as it relates to manatees, was addressed by Domning (1991); general stewardship of Florida's environmental resources is the cornerstone of the state's ecosystem management program (Barnett et al. 1995).

It should also be noted that humans who kill, injure, or harass manatees violate federal and state laws protecting manatees specifically or marine mammals or endangered species in general. In some ways, "incidental take" of manatees by boaters is not very different from incidental take of manatees and other marine mammals by fishermen; in the latter case, there has been considerable effort in the United States and elsewhere to monitor fishing activities, change gear or methods, and otherwise reduce the take (Marine Mammal Commission 1996). The Marine Mammal Protection Act, for example, places the burden of proof (Hofman 1989) on fishermen to reduce incidental take to "insignificant levels." Boating kills approximately 50 manatees a year (Fig. 12-5), seriously injures an undetermined number, and harasses even more manatees, perhaps causing them to abandon preferred habitats. The burden of proof should be on the boating community (not conservationists or government agencies) to reduce this "take" of manatees.

In this chapter, I have referred repeatedly to the link between species conservation and habitat integrity. Boating causes seagrass scarring (more than 6% of Florida's 1.1 million ha of seagrasses have some scarring, and certain local seagrass beds have extensive scarring [Sargent et al. 1995]). The dredging of channels and boating itself increase suspended sediments in waterways and thereby impair seagrass productivity by reducing light penetration (see Gucinski 1982, various papers in Kenworthy and Haunert 1991, review of human impacts in Zieman 1982). In addition, boat wakes create bottom-shear stress that erodes seagrass beds (Kenworthy et al. 1988, Kruer 1994, both cited in Sargent et al. 1995). In fact, Gucinski (1982) noted for submerged aquatic vegetation (SAV) in Chesapeake Bay that "areas of least SAV distribution and slowest recovery are also areas of greatest boating congestion." Thus, boats influence manatee health and well-being, both directly and indirectly, by diminishing sea grass ecosystem health and productivity. Of course, declines in sea grasses have economic, esthetic, and other consequences too.

Supporters of boat speed regulations point out that speed zones are necessary for human safety as much as for manatee safety. When assessed in terms of number of human deaths and injuries per 100,000 registered boats, Florida is the most dangerous state in which to boat (Anonymous 1996). Improper training, excessive speed, alcohol, and overcrowded waterways all contribute to this alarming statistic. A survey sponsored by the Marine Industries Association (Baker et al. 1992) found that most (59%) registered boaters in Broward County (the Fort Lauderdale area) favored county-line-to-county-line seasonal boat speed restrictions on weekends and holidays; 84% of the registered boaters who responded to the survey favored speed limits for boats in manatee protection zones.

Issues to Be Resolved

In considering both of these real-life situations, there are several issues that must be resolved.

What is the proper balance between human use and stewardship of natural resources? A related question is how do we control human population size and resource use to permit both the well-being of our species and the survival of other species and ecosystems?

How are intrinsic values (values associated simply with existence of a resource) to be figured into economic decisions? How does destruction of natural resources enter the overall economic audit at the local, state, and national levels?

How do or should legislators respond when powerful interest groups bring pressure to bear to advance positions with which most citizens may be uncomfortable?

What avenues for communication exist to permit people with diametrically opposed points of view to speak rationally and to reach mutually beneficial solutions?

At what point will the boating industry, like other industries that take marine mammals, be held to the legal requirement to reduce mortality to insignificant levels? That is, when will the burden be shifted to the boating industry to prove that its activities do not harm manatees, rather than requiring others to prove that they do?

Conclusion

The conservation of manatees in Florida provides an instructive example of how a broad and inclusive program for saving an endangered species in the United States has evolved. The story is marked by successes and failures, new and unforeseen challenges, conflicting interests, and new insights. An important lesson to bear in mind is that the battle to save the Florida manatee will never end. It requires, and will continue to require, the vigilance and passionate caring of individual citizens, as well as the conscientious efforts of people working in public agencies and private enterprises. Few of the important questions can be answered once and for all; they require endless reasking and rethinking.

Acknowledgments

John R. Twiss Jr. conceived this chapter and provided valuable direction and focus. Lynn W. Lefebvre and Patrick M. Rose provided helpful comments on an early draft, and Rose added specific information regarding boat use in Florida. Leslie Ward-Geiger provided the maps, and Scott D. Wright the graphs illustrating manatee mortality used in the chapter. J. Ross Wilcox provided background information regarding power plant operations. Samantha D. Eide, Suzanne Montgomery, Randall R. Reeves, and Sentiel A. Rommel, together with several anonymous reviewers, provided a number of useful comments and reminded me of my audience.

Literature Cited

Ackerman, B. B., S. D. Wright, R. K. Bonde, D. K. Odell, and D. J. Banowetz. 1995. Trends and patterns in mortality of manatees in Florida, 1974–1992. Pages 223–258 *in* T. J. O'Shea, B. B. Ackerman, and H. F. Percival (eds.), Population Biology of the Florida Manatee. U.S. Department of the Interior, National Biological Service, Information and Technology Report 1.

Anonymous. 1996. Department of Environmental Protection Law Enforcement Report. Supplement for the Florida Legislature, Tallahassee, FL.

Baker, E. K., M. E. Vallanueva, T. W. Minton, and M. De Amicis. 1992. Potential economic impact of a seasonal county line to county line slow speed limit in Broward County. Final report to South Florida Marine Industries Association, Miami, FL.

Barnett, E., J. Lewis, J. Marx, and D. Trimble (eds.). 1995. Ecosystem Management Implementation Strategy. An action plan for the Department of Environmental Protection. Developed by the Ecosystem Management Implementation Strategy Committee and Florida Department of Environmental Protection, Tallahassee, FL.

Beck, C. A., and J. P. Reid. 1995. An automated photo-identification catalog for studies of the life history of the Florida manatee. Pages 120–134 *in* T. J. O'Shea, B. B. Ackerman, and H. F. Percival (eds.), Population Biology of the Florida Manatee. U.S. Department of the Interior, National Biological Service, Information and Technology Report 1.

Bendle, B. J., and F. W. Bell. 1995. An estimation of the total willingness to pay by Floridians to protect the endangered West Indian manatee through donations. Florida Department of Environmental Protection and Florida State University, Tallahassee, FL.

Best, R. C. 1983. Apparent dry-season fasting in Amazonian manatees (Mammalia: Sirenia). Biotropica 15 (1): 61–64.

Bolen, M. E. 1997. Age determination of the Florida manatees,

Trichechus manatus latirostris, killed by the 1996 red tide epizootic in southwestern Florida. Senior thesis, Eckerd College, St. Petersburg, FL. 43 pp.

Bossart, G. D., D. G. Baden, R. Y. Ewing, B. Roberts, and S. D. Wright. 1998. Brevetoxicosis in manatees (*Trichechus manatus latirostris*) from the 1996 epizootic: Gross, histologic, and immunohistochemical features. Toxicologic Pathology 26:276–282.

Boyd, I. A., C. Lockyer, and H. D. Marsh. 1999. Reproduction in marine mammals. *In* J. E. Reynolds III and S. A. Rommel (eds.), Biology of Marine Mammals. Smithsonian Institution Press, Washington, DC (in press).

Burgess, J. C. 1995. Biodiversity loss through tropical deforestation: The role of timber production and trade. Pages 237–255 *in* C. A. Perrings, K. G. Maler, C. Folke, C. S. Holling, and B. O. Jansson (eds.), Biodiversity Conservation. Kluwer Academic Publishers, Dordrecht, the Netherlands.

Carr, T. 1994. The manatees and dolphins of the Miskito Coast Protected Area, Nicaragua. Report to the Marine Mammal Commission. (Available from National Technical Information Service, Springfield, VA. PB94-170354.) 23 pp.

Craig, B. A., M. A. Newton, R. A. Garrott, J. E. Reynolds III, and J. R. Wilcox. 1997. Analysis of aerial survey data on *Trichechus manatus* using Markov chain Monte Carlo. Biometrics 53:524–541.

Davis, S. M., and J. C. Ogden. 1994. Introduction. Pages 3–8 *in* S. M. Davis and J. C. Ogden (eds.), Everglades: The Ecosystem and Its Restoration. St. Lucie Press, Delray Beach, FL.

Domning, D. P. 1982. Commercial exploitation of manatees *Trichechus* in Brazil *c.* 1785–1973. Biological Conservation 22:101–126.

Domning, D. P. 1991. Why Save the Manatee? Pages 168–173 *in* J. E. Reynolds III and D. K. Odell, Manatees and Dugongs. Facts on File, Inc., New York, NY.

Domning, D. P., and L. C. Hayek. 1986. Interspecific and intraspecific morphological variation in manatees (Sirenia: *Trichechus*). Marine Mammal Science 2:87–144.

Douglas, M. S. 1947. The Everglades: River of Grass. Rinehart and Company, New York, NY.

Eberhardt, L. L., and T. J. O'Shea. 1995. Integration of manatee life-history data and population modeling. Pages 269–279 *in* T. J. O'Shea, B. B. Ackerman, and H. F. Percival (eds.), Population Biology of the Florida Manatee. U.S. Department of the Interior, National Biological Service, Information and Technology Report 1.

Florida Center for Public Management. 1995. Florida Assessment of Coastal Trends FACT. Prepared for the Florida Coastal Management Program and Florida Department of Community Affairs, Tallahassee, FL.

Florida Conservation Foundation. 1993. Guide to Florida Environmental Issues and Information. Florida Conservation Foundation, Winter Park, FL.

Florida Department of Environmental Protection. 1995. Fiscal Year 1994–95 Annual Report, Save the Manatee Trust Fund. Prepared for the Florida State Senate and The Florida House of Representatives, Tallahassee, FL. 41 pp. + appendices.

Franklin, T. M. 1995. Putting wildlife science to work: Influencing public policy. Wildlife Society Bulletin 23:322–326.

Garrott, R. A., B. B. Ackerman, J. R. Cary, D. M. Heisey, J. E. Reynolds III, and J. R. Wilcox. 1995. Assessment of trends in sizes of manatee populations at several Florida manatee aggregation sites. Pages 34–55 *in* T. J. O'Shea, B. B. Ackerman, and H. F. Percival (eds.), Population Biology of the Florida Manatee. U.S. Department of the Interior, National Biological Service, Information and Technology Report 1.

Grigione, M. M. 1996. Observations on the status and distribution of the West African manatee in Cameroon. African Journal of Ecology 34:189–195.

Gucinski, H. 1982. Sediment suspension and resuspension from small craft induced turbulence. Project summary, EPA-600/S3-82-084, Chesapeake Bay Program, Annapolis, MD. 2 pp.

Hartman, D. S. 1979. Ecology and behavior of the manatee (*Trichechus manatus*) in Florida. Special Publication No. 5, American Society of Mammalogists. 153 pp.

Hefner, J. M. 1986. Wetlands in Florida 1950's to 1970's. Pages 23–32 *in* E. D. Estevez, J. Miller, J. Morris, and R. Hamman (eds.), Proceedings of the Conference: Managing Cumulative Effects in Florida Wetlands, held in October 1985, Sarasota, FL. New College Environmental Studies Program Publication No. 37. Omnipress, Madison, WI.

Hernandez, P., J. E. Reynolds III, H. Marsh, and M. Marmontel. 1995. Age and seasonality in spermatogenesis of Florida manatee. Pages 84–97 *in* T. J. O'Shea, B. B. Ackerman, and H. F. Percival (eds.), Population Biology of the Florida Manatee. U.S. Department of the Interior, National Biological Service, Information and Technology Report 1.

Hofman, R. J. 1989. The Marine Mammal Protection Act: A first of its kind anywhere. Oceanus 32 (1): 21–25.

Horwich, R. H., D. Murray, E. Saqui, J. Lyon, and D. Godfrey. 1993. Ecotourism and community development: A view from Belize. Pages 152–168 *in* K. Lindberg and D. E. Hawkins (eds.), Ecotourism: A Guide for Planners and Managers. The Ecotourism Society, North Bennington, VT.

Kenworthy, W. J., and D. E. Haunert (eds.). 1991. The light requirements of seagrasses: Proceedings of a Workshop to Examine the Capability of Water Quality Criteria, Standards and Monitoring Programs to Protect Seagrasses. NOAA Technical Memorandum NMFS-SEFC-287.

Kenworthy, W. J., M. S. Fonseca, and G. W. Thayer. 1988. A comparison of wind-wave and boat wake-wave energy in Hobe Sound: Implications for seagrass growth. Annual Report to U.S. Fish and Wildlife Service, Sirenia Project, Gainesville, FL. 21 pp.

Kruer, C. R. 1994. Mapping assessment of vessel damage to shallow seagrasses in the Florida Keys. Final report to Florida Department of Natural Resources and University of South Florida, Florida Institute of Oceanography. FIO Contract no. 47-10-123-L3.

Lefebvre, L. W., and T. J. O'Shea. 1995. Florida Manatees. Pages 267–269 *in* E. T. LaRoe, G. S. Farris, C. E. Puckett, P. D. Doran, and M. J. Mac (eds.), Our Living Resources: A Report to the Nation on the Distribution, Abundance, and Health of U.S. Plants, Animals, and Ecosystems. U.S. Department of the Interior, National Biological Service, Washington, DC.

Lefebvre, L. W., T. J. O'Shea, G. B. Rathbun, and R. C. Best. 1989. Distribution, status, and biogeography of the West Indian manatee. Pages 567–610 *in* C. A. Woods (ed.), Biogeography of the West Indies. Sandhill Crane Press, Gainesville, FL.

Lindberg, K., and D. E. Hawkins (eds.). 1993. Ecotourism: A Guide for Planners and Managers. The Ecotourism Society, North Bennington, VT. 175 pp.

Mangel, M., L. M. Talbot, G. K. Meffe, M. T. Agardy, D. L. Alverson,

J. Barlow, D. B. Botkin, G. Budowski, T. Clark, J. Cooke, R. H. Crozier, P. K. Dayton, D. L. Elder, C. W. Fowler, S. Funtowicz, J. Giske, R. J. Hofman, S. J. Holt, S. R. Kellert, L. A. Kimball, D. Ludwig, K. Magnusson, B. S. Malayang III, C. Mann, E. A. Norse, S. P. Northridge, W. F. Perrin, C. Perrings, R. M. Peterman, G. B. Rabb, H. A. Regier, J. E. Reynolds III, K. Sherman, M. P. Sissenwine, T. D. Smith, A. Starfield, R. J. Taylor, M. F. Tillman, C. Toft, J. R. Twiss Jr., J. Wilen, and T. P. Young. 1996. Principles for the conservation of wild living resources. Ecological Applications 6:338–362.

Marine Mammal Commission. 1986. Habitat protection needs for the subpopulation of West Indian manatees in the Crystal River area of Northwest Florida. (Available from National Technical Information Service, Springfield, VA. PB86-200 250.) 46 pp.

Marine Mammal Commission. 1989. Preliminary assessment of habitat protection needs for West Indian manatees on the east coast of Florida and Georgia. (Available from National Technical Information Service, Springfield, VA. PB89-162 002.) 120 pp.

Marine Mammal Commission. 1994. Annual report to Congress for 1993. (Available from National Technical Information Service, Springfield, VA. PB95-154530.) 260 pp.

Marine Mammal Commission. 1996. Annual report to Congress for 1995. (Available from National Technical Information Service, Springfield, VA. PB96-157482.) 235 pp.

Marmontel, M. 1993. Age determination and population biology of the Florida manatee, *Trichechus manatus latirostris*. Ph.D. dissertation, University of Florida, Gainesville, FL. 408 pp.

Marmontel, M. 1994. Regional management plan for the West Indian manatee, *Trichechus manatus*. Revised draft, Working Document 3, Regional Workshop on the Conservation of the West Indian Manatee in the Wider Caribbean Region. 1–4 March 1994, Kingston, Jamaica. 67 pp.

Marmontel, M. 1995. Age and reproduction in female Florida manatees. Pages 98–119 *in* T. J. O'Shea, B. B. Ackerman, and H. F. Percival (eds.), Population Biology of the Florida Manatee. U.S. Department of the Interior, National Biological Service, Information and Technology Report 1.

Marmontel, M., S. R. Humphrey, and T. J. O'Shea. 1997. Population viability analysis of the Florida manatee (*Trichechus manatus latirostris*), 1976–1991. Conservation Biology 11:467–481.

Marsh, H., and L. W. Lefebvre. 1994. Sirenian status and conservation efforts. Aquatic Mammals 20 (3): 155–170.

Meffe, G. K., and S. Viederman. 1995. Combining science and policy in conservation biology. Wildlife Society Bulletin 23:327–332.

Mitchell, J. 1976. Age determination in the dugong *Dugong dugon* (Muller). Biological Conservation 9:25–28.

Myers, N. 1988. Tropical forests and their species: Going, going . . . ? Pages 28–35 *in* E. O. Wilson (ed.), Biodiversity. National Academy Press, Washington, DC. 521 pp.

National Biological Service, Sirenia Project. 1993. Atlantic coast manatee telemetry, 1986–1993 progress report. Vol. 1. 232 pp.

Norris, K. S. 1978. Marine mammals and man. Pages 320–338 *in* H. P. Brokaw (ed.), Wildlife and America. Council on Environmental Quality, Washington, DC.

Norse, E. A. 1993. Global Marine Biodiversity Strategy. Island Press, Washington, DC. 383 pp.

Odell, D. K. 1982. West Indian manatee *Trichechus manatus*. Pages 828–837 *in* J. A. Chapman and G. A. Feldhamer (eds.), Wild Mammals of North America: Biology, Management and Economics. The Johns Hopkins University Press, Baltimore, MD.

O'Hara, S. U. 1996. Discursive ethics in ecosystems valuation and environmental policy. Ecological Economics 16:95–107.

O'Shea, T. J. 1995. Waterborne recreation and the Florida manatee. Pages 297–311 *in* R. L. Knight and K. J. Gutzwiller (eds.), Wildlife and Recreationists: Coexistence through Management and Research. Island Press, Washington, DC.

O'Shea, T. J., and W. C. Hartley. 1995. Reproduction and early-age survival of manatees at Blue Spring, upper St. Johns River, Florida. Pages 157–170 *in* T. J. O'Shea, B. B. Ackerman, and H. F. Percival (eds.), Population Biology of the Florida Manatee. U.S. Department of the Interior, National Biological Service, Information and Technology Report 1.

O'Shea, T. J., and C. A. Langtimm. 1995. Estimation of survival of adult Florida manatees in the Crystal River, at Blue Spring, and on the Atlantic coast. Pages 194–222 *in* T. J. O'Shea, B. B. Ackerman, and H. F. Percival (eds.), Population Biology of the Florida Manatee. U.S. Department of the Interior, National Biological Service, Information and Technology Report 1.

O'Shea, T. J., and C. A. Salisbury. 1991. Belize—a last stronghold for manatees in the Caribbean. Oryx 25:156–164.

O'Shea, T. J., B. B. Ackerman, and H. F. Percival (eds.). 1995. Population Biology of the Florida Manatee. U.S. Department of the Interior, National Biological Service, Information and Technology Report 1. 289 pp.

Packard, J. M. 1981. Abundance, distribution, and feeding habits of manatees (*Trichechus manatus*) wintering between St. Lucie and Palm Beach Inlets, Florida. U.S. Fish and Wildlife Contract Report No. 14-16-004-80-105. 139 pp.

Packard, J. M., and O. F. Wetterquist. 1986. Evaluation of manatee habitat on the northwestern Florida coast. Coastal Zone Management Journal 14 (4): 279–310.

Packard, J. M., D. B. Siniff, and J. A. Cornell. 1986. Use of replicate counts to improve indices of trends in manatee abundance. Wildlife Society Bulletin 14:265–275.

Parker, S., and K. Wang. 1996. Report on a survey of the Florida public on manatee protection and other topics related to Florida's environment. Unpublished report to Save the Manatee Club, Maitland, FL. 64 pp.

Pearce, D. W., and C. A. Perrings. 1995. Biodiversity conservation and economic development: Local and global dimensions. Pages 23–40 *in* C. A. Perrings, K. G. Maler, C. Folke, C. S. Holling, and B. O. Jansson (eds.), Biodiversity Conservation. Kluwer Academic Publishers, Dordrecht, the Netherlands.

Ralls, K., and A. M. Starfield. 1995. Choosing a management strategy: Two structured decision-making methods for evaluating the predictions of stochastic simulation models. Conservation Biology 9:175–181.

Rathbun, G. B., J. A. Powell, and G. Cruz. 1983. Status of the West Indian manatee in Honduras. Biological Conservation 26:301–308.

Rathbun, G. B., J. P. Reid, R. K. Bonde, and J. A. Powell. 1995. Reproduction in free-ranging Florida manatees. Pages 135–156 *in* T. J. O'Shea, B. B. Ackerman, and H. F. Percival (eds.), Population Biology of the Florida Manatee. U.S. Department of the Interior, National Biological Service, Information and Technology Report 1.

Ray, G. C., J. A. Dobbin, and R. V. Salm. 1978. Strategies for protecting marine mammal habitats. Oceanus 21 (3): 55–67.

Reeves, R. R., D. Toboku-Metzger, and R. A. Kapindi. 1988. Distribution and exploitation of manatees in Sierra Leone. Oryx 22:75–84.

Reeves, R. R., S. Leatherwood, T. A. Jefferson, B. E. Curry, and

T. Henningsen. 1996. Amazonian manatees, *Trichechus inunguis*, in Peru: Distribution, exploitation, and conservation status. Interciencia 21 (6): 246–254.

Reynolds, J. E., III. 1995. Florida manatee population biology: Research progress, infrastructure, and applications for conservation and management. Pages 6–12 *in* T. J. O'Shea, B. B. Ackerman, and H. F. Percival (eds.), Population Biology of the Florida Manatee. U.S. Department of the Interior, National Biological Service, Information and Technology Report 1.

Reynolds, J. E., III, and C. J. Gluckman. 1988. Protection of West Indian Manatees (*Trichechus manatus*) in Florida. Report to Marine Mammal Commission. (Available from National Technical Information Service, Springfield, VA. PB88-222922.) 85 pp.

Reynolds, J. E., III, and K. D. Haddad (eds.). 1990. Report of the Workshop on Geographic Information Systems as an Aid to Managing Habitat for West Indian Manatees in Florida and Georgia. Florida Marine Research Publication 49. 98 pp.

Reynolds, J. E., III, and D. K. Odell. 1991. Manatees and Dugongs. Facts on File, Inc., New York, NY. 192 pp.

Reynolds, J. E., III, and S. A. Rommel (eds.). 1999. Biology of Marine Mammals. Smithsonian Institution Press, Washington, DC (in press).

Reynolds, J. E., III, and J. R. Wilcox. 1986. Distribution and abundance of the West Indian manatee (*Trichechus manatus*) around selected Florida power plants following winter cold fronts: 1984–1985. Biological Conservation 38:103–113.

Reynolds, J. E., III, and J. R. Wilcox. 1994. Observations of Florida manatees (*Trichechus manatus latirostris*) around selected power plants in winter. Marine Mammal Science 10:163–177.

Reynolds, J. E., III, W. A. Szelistowski, and M. A. Leon. 1995. Status and conservation of manatees (*Trichechus manatus manatus*) in Costa Rica. Biological Conservation 71:193–196.

Ricklefs, R. E. 1990. Ecology, 3d ed. W. H. Freeman and Company, New York, NY. 896 pp.

Rosas, F. C. W. 1994. Biology, conservation and status of the Amazonian manatee *Trichechus inunguis*. Mammal Review 24 (2): 49–59.

Salisbury, C. L., and C. A. Beck. 1992. Regional West Indian manatee studbook 1992. Lowry Park Zoological Garden, Tampa, FL. 38 pp.

Sargent, F. J., T. J. Leary, D. W. Crewz, and C. R. Kruer. 1995. Scarring of Florida's seagrasses: Assessment and management options. Florida Department of Environmental Protection, Florida Marine Research Institute Technical Report TR-1. 46 pp. + appendices.

Soileau, D. M., J. D. Brown, and D. W. Fruge. 1985. Mitigation banking: A mechanism for compensating unavoidable fish and wildlife habitat losses. Pages 465–474 *in* Transactions of the Fiftieth North American Wildlife and Natural Resources Conference.

Talbot, L. M. 1996. Living Resource Conservation: An International Overview. A report to the Marine Mammal Commission, Washington, DC. 56 pp.

Thayer, G. W., D. A. Wolfe, and R. B. Williams. 1975. The impact of man on seagrass systems. American Scientist 63:288–296.

Thornback, J., and M. Jenkins. 1982. The IUCN Red Data Book, Part 1. Threatened Mammalian Taxa of the Americas and Australasian Zoogeographic Region (Excluding Cetacea). International Union for the Conservation of Nature and Natural Resources, Gland, Switzerland. 516 pp.

Timm, R. M., L. Albuja V., and B. L. Clauson. 1986. Ecology, distribution, harvest, and conservation of the Amazonian manatee *Trichechus inunguis* in Ecuador. Biotropica 18 (2): 150–156.

U.S. Fish and Wildlife Service. 1989. Florida Manatee (*Trichechus manatus latirostris*) Recovery Plan. Prepared by the Florida Manatee Recovery Team for the U.S. Fish and Wildlife Service, Atlanta, GA. 98 pp.

U.S. Fish and Wildlife Service. 1996. Florida Manatee Recovery Plan, Second Revision. U.S. Fish and Wildlife Service, Atlanta, GA. 160 pp.

Wallace, R. L. 1994. The Florida manatee recovery program: Organizational learning and a model for improving recovery programs. Pages 131–156 *in* T. W. Clark, R. P. Reading, and A. Clarke (eds.), Saving Endangered Species: Professional and Organizational Lessons for Improvement. Island Press, Covelo, CA. 450 pp.

Ward, L. I., and B. L. Weigle. 1993. To save a species: GIS for manatee research and management. GIS World 6 (8): 34–37.

Wilson, E. O. 1987. Biological diversity as a scientific and ethical issue. Pages 29–48 *in* Papers read at the Joint Meeting of the Royal Society and the American Philosophical Society, Vol. 1. Meeting held 24 April 1986 in Philadelphia. American Philosophical Society, Philadelphia, PA.

World Resources Institute, The World Conservation Union, and United Nations Environment Programme. 1992. Global Biodiversity Strategy. World Resources Institute, Washington, DC.

Wright, S. D., B. B. Ackerman, R. K. Bonde, C. A. Beck, and D. J. Banowetz. 1995. Analysis of watercraft-related mortality of manatees in Florida, 1979–1991. Pages 259–268 *in* T. J. O'Shea, B. B. Ackerman, and H. F. Percival (eds.), Population Biology of the Florida Manatee. U.S. Department of the Interior, National Biological Service, Information and Technology Report 1.

Zeiller, W. 1992. Introducing the Manatee. University Press of Florida, Gainesville, FL. 151 pp.

Zieman, J. C. 1982. The ecology of the seagrasses of South Florida: A community profile. U.S. Fish and Wildlife Service, Office of Biological Services, Washington, DC. FWS/OBS-82-25. 182 pp.

13

WILLIAM F. PERRIN

Selected Examples of Small Cetaceans at Risk

Problems of conservation and management exist for nearly all of the 68 currently recognized small cetaceans (Brownell et al. 1989, Perrin 1989, Klinowska 1991, Reeves and Leatherwood 1994). In this chapter, I first describe a few examples drawn from hundreds of problems that afflict dolphins, porpoises, and small whales in the waters of both the developing and the more developed nations. I then discuss the special nature of problems facing small cetaceans; finally I briefly discuss some lessons learned about their conservation.

The species discussed here include all the cetacean species except the baleen whales and the sperm whale (collectively called the "great whales"). The dichotomy of terminology arose during the early days of the International Whaling Commission when the "great" whales were those species of most interest to the whaling industry. Everything else was considered a "small" cetacean even though some species, such as Baird's beaked whale, may be as large as or larger than some of the "great" whales (Jefferson et al. 1993).

The Vaquita

The vaquita ("little cow" in Spanish) (*Phocoena sinus*) has the smallest range of any marine small cetacean and is the most endangered, as a result of incidental kill in gillnet fisheries (Brownell 1986, Gerrodette et al. 1995, Vidal 1995). It is a small porpoise (Fig. 13-1) that lives only in a portion of the upper Gulf of California, the sea that separates Baja California from the mainland of northern Mexico (Gerrodette et al. 1995). The species was not known to science until 1958 (Table 13-1). The other members of its genus—the harbor porpoise (*P. phocoena*), Burmeister's porpoise (*P. spinipinnis*), and the spectacled porpoise (*P. dioptrica*)—are denizens of cool- to cold-temperate waters, but the vaquita inhabits waters that can exceed 28°C. It is part of an originally cool-water fauna that is thought to have become trapped in the northern gulf when the tropical zone to the south expanded northward during a geological warming period (Norris and McFarland 1958); its closest relative is Burmeister's porpoise in the Southern Hemisphere (Rosel et al. 1995).

The most recent population estimates for the vaquita range from only 224 to 885 (Barlow et al. 1997), and continuing incidental fishery kills (D'Agrosa et al. 1995) are almost certainly unsustainable (International Whaling Commission 1995, 1997).

Awareness about the vaquita's plight has not resulted in sufficient efforts to stop the killing, and the species seems headed for extinction. Why is this so? The most basic answer is that people in the region are trying to make a living under difficult conditions. Mexico is still a developing nation, and

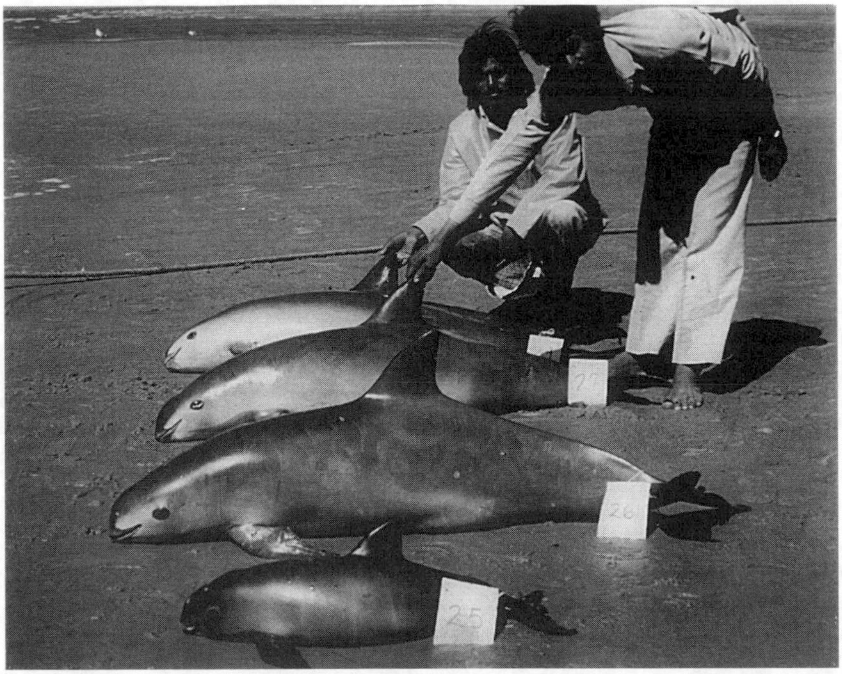

Figure 13-1. Four vaquitas (*Phocoena sinus*) captured and killed accidentally near El Golfo de Santa Clara, Sonora, Gulf of California, Mexico, during experimental gillnet fishing for totoaba, March 1985. (Photograph by Alejandro Robles)

rural poverty is a severe problem. Fishing has long been a primary industry in the northern Gulf of California; it requires little capital, exploits common resources, and can be lucrative. Unfortunately, the fisheries, including banned but continuing fisheries for the endangered totoaba (a large member of the croaker and drum family, *Cynoscion macdonaldi*) as well as shark, croaker, and mackerel fisheries, kill vaquitas (Vidal et al. 1994, D'Agrosa et al. 1995).

Mexico is a democracy, and elected officials there must respond to the needs and wishes of the electorate. So far, the most pressing needs have been for jobs and economic opportunity. Many Mexicans, of course, realize the importance of conservation, and Mexico has made large advances in conservation law and policy (e.g., in preserving gray whale habitat). But the highest priority perforce has been placed on achieving a decent standard of living for everyone. The implementation and enforcement of legal measures to protect wildlife cannot ignore these political and economic exigencies. When a fisherman tries to feed his family, he cannot reasonably be expected to stop fishing because he kills an occasional vaquita unless he is offered a viable economic alternative (Vidal 1993). Indubitably, unregulated, all-out exploitation of the local marine resources will likely eventually deprive him of a livelihood completely, but it is difficult for a breadwinner to balance what is to him a remote eventuality against the immediate need for food or money. (These comments apply equally to situations of incidental kill in other developing nations, where fishing often provides needed protein and cash income at a subsistence level.)

Incidental catches in gillnets may not be the only factor threatening the existence of the vaquita. Some mortality has been reported to be caused by shrimp trawls (Vidal 1995), and ecological depletion of the resources of the upper gulf by fisheries of all kinds could be affecting the vaquita's food base (Vidal 1995).

Most now agree that the only measure that would completely protect the vaquita and possibly allow it to recover would be an enforced total ban on gillnetting and trawling activities in the northern Gulf of California (International Whaling Commission 1995). This is not likely to happen, for the reasons outlined above, and so it seems that the vaquita may continue to decline. One very recent encouraging sign is recognition by the Mexican government, in outlining its recovery strategy for the vaquita to the International Whaling Commission (Table 13-1), that the problem is of international importance and concern, even though it is centered entirely within Mexican waters.

A plan does exist in Mexico for preserving the habitat of the vaquita. The general objective for managing the upper Gulf of California and Colorado River Delta Biosphere Reserve established in 1993 is to "conserve for present and future use and sustainable advantage, the diversity and integrity of wild and aquatic flora and fauna in their natural ecosystems" (L. Rojas, pers. comm.). Specific objectives of the plan include to identify and protect critical areas for endemic species like the totoaba, vaquita, and others. However, it remains to be seen whether the Mexican government will have the resources and resolve to implement and enforce the provisions of its plan for recovery of the vaquita. International moral support and financial and

Table 13-1. Chronology of the Vaquita

Year	Event
1942	Peak of the totoaba fishery (which killed vaquitas incidentally): 2,261 tons of meat in 1975 (Flanagan and Hendrickson 1976)
1958	First scientific description of the species (Norris and McFarland 1958)
1961	First data on incidental kills in totoaba gillnet fishery (Norris and Prescott 1961)
1968	First data on ecology (feeds on small, bottom-dwelling fishes [Fitch and Brownell 1968])
1975	Ban on totoaba fishing because of great decline in abundance of the fish stock (only 59 tons of meat harvested), but other fisheries dangerous to vaquitas continue
1976	First expressions of concern about population status (Villa-R. 1976; see also Brownell 1982)
1978	Placed in IUCN Red Data Book as "vulnerable" (Goodwin and Holloway 1978)
	Placed on Mexico's list of wildlife species that are rare or in danger of extinction (Villa-R. 1978)
1979	First proposal for a cetacean sanctuary in the Gulf of California to protect, inter alia, the vaquita (Anonymous 1979)
	Listed in Appendix I (species fully protected) of CITES (Convention on International Trade in Endangered Species of Wild Fauna and Flora)
1983	"Experimental" totoaba gillnet fisheries begin, ostensibly to assess stocks; about 70 tons taken each year, with concomitant incidental kills of vaquitas (Vidal 1995)
1985	Vaquita listed as endangered under U.S. Endangered Species Act, mandating cooperative work by the United States with Mexico to aid recovery
1986	First data on external appearance (Robles et al. 1986, Brownell et al. 1987)
	First extended field studies of the species begin (Silber 1990, Silber et al. 1994)
1990	IUCN (World Conservation Union) status changed from"vulnerable" ("Taxa believed likely to move into the endangered category in the near future if the causal factors continue operating") to "endangered" ("Taxa in danger of extinction and whose survival is unlikely if the causal factors continue operating") (World Conservation Monitoring Centre 1990, Klinowska 1991)
1992	Mexico establishes Technical Committee for the Preservation of the Totoaba and Vaquita, with international consultants
1993	First line-transect survey of abundance results in population estimate of 316, with 95% confidence limits of 118 to 847 (Gerrodette 1994, Gerrodette et al. 1995); later revised to 224–885 based on pooled analyses of several surveys (Barlow et al. 1997)
	Vaquita recovery plan developed by Mexico with assistance from U.S. Marine Mammal Commission (Marine Mammal Commission 1994a)
	Mexico creates Biosphere Reserve in northern Gulf of California (Reeves and Leatherwood 1994), but parts of vaquita range not included in core area
1994	First studies of life history indicate that rate of increase is likely lower than for other porpoises (Hohn et al. 1996)
	Incidental mortality that is likely unsustainable continues in wide range of gillnet fisheries, with levels probably above the 35 per year estimated earlier (D'Agrosa et al. 1995)
1995	Management Plan for the Biosphere Reserve of the Upper Gulf of California and the Colorado River Delta published by Mexican government and submitted to IWC (International Whaling Commission 1997); includes ban on fishing in Colorado River Delta and the "Nucleus Zone" of the Reserve (this ban remained unenforced through early 1999)
1996	Listed by IUCN as "critically endangered" (International Union for the Conservation of Nature and Natural Resources 1996)

technical assistance may make the difference and should be augmented at this critical juncture. Most recently, the International Committee for the Recovery of the Vaquita, constituted under the recovery plan, met and agreed inter alia on the likely very small size of the remaining population (low 100s) and the need for better estimates of abundance and incidental fishery takes.

The Baiji

What is most remarkable about the baiji (*Lipotes vexillifer*) is that it still exists at all. It is a river dolphin (Fig. 13-2) that shares the Yangtze River drainage with approximately 10% of the world's human population and suffers from all the attendant river traffic, overexploitation of fish and water resources, and pollution. Its range has contracted; it formerly occurred in nearly 2,000 km of the river, in tributaries, and in adjacent lakes. Now it is found only in small groups in limited stretches of the lower and middle Yangtze (Chen and Hua 1989a). Nobody knows how many there were originally, and there are no reliable estimates of current abundance, but the most optimistic estimates place the population in the low hundreds (Table 13-2). In the most recent efforts to estimate abundance, in 1993 and 1994 (Liu and Wang 1996), only 15 baiji were sighted during six surveys lasting 150 days and covering some 800 km of the middle reaches of the Yangtze, about half of the range of the species (the total of 2,938 km of search track included portions of the river surveyed more than once, in different surveys). The greatest number seen at one time during a single survey was five. Larger groups of up to 16 baiji were seen in surveys in the late 1970s and 1980s (Liu and Wang 1996). There is wide agreement that abundance has decreased during the past 20 years and fear that the number remaining may be very small indeed.

Although the baiji has always been captured in small numbers for its oil (the flesh is considered inedible), its main enemy is a fishing method called "rolling hooks" (Klinowska

Figure 13-2. This adult male, the only baiji now in captivity, has been at a research facility in Wuhan, China, since 1980. This odd and fascinating river dolphin, endemic to the Yangtze River, is very near extinction. (Photograph by Steve Leatherwood)

Table 13-2. Chronology of the Baiji

Year	Event
200 B.C.	First appearance in Chinese literature in the *Er-Ya* (Zhou and Zhang 1991)
1918	Discovery by western science (Miller 1918)
1978	First field investigations of distribution, abundance, and ecology (Zhou 1989)
1979	Protected as "rare and precious aquatic animal" by Chinese law (Wang 1989)
1983–1986	Additional protection under various laws and decrees
1985	First national meeting on protection of the baiji, in Wuhan
1986	Population estimated at 300 (Chen and Hua 1989a)
	International workshop in China generates recommendations for assessment and management (Perrin and Brownell 1989)
1988	Listed as endangered by IUCN
1989	Listed as endangered under the U.S. Endangered Species Act
1993	Second international workshop in China; noted that harmful fishing activities continue and concluded that baiji declining and at very high risk of extinction within 25 years (Zhou et al. 1994)
1994	IUCN Cetacean Specialist Group and others urge that all surviving baiji be brought into captivity in a "seminatural reserve" to create a captive breeding population and preserve the species (Reeves and Leatherwood 1994, Liu and Wang 1996); Chinese government begins this program
1995	First baiji placed in seminatural reserve at Shishou (animal dies in 1996, see text)
1996	IUCN classifies baiji as "critically endangered" (International Union for the Conservation of Nature and Natural Resources 1996)

1991, Zhou 1992) that catches dolphins accidentally. The gear consists of very finely pointed hooks attached at small intervals along a long, slack, bottom setline. The supersharp hooks snag fish feeding on the bottom. Baiji are thought to be attracted to the snagged fish and themselves become entangled and die. The drastic impact of this fishing gear on the baiji is well known, and the gear has been banned on the river, but its use continues (Zhou et al. 1994). There are at least three reasons for this continued use: (1) The river is very long and resources for enforcement (vessels, wardens, and funds for fuel) are meager. (2) The population of China continues to grow, with industrialization of the Yangtze River valley and overuse of water and living resources increasing concomitantly. In this context, the ordinary fisherman trying to make a living is under greater and greater pressure to do things that, although illegal, may give him a fish catch. (3) Perhaps the most important factor is that China is not a monolithic nation but rather a complex mosaic of semiautonomous provinces, regions, and various extralegal fiefdoms with differing and sometimes overlapping and conflicting authorities, interests, perceptions, and motives. This makes collective conservation action problematic and often ineffective. As has been described for the giant panda in China (Schaller 1993), real progress, as opposed to progress in theory or on paper, is almost nonexistent.

Other sources of human-caused mortality of baiji include explosions during riverbank construction projects and collisions with large vessels (Klinowska 1991); both kill baiji directly. Threats to baiji habitat include increasing impoundment of tributary waters that support spawning runs of important prey fishes, overfishing, industrial pollution, and construction of large new dams, such as the Ghezouba Dam (Hua and Chen 1992) and the Three Gorges Dam. The latter is now under construction despite protests within China and internationally that the dam will likely wipe out a major portion of dolphin habitat because of downstream scouring of the riverbed (Fearnside 1988, Chen and Hua 1989b, Topping 1995).

Although many well-meaning and able people in China and abroad are working hard to save the baiji, it seems unlikely that it will survive far into the next century. At this writing, efforts are being made to bring as many as possible of the remaining baiji into "seminatural reserves" to protect them from fisheries and other sources of mortality on the river proper (Reeves and Leatherwood 1994, Liu et al. 1995, Zhou and Gao 1995, Liu and Wang 1996). The idea is to allow them to breed and multiply in the reserves and to restock the river with dolphins at some time in the far future when habitat conditions have improved. One of the two reserves built to date is an ancient bend (oxbow) of the Yangtze at Shishou in Hubei Province that has been fenced off. Studies have shown the water quality and forage in the oxbow to be adequate to support a captive group of finless porpoises (*Neophocaena phocaenoides*). If the finless porpoises are removed and if fishing is successfully banned in the reserve, it may be a suitable place to put baiji removed from the main river (Reeves and Leatherwood 1994). The other seminatural reserve is a blocked-off channel between two parts of the Yangtze at Tongling in Anqing Province, but it has problems of water quality and low forage-fish population (Reeves and Leatherwood 1994).

However, it has proven very difficult to find and capture the few remaining baiji in the wild (Liu and Wang 1996). One baiji that was captured and placed in the reserve in December 1995 reportedly became sick and subsequently died after becoming entangled in a net (Beijing Xinhua [newspaper], 23 July 1996). Against all advice, the finless porpoises were allowed to remain in the reserve, possibly contributing to the debilitation and demise of the lone baiji. The results to date of the concerted rescue effort for the species have not been good, and there is little reason for optimism.

The Eastern Spinner Dolphin

The story of the eastern spinner dolphin is one of a hard-won victory for conservation of a marine mammal.

The eastern spinner (Fig. 13-3) (*Stenella longirostris orientalis*) is endemic to the eastern tropical Pacific off Mexico and Central America (Perrin 1990). It differs sharply from spinner dolphins in other parts of the world's Tropics in coloration and in shape of body and dorsal fin, and in adult males the fin is canted forward; this is correlated with presence of a large postanal ventral hump. Such pronounced morphological differences are usually assumed in mammals to indicate that an animal has evolved to be uniquely adapted to its particular habitat, in this case the oceanographically distinct far-eastern tropical Pacific (Reilly 1990). As such, the eastern spinner dolphin population represents an "evolutionarily significant unit," worthy of preservation as a unique entity, part of our heritage of biological diversity (Dizon et al. 1994). Since the first records of the eastern spinner's existence in the 1960s (Perrin 1975), its fate has been linked with the development and resolution of the tuna-dolphin problem, the controversial netting of dolphin schools in the eastern tropical Pacific by tuna purse seiners to catch the yellowfin tuna (*Thunnus albacares*) that associate with them (Perrin 1968, 1969, 1970; Allen 1985; Joseph 1994; see Gosliner, this volume, for more details). The dolphins are of several species: the spinner dolphin (several populations), the pantropical spotted dolphin (*Stenella attenuata*), the short-beaked common dolphin (*Delphinus delphis*), the long-beaked common dolphin (*Delphinus capensis*), and the striped dolphin (*Stenella coeruleoalba*). The reason for the tuna-dolphin association is not known but may be related to the tendency of tuna to gather under floating objects and/or with foraging efficiency; either the tuna or the dolphins or both may benefit from increased efficiency in finding and catching prey because they travel and hunt together (Edwards 1992). U.S. fishermen began exploiting the association in the late 1950s when they shifted from pole-and-line fishing to the use of large purse seine nets (McNeely 1961; Green et al. 1971; Perrin 1968, 1969).

From the time that it first became known that very large numbers of eastern spinners were dying in tuna nets (1968–1969 [see Perrin 1970]), it took approximately 25 years for the subspecies to be protected to the extent that its survival is assured. This great delay, or slow progress, which resulted in reduction of the population to 32–58% (best estimate 44%) of its original size (Wade 1993) or less (Wade 1994), was due to at least two factors: the tuna fishery was very large, economically important, and politically influential; and the fishery took place out of view on the high seas. Progress in reducing mortality and halting the decline was achieved only after great pressure and adverse publicity were generated by environmental organizations. Government did not move until it was forced to do so by public opinion; awareness of the problem and availability of the means to solve it were not enough. The issue has involved dozens of lawsuits, countersuits, injunctions, appeals, resolutions, and protracted negotiations among government, environmental organizations, and the industry (see Gosliner, this volume), as well as 25 years of intensive and

A

B

Figure 13-3. With its monochrome coloration, reversed dorsal fin (in adult males), and large postanal hump, the eastern spinner dolphin (*Stenella longirostris orientalis*) from the far-eastern tropical Pacific (*A*) is very different from other subspecies of spinner dolphins elsewhere in the Pacific and the world (*B*). Its uniqueness deserves protection. (Photographs by Robert Pitman)

large-scale research costing more than $100 million, not including legal fees. Unfortunately, resources of this scale are not likely to be available in most other countries where serious problems of incidental kill in fisheries exist.

Another important factor leading to a reduced mortality has been the shift in the fleet from the U.S. flag to the flags of Mexico, Venezuela, Ecuador, Vanuatu, and other nations (Bonanno and Constance 1996). Restrictions placed on operations of U.S. tunaboats in the 1970s achieved approximately a 90% reduction in deaths of dolphins of all species. However, as the fleet moved to non-U.S. flags, the issue moved out of U.S. control, and the kills increased again, totaling more than 100,000 dolphins (of all species) in 1986 (Joseph 1994). This was followed by increased consideration of U.S. sanctions on tuna imports. Because the United States is a major tuna market, the non-U.S. tuna producers became alarmed and set out to reduce their dolphin kills by using methods developed in the U.S. fishery. This effort was organized and orchestrated by the Inter-American Tropical Tuna Commission (funded largely by the United States) in a very successful program of research, education, and technical assistance and with an emphasis on individual responsibility by the boat captains and owners for their dolphin kills. The kill of dolphins of all species again declined rapidly to levels in the mid-1990s of a few thousand a year (Joseph 1994); in 1995 only 664 eastern spinners were known to have been killed in the fishery, about one-tenth of 1% of the estimated total population of 631,800 (Lennert and Hall 1996); this is in comparison with an estimated mortality of 15,000 to 16,000 in 1986 (Hall and Boyer 1988). Legislation enacted in 1997 in the United States Congress will allow nations participating in this successful international program to reenter the U.S. tuna market after it has been formalized under a binding international agreement.

This is one of the few examples of success in conserving small cetaceans. The urgent conservation problem has almost certainly been solved, although issues remain of appropriate target rates of population recovery, possible unobserved or unreported mortality or disruption of reproduction caused by chase and capture, and humane treatment of the dolphins. In addition, there is the issue of animal rights. Many believe that dolphins should not be deliberately chased, captured, and exposed to danger of death in this manner for any reason. So far this has been a minority view, especially in other nations, but that may change in the future; perhaps some day the dolphins will be left in peace.

The Striped Dolphin in Japan

What has happened to the striped dolphin in Japan is very much like what happened to the great whales in the Southern Ocean in the 1960s. A directed fishery has been allowed to continue in the face of evidence of sharp reduction of the population and repeated strong recommendations by scientists (e.g., the International Whaling Commission's Scientific Committee [references below]) that the fishery be stopped.

The striped dolphin (Fig. 13-4) (*Stenella coeruleoalba*) occurs around the world in many locations in tropical and warm-temperate waters (Perrin et al. 1994b). Population structure is not well known, but it can be assumed that regional populations exist as for other pelagic dolphins (Perrin and Brownell 1994). In Japanese waters, the species appears seasonally, associated with the advancing northern periphery of the warm Kuroshio Current. The northern boundary of the range extends to 46°N latitude in summer and retreats to 33°N latitude in winter. It has recently been suggested that there may be separate coastal and offshore stocks of striped dolphins off Japan (International Whaling Commission 1992).

Catches of dolphins in directed Japanese drive and harpoon fisheries date back to at least the Genruko period (1688–1703), but the types of dolphins caught were not recorded in the earlier centuries (International Whaling Commission 1994). The first known catches of striped dolphins occurred in 1888 in a drive fishery on the Izu Peninsula. The catches in this century reached very high levels during the peak years of the fishery: more than 22,000 in 1942, about 22,000 in 1959, and 16,492 in 1980 (Perrin et al. 1994a). These catches are thought to have been unsustainable and to have caused the population to decline (Kasuya 1985). Voluntary reductions in catch began in 1982 (a quota of 5,000 for the main drive fishery in Taiji), and catches during the period 1981–1987 ranged from 358 to 4,833, averaging 2,830. Official limits on catches set by prefectural governments and later by the national government began in 1989. In the period 1989–1993 the average catch dropped to 1,028. Catch quotas have not been filled, despite continued demand for dolphin meat. This supports the hypothesis of a long-term decline in abundance, a decline that has been noted by the drive fishermen themselves (International Whaling Commission 1993). Based on these lines of evidence, the Scientific Committee of the International Whaling Commission in 1992 concluded that the striped dolphin population in Japanese coastal waters cannot support continued exploitation and strongly recommended that the fishery be halted pending a complete assessment of the population (International Whaling Commission 1993). The recommendation was not binding because of the lack of a mandate by the International Whaling Commission for management of small cetaceans. The advice, repeated in 1993 (International Whaling Commission 1994), was not followed by Japan although the catch limit was reduced (to 725 in 1993 [National Research Institute of

Figure 13-4. The striped dolphin (*Stenella coeruleoalba*) has been harvested intensively in Japan in recent decades at rates that are probably unsustainable. (Photograph by William E. Schevill)

Far Seas Fisheries 1995]). Again, the quota was not taken in 1993 despite continued demand. Catches from 1992 to 1995 were 1,122, 544, 545, and 619, respectively (International Whaling Commission 1995, 1996; National Research Institute of Far Seas Fisheries 1997).

Other small cetaceans are taken in drives and by harpoon and crossbow in Japan. These include pantropical spotted dolphins, spinner dolphins, bottlenose dolphins (*Tursiops truncatus*), short-beaked common dolphins, rough-toothed dolphins (*Steno bredanensis*), short-finned pilot whales (*Globicephala macrorhynchus*), Risso's dolphins (*Grampus griseus*), melon-headed whales (*Peponocephala electra*), false killer whales (*Pseudorca crassidens*), Pacific white-sided dolphins (*Lagenorhynchus obliquidens*), Dall's porpoises (*Phocoenoides dalli*), Baird's beaked whales (*Berardius bairdii*), and others (International Whaling Commission 1993, 1994, 1995). As catches of the striped dolphin (and of the great whales) have declined, catches of some other species have increased. The International Whaling Commission's Scientific Committee has expressed concern that there is insufficient information on the status of the exploited populations and also that low catches of one species (the striped dolphin) have resulted in the shifting of effort to other species, notably the bottlenose dolphin and Risso's dolphin (International Whaling Commission 1993).

Although the striped dolphin fishery has not been halted, Japan has acted on other advice (International Whaling Commission 1993) to set catch limits on small cetaceans by species and to conduct research aimed at providing reliable estimates of abundance and stock identity for all the species (National Research Institute of Far Seas Fisheries 1995). Thus, although the International Whaling Commission does not have a direct mandate to manage small cetaceans (as discussed below), it has been successful in some instances in influencing the actions of nations exploiting them. However, the continuing fishery for the greatly depleted striped dolphin points out the need for international mechanisms for conservation of dolphins, porpoises, and small whales.

The Special Problems of Small Cetaceans

As compared with the great whales, the small cetaceans have several special problems.

Ease of Capture

Dolphins, porpoises, and small whales are highly vulnerable to hunting because of their small size and, in some species, their habit of riding the bow waves of vessels. They can be captured with small-scale equipment (e.g., hand-held harpoons and rifles) and often are not big or strong enough to endanger their captors. They are more easily killed in gillnets and other fishing gear than the larger whales because they usually do not have enough strength to break loose (Perrin et al. 1994a). They are also more vulnerable to entanglement in small-mesh nets because they are more easily snagged by their teeth or appendages (Barham et al. 1977); the larger appendages of the great whales do not fit into the mesh, and the baleen whales have no teeth. Small cetaceans can also be driven ashore in large numbers, as is done with long-finned pilot whales (*Globicephala melas*) in the Faroe Islands (Reeves and Leatherwood 1994) and several species in Japan (discussed above).

Vulnerable Habitats

Many small cetaceans are also relatively vulnerable because of their habitats. A river can be dammed, water flow can be diverted, rivers and estuaries are easily polluted, and coastal development can alter or degrade adjacent habitats (Perrin and Brownell 1989, International Whaling Commission 1994, Reeves and Leatherwood 1994). The species occurring in such habitats include the river dolphins proper (the baiji, the Ganges river dolphin [*Platanista gangetica*], the Indus river dolphin [*Platanista minor*], the boto [*Inia geoffrensis*], and the franciscana [*Pontoporia blainevillei*]), the tucuxi (*Sotalia fluviatilis*), the hump-backed dolphins (*Sousa chinensis* and *S. teuszii*), the bottlenose dolphin, the Irrawaddy dolphin (*Orcaella brevirostris*), the finless porpoise, the harbor porpoise, Burmeister's porpoise, and the white whale or beluga (*Delphinapterus leucas*), all inhabitants of rivers or shallow coastal and estuarine waters.

Development of New Markets

Another special problem for the small cetaceans is the conversion of incidental kills to directed fisheries. Once a small cetacean has been killed by accident in a fishing net, a fisherman or fish buyer can easily transport it to market to see if it can be sold. If the buying public decides it likes the meat and substantial demand develops, the fishermen can then switch to catching the animals deliberately. This has happened on a large scale in Peru; incidental catches there of dolphins and porpoises in gillnets led quickly to development of a large market and directed fisheries using purse seines, harpoons, gillnets, and dynamite. A government decree banned the capture of small cetaceans and trade in their products in 1990, but this law was largely ignored or circumvented, and the annual catch in the early to mid-1990s was estimated at 17,600, mainly dusky dolphins (*Lagenorhynchus obscurus*) but also long-beaked common dolphins, Burmeister's porpoises, bottlenose dolphins, and others (Van Waerebeek and Reyes 1994). Most recently, a law was passed declaring seven species of small cetaceans, including those taken commonly in fisheries, to be protected in Peruvian waters (International Whaling Commission 1997). Accurate monitoring of the kill is difficult, if not impossible, because the kill is illegal, and fishermen are reluctant to report their takes. Similar conversion of incidental kills to covert directed fisheries has occurred in Sri Lanka (Leatherwood and Reeves 1989) (Fig. 13-5) and the Philippines (Dolar et al. 1994) and can be assumed to have taken place elsewhere. In the Philippines, where a legal ban on killing dolphins also exists, the shift has been exacerbated by growing depletion of fish stocks. Unless other steps are taken to increase the supply of affordable protein, cetaceans will be increasingly exploited, legally or illegally.

Figure 13-5. Dolphins killed accidentally in fishing nets often make their way to market in some countries. Here a spotted dolphin is being transported from the main fish market at Galle, Sri Lanka, 1985. (Photograph by Steve Leatherwood)

Difficulties of Monitoring and Regulation

Incidental kills and small directed takes of dolphins and porpoises are difficult to monitor and regulate. The animals are often killed or caught by a large number of small vessels—literally thousands in some countries (e.g., China [Zhou and Wang 1994])—that operate independently and land their catches in a large number of places, including undeveloped beaches. The small carcasses can be hidden or cut up at sea and smuggled ashore as meat. In some cases, monitoring by inspection is impossible; it would require almost as many inspectors as fishermen. And, of course, if small cetaceans caught during fishing operations are of no use to the fishermen, they can simply be discarded over the side with no one the wiser. From personal experience, I can say that fishermen quickly learn that cooperating in gathering data on incidental catches can lead directly to restrictions on fishing. Unless the fishermen and the local community are fully committed to conservation of the resources they are exploiting, there is no hope for monitoring or controlling many takes of small cetaceans.

Lack of International Means of Management

Small cetaceans have been the "forgotten whales" in international conservation and management (Brownell et al. 1989). The International Whaling Commission manages exploitation of the great whales, including those within the territorial waters of member nations (see Gambell, this volume). However, the small cetaceans fall outside the International Whaling Commission's competence, or at least this is the current working interpretation of the Convention. Not all member nations agree with this; it has been the source of much controversy within the Commission and has been included on the annual agenda since the late 1980s. The International Whaling Commission's Scientific Committee proposed as early as 1979 that at least some small cetaceans (the white whale and the narwhal [*Monodon monoceros*]) be added to the Schedule (the agreed source document mandating competence and responsibilities within the Convention) (International Whaling Commission 1980:57). The reasoning by its sub-committee on small cetaceans was as follows:

> . . . management of the aboriginal / subsistence fisheries for white whales and narwhals should be considered by the Commission in the same manner as the bowhead fishery in the Bering Sea and Arctic Ocean. White whales of some stocks and narwhals on the one hand and bowhead whales on the other both undergo long migrations, crossing national territorial boundaries. Both are taken by indigenous peoples using light craft and harpoons, with various modifications derived from modern technology. Whaling efforts for the two are interrelated, and scientific analysis of catch

data should take this multispecies aspect of aboriginal whaling into consideration. . . . The only substantive differences between the fisheries are in size of the whales and size of and organization of the whaling crews involved, differences not justifying the radically different treatment presently given them (International Whaling Commission 1980:124).

However, these initiatives failed. Some member nations, such as Canada (no longer a member), Russia, Mexico, and Japan, have large-scale small-cetacean fisheries or large incidental kills of small cetaceans and have resisted extension of the competence of the International Whaling Commission to manage small cetaceans on the grounds of preserving national sovereignty. This argument is inconsistent with the current agreed purview of the International Whaling Commission covering large whales in territorial waters.

Although the member nations have not been able to agree to extend the Commission's authority to small cetaceans, they have agreed to provide data on directed and incidental takes for consideration by the Scientific Committee and to consider small-cetacean issues in the workings of the Commission. As noted above, the Scientific Committee in recent years has frequently offered nonbinding recommendations and advice to member nations on research and actions to conserve small cetaceans. For the most part, these recommendations have been followed, establishing a de facto extension of the International Whaling Commission umbrella to small cetaceans.

Another attempt to compensate for the lack of international mechanisms to conserve small cetaceans has been the focus by the Cetacean Specialist Group of IUCN–The World Conservation Union (an intergovernmental body) on small-cetacean issues. The group's action plan for 1988–1992 (Perrin 1989, Reeves and Leatherwood 1994) contained a list of 45 recommended conservation actions; of these, all but three dealt solely with small cetaceans, with special emphasis on the highly vulnerable river dolphins. Most of these projects have been funded and are under way or completed. The new action plan for 1994–1998 (Reeves and Leatherwood 1994) again focuses primarily on the small cetaceans.

A consortium composed of the United Nations Environment Programme (UNEP), the Food and Agriculture Organization (FAO), the World Conservation Union, and other intergovernmental organizations has also tried to fill the gap for small cetaceans in the Global Plan of Action for the Conservation, Management, and Utilization of Marine Mammals (Food and Agriculture Organization/United Nations Environment Programme 1985, Meith 1988).

A recent development has been the trend toward establishment of regional agreements on conservation of small cetaceans under the Convention on Migratory Species of Wild Animals (commonly known as the Bonn Convention). The Agreement on the Conservation of Small Cetaceans of the Baltic and North Seas (known as ASCOBANS) was ratified and put in place in 1994. A secretariat has been established in Germany, and the parties to the agreement (the United Kingdom, Sweden, Finland, the Netherlands, Belgium, Germany, Denmark, and the European Community) are developing plans for joint assessment and protection of small cetaceans in the region. Priority is being given to assessment and reduction of incidental mortality of cetaceans in fishing gear (International Whaling Commission 1996). The agreement may be expanded in the future to include the waters around Ireland and the Bay of Biscay, which would allow membership by Ireland and Spain. A second regional agreement is in ratification, the Agreement on the Conservation of Cetaceans of the Black Sea, Mediterranean Sea and Contiguous Atlantic Area, and a possible agreement covering Southeast Asia is being considered (International Whaling Commission 1996).

The texts of the various international conventions and agreements discussed here can be found in the U.S. Marine Mammal Commission's compendium of international agreements (Marine Mammal Commission 1994b, 1997).

Some Lessons Learned along the Way

General principles for the conservation of marine mammals are discussed in Chapter 20, and some of the efforts to address the special problems of conserving small cetaceans are described above. This section relates some of the conclusions that I have reached during my 35 years spent studying small cetaceans and the problems of their conservation. My perspective has been mainly from inside a U.S. federal agency, although I have also worked with various international organizations.

Laws without the Will and Resources to Enforce Them Are Worse than No Laws at All

This is particularly true of laws relating to incidental kills of small cetaceans in fisheries where the bycatch is discarded at sea. In other situations where incidentally caught dolphins are kept for human consumption, the creation of a market has led to directed takes. In such cases, a legal ban without meaningful enforcement can simply drive the traffic in dolphin meat underground. This has occurred in Peru (Van Waerebeek and Van Bressem 1995) and the Philippines (personal observations). As noted above, an unfortunate side effect of such an ineffectual ban often has been to close the de facto "dolphin fisheries" to scientific investigation and government scrutiny. Because the fisheries legally do not exist, fishermen (and local officials) are not eager to allow access to anyone. Thus, an ill-considered ban or one without the resources and the will to back it up can have a negative net effect.

Incidental Mortality Cannot Always Be Totally Eliminated

After 20-some years of experience under the U.S. Marine Mammal Protection Act of 1972, it was finally recognized that many valuable fisheries cannot operate without causing some incidental mortality of marine mammals, despite every attempt to avoid it. This has led to a reconciliation of conservation and economic needs (see Baur et al., this volume) that, it is hoped, will serve as a model for other countries where the existing laws are not working. For example, in the Philippines it is illegal to catch or kill a dolphin by any means, including during operation of a fishery directed at other species (Dolar 1994). However, closing down the fisheries that take dolphins incidentally would have extreme economic impacts, perhaps even literally causing starvation in some regions. Obviously that is not going to happen, and, in fact, the law is considered a bad law and widely ignored. What is the answer? As discussed elsewhere (see Meffe et al., this volume), all stakeholders in such a situation must be involved in developing a conservation regime if it is to work. Experience in the United States has shown that in most cases involving small cetaceans there is some level of incidental kill that is acceptable both to the fishermen and to those charged with conserving the marine mammals. In other words, a consensus of limits can be reached, and, with commitment, excessive kills can be reduced to these limits.

"Sustainable Development" Probably Will Not Work for Small Cetaceans

Sustainable development and utilization of all resources has become a prevalent international theme since the United Nations Conference on Environment and Development in 1992 (the "Rio Summit," which produced Agenda 21 [United Nations Conference on Environment and Development 1992]). Although some incidental mortality in fisheries may be sustainable, populations of small cetaceans are not good candidates for sustainable development in the sense of Agenda 21. A resolution that came out of a recent workshop on marine mammals of Southeast Asia is pertinent (Perrin et al. 1996:60):

> The characteristics and difficult-to-study habits of marine mammals do not suit them well for sustainable exploitation. All these species are long-lived animals with very low rates of natural increase. Absolute population estimates are technically difficult to obtain, and it is very difficult to monitor trends in population size at spatial and temporal scales which are useful to management. Thus it is very difficult to determine whether a take is sustainable. History suggests that non-subsistence takes will be unsustainable.
>
> Considering the current pressures and the projected increases in human populations with their consequent developments in the region, . . . substantive sustainable development is not a viable option and . . . countries in the region should be urged to take steps to minimize the incidental capture of small cetaceans and dugongs, take steps to protect their important marine and riverine habitats, consider the banning of sales of products from incidental catches, and allow takes of marine mammals for oceanaria only where they can be shown to be sustainable.

These comments apply to any of the less-developed regions of the world; increased exploitation of marine mammals for nonsubsistence use is not an appropriate option in a development plan.

The Environmental Organizations Are Indispensable

When I was involved in bringing to light the tuna-dolphin problem in the late 1960s (Perrin 1968, 1969, 1970), I soon came to appreciate the value of nongovernmental groups, commonly referred to as NGOs. Although the scientific community was alert to the problem, it was not until several environmental groups became involved that things began to happen—that is, funds became available for research to reduce dolphin mortality in purse seines and to assess the population impacts of the mortality. In my experience, this pattern is repeated in every instance of crisis or concern about the conservation of small cetaceans. The NGOs (along with the governmental oversight agencies such as the U.S. Marine Mammal Commission) help keep us as scientists accountable and focused in the right direction. They also play a valuable role in educating the public and the Congress. The positions taken by these groups can sometimes be extreme, but they often help counterbalance the obduracy and vested interests found at the other end of the spectrum. The resulting governmental policies and legislative solutions are usually just about right. Without the NGOs, the small cetaceans would be much worse off than they are.

Oceanariums and Whale Watching Offer Important Educational Opportunities and Should Be Encouraged

In the United States the public's concern about the welfare of dolphins, porpoises, and small whales can be linked with its familiarity with them through the television show *Flipper* and the introduction of killer whales into captivity in the

1960s (see Reeves and Mead, this volume). In countries where there are no oceanariums, such as, for example, Peru, Sri Lanka, and the Philippines, small cetaceans are perceived primarily as "another kind of fish," and there is little public appreciation of them or concern about their conservation. This may be in part a simplistic point, of course, because the presence of an affluent middle class, as exists in the United States and other more developed countries, must be an important factor in public concern about conservation in general. But the fact remains that most Peruvians, Sri Lankans, and Filipinos have no opportunity to see live cetaceans at close hand but know them only from carcasses at the fishing ports or in the markets. Many are not even aware that cetaceans occur in the waters of their countries. My experience with nascent whale-watching operations in the Philippines has shown me that a close encounter with live dolphins or whales can change an individual's perceptions and evoke active concern about marine mammal conservation. Oceanariums, especially in the more affluent countries, have given millions of people the opportunity for such experiences. Introduction of similar opportunities in the less-developed countries could do much to foster an awareness of small cetaceans and a commitment to their conservation. Simply stated, a few well-cared-for animals in tanks could save thousands or millions in the sea.

In the establishment and operation of any oceanarium, of course, it is to be hoped that competent professionals will be enlisted in assessing acceptable levels of removals from wild populations; in capturing, transporting, and acclimating animals humanely; and in ensuring that training and care are the best attainable. Strict laws and regulations to ensure this are in place in Europe (most nations), North America, Australia, and New Zealand, but currently are lacking in most other places.

Summary

Many populations of small cetaceans face serious problems of conservation, even of survival. Small cetaceans are especially vulnerable to incidental mortality in fisheries and destruction of their habitats. They are extremely difficult to assess and monitor and are therefore easily overexploited. There is currently no agreed international approach to their conservation and management. Effective conservation requires meaningful national laws and the will and resources to enforce them, recognition and management of incidental mortality within sustainable limits, continued attention by nongovernmental groups, and greater efforts to make the public in the less-developed countries aware of the value and vulnerability of their dolphins, porpoises, and small whales.

Literature Cited

Allen, R. L. 1985. Dolphins and the purse-seine fishery for yellowfin tuna. Pages 236–252 *in* J. R. Beddington, R. J. H. Beverton, and D. M. Lavigne (eds.), Marine Mammals and Fisheries. George Allen and Unwin, Boston and Sydney.

Anonymous. 1979. Proceedings, Workshop on Cetacean Sanctuaries, 4–9 February 1979, Tijuana and Guerro Negro, B.C. [Mexico]. International Union for Conservation of Nature and Natural Resources, Gland, Switzerland.

Barham, E. G., W. K. Taguchi, and S. B. Reilly. 1977. Porpoise rescue methods in the yellowfin purse seine fishery and the importance of Medina panel mesh size. Marine Fisheries Review 39 (5): 1–10.

Barlow, J., T. Gerrodette, and G. Silber. 1997. First estimates of vaquita abundance. Marine Mammal Science 13:44–58.

Baur, D. C., M. J. Bean, and M. L. Gosliner. 1999. The laws governing marine mammal conservation in the United States. (This volume)

Bonanno, A., and D. Constance. 1996. Caught in the Net: The Global Tuna Industry, Environmentalism, and the State. University Press of Kansas, Lawrence, KS.

Brownell, R. L., Jr. 1982. Status of the cochito, *Phocoena sinus*, in the Gulf of California. Pages 85–90 *in* FAO Advisory Committee on Marine Resources Research, Working Party on Marine Mammals, Mammals in the Seas. Vol. 4. Small Cetaceans, Seals, Sirenians and Otters. Food and Agriculture Organization Fisheries Series 4. Food and Agriculture Organization, Rome, Italy.

Brownell, R. L., Jr. 1986. Distribution of the vaquita, *Phocoena sinus*, in Mexican waters. Marine Mammal Science 2:299–305.

Brownell, R. L., Jr., L. T. Findley, O. Vidal, A. Robles, and S. Manzanilla N. 1987. External morphology and pigmentation of the vaquita, *Phocoena sinus* (Cetacea: Mammalia). Marine Mammal Science 3:22–30.

Brownell, R. L., Jr., K. Ralls, and W. F. Perrin. 1989. The plight of the 'forgotten' whales. Oceanus 32 (1): 5–11.

Chen, P., and Y. Hua. 1989a. Distribution, population size and protection of *Lipotes vexillifer*. Occasional Papers of the Species Survival Commission (SSC) 3:81–85.

Chen, P., and Y. Hua. 1989b. Projected impacts of the Three Gorges Dam on the baiji, *Lipotes vexillifer*, and the needs for the conservation of the species. [Translation of 1987 unpublished report]. Southwest Fisheries Center Administrative Report LJ-89-23. 15 pp.

D'Agrosa, C., O. Vidal, and W. C. Graham. 1995. Mortality of the vaquita (*Phocoena sinus*) in gillnet fisheries during 1993–94. Reports of the International Whaling Commission (Special Issue 16): 283–291.

Dizon, A. E., W. F. Perrin, and P. A. Akin. 1994. Stocks of dolphins (*Stenella* spp. and *Delphinus delphis*) in the eastern tropical Pacific: A phylogeographic classification. NOAA Technical Report NMFS 119. 20 pp.

Dolar, M. L. L. 1994. Incidental takes of small cetaceans in fisheries in Palawan, central Visayas and northern Mindanao in the Philippines. Reports of the International Whaling Commission (Special Issue 15): 355–363.

Dolar, M. L. L., S. Leatherwood, C. J. Wood, C. L. Hill, M. N. R. Alava, and L. V. Aragones. 1994. Directed fisheries for cetaceans in the Philippines. Reports of the International Whaling Commission 44:439–449.

Edwards, E. F. 1992. Energetics of associated tunas and dolphins in the eastern tropical Pacific Ocean: A basis for the bond. Fishery Bulletin (U.S.) 90:678–702.

Fearnside, P. M. 1988. China's Three Gorges Dam: Fatal project or step toward modernization? World Development 16:615–630.

Fitch, J. E., and R. L. Brownell Jr. 1968. Fish otoliths in cetacean stomachs and their importance in interpreting feeding habits. Journal of the Fisheries Research Board of Canada 25:2561–2574.

Flanagan, C. A., and J. R. Hendrickson. 1976. Observations on the commercial fishery and reproductive biology of the totoaba *Cynoscion macdonaldi* in the northern Gulf of California, Mexico. Fishery Bulletin (U.S.) 74:531–544.

Food and Agriculture Organization / United Nations Environment Programme. 1985. Marine mammals: Global plan of action. UNEP Regional Seas Reports and Studies 55. 115 pp.

Gambell, R. 1999. The International Whaling Commission and the contemporary whaling debate. (This volume)

Gerrodette, T. 1994. Estimate of population size for the vaquita, *Phocoena sinus*. International Whaling Commission meeting document SC / 46 / SM23. 9 pp.

Gerrodette, T., L. A. Fleischer, H. Pérez-Cortés, and B. Villa Ramírez. 1995. Distribution of the vaquita, *Phocoena sinus,* based on sightings from systematic surveys. Reports of the International Whaling Commission (Special Issue 16): 273–281.

Goodwin, H. A., and C. W. Holloway (compilers). 1978. International Union for Conservation of Nature and Natural Resources Red Data Book. Vol. 1. Mammalia. IUCN, Morges, Switzerland.

Gosliner, M. L. 1999. The tuna-dolphin controversy. (This volume)

Green, R. E., W. F. Perrin, and B. P. Petrich. 1971. The American tuna purse seine fishery. Pages 182–194 *in* H. Kristjonsson (ed.), Modern Fishing Gear of the World. 3. Fish Finding, Purse Seining, Aimed Trawling. Fishing News (Books), London.

Hall, M. A., and S. D. Boyer. 1988. Incidental mortality of dolphins in the eastern tropical Pacific tuna fishery in 1986. Reports of the International Whaling Commission 38:439–441.

Hohn, A. A., A. J. Read, S. Fernandez, O. Vidal, and L. Findley. 1996. Life history of the vaquita, *Phocoena sinus*. Journal of Zoology (London) 239:235–251.

Hua, Y., and P. Chen. 1992. Investigation for impacts of changes of the lower reach of Ghezouba Dam between Yichang and Chenglingji on the baiji, *Lipotes vexillifer* after its key water control project founded. Journal of Fisheries of China 16:322–329. [In Chinese, with English summary.]

International Union for the Conservation of Nature and Natural Resources. 1996. IUCN Red List of Threatened Animals. IUCN, Gland, Switzerland.

International Whaling Commission. 1980. Report of the Scientific Committee. Reports of the International Whaling Commission 30:42–137.

International Whaling Commission. 1992. Report of the Scientific Committee. Reports of the International Whaling Commission 42:51–270.

International Whaling Commission. 1993. Report of the Scientific Committee. Reports of the International Whaling Commission 43:55–219.

International Whaling Commission. 1994. Annex F. Report of the sub-committee on small cetaceans. Reports of the International Whaling Commission 44:108–119.

International Whaling Commission. 1995. Report of the Scientific Committee. Reports of the International Whaling Commission 45:53–103.

International Whaling Commission. 1996. Report of the Scientific Committee. Reports of the International Whaling Commission 46:49–106.

International Whaling Commission. 1997. Report of the Scientific Committee. Reports of the International Whaling Commission 47.

Jefferson, T. A., S. Leatherwood, and M. A. Webber. 1993. Marine Mammals of the World. FAO Species Identification Guide. UNEP / FAO, Rome.

Joseph, J. 1994. The tuna-dolphin controversy in the eastern Pacific Ocean: Biological, economic, and political impacts. Ocean Development and International Law 25:1–30.

Kasuya, T. 1985. Effect of exploitation on reproductive parameters of the spotted and striped dolphins off the Pacific coast of Japan. Scientific Reports of the Whales Research Institute Tokyo 36:107–138.

Klinowska, M. 1991. Dolphins, Porpoises, and Whales of the World. The IUCN Red Data Book. IUCN, Gland, Switzerland, and Cambridge, U.K.

Leatherwood, S., and R. R. Reeves. 1989. Marine mammal research and conservation in Sri Lanka 1985–1986. United Nations Environment Programme, Oceans and Coastal Areas, Marine Mammal Technical Report 1. 138 pp.

Lennert, C., and M. A. Hall. 1996. Estimates of incidental mortality of dolphins in the eastern Pacific Ocean tuna fishery in 1994. Reports of the International Whaling Commission 46:555–558.

Liu, R., and D. Wang. 1996. Studies on population size and activities alteration regularities of *Lipotes vexillifer* and *Neophocaena phocaenoides* in the Yangtze River. IBI Reports [International Marine Biological Research Institute, Kamogawa, Japan] 6:1–8.

Liu, R., Q. Zhao, Z. Wei, and D. Chen. 1995. New progress of conservation of baiji (*Lipotes vexillifer*) and finless porpoise (*Neophocaena phocaenoides*) in China. IBI Reports [International Marine Biological Research Institute, Kamogawa, Japan] 5:45–55.

Marine Mammal Commission. 1994a. Annual report to Congress for 1993. (Available from National Technical Information Service, Springfield, VA. PB95-154530.) 260 pp.

Marine Mammal Commission. 1994b. The Marine Mammal Commission Compendium of Selected Treaties, International Agreements, and Other Relevant Documents on Marine Resources, Wildlife, and the Environment, R. L. Wallace, compiler. Marine Mammal Commission, Washington, DC. 3,547 pp.

Marine Mammal Commission. 1997. The Marine Mammal Commission Compendium of Selected Treaties, International Agreements, and other Relevant Documents on Marine Resources, Wildlife, and the Environment. First update. Marine Mammal Commission, Washington, DC. 1,017 + xix pp.

McNeely, R. L. 1961. The purse seine revolution in tuna fishing. Pacific Fisherman 59 (7): 27–58.

Meith, N. 1988. Marine Mammals, 2d ed. United Nations Environment Programme, Nairobi, Kenya. 40 pp.

Meffe, G. K., W. F. Perrin, and P. K. Dayton. 1999. Marine mammal conservation: Guiding principles and their implementation. (This volume)

Miller, G. S., Jr. 1918. A new river-dolphin from China. Smithsonian Miscellaneous Collections 68(9). 12 pp. and 13 plates.

National Research Institute of Far Seas Fisheries. 1995. Japan. Progress report on cetacean research April 1993 to March 1994. Reports of the International Whaling Commission 45:239–244.

National Research Institute of Far Seas Fisheries. 1997. Japan. Progress report on cetacean research April 1995 to March 1996. Reports of the International Whaling Commission 47.

Norris, K. S., and W. N. McFarland. 1958. A new harbor porpoise of the genus *Phocoena* from the Gulf of California. Journal of Mammalogy 39:22–39.

Norris, K. S., and J. H. Prescott. 1961. Observations on Pacific cetaceans of Californian and Mexican waters. University of California Publications in Zoology 63:291–402, pl. 27–41.

Perrin, W. F. 1968. The porpoise and the tuna. Sea Frontiers 14:166–174.

Perrin, W. F. 1969. Using porpoises to catch tuna. World Fishing 18:42–45.

Perrin, W. F. 1970. The problem of porpoise mortality in the U.S. tropical tuna fishery. Pages 435–448 *in* Proceedings of the Sixth Annual Conference on Biological Sonar and Diving Mammals, Stanford Research Institute, Palo Alto, CA, 1969.

Perrin, W. F. 1975. Variation of spotted and spinner porpoise (genus *Stenella*) in the eastern Pacific and Hawaii. Bulletin of the Scripps Institution of Oceanography 21. 206 pp.

Perrin, W. F. (compiler). 1989. Dolphins, porpoises, and whales. An action plan for the conservation of biological diversity: 1988–1992. International Union for the Conservation of Nature and Natural Resources, Gland, Switzerland. 29 pp.

Perrin, W. F. 1990. Subspecies of *Stenella longirostris* (Mammalia: Cetacea: Delphinidae). Proceedings of the Biological Society of Washington 103:453–463.

Perrin, W. F., and R. L. Brownell Jr. (eds.). 1989. Report of the workshop. Pages 1–22 *in* W. F. Perrin, R. L. Brownell Jr., K. Zhou, and J. Liu (eds.), Biology and Conservation of the River Dolphins. Occasional Papers of the IUCN Species Survival Commission No. 3.

Perrin, W. F., and R. L. Brownell Jr. 1994. A brief review of stock identity in small marine cetaceans in relation to assessment of driftnet mortality in the North Pacific. Reports of the International Whaling Commission (Special Issue 15): 393–401.

Perrin, W. F., G. P. Donovan, and J. Barlow (eds.). 1994a. Gillnets and Cetaceans. Proceedings of the Conference on Mortality of Cetaceans in Passive Fishing Nets and Traps, 20–25 October 1990, La Jolla, CA. Reports of the International Whaling Commission (Special Issue 15): 1–629.

Perrin, W. F., C. E. Wilson, and F. I. Archer II. 1994b. Striped dolphin, *Stenella coeruleoalba* (Meyen, 1833). Pages 129–159 *in* S. H. Ridgway and R. Harrison (eds.), Handbook of Marine Mammals. Vol. 5. The First Book of Dolphins. Academic Press, London.

Perrin, W. F., M. L. L. Dolar, and M. N. R. Alava. 1996. Report of the Workshop on the Biology and Conservation of Small Cetaceans and Dugongs of Southeast Asia, 27–30 June 1995, Dumaguete [Philippines]. UNEP(W)/EAS WG.1/2. UNEP, Bangkok. 101 pp.

Reeves, R. R., and S. Leatherwood (compilers). 1994. Dolphins, porpoises, and whales. 1994–1998 Action Plan for the Conservation of Cetaceans. International Union for the Conservation of Nature and Natural Resources, Gland, Switzerland.

Reeves, R. R., and J. G. Mead. 1999. Marine mammals in captivity. (This volume)

Reilly, S. B. 1990. Seasonal changes in distribution and habitat differences among dolphins in the eastern tropical Pacific. Marine Ecology Progress Series 66:1–11.

Robles, R., L. T. Findley, O. Vidal, R. L. Brownell, Jr., and S. Manzanilla N. 1986. Registros recientes y apariencia externa de la marsopa del Golfo de California, o vaquita, *Phocoena sinus* Norris and McFarland, 1958. Resúmenes (abstracts) XI Reunion Internacional Sobre Mamíferos Marinos, 2–6 April 1986, Guaymas, Sonora, Mexico.

Rosel, P. E., M. G. Haygood, and W. F. Perrin. 1995. Phylogenetic relationships among the true porpoises (Cetacea: Phocoenidae). Molecular Phylogenetics and Evolution 4:463–474.

Schaller, G. B. 1993. The Last Panda. University of Chicago Press, Chicago, IL. 291 pp.

Silber, G. K. 1990. Occurrence and distribution of the vaquita *Phocoena sinus* in the northern Gulf of California. Fishery Bulletin (U.S.) 88:339–346.

Silber, G. K., M. W. Newcomer, P. C. Silber, H. Perez-Cortes M., and G. M. Ellis. 1994. Cetaceans of the northern Gulf of California: Distribution, occurrence, and relative abundance. Marine Mammal Science 10:283–298.

Topping, A. R. 1995. Ecological roulette: Damming the Yangtze. Foreign Affairs 74:132–146.

United Nations Conference on Environment and Development. 1992. Agenda 21: Programme of action for sustainable development. United Nations Publications, New York, NY.

Van Waerebeek, K., and J. C. Reyes. 1994. Post-ban small cetacean takes off Peru: A review. International Whaling Commission meeting document SC/46/SM16. International Whaling Commission, Histon, Cambridge, U.K. 24 pp.

Van Waerebeek, K., and M. F. Van Bressem. 1995. Preliminary notes on cetacean mortality in fisheries off Peru and Ecuador in 1994. International Whaling Commission meeting document SC/47/SM38. International Whaling Commission, Histon, Cambridge, U.K.

Vidal, O. 1993. Aquatic mammal conservation in Latin America: Problems and perspectives. Conservation Biology 7:788–795.

Vidal, O. 1995. Population biology and incidental mortality of the vaquita, *Phocoena sinus*. Reports of the International Whaling Commission (Special Issue 16): 247–272.

Vidal, O., K. Van Waerebeek, and L. T. Findley. 1994. Cetaceans and gillnet fisheries in Mexico, Central America and the wider Caribbean. Reports of the International Whaling Commission (Special Issue 15): 221–237.

Villa-R., B. 1976. Report on the status of *Phocaena sinus* [*sic*], Norris and McFarland 1958, in the Gulf of California. Anales del Instituto Biológico, Universidad Nacional Autónoma de México 47, Seria Zoológica: 203–208.

Villa-R., B. 1978. Especies mexicanos de vertebrados silvestres raras o en peligro de extinción. Anales del Instituto Biológico, Universidad Nacional Autónoma de México, Seria Zoológica: 303–320.

Wade, P. R. 1993. Estimation of historical population size of the eastern stock of spinner dolphin (*Stenella longirostris orientalis*). Fishery Bulletin (U.S.) 91:775–787.

Wade, P. R. 1994. Abundance and population dynamics of two eastern Pacific dolphins, *Stenella attenuata* and *Stenella longirostris orientalis*. Ph.D. dissertation, University of California at San Diego, CA. 255 pp.

Wang, X. 1989. Conservation and management of *Lipotes vexillifer* in China: Experiences, lessons and tentative plans for the future. Occasional Papers of the Species Survival Commission (SSC) 3:157–173.

World Conservation Monitoring Centre. 1990. 1990 Iucn Red List of Threatened Animals. World Conservation Monitoring Centre, IUCN–The World Conservation Union, Cambridge, U.K.

Zhou, K. 1989. Brief review of studies on baiji, *Lipotes vexillifer*. IBI Reports [International Marine Biological Research Institute, Kamogawa, Japan] 1:33–36.

Zhou, K. 1992. Relation between human activities and marine mammals in China. IBI Reports [International Marine Biological Research Institute, Kamogawa, Japan] 3:15–23.

Zhou, K., and A. Gao. 1995. Semi-natural reserve is the best possible approach to rescue the baiji. IBI Reports [International Marine Biological Research Institute, Kamogawa, Japan] 5:57–61.

Zhou, K., and X. Wang. 1994. A brief review of passive fishing gears and incidental catches of small cetaceans in Chinese waters. Reports of the International Whaling Commission (Special Issue 15): 347–354.

Zhou, K., and X. Zhang. 1991. Baiji: The Yangtze River Dolphin and Other Endangered Animals of China. The Stonewall Press, Washington, DC.

Zhou, K., S. Ellis, S. Leatherwood, M. Bruford, and U. Seal (eds.). 1994. Baiji (*Lipotes vexillifer*) population and habitat viability assessment. IUCN/SCC Captive Breeding Specialist Group. 252 pp.

14

STEVEN K. KATONA AND SCOTT D. KRAUS

Efforts to Conserve the North Atlantic Right Whale

The right whales of the genus *Eubalaena,* including those in the North Atlantic, North Pacific, and Southern Oceans, are among the rarest baleen whales in the world. This chapter focuses on the North Atlantic right whale (*Eubalaena glacialis*), of which only 300 remain in the entire North Atlantic Ocean, making it the rarest large whale in the Atlantic Ocean (Fig. 14-1).

Despite its small remaining population, much is known about the North Atlantic right whale and about steps that could be taken to save it. This chapter presents a review of human activities that put these whales in peril of extinction, a summary of the species' biology with emphasis on aspects that put it at particular risk, the history of actions taken to protect right whales, and a summary of recommended future research and conservation actions.

Early History of Exploitation

The North Atlantic right whale was one of the baleen whale species first hunted by humans. Directed exploitation of this species began at least 1,000 years ago along the Atlantic shores of southern Europe. How early hunters learned their skills or whether hunting evolved as an outgrowth of scavenging carcasses of whales stranded along the shore will never be known. Furthermore, because no written records exist of the number of whales killed or the places and manner in which they were taken, early hunting can only be described in general terms.

Basque fishermen began hunting right whales not long after A.D. 1000 at a time when commerce and trade were expanding throughout Europe and neighboring areas. They may have caught whales as a seasonal supplement to fishing, with the main objective of obtaining blubber oil for illumination. Some meat, such as tongues, may also have been used. Basques hunted in the Bay of Biscay off northern Spain and western France. Nearly 50 whaling settlements have been identified, each of which probably took one whale every year or two (Aguilar 1986).

The Basque voyages ranged north and west during succeeding decades and centuries, perhaps in response to local declines in populations of fish or whales, changing weather conditions, or changing economic factors. By the early 1500s the Basques had reached the coasts of Newfoundland and Labrador, where the abundance of fish and whales made such long voyages worthwhile. From at least the 1530s into the early 1600s Basques hunted right whales and bowhead whales (*Balaena mysticetus*) near Red Bay, Labrador, and elsewhere in the Strait of Belle Isle every year from about June through November (Cumbaa 1986). Between 20 and 30 Basque galleons probably worked

Figure 14-1. The right whale, *Eubalaena glacialis,* has been exploited by humans for more than 1,000 years. It is now the rarest large whale in the North Atlantic Ocean; only 300 animals may remain. (Photograph by Chris Slay, courtesy of New England Aquarium)

Newfoundland waters every season. Aguilar (1986) calculated average catches of about 12 whales per boat, 300–500 whales per season, and an estimated cumulative kill of 25,000–40,000 whales between the years 1530 and 1610. Most of those whales were probably North Atlantic right whales, and the total kill was certainly greater than estimated, owing to the death of whales struck but not landed. After about 1610 North Atlantic right whales appear to have become scarce in Newfoundland and Labrador. It is also possible that the decreased catch resulted from decreased effort for other reasons. Barkham (1977 [cited in Schevill et al. 1986]) hypothesized that Basque whaling declined because the whalers and their ships were conscripted into Spanish naval campaigns and the Spanish Armada. However, the fact that sightings of the species are still rare today in those waters suggests that overhunting did occur.

After the decline of Basque whaling in Newfoundland, merchants from a number of European countries invested in numerous voyages to hunt right whales throughout the northeastern Atlantic. The expeditions eventually penetrated into the remote, frigid waters off Norway, around Spitzbergen, and west to Greenland and into Hudson Bay in search of bowhead whales, walruses, and other arctic species. British, Dutch, Danish, and Norwegian vessels were the most numerous, but Spanish whalers also took part. Basques are said to have served as harpooners on many of the vessels. By the late 1800s these fleets appeared to have almost extirpated bowhead whales throughout the arctic portion of the northeastern and northwestern Atlantic Ocean and to have depleted the numbers of North Atlantic right whales nearly everywhere except in waters off Nova Scotia, New England, and the southeastern United States.

North Atlantic right whales may have survived off Nova Scotia and New England only because few European whalers ventured farther south along the American coast than northern Nova Scotia. Consequently, North Atlantic right whales were abundant on the Scotian Shelf and along the eastern seaboard of what is now the United States when European colonists arrived in the early 1600s.

Written accounts from the period summarized in Allen (1916) give the impression that right whales were plentiful in Massachusetts Bay and adjacent waters, although it is possible that reports were biased toward days or seasons when the whales were present in highest numbers. An entry in the journal of Bradshaw and Winslow for 1620 (included in Allen 1916:132*ff*) noted: "Our master [of the *Mayflower*] and his mate, and others, experienced in fishing, professed we might have made three or four thousand pounds worth of oil. They preferred it before Greenland whale-fishing, and purpose the next winter to fish for whale here." The *Mayflower* did not have the tools for whale hunting, and it is uncertain where and when the English colonists began whale hunting. The first big catch recorded by Allen (1916) took place in January 1700, when "all the boates round [Cape Cod Bay] killed twenty nine whales in one day" (Schevill et al. 1986). By that time, the colonists were exporting large quantities of whale oil and baleen ("whalebone") to England (Reeves 1991).

The actual population abundance of right whales along the coast of New England during early colonial times is not known. During the late 1600s colonial hunters sighted North Atlantic right whales from shore stations, then launched small boats to pursue and harpoon them. Schevill et al. (1986) contended that there was no evidence to indicate that the species was more abundant in Cape Cod Bay during the early 1600s than during the early 1970s, but the intensity and success of the hunt, as described in literature from colonial times and subsequently, make it extremely hard for us to accept their conclusion (see also Blaylock et al. 1995).

By the early 1700s North Atlantic right whales were hunted from numerous shore stations along the coast from New York to Gloucester, Massachusetts. Examples of the catches include the 29 right whales killed in one day during January 1700 in Cape Cod Bay, 86 right whales caught by 28 boats at Nantucket during 1726 (Schevill et al. 1986), and approximately 110 whales taken by Long Island shore whalers during 1707 (Reeves and Mitchell 1986a). By the mid-1700s shore-based whalers were taking very few right whales and most had ceased to operate, but several whale-hunting operations persisted along the shores of Long Island, New York, and the Outer Banks of North Carolina (Reeves and Mitchell 1988) until the early 1900s.

As the population of North Atlantic right whales declined, New Englanders constructed ships for hunting right whales and other species farther offshore. From the mid-1700s through much of the 1800s Yankee whalers, as well as French and British whalers, hunted right, humpback (*Megaptera novaeangliae*), and sperm whales (*Physeter catodon*) and other species in the Atlantic Ocean; then gray whales (*Eschrichtius robustus*), bowhead whales, and others in the Pacific Ocean, Arctic Ocean, and more distant waters (Starbuck 1878). Up to six boats could be launched from each ship, pursuing whales by sail and oar. Right whales were too rare to be the main quarry of the hunt, but they were pursued whenever they were encountered.

The discovery of petroleum in Pennsylvania in 1859 soon reduced the demand for whale oil as fuel for lamps and as a lubricant. However, baleen remained in great demand well into the 1900s, and right whales continued to be hunted. Reeves and Mitchell's (1986b) painstaking analysis of logbooks and other historical documents demonstrated that North Atlantic right whales continued to be taken into the late 1800s, both opportunistically and on grounds recognized for right whale hunting by hunters of the period. According to those authors, substantial catches were made southeast of Cape Farewell, Greenland (at least 25 whales between 1868 and 1897); along the southeastern coast of the United States, especially off South Carolina and Georgia (at least 25–30 whales from 1876 to 1882); along the west coast of Africa between about 15°N and 23°N latitude (at least 82 whales from 1855 to 1858); and off the northwest coast of Iceland (no estimate given; Brown [1986] listed eight or nine whales from 1900 to 1982). Because right whales are absent or very rare in all of those locations except along the southeastern coast of the United States, one must assume that they were eliminated by the American pelagic whaling fleet.

The aboriginal population abundance before hunting started will never be known with certainty. What is certain is that approximately 1,000 years of hunting, directed and intensive at first, then occasional and opportunistic, was more than populations of this species could sustain. Based primarily on the amounts of oil and baleen exported to England from the American colonies, calculations by Reeves et al. (1992) suggest that there could have been less than 100 North Atlantic right whales alive by the end of the 1700s. If those calculations are right, the catches documented by Reeves and Mitchell (1986b) represented a large proportion of the North Atlantic right whales then in existence.

It is likely that by 1900 only a few dozen right whales remained in the western North Atlantic, with perhaps not many more in the eastern North Atlantic. Catches during the early part of this century took place off the Faroe Islands (7 or 9 whales), West Norway (1 whale), Shetland Islands (6 whales), Ireland (18 whales), the Hebrides (94 whales), the Azores (1 whale), and Madeira (3 whales) (Brown 1986). Right whales are probably not extinct in the northeastern Atlantic, but they are extremely rare. The paucity of recent sightings in the eastern Atlantic suggests that right whales from the western and eastern North Atlantic probably comprised two distinct stocks, as Reeves and Mitchell (1986b) hypothesized.

The last documented capture of a right whale by whalers in the northeastern United States occurred in 1918 at East Hampton, Long Island. A calf killed in 1935 off the coast of Florida was the last right whale intentionally killed in U.S. waters. The last right whale taken by hunters in the western North Atlantic was killed in 1951 in Trinity Bay, Newfoundland (Sergeant 1966).

Research Methods

Classical accounts of North Atlantic right whales (e.g., Andrews 1908) were based on gross anatomical descriptions of specimens or on compilation of published hunting records (Collett 1909). The first dedicated scientific observations of these whales at sea were done in Cape Cod Bay by W. E. Schevill and his colleagues from the Woods Hole Oceanographic Institution during the 1950s (e.g., Schevill 1959). Beginning in the late 1970s E. D. Mitchell and R. R. Reeves pioneered the detailed inspection of logbooks, newspaper accounts, and commercial records, supplemented by occasional reports of serendipitous sightings of the species (e.g., Reeves and Mitchell 1986a,b). The discovery in the early 1980s of several locations where right whales gather seasonally to feed and reproduce was the major impetus for development of a dedicated, comprehensive research program to study the biology of North Atlantic right whales.

Field studies of North Atlantic right whales now involve a number of field techniques. Surveys are conducted from boats, ships, airplanes, and, on occasion, blimps to assess distribution and abundance and to study ecology and behavior. Shipboard and aerial surveys are conducted annually in most known habitats of North Atlantic right whales, although sampling is less frequent in the more remote areas, including the Great South Channel (southeast of Cape Cod), Scotian Shelf (continental shelf waters of Nova Scotia), and waters more than 32 km (20 miles) off the coast of Georgia and Florida.

One of the most valuable techniques for learning about right whales has been the ability to identify individuals. Southern right whales (*E. australis*) were the first cetaceans to be identified individually (Payne 1972, Payne et al. 1983); the same technique has proved useful for North Atlantic right whales (Kraus, Prescott et al. 1986). Identifications are made from photographs of the individually distinctive arrangements of raised, rough epidermal tissue (callosities) located on the heads of right whales more or less in the locations where humans have hair (i.e., eyebrows, moustache, sideburns). New photographs are matched with photographs in the North Atlantic right whale catalog, a collection to which all researchers submit photographs (Kraus, Moore et al. 1986). As of January 1994 the catalog contained 331 individually identified right whales from the entire North Atlantic Ocean (Knowlton et al. 1994). Some cataloged whales are known to be dead and others are probably dead. Photographs of individuals known to be dead may still be useful for various purposes and are retained in the catalog. Photographic comparisons provide data on the age and sex of individuals, long-distance migrations, reproductive and mortality rates, and the impacts of human activities on the population.

Researchers also work from boats, using a crossbow and hollow-tipped arrow to collect small skin samples from identified individuals (Brown et al. 1991) (Fig. 14-2). The DNA extracted from the samples has been used to identify the sex of individuals, compare genetic information with observed patterns of migration and habitat use, and evaluate genetic variability. By linking genetic information on each whale with individual identification, age, sex, reproductive status, and pollutant levels (Crone and Kraus 1990), demographic analyses should ultimately enable us to judge how different habitats are used by different components of the population. In addition, the small amounts of blubber frequently attached to skin samples have been used to study organochlorine contaminants in this population (Woodley et al. 1991).

Satellite telemetry is being used to investigate right whale movements among areas and to help locate additional areas visited by the whales. A tag attached directly to a whale's back provides frequent sampling of date, time, and location. Correlation of swimming path with data on temperature, productivity, location of fronts, or other factors determined by remote-sensing satellites provides important information on habitat use and preference. Remote-sensing data can then be used to locate areas with oceanographic features comparable with those already known to be important for right whales (Mate et al. 1992).

These new techniques should help us close some of the gaps in our understanding of habitat use, migration patterns, and the relationships among sex, age, and behavior.

Summary of Current Knowledge

Taxonomy

Three closely related populations of right whales exist today: the North Atlantic right whale, the North Pacific right whale, and the southern right whale. However, there is uncertainty about how to classify them (Schevill 1986). Rice (in press) included all the populations within *Balaena glacialis* Müller, 1776 and questioned the validity of recognizing any subspecies. Cummings (1985) classified all populations north of the equator as *Eubalaena glacialis* (Müller, 1776) and all populations south of the equator as *Eubalaena australis* (Desmoulins, 1822). Others (e.g., Hershkovitz 1966) have also distinguished the North Atlantic population as *E. g. glacialis* and the North Pacific population as *E. g. japonica*.

Comparison of the mitochondrial DNA (mtDNA) of North Atlantic right whales with samples taken from South Atlantic right whales near Argentina showed that the two populations did not have any shared patterns. The genetic differences between the northern and southern Atlantic populations suggested a separation time of nearly one million years (Schaeff et al. 1991). Because the mtDNA data reflect the behavior of females only, they do not necessarily imply complete population separation over that entire period of time.

Regardless of the disagreements over taxonomy and any uncertainty about interpretation of genetic difference, it is generally agreed that the right whale population in the North Atlantic is extremely small and that it has been geographically isolated from other right whales for a very long time. Moreover, we are all but certain that North Atlantic right whales do not interbreed with right whales from other ocean basins. Thus, the North Atlantic population should be conserved and managed as a separate "evolutionarily significant unit" (terminology from Ryder 1986, Dizon et al. 1994).

Anatomy

North Atlantic right whales were depleted before zoologists had many opportunities to examine them, and studies of

Figure 14-2. A researcher prepares to shoot a dart into a right whale to obtain a small sample of skin for genetic and other analyses. Lower Bay of Fundy, 8 September 1991. (Photograph by Chris Slay, courtesy of New England Aquarium)

anatomy and physiology have been limited by the lack of fresh specimens. Cope (1865), True (1904), and Allen (1908) described the external appearance and skeletal features of North Atlantic right whales, but most information on right whale anatomy comes from the North Pacific species (Omura 1958, Klumov 1962, Omura et al. 1969). In the North Atlantic, some new work is under way resulting from enhanced stranding response efforts to determine causes of death in right whales (see Wilkinson and Worthy, this volume).

Distribution

The distribution of North Atlantic right whales was historically known to have included a broad arc extending from northern Florida, north along the east coast of North America, including waters of the Gulf of St. Lawrence and Atlantic Canada, east to western Greenland, Iceland, Spitzbergen, and Norway, and south along the European coast to the Saharan coast of Africa. Separate stocks probably occupied the western and eastern portions of the North Atlantic Ocean (Reeves and Mitchell 1986b).

Seasonal Habitat Use and Movements

Too few individuals remain to describe the current distribution, habitat use, or movements of the northeastern Atlantic stock of right whales. In contrast, data from the long-term study of identified individuals and the use of satellite-monitored radio tags have supplemented historical records to provide considerable information on seasonal patterns of distribution and movements of the northwestern Atlantic stock. Seasonal distribution and movements show some segregation by sex. Most cows give birth in the coastal waters of the southeastern United States during the winter months (Knowlton et al. 1994). The mothers and calves are frequently seen within 8 to 16 km (5 to 10 miles) of the coast, sometimes within 1.6 km (1 mile) of the beach in very shallow water, but also, at least on occasion, more than 48 km (30 miles) from shore. Males and noncalving females are rarely seen in that area, and their whereabouts during the winter remain unknown (Kraus et al. 1988).

In the spring, aggregations of North Atlantic right whales are observed feeding in the Great South Channel east of Cape Cod and in Massachusetts Bay (Winn et al.

1986, Hamilton and Mayo 1990, Kenney et al. 1995). In the summer and autumn, they are observed nursing, feeding, and courting in the Bay of Fundy between Maine and Nova Scotia, and feeding and courting in an area on the Scotian Shelf 50 km (31 miles) south of Nova Scotia (Stone et al. 1988, Kraus and Brown 1992). Several outlying sightings of North Atlantic right whales have been reported, including individuals at Bermuda (Payne 1972), in the Gulf of Mexico (Moore and Clark 1963), and off Greenland and Newfoundland (Knowlton et al. 1992).

Tracking of individual North Atlantic right whales equipped with satellite-monitored radio tags has revealed excursions of surprising speed and distance (Mate et al. 1992). One mother and her calf traveled more than 3,200 km (2,000 miles) during a 43-day period.

Feeding Ecology

North Atlantic right whales migrate into high-latitude waters to feed. Their primary prey is the copepod *Calanus finmarchicus*, especially the larger, oil-rich developmental stages (C-IV and C-V) and adults (Murison and Gaskin 1989, Mayo and Marx 1990, Kenney and Wishner 1995). Other small zooplankton, such as *Pseudocalanus minutus*, *Centropages* spp., and barnacle larvae, are eaten at times (Mayo and Marx 1990). The euphausiid *Meganyctiphanes norvegica* is frequently abundant in Gulf of Maine habitats where right whales feed, but right whales have not been seen feeding on surface swarms, and euphausiid parts have been found only infrequently in fecal remains collected in the Bay of Fundy (Murison and Gaskin 1989).

The whales filter-feed by swimming continuously with the mouth open at the surface (skim-feeding) or at depth. Feeding bouts at the surface can last for hours. When feeding at depth (down to 150 m) dives of up to 20 minutes or more may be repeated for hours. North Atlantic right whales must at times feed very near the bottom in the Bay of Fundy, because they sometimes surface with mud on their snouts. Video observations made using a remotely operated vehicle in an area used by feeding whales showed whale-sized marks in the ocean bottom (G. S. Stone and M. J. Crone, pers. comm.). As many as 270 finely fringed baleen plates, measuring as long as 2.4 m (8 feet), are located on each side of the jaw and allow the whale to filter small zooplankton from the water. The mouth is opened and the baleen exposed only when the concentration of plankton animals in the water is above a threshold value. North Atlantic right whales observed in Cape Cod Bay did not skim-feed unless more than 1,000 zooplankton organisms per cubic meter were present (Mayo and Marx 1990). In the Bay of Fundy, where observations using sonar have shown whales diving to depths of 90–150 m in areas of high copepod biomass, whales did not make feeding dives unless at least 820 copepods per cubic meter (170 mg/m^3) were present (Murison and Gaskin 1989).

Kenney et al. (1986) used estimates of body weight, metabolic rate, assimilation efficiency, time spent feeding, mouth size, and swimming speed to calculate that a North Atlantic right whale must feed in prey patches containing energy densities of 7.57 to 2,394 kcal/m^3 if it is to remain in energy balance. Those values are from 10 to 1,000 times greater than the densest concentration of zooplankton sampled in the vicinity of North Atlantic right whales in the Great South Channel. Kenney et al. (1986) suggested that the explanation of this conundrum was the inability of scientists to sample zooplankton patches as precisely as do the whales. Zooplankton organisms are neither homogeneously nor randomly distributed in the water column, but instead usually occur in "patches" (Wu and Loucks 1995). Dense patches of copepods and other small zooplankters form where the animals are brought together by tide or wind. The copepods become concentrated vertically or horizontally at convergences or at fronts where water parcels of different temperature, salinity, and density meet (Wishner et al. 1988, Kenney and Wishner 1995). Concentration may be further enhanced as the animals seek preferred intensities of light or other physical factors during diurnal or seasonal vertical migration.

Mayo and Marx (1990) observed that right whales in a plankton patch with a density above the threshold for feeding swam in convoluted paths, often making abrupt turns. Whales swimming outside a patch moved faster and in straighter paths.

How whales find patches is not known. Possibilities include random search, search for physical or biological characteristics of convergences or fronts, detection of taste or smell of the water associated with plankton abundance, visual or tactile assessment of plankton abundance, detection of bioluminescence, or detection of diminished background noise caused by the "acoustic shadow" created by a dense patch (T. Ford, pers. comm.).

Recent high-precision assessments of the biomass of patches have attempted to resolve the issue of whether plankton patches are dense enough to fulfill the energetic requirements of right whales (Kenney et al. 1986). Using a pump to sample plankton at very precise depth intervals (0.1 m) near the surface in Cape Cod Bay, C. A. Mayo (pers. comm.) has recently detected microlayers of copepods, sometimes only a few centimeters thick, that can contain in excess of one million copepods per cubic meter. In the Great South Channel, Wishner et al. (1988) used sonar imagery and specialized plankton tows to sample a very large, nearly monospecific patch of *Calanus finmarchicus* possibly covering 2,500 km^2 in extent. The patch had relatively sharp horizontal boundaries, and highest copepod abundance was in the top 20 m. Maximal abundance was 41,600 copepods per cubic meter. *Calanus* abundance inside the patch was about 83 times higher than immediately below it and 311 times greater than in surface samples just outside the patch. Equally precise descriptions of patches at greater depths will be more difficult to achieve, but new techniques, including deep-diving submersibles, remotely operated vehicles, and in situ videography, offer much promise.

The four critical habitats where North Atlantic right whales are most frequently seen are among the few places where extremely concentrated patches of copepods have been found. Three of them (Browns-Baccaro Bank, Bay of Fundy, and Great South Channel) are places where deep basins (approximately 150 m) are flanked by relatively shoal water. Copepods are concentrated by convergences and upwellings driven by tidal currents. Upwelling driven by tidal currents also produces the dense patches of plankton in Cape Cod Bay, although no deep basin is present. Because the summer distribution of North Atlantic right whales is so tightly coupled with their primary prey, *Calanus finmarchicus,* the whales are not seen when copepod populations are abnormally low. For example, during spring 1992 hydrographic anomalies, perhaps associated with decreased temperatures in the Northern Hemisphere caused by the eruption of Mount Pinatubo or by the 1991–1992 El Niño event, resulted in very low abundance of copepods in the Great South Channel. No right whales were seen (Kenney 1994).

Reproduction

Although one North Atlantic right whale female was observed to calve as early as five years of age and another at age 6, the mean age at first parturition observed for 86 females was 7.57 years (Knowlton et al. 1994). That number is certain to rise as the length of observation increases. Except for postmortem anatomical examination of the testes, no unequivocal criterion for sexual maturity in males is available. Males of all ages, including young individuals who cannot possibly be sexually mature, have been seen in courtship groups. However, it appears that only males that are more than 10 years of age can get close enough to a female to have an opportunity for mating. The age of first reproduction for males will only become known from back calculation after analyzing the paternity of calves using genetic techniques. This work has just begun. Brown et al. (1994) used genetics to show that the sex ratio in this population is 1:1.

Courtship is the most energetic and spectacular behavior displayed by this species. Male right whales are "sperm competitors" (Brownell and Ralls 1986), devoting energy to gamete production and delivery rather than physical aggression. Sperm competitors typically have large testes and elaborate penises compared with those of related species that compete in other ways (Parker 1984). Male right whales have the largest testes (up to 980 kg total weight) and longest penises (up to 3.35 m or 11 feet) in the world. In courtship groups, which may include 40 animals or more, males do not behave aggressively toward each other but instead try to get close enough to the focal female to be able to mate. Females may incite males by making groaning sounds, resembling the mooing of a cow, that can be heard underwater for several miles. Males can be seen swimming quickly in a beeline for a groaning female. A female can avoid copulation by rolling onto her back with her belly out of the water. However, the long penis of the male at her side can reach her genital area. A female may have intromission with several males during a courtship bout. The criteria a female uses for discriminating between males are not known. Also unknown is whether pairs or groups of males cooperate to gain access to females.

The seasonal timing and duration of the courtship season, which extends from August through September in the western North Atlantic right whale population, are puzzling. Because mothers with calves are first seen in December in waters off Georgia and Florida, Best's (1994) estimate of a 12-month gestation period in southern right whales cannot apply to this species unless one of the following hypotheses is also true: (1) courtship in the Bay of Fundy is merely foreplay and insemination occurs elsewhere during December, or (2) calves are born before December at an unknown location. Alternatively, (3) gestation is longer than 12 months, or (4) implantation is delayed.

A female gives birth to a single calf. The mean interval between births was 3.67 years (n = 86) (Knowlton et al. 1994), with a range of from 2 to 7 years. One female accompanied by a calf was resighted more than 24 years later with another calf, suggesting that the reproductive lifespan of North Atlantic right whales is at least that long (P. Hamilton, pers. comm.).

Genetic studies offer the promise of one day being able to identify every right whale's paternity. This would allow the reconstruction of complete genealogies, estimation of age at first reproduction for males, and possibly the assessment of relative reproductive success among males and females. Ironically, it is only the small size of the population that permits such detailed genetic investigations because sampling of most individuals is feasible.

Most calves are thought to be born in the coastal waters of the southeastern United States (Kraus and Kenney 1991).

Either the number of calves produced by this population fluctuates irregularly or scientists have not been able to sample the number of calves reliably. From 1980 to 1992 between 5 and 17 calves per year were sighted during studies in waters of the Georgia-Florida bight (Knowlton et al. 1994). No significant increase or decrease was found in the number of calves per year over the period from 1984 to 1992. Twenty-one calves were observed during winter 1996, the highest number seen during 14 seasons of investigation. Because some cows with newborn calves are missed during the winter surveys off Georgia and Florida, a complete assessment of a year's calf production requires surveys in the northern critical habitats, particularly Cape Cod Bay and the Bay of Fundy.

Mothers and calves migrate north for spring feeding in the Great South Channel and Cape Cod Bay, then on to the only well-defined summer nursery area, in the lower Bay of Fundy, where, along with juveniles, they feed from late July to mid-October. However, Schaeff et al. (1993) inferred from genetic and photo-identification data that one group of cows does not bring its calves to the Bay of Fundy each year. Therefore, another summer and fall nursery area must exist although its location is unknown. This unidentified nursery is not in the high-use area of the Scotian Shelf near Browns Bank because cow / calf pairs have been seen there only four times in 1,059 sightings over eight field seasons (Knowlton et al. 1994). Knowlton et al.'s (1992) report of a cow and calf off Greenland in 1992 is suggestive. Locating the unidentified nursery would be an important contribution to further protection of North Atlantic right whales.

Data on mean longevity are not yet available. An indication that potential longevity can be very long was obtained by serendipity. A right whale calf accompanied by its mother was killed in Florida in 1935, and a photograph of the pair was published in the New York *Herald Tribune.* The newspaper article was included in the collection of whaling memorabilia assembled by Col. Eugene Clark. Whale biologist Frederick Wenzel looked through that collection some time after Col. Clark's death, found the photograph, and sent it to one of us (S.D.K.) at the New England Aquarium in 1987. Several years later an aquarium researcher recognized the mother whale in the photograph as whale number 1045 in the right whale catalog. The animal was seen in 1959 off Cape Cod by Woods Hole Oceanographic Institution researchers and was seen irregularly until summer 1995 when personnel from the National Marine Fisheries Service observed her near Georges Bank, badly wounded with cuts from a ship's propeller. Assuming that the calf killed in 1935 was No. 1045's first calf and that she gave birth at age eight (the mean for North Atlantic right whales), the whale would have been 67 years old when last seen in summer 1995. The fact that she was never seen with a calf during the aquarium's study could indicate that she was reproductively senescent.

Mortality

Analyses of stranding, entanglement, and photographic data have provided estimates of mortality for North Atlantic right whales. Known mortality is particularly high during the first three years of life, ranging from 5 to 18% based on documented deaths (Kraus 1990). "Natural" mortality appears to account for about two-thirds of total mortality at this time. The remaining 33% of mortality in this population is caused by human activities, primarily ship collisions and entanglement in fishing gear (Kenney and Kraus 1993). Unfortunately, the deep basins of the Bay of Fundy and Great South Channel concentrate not only the food that sustains right whales, but also the primary threat to their survival—ships (Fig. 14-3). The Bay of Fundy shipping lanes go directly through the Grand Manan Basin feeding and courtship area. Similarly, all ship traffic between Boston (or other Gulf of Maine ports) and southern destinations must transit through the Great South Channel to avoid Georges Bank. Collision with ships is the greatest source of human-induced mortality for this species (Kraus 1990), claiming at least one or two North Atlantic right whales annually along the east coast of North America (Fig. 14-4). This may account for a significant reduction in the growth rate of the remaining population of North Atlantic right whales.

In late 1995 and early 1996 human-induced mortality was particularly high, with eight deaths recorded between November 1995 and March 1996. Three of the carcasses showed signs of having been hit by ships. More puzzling were carcasses of three calves found offshore of Florida. Suspicion arose that the animals might have been killed by pressure-induced trauma as a result of explosions by artillery or other munitions used in training exercises conducted by the U.S. Navy. Postmortem examinations of the carcasses did not provide unequivocal proof of pressure-induced trauma. A workshop at the Mayport (Florida) Naval Station and aboard the Aegis class missile cruiser USS *Leyte Gulf* attended by one of us (S.K.K.) made a good case that artillery fire did not harm the whales. During such exercises, no live rounds are fired and the guns are not directly over the water. However, the deaths of two of the three calves coincided with the 16 February 1996 detonation of twelve 500-pound (227-kg) bombs dropped from airplanes approximately 35 miles (56 km) offshore. This was the only instance in which live bombs were dropped at sea in this region during winter 1996. Pressure fronts from explosions may attenuate relatively slowly in the shallow water over the gradually sloping

Figure 14-3. A right whale narrowly misses being struck by a container ship in the lower Bay of Fundy, 2 August 1995. (Photograph by Lisa Conger, courtesy of New England Aquarium)

Figure 14-4. A young right whale that was killed by a ship strike near the Florida coast in January 1993. The propeller cuts were the outwardly visible signs of trauma; broken bones and internal bleeding, documented during the necropsy, provided further evidence concerning the cause of death. (Photograph by Robert K. Bonde)

continental shelf off Mayport, which is only 40 m deep at distances of 80 km (50 miles) or more offshore, and could harm nearby whales. Even if the exact cause of death of the three calves is never established with certainty, caution suggests that no bombs or other high-pressure explosives should be detonated in those waters.

Population Size and Rate of Growth

There is little doubt that the North Atlantic right whale population was even smaller in the past than it is today. Schaeff et al. (1993) found only three matrilines represented in the mitochondrial DNA (mtDNA) from more than 100 animals sampled in the western North Atlantic population. Because mtDNA is inherited only from the mother, this suggests that the population did indeed go through a very small genetic "bottleneck" at some time in the recent past (although it could have been thousands of years ago). Schaeff et al.'s (1993) result does not imply that only three female North Atlantic right whales existed at some point in the past; each mtDNA haplotype could have been represented by more than one female. However, their conclusion does not contradict Reeves et al.'s (1992) suggestion that the population of North Atlantic right whales may have been reduced to as few as a dozen animals by hunting.

Annual estimates of population size back-calculated from data on calving and mortalities showed steady increase from 255 individuals in 1986 to 295 in 1992. The mean net growth from one year to the next was 2.5% (Knowlton et al. 1994). The highest population estimate for right whales obtained during aerial surveys conducted between 1979 and 1981 was 380 ± 688 (Winn 1982).

If there is good news, it is that the right whale population is probably larger than in 1935 when the species first received international protection, but this statement cannot be proved because we know so little about historical population size.

The bad news is that the estimated 2.5% annual rate of population growth (Knowlton et al. 1994) is much lower than the growth rates of 6–7% per year recorded for populations of southern right whales in Argentina and South Africa (Best 1993). At the time of this writing, the 2.5% growth rate calculated by Knowlton et al. (1994) is probably overly optimistic. A recent increase in known mortalities and a sharp decline in reproduction for the 1993–1995 period (an average of 7 calves per year compared with an average of 14 calves per year between 1988 and 1992) have caused consternation among right whale researchers and managers. The 1996 peak of 21 calves has not alleviated this concern because only 10 of those calving females had calved previously. In other words, it is encouraging to be recruiting new mothers to this population, but real population growth will only derive from both recruitment and continued calving of the existing reproductive pool. In 1996 researchers expected that more than 40 females that had previously borne calves would give birth again; less than a quarter of that number did so.

In addition, mortalities estimated by counting long-term (six-year) disappearances from the identified pool of right whales have shown a precipitous increase in the past two years. These factors strongly suggest that the North Atlantic right whale population is currently declining in size.

Possible Reasons for Low Rate of Population Growth

Several factors may be influencing the recovery rate of the North Atlantic right whale population.

SHIP STRIKE AND ENTANGLEMENT. Of the possible factors that may be depressing the growth rate of the North Atlantic right whale population, among the most important are strikes by large ships and entanglement in fixed fishing gear. Recent analyses suggest that those two factors account for one-third of all mortality in this population (Kraus 1990, Kenney and Kraus 1993). No similar estimate is available for the effect of any other factor on the rate of growth of this population.

POLLUTION. Two types of pollution could affect right whales (although we hasten to say that we have no evidence that either is affecting the North Atlantic population). First, chemical contaminants enter the whales' tissues via their food; however, the low trophic level on which right whales feed might minimize the effects of such bioconcentration. Second, nonfood items or chemical contaminants might be ingested directly during feeding. Right whales feed in convergence zones and slicks where surface currents concentrate anything that floats, including not only prey items, but also oil, contaminants associated with the surface microlayer, and floating trash (Carr 1985). Contact with floating oil during skim-feeding could foul the baleen plates, but this has not been observed. No nonfood items have been found in the few stomachs of North Atlantic right whales that have been examined; however, observations have been made of rope becoming entangled in the mouthparts, presumably as the whale fed open-mouthed.

An analysis of blubber samples taken from right whales revealed measurable levels of DDT, other organochlorine pesticides, and PCBs (Woodley et al. 1991), but the reported levels were considered low relative to those of other marine mammals (see also Gauthier et al. 1997). The number of samples available for study could be increased if the very small amounts of blubber obtained in biopsy samples could be analyzed. However, interpretation of such results would necessitate consideration of the manner in which contaminants are distributed within the blubber layer and within other tissues, as noted by Aguilar and Borrell (1994) and recognized by Woodley et al. (1991).

FOOD SUPPLY. Possible reduction in the abundance of copepods, caused either by competition or by oceanographic changes, has also been invoked to explain the low population growth rate. Mitchell (1975) hypothesized that competition from sei whales (*Balaenoptera borealis*) may have limited the ability of right whale populations to increase. Payne et al. (1990) considered competition from sei whales less important than potential competition from planktivorous fishes, such as sand lance (*Ammodytes americanus*), herring (*Clupea harengus*), basking sharks (*Cetorhinus maximus*), and others. R. Kenney (pers. comm.) hypothesized that temporary, large-scale climatic changes may have altered currents and prevented the formation of dense patches of copepods in the Great South Channel during 1992, a year when right whales were absent. We appreciate the fundamental importance of very dense patches of plankton prey to North Atlantic right whales and the crucial importance of identified critical habitats in the feeding range where those concentrations are usually available. However, we have not yet seen convincing data that North Atlantic right whales are food-limited at this time. Although competition or oceanographic changes may locally and temporarily limit the food intake of right whales, we believe that the copepods on which North Atlantic right whales primarily feed are far too abundant for them to be limiting this population to fewer than 300 individuals.

WHALE WATCHING. Whale watching has also evoked concern with regard to right whales (Fig. 14-5). However, whale watching only began in the 1970s in New England and Canada and thus could not be a primary cause of the slow recovery of the North Atlantic right whale population. Although whale watching could have some effect on the whales by distracting them, displacing them from rich food patches, dispersing food patches with wake or propeller wash, or in other ways, it is probably inconsequential compared with the lethal threats posed by large ships and fixed fishing gear. We also see no evidence that noise from boats or other sources (except for powerful explosions) is problematic at this time, although we strongly believe that the amount of noise injected by humans into the ocean should be reduced at every opportunity.

HABITAT REDUCTION. Reeves et al. (1978) hypothesized that intensive use of Delaware and Chesapeake Bays by humans had preempted their use by right whales, thereby diminishing the potential recovery of the population. Not enough is known about precolonial use of those bays by the whales to permit evaluation of this effect.

INBREEDING. The small size of the North Atlantic right whale population has provoked discussion about whether "inbreeding" might be retarding its recovery. Schaeff et al. (1997) demonstrated from the nuclear DNA (which is inherited from both parents) that the proportion of genetic material shared among unrelated North Atlantic right whales (i.e., not siblings, parents, or offspring) is significantly higher than that shared among unrelated right whales (*E. australis*) in the South Atlantic. Correlating this reduced genetic diversity with actual effects on reproduction or mortality will not be easy. To date, no such effects have been identified, nor is there general agreement on how much genetic variation is sufficient in a mammal population. Even if such a relationship were confirmed, no mitigation is possible. The only beneficial action is to reduce mortality from other causes, where possible, to maximize the number of calves recruited into the population.

CARRYING CAPACITY. Finally, it could be argued that the current population, which was estimated to be 295 whales in 1992 (Knowlton et al. 1994), may represent the approximate carrying capacity (K) for today's environment.

Figure 14-5. Whale-watching enterprises in Nova Scotia and New Brunswick, Canada, depend on opportunities of seeing right whales up close. Lower Bay of Fundy, 31 August 1995. (Photograph by Amy Knowlton, courtesy of New England Aquarium)

Based entirely on intuition, we believe that this is not the case and that the population could grow substantially if the whales could be protected from collisions with ships and entanglement in fishing gear.

History of Protective Legislation

The steady westward progression of the hunting grounds for North Atlantic right whales should have suggested to the early whalers that their predatory success was decreasing the whale population. Perhaps they realized it and did not care. Such an attitude would not be surprising, given the exploitative perspectives typical of past times and the belief that the ocean contained unlimited resources. In any case, neither the hunters nor European chroniclers recorded such an awareness.

Even when writers began to note the increasing difficulty of finding right whales to kill, no protective actions could have been taken. Until the 1900s societies lacked any conceptual or legal framework for conserving species that were not confined to national borders. Designing and implementing protection for a pelagic species would have been impossible.

The first two decades of the 1900s brought improvement in the context for such conservation. World War I caused a temporary decrease in whaling, but more important, it was a powerful demonstration that peacekeeping and certain other issues, including conservation, could only be achieved by an international forum. The League of Nations, created primarily for peacekeeping in 1919, also provided the arena for the first actions to protect right whales. In 1931 the League of Nations responded to an enormous increase in pelagic whale hunting, particularly in the Southern Ocean, and concluded the first international Convention for the Regulation of Whaling, which entered into force in 1935. Because it was clear that right whales (which were classified as a single species at that time) had declined to alarmingly low numbers, the Convention included a total ban on commercial hunting of that group. The North Atlantic right whale thus became one of the first baleen whales to receive international protection.

Unfortunately, League of Nations protection was not completely effective for several likely reasons: conservation measures were not based on adequate scientific knowledge, some important whaling nations refused to sign the Convention, and there was no mechanism to enforce the ban on hunting (Rose and Crane 1995). For example, 36 right whales are known to have been taken from waters off Korea and Japan between 1935 and 1938, and four more were taken in the North Pacific in the early 1940s (Omura 1986).

During World War II the threat of submarines discouraged whaling ships from putting to sea, and commercial catches of all whale species dropped to nearly zero. Furthermore, as the war continued, every available ship and sailor was drawn into the war effort. The whales' respite from hunting may have been interrupted on occasion by war-related activities. Anecdotal reports suggest that some whales may have been killed by torpedoes or depth charges either as target practice or accidentally. The tendency of right whales to remain still at the surface could have made them particularly vulnerable targets.

After World War II, whale hunting resumed. As part of its efforts to rebuild the Japanese economy and meet a protein shortage, the United States encouraged and assisted Japan in developing a capability for pelagic whaling. European and North American nations with histories of hunting whales resumed those activities. The Soviet Union entered the whaling industry by taking the German Antarctic fleet as war reparations.

With the increase in hunting came the realization that catch regulation was required. In 1946 fifteen nations formed a new International Convention for the Regulation of Whaling, of which one element was the creation of the International Whaling Commission (IWC).

Since its formation, the IWC has been strained by several factors: its conflicting objectives of conserving whales and preserving the whaling industry, ambiguity in the scope of its responsibilities (Rose and Crane 1995), and decades of contentious negotiations about blue whale units, quotas, maximum sustainable yields, and even more technically arcane methods of limiting or allocating catches (see Gambell, this volume). Nevertheless, its member nations have never wavered in their commitment to prohibit commercial hunting of right whales.

It appeared until recently that the nations that were party to the Convention had, for the most part, cooperated with the ban. Well-known exceptions were the takes of 10 North Pacific right whales by the Soviet Union in 1955 and 13 by Japan between 1956 and 1968, all covered by scientific permits issued by the respective governments (Scarff 1986). Also, one right whale was killed at a British Columbia shore station in 1951 (Pike and McAskie 1969), another at a Newfoundland shore station in the same year (Sergeant 1966), and one off Kamchatka in 1964 (Scarff 1986). Several right whales were taken in the postwar period by non-IWC members, including two in China in 1965 and at least one in Korea in the 1960s (Scarff 1986), another in Korea in the mid-1970s (Park 1987), and three at Madeira, Portugal (one in 1959 and two in 1967 [Brown 1986]).

Only recently was it revealed that Soviet whalers took several hundred right whales in the Okhotsk Sea, and possibly others elsewhere in the North Pacific, during the 1950s and 1960s (Yablokov 1994, Brownell et al. in press). In addition, the Soviet whaling fleet covertly killed more than 700 right whales in the Southern Ocean during the 1960s (Yablokov 1994, Zemsky et al. 1995). These reports indicate how easily substantial catches can be missed or concealed.

With the exceptions noted above, right whales have been continuously protected from hunting more or less successfully since 1931, but the powers of the IWC did not extend to any other types of protection. The scope of protection for right whales and other marine mammals in the United States was considerably broadened in the early 1970s when the U.S. Congress passed two sweeping laws, the Marine Mammal Protection Act in 1972 and the Endangered Species Act in 1973 (see Baur et al., this volume).

The marine mammal law provides a potentially broad suite of protection measures by making it illegal to "take" a marine mammal in U.S. waters without a permit or other authorization. The act defines "take" as "to harass, hunt, capture or kill, or attempt to harass, hunt, capture or kill any marine mammal." As a result, since 1972 right whales and all other marine mammals have, in theory, been protected from nearly any type of disturbance or harm that people could inflict. Exceptions include the incidental capture of animals in fishing gear; other forms of incidental take; collection of marine mammals for scientific research, public display, or enhancement of the species; as well as certain types of unauthorized "take," such as ship strikes.

The Endangered Species Act provides a different foundation for protecting plants or animals that are listed as endangered or threatened. Responsibility for administering the act is shared by the National Marine Fisheries Service, which oversees management of populations of cetaceans and most pinnipeds, and the U.S. Fish and Wildlife Service, which has responsibility for sea otters, walruses, sirenians, and polar bears. Right whales are listed as endangered under the act.

The Endangered Species Act also prohibits the "take" of any listed species as well as the import of its parts or products into the United States except for "scientific purposes or to enhance the propagation or survival of the affected endangered species." More important, the Endangered Species Act also can be used to protect the habitat of listed species, including, in some cases, areas that are no longer used by the species. Increased management, research, and law enforcement dedicated to listed species are also provided through cooperative agreements between states and the federal government executed under section 6 of the act. Section 7 is particularly important, because it requires federal agencies to consult with the National Marine Fisheries Service to ensure that any action taken, permitted, or funded is not likely to jeopardize the continued existence of the species or result in the destruction or adverse modification of the critical habitats of listed species. Because actions by the federal government are required for many activities that could affect right whales or their habitats, including dredging, waste disposal, petroleum or mineral extraction, construction of piers, platforms or other structures, and discharge of explosives, the Endangered Species Act can have important benefits for this species. Protection of habitat may be especially important in efforts to protect depleted populations. A depleted, small population may not occupy its full potential or historic range, and deleterious alteration of habitat that might eventually be repopulated could jeopardize recovery of the population.

However, identifying critical habitat for a migratory species, such as the North Atlantic right whale, is difficult. Distribution can vary considerably between years resulting from short-term changes in physical oceanography and in the abundance and distribution of food resources or competitors. Because of the species' wide range, long-distance migrations, and offshore distribution during much of the year, adequate data were not available on right whales until recently, and critical habitats were not formally designated until 1994.

Defining critical habitat for right whales entailed an additional complication because the animals routinely spend portions of the year in waters off Canada. Fortunately, both section 8 of the Endangered Species Act and section 108 of the Marine Mammal Protection Act anticipate such situations and encourage agreements with other nations for the protection and conservation of endangered species. Canada has cooperated in some ways to protect North Atlantic right whales despite the fact that no special marine mammal legislation exists in that country and no species-specific or taxon-specific marine mammal protection regulations currently exist under its Fisheries Act. Right whales are classified as "endangered" by the Committee on the Status of Endangered Wildlife in Canada, but this designation has no legal status or direct effect on protection. The Canadian federal government is developing an endangered species act, but the legislation is still in a preliminary stage.

The Endangered Species Act and informal Canadian cooperation offer a good framework for legally protecting all five habitat areas thought to be essential to the survival and recovery of the North Atlantic right whale. Three areas in the United States (the Georgia-Florida calving grounds, Great South Channel spring feeding area, and Cape Cod–Massachusetts Bay late winter feeding/nursery area) were designated as critical habitat by the National Marine Fisheries Service in 1994 on the basis of a petition from the Right Whale Recovery Team. Two other areas in Canada (lower Bay of Fundy summer feeding/nursery area and southern Scotian Shelf summer feeding area) were designated as "conservation areas" by Canada's Department of Fisheries and Oceans in 1993. The currently designated geographic boundaries of critical habitat may need to be modified as more information accumulates. Additional research may also reveal additional critical habitat south of Iceland and Greenland or elsewhere, the protection of which would require agreements with other nations.

Several U.S. states have also enacted legislation to protect right whales within their jurisdictions. North Atlantic right whales are classified as "endangered" under state laws in Georgia and Massachusetts and have also been designated as the state marine mammal in those states. Massachusetts has adopted regulations that prohibit vessels within its waters from approaching right whales closer than 457 m (500 yards) without a permit.

Right whales also benefit from a final broad layer of protection, namely the species' listing in Appendix I of the Convention on International Trade in Endangered Species of Wild Fauna and Flora (CITES), established in 1973. The measure prohibits international commercial trade of any part or product of Appendix I species between signatories. Parts or products for research purposes require permits from the governments of both the originating and receiving countries before the material can be shipped.

Even though the population may be growing very slowly, it is discouraging that North Atlantic right whales are still so rare despite 50 years of international and national protection. Two main factors may account for this slower-than-expected response. First, as mentioned above, very few reproductively active females may have escaped hunters and remained alive when whaling stopped. Second, conservation actions have protected North Atlantic right whales from harpoons but not from collisions with ships and fishing gear. As the number of large, fast cargo and military ships increased after World War II, and as the amount of fixed fishing gear, especially gillnets and deep-water lobster traps, proliferated in offshore waters, these dangers became—unbeknownst to scientists or managers—the primary immediate factors retarding the recovery of this whale population.

It is also worth noting that not until 15 years after the passage of the Endangered Species Act did the National Marine Fisheries Service apply the full weight of its provisions to assist the recovery of right whales. Section 4(f) of the act directs the agency responsible for an endangered species to develop and implement a recovery plan if doing so will promote the conservation of a species. The National Marine Fisheries Service formed a 10-person recovery team in 1988 to produce a recovery plan for right whales. Among the factors contributing to the slow pace of the agency's response may have been assignment of lower priority to its relatively new responsibility for overseeing conservation of marine mammals in addition to its historical core mission of supporting fisheries. Intraagency competition for attention and funding also came from issues related to such things as bowhead whales, bottlenose dolphins, and tuna-dolphin conflicts. It may be equally true that the agency did not immediately know how to put into practice the new concepts of ecosystem- and population-based management that the Congress had incorporated into the Marine Mammal Protection Act and the Endangered Species Act.

After extensive review by the public and by all appropriate federal and state agencies, the final recovery plan for right whales was accepted by the National Marine Fisheries Service and published in December 1991 (National Marine Fisheries Service 1991). The plan promulgates a far-reaching, inclusive approach to conservation of right whales. It recommends a broad range of actions and activities, including research, public education, habitat protection, new legislation, and others, each of which may benefit the species to some degree but all of which together should improve its chances of increasing.

The agency also appointed two teams to coordinate implementation of the plan. The Northeastern Right Whale Implementation Team was established to coordinate actions needed in the species' spring and summer range, and the Southeastern Right Whale Implementation Team was established to coordinate actions needed for the winter range. It remains to be seen whether Congress and the National Marine Fisheries Service will provide the money necessary to help the teams perform the most important of those far-reaching tasks.

Research Leading to New Conservation Measures

Since the late 1970s many investigations of North Atlantic right whales have been driven by proposals from government agencies contemplating activities such as mining, oil drilling, and military exercises within right whale habitat. Sections 6 and 7 of the Endangered Species Act require that the National Marine Fisheries Service examine the potential impacts of those activities.

In 1979, responding to the Pittston Oil Company's proposal to build a refinery and supertanker port in Eastport, Maine, the National Marine Fisheries Service supported the first aerial surveys of whales in the Bay of Fundy. Those surveys led to the serendipitous discovery that the lower part of the bay was a summer and autumn nursery for right whales (Kraus et al. 1982). Pittston's proposal eventually was withdrawn, partly because of the economics of the oil industry but also because the presence of right whales and bald eagles, both of which were listed as endangered under the Endangered Species Act, delayed the granting of exemptions to the Clean Water and Clean Air Acts that the company needed.

From 1979 to 1982 the Cetacean and Turtle Assessment Program at the University of Rhode Island conducted aerial surveys for whales, dolphins, and sea turtles from Cape Hatteras to Nova Scotia and out to the continental shelf edge (Winn 1982). Those surveys were supported by the U.S. Bureau of Land Management as a prelude to leasing the rights for undersea oil exploration and development along the east coast of the United States. The Marine Mammal Protection Act and the Endangered Species Act both required that the bureau provide additional information on potential impacts of such activities. A major component of the assessment program was a series of surveys focused on right whales. Those surveys produced new information on the distribution of right whales in the Great South Channel and off Nova Scotia. The findings ultimately led to the cancellation of oil leasing programs in the Great South Channel.

After the identification of important feeding and nursery areas for right whales by the surveys, field-based research programs focused on that species were initiated at the New England Aquarium in Boston and the Center for Coastal Studies in Provincetown, Massachusetts. In 1986 scientists from the two institutions and from the University of Rhode Island and Woods Hole Oceanographic Institution formed the Right Whale Consortium, a cooperative research agreement by which data on observations of North Atlantic right whales throughout their summer range would be exchanged and entered into a single comprehensive database and catalog of photographs for individual identification (the Right Whale Catalog).

In the late 1980s the Minerals Management Service supported surveys to estimate the distribution and abundance of whales in the coastal waters of the southeastern United States from Cape Hatteras, North Carolina, to Miami, Florida. Right whales were seen during those surveys, confirming that the coastal zone of the southeastern United States is important habitat and a migratory corridor for right whales during the winter months.

Dredging activities in the southeastern United States provide a good example of the complex, interrelated issues involved in right whale conservation. During the late 1980s dredging activities for the ports of Brunswick and Kings Bay, Georgia, and Fernandina Beach and Jacksonville, Florida, were discovered to be killing endangered sea turtles, particularly during late spring to autumn. Shutting down dredging was not an option because the ports in question are in a region characterized by a high rate of siltation, and the harbors would become impassable without maintenance. Therefore, restriction of dredging to winter months was proposed as a way to reduce turtle mortality. The Army Corps of Engineers, which was responsible for conducting dredging operations, was required under section 7 of the Endangered Species Act to consult with the National Marine Fisheries Service to determine if dredging during winter would jeopardize the survival of any endangered species.

A conflict was quickly identified. Beginning in 1984 researchers from the New England Aquarium, assisted by a group of Delta Airlines pilots who volunteered use of their private aircraft, had conducted surveys for right whales off the coast of Georgia and Florida. Their observations of mothers with calves confirmed earlier reports (Allen 1916; Layne 1965; Caldwell and Caldwell, summarized in Winn 1984; Mead 1986) that those waters might be a calving ground. Based on the preliminary survey data and subsequent research showing that nearly one-third of all right whale deaths were due to ship/whale collisions (Kraus 1990), the National Marine Fisheries Service concluded that the proposed actions jeopardized right whales.

The agreed solution was to allow dredging to proceed while providing the vessel operators with near "real-time" information on right whale distribution in the dredging zone. This was done by flying aircraft in a systematic search pattern with observers reporting daily to the dredge operators the position of all right whales sighted. In addition, dredge boats were required to carry whale observers to look out for whales during transits between the channels and the dump sites offshore. Eventually, an agreement was reached whereby the dredges slowed to speeds of less than 5 km/hour during the transits when visibility was impaired, at night, or whenever a right whale had been sighted within 16 km (10 miles) of the transit and dumping zones.

These operating standards are currently in force for all dredges working within the right whale critical habitat in the southeastern United States coastal zone. However, they apply only to dredges. Because right whales are vulnerable to any large vessel traveling at high speed, commercial and military vessels need to be included in the slow-speed restrictions within right whale critical habitat. Both the U.S. Navy and the U.S. Coast Guard have voluntarily mandated that their vessels operate at reduced speed when transiting waters within the Georgia-Florida critical habitat for right whales. The agencies also conduct training sessions for all bridge personnel at the beginning of winter, providing them with information on how to identify North Atlantic right whales and report sightings. That information is also posted on the bridges of Navy and Coast Guard vessels throughout winter. The Southeastern Right Whale Implementation Team is considering further recommendations along these lines, but mandating speed limits for ships at sea is a complicated process that must be carried out under admiralty law.

One of the curious features of this history of research and protection is that both researchers and managers have frequently needed to act on the basis of incomplete information. Usually scientists stake their findings on a level of statistical significance whereby one is at least 95% confident in the result; that is, there is a less than 5% probability that the findings occurred by chance. However, because of the extremely small size of the right whale population, the sample size for most quantities measured (such as numbers of sightings, calves, mothers, rate of mortality, etc.) was very small, rendering some statistical tests nearly meaningless.

Further estimation of population size is complicated by the highly aggregated distribution of the species, which results in many sample values of "zero" and a few large values when groups of whales are sighted. For example, the weighted mean estimate for population size of North Atlantic right whales based on data from all three years of the cetacean/turtle assessment surveys was 380 with a 95% confidence interval of plus or minus 688 (Winn 1982)! Because of the very small remaining population, researchers and managers both recognized the need to act quickly and intuitively, taking actions before defining problems with the statistical exactitude they would usually require.

Future Conservation Needs and Options

The survival of right whales probably depends on the timeliness with which recommendations of the recovery plan and the implementation teams can be carried out. It certainly depends upon the survival of the Endangered Species Act because that act has been the foundation of most management actions to date. Any revision of the act that emphasizes economic considerations and seeks to reduce the impacts of conservation measures on human beings, rather than focusing on the survival of a wild species, might well result in the extinction of the North Atlantic right whale.

Assuming that the act and right whale implementation teams survive in their current forms, the clear first priority is the reduction in ship/whale collisions. Other important actions will include reducing the incidence of entanglement in fishing gear and determining whether reduced habitat availability and quality, chronic pollutant impacts, whale watching, and acoustic disturbance from vessel traffic are slowing the population's recovery.

The implementation teams have already made some progress. A mariner education program has been started in the southeastern United States, notices to mariners regarding the seasonal presence of right whales are published annually and issued over the Coast Guard marine broadcasts (Notices to Mariners), and right whale critical habitats will be outlined on nautical charts. Work on identifying high-risk areas and slowing vessels within those areas is under way. Additional strategies may also need to be explored, including mounting acoustic deterrents on ships, detecting whales underwater using side-scanning sonar or other methods still to be developed, and designing "whale-safe" ships. For example, computer modeling has recently been used to investigate how hydrodynamic forces produced by moving ships might suck right whales toward the ship or push them away (Knowlton et al. 1995). Such insights could be used in designing new ships. Also, replacement of propellers with new propulsion systems, such as enclosed turbojet hydraulic drives or magnetohydrodynamic drives, could eliminate the kind of injury responsible for most right whale deaths; however, because these systems operate at high speeds, additional risks may result.

The gear entanglement problem frustrates managers and scientists as much as the problem of ship/whale collisions does. The only consolation may be that many of the animals have been able to escape from entanglements on their own, although it is not known whether injuries sustained during those entanglements have compromised long-term survival. The potential magnitude of the problem is demonstrated by the fact that approximately 57% of 118 animals in the right whale catalog photographed while they were alive show scars apparently caused by ropes or nets (Kraus 1990). It is considerably more difficult to identify particular locations where whales are at increased risk of entanglement than it is to identify locations of increased risk of ship strike. This is because fixed fishing gear is broadly distributed both nearshore and offshore all along the coast of North America (as well as in other places historically used by populations of right whales). Records of entanglements from Newfoundland to Florida show no clear pattern that might inform a management strategy, other than seasonally prohibiting the use of heavy fixed fishing gear such as ganged lobster traps and anchored gillnets in high-use right whale habitats during periods when right whales are present. Such gear is believed to be responsible for the known mortalities due to entanglement.

That strategy is recommended in the recovery plan and is currently under review by regional implementation teams and the National Marine Fisheries Service. Closing all fisheries along the entire east coast would be neither economically nor politically acceptable, nor would it necessarily be more effective than seasonal closure of a few relatively small areas during the times when they are used intensively by right whales. For example, the New England Fishery Management Council and the Fisheries Service have already restricted gillnets in part of the Great South Channel critical habitat, and Georgia and Florida have prohibited gillnets within their state waters. Coincidentally, the low current abundance of groundfish in the North Atlantic off Canada and New England may have the beneficial result of reducing the incidental take of many species of marine mammals, including North Atlantic right whales, because fishery management agencies are mandating sharp reductions in fishing effort.

The potential impacts of pollution, habitat modification, acoustic disturbance, and whale watching are complex and interrelated. As the scale of urbanization increases in coastal zones, these factors could become more troublesome (Fig. 14-6). Whether they affect right whales or any other whale species is still a matter of largely emotional debate because the few studies that have been done are inconclusive. For example, pollutants are present in measurable amounts in nearly every mammal (including humans), but direct causal links between various compounds and changes in pathology, health, or behavior have rarely been established unequivocally. Measuring the responses of populations or of individual whales to pollutants, acoustic disturbance, habitat degradation, and whale watching is nearly impossible, partly because we lack baseline information with which to compare the contemporary situation and partly because it is difficult to separate the multiple potential effects of several variables.

In our view, the best we can do is to work toward a conservative (risk averse) management approach to unknown impacts of this type by making every effort to minimize the ocean urbanization process whenever and wherever possible. By doing so, we improve the chances of a healthy future for both right whales and our own descendants. The North Atlantic right whale is about as close to extinction as a large mammal can get and still have a whisker of a chance at survival. Because no other whales within its range are related to it or resemble it closely, we would notice its extinction considerably more than the disappearance of a sparrow, warbler, or salamander, for example. Its closest relative, the southern right whale, lives in the Southern Hemisphere and would probably not migrate into the North Atlantic Ocean to colonize the "vacant" range except possibly in the course of geological time.

Figure 14-6. As a species that regularly uses nearshore waters, the right whale is particularly vulnerable to disturbance and contamination from human activities in the coastal zone. Here, a right whale surfaces within only a few tens of meters of a Florida beach development, 12 February 1989. (Photograph by Chris Slay, courtesy of New England Aquarium)

Lessons for Other Species

The history of research on and conservation of North Atlantic right whales provides a number of lessons that may be applicable to other endangered species.

First, development of an effective management program requires sufficient funding to carry out a sound research program that will provide data for identifying, justifying, and evaluating actions for conservation of the species. Accurate descriptions of habitat-use patterns, mortality sources and trends, and population recruitment trends are particularly important. Inadequate funding has severely compromised right whale research by limiting the scheduling and scope of investigations.

Second, developing and implementing effective research and management programs is a long, slow process that requires a great deal of persistence and patience. Although it took many years to initiate, the Right Whale Recovery Plan has become the most important instrument for setting priorities and coordinating implementation of activities for the benefit of these whales. It is appropriate to mention the special role that one independent federal agency, the Marine Mammal Commission, has played in this regard. The Commission is a small (budget approximately $1 million annually) watchdog agency, which makes recommendations to Congress and the federal agencies on any federal activities that affect marine mammals; comments and provides guidance to the Department of State on international activities that affect marine mammals; and reviews proposals submitted to the National Marine Fisheries Service and the Fish and Wildlife Service for permits to conduct research on marine mammals. It was the first agency to call for a recovery plan for right whales, has offered uniquely informed guidance during all phases of plan construction, has helped coordinate the roles of many agencies involved in right whale recovery efforts, and has worked to make funds available for needed research. Its power to "cajole and coerce" stems from the fact that, by statute, agencies must heed its recommendations or make known to Congress, in detail, their reasons for not doing so. The Commission has also played a strong role in guiding implementation of the plan. In the absence of such an agency, the concerted efforts to save the North Atlantic right whale might have suffered further delay or perhaps not exist at all.

Third, because sample sizes are so small, even with the best data available on an extremely endangered species, studies may not meet traditional scientific standards of proof. The only remedy is to continue investigations for many years. For example, during the years 1993 through 1995 the annual count of the number of North Atlantic right whale calves in Georgia-Florida waters was approximately half of that during the years from 1984 through 1992. These low counts suggested to many that the reproduction of North Atlantic right whales was failing. But the number of calves counted in 1996 by New England Aquarium scientists (21) was the largest ever obtained since studies began in 1980. Reasons for the variability in annual calf production are incompletely known, but understanding the mix of new and old calving females is critical for assessing the population's reproductive status and, to do that, a long time-series of data on individuals is clearly essential.

Fourth, an effective conservation program will require cooperation and action from many federal and state agencies and nongovernmental conservation groups. International cooperation is essential when population ranges span national boundaries. The contributions of dedicated private volunteers can also make a difference. For example, the North Atlantic right whale has benefitted from the assistance of a group of Delta Airlines pilots, without whom the identification, understanding, and protection of the Georgia-Florida calving ground might be 10 years behind what it is now. Contributions of photographs by marine biologists and others from many parts of the United States and Canada, and as far away as Iceland, have been crucial to research efforts.

Fifth, incidental take of a species may be much more difficult to regulate than directed take by hunting. In the case of the North Atlantic right whale, the prohibition on hunting has been very effective, but accidental losses due to collisions with ships and entanglements in fixed fishing gear could very well push the species to extinction. In this case, the responsibility for killing North Atlantic right whales has broadened from a relatively small group of hunters seeking oil and baleen to a very diffuse group that includes most of us who eat seafood; purchase foreign autos, petroleum, appliances, or other products that arrive on ships; profit from the export of goods by sea; or benefit from the services of the Navy or Coast Guard.

Finally, the events of 1996 reinforce the important lesson that we should not become complacent about the state of our knowledge. Before February 1996 it had been assumed that during winter North Atlantic right whale mothers and calves were distributed within 24 km (15 miles) or less of the Georgia-Florida coast, and the description and designation of critical habitat was based on that assumption. After the carcass of a right whale calf was found 40 km (25 miles) offshore from the Kings Bay Naval Base on 19 February 1996 and another on 22 February about 32 km (20 miles) northeast of the first carcass, aerial surveys out to 80 km (50 miles) offshore were initiated and several right whales were observed at least 40 km (25 miles) offshore. In retrospect, it is clear that researchers did not know about offshore whale distributions because they had not looked systematically. They had never looked because funding, which was often not assured until well into the research season, was so limited that they could not charter airplanes with sufficient range to survey 80 km (50 miles) offshore and could not afford the cost of the flight hours needed to accomplish the task. It is fair to say that the current description of the winter habitat of North Atlantic right whales along the southeastern coast of the United States is biased by that constrained effort.

In conclusion, it will take decades before one can judge whether the North Atlantic right whale has been saved from imminent extinction. The best of human efforts may not be enough to save it. Nevertheless, commitment to the task has grown steadily. It is gratifying to see willing participation from individual scientists and their institutions, states, and relevant sectors of the federal government. During the 1970s and early 1980s it would have been difficult to imagine that the U.S. Navy, U.S. Coast Guard, ship traffic controllers in major shipping lanes, and others would actually modify their activities to help protect right whales, but they are now beginning to do so. We cannot yet predict the future of the North Atlantic right whale, but we are confident that the dedication of people everywhere to helping the species survive has never been stronger.

Acknowledgments

We thank the following reviewers for their careful and insightful comments on early drafts of this chapter: Phillip Clapham, Robert Kenney, Randall Reeves, Tim Smith, and four anonymous reviewers. Their suggestions have substantially improved it.

Literature Cited

Aguilar, A. 1986. A review of old Basque whaling and its effect on the right whales (*Eubalaena glacialis*) of the North Atlantic. Reports of the International Whaling Commission (Special Issue 10): 191–200.

Aguilar, A., and A. Borrell. 1994. Assessment of organochlorine pollutants in cetaceans by means of skin and hypodermic biopsies. Pages 245–267 *in* M. C. Fossi and C. Leonzio (eds.), Nondestructive Biomarkers in Vertebrates. Lewis Publishers, Boca Raton, FL.

Allen, J. A. 1908. The North Atlantic right whale and its near allies. Bulletin of the American Museum of Natural History 24:277–329 + plates 19–24.

Allen, J. A. 1916. The whalebone whales of New England. Memoirs of the Boston Society of Natural History 8 (2): 107–322.

Andrews, R. C. 1908. Notes upon the external and internal anatomy of *Balaena glacialis*. Bulletin of the American Museum of Natural History 24:171–182.

Barkham, S. H. 1977. Guipuzcoan shipping in 1571, with particular reference to the decline of the transatlantic fishing industry. University of Nevada, Reno, NV. Desert Research Institute, Publications in the Social Sciences 13:73–81.

Baur, D. C., M. J. Bean, and M. L. Gosliner. 1999. The laws governing marine mammal conservation in the United States. (This volume)

Best, P. B. 1993. Increase rates in severely depleted stocks of baleen whales. ICES Journal of Marine Science 50:169–186.

Best, P. B. 1994. Seasonality of reproduction and the length of gestation in southern right whales *Eubalaena australis*. Journal of Zoology (London) 232:175–189.

Blaylock, R. A., J. W. Hain, L. J. Hansen, D. L. Palka, and G. T. Waring. 1995. U.S. Atlantic and Gulf of Mexico Marine Mammal Stock Assessments. U.S. Department of Commerce, NOAA Technical Memorandum NMFS-SEFSC-363. 211 pp.

Brown, M. W., S. D. Kraus, and D. E. Gaskin. 1991. Reaction of North Atlantic right whales (*Eubalaena glacialis*) to skin biopsy sampling for genetic and pollutant analysis. Reports of the International Whaling Commission (Special Issue 13): 81–89.

Brown, M. W., S. D. Kraus, D. E. Gaskin, and B. N. White. 1994. Sexual composition and analysis of reproductive females in the North Atlantic right whale (*Eubalaena glacialis*) population. Marine Mammal Science 10:253–265.

Brown, S. G. 1986. Twentieth-century records of right whales (*Eubalaena glacialis*) in the northeast Atlantic Ocean. Reports of the International Whaling Commission (Special Issue 10): 121–127.

Brownell, R. L., and K. Ralls. 1986. Potential for sperm competition in baleen whales. Reports of the International Whaling Commission (Special Issue 8): 97–112.

Brownell, R. L., Jr., P. J. Clapham, T. Kasuya, and T. Miyashita. In press. Conservation status of North Pacific right whales. Reports of the International Whaling Commission (Special Issue 18).

Carr, A. F. 1985. Rips, FADS, and little loggerheads. BioScience 36:92–100.

Collett, R. 1909. A few notes on the whale *Balaena glacialis* and its capture in recent years in the North Atlantic by Norwegian whalers. Proceedings of the Zoological Society of London 1909: 91–98.

Cope, E. D. 1865. Note on a species of whale occurring on the coasts of the United States. Proceedings of the Academy of Natural Sciences, Philadelphia 17:168–169.

Crone, M. J., and S. D. Kraus. 1990. Right whales (*Eubalaena glacialis*) in the western North Atlantic: A catalog of identified individuals. New England Aquarium, Boston, MA. 223 pp.

Cumbaa, S. L. 1986. Archaeological evidence of the 16th century Basque right whale fishery in Labrador. Reports of the International Whaling Commission (Special Issue 10): 187–190.

Cummings, W. C. 1985. Right whales *Eubalaena glacialis* (Müller, 1776) and *Eubalaena australis* (Desmoulins, 1822). Pages 275–304 *in* S. H. Ridgway and R. Harrison (eds.), Handbook of Marine Mammals. Vol. 3. The Sirenians and Baleen Whales. Academic Press, London.

Dizon, A. E., W. F. Perrin, and P. A. Akin. 1994. Stocks of dolphins (*Stenella* spp. and *Delphinus delphis*) in the eastern tropical Pacific: A phylogeographic classification. NOAA Technical Report NMFS 119:1–20.

Gambell, R. 1999. The International Whaling Commission and the contemporary whaling debate. (This volume)

Gauthier, J. M., C. D. Metcalfe, and R. Sears. 1997. Chlorinated organic contaminants in blubber biopsies from northwestern Atlantic balaenopterid whales summering in the Gulf of St. Lawrence. Marine Environmental Research 44:201–223.

Hamilton, P. K., and C. A. Mayo. 1990. Population characteristics of right whales (*Eubalaena glacialis*) observed in Cape Cod and

Massachusetts Bays, 1978–1986. Reports of the International Whaling Commission (Special Issue 12): 203–208.

Hershkovitz, P. 1966. Catalog of Living Whales. U.S. National Museum Bulletin No. 246. 256 pp.

Kenney, R. D. 1994. Anomalous 1992 spring and summer distributions of right whales (*Eubalaena glacialis*) and other cetaceans in continental shelf waters off the northeastern Unites States and adjacent Canada. Report to the Marine Mammal Commission. (Available from National Technical Information Service, Springfield, VA. PB99-102493.) 68 pp.

Kenney, R. D., and S. D. Kraus. 1993. Right whale mortality—a correction and an update. Marine Mammal Science 9:445–446.

Kenney, R. D., and K. F. Wishner. 1995. The South Channel ocean productivity experiment. Continental Shelf Research 15:373–384.

Kenney, R. D., M. A. M. Hyman, R. E. Owen, G. P. Scott, and H. E. Winn. 1986. Estimation of prey densities required by western North Atlantic right whales. Marine Mammal Science 2:1–13.

Kenney, R. D., H. E. Winn, and M. C. Macaulay. 1995. Cetaceans in the Great South Channel, 1979–1989: Right whale (*Eubalaena glacialis*). Continental Shelf Research 15:385–414.

Klumov, S. K. 1962. Gladkie (Yaponskie) kity Tikhogo Okeana [The right whale in the Pacific Ocean]. Pages 202–297 *in* P. I. Usachev (ed.), Biologicheskie Issledovaniya Marya (Plankton) [Biological Marine Studies "plankton"]. Trudy Instituta Okeanologii Akademii Nauk SSSR, Moscow.

Knowlton, A. R., J. Sigurjønsson, J. N. Ciano, and S. D. Kraus. 1992. Long-distance movements of North Atlantic right whales (*Eubalaena glacialis*). Marine Mammal Science 8:397–405.

Knowlton, A. R., S. D. Kraus, and R. D. Kenney. 1994. Reproduction in North Atlantic right whales (*Eubalaena glacialis*). Canadian Journal of Zoology 72:1297–1305.

Knowlton, A. R., F. T. Korsmeyer, J. E. Kerwin, H.-Y. Wu, and B. Hynes. 1995. The hydrodynamic effects of large vessels on right whales. Final report to the National Marine Fisheries Service, Northeast Fisheries Science Center, Woods Hole, MA.

Kraus, S. D. 1990. Rates and potential causes of mortality in North Atlantic right whales (*Eubalaena glacialis*). Marine Mammal Science 6:278–291.

Kraus, S. D., and M. W. Brown. 1992. A right whale conservation plan for the waters of Atlantic Canada. Pages 79–85 *in* J. H. M. Willison, S. Bondrup-Nielsen, C. Drysdale, T. B. Herman, N. W. P. Munro, and T. L. Pollock (eds.), Science and the Management of Protected Areas: Developments in Landscape Management and Urban Planning. Vol. 7. Elsevier, London.

Kraus, S. D., and R. D. Kenney. 1991. Information on right whales (*Eubalaena glacialis*) in three proposed critical habitats in United States waters off the western North Atlantic Ocean. Report to the Marine Mammal Commission. (Available from National Technical Information Service, Springfield, VA. PB91-194431.) 65 pp.

Kraus, S. D., J. H. Prescott, P. V. Turnbull, and R. R. Reeves. 1982. Preliminary notes on the occurrence of the North Atlantic right whale, (*Eubalaena glacialis*), in the Bay of Fundy. Reports of the International Whaling Commission 32:407–411.

Kraus, S. D., K. E. Moore, C. E. Price, M. J. Crone, W. A. Watkins, H. E. Winn, and J. H. Prescott. 1986. The use of photographs to identify individual North Atlantic right whales (*Eubalaena glacialis*). Reports of the International Whaling Commission (Special Issue 10): 145–151.

Kraus, S. D., J. H. Prescott, A. R. Knowlton, and G. S. Stone. 1986. Migration and calving of right whales (*Eubalaena glacialis*) in the western North Atlantic. Reports of the International Whaling Commission (Special Issue 10): 139–144.

Kraus, S. D., M. J. Crone, and A. R. Knowlton. 1988. The North Atlantic right whale. Pages 684–698 *in* W. J. Chandler (ed.), Audubon Wildlife Report 1988/1989. Academic Press, New York, NY.

Layne, J. N. 1965. Observations on marine mammals in Florida waters. Bulletin of the Florida State Museum 9:131–181.

Mate, B. R., S. Nieukirk, R. Mesecar, and T. Martin. 1992. Application of remote sensing methods for tracking large cetaceans: North Atlantic right whales (*Eubalaena glacialis*). Final report to the Minerals Management Service. Report no. 01-0069. 167 pp.

Mayo, C. A., and M. K. Marx. 1990. Surface foraging behavior of the North Atlantic right whale and associated plankton characteristics. Canadian Journal of Zoology 68:2214–2220.

Mead, J. G. 1986. Twentieth-century records of right whales (*Eubalaena glacialis*) in the northwestern Atlantic Ocean. Reports of the International Whaling Commission (Special Issue 10): 109–119.

Mitchell, E. 1975. Trophic relationships and competition for food in northwest Atlantic whales. Proceedings of the Canadian Society of Zoology (Annual Meeting): 123–132.

Moore, J. C., and E. Clark. 1963. Discovery of right whales in the Gulf of Mexico. Science 141:269.

Murison, L. D., and D. E. Gaskin. 1989. The distribution of right whales and zooplankton in the Bay of Fundy, Canada. Canadian Journal of Zoology 67:1411–1420.

National Marine Fisheries Service. 1991. Recovery plan for the northern right whale (*Eubalaena glacialis*). National Marine Fisheries Service, Silver Spring, MD. 86 pp.

Omura, H. 1958. North Pacific right whales. Scientific Reports of the Whales Research Institute Tokyo 13:1–52.

Omura, H. 1986. History of right whale catches in the waters around Japan. Reports of the International Whaling Commission (Special Issue 10): 35–41.

Omura, H., S. Ohsumi, T. Nemoto, K. Nasu, and T. Kasuya. 1969. Black right whales in the North Pacific. Scientific Reports of the Whales Research Institute Tokyo 21:1–78.

Park, K. 1987. History of Korean Coastal Whaling. Taiwa Press, Seoul. 562 pp. [In Korean.]

Parker, E. D. 1984. Sperm competition and the evolution of animal mating strategies. Pages 1–60 *in* R. L. Smith (ed.), Sperm Competition and the Evolution of Animal Mating Systems. Academic Press, New York, NY.

Payne, M., D. Wiley, S. Young, S. Pittman, P. Clapham, and J. Jossi. 1990. Recent fluctuations in the abundance of baleen whales in the southern Gulf of Maine in relation to changes in selected prey. Fishery Bulletin 88:687–696.

Payne, R. 1972. Swimming with Patagonia's right whales. National Geographic 142 (4): 576–587.

Payne, R., O. Brazier, E. M. Dorsey, J. S. Perkins, V. J. Rowntree, and A. Titus. 1983. External features in southern right whales (*Eubalaena australis*) and their use in identifying individuals. Pages 371–445 *in* R. Payne (ed.), Communication and Behavior of Whales. Westview Press, Boulder, CO.

Pike, G. C., and I. B. McAskie. 1969. Marine mammals in British Columbia. Fisheries Research Board of Canada Bulletin No. 171:1–54.

Reeves, R. R. 1991. Pre-exploitation abundance of right whales: Clues from historical records. Whalewatcher 25 (3): 3–5.

Reeves, R. R., and E. D. Mitchell. 1986a. American pelagic whaling for right whales in the North Atlantic. Reports of the International Whaling Commission (Special Issue 10): 221–254.

Reeves, R. R., and E. D. Mitchell. 1986b. The Long Island, New York, right whale fishery: 1650–1924. Reports of the International Whaling Commission (Special Issue 10): 201–220.

Reeves, R. R., and E. Mitchell. 1988. History of whaling in and near North Carolina. NOAA Technical Report NMFS 65. 28 pp.

Reeves, R. R., J. G. Mead, and S. K. Katona. 1978. The right whale, *Eubalaena glacialis,* in the western North Atlantic. Reports of the International Whaling Commission 28:303–312.

Reeves, R. R., J. M. Breiwick, and E. Mitchell. 1992. Pre-exploitation abundance of right whales off the eastern United States. Pages 5–7 *in* J. Hain (ed.), The Right Whale in the Western North Atlantic: A Science and Management Workshop. 14–15 April 1992, Silver Spring, MD. Northeast Fisheries Science Center Reference Document 92-05.

Rice, D. W. In press. Marine Mammals of the World: Systematics and Distribution. Society for Marine Mammalogy, Special Publication no. 4, Lawrence, KS.

Rose, G., and S. Crane. 1995. The evolution of international whaling law. Pages 159–181 *in* P. Sands (ed.), Greening International Law. The New Press, New York, NY.

Ryder, O. A. 1986. Species conservation and systematics: The dilemma of subspecies. Trends in Ecology and Evolution 1:9–10.

Scarff, J. E. 1986. Historic and present distribution of the right whale (*Eubalaena glacialis*) in the eastern North Pacific south of 50°N and east of 180°W. Reports of the International Whaling Commission (Special Issue 10): 43–63.

Schaeff, C., S. D. Kraus, M. Brown, J. Perkins, R. Payne, D. Gaskin, P. Boag, and B. White. 1991. Preliminary analysis of mitochondrial DNA variation within and between the right whale species *Eubalaena glacialis* and *Eubalaena australis.* Reports of the International Whaling Commission (Special Issue 13): 217–223.

Schaeff, C. M., S. D. Kraus, M. W. Brown, and B. N. White. 1993. Assessment of the population structure of western North Atlantic right whales (*Eubalaena glacialis*) based on sighting and mtDNA data. Canadian Journal of Zoology 71:339–345.

Schaeff, C. M., S. D. Kraus, M. W. Brown, J. S. Perkins, R. Payne, and B. N. White. 1997. Comparison of genetic variability of North and South Atlantic right whales (*Eubalaena*), using DNA fingerprinting. Canadian Journal of Zoology 75:1073–1080.

Schevill, W. E. 1959. Return of the right whale to New England waters. Journal of Mammalogy 40:639.

Schevill, W. E. 1986. Right whale nomenclature. Reports of the International Whaling Commission (Special Issue 10): 19.

Schevill, W. E., W. A. Watkins, and K. E. Moore. 1986. Status of *Eubalaena glacialis* off Cape Cod. Reports of the International Whaling Commission (Special Issue 10): 79–82.

Sergeant, D. E. 1966. Populations of large whale species in the western North Atlantic with special reference to the fin whale. Fisheries Research Board of Canada, Arctic Biological Station Circular No. 9. 13 pp.

Starbuck, A. 1878. I. History of the American whale fishery from its earliest inception to the year 1876. U.S. Commission of Fish and Fisheries. Part IV. Report of the Commissioner for 1875–1876. II. Appendix to Report of Commissioner. Appendix A. The Sea Fisheries. 768 pp. + plates. Commission of Fish and Fisheries, Washington, DC.

Stone, G. S., S. D. Kraus, J. H. Prescott, and K. W. Hazard. 1988. Significant aggregations of the endangered right whale, *Eubalaena glacialis,* on the continental shelf of Nova Scotia. Canadian Field-Naturalist 102:471–474.

True, F. 1904. The Whalebone Whales of the Western North Atlantic. Smithsonian Contributions to Knowledge 33:1–332 + plates 1–50.

Wilkinson, D., and G. A. J. Worthy. 1999. Marine mammal stranding networks. (This volume)

Winn, H. E. 1982. A characterization of marine mammals and turtles in the mid- and North Atlantic areas of the U.S. outer continental shelf. Final report of the Cetacean and Turtle Assessment Program, University of Rhode Island, to Department of the Interior, Bureau of Land Management, Washington, DC. Contract No. AA551-CT8-48. 450 pp. + appendices.

Winn, H. E. 1984. Development of a right whale sighting network in the southeastern United States. (Available from National Technical Information Service, Springfield, VA. PB84 240548.) 12 pp.

Winn, H. E., C. A. Price, and P. W. Sorensen. 1986. The distributional biology of the right whale (*Eubalaena glacialis*) in the western North Atlantic. Reports of the International Whaling Commission (Special Issue 10): 129–138.

Wishner, K., E. Durbin, A. Durbin, M. Macaulay, H. E. Winn, and R. D. Kenney. 1988. Copepod patches and right whales in the Great South Channel off New England. Bulletin of Marine Science 43:825–844.

Woodley, T. H., M. W. Brown, S. D. Kraus, and D. E. Gaskin. 1991. Organochlorine levels in North Atlantic right whale (*Eubalaena glacialis*) blubber. Archives of Environmental Contamination and Toxicology 21:141–145.

Wu, J., and O. L. Loucks. 1995. From balance of nature to hierarchical patch dynamics: A paradigm shift in ecology. Quarterly Review of Biology 70:439–466.

Yablokov, A. V. 1994. Validity of whaling data. Nature 367:108.

Zemsky, V. A., A. A. Berzin, Y. A. Mikhalyev, and D. D. Tormosov. 1995. Materials on whaling by Soviet Antarctic whaling fleets (1947–1972). Center for Russian Environmental Policy, Moscow. 320 pp.

15

DARYL P. DOMNING

Endangered Species
The Common Denominator

The foregoing chapters have examined several marine mammal species that are especially endangered. They illustrate the diversity of problems encountered in marine mammal conservation. It is important to realize, however, that these species and their problems are no more than special cases drawn from a much wider reality encompassing countless plants and animals. The fact that these diverse species share so many problems points to a common cause: the growing domination of Earth's biosphere by a single species, our own. On an increasingly crowded planet, biologists who wish to be effective conservationists must attend not only to the biological needs of endangered species, but even more to the complexities of managing people. We are thus forced to consider social issues that lie well outside the biologist's usual interests and concerns. However distant from our professional specialties and however far beyond our influence these matters may seem, they are relevant to everything we do.

The Nature of the Threat to Nature

The global loss of biodiversity now under way will probably dwarf in scale any previous mass extinction on this planet (Heywood 1995). The causes of most past extinctions are unknown, but the current wave of extinctions is clearly the result of massive rearrangement and rerouting of matter and energy by an exploding human population. The impact of this explosion is less violent than that of an incoming asteroid, but many of its effects will be at least as pervasive and perhaps longer lasting. The suburbs expanding outward from cities, the dams thrown across river valleys, the motorboats barreling across sea grass flats, the driftnets scattered on the high seas, the poisons cast abroad on wind and water are just as surely shrapnel from this single explosion as is a harpoon fired into the flank of a whale. If this human-caused event were not happening, few of the organisms now labeled "endangered" would be in peril.

It is necessary to grasp the singular nature of this event in human and planetary history for the pieces of the ecocrisis puzzle to fall into place. It is simplistic to view each endangered species, habitat, or ecosystem as a problem or set of problems to be solved in isolation. Yet conservation campaigns built around "flagship species," our bureaucratic apparatus of species-specific recovery plans and recovery teams, and even the recent calls for ecosystem management in conservation serve to reinforce our compartmentalized thinking. Such tools and tactics can be necessary and useful in their place, but we need to acknowledge their limitations and not lose sight of the larger context.

The pervasive effects of the human population explosion

are unmistakably clear from the four preceding chapters; in each case, people are the problem. Species as diverse and distant as right whales (*Eubalaena glacialis*) in the North Atlantic, monk seals (*Monachus schauinslandi*) in Hawaii, and dolphins and porpoises worldwide all suffer competition from human fisheries or have been directly exploited by them. Entanglement in fishing gear and collisions with watercraft threaten right whales and Florida manatees (*Trichechus manatus*) alike. Overhunting in the nineteenth century still casts the shadow of genetic impoverishment over right whales and, possibly, Hawaiian monk seals. Human appropriation of space and resources in Delaware and Chesapeake Bays and in the Northwestern Hawaiian Islands may have reduced the environmental carrying capacity for right whales and monk seals, respectively. Slight human disturbance can affect monk seal reproduction, yet even a more human-tolerant species like the manatee has difficulty coexisting with Florida's skyrocketing human population. Hunting and deliberate or incidental netting have devastated once numerous populations of harbor porpoises (*Phocoena phocoena*), striped dolphins (*Stenella coeruleoalba*), and spinner dolphins (*S. longirostris*). What Katona and Kraus (this volume) call the accelerating rate of urbanization in coastal zones is already a global reality.

No group of biologists is in a better position than marine mammalogists to testify about human threats to the biosphere. In case after case, we can show that the problems stem from people and not from any deficiency in the animals themselves, nor from human-independent processes in the environment. And when we seek remedies for these problems, we must recall, as Reynolds (this volume) emphasizes, that it is human and not animal behavior that is subject to modification.

What is the nature of this destructive human behavior? Every living thing is programmed by natural selection to maximize its control over matter and energy, redirecting them to its own growth and reproduction. Without this active self-preservation, no life could survive. For as long as we have been human, we too have obeyed this innate urge to selfish behavior.

The fossil record shows the results: wherever the most able of animals has wandered, extinctions of other species have marked its path as it has appropriated their living space, their food, or their very bodies for its own needs. To this cause many scholars have ascribed the demise of the great Pleistocene land mammals, the loss of which decimated the mammalian fauna of every continent but Antarctica (Martin and Klein 1984, Crosby 1986). Ancient humans are even more surely to blame for the more recent extinctions of moas (families Dinornithidae and Anomalopterygidae), elephant birds (family Aepyornithidae), and other animals in places like New Zealand and Madagascar (Cassels 1984, Dewar 1984). In the Hawaiian and many other Pacific islands, prehistoric Polynesians drove the great majority of the native birds to extinction, further belying the myth of the Noble Savage living in perfect harmony with nature (Olson 1990). European explorers, in a later age, devoured the last dodos (*Raphus cucullatus*), auks (*Alca impennis*), Steller's sea cows (*Hydrodamalis gigas*), and other indigenous animals on many a new-found island—leaving in their place goats, pigs, cats, and rats to carry on the destruction of other native species in ways never foreseen (Crosby 1986). In short, our impact on nature was seldom, if ever, limited by anything but our cunning, our technology, our appetite, or our numbers.

With this history in mind, we should not make the mistake of imagining that our daily assaults on nature began with the scientific or industrial revolutions, let alone with modern capitalism, communism, or consumerism. These only increased our numbers and our power to do that for which we have never lacked the will.

As in time, so in space: the problem is no more local than it is recent. When we hear that the list of endangered species has grown by a butterfly, or a cactus, or a desert pupfish, or a rain forest frog, we will not be so myopic as to search for the cause with a magnifying glass in that creature's microhabitat. Great effects bespeak great causes, and the key is to recognize that these many obliterations of lowly, far-flung species, coincident as they are in our brief lifetimes, are indeed but the fallout from a singular event—one as great, as obvious, and sometimes as invisible to us as the ocean is to the fish. Yet it is not a force of inanimate nature, let alone an act of God. We bear the blame and have the power to choose a different course, but only by subordinating our ancient selfishness to a vision of a whole greater than ourselves—a whole that, we now see, depends on us as much as we have always depended on it.

Thus, when we come to focus on marine mammals, it must be with a view larger than a whale's narrow slice of the world, however wide the ocean it swims. If from here on we examine only marine mammals and their problems, we must not lose sight of the myriad other species with similar problems or of the erratically intelligent species that is causing the problems. We must not expect to find solutions that stop short of changing the way we ourselves behave. We must instead face the necessity of setting limits to our appropriation of Earth's finite matter, energy, and space before our time also runs out. We must see that such limits will necessarily arise, at least in part, from motivations transcending the ancient selfishness that led us to this situation in the first place.

What is needed is a more enlightened self-interest—

more enlightened and less self-interested than most of the traditional, pragmatic rationales for conservation, valid though these remain. We do well to argue in political debate that this tree may one day cure our cancers, or this panda will reliably attract tourist dollars, or this forest will renew the air we breathe. Any good deed can have many justifications, and the course of the campaign must dictate the tactics of the moment. But we risk ultimate defeat if there is not, beneath all such arguments, a moral certainty that preserving the biosphere intact is a good thing to do in itself.

Origins of the Environmental Conscience

Fortunately, this moral foundation is already laid, and is being extended, even as the tide of selfishness seems to rise higher against it than ever before. It is fashionable to deny the moral progress of civilization, yet history may provide no clearer examples of such progress than in our attitudes toward the living world in general and marine mammals in particular.

Europe's Age of Exploration was an age of ruthless exploitation of marine mammals and other species. (Indeed, in the language of the Portuguese, who ushered in that age, "exploration" and "exploitation" are the same word.) This exploitation was not only ruthless but heedless: the extermination of the Atlantic population of gray whales (*Eschrichtius robustus*) (Mead and Mitchell 1984) during the seventeenth and early eighteenth centuries left scarcely more of a historical record than did the great extinctions of the Late Pleistocene. The science of biology was then in its infancy, and many areas of human activity and of the globe were beyond the ken of systematic observation or record.

By the late eighteenth century, however, the increasing maturity of natural history as a science had begun to spark reflection on the mortality of our fellow species. The possibility of biological extinctions entered the Western consciousness—more, admittedly, from discoveries in paleontology than from observations of contemporary human rapacity, but the possibility dawned on us nevertheless (Rudwick 1972). Warnings of imminent resource depletion even found their way into government reports on Steller's sea cows (1755) and Amazonian manatees (*Trichechus inunguis*) (1786), although the day was still far distant when such warnings were apt to change policy (Domning 1978, 1982). By then, time had run out for relict, localized species like the Steller's sea cow. Manatees were saved not by human foresight but by their own numbers, wide range, and cryptic habits. It just was not possible to find and kill all of them. As the spaces and snows of Russia saved that nation from the Napoleonic and Nazi armies, the great waters of the world were the salvation of manatees, whales, and the other sea mammals pursued so doggedly for human commerce. This was still the situation a century ago when Rudyard Kipling penned "The White Seal" (1894), and it seemed that marine mammals could survive the human onslaught only by hiding in the trackless ocean.

Then something changed. Historical forces that had developed together throughout the nineteenth century—natural science, the Industrial Revolution, and the exponential growth of the human population—interacted in the twentieth century to spark a breakthrough in our thought. We scientists would like to think that it was our growing perceptiveness that brought this about, but the spreading damage wrought by technology, and by a rising living standard multiplied by population, simply made the problems too obvious to ignore.

This dawn of what we might call the modern environmental conscience revealed a beleaguered biosphere. Sea otters (*Enhydra lutris*), northern elephant seals (*Mirounga angustirostris*), right whales, and other species had been hunted to near-extinction; Caribbean monk seals (*Monachus tropicalis*) would be lost altogether before the twentieth century was out. Alarm over depletion of northern fur seals (*Callorhinus ursinus*) led first to government regulation, then to international treaties (Bean 1983). This was followed by attempts to regulate commercial exploitation of whales and other species and, after World War II, by creation of the International Whaling Commission (Bean 1983; Gambell, this volume). These essentially self-interested attempts to perpetuate our exploitation of valuable commercial resources were part of an ancient tradition that is still going strong today as the so-called "wise use movement." The novelty was the newfound synergy that developed after midcentury between this old utilitarian, anthropocentric motive and the biocentric view pioneered by John Muir and others in the nineteenth century. The result, what we now call the ecological movement, transformed the previous regulatory efforts and took on a new life of its own. The spotlight of public opinion was suddenly thrown on what had been an academic and economic issue of some obscurity, and environmentalists found a new and stirring battle cry: "Save the Whales!"

The modern environmental conscience had come of age, and Western civilization had discovered a new moral imperative: species and their habitats were to be preserved for their own sake. Beginning as an explicit emotional and intellectual conviction in the affluent West and North, this idea (reinforced by longstanding Eastern traditions and by the experience and intuition of indigenous peoples) is gradually spreading, not without resistance, to the less "developed" regions of the world. There, to the extent that it has been accepted, the environmental ethic is seen more pragmatically as a necessary means of development and of preserving the human life-support system against the increasingly terrifying prospect of human overpopulation (e.g., Smith 1996).

The pragmatic perspective on species preservation is certainly not lacking in the First World, but here it is accompanied (sometimes even eclipsed) by intellectual currents that range from sober moral discernment to enthusiasms transcending reason and even legality. One initially sensational theme, the supposedly superior intelligence of cetaceans, is no longer embraced uncritically, thanks to advances in scientific knowledge. As Roger Payne puts it, whales probably do not have advanced religions! This, however, has not diminished their appeal to assorted "New Age" cultists. Although one could argue that public concern for endangered species is to be welcomed regardless of its motivation, in the long run only attitudes grounded in reality will provide secure foundations for public policy.

Another such current, the animal welfare movement, spans the spectrum from simple concern for humane treatment of animals to radical opposition by animal rights activists to any human use of them whatsoever. From the early Greenpeace actions against whalers and sealers to continuing debates over display of killer whales and other species in oceanariums (Reeves and Mead, this volume), marine mammals have been a central focus of animal welfare concerns. Biologists and managers do well to give serious thought to these concerns despite the reprehensible vandalism and violence occasionally associated with extremes of this movement, which only serve to obscure moral issues that sooner or later must be addressed.

Educating the Public

Because of our familiarity with the facts and the issues, we biologists have a responsibility to help shape the public's moral conscience in regard to animal welfare. For example, misguided media attention sometimes results in misplaced expenditure of scarce resources in response to perceived emergencies, as in the case of the famous trio of gray whales trapped in arctic ice in 1988 (Rose 1989). At a minimum, such events should be used as "teachable moments" to give the public a more accurate view of natural history, species status, and responsible wildlife stewardship. Better, the scientific community should become more skilled at getting its message across to the news media and redirecting sentiment-driven attention and effort to the more substantive biological emergencies that confront us. Recent coverage of the biodiversity crisis shows that serious issues can be compelling news if only journalists are educated (by us) to see beneath the superficialities.

Such education will not always be a simple matter of providing the facts. The "facts" about the status of wild species are often hard enough to determine; they are harder still to forge into arguments for protection that are convincing to a nonscientific and perhaps hostile audience. Katona and Kraus (this volume) note that, precisely in the cases of those species (like the right whale) that are least numerous and therefore most endangered, the standard scientific concept of "statistical significance" becomes irrelevant because of small sample sizes. In the case of the right whale, "researchers and managers both recognized the need to act quickly and intuitively, taking actions before defining problems with the statistical exactitude they would usually require." Provided that one had more time than the usual media sound bite allows, such a situation could be turned into an opportunity for a useful lesson in statistical inference, or even on the inherent limitations of scientific inquiry. Nonscientist critics, however, are likely to argue that a threat has not been "scientifically proven."

Some scientific conclusions naturally lend themselves to misinterpretation. Is it not, after all, a hopeful sign that Hawaiian monk seals at French Frigate Shoals seem to have approached their habitat's carrying capacity (as suggested by Ragen and Lavigne, this volume)? And doesn't this show that they are coexisting peacefully with the nearby lobster fishery? Yes and no. Certainly the period of population growth and recovery was encouraging, but the carrying capacity of the habitat in question may well have been artificially depressed by the fishery, thereby decreasing juvenile survival and destabilizing the age structure, and further reducing the population's ability to recover. But these vital points could easily be overlooked in a news report, and they need to be emphasized in communicating with the public.

A still more complicated public relations dilemma of this kind is developing around the Florida manatee (Reynolds, this volume). The results of decades of effort at determining manatee numbers and status have recently been published (O'Shea et al. 1995). Taken at face value, the data show that the manatee population is stable and probably increasing; in fact, statewide aerial surveys conducted (and well publicized) in January and February 1996 counted many more manatees than were previously thought to exist. So, can we not conclude that recovery efforts have succeeded and that no further restrictions on boaters or developers are necessary? If manatee numbers have grown along with human numbers in Florida, does that not show that human population growth is harmless to wildlife, maybe even beneficial?

The scientists' figures, even statistically significant figures, do not tell the whole story. The larger context, the specifically human context, is essential. The audience needs to know that Florida manatees have indeed benefitted from some human activities, even activities that are otherwise environmentally harmful (introduction of exotic weeds like *Eichhornia* and *Hydrilla;* and construction of warm-water discharges like those of power plants, which have expanded the manatees' winter range) as well as ones designed to be helpful (enactment of laws to preserve habitat and regulate boat speeds). All these have cushioned manatees against the negative effects of human encroachment, but the inherent limits of these beneficial activities are now being reached while the human and boat populations continue to grow without limit. As long as this growth continues, the long-range outlook for manatees is grim.

Looked at closely, the data show that it is precisely in the best-protected areas (Crystal River and Blue Spring) that manatees have increased (through births as well as immigration), and not along Florida's heavily developed Atlantic coast. The overall situation is, in fact, an inadvertent experiment to determine what level of human harassment manatee populations can tolerate. The results neatly demonstrate both their ability to flourish, given reasonable protection, and their likely inability to survive much longer, given the pace and direction of change in Florida's human-dominated environment. The challenge for environmentalists will be to present this complex case clearly to the public. As it happened, the publicity in January and February 1996 over the record results of the aerial surveys was swept from the headlines in March and April by a massive die-off of more than 150 manatees in southwest Florida caused by a red tide. At this writing, media portrayals of manatee status have turned back toward pessimism. But the public relations roller coaster of spring 1996 only underlines the enduring need for balanced, in-depth information to buffer public perceptions against such unpredictable events.

Animals Versus People

Education about the moral and practical dimensions of endangered species dilemmas will not, by itself, make the problems go away. I once wrote that we have an obligation to ensure the survival of other species; whereupon I was asked on what philosophical basis I could argue that a starving village should spare the last African manatee. My answer was that the question should not even arise. Why is the village starving in the first place? Our moral responsibility as the de facto stewards of the planet is to foresee and forestall such ultimate confrontations, which end in tragedy no matter how they are resolved. In other words, I prefer to think less in terms of animal rights than of human responsibilities, which are philosophically less problematic.

Why drag in moral arguments at all? Because most of the other arguments for preserving species potentially founder on the fact that if our practical need for a species ends, so does the justification for preserving it. If fur is out of fashion, why protect fur seals from marine debris, especially if they compete with fishermen? If sperm whales are kept around just for their spermaceti, then jojoba oil renders them redundant. Jojoba plants will become redundant too as soon as we learn to make the oil synthetically at less cost and with higher purity. The tendency of all our industry, after all, is to replace natural products with synthetic ones wherever possible. Once the DNA of a species has been read and recorded, won't the species itself be expendable?

Of course, the species may have esthetic value that can be used to turn a profit through books, videos, or whale-watching cruises, but a government may still decide that a flood-control dam is more vital (to humans) than a river dolphin's habitat. Exploitation of a species may help preserve an aboriginal culture and its traditions of hunting—or undermine that same culture by increasing its dependence on a cash economy. A species may play a key role in its ecosystem, from which we derive indirect benefit—or, like some marine mammals, it may compete directly with our fisheries. If the justification for an animal's existence depends only on what it can do for us, what happens if the cost-benefit ratio reverses?

Hence, species need a principle by which their autonomous existence can be secured. Whether this principle is expressed in terms of animal rights or human responsibilities, it is irreducibly moral in that it transcends human needs and desires. Without such a principle and its acceptance by most people, the odds are against any endangered species' survival in the long run.

Of those who already accept such a moral principle, some ground it in religious belief, and others do not. Religions must bear their share of blame for the environmental abuses of the past. In contrast to their encouragement of morality in other areas, most religious institutions in the West have, until recently, remained scandalously silent about the ecological and population crisis, and some continue to make obstructive statements on these topics even today. Yet this century's secular progress in environmental consciousness and moral awareness is becoming evident across the religious spectrum as well; "creation-centered spirituality" (not to be confused with special creationism!) is a major new theme in mainstream Western theology. It views the natural world not as something expendable, for humans to dominate and exploit however they wish, but as something good and valuable in itself, to be used only in ecologically sustainable ways and to be cared for and nurtured as a religious duty (e.g., see Fox 1983, Berry 1988, Boff 1995). For once, organized Western religions are learning lessons of moral and spiritual importance not only from natural science, but also from observing the condition of Earth itself. One might almost see in this development a fulfillment of the Biblical prophecy that if the disciples were to keep silence, the very stones would cry out (Luke 19:40).

Unlikely Partners

Developments in the religious realm are social realities to which marine mammalogists (and other scientists) should attend. We and the animals we study have played conspicuous roles in the events and controversies that stimulated these developments: "Save the Whales" bumper stickers and "dolphin-safe" tuna labels are not just icons of popular culture, but genuine milestones in the history of philosophy and theology. Moreover, it is increasingly necessary to appeal to moral arguments to justify setting aside space and resources for wild animals on our crowded planet. No single group in society will be able to accomplish this alone; science, government, business, and religion must all cooperate if we are to gain the universal acceptance of a principle that transcends both science and pragmatic policy.

It is not to be expected, of course, that a team such as this will pull together in perfect harmony; four more mutually suspicious sectors could not be selected from our society! Nor are science, government, business, and religion apt to agree on the idea of promoting such a thing as a moral principle, let alone on its content. Fortunately, however, they do not need to agree on motives or principles. All they need to share is a common goal. Any good deed can have many justifications, and not all of them need to be good, or even (at first glance) mutually compatible.

Governments in the North, for their own selfish reasons as well as for altruistic reasons, seek to restrain population growth in the South, whereas those in the South call for an end to wasteful consumption by the North (and let us hope they both succeed). Nations everywhere would prefer their own pollution to find its way into some other jurisdiction, but, failing that, they might settle for reducing it at the source. Profit-making enterprises (the very embodiments of human selfishness, yet the source of most of our material comforts) see the exploding populations of the Third World as potential markets, but they also realize that the standards of living in such countries must rise so that their people can afford manufactured goods. Fossil-fuel producers still deny the reality of global warming, but banks and insurance companies, fearing the costs of climate change, are already starting to finance greener technologies.

Religious leaders of one stripe decry inroads on the "right to life," generally quite narrowly defined; those of another persuasion struggle to liberate the politically and economically oppressed; still others, whether Hindu or animist, worshipers of Christ or of the Great Mother Goddess, uphold the sacredness (in some sense) of the entire Cosmos. Some churchmen say overpopulation causes poverty; others say the reverse. Here too there is more common ground than many of the protagonists admit. Scientists, for their part, disagree about global warming and about the number of species at risk from deforestation. Proponents of space stations, green revolutions, genome projects, and biological surveys fault one another's priorities, but the consensus that the planet is in crisis has never been stronger. Meanwhile, countless ordinary citizens throughout the world band together in nongovernmental organizations advocating the most exuberantly diverse, even contradictory, solutions, but they are united in raising an ever-louder cry of alarm over their worsening environment and the timidity of their leaders.

Some might see all this as a portrait of chaos, of madmen fighting aboard a sinking ship. I see in it a hopeful pattern. The debaters are in fact not mad but (mostly) rational; even the blindest have an accurate perception of some part of the elephant. Most encouraging is the role played by the newly evolved nongovernmental sector: this great pool of talent and determination, self-organized like a primordial soup into myriad affinity and pressure groups, surrounds and lubricates the scientific, governmental, commercial, and religious wheels and increasingly drives them as well. Obstacles to the free flow of information are being irreversibly broken down by alternative media and electronic communications, and the marketplace of ideas is more genuinely democratic than ever before. The more people talk to one another, the more real the "global village" becomes and the more consensus about the problems crystallizes. Where disagreements remain, there are usually enough problems needing attention for everyone to be able to work on his or her favorite; even where world views are irreconcilable, common goals can be found when all people are at ecological risk—and demanding that their leaders get on with it.

How can this rosy vision be translated into reality? And how can marine mammals and other species best be conserved and studied in this fast-changing social and intellectual milieu? Once again, marine mammalogy itself is at the forefront. As sketched by Reynolds (this volume), the case of the Florida manatee offers an outstanding example of how disparate entities can collaborate effectively for the benefit of an endangered species and its habitat.

Central to this collaboration has been the generally amicable relationship between federal and state government agencies and among research, management, and enforcement units within these agencies. The close partnership between the U.S. Fish and Wildlife Service (with, more recently, the U.S. Geological Survey) and the Florida

Department of Environmental Protection has allowed mutual support and shifting of responsibilities in response to temporary funding shortfalls on one side or the other—demonstrating the value of a diversified support base. Several other Florida state agencies, the Georgia Department of Natural Resources, and local governments, as well as the Army, Navy, Coast Guard, and National Aeronautics and Space Administration, also play vital roles on the front lines of manatee protection, with the help (and, of course, prodding) of the primary state and federal players.

Lest all this cozy inter- and intragovernmental cooperation become incestuous, university-based and other independent scientists provide outside perspectives and independent peer review. Further tangible support comes from sources one might not have anticipated: supplementary (usually in-kind) assistance in research, management, and public education has regularly and generously been furnished by private enterprises such as the Miami Seaquarium, SeaWorld, Inc., Lowry Park Zoo, and the Florida Power & Light Company.

A recovery team with broad representation (even including the Marine Industries Association!) provides high-level vision and coordination through its recovery plan. Exercising critical oversight, enforcing cooperation, and exerting pressure where needed are, at the federal extreme, the U.S. Marine Mammal Commission, and, at the nongovernmental level, the energetic and vocal Save the Manatee Club, which also funds basic and applied research to a surprising degree. The general public provides substantial direct support for manatee programs by voluntary donations to the state and the Save the Manatee Club, and is often mobilized by the latter to press the state legislature for stronger manatee protection.

This healthy diversity of coworkers and their spirit of cooperation are, I believe, largely responsible for giving the Florida manatee the fighting chance for survival that it now has—and this diversity and spirit are not to be taken for granted. In fact, they contrast dramatically with the situation of the Hawaiian monk seal (Lavigne, this volume). The monk seal recovery effort has been almost entirely in the hands of one federal agency, the National Marine Fisheries Service (NMFS). Charged as it is with both fostering commercial fisheries and facilitating the recovery of monk seals, NMFS has a built-in conflict of interest. Although the Hawaiian monk seal is even more exclusively a resident of Hawaii than the Florida manatee is of Florida, the Hawaii state government has been all but absent from the recovery effort and has also tended to take the side of fisheries in seal-fishery conflicts. Apart from minor military and Coast Guard assistance, the Hawaiian scene is practically devoid of the diversity of constructive players seen in Florida; until recently, even the recovery team has functioned only sporadically. The recovery effort's narrow institutional base has left it vulnerable to funding shortfalls; indeed, much of its funding over the years has had to come by direct congressional appropriation, and that only at the strenuous urging of the Marine Mammal Commission. It is thus no surprise that the Hawaiian monk seal could well become the first intensively managed marine mammal species to go extinct—perhaps even before the much less intensively managed Mediterranean monk seal or the vaquita.

Poverty: Common Threat, Common Ground?

The Florida manatee recovery effort is an encouraging model, but it must be admitted that in most areas of environmental protection, such a meeting of disparate minds is exceptional. Adversarial relations are more typical. True, the rate of change in public opinion, catalyzed by Earth Days and Earth Summits, is accelerating, and we may yet be pleasantly surprised by breakthroughs in global consciousness. Meanwhile, however, progress is likely to depend more on hard work and practical strategies of consensus building. In the search for common ground, it may prove true that the proper study of mankind is man: just as people are the cause of the crisis and people will have to implement whatever solutions are tried, so we will only find appropriate solutions when we focus our attention on people as the victims of the crisis. To understand the mechanics of humanity's collision with its environment, we should look where the impact is most obvious, violent, and damaging to both—and that is in the lives of the poor.

Because it is our material culture that insulates us from the rougher bits of our surroundings, the materially poor are by definition those who are closest to their physical and biological environment and hence suffer the most when the environment suffers. Often, they are forced in turn by their destitution to inflict serious damage on that same environment, through poaching, overfishing, overgrazing, deforestation, and other unsustainable practices. The affluent do indeed command more damaging technology; as noted by Katona and Kraus (this volume), "the responsibility for killing North Atlantic right whales has broadened from a relatively small group of hunters seeking oil and baleen to a very diffuse group that includes most of us who eat seafood; purchase foreign autos, petroleum, appliances, or other products that arrive on ships; profit from the export of goods by sea; or benefit from the services of the Navy or Coast Guard." However, the sheer numbers of the poor and their rapid increase (itself both cause and effect of their poverty) make their impact substantial—and, ironically, it will be multiplied to the extent that their standard of living rises. Collisions with motorboats as a cause of manatee deaths are no longer confined to affluent Florida but have begun to spread with "development" throughout Latin America and the Caribbean (Estrada and Ferrer 1987, O'Shea et al. 1988).

From these and all the other dilemmas of economic "progress," it follows that the poor are at the center of "development," humanitarian, and human rights concerns on the part of governmental, commercial, and religious bodies. They are therefore the point at which the interests of environmental science, government, business, and religion most dramatically intersect—or, too often, collide.

Population growth is now adding some 95 million people a year to this planet, and most of them are poor. At the same time, the world is becoming more economically polarized than ever before, with wealth (in both developed and developing countries) being concentrated in proportionately fewer and fewer hands. Our global polity is increasingly dominated by transnational corporations that wield more power than most governments, and, through entities such as the World Trade Organization, they are using that power systematically to dismantle (in the name of "free trade") all governmental restraints on profit seeking (Korten 1995). One of the more obscure results of this ominous trend is a renewed threat to eastern tropical Pacific dolphins as a consequence of new international trade agreements such as the General Agreement on Tariffs and Trade (GATT), following years of hard-won progress in ameliorating the "tuna-dolphin problem" (Gosliner, this volume; Perrin, this volume). A much larger and more worrisome result of this resurrected laissez-faire capitalism is increasing economic insecurity for most of the human race, with ever-deepening poverty that is destabilizing both societies and ecosystems worldwide.

The crucial relevance of the poor to most environmental conflicts (and vice versa), the rapidly increasing numbers of the impoverished, and the increasing pressure exerted on them and their environments by unrestrained profit seeking are facts of life today whose importance to conservation cannot be overstated. The practical implication is that efforts to help the environment will have the most strategic effects, and will yield the most profound and long-lasting benefits, when they serve the poorest members of each society.

Hence, while not neglecting to support efforts at saving endangered species and their habitats, or cleanups of toxic waste, or other urgent activities, we will be wise to give still greater attention to well-designed programs that eradicate poverty. For example, it has been repeatedly shown that one of the most powerful catalysts of social and economic development is the education of girls. Enabling girls to stay in school longer delays marriage and childbearing; it gives women marketable skills, thereby raising their economic and social status relative to men; and by giving them both career options outside the home and better knowledge of home economics and hygiene, it leads directly to a desire for fewer, healthier, and better-cared-for children. Better-educated women voluntarily seek out the family-planning and other services that they need, thereby braking population growth and pressures on the local ecosystem and raising the community's overall level of education, health, productivity, self-sufficiency, and self-determination. Enhancing (through better access to health care and credit as well as to education) the status of rural women (who in many countries are major users and de facto managers of forests) can even have immediate benefits in preserving forests and biodiversity (Jacobson 1992). Thus, whereas hiring and equipping game wardens might be needed as a stopgap solution to poaching in a national park, history may well show that the money spent on the local school for girls actually did more to enhance the long-term survival of the wildlife.

While fostering such genuinely wise efforts to end poverty, however, we must keep a skeptical eye on schemes of development by "sustainable utilization," which often sport the label of "wise use." The danger is typically that the sustainability is conjectural, but the utilization is certain. The remedy is to keep the burden of proof of sustainability and wisdom where it belongs, on the would-be developers. Otherwise, by seeking quick fixes for poverty, we will lose the chance of finding lasting solutions.

Organizations and people who find it hard to concur on the urgency of protecting "useless" plants or animals might find it even harder to differ (publicly, at least) on the value of education and public health programs. Even mutually antagonistic religions can generally agree that aid to the poor is a good thing. Governments are often more open to acceptance of people-directed aid than they are to acceptance of pro-environment initiatives that smack of interference in "internal affairs" or infringement on "private property rights." International pressure on corrupt, authoritarian regimes can be more readily brought to bear when humanitarian rather than environmental needs are at issue. Businesses can get tax write-offs as well as favorable publicity for humanitarian acts (in place of bad publicity, even boycotts, for violations of human rights). What is needed is for scientists and conservationists to grasp more clearly that a dollar intelligently spent to relieve poverty is not just a dollar diverted from a species-recovery program; in the long run it may be the investment best suited to achieve both ends.

Framing it in a more general context, we contribute to the stability of both the human and the nonhuman worlds when we lower the center of gravity, as it were, of power in human societies. In economic terms, this means increasing the wealth of those at the bottom (which implies less consumption and waste by those of us at the top, so that there will be something to spare for the others). In social and political terms, it implies their overall empowerment, both as individuals (through education, gender equality, democratization, and decentralization of decision making) and as communities (through the protection of community rights and the preservation of traditional cultures and local authority structures). These sorts of empowerment often require no financial aid at all and are more effective than simply throwing money at problems. Just as those in closest contact with the land are the first to suffer from environmental degradation, they are also (in those cases where they have preserved a tradition of sustainable resource use) often the best judges of how to prevent or heal such degradation, and they have the strongest incentives to do so. (Dugongs [*Dugong dugon*] in Palau are a potential example [see Johannes 1981].) Obviously, decentralized management is not the solution to all problems. High-seas whaling could not be managed locally, and the increasing technological sophistication of much wildlife biology is beyond the reach of local communities. Management must be at the appropriate scale to the problem at hand, but even where the scale is large, there often remains a useful role for the small.

Where environmentally friendly traditions do survive, the indigenous religions can often provide powerful motivation to responsible stewardship as well as direct aid in conservation work and should not be overlooked when partnerships with religious bodies are sought (cf. Ortiz 1996). An interesting example is provided by the "whale temples" on the coast of Vietnam, whose keepers have collected and preserved skulls of stranded cetaceans and made them available to biologists conducting surveys of species distribution (Smith et al. 1997). Even indigenous myths, legends, and folk beliefs can contribute to conservation, for example, of the river dolphins *Inia* and *Sotalia* and of natural resources in general in the Amazon Basin (Smith 1996). Governments and scientists, therefore, are well advised to respect and foster the hard-won wisdom of traditional societies, just as they would preserve the native vegetation that prevents erosion of a hillside.

This is the resolution of the false dichotomy between environmental protection and "sustainable development." Once we realize that "growth" in any quantitative sense is inherently unsustainable on a finite planet, and that growth in human numbers must entail decline in (our) per-capita consumption—once we understand "development" in a qualitative sense that starts with improving the lives of the most desperately poor—then we will see that the paths to ecological sanity and human development inevitably converge. Likewise convergent are the pragmatic and moral reasons to value the natural world, as well as the moral imperatives to care for our neighbor and to care for the Earth. Each individual, each organization will act out of a different mix of these motives; what matters is that they recognize the commonality of their interests and the convergence of their aims.

Yes, there is a moral dimension to our work; yes, there is progress in our moral sense, as in our science; and yes, there is hope for saving and enhancing life on Earth through synergies among science, government, business, and religion, whenever citizens demand such action. It is in fact only through such alliances and such demands, down through the ages, that much of the human race has grudgingly been made to admit that certain things are simply wrong: human sacrifice, slavery, child abuse, genocide, racism, even cruelty to animals. In our work with endangered species, we are on a cutting edge of whatever moral progress our own species can claim to be making. Let us step into the twenty-first century with the confidence, determination, humility, and hope that that awareness inspires.

Literature Cited

Bean, M. J. 1983. The Evolution of National Wildlife Law. Praeger, New York, NY.

Berry, T. 1988. The Dream of the Earth. Sierra Club Books, San Francisco, CA.

Boff, L. 1995. Ecology and Liberation. Orbis Books, Maryknoll, NY.

Cassels, R. 1984. The role of prehistoric man in the faunal extinctions of New Zealand and other Pacific islands. Pages 741–767 *in* P. S. Martin and R. G. Klein (eds.), Quaternary Extinctions: A Prehistoric Revolution. University of Arizona Press, Tucson, AZ.

Crosby, A. W. 1986. Ecological Imperialism: The Biological Expansion of Europe, 900–1900. Cambridge University Press, Cambridge, U.K.

Dewar, R. E. 1984. Extinctions in Madagascar: The loss of the subfossil fauna. Pages 574–593 *in* P. S. Martin and R. G. Klein (eds.), Quaternary Extinctions: A Prehistoric Revolution. University of Arizona Press, Tucson, AZ.

Domning, D. P. 1978. Sirenian evolution in the North Pacific Ocean. University of California Publications in Geological Sciences 118:xi + 176.

Domning, D. P. 1982. Commercial exploitation of manatees *Trichechus* in Brazil *c.* 1785–1973. Biological Conservation 22:101–126.

Estrada, A. R., and L. T. Ferrer. 1987. Distribucion del manati antillano, *Trichechus manatus* (Mammalia: Sirenia), en Cuba. I. Region occidental. Poeyana No. 354:1–12.

Fox, M. 1983. Original Blessing: A Primer in Creation Spirituality. Bear and Company, Santa Fe, NM.

Gambell, R. 1999. The International Whaling Commission and the contemporary whaling debate. (This volume)

Gosliner, M. L. 1999. The tuna-dolphin controversy. (This volume)

Heywood, V. H. (ed.). 1995. Global biodiversity assessment. Published for the United Nations Environment Programme. Cambridge University Press, Cambridge and New York, NY.

Jacobson, J. L. 1992. Gender bias: Roadblock to sustainable development. Worldwatch Paper 110:1–60.

Johannes, R. E. 1981. Words of the Lagoon: Fishing and Marine Lore in the Palau District of Micronesia. University of California Press, Berkeley, CA.

Katona, S. K., and S. D. Kraus. 1999. Efforts to conserve the North Atlantic right whale. (This volume)

Kipling, R. 1894. The Jungle Book. Macmillan and Company, London.

Korten, D. C. 1995. When Corporations Rule the World. Kumarian Press/Berrett-Koehler Publishers, San Francisco, CA.

Lavigne, David M. 1999. The Hawaiian monk seal: Management of an endangered species. (This volume)

Martin, P. S., and R. G. Klein (eds.). 1984. Quaternary Extinctions: A Prehistoric Revolution. University of Arizona Press, Tucson, AZ.

Mead, J. G., and E. D. Mitchell. 1984. Atlantic gray whales. Pages 33–53 *in* M. L. Jones, S. L. Swartz, and S. Leatherwood (eds.), The Gray Whale *Eschrichtius robustus*. Academic Press, Orlando, FL.

Olson, S. L. 1990. The prehistoric impact of man on biogeographical patterns of insular birds. Atti dei Convegni Lincei (Accademia Nazionale dei Lincei, Rome) 85:45–51.

Ortiz, A. 1996. American Indian religious freedom: First People and the First Amendment. Cultural Survival Quarterly 19 (4): 26–29.

O'Shea, T. J., M. Correa-Viana, M. E. Ludlow, and J. G. Robinson. 1988. Distribution, status, and traditional significance of the West Indian manatee *Trichechus manatus* in Venezuela. Biological Conservation 46:281–301.

O'Shea, T. J., B. B. Ackerman, and H. F. Percival (eds.). 1995. Population Biology of the Florida Manatee. U.S. Department of the Interior, National Biological Service, Information and Technology Report 1:1–289.

Perrin, W. F. 1999. Selected examples of small cetaceans at risk. (This volume)

Ragen, T. J., and D. M. Lavigne. 1999. The Hawaiian monk seal: Biology of an endangered species. (This volume)

Reeves, R. R., and J. G. Mead. 1999. Marine mammals in captivity. (This volume)

Reynolds, J. E., III. 1999. Efforts to conserve the manatees. (This volume)

Rose, T. 1989. Freeing the Whales: How the Media Created the World's Greatest Non-Event. Carol Publishing Group, New York, NY.

Rudwick, M. J. S. 1972. The Meaning of Fossils: Episodes in the History of Palaeontology. Macdonald, London, and American Elsevier, New York, NY.

Smith, B. D., T. A. Jefferson, S. Leatherwood, D. T. Ho, C. V. Thuoc, and L. H. Quang. 1997. Investigations of marine mammals in Vietnam. Asian Marine Biology 14:145–172.

Smith, N. J. H. 1996. The Enchanted Amazon Rain Forest: Stories from a Vanishing World. University Press of Florida, Gainesville, FL.

16

DAVID W. LAIST, JAMES M. COE, AND KATHRYN J. O'HARA

Marine Debris Pollution

Over the past five decades the disposal and loss of trash into the world's oceans have become a pervasive new form of pollution known as marine debris. Marine debris includes items ranging in size from minute plastic pellets, no more than a few millimeters in diameter, to derelict fishing nets, hundreds or thousands of meters long. Marine mammals, seabirds, turtles, crabs, and other species are injured or killed when they become entangled in marine debris or when they ingest it. For beach users and coastal residents, debris poses a threat to human health and safety. It also has substantial economic impact on fishermen by reducing fish and shellfish stocks, and on coastal communities by befouling shorelines and coastal waters, which adversely affects tourism.

At least three factors account for the recent increase in marine debris: (1) disposal practices rooted in the outdated notion that the ocean's enormous size enables it to absorb all kinds of human waste without harm; (2) proliferation of synthetic materials resistant to degradation in the marine environment; and (3) increasing numbers of mariners and coastal residents using and discarding more and more synthetic items.

Until the mid-1900s most products of human industry were made of natural fibers and materials that, when lost or thrown into the ocean, tended to sink or degrade quickly. As a result, the accumulation of floating and beach-cast debris at any one time was equal to the total amount of cotton or hemp rope, cloth, wood, and other materials discarded or lost over a period of days or weeks by a comparatively small maritime community.

In the 1940s, however, plastics and other synthetics began to replace natural materials in both the fabrication and packaging of everyday items. Their low cost, light weight, durability, and ease of molding or extruding into myriad shapes favored their use in manufacturing single-use items, such as plastic bags, packaging, and bottles, and made other items such as rope, line, and net more expendable. As new applications evolved, plastic production in the United States alone increased from 2.72 billion kg/year (6 billion pounds/year) in 1960 to 27.2 billion kg/year (60 billion pounds/year) in 1980 (Weisskopf 1988). Because many synthetic materials are buoyant and degrade slowly, discarded plastic objects also tend to migrate long distances and collect along beaches and ocean drift lines. As a result, the accumulated mass of floating and beach-cast debris gradually expanded to include the total amount of plastics and other persistent materials discarded or lost in the ocean over periods of many months or years by a burgeoning human population.

As the numbers of plastic items and people using them

increased, plastic rope, bags, sheeting, fishing nets and line, bottles, and the like came to dominate marine debris. At first, marine debris was viewed—and largely dismissed—as an extension of land-based litter. Then, early in the 1980s, scientists puzzled by an alarming and unexplained decline in northern fur seals (*Callorhinus ursinus*) in the Bering Sea began to suspect that entanglement of young seals in marine debris was the primary cause (Fowler 1982). Initially, the conjecture was met with skepticism, and many resource managers balked at considering it. Nevertheless, this tentative link between floating trash and the decline of a marine species was like a sentinel's call for a closer examination of possible effects on other species. It soon became apparent that the effects of marine debris were far more widespread, both geographically and biotically, than previously thought. This insight—combined with marine debris' increasingly apparent esthetic impacts and beach closures due to hazardous debris items, such as medical wastes—catalyzed action around the world to control the sources of debris (O'Hara 1988, Baur and Iudicello 1990, Shomura and Godfrey 1990, Committee on Shipborne Wastes 1995).

Since the mid-1980s efforts have proceeded on many fronts to identify and reduce both the sources and impacts of marine debris. These efforts are instructive for several reasons. First, they address a significant form of marine pollution that affects marine mammals and other marine life throughout the world. Second, they illustrate how marine mammals can serve as indicators of the health of marine ecosystems. Third, they provide a fascinating case study on the evolution of responsive management programs. And fourth, they underscore the important need for cooperation among public, industry, and governmental organizations, at both the national and international levels, to effectively address marine mammal conservation issues.

Types, Sources, and Amounts of Marine Debris

Marine debris is a broad term covering virtually any manufactured item that may be lost or discarded in the marine environment. The kinds of objects most commonly encountered include plastic bags, wrappers, bottles, and cups; synthetic rope and line; glass bottles; metal cans; lumber; and cigarette butts. Another form of marine debris that is ubiquitous in the world's oceans, yet inconspicuous because of its small size, is raw plastic pellets—the initial form in which plastic is shipped to manufacturers for shaping into final products.

The sources of marine debris are both land-based and sea-based. Major land-based sources are industrial outfalls, sewage and storm drains, beachgoers, coastal dumps, and upland runoff into rivers and bays. The principal at-sea sources are all types of watercraft (e.g., cargo, commercial fishing, military, passenger, and recreational vessels) and offshore platforms. Clearly, marine debris is largely caused by the overt or accidental actions of innumerable people who individually discard small amounts of material into the ocean. Separately their contributions may be insignificant, but collectively they are not.

Although broad categories of sources are generally apparent, neither the total amount nor the relative contribution of different sources is clear (Pruter 1987). A study of ocean pollution by the National Academy of Sciences (1975) estimated the total amount of garbage discharged from ships and offshore platforms worldwide at 6.4 million mt/year, representing perhaps 90% of the trash entering the ocean. Although this estimate is often cited to illustrate the scale of the problem, its accuracy is doubtful. Reliable data broadly representative of waste generation rates from contributing sources were not, and still are not, available. Researchers seeking to place the issue in a broad context therefore have had to extrapolate small, unrepresentative data sets (e.g., waste generation rates from a few ships in one or two ports) using large, vaguely defined source categories (e.g., the number of fishing vessels worldwide). Thus, although the academy estimated the loss and discard of derelict fishing gear from all commercial fishing vessels at 1,350 mt/year worldwide, Merrell (1980) estimated that 1,650 mt/year of fishing gear were discarded or lost off Alaska alone and that the global total was 135,000 mt/year.

Marine debris includes items made of paper, cloth, wood, concrete, metal, glass, rubber, leather, and plastic. The relative proportions of these materials entering the ocean are uncertain but may be similar to those of land-based municipal solid waste (Fig. 16-1). In landfills, plastics have recently been estimated to contribute about 10% of all wastes by weight and 21% by volume. However, because plastics resist corrosion in the marine environment and, for this reason, may be used more frequently by mariners, plastics may make up a greater percentage of marine-generated solid wastes. Because many plastics float and degrade slowly, they may be carried by winds and currents thousands of miles from their entry point and circulate in the world's oceans for years (Fig. 16-2).

For example, in May 1990 some 80,000 athletic shoes being shipped to the United States were lost overboard in the North Pacific northwest of Hawaii during a severe storm (Ebbesmeyer and Ingraham 1992). Six to 12 months later, thousands of shoes, many still wearable, were found by beachcombers in British Columbia, Washington, and Oregon. By the end of 1991 shoes from the spill began to appear in Hawaii, apparently having moved with the California Current south and then west. Similarly, plastic pellets are

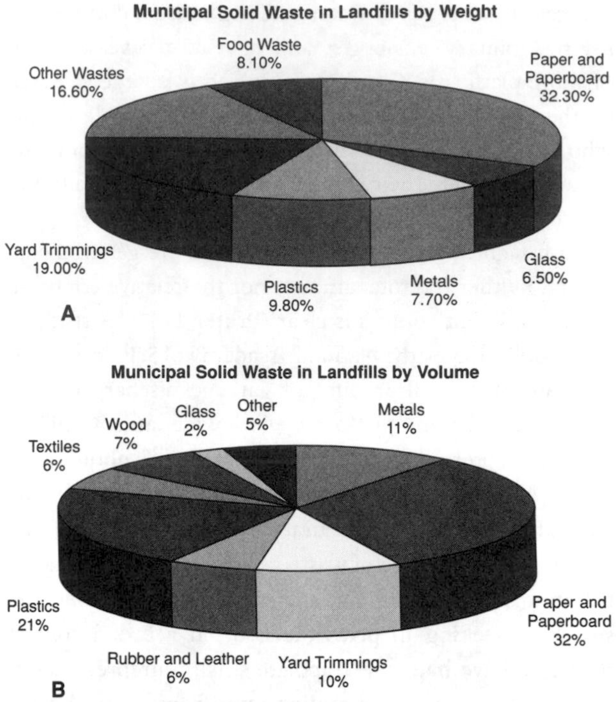

Figure 16-1. The composition of waste materials in the U.S. municipal solid waste stream by weight (*A*) and volume (*B*) in 1990 (Environmental Protection Agency 1992a).

now collected routinely in plankton tows in the Southern Ocean, thousands of miles from the nearest plastic manufacturing plant.

Because of their buoyancy and persistence, plastic items contribute disproportionately to the overall impact of marine debris. Most of the debris that either entangles animals or is found in their stomachs is made of plastic (Laist 1997). Most of the debris found on beaches is also made of plastic. The Center for Marine Conservation has organized and conducted beach cleanups in the United States since 1986 and internationally since 1989. Data from these cleanups indicate that plastic items compose about 60% of beach-cast debris (Table 16-1). Marine debris monitoring studies at selected U.S. national seashores indicate even higher percentages of plastic—92% of all debris items (Cole et al. 1992). In fact, the prevalence of plastics has led some scientists and resource managers to use the term "plastic pollution" interchangeably with "marine debris pollution."

Biological Impacts of Marine Debris

Marine mammals, seabirds, turtles, fish, and crustaceans can be injured or killed by entanglement in the loops and openings of marine debris and by ingesting all sorts of objects (Laist 1987) (Table 16-2). Entangled animals may exhaust themselves and drown, lose their ability to catch food

Figure 16-2. Beach-cast bottles, fishing floats, and other marine debris on Laysan Island, an uninhabited island in the Northwestern Hawaiian Islands more than 1,125 km (700 miles) northwest of the nearest center of human population in the main Hawaiian Islands. (Photograph by M. Burcham)

Table 16-1. Range of Percentage Composition of Marine Debris Items Collected during Beach Cleanups in the United States (1988–1995) and Internationally (1990–1995)

Debris Category	% of Items Reported in U.S. Beach Cleanups (1988–1995)	% of Items Reported in International Beach Cleanups (1990–1995)
Plastic	53.19–63.98	58.83–66.84
Metal	10.23–12.56	10.09–16.79
Glass	9.54–11.83	6.95–12.64
Paper	9.85–15.83	3.60–15.19
Wood	2.34–3.37	2.67–4.15
Rubber	1.77–2.52	1.60–2.53
Cloth	1.15–1.71	0.38–1.74

Sources: O'Hara and Debenham (1989), O'Hara and Younger (1990), Debenham and Younger (1991), Younger and Hodge (1992), Hodge and Glen (1993, 1994), Hodge et al. (1993), Halperin and Lewis (1994), Sheavly (1995, 1996), Center for Marine Conservation (1997).

Table 16-2. Number and Percentage of Marine Wildlife Species Worldwide for Which There Is Available Evidence of Debris Entanglement and Ingestion

Species Group	Total No. of Extant Species Worldwide	No. and Percentage of Species with Entanglement Records		No. and Percentage of Species with Ingestion Records		Species with Entanglement and/or Ingestion Records	
		No.	(%)	No.	(%)	No.	(%)
Marine mammals	115	32	(28%)	26	(23%)	49	(43%)
Mysticeti (baleen whales)	10	6	(60%)	2	(20%)	6	(60%)
Odontoceti (toothed whales)	65	5	(8%)	21	(32%)	22	(34%)
Otariidae (fur seals and sea lions)	14	11	(79%)	1	(7%)	11	(79%)
Phocidae (true seals)	19	8	(42%)	1	(5%)	8	(42%)
Sirenia (manatees and dugongs)	4	1	(25%)	1	(25%)	1	(25%)
Mustelidae (sea otter)	1	1	(100%)	0	(0%)	1	(100%)
Seabirds	312	51	(16%)	111	(36%)	138	(44%)
Sphenisciformes (penguins)	16	6	(38%)	1	(6%)	6	(38%)
Podicipediformes (grebes)	19	2	(10%)	0	(0%)	2	(10%)
Procellariiformes (albatrosses, petrels, and shearwaters)	99	10	(10%)	62	(63%)	63	(64%)
Pelecaniformes (pelicans, boobies, gannets, cormorants, frigatebirds, and tropicbirds)	51	11	(22%)	8	(16%)	17	(33%)
Charadriiformes (shorebirds, skuas, gulls, terns, auks)	122	22	(18%)	40	(33%)	50	(41%)
Sea turtles	7	6	(86%)	6	(86%)	6	(86%)
Other birds	—	5		0		5	
Fish	—	34		33		60	
Crustaceans	—	8		0		8	
Squid	—	0		1		1	
Species total		136		177		267	

Source: Laist (1996a).

or avoid predators, incur wounds and infections from abrasion by attached debris, or adopt aberrant behavior patterns that place them at a competitive disadvantage. Animals that ingest debris may have their digestive tracts blocked, irritated, or punctured; their food intake may be reduced by a false sense of satiation; or their nutrient absorption rates may be diminished. Such impacts were largely unrecognized until research on northern fur seals revealed their potential magnitude early in the 1980s.

At that time, scientists with the National Marine Fisheries Service were investigating an alarming, unexplained decline of northern fur seals on the Pribilof Islands in the Bering Sea (Scheffer and Kenyon 1989). Judging by the robust physical condition of the seals, food availability did not appear to be a problem. Various studies also ruled out other possible causes, such as disease, toxic chemicals, and predation. Based on the decreased rate of return of tagged juveniles and steady return rates of older animals, the decline was judged to be related to an increased at-sea mortality of juveniles, which remain at sea for the first two or three years of life.

At the same time, the National Marine Fisheries Service had been monitoring the number of fur seals returning to haul-out beaches entangled in small trawl net scraps and other debris. Almost all observed entanglements involved juveniles. The annual entanglement rates among juvenile males observed in annual harvests since 1967 ranged from about 0.2 to 0.7% (Fowler et al. 1993) (Fig. 16-3). Although this rate was far too small to account directly for the decline, the number of seals entangled and killed at sea was unknown. With no data to directly assess at-sea mortality, indirect analytic approaches were necessary. Trends in observed entanglement rates on land were found to be positively correlated to both the unexplained high mortality of

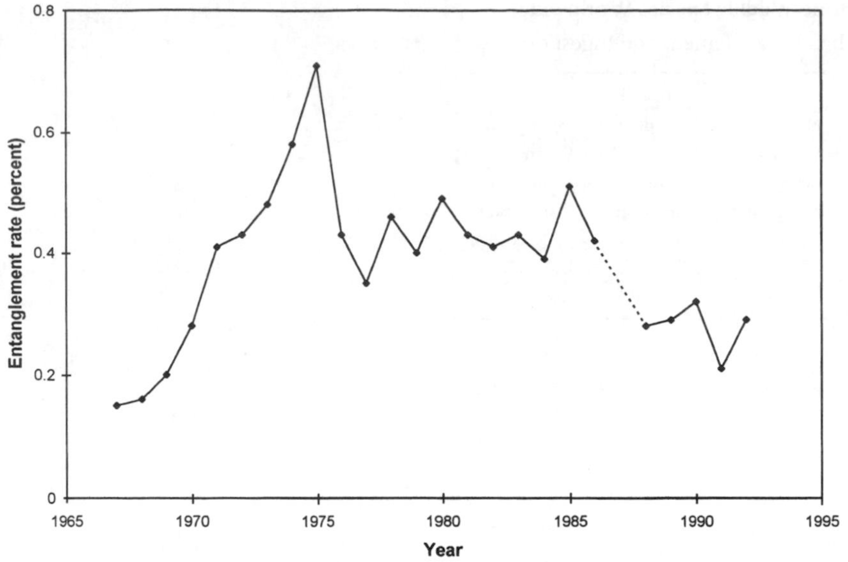

Figure 16-3. Percentage of juvenile male northern fur seals with entangling debris in commercial seal harvests from 1967 to 1992 and the research roundups from 1985 to 1992 on St. Paul Island, Alaska (Fowler et al. 1993).

juveniles at sea and the number of pups born (Fowler 1982). Also, most of the net debris found on Alaska beaches included much larger and heavier material than that found on animals during culls (usually less than 150 g), and the few dead seals recovered at sea were usually entangled in large net fragments. From these correlations and observations, Fowler (1982) postulated that in the late 1970s, 50,000 fur seals were entangled and killed annually at sea by marine debris.

Other studies soon provided additional indirect evidence linking debris to the population's decline. For example, observations showed that captive juvenile fur seals—but not the older, larger animals—exhibit a penchant for approaching and entangling themselves in floating trawl net fragments (Yoshida et al. 1985, Bengtson et al. 1988). Studies of captive fur seals showed that juveniles entangled in debris weighing 225 g spent 75% less time swimming than did unencumbered animals, and that the drag of attached debris imposed high energetic demands (Feldkamp et al. 1989). Theoretical estimates of the amounts of discarded webbing present in the northern fur seal range suggested that net debris was sufficiently abundant to cause the estimated number of entanglement mortalities (Lenarz 1985). Field studies found that animals entangled in small net fragments spent twice as much time foraging at sea as did nonentangled animals. After a year, the former were resighted only half as often as the latter (DeLong et al. 1988).

Fowler's (1982) deduction that marine debris could cause an unknown yet substantial level of mortality sparked vigorous debate and precipitated investigations of interactions involving other species. A colony of Australian fur seals (*Arctocephalus pusillus*) in Tasmania had an entanglement rate of 1.9% (± 0.7) (Pemberton et al. 1992); colonies of northern elephant seals (*Mirounga angustirostris*) in the California Channel Islands had entanglement rates of 0.10 to 0.16% (Stewart and Yochem 1990); Antarctic fur seal (*Arctocephalus gazella*) rookeries on Bird Island, South Georgia, had an average entanglement rate of 0.11% (Croxall et al. 1990); rookeries of Cape (Australian) fur seals (*Arctocephalus pusillus*) in South Africa and Namibia had observed rates of 0.11 to 0.22% (Shaughnessy 1980); and endangered Hawaiian monk seals (*Monachus schauinslandi*) had entanglement rates of 0.18 to 0.85% (Henderson 1990).

Data from beach-cast and salvaged carcasses have also provided evidence that marine mammals die from entanglement in debris and suffer from the effects of ingesting it. An examination of 439 stomachs collected from Florida manatees (*Trichechus manatus*) salvaged from 1978 through 1985 revealed that 63 (14.4%) contained ingested debris. Sixteen of 940 (1.7%) manatees recovered from 1974 to 1985 also had entanglement injuries or attached debris (Beck and Barros 1991). Within these samples, four deaths had clearly been caused by ingested debris and six by entanglement. For cetaceans and pinnipeds, stranding data suggest that ingestion of debris is uncommon or rare for most species. However, a sample of 32 stomachs collected from pygmy sperm whales (*Kogia breviceps*) stranded along the U.S. Atlantic and Gulf of Mexico coasts between 1971 and 1996 includes six (18%) with substantial amounts of plastic, including plastic sheeting (J. Mead, Smithsonian Institution, pers. comm.). Seven percent (2 of 30) of the documented mortality of northern right whales in the western North Atlantic from 1970 to 1993 has been attributed to entanglement in fishing gear (Kraus 1990, Kenney and Kraus 1993) although most or all of these entanglements may have been with active rather than derelict fishing gear.

Scientists studying species other than marine mammals also began to look more closely for evidence that marine debris was having an impact. For sea turtles, numerous anecdotal reports from the 1960s and 1970s suggested that ingestion of debris was both common and lethal (Balazs 1985). Sea turtles appeared predisposed to ingestion-related impacts because they are indiscriminate feeders (Carr 1987) with anatomical features such as esophageal papillae that prevent regurgitation and highly convoluted intestines that increase risks of blockage and abrasion by debris (Lutz and Alfaro-Schulman 1987).

Subsequent studies of stranded turtles supported this concern. Stomachs of sea turtles that stranded along the U.S. Atlantic and Gulf of Mexico coasts between 1980 and 1992 also revealed ingested materials. Hard plastic pieces, plastic sheeting, line, and pieces of rubber were found in 44% (8 of 18) of hawksbill turtles, 13% (15 of 115) of leatherback turtles, 6.9% (18 of 262) of green turtles, and 6.6% (59 of 896) of loggerhead turtles (W. Teas and W. Witzell, National Marine Fisheries Service, Southeast Fisheries Science Center, pers. comm.). Plastics were found in the guts of 56% (24 of 43) of small green sea turtles found dead in Florida, at least 2 of which (5%) clearly died as a result of the ingested plastic (Bjorndal et al. 1994). Sea turtles also appear to be prone to entanglement in debris, which may occur when they try to eat it. In perhaps the only large data set collected at sea on entanglement for any species, 6% of some 800 loggerhead sea turtles captured and tagged off the Azores from 1990 to 1993 were found entangled in debris (Bjorndal and Bolton 1994).

High percentages of certain shearwaters, storm petrels, fulmers, and phalaropes also ingest plastics (Robards et al. 1996, Laist 1996a), although the effects are not clear. Unlike sea turtles, adults of many seabird species can regurgitate indigestible items, presumably including plastics. Despite this ability, there is evidence to suggest that the ingestion of plastics may adversely affect the biological fitness of some seabirds. A sampling project in the tropical Pacific found that individual seabirds with large amounts of plastics in their stomachs tended to have lower body weights than individuals of the same species containing little or no plastic (Spear et al. 1995). Also, plastic debris ingested by adults can be fed to chicks and cause their death (Sileo et al. 1990). For species such as cormorants (Podolsky and Kress 1989) and gannets (Montevecchi 1991) that collect netting and line to build nests, and for some plunge-feeding and scavenging seabirds, entanglement also poses a mortality threat.

Lost or discarded fishing gear, mostly derelict pots, traps, and gillnets, also catch commercially valuable fish and shellfish. Called "ghost fishing," the catch of marine life by derelict gear is a poorly quantified but potentially significant problem (Laist 1996). Participants in many trap fisheries typically lose 10 to 30% of their traps annually. Attempts to quantify ghost fishing related to these losses include estimates of 670 mt of American lobster caught in lost lobster pots off the northeastern United States in 1978 (Smolowitz 1978); 300 mt of sablefish (7.5 to 30% of the amount landed) caught in lost traps off British Columbia from 1977 to 1983 (Scarsbrooke et al. 1988); and 93,169 kg (205,400 pounds) of king crab caught in lost traps in Bristol Bay, Alaska, in 1990 and 1991 (Kruse and Kimker 1993).

A review of entanglement and ingestion records reveals that at least 267 species of marine wildlife interact with marine debris, including 58% of the world's pinniped species and 15% of the world's cetacean species (Laist 1996a). The frequency of the interactions varies greatly by species. Entanglement in debris also appears far more likely to kill animals than does ingestion, and virtually all animals that are unable to free themselves quickly probably die eventually from related effects (Laist 1996a). Although most entanglements involve derelict fishing gear, monofilament line, netting, and strapping bands, the most commonly ingested materials are plastic bags and small pieces of hard plastic.

The significance of interactions at a population level remain subject to debate because there is no direct means of sampling total debris-related mortality, particularly deaths at sea, for any species, including the northern fur seal. Nevertheless, species known to experience debris-related deaths include several that have been formally designated as endangered or depleted (e.g., Hawaiian monk seals, West Indian manatees, the northern fur seals, and the various sea turtle species). For these and perhaps other species, marine debris may reduce and then limit population size, much as the effects of polychlorinated biphenyls (PCBs) on the shells of osprey and pelican eggs resulted in the reduction of population sizes of those species. For example, the Pribilof Islands' population of northern fur seals has shown little sign of recovering since the early 1980s when its decline ebbed, and it may be that continuing interactions with marine debris are now preventing recovery. That is, a new equilibrium may have been established between pup production and mortality from entangling debris and other causes that has effectively reduced the species' carrying capacity (Fowler and Siniff 1992).

Defining and Characterizing the Problem

Management actions begin with the identification and characterization of a problem. In the field of natural resource management, scientists play a central role, serving as the eyes and ears of resource managers. Although problem identification must precede management action, the process of defining a problem too often receives inadequate attention. At one extreme, uninterested managers may give inadequate support to investigate research findings that suggest potential problems, thereby causing significant problems to be overlooked; at the other extreme, some problems are "studied to death," with management action deferred pending conclusive scientific proof of a particular hypothesis.

In the case of marine debris, recognition of the issue came gradually, beginning with anecdotal accounts by scientists who noticed and reported debris in unexpected places. As noted above, scientists monitoring the northern fur seal harvest on the Pribilof Islands began finding debris on fur seals in the 1960s. Similarly, Kenyon and Kridler (1969) found plastics in decomposed carcasses of albatrosses while surveying fauna in the Northwestern Hawaiian Islands; Carpenter and Smith (1972) discovered that small egg-shaped spheres in their plankton tows from the Sargasso Sea were actually plastic pellets; Venrick et al. (1973) observed the widespread occurrence of floating plastic debris in the central North Pacific Ocean during biological oceanographic surveys; Merrell (1980), while studying the recovery of biota after atomic weapons tests, found large quantities of net debris fouling remote beaches in the Aleutian Islands; Morris (1980) reported that plastic items composed most of the floating trash in the South Atlantic Ocean; and Bonner and McCann (1982) described plastic "neck collars" on Antarctic fur seals on remote islands in the Southern Ocean.

With such observations came a recognition that more and more ship crews, following the standard practice of dumping their garbage over the side, were introducing increasing amounts of solid waste into the oceans. In the early years of the environmental movement, this prompted the Intergovernmental Maritime Consultative Organization (now the International Maritime Organization) to include regulations limiting the discharge of vessel garbage as an annex (Annex V) to the 1973 International Convention for the Prevention of Pollution from Ships (commonly called the MARPOL Convention). Shortly thereafter, a review of ocean pollution by the U.S. National Academy of Sciences (1975) examined the issue in a chapter entitled "Marine Litter." Likening trash in the ocean to land-based litter, the chapter title succinctly depicted trash in the ocean as an esthetic annoyance. Given the paucity of information to suggest otherwise, this characterization is understandable; however, it also conveyed and perhaps solidified the perception of the issue as an inconvenience rather than an issue of biological significance.

This perception may have biased both assessments of and responses toward trash in the ocean, even after Fowler's work early in the 1980s had suggested that debris could affect species at population levels. Fowler's own agency, the National Marine Fisheries Service, largely dismissed his conclusions as speculative and was unwilling to act on his findings. There the issue might have languished except for the involvement of concerned public interest groups and the Marine Mammal Commission, an independent agency of the U.S. government with broad authority to review federal actions related to marine mammal conservation.

The Commission judged that Fowler's conclusions deserved closer examination, and in 1982 it recommended that the Service hold a workshop to review the problem and identify possible actions to reduce the amounts of lost fishing net and strapping bands in the oceans. Although some National Marine Fisheries Service officials supported the recommendation, the agency's leadership resisted on grounds that funding was limited and the problem's importance was doubtful. The Commission, however, continued to raise the matter, and in the spring of 1983, the Service convened a meeting with officials of other North Pacific fishing nations to solicit their views on the need for a possible workshop.

At the meeting, Fowler presented results of the entanglement studies and the Marine Mammal Commission proposed draft terms of reference for an international workshop on marine debris. The officials present unanimously concluded that the workshop was warranted "as a matter of conscience." The Commission subsequently contributed seed money and recommended persons to serve on a steering committee to plan the workshop. Under these circumstances, the Service reluctantly came to support the proposal, and the first international workshop on the fate and impact of marine debris was held in November 1984. To help identify management options before the workshop, the Commission contracted for a legal analysis of relevant U.S. laws and international agreements to serve as a workshop background document. The report (Bean 1984) identified the importance of MARPOL Annex V and the need for the United States to ratify its provisions and promote its entry into force.

Fowler's conclusions about the effects of marine debris on fur seals also kindled an immediate response from ocean-oriented environmental groups and the public. Early in 1984, as the above-mentioned workshop was being planned, several nongovernmental organizations (NGOs) formed the Entanglement Network to alert their constituencies to the problem and to lobby government officials.

The involvement of the Entanglement Network was crucial both in stimulating government action and in helping to mitigate the problem directly. By communicating with government officials and by generating public awareness through newsletters, magazines, brochures, and other outreach efforts, the NGOs effectively increased pressure on the National Marine Fisheries Service to proceed with the workshop. Perhaps even more important, they provided support for a review of information (Wallace 1985) that served to broaden appreciation of the problem from an esthetic problem to one posing a threat to the conservation of marine life. Their lobbying efforts also prompted Congress in 1985 to appropriate $1 million to the National Marine Fisheries Service for development of a research and management program on discarded netting and other debris.

Because of the particular concern for northern fur seals, the 1984 workshop focused principally, but not exclusively, on the North Pacific Ocean. To reflect the scope of the issue and to avoid the connotations of the term *marine litter*, workshop organizers coined a new term: *marine debris*.

Participants in the workshop included representatives of the gear manufacturing and fishing industries and environmental groups, as well as physical oceanographers, biologists, resource managers, and other government officials. For the first time, information was compiled on the sources, amounts, and biological impacts of derelict fishing gear and other trash in the marine environment. This compilation provided clear evidence of increasing amounts of debris, particularly plastic items, in all the world's oceans. It also illustrated the wide variety of debris present and the surprising number of marine species affected (Shomura and Yoshida 1985). Most important, however, the evidence provided a surprisingly convincing case that marine debris could, in fact, be creating biological impacts on a population level. The support for this possibility prompted a shift in perceptions of marine debris from that of a local litter problem to a significant global marine pollution issue.

Developing a Management Response

Because of the many sources and types of marine debris, its potential to be carried thousands of miles by winds and currents, and the fact that no single national or international agency has a clear responsibility for addressing the issue, the prospect of developing an effective management response was daunting.

However, with the workshop proceedings, the congressional directive and funding, and the commitment of a few agencies, groups, and individuals, it was possible over the next decade to mount a constructive response. Among many factors that contributed to that response, five areas were particularly important and serve to illustrate the steps involved in building a cooperative management program: public awareness and involvement, U.S. legislative and executive leadership in government, involvement of international agencies and organizations, national-level programs, and scientific research. Because the United States has been at the forefront of efforts to deal with marine debris and because we are most familiar with efforts in that country, the following discussion draws heavily on U.S. experience. The points illustrated below could, however, probably be made equally well with examples from other countries and international organizations.

Public Awareness and Involvement

Probably nothing was more important in crafting a response to marine debris than public awareness and involvement. In a sense, the public is both the cause of and the solution to the problem. Trash discarded or lost by beachgoers, recreational boaters, and sport fishermen is a major source of marine debris. Education programs to modify the attitudes and behavior of individuals are a fundamental need. On the other hand, as the major beneficiaries and potent advocates of clean coasts and oceans, members of the public, through letters to government officials and the work of NGOs, provided the motivating force for government action.

Since the mid-1980s public awareness efforts have been phenomenally successful. The nature of the issue itself contributed to this success. First, debris is easily recognized and understood. Virtually everyone has encountered a littered landscape and experienced exasperation at someone's careless, irresponsible action. Familiarity with the issue probably predisposes the public to take actions to mitigate it. Second, marine debris is a photogenic form of pollution. Photographs of wildlife, particularly marine mammals, killed or otherwise debilitated by debris, provided compelling images that touched people (Fig. 16-4). Pictures in the media epitomized the problem in a way that instantly linked cause and effect. Third, the solution is straightforward and noncontroversial; few would argue that throwing garbage into the ocean is either a good idea or unavoidable.

Public awareness efforts often are most successful when people are offered constructive opportunities to help solve a problem. The first volunteer beach cleanup was organized in 1984 by Judie Neilson, a private citizen who sought to help the Oregon Department of Fish and Wildlife gather data on the types and amounts of trash along the Oregon coast (Neilson 1985). After the planned cleanup was announced, local businesses and newspapers eagerly donated equipment and services, and despite poor weather on the scheduled day, more than 2,000 volunteers turned out and filled more than 2,400 bags of trash. More than 1,600 participants also completed and returned questionnaires listing what they found.

Figure 16-4. Photographs like this one of a Hawaiian monk seal with a plastic band around its muzzle help draw public attention to the problems of marine debris. (Photograph by D. J. Alcorn)

Since then, literally millions of people have participated in annual beach cleanups organized by the Center for Marine Conservation and state and local agencies throughout the United States and abroad. In 1986, 2,700 participants spent three hours removing debris from beaches in Texas and recording data on what they found (O'Hara, Maraniss et al. 1987). By 1988 beach cleanups were scheduled in 25 states as part of "Coastweeks," an annual fall celebration of coastal environments (O'Hara and Debenham 1989). In 1994 the Center helped organize fall cleanups in 35 U.S. states and territories and in 60 countries around the world (Sheavly 1995). In many areas, annual cleanups have evolved into year-round adopt-a-beach programs, and similar programs have been launched for rivers and other inland waters.

Beach cleanups can further several disparate objectives, and this is one reason that they are so successful and important. Most obviously, they provide a community service by removing large amounts of unsightly trash at little or no cost to taxpayers. In 1993, 222,116 volunteers, working three hours each, removed 2.36 million kg (5.2 million pounds) of trash from 2,254 km (5,570 miles) of coastline (Halperin and Lewis 1994). If those volunteers had been paid minimum wage, the total cost of the 1993 cleanup would have been about $2.8 million (excluding time spent planning and the costs of donated bags, gloves, etc.). Perhaps more important, however, beach cleanups provide a springboard for other action. They provide topics for news and feature stories, which further promote public awareness. Beach cleanups also attract politicians whose personal involvement may be translated into essential support for related government programs. Cleanup events also encourage individuals to contact members of Congress and other policy makers. For example, reports of large numbers of balloons found during coastal cleanups led groups, including schoolchildren, to successfully petition state legislators for laws banning mass balloon launches.

Beach cleanups also provide data on the types, amounts, and sources of marine debris. Data compiled by the Center for Marine Conservation from the 1986 beach cleanup in Texas were presented to Congress during ratification hearings on MARPOL Annex V. Based in part on those data, Congress directed the President to seek an amendment to Annex V adding the Gulf of Mexico to its list of special areas (see below). Data from beach cleanups have been recorded on standardized data cards and entered by the Center into an international marine debris database.

The public has also become directly involved in enforcement. The maritime industry, and the cruise ship component in particular, received a jolt in April 1993 when the largest fine ever imposed for unlawfully discharging plastics at sea was levied against a cruise ship line. The $500,000 fine, the maximum allowed under U.S. law, was assessed after the company pleaded guilty to a felony charge of dumping more than 20 bags of garbage from one of its ships off the Florida Keys. The widely publicized case was based on a videotape filmed by two passengers and turned over to the U.S. Coast Guard. At its discretion, the court awarded half the fine to the two passengers. The negative publicity almost certainly was a far stronger compliance incentive to the industry than the substantial fine itself. Knowledge that crew, passengers, or other people may document and report illegal discharges now provides a strong stimulus for cruise ship operators, as well as other vessel operators, to heed garbage discharge restrictions.

In most cases, however, individuals must take the responsibility for marine debris. Even when reference is made to "commercial fisheries," "cruise lines," "sewer systems," or "storm drains," it was some individual who threw the trash over the rail, into the street, down the toilet, or into a ditch. For this reason, public education and awareness must be fundamental to any mitigation strategy.

Agreement on this point has led to cooperation among groups that traditionally have found themselves on opposing sides of an issue. An example is a tripartite relationship formed in the mid-1980s among the Center for Marine Conservation, the Society for the Plastics Industry (a trade organization), and the National Marine Fisheries Service (O'Hara 1988). By focusing on a common objective—educating people to dispose of plastic products properly—the three groups were able to pool their talents and resources. The result was a major public awareness campaign featuring a series of high-quality public service announcements for the print media (produced by an advertising agency at no charge), brochures on marine debris relevant to constituencies of each group, a citizen's guide to marine debris (O'Hara, Atkins et al. 1987; O'Hara et al. 1994), a television public service announcement featuring Popeye (use of the character was donated by King Features, Inc.), a toll-free response number, and many other materials (Bruner 1990).

Another example was in Newport, Oregon, where local port officials, with a grant from the National Marine Fisheries Service, and local fishing industry leaders joined forces with Fran Recht, an energetic graduate student, in 1987 to organize a port reception facility for ship-generated garbage. Fishermen, who were encouraged to return their plastic wastes and old fishing gear to port, initially viewed the project with skepticism. However, the enthusiasm of the project coordinator, who solicited and implemented suggestions from fishermen, proved so successful that it became a model for other U.S. ports (Recht 1988). To extend support to other fishing communities, the fishing industry, supported by the National Marine Fisheries Service, sponsored the North Pacific Rim Fishermen's Conference on Marine Debris in October 1987 involving 60 participants from villages, towns, and cities in five North Pacific fishing nations (Alverson and June 1988).

In the spring of 1987 the national media followed the two-month odyssey of a New York City garbage barge. Prohibited from dumping garbage at sea, the barge sailed to ports as far away as South America in an unsuccessful attempt to find a landfill willing to accept its cargo. That summer, syringes and other medical wastes washed ashore in New Jersey and New York, prompting local officials to briefly close beaches to protect public health. More medical waste washed ashore in the northeastern United States in 1988. These events drew attention to what was portrayed as a crisis related to the disposal of solid waste.

Time and *Newsweek* both ran cover stories on these events, and articles appeared in *U.S. News and World Report*, *Smithsonian*, and hundreds of other national and local publications. This attention put those industries whose products were linked to marine debris in an unflattering public spotlight. Motivated by the dual forces of public image and an obligation "to do the right thing," many industry groups acted to demonstrate their concern. For example, Morton Salt, which packages salt for commercial fisheries in the Gulf of Mexico, converted from plastic to paper bags after it was brought to its attention that these bags were helping foul Gulf beaches. Other companies whose products were identified as components of marine debris began labeling their merchandise with messages urging proper disposal.

In some cases, public concern can lead to new marketing strategies that are far more effective in bringing about change than any laws, regulations, or other tools in a resource manager's arsenal. For example, Berkley, a major producer of monofilament fishing line, created a national program to recycle used line to enhance its reputation as a responsible industry leader. It provided recycling bins to retailers and paid for shipping used line that could be recycled into bicycle seats, tackle boxes, and other new items. Similarly, when the media published photographs of wildlife entangled in six-pack beverage rings (and while Congress was considering requirements for the use of degradable plastic), Illinois Tool Works, a large manufacturer of ring connectors, switched to photodegradable plastic for making six-pack yokes. Later, when photodegradation of plastics in the marine environment was questioned, the company introduced "tear tab" rings that break the loops when cans are removed and promoted efforts to recycle carrier yokes.

Legislative and Executive Leadership in Government

Not coincidentally, in the mid-1980s marine debris began to draw attention at the highest levels of government at the same time that public concern and media coverage surged. For politicians, marine debris offered an opportunity to demonstrate their commitment to environmental protection, capitalizing on an issue that enjoyed virtually unanimous support. During the 1988 presidential campaign, both candidates expressed concern for the issue, and President George Bush cited marine debris in his inaugural speech and in the State of the Union address. It is also no coincidence that most of the effort by U.S. agencies to address marine debris issues in the late 1980s was in direct response to actions, directives, and advice from Congress and the President.

Congressional influence—wielded through the appropriation of funds for specific programs, legislation establishing agency authorities and mandates, and other forms of advice and direction to the Executive Branch—was especially important. In April 1987, after a series of hearings on the issue (Committee on Merchant Marine and Fisheries 1986), 30 U.S. senators jointly wrote to President Ronald Reagan, citing the effects of marine debris on northern fur seals and other marine species and calling for formation of a high-level interagency task force on marine debris (O'Hara 1988). In so doing, the senators recognized that responsive measures would cut across the functions of many federal agencies and that addressing the problem would entail both high-level agency commitment and interagency coordination. The President promptly created such a body—the Interagency Marine Debris Task Force under the White House Domestic Policy Council—and charged it with developing a plan of action. Composed of high-level officials from 12 federal departments and agencies, the task force met several times over the next year.

In May 1988 the task force produced a report (Cottingham 1988, Interagency Task Force on Persistent Marine Debris 1988) recommending various research, public education, and mitigation actions to be taken jointly and separately by involved agencies. After completing its report, however, the task force was never reconvened, and no mechanism remained to coordinate agency work, monitor progress, follow up on new findings, or generally maintain agency interest and attention. By the mid-1990s related efforts in many federal agencies had faded, and little was done to redirect efforts in light of progress and new information.

Congressional attention was also directed toward Annex V of the International Convention for the Prevention of Pollution from Ships (see below). The annex, which calls for measures to regulate the disposal of ship-generated garbage, was ratified by the U.S. Senate in November 1987. Because of particularly large amounts of debris found on Texas beaches, the Senate also directed the President to seek an amendment to the annex to add the Gulf of Mexico to its list of "special areas" where more stringent discharge standards apply. Shortly after ratification, Congress passed the Marine Plastic Pollution Research and Control Act of 1987 (Public Law 100-220) to implement the requirements of the annex. This legislation exceeded Annex V provisions in two areas. First, Congress applied the discharge restrictions of Annex V to all navigable waters in the United States, including rivers and lakes, rather than just waters seaward of the baseline for the territorial sea. Second, it limited a provision in Annex V that permanently exempts government ships from compliance obligations; instead U.S. government vessels must comply within five years (see below).

The implementing law also mandated certain action by other federal agencies (Baur and Iudicello 1990). It directed the National Oceanic and Atmospheric Administration and the Environmental Protection Agency to prepare reports on the effects of plastic debris on the marine environment and on ways to reduce plastic pollution. It also directed interagency support for a public outreach program and the formation of "citizen pollution patrols" to help clean beaches, monitor marine debris trends, and report illegal discharges. As noted above, however, Congress failed to provide a mechanism for sustained leadership in carrying out tasks related to Annex V. In a recent National Research Council review of U.S. efforts to implement Annex V (Committee on Shipborne Wastes 1995), this oversight prompted a recommendation that Congress establish a permanent independent federal commission to oversee related interagency work. Congress, however, has shown little interest in acting on this recommendation.

Congress also addressed issues related to marine debris under other statutes, such as the Medical Waste Tracking Act of 1988, the U.S. Public Vessel Medical Waste Anti-Dumping Act of 1988, the Degradable Plastic Ring Carriers Act of 1988, and the Shore Protection Act of 1988 (Baur and Iudicello 1990). The first three of these acts called for actions to address problems that had been given high profiles in the media (i.e., medical wastes that had prompted beach closures in New York and New Jersey and the entanglement of wildlife in six-pack rings). The Shore Protection Act, which required a national program for monitoring coastal environmental quality, identified floatable debris as one of the pollutants to be monitored. As the initial surge of public attention passed, however, congressional attention to such specific actions diminished.

Although its various directives and mandates to federal agencies may reflect the breadth of Congress's concern, its appropriation of funds to implement necessary actions may be a better reflection of the depth of that concern. In this regard, between 1986 and 1995 Congress continued to provide annual appropriations of $650,000 to $750,000 to the National Marine Fisheries Service for its program on derelict fishing gear and other debris. However, this was the only regular source of funds earmarked by Congress for work on marine debris. Funding to carry out most mandates to other agencies was neither explicitly authorized nor appropriated.

As a result, many of the agencies assigned new responsibilities found themselves in a familiar position of having to do more with less. Most involved agencies had to stretch appropriations for related programs, use scarce discretionary funds, pool limited funding with other agencies and groups, or limit work to that which could be done by existing personnel with no capital expenditures. As most agency budgets decreased in the 1990s, even modest agency efforts declined. And in 1996, amid intense pressure to reduce federal spending, Congress eliminated funding for the National Marine Fisheries Service marine debris program, substantially limiting federal efforts to undertake relevant work.

Thus, although Congress and the President provided essential direction for initiating a broad response to marine debris, appropriations for agencies, inadequate interagency coordination, and a lack of high-level leadership hobbled efforts by most federal agencies to sustain a response.

International Agencies and Organizations

Marine debris enters the oceans from shorelines and ships of all coastal nations and may be carried by winds, storms, and ocean currents thousands of miles from its point of origin. As a result, no area, regardless of how remote or protected, is immune. The international nature of the challenge to control this pollution was recognized at the 1984 workshop, and the need for follow-up actions by international organizations and national governments around the world received immediate attention (Baur and Iudicello 1990).

The International Maritime Organization has lead responsibility for two key international treaties (Bean 1984, Marine Mammal Commission 1994): the 1973/1978 Convention for the Prevention of Pollution from Ships (usually referred to as the MARPOL Convention) and the 1972 Convention on the Prevention of Marine Pollution by Dumping of Wastes and Other Matter (commonly called the London Dumping Convention). Like most international conventions, both set forth basic provisions that signatory nations agree to adopt as part of their domestic legal authorities. For these two conventions, their provisions apply to all ships (foreign and domestic) operating in a signatory nation's jurisdiction (usually out to 200 nautical miles [370.4 km] from shore) and to all ships registered in a signatory nation, wherever they travel.

The London Dumping Convention prohibits ships from carrying land-generated garbage to sea for purposes of dumping. Concluded in 1972, this convention entered into force in 1975 after acceptance by the requisite number of countries. However, the part of the MARPOL Convention relevant to marine debris, Annex V, did not progress as quickly. The original MARPOL Convention addressed specific types of ship-generated pollution under five annexes, the last of which, Annex V, deals with garbage generated during routine ship operations. The principal features of Annex V are (1) discharge standards for the disposal of ship-generated garbage at sea, including a ban on all disposal of plastics (Table 16-3), (2) the designation of "special areas" in which more stringent discharge restrictions apply, and (3) requirements that ports in party nations have suitable, convenient port reception facilities to receive ship-generated garbage.

Although certain mandatory obligations of the MARPOL Convention entered into force in 1983, Annex V is an optional annex. As such, its provisions are binding only for those MARPOL parties that also choose to ratify Annex V separately. To enter into force, Annex V had to be ratified by MARPOL parties representing at least 50% of the world's commercial shipping tonnage. By the early 1980s nations representing less than 40% of the world's tonnage had ratified Annex V. The United States and several other major shipping nations were among those that had not yet done so.

With new analyses suggesting significant effects of marine debris on seals and other marine life that came to light in the 1984 workshop, some U.S. government agencies, particularly the U.S. Coast Guard, recognized the need to accelerate the Annex V implementation process. The Coast Guard serves as the lead agency representing the United States in the International Maritime Organization and its subsidiary bodies, including the Marine Environment Protection Committee (MEPC), which oversees the MARPOL Convention. And while the Coast Guard worked to speed up the U.S. ratification process, it also worked with the Marine Mammal Commission and the National Oceanic and Atmospheric Administration to encourage similar action by other nations.

In 1986 the three U.S. agencies jointly prepared papers for the MEPC describing new information on the biological impact of marine debris, the importance of implementing Annex V, and efforts in the United States to speed ratification (Marine Mammal Commission 1987). In response to a U.S. recommendation, MEPC also agreed to develop guidelines for implementing Annex V. With drafting help from the National Oceanic and Atmospheric Administration and the Marine Mammal Commission, the Coast Guard subsequently submitted proposed guidelines to MEPC for ship owners, government agencies, and port operators (Marine Mammal Commission 1988). The guidelines recommended advice on training and educating seafarers, on handling and processing garbage aboard ships, on provisioning ships to minimize potential garbage, advising ship operators and others about Annex V requirements, and developing port reception facilities. With some changes, they were adopted by MEPC in 1988.

These efforts encouraged several other countries to speed their ratification processes. The United States represents about 4% of the world's commercial ship tonnage, and when the United States filed its instrument of ratification for Annex V on 30 December 1987, the last criterion needed for entry into force was satisfied. The 39 nations that had ratified the annex then had one year to put their domestic programs into place. Thus, Annex V became a binding

Table 16-3. Summary of Garbage Discharge Limitations under the International Convention for the Prevention of Pollution from Ships (1973–1978) and the U.S. Act to Prevent Pollution from Ships, as Amended

	Discharge Prohibitions for All Vessels		Discharge Prohibitions for Offshore Platforms and Associated Vessels[c]
Type of Garbage	Outside Special Areas[a]	Inside Special Areas[b]	
Plastics, including synthetic ropes and fishing nets and plastic bags	Disposal prohibited	Disposal prohibited	Disposal prohibited
Dunnage, lining, and packing materials that float	Disposal prohibited less than 25 nautical miles (46.3 km) from nearest land	Disposal prohibited	Disposal prohibited
Paper, rags, glass, metal bottles, crockery, and similar refuse	Disposal prohibited less than 12 nautical miles (22.2 km) from nearest land	Disposal prohibited	Disposal prohibited
Paper, rags, glass, etc., comminuted or ground[d]	Disposal prohibited less than 3 nautical miles (5.5 km) from nearest land	Disposal prohibited	Disposal prohibited
Food waste not comminuted or ground	Disposal prohibited less than 12 nautical miles (22.2 km) from nearest land	Disposal prohibited less than 12 nautical miles (22.2 km) from nearest land	Disposal prohibited
Food waste comminuted or ground[d]	Disposal prohibited less than 3 nautical miles (5.5 km) from nearest land	Disposal prohibited less than 12 nautical miles (22.2 km) from nearest land[e]	Disposal prohibited less than 12 nautical miles (22.2 km) from nearest land
Mixed refuse types	Apply most stringent disposal restriction	Apply most stringent disposal restriction	Apply most stringent disposal restriction

[a]Under the Act to Prevent Pollution from Ships, discharge limitations in the United States apply within all navigable waters, including rivers, lakes, and other inland waters.

[b]Special Areas listed in Annex V are the Mediterranean, Baltic, Red, Black, and North Seas; the Persian Gulf/Gulf of Oman; the Wider Caribbean Region; and the Antarctic Ocean. However, at the end of 1995 only the North Sea, the Baltic Sea, and the Antarctic Ocean Special Areas were actually in effect because nations bordering the other listed areas had not yet affirmed to the International Maritime Organization that adequate port reception facilities were in place.

[c]Offshore platforms and associated vessels include all fixed or floating platforms engaged in exploitation or exploration of seabed mineral resources and all vessels alongside or within 500 m of such platforms.

[d]Comminuted or ground garbage must be able to pass through a 25-mm (1-inch) mesh screen.

[e]For the Special Area in the Wider Caribbean Region only, disposal is prohibited within 3 nautical miles (5.5 km) rather than 12 nautical miles (22.2 km) from the nearest land.

obligation for all its parties on 31 December 1988. Other nations have since signed Annex V and, as of May 1996, it had been ratified or otherwise accepted by 79 nations representing more than 82% of the world's commercial shipping tonnage.

Since 1988 several amendments have been adopted to refine Annex V, including some proposed by the United States. One amendment, prompted largely by the entanglement of seals in net fragments, eliminated an exemption allowing commercial fishermen to discard net debris generated while repairing fishing gear at sea. Another, prompted by the U.S. Senate directive referred to earlier, added the Wider Caribbean Region, including the Gulf of Mexico, to the list of Annex V special areas. A third amendment, offered by the Coast Guard based on its experience in implementing Annex V (see below), added requirements for vessels over certain sizes to post placards describing garbage discharge restrictions, to maintain garbage disposal record books, and to carry solid waste management plans.

Particularly important to Annex V are provisions requiring adequate port reception facilities. The importance of these provisions stems not only from the obvious need for alternative means of disposing of waste that cannot be discarded at sea, but also from a prerequisite in the annex for implementing listed special areas. That is, Annex V requires that nations bordering special areas notify the International Maritime Organization that such facilities are in place before they can enforce the more stringent special area standards. Nations bordering special areas have been slow to act. This prerequisite had been met for only two of the annex's eight listed areas by the end of 1996. For one other area, the Antarctic, this requirement was waived in view of restrictions under other treaties on the disposal of solid wastes on the Antarctic continent. All solid wastes generated by ships in the Southern Ocean must be brought out of the area. Thus, five of the eight listed special areas remain unimplemented until bordering nations can ensure that reception facilities are available.

Assuring that port reception facilities are widely available is a challenging task. In some listed special areas, such as the Caribbean, some bordering nations have ratified neither Annex V nor the MARPOL Convention. In addition, many small island states are reluctant to take on the obligation of accepting solid waste from ships because of limited space and poor terrain for landfills, a lack of other facilities to handle large amounts of trash, and frequent visits by large cruise ships that can generate large amounts of garbage. To help address these problems, international banks, such as the World Bank, the Inter-American Development Bank, and the Asian Development Bank, have offered support. For example, in the Caribbean area, the World Bank has funded two projects: one for $34 million to help plan and construct solid waste management infrastructure in six small island nations in the eastern Caribbean, and the other for $5.5 million to help national governments develop laws and compliance strategies needed to meet MARPOL requirements.

Another problem for port reception facilities arises from inconsistent user fees. Port charges to off-load garbage have been highly variable and sometimes excessive. When such fees are assessed only to vessels actually off-loading garbage, ships may avoid using the facilities to cut costs. This encourages illegal dumping at sea and overuse of facilities in other ports with limited capabilities. Although a few ports charge a mandatory handling fee to all ships entering them and others incorporate the costs into basic vessel dockage fees, such practices are not widespread. Identifying and resolving such implementation problems has been, and will continue to be, a slow process. For Annex V, however, the key to effective implementation will probably be the wide availability of convenient, fairly priced port reception facilities backed by visible enforcement.

Through interventions similar to those made with the International Maritime Organization, federal agencies also encouraged responsive actions by other international organizations. The Marine Mammal Commission and the National Oceanic and Atmospheric Administration, for example, encouraged the Intergovernmental Oceanographic Commission's Scientific Committee on Global Investigation of Pollution in the Marine Environment to adopt a manual on procedures for monitoring marine debris (Marine Mammal Commission 1993). The State Department, with assistance from the Marine Mammal Commission, also brought marine debris to the attention of the international Commission and Committee for the Conservation of Antarctic Marine Living Resources. In so doing, it helped encourage scientists in Antarctic Treaty nations to begin routine monitoring of marine debris and related impacts in the Antarctic and to seek listing of the Southern Ocean as a special area under Annex V.

The National Oceanic and Atmospheric Administration, in cooperation with the Intergovernmental Oceanographic Commission's regional Commission for the Caribbean (IOCARIBE), also supported a series of regional workshops on marine debris. Workshop participants successfully completed a regional marine debris action plan (Intergovernmental Oceanographic Commission 1994) approved by parties to the Caribbean Environment Program, a regional seas program organized under auspices of the United Nations Environment Programme.

A wide array of other international organizations and programs has mandates well suited for addressing specific research and management needs related to marine debris (Baur and Iudicello 1990). They offer an effective means for initiating parallel actions in many countries. When provided with good information substantiating a problem, most have been willing to use their authorities and expertise. However, a great deal of work and time is usually required to reach agreement, organize, and fine-tune initiatives. This, in turn, requires the interest, energy, and resources of motivated agencies in member governments. It also demands a long-term perspective (i.e., 10 to 20 years) that is difficult to sustain as people in key positions come and go, priorities change, and resources are stretched to meet competing demands. These are probably the greatest challenges with respect to engaging international authorities in efforts to reduce marine debris pollution.

National Programs in the United States

Although congressional laws and funding decisions provide guidance for federal agencies, other factors also play a role in shaping agency actions. Administrators and program managers recommend, fight for, and determine funding priorities within an agency. In doing so, they share a substantial part of the responsibility for what is, and what is not, supported. Entrenched perceptions of marine debris as a secondary litter problem have probably substantially impeded work by some agencies. In other agencies, this problem has not existed or it has been overcome, allowing effective programs to flourish.

Marine Entanglement Research Program

Under the Marine Mammal Protection Act, the Endangered Species Act, and other statutes, the National Marine Fisheries Service has lead responsibility for conserving many marine species affected by marine debris. Because of this charge, Congress provided the National Oceanic and Atmospheric Administration, as the Service's parent organization, $1 million in 1984 to develop and implement, in consultation with the Marine Mammal Commission, a research and management program on discarded fishing gear and other debris. As had occurred during planning for the

1984 workshop, Service leadership demonstrated little enthusiasm or commitment to the task, despite the congressional directive.

Early in 1985, nearly halfway through the fiscal year and without consulting the Marine Mammal Commission, the National Marine Fisheries Service committed a quarter of the funds earmarked by Congress for marine debris to cover unrelated agency expenses. The agency also had done little to identify work on marine debris that might be undertaken. The Commission immediately objected to the reallocation of funds and assumed the lead for preparing a program plan. After meeting with National Marine Fisheries Service staff members and others, it developed and provided the Service with a recommended plan for allocating the entire congressional appropriation. The plan identified specific tasks, such as developing a public information program, supporting beach cleanups, studying factors related to the entanglement of northern fur seals, assessing specific sources of fishing debris, supporting a full-time program manager to oversee related work, and covering expenses for the 1984 workshop (Marine Mammal Commission 1986).

Upon receiving the recommended plan, the Service proceeded to provide only $750,000 for its implementation, claiming that it was too late in the fiscal year to restore full funding. After further objections from the Commission, however, the agency increased funding for the 1985 program to $900,000. No new funding was requested by the Service to carry the program forward in 1986. In light of these actions and anxious to see work continued, Congress provided $750,000 to the Service for work in 1986. Funding for the program in 1987 and 1988 was also omitted from Service budget requests but provided by Congress. Almost entirely through the dedicated efforts of the program manager assigned to oversee expenditure of the congressional appropriations, the Service forged a constructive program, the Marine Entanglement Research Program, designed to address a broad range of related research and management tasks.

From this rocky beginning, the program became a cornerstone of the federal government response to marine debris pollution. Over the next decade, it was the only federal program dedicated exclusively to work on the full range of sources and impacts of marine debris. Building on the initial program plan developed by the Commission, the program emphasized several major themes: (1) improving information on the nature, extent, and effects of marine debris; (2) enhancing public awareness of the impacts of marine debris to change the attitudes and behavior of individuals regarding the disposal of garbage; (3) encouraging actions that would offer fishermen and other seafarers convenient, practical alternatives to improper disposal of ship-generated garbage at sea; and (4) encouraging other agencies and groups to use their authorities and expertise to address aspects of the marine debris issue.

Because of the multifaceted nature of the marine debris problem, the fourth point is particularly important. The program sought to involve other federal and state agencies, industry groups, the public, academic institutions, and international organizations in cooperative research, education, and mitigation projects. To do this, several techniques were used. Most program funds were used to support projects that required matching funds or "in kind" support (e.g., salaries or use of equipment) from cooperating groups. This effectively encouraged other agencies and international organizations to start projects that they otherwise would have been reluctant or unable to undertake, and it also allowed the program to accomplish far more than would otherwise have been possible.

Examples of projects supported in this way were marine debris monitoring surveys (Johnson and Merrell 1988, Cole et al. 1992, Ribic et al. 1992), studies of entanglement and ingestion rates among seals (DeLong et al. 1988, Stewart and Yochem 1990) and sea turtles (Lutz and Alfaro-Schulman 1987), work to disentangle Hawaiian monk seals and destroy entangling debris on their breeding beaches (Henderson 1990), demonstration of port recycling projects (Recht 1988), printing and distribution of placards and brochures, organization and promotion of volunteer beach cleanups (Hodge and Glen 1993), organizing and hosting periodic international workshops to review and analyze efforts worldwide to address marine debris pollution (Shomura and Yoshida 1985, Wolfe 1987, Shomura and Godfrey 1990, Coe and Rogers 1996), conducting a detailed review of U.S. efforts to implement Annex V (Committee on Shipborne Wastes 1995), development of international guidelines for port facilities receiving ship-generated garbage, and convening and organizing meetings to facilitate implementation of a Caribbean special area under Annex V. These projects helped address many of the congressional mandates assigned not only to the National Oceanic and Atmospheric Administration, but also to other federal agencies.

Periodic public and interagency meetings were also held to help broaden support for needed activities. Late in the 1980s the program manager began a series of informal meetings open to representatives of concerned agencies, congressional staff, industry leaders, and environmental groups. The meetings provided an opportunity to review ongoing projects, discuss priorities, and formulate cooperative projects. Unfortunately, without a formal charter, mandate, or means of support, participation in the meetings could not be sustained. The program manager also convened an ad hoc interagency advisory committee to help identify program funding priorities. Meetings were held early in the annual budget cycle and involved staff members from the National Marine Fisheries Service, the Marine Mammal Commission, the Coast Guard, the National Sea Grant College Program, and other agencies.

For the first few years of the program, Congress provided funds even though none were requested by the Administration. Then, after the report of the Interagency Task Force on Persistent Marine Debris in 1988, a specific line item for the program was included in the Administration's annual budget requests, and Congress continued to appropriate $750,000 per year to carry the program forward. As noted above, however, in 1995 when public and media attention to the issue had subsided, Congress denied the Administration's funding request for the program. The National Oceanic and Atmospheric Administration made no effort to reprogram funds to support core tasks, such as public education and beach cleanups, and it immediately deleted a request for funds from its proposed 1997 budget. Because of the fundamental relationship between marine debris pollution and the agency's mission as steward for living marine resources, the Marine Mammal Commission recommended that the National Marine Fisheries Service reprogram and continue to request funds to maintain a minimal marine debris program. However, the agency neither requested nor provided any further funding in 1996 or 1997 and the program was terminated. This ended the Service's leadership role in the issue and, since then, no other agency has stepped forward to fill that void.

Controlling Ship-Generated Garbage Discharges

The Coast Guard, by virtue of its role in enforcing marine environmental protection laws, has been one of the most active and important federal agencies in addressing marine debris (Committee on Shipborne Wastes 1995). It worked closely with Congress to draft domestic implementing legislation (i.e., the Marine Plastic Pollution Research and Control Act of 1987), helped develop and refine related regulatory and enforcement measures, and demonstrated a high level of commitment. The Coast Guard thus became established as an international leader in the implementation of Annex V.

When the U.S. implementing legislation for Annex V was adopted late in 1987, the Coast Guard set to work developing domestic regulations to give effect to the new requirements. Although final rules were available by the end of 1990, no additional money had been authorized to implement Annex V. Because of its existing responsibilities for search and rescue, drug interdiction, immigration control, and other activities, the Coast Guard was unable to implement the new regulations. This inability was the subject of congressional oversight hearings in the fall of 1992, after which Congress gave the Coast Guard additional money, enabling it to increase attention and resources on implementing Annex V.

Early in 1993 the Coast Guard took several highly publicized enforcement actions (e.g., the case cited earlier of dumping by a cruise ship) signaling its intention to vigorously enforce the new garbage discharge regulations. It also enlisted help from the Department of Agriculture's Animal and Plant Health Inspection Service, whose inspectors routinely board vessels arriving from foreign ports to check for exotic disease, pests, and other potentially dangerous plants and animals in ship cargo and garbage. Under a cooperative agreement, inspectors would also check vessels for violations of Annex V (e.g., an absence of plastic garbage despite a lengthy voyage) and turn evidence of infractions over to the Coast Guard for prosecution.

Although these actions helped the Coast Guard detect and prosecute violations, success in this regard still hinged on firsthand accounts or other direct evidence of illegal discharges, which were rarely available. The need for other means of detecting violations, as well as for promoting compliance, was apparent. Recognizing these needs, the Coast Guard's interim rules had included requirements that vessels above certain sizes post placards on discharge limits and carry solid waste management plans listing procedures and crew responsibilities for handling garbage. They also called for large ships to maintain garbage discharge record books that boarding enforcement officers could check and compare against garbage stowed aboard ship to help verify compliance. The proposed rules, however, were not approved by the Office of Management and Budget, which was then operating under a directive to limit new regulations. After taking steps to add these provisions to Annex V (see above) and also attempting to clarify authority for these actions under domestic law, the Coast Guard was able to include them in its regulations.

Another difficulty has been bringing enforcement actions against foreign vessels. The MARPOL Convention relies on a "flag-state" enforcement system under which parties are to refer violations involving foreign vessels to the government of the country in which the ship is registered. Follow-up by the flag-state nations, however, was very poor. As of 1992 most referrals were never acknowledged and fewer than 2% resulted in fines (Committee on Shipborne Wastes 1995). Because of this deficiency, as well as the advantages of the record-keeping requirements, the Coast Guard brought the problem to the attention of the International Maritime Organization's Marine Environment Protection Committee. The committee subsequently took steps to improve the tracking of flag-state responses to referrals and added a record-keeping requirement to Annex V. After advising the committee of its intention to institute a new port-nation enforcement policy for Annex V in U.S. waters, the Coast Guard also began taking direct enforcement action against foreign ships suspected of having violated Annex V restrictions within the U.S. 200-mile (370.4-km) exclusive economic zone.

As the Coast Guard gained experience in implementing the annex, it became apparent that certain authorities under the U.S. implementing legislation needed to be clarified. In addition to the need for stronger mandates for placards, solid waste management plans, and garbage record books, the Coast Guard identified a need for stronger directives related to establishing an interagency coordinating group, implementing public outreach programs, imposing civil penalties, and maintaining a toll-free hotline for violation reports. The Coast Guard worked closely with Congress beginning in the early 1990s to develop legislation on these matters; to date, however, most have not been adopted.

Among the many other notable actions by the Coast Guard to help implement Annex V have been support for public outreach programs (both jointly with the Marine Entanglement Research Program and through its own programs, such as the Coast Guard Auxiliary), convening informal interagency coordination meetings on matters relating to Annex V, advising ship and port operators on how to comply with Annex V, helping Caribbean nations develop programs related to Annex V and other MARPOL annexes, and leading U.S. efforts through the International Maritime Organization to spur implementation of Annex V internationally.

Navy Shipboard Solid Waste Program

As noted above, Annex V explicitly exempts government ships from its garbage discharge standards. However, when Congress passed U.S. implementing legislation, it limited the exemption for U.S. government ships to five years from the date of the law's enactment. It also required that federal agencies report to Congress on efforts to bring fleets into compliance or, if compliance was not possible, that they advise Congress as to the reason and propose an alternative schedule for complying. Most federal agencies brought their ships into compliance by the end of the exemption period in 1994. However, for the U.S. Navy, the challenge was particularly difficult because of unique space constraints on military ships, the need for extended voyages away from port, and the sheer number of ships.

Recognizing these difficulties, the Navy made a high-level commitment to work toward compliance (Alig et al. 1990). First, the Navy issued a fleet-wide order requiring its surface ships to retain plastic wastes for land-based disposal except on the longest voyages when storage space, fire, and health concerns precluded this. Second, it began selectively provisioning ships to minimize plastic packaging and to reduce the amount of nonreusable items brought on board. The Navy estimated that by these means it had reduced plastic waste discharges by 70%. Finally, it supported an intensive research and development program to design shipboard solid waste processing equipment. At a cost of $22.5 million, Navy engineers developed designs for an innovative waste processor for melting shipboard plastic wastes into sanitary, storable blocks. They also developed improved designs for shipboard pulpers to macerate paper and food waste and for shredders to grind glass and metal into small shards.

With these measures, the Navy determined that it would meet all Annex V discharge standards except for those in special areas where only food waste could be discharged. The Navy advised Congress of its efforts in 1993 and suggested that an amendment to Annex V be sought to allow the discharge of pulped and shredded wastes in special areas. Later that year, after considering the Navy's report, Congress rejected the Navy's recommended amendment, directed the Navy to install the new plastic processors aboard its ships, extended the Navy's compliance deadline, and directed that it submit a report in 1996 on steps needed to achieve compliance by the new dates or, if not feasible, to recommend an alternative approach. For Navy surface ships, Congress directed that plastic processors be installed by 1998 to meet the Annex V prohibition on plastic discharges and that compliance with all other discharge standards, including those for special areas, be met by 2000. For submarines, full compliance was to be achieved by 2008.

Projecting a need to retrofit about 200 ships with plastic processors, the cost estimates for purchasing and installing the new equipment was $300 million. In its draft 1996 report to Congress, the cost for partial compliance (i.e., allowing the discharge of pulped and shredded waste in special areas) was estimated at an additional $350 million, and full compliance, which would require installing incinerators, would cost more than one billion dollars (Department of the Navy 1996). The vast majority of these costs involve reconfiguring space to retrofit new equipment, relocating existing equipment, and providing waste storage. Presumably, they are far higher than costs for other ships because of unique space and siting needs for military equipment, and significantly higher than costs that would be incurred if equipment and space were incorporated into ship designs before they were built.

The Navy's review and development of technology for shipboard waste processing equipment represent the most thorough examination of shipboard processing alternatives that exists. As the new technology is transferred to other fleets, the value of the Navy's efforts should increase many times over. Although the Navy's cost estimates for retrofitting its own equipment are undoubtedly much higher than should the case for nonmilitary ships, they underscore the economic importance of factoring the required waste-processing equipment and other needs, including storage space, into the design of new ships.

Pollution Control and Solid Waste Management Programs

Under the Clean Water Act; the Marine Protection, Research, and Sanctuaries Act; and many other statutes, the Environmental Protection Agency is responsible for managing solid waste disposal and for controlling both point- and nonpoint-source pollution generally. Although the agency's overall mission suggests that it should have a major role in addressing marine debris pollution, none of the acts under which it operates directs it to develop a strategy for marine debris. Before the mid-1990s the agency had made little effort to do so on its own initiative. For example, it had not used its authority to reduce solid wastes discharged from storm drains. Nor had the agency integrated port reception facilities for garbage into its land-based solid waste disposal and recycling programs.

For the most part, the Environmental Protection Agency focused on specific congressional directives. For example, it completed studies mandated by the Marine Plastic Pollution Research and Control Act on methods to manage plastic wastes (Environmental Protection Agency 1990) and on plastics in the New York Bight (Environmental Protection Agency 1989). Pursuant to the Medical Waste Tracking Act of 1988, it also developed regulations to track the disposal of medical wastes. Perhaps its most noteworthy efforts, however, have been undertaken at the initiative of individual staff members. For example, in cooperation with the Society for the Plastics Industry, the agency's Office of Water completed a comprehensive report on steps to prevent discharges of plastic pellets into aquatic ecosystems (Environmental Protection Agency 1992b), and it guided the development of a national marine debris monitoring plan (Escardo-Boomsma et al. 1996). Similarly, staff members in the agency's Gulf of Mexico regional office, in cooperation with coastal states, helped organize regional beach cleanups and developed a public outreach program targeting recreational boaters.

Although these actions met and exceeded congressional directives, they do not reflect assumption of a strong federal leadership role. Because of the agency's mission and the leadership vacuum created after the Federal Task Force on Persistent Marine Debris was terminated in 1988, the Marine Mammal Commission and the Coast Guard asked the Environmental Protection Agency to exercise a more prominent role in coordinating federal marine debris activities. Although slow to respond, the agency convened an interagency meeting in June 1996 to discuss formation of a federal interagency marine debris coordinating committee. However, during the following year, the agency announced no plans to reconvene the group. If this group had been formally established and maintained, the agency would have made a significant contribution toward addressing a fundamental weakness in the federal response to marine debris.

Scientific Research

Scientists have played a pivotal role by alerting resource managers to marine debris pollution. Their findings, first compiled in the 1984 Workshop on the Fate and Impact of Marine Debris (Shomura and Yoshida 1985), were followed by proceedings from a special session on marine debris at the Sixth International Ocean Disposal Symposium in 1986 (Wolfe 1987). Together, papers and reports from these two meetings provided compelling, if circumstantial, evidence of a significant problem. In so doing, they also inspired an era of intensive research on marine debris that would provide a strong foundation for initiating a management response.

Initially, this new wave of research refined data on the sources, types, amounts, and distribution of marine debris and the nature and extent of its impact on marine biota. It soon expanded to include studies of economic impacts and technological solutions. Although a great deal of new information has been obtained, stubborn obstacles have prevented the resolution of fundamental uncertainties. In only a few cases has research provided conclusive results.

For example, after the 1984 workshop, a spate of beach surveys was undertaken around the world to assess the composition of marine debris (Shomura and Godfrey 1990). A major objective was to identify items and sources so that managers could target mitigation efforts more effectively. Some items could be easily linked to specific industries. These included trawl net fragments in Alaska (Merrell 1985, Johnson and Merrell 1988), plastic pellets (Cole et al. 1990, Trulli et al. 1990), and hard hats, 55-gallon (26.4-liter) drums, and white plastic sheeting used on offshore oil drilling platforms in the Gulf of Mexico (O'Hara, Maraniss et al. 1987).

In these cases, the survey findings helped spur corrective measures. As noted above, efforts were made in North Pacific fishing communities to collect discarded trawl net fragments that were entangling northern fur seals (Alverson and June 1988), and measures were taken to reduce the loss of plastic pellets from manufacturing plants and transshipment facilities (Environmental Protection Agency 1992b).

To reduce debris generated by offshore oil workers, mandatory education programs were instituted to make workers aware of marine debris and related discharge restrictions (Minerals Management Service 1986). Also, the oil industry took steps to reduce the amount of packaging by switching to bulk sizes (Minerals Management Service 1992).

Occasionally it has been possible to identify debris sources by correlating the seasonal appearance of certain items with local activities. For example, the occurrence of onion bags, egg cartons, salt bags, rubber gloves, and certain other items has been correlated with seasonal pulses in coastal shrimp fishing off southern Texas (Miller et al. 1995), prompting directed education and enforcement efforts. In a few cases, sources have been identified from corporate logos or vessel names printed on discarded glasses, shampoo bottles, balloons, and other items. Bar codes and labels also have been used to identify manufacturers and approximate the age of some items (Dixon and Dixon 1983).

Unfortunately, the sources of most items have been untraceable. A soda bottle, six-pack ring, plastic bag, or length of rope found in a debris survey could have come from a fishing vessel, a recreational boat, a careless coastal resident, or even an inland trash truck whose wind-blown garbage landed in a roadside ditch from which it was carried by runoff down a river to the sea.

Another major objective of surveys has been to detect trends in the occurrence of certain items over time, thus making it possible to evaluate the effectiveness of management actions (Ribic et al. 1996). Again, only limited success has been achieved. Daily surveys by the National Park Service at Padre Island, Texas, indicated a decreased occurrence of debris from offshore oil platforms and vessels during the early 1990s, but trash from shrimp trawlers has not decreased (J. Miller, National Park Service, Padre Island National Seashore, pers. comm.). The implication is that oil workers have responded positively to management efforts, but local shrimp fishermen have not. Beach surveys in Alaska also suggest that trawl net debris has decreased as a result of industry outreach efforts and the entry into force of Annex V (Johnson 1990).

In most cases, however, statistically valid evidence of trends has been difficult to obtain. Enormous, unpredictable fluctuations occur in debris at sampling sites because of such things as changes in storm, wind, and current conditions; inconsistencies in the way people dispose of trash; redeposit and exposure of buried debris; and differences in beach orientation, size, slope, and exposure. In addition, researchers seldom use standardized survey methods, and few studies have lasted longer than a year. For logistic and economic reasons, beach studies have almost always involved monthly or less-frequent sampling. At-sea surveys suffer from similar deficiencies and are further limited by the difficulty of sighting and collecting debris at sea and the high cost of shiptime. The cost factor has meant that most at-sea sampling has had to be from "platforms of opportunity" whose schedules and routes are not ideal for debris surveys. All of these factors confound the interpretation of survey data and make comparison among surveys difficult or impossible.

Several efforts have been made to overcome such problems. To standardize survey methods, the National Oceanic and Atmospheric Administration developed a marine debris survey manual describing procedures for shipboard sighting surveys of large floating debris, trawl surveys for small debris, beach surveys for both large and small debris, and surveys for debris on the seafloor (Ribic et al. 1992). Interagency support was provided for quarterly surveys of marine debris over a five-year period at selected national seashores in the United States (Cole et al. 1992). The results of these and other long-term surveys were used to evaluate different survey sampling schemes (Ribic and Ganio 1996) and the development of a national marine debris monitoring program for the United States (Escardo-Boomsma et al. 1996). Initial sampling efforts under this program were launched in April 1996.

Another area of intense study since the 1984 workshop has been biological impact assessment. A large number of studies were undertaken throughout the world to identify debris items and the geographic areas where biological interactions occur, and to resolve uncertainties about the impacts of marine debris on individual species. As indicated above, these studies have consistently found that the vast majority of lethal interactions involve derelict fishing gear (particularly netting and monofilament line), strapping bands, and plastic bags (Laist 1996a). Limited success has been achieved, however, in quantifying the impacts on individual species.

Like Fowler's work on northern fur seals, most entanglement and ingestion studies have been based on observations of animals that congregate on shore to rest, breed, molt, nest, etc., or animals that washed ashore dead. However, live entangled animals seen on shore probably include only those that were caught in relatively light material or that became entangled close enough to shore to allow them to swim or fly back to land. It has been almost impossible to determine the extent to which entangling line or ingested debris has contributed to the death of a stranded animal. As a result, incidents observed on land represent an unknown proportion of the total.

A proper assessment of total mortality requires information on rates of entanglement at sea and a better understanding of the proportion of entanglements that leads to mortality. Because animals may encounter marine debris and die anywhere within their range, the chances are extremely small of finding them before they are scavenged, decompose, or sink. Until ways are found to estimate the rates at which animals interact with marine debris and die at sea, uncertainty about the impacts of such mortality will continue to blunt the sense of urgency among managers.

Derelict fishing gear is the one type of marine debris that should be amenable to studies of at-sea mortality. Major fishing areas where gear is lost are well known, and it should be possible to locate lost nets and traps to investigate their catch of fish, shellfish, and other species. Unfortunately, fishery managers appear to have dismissed such impacts as either unavoidable or insignificant. Their reasoning rests on unsupported or poorly examined assumptions that gear loss is inevitable and that derelict gear quickly loses its ability to catch marine life because of degradation, collapse, burial, or other factors (Marine Mammal Commission 1996). Of the few studies on ghost fishing, most have involved derelict fish and crab traps and the development of degradable time-release escape panels for traps. However, little has been done to assess the effectiveness of escape panels or mortality in disabled traps over the long term, and almost no work has been done to assess ghost fishing by lost gillnets (Laist 1996b). Here, the principal research obstacles have been inadequate funding and a lack of resolve on the part of fishery agencies, rather than fundamental sampling difficulties.

Attempts have been made to measure the direct costs of marine debris (e.g., cleaning beaches, repairing debris-damaged vessels and fishing gear, and operating shipboard and port waste reception systems) as well as the indirect costs (e.g., lost sailing time, lost tourist revenues, esthetic damage, and lost wildlife enjoyment). Although direct costs are relatively easy to measure, indirect costs have been subject to considerable debate. Determining indirect costs, which involves measuring the benefits lost to society as a result of pollution, has been an elusive problem for economists under much less complex conditions than those posed by marine debris (Dorfman and Dorfman 1993). On the other hand, recent work on the value of clean beaches, which involves estimating the benefits of less pollution, suggests that the public's willingness to pay to ensure litter-free beaches is quite high (Smith et al. 1996).

Considerable attention has been given to the development of technology. As noted above, the U.S. Navy developed an innovative design for shipboard processing of plastic wastes and reviewed evolving technologies, such as plasma-arc thermal destruction and supercritical water oxidation, to address other waste disposal needs (Department of the Navy 1996). Some manufacturers have also altered packaging and product designs or begun to use degradable plastic to address concerns related to marine debris. Although it has received little attention from fisheries managers, new fishing gear may offer opportunities to reduce the impacts of derelict gear through the use of degradable float releases for gillnets, greater use of degradable netting and line, and new technology to help relocate lost gear and reduce the likelihood of losing gear in the first place (Laist 1996b).

Although the tasks confronting scientists studying marine debris are complex and challenging, the role of scientists and the importance of their data are clear. Defensible scientific analyses were essential for recognizing marine debris as a significant marine pollutant, and they remain a fundamental need to guide and justify future control measures. By the same token, improvements in technology have helped to address some problems and could make important future contributions if requisite attention and resources are made available.

Conclusions

The responses to marine debris pollution illustrate many important principles inherent to the management of natural resources. First, virtually all efforts to mitigate environmental problems involve a constant interplay between scientists, resource managers, conservationists, the public, and industry. Second, fundamental changes often hinge on the dedication of a few individuals willing to act on their convictions. Third, despite inherent constraints imposed by annual budget cycles and periodic staff turnover, the management of natural resources requires persistence and a long-term perspective best measured in terms of decades rather than years and in programs rather than projects. Fourth, problems must not be ignored simply because they appear enormous or even insurmountable; rather, they should be broken into manageable tasks that can provide a basis for building a broader effort. And fifth, management actions should begin with a clear statement of the problem supported by thorough analysis of available information, usually by scientists. This should define as accurately as possible not only the nature and scope of the problem, but just as important, the uncertainties that have not or cannot be resolved.

Managers must be prepared to take appropriate action based both on what is known and what is not known. Too often, decision makers are willing to act only on what is known and can be proven. In the marine environment, knowing or proving anything with certainty is the exception rather than a reasonable expectation. And although a strong, fact-based rationale is needed to justify any management action, ignoring a suspected or suggested problem because it cannot be immediately documented or precisely measured can lead to disastrous consequences for the resources. Thus, good management, like good science, must proceed not only on the basis of what the data prove, but also on the basis of what they imply.

At almost every step, efforts to address marine debris have met extraordinary challenges. Fowler's initial conclusions in the early 1980s that marine debris was a significant conservation threat could only have been reached with ingenious, deductive analysis requiring a willingness to consider not only what could be documented, but what was implied. Also, it was probably possible only because, at that time, the northern fur seal was one of the most thoroughly studied marine mammal species in the world. However, as intellectually compelling as Fowler's analysis may have been, direct evidence of population-level impacts from marine debris was, and remains, scant, leaving ample room for skepticism and scientific challenge.

The issue easily could have been buried right there. In fact, it would have been if matters had been left in the hands of National Marine Fisheries Service leadership. It was clear that marine debris came from innumerable sources and that its control would be a daunting task beyond the scope of the Service's management authority. The Service used uncertainty about the role of marine debris in the decline of fur seals as grounds for inaction. Fortunately, others found the evidence sufficiently convincing to demand a thorough assessment of the problem. Through persistent pressure from a few Service scientists, the Marine Mammal Commission, and nongovernmental groups, the National Marine Fisheries Service finally agreed to convene the 1984 workshop. The data presented on the amounts of fishing gear in use and being lost, the amounts of debris observed on beaches and in the open ocean, and the impacts on many marine species indicated a problem of global scale that could not be ignored.

Since 1984 research has been done on affected species throughout the world. Efforts to obtain the kinds of evidence needed for assessing the population-level impacts of and trends in marine debris have been frustrating, and definitive results remain elusive. Scientists studying biological effects have found plenty of evidence that debris is harmful to individuals of many species. Nevertheless, they have been unable to establish firmly when, where, and how often animals at sea are affected. Similarly, scientists monitoring the amounts of marine debris in the ocean have had limited success in determining the relative importance of different sources or in detecting even broad trends in occurrence. The tremendous variability in human waste disposal patterns, currents, winds, and other factors makes statistically valid data collection and analysis exceedingly difficult.

As formidable as the research challenges have proven to be, those facing managers have been even greater. In part, this is because of the circumstantial nature of evidence documenting biological impacts and a reluctance to act on less than conclusive proof of a problem. In addition, because virtually everyone in coastal and ocean areas is a potential polluter, officials at all levels of government, local to international, as well as people in industry and private organizations, have legitimate and important roles to play. As a result, there has been a tendency to view marine debris as someone else's problem and to conclude that the allocation of limited resources from one's own agency or group to help solve it would be ineffective or unproductive.

The corollary, however, is that the management of marine debris is a composite of independent decisions about what each relevant agency or group can and should do to address the problem. When constructive actions have been taken, at least three key factors have figured prominently in the decision making: (1) a judgment as to the importance of the problem, (2) ethical responsibility, and (3) public pressure. As indicated above, the first factor involves a willingness to act on what the best available information suggests, but does not necessarily prove. The second factor is important because most people feel an obligation to join in mitigation efforts. And this point underpins the third factor—public pressure. The concern and activism of individual citizens, often but not always expressed through a nongovernmental organization, have been highly effective in motivating policy makers, particularly those most sensitive to public image, such as politicians who depend on the public for support and corporate executives whose businesses depend on the public's perception and consumption of goods or services.

In light of these factors, some agencies and groups in the United States, most notably the Center for Marine Conservation, the Marine Mammal Commission, the Coast Guard, the Navy, and certain industries, have responded quickly and with sustained vigor through high-level leadership and commitment. Agencies such as the Coast Guard and the Navy committed substantial funding and personnel to address the issue, and other groups, such as the Marine Mammal Commission and Center for Marine Conservation accomplished much with more limited resources.

In other agencies and groups, such as the U.S. Congress, the National Oceanic and Atmospheric Administration, the Environmental Protection Agency, and the components of the commercial fishing industry, leadership has been inconsistent. For example, although the Marine Entanglement Research Program in the National Oceanic and Atmospheric Administration became a major force in facilitating needed work, domestically and internationally, before it was ended abruptly; fisheries managers have done little to address problems related to lost or discarded gear. Some individual fisheries have made strong efforts to reduce marine debris, but others, such as the shrimp fishery in Texas, have done little. Although the U.S. Congress has provided clear mandates and direction, it has been reluctant to provide sustained funding for core programs and has neglected the need for long-term interagency coordination and leadership.

In virtually all cases in which earnest efforts to address marine debris pollution have been made, however, decisions to act have hinged on the commitment of a few dedicated individuals who were willing to act on good sense rather than await indisputable scientific proof and who were unwilling to be deterred by seemingly impossible challenges.

Literature Cited

Alig, C. S., L. Koss, T. Scarano, and F. Chitty. 1990. Control of plastic wastes aboard naval ships at sea. Pages 879–894 *in* R. S. Shomura and M. L. Godfrey (eds.), Proceedings of the Second International Conference on Marine Debris. 2–7 April 1989, Honolulu, HI. Vol. 2. U.S. Department of Commerce, NOAA Technical Memorandum NMFS-SWFSC-154.

Alverson, D. L., and J. A. June (eds.). 1988. Proceedings of the North Pacific Rim Fishermen's Conference on Marine Debris. 13–16 October 1987, Kailua-Kona, HI. Natural Resources Consultants, Seattle, WA. 460 pp.

Balazs, G. H. 1985. Impact of ocean debris on marine turtles: Entanglement and ingestion. Pages 387–429 *in* R. S. Shomura and H. O. Yoshida (eds.), Proceedings of the Workshop on the Fate and Impact of Marine Debris. 26–29 November 1984, Honolulu, HI. U.S. Department of Commerce, NOAA Technical Memorandum NMFS-SWFC-54.

Baur, D. C., and S. Iudicello. 1990. Stemming the tide of marine debris pollution: Putting domestic and international control authorities to work. Ecology Law Quarterly 17:71–142.

Bean, M. J. 1984. United States and international authorities applicable to entanglement of marine mammals and other organisms in lost and discarded fishing gear and other debris. A report to the Marine Mammal Commission, Washington, DC. 56 pp.

Beck, C. A., and N. B. Barros. 1991. The impact of debris on the Florida manatee. Marine Pollution Bulletin 22:508–510.

Bengtson, J. L., C. W. Fowler, H. Kajimura, R. L. Merrick, K. Yoshida, and S. Nomura. 1988. Fur seal entanglement studies: Juvenile males and newly weaned pups, St. Paul Island, Alaska. Pages 34–57 *in* P. Kozlof and H. Kajimura (eds.), Fur Seal Investigations. U.S. Department of Commerce, NOAA Technical Memorandum NMFS F/NWC-146.

Bjorndal, K. A., and A. B. Bolton. 1995. Effects of marine debris on sea turtles. Pages 29–30 *in* Poster Abstracts and Manuscripts, Third International Conference on Marine Debris. 8–13 May 1994, Miami, FL. U.S. Department of Commerce, NOAA Technical Memorandum NMFS-AFSC-51.

Bjorndal, K. A., A. B. Bolton, and C. J. Lagueux. 1994. Ingestion of marine debris by juvenile sea turtles in coastal Florida habitats. Marine Pollution Bulletin 28:154–158.

Bonner, W. N., and T. S. McCann. 1982. Neck collars on fur seals, *Arctocephalus gazella,* at South Georgia. British Antarctic Survey Bulletin 57:73–77.

Bruner, R. G. 1990. The plastics industry and marine debris: Solutions through education. Pages 1077–1089 *in* R. S. Shomura and M. L. Godfrey (eds.), Proceedings of the Second International Conference on Marine Debris. 2–7 April 1989, Honolulu, HI. Vol. 2. U.S. Department of Commerce, NOAA Technical Memorandum NMFS-SWFSC-154.

Carpenter, E. J., and K. L. Smith Jr. 1972. Plastics on the Sargasso Sea surface. Science 175:1240–1241.

Carr, A. 1987. Impact of nondegradable marine debris on the ecology and survival outlook of sea turtles. Marine Pollution Bulletin 18:352–356.

Center for Marine Conservation. 1997. 1996 Coastal Cleanup Results. Center for Marine Conservation, Washington, DC. 104 pp.

Coe, J. M., and D. R. Rogers (eds.). 1996. Marine Debris: Sources, Impacts, and Solutions. Springer-Verlag, New York, NY. 432 pp.

Cole, C. A., J. P. Kumer, D. A. Manski, and D. V. Richards. 1990. Annual Report of National Park Marine Debris Monitoring Program, 1989 Marine Debris Surveys. National Park Service Technical Report NPS/NRWV/NRTR-90/04. Natural Resources Publication Office, Denver, CO. 31 pp.

Cole, C. A., W. P. Gregg, D. V. Richards, and D. A. Manski. 1992. Annual Report of National Park Marine Debris Monitoring Program, 1991 Marine Debris Surveys with summary of data from 1988 to 1991. National Park Service Technical Report NPS/NRWV/NRTR-92/10. Natural Resources Publication Office, Denver, CO. 56 pp.

Committee on Merchant Marine and Fisheries. 1986. Plastic pollution in the marine environment. Hearing before the Subcommittee on Coast Guard and Navigation, 12 August 1986, House of Representatives. Serial No. 99-47. Government Printing Office, Washington, DC. 210 pp.

Committee on Shipborne Wastes. 1995. Clean Ships, Clean Ports, Clean Oceans: Controlling Garbage and Plastic Wastes at Sea. Marine Board, National Research Council. National Academy Press, Washington, DC. 355 pp.

Cottingham, D. 1988. Persistent Marine Debris: Challenge and Response: The Federal Perspective. National Oceanic and Atmospheric Administration, Office of the Chief Scientist, Washington, D.C. 41 pp.

Croxall, J. P., S. Rodwell, and I. L. Boyd. 1990. Entanglement in man-made debris of Antarctic fur seals at Bird Island, South Georgia. Marine Mammal Science 6:221–233.

Debenham P., and L. K. Younger. 1991. Cleaning North America's Beaches: 1990 Beach Cleanup Results. Center for Marine Conservation, Washington, DC. 291 pp.

DeLong, R. L., P. Dawson, and P. J. Gearin. 1988. Incidence and impact of entanglement in netting debris on northern fur seal pups and adult females, St. Paul Island, Alaska. Pages 58–68 *in* P. Kozlof and H. Kajimura (eds.), Fur Seal Investigations. U.S. Department of Commerce, NOAA Technical Memorandum NMFS F/NWC-146. 189 pp.

Department of the Navy. 1996. U.S. Navy Solid Waste Management Plan for MARPOL Annex V Special Areas. Draft report to Congress. Office of the Chief of Naval Operations, Washington, DC. 60 pp.

Dixon, T. R., and T. J. Dixon. 1983. Marine litter research program, stage 5. Keep Britain Tidy Group, Buckinghamshire College of Higher Education, Brighton, U.K.

Dorfman, R., and N. S. Dorfman (eds.). 1993. Economics of the Environment: Selected Readings, 3d ed. W. W. Norton and Company, New York, NY. 517 pp.

Ebbesmeyer, C. C., and W. J. Ingraham Jr. 1992. Shoe spill in the North Pacific. EOS, Transactions, American Geophysical Union 73:361–365.

Environmental Protection Agency. 1989. Report to Congress on New York Bight plastics study. Washington, DC.

Environmental Protection Agency. 1990. Methods to manage and control plastic wastes: A report to Congress. EPA530-SW-89-051. Washington, DC.

Environmental Protection Agency. 1992a. Characterization of Municipal Solid Waste in the United States: 1992 Update. EPA/530-R-92-019. Office of Solid Waste Management, Washington, DC.

Environmental Protection Agency. 1992b. Plastic pellets in the aquatic environment: Sources and recommendations. Final report. EPA 842/B-92/010. EPA Information Clearinghouse, Cincinnati, OH.

Escardo-Boomsma, J., J. Goodman, K. J. O'Hara, and C. A. Ribic. 1996. National Marine Debris Monitoring Program. Center for Marine Conservation, Washington, DC. 93 pp.

Feldkamp, S. D., D. P. Costa, and G. K. DeKrey. 1989. Energetic and behavioral effects of net entanglement on juvenile northern fur seals, *Callorhinus ursinus*. Fishery Bulletin 87:85–94.

Fowler, C. W. 1982. Interactions of northern fur seals and commercial fisheries. Pages 278–292 *in* Transactions of the 47th North American Wildlife and Natural Resources Conference. Wildlife Management Institute, Washington, DC.

Fowler, C. W., and D. B. Siniff. 1992. Determining population status and the use of biological indices from the management of marine mammals. Pages 1051–1061 *in* D. R. McCullough and R. H. Reginals (eds.), Wildlife 2000: Populations. Elsevier Science Publishers, London.

Fowler, C. W., J. Baker, R. Ream, B. Robson, and N. Kiyota. 1993. Entanglement studies, St. Paul Island, 1992 juvenile male northern fur seals. AFSC Processed Report 93-03. Alaska Fisheries Science Center, National Marine Fisheries Service, Seattle, WA. 42 pp.

Halperin, L. A., and D. L. Lewis. 1994. 1993 International Coastal Cleanup Results. Center for Marine Conservation, Washington, DC. 187 pp.

Henderson, J. R. 1990. Recent entanglements of Hawaiian monk seals in marine debris. Pages 540–553 *in* R. S. Shomura and M. L. Godfrey (eds.), Proceedings of the Second International Conference on Marine Debris. 2–7 April 1989, Honolulu, HI. Vol. 1. U.S. Department of Commerce, NOAA Technical Memorandum NMFS-SWFSC-154.

Hodge, K. L., and J. Glen. 1993. 1992 National Coastal Cleanup Report. Center for Marine Conservation, Washington, DC. 330 pp.

Hodge, K. L., and J. Glen. 1994. 1993 International Coastal Cleanup Results. Center for Marine Conservation, Washington, DC. 187 pp.

Hodge, K. L., J. Glen, and D. Lewis. 1993. 1992 International Coastal Cleanup Results. Center for Marine Conservation, Washington, DC. 217 pp.

Interagency Task Force on Persistent Marine Debris. 1988. Report of the Interagency Task Force on Persistent Marine Debris. National Oceanic and Atmospheric Administration, Office of the Chief Scientist, Washington, DC. 170 pp. + appendices.

Intergovernmental Oceanographic Commission. 1994. Marine Debris: Solid Waste Management Action Plan for the Wider Caribbean. IOC Technical Series 41. UNESCO, Paris, France. 21 pp.

Johnson, S. W. 1990. Entanglement debris on Alaskan beaches, 1990. U.S. Department of Commerce NWAFC Processed Report 90-10. 16 pp.

Johnson, S. W., and T. H. Merrell. 1988. Entanglement Debris on Alaskan Beaches 1986. U.S. Department of Commerce, NOAA Technical Memorandum NMFS F/NWC-126. 26 pp.

Kenney, R. D., and S. D. Kraus. 1993. Right whale mortality—a correction and an update. Marine Mammal Science 9:445–446.

Kenyon, K. W., and E. Kridler. 1969. Laysan albatross swallow indigestible matter. Auk 86:339–343.

Kraus, S. D. 1990. Rates and potential causes of mortality in North Atlantic right whales (*Eubalaena glacialis*). Marine Mammal Science 6:278–291.

Kruse, G. H., and A. Kimker. 1993. Degradable escape mechanisms for pot gear: A summary report to the Alaska Board of Fisheries. Regional Information Report No. 5J93-01. Alaska Department of Fish and Game, Juneau, AK. 23 pp.

Laist, D. W. 1987. Overview of the biological effects of lost and discarded plastic debris in the marine environment. Marine Pollution Bulletin 18:319–326.

Laist, D. W. 1996a. Impacts of marine debris: Entanglement of marine life in marine debris including a comprehensive list of species with entanglement and ingestion records. Pages 99–139 *in* J. M. Coe and D. R. Rogers (eds.), Marine Debris: Sources, Impacts, and Solutions. Springer-Verlag, New York, NY.

Laist, D. W. 1996b. Marine debris entanglement and ghost fishing: A cryptic and significant type of bycatch? Pages 33–39 *in* Proceedings of the Solving Bycatch Workshop: Considerations for Today and Tomorrow. 25–27 September 1995, Seattle, WA. Report No. 96-03. Alaska Sea Grant College Program, Fairbanks, AK.

Lenarz, W. H. 1985. Theoretical first approximations of densities of discarded webbing in the eastern North Pacific Ocean and Bering Sea. Pages 213–217 *in* R. S. Shomura and H. O. Yoshida (eds.), Proceedings of the Workshop on the Fate and Impact of Marine Debris. 26–29 November 1984, Honolulu, HI. U.S. Department of Commerce, NOAA Technical Memorandum NMFS-SWFC-54.

Lutz, P. L., and A. A. Alfaro-Schulman. 1987. The effects of chronic plastic ingestion on green sea turtles. Final report to the Marine Entanglement Research Program, National Marine Fisheries Service, Northwest and Alaska Fisheries Science Center, Seattle, WA. 49 pp.

Marine Mammal Commission. 1986. Annual report to Congress for 1985. (Available from National Technical Information Service, Springfield, VA. PB86-216 249.) 180 pp.

Marine Mammal Commission. 1987. Annual report to Congress for 1986. (Available from National Technical Information Service, Springfield, VA. PB87-154092.) 193 pp.

Marine Mammal Commission. 1988. Annual report to Congress for 1987. (Available from National Technical Information Service, Springfield, VA. PB88-168984.) 209 pp.

Marine Mammal Commission. 1993. Annual report to Congress for 1992. (Available from National Technical Information Service, Springfield, VA. PB95-154995.) 241 pp.

Marine Mammal Commission. 1994. The Marine Mammal Commission Compendium of Selected Treaties, International Agreements, and Other Relevant Documents on Marine Resources, Wildlife, and the Environment, R. L. Wallace, compiler. Vol. 2. Marine Mammal Commission, Washington, DC.

Marine Mammal Commission. 1996. Annual report to Congress for 1995. (Available from National Technical Information Service, Springfield, VA. PB96-157482.) 235 pp.

Merrell, T. R., Jr. 1980. Accumulation of plastic litter on beaches of Amchitka Island, Alaska. Marine Environmental Research 3:171–384.

Merrell, T. R., Jr. 1985. Fishnets and other plastic litter on Alaska beaches. Pages 160–182 *in* R. S. Shomura and H. O. Yoshida (eds.), Proceedings of the Workshop on the Fate and Impact of Marine Debris. 26–29 November 1984, Honolulu, HI. U.S. Department of Commerce, NOAA Technical Memorandum NMFS-SWFC-54.

Miller, J. E., S. W. Baker, and D. L. Echols. 1995. Marine Debris Point Source Investigation 1994–1995, Padre Island National Seashore. National Park Service. 40 pp.

Minerals Management Service. 1986. Guidelines for reducing or eliminating trash and debris in the Gulf of Mexico. Notice to lessees and operators of federal oil and gas leases in the Outer Continental Shelf, Gulf of Mexico OCS Region. NTL No. 86-11. Mineral Management Service, Gulf of Mexico OCS Office, New Orleans, LA.

Minerals Management Service. 1992. Proceedings: Twelfth Annual Gulf of Mexico Information Transfer Meeting. 5–7 November 1991, New Orleans, LA. OCS Study MMS 92-007. Minerals Management Service, Gulf of Mexico OCS Region, New Orleans, LA.

Montevecchi, W. A. 1991. Incidence and types of plastic in gannets' nests in the northwest Atlantic. Canadian Journal of Zoology 69:295–297.

Morris, R. J. 1980. Plastic debris in the surface waters of the South Atlantic. Marine Pollution Bulletin 11:164–166.

National Academy of Sciences. 1975. Marine litter (chapter 8). Pages 405–438 *in* Assessing Potential Ocean Pollutants: A Report of the Study Panel on Assessing Potential Ocean Pollutants. Ocean Affairs Board, National Research Council, National Academy of Sciences Printing and Publishing Office (now National Academy Press), Washington, DC.

Neilson, J. 1985. The Oregon experience. Pages 154–159 *in* R. S. Shomura and H. O. Yoshida (eds.), Proceedings of the Workshop on the Fate and Impact of Marine Debris. 26–29 November 1984, Honolulu, HI. U.S. Department of Commerce, NOAA Technical Memorandum NMFS-SWFC-54.

O'Hara, K. J. 1988. Plastic debris and its effects on wildlife. Pages 395–434 *in* W. J. Chandler, L. Labate, and C. Wille (eds.), Audubon Wildlife Report 1988/1989. Academic Press, San Diego, CA.

O'Hara, K. J., and P. Debenham. 1989. Cleaning America's Beaches: 1988 National Beach Cleanup Results. Center for Marine Conservation, Washington, DC. 202 pp.

O'Hara, K. J., and L. K. Younger. 1990. Cleaning North America's Beaches: 1989 Beach Cleanup Results. Center for Marine Conservation, Washington, DC. 310 pp.

O'Hara, K. J., N. Atkins, and S. Iudicello. 1987. Plastics in the Ocean: More Than a Litter Problem. Center for Marine Conservation, Washington, DC. 128 pp.

O'Hara, K., L. Maraniss, J. Deichmann, J. Perry, and R. Bierce. 1987. 1986 Texas Coastal Cleanup Report. Center for Marine Conservation, Washington, DC. 105 pp.

O'Hara, K. J., S. Iudicello, and J. Zilligen. 1994. A Citizen's Guide to Plastics in the Ocean: More Than a Litter Problem. Center for Marine Conservation, Washington, DC. 128 pp.

Pemberton, D., N. P. Brothers, and R. Kirkwood. 1992. Entanglement of Australian fur seals in man-made debris in Tasmanian waters. Wildlife Research 19:151–159.

Podolsky, R. H., and S. W. Kress. 1989. Plastic debris incorporated into double-crested cormorant nests in the Gulf of Maine. Journal of Field Ornithology 60:248–250.

Pruter, A. T. 1987. Sources, quantities and distribution of persistent plastics in the marine environment. Marine Pollution Bulletin 18:305–310.

Recht, F. 1988. Dealing with Annex V—Reference Guide for Ports. U.S. Department of Commerce, NOAA Technical Memorandum NMFS F/NWR-23. 132 pp.

Ribic, C. A., and L. M. Ganio. 1996. Power analysis for beach surveys of marine debris. Marine Pollution Bulletin 32:554–557.

Ribic, C. A., T. R. Dixon, and I. Vining. 1992. Marine Debris Survey Manual. U.S. Department of Commerce, NOAA Technical Report NMFS 108. 92 pp.

Ribic, C. A., S. W. Johnson, and C. A. Cole. 1996. Distribution, type, accumulation, and sources of marine debris in the United States, 1989–1993. Pages 35–47 *in* J. M. Coe and D. R. Rogers (eds.), Marine Debris: Sources, Impacts, and Solutions. Springer-Verlag, New York, NY.

Robards, M. D., T. J. Gould, and J. F. Piatt. 1996. The highest global concentrations and increased abundance of oceanic plastic debris in the North Pacific: Evidence from seabirds. Pages 71–80 *in* J. M. Coe and D. R. Rogers (eds.), Marine Debris: Sources, Impacts, and Solutions. Springer-Verlag, New York, NY.

Scarsbrooke, J. R., G. A. McFarlane, and W. Shaw. 1988. Effectiveness of experimental escape mechanisms in sablefish traps. North American Journal of Fisheries Management 8:158–161.

Scheffer, V. B., and K. W. Kenyon. 1989. The rise and fall of a seal herd. Animal Kingdom 92 (2): 14–19.

Shaughnessy, P. D. 1980. Entanglement of cape fur seals with man-made objects. Marine Pollution Bulletin 11:332–336.

Sheavly, S. B. 1995. 1994 International Coastal Cleanup Results. Center for Marine Conservation, Washington, DC. 85 pp.

Sheavly, S. B. 1996. 1995 International Coastal Cleanup: U.S. Results. Center for Marine Conservation, Washington, DC. 102 pp. + appendices.

Shomura, R. S., and M. L. Godfrey (eds.). 1990. Proceedings of the Second International Conference on Marine Debris. 2–7 April 1989, Honolulu, HI. Vols. 1 and 2. U.S. Department of Commerce, NOAA Technical Memorandum NMFS-SWFSC-154. 1,274 pp.

Shomura, R. S., and H. O. Yoshida (eds.). 1985. Proceedings of the Workshop on the Fate and Impact of Marine Debris. 26–29 November 1984, Honolulu, HI. U.S. Department of Commerce, NOAA Technical Memorandum NMFS-SWFC-54. 580 pp.

Sileo, L., P. R. Sievert, and M. D. Samuel. 1990. Causes of mortality of albatross chicks at Midway Atoll. Journal of Wildlife Diseases 26:329–338.

Smith, K. V., X. Zhang, and R. B. Palmquist. 1996. The economic value of controlling marine debris. Pages 187–202 *in* J. M. Coe and D. R. Rogers (eds.), Marine Debris: Sources, Impacts, and Solutions. Springer-Verlag, New York, NY.

Smolowitz, R. J. 1978. Trap design and ghost fishing: Discussion. Marine Fisheries Review 40 (5–6): 59–67.

Spear, L. B., D. G. Ainley, and C. A. Ribic. 1995. Incidence of plastic in seabirds from the tropical Pacific, 1984–1991: Relation with distribution of species, sex, age, season, year and body weight. Marine Environmental Reseach 40:123–146.

Stewart, B. S., and P. K. Yochem. 1990. Pinniped entanglement in synthetic materials in the Southern California Bight. Pages 554–561 *in* R. S. Shomura and M. L. Godfrey (eds.), Proceedings of the Second International Conference on Marine Debris. 2–7 April 1989, Honolulu, HI. Vol. 1. U.S. Department of Commerce, NOAA Technical Memorandum NMFS-SWFSC-154.

Trulli, W. R., H. K. Trulli, and D. P. Redford. 1990. Characterization of marine debris in selected harbors of the United States. Pages 309–324 *in* R. S. Shomura and M. L. Godfrey (eds.), Proceedings of the Second International Conference on Marine Debris. 2–7 April 1989, Honolulu, HI. Vol. 1. U.S. Department of Commerce, NOAA Technical Memorandum NMFS-SWFSC-154.

Venrick, E. L., T. W. Backman, W. C. Bartram, C. J. Platt, M. S. Thornhill, and R. E. Yates. 1973. Man-made objects on the surface of the central North Pacific Ocean. Nature 246:30–32.

Wallace, N. 1985. Debris entanglement in the marine environment: A review. Pages 259–277 *in* R. S. Shomura and H. O. Yoshida (eds.), Proceedings of the Workshop on the Fate and Impact of Marine Debris. 27–29 November 1984, Honolulu, HI. U.S. Department of Commerce, NOAA Technical Memorandum NMFS-SWFC-54.

Weisskopf, M. 1988. Plastic reaps a grim harvest in the oceans of the world. Smithsonian 18 (12): 58–69.

Wolfe, D. A. (ed.). 1987. Plastics in the sea: Selected papers from the Sixth International Ocean Disposal Symposium. Marine Pollution Bulletin 18:303–365.

Yoshida, K., N. Baba, M. Nakajima, Y. Fujimaki, A. Furuta, S. Nomura, and K. Takahashi. 1985. Fur seal entanglement survey report: Test study at a breeding facility, 1983. Document submitted to the 28th Meeting of the Standing Scientific Committee of the North Pacific Fur Seal Commission. 4–12 April 1985, Tokyo, Japan.

Younger, K. L., and K. Hodge. 1992. 1991 International Coastal Cleanup Overview. Center for Marine Conservation, Washington, DC. 114 pp.

17

JOSEPH R. GERACI, JOHN HARWOOD,
AND VALERIE J. LOUNSBURY

Marine Mammal Die-Offs

Causes, Investigations, and Issues

During the 1980s and 1990s there was an unprecedented series of events in which large numbers of marine mammals died. These episodes provoked widespread public and scientific concern that the die-offs were a consequence of habitat degradation and growing human pressure on the marine environment. Because previously unknown disease agents were involved in several of these events, fear for public health became an issue. Today die-offs have assumed a new importance to scientists, policy makers, and managers alike, and the pressure to "solve the problem" is great. An effective and responsible plan of action requires, in addition to a multitude of practical considerations, a solid understanding of the biological and environmental processes that may be involved.

In this chapter, we first try to place marine mammal die-offs in their ecological context. To do this, we review some of the more common causes of death in these species. We distinguish between background mortality—caused by agents or circumstances to which an animal is exposed almost every day—and episodic mortality caused by unusual environmental conditions or outbreaks of disease. We then discuss some of the more spectacular die-offs that have occurred in the past two decades and show that, although each event had a primary cause, a number of other factors may have contributed to their scale.

Because the events are complex, it is important that experts from a range of disciplines be involved in their investigation. To succeed requires good planning, unusual cooperation between government agencies, and generous funding. In the section titled "Responding to a Die-Off," we examine studies of die-offs and show that a prepared protocol is a guideline at best, and that the course of any investigation is ultimately shaped by the unique circumstances surrounding each event—the science, politics, and economics, and the way in which the public exerts its role. Every die-off is a singular opportunity to learn more about the animals and how to manage their populations. Each investigation, whether or not the outcome is considered successful, generates insights and experience that may hold the key to future response actions. In the final section of this chapter, we consider whether mass mortalities are more or less likely to occur in the future, and whether any efforts can or should be made to moderate their impacts. The latter is a question for both the scientist, who might argue that nature should run its course, and the policy maker, who may be moved by other imperatives to intervene.

Normal Background Mortality

Every day marine mammals die as a result of starvation, predation, trauma, and disease. The results of population studies over the past few decades allow us to make some generalizations about average levels of mortality for many species. As is typical of many large mammals (Ralls et al. 1980, Fowler 1987), mortality in marine mammals is generally highest in the youngest (i.e., first year) and oldest age classes. Half or more of the pinnipeds born in certain populations may not survive their first year. During the 1950s about 60,000 to 80,000 northern fur seal (*Callorhinus ursinus*) pups (from an estimated 450,000 born annually [York 1987]) died from starvation, trauma, and disease during each pupping season on St. Paul Island in the U.S. Pribilof Islands (Jellison and Milner 1958, Keyes 1965). By contrast, episodic events are more likely to affect one or more segments of a population (e.g., independent juveniles, adults) because of factors such as segregation by age or sex, or differences in behavior, food, or habitat preference, or, perhaps, contaminant burdens (Geraci et al. 1982, Calzada et al. 1994). Only by understanding the causes and patterns of normal mortality can we recognize unusual events and determine their cause and impacts on a population (Fig. 17-1).

Prenatal and Neonatal Mortality

The picture of mortality begins with abortions, premature and stillbirths, and neonatal deaths (i.e., within hours or days of birth). First-time breeders produce fewer young that survive the neonatal period than do older animals, possibly because of their smaller size, inexperience, or low social status (Le Boeuf et al. 1972, Lunn and Boyd 1993). In the usual course of events, some diseases, such as leptospirosis and calicivirus infections (Smith et al. 1973, 1974), can also lead to the death of fetuses and neonates. Exceptionally high early mortality—due to trauma, disease, starvation, and severe weather—is often associated with episodic events. This is discussed more fully in the section on episodic mortality.

Starvation

Starvation is one of the most common causes of death of young marine mammals that are dependent on their mothers for food, and it is the single most important cause of pup mortality in many species of pinnipeds (Keyes 1965, Le Boeuf et al. 1972). Seal pups on a crowded breeding beach can easily become separated from their mothers during storms or disturbances and subsequently starve. A mother may desert her pup because she is debilitated, ill, or injured (Trillmich et al. 1991, Hiruki et al. 1993). Such desertion may become more common as per capita food availability for adults decreases.

Starvation is generally less common in the young of species with prolonged (i.e., >1 year) lactation periods, such as sirenians and most odontocetes. Even in these groups, widespread disease among adult females may influence calf survival (Geraci, Dailey et al. 1978). Pacific walrus (*Odobenus rosmarus rosmarus*) calf mortality nearly quadrupled in the decade between 1970 and 1980 as a presumed consequence of maternal malnutrition (Fay et al. 1986, 1989).

Recently weaned animals with poorly developed foraging skills may starve when prey are scarce or hard to find. Starvation is common, for example, in juvenile sea otters (*Enhydra lutris*) that occupy long-colonized areas depleted of energy-rich prey (Monnett and Rotterman 1988).

Malnourished animals may not live long enough to starve but may die of related conditions, such as hypothermia, electrolyte disturbances, or disease. These conditions can obscure the primary cause of death. When a population gradually approaches the carrying capacity of its environ-

Figure 17-1. Only careful examination of these gray seal pup carcasses, combined with knowledge of normal patterns and causes of mortality, can verify the occurrence of an episodic event. (Photograph by J. Harwood)

ment, the effects of nutritional stress may only be noticeable as a slow decline in numbers, decreased birth rate, or reduced juvenile survival. Such demographic changes have been observed in the Pacific walrus population (Fay et al. 1989). By contrast, an episodic event, such as the sudden disappearance of prey, would be expected to have more immediate and dramatic consequences, sometimes on all segments of the population (see the discussion of the 1982–1983 El Niño event, below).

Direct Environmental Effects

Marine mammals as a group have adapted to cope with varying and often extreme climatic conditions. Still, many individual animals die as a direct consequence of environmental factors. A seal pup may be swept away by heavy surf, and a cetacean or a Florida manatee (*Trichechus manatus latirostris*) might lag behind in a seasonal migration to warmer waters and suffer hypothermia. Ice accidents are a common hazard for cold-water species: a sudden freeze might trap a few whales in the ice or force them to strand, or, by closing a breathing hole, cause a seal to suffocate. Unusual environmental conditions—severe storms, early breakup of ice floes, or prolonged cold—can have a much greater impact. These are discussed more fully later in this chapter.

Trauma

Marine mammals risk injury from many sources. Pinniped pups in crowded colonies may suffer trauma from trampling, bite wounds, or storms (Keyes 1965, Le Boeuf et al. 1972). Pacific walruses sometimes react to disturbance with panic and stampede. One incident on St. Lawrence Island in 1978 apparently resulted in the death of about 1,000 individuals, mostly females and calves (Fay and Kelly 1980). Groups of adult male Hawaiian monk seals (*Monachus schauinslandi*) may seriously injure or kill adult females and juveniles of both sexes in mass-mating (so-called "mobbing") attempts (Johnson and Johnson 1981, Banish and Gilmartin 1992). Territorial contests among adult male otariids and elephant seals (*Mirounga* spp.) may result in mortality rates that are far higher than those for females of the same age (Johnson 1968, Baker and McCann 1989).

Although commercial hunting of marine mammals has declined greatly in the late twentieth century, mortality caused by other human activities, particularly fishing, has risen substantially over the past few decades. In spite of growing public concern and protective legislation, marine mammal deaths worldwide due to fishery interactions and entanglement in lost or discarded gear continue on a large scale (see Northridge and Hofman, this volume, and Laist et al., this volume).

Collision with vessels can be an important cause of death. About 35–50 Florida manatees are killed by boats each year; this accounts for about 25% of the total annual mortality in this population (O'Shea et al. 1985, Ackerman et al. 1995). The few northern right whales (*Eubalaena glacialis*) killed in shipping lanes along the U.S. Atlantic coast may be enough to jeopardize stock recovery (Kraus 1990). As in most large mammals with low reproductive rates, the persistence of these populations depends on a high survival rate among adults (Eberhardt and Siniff 1977), and thus such losses are unlikely to be sustainable (Eberhardt and O'Shea 1995).

Predation

Young animals and those weakened by illness or injury are most at risk from predation by a variety of carnivores including coyotes, foxes, eagles, sharks, polar bears (*Ursus maritimus*), killer whales (*Orcinus orca*), and leopard seals (*Hydrurga leptonyx*), among others. Pinniped pups are particularly vulnerable because they are born at predictable locations and times (see Riedman 1990 for review). For some species, such as the crabeater seal (*Lobodon carcinophagus*) (Siniff and Bengtson 1977, Laws 1984), predation, in this case by leopard seals, may be the greatest single cause of pup mortality.

Predation can be a serious threat to endangered or vulnerable species. If a marine mammal is not the principal prey species of the predator, that predator may continue to take a constant number of individuals (rather than a constant proportion of the population) as the population declines. As a result, the proportion of mortality due to predation steadily rises. Shark predation is considered to be a minor, but contributory, factor in the continuing decline of the Hawaiian monk seal (Johnson and Johnson 1981, Westlake and Gilmartin 1990). Most of the Galápagos fur seals (*Arctocephalus galapagoensis*) on southern Isabela Island were killed by feral dogs (Trillmich 1987). Besides killing animals outright, such terrestrial predators may introduce pathogens (e.g., morbillivirus) that can have far-reaching effects on the population.

Infection with Parasites

Anderson and May (1992) have made a useful distinction between microparasites and macroparasites, and we follow their terminology here. Microparasites are generally small and reproduce within their hosts. Hosts that recover from infection usually acquire long-lasting immunity against reinfection. Macroparasites are typically large and require an intermediate host; any acquired immunity to reinfection is short-lived.

Macroparasites

Marine mammals harbor a wide range of macroparasites, which are frequently predictable in their occurrence and severity (Geraci and St. Aubin 1987). Heavy burdens of macroparasites may have little effect on a host unless it is also stressed by illness, injury, or starvation. Then, usually harmless parasites, such as nematodes in the lungs or stomach, can become pathogenic.

A few macroparasites are more commonly associated with illness. The nematode *Uncinaria lucasi* has periodically caused high mortality (due to hemorrhagic diarrhea and anemia) of northern fur seal pups in the Pribilof Islands (Keyes 1965). Nematodes of the genus *Crassicauda* are serious pathogens of cetaceans. In odontocetes they destroy mammary gland tissue (Geraci, Dailey et al. 1978) and cause potentially fatal cranial bone lesions (Perrin and Powers 1980). In rorquals they infect the urogenital tract, sometimes causing renal failure (Lambertsen et al. 1986). In North Atlantic fin whales (*Balaenoptera physalus*), the resulting calf mortality may be high enough to impede population recovery (Lambertsen 1992). The trematode *Nasitrema* in the cranial sinuses of cetaceans is common and relatively innocuous. Occasionally, one of these trematodes migrates to the brain, critically damaging tissues along the way (Ridgway and Dailey 1972). This macroparasite is one of the few that has been directly linked to strandings (Dailey and Walker 1978; Morimitsu et al. 1987, 1992).

Microparasites

Microparasites flourish in marine mammal habitats, but most of them pose little threat to a healthy animal. Opportunistic pathogens, such as the bacteria *Streptococcus* sp., *Vibrio* sp., and *Corynebacterium* sp., may invade and overwhelm those weakened by malnutrition, injury, or infection with other parasites (Stroud and Roffe 1979, Baker 1984, Baker and McCann 1989). Leptospirosis, caused by the spirochete *Leptospira* sp., occurs in domestic and wild animals throughout the world, including California sea lions (*Zalophus californianus*) and, to a lesser extent, northern fur seals. Some bacteria previously thought to be restricted to terrestrial mammals, including mycobacteria of the complex associated with tuberculosis (*Mycobacteria bovis, M. tuberculosis*) (Forshaw and Phelps 1991, Cousins et al. 1993, Woods et al. 1995) and an apparently new strain or species of *Brucella* (Ewalt et al. 1994, Ross et al. 1994), are now being found in marine species. The effects of these organisms at the population level are as yet unknown.

By the end of the 1970s only a few viruses had been isolated from marine mammals (Smith and Skilling 1979), and they were generally considered to play only a minor role in natural mortality. Since 1980 the list of viruses has grown rapidly; so has our understanding of their significance to individual animals and populations. For example, caliciviruses infect many North Pacific species. Although they may cause skin lesions and perhaps reproductive failure in some individuals (Smith et al. 1986), their effect on population dynamics remains speculative (Fay et al. 1986, Merrick et al. 1987). Infection with herpesvirus may also be common (Stenvers et al. 1992, Stuen et al. 1994) and is sometimes fatal (Borst et al. 1986, Kennedy et al. 1992), but this virus has yet to be linked to widespread disease. Other viruses, many with little or no recognized effects, are continually being identified (Bossart 1990, Kennedy-Stoskopf 1990, Osterhaus et al. 1993, Bossart et al. 1996), and more will be found as investigators become increasingly alert to their presence and as techniques to isolate and identify them continue to improve.

The most important ecological role of microparasites, particularly viruses (e.g., morbillivirus, influenza virus), is probably their association with die-offs; this is discussed more fully later in this chapter.

Strandings

A stranded marine mammal is one that is unable to return to the water because it is ill or injured or is trapped in a perilous setting. In any area, strandings of coastal animals tend to occur in somewhat predictable patterns that reflect the numbers and species that live there. Most strandings are of animals that come ashore alone, or as mother-young pairs, already in weakened condition (Geraci and St. Aubin 1979, Bossart et al. 1985, Banish and Gilmartin 1992); in these cases, stranding may hasten death but is seldom the underlying cause.

As opposed to die-offs, which may affect more than one species and occur over a larger area and period of time, mass strandings can be defined as two or more cetaceans (excluding parent-calf pairs) coming ashore alive at the same time and place (Geraci and Lounsbury 1993). These events usually involve pelagic, social odontocetes (e.g., pilot whales [*Globicephala* sp.], Atlantic white-sided dolphins [*Lagenorhynchus acutus*]) (Fig. 17-2). In some cases, individuals within the group may be weakened by disease (Geraci, Testaverde et al. 1978; Walsh et al. 1990; Bossart et al. 1991; Duignan, House, Geraci, Duffy et al. 1995; Duignan, House, Geraci, Early et al. 1995).

Why do animals mass strand? Many individuals within a typical mass-stranded group come ashore in apparently

Figure 17-2. Mass strandings typically involve pelagic, social odontocetes. Of the more than 200 long-finned pilot whales that stranded in Bonavista Bay, Newfoundland, on 29 September 1975, about 125 died. The rest returned to sea on the next tide. (Photograph by D. St. Aubin)

good health (Geraci and St. Aubin 1979, Gales 1992), a fact that has sparked considerable debate (Geraci and Lounsbury 1993). Some events are evidently related to local coastal conditions: areas with broad tidal flats, strong or unusual currents, or extreme tidal volume may function as "whale traps" for unwary visitors (Brabyn and McLean 1992). Some scientists suggest that pelagic species run aground because their echolocation is impaired in shallow water (Dudok van Heel 1966). Others believe that cetaceans use the earth's magnetic field as a cue for navigation and are sometimes led astray by geomagnetic anomalies or disturbances (Klinowska 1985, 1986; Kirschvink et al. 1986). Mass strandings have also been proposed to be a natural mechanism for population regulation (Sergeant 1982a). Although some strandings occur in areas or under conditions that might support such hypotheses, others do not (Geraci and Lounsbury 1993). The only apparent common factor in all events is social cohesion—a force strong enough to ensure that when a single animal comes ashore, for whatever reason, others in the pod are likely to follow.

Most mass strandings involve small numbers (<15) of cetaceans (Geraci and Lounsbury 1993) although some species, notably pilot whales, false killer whales (*Pseudorca crassidens*), and melon-headed whales (*Peponocephala electra*), occasionally strand in groups of 50 to 150 or more. Even these numbers probably represent a modest loss to most populations.

Habitat Degradation and Disturbance

Contamination and other forms of habitat degradation have assumed a controversial role in marine mammal mortality. Some events, such as the *Exxon Valdez* oil spill, have obvious and dramatic effects (Loughlin 1994). In most cases, however, the influences of contaminants and disturbance are more likely to be indirect (e.g., through their effects on prey availability or by increasing susceptibility to disease as a result of changes in hormonal balance and immune function [Safe 1984, Bergman et al. 1992, De Swart et al. 1995, Lahvis et al. 1995, Ross et al. 1996, O'Shea 1999]).

Oil spills have received widespread attention as a cause of marine mammal deaths. There was little hard evidence for that belief, however, before the 1989 *Exxon Valdez* spill in Prince William Sound, Alaska (Geraci and St. Aubin 1990). Between 3,500 and 5,500 sea otters were estimated to have died in that event (Hofman 1994), which left little doubt about the vulnerability of that species to oil or any other substance that might foul its fur. About 300 harbor seals (*Phoca vitulina*) also died (Spraker et al. 1994), far more pinnipeds than had ever been documented in any previous spill (St. Aubin 1990).

The long-term impacts of oil spills are poorly understood and undoubtedly complex. The ultimate fate of the sea otters that survived the fresh and residual oil in Prince William Sound may depend largely on the oil's effect on the abundance of prey species, such as mussels and clams, and the health effects of consuming prey contaminated by petroleum residues (Neff 1990, Doroff and Bodkin 1994). The persistence of abnormal sea otter mortality patterns in some areas in the years following the spill (Burn 1994) suggests that long-term effects have occurred in this population.

Marine debris is a greater hazard for many marine mammals. Pinnipeds and baleen whales become entangled in discarded nets, ropes, packing bands, and monofilament line

(Laist 1987, Croxall et al. 1990). Florida manatees and some odontocetes (e.g., *Kogia* sp.) are more likely to ingest trash, especially plastics, often with fatal results (Laist 1987, Weisskopf 1988, Beck and Barros 1991). See Laist et al. (this volume) for a complete review.

Episodic Mortality

Certain factors, particularly infectious agents and environmental conditions, occasionally cause the deaths of large numbers of marine mammals, sometimes in a matter of days or perhaps over a period of months. The gravity of these events may not be immediately apparent, particularly when they are spread over time or a large area or if they occur in remote locations. In this section, we review factors that can cause such die-offs and briefly address several examples. In the following section, we discuss some recent events in more detail.

Unusual Environmental Conditions

Unusual environmental conditions probably account for most die-offs. Colonially breeding pinnipeds are especially vulnerable to extreme weather. During the winter of 1982–1983, for example, severe storms—coinciding with the highest tides of the year—hit the California coast during the peak of the northern elephant seal (*Mirounga angustirostris*) pupping season. At some sites, more than 80% of the pups died from drowning and trauma; at least 2,000 were lost from San Miguel and San Nicolas Islands alone (Le Boeuf and Condit 1983, Le Boeuf and Reiter 1991). Severe storms occasionally cause mass mortality in other groups of marine mammals. Cyclones in northern Australia have killed dugongs (*Dugong dugon*) by leaving them stranded out of water (Marsh 1989) and indirectly by depleting food resources. In 1992 a cyclone caused freshwater flooding that destroyed most of the sea grass beds in Hervey Bay (Queensland). Many dugongs left the area, but over the next few months, more than 100 died from starvation (Preen and Marsh 1995).

Protracted or intense cold spells in the southeastern United States periodically kill large numbers of Florida manatees, particularly independent juveniles, which may be nutritionally stressed and inexperienced at finding warm-water refuges (Campbell and Irvine 1981, O'Shea et al. 1985). Following a week of extreme cold in the winter of 1989–1990, about 56 manatees, representing 2–3% of the population as estimated at that time, died from cold stress (Ackerman et al. 1995).

Ice can be a real hazard, even for species whose evolution has been shaped by it. Beluga whales (*Delphinapterus leucas*) and narwhals (*Monodon monoceros*), usually in groups of 20 to 200, but sometimes thousands at a time, occasionally become trapped in ice by an early fall or late spring freeze (Freeman 1968, Sergeant and Williams 1983, Burns and Seaman 1985, Ivashin and Shevlyagin 1987, Siegstad and Heide-Jørgensen 1994). Some may remain there for months, starving and being taken by natural predators and human hunters. Several hundred sea otters were actually prevented from entering the water by heavy ice along the Alaska Peninsula during 1971 and 1972. Unable to forage, the otters died of hypothermia and shock (Schneider and Faro 1975). Prolonged spring ice that prevents land-breeding pinnipeds from reaching traditional pupping grounds (Kogai 1968), or the early breakup of floes used by ice-breeding seals (Geraci and Lounsbury 1993), can cause massive mortality of pups and, in the latter case, of their mothers as well. Along southern Newfoundland, blue whales (*Balaenoptera musculus*) and herds of white-beaked dolphins (*Lagenorhynchus albirostris*) are sometimes forced ashore by wind-driven ice (Sergeant 1982b); in the harsh winter of 1982–1983, hundreds of cetaceans died in ice-clogged bays and coves (Buck and Spotte 1986a, Hai et al. 1996).

Microparasite Outbreaks

In the context of this chapter, the term *microparasites* refers to bacteria and viruses, although other microorganisms, including yeasts, also fall within this category. As far as we know, bacteria have been responsible for very few large-scale die-offs, whereas viruses have been implicated in nearly all of the mass mortalities attributed to infectious disease since about 1980.

Determining whether a microparasite is a primary pathogen or merely appears later as a secondary invader in an animal already weakened is not always easy. The classical approach required to establish an organism as the cause of a particular disease (in humans) was first defined by Robert Koch in 1884. "Koch's postulates" stipulate that (1) the same microorganism must be found in every case of disease and not in healthy individuals, (2) the microorganism must be isolated and grown in the laboratory, (3) it must reproduce the disease when inoculated by itself into healthy individuals, and (4) the same organism must be found again in these individuals and recovered in laboratory culture.

The requirements to fulfill Koch's postulates cannot always be met. Obtaining this kind of information is often difficult in well-studied human disease outbreaks; it is much more so in the case of die-offs of marine mammals. Their populations are large, complex, and generally inaccessible. Controlled studies are unfeasible because of the size of the animals and the numbers that would be required. Public and political pressure are unlikely to allow the kinds of studies necessary on marine mammals, and results gained from investigations of laboratory animals are not always transferrable to species (which may be 10,000 times their mass) from a different realm. Thus, we often reach a decision through a relentless process of eliminating other plausible causes, one by one, until the burden of proof favors a microparasite that (1) is consistently isolated from infected animals, (2) has the potential to produce the observed lesions or clinical conditions, and (3) could spread in a manner that would explain the observed pattern of mortality. Complicating the matter, we recognize that pathogens do not always cause illness, and that the expression of disease is, in large part, determined by attributes of the host, such as age, general health, and history of exposure. Individuals, even populations, may harbor (and spread) infectious agents while showing no signs of illness themselves.

What outbreaks have been attributed to bacteria? Pneumonia, apparently caused by *Pneumococcus* sp., killed up to 50% of gray seal (*Halichoerus grypus*) pups at St. Kilda, Scotland, in 1960 (Gallacher and Waters 1964). Periodic outbreaks of leptospirosis, endemic in California sea lions, have killed at least a few hundred animals since it was first recognized in 1970 (Vedros et al. 1971, Dierauf et al. 1985).

The first mass mortality attributed to a virus (Influenza A) occurred along the New England coast between December 1979 and October 1980 (Geraci et al. 1982). Unusually warm conditions, crowding, and a concurrent respiratory infection with mycoplasma may have triggered this epidemic, which first appeared in dense aggregations of harbor seals in Cape Cod Bay (Massachusetts) and gradually moved northward through the spring and summer. At least 450 harbor seals, an estimated 3–5% of the New England population (Payne and Schneider 1984), died of acute pneumonia. Periodic outbreaks continue to cause low-level mortality in this population (Callan et al. 1995).

Of greater concern are the morbilliviruses, which are potentially lethal and widely distributed among marine mammals (Dietz et al. 1989; Bengtson et al. 1991; Duignan, House, Geraci, Duffy et al. 1995; Duignan, Saliki et al. 1995). In 1987–1988, an outbreak of canine distemper, which was possibly transmitted from sled dogs, killed thousands of Baikal seals (*Phoca sibirica*) (Grachev et al. 1989). This episode was followed by outbreaks caused by related morbilliviruses that swept through populations of harbor seals in Europe in 1988 and striped dolphins (*Stenella coeruleoalba*) in the Mediterranean in 1990 through 1992 (see later discussion). Studies following these outbreaks exposed the possible role of morbilliviruses in earlier die-offs. The discovery of antibodies to canine distemper virus in crabeater seals (Bengtson et al. 1991) suggested that this virus may have caused a previously unexplained illness that killed about 2,500 seals along the Antarctic Peninsula in 1955 (Laws and Taylor 1957). The presence of antibodies to morbillivirus in bottlenose dolphins (*Tursiops truncatus*) sampled during the 1987–1988 U.S. Atlantic coast die-off (Geraci 1989) and the subsequent finding of viral antigen in preserved tissues (Lipscomb, Schulman et al. 1994; Duignan, House, Geraci, Duffy et al. 1995; Duignan et al. 1996) are evidence that morbillivirus also played a role in that event.

Morbillivirus infection, without associated mortality, is now known to be common in many species of marine mammals (Duignan et al. 1994; Duignan, House, Geraci, Duffy et al. 1995; Duignan, House, Geraci, Early et al. 1995; Duignan, House, Walsh et al. 1995; Duignan, Saliki et al. 1995). In populations in which the virus is endemic, such as it is in long-finned pilot whales (*Globicephala melas*) of the western North Atlantic, infection is presumably widespread but of little consequence because the animals have developed immunity through frequent exposure. Outbreaks of illness are more likely to follow the introduction of the virus into naive (previously unexposed) populations.

Mass Strandings

Deaths in mass strandings that appear to be a consequence of social cohesion, and deaths due to ice entrapment, are simply part of normal background mortality. Social odontocetes are also susceptible to conditions, such as starvation and disease, that might lead to episodic mortality. An affected animal may come ashore as part of a mass stranding, or perhaps even initiate one. In this way, a mass stranding might conceivably reflect a die-off. Distinguishing an event of this nature from one caused by a navigational error would require a rigorous study. Is there a greater than expected frequency of events or number of animals coming ashore? Are strandings occurring in unusual locations or patterns? Are other marine animals dying in the same area? Have there been any coincident environmental disruptions such as a red tide or a toxic spill? Such clues may suggest the need for an investigation that is broader in scope than the response to a "typical" mass stranding.

Over the past two decades, stranding networks have been established in many countries, and specimen and data collection protocols developed to gain biological information (Geraci and St. Aubin 1979, Reynolds and Odell 1991, Wilkinson 1991, Geraci and Lounsbury 1993; see Wilkinson and Worthy, this volume). Specimen banks make it possible to reevaluate, years later, the condition of animals at the time of their deaths and may help further explain some of the more unusual stranding events long after they have occurred.

For example, between 1981 and 1991 there were 10 separate mass strandings of long-finned pilot whales, totaling 476 animals, within a 32-km (20-mile) radius on Cape Cod (Massachusetts), in an area where only one incident had been reported in the previous 20 years (Geraci and Lounsbury 1993). Retrospective studies (Duignan, House, Geraci, Early et al. 1995) have shown that these whales were exposed to morbillivirus as early as 1982. In 1989 a stranded calf was found with clinical disease. These findings, as well as the presence of infection in other social odontocetes (notably false killer whales and short-finned pilot whales [*Globicephala macrorhynchus*]) in the western Atlantic, suggest that scientists may need to investigate the possible role of morbilliviruses in some mass strandings (Duignan, House, Geraci, Duffy et al. 1995).

Over evolutionary history, the strong social cohesion that is characteristic of many dolphin species obviously must convey advantages in survival and reproduction that outweigh the risks of an occasional mass stranding; these events are usually relatively rare. However, if disease outbreaks and other episodic phenomena are becoming more frequent, as some authors suggest, these risks may be magnified if healthy members of a stable social group tend to follow sick members ashore.

Phycotoxins

Certain algae and protozoa, particularly dinoflagellates, produce toxins that can accumulate in fish and invertebrates and eventually poison predators higher up the food chain. These compounds are difficult to detect and may leave little evidence of their presence. Thus their role in marine mammal mortality is often uncertain and may have gone unrecognized in the past.

Phycotoxins have been implicated in a number of marine mammal mortalities. Unusual dinoflagellate blooms (red tides) off western Florida over an eight-month period in 1946–1947 killed invertebrates, turtles, and tremendous numbers of fish, and were circumstantially linked to the deaths of several bottlenose dolphins (Gunter et al. 1948). Sand lance (*Ammodytes* sp.) contaminated with dinoflagellate toxin were suspected to have caused occasional die-offs of northern fur seals in the Pribilof Islands in the early 1960s (Keyes 1965). In 1978 more than 25% of the Hawaiian monk seal population on Laysan Island was apparently poisoned by fish containing ciguatoxin and subsequently died from starvation and macroparasite infection (Banish and Gilmartin 1992). The link between dinoflagellate blooms in the western Bering Sea and high sea otter mortality in 1977 and 1981 (Sidorov 1987) was circumstantial, as was the association between the deaths of more than 30 sea otters at Kodiak Island (Alaska) and high levels of paralytic shellfish poison (saxitoxin) in local mussels and clams during the summer of 1987 (DeGange and Vacca 1989). In late 1987, 14 humpback whales (*Megaptera novaeangliae*) in Cape Cod Bay (Massachusetts) died after eating Atlantic mackerel (*Scomber scombrus*) contaminated with saxitoxin (Geraci et al. 1989) (Fig. 17-3); this number is equivalent to 50 years' "typical mortality" in this population (Anderson and White 1992). Brevetoxin-contaminated ascidians were implicated in the deaths of at least 37 manatees in southwestern Florida in April 1982 (O'Shea et al. 1991), and the same toxin, perhaps ingested or encountered as an aerosol during an unusually strong red tide, may have caused the more serious manatee die-off that occurred in the same region in early 1996 (see Reynolds, this volume). The devastating potential of such events was fully realized between mid-May through early June 1997 when perhaps 50% or more of the largest remaining colony of Mediterranean monk seals (*Monachus monachus*) (estimated at 270 animals in 1996) died at Cap Blanc, Mauritania. Although unproven, strong evidence points to saxitoxin poisoning as the cause (Hernández et al. 1998).

Evidence for the role of phycotoxins in the deaths of more than 740 bottlenose dolphins on the U.S. Atlantic coast between June 1987 and March 1988 is less clear-cut. Geraci (1989) concluded that sublethal exposure to brevetoxin may have left the dolphins emaciated, exhausted, thermally stressed, and vulnerable to the various bacterial and viral infections that finally killed them.

Dinoflagellate and algal blooms are becoming more numerous, and their geographic range is expanding, perhaps exacerbated by pollution and other environmental changes (Anderson 1994). Thus the risks to marine mammals from exposure to phycotoxins may be increasing. Small, relatively localized populations, such as the endangered monk seals and the Florida manatee, are especially vulnerable.

Environmental Change

Sudden changes in oceanic conditions, such as those associated with El Niño southern oscillation events, can dramatically alter the availability of particular species of prey for marine mammals. A decrease in food abundance has a direct effect on population productivity in species that feed during lactation and that are constrained by the location of their breeding sites to feed within a relatively restricted area. For example, the 1982–1983 El Niño event resulted in increased abortions and pup mortality in eastern Pacific fur seal and sea lion populations (Trillmich et al. 1991). Effects were evident even in populations of seals in the Antarctic (Testa et al. 1991). For species or populations with a restricted range,

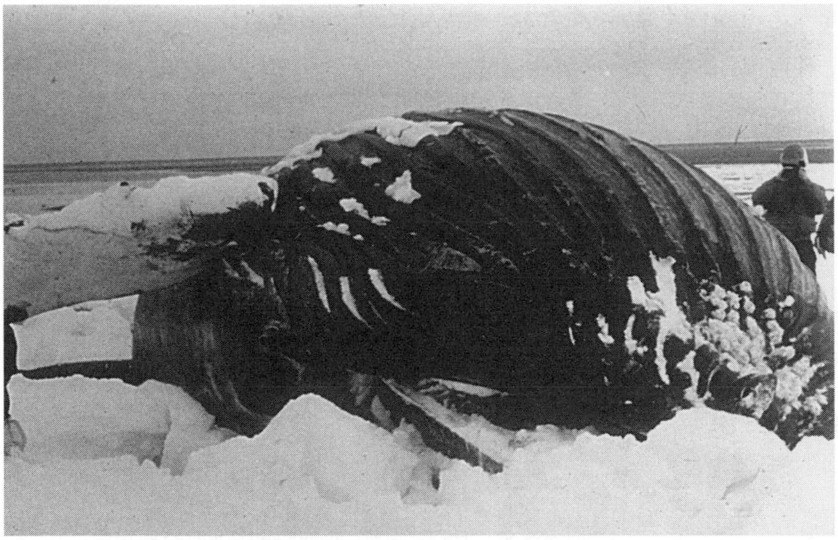

Figure 17-3. Large cetaceans most often die at sea and wash ashore decomposed, making it difficult to determine the cause of death. The stomach contents of this humpback whale, recovered in Cape Cod Bay during the winter of 1987–1988, showed that death was due to ingestion of saxitoxin-contaminated mackerel. (Photograph courtesy of New England Aquarium, Boston, MA)

such as the Hawaiian monk seal on French Frigate Shoals (Northwestern Hawaiian Islands) (Gilmartin and Eberhardt 1995) or population subgroups (e.g., breeding females, territorial males) unwilling to leave an area, extreme events can cause widespread starvation.

Recent Episodic Events

In this section we describe some of the more spectacular die-offs of marine mammals, consider the biological and environmental circumstances under which they occurred, and analyze their impact on the populations (Table 17-1). The fact that many of these events were reported during the late 1980s and 1990s prompted suggestions that they were becoming more common (Lavigne and Schmitz 1990). Other reviews (e.g., Harwood and Hall 1990) indicate that die-offs of this kind have occurred frequently in the past, but that, for a variety of reasons (e.g., remote locations), the events were poorly documented. In many cases, such as in the 1955 crabeater seal die-off (Laws and Taylor 1957), appropriate technologies were unavailable at the time for either detecting or characterizing the processes at work. We concentrate on recent events because they have been more thoroughly documented and, in most cases, were the focus of intensive scientific and public attention. To begin, we provide a brief chronology of each event and describe the speculations that were prevalent at the time. We include examples of mass mortality resulting from human activities, in one case, to demonstrate some of the differences involved in responding to such an event and, in the other, to illustrate how altered environmental conditions can lead to unexpected consequences. We then describe how the primary cause of each event was finally identified; the roles of other factors that may have contributed to the mortality are considered in more detail. Finally, we consider the importance of mass mortalities in the dynamics of marine mammal populations.

Chronology of Die-Off Events

During the past 15 years, scientists have had the opportunity to document and study a number of events involving the mass mortality of various species of marine mammals.

The 1982–1983 El Niño Southern Oscillation Event

Periodically, the pattern of currents in the South Pacific Ocean alters, causing massive changes in productivity, especially along the west coast of South America. These events are well known, and the phenomenon is called "El Niño." The 1982–1983 event caused widespread mortality of pups in colonies of fur seals and sea lions in the Galápagos Islands, Ecuador, and on mainland Peru. Galápagos fur seals were particularly hard hit; in addition to the loss of pups and juveniles, an estimated 50% of adult females and 100% of territorial males died during the event (Trillmich and Dellinger 1991). There was little controversy about the effects on Galápagos Island and other South American populations, but these mortalities were followed by similar events in the North Pacific affecting many other pinniped species. Detailed descriptions can be found in Trillmich and Ono (1991).

Bottlenose Dolphins along the U.S. Atlantic Coast, 1987–1988

Between July and December 1987 large numbers of bottlenose dolphin carcasses washed ashore along the Atlantic coast of the United States. The earliest strandings occurred along the New Jersey shore in June. When the unusual nature of the event become evident, the U.S. government launched a multidisciplinary investigation (Geraci 1989),

Table 17-1. Mass Mortalities of Marine Mammals

Year	Species/Location	Number killed	Cause	References
ca. 1825	Cape fur seals Namibia	~500,000	Biotoxins?, starvation?	Wyatt (1980)
1955	Crabeater seals Antarctic Peninsula	~2,500	Viral disease Morbillivirus?	Laws and Taylor (1957) Bengtson et al. (1991)
1970	California sea lions California	Several hundred	Leptospirosis	Vedros et al. (1971)
1971	Galápagos sea lions Galápagos Islands	~10,000–25,000 (est. 50% of population	Undetermined	Rand (1971), Gentry and Kooyman (1986)
1971, 1972	Sea otters Alaska Peninsula	Hundreds to thousands	Starvation/shock (heavy ice)	Schneider and Faro (1975)
1973	Harp seals Gulf of St. Lawrence	Hundreds to thousands	Crushing, drowning (storms, ice breakup)	Geraci and Lounsbury (1993)
1976–1977	Florida manatees Florida	~40	Cold stress	Campbell and Irvine (1981), O'Shea et al. (1985)
1978	Hawaiian monk seals Laysan Island	~50	Ciguatoxin poisoning, emaciation, parasites	Banish and Gilmartin (1992)
1978	Pacific walruses St. Lawrence Island	~1,000	Trauma/trampling	Fay and Kelly (1980)
1979–1980	Harbor seals New England	450+	Viral influenza	Geraci et al. (1982)
1982	Florida manatees SW Florida	37+	Brevetoxin poisoning	O'Shea et al. (1991)
1982–1983	Galápagos fur seals Galápagos Islands	100% of pups, juveniles, territorial males; 50% of adult females	Starvation (El Niño–related)	Trillmich (1985), Trillmich and Dellinger (1991)
1983	Northern elephant seals California	2,400+ pups	Drowning/trauma/starvation (El Niño–related storms)	Le Boeuf and Condit (1983), Le Boeuf and Reiter (1991)
1984–1985	Beluga whales NW Bering Sea	Est. 500–3,000	Ice entrapment	Burns and Seaman (1985), Ivashin and Shevlyagin (1987)
1987	Sea otters Alaska Peninsula	30+	Saxitoxin poisoning?	DeGange and Vacca (1989)
1987	Humpback whales Cape Cod Bay	14	Saxitoxin poisoning	Geraci et al. (1989)
1987–1988	Baikal seals Lake Baikal	5,000–10,000	Morbillivirus (CDV)	Grachev et al. (1989)
1987–1988	Bottlenose dolphins U.S. mid-Atlantic	750+	Morbillivirus?, biotoxins?, bacterial infections	Geraci (1989); Lipscomb, Schulman et al. (1994); Duignan, House, Geraci, Duffy et al. (1995)
1987–1988	Harbor seals Europe	~17,000	Morbillivirus (PDV)	Hall et al. (1992), Heide-Jørgensen et al. (1992)
1989	Sea otters Alaska	3,500–5,500	Oil spill	Loughlin (1994)
1990–1992	Striped dolphins Mediterranean Sea	Several thousand	Morbillivirus (DMV)	Duignan et al. (1992), Calzada et al. (1994)
1992	Dugongs Queensland, Australia	100+	Starvation	Preen and Marsh (1995)
1994	Cape fur seals Namibia	120,000+	Starvation	This chapter
1996	Florida manatees SW Florida	~150	Brevetoxin poisoning	Bossart et al. (1998)

with response teams moving from Virginia, to South Carolina, and finally to Florida as mortality advanced southward in conjunction with normal dolphin migratory movements. Peak mortality occurred from July through September 1987, although the die-off continued until March 1988. Public speculation centered on a link to sewage and the discharge of toxic waste, and on the possibility that a retrovirus causing an AIDS-like condition might be emerging in dolphins.

Early in the investigation, evidence pointed to immunosuppression due either to an infectious agent or to some type of toxin. A variety of microbial agents was found in the animals but none consistently enough to mark it as the cause. The contaminant picture also showed no clear pattern. Unusually warm water temperatures and brevetoxin contamination of coastal shellfish beds in the region stimulated analyses for biotoxins. Meanwhile, environmentalists remained adamant that pollution was responsible. The potential role of morbillivirus, recorded but considered insignificant at the time, gained renewed attention (Lipscomb, Schulman et al. 1994; Duignan, House, Geraci, Duffy et al. 1995; Duignan et al. 1996) after the morbillivirus outbreaks in Europe (see later discussion). By March 1988 more than 740 carcasses had been recovered; an unknown number of dolphins died at sea.

The Harp Seal Invasion of Norway, 1987

In the northeastern Atlantic, harp seals (*Phoca groenlandica*) give birth on ice in the White Sea and around the island of Jan Mayen. Outside the pupping season, they disperse widely in the Barents and Norwegian Seas. From 1985 onward, large numbers of harp seals began to appear off the north coast of Norway. Many became entangled in fishing nets and subsequently drowned. In 1987 this invasion was so large that harp seals were reported throughout the North Sea and as far south as the coast of Spain, and the Norwegian government agreed to pay fishermen for damages to nets caused by entangled seals. In 1987 and 1988 compensation was paid for 79,000 seals (Haug et al. 1991), although one observer (Wiig 1988) estimated that more than 100,000 drowned in fishing nets in 1987 alone.

Harbor Seals in the North Sea, 1988

During April 1988 large numbers of dead and dying, prematurely born harbor seal pups were reported from the Kattegat / Skagerrak (the neck of water that joins the North Sea to the Baltic). Soon, dead adult female seals were also reported from the same area. These deaths coincided with the presence of large blooms of toxic and nontoxic algae (Rosenberg et al. 1988). Deaths were then reported from the Wadden Sea, an area of partially enclosed water along the North Sea coast of Holland, Germany, and Denmark, away from the area of the bloom. Reports of deaths spread across the North Sea to the east coasts of England and Scotland and to the west coast of Norway. Finally, deaths spread to the Atlantic coast of Scotland and to Ireland. Because seals in the Wadden Sea are known to carry high levels of contaminants, there was much speculation that the deaths were the result of pollution, and this remained an obsession for the media throughout 1988. As deaths spread throughout the North Sea, it became clear that the pattern of mortality was consistent with that caused by an infectious disease, and a number of potential disease agents were proposed before the primary cause, a morbillivirus, was finally identified. In total, more than 18,000 dead harbor seals were reported along European coasts in 1988. Very few deaths were reported in 1989. More detailed histories of this event can be found in Dietz et al. (1989), Harwood (1989), Kennedy (1990), and Heide-Jørgensen et al. (1992).

Sea Otters in Prince William Sound, Alaska, 1989

On 24 March 1989 the *Exxon Valdez* ran aground in Prince William Sound, Alaska, spilling an estimated 11 million gallons (42×10^6 liters) of oil in less than five hours (Morris and Loughlin 1994, Zimmerman et al. 1994). Although industry response plans for this type of disaster were in place, no one was actually prepared. The oil remained in a relatively small area for the first three days, but by the time the response was organized, a winter storm had spread the oil over hundreds of square kilometers; more than 1,100 km of coastline were eventually contaminated. Massive clean-up efforts lasted months and continued intermittently until 1992; residues remain even today. Sea otter rescue effort peaked in May and ended in late July 1989. An estimated 3,500 to 5,500 sea otters died during this time from the combined effects of inhalation of volatile fractions, ingested oil, hypothermia, and shock (Osborn and Williams 1990, Lipscomb, Harris et al. 1994). Of the approximately 360 sea otters treated in rescue centers, more than one-third died, despite intensive (and expensive) medical treatment. See Loughlin (1994) for a review of this event.

Striped Dolphins in the Mediterranean Sea, 1990–1992

From July through November 1990 large numbers of dead striped dolphins were found along the Mediterranean coasts of Spain, France, and northern Italy. Many animals had been in poor condition before death, and the carcasses carried high levels of contaminants. Again, there was speculation that pollution may have been the cause (Aguilar and Borrell 1994). Aguilar and Raga (1993) provided a detailed description of the event in the western Mediterranean, during which at least 1,000 carcasses were recovered. The mortality spread across the Mediterranean and affected southern Italy and the eastern Mediterranean in 1991, and was especially high around Greece between July 1991 and December 1992 (Cebrian 1995).

Cape Fur Seals in Namibia, 1994

The following summary is taken from Roux (in United Nations Environment Programme 1995). Throughout 1994 almost all colonies of Cape fur seals (*Arctocephalus pusillus pusillus*) in Namibia suffered the highest levels of pup mortality ever observed, resulting from abandonment and starvation. Those females that continued to feed their young became very thin, and there was a high mortality of subadult males, which were also present on the breeding grounds. By the end of May, all sex and age groups had suffered unprecedented mortality and approximately 120,000 pups had died. In June and July, there was a high rate of abortion among surviving females.

The Cape fur seal population had been increasing steadily since the 1970s (Punt and Butterworth 1995) after the virtual cessation of commercial hunting. There was some evidence that pup production had begun to level off, and there was considerable speculation in the popular press that the events of 1994 were indications that the population had exceeded its carrying capacity.

Florida Manatees, 1996

From early March through April 1996 more than 155 manatee carcasses were recovered from southwestern Florida; only 33 had been reported from the same area in the previous two-month period. The number of deaths in this single event exceeded the average annual mortality for the Florida population from 1982 through 1992 (Ackerman et al. 1995). Most of the manatees had been in good health before death, and there were no signs of cold stress. Early evidence pointed to the possible involvement of a virus or toxin. There was suspicion that animals may have been exposed to high levels of herbicides or pesticides from agricultural runoff. The presence of an unusually strong and persistent red tide with associated fish kills and increased cormorant mortality, and similarities to the 1982 brevetoxin-related manatee deaths pointed to the possibility of a biotoxin (Scott Wright, Florida Department of Environmental Protection, pers. comm.).

Primary Causes of the Mass Mortalities

Of the events described above, the mass mortality of sea otters was the only one for which the cause was known from the outset. Experimental studies had demonstrated the extreme vulnerability of this species to spilled oil (Costa and Kooyman 1982). In a sense, this event was an accident waiting to happen. Of the remaining die-offs, the harbor seal mortality in the North Sea and the striped dolphin mortality in the Mediterranean provide the best evidence for a primary cause. In the case of the harbor seal (Harwood and Reijnders 1988, Heide-Jørgensen et al. 1992), there was initially much speculation about the link between seal deaths and an algal bloom. Within a month, however, deaths were reported from areas unaffected by the bloom. Attention then focused on the possible effects of chemical pollution and on the involvement of a microparasite. The occurrence of deaths on relatively unpolluted coasts ruled out pollution as the primary cause, and the investigation shifted to search for a microparasite that could have caused the deaths. The search was made easier by the fact that many sick and dying seals were brought into rescue centers where there were opportunities to obtain good-quality samples.

There were early reports in July 1988 (Osterhaus 1988) that the harbor seal deaths were caused by either a herpesvirus or a picornavirus (the best known picornavirus is polio), but the data from dead and sick animals did not satisfy any of Koch's postulates. However, over the course of the next three months, a pathogen that did meet these demands was found (Osterhaus and Vedder 1988). At first it was believed to be the canine distemper virus (Osterhaus et al. 1988), a microorganism that causes fatal illness in domestic dogs and some wild carnivores. Closer analysis of the virus structure indicated that this was a new virus—phocine distemper virus (PDV) (Cosby et al. 1988, Mahy et al. 1988). The epidemiology and clinical signs of phocine distemper are similar to those of canine distemper (Bergman et al. 1990). Animals die within about 20 days of contracting the disease, but probably shed infective virus particles for only a few days during that period. The most common route for transmission is the aerosol produced by the coughing and sneezing of infected animals. Most of the viral transfer in seals probably occurs when they are hauled out in large aggregations on land. The source of phocine distemper infection in 1988 is not entirely clear, but there is little evidence of its presence among North Sea seals before the outbreak (Harwood et al. 1989, Osterhaus et al. 1989). In 1987 and 1988 there were substantial invasions of harp seals into the North Sea, prompting speculation that these seals may have introduced the virus into naive populations (Goodhart 1988). Although this suggestion was dismissed by some authors (Dietz et al. 1989, Lavigne and Schmitz 1990), we now know that PDV was present in harp seals from Greenland before 1988 (Markussen and Have 1992) and is probably a persistent infection in the population from which the invaders originated (Stuen et al. 1994); we also know that such invasions have occurred at irregular intervals in the past

(Sergeant 1991). In 1988 about 60% of the infected harbor seals died.

The striped dolphin die-off occurred shortly after the phocine distemper epidemic in the North Sea, and after another new virus (now known as dolphin morbillivirus) very similar to phocine distemper virus had been identified in several harbor porpoises (*Phocoena phocoena*) found dead in the Irish Sea during 1988 (Kennedy et al. 1988). Evidence of infection with the same or a very closely related virus was found in most of the dead dolphins from the Mediterranean that were examined (Van Bressem et al. 1991, Domingo et al. 1992, Duignan et al. 1992). Although only one of Koch's postulates could be met in this case, the pattern of illness suggested that the underlying cause of death was the morbillivirus. The animals finally succumbed to often overwhelming infection by secondary invaders.

Determining the cause of the 1987–1988 bottlenose dolphin die-off was complicated (Fig. 17-4). Many of the carcasses examined were badly decomposed. Dolphins dying early in the event showed a variety of skin lesions, some suspected to be of viral origin; and some animals had lost large sheets of epidermis. As time passed, many dolphins showed more advanced, often chronic forms of lung and liver disease, suggesting that they had overcome the initial illness and were dying of secondary causes. The event was dramatic, unprecedented at that time, and the subject of intense scientific and public concern. Early findings led away from microbial agents as the principal cause of death because no single one that was isolated could produce the array of conditions observed. The numerous bacterial and fungal pathogens found were considered to be secondary invaders. Evidence of virus infection in a few animals, including the finding of antibodies to morbillivirus in sera of 6 of 13 dolphins captured off the coast of Virginia in 1988, was not considered significant at that time. The transmission of a highly contagious viral pathogen over such a broad range, in an environment where airborne transmission was limited, was thought unlikely. Yet, fear that an AIDS-like condition might be involved created pressure to screen samples for human immunodeficiency virus (HIV). Concern that the dolphins had been poisoned by toxic wastes led to analyses for radioactivity, heavy metal, and organochlorine contamination. Organochlorine levels were highly variable—among the highest ever detected in cetaceans in some samples, but low in others. Shellfish beds in the region contained enough brevetoxin for them to be closed to commercial harvesting. The few dolphin specimens suitable for brevetoxin analysis showed the toxin to be present in 8 of 17 liver samples taken from animals that died at various points in the outbreak, as well as in a menhaden (*Brevoortia* sp.) recovered from the stomach of one dead dolphin. No toxin was detected in dolphins that had stranded in the same location in previous years or in other regions at the time of the outbreak. This was taken as evidence that brevetoxin poisoning was the underlying cause of the illness that eventually led to overwhelming bacterial and viral infections (Geraci 1989).

Retrospective studies using techniques developed and refined after this die-off (Lipscomb, Schulman et al. 1994; Duignan, House, Geraci, Duffy et al. 1995; Duignan et al. 1996) have demonstrated a high prevalence of morbillivirus infection, both in dolphins that died and in free-ranging animals sampled during the outbreak. Duignan et al. (1996) presented evidence that epidemics caused by a morbillivirus very similar to dolphin morbillivirus have occurred sporadically in the U.S. southeast coastal bottlenose dolphin population: in 1982 on the east coast of Florida, in 1987–1988 on the U.S. Atlantic coast, and in the Gulf of Mexico between

Figure 17-4. Bottlenose dolphin carcasses recovered during the 1987–1988 U.S. Atlantic coast die-off showed a baffling range of conditions. Most dolphins died from overwhelming secondary infections. (Photograph courtesy of U.S. Department of Agriculture)

1992 and 1994 (Lipscomb, Kennedy et al. 1994). The influence of brevetoxin in the 1987–1988 die-off remains uncertain.

The deaths associated with the 1982–1983 El Niño were clearly the result of environmental change. This also appears to have been the cause of the Cape fur seal die-off in 1994. Although evidence of exposure to morbillivirus was found in some animals, the primary cause of death for all fur seal pups was chronic starvation (Anselmo et al. 1995). A mass of low-oxygen-content water intruded onto the northern continental shelf of Namibia in the first half of 1993 and remained there at least through August 1994. All pelagic and epipelagic fish species (the principal prey of Cape fur seals) displayed abnormal distributions or behavior in 1994; myctophids disappeared, and anchovy and pilchard stocks decreased sharply (Roux in United Nations Environment Programme 1995).

The 1987 harp seal invasion also coincided with unusual ecological conditions in the Barents Sea, where herring and capelin stocks were dramatically reduced in abundance. There is controversy about the role of commercial fishing in this reduction. Both species of fish are known to show wide fluctuations in abundance, even in the absence of fishing pressure. The main cause of harp seal mortality was trauma following entanglement in fishing gear. Although these seals were thin at the time of death, they were not emaciated. It is doubtful whether mortality would have been as high if large amounts of static fishing gear had not been deployed along the Norwegian coast at the time.

By the time this volume is published, the story of the 1996 Florida manatee die-off may be complete. Although suspicion first focused on the unusually strong red tide that coincided with the timing and location of the die-off, difficulties in proving biotoxin as the cause of death, widespread involvement of morbilliviruses in other recent mass mortalities, and concerns for coastal water quality compelled a wide range of investigations. The results of these analyses did not support a role for either contaminants or infectious agents. The process of elimination left biotoxins, probably brevetoxin, as the most likely cause of the die-off. The pattern of mortality, the neurological symptoms observed in rescued animals, the pathologic evidence, and the detection of brevetoxin in manatee tissue provide strong evidence to support this conclusion (Bossart et al. 1998).

Contributing Factors

As shown in the previous section, the primary causes of most marine mammal die-offs reported in the past decade are reasonably well understood. Still, in most of these events there was widespread scientific and public concern that anthropogenic factors, such as pollution and overfishing, were the underlying causes. This was certainly true for the 1988 phocine distemper outbreak, which we will use as an example to show how contributory factors may operate and how we can assess the evidence for their effects.

Mortality rates during the 1988 phocine distemper epidemic were not the same in different parts of the North Sea: a far higher proportion of animals died in the southern areas (Harwood et al. 1991) where contaminant burdens are known to be high. Basic epidemiological modeling carried out by Grenfell et al. (1992) indicated that this disparity could be due to either different contact rates between infectious and susceptible individuals or different mortality rates after infection. If the first explanation is correct, there should also be differences in the proportion of surviving animals with antibodies to phocine distemper virus. However, a survey carried out in 1989 found that prevalence rates were similar throughout the United Kingdom (Harwood et al. 1989), thus indicating differential mortality. Why should this occur? The potential contributory factors include the presence of macroparasites, algal blooms, organochlorine pollution, variations in body condition, the presence of sewage-related bacteria in the water, and previous exposure of the population to the virus. Some of these proposed factors can be ruled out: seals found dead in 1988 did have high levels of macroparasites, but this was not a universal phenomenon and was probably a consequence of immunosuppression related to phocine distemper; although there was an algal bloom in the Kattegat / Skagerrak at the start of the epidemic, it soon moved off in a direction away from the path of the virus. Similarly, although the highest mortality did occur in areas where raw sewage is still discharged into the sea, the species of bacteria associated with the outbreak are not routinely found in sewage.

In the seal, striped dolphin, and bottlenose dolphin die-offs, popular attention also focused on the role of pollution, a factor we examine in more detail. A number of environmental contaminants (particularly organochlorine compounds and certain heavy metals) are known to have an immunosuppressive effect on laboratory animals (Safe 1984). These compounds are bioaccummulative and thus often found in high concentrations in top predators, such as many marine mammals (for an extensive review, see O'Shea 1999). In addition, organochlorines are preferentially soluble in lipids and occur in particularly high concentrations in the blubber. The evidence for a causal relationship or compounding effect between high contaminant levels and susceptibility to disease in marine mammals is inconclusive (Brouwer et al. 1989, Muir et al. 1990, Kendall et al. 1992). Some of the bottlenose dolphins sampled during the 1987–1988 die-off had levels of organochlorines among the highest ever recorded for cetaceans (Geraci 1989), and animals that died during the European phocine distemper and the Mediterranean dolphin morbillivirus epidemics had higher concentrations of organochlorines than apparently healthy animals sampled before or after the events (Hall et al. 1992, Aguilar and Raga 1993, Aguilar and Borrell 1994). It should be noted, however, that (except for striped dolphins late in the Mediterranean die-off [Aguilar and Borrell 1994]) these animals were also in far worse physical condition. Because the critical pollutants (the polychlorinated biphenyls) are stored primarily in the blubber and become more concentrated as fat is used up during fasting or starvation, it is possible that the difference in levels at the outset of infection in most seals and dolphins was small.

Studies to determine the association between contaminants and immunosuppression in harbor seals are ongoing. Harder et al. (1992) found no difference in response to phocine distemper virus in harbor seals fed fish supplemented with organochlorines—to mimic the contaminant burden of fish in the Wadden Sea—as compared with those fed clean fish. Recent experiments by other scientists (De Swart et al. 1994, 1995; Ross et al. 1996) had different results: seals fed fish from polluted areas showed an impaired immune response compared with those fed clean fish. The link between pollution and the 1988 harbor seal die-off remains unresolved and the subject of controversy.

Starvation and malnutrition can affect a marine mammal's susceptibility to disease by more than one mechanism (Suskind 1977, Seth and Beotra 1986). For example, the associated weakness and stress might result in immunosuppression and increased likelihood of secondary infection. The utilization of blubber may lead to the release of fat-soluble toxins into the bloodstream, with possible consequences to immune function. There were suggestions that the 1990 dolphin morbillivirus outbreak in the western Mediterranean was triggered by reduced food resources, because many of the animals were in poor condition with thin blubber. This, however, might have been the result of the long course of morbillivirus infection.

The lowest mortality in the phocine distemper outbreak occurred in northern areas. If harp seals are the usual vector for introducing the phocine distemper virus into harbor seal populations, at least in the northeastern Atlantic, then the more northerly stocks have probably been challenged more frequently with this virus and may have become more resistant. Social organization and behavior may also have been important in determining the force of infection (i.e., the number of susceptible hosts that an infectious individual contacts while it is capable of transmitting the virus) in different areas. The highest mortalities occurred in May–June, at the start of the pupping season, and in August, when most seals molt. These are periods when seals spend much of their time out of water and are therefore more likely to come into contact with infectious individuals.

Thus, although some of the proposed contributory factors can be ruled out, it appears likely that others did affect the level of mortality in particular areas. It is, however, currently impossible to determine the extent of additional mortality attributable to any or all of these factors, and this uncertainty continues to generate controversy. Clearly, the role of contaminants, in particular, needs to be clarified. This can only be accomplished through continued laboratory investigations.

Long-Term Consequences of Die-Offs

Losses to the populations involved in these recent mass mortalities were high: 30% of the northeastern Atlantic harbor seal population in 1988; all of the Cape fur seal pups born in 1993 and 1994 (Roux in United Nations Environment Programme 1995); 50% of the U.S. Atlantic coastal migratory stock of bottlenose dolphins in 1987–1988 (Scott et al. 1988); through entanglement in nets, most of the harp seal pups born in the Barents Sea population in 1986, 1987, and 1988 (Kjellqwist et al. 1995); and perhaps 7–8% of the Florida manatee population in 1996. Are these mass mortalities important?

Harwood and Hall (1990) concluded that such events could have a substantial effect on long-term dynamics and population genetics, a view supported by theoretical analysis of the potential impact of episodic mortalities (Mangel and Tier 1994). In the North Sea, mass mortalities of harbor seals have probably occurred at approximately 50-year intervals. Yet, large populations seem to recover surprisingly rapidly. For example, by 1994, the North Sea harbor seal population had returned to levels approaching those observed before 1988 (International Council for the Exploration of the Sea 1994).

In many cases, marine mammal die-offs have taken the highest toll on the youngest age classes—the segment that usually suffers the highest natural mortality and is the most easily replaced—thus reducing the impact on population dynamics (Fowler 1987). Populations of species with long pupping or calving intervals would probably recover more slowly from such a loss. The Florida manatee, for example, has a calving interval of at least two to three years (Marmontel 1995, Rathbun et al. 1995). The high rate of perinatal death observed in this population (Ackerman et al. 1995) might further prolong the recovery period after a high mortality of calves. For mammals in general, episodic events that kill large numbers of adults, especially females, have the greatest long-term impacts (Eberhardt and Siniff 1977).

Thus recovery of the Galápagos fur seal (Trillmich and Dellinger 1991) and Mediterranean striped dolphin (Calzada et al. 1994) populations may take many years. Recovery of the fur seal population will be further delayed by continued decreased recruitment due to the high mortality of pups and juveniles (Trillmich and Dellinger 1991). The large number of adult manatees involved in the 1996 die-off underscores the vulnerability of small, restricted populations to catastrophic events (Ackerman et al. 1995) (Fig. 17-5).

These observations suggest that episodic mortality can have serious and lasting effects. In fact, very small populations, such as those of the highly endangered Mediterranean or Hawaiian monk seals, or Florida manatees, may be at risk of extinction from such events. The greatest threat to these populations is probably viruses, particularly morbilliviruses, many of which have multiple hosts. Large populations in which infection is prevalent can act as a reservoir for transmitting viruses to rare and vulnerable species. This is a special case of "shared enemies," a form of competition that can lead to the displacement or removal of species from ecosystems (Holt and Lawton 1994). The Mediterranean monk seal may be susceptible to both canine distemper and phocine distemper infection and thus at particular risk from such processes (Osterhaus et al. 1992).

Responding to a Die-Off

Die-offs can extend over periods of weeks or months, take place over a broad geographic range, and involve species that are difficult to study. Sick animals may be too far at sea for investigators to study their condition or even to obtain a reliable estimate of mortality. Die-offs respect no international borders. A response team may find itself unwelcome in the waters of a neighboring country, which itself may lack resources or the interest to pursue its own investigation. The expression and outcome of a die-off may be influenced by elusive factors that have their own pattern in time and space. An event may have different effects among species or population subgroups that share the same range because of such factors as age, sex, previous exposure to pathogens, and, at a more basic level, size, anatomy, and physiology. Thus we cannot expect that a single study protocol will be appropriate for all cases. On the other hand, we can assume that for most events, the cause will not be established at the outset, and that certain issues will repeatedly arise among scientists, policy makers, and the public. An effective response demands careful organization and continuous cooperation among numerous agencies if the kinds of information, samples, and data necessary are to be collected. These data can only be interpreted in the context of baseline information on the relevant species. Finally, we consider some of the problems investigators face in any event that draws widespread scientific and public attention.

What Are the Issues?

Die-offs affect more than the health and lives of the animals involved. What drives the initial response is legal responsibility, animal welfare, and scientific interest. As the event takes on larger dimensions, there may be fears for the entire population or even other species. Public health issues arise: potentially transmissible diseases, contamination of commercial food species, and significance to the recreational use of coastal waters. Most die-offs in recent years have raised serious questions about ecosystem health, particularly when biotoxins, pollutants, and human activities are sus-

Figure 17-5. Brevetoxin from the red tide organism *Gymnodinium breve* can accumulate in marine organisms and disperse in air. Both sources of brevetoxin have been implicated in the deaths of West Indian manatees on Florida's southwestern coast. (Photograph courtesy of Florida Department of Environmental Protection)

pected as the cause. With growing public awareness, these issues, whether based on fact or speculation, have gained tremendous political importance.

Thus, the response team must be prepared to determine the cause of the event, its impact on the population, and the implications for ecosystem health, and address any public health concerns. Although such a complex study may do little for the animals beyond providing an explanation for their deaths, the information gained may help shape response programs and environmental policies that will abate the effects of future events and perhaps even reduce their frequency.

Elements of Planning

The key to a die-off investigation is organization, preplanning, and a strong spirit of cooperation. A large event requires the collaboration of local, regional, and federal agencies; laboratories with expertise in microbiology, pathology, and contaminant and biotoxin analysis; stranding network members and volunteers; and the media, among others.

Contingency Plans

In any region where die-offs are likely to occur, a mechanism for rapidly deploying a well-trained response team should be in place. This assumes that (1) a contingency plan exists, (2) the agency responsible for initiating action has been determined, (3) the roles of all collaborating parties are clearly defined, and (4) ample funding is available. Ideally, each region will have its own plans, based on the kinds of die-offs that are apt to occur there. Where jurisdiction over an area or species is vague, conflicting, or overlapping, managers must develop an interagency approach. A die-off across a national border will certainly need some kind of agreement. Managers must consider that local regulations might restrict response activities. For example, vehicle and vessel use may be prohibited in areas designated as critical habitats. In any case, plans must be developed that aim to minimize the damage or disturbance to the local environment and other animal species. Each category of event will require a different strategy. An oil spill plan will emphasize immediate cleanup and rescue, whereas an array of analytical studies will be required for a die-off of unknown cause.

Even with all this in place, a response rarely, if ever, proceeds according to plan. There were eight oil-spill contingency plans for Prince William Sound when the *Exxon Valdez* ran aground, but none for a spill of that scale (Morris and Loughlin 1994, Zimmerman et al. 1994). The company initially charged with containing the oil was unprepared. By the time a response was organized, a winter storm had spread the oil far beyond the original site. Personnel from federal and state agencies and the oil industry arrived within hours, but not all were familiar with the plans. It was not clear who was responsible, what should be done and under whose authority, and where the funds would come from. Responsibility for animal management became a conflicting issue. The U.S. Fish and Wildlife Service is responsible for sea otters, walruses, and polar bears; the National Marine Fisheries Service for pinnipeds and cetaceans; and, according to Alaska statute, the Alaska Department of Fish and Game is charged with managing and conserving all wildlife. Collecting and treating oiled marine mammals in U.S. waters requires permits from the appropriate management agency. The location itself presented tremendous logistic difficulties. The town of Valdez was unprepared for the influx of people; limited road access, aircraft, vessels, and work space led to intense competition for these resources. (See Loughlin [1994] for a complete review.) Nearly every die-off has had a comparable story; the problems, although not identical, have been nonetheless disabling. These experiences may be the best teachers when it comes to planning and training for future responses.

How is a response funded? Ideally, any plan should include a budget to support even a modest operation through the first few days or weeks. That is not always the case. Sometimes private institutions, perhaps because they are close by, have launched forth at their own cost, using personnel, vehicles, and other resources, expecting reimbursement and, eventually, continuing support. The New England Aquarium bore almost the entire cost of the 1979–1980 influenza study and the 1988 finding of saxitoxin in humpback whales. Fortunately, these were both relatively low-cost investigations. Not every institution is willing or capable of undertaking even this level of action. Underfunding has the greatest potential to sabotage an investigation. It leads to interruptions, frustration, shortcuts, cost-cutting measures that reduce the quality of work, and delay in the analyses that may hold the answer. Long-term studies are an even greater challenge.

The *Exxon Valdez* incident took place in March 1989, and its effects will continue to be studied well into the next century. This will require long-range planning and substantial commitments of money, resources, and personnel. Government funding, which is typically short-term, will, for die-offs, have to be reviewed in a different context.

When to Respond

Policy makers and managers must be alert to the presence of a die-off, well-informed as to its scale and characteristics, and prepared (i.e., authorized and willing)—in terms of funding and logistics—to initiate action. The first step in this process is determining that the need for response exists (in other words, that a die-off is taking place). The early stages may be marked by nothing more than a few animals coming ashore in a pattern indistinguishable from those of previous years. There is no specific number of casualties that constitutes a die-off. At some point however, the local person in charge must make the decision to alert the responsible agency, as early as possible, that something unusual may be happening. This will allow time for staging the response. It is easier to call off an action for an event that turns out to be insignificant than it is to begin one when a die-off is well under way.

The lines for making these decisions are not always clear, and not all large-scale mortalities call for action. A team would certainly respond rapidly if 100 seals were affected by an oil spill. What would be the point of a response if the same pups were killed or injured by a severe storm that swept them off their rookeries? In such a case, the cause of death is clear, and little can be done to help injured animals beyond rescuing the few that might be accommodated in rehabilitation facilities. In the United States and many other countries, this type of event is already dealt with by organized stranding networks. On the other hand, there may be instances, such as a toxic spill, in which no animals have yet been affected but for which the potential for harm is great. In such a case, the decision to intervene may be appropriate before any casualties have occurred.

The Response Team

The response team should consist of persons with collective expertise in life history and ecology, clinical medicine, anatomy and pathology, infectious diseases, and toxicology. This expertise aside, the investigators' ability to get the job done depends on the support and services of individuals skilled in media relations, personnel management, and resource acquisition. A team member familiar with pertinent local laws and regulations, regional oceanographic conditions, and potential sources of logistic support is critical to efficiency. During the course of the response, investigators should maintain constant communication with outside scientists in relevant disciplines to provide another level of insight and objectivity, which pressure, chaos, and fatigue can easily erode. Maintaining a roster of qualified scientists willing to provide this service will save time and effort (needed elsewhere) once action is under way.

Very few persons, if any, are employees of a response team. Members are drawn from various institutions and agencies, largely as volunteers or because their services are available, not necessarily because of their training. Even the core group will have to balance its team activity with other commitments, more so as the investigation continues. At some point, one or more persons may be forced to withdraw from the team to resume their usual responsibilities. Disruption can be minimized by providing broad training so that other team members can fill a short-term gap, and by creating a reserve team for critical positions.

Obviously, the chain of command and roles and responsibilities must be clearly established at the outset of a response action. The coordinator must keep the team working together and focused, remain objective throughout the investigation, and be able to do this under extreme pressure. Although scientific expertise may be a plus, perhaps the most essential attributes of a coordinator are leadership, personality, and administrative capability.

Investigating the Event

The central mission of the response team is to determine the cause of the die-off, how it affects the population, and whether the event has broader implications for public and environmental health. The field activities associated with the response can themselves potentially injure the habitat and species already threatened by the event. Managers and policy makers must strive to maintain a balance between the needs of the study and those of the environment.

Determining the Cause

What does it mean when debilitated seals have been observed for nearly a month on a rookery and in nearby waters; when a cluster of whale carcasses, in too poor condition for even gross dissection, appears after an onshore wind; or when a few dozen manatees are found dead along with large numbers of fish and cormorants? Although each incident can present a formidable challenge to an investigating team, there are certain rules of thumb, based on the mortality pattern alone, that can help guide the first stages of the study.

The sudden appearance of whale carcasses suggests that they probably died around the same time, a situation for which there are few likely causes. Some viruses can kill quickly; not many other infectious agents known from marine mammals have this potential. Macroparasitic disease can be virtually ruled out. Other possibilities might include an environmental event such as ice entrapment leading to suffocation; human interaction such as net entanglement, shooting, or an underwater explosion; or poisoning, perhaps by a contaminant or a biotoxin from an algal bloom. The manatee scenario similarly rules out bacteria and parasites, but viruses as well, because few, if any, are known to cross as many vertebrate classes. An investigator might consider, instead, an environmental event, a biotoxin perhaps, or poisoning by an extraordinarily potent anthropogenic substance. The pattern of illness in seals offers no real clues.

Whether or not a particular die-off reveals conspicuous signs that broadly suggest the cause, carrying the study to conclusion will require the diligent collection and analysis of vast amounts of data and samples. Even when the cause seems clear—northern elephant seals swept off a rookery by a storm (Le Boeuf and Condit 1983)—samples are needed to determine whether contributing factors, such as starvation or disease, might have been involved. Everything that can be learned from one die-off—biology, life history, contaminants—enriches baseline information for better understanding the next. The range of data gathered during the 1987–1988 bottlenose dolphin die-off (Geraci 1989) serves as an example. Signs early in the event pointed to the action of an infectious agent or toxin. Tissue and fluid samples from every suitable carcass were taken to isolate any bacteria, chlamydia, mycoplasma, fungi, and viruses, and to analyze for a wide range of contaminants, including heavy metals and organic compounds. Samples from lesions and organs were taken for histopathology and electron microscopy, and liver and other organs were analyzed for biotoxins. On two occasions free-ranging dolphins were captured for blood studies that might offer important clues to their clinical condition and the pathogens they might have encountered.

The results of a study depend as much on how the specimens are handled, transported, and analyzed as they do on the quantity of samples and how they are obtained (Geraci and Lounsbury 1993, Becker et al. 1994). Continuity demands that the material be analyzed as soon as possible, especially when searching for microparasites, toxins, or contaminants that perish or deteriorate quickly or that could be a risk to public health. Questions regarding the validity of a particular analysis can be avoided by sending critical samples to different laboratories for duplicate testing. Samples to be analyzed for saxitoxin, suspected of poisoning humpback whales, were sent to three separate laboratories; results within three days confirmed its presence and prompted authorities to issue a public health advisory. Would that step have been taken if only one laboratory had been involved? A record of all sample transfers, from collection through analysis, will be required to trace their path, establish accountability, and accurately correlate specific samples with their results. This is known as the "chain of custody," and failure to maintain it can destroy the credibility of an investigation.

Investigating the contribution of ecosystem health to a die-off demands even more data. Water and sediment samples may be needed to determine the presence of dinoflagellates, human and domestic wastes, contaminants such as pesticides, herbicides, fertilizers, and petroleum hydrocarbons, and any substances suspected to have been spilled in the area or introduced in runoff. Analyzing meteorological and oceanographic patterns for the preceding days, weeks, or months may reveal evidence of unusual conditions. Some of these factors may be interrelated and linked in a long sequence. For example, unusual amounts of rainfall might lead to increased runoff, causing a high influx of nitrates and phosphates that, combined with warm water temperatures, may trigger a bloom of dinoflagellates whose toxins accumulate up the food chain to finally poison a whale. Determining whether environmental agents might have contributed to the 1987–1988 bottlenose dolphin die-off required a review of the types and amounts of wastes discharged into central U.S. east coast waters, the weather and ocean current patterns that might have affected the movement of those wastes, and the occurrence and distribution of plankton blooms. Unfortunately, much of this information was unavailable or incomplete. Only thorough environmental sampling will reveal the relationship between die-offs and ecosystem conditions.

Assessing Population Effects

The consequences of a die-off at the population level depend on the age and sex distribution and total number of animals lost. Obtaining this information may require beach and vessel surveys, as well as onshore and offshore aerial observations, to locate carcasses and identify trends in the overall mortality pattern. Surveys to obtain this kind of information are often the most costly element of a study. Analysis of life history data collected from carcasses will show how each sex and age class was affected by the die-off.

Differential mortality may occur for a number of reasons. For example, the influenza outbreak in New England harbor seals predominantly affected juveniles (Geraci et al. 1982). This might have suggested that either they lacked immunity to the virus or they were predisposed to infection by previous illness, malnutrition, or parasitism, or social factors (i.e., distribution) that might have brought juveniles in closer contact with the virus. In this case, the young seals had aggregated at haul-out sites where the opportunity for viral transmission through aerosols was magnified. Adult seals were dispersed to the north and, for the most part, escaped infection. Thus the apparent absence of a particular age group from mortality statistics may not necessarily indicate immunity or resistance to the infectious agent, toxin, or whatever else might have caused the die-off, but simply that they were not there at the time. Knowing the species' life history and patterns of habitat use helps to interpret the significance of how and why a certain segment of the population is affected. Communicating with neighboring agencies or stranding networks may confirm that the "missing" population groups have, in fact, been sighted elsewhere.

Public Health Issues

When sick marine mammals come ashore in full view of the public, the question often asked is whether the "disease" can be transmitted to humans and domestic animals. In fact, the risk to humans is generally assumed to be low for those who take reasonable precautions (Geraci and Ridgway 1991, Geraci and Lounsbury 1993). This may be difficult for investigators, as it was for 11 team members who developed conjunctivitis (inflammation of the soft tissues of the eye) after handling carcasses of seals that had died of influenza (Webster et al. 1981). One calicivirus, from the many that affect marine mammals, may have been transmitted to a laboratory technician (Smith et al. 1986). Microbes commonly isolated from bottlenose dolphin carcasses examined during the 1987–1988 die-off included various species of *Vibrio* (Geraci 1989), many of which are commonly found in healthy, free-ranging cetaceans (Buck and Spotte 1986b). Although there have been no known cases of handlers acquiring an infection through contact with marine mammals (Wilkinson 1991), some species of *Vibrio* cause serious illness in humans.

These are but a few examples. Prudent policy suggests that those handling sick animals or carcasses take adequate precautions to prevent infection, and that the public be urged to avoid contact. This policy should also extend to pets and domestic animals. A dog roaming the beach could be exposed to canine distemper from an infected seal. After a disease agent has been isolated, laboratory tests may determine the potential risk to other species. While these studies are under way, it may be necessary to restrict the distribution of tissues to collaborating scientists. This is, however, guaranteed to cause dissention among others who may see this restriction as a personal denial of access to a public resource.

The finding of a poison, contaminant, or toxin may generate an action by health authorities, such as closing local shellfish beds or warning the public to temporarily avoid eating fish species known to carry the toxin. The public and investigators working on the gulf coast of Florida where red tides occur should be alerted to the irritating effects of brevetoxin aerosols on the eyes and respiratory tissues. Evidence of contamination by toxic or human wastes may require closure of public bathing areas or legal action to enforce environmental regulations that protect coastal and marine waters.

Sources of Baseline Information

Data collected during an investigation can only be interpreted in the context of baseline information. There are a number of sources to consider, each with its own advantages and limitations.

Free-Ranging Animals

Studies (especially long-term) of free-ranging animals provide a wealth of information on normal patterns of behavior and habitat use. Some pinnipeds, with their close ties to shore, are easily observed. For such species, we have a good understanding of the typical patterns of illness and mortality and many of the factors that influence them, such as weather conditions, maternal behavior, and aggressive interactions. Occasionally, biologists on a rookery may actually witness a die-off (Le Boeuf and Condit 1983). Coastal cetaceans, more than pelagic species, as well as sirenians and sea otters, lend themselves to photographic identification programs and other noninvasive methods to study populations, behavior, longevity, and habitat use. Such data are vital for developing management strategies and may be especially critical in the event of a die-off.

Sampling and tagging studies provide opportunities to learn about genetic and health profiles, animal movements, dive patterns, stock identity, diet, reproductive condition, milk composition, and physiology (e.g., hematology, water balance). Baseline data on contaminant burdens are especially vital. These allow us not only to monitor trends in marine pollution, but also provide a standard for comparison with levels found in sick or dead marine mammals. In recent years, studies of free-ranging animals have, for example, added tremendously to knowledge about the nature of morbillivirus infections in marine mammals. Research that combines data on serology, life history, and behavior is further clarifying the patterns of infection within and between populations (Duignan, Saliki et al. 1995; Duignan et al. 1996). This knowledge may help to predict which groups are at greater risk during a disease outbreak and improve the response to future events.

Studies on free-ranging animals have their limitations. Logistics and safety can be a nightmare. Consider the difficulties involved in finding and capturing a wild pilot whale, for example, and add to that the number needed to conduct a credible study. If these obstacles were not formidable enough, the costs would be. The public mood may not be entirely sympathetic to investigators chasing a pod of healthy dolphins and wrestling each one on deck to examine it. Even scientists would have difficulty justifying the risks involved in pursuing and capturing a healthy but endangered monk seal.

Accidental and Fishery-Related Mortality

Every year marine mammals worldwide are killed in fishing gear, and most of the carcasses are simply discarded. Provided that the samples are fresh, animals killed in these and other accidents offer a unique opportunity to study the normal range of health conditions found in a cross section of a population. Samples taken for contaminant analysis from animals that were robust before death provide a far more accurate picture of typical tissue burdens and ecosystem health than samples taken from marine mammals that come ashore ill or emaciated.

Strandings

Stranded animals can provide valuable data on distribution and abundance, biology, life history, and health, depending on the quality of the specimens and the care with which they are collected (Geraci and Lounsbury 1993; Wilkinson and Worthy, this volume). The pattern of stranded neonates may indicate the presence of nearby calving grounds, information that may be useful in management programs. Tissue and blood samples yield information on contaminants and the causes of illness. Banked samples can be analyzed years later with the help of advanced technology to study epidemiology and trends in toxicology.

Regional stranding records can be critical to an investigation of an unusual event. The best way to assess the effect of a die-off is by comparing population numbers from before and after the event, but this kind of information is not always available. It is also possible, however, to obtain an estimate by comparing the total mortality with the average stranding rate for the years preceding the event. Using this method, Scott et al. (1988) were able to determine that the 742 bottlenose dolphin carcasses retrieved during 1987–1988 represented a 10-fold increase over the previous average yearly mortality.

Stranded animals, mostly pinnipeds, are treated in rehabilitation centers for conditions ranging from simple malnourishment to serious injury or disease. Studies on these animals allow us to gain a reasonable understanding of disease processes in action and of the limits of their adaptive mechanisms.

Mass strandings offer a burst of information in a very short time. Such events can provide data and samples from both sexes that span the full range of ages and health conditions. The potential value of this material depends on maintaining stringent collection and processing standards that are not always achievable under the chaotic circumstances surrounding these events. A mass stranding investigation is a true test of how well a response team is organized (Fig. 17-6).

Captive Marine Mammals

Captive marine mammals are a singular resource for long-term observational and physiological studies, recognizing that their behavior and physiology may be altered under these conditions. They present an unparalleled opportunity to learn about the day-to-day progress of illness and recovery, behavioral and other clinical features of disease, functional impairment of organ systems, and dietary requirements that can be extrapolated to a wild population.

The Comparative Approach

Health depends on the harmonious interplay of all organ systems responding to an ever-changing environment, a process that begins at the cellular level. In every organ, the cells of a humpback whale look and function much the same as those of a dog, cat, or any other mammal. In this sense, mammals are remarkably similar. However, marine mammals have specialized anatomical and physiological adaptations for living at sea—the breathing reflex, diving and stress responses, skin structure, and mechanisms for maintaining salt and water balance—that affect the expression of illness and its outcome. Yet because so few animals are available for study, we must often apply findings from one species or group to another. The approach can be effective but must be used with caution. For example, we have a reasonable understanding of the actions and lethal dosage levels of some biotoxins in humans and laboratory animals, but some of the same adaptations that allow a marine mammal to feed below the surface may actually increase its vulnerability to poisoning: during a dive, blood is selectively channeled to the heart and brain, perhaps potentiating the effects of biotoxins on vital organs. For animals that must surface to breathe, any condition that seriously impairs coordination for even a few minutes could be fatal. A sampling protocol is needed to gather each piece of information, but only a team that understands the animals can put it all together.

Public Reaction and Presentation of Results

The intense public interest that marine mammal die-offs generate can be advantageous. For example, it is widely believed that the British prime minister of the day was convinced of the political importance of environmental issues by the fact that even right-wing newspapers devoted pages of coverage to the deaths of North Sea harbor seals in 1988. When influenza virus was found in New England harbor seals in 1979, the public's anxiety over the potential threat to other species virtually ensured that every conceivable study needed to allay this fear would be funded. All too often, however, the constant pressure from reporters, the public, and government officials for explanations of these events can tempt investigators to speculate prematurely. As a result, there is still a widespread perception, even among scientists, that the die-offs of seals in the North Sea and dolphins in the Mediterranean were caused by pollution. As we have seen, this was not the case. From a different viewpoint, many southern African newspapers presented the die-off of Cape fur seals as evidence that the species was exceeding the carrying capacity of its environment and that this was a good reason for increasing the size of the commercial seal harvest. Again, the facts do not support this belief.

It is not immediately obvious what can be done to prevent such misconceptions. Speculation is the lifeblood of science: it is the way in which testable hypotheses are formed.

Figure 17-6. Mass strandings yield valuable data on health and life history but are difficult to investigate thoroughly. (Photograph by S. Heaslip, *Cape Cod Times*)

In the case of events like marine mammal die-offs, in which experts from a variety of disciplines are involved, each group inevitably, if not aggressively, stresses the importance of its own results. In the extreme, this competition can undermine the credibility of the investigation and promote misunderstanding. Only by presenting a united front can the response team inspire any measure of public confidence.

Outside the scientific community, various interest groups, some with narrow focus, often and without scruple attempt to use the opinions of different scientists to further their own aims. Because the media prefer clear-cut stories, they tend to endorse those explanations that are presented most forcibly and, perhaps in some cases, those that might draw the largest audience. This is especially so for large-scale events for which the public demands an immediate answer. The longer the investigation, the more opportunity for breaks in continuity that leave time gaps for breeding speculation.

Clearly it would be unethical, and even counterproductive, to withhold information from the public. The harmful effect of unwarranted speculation underscores the importance of a well-organized investigation, as well as the need to appoint a single spokesperson to deal with all media inquiries. Still, a reporter will, at some point, insist on interviewing the "scientist." Keeping the media accurately informed of all new findings consumes valuable time, but not doing so invites others to render a less-informed opinion. Because most scientific research is funded by the government—and thus by the taxpayers—scientists and managers have an obligation, which some find trying, to be responsive and responsible when dealing with public concerns.

What Lies Ahead?

For most marine mammals, viruses are the most probable cause of a major die-off. The greatest impact would likely follow the introduction of a novel pathogen into a naive population. A variety of human activities could promote such introductions. The most obvious is the increase in international and intercontinental movements of wild and domestic animals. The risks this poses to terrestrial organisms are already well recognized. There are also risks from the rescue, rehabilitation, and release of sick, vagrant marine mammals. We have already suggested that harp seals introduced phocine distemper virus into the North Sea; such wanderers may be an important source of newly emerging infections. The release of rehabilitated animals outside their usual range may introduce new pathogens to unrelated marine mammal populations, and those returned to their home range may carry pathogens acquired in captivity. Responsible rehabilitation centers will have criteria for releasing such animals as one way to minimize these risks (St. Aubin et al. 1996).

Climatic changes will influence marine mammal behavior, and this may in turn affect the transmission rate of some pathogens. For example, ringed seals (*Phoca hispida*) in the Baltic Sea normally haul out in a widely dispersed pattern on spring sea ice. In recent years ice cover has been limited, resulting in denser aggregations of seals on the haul-out areas (Härkönen and Lunneryd 1992), a situation that would increase the contact rate between susceptible and infectious individuals in the event of a disease outbreak. By influencing the location and abundance of prey, climatic variation will also affect the distribution of microparasites and their hosts. Consequent to climate change, individual marine mammals may wander more widely than before, with greater risk of transferring pathogens between populations. Changes in prey abundance or distribution may lead to poor physical condition and physiological stress among large segments of a population, increasing the potential for a virus to strike with devastating effect. For polar species, climate change over the next few decades may lead to more extreme and less predictable environmental conditions; ice accidents will likely increase.

In contrast to die-offs caused by pathogens and climatic disturbances, actions can be taken to reduce the risk of some events that result from human activities. No one would argue against committing all the resources necessary to prevent an ecological disaster such as the *Exxon Valdez* spill. However, there might be less pressure (and more resistance) to do so for a die-off whose link to human enterprise is not as definite. For example, it would be difficult to further regulate agricultural runoff into Florida's coastal waters based simply on the suspicion that the red tides that killed the manatees were the result of pollution-associated nutrient enrichment. There are many such instances in which commercial and environmental interests conflict—perhaps an inevitable consequence of our desire to protect and, at the same time, exploit marine habitats. Realistically, such measures are more likely to be taken in areas of the world where conservation efforts are assumed important and are affordable—better yet, profitable. The whale-watching industry itself provides a good example of environmental protection through profit: healthy whales keep the books balanced. These industries have influenced the creation of marine sanctuaries where harmful activities are restricted.

In general, it is not clear if anything can, or should, be done to reduce the risks of die-offs in the future. As we have seen in our previous discussion, identifying a single cause of an event is often difficult. Direct intervention, whether to vaccinate against a disease or to rehabilitate sick or starving animals, is rarely successful and often extremely expensive. These actions may also run counter to natural selection by increasing the survival rate of unfit animals. Such intervention might be justified for an endangered species at risk of extinction or a highly valued local population. For instance, the red tide organism cannot flourish in water of salinities less than about 30 parts per thousand. Thus it may be possible to weaken a dinoflagellate bloom that threatens manatees in an estuary by releasing freshwater from an upstream floodgate (O'Shea et al. 1991). In every case, the long-term consequences of such intervention for the rest of the population, and for the environment, must be evaluated.

We may never know the extent to which human activities influence either the frequency or the severity of die-offs. For many species, especially the otariid seals, die-offs have almost certainly been a feature of their evolutionary history; they have adapted to this with reproductive strategies that allow rapid population recovery. Historically, these populations have been resilient, but cumulative, perhaps synergistic, effects of multiple insults may change their recovery rates in the future.

Studies will continue to furnish information for upgrading contingency plans, analytical techniques, and baseline knowledge of marine mammal species—all needed to better understand the nature of die-offs. Policy makers and managers must balance this information with realities and public attitudes. Every die-off has drawn attention, deservedly or not, to marine contaminants and habitat degradation. Although scientists insist on more studies to establish the link, the public may be prepared to disregard that step in their desire for swift action. On one hand, this pressure could drive environmental measures that would ultimately benefit all marine species; on the other, these measures will only endure if the decisions are based on sound information. In this context, the policy maker's—and the marine mammal's—best ally is an informed public.

We can predict with certainty that die-offs will continue to occur. Each will provide an opportunity to learn and thereby improve policies for the conservation of marine mammal populations and ocean resources.

Literature Cited

Ackerman, B. B., S. D. Wright, R. K. Bonde, D. K. Odell, and D. J. Banowetz. 1995. Trends and patterns in mortality of manatees in Florida, 1974–1992. Pages 223–258 *in* T. J. O'Shea, B. B. Ackerman, and H. F. Percival (eds.), Population Biology of the Florida

Manatee. U.S. Department of the Interior, National Biological Service, Information and Technology Report 1.

Aguilar, A., and A. Borrell. 1994. Abnormally high chlorinated biphenyl levels in striped dolphins (*Stenella coeruleoalba*) affected by the 1991–1992 Mediterranean epizootic. The Science of the Total Environment 154:237–247.

Aguilar, A., and J. A. Raga. 1993. The striped dolphin epizootic in the Mediterranean Sea. Ambio 22:524–528.

Anderson, D. M. 1994. Red tides. Scientific American 271 (2): 62–68.

Anderson, D. M., and A. W. White. 1992. Marine biotoxins at the top of the food chain. Oceanus 35 (3): 55–61.

Anderson, R. M., and R. M. May. 1992. Infectious diseases of humans: Dynamics and control. Oxford University Press, Oxford and New York, NY.

Anselmo, S., P. 't Hart, H. Vos, J. Groen, and A. D. M. E. Osterhaus. 1995. Mass mortality of Cape fur seals *Arctocephalus pusillus pusillus* in Namibia, 1994. Seal Rehabilitation and Research Centre Publication. Pieterburen, Netherlands. 9 pp.

Baker, J. R. 1984. Mortality and morbidity in grey seal pups (*Halichoerus grypus*). Studies on its causes, effects of environment, the nature and sources of infectious agents and the immunological status of pups. Journal of Zoology (London) 203:23–48.

Baker, J. R., and T. S. McCann. 1989. Pathology and bacteriology of adult male Antarctic fur seals, *Arctocephalus gazella,* dying at Bird Island, South Georgia. British Veterinary Journal 145:263–275.

Banish, L. D., and W. G. Gilmartin. 1992. Pathological findings in the Hawaiian monk seal. Journal of Wildlife Diseases 28:428–434.

Beck, C. A., and N. B. Barros. 1991. The impact of debris on the Florida manatee. Marine Pollution Bulletin 22:508–510.

Becker, P. R., D. Wilkinson, and T. I. Lillestolen. 1994. Marine Mammal Health and Stranding Response Program: Program Development Plan. U.S. Department of Commerce, NOAA Technical Memorandum NMFS-OPR-94-2. 35 pp.

Bengtson, J. L., P. Boveng, U. Franzén, P. Have, M. P. Heide-Jørgensen, and T. J. Härkönen. 1991. Antibodies to canine distemper virus in Antarctic seals. Marine Mammal Science 7:85–87.

Bergman, A., B. Järplid, and B.-M. Svensson. 1990. Pathological findings indicative of distemper in European seals. Veterinary Microbiology 23:331–342.

Bergman, A., M. Olsson, and S. Reiland. 1992. Skull-bone lesions in the Baltic grey seal (*Halichoerus grypus*). Ambio 21:517–519.

Borst, G. H. A., H. C. Walvoort, P. J. H. Reijnders, J. S. van der Kamp, and A. D. M. E. Osterhaus. 1986. An outbreak of a herpesvirus infection in harbor seals (*Phoca vitulina*). Journal of Wildlife Diseases 22:1–6.

Bossart, G. D. 1990. Acute necrotizing enteritis associated with suspected coronavirus infection in three harbor seals (*Phoca vitulina*). Journal of Zoo and Wildlife Medicine 21:84–87.

Bossart, G. D., D. K. Odell, and N. H. Altman. 1985. Cardiomyopathy in stranded pygmy and dwarf sperm whales. Journal of the American Veterinary Medical Association 187:1137–1140.

Bossart, G. D., M. T. Walsh, D. K. Odell, J. D. Lynch, D. O. Buesse, R. Friday, and W. G. Young. 1991. Histopathologic findings of a mass stranding of pilot whales, *Globicephala macrorhynchus.* Pages 85–90 *in* J. E. Reynolds III and D. K. Odell (eds.), Marine Mammal Strandings in the United States: Proceedings of the Second Marine Mammal Stranding Workshop. 3–5 December 1987, Miami, FL. NOAA Technical Report NMFS-98.

Bossart, G. D., C. Cray, J. L. Solorzano, S. J. Decker, L. H. Cornell, and N. H. Altman. 1996. Cutaneous papillomaviral-like papillomatosis in a killer whale (*Orcinus orca*). Marine Mammal Science 12:274–281.

Bossart, G. D., D. G. Baden, R. Y. Ewing, B. Roberts, and S. D. Wright. 1998. Brevetoxicosis in manatees (*Trichechus manatus latirostris*) from the 1996 epizootic: Gross, histologic, and immunohistochemical features. Toxicologic Pathology 26:276–282.

Brabyn, M. W., and I. G. McLean. 1992. Oceanography and coastal topography of herd-stranding sites for whales in New Zealand. Journal of Mammalogy 73:469–476.

Brouwer, A., P. J. H. Reijnders, and J. H. Koeman. 1989. Polychlorinated biphenyl (PCB)–contaminated fish induces vitamin A and thyroid hormone deficiency in the common seal (*Phoca vitulina*). Aquatic Toxicology 15:99–106.

Buck, J. D., and S. Spotte. 1986a. Microbiology of captive white-beaked dolphins (*Lagenorhynchus albirostris*) with comments on epizootics. Zoo Biology 5:321–329.

Buck, J. D., and S. Spotte. 1986b. The occurrence of potentially pathogenic vibrios in marine mammals. Marine Mammal Science 2:319–324.

Burn, D. 1994. Boat-based population surveys of sea otters (*Enhydra lutris*) in Prince William Sound, Alaska, following the *Exxon Valdez* spill. Pages 61–80 *in* T. R. Loughlin (ed.), Marine Mammals and the *Exxon Valdez*. Academic Press, San Diego and London.

Burns, J. J., and G. A. Seaman. 1985. Investigation of belukha whales in coastal waters of western and northern Alaska: II. Biology and ecology. Final report to U.S. Department of Commerce, NOAA, contract NA81RAC00049. Alaska Department of Fish and Game, Fairbanks, AK. 129 pp.

Callan, R. J., G. Early, H. Kida, and V. S. Hinshaw. 1995. The appearance of H3 influenza viruses in seals. Journal of General Virology 76:199–203.

Calzada, N., C. H. Lockyer, and A. Aguilar. 1994. Age and sex composition of the striped dolphin die-off in the western Mediterranean. Marine Mammal Science 10:299–310.

Campbell, H. W., and A. B. Irvine. 1981. Manatee mortality during the unusually cold winter of 1976–77. Pages 86–91 *in* R. L. Brownell Jr. and K. Ralls (eds.), The West Indian Manatee in Florida: Proceedings of a Workshop Held in Orlando, FL, 27–29 March 1978. Florida Department of Natural Resources, Tallahassee, FL.

Cebrian, D. 1995. The striped dolphin *Stenella coeruleoalba* epizootic in Greece, 1991–1992. Biological Conservation 74:143–145.

Cosby, S. L., S. McQuaid, N. Duffy, C. Lyons, B. K. Rima, G. M. Allan, S. J. McCulloch, S. Kennedy, J. A. Smyth, F. McNeilly, C. Craig, and C. Örvell. 1988. Characterization of a seal morbillivirus. Nature 336:115–116.

Costa, D. P., and G. L. Kooyman. 1982. Oxygen consumption, thermoregulation, and the effect of fur oiling and washing on the sea otter, *Enhydra lutris.* Canadian Journal of Zoology 60:2761–2767.

Cousins, D. V., S. N. Williams, R. Reuter, D. Forshaw, D. Chadwick, D. Coughran, P. Collins, and N. Gales. 1993. Tuberculosis in wild seals and characterisation of the seal bacillus. Australian Veterinary Journal 70:92–97.

Croxall, J. P., S. Rodwell, and I. L. Boyd. 1990. Entanglement in man-made debris of Antarctic fur seals at Bird Island, South Georgia. Marine Mammal Science 6:221–233.

Dailey, M. D., and W. A. Walker. 1978. Parasitism as a factor (?) in single strandings of southern California cetaceans. Journal of Parasitology 64:593–596.

DeGange, A., and M. M. Vacca. 1989. Sea otter mortality at Kodiak

Island, Alaska, during summer 1987. Journal of Mammalogy 70:836–838.

De Swart, R. L., P. S. Ross, L. J. Vedder, H. H. Timmerman, S. Heisterkamp, H. Van Loveren, J. G. Vos, P. J. H. Reijnders, and A. D. M. E. Osterhaus. 1994. Impairment of immune function in harbour seals (*Phoca vitulina*) feeding on fish from polluted waters. Ambio 23:155–159.

De Swart, R. L., P. S. Ross, H. H. Timmerman, H. W. Vos, P. J. H. Reijnders, J. G. Vos, and A. D. M. E. Osterhaus. 1995. Impaired cellular immune response in harbour seals (*Phoca vitulina*) feeding on environmentally contaminated herring. Clinical and Experimental Immunology 101:480–486.

Dierauf, L. A., D. Vandenbroek, J. Roletto, M. Koski, L. Amaya, and L. J. Gage. 1985. An epizootic of leptospirosis in California sea lions. Journal of the American Veterinary Medical Association 187:1145–1148.

Dietz, R., M.-P. Heide-Jørgensen, and T. Härkönen. 1989. Mass deaths of harbor seals (*Phoca vitulina*) in Europe. Ambio 18:258–264.

Domingo, M., J. Visa, M. Pumarola, A. J. Marco, L. Ferrer, R. Rabanal, and S. Kennedy. 1992. Pathologic and immunocytochemical studies of morbillivirus infection in striped dolphins (*Stenella coeruleoalba*). Veterinary Pathology 29:1–10.

Doroff, A. M., and J. L. Bodkin. 1994. Sea otter foraging behavior and hydrocarbon levels in prey. Pages 193–208 *in* T. R. Loughlin (ed.), Marine Mammals and the *Exxon Valdez*. Academic Press, San Diego and London.

Dudok van Heel, W. H. 1966. Navigation in Cetacea. Pages 597–606 *in* K. S. Norris (ed.), Whales, Dolphins and Porpoises. University of California Press, Berkeley, CA.

Duignan, P. J., J. R. Geraci, J. A. Raga, and N. Calzada. 1992. Pathology of morbillivirus infection in striped dolphins (*Stenella coeruleoalba*) from Valencia and Murcia, Spain. Canadian Journal of Veterinary Research 56:242–248.

Duignan, P. J., J. T. Saliki, D. J. St. Aubin, J. A. House, and J. R. Geraci. 1994. Neutralizing antibodies to phocine distemper virus in Atlantic walruses (*Odobenus rosmarus rosmarus*) from Arctic Canada. Journal of Wildlife Diseases 30:90–94.

Duignan, P. J., C. House, J. R. Geraci, N. Duffy, B. K. Rima, M. T. Walsh, G. Early, D. J. St. Aubin, S. Sadove, H. Koopman, and H. Rhinehart. 1995. Morbillivirus infection in cetaceans of the western Atlantic. Veterinary Microbiology 44:241–249.

Duignan, P. J., C. House, J. R. Geraci, G. Early, H. Copland, M. T. Walsh, G. D. Bossart, C. Cray, S. Sadove, D. J. St. Aubin, and M. Moore. 1995. Morbillivirus infection in two species of pilot whales (*Globicephala* sp.) from the western Atlantic. Marine Mammal Science 11:150–162.

Duignan, P. J., C. House, M. T. Walsh, T. Campbell, G. D. Bossart, N. Duffy, P. J. Fernandes, B. K. Rima, S. Wright, and J. R. Geraci. 1995. Morbillivirus infection in manatees. Marine Mammal Science 11:441–451.

Duignan, P. J., J. T. Saliki, D. J. St. Aubin, G. Early, S. Sadove, J. A. House, K. Kovacs, and J. R. Geraci. 1995. Epizootiology of morbillivirus infection in North American harbor (*Phoca vitulina*) and gray seals (*Halichoerus grypus*). Journal of Wildlife Diseases 31:491–501.

Duignan, P. J., C. House, D. K. Odell, R. S. Wells, L. J. Hansen, M. T. Walsh, D. J. St. Aubin, B. K. Rima, and J. R. Geraci. 1996. Morbillivirus infection in bottlenose dolphins: Evidence for recurrent epizootics in the western Atlantic and Gulf of Mexico. Marine Mammal Science 12:499–515.

Eberhardt, L. L., and T. J. O'Shea. 1995. Integration of manatee life-history data and population modeling. Pages 269–279 *in* T. J. O'Shea, B. B. Ackerman, and H. F. Percival (eds.), Population Biology of the Florida Manatee. U.S. Department of the Interior, National Biological Service, Information and Technology Report 1.

Eberhardt, L. L., and D. B. Siniff. 1977. Population dynamics and marine mammal management policies. Journal of the Fisheries Research Board of Canada 34:183–190.

Ewalt, D. R., J. B. Payeur, B. M. Martin, D. R. Cummins, and W. G. Miller. 1994. Characteristics of a *Brucella* species from a bottlenose dolphin (*Tursiops truncatus*). Journal of Veterinary Diagnostic Investigation 6:448–452.

Fay, F. H., and B. P. Kelly. 1980. Mass natural mortality of walruses (*Odobenus rosmarus*) at St. Lawrence Island, Bering Sea, autumn 1978. Arctic 33:226–245.

Fay, F. H., B. P. Kelly, P. H. Gehnrich, J. L. Sease, and A. A. Hoover. 1986. Modern populations, migrations, demography, trophics, and historical status of the Pacific walrus. U.S. Department of Commerce, NOAA, Outer Continental Shelf Environmental Assessment Program, Final Reports of the Principal Investigators 37:231–376. NOAA, National Ocean Service, Anchorage, AK.

Fay, F. H., B. P. Kelly, and J. L. Sease. 1989. Managing the exploitation of Pacific walruses: A tragedy of delayed response and poor communication. Marine Mammal Science 5:1–16.

Forshaw, D., and G. R. Phelps. 1991. Tuberculosis in a captive colony of pinnipeds. Journal of Wildlife Diseases 27:288–295.

Fowler, C. W. 1987. A review of density dependence in populations of large mammals. Pages 401–441 *in* H. H. Genoways (ed.), Current Mammalogy. Vol. 1. Plenum Press, New York and London.

Freeman, M. M. R. 1968. Winter observations on beluga whales (*Delphinapterus leucas*) in Jones Sound, N.W.T. Canadian Field-Naturalist 82:276–286.

Gales, N. J. 1992. Mass stranding of striped dolphins, *Stenella coeruleoalba*, at Augusta, Western Australia: Notes on clinical pathology and general observations. Journal of Wildlife Diseases 28:651–655.

Gallacher, J. B., and W. E. Waters. 1964. Pneumonia in grey seal pups at St. Kilda. Journal of Zoology (London) 142:177–180.

Gentry, R. L., and G. L. Kooyman. 1986. Introduction. Pages 3–27 *in* R. L. Gentry and G. L. Kooyman (eds.), Fur Seals: Maternal Strategies on Land and at Sea. Princeton University Press, Princeton, NJ.

Geraci, J. R. 1989. Clinical investigation of the 1987–88 mass mortality of bottlenose dolphins along the U.S. central and south Atlantic coast. Final Report to National Marine Fisheries Service, U.S. Navy (Office of Naval Research), and Marine Mammal Commission. 63 pp.

Geraci, J. R., and V. J. Lounsbury. 1993. Marine mammals ashore: A field guide for strandings. Texas A&M University Sea Grant College Program, Galveston, TX. 305 pp.

Geraci, J. R., and S. H. Ridgway. 1991. On disease transmission between cetaceans and humans. Marine Mammal Science 7:191–194.

Geraci, J. R., and D. J. St. Aubin. 1979. Stranding workshop summary report: Analysis of marine mammal strandings and recommendations for a nationwide stranding salvage program. Pages 1–33 *in* J. R. Geraci and D. J. St. Aubin (eds.), Biology of Marine Mammals: Insights Through Strandings. Report no. MMC-77/13. Marine Mammal Commission. (Available from National Technical Information Service, Springfield, VA. PB-293 890.)

Geraci, J. R., and D. J. St. Aubin. 1987. Effects of parasites on marine mammals. International Journal for Parasitology 17:407–414.

Geraci, J. R., and D. J. St. Aubin. 1990. Summary and conclusions. Pages 253–256 *in* J. R. Geraci and D. J. St. Aubin (eds.), Marine Mammals and Oil: Confronting the Risks. Academic Press, San Diego, CA.

Geraci, J. R., M. D. Dailey, and D. J. St. Aubin. 1978. Parasitic mastitis in the Atlantic white-sided dolphin, *Lagenorhynchus acutus,* as a probable factor in herd productivity. Journal of the Fisheries Research Board of Canada 35:1350–1355.

Geraci, J. R., S. A. Testaverde, D. J. St. Aubin, and T. H. Loop. 1978. A mass stranding of the Atlantic white-sided dolphin (*Lagenorhynchus acutus*): A study into pathobiology and life history. Report no. 75/12. Marine Mammal Commission. (Available from National Technical Information Service, Springfield, VA. PB-289 361.)

Geraci, J. R., D. J. St. Aubin, I. K. Barker, R. G. Webster, V. S. Hinshaw, W. J. Bean, H. L. Ruhnke, J. H. Prescott, G. Early, A. S. Baker, S. Madoff, and R. T. Schooley. 1982. Mass mortality of harbor seals: Pneumonia associated with influenza A virus. Science 215:1129–1131.

Geraci, J. R., D. M. Anderson, R. J. Timperi, D. J. St. Aubin, G. A. Early, J. H. Prescott, and C. A. Mayo. 1989. Humpback whales (*Megaptera novaeangliae*) fatally poisoned by dinoflagellate toxin. Canadian Journal of Fisheries and Aquatic Sciences 46:1895–1898.

Gilmartin, W. G., and L. L. Eberhardt. 1995. Status of the Hawaiian monk seal (*Monachus schauinslandi*) population. Canadian Journal of Zoology 73:1185–1190.

Goodhart, C. B. 1988. Did virus transfer from harp seals to common seals? Nature 336:21.

Grachev, M. A., V. P. Kumarev, L. V. Mamaev, V. L. Zorin, L. V. Baranova, N. N. Denikina, S. I. Belikov, E. A. Petrov, V. S. Kolesnik, R. S. Kolesnik, V. M. Dorofeev, A. M. Beim, V. N. Kudelin, F. G. Nagieva, and V. N. Sidorov. 1989. Distemper virus in Baikal seals. Nature 338:209.

Grenfell, B. T., M. E. Lonergan, and J. Harwood. 1992. Quantitative investigations of the epidemiology of phocine distemper virus (PDV) in European common seal populations. The Science of the Total Environment 115:15–29.

Gunter, G., F. G. W. Smith, C. C. Davis, and R. H. Williams. 1948. Catastrophic mass mortality of marine animals and coincident phytoplankton bloom on the west coast of Florida, November 1946 to August 1947. Ecological Monographs 18:309–324.

Hai, D. J., J. Lien, D. Nelson, and K. Curren. 1996. A contribution to the biology of the white-beaked dolphin, *Lagenorhynchus albirostris,* in waters off Newfoundland. Canadian Field-Naturalist 110:278–287.

Hall, A. J., R. J. Law, D. E. Wells, J. Harwood, H. M. Ross, S. Kennedy, C. R. Allchin, L. A. Campbell, and P. P. Pomeroy. 1992. Organochlorine levels in common seals (*Phoca vitulina*) which were victims and survivors of the 1988 phocine distemper epizootic. The Science of the Total Environment 115:145–162.

Harder, T. C., T. Willhaus, W. Leibold, and B. Liess. 1992. Investigations on course and outcome of phocine distemper virus infection in harbour seals (*Phoca vitulina*) exposed to polychlorinated biphenyls. Journal of Veterinary Medicine 39:19–31.

Härkönen, T., and S. G. Lunneryd. 1992. Estimating abundance of ringed seals in the Bothnian Bay. Ambio 21:497–503.

Harwood, J. 1989. Lessons from the seal epidemic. New Scientist 121 (1652): 38–41.

Harwood, J., and A. J. Hall. 1990. Mass mortality in marine mammals: Its implications for population dynamics and genetics. Trends in Ecology and Evolution 5:254–257.

Harwood, J., and P. Reijnders. 1988. Seals, sense and sensibility. New Scientist 120 (1634): 26–28.

Harwood, J., S. D. Carter, D. E. Hughes, S. C. Bell, J. R. Baker, and H. J. C. Cornwell. 1989. Seal disease predictions. Nature 339:670.

Harwood, J., A. R. Hiby, D. Thompson, and A. Ward. 1991. Seal stocks in Great Britain. Surveys conducted between 1986 and 1989. Natural Environment Research Council (NERC) News (January): 11–15.

Haug, T., A. B. Krøyer, K. T. Nilssen, K. I. Ugland, and P. E. Aspholm. 1991. Harp seal (*Phoca groenlandica*) invasions in Norwegian coastal waters: Age composition and feeding habits. ICES Journal of Marine Science 48:363–371.

Heide-Jørgensen, M.-P., T. Härkönen, R. Dietz, and P. M. Thompson. 1992. Retrospective of the 1988 European seal epizootic. Diseases of Aquatic Organisms 13:37–62.

Hernández, M., I. Robinson, A. Aguilar, L. M. González, L. F. López-Jurado, M. I. Reyero, E. Cacho, J. Franco, V. Lopez-Rodas, and E. Costas. 1998. Did algal toxins cause monk seal mortality? Nature 393:28–29.

Hiruki, L. M., I. Stirling, W. G. Gilmartin, T. C. Johanos, and B. L. Becker. 1993. Significance of wounding to female reproductive success in Hawaiian monk seals (*Monachus schauinslandi*) at Laysan Island. Canadian Journal of Zoology 71:469–474.

Hofman, R. 1994. Foreword. Pages xiii–xvi *in* T. R. Loughlin (ed.), Marine Mammals and the *Exxon Valdez*. Academic Press, San Diego and London.

Holt, R. D., and J. H. Lawton. 1994. The ecological consequences of shared natural enemies. Annual Review of Ecology and Systematics 24:495–520.

International Council for the Exploration of the Sea. 1994. Report of the study group on seals and small cetaceans in European seas. ICES C.M. 1994/N:2.

Ivashin, M. V., and K. V. Shevlyagin. 1987. The white whale (*Delphinapterus leucas* Pallas, 1776): Entrapment and escape in the ice of Senjavin Strait, USSR. Reports of the International Whaling Commission 37:357–359.

Jellison, W. L., and K. C. Milner. 1958. Salmonellosis (bacillary dysentery) of fur seals. Journal of Wildlife Management 22:199–200.

Johnson, A. M. 1968. Annual mortality of territorial male fur seals and its management significance. Journal of Wildlife Management 32:94–99.

Johnson, B. W., and P. A. Johnson. 1981. The Hawaiian monk seal on Laysan Island: 1978. Report no. MMC-78/15. Marine Mammal Commission. (Available from National Technical Information Service, Springfield, VA. PB82-109661.) 17 pp.

Kendall, M. D., B. Safieh, J. Harwood, and P. P. Pomeroy. 1992. Thymulin plasma concentrations, the thymus and organochlorine contaminant levels in seals infected with phocine distemper virus. The Science of the Total Environment 115:133–144.

Kennedy, S. 1990. Review of the 1988 European seal morbillivirus epizootic. Veterinary Record 127:563–567.

Kennedy, S., J. A. Smyth, P. F. Cush, S. J. McCullough, G. M. Allan, and S. McQuaid. 1988. Viral distemper now found in porpoises. Nature 336:21.

Kennedy, S., I. J. Lindstedt, M. M. McAliskey, S. A. McConnell, and S. J. McCullough. 1992. Herpesviral encephalitis in a harbor porpoise (*Phocoena phocoena*). Journal of Zoo and Wildlife Medicine 23:374–379.

Kennedy-Stoskopf, S. 1990. Viral diseases in marine mammals. Pages 97–113 *in* L. A. Dierauf (ed.), CRC Handbook of Marine Mammal Medicine: Health, Disease, and Rehabilitation. CRC Press, Boca Raton, FL.

Keyes, M. C. 1965. Pathology of the northern fur seal. Journal of the American Veterinary Medical Association 147:1090–1095.

Kirschvink, J. L., A. E. Dizon, and J. A. Westphal. 1986. Evidence from strandings for geomagnetic sensitivity in cetaceans. Journal of Experimental Biology 120:1–24.

Kjellqwist, S. A., T. Haug, and T. Øritsland. 1995. Trends in age-composition, growth and reproductive parameters of Barents Sea harp seals, *Phoca groenlandica*. ICES Journal of Marine Science 52:197–208.

Klinowska, M. 1985. Cetacean live stranding sites relate to geomagnetic topography. Aquatic Mammals 1:27–32.

Klinowska, M. 1986. Cetacean live stranding dates relate to geomagnetic disturbances. Aquatic Mammals 11:109–119.

Kogai, V. M. 1968. Present condition and dynamics of the fur seal population of Tyuleni (Robben) Island. Pages 39–48 *in* V. A. Arsen'ev and K. I. Panin (eds.), Pinnipeds of the North Pacific. All-Union Research Institute of Marine Fisheries and Oceanography (VNIRO). (Translated from Russian by the Israel Program for Scientific Translations, 1971.)

Kraus, S. D. 1990. Rates and potential causes of mortality in North Atlantic right whales (*Eubalaena glacialis*). Marine Mammal Science 6:278–291.

Lahvis, G. P., R. S. Wells, D. W. Kuehl, J. L. Stewart, H. L. Rhinehart, and C. S. Via. 1995. Decreased lymphocyte responses in free-ranging bottlenose dolphins (*Tursiops truncatus*) are associated with increased concentrations of PCBs and DDT in peripheral blood. Environmental Health Perspectives 103 (Suppl. 4): 67–72.

Laist, D. W. 1987. Overview of the biological effects of lost and discarded plastic debris in the marine environment. Marine Pollution Bulletin 18:319–326.

Laist, D. W., J. M. Coe, and K. J. O'Hara. 1999. Marine debris pollution. (This volume)

Lambertsen, R. H. 1992. Crassicaudiosis: A parasitic disease threatening the health and population recovery of large baleen whales. Revue Scientifique et Technique (International Office of Epizootics) 11:1131–1141.

Lambertsen, R. H., B. Birnir, and J. E. Bauer. 1986. Serum chemistry and evidence of renal failure in the north Atlantic fin whale population. Journal of Wildlife Diseases 22:389–396.

Lavigne, D. M,. and O. J. Schmitz. 1990. Global warming and increased population densities: A prescription for seal plagues. Marine Pollution Bulletin 21:280–284.

Laws, R. M. 1984. Seals. Pages 621–715 *in* R. M. Laws (ed.), Antarctic Ecology. Vol 2. Academic Press, London and New York, NY.

Laws, R. M., and R. J. F. Taylor. 1957. A mass mortality of crabeater seals *Lobodon carcinophagus* (Gray). Proceedings of the Zoological Society of London 129:315–325.

Le Boeuf, B. J., and R. S. Condit. 1983. The high cost of living on the beach. Pacific Discovery 36 (3): 12–14.

Le Boeuf, B. J., and J. Reiter. 1991. Biological effects associated with El Niño Southern Oscillation, 1982–83, on northern elephant seals breeding at Año Nuevo, California. Pages 206–218 *in* F. Trillmich and K. A. Ono (eds.), Pinnipeds and El Niño: Responses to Environmental Stress. Springer-Verlag, Berlin.

Le Boeuf, B. J., R. J. Whiting, and R. F. Gantt. 1972. Perinatal behavior of northern elephant seal females and their young. Behaviour 43:121–156.

Lipscomb, T. P., R. K. Harris, A. H. Rebar, B. E. Ballachey, and R. J. Haebler. 1994. Pathology of sea otters. Pages 265–279 *in* T. R. Loughlin (ed.), Marine Mammals and the *Exxon Valdez*. Academic Press, San Diego and London.

Lipscomb, T. P., S. Kennedy, D. Moffett, and B. K. Ford. 1994. Morbilliviral disease in an Atlantic bottlenose dolphin (*Tursiops truncatus*) from the Gulf of Mexico. Journal of Wildlife Diseases 30:572–576.

Lipscomb, T. P., F. Y. Schulman, D. Moffett, and S. Kennedy. 1994. Morbilliviral disease in Atlantic dolphins (*Tursiops truncatus*) from the 1987–1988 epizootic. Journal of Wildlife Diseases 30:567–571.

Loughlin, T. R. (ed.). 1994. Marine Mammals and the *Exxon Valdez*. Academic Press, San Diego and London.

Lunn, N. J., and I. Boyd. 1993. Effects of maternal age and condition on parturition and the perinatal period of Antarctic fur seals. Journal of Zoology (London) 229:55–67.

Mahy, B. W. J., T. Barrett, S. Evans, E. C. Anderson, and C. J. Bostock. 1988. Characterization of a seal morbillivirus. Nature 336:115.

Mangel, M., and C. Tier. 1994. Four facts every conservation biologist should know about persistence. Ecology 75:607–614.

Markussen, N. H., and P. Have. 1992. Phocine distemper virus infection in harp seals, *Phoca groenlandica*. Marine Mammal Science 8:19–26.

Marmontel, M. 1995. Age and reproduction in female Florida manatees. Pages 98–119 *in* T. J. O'Shea, B. B. Ackerman, and H. F. Percival (eds.), Population Biology of the Florida Manatee. U.S. Department of the Interior, National Biological Service, Information and Technology Report 1.

Marsh, H. 1989. Mass stranding of dugongs by a tropical cyclone in northern Australia. Marine Mammal Science 5:78–84.

Merrick, R. L., T. R. Loughlin, and D. G. Calkins. 1987. Decline in abundance of the northern sea lion, *Eumetopias jubatus,* in Alaska, 1956–1986. Fishery Bulletin 85:351–365.

Monnett, C., and L. Rotterman. 1988. Sex-related patterns in the post-natal development and survival of sea otters in Prince William Sound, Alaska. Pages 162–190 *in* D. B. Siniff and K. Ralls (eds.), Population Status of California Sea Otters. U.S. Department of the Interior, Minerals Management Service, Pacific OCS Region, Los Angeles, CA. OCS Study MMS 88-0021.

Morimitsu, T., T. Nagai, M. Ide, H. Kawano, A. Naichuu, M. Koono, and A. Ishii. 1987. Mass stranding of Odontoceti caused by parasitogenic eighth cranial neuropathy. Journal of Wildlife Diseases 23:586–590.

Morimitsu, T., H. Kawano, K. Torihara, E. Kato, and M. Koono. 1992. Histopathology of eighth cranial nerve of mass stranded dolphins at Goto Islands, Japan. Journal of Wildlife Diseases 28:656–658.

Morris, B. F., and T. R. Loughlin. 1994. Overview of the *Exxon Valdez* oil spill 1989–1992. Pages 1–22 *in* T. R. Loughlin (ed.), Marine Mammals and the *Exxon Valdez*. Academic Press, San Diego and London.

Muir, D. C. G., C. A. Ford, R. E. A. Stewart, T. G. Smith, R. F. Addison, M. E. Zinck, and P. Béland. 1990. Organochlorine contaminants in belugas, *Delphinapterus leucas,* from Canadian waters. Pages 165–190 *in* T. G. Smith, D. J. St. Aubin, and J. R. Geraci (eds.), Advances in Research on the Beluga Whale, *Delphinapterus leucas.* Canadian Bulletin of Fisheries and Aquatic Sciences No. 224. Department of Fisheries and Oceans, Ottawa.

Neff, J. M. 1990. Composition and fate of petroleum and spill-treating agents in the marine environment. Pages 1–33 *in* J. R. Geraci and D. J. St. Aubin (eds.), Marine Mammals and Oil: Confronting the Risks. Academic Press, San Diego, CA.

Northridge, S. P., and R. J. Hofman. 1999. Marine mammal interactions with fisheries. (This volume)

Osborn, K., and T. M. Williams. 1990. Postmortem examination of sea otters. Pages 134–146 *in* T. M. Williams and R. W. Davis (eds.), Sea Otter Rehabilitation Program: 1989 *Exxon Valdez* Oil Spill. International Wildlife Research.

O'Shea, T. J. 1999. Environmental contaminants and marine mammals. *In* J. E. Reynolds III and S. Rommel (eds.), Biology of Marine Mammals. Smithsonian Institution Press, Washington, DC (in press).

O'Shea, T. J., C. A. Beck, R. K. Bonde, W. I. Kochman, and D. K. Odell. 1985. An analysis of manatee mortality patterns in Florida, 1976–81. Journal of Wildlife Management 49:1–11.

O'Shea, T. J., G. B. Rathbun, R. K. Bonde, C. D. Buergelt, and D. K. Odell. 1991. An epizootic of Florida manatees associated with a dinoflagellate bloom. Marine Mammal Science 7:165–179.

Osterhaus, A. D. M. E. 1988. Seal death. Nature 334:301–302.

Osterhaus, A. D. M. E., and E. J. Vedder. 1988. Identification of a virus causing recent seal deaths. Nature 335:20.

Osterhaus, A. D. M. E., J. Groen, P. de Vries, F. G. C. M. UytdeHaag, B. Klingeborn, and R. Zarnke. 1988. Canine distemper virus in seals. Nature 335:403–404.

Osterhaus, A. D. M. E., J. Groen, F. G. C. M. UytdeHaag, I. K. G. Visser, E. J. Vedder, J. Crowther, and C. J. Bostock. 1989. Morbillivirus infections in European seals before 1988. Veterinary Record 125:326.

Osterhaus, A. D. M. E., I. K. G. Visser, R. L. De Swart, M. F. Van Bressem, M. W. G. van de Bildt, C. Örvell, T. Barrett, and J. A. Raga. 1992. Morbillivirus threat to Mediterranean monk seals? Veterinary Record 130:141–142.

Osterhaus, A. D. M. E., H. W. J. Broders, J. S. Teppema, T. Kuiken, J. A. House, H. W. Vos, and I. K. G. Visser. 1993. Isolation of a virus with rhabdovirus morphology from a white-beaked dolphin (*Lagenorhynchus albirostris*). Archives of Virology 133:189–193.

Payne, P. M., and D. C. Schneider. 1984. Yearly changes in abundance of harbor seals, *Phoca vitulina,* at a winter haul-out site in Massachusetts. Fishery Bulletin 82:440–442.

Perrin, W. F., and J. E. Powers. 1980. Role of a nematode in natural mortality of spotted dolphins. Journal of Wildlife Management 44:960–963.

Preen, A. R., and H. Marsh. 1995. Response of dugongs to large-scale loss of seagrass from Hervey Bay, Queensland, Australia. Wildlife Research 22:507–519.

Punt, A. E., and D. S. Butterworth. 1995. The effects of future consumption by the Cape fur seal on catches and catch rates of the Cape hakes. 4. Modelling the biological interactions between Cape fur seals *Arctocephalus pusillus pusillus* and the Cape hakes *Merluccius capensis* and *M. paradoxus.* South African Journal of Marine Science 16:255–286.

Ralls, K., R. L. Brownell Jr., and J. Ballou. 1980. Differential mortality by sex and age in mammals, with specific reference to the sperm whale. Reports of the International Whaling Commission (Special Issue 2): 233–243.

Rand, C. S. 1971. Nodular suppurative cutaneous cellulitis in a Galapagos sea lion. Journal of Wildlife Diseases 11:325–330.

Rathbun, G. B., J. P. Reid, R. K. Bonde, and J. A. Powell. 1995. Reproduction in free-ranging Florida manatees. Pages 135–156 *in* T. J. O'Shea, B. B. Ackerman, and H. F. Percival (eds.), Population Biology of the Florida Manatee. U.S. Department of the Interior, National Biological Service, Information and Technology Report 1.

Reynolds, J. E., III. 1999. Efforts to conserve the manatees. (This volume)

Reynolds, J. E., III, and D. K. Odell (eds.), 1991. Marine Mammal Strandings in the United States: Proceedings of the Second Marine Mammal Stranding Workshop. 3–5 December 1987, Miami, FL. NOAA Technical Report NMFS-98.

Ridgway, S. H., and M. D. Dailey. 1972. Cerebral and cerebellar involvement of trematode parasites in dolphins and their possible role in stranding. Journal of Wildlife Diseases 8:33–43.

Riedman, M. 1990. The Pinnipeds: Seals, Sea Lions, and Walruses. University of California Press, Berkeley, CA. 439 pp.

Rosenberg, R., O. Lindahl, and H. Blanck. 1988. Silent spring in the sea. Ambio 17:289–290.

Ross, H. M., G. Foster, R. J. Reid, K. L. Jahans, and A. P. MacMillan. 1994. *Brucella* species infection in sea-mammals. Veterinary Record 134:359.

Ross, P. S., R. L. De Swart, H. H. Timmerman, P. J. H. Reijnders, J. G. Vos, H. Van Loveren, and A. D. M. E. Osterhaus. 1996. Suppression of natural killer cell activity in harbour seals (*Phoca vitulina*) fed Baltic Sea herring. Aquatic Toxicology 34:71–84.

Safe, S. 1984. Polychlorinated biphenyls (PCBs) and polybrominated biphenyls (PBBs): Biochemistry, toxicology and mechanism of action. Critical Reviews in Toxicology 13:319–395.

Schneider, K. B., and J. B. Faro. 1975. Effects of sea ice on sea otters (*Enhydra lutris*). Journal of Mammalogy 56:91–101.

Scott, G. P., D. M. Burn, and L. J. Hansen. 1988. The dolphin die-off: Long-term effects and recovery of the population. Oceans '88 Proceedings 3:819–823.

Sergeant, D. E. 1982a. Mass strandings of toothed whales (Odontoceti) as a population phenomenon. Scientific Report of the Whales Research Institute Tokyo 34:1–47.

Sergeant, D. E. 1982b. Some biological correlates of environmental conditions around Newfoundland during 1970–79: Harp seals, blue whales and fulmar petrels. North Atlantic Fisheries Organization (NAFO) Scientific Council Studies 5:107–110.

Sergeant, D. E. 1991. Harp seals, man and ice. Canadian Special Publication of Fisheries and Aquatic Sciences 114. 153 pp.

Sergeant, D. E., and G. A. Williams. 1983. Two recent entrapments of narwhals, *Monodon monoceros,* in arctic Canada. Canadian Field-Naturalist 97:459–460.

Seth, V., and A. Beotra. 1986. Malnutrition and the immune system. Indian Pediatrics 23:277–302.

Sidorov, K. S. 1987. Activity of Kurile-Kamchatka Chain volcanoes as the cause of "red tides" and toxic phenomena in the Commander Islands. Pages 25–30 *in* Sea Otters and Fur Seals of the Commander Islands. VNIRO. Far East Press, Petropavlovsk, Kamchatka.

Siegstad, H., and M. P. Heide-Jørgensen. 1994. Ice entrapments of narwhals (*Monodon monoceros*) and white whales (*Delphinapterus leucas*) in Greenland. Meddelelser om Grønland, Bioscience 39:151–160.

Siniff, D. B., and J. L. Bengtson. 1977. Observations and hypotheses concerning the interactions among crabeater seals, leopard seals, and killer whales. Journal of Mammalogy 58:414–416.

Smith, A. W., and D. E. Skilling. 1979. Viruses and virus diseases of marine mammals. Journal of the American Veterinary Medical Association 175:918–920.

Smith, A. W., T. G. Akers, S. H. Madin, and N. A. Vedros. 1973. San

Miguel sea lion virus isolation, preliminary characterization and relationship to vesicular exanthema of swine virus. Nature 244:108–110.

Smith, A. W., R. J. Brown, D. E. Skilling, and R. DeLong. 1974. *Leptospira pomona* and reproductive failure in California sea lions. Journal of the American Veterinary Medical Association 165:996–998.

Smith, A. W., D. E. Skilling, J. E. Barlough, and E. S. Berry. 1986. Distribution in the North Pacific Ocean, Bering Sea, and Arctic Ocean of animal populations known to carry pathogenic caliciviruses. Diseases of Aquatic Organisms 2:73–80.

Spraker, T. R., L. F. Lowry, and K. J. Frost. 1994. Gross necropsy and histopathologic lesions found in harbor seals. Pages 281–311 *in* T. R. Loughlin (ed.), Marine Mammals and the *Exxon Valdez*. Academic Press, San Diego and London.

St. Aubin, D. J. 1990. Physiologic and toxic effects on pinnipeds. Pages 103–127 *in* J. R. Geraci and D. J. St. Aubin (eds.), Marine Mammals and Oil: Confronting the Risks. Academic Press, San Diego, CA.

St. Aubin, D. J., J. R. Geraci, and V. J. Lounsbury (eds.). 1996. Rescue, Rehabilitation and Release of Marine Mammals: An Analysis of Current Views and Practices. Proceedings of a Workshop Held in Des Plaines, IL, 3–5 December 1991. U.S. Department of Commerce, NOAA Technical Memorandum NMFS-OPR-8. 65 pp.

Stenvers, O., J. Plotz, and H. Ludwig. 1992. Antarctic seals carry antibodies against seal herpesvirus. Archives of Virology 123:421–424.

Stroud, R. K., and T. J. Roffe. 1979. Causes of death in marine mammals stranded along the Oregon coast. Journal of Wildlife Diseases 15:91–97.

Stuen, S., P. Have, A. D. M. E. Osterhaus, J. M. Arnemo, and A. Moustgaard. 1994. Serological investigation of virus infections in harp seals (*Phoca groenlandica*) and hooded seals (*Cystophora cristata*). Veterinary Record 134:502–503.

Suskind, R. M. (ed.). 1977. Malnutrition and the Immune Response. Raven Press, New York, NY.

Testa, J. W., G. Oehlert, D. G. Ainley, J. L. Bengtson, D. B. Siniff, R. M. Laws, and D. Rounsevell. 1991. Temporal variability in Antarctic marine ecosystems: Periodic fluctuations in phocid seals. Canadian Journal of Fisheries and Aquatic Sciences 48:631–639.

Trillmich, F. 1985. Effects of the 1982/83 El Niño on Galapagos fur seals and sea lions. Noticias de Galapagos 42:22–23.

Trillmich, F. 1987. Galapagos fur seal, *Arctocephalus galapagoensis*. Pages 23–27 *in* J. P. Croxall and R. L. Gentry (eds.), Status, Biology, and Ecology of Fur Seals: Proceedings of an International Symposium and Workshop, Cambridge, England, 23–27 April 1984. U.S. Department of Commerce, NOAA Technical Report NMFS-51.

Trillmich, F., and T. Dellinger. 1991. The effects of El Niño on Galapagos pinnipeds. Pages 66–74 *in* F. Trillmich and K. A. Ono (eds.), Pinnipeds and El Niño: Responses to Environmental Stress. Springer-Verlag, Berlin.

Trillmich, F., and K. A. Ono (eds.). 1991. Pinnipeds and El Niño: Responses to Environmental Stress. Springer-Verlag, Berlin. 293 pp.

Trillmich, F., K. A. Ono, D. P. Costa, R. L. DeLong, S. D. Feldkamp, J. M. Francis, R. L. Gentry, C. B. Heath, B. J. Le Boeuf, P. Majluf, and A. E. York. 1991. The effects of El Niño on pinniped populations in the Eastern Pacific. Pages 247–270 *in* F. Trillmich and K. A. Ono (eds.), Pinnipeds and El Niño: Responses to Environmental Stress. Springer-Verlag, Berlin.

United Nations Environment Programme. 1995. Marine mammal / fishery interactions: Analysis of cull proposals. UNEP(OCA) / MM.SAC.3 / 1. United Nations Environment Programme, Nairobi.

Van Bressem, M. F., I. K. G. Visser, M. W. G. van de Bilt, J. S. Teppema, J. A. Raga, and A. D. M. E. Osterhaus. 1991. Morbillivirus infection in Mediterranean striped dolphins (*Stenella coeruleoalba*). Veterinary Record 129:471–472.

Vedros, N. A., A. W. Smith, J. Schonewald, G. Migaki, and R. C. Hubbard. 1971. Leptospirosis epizootic among California sea lions. Science 172:1250–1251.

Walsh, M. T., D. K. Odell, G. Young, E. D. Asper, and G. Bossart. 1990. Mass strandings of cetaceans. Pages 673–692 *in* L. A. Dierauf (ed.), CRC Handbook of Marine Mammal Medicine: Health, Disease, and Rehabilitation. CRC Press, Boca Raton, FL.

Webster, R. G., J. Geraci, and G. Petursson. 1981. Conjunctivitis in human beings caused by influenza A virus of seals. New England Journal of Medicine 304:911.

Weisskopf, M. 1988. Plastic reaps a grim harvest in the oceans of the world. Smithsonian 18 (12): 58–69.

Westlake, R. L., and W. G. Gilmartin. 1990. Hawaiian monk seal pupping locations in the Northwestern Hawaiian Islands. Pacific Science 44:366–383.

Wiig, O. 1988. Gronlandssel og selinvasjon. Naturen 2:35–41.

Wilkinson, D. M. 1991. Report to Assistant Administrator for Fisheries: Program review of the marine mammal stranding networks. U.S. Department of Commerce, NOAA, National Marine Fisheries Service. (Available from Office of Protected Resources, National Marine Fisheries Service, Silver Spring, MD.) 171 pp.

Wilkinson, D., and G. A. J. Worthy. 1999. Marine mammal stranding networks. (This volume)

Woods, R., D. V. Cousins, R. Kirkwood, and D. L. Obendorf. 1995. Tuberculosis in a wild Australian fur seal (*Arctocephalus pusillus doriferus*) from Tasmania. Journal of Wildlife Diseases 31:83–86.

Wyatt, T. 1980. Morrell's seals. Journal du Conseil Conseil International pour l'Exploration de la Mer 39:1–6.

York, A. E. 1987. Northern fur seal, *Callorhinus ursinus*, eastern Pacific population (Pribilof Islands, Alaska, and San Miguel Island, California). Pages 9–21 *in* J. P. Croxall and R. L. Gentry (eds.), Status, Biology and Ecology of Fur Seals: Proceedings of an International Symposium and Workshop, Cambridge, England, 23–27 April 1984. U.S. Department of Commerce, NOAA Technical Report NMFS-51.

Zimmerman, S. T., C. S. Gorbics, and L. F. Lowry. 1994. Response activities. Pages 23–45 *in* T. R. Loughlin (ed.), Marine Mammals and the *Exxon Valdez*. Academic Press, San Diego and London.

18

DEAN WILKINSON AND
GRAHAM A. J. WORTHY

Marine Mammal Stranding Networks

The popular perception of a response to a marine mammal stranding is of people taking heroic measures to rescue a group of live pilot whales stranded on a beach (Fig. 18-1). In several respects, this is a mistaken picture of the typical marine mammal stranding. The definition adopted by the U.S. National Marine Fisheries Service gives a sense of the difference between reality and popular perception: "A stranded marine mammal is: Any dead marine mammal on a beach or floating nearshore; Any live cetacean on a beach or in water so shallow that it is unable to free itself and resume normal activity; or Any live pinniped which is unable or unwilling to leave the shore because of injury or poor health" (Wilkinson 1991).

Although the U.S. Fish and Wildlife Service has not adopted a formal definition of a stranding for species under its jurisdiction (i.e., sea otters, manatees, walruses, and polar bears), the functional definitions are virtually identical to those for pinnipeds and cetaceans.

The most commonly stranded marine mammal is a dead, beach-cast, often decomposed animal (Fig. 18-2). In the United States, far more pinnipeds strand each year than cetaceans, and mass strandings are rare. Even in the case of live stranded cetaceans, single stranded animals that are ill or injured are more common than mass strandings.

From 1989 through 1994 a total of 21,228 marine mammal strandings was reported in the United States—an annual mean of 3,538 animals. Of these, 12,681 (mean, 2,113) were pinnipeds (National Marine Fisheries Service, unpublished data), 6,768 (mean, 1,128) were cetaceans (National Marine Fisheries Service, unpublished data), 649 were southern sea otters (*Enhydra lutris*) (mean, 108) (California Department of Fish and Game, Monterey Bay Aquarium, unpublished data), and 1,130 were West Indian manatees (*Trichechus manatus*) (mean, 188) (Florida Department of Environmental Protection, unpublished data). The data shown in Figure 18-3 are the result of the efforts of a large body of volunteers involved in stranding response networks administered by the National Marine Fisheries Service and the Fish and Wildlife Service.

Although the means are significantly higher than those reported for the six years from 1983 to 1988 (Wilkinson 1991), this trend is, at least in part, attributable to increased effort and not solely the result of increased numbers of stranded animals. Because of the difficulty in covering the Alaska coast, little concerted effort has been made to record pinniped strandings there.

The 1992–1993 pinniped totals are inflated by occurrence of an El Niño event. Such meteorological events originate in the South Pacific with weakened easterly winds. They cause changes in both climate and sea temperatures. The increase

Figure 18-1. Part of a pod of long-finned pilot whales that stranded alive on Cape Cod near Eastham, Massachusetts. The animals, some draped with sheets, are being kept cool by volunteers bringing buckets of water. (Photograph courtesy of Center for Coastal Studies, Provincetown, Massachusetts)

Figure 18-2. A humpback whale being towed from the surf, Virginia Beach, Virginia, 4 June 1995. (Photograph by C. Driscoll)

in water temperature changes the abundance and distribution of fish populations and has a significant impact on pinniped mortality rates due to reductions in prey populations (Trillmich and Ono 1991).

It is statistically possible to predict with some certainty which species are most likely to strand. During the 1989–1994 period, the most commonly stranded pinniped was the California sea lion (*Zalophus californianus*), with 5,812 animals recorded. The most commonly stranded cetacean was the bottlenose dolphin (*Tursiops truncatus*), with 3,676 recorded. Other pinniped species that often stranded were harbor seals (*Phoca vitulina*) (3,426) and northern elephant seals (*Mirounga angustirostris*) (1,598). Other frequently stranded cetaceans were harbor porpoises (*Phocoena phocoena*) (485), long-finned pilot whales (*Globicephala melas*) (222), gray whales (*Eschrichtius robustus*) (234), and pygmy sperm whales (*Kogia breviceps*) (195). Because the species is often involved in mass strandings, there is considerable year-to-year variation in the numbers of pilot whales recorded.

Development of Stranding Networks

Wherever marine mammals strand, people take notice. In many areas, this has prompted groups of people to organize themselves into informal networks to help the animals. Researchers also have recognized that stranded animals are a source of information that otherwise could be difficult to obtain. The nature and composition of stranding networks vary from country to country, as well as within countries. In

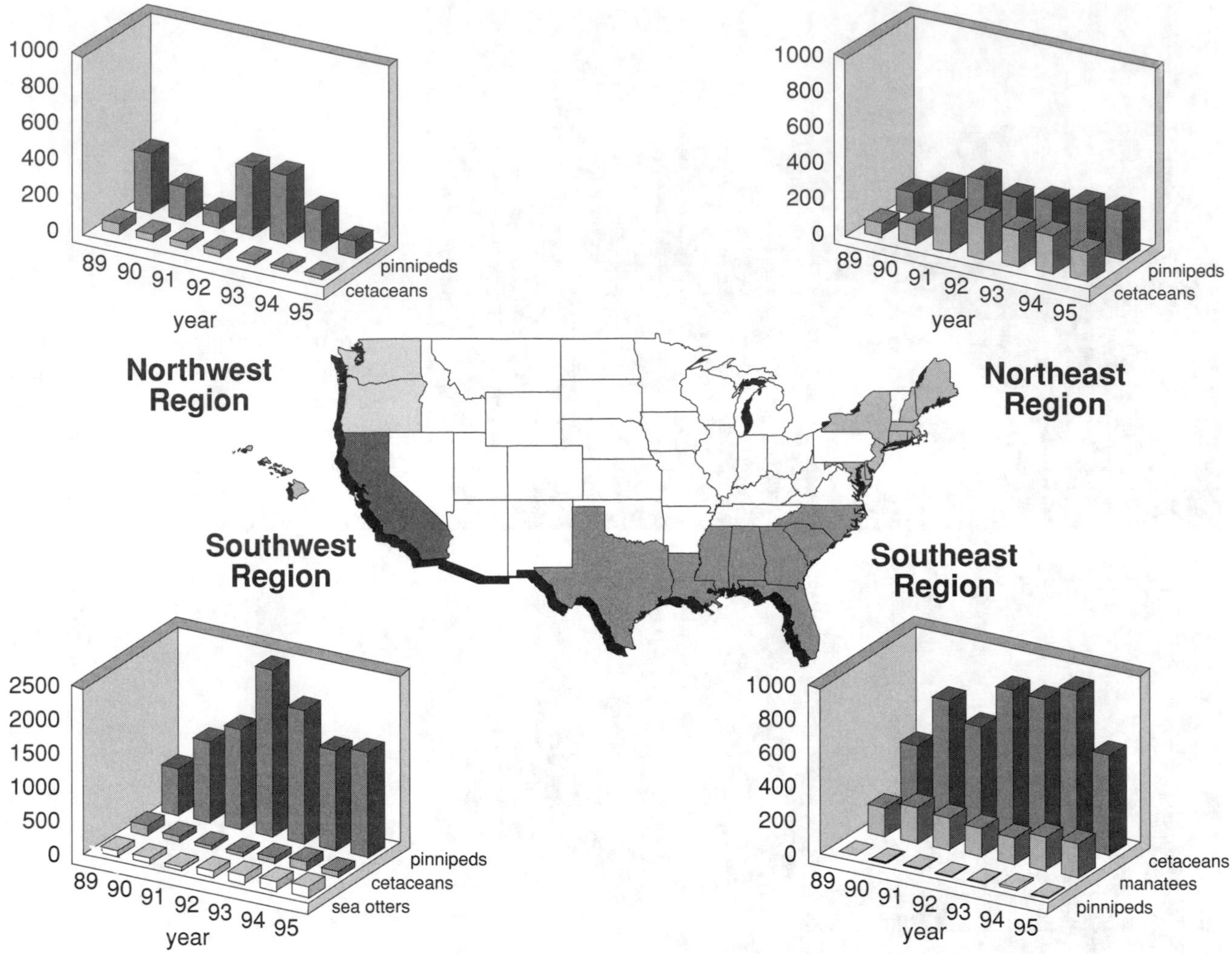

Figure 18-3. Map of the United States showing the four geographic regions that compose the stranding network. Insets illustrate stranding frequency by taxonomic group and by year, based on data collected through the stranding network.

some cases, they are sponsored by governments; in others, they primarily involve people motivated by academic interest. In southern Argentina, a single individual, Nathalie Rae Goodall, has functioned as a one-person stranding network (Goodall 1978, 1989).

Levels of effort also vary. In some countries, only cetaceans are recorded; in others, such as the Netherlands, extensive efforts have been made to document both pinnipeds and cetaceans. In New Zealand and Australia, detailed protocols for handling mass strandings have been prepared (Anonymous 1984, Baker 1986). Cetacean strandings have been recorded systematically in the United Kingdom since 1913 (Sheldrick 1979). In many ways the U.S. stranding network is unique, in terms of both government involvement with an extensive volunteer network and the range of activities involved.

Although individuals and institutions in various parts of the United States had made efforts to monitor strandings in their own areas, no systematic effort was made to collect such information nationwide until 1972. The U.S. network had its genesis when James G. Mead of the Smithsonian Institution in Washington, D.C., began to compile stranding records from researchers throughout the country. This effort eventually led to the standardization of the way stranding data were collected.

Legal authority for the U.S. stranding response network is contained in the Marine Mammal Protection Act (Public Law 92-522, as amended), which is discussed below. The National Marine Fisheries Service's original interpretation of the Marine Mammal Protection Act caused some scientists to become concerned that access to tissues and other research opportunities involving stranded animals could be unduly restricted. To address this issue and others related to strandings, the Marine Mammal Commission sponsored a workshop in 1977. Among the recommendations of the workshop was that a regional stranding response system, coordinated by the National Marine Fisheries Service, be established (Geraci and St. Aubin 1979).

It was not until 1981 that the regional apparatus was in place and the procedures for network participation and reporting were established. Between 1981 and 1991 regional networks administered by the National Marine Fisheries Service's regional offices operated virtually independently. A massive mortality of bottlenose dolphins in 1987–1988, and the attendant public concern, led to the realization that what had been, in many ways, a laissez-faire approach toward strandings was inadequate.

In 1991 a National Marine Fisheries Service–sponsored program review identified inconsistencies in policies among the regions and made recommendations to address this and other problems (Wilkinson 1991). Soon thereafter, the Service created the position of national stranding coordinator. The coordinator's chief responsibilities are to define national stranding policy, standardize network operations, and enhance the capabilities of network members.

Network members are issued letters of authorization by the Service's regional offices. Although there are some gaps in coverage, network members can be found in all the coastal states, and thousands of individuals from various backgrounds participate. Members include government entities, aquariums, rehabilitation centers, academic institutions, research organizations, individual scientists, veterinarians, and nonspecialists with appropriate interests and skills. Virtually everyone involved has expertise in some area of marine mammal science or has received training to supplement a background in biology. Some institutions make extensive use of volunteers. As an example, several hundred volunteers work with the Marine Mammal Center in Sausalito, California (Fig. 18-4). In Massachusetts, more than 500 potential volunteers help respond to mass strandings on Cape Cod.

Members of the stranding networks are not reimbursed for their time or expenses. Lack of stable financial support has often created problems for the stranding networks, and many inevitably operate on inadequate budgets. Members respond to stranded animals at inconvenient times. As any experienced network member can attest, the stench from a dead stranded cetacean can be almost overwhelming. Even worse, the smell clings to a person's skin and clothing for many days regardless of how thoroughly they are washed. In light of such negative aspects, one is tempted to ask why anybody would undertake such a task. Considering the costs, inconveniences, and discomfort involved, there seems little doubt that the volunteers are motivated by genuine concern for the animals and a desire to learn as much as possible about them.

Legal Background for Stranding Operations

Two provisions of the Marine Mammal Protection Act deal with the rescue of stranded marine mammals in the United States. Section 109(h) states:

> (1) Nothing in this title or title IV shall prevent a Federal, State or local government official or employee or a person designated under section 112(c) from taking, in the course of his or her duties as an official, employee or designee, a marine mammal in a humane manner (including euthanasia) if such taking is for—
>
> (A) the protection or welfare of the mammal,
>
> (B) the protection of the public health and welfare, or
>
> (C) the nonlethal removal of nuisance animals.
>
> . . . (3) In any case in which it is feasible to return to its natural habitat a marine mammal taken . . . under circumstances described in this subsection, steps to achieve that result shall be taken.

Letters of authorization are issued under provisions of section 112(c) that allow the Secretary of Commerce to enter into cooperative agreements to carry out the purposes of the Act.

In 1992 the stranding networks received explicit recognition within the Marine Mammal Protection Act with the addition of Title IV, the Marine Mammal Health and Stranding Response Act (Public Law 102-587). Among other things, Title IV requires the National Marine Fisheries Service to collect and disseminate information regarding the health of marine mammals and health trends of wild populations. The Service is also specifically required to collect information on strandings; to "monitor species, numbers, conditions, and causes of illnesses and deaths of stranded animals"; and to collect "other life history and reference level data, including marine mammal tissue analyses, that would allow comparison of the causes of illness and deaths in stranded marine mammals with physical, chemical, and biological environmental parameters."

The two sections of the Marine Mammal Protection Act reflect different objectives regarding the stranding networks. Section 109 has as its primary purpose the rehabilitation of stranded animals and their return to wild populations. Title IV is intended to ensure that as much scientific information as possible is obtained from stranded animals. Although the aims are not mutually exclusive, they relate to different issues.

The letters of authorization issued to stranding network members have two levels of authority. All members are authorized to collect information from dead stranded marine mammals. Because physical facilities and veterinary expertise are necessary to successfully rehabilitate live animals, the issuance of authority for this level of activity is more limited. Most of the letters of authorization dealing with rehabilitation have been issued to institutions such as aquariums and facilities specifically set up to handle live stranded animals.

Network Activities: The Texas Marine Mammal Stranding Network as an Illustration

The extent of coverage and the organizational structure of the networks vary widely, depending on numbers and types of animals that strand in each area, the availability of physical and financial resources, and scientific expertise present. In the southeast region, for example, coverage and involvement range from virtually no coverage in Louisiana to a statewide organization in Texas with hundreds of volunteers. The Alabama network is essentially a single person, whereas Florida's consists of many interactive, but independent, groups of academics, aquariums, and trained members of the general public. The network in South Carolina is administered by the state government. This range of organizational size and structure has resulted in a variety of solutions to funding needs.

The Texas Marine Mammal Stranding Network is one of the most active participants in the national network system, and a review of its evolution and activities, and the difficulties it has faced, may be useful. In addition to responding to strandings, the Texas network has developed major fund-raising and education programs.

Before 1980 sporadic responses to strandings in Texas were coordinated by David J. Schmidly of Texas A&M University. Activities were at a relatively low level with little public awareness. In 1980 Raymond J. Tarpley and Gregg Schwabb formally founded the Texas network as part of the southeast regional stranding program. It was designed to cover the entire Texas coast.

During the 1980s the Texas network grew tremendously, and large numbers of volunteers came forward to help. The growth in public awareness of the program and its purposes is reflected in the dramatic increase in the number of animals recovered, from 14 in 1981 to an average of 160 animals annually from 1986 through 1993. Most of the increase in the early years was a result of increased surveillance and not increased mortality rates.

A board of directors for the network was established in 1989, and it was formally incorporated as a nonprofit organization. This allowed it to solicit tax-deductible donations from individuals and to apply to foundations for financial support.

Organizationally, the salvage component and the fund-raising component of the organization have independent roles. The aims with respect to salvage are to respond to all marine mammal strandings within the state of Texas, to care for live stranded animals, to perform necropsies and collect selected tissues for scientific research, and to maintain a database and tissue archives that are available to all researchers. The major goals of the fund-raising component are to raise funds to support the salvage network, to promote public education, and to support student projects through scholarships and grants-in-aid for research.

Network coverage extends from the Texas-Louisiana state line to the Mexican border, a coastline of more than 1,600 km (1,000 miles), including the barrier islands. Six network regions have been designated along the coast: Sabine Pass, Galveston, Port O'Connor, Port Aransas, Corpus Christi, and South Padre Island. Each has a regional coordinator who organizes local volunteers to assist with recoveries and necropsies, contacts local businesses for donations, and communicates with the local media. The regional coordinators work with the state operations coordinator based at Texas A&M University-Galveston—the Texas network's only full-time paid position.

The state operations coordinator is responsible for coordinating and storing all data and samples collected, coordinating responses to live strandings, communicating with the Service, organizing public education services, and overseeing large-scale fund-raising. Because good communications are vital for timely responses, the operations coordinator's office is equipped with a statewide paging system, a toll-free telephone line to receive reports, and two cellular telephones. A four-wheel-drive truck is available for recovering animals.

A special response team of trained volunteers works out of the state office. The team is dispatched immediately to respond to fresh strandings or live strandings anywhere in the state and to transport all freshly dead animals to Galveston, where a detailed necropsy is performed. The necropsy includes sampling for histopathology, toxicology, infectious diseases, life history data, and anatomical studies. The response team also assists local volunteers with primary care for live stranded animals. The Texas network has three portable holding tanks that can be set up to hold dolphins temporarily. Longer-term care is provided at several cooperating facilities along the coast.

During the period 1989 through 1994 the Texas network recovered 1,163 marine mammals, 94% of which were bottlenose dolphins. This figure accounts for 17% of all cetacean strandings and 28% of all bottlenose dolphin strandings recorded in the United States during that time. In 1994 the Texas network responded to nine live strandings. One pygmy sperm whale required euthanasia on the beach and three other animals—a striped dolphin (*Stenella coeruleoalba*), a Fraser's dolphin (*Lagenodelphis hosei*), and a bottlenose dolphin—died immediately after stranding. Four

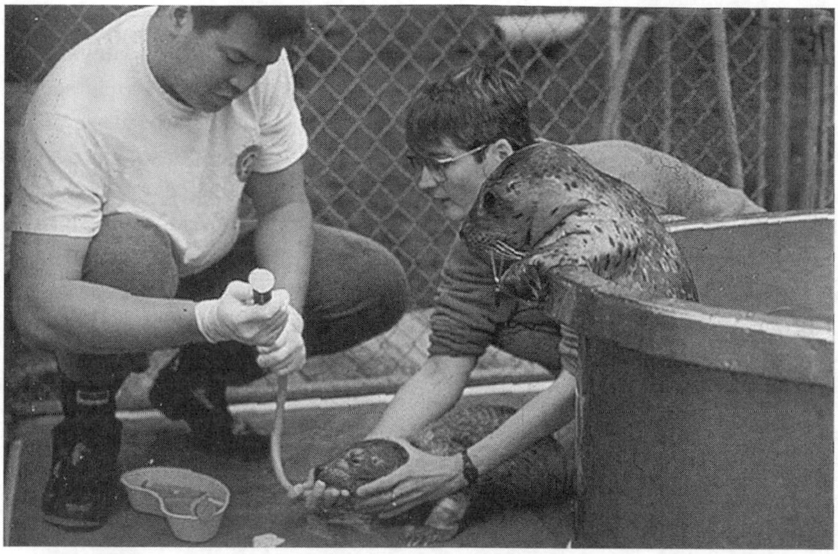

Figure 18-4. Tube-feeding a harbor seal during rehabilitation. (Photograph courtesy of the Marine Mammal Center, Sausalito, California)

adult bottlenose dolphins were rehabilitated and released, and one very young bottlenose dolphin was transferred to Sea World of Texas for extended care.

Unusual mortality events occurred in the Texas area in 1990, 1992, and again in 1994. The Texas network responded to more than 200 dolphin strandings each in 1990 and 1992 and 296 in 1994. In March 1994 as many as 50 dolphins a week washed ashore along a 62-km (100-mile) stretch of coastline near Galveston.

In addition to responding to strandings, the Texas network has become increasingly involved in public education. Ultimately, the program depends on public support. At the operating level, the general public is likely to be the source of most stranding reports. An informed public also is much more likely to make individual donations and encourage government support. Without such funding, the networks would not be able to survive.

The Texas network is involved with educating people through lectures, training sessions, and a traveling museum display. During 1994 more than 70 public seminars, presentations, and training necropsy sessions were conducted for audiences ranging from elementary schools to Elderhostel groups. These presentations covered general marine mammal biology as well as specific topics related to strandings. Actual necropsies were undertaken by some groups, and role-playing activities were provided for the younger ones. The network is completing production of a training video on proper necropsy techniques to help train members who respond to strandings.

Rehabilitation Issues

The definition of "rehabilitation" commonly used by the stranding networks differs from the general definition of the term. It refers to the period of time during which a marine mammal requires treatment. After an animal has recovered, it is deemed to be rehabilitated, whether it is returned to the wild or retained in captivity.

The rehabilitation of abandoned, injured, or sick marine mammals is consistent with humane concern for wild animals. With very limited exceptions, however, one should not be misled into believing that such rehabilitation contributes to the maintenance of healthy wild populations. Just as people may place a value on the treatment of injured songbirds, even though it is known that this makes no significant contribution to the overall health of songbird populations, the rehabilitation of stranded marine mammals is regarded by many as a humane and responsible gesture toward individual animals.

Rehabilitation has the potential to contribute to the conservation of only two marine mammal species in U.S. waters—Hawaiian monk seals (*Monachus schauinslandi*) and West Indian manatees. For both of these species, directed rehabilitation programs are part of official recovery programs. In Hawaii, a "head-start" program has been set up to increase the survival rate of monk seal pups. Although the pups in question are not ones that have stranded, the program has potential implications for stranded animals (see Ragen and Lavigne, this volume). A U.S. Fish and Wildlife Service program in Florida has successfully rehabilitated and released a number of manatees back into the wild (see Reynolds, this volume).

There are two main reasons why rehabilitation efforts for other species are not likely to contribute significantly to their conservation. First, the number of animals successfully rehabilitated is relatively small. Second, the size of most wild populations is large when compared with the number of live strandings.

Between 1972 and 1995 only 65 cetaceans were successfully rehabilitated. There are several reasons for this low number. Cetaceans are exclusively aquatic and typically strand alive only when extremely ill or seriously injured. Second, the facilities required for treating such animals are much more elaborate than those needed for treating most terrestrial animals or pinnipeds, and the number of such facilities is limited. Finally, knowledge has come slowly for those involved in the care and treatment of cetaceans. For example, only within the past few years have formulas been developed that allow for successful feeding of unweaned calves. For species such as the pygmy sperm whale, only recently has enough been learned to permit successful rehabilitation. Before 1990 stranded pygmy sperm whales almost inevitably died before treatment could be initiated. As knowledge increased, efforts were more successful, and several pygmy sperm whales have now been successfully rehabilitated and released.

In contrast, each year several hundred pinnipeds are successfully rehabilitated and returned to the wild. The largest number for any one species was 525 California sea lions rehabilitated in 1992, but this number is relatively insignificant when compared with an estimated U.S. population of up to 160,000 animals (Barlow et al. 1995). Even those pinniped populations that are designated as depleted exist in large enough numbers that rehabilitation is unlikely to contribute to their recovery. For example, the Pribilof Islands stock of northern fur seals (*Callorhinus ursinus*) is estimated at about 982,000 animals (National Marine Fisheries Service 1993). Even if a large-scale rehabilitation project were possible, its effect on the population would be minuscule.

Although rehabilitation and release of stranded marine mammals have limited value in terms of population conservation, the care of live stranded animals can provide useful information applicable both to maintenance of captive animals and management of wild populations. Stranded animals are often ill and thus can provide information on the pathogens and parasites that affect wild populations. By treating stranded animals, veterinarians can obtain information and experience that can be applied to captive populations. Treatment of live animals can also provide information on the physiology, life history, and behavior of marine mammals—information that can be gained only with difficulty in the wild.

Apart from the issue of whether rehabilitation programs contribute to the conservation of wild populations, it is appropriate to ask whether rehabilitated animals can resume a normal life after release. Confirmation of an animal's survival after release back to the wild is critical, and limited data are available on this point. The National Marine Fisheries Service has required that released animals be marked or tagged so that they can be identified if they strand again. However, because of the difficulty and cost of monitoring cetaceans and pinnipeds in the marine environment, only a few serious efforts have been made to confirm survival. Seagars (1988) reported tag resighting data on California pinnipeds. Studies done on released rehabilitated or captive pinnipeds and cetaceans using radio or satellite tags include Payne and Rimmer (1982), Mate (1989), Harvey (1991), Gales and Waples (1993), Mate et al. (1994), and Davis et al. (1996). Because the species is endangered, a more extensive effort has been made to track released manatees using tether tags (Rathbun et al. 1990, Reid et al. 1995).

The use of such technology has been increasing, but it is expensive. Such efforts should be encouraged for reasons beyond the question of whether an individual animal survives. Transmitter tags can also provide behavioral information such as dive times, depth of dives, and movement. Although continued receipt of signals in such circumstances is confirmation of survival, the opposite is not necessarily an indication that an animal has perished. Without routine verification of survival, the effectiveness of rehabilitation programs will continue to be uncertain. To many people, however, success will continue to be gauged by numbers of animals successfully treated and released.

The issue of survival introduces an ethical element—should animals be released if their chance of survival is low or unknown? Because of limited capacity, a rehabilitation facility may have to choose between the release of a less-than-completely-healthy animal or euthanasia. Premature release can be justified by the argument that the animal will have at least a chance to survive. Because of the Marine Mammal Protection Act's requirement that animals be treated humanely, the question is whether releasing an animal with a low chance of survival may contribute to its suffering. Very young animals, even healthy ones, may not have acquired the skills needed to forage or avoid predators. In light of these uncertainties, no single policy can apply in every case. Those engaged in rehabilitation and management simply have to exercise their best judgment.

Issues also arise with respect to the possible impacts of released animals on wild populations. In 1991 the Marine Mammal Commission and the National Marine Fisheries Service cosponsored a workshop to examine these issues (St. Aubin et al. 1996). Participants agreed that the health of a wild population outweighs the welfare of an individual animal. During the workshop, two issues received particular attention: the introduction of diseases into wild populations and the possible genetic consequences of releasing stranded animals.

Marine mammals are often ill when they strand, and such animals may function as reservoirs for disease if they are returned to the wild. Also, an animal may contract diseases during its rehabilitation period and then carry them into the wild.

Some scientists have argued that the least fit members of a population are those that strand. If these animals are released back into a wild population, they argue, the overall health of that population could be affected and the natural selection process could be altered. For example, one of the most common afflictions of stranded pinnipeds is lungworm. Although a lungworm condition is treatable, a genetic factor could make some animals more vulnerable than others. If rehabilitated animals are released, the genetic fitness of entire populations could be affected.

A fallacy of such an argument is that virtually any physical condition may be linked to genetics. Our knowledge of genetically caused health problems in marine mammals is extremely limited, however. Without at least some evidence that a particular condition has a genetic basis, the decision usually should be in favor of the individual animal.

A point to consider is the level of scientific certainty that must be reached before an action is taken. If the requirement is to prove an absolute cause-and-effect relationship, a problem may be exacerbated and corrective action may be either precluded or not taken in a timely manner.

Translation of science into policy may present a dilemma. Management decisions often have to be made based on scientific evidence that is less than definitive. As an example, the Endangered Species Act (Public Law 93-205, as amended) provides that individuals may petition an agency to designate a species as threatened or endangered. The agency responsible for the decision must act on the basis of the "best scientific and commercial data available." In some cases, the "best" information may be less than definitive, but the agency is required to make a decision.

Two release decisions illustrate this dilemma and how different determinations may be made in similar circumstances. In 1991 stranding network members found antibodies to phocine distemper virus in pinnipeds that stranded along the U.S. Atlantic coast. The decision was made that no animal showing positive antibody titers to the virus could be released into the wild population, even if the individual appeared to be healthy. This decision was based, at least in part, on the fact that the same disease had previously been responsible for the deaths of more than 17,000 pinnipeds in Europe (Osterhaus and Vedder 1988), and there was uncertainty as to the etiology of the disease and its prevalence in populations in the western Atlantic. In a similar case, a number of sea otters being rehabilitated after the 1989 *Exxon Valdez* oil spill were found to have a herpesvirus, and a decision was made that they could be released (R. Keith Harris, pers. comm.).

Despite their controversial aspects, it is clear that rehabilitation and release programs have helped foster much of the support, in terms of both public sentiment and finances, for stranding network operations. The Marine Mammal Protection Act also provides an unambiguous mandate for rehabilitating stranded animals.

Strandings and Science

In the Marine Mammal Health and Stranding Response Act, Congress observed that stranding networks have the potential of gaining valuable information but that realization of this potential depends on the training and education of network members. When setting up network operations, it is important to recognize that there is a trade-off between the extent of coverage and the amount of scientific information that can be obtained. It is not possible to deploy highly trained professional personnel throughout all the coastal areas where animals may strand. However, nonspecialists with scientific backgrounds can be given the training and field resources needed to collect basic information.

To enhance the abilities of network members, the National Marine Fisheries Service and the Fish and Wildlife Service have developed a series of documents to distribute to volunteers. The primary reference is a field guide that includes a species identification key, treatment protocols for live stranded animals, and basic information on tissue collection (Geraci and Lounsbury 1993). A more detailed manual covering pinnipeds has also been developed. It provides information on methods for gross necropsy and instructions on collecting life history data and collecting and preparing tissues for pathogen detection, histopathology, and contaminant and toxicological analyses (Dierauf 1994). The Fish and Wildlife Service prepared a similar manual on manatees (Bonde et al. 1983). With support from the Marine Mammal Commission, an instructional video was prepared by Sea World, Orlando, Florida, and distributed to network members.

From a management perspective, it is important to have baseline data with which to make comparisons. To develop this baseline, the National Marine Fisheries Service requires the collection of a minimum set of data from each stranding. The standardized data collection form is reproduced in Figure 18-5. The Service may make requests for additional information, but such information is not required as a condition of network participation. Network members are also encouraged to provide tissues to scientific investigators.

Observations of dead stranded animals can reveal much about their lives and, with a sufficient sample size, about the species as a whole. Much of the professional literature on marine mammals has been the result of information gained from stranded animals. Species such as the pygmy sperm whale strand commonly but are seldom observed in the wild, and most of our knowledge of this species has come from stranded animals. More may have been learned about the life history of the Atlantic white-sided dolphin (*Lagenorhynchus acutus*) from a single mass stranding than from all of the previous work on this species (Geraci et al. 1978).

Even the basic information requested on the stranding data sheet can be useful for management decisions. Knowing the species and location of a stranding may provide information on a species' range and distribution. For instance, stranding data from the early 1990s indicate that some pinniped species on the Atlantic coast may be expanding their range south. Previous strandings of seals in the southeast region of the United States have been considered anomalous, but that assessment may change based on evidence that several harbor seals strand each year in North Carolina. Farther north, strandings of arctic seals such as harp seals (*Phoca groenlandica*) and hooded seals (*Cystophora cristata*) have become more common in New England and the mid-Atlantic states. This is most dramatically illustrated by the number of harp seal strandings, which has increased steadily from three animals in 1989 to 78 in 1995. Expansion of range may be coincident with increases in population abundance.

Changes in the length and sex distribution of stranded animals may indicate that something unusual is occurring. In some marine mammals, length measurements correlate roughly with age. A change in the length distribution of stranded animals may indicate a change in mortality patterns or the age structure of the population.

Similarly, a change in the sex distribution of stranded animals may warrant investigation. As an example, when a leptospirosis epizootic occurred in 1984, a disproportionate number of male California sea lions stranded. There was

MARINE MAMMAL STRANDING REPORT SID#____ (NMFS USE)

FIELD NO.:____ NMFS REGISTRATION NO.____

COMMON NAME:____ GENUS:____ SPECIES:____

EXAMINER
Name:____ Agency:____ Phone:____
Address:____

LOCATION
State:____ County:____
City:____
Locality Details:____
*Latitude:____N
*Longitude:____W

TYPE OF OCCURRENCE
Mass Stranding: (Yes) / (No) # Animals____
Human Interaction: (Yes) / (No) / (?)
Check one: __1. Boat collision
__2. Shot
__3. Fishery interaction
__4. Other____
How determined: ____
Other Causes (if known):____

DATE OF INITIAL OBSERVATION:
Yr ____ Mo ____ Day ____
CONDITION: Check one:__1.Alive
__2.Fresh dead
__3.Moderate decomp.
__4.Advanced decomp.
__5.Mummified
__? Unknown

DATE OF EXAMINATION:
Yr ____ Mo ____ Day ____
CONDITION: Check one:__1.Alive
__2.Fresh dead
__3.Moderate decomp.
__4.Advanced decomp.
__5.Mummified
__? Unknown

LIVE ANIMAL - Condition and Disposition:
Check one or more: __1.Released at site
__2.Sick
__3.Injured
__4.Died
__5.Euthanized
__6.Rehabilitated and released
__? Unknown
Transported to: ____
(Died) / (Released) Date:____

TAGS APPLIED?: (Yes) / (No)
TAGS PRESENT?: (Yes) / (No)

	Dorsal	Left	Right
Tag No.(s):	____	____	____
Color(s):	____	____	____
Type: Placement	____	Front/Rear	Front/Rear

CARCASS - Disposition, check one:
Check one: __1.Left at site
__2.Buried
__3.Towed
__4.Sci. collection (see below)
__5.Edu. collection (see below)
__6.Other ____
__? Unknown
NECROPSIED? (Yes) / (No)

MORPHOLOGICAL DATA:
Sex - Check one: __1.Male
__2.Female
__? Unknown
Straight Length:____(cm)/(in)/(est)
*Weight:____(kg)/(lb)/(est?)
PHOTOS TAKEN? (Yes) / (No)

REMARKS: ____

DISPOSITION OF TISSUE/SKELETAL MATERIAL: ____

*Record data if available

It is estimated that completion of this form requires 20 minutes.

OMB#0648-0178, expires 01/31/97

Figure 18-5. Standard data reporting form used by the stranding network to obtain information on every stranded marine mammal.

also a change in the age distribution of stranded animals. The majority of the animals were either juveniles or subadults (Dierauf et al. 1985).

It might seem that the most obvious information that could be obtained from dead marine mammals would relate to the causes of death and rates of mortality. Without baseline information, however, the significance of such information is limited. In other words, without an adequate sample to define normal conditions, it is difficult to detect the abnormal. Detection of the abnormal is important in evaluating epizootic events. By providing baseline information, stranding networks contribute to the ability to detect such events.

Although stranding data cannot provide absolute mortality levels, they can help detect changes in mortality rates (Hersh et al. 1990). Because stranding coverage had been consistent over time along several areas of the east coast, the Service was able to use historic stranding rates as an index to determine that the epizootic affecting the coastal migratory stock of bottlenose dolphins during 1987–1988 had caused the death of more than 50% of the population over a 10-month period (Scott et al. 1988).

Many members of the stranding networks do more than collect the basic data required, conduct gross necropsies, and collect tissues for analysis. Their efforts have provided information on the parasites and diseases affecting marine mammal populations. Treatment of live stranded animals has provided similar information. A large body of literature has been produced on the pathogens and parasites affecting marine mammals, much of which has been the result of work with stranded animals.

If there has been a weakness in this area, it is the tendency by researchers to report only new and unusual findings in the scientific literature. A wealth of information on marine mammal diseases exists in the gray literature and on forms stashed away in filing cabinets. There have been relatively few efforts to systematically survey the causes of morbidity and mortality in stranded animals (Schroeder et al. 1973, Stroud and Roffe 1979, Cowan et al. 1986, Steiger et al. 1989, Dieter 1991, Gerber et al. 1993). For example, most stranding network members involved in the rehabilitation of pinnipeds state that among the most common pinniped pathologies are lungworms and heartworms, but there have been few efforts to quantify such findings (van der Kamp 1987, Gerber et al. 1993).

Strandings and Management

Systematic efforts to gather information from stranded animals have potential for improving management capabilities. In addition to providing an indication of mortality rates, stranding data can provide insights about stock identity, life history and population dynamics, and human–marine mammal interactions.

If the total number of bottlenose dolphins in U.S. waters remained constant, yet the species became extinct in the Gulf of Mexico, management would be judged to have failed. A central goal of management is to prevent populations from becoming severely depleted or extinct within specific parts of their range. To achieve this goal, a good understanding of stock identity and boundaries is necessary. The importance of stock differentiation was demonstrated during the 1987–1988 die-off of bottlenose dolphins on the U.S. Atlantic coast. There are two stocks of bottlenose dolphins in the area: a coastal stock that migrates seasonally along the coast and a more abundant offshore stock (Scott et al. 1988, Kenney 1990). When carcasses found on beaches from New Jersey to Florida were examined for morphological features, it was discovered that virtually all the animals were from the coastal stock. This raised concern that the stock may have been seriously depleted by the die-off.

Traditionally, morphology has been the primary standard for evaluating systematic differences between species. It can also be used to define stocks, and information from strandings can provide key information. By comparing cranial measurements, tooth and vertebral counts, and color patterns, scientists were able to differentiate the Baja California neritic (coastal) stock of common dolphins (*Delphinus delphis*) from other common dolphins in the eastern Pacific. As a result of these studies, a separate species, *D. capensis,* has been established (Heyning and Perrin 1994).

Differences in parasite infestation can reflect differences in species distribution and prey species and help define populations. For example, there are marked differences between the parasites of inshore and offshore western North Atlantic bottlenose dolphins (Mead and Potter 1990, 1995). Coastal animals commonly have *Braunina* in the stomach and do not have *Phyllobothrium* and *Monorhygma* in other tissues. The situation is reversed with the offshore stock.

It may be a tragic commentary, but the presence of specific contaminants or the ratio of contaminant burdens also can help define stocks (Aguilar 1987). As in the case of parasites, differences may indicate either spatial segregation or differences of contaminant levels in prey. One study of stranded animals on the west coast of North America indicated that the ratio of DDT metabolites to PCBs was higher in harbor porpoises from California than in those from Washington and Oregon, suggesting that porpoises in the two regions were from different stocks (Calambokidis 1986).

Another tool for distinguishing populations is genetic analysis. DNA can be obtained from a small piece of skin or other tissue. By sequencing mitochondrial or nuclear DNA, it may be possible to define specific populations (Amos et al.

1992). The importance of such information is illustrated by the status of harbor porpoises in the western North Atlantic. The impact of incidental mortality from fisheries would, in this instance, be much more serious if there are three or four reproductively isolated populations of harbor porpoise than if there is one large population. A workshop on the status of the species strongly recommended that additional genetic analyses be undertaken to address the issue of stock definition (National Marine Fisheries Service 1992).

Life History and Population Dynamics

Stranded animals can also serve as a source of information on life history and population dynamics. Before it can be determined if special management action is needed for specific populations, such parameters as longevity, age at sexual maturity, reproductive rates, and mortality rates can provide the information necessary to develop population models.

Although the length of an animal can be used to infer its maturity status, there are much more exact methods of determining age. In pinnipeds and most odontocetes, teeth can be processed and growth layer groups counted to provide an estimation of age (Laws 1953, Hohn 1980). Growth layer groups in the periotic bone have been used to estimate age in manatees (Marmontel et al. 1996). For some baleen whales, ear plugs have been used to estimate age (Lockyer 1974). Accurate age determinations and a sufficient sample can provide information on the longevity of a species. Using the same technique, it also may be possible to determine the age at which a female dolphin became sexually mature (Hohn et al. 1991).

Similarly, reproductive status often can be determined from stranded animals. In the case of male pinnipeds and cetaceans, it is possible to determine sexual maturity. In female cetaceans, ovulations leave permanent corpora, and examination of ovaries may help reconstruct an animal's reproductive history (Collet and Harrison 1981).

Stranded animals are also a potential source of information on the prey species of marine mammals. In addition to identifying intact prey items, researchers can identify prey species using fish otoliths (ear bones) and squid mouthparts (Seltzer et al. 1986, Barros and Odell 1990, Barros 1992, Schwartz et al. 1992). Changes in prey composition may reflect changes in prey abundance or environmental problems. Although studies were not conducted on stranded animals, scat analysis of pinnipeds during the 1983 El Niño event mirrored changes in fish populations along the west coast (Trillmich and Ono 1991).

Diseases and Causes of Mortality

Gross necropsies, histopathologic examinations, and other analyses can provide information on the diseases and parasites afflicting marine mammals. Stranding networks played a key role in detecting phocine distemper virus in seals in the North Sea and the northeastern United States. After the disease was detected in the United States, analysis of blood serum that had been banked by network members indicated that the disease was present in the population as early as 1986 and is probably enzootic (Geraci et al. 1993). This indicated that the disease was present before the 1988 epizootic in Europe. Tissues collected by network members also enabled researchers to determine that a morbillivirus was present in bottlenose dolphins in the Gulf of Mexico and was the probable cause of a mortality event on the Texas coast in 1994 (Lipscomb et al. 1994, 1996).

Under the Marine Mammal Protection Act, the National Marine Fisheries Service has the task of reducing the impact of human activities on marine mammals, specifically the impact of fisheries. To accomplish this, data are needed on where and when such interactions occur. Although data on stranded animals cannot be extrapolated to provide total mortality levels from interactions, they can provide an indication that specific problems require further investigation. Examination of stranded animals by trained observers can provide information on human interactions (Hare and Mead 1987).

Stranding data have shown that ship collisions cause a significant number of deaths of the critically endangered northern right whale, *Eubalaena glacialis* (Kraus 1990). Based on this information, the Right Whale Recovery Team listed this problem as the top recovery priority (National Marine Fisheries Service 1991).

In recent years, direct observation indicated that the groundfish set gillnet fishery was having a significant impact on harbor porpoises in the western North Atlantic (Read and Gaskin 1990). However, strandings of 49 animals in the spring of 1993, some of which had evidence of entanglement, provided evidence that a second fishery, about which little was known, was also affecting the population. This information led to placement of government observers in the fishery in an effort to improve reporting of mortalities. Similarly, increases in the number of stranded harbor porpoises on the California coast in the mid-1980s alerted managers to a serious problem with a halibut gillnet fishery, and this led to area closures in the fishery (Seagars et al. 1986).

Stranded Marine Mammals and Contaminants

The massive mortality of bottlenose dolphins along the U.S. Atlantic coast in 1987–1988 rekindled interest in the health of marine mammals generally and in the information that could be collected from stranded animals. Although high levels of organochlorine contaminants were found in some animals, it was not possible to determine whether the contaminants played a role in the die-off. Because of the lack of baseline information and methodological differences in the information that was available, it could not be determined whether the contaminant loads were anomalous. To complicate the matter, the most likely impact of such contaminants was not direct toxicity but more subtle effects on the animals.

Some studies have raised interesting questions as to whether there is a causal relationship between a reduction in reproductive rates and organochlorine contaminants. Helle (1980) found a correlation between reduced reproductive rates in ringed seals, *Phoca hispida,* in the Baltic Sea and high levels of PCBs. Reijnders (1984) questioned the methodology of this study but found a similar correlation between contaminant levels and lack of reproductive success in harbor seals in the Wadden Sea. He showed experimentally that a diet higher in PCBs had an impact on reproduction in harbor seals that was not exhibited in control animals and hypothesized that the contaminants affected hormonal balance (Reijnders 1986). The author of a study on contaminants in harbor seals in Puget Sound noted that reproductive success was lower and juvenile mortality higher in the southern area of the sound and that seals in that area had higher levels of PCBs (Calambokidis et al. 1984).

Another potential impact of contaminants on marine mammals is immunological dysfunction. A cause-and-effect relationship is difficult to prove, however. Because the direct cause of death in such a situation is usually a pathogen that the animal might have successfully overcome, it is difficult to prove that contaminants were a contributing factor. In the case of marine mammals, details on locations, numbers of mortalities, actual causes of death, and a number of other variables may not be available. Recent efforts to characterize marine mammal immune systems have provided the first step in addressing this issue (De Swart et al. 1993, DiMolfetto-Landon et al. 1995, Erickson et al. 1995). In addition, studies in Europe indicate a correlation between reduced immunological function and pollutants (Brouwer et al. 1989, De Swart et al. 1994, Ross et al. 1995).

In both the reproductive and immunological studies, correlations were noted. Correlations alone do not establish a cause-and-effect relationship. For definitive scientific proof, adequate controls and sample size are necessary. Ideally, the mechanism by which a phenomenon occurs should be fully explained.

Stranded animals offer the potential of addressing some of the issues related to the impacts of pollutants on marine mammals, but there are limitations that must be taken into account. First, extreme care needs to be taken in collecting and preserving samples for contaminant analysis to avoid contamination. Differences as small as parts per billion may be significant for certain compounds. Therefore, extremely rigorous protocols for collecting and storing tissues are required (Geraci and Lounsbury 1993, Becker et al. 1994).

Second, the time of death usually cannot be determined for animals that wash onto the beach, and this creates uncertainty about the effects of tissue decomposition on the measurements of contaminants. Although one study monitored organochlorine levels over time in a decomposing striped dolphin, the time intervals (6, 13, 21, 29, 41, and 55 days) were longer than one usually would expect for a beach-cast animal (Borrell and Aguilar 1990). The time during which a dead animal may be useful for contaminant analysis ranges from a few hours to about a week after death. Time postmortem is not the only variable to be considered. Ambient air and water temperatures can also affect the rate of decomposition.

Third, it is important to consider the possibility that variability in the distribution of contaminants within individual tissues will influence results. Selective partitioning or seasonal differences within tissues mean that protocols on sample locations are critical. If contaminants are nonuniformly distributed within tissues, protocols must be set up to minimize bias and variability in analytical results. An analysis of the intraorgan distribution of contaminants in harbor porpoises indicated that for liver and blubber the sampling location contributed little to variation in measured levels of chlorinated hydrocarbons and heavy metals (Stein et al. 1992). Because blubber of harbor porpoises may be less metabolically active than that of other species, tests on additional species are needed.

Finally, the question of whether singly stranded animals are representative of populations as a whole must be considered. Many strand because of illness and may be debilitated. An emaciated animal that has metabolized most of its blubber reserve might have a different contaminant profile than a more robust individual.

Although there has been considerable speculation about the impacts of contaminants on marine mammals, our level of knowledge and the science needed to address questions are both still in the developmental stage.

Mortality Events

The stranding networks play another key role in detection and response to unusual mortality events. The Marine Mammal Health and Stranding Response Act sets up procedures to be followed when such events occur. The law establishes an advisory group—the Working Group on Marine Mammal Unusual Mortality Events. The working group is composed of specialists from a number of scientific disciplines and is to be consulted when an unusual mortality event is suspected. It also provides guidance on specific investigative directions.

The working group established criteria for determining whether an unusual mortality event is occurring and thus whether a response is appropriate. These are as follows:

1. A marked increase is observed in the magnitude of strandings when compared with prior records. Magnitude by itself may not be an indication of an unusual mortality event and should be weighed against other knowledge.
2. Animals are stranding at a time of the year when strandings are unusual.
3. An increase in strandings is occurring in a very localized area (possibly suggesting a localized problem), is occurring throughout the geographical range of the species/population, or is spreading geographically with time.
4. The species, age, or sex composition of the stranded animals is different than that of animals that normally strand in the area at a specific time of the year.
5. Stranded animals exhibit similar or unusual pathologic findings or the general physical condition (e.g., blubber thickness) of stranded animals is different from what is normally seen.
6. Mortality is accompanied by behavioral patterns observed among living individuals in the wild that are unusual, such as their presence in habitats normally avoided or abnormal patterns of swimming and diving.
7. Unusual or severely endangered species are stranding. Stranding of three or four right whales (*Eubalaena glacialis*), for example, may be cause for great concern, whereas stranding of a similar number of fin whales (*Balaenoptera physalus*) may not.

The application of these criteria is dependent on the contributions of the stranding networks in two ways. First, the networks are the initial source of the information. Second, that information must be compared with historic baseline information before a judgment can be made. Without accurate data and consistent effort on the part of the networks, such baseline information will not be available.

The networks also can play a key role in the response to unusual mortality events. If live animals are involved, network members are usually best qualified to provide treatment, although a major event can quickly overwhelm local facilities. At best, facilities can accommodate only a few cetaceans. Although the physical facilities required to treat live pinnipeds are less complex, even they can be stretched to capacity, as happened during the 1992–1993 El Niño and the outbreak of leptospirosis in California sea lions in 1984.

Institutional members of the networks also have the personnel and equipment to respond rapidly to stranded dead marine mammals. As Geraci et al. (this volume) point out, there are numerous possible causes for mortality events. These include parasites or other serious infectious agents, changes in environmental conditions such as an El Niño or a sudden change in water temperature, naturally occurring biotoxins, and fouling or toxicity caused by oil or chemical spills or toxic runoff of chemicals.

If the cause of a mortality event is not known, all possibilities may have to be investigated. Because the analyses required for each of them vary, tissue collection and preservation protocols also differ. For example, liver collected for contaminant analysis should be frozen, and liver collected for histopathologic analysis should be fixed in formalin. Improper collection or preservation could render a tissue useless for a particular type of analysis. Network members can collect tissues for such analyses, but only if they have adequate information and training.

When the die-off of bottlenose dolphins occurred in 1987–1988, it was viewed as an anomalous event. In fact, such events may be more common than previously believed. During the three-year period beginning in April 1991, there were 11 consultations with the advisory group. The events reflect the range of possible causes, including environmental conditions in the case of the El Niño, serious pathogens such as phocine distemper virus (Duignan et al. 1993) and dolphin morbillivirus (Lipscomb et al. 1994, 1996), and two events that turned out to be human interactions but that were initially investigated as mortality events.

Summary

Each year in the United States, substantial numbers of marine mammals strand. A network of volunteers has been set up to respond to these strandings. The network is responsible for the rescue and rehabilitation of live stranded animals and the collection of basic biological data from dead stranded animals.

Stranded marine mammals have contributed much to what is known about some species. Even the most basic data can provide important information, especially if the effort to detect and report strandings is consistent. Stranded animals can provide considerably more scientific information if those who respond to strandings have been adequately trained and follow standard protocols for collecting data and tissues. Because the network is made up of volunteers, there are practical limitations on the amount of effort that can be expected. As information demands increase, the willingness of network members to respond may be reduced.

In the Marine Mammal Health and Stranding Response Act, the Congress made it national policy to monitor the various factors affecting the health of marine mammal populations. Stranding networks have played a key role in this area in the past, and the role is likely to be enhanced in the future. Although stranding records usually do not provide an adequate basis for estimating actual mortality rates, they can provide many kinds of valuable information. They help document human–marine mammal interactions that warrant further investigation, and they provide information on the parasites and pathogens that affect marine mammal populations. The act requires an accelerated response to unusual mortality events, and stranding networks are likely to provide initial information that helps identify such events. Network members also participate in the collection and preparation of the tissues needed to determine the causes of such events.

Anthropogenic contaminants are ubiquitous, and some chemicals have been detected in relatively high levels in marine mammals. Before it can be determined with certainty whether such levels have a deleterious impact on marine mammals, a baseline needs to be established.

Stranded animals also can contribute information on life history and population dynamics. Morphological, genetic, and other data can help define discrete populations for management purposes.

Stranding networks around the world have made substantial contributions to our knowledge of marine mammals. The potential is even greater. These efforts have been made by dedicated volunteers receiving little government support and little recognition for their efforts. Marine mammals have assumed a special status with the public (see Lavigne et al., this volume), but, for the most part, the public is unaware of the cadre of people who rescue and treat animals and collect information that contributes to their protection.

Literature Cited

Aguilar, A. 1987. Using organochlorine pollutants to discriminate marine mammal populations: A review and critique of methods. Marine Mammal Science 3:242–262.

Amos, W., H. Whitehead, M. J. Ferrari, D. A. Glockner-Ferrari, R. Payne, and J. Gordon. 1992. Restrictable DNA from sloughed cetacean skin; its potential for use in population analysis. Marine Mammal Science 8:275–283.

Anonymous. 1984. Victorian whale rescue plan: A contingency plan for strandings of cetaceans (whales, dolphins, and porpoises) on the Victorian coastline. Fisheries and Wildlife Service, Department of Conservation, Forest and Lands, Victoria (Australia). 70 pp.

Baker, V. (ed.). 1986. Marine mammal rescue. New Zealand Department of Conservation. 103 pp.

Barlow, J., R. L. Brownell Jr., D. P. DeMaster, K. A. Forney, M. S. Lowry, S. Osmek, T. J. Ragen, R. R. Reeves, and R. J. Small. 1995. U.S. Pacific Marine Mammal Stock Assessments. U.S. Department of Commerce, NOAA Technical Memorandum NMFS-SWFSC-219. 162 pp.

Barros, N. B. 1992. Food habits. Pages 29–34 *in* L. J. Hansen (ed.), Report on investigation of the 1990 Gulf of Mexico bottlenose dolphin strandings. National Marine Fisheries Service, Southeast Fisheries Science Center Contribution MIA-92/93-21.

Barros, N. B., and D. K. Odell. 1990. Food habits of bottlenose dolphins (*Tursiops truncatus*) in the southeastern United States. Pages 309–328 *in* S. Leatherwood and R. R. Reeves (eds.), The Bottlenose Dolphin. Academic Press, San Diego, CA.

Becker, P. R., D. Wilkinson, and T. I. Lillestolen. 1994. Marine Mammal Health and Stranding Response Program: Program Development Plan. U.S. Department of Commerce, NOAA Technical Memorandum NMFS-OPR-94-2. 35 pp.

Bonde, R. K., T. J. O'Shea, and C. A. Beck. 1983. Manual of procedures for the salvage and necropsy of carcasses of the West Indian manatee (*Trichechus manatus*). Sirenia Project, Department of the Interior. (Available from National Technical Information Service, Springfield, VA. PB 83-255273.) 175 pp.

Borrell, A., and A. Aguilar. 1990. Loss of organochlorine compounds in the tissues of a decomposing stranded dolphin. Bulletin of Environmental Contamination and Toxicology 45:46–53.

Brouwer, A., P. J. H. Reijnders, and J. H. Koeman. 1989. Polychlorinated biphenyl (PCB)–contaminated fish induces vitamin A and thyroid hormone deficiency in the common seal (*Phoca vitulina*). Aquatic Toxicology 15:99–106.

Calambokidis, J. 1986. Chlorinated hydrocarbons in harbor porpoise from Washington, Oregon, and California: Regional differences in pollutant ratios. National Marine Fisheries Service, Southwest Fisheries Science Center Administrative Report LJ-86-35C. 29 pp.

Calambokidis, J., J. Peard, G. H. Steiger, and J. C. Cubbage. 1984. Chemical Contaminants in Marine Mammals from Washington State. U.S. Department of Commerce, NOAA Technical Memorandum NOS-OMS 6. 167 pp.

Collet, A., and R. J. Harrison. 1981. Ovarian characteristics corpora lutea and corpora albicantia in *Delphinus delphis* stranded on the Atlantic coast of France. Aquatic Mammals 8:69–76.

Cowan, D. F., W. A. Walker, and R. L. Brownell Jr. 1986. Pathology of small cetaceans stranded along southern California beaches. Pages 323–367 *in* M. M. Bryden and R. Harrison (eds.), Research on Dolphins. Clarendon Press, Oxford, U.K.

Davis, R. W., G. A. J. Worthy, B. Würsig, S. K. Lynn, and F. I. Townsend. 1996. Diving behavior and at-sea movements of an Atlantic spotted dolphin in the Gulf of Mexico. Marine Mammal Science 12:569–581.

De Swart, R. L., R. M. G. Kluten, C. J. Huizing, L. J. Vedder, P. J. H. Reijnders, I. K. G. Visser, F. G. M. C. UytdeHaag, and A. D. M. E. Osterhaus. 1993. Mitogen and antigen induced B and T cell responses of peripheral blood mononuclear cells from the harbour seal (*Phoca vitulina*). Veterinary Immunology and Immunopathology 37:217–230.

De Swart, R. L., P. S. Ross, L. J. Vedder, H. H. Timmerman, S. Heisterkamp, H. Van Loveren, J. G. Vos, P. J. H. Reijnders, and A. D. M. E. Osterhaus. 1994. Impairment of immune function in harbour seals (*Phoca vitulina*) feeding on fish from polluted waters. Ambio 23:155–159.

Dierauf, L. A. 1994. Pinniped Forensic, Necropsy and Tissue

Collection Guide. U.S. Department of Commerce, NOAA Technical Memorandum NMFS-OPR-94-3. 80 pp.

Dierauf, L. A., D. J. Vandenbroek, J. Roletto, M. Koski, L. Amaya, and L. J. Gage. 1985. An epizootic of leptospirosis in California sea lions. Journal of the American Veterinary Medical Association 187:1145–1148.

Dieter, R. L. 1991. Recovery and necropsy of marine mammal carcasses in and near Point Reyes National Seashore, May 1982–March 1987. Pages 123–141 *in* J. E. Reynolds III and D. K. Odell (eds.), Marine Mammal Strandings in the United States. U.S. Department of Commerce, NOAA Technical Report NMFS-98.

DiMolfetto-Landon, L., K. L. Erickson, M. Blanchard-Channell, S. J. Jeffries, J. T. Harvey, D. A. Jessup, D. A. Ferrick, and J. L. Stott. 1995. Blastogenesis and interleukin-2 receptor expression assays in the harbor seal (*Phoca vitulina*). Journal of Wildlife Diseases 31:150–158.

Duignan, P. J., S. Sadove, J. T. Saliki, and J. R. Geraci. 1993. Phocine distemper in harbor seals (*Phoca vitulina*) from Long Island, New York. Journal of Wildlife Diseases 29:465–469.

Erickson, K. L., L. DiMolfetto-Landon, R. S. Wells, T. Reidarson, J. L. Stott, and D. A. Ferrick. 1995. Development of an interleukin-2 receptor expression assay and its use in evaluation of cellular immune responses in bottlenose dolphin (*Tursiops truncatus*). Journal of Wildlife Diseases 31:142–149.

Gales, N., and K. Waples. 1993. The rehabilitation and release of bottlenose dolphins from Atlantis Marine Park, Western Australia. Aquatic Mammals 19:49–59.

Geraci, J. R., and V. J. Lounsbury. 1993. Marine mammals ashore: A field guide for strandings. Texas A&M University Sea Grant College Program, Galveston, TX. 305 pp.

Geraci, J. R., and D. J. St. Aubin (eds.). 1979. Biology of Marine Mammals: Insights through Strandings. Report no. MMC-77/13. Marine Mammal Commission. (Available from National Technical Information Service, Springfield, VA. PB-293 890.) 351 pp.

Geraci, J. R., S. A. Testaverde, D. J. St. Aubin, and T. H. Loop. 1978. A mass stranding of the Atlantic white-sided dolphin (*Lagenorhynchus acutus*): A study into pathobiology and life history. Report no. 75-12. Marine Mammal Commission. (Available from National Technical Information Service, Springfield, VA. PB-289 361.) 141 pp.

Geraci, J. R., P. J. Duignan, and G. Early. 1993. Survey for morbillivirus in pinnipeds along the northeastern coast. Final Report to the National Marine Fisheries Service. (Available from Office of Protected Resources, National Marine Fisheries Service, Silver Spring, MD.) 95 pp.

Geraci, J. R., J. Harwood, and V. J. Lounsbury. 1999. Marine mammal die-offs: Causes, investigations and issues. (This volume)

Gerber, J. A., J. Roletto, L. E. Morgan, D. M. Smith, and L. J. Gage. 1993. Findings in pinnipeds stranded along the central and northern California coast, 1984–1990. Journal of Wildlife Diseases 29:423–433.

Goodall, R. N. P. 1978. Report on the small cetaceans stranded on the coasts of Tierra del Fuego. Scientific Reports of the Whales Research Institute Tokyo 30:197–230.

Goodall, R. N. P. 1989. The lost whales of Tierra del Fuego. Oceanus 32 (1): 89–95.

Hare, M. P., and J. G. Mead. 1987. Handbook for determination of adverse human–marine mammal interactions from necropsies. National Marine Fisheries Service, Northwest and Alaska Fisheries Center Processed Report 87-06. 35 pp.

Harvey, J. T. 1991. Survival and behavior of previously captive harbor seals after release into the wild. Pages 117–122 *in* J. E. Reynolds III and D. K. Odell (eds.), Marine Mammal Strandings in the United States. U.S. Department of Commerce, NOAA Technical Report NMFS-98.

Helle, E. 1980. Lowered reproductive capacity in female ringed seals (*Pusa hispida*) in the Bothnian Bay, northern Baltic Sea, with special reference to uterine occlusions. Annales Zoologici Fennici 17:147–158.

Hersh, S. L., D. K. Odell, and E. D. Asper. 1990. Bottlenose dolphin mortality patterns in the Indian/Banana River system of Florida. Pages 155–164 *in* S. Leatherwood and R. R. Reeves (eds.), The Bottlenose Dolphin. Academic Press, San Diego, CA.

Heyning, J. E., and W. F. Perrin. 1994. Evidence for two species of common dolphins (Genus *Delphinus*) from the eastern north Pacific. Natural History Museum of Los Angeles County Contributions in Science No. 442. 35 pp.

Hohn, A. A. 1980. Age determination and age related factors in the teeth of western North Atlantic bottlenose dolphins. Scientific Reports of the Whales Research Institute Tokyo 32:39–66.

Hohn, A. A., M. D. Scott, and R. S. Wells. 1991. Evidence of age at maturation in dolphin teeth. Page 34 *in* Proceedings, Ninth Biennial Conference on the Biology of Marine Mammals, Chicago, IL (abstract only).

Kenney, R. D. 1990. Bottlenose dolphins off the northeastern United States. Pages 369–386 *in* S. Leatherwood and R. R. Reeves (eds.), The Bottlenose Dolphin. Academic Press, San Diego, CA.

Kraus, S. D. 1990. Rates and potential causes of mortality in North Atlantic right whales (*Eubalaena glacialis*). Marine Mammal Science 6:278–291.

Lavigne, D. M., V. B. Scheffer, and S. R. Kellert. 1999. The evolution of North American attitudes toward marine mammals. (This volume)

Laws, R. M. 1953. A new method of age determination in mammals with reference to the elephant seal (*Mirounga leonina,* Linn.). Falkland Islands Dependencies Survey Scientific Reports 2:1–11.

Lipscomb, T. P., S. Kennedy, D. Moffett, and B. K. Ford. 1994. Morbilliviral disease in an Atlantic bottlenose dolphin (*Tursiops truncatus*) from the Gulf of Mexico. Journal of Wildlife Diseases 30:572–576.

Lipscomb, T. P., S. Kennedy, D. Moffett, A. Krafft, B. A. Klaunberg, J. H. Lichy, G. T. Regan, G. A. J. Worthy, and J. K. Taubenberger. 1996. Morbilliviral epizootic in Atlantic bottlenose dolphins in the Gulf of Mexico. Journal of Veterinary Diagnostic Investigations 8:283–290.

Lockyer, C. 1974. Investigation of the ear plug of the southern sei whale *Balaenoptera borealis* as a valid means of determining age. Journal du Conseil Conseil International pour l'Exploration de la Mer 36:71–81.

Marmontel, M., T. J. O'Shea, H. I. Kochman, and S. R. Humphrey. 1996. Age determination in manatees using growth-layer group counts in bone. Marine Mammal Science 12:54–88.

Mate, B. R. 1989. Watching habits and habitats from earth satellites. Oceanus 32 (1): 14–18.

Mate, B. R., K. M. Stafford, R. Nawojchik, and J. L. Dunn. 1994. Movements and dive behavior of a satellite-monitored Atlantic white-sided dolphin (*Lagenorhynchus acutus*) in the Gulf of Maine. Marine Mammal Science 10:116–121.

Mead, J. G., and C. W. Potter. 1990. Natural history of bottlenose dolphins along the central Atlantic coast of the United States. Pages 165–195 *in* S. Leatherwood and R. R. Reeves (eds.), The Bottlenose Dolphin. Academic Press, San Diego, CA.

Mead, J. G., and C. W. Potter. 1995. Recognizing two populations of the bottlenose dolphin (*Tursiops truncatus*) off the Atlantic coast of North America: Morphologic and ecologic considerations. IBI Reports 5:31–44.

National Marine Fisheries Service. 1991. Recovery plan for the northern right whale (*Eubalaena glacialis*). Prepared by the Right Whale Recovery Team for the National Marine Fisheries Service, Silver Spring, MD. 86 pp.

National Marine Fisheries Service. 1992. Harbor porpoise in eastern North America: Status and research needs. National Marine Fisheries Service, Northeast Fisheries Science Center Reference Document 92-06. (Available from Office of Protected Resources, National Marine Fisheries Service, Silver Spring, MD.) 28 pp.

National Marine Fisheries Service. 1993. Final conservation plan for the northern fur seal (*Callorhinus ursinus*). Prepared by the National Marine Mammal Laboratory / Alaska Fisheries Science Center, Seattle, WA, and the Office of Protected Resources, National Marine Fisheries Service, Silver Spring, MD. 80 pp.

Osterhaus, A. D. M. E., and E. J. Vedder. 1988. Identification of a virus causing recent seal deaths. Nature 335:20.

Payne, P. M., and C. C. Rimmer. 1982. Radio-telemetry of a rehabilitated harbor seal during the winter 1982 with comments on movements and numbers of the harbor seal in Massachusetts. Report to the National Marine Fisheries Service. (Available from Office of Protected Resources, National Marine Fisheries Service, Silver Spring, MD.) 46 pp.

Ragen, T. J., and D. M. Lavigne. 1999. The Hawaiian monk seal: Biology of an endangered species. (This volume)

Rathbun, G. B., J. P. Reid, and G. Carowan. 1990. Distribution and movement patterns of manatees (*Trichechus manatus*) in northwestern peninsular Florida. Florida Marine Research Publications 48:1–33.

Read, A. J., and D. E. Gaskin. 1990. The effects of incidental catches on harbour porpoises (*Phocoena phocoena*) in the Bay of Fundy and Gulf of Maine. International Whaling Commission SC / 42 / SM21. 18 pp.

Reid, J. P., R. K. Bonde, and T. J. O'Shea. 1995. Reproduction and mortality of radio-tagged and recognizable individual manatees on the Atlantic coast of Florida. Pages 171–191 *in* T. J. O'Shea, B. B. Ackerman, and H. F. Percival (eds.), Population Biology of the Florida Manatee. U.S. Department of the Interior, National Biological Service, Information and Technology Report 1.

Reijnders, P. J. H. 1984. Man-induced environmental factors in relation to fertility changes in pinnipeds. Environmental Conservation 11:61–65.

Reijnders, P. J. H. 1986. Reproductive failures in common seals feeding on fish from polluted coastal waters. Nature 324:456–457.

Reynolds, J. E., III. 1999. Efforts to conserve the manatees. (This volume)

Ross, P. S., R. L. De Swart, P. J. H. Reijnders, H. Van Loveren, J. G. Vos, and A. D. M. E. Osterhaus. 1995. Contaminant-related suppression of delayed-type hypersensitivity and antibody responses in harbor seals fed herring from the Baltic Sea. Environmental Health Perspectives 103:162–167.

Schroeder, R. J., C. A. Delli Quadri, R. W. McIntyre, and W. A. Walker. 1973. Marine animal disease surveillance program in Los Angeles County. Journal of the American Veterinary Medical Association 163:580–581.

Schwartz, M., A. Hohn, H. Bernard, S. Chivers, and K. Peltier. 1992. Stomach contents of beach cast cetaceans collected along the San Diego County coast of California, 1972–1991. National Marine Fisheries Service, Southwest Fisheries Science Center Administrative Report LJ-92-18. 18 pp.

Scott, G. P., D. M. Burn, and L. J. Hansen. 1988. The dolphin die-off: Long-term effects and recovery of the population. Oceans '88 Proceedings 3:819–823.

Seagars, D. 1988. The fate of released rehabilitated pinnipeds based on tag-resight information: A preliminary assessment. National Marine Fisheries Service, Southwest Region Administrative Report SWR-88-1. 31 pp.

Seagars, D. J., J. Lecky, J. Lawson, and H. Stone. 1986. Evaluation of the California Marine Mammal Stranding Network as a management tool based on records for 1983 and 1984. National Marine Fisheries Service, Southwest Region Administrative Report SWR-86-5. 34 pp.

Seltzer, L. A., G. Early, P. M. Fiorelli, P. M. Payne, and R. Prescott. 1986. Stranded animals as indicators of prey utilization by harbor seals, *Phoca vitulina concolor,* in southern New England. Fishery Bulletin 84:217–220.

Sheldrick, M. C. 1979. Cetacean strandings along the coasts of the British Isles 1913–1977. Pages 35–53 *in* J. R. Geraci and D. J. St. Aubin (eds.), Biology of Marine Mammals: Insights through Strandings. Report no. MMC-77 / 13. Marine Mammal Commission. (Available from National Technical Information Service, Springfield, VA. PB-293 890.)

St. Aubin, D. J., J. R. Geraci, and V. J. Lounsbury (eds.). 1996. Rescue, Rehabilitation and Release of Marine Mammals: An Analysis of Current Views and Practices. Proceedings of a Workshop Held in Des Plaines, Illinois, 3–5 December 1991. U.S. Department of Commerce, NOAA Tecnical Memorandum NMFS-OPR-8. 65 pp.

Steiger, G. H., J. Calambokidis, J. C. Cubbage, D. E. Skilling, A. W. Smith, and D. H. Gribble. 1989. Mortality of harbor seal pups at different sites in the inland waters of Washington. Journal of Wildlife Diseases 25:319–328.

Stein, J. E., K. L. Tilbury, D. W. Brown, C. A. Wigren, J. P. Meador, P. A. Robisch, S.-L. Chan, and U. Varanasi. 1992. Intraorgan Distribution of Chemical Contaminants in Tissues of Harbor Porpoises (*Phocoena phocoena*) from the Northwest Atlantic. U.S. Department of Commerce, NOAA Technical Memorandum NMFS-NWFSC-3. 76 pp.

Stroud, R. K., and T. J. Roffe. 1979. Causes of death in marine mammals stranded along the Oregon coast. Journal of Wildlife Diseases 15:91–97.

Trillmich, F., and K. A. Ono (eds.). 1991. Pinnipeds and El Niño: Responses to Environmental Stress. Springer-Verlag, Berlin.

van der Kamp, J. S. 1987. Pulmonary diseases in seals: A histopathological review. Aquatic Mammals 13:122–124.

Wilkinson, D. M. 1991. Report to Assistant Administrator for Fisheries: Program review of the marine mammal stranding networks. U.S. Department of Commerce, NOAA, National Marine Fisheries Service. (Available from Office of Protected Resources, National Marine Fisheries Service, Silver Spring, MD.) 171 pp.

19

RANDALL R. REEVES AND JAMES G. MEAD

Marine Mammals in Captivity

As recently as the mid-1960s, killer whales (*Orcinus orca*) were feared and despised. Programs to exterminate them were implemented without public opposition. Yet scarcely 10 years after "Moby Doll" became the first captive killer whale (Newman and McGeer 1966), a vigorous anticaptivity campaign had arisen in the Pacific Northwest, effectively closing down all live-capture operations in Washington and British Columbia waters (Hoyt 1990). Thus, having transformed the public image of the killer whale, oceanariums now find it difficult to catch more. Even if a permit could be obtained, the negative publicity guaranteed to attend any capture operation would act as a powerful disincentive to proceed. At least some of the public's widespread fascination and sympathy with other cetaceans, in addition to killer whales, are a result of exposure to animals in captivity.

The questions posed in this chapter are complicated and controversial. Like many other subjects in public policy that are driven and shaped as much by attitudes and beliefs as by scientific evidence, few aspects of marine mammals in captivity are amenable to conclusive, unambiguous commentary. Scientific evidence plays a role but, more often than not, it is subject to countervailing interpretations, its relevance is questionable, or it is simply inconclusive. Is it possible to measure the nonmonetary costs and benefits—to the animals, to those who pay to see them, and to those whose livelihoods are at stake? On what grounds do we decide that the interests of a species or population transcend those of an individual animal? How much more alien would these animals seem to most of us, were it not for the first-hand exposure provided by zoos and oceanariums? Depending on how these and other questions raised in this chapter are answered, an oceanarium might be regarded as an amusement park, an educational center, a research laboratory, a genetic bank, or a prison.

We begin the chapter with a brief review of the history of marine mammals in captivity and a summary of developments in the regulation of the live-capture industry, particularly in the United States. We then address some of the arguments used to justify the keeping of marine mammals in captivity, as well as arguments that have been used against the practice. In each case, we attempt to give equal time to the counterarguments.

Background Comment

This chapter focuses mainly on cetaceans because they are the marine mammals that fuel the most controversy. Although many pinnipeds, otters, sirenians, and polar bears (*Ursus maritimus*) are kept in zoos and oceanariums, these species do not inspire the same passion as cetaceans. They are, however, part of a larger controversy concerning the role of zoos and zoolike institutions in today's world.

During the past 25 years, cetaceans have become a symbol of the animal liberation movement (Scheffer 1991). To many people their significance transcends any ecological or economic value that they might have. In the views of Scheffer (1991) and Barstow (1991), the mystique and beauty of cetaceans cannot, and need not, be measured by science. It is enough to care about their welfare simply because of how we feel toward them or because of what we believe about them. A contrary view has been expressed by Freeman (1990), Kalland (1993), and Peterson (1993), who point to the distortion of scientific evidence that has led to the creation of a "super whale," larger than life, a composite of all the favorable attributes that have been ascribed to cetaceans over the past several decades.

The two camps—Scheffer, Barstow, and other whale protectionists on one side and Freeman, Kalland, and other advocates of "sustainable whaling" on the other—have engaged mostly in a debate centered on whaling, yet the essence of their differences is closely related to the controversy about cetaceans in captivity. Freeman (1990:112) argued that the appeal of dolphins in captivity—"from the jaw configuration that gives the appearance of a fixed smile, to the tricks they have been taught to perform for the delight of their human audiences"—has contributed to the momentum against whaling. Similarly, the emotive images provided by whaling, along with the fact that commercial whaling has seriously depleted many of the world's stocks of whales, provided initial inspiration for people who now campaign to close oceanariums and return captive cetaceans to the wild. Whatever the evidence, and however it is interpreted, the furor over cetaceans in captivity has become a feature of our lives as marine mammalogists. The "special place [of cetaceans] in public affections" (Klinowska and Brown 1986:8) is something that underlies the more general discussion about the changing role of zoos and other institutions that maintain wild animals in captivity.

History of Marine Mammals in Captivity

Table 19-1 lists each species of marine mammal that has been represented in captivity and provides information on (1) whether the animals were deliberately captured alive, salvaged after stranding or being removed from fishing gear, or taken in a drive hunt; (2) the year when first brought into captivity; (3) the year of the first captive birth; and (4) the maximum length of time in captivity. The table is not exhaustive. Some relevant information has certainly escaped our notice. Also, during the period between this chapter's submission and its publication, longevity records are likely to have been exceeded, new species to have been brought into captivity, and other species to have given birth in captivity for the first time.

The keeping of wild animals in menageries and zoos has a long history, and certain marine mammals have figured in that history for hundreds of years. Live polar bears were treasured by royalty and potentates in ancient times (Larsen 1978). During the reign of the Roman emperor Claudius (A.D. 41–54), a live-stranded killer whale was kept in a netted enclosure while the praetorian guards attacked it with lances (Pliny 1967:173) (Fig. 19-1). This spectacle foreshadowed today's nonbrutal, but still stirring, killer whale shows in oceanariums. Arctic whalers and sealers occasionally brought home orphaned polar bear cubs and walrus calves (*Odobenus rosmarus*) for private collections and zoos (Lubbock 1937:436). The first recorded Mediterranean monk seal (*Monachus monachus*) was brought into captivity in 1760 (Maxwell 1967) and the first Caribbean, or West Indian, monk seal (*M. tropicalis*) in 1843 (Rice 1973). These are among the earliest records of marine mammals in captivity. The relative ease of catching and maintaining bears (young ones, at least) and pinnipeds explains why so many more seals, sea lions, and polar bears have been kept in zoos and aquariums and why they generally appeared in captivity earlier than cetaceans.

Otariids, particularly sea lions, have long dominated the world population of captive pinnipeds. The California sea lion (*Zalophus californianus*) is the most popular, owing to its easy availability, capacity for learning to perform, hardiness, and readiness to breed in captivity. Many facilities in the Northern Hemisphere have also kept harbor seals (*Phoca vitulina*) on display, but these animals are seldom trained to perform. Of the pinnipeds acquired by zoos and oceanariums in North America during 1983–1990, 84% were "captive-bred" (Asper et al. 1990). In recent years, captive births and rehabilitated stranded animals (see Wilkinson and Worthy, this volume) have met virtually all of the demand for pinnipeds in North American institutions.

A few cetaceans, probably most of them harbor porpoises (*Phocoena phocoena*), were introduced to private collections in France as early as the 1400s (Collet and Duguy 1987:17). Beginning in the 1860s, sporadic attempts were made to maintain live belugas (*Delphinapterus leucas*), "porpoises" (probably harbor porpoises), and "dolphins" (probably bottlenose dolphins, *Tursiops truncatus*) in tubs or tanks in eastern North America and Europe (Collet 1984, Reeves and Leatherwood 1984, Bryden and Harrison 1986). The main purpose in keeping the animals was to display them as curiosities. Occasionally, however, nineteenth-century scientists also studied captive cetaceans.

John Anderson, a British surgeon and naturalist, secured

Table 19-1. Records of Marine Mammals in Captivity

Species	Obtained by[a]	First Captivity[b]	First Birth[c]	Maximal Time in Captivity	Sources[d]
Sirenia					
West Indian manatee (*Trichechus manatus*)	LC, SA	1866–1870	1975	>44 years	1, 6, 7, 8, 70
West African manatee (*Trichechus senegalensis*)	LC	1923	—	16 years	1, 9, 82
Amazonian manatee (*Trichechus inunguis*)	SA	1896	—	19 years	1, 10, 82
Dugong (*Dugong dugon*)	LC, SA	1955	—	20 years	1, 8, 11, 82
Cetacea-Odontoceti					
Platanistidae					
Susu (*Platanista gangetica*)	LC, SA	1873	—	299 days	12, 13, 14, 15
Bhulan (*Platanista minor*)	LC	1968	—	5 years	14, 16
Baiji (*Lipotes vexillifer*)	LC, SA	1980	—	>18 years	14
Franciscana (*Pontoporia blainvillei*)	SA	1950s	—	days	14, 17
Boto (*Inia geoffrensis*)	LC	1956	1968	26 years, 6 months	14, 18, 19
Monodontidae					
White whale (*Delphinapterus leucas*)	LC, SA	1860s	1972	27 years	20, 21, 26, 82
Narwhal (*Monodon monoceros*)	LC	1969	—	4 months	14
Phocoenidae					
Harbor porpoise (*Phocoena phocoena*)	LC, SA	≤1859	—	>12 years, 7 months	22, 23, 24, 85
Burmeister's porpoise (*Phocoena spinipinnis*)	SA	1984	—	9 days	25
Finless porpoise (*Neophocaena phocaenoides*)	LC, SA	<1963	1976	>23 years, 3 months	26, 27, 28, 85
Dall's porpoise (*Phocoenoides dalli*)	LC	1956	—	21 months	29, 31, 32
Delphinidae					
Rough-toothed dolphin (*Steno bredanensis*)	LC, SA, DR	1950s	1963(h)	>12 years	16, 26, 33, 34
Indo-Pacific hump-backed dolphin (*Sousa chinensis*)	LC, SA	1963	+(h)	>25 years	30, 33, 35, 36
Tucuxi (*Sotalia fluviatilis*)	LC	1965	?	~20 years	33, 37, 82
White-beaked dolphin (*Lagenorhynchus albirostris*)	LC, SA	1977	—	101 days	64, 65, 66
Atlantic white-sided dolphin (*Lagenorhynchus acutus*)	SA	1970s	—	8 months	58, 67
Pacific white-sided dolphin (*Lagenorhynchus obliquidens*)	LC, SA, DR	1934	1983–1990	21 years	26, 68, 76, 85
Dusky dolphin (*Lagenorhynchus obscurus*)	LC	1961	—	>7 years	35
Risso's dolphin (*Grampus griseus*)	LC?, DR, SA	1957 (1875?)	1962	>35 years, 8 months	20, 26, 82, 85
Bottlenose dolphin (*Tursiops truncatus*)	LC, SA, DR	≤1913	1947	>46 years	20, 21, 26, 31, 80, 82
Atlantic spotted dolphin (*Stenella frontalis*)	LC, SA	~1952	—	>10 years	33, 83
Pantropical spotted dolphin (*Stenella attenuata*)	LC, SA, DR	1958	1973	6 years, 6 months	20, 47, 82, 85
Spinner dolphin (*Stenella longirostris*)	LC, SA, DR?	1963?	?	>10 years	33, 44
Clymene dolphin (*Stenella clymene*)	SA	1965	—	5 days	33
Striped dolphin (*Stenella coeruleoalba*)	LC?, SA	1950	—	>14 months	82, 85
Short-beaked common dolphin (*Delphinus delphis*)	LC, SA	1957	<1960	22 years	33, 52, 82, 85
Long-beaked common dolphin (*Delphinus capensis*)	DR	1990s	—	5 years	40
Fraser's dolphin (*Lagenodelphis hosei*)	LC, SA	1974	—	100 days	33
Northern right whale dolphin (*Lissodelphis borealis*)	LC	1969	—	15 months	32
Irrawaddy dolphin (*Orcaella brevirostris*)	LC, SA	1974	1979	17 years	46, 82
Commerson's dolphin (*Cephalorhynchus commersonii*)	LC	1978	1985	17 years	33, 45, 82
Heaviside's dolphin (*Cephalorhynchus heavisidii*)	LC	1975	—	7 days	33
Hector's dolphin (*Cephalorhynchus hectori*)	LC	1970	—	2 years, 6 months	33
Melon-headed whale (*Peponocephala electra*)	LC, DR	1965	—	~17 months	26, 33, 82
Pygmy killer whale (*Feresa attenuata*)	LC, SA, DR	1963	—	22 days	33, 48
False killer whale (*Pseudorca crassidens*)	LC, SA, DR	1937	1983–1990	>26 years	26, 44, 76, 82, 85
Killer whale (*Orcinus orca*)	LC, SA, DR	1964	1977	27 years	26, 69, 74
Long-finned pilot whale (*Globicephala melas*)	SA, DR	1960	—	~3 years	49, 61
Short-finned pilot whale (*Globicephala macrorhynchus*)	LC, SA, DR	1935	<1983	>30 years	26, 72, 73, 75, 76, 82

Table 19-1 continued

Species	Obtained by[a]	First Captivity[b]	First Birth[c]	Maximal Time in Captivity	Sources[d]
Ziphiidae					
Blainville's beaked whale (*Mesoplodon densirostris*)	SA	1969	—	3 days	41, 58
Gervais' beaked whale (*Mesoplodon europaeus*)	SA	1983	—	19 days	55
Ginkgo-toothed beaked whale (*Mesoplodon ginkgodens*)	SA	1982	—	6 hours	26, 85
Hubbs' beaked whale (*Mesoplodon carlhubbsi*)	SA	1989	—	25 days	84
Cuvier's beaked whale (*Ziphius cavirostris*)	SA	1956	—	1 month	82
Physeteridae					
Sperm whale (*Physeter catodon*)	SA	1932	—	weeks	14
Pygmy sperm whale (*Kogia breviceps*)	SA	≤1948	—	6 months	57, 79
Dwarf sperm whale (*Kogia simus*)	SA	≤1978	—	4 days	57
Cetacea-Mysticeti					
Eschrichtiidae					
Gray whale (*Eschrichtius robustus*)	LC	1971	—	1 year	8
Balaenopteridae					
Minke whale (*Balaenoptera acutorostrata*)	LC, SA	1938	—	~3 months	38, 85
Bryde's whale (*Balaenoptera edeni*)	SA	1988	—	41 days	39
Humpback whale (*Megaptera novaeangliae*)	SA	1981	—	~1 week	20
Carnivora					
Odobenidae					
Walrus (*Odobenus rosmarus*)	LC	1608	1975	>26 years	1, 42, 50, 75, 76, 85
Otariidae					
New Zealand sea lion (*Phocarctos hookeri*)	LC	1887	—	2 years, 10 months	59, 82
South American sea lion (*Otaria byronia*)	LC	1866	1937	22 years, 10 months	1, 76, 82
California sea lion (*Zalophus californianus*)	LC, SA	1867	≤1905	40 years	1, 56, 75, 82
Australian sea lion (*Neophoca cinerea*)	LC, SA	1965	1981	23 years	59, 60, 62, 78, 85
Steller sea lion (*Eumetopias jubatus*)	LC	1861	1968	26 years, 11 months	1, 76, 82, 85
Northern fur seal (*Callorhinus ursinus*)	LC	1909	1932	14 years	1, 76, 82
Cape fur seal (*Arctocephalus pusillus*)	LC, SA	1871	1939, 1913(h)	23 years	1, 54, 59, 78, 81, 82
Antarctic fur seal (*Arctocephalus gazella*)	?	1958	<1981	≥4 years	59, 82
New Zealand fur seal (*Arctocephalus forsteri*)	LC, SA	1887	1929	21 years	52, 62, 82
Subantarctic fur seal (*Arctocephalus tropicalis*)	SA	1962	<1981	10 years	59, 78, 82
Galápagos fur seal (*Arctocephalus galapagoensis*)	LC	1931	<1981	4 years	59, 63, 82
Guadalupe fur seal (*Arctocephalus townsendi*)	LC	1922	—	2 years	1:735, 82
South American fur seal (*Arctocephalus australis*)	LC	1909	<1981	15 years	1, 59, 76
Phocidae					
Harbor seal (*Phoca vitulina*)	LC	1831	1868	45 years	1, 55, 75, 82
Spotted seal (*Phoca largha*)	LC, SA	1933	1972	>33 years, 2 months	75, 85
Ringed seal (*Phoca hispida*)	LC	1902	1929(h)	15 years	1, 50, 82
Baikal seal (*Phoca sibirica*)	LC	<1959	?	>11 years, 9 months	71, 82, 85
Caspian seal (*Phoca caspica*)	?	1962	1990	?	82, 85
Harp seal (*Phoca groenlandica*)	LC	1853	1861	10 years	1, 76, 82
Ribbon seal (*Phoca fasciata*)	SA	1962	—	7 years, 11 months	82, 85
Gray seal (*Halichoerus grypus*)	LC	1871	1931	41 years	1, 82
Bearded seal (*Erignathus barbatus*)	SA	1908	—	>9 years, 10 months	82, 85
Hooded seal (*Cystophora cristata*)	SA	1870	<1976	7 years	56, 76, 82, 85
Mediterranean monk seal (*Monachus monachus*)	LC, SA	1760	1962	24 years	50, 53
Caribbean monk seal (*Monachus tropicalis*)	LC	1897	—	6 years	1
Hawaiian monk seal (*Monachus schauinslandi*)	LC	1951	—	8–10 years	1, 76, 82
Crabeater seal (*Lobodon carcinophagus*)	LC	<1931	—	3 months	51, 82
Leopard seal (*Hydrurga leptonyx*)	LC, SA	1912	—	12 years	1, 52
Weddell seal (*Leptonychotes weddelli*)	LC	1910	—	7 months	1:736, 82

Continued on next page

Table 19-1 continued

Species	Obtained by[a]	First Captivity[b]	First Birth[c]	Maximal Time in Captivity	Sources[d]
Phocidae (continued)					
Southern elephant seal (*Mirounga leonina*)	LC	1910	1926	>22 years	1, 50, 82
Northern elephant seal (*Mirounga angustirostris*)	LC, SA	1882	1958	>13 years, 5 months	1, 50, 75, 82, 85
Ursidae					
Polar bear (*Ursus maritimus*)	LC	≤1060	≤1889	43 years	1, 2, 77, 82
Mustelidae					
Sea otter (*Enhydra lutris*)	LC, SA	1932	1960s	~20 years	3, 4, 5, 43, 82

[a]LC, direct live capture; SA, salvaged from stranding or fishing gear; DR, taken from a deliberate drive hunt.

[b]Symbol "≤" means in the year stated or earlier; "<" means before the year stated.

[c]Symbol "≤"means in the year stated or earlier; "<" means before the year stated; "?" means we suspect that captive births have occurred but cannot confirm it; "+" means we know that at least one birth has occurred but have no details; "(h)" means the first birth was of a hybrid. Note that we have tried to establish whether the newborn was conceived in captivity and have not included those known to have been conceived in the wild.

[d]1, Crandall (1964); 2, Larsen (1978); 3, Barabash-Nikiforov (1962); 4, Riedman and Estes (1990); 5, S. A. D. Harkness, pers. comm.; 6, Blunt (1976); 7, Bertram and Bertram (1977); 8, Ridgway and Harrison (1985); 9, unpublished data from Royal Zoological Society, Antwerp; 10, Rosas (1994); 11, H. Marsh, pers. comm.; 12, Anderson (1878); 13, Pelletier and Pelletier (1986); 14, Ridgway and Harrison (1989); 15, Tobayama and Kamiya (1989); 16, Collet (1984), 17, Monzón and Corcuera (1991); 18, Huffman (1970); 19, Caldwell et al. (1989); 20, Reeves and Leatherwood (1984); 21, Jones (1992); 22, Buckland (1868), 23, Spotte et al. (1978); 24, Collet and Duguy (1987); 25, Loureiro (1985); 26, Kasuya et al. (1984); 27, Kasuya et al. (1986); 28, T. Kasuya (pers. comm.); 29, Norris and Prescott (1961); 30, S. H. Ridgway (pers. comm.); 31, Wood (1973); 32, Walker (1975); 33, Ridgway and Harrison (1994); 34, Dohl et al. (1974); 35, Best and Ross (1984); 36, Smith (1991); 37, Spotte (1967); 38, Kimura and Nemoto (1956); 39, D. K. Odell (pers. comm.); 40, T. A. Jefferson (pers. comm.); 41, Caldwell and Caldwell (1971); 42, R. A. Kastelein (pers. comm.); 43, Woolfenden (1979); 44, Brown et al. (1966); 45, Joseph et al. (1987); 46, Tas'an and Leatherwood (1984); 47, Nishiwaki, Nakajima, and Kamiya (1965); 48, Nishiwaki, Kasuya, et al. (1965); 49, Medway and Moldovan (1966); 50, Maxwell (1967); 51, Ross et al. (1976); 52, Alan Baker (pers. comm.); 53, Rigas and Ronald (1985); 54, Nowak and Paradiso (1983); 55, Caldwell and Caldwell (1991); 56, Ehlers (1965); 57, Sylvestre (1983); 58, J. G. Mead (unpublished data); 59, Ridgway and Harrison (1981a); 60, J. K. Ling (pers. comm.); 61, W. Medway (pers. comm.); 62, Augee (1988); 63, Townsend (1934); 64, Andrésson (1978); 65, Buck and Spotte (1986); 66, Klinowska and Brown (1986); 67, Mate et al. (1994); 68, Brown and Norris (1956); 69, Duffield et al. (1995); 70, Marmontel (1995); 71, Ridgway and Harrison (1981b); 72, Kritzler (1949); 73, Kritzler (1952); 74, Duffield and Miller (1988); 75, Asper et al. (1988); 76, Asper et al. (1990); 77, Malev et al. (1991); 78, S. Johnson (pers. comm.); 79, Marine Mammal Events Program, Smithsonian Institution (Record MME10059); 80, Wood (1977); 81, Mohr (1952); 82, M. L. Jones (pers. comm.); 83, Wood (1953); 84, Lynn and Reiss (1992); 85, T. Tobayama (pers. comm.).

a Ganges River dolphin (*Platanista gangetica*) that had been caught in fishing gear and transported to Calcutta by ship in a bathtub (Anderson 1878). The dolphin did not eat live fish placed in its tank during the day, but some fish disappeared during the night, suggesting that it was a nocturnal feeder. Because Anderson had established from dissections that this species was functionally blind, he concluded that the river dolphin depended on "the tactile sensibility of its long snout" to find and capture prey. Later, investigators working with captive Indus River dolphins (*P. minor*) discovered that the *Platanista* dolphins swim on their side and continuously scan their environment using echolocation clicks (Herald et al. 1969) (Fig. 19-2).

The first serious attempt to establish a captive colony of dolphins in North America was in 1914 when several bottlenose dolphins salvaged from a net fishery in North Carolina were shipped to the New York Aquarium (Townsend 1914). The world's first oceanarium was Marine Studios (later called Marineland of Florida), which opened in 1938 with bottlenose dolphins caught in local waters as the star attractions (Wood 1973, Norris 1991). During the next several decades, and especially since the 1960s, exhibition of dolphins and whales in captivity has proliferated around the world. Facilities holding cetaceans are now found on all continents except Antarctica. Dolphins are kept in sea pens or lagoons at exclusive resort hotels and other facilities where guests can swim and interact with them (see Samuels and Spradlin 1995). Performing killer whales are the main attractions at Sea World's sprawling theme parks, and many smaller institutions depend on dolphin or whale shows to attract customers. Although the principal motivation behind such displays is commercial, most institutions also support programs of scientific research, education, and conservation. The U.S. Navy has its own large stock of captive dolphins and whales for use in research and various applied programs (e.g., Wood 1973, Anonymous 1992b, Au 1993).

As of 1990 (the year of the most recent published census of captive marine mammals in North America) 102 institutions in the United States and Canada had 1,550 marine mammals representing 32 species on display, not including the Navy's holdings (Asper et al. 1990). The vast majority of these animals were California sea lions, harbor seals, and bottlenose dolphins. The bottlenose dolphin has always had the largest and most widespread captive population of all the cetaceans. In North America alone (including Mexico, the United States, and the Bahamas), some 1,500 bottle-

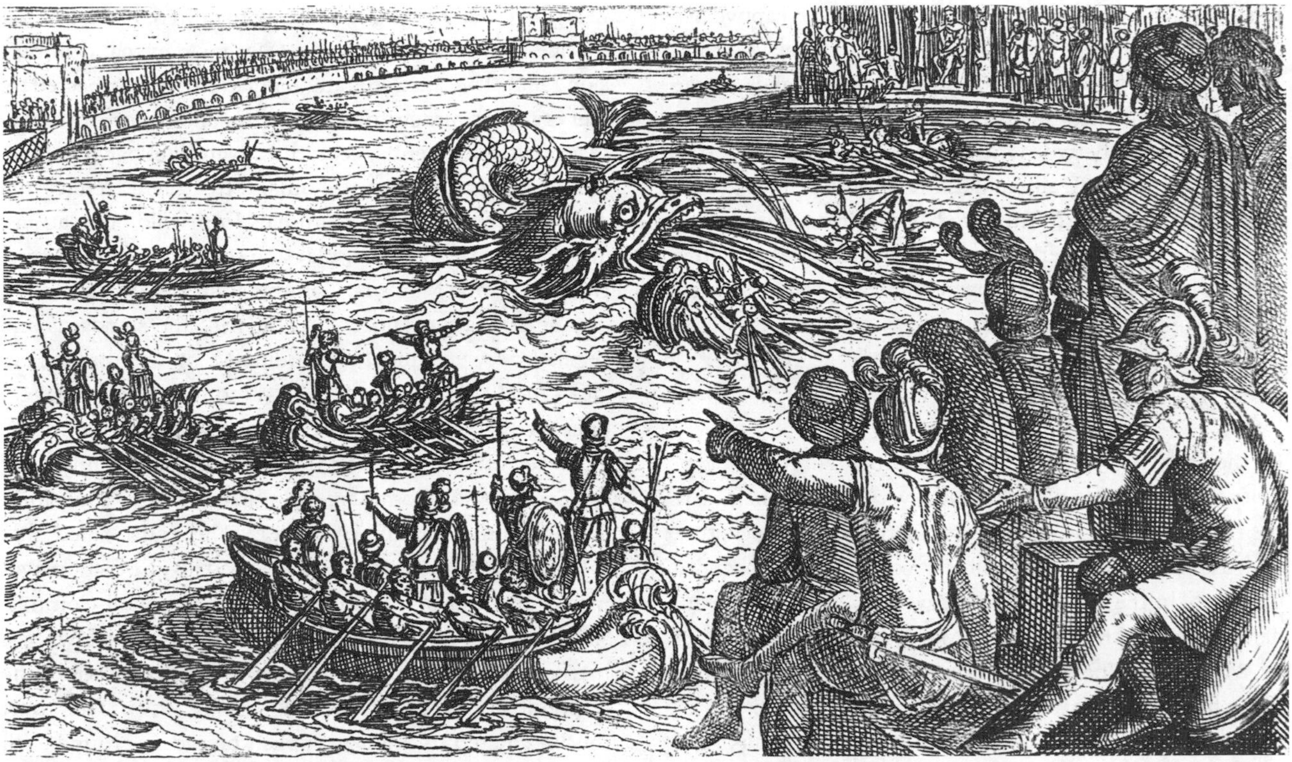

Figure 19-1. An imaginative depiction by Antonio Tempesta (1602) of what was perhaps the world's first killer whale show. A whale stranded alive in the harbor at Ostia (the mouth of the Tiber, near Rome) during the first century A.D. After the area around it was netted off, the whale was attacked by praetorian guards, to the amusement of spectators (Pliny 1967). (Drawing courtesy of Kendall Whaling Museum, Sharon, Massachusetts, Cat. No. Sign. P-B 2621)

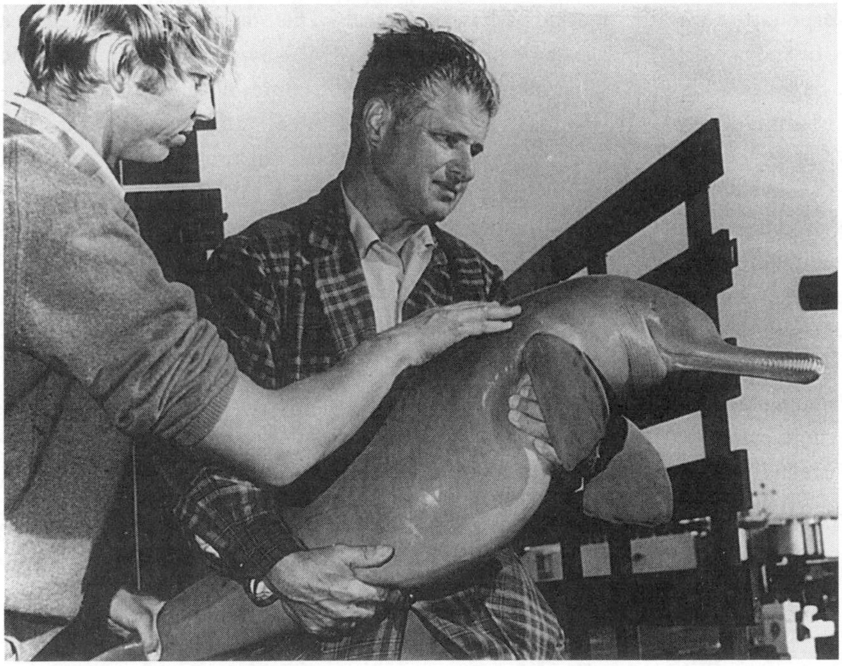

Figure 19-2. E. S. Herald of the Steinhart Aquarium, San Francisco, holds a young susu captured in the Indus River in 1969 for shipment to North America. R. L. Brownell Jr. looks on. (Photograph courtesy of Smithsonian Institution)

nose dolphins were removed from the wild for captive display or research between 1938 and 1980 (Leatherwood and Reeves 1982). More than 500 were captured alive in the southeastern United States between 1973 and 1988 (Scott 1990). However, between August 1989 and August 1996 (the time of this writing), all replenishment of the captive stock of this species in North America has been by captive breeding (S. H. Ridgway, pers. comm.). Increasingly, the captive stocks of many species have been supplemented by animals born in captivity.

Regulation of Live-Capture Activities

By the early 1970s the holding of marine mammals in captivity had become so popular that government agencies saw the need to develop and apply standards regarding capture and transport methods, facilities, and care or husbandry practices. In the United States, development of such standards began with the Marine Mammal Protection Act of 1972 (MMPA). The Act authorizes marine mammals to be taken for purposes of scientific research or public display or to enhance the survival of a species or stock. Such taking is regulated by a permit system. Permits may be issued by the Secretary of Commerce or the Secretary of the Interior, depending on the species involved. Permit applications are subject to public review and to review by the Marine Mammal Commission and its Committee of Scientific Advisors on Marine Mammals. The history of the interpretation, implementation, amendment, and evolution of the MMPA with respect to captivity-related issues can be followed by reference to annual reports of the Marine Mammal Commission (Marine Mammal Commission 1974 et seq.).

The regulatory process operates essentially on two levels: (1) to ensure that wild populations are conserved, and (2) to ensure that individual animals are treated humanely from the time of their capture throughout their confinement. Responsibility for assessing the impacts of removal of animals on wild populations clearly rests with the Department of Commerce's National Marine Fisheries Service (NMFS) in cases involving cetaceans and most pinnipeds and with the Department of the Interior's Fish and Wildlife Service (FWS) in those involving walruses, sirenians, polar bears, and otters.

Responsibility for the welfare of captive animals has traditionally been less clear-cut than the responsibility for conserving wild populations. The Department of Agriculture's Animal and Plant Health Inspection Service (APHIS) is authorized under the Animal Welfare Act to regulate matters affecting animals in captivity. APHIS's Standards and Regulations for the Humane Handling, Care, Treatment, and Transportation of Marine Mammals took effect in 1979 after nearly five years of negotiations with NMFS, FWS, and the Marine Mammal Commission (Marine Mammal Commission 1980). The standards and regulations were expected to: "serve to encourage the care and maintenance of marine mammals so as to enhance the health and life span of captive marine mammals, ensure humane treatment, reduce the need to remove marine mammals from wild populations, and enhance the public display and scientific research experience" (Marine Mammal Commission 1976:28).

Administration and enforcement of the standards and regulations were initially coordinated by the three agencies—APHIS, NMFS, and FWS—according to a formal cooperative agreement (Marine Mammal Commission 1980). However, in 1992 a resort hotel in Nevada successfully sued the Secretary of Commerce to obtain authorization for a swim-with-the-dolphin enterprise. The court ruled that NMFS (and by inference also FWS) had no jurisdiction over marine mammals in captivity (Marine Mammal Commission 1994). Once a decision has been made allowing a marine mammal to be removed from the wild, the responsibility of the permitting agency ends. The court thus attempted to draw an explicit boundary around each agency's responsibilities and to distinguish APHIS as having sole responsibility for captive animals. The 1994 amendments to the MMPA turned this into law.

Hoyt (1992:25) pointed out that the "reach" of the MMPA extended, "in one way or another, to almost every marine park in the world." This statement is reflected in a 1994 amendment to the MMPA that explicitly imposes the same standards on foreign facilities wishing to import marine mammals from the United States as apply to institutions within the United States. In other words, a foreign facility must demonstrate that it (a) offers "a program for education or conservation purposes that is based on professionally recognized standards of the public display community," (b) meets APHIS licensing standards, and (c) is open to the public (Marine Mammal Commission 1995:231). It remains unclear how this measure can be enforced without an international inspection protocol.

The extent to which activities related to marine mammals in captivity are regulated in other countries varies. Hoyt (1992), in a wide-ranging critique of the "captive orca industry," summarized the situations in Canada, Iceland, the United Kingdom (UK), Europe (European Community), and Japan. Governments in Australia, the UK, and Canada have undertaken reviews and public inquiries of their cetacean display and live-capture operations (Australia: Anonymous 1985; UK: Klinowska and Brown 1986, Anonymous 1988; Canada: Anonymous 1992a). After a public debate in Australia in 1984 and 1985 (Anonymous 1985), the state of Victoria banned any new permits for keeping cetaceans in captivity or catching them for export (Steuer 1989). The UK standards for keeping cetaceans were judged by Hoyt (1992) to be more stringent, in certain respects, than those in the United States. For example, the minimum pool size for killer whales in the UK is four times the size required in the United States (Hoyt 1992:24). The UK standards, however, are only guidelines, not regulations. In any event, all British institutions with cetaceans on display had closed by 1994.

Following principles and guidelines issued in 1992, Canada prohibits the live capture of killer whales and accords priority to Canadian institutions in decisions about live-capture permits for belugas (Anonymous 1992a). A permit system to control live-capture operations has been in effect in the Republic of South Africa since 1974 (Best and Ross 1984). As far as is known, Japan has no national standards for the care and maintenance of marine mammals in captivity. In all of these countries, live-capture activities are subject to regulation under relevant fishery laws, and any exports of marine mammals must meet the requirements of the Convention on International Trade in Endangered Species of Wild Fauna and Flora.

The International Whaling Commission (IWC) has no direct role in decisions related to live-capture operations. It was suggested in 1982 that, as a condition of IWC membership, nations should be required to provide basic information on captive cetaceans (Anonymous 1983:18). The question of whether the IWC has the legal competence to manage any aspect of the exploitation of small and medium-sized odontocetes (toothed cetaceans) has been controversial. The IWC Scientific Committee's Sub-committee on Small Cetaceans attempted a worldwide review of live-capture operations at its 1983 annual meeting and concluded that certain stocks of five species were of particular concern: killer whale, bottlenose dolphin, short-finned pilot whale (*Globicephala macrorhynchus*), tucuxi (*Sotalia fluviatilis*), and Commerson's dolphin (*Cephalorhynchus commersonii*) (International Whaling Commission 1984:148). It called for more information on these stocks and endorsed the concept of a percentage rule for limiting annual removals from regional populations. U.S. guidelines restricting total removals from bottlenose dolphin stocks in the southeastern United States to no more than 2% of the minimum estimated population (see Scott 1990) were cited as constituting a "prudent" approach that could be "safely followed pending results of other assessments" (International Whaling Commission 1984:150). The live-capture fisheries for killer whales off western North America and Iceland, bottlenose dolphins off the southeastern United States, and belugas off Canada and Russia were cited in a world review of exploitation of small cetaceans prepared for the 1992 United Nations Conference on Environment and Development in Rio de Janeiro (International Whaling Commission 1992). Attention was also drawn to the less-well-documented captures of small cetaceans in Japan; bottlenose dolphins (mainly for export) in Cuba; and bottlenose dolphins, common dolphins (*Delphinus* sp.), and harbor porpoises in the Black Sea (International Whaling Commission 1992). Although it seems unlikely that the IWC will become directly involved in managing live-capture fisheries, the Scientific Committee, through its Sub-committee on Small Cetaceans, will continue to provide an international forum for focusing attention on conservation concerns arising from such fisheries.

Arguments For and Against Captivity

In this section we discuss some of the arguments that have been made for and against holding marine mammals, particularly cetaceans and pinnipeds, in captivity.

Arguments in Favor of Captivity

Argument: Marine mammals in captivity are ambassadors for their species. By providing opportunities for close observation by masses of people, they educate, raise awareness, and generate concern about the conservation of wild populations. Thus, the benefit to entire species or populations offsets the loss of freedom experienced by individual animals.

This argument is intuitively attractive but not easy to evaluate with data. Zoos and oceanariums have enormous potential for increasing awareness and conveying information. A recent poll conducted by the Roper Organization, entitled "Public Attitudes toward Aquariums, Animal Theme Parks, and Zoos," found that a large majority of the 1,987 respondents believed that these institutions performed valuable educational functions and contributed to conservation (S. H. Ridgway, in litt., 7 July 1995).

Most institutions displaying marine mammals have for some time offered educational programs and supported a variety of activities intended to promote conservation. A 1988 amendment to the MMPA explicitly requires public display permit holders to offer programs of education and conservation meeting professionally recognized standards, and, as mentioned above, this requirement now applies to foreign institutions that import marine mammals from the United States.

A public display facility's commitment to education and conservation has traditionally been assessed by reference to attendance records, the number and types of outreach programs offered, the size of the program staff, and the amount of money invested in noncommercial activities (Evans and Wolfson 1984). Such measures, however, do not reflect the quality of what is being presented (e.g., see Hoyt 1992). Nor do they necessarily address the difficult question of whether any particular aspect of the total offering makes a positive difference in terms of education or conservation. Rigorous studies in the realm of social science are needed to evaluate the true benefits of captive animal displays. The same is true, of course, of books, videotapes, television documentaries, and whale-watching activities, the benefits of which are often implicitly assumed but rarely well documented.

The intrinsic educational value of displaying wild animals in captivity seems self-evident to most people associated with the public display industry (e.g., Anonymous 1984, Duffield and Dimeo-Ediger 1984). Critics claim that many, if not all, of the same educational benefits could be provided by other forms of presentation such as books, videotapes, field trips to observe the animals in nature, even "virtual reality" presentations (Hoyt 1992). They also claim that the public display of marine mammals in captivity can be countereducational (e.g., when performances convey anthropomorphic images or provide false or misleading information [Klinowska and Brown 1986, Hoyt 1992]). Captive animals frequently exhibit aberrant behavior, and their appearance may differ from that of their wild kin (DeBlieu 1990). An example of the latter is what Hoyt (1992:52–53) called the "drooping fin syndrome" in killer whales. The tall, erect dorsal fin of an adult male typically bends to the side and collapses after a few years in captivity. This syndrome is apparently not a health problem for the animal (wild whales occasionally have bent fins as well), but it definitely creates a problem for anyone trying to convince those opposed to public display that captive whales are perfectly "normal." The unintended message received by someone who is exposed to bored, neurotic, or disfigured animals is likely to be that there is something wrong with captivity.

Argument: Many aspects of marine mammal biology, physiology, and behavior can only be studied, or at least can be studied most efficiently, using captive subjects.

The opportunity to do research is a common justification for bringing marine mammals into captivity. Much of the literature on the biology, physiology, and behavior of marine mammals is based on studies using captive subjects (e.g., in the case of small cetaceans, Herman 1980, Kanwisher and Ridgway 1983, Schusterman et al. 1986, Nachtigall and Moore 1988, Leatherwood and Reeves 1990, Au 1993). Controversy on this point stems not from whether research has been done, but rather from whether the results are meaningful, and, if so, whether they are worth the costs to animal welfare and conservation.

Animals in artificial environments are unable to exhibit their full range of behavior. However "enriched" an enclosure may be, it cannot offer the variability of natural habitat. Social interactions are limited by the numbers and types of individuals present. Space severely constrains an animal's ability to avoid contact with others or to act independently. The ability of cetaceans to find and capture prey in the wild cannot be fully demonstrated in captivity, even with carefully controlled experimentation. Some aspects of an animal's behavior simply vanish from its repertoire in captivity while other characteristics can become exaggerated. In a broad sense, however, animals tend to exhibit species-specific differences in their behavior in captivity, and these differences correlate reasonably well with what is known about social and behavioral differences between species in the wild (Defran and Pryor 1980). Bottlenose dolphins tend to maintain similar daily cycles in the wild and in captivity (Saayman et al. 1973).

Much of what is known about the acoustic abilities of odontocete cetaceans has been learned through experiments with captive animals. However, it is not always clear whether the results of such work represent how the organisms function in nature. Perhaps the most compelling example of work that could not have been done without captive subjects is the study of biosonar in dolphins. After reviewing the state of knowledge about dolphin biosonar, however, Au (1993:271), a U.S. Navy researcher, concluded: "Our perception of how dolphins utilize their sonar in the wild is based on extrapolation of knowledge obtained in 'laboratory' experiments—we do not have the foggiest idea of how dolphins utilize their sonar in a natural environment." He described an experiment in which a captive bottlenose dolphin was blindfolded with eyecups for a series of target-detection trials. An array of hydrophones, mounted with suction cups on the animal's head, confirmed that it produced echolocation signals during the experiment. After the session, a live fish was introduced into the tank. The dolphin had not encountered live fish during the several years of its confinement. While still blindfolded, the animal positioned itself near the fish and maintained its position relative to the fish as both swam around the pool. The dolphin caught the fish five times, returning it to the trainer each time. At no time during the experiment were sonar signals detected by the hydrophones. Apparently the dolphin used only its hearing and passive localization capability to detect, track, and capture the fish. Thus, although experimentation with captive dolphins has established that they have a sophisticated biosonar system, it has revealed little about how they employ this ability in the wild. Such understanding will probably require either work with trained animals in the open sea or the monitoring of wild animals with satellite-linked radiotelemetry.

It is important to acknowledge the limitations attached to studies of captive animals, particularly in regard to the degree to which their behavior is representative or aberrant, but it is equally important to recognize that much has been learned (e.g., about dolphin sonar and other sensory and physiological processes) through research involving captive marine mammals. The work of Pryor and Shallenberger (1991), in which they used experience with captive spinner and pantropical spotted dolphins (*Stenella longirostris* and *S. attenuata,* respectively) to interpret observations of wild dolphins caught in tuna purse seines, is an example of how research in captivity can help address conservation problems for wild populations.

The late Kenneth Norris, whose career encompassed work with captive cetaceans and wild dolphin communities (Norris 1974, Norris et al. 1994), provided a unique perspective on captivity issues. As curator at Marineland of the Pacific in the 1950s, Norris led collecting expeditions and witnessed the high mortality of animals (e.g., see Norris and Prescott 1961, Walker 1975). His later role as a university professor and outspoken conservationist reflected a transformation in attitude brought about, at least in part, by experiences with the public display industry. Those opposed to keeping cetaceans in captivity often quote Norris to buttress their arguments: "Confinement compresses a porpoise's activity, no matter how large the tank. . . . In fact, confinement compresses natural activity so tightly that it may be distorted virtually beyond recognition. The captive porpoise forms unnatural life patterns, like the antelope in the zoo, used to ranging many miles a day, who comes to promenade in a stereotyped figure eight around his cage until the single track is rutted a foot below the surrounding soil" (Norris 1974:165). Yet Norris has also been quoted as saying that captive animals "have told us all we know about the dolphin mind, . . . how their senses work, how they echolocate, how they dive, and much of what we know about how their societies work" (Brownlee 1986:12).

In one essay, Norris (1991) suggested that studies in captivity and in the wild could be complementary and synergistic. He conceived the idea of a "dolphin sabbatical," in which carefully selected individuals are brought into captivity for periods of experimental research, then released back into the wild, as a way of realizing that potential without sacrificing the animals' welfare or preventing them from functioning in their natural populations (Mlot 1984, Wells 1989, Howard 1995; also see below for more discussion).

Argument: Marine mammals housed in high-quality oceanariums are actually better off in some ways than they would be in the wild. Their health status is carefully monitored; they are treated for disease or injury; they experience none of the stress associated with finding and capturing prey; they are spared from predation, entanglement in fishing gear, and collisions with vessels—the kinds of hazards that regularly confront wild marine mammals; and their abundant leisure time is punctuated by stimulating interactions with trainers and appreciative crowds of people.

Advocates of captive display frequently point out the "benefits" enjoyed by individual cetaceans (and, by inference at least, other marine mammals) in captivity: high-quality medical care, a reliable food supply, freedom from predation. They argue that these offset the loss of freedom, space, and stimulation (e.g., M. Stoskopf and B. Andrews, as quoted in Riley 1993; K. Pryor as quoted in Brownlee 1986). As Brownlee (1986:17) observed, "Much of this disagreement seems specious since nobody really knows how the animals themselves feel about it."

Different species, and even different individuals of the same species, respond differently to captivity. Coastal bottlenose dolphins, and probably other coastal animals such as hump-backed dolphins (*Sousa* spp.) and Irrawaddy dolphins (*Orcaella brevirostris*), adapt relatively well to captive conditions (although suppositions about the latter two species are based on limited experience) (Fig. 19-3). In contrast, some oceanic species, such as spinner and pantropical spotted dolphins, do not adapt readily. However, the ease with which a dolphin adapts to capture and captivity is more than a question of whether its natural habitat is inshore rather than offshore or whether it is accustomed to living in shallow, semienclosed waters rather than the deep, open sea. Harbor porpoises, for example, inhabit shallow water near shore, but they have generally done less well in captivity (Andersen 1978, Klinowska 1991) than rough-toothed dolphins (*Steno bredanensis*), which have an oceanic distribution (Pryor 1975, Shallenberger 1981). Limited experience with some species, such as Dall's porpoise (*Phocoenoides dalli*) (Ridgway 1966, Walker 1975) and the pygmy killer whale (*Feresa attenuata*) (Pryor et al. 1965), suggests that they are poorly suited to a captive existence.

This argument's validity depends, ultimately, on the demands that a particular animal faces in the wild and on the quality of the facilities and care that are provided in a given captive environment. It might be fair to suggest, for example, that animals living in severely polluted waters would be better off in a high-quality oceanarium. It is also important to emphasize that any statement about the "adaptability" of a particular species must be evaluated in the light of how much, and what kind, of experience the care-giving staff has. For example, Shallenberger (1981:57) reported that,

Figure 19-3. An Irrawaddy dolphin at Jaya Ancol Oceanarium, Jakarta, Indonesia, May 1983, expels water from its mouth, a typical behavior of the species both in the wild and in captivity. (Photograph by Steve Leatherwood)

although spinner dolphins are difficult to maintain in captivity, some success (i.e., improved longevity, some captive births) was eventually achieved at Sea Life Park in Hawaii once the animals were "being cared for by people with *Stenella* experience." In the case of harbor porpoises, the vast majority brought into captivity (probably totaling at least 150 worldwide) have been caught incidentally in fisheries and kept for rehabilitation or research (Andersen 1978, Collet 1984, Klinoswka 1991, Nachtigall et al. 1995). The poor survival record can be attributed in large part to diseases contracted in the wild and to injuries sustained during capture and transit. The fact that most porpoises have been housed singly helps explain the lack of captive breeding. At least until the early 1990s, no attempt had been made to select and maintain a healthy group of harbor porpoises "of appropriate age and sex" for a captive breeding program (Klinowska 1991:98).

To challenge the argument that captivity is "good for" individual animals, Pilleri (1983) claimed that the brains of dolphins shrink by as much as 30% in captivity. The available evidence, however, does not support that claim. Using postmortem records, Ridgway (1990) regressed the brain weight:body length ratio against years in captivity for 18 adult bottlenose dolphins. No significant difference was found between newly captured dolphins and those that died after being held in captivity for 5, 10, and up to 13 years.

Most captive facilities, with their concrete tanks and chemically treated water, provide environments that are extremely different from natural environments. Wild animals are suited by evolution to the stresses experienced in nature. They do not "need" veterinary care, and the "stress" of foraging is a natural pressure. To suggest that artificial environments are somehow better for the animals than natural environments is inescapably anthropocentric. It may also have ominous implications. If captivity were an appropriate substitute for nature, what would be the impetus for preserving biologically diverse natural systems?

Argument: A sophisticated, well-organized network of marine mammal holding facilities makes it possible to salvage, rehabilitate, maintain, and in some cases release animals that are stranded, sick, or injured. Without the large subsidy provided by animal display operations, such facilities either would not exist or would have much lower standards of care.

The rescue and rehabilitation of marine mammals found stranded, orphaned, or in some way incapacitated are properly viewed as a distinct branch of captivity. Rehabilitation of severely sick or injured animals is possible only if they can be moved to a suitable facility, whether temporary or permanent (Fig. 19-4). It is no coincidence that the sense of obligation to rescue and rehabilitate marine mammals has developed concurrently with the proliferation of captive maintenance facilities. Improvements in facilities and procedures have made it increasingly feasible to rescue and rehabilitate animals. Exposure to animals in captivity has probably also increased the public's willingness to invest in such efforts. In addition to the long-standing participation by established oceanariums, a number of institutions have been established in recent years with rescue and rehabilitation as their primary mission (see Wilkinson and Worthy, this volume).

Two aspects are important to consider. First, does a release program contribute to the conservation of wild populations? Second, can rescue and rehabilitation efforts help stock zoos and oceanariums, thus reducing the need to remove additional animals from the wild? We discuss each of

Figure 19-4. One of the earliest attempts to rescue and rehabilitate a beaked whale began in January 1973 when a Blainville's beaked whale (*Mesoplodon densirostris*) stranded alive on a New Jersey beach. The animal was initially held in a swimming pool that had been drained and filled with seawater, then later was transported to the New York Aquarium. Efforts to force-feed the whale were generally unsuccessful, and it lived for only three days. (Photograph courtesy of Smithsonian Institution)

these briefly here; a separate discussion of Florida manatees (*Trichechus manatus*) appears later in the chapter.

Contribution to the Conservation of Wild Populations

Rescue and rehabilitation programs are likely to be of direct conservation benefit only in cases where the wild population is small and threatened (St. Aubin, Geraci et al. 1996). Monk seals, California sea otters (*Enhydra lutris*), and manatees are possible examples. For wild populations that are reasonably large, reproducing normally, and not experiencing excessive mortality, conservation is not a valid reason for rehabilitating and releasing animals. In fact, it could be argued that such efforts actually interfere with natural selection and evolution.

Whatever the potential benefits, several serious risks need to be considered. Well-intentioned releases could (1) put animals with "maladaptive traits" back into the wild gene pool, (2) destabilize the social order (e.g., by changing the adult sex ratio and jeopardizing the health of reproductive females), and (3) exacerbate political conflicts between fishermen and marine mammals in specific areas (St. Aubin, Geraci et al. 1996). Also, it is critically important to avoid introducing exotic diseases to wild populations through release programs (see Geraci et al., this volume).

Using Rescued Animals to Replenish Captive Stocks

If sick, injured, or stranded animals can be rehabilitated, there should be little argument against using them as substitutes for live-caught animals. This is particularly valuable in instances where capture programs may negatively affect wild populations. In fact, since 1977 NMFS has encouraged facilities to depend almost entirely on rehabilitated and captive-born pinnipeds (Hohn and Wilkinson 1996). As a result, the pressure to capture California sea lions and harbor seals, the two most common pinnipeds in captivity in North America, has declined.

Argument: Captive maintenance (and propagation) of marine mammals provides a form of insurance against species extinction and can be used to support reintroductions, restocking, and other direct conservation efforts. It is important to develop methods and facilities using species that are abundant and easily accessible so that the techniques and technology will be available for use with threatened or endangered populations.

This is by now a familiar justification for the existence of zoos, which can contribute to preserving biotic and genetic diversity in six main ways (Foose 1983):

1. By serving as refugia for taxa destined for extinction in the wild;
2. By providing propagules for repopulation of natural habitats;
3. By reinforcing natural populations that are so small and fragmented that they are not genetically and demographically viable;
4. By maintaining repositories for germ plasm as an adjunct or an alternative to populations of living animals;
5. By conducting research that will improve management for wild as well as for captive populations; and
6. By educating the public to support conservation of wildlife in natural habitats.

Reintroduction or restocking programs (see International Union for the Conservation of Nature and Natural

Resources [1987] for definitions of terms) involving captive propagules have a mixed record of success and failure (Griffith et al. 1989). Arabian oryxes (*Oryx leucoryx*), red wolves (*Canis rufus*), California condors (*Gymnogyps californianus*), peregrine falcons (*Falco peregrinus*), golden lion tamarins (*Leontopithecus rosalia*), and black-footed ferrets (*Mustela nigripes*) are among the most highly publicized of many examples (Kleiman 1989, Beck 1995, Loftin 1995).

Captive breeding for purposes of conservation has only recently been put forward as a major justification for holding cetaceans in captivity (Ames 1991). At an international meeting on river dolphins in 1986, consideration was given to the need for, and feasibility of, a captive breeding program for China's endangered Yangtze River dolphin, or baiji (*Lipotes vexillifer*) (Perrin and Brownell 1989; also see Perrin, this volume). Since then, two approaches have been pursued—one the building of concrete tanks in which to maintain baiji, the other the development of a "seminatural reserve" for them. Although germ plasm "banking," research, and public education (Foose's points 4–6, above) have been touted as part of the justification for keeping baiji in captivity (Liu 1991), the main emphasis has increasingly been placed on Foose's points 1–3. Since the mid-1980s the baiji's situation has continued to deteriorate rapidly, and the seminatural reserve is increasingly viewed as a permanent refugium for a species that is doomed in the wild.

According to Ralls (1989), the goals of a breeding program should be to (1) achieve routine breeding in captivity or semicaptivity, (2) assure the security of the captive or semicaptive population by allowing it to expand as rapidly as possible and by founding subpopulations, and (3) preserve genetic diversity through careful and intensive management of the captive or semicaptive population. She suggested that a successful program for baiji would require an effective founding population size of 20–25 animals, with the goal of attaining a final effective population size of 200–300. (Note that the term *effective* refers to the component of the total population that is sexually mature and contributing to reproduction.)

In spite of an aggressive effort during the past several years to locate and capture baiji, only one animal (a male rescued from fishing gear in January 1980) is currently alive in a tank.

At least two major reservations arise when considering captive breeding as a strategy for baiji conservation:

1. Efforts to breed the baiji in captivity might profit from lessons learned with other cetaceans in captivity. However, experience with its near relative, the Amazon River dolphin, or boto (*Inia geoffrensis*), is not cause for optimism. More than 70 botos were imported to the United States between 1956 and 1966, yet by 1966 only 19 remained alive. Three live births occurred, but none of the calves lived for more than two weeks (Caldwell et al. 1989). "Few platanistoid dolphins have been born in captivity and no established record of husbandry or research provides guidelines for propagating river dolphins" (Ridgway et al. 1989:160).

   Experience with other species, such as the bottlenose dolphin, killer whale, and beluga, has shown that a long-term commitment of resources is essential. Some captured individuals will fail to reproduce, whether because of their advanced age, social incompatibility with other animals, or premature death. If one accepts the premise of Foose (1983) and Ralls (1989) that an effective founding population of at least 5–10 pairs is required for a viable captive stock, it is difficult to envision how this level could be reached with baiji. During recent surveys to locate animals for capture, only a few small pods were observed, and most of these proved impossible to approach (Liu Renjun and Wang Ding, pers. comm.).
2. By offering the option of captive maintenance and propagation, one runs the risk of weakening the social and political commitment to preserve healthy aquatic or marine habitats. It could be argued that, without a realistic expectation of eventually reestablishing a viable population in the wild, investment of resources in captive breeding programs is either pointless or counterproductive. Obtaining a sufficiently large and demographically appropriate group of animals to form a captive breeding stock can work against efforts to protect a viable population in the wild. In the case of baiji, the decision to pursue conservation through captive programs has meant, from a practical standpoint, that efforts to protect dolphins in "natural reserves" have been essentially abandoned. The few areas of the Yangtze that still have animals, and thus would be worth managing as reserves, are also, of necessity, the most attractive sites for capturing dolphins to stock the seminatural reserve.

Schroeder and Keller (1990) suggested that experience with techniques for improving reproductive efficiency in captive bottlenose dolphins (e.g., artificial insemination and embryo transplantation) could provide a model for endangered species such as the baiji. The application of advanced reproductive technologies to cetaceans, however, is still far from routine. According to Robeck et al. (1994:332), "present realities indicate that species currently endangered and without a successful captive breeding program may not benefit from these techniques."

During the years 1976–1979 only 12% of the pinnipeds acquired by North American institutions were captive-born. From 1983 through 1990, 84% of those acquired were captive-born. The captive populations of California sea lions and harbor seals in North America are now essentially self-sustaining. Captive-born and rescued/rehabilitated harbor seals have been used to restock the wild population in the Wadden Sea (Reijnders et al. 1996). A novel type of intervention, involving live capture, several months of nurturing, and later release of young females, has aided the recovery of Hawaiian monk seals at several haul-out sites (Gerrodette and Gilmartin 1990; Ragen and Lavigne, this volume).

In contrast to these positive developments with other pinnipeds, plans to develop a "breeding center" for Mediterranean monk seals at Antibes Marineland on the French Riviera have been severely criticized. Johnson (1994) noted, among other things, that the record of maintaining this species in captivity was dismal and that no monk seals had ever been born in captivity. Because the principal source of animals for the Antibes facility would be the population residing along the northwest coast of Africa, the animals would need to be transported long distances and held far from their natural setting. The expenditure of resources for captive breeding would preclude the use of those resources for enhancing protection of wild seals and their habitat.

Thus, many of the same arguments apply to the Mediterranean monk seal as apply to the baiji. In both cases, captive breeding initiatives have come at a late, and probably critical, time for the dwindling wild populations. Advocates of captive breeding find themselves in a "catch-22" position. If captures are not permitted, the husbandry record will not improve and there will be no captive births.

Arguments against Captivity

Argument: Removal of animals from wild populations to supply captive facilities constitutes an additional stress on those populations, thus contributing to their decline.

Advocates of public display frequently point out that many more marine mammals are killed or injured by hunters and fishermen every year than are removed by live capture (e.g., Ames 1991, Riley 1993). In North America at least, the direct effect of current live-capture operations on the conservation status of wild populations is probably negligible. For example, the beluga population in western Hudson Bay, at more than 23,000 animals (Richard et al. 1990), should have been large enough to sustain the documented live capture of 68 whales between 1967 and 1992 (Anonymous 1992a) even when the substantial kill by Inuit is taken into account.

In Japan, and to some extent elsewhere in Asia, many of the cetaceans that have ended up in oceanariums were taken from drives (Kasuya et al. 1984, Reeves et al. 1994) (see Table 19-1). In most instances, the animals sold to oceanariums would have been killed otherwise. Thus, the live removals could be viewed as a substitute, rather than an addition, in terms of mortality in the wild population. On the other hand, money gained from the sale of live animals might add to the incentive for continuing or expanding the hunt. In 1993 Marine World Africa USA in Vallejo, California, obtained four false killer whales (*Pseudorca crassidens*) from the drive at Iki Island, Japan, and were promptly condemned for doing so by several animal rights groups (In Defense of Animals, Humane Society of the United States, and Earth Island Institute). A spokesman for the oceanarium argued that his institution had "rescued the whales from death," while the president of In Defense of Animals accused Marine World of giving "tacit approval" to the hunt (Morris 1993).

Most of the walruses brought into captivity have been pups orphaned by hunters. This practice creates the same dilemma as the salvaging of cetaceans from drives. The pups clearly would die if they were not "adopted" by oceanariums and zoos, yet if institutions purchased them from hunters, this might add legitimacy and profitability to the continued killing of adult walruses by Inuit. To preclude this effect, recent permits for the taking of young walruses in Alaska have been issued with the condition that no payment be made (A. G. Kirk, pers. comm.).

Killer whales in inshore waters of British Columbia and Washington probably provide the best-known example of live-capture operations depleting a local wild population of marine mammals. At least 62 individuals were permanently removed from these waters between 1962 and 1973 (Bigg and Wolman 1975), and this seems to have had a substantial impact on the resident "southern community" of whales (Olesiuk et al. 1990). Since the banning of further removals in both British Columbia and Washington in the mid-1970s (Hoyt 1990), most captive killer whales have been caught near Iceland or born in captivity (Duffield et al. 1995). Fifty-one whales were taken from the wild in Iceland between 1976 and 1988, and this catch rate was judged to be "within the reproductive capacity of the overall Icelandic stock(s)" (Sigurjónsson and Leatherwood 1988:315).

Unregulated catches to stock new dolphinariums in Thailand have been made from coastal populations of hump-backed dolphins and Irrawaddy dolphins that were probably already depleted (Smith 1991, International Whaling Commission 1994). Similar situations have undoubtedly arisen, and more will arise, in other parts of Asia. In the southeastern United States, where collectors took most of the captive bottlenose dolphins held in Europe and North America, such operations apparently reduced some local stocks before the live-capture fishery was regulated under a quota scheme (Scott 1990). It is important to bear in mind that some live-capture fisheries have tended to target relatively young females (Walker 1975, Sigurjónsson and Leatherwood 1988, Scott 1990). Such selectivity results in greater impacts than if the removals were more balanced or were skewed in another way with respect to age and sex.

Argument: Marine mammals do not survive as well in captivity as they do in the wild.

This argument has been advanced by most anticaptivity groups, and numerous studies have investigated its merits (e.g., DeMaster and Drevenak 1988, Woodley et al. 1994, Small and DeMaster 1995a). The question of whether marine mammals survive as well in captivity as in the wild is complex and difficult to answer conclusively. Although most of the discourse related to this argument has focused on cetaceans, several investigators have also analyzed data on survivorship of captive sea lions.

It has been virtually impossible to obtain unbiased estimates of natural mortality rates for most wild cetacean populations. An animal's probability of dying changes during the course of its life; young animals generally have higher mortality rates than older animals. In polygynous species particularly, males tend to have higher mortality rates than females (Kasuya and Marsh 1984, Olesiuk et al. 1990). Long-term field studies of killer whales and bottlenose dolphins, using photo-identification and mark-recapture techniques, provide the best data available for estimating natural mortality rates of odontocete cetaceans. Bigg (1982) reported annual natural mortality rates of 0.028 for adult males, 0.007 for adult females, and 0.023 for juveniles in the inshore population of killer whales off Vancouver Island, British Columbia. Reanalysis of the same data gave a combined overall estimate of 0.02 (95% confidence interval 0.01–0.03) for this population (DeMaster and Drevenak 1988:308). Wells and Scott (1990) estimated annual survival rates (following the method of DeMaster and Drevenak 1988, see below) of 0.803 (± SD 0.0703) for young of the year and 0.961 (± SD 0.0079) for older animals in the Sarasota Bay, Florida, population of bottlenose dolphins. They cautioned that these estimates were likely biased upward because some undocumented mortality probably occurred. In this regard, it should be noted that Hersh et al. (1990) estimated annual natural mortality rates of bottlenose dolphins in the Indian/Banana River complex, eastern Florida, with data from an intensive eight-year carcass-salvage program, in combination with population estimates derived from aerial surveys. Their mortality estimates for the population overall ranged from 0.07 to 0.09.

A standard method of assessing survivorship is necessary for making meaningful comparisons between institutions and between captive and wild populations. Such a method was developed by DeMaster and Drevenak (1988) as follows. First, a daily survival rate (DSR) is calculated by the formula:

$$\text{DSR} = 1 - \frac{\sum_{i=1}^{K} (y_i)}{\sum_{i=1}^{K} (x_i)}$$

where y_i is one if the ith individual died during the reporting period and zero if the ith individual survived through the entire reporting period; x_i is the total number of days, including any days on which deaths may have occurred, in the reporting period for the ith individual; and K is the number of animals in the sample. The summation of y over all animals is the total number of deaths that occurred; the summation of x over all animals is the total number of animal-days observed. This DSR is then converted to an annual survival rate (ASR) by raising the DSR to the 365.25th power.

DeMaster and Drevenak (1988) used data from the NMFS inventory of acquisitions and deaths of animals held in United States and other institutions between 1975 and 1984 (see Temte 1993) in an initial attempt to estimate post-capture survival rates of three species. The overall ASRs were 0.93 for bottlenose dolphins and killer whales and 0.94 for belugas. DeMaster and Drevenak did not consider their results conclusive with regard to whether life expectancies of captive animals were better or worse than those of free-ranging animals. They did, however, reduce much of the previous confusion caused by inappropriate comparisons. Their results indicated significant differences in survivorship of bottlenose dolphins between institutions. A preliminary attempt to correlate ASRs with particular characteristics of the institutions, such as pool sizes, water filtration systems, numbers of animals per pool, and frequency and duration of performances, illustrated the difficulty of determining the relative importance of various factors to survivorship (Steuer 1989).

An important finding of the study by DeMaster and Drevenak (1988, also see Steuer 1989) is that a large-scale captive breeding program causes an institution's calculated overall ASR to decrease. This is because the survival rate of captive-born calves is significantly less than that of non-calves. To reduce the effect of this bias, Small and DeMaster (1995a) introduced the concept of an "acclimation period," arbitrarily set at three days so as to exclude from analyses any stillbirths or calves that died from birth-related complications. In a further analysis based on survival of bottlenose dolphins and California sea lions, the same authors proposed that a 60-day acclimation period be recognized as "a distinct interval of relatively high mortality that should be treated separately from long-term survival estimates when evaluating husbandry practices of oceanaria and zoos" (Small and DeMaster 1995b:510).

Small and DeMaster (1995a) analyzed NMFS survival data for California sea lions and northern sea lions (*Eumetopias jubatus*) as well as bottlenose dolphins, killer whales, and belugas through 1992. Overall ASRs for the captive populations of all five species were between 0.937 and 0.968. The ASRs of bottlenose dolphins and California sea lions for the most recent five years (1988–1992) were significantly higher than the ASRs for pre-1988 (from 0.931 to 0.951 and from 0.935 to 0.952, respectively; in both cases $P < 0.001$). Small and DeMaster concluded that husbandry practices for these two species had improved in recent years, but they also noted the need for improved survivorship at several institutions. The ASR of belugas increased, but this increase was not statistically significant. The ASRs of killer whales and northern sea lions showed no trend. As pointed out by Small and Demaster (1995a), the estimated survival rate of noncalf killer whales in the wild population off Washington and British Columbia (Olesiuk et al. 1990) was significantly higher than that of noncalf captives through 1992 (0.976 vs. 0.938, $P < 0.001$). In contrast, York's (1994) highest age-specific annual survival rate for wild northern sea lions, 0.930 during year 4, was lower than the estimate of 0.968 for captive northern sea lions (males and females, combined) reported by Small and DeMaster (1995a). A definitive answer to the basic question of how survival of marine mammals in captivity compares with that in the wild remains elusive, but it is preferable that the question be answered species by species.

An alternative approach for comparing captive and wild populations is to use a suite of parameters, including age distribution, maximal longevity, average age of currently living members of the population, average age at death, crude birth rate, fecundity rate, recruitment rate, and mortality rate (Duffield and Wells 1993). Data from the wild currently are insufficient for broad-scale application of this approach for most species. For the bottlenose dolphin, however, the long-term study in Sarasota Bay provides the needed data (Wells and Scott 1990), and similar potential resides in the long-term data on killer whales in inshore waters of British Columbia and Washington (Bigg et al. 1990, Olesiuk et al. 1990). The data needed for estimating these parameters in captive populations are not readily available from NMFS but rather must come from industry sources (e.g., see Asper et al. 1988, 1990). A preliminary comparison of the Sarasota bottlenose dolphin population with the captive population in North America revealed some similarities (e.g., in age distributions, maximal longevities, and average ages of currently living animals) as well as some differences (e.g., in crude birth and fecundity rates) (Duffield and Wells 1993). We are uncertain of the appropriateness of comparing so many aspects of a managed captive metapopulation involving many different institutions with those of an unmanaged wild stock. As noted by Duffield and Wells, the captive population may be subject to the effects of uncoordinated husbandry decisions by the different institutions, particularly in regard to those parameters related to reproduction. The recent trend toward single-sex or single-animal displays (Asper et al. 1990) would, for example, strongly affect birth and fecundity rates.

Argument: Marine mammals (cetaceans in particular) have rights equivalent to those of humans, and holding these animals in captivity is an abuse of those rights, regardless of whether their treatment and care are judged acceptable by current standards of humaneness. With the proliferation of media presentations of marine mammals in the wild and increased opportunities for people to observe the animals outside captivity (e.g., "whale watching"), a transition away from captive display is both appropriate and feasible.

This animal rights argument against captivity can be applied to many wild animals, not just marine mammals. It has been invoked with particular force, however, in the case of cetaceans (Jamieson and Regan 1984), which some people consider special because of their intelligence and sociability (e.g., see Klinowska and Brown 1986, Barstow 1991, Scheffer 1991). The animal rights argument, of all those discussed in this chapter, is least amenable to scientific discourse. It resides in an epistemologically separate universe—the realm of philosophy or religion. However disinclined those defending captivity may be to engage in serious debate with proponents of animal rights, they seem to have no choice. Cartmill (1994:1082), writing in the *Journal of Mammalogy,* stated:

> [The animal rights position] deserves to be examined critically and attacked where it is weak or inconclusive. It does not deserve to be brushed aside as a crazy delusion that can be dispelled by better science education. Doing so will not have a positive effect on the thoughtless or fanatical supporters of the doctrine of animal rights, and it is bound to have a negative effect on the ones that have given serious thought to these questions.

At the Global Conference on the Non-consumptive Utilisation of Cetacean Resources (also known as the "Whales

Alive" conference) held in Boston, Massachusetts, in 1983, participants acknowledged that experience with animals in captivity had "contributed to the present understanding of and benevolent feeling towards cetaceans" (Anonymous 1983:17). Nevertheless, this group, most of whom favored a ban on commercial whaling, had difficulty reaching a consensus on the captivity issue. It was "the most volatile and divisive subject" discussed at the conference (Barstow 1986:161). Captivity-related recommendations in the conference report dealt mainly with the need for uniform standards in capture and transport techniques, facilities, and animal care; better documentation of the impacts of live-capture operations on wild populations; and more research on "emotional behavior" of cetaceans to interpret the effects of captivity (e.g., see Hindley 1984). It also recommended, however, that efforts be made:

> to bring to an end in due course the keeping of cetaceans in captivity, with a view to the ultimate replacement of dolphinaria by facilities for observation, educational studies and enjoyment of *wild* cetaceans, including special exposure to audiovisual media representing them, and the establishment of facilities to which cetaceans may voluntarily make themselves available for interaction with, or observation by, humans (Anonymous 1983:18).

The report acknowledged that observing animals in the wild (e.g., whale watching) carries some risk for the animals. If as many people joined whale-watching cruises as visit oceanariums, some impact on wild cetacean populations (in the form of stress at least, if not injury and mortality) could be expected (e.g., see Beach and Weinrich 1989, Tyack 1989, Duffus and Dearden 1990). In many instances, wild dolphin watching has evolved into dolphin feeding, with attendant problems such as "alteration of natural foraging patterns, dependence on an artificial food supply, and death from contaminated and toxic fish" (Frohoff and Packard 1995:47; also see Bryant 1994, Orams 1995). The promotion of manatee watching in Florida has led to concern about the effects of additional vessel traffic and of efforts by divers to follow, stroke, and even ride the manatees (Shackley 1992).

Considerable momentum aimed at eliminating cetaceans from captive displays has developed in some Western countries since 1983. The Australian parliamentary committee, mentioned earlier, concluded in 1985 that, although existing oceanariums in Australia should be allowed to continue in operation, no new facilities should be established and the keeping of cetaceans should eventually be phased out unless further research justifies its continuance (Anonymous 1985). Again as mentioned above, the last dolphinarium in the United Kingdom closed in 1993, thus completing the "phase-out" of captive displays of cetaceans in that country, approximately 10 years after "Whales Alive."

In the United States, much attention has been given in recent years to the question of whether, and how, to release cetaceans back into the wild (i.e., "giving them back their freedom"). According to Brill (1994), the campaigns calling for such releases are based on the premise that captivity of any kind is morally offensive. In considering animal releases, it is important to distinguish between "reintroduction" and "return to the wild." Reintroduction refers to "the intentional movement of an organism into a part of its native range from which it has disappeared or become extirpated in historic times as a result of human activities" (International Union for the Conservation of Nature and Natural Resources 1987:1). Brill's (1994:337) definition of return to the wild is that it implies a "scientific process, similar to reintroduction," but with the principal aim of simply allowing the animal to resume a life "free of any further intervention by or dependence upon humans." In other words, reintroduction is to benefit conservation, whereas return to the wild is to benefit the individual animal.

The statement of the International Union for the Conservation of Nature and Natural Resources (1987:3) on translocation of living organisms urges that "no alien species should be deliberately introduced into any natural habitat." Any release of captive marine mammals into the wild needs to be carefully considered to avoid introduction of exotic (nonendemic) species. Some have already occurred. For example, in 1991 three bottlenose dolphins that had been in captivity for at least 12 years were released off the Turks and Caicos Islands in the Bahamas (McKenna 1992). Two of the animals had been caught originally off the southeastern United States (probably Florida), but one had been taken from waters off Taiwan in the western Pacific. This well-intentioned gesture apparently was "successful" because all three animals were resighted "numerous times" after their release (Balcomb 1994). The genus *Tursiops* exhibits considerable morphological variability. Two well-differentiated forms, offshore and coastal, have been described for the western North Atlantic (Mead and Potter 1995). Clear differentiation also exists in other regions (Curry and Smith 1997), including Taiwan (Ross and Cockcroft 1990, Reeves et al. 1994). Because *Tursiops* systematics are currently complicated and provisional, the safest course for releasing captives into the wild, at least from the standpoint of maintaining the genetic and ecological "purity" of regional populations, is to ensure that animals are returned as close as possible to their original capture site.

The Warner Brothers movie *Free Willy,* released in 1993, gave enormous impetus to the idea of releasing captive killer whales (Bock 1994, Rose 1994). Balcomb (1994) compiled information on more than 25 releases of dolphins and whales that had been in captivity for a year or longer and on various other releases of shorter-term captives. Most releases have been poorly documented, with little or no follow-up to determine how well the animals adjusted to life outside captivity. In a few instances, the animals have been tagged or instrumented for postrelease monitoring (e.g., Early and Rumage 1988, Gales and Waples 1993, Mate et al. 1994, Davis et al. 1996). The most rigorously planned and executed capture-maintenance-release project to date was based on Kenneth Norris's concept of a "dolphin science sabbatical." Two young male bottlenose dolphins, removed in 1988 from the well-studied coastal population on the west coast of Florida, were maintained in captivity for two years of research in California and then released in 1990 into the same area where one of them had been caught (Wells 1989, Bassos 1993). Norris (1995:xii) judged the sabbatical a failure, noting that two years of captivity was an insufficient time for the dolphins to make the expected "connection" with the researchers: "In the end, however much I wanted to open the channel between us and then explore a little, this was, I concluded, not the way it should be done."

Norris's two dolphins experienced a "hard release" although they were given the benefit of acclimation in a sea pen and phased introduction to live food. Once released, they had no "half-way house" to which they could return for provisions. Protocols for selecting and preparing animals, conducting releases, and monitoring animals after release were developed for marine mammals by two workshops of experts in 1992 (Brill and Friedl 1993).

Sirenians

Sirenians, unlike cetaceans and pinnipeds, have not been trained to perform in captivity. Their presence in zoological parks outside North America has generally been motivated by the menagerie tradition (i.e., the desire to collect and exhibit the exotic or unusual). Manatees (*Trichechus* spp.) and dugongs (*Dugong dugon*) tend to appeal more to people's curiosity about nature than to their desire to be entertained and impressed by trained behavior (Fig. 19-5). The situation

Figure 19-5. Steve Leatherwood gets a close-up look at a manatee in Homosassa Springs, Florida, a state-owned facility where manatees and other aquatic fauna (see jacks in the background) live in an enclosed, but natural environment. (Photograph by Howard Hall)

in the southeastern United States, where rehabilitation of injured and orphaned manatees has come to play a central role in conservation (see Reynolds, this volume), differs from that in Europe and Asia. Several institutions in Florida have integrated the rescue and rehabilitation of manatees into their overall operations (Reynolds and Odell 1991; Reynolds, this volume). Thus, a given facility's captive display and educational offering is actually the rescue and rehabilitation program itself, with public service, research, and conservation dimensions. To illustrate the scale of these efforts, Sea World of Florida responded to 160 requests for assistance with distressed manatees between 1976 and October 1995. Fifty-seven of the animals were eventually released, including 10 at the rescue site. Sixty-eight animals died during rehabilitation, 36 of them within the first week because of the severity of their injuries or disease. An additional 10 died before their arrival at the rehabilitation center (information supplied by Sea World of Florida).

Currently, the Florida manatee (*Trichechus manatus manatus*) seems to represent a special case of marine mammals in captivity. Rather than taking from wild populations to stock their displays, oceanariums are helping to maintain the subspecies in the wild while at the same time developing on-site exhibits that are both popular and educational (Marshall and Henry, n.d.). Thus, the drawbacks mentioned above in connection with last-ditch interventions with baiji and monk seals do not apply. A side benefit of the manatee program is that curators and veterinarians working with stranded animals have gained valuable experience of the kind that would be needed for a captive breeding effort.

Possibilities of Domestication

It has been suggested that the bottlenose dolphin could be the first cetacean to become "domesticated" (Pryor 1975) and even that this species might come to be regarded as the "white rat" of the cetaceans (Leatherwood and Reeves 1978). In some ways, marine mammals have already been domesticated. Sea lions and odontocete cetaceans have been trained to locate and recover objects from the seafloor (Bowers and Henderson 1972, Conboy 1975) and to cooperate in at-sea research (Wood 1973, Kanwisher and Ridgway 1983, Ridgway 1987). In New York City, consideration has been given to the idea of training harbor seals for public security work, such as underwater photography for bridge inspection and the detection and recovery of weapons, drugs, and human corpses in waterways (Riedman 1990:315). Captive dolphins are believed by some to have therapeutic value for humans. One person has used her own interactions with captive dolphins to improve her ability to help autistic children (St. John 1986). These practical uses are in addition to those mentioned or implied elsewhere in this chapter, and we could have included them among the arguments in favor of marine mammals in captivity.

Actual domestication still seems somewhat futuristic to us, although not everyone shares that view. St. Aubin, Ridgway et al. (1996:3) chose to refer to the bottlenose dolphins held in natural seawater enclosures at U.S. Navy laboratories as "semidomesticated." They noted that the term *captive* was not appropriate for animals that "voluntarily accompany humans on exercises at sea and choose to remain with their handlers." Selective breeding of marine mammals to enhance particular characteristics (e.g., docility, trainability, reproductive performance) has not been widely reported or discussed, but this may occur inadvertently as captive breeding programs develop. Genetic alteration would be simple, judging from the fact that hybridism, including intergeneric and even interfamilial crossing, has been reported occasionally among captive marine mammals (Nishiwaki and Tobayama 1982, King 1983, Sylvestre and Tasaka 1985). In fact, a "wholphin," a bottlenose dolphin–false killer whale cross at Sea Life Park in Hawaii, has produced two calves, indicating that such hybrids can be fertile (Ridgway 1995).

Concluding Remarks

The issues raised by maintaining marine mammals in captivity are embedded within broader subjects, such as human-animal relations, environmental ethics, the worth and relevance of basic scientific inquiry, and the survival and recovery of endangered species. Science has not provided, and is not likely to provide in the immediate future, definitive support for any of the arguments raised for or against maintaining marine mammals in captivity. Some of the controversy may be rooted in technical differences of opinion about how data should be analyzed and interpreted. Much more of it probably comes from differences in values, belief systems, or worldviews.

A large number of people make at least part of their living from marine mammals in captivity. This includes not only those who own or work at zoos and oceanariums, but also those who work for regulatory agencies and nongovernmental organizations and those whose research is funded or otherwise subsidized by such institutions or groups. Vested interests abound on all sides. The public hearings, the contract reports, the strategy sessions of anticaptivity campaigners on the one hand and industry lobbyists on the other, even the scientific papers and book chapters such as this one, all provide work for people. In some respects, the more controversy there is, the more work (of certain kinds) that becomes available. It may not be entirely coincidental that large-scale commercial whaling and sealing came to an end in the mid-1980s at about the same time that controversy about marine mammals in captivity became heated. Many of the same organizations and the same people who earlier devoted energy and resources to the antiwhaling and antisealing movements have now directed their attention to the captive display industry.

With the whaling and sealing industries now remnants of what they were in the 1960s when "save the whale" and "save the seal" campaigns were born, it is now the curators, collectors, and zoological park developers who are on the defensive (Norton et al. 1995). This shift, however, has necessitated a change in emphasis. Opposition to whaling and sealing was driven by concern about both species conservation and animal welfare (e.g., the humaneness of killing methods). Today, we recognize that fishery bycatches, "subsistence" or "community-based" whaling and sealing, pollution, and habitat degradation also threaten populations and cause animals to suffer. Live-capture operations, in contrast, have generally not depleted wild populations, and exposure to captive marine mammals has certainly made some people more sympathetic and informed. The most serious opposition to marine mammals in captivity is rooted in concern about the welfare of individual animals rather than species conservation.

Acknowledgments

The following people helped us by providing literature, illustrations, or data: Alison Smith, Thomas Woodley, Thomas Jefferson, Daniel Odell, Alan Baker, William Medway, Toshio Kasuya, Steve Leatherwood, Suzanne Harkness, Peter Shaughnessy, and Sue Johnson. We are grateful to all of them. We are especially indebted to Marvin L. Jones, whose extensive compilation of information on animals in captivity helped us fill in many of the gaps in Table 19-1. Critical reviews by Sam Ridgway, Robert Hofman, Alison Kirk, Jan Sechrist, Kris Karmon, John Reynolds, Richard Wallace, and four anonymous reviewers significantly improved the manuscript.

Literature Cited

Ames, M. H. 1991. Saving some cetaceans may require breeding in captivity. BioScience 41:746–749.

Andersen, S. H. 1978. Experiences with harbour porpoises, *Phocoena phocoena,* in captivity: Mortality, autopsy findings and influence of the captive environment. Aquatic Mammals 6 (2): 39–49.

Anderson, J. 1878. Anatomical and zoological researches: Comprising an account of the zoological results of the two expeditions to Western Yunnan in 1868 and 1875; and a monograph of the two cetacean genera *Platanista* and *Orcella*. 2 vols. Bernard Quaritch, London.

Andrésson, G. 1978. Chasing the elusive dolphin. Atlantica and Iceland Review 16 (2): 28–31.

Anonymous. 1983. Whales Alive: Report of Global Conference on the Non-Consumptive Utilisation of Cetacean Resources. 7–11 June 1983, New England Aquarium, Boston, MA. Connecticut Cetacean Society, Wethersfield, CT; Animal Welfare Institute, Washington, DC. 49 pp.

Anonymous. 1984. Report of a Workshop on Animals on Display: Educational and Scientific Impact. John G. Shedd Aquarium, 12–16 February, Chicago, IL. Convened by American Association of Zoological Parks and Aquariums. Unpublished.

Anonymous. 1985. Dolphins and whales in captivity. Report by the Senate Select Committee on Animal Welfare. Australian Government Publishing Service, Canberra. 117 pp.

Anonymous. 1988. Dolphinaria. Report of the Steering Group. Department of the Environment, U.K. 117 pp.

Anonymous. 1992a. Capture and maintenance of cetaceans in Canada. A report prepared by the Advisory Committee on Marine Mammals for the Minister of Fisheries and Oceans. Ottawa, Canada. 52 pp.

Anonymous. 1992b. Annotated bibliography of publications from the U.S. Navy's marine mammal program. Naval Command, Control and Ocean Surveillance Center, San Diego, CA. NRaD Technical Document 627, Revision C. 91 pp.

Asper, E. D., L. H. Cornell, D. A. Duffield, and N. Dimeo-Ediger. 1988. Marine mammals in zoos, aquaria and marine zoological parks in North America: 1983 census report. International Zoo Yearbook 27:287–294.

Asper, E. D., D. A. Duffield, N. Dimeo-Ediger, and E. D. Shell. 1990. Marine mammals in zoos, aquaria and marine zoological parks in North America: 1990 census report. International Zoo Yearbook 29:179–187.

Au, W. W. L. 1993. The Sonar of Dolphins. Springer-Verlag, New York, NY. 277 pp.

Augee, M. L. (ed.). 1988. Marine Mammals of Australasia: Field Biology and Captive Management. Royal Zoological Society of New South Wales, Mosman, New South Wales, Australia.

Balcomb, K. C., III. 1994. Cetacean releases: A list of examples. Unpublished manuscript. On file at Marine Mammal Commission, Bethesda, MD.

Barabash-Nikiforov, I. I. 1962. The sea otter (*Enhydra lutris* L.)—biology and economic problems of breeding. Israel Program for Scientific Translations, Jerusalem (Translated from Russian).

Barstow, R. 1986. Non-consumptive utilization of whales. Ambio 15:155–163.

Barstow, R. 1991. Whales are uniquely special. Pages 4–7 *in* N. Davies, A. M. Smith, S. R. Whyte, and V. Williams (eds.), Why Whales? Whale and Dolphin Conservation Society, Bath, U.K.

Bassos, M. K. 1993. A behavioral assessment of the reintroduction of two bottlenose dolphins. M.S. thesis, University of California, Santa Cruz, CA. 84 pp.

Beach, D. W., and M. T. Weinrich. 1989. Watching the whales: Is an educational adventure for humans turning out to be another threat for endangered species? Oceanus 32 (1): 84–88.

Beck, B. 1995. Reintroduction, zoos, conservation, and animal welfare. Pages 155–163 *in* B. G. Norton, M. Hutchins, E. F. Stevens, and T. L. Maple (eds.), Ethics on the Ark: Zoos, Animal Welfare, and Wildlife Conservation. Smithsonian Institution Press, Washington, DC.

Bertram, G. C. L., and C. K. Ricardo Bertram. 1977. The status and husbandry of manatees *Trichechus* spp. International Zoo Yearbook 17:106–108.

Best, P. B., and G. J. B. Ross. 1984. Live-capture fishery for small cetaceans in South African waters. Reports of the International Whaling Commission 34:615–618.

Bigg, M. A. 1982. An assessment of killer whale (*Orcinus orca*) stocks off Vancouver Island, British Columbia. Reports of the International Whaling Commission 32:655–666.

Bigg, M. A., and A. A. Wolman. 1975. Live-capture killer whale (*Orcinus orca*) fishery, British Columbia and Washington, 1962–73. Journal of the Fisheries Research Board of Canada 32:1213–1221.

Bigg, M. A., P. F. Olesiuk, G. M. Ellis, J. K. B. Ford, and K. C. Balcomb III. 1990. Social organization and genealogy of resident killer whales (*Orcinus orca*) in the coastal waters of British Columbia and Washington State. Reports of the International Whaling Commission (Special Issue 12): 383–405.

Blunt, W. 1976. The Ark in the Park: The Zoo in the Nineteenth Century. Hamish Hamilton and The Tryon Gallery, London.

Bock, P. 1994. Whale watcher. The Seattle Times, Pacific, 23 October, pp. 14–23.

Bowers, C. A., and R. S. Henderson. 1972. Project Deep Ops: Deep object recovery with pilot and killer whales. Report NUC TP 306. Naval Undersea Center, San Diego, CA.

Brill, R. L. 1994. Return to the wild as an option for managing Atlantic bottlenose dolphins. Pages 337–342 *in* American Zoo and Aquarium Association Annual Conference Proceedings.

Brill, R. L., and W. A. Friedl. 1993. Reintroduction to the wild as an option for managing Navy marine mammals. Naval Command, Control and Ocean Surveillance Center, San Diego, CA. Technical Report 1549. 16 pp. + appendices.

Brown, D. H., and K. S. Norris. 1956. Observations of captive and wild cetaceans. Journal of Mammalogy 37:311–326.

Brown, D. H., D. K. Caldwell, and M. C. Caldwell. 1966. Observations on the behavior of wild and captive false killer whales, with notes on associated behavior of other genera of captive dolphins. Los Angeles County Museum Contributions in Science 95:1–32.

Brownlee, S. 1986. Ambassadors for their species. Pacific Discovery 39 (4): 7–19.

Bryant, L. 1994. Report to Congress on results of feeding wild dolphins: 1989–1994. National Marine Fisheries Service, Office of Protected Resources, Silver Spring, MD.

Bryden, M. M., and R. Harrison. 1986. Preface. Pages v–viii *in* M. M. Bryden and R. Harrison (eds.), Research on Dolphins. Clarendon Press, Oxford, U.K. 478 pp.

Buck, J. D., and S. Spotte. 1986. Microbiology of captive white-beaked dolphins (*Lagenorhynchus albirostris*) with comments on epizootics. Zoo Biology 5:321–329.

Buckland, F. T. 1868. Curiosities of Natural History, 3d series, 2d ed. Vol. 1. Richard Bentley, London. 352 pp.

Caldwell, D. K., and M. C. Caldwell. 1971. Sounds produced by two rare cetaceans stranded in Florida. Cetology 4:1–6.

Caldwell, M. C., and D. K. Caldwell. 1991. A note describing sounds recorded from two cetacean species, *Kogia breviceps* and *Mesoplodon europaeus*, stranded in northeastern Florida. Pages 151–154 *in* J. E. Reynolds III and D. K. O'Dell (eds.), Marine Mammal Strandings in the United States. NOAA Technical Report NMFS-98.

Caldwell, M. C., D. K. Caldwell, and R. L. Brill. 1989. *Inia geoffrensis* in captivity in the United States. Pages 35–41 *in* W. F. Perrin, R. L. Brownell Jr., K. Zhou, and J. Liu (eds.), Biology and Conservation of the River Dolphins. Occasional Papers of the IUCN Species Survival Commission No. 3.

Cartmill, M. 1994. Animal rights: A reply to Howard. Journal of Mammalogy 75:1080–1082.

Collet, A. 1984. Live-capture of cetaceans for European institutions. Reports of the International Whaling Commission 34:603–607.

Collet, A., and R. Duguy. 1987. Les Dauphins: Historique et Biologie. Science et Decouvertes, Le Rocher, Monaco. 123 pp.

Conboy, M. E. 1975. Project 'Quick Find': A marine mammal system for object recovery. Rapports et Proces-Verbaux des Réunions Conseil International pour l'Exploration de la Mer 169:487–500.

Crandall, L. S. 1964. The Management of Wild Mammals in Captivity. University of Chicago Press, Chicago, IL. 769 pp.

Curry, B. E., and J. Smith. 1997. Phylogeographic structure of the bottlenose dolphin (*Tursiops truncatus*): Stock identification and implications for management. Pages 227–247 *in* A. E. Dizon, S. J. Chivers, and W. F. Perrin (eds.), Molecular Genetics of Marine Mammals. Society for Marine Mammalogy, Special Publication No. 3.

Davis, R. W., G. A. J. Worthy, B. Würsig, S. K. Lynn, and F. I. Townsend. 1996. Diving behavior and at-sea movements of an Atlantic spotted dolphin in the Gulf of Mexico. Marine Mammal Science 12:569–581.

DeBlieu, J. 1990. The polar bear's dance: Thoughts on wildness and captivity. Orion 9 (2): 24–31.

Defran, R. H., and K. Pryor. 1980. The behavior and training of cetaceans in captivity. Pages 319–362 *in* L. M. Herman (ed.), Cetacean Behavior: Mechanisms and Functions. John Wiley and Sons, New York, NY.

DeMaster, D. P., and J. K. Drevenak. 1988. Survivorship patterns in three species of captive cetaceans. Marine Mammal Science 4:297–311.

Dohl, T. P., K. S. Norris, and I. Kang. 1974. A porpoise hybrid: *Tursiops* × *Steno*. Journal of Mammalogy 55:217–221.

Duffield, D., and N. Dimeo-Ediger. 1984. Marine mammals in captivity: Census and significance. Whalewatcher 18 (4): 14–15.

Duffield, D. A., and K. W. Miller. 1988. Demographic features of killer whales in oceanaria in the United States and Canada, 1965–1987. Rit Fiskideildar 11:297–306.

Duffield, D. A., and R. S. Wells. 1993. A discussion on comparative data of wild and oceanarium *Tursiops* populations. Pages 28–39 *in* N. F. Hecker (ed.), Proceedings of the 18th International Marine Animal Trainers Association Conference. 4–9 November 1990, Chicago, IL.

Duffield, D. A., D. K. Odell, J. F. McBain, and B. Andrews. 1995. Killer whale (*Orcinus orca*) reproduction at Sea World. Zoo Biology 14:417–430.

Duffus, D. A., and P. Dearden. 1990. Non-consumptive wildlife-oriented recreation: A conceptual framework. Biological Conservation 53:213–231.

Early, G., and T. Rumage. 1988. A whale's fancy and the three that got away. Whalewatcher 22 (1): 3–5.

Ehlers, K. 1965. Records of the hooded seal, *Cystophora cristata* Erxl, and other animals at Bremerhaven Zoo. International Zoo Yearbook 5:148–149.

Evans, W. E., and F. H. Wolfson. 1984. Cetaceans in captivity: Attitudinal impact and value as an educational resource. Whalewatcher 18 (4): 16–18.

Foose, T. J. 1983. The relevance of captive populations to the conservation of biotic diversity. Pages 374–401 *in* C. M. Schonewald-Cox, S. M. Chambers, B. MacBryde, and W. L. Thomas (eds.), Genetics and Conservation: A Reference for Managing Wild Animal and Plant Populations. Benjamin/Cummings, Menlo Park, CA.

Freeman, M. M. R. 1990. A commentary on political issues with regard to contemporary whaling. North Atlantic Studies 2 (1–2): 106–116.

Frohoff, T. G., and J. M. Packard. 1995. Human interactions with free-ranging and captive bottlenose dolphins. Anthrozoös 8:44–53.

Gales, N., and K. Waples. 1993. The rehabilitation and release of bottlenose dolphins from Atlantis Marine Park, Western Australia. Aquatic Mammals 19:49–59.

Geraci, J. R., J. Harwood, and V. J. Lounsbury. 1999. Marine mammal die-offs: Causes, investigations, and issues. (This volume)

Gerrodette, T., and W. G. Gilmartin. 1990. Demographic consequences of changed pupping and hauling sites of the Hawaiian monk seal. Conservation Biology 4:423–430.

Griffith, B., J. M. Scott, J. W. Carpenter, and C. Reed. 1989. Translocation as a species conservation tool: Status and strategy. Science 245:477–480.

Herald, E. S., R. L. Brownell Jr., F. L. Frye, E. J. Morris, W. E. Evans, and A. B. Scott. 1969. Blind river dolphin: First side-swimming cetacean. Science 166:1408–1410.

Herman, L. M. (ed.). 1980. Cetacean Behavior: Mechanisms and Functions. John Wiley and Sons, New York, NY.

Hersh, S. L., D. K. Odell, and E. D. Asper. 1990. Bottlenose dolphin mortality patterns in the Indian/Banana River system of Florida. Pages 155–164 *in* S. Leatherwood and R. R. Reeves (eds.), The Bottlenose Dolphin. Academic Press, San Diego, CA.

Hindley, M. P. 1984. Psychological aspects of cetaceans in captivity. Whalewatcher 18 (4): 4–7.

Hohn, A. A., and D. M. Wilkinson. 1996. Rehabilitating stranded cetaceans and pinnipeds: Management issues and data summary. Pages 30–42 *in* D. J. St. Aubin, J. R. Geraci, and V. J. Lounsbury (eds.), Rescue, Rehabilitation, and Release of Marine Mammals: An Analysis of Current Views and Practices. Proceedings of a Workshop Held in Des Plaines, Illinois, 3–5 December 1991. U.S. Department of Commerce, NOAA Technical Memorandum NMFS-OPR-8.

Howard, C. J. 1995. Dolphin Chronicles. Bantam Books, New York, NY. 304 pp.

Hoyt, E. 1990. Orca the whale called killer. Camden House, Camden East, Ontario, Canada. 291 pp.

Hoyt, E. 1992. The performing orca—why the show must stop. An in-depth review of the captive orca industry. Whale and Dolphin Conservation Society, Bath, U.K. 102 pp.

Huffman, W. E. 1970. Notes on the first captive conception and live birth of an Amazon dolphin in North America. Underwater Naturalist 6 (3): 9–11.

International Union for the Conservation of Nature and Natural Resources. 1987. The IUCN position statement on translocation of living organisms: Introductions, re-introductions and restocking. International Union for the Conservation of Nature and Natural Resources, Gland, Switzerland.

International Whaling Commission. 1984. Report of the Scientific Committee. Reports of the International Whaling Commission 34:35–181.

International Whaling Commission. 1992. Report of the Scientific Committee. Reports of the International Whaling Commission 42:51–270.

International Whaling Commission. 1994. Report of the Scientific Committee. Reports of the International Whaling Commission 44:41–201.

Jamieson, D., and T. Regan. 1984. Whales are not cetacean resources—an animal rights view. Whalewatcher 18 (4): 8–10.

Johnson, W. M. 1994. Captive breeding and the Mediterranean monk seal: A focus on Antibes Marineland. International Marine Mammal Association, Guelph, Ontario, Canada. 44 pp.

Jones, M. L. 1992. Longevity of mammals in captivity—an update. In Vivo 6:363–366.

Joseph, B. E., J. E. Antrim, and L. H. Cornell. 1987. Commerson's dolphin (*Cephalorhynchus commersonii*): A discussion of the first live birth within a marine zoological park. Zoo Biology 6:69–77.

Kalland, A. 1993. Management by totemization: Whale symbolism and the anti-whaling campaign. Arctic 46:124–133.

Kanwisher, J. W., and S. H. Ridgway. 1983. The physiological ecology of whales and porpoises. Scientific American 248 (6): 110–120.

Kasuya, T., and H. Marsh. 1984. Life history and reproductive biology of the short-finned pilot whale, *Globicephala macrorhynchus,* off the Pacific coast of Japan. Reports of the International Whaling Commission (Special Issue 6): 259–310.

Kasuya, T., T. Tobayama, and S. Matsui. 1984. Review of the live-capture of small cetaceans in Japan. Reports of the International Whaling Commission 34:597–601.

Kasuya, T., T. Tobayama, T. Saiga, and T. Kataoka. 1986. Perinatal growth of delphinoids: Information from aquarium reared bottlenose dolphins and finless porpoises. Scientific Reports of the Whales Research Institute Tokyo 37:85–97.

Kimura, S., and T. Nemoto. 1956. Note on a minke whale kept alive in aquarium. Scientific Reports of the Whales Research Institute Tokyo 11:181–184.

King, J. E. 1983. Seals of the World, 2d ed. British Museum (Natural History) and Cornell University Press, Ithaca, NY. 240 pp.

Kleiman, D. G. 1989. Reintroduction of captive mammals for conservation. BioScience 39:152–161.

Klinowska, M. 1991. Dolphins, Porpoises and Whales of the World. The IUCN Red Data Book. IUCN, Gland, Switzerland, and Cambridge, U.K.

Klinowska, M., and S. Brown. 1986. A review of dolphinaria. Report prepared for the Department of the Environment, U.K. 247 pp.

Kritzler, H. 1949. The pilot whale at Marineland. Natural History 58:302–308, 331–332.

Kritzler, H. 1952. Observations on the pilot whale in captivity. Journal of Mammalogy 33:321–334.

Larsen, T. 1978. The World of the Polar Bear. Hamlyn, London. 96 pp.

Leatherwood, S., and R. R. Reeves. 1978. Porpoises and dolphins. Pages 96–111 *in* D. Haley (ed.), Marine Mammals of Eastern North Pacific and Arctic Waters. Pacific Search Press, Seattle, WA. 256 pp.

Leatherwood, S., and R. R. Reeves. 1982. Bottlenose dolphin *Tursiops truncatus* and other toothed cetaceans. Pages 369–414 *in* J. A. Chapman and G. A. Feldhamer (eds.), Wild Mammals of North America: Biology, Management, and Economics. Johns Hopkins University Press, Baltimore, MD.

Leatherwood, S., and R. R. Reeves (eds.). 1990. The Bottlenose Dolphin. Academic Press, San Diego, CA.

Liu, R. 1991. New advances on population status and protective measures for *Lipotes vexillifer* and *Neophocaena phocaenoides* in the Changjiang River. Aquatic Mammals 17:181–183.

Loftin, R. 1995. Captive breeding of endangered species. Pages 164–180 *in* B. G. Norton, M. Hutchins, E. F. Stevens, and T. L. Maple (eds.), Ethics on the Ark: Zoos, Animal Welfare, and Wildlife Conservation. Smithsonian Institution Press, Washington, DC.

Loureiro, J. E. 1985. Stranding of a black porpoise (*Phocoena spinipinnis*) (Cetacea, Phocoenidae) in Bahia Samborombon, Prov. of Bs. Aires. Page 30 *in* Primera Reunion de Trabajo de Expertos en Mamiferos Acuaticos de America del Sur, Conclusiones. 25–29 June 1984, Buenos Aires, Argentina.

Lubbock, B. 1937. The Arctic Whalers. Brown, Son and Ferguson, Glasgow. 483 pp.

Lynn, S. K., and D. L. Reiss. 1992. Pulse sequence and whistle production by two captive beaked whales, *Mesoplodon* species. Marine Mammal Science 8:299–305.

Malev, A. V., V. S. Andreyevskaya, I. V. Egorov, G. M. Nekrasova, T. M. Golubetseva, E. D. Tkachenko, and T. E. Lysenko. 1991. Breeding of polar bears (*Ursus maritimus*) in the zoos of the Soviet Union. Page 89 *in* S. C. Amstrup and O. Wiig (eds.), Polar Bears. Proceedings of the 10th working meeting of the IUCN/SSC Polar Bear Specialist Group. Occasional Papers of the IUCN Species Survival Commission No. 7.

Marine Mammal Commission. 1974. Annual report to Congress for 1973. (Available from National Technical Information Service, Springfield, VA. PB-269 709.) 14 pp.

Marine Mammal Commission. 1976. Annual report to Congress for 1975. (Available from National Technical Information Service, Springfield, VA. PB 269-711.) 50 pp.

Marine Mammal Commission. 1980. Annual report to Congress for 1979. (Available from National Technical Information Service, Springfield, VA. PB81-247-892.) 100 pp.

Marine Mammal Commission. 1994. Annual report to Congress for 1993. (Available from National Technical Information Service, Springfield, VA. PB95-154530.) 260 pp.

Marine Mammal Commission. 1995. Annual report to Congress for 1994. (Available from National Technical Information Service, Springfield, VA. PB95-173233.) 270 pp.

Marmontel, M. 1995. Age and reproduction in female Florida manatees. Pages 98–119 *in* T. J. O'Shea, B. B. Ackerman, and H. F. Perceval (eds.), Population Biology of the Florida Manatee. U.S. Department of the Interior, National Biological Service, Information and Technology Report 1.

Marshall, J., and B. R. Henry. N.d. Manatees: The last generation? An evaluation and interpretive elements study. Report prepared for Sea World of Florida, Orlando, FL.

Mate, B. R., K. M. Stafford, R. Nawojchik, and J. L. Dunn. 1994. Movements and dive behavior of a satellite-monitored Atlantic white-sided dolphin (*Lagenorhynchus acutus*) in the Gulf of Maine. Marine Mammal Science 10:116–121.

Maxwell, G. 1967. Seals of the World. Houghton Mifflin, Boston, MA. 151 pp.

McKenna, V. 1992. Into the Blue. Harper, San Francisco, CA. 144 pp.

Mead, J. G., and C. W. Potter. 1995. Recognizing two populations of the bottlenose dolphin (*Tursiops truncatus*) off the Atlantic coast of North America: Morphologic and ecologic considerations. IBI Reports [International Marine Biological Research Institute, Kamogawa, Japan] 5:31–44.

Medway, W., and F. Moldovan. 1966. Blood studies in the North Atlantic pilot (pothead) whale, *Globicephala melaena* (Traill, 1809). Physiological Zoology 39:110–116.

Mlot, C. 1984. The dolphin science sabbatical. Whalewatcher 18 (3): 17,19.

Mohr, E. 1952. Die Robben der europäischen Gewässer. Monographien der Wildsäugetiere. Band 12. Paul Schöps, Frankfurt am Main. 283 pp.

Monzón, F., and J. Corcuera. 1991. Franciscana *Pontoporia blainvillei* (Gervais & d'Orbigny, 1844). Pages 16–22 *in* H. L. Capozzo and M. Junín (eds.), Estado de Conservación de los Mamíferos Marinos del Atlántico Sudoccidental. Informes y Estudios del Programa de Mares Regionales del PNUMA (UNEP) 138.

Morris, J. 1993. Marine World raked for taking whales from Japanese roundup. Contra Costa Times, 9 April.

Nachtigall, P. E., and P. W. B. Moore (eds.). 1988. Animal Sonar: Processes and Performance. Plenum Press, New York, NY. 862 pp.

Nachtigall, P. E., J. Lien, W. W. L. Au, and A. J. Read (eds.). 1995. Harbour Porpoises: Laboratory Studies to Reduce Bycatch. De Spil Publishers, Woerden, the Netherlands.

Newman, M. A. 1971. Capturing narwhals for the Vancouver Public Aquarium, 1970. Polar Record 15:922–923.

Newman, M. A., and P. L. McGeer. 1966. The capture and care of a killer whale, *Orcinus orca,* in British Columbia. Zoologica 51 (5): 59–70.

Nishiwaki, M., and T. Tobayama. 1982. Morphological study on the hybrid between *Tursiops* and *Pseudorca.* Scientific Reports of the Whales Research Institute Tokyo 34:109–121.

Nishiwaki, M., M. Nakajima, and T. Kamiya. 1965. A rare species of dolphin (*Stenella attenuata*) from Arari, Japan. Scientific Reports of the Whales Research Institute Tokyo 19:53–64.

Nishiwaki, M., T. Kasuya, T. Kamiya, T. Tobayama, and M. Nakajima. 1965. *Feresa attenuata* captured at the Pacific coast of Japan in 1963. Scientific Reports of the Whales Research Institute Tokyo 19:65–90.

Norris, K. S. 1974. The Porpoise Watcher. W. W. Norton, New York, NY. 250 pp.

Norris, K. S. 1991. Looking at captive dolphins. Pages 293–303 *in* K. Pryor and K. S. Norris (eds.), Dolphin Societies: Discoveries and Puzzles. University of California Press, Berkeley, CA.

Norris, K. S. 1995. Foreword. Pages ix–xiii *in* C. J. Howard, Dolphin Chronicles. Bantam Books, New York, NY.

Norris, K. S., and J. H. Prescott. 1961. Observations on Pacific cetaceans of Californian and Mexican waters. University of California Publications in Zoology 63:291–402.

Norris, K. S., B. Würsig, R. S. Wells, and M. Würsig. 1994. The Hawaiian Spinner Dolphin. University of California Press, Berkeley, CA.

Norton, B. G., M. Hutchins, E. F. Stevens, and T. L. Maple (eds.). 1995. Ethics on the Ark: Zoos, Animal Welfare, and Wildlife Conservation. Smithsonsian Institution Press, Washington, DC. 330 pp.

Nowak, R. M., and J. L. Paradiso. 1983. Walker's Mammals of the World, 4th ed. Johns Hopkins University Press, Baltimore, MD.

Olesiuk, P. F., M. A. Bigg, and G. M. Ellis. 1990. Life history and population dynamics of resident killer whales (*Orcinus orca*) in the coastal waters of British Columbia and Washington State. Reports of the International Whaling Commission (Special Issue 12): 209–243.

Orams, M. B. 1995. Tourism and marine wildlife: The wild dolphins of Tangalooma, Australia: A case report. Anthrozoös 7:195–201.

Pelletier, C., and F. Pelletier. 1986. Bhulan, dauphin sacré. L'univers du Vivant 3:8–19.

Perrin, W. F. 1999. Selected examples of small cetaceans at risk. (This volume)

Perrin, W. F., and R. L. Brownell Jr. (eds.). 1989. Report of the Workshop. Pages 1–22 *in* W. F. Perrin, R. L. Brownell Jr., K. Zhou, and J. Liu (eds.), Biology and Conservation of the River Dolphins. Occasional Papers of the IUCN Species Survival Commission No. 3.

Peterson, J. H., Jr. 1993. Epilogue: Whales and elephants as cultural symbols. Arctic 46:172–174.

Pilleri, G. 1983. Cetaceans in captivity. Investigations on Cetacea 15:221–249.

Pliny. 1967. Pliny natural history with an English translation in 10 volumes. Vol. 3. By H. Rackham. Harvard University Press, Cambridge, MA.

Pryor, K. 1975. Lads before the Wind: Adventures in Porpoise Training. Harper and Row, New York, NY. 278 pp.

Pryor, K., and I. K. Shallenberger. 1991. Social structure in spotted dolphins (*Stenella attenuata*) in the tuna purse seine fishery in the eastern tropical Pacific. Pages 160–196 *in* K. Pryor and K. S. Norris (eds.), Dolphin Societies: Discoveries and Puzzles. University of California Press, Berkeley, CA.

Pryor, T., K. Pryor, and K. S. Norris. 1965. Observations on a pygmy killer whale (*Feresa attenuata* Gray) from Hawaii. Journal of Mammalogy 46:450–461.

Ragen, T. J., and D. M. Lavigne. 1999. The Hawaiian monk seal: Biology of an endangered species. (This volume)

Ralls, K. 1989. A semi-captive breeding program for the baiji, *Lipotes vexillifer:* Genetic and demographic considerations. Pages 150–156 *in* W. F. Perrin, R. L. Brownell Jr., K. Zhou, and J. Liu (eds.), Biology and Conservation of the River Dolphins. Occasional Papers of the IUCN Species Survival Commission No. 3.

Reeves, R. R., and S. Leatherwood. 1984. Live-capture fisheries for cetaceans in USA and Canadian waters, 1973–1982. Reports of the International Whaling Commission 34:497–507.

Reeves, R. R., D. P. DeMaster, C. L. Hill, and S. Leatherwood. 1994. Survivorship of odontocete cetaceans at Ocean Park, Hong Kong, 1974–1994. Asian Marine Biology 11:107–124.

Reijnders, P. J. H., S. M. J. M. Brasseur, and E. H. Ries. 1996. The release of seals from captive breeding and rehabilitation programs: A useful conservation tool? Pages 54–57 *in* D. J. St. Aubin, J. R. Geraci, and V. J. Lounsbury (eds.), Rescue, Rehabilitation, and Release of Marine Mammals: An Analysis of Current Views and Practices. Proceedings of a Workshop Held in Des Plaines, Illinois, 3–5 December 1991. U.S. Department of Commerce, NOAA Technical Memorandum NMFS-OPR-8.

Reynolds, J. E., III. 1999. Efforts to conserve the manatees. (This volume)

Reynolds, J. E., III, and D. K. Odell. 1991. Manatees and dugongs. Facts on File, Inc., New York, NY. 192 pp.

Rice, D. W. 1973. Caribbean monk seal (*Monachus tropicalis*). Pages 98–112 *in* C. W. Holloway (ed.), Seals: Proceedings of a working meeting of seal specialists on threatened and depleted seals of the world, held under the auspices of the Survival Service Commission of IUCN, 18–19 August 1972, University of Guelph, Guelph, Ontario, Canada. International Union for Conservation of Nature and Natural Resources, Morges, Switzerland.

Richard, P. R., J. R. Orr, and D. G. Barber. 1990. The distribution and abundance of belugas, *Delphinapterus leucas,* in eastern Canadian subarctic waters: A review and update. Canadian Special Publication of Fisheries and Aquatic Sciences 224:23–38.

Ridgway, S. H. 1966. Dall porpoise, *Phocoenoides dalli* (True): Observations in captivity and at sea. Norsk Hvalfangst-tidende 55:97–110.

Ridgway, S. H. 1987. The Dolphin Doctor. Yankee Books, Dublin, NH. 159 pp.

Ridgway, S. H. 1990. The central nervous system of the bottlenose dolphin. Pages 69–97 *in* S. Leatherwood and R. R. Reeves (eds.), The Bottlenose Dolphin. Academic Press, San Diego, CA.

Ridgway, S. H. 1995. The tides of change: Conservation of marine mammals. *In* J. Demarest, B. Durrant, and E. Gibbons (eds.), Conservation of Endangered Species in Captivity: An Integrated Approach. State University of New York Press, Albany, NY.

Ridgway, S. H., and R. J. Harrison (eds.). 1981a. Handbook of Marine Mammals. Vol. 1. The Walrus, Sea Lions, Fur Seals and Sea Otter. Academic Press, London.

Ridgway, S. H., and R. J. Harrison (eds.). 1981b. Handbook of Marine Mammals. Vol. 2. Seals. Academic Press, London.

Ridgway, S. H., and R. Harrison (eds.). 1985. Handbook of Marine Mammals. Vol. 3. The Sirenians and Baleen Whales. Academic Press, London.

Ridgway, S. H., and R. Harrison (eds.). 1989. Handbook of Marine Mammals. Vol. 4. River Dolphins and the Larger Toothed Whales. Academic Press, London.

Ridgway, S. H., and R. Harrison (eds.). 1994. Handbook of Marine Mammals. Vol. 5. The First Book of Dolphins. Academic Press, London.

Ridgway, S. H., K. S. Norris, and L. H. Cornell. 1989. Some considerations for those wishing to propagate platanistoid dolphins. Pages 159–167 *in* W. F. Perrin, R. L. Brownell Jr., K. Zhou, and J. Liu (eds.), Biology and Conservation of the River Dolphins. Occasional Papers of the IUCN Species Survival Commission No. 3.

Riedman, M. 1990. The Pinnipeds: Seals, Sea Lions, and Walruses. University of California Press, Berkeley, CA. 439 pp.

Riedman, M. L., and J. A. Estes. 1990. The sea otter (*Enhydra lutris*): Behavior, ecology, and natural history. U.S. Department of the Interior, Fish and Wildlife Service, Biological Report 90 (14): 1–127.

Rigas, G., and K. Ronald. 1985. Observations on the biology and behaviour of the Mediterranean monk seal. Aquatic Mammals 11:23–26.

Riley, D. 1993. Our love of dolphins has turned into a questionable affair. Smithsonian 23 (10): 58–67.

Robeck, T. R., B. E. Curry, J. F. McBain, and D. C. Kraemer. 1994. Reproductive biology of the bottlenose dolphin (*Tursiops truncatus*) and the potential application of advanced reproductive technologies. Journal of Zoo and Wildlife Medicine 25:321–336.

Rosas, F. C. W. 1994. Biology, conservation and status of the Amazonian manatee *Trichechus inunguis.* Mammal Review 24 (2): 49–59.

Rose, N. A. 1994. Keiko update. Whalewatcher 28 (1): 22.

Ross, G. J. B., and V. G. Cockcroft. 1990. Comments on Australian bottlenose dolphins and the taxonomic status of *Tursiops aduncus* (Ehrenberg, 1832). Pages 101–128 *in* S. Leatherwood and R. R. Reeves (eds.), The Bottlenose Dolphin. Academic Press, San Diego, CA.

Ross, G. J. B., F. Ryan, G. S. Saayman, and J. Skinner. 1976. Observations on two captive crabeater seals *Lobodon carcinophagus.* International Zoo Yearbook 16:160–164.

Saayman, G. S., C. K. Tayler, and D. Bower. 1973. Diurnal activity cycles in captive and free-ranging Indian Ocean bottlenose dolphins (*Tursiops aduncus* Ehrenburg). Behaviour 44:212–233.

Samuels, A., and T. R. Spradlin. 1995. Quantitative behavioral study of bottlenose dolphins in swim-with-dolphin programs in the United States. Marine Mammal Science 11:520–544.

Scheffer, V. 1991. Why should we care about whales? Pages 17–19 *in* N. Davies, A. M. Smith, S. R. Whyte, and V. Williams (eds.), Why Whales? Whale and Dolphin Conservation Society, Bath, U.K.

Schroeder, J. P., and K. V. Keller. 1990. Artificial insemination of bottlenose dolphins. Pages 447–460 *in* S. Leatherwood and R. R. Reeves (eds.), The Bottlenose Dolphin. Academic Press, San Diego, CA.

Schusterman, R. J., J. A. Thomas, and F. G. Wood (eds.). 1986. Dolphin Cognition and Behavior: A Comparative Approach. Lawrence Erlbaum Associates, Hillsdale, NJ. 393 pp.

Scott, G. P. 1990. Management-oriented research on bottlenose dolphins by the Southeast Fisheries Center. Pages 623–639 *in* S. Leatherwood and R. R. Reeves (eds.), The Bottlenose Dolphin. Academic Press, San Diego, CA.

Shackley, M. 1992. Manatees and tourism in southern Florida: Opportunity or threat? Journal of Environmental Management 34:257–265.

Shallenberger, E. W. 1981. The status of Hawaiian cetaceans. Report prepared for Marine Mammal Commission. (Available from National Technical Information Service, Springfield, VA. PB82-109398.) 79 pp.

Sigurjónsson, J., and S. Leatherwood. 1988. The Icelandic live-capture fishery for killer whales, 1976–1988. Rit Fiskideildar 11:307–316.

Small, R. J., and D. P. DeMaster. 1995a. Survival of five species of captive marine mammals. Marine Mammal Science 11:209–226.

Small, R. J., and D. P. DeMaster. 1995b. Acclimation to captivity a quantitative estimate based on survival of bottlenose dolphins and California sea lions. Marine Mammal Science 11:510–519.

Smith, A. M. 1991. Prisoners in paradise. Sonar 6:14–15.

Spotte, S. H. 1967. Intergeneric behavior between captive Amazon river dolphins *Inia* and *Sotalia*. Underwater Naturalist 4 (2): 9–13.

Spotte, S., J. L. Dunn, L. E. Kezer, and F. M. Heard. 1978. Notes on the care of a beach-stranded harbor porpoise (*Phocoena phocoena*). Cetology 32:1–6.

St. Aubin, D. J., J. R. Geraci, and V. J. Lounsbury (eds.). 1996. Rescue, Rehabilitation, and Release of Marine Mammals: An Analysis of Current Views and Practices. Proceedings of a Workshop Held in Del Plaines, Illinois, 3–5 December 1991. U.S. Department of Commerce, NOAA Technical Memorandum NMFS-OPR-8.

St. Aubin, D. J., S. H. Ridgway, R. S. Wells, and H. Rhinehart. 1996. Dolphin thyroid and adrenal hormones: Circulating levels in wild and semidomesticated *Tursiops truncatus,* and influence of sex, age, and season. Marine Mammal Science 12:1–13.

Steuer, K. L. 1989. A comparative institutional survey of factors influencing mortality of cetaceans in U.S. zoos and aquaria. Unpublished report prepared by the Center for Coastal Studies, Provincetown, MA, for Animal Protection Institute of America, International Wildlife Coalition, and Humane Society of the United States.

St. John, P. 1986. Dolphins, autistic children and non-verbal communication. Whalewatcher 20 (4): 23–25.

Sylvestre, J. P. 1983. Review of *Kogia* specimens (Physeteridae, Koginae) kept alive in captivity. Investigations on Cetacea 15:201–219.

Sylvestre, J.-P. and S. Tasaka. 1985. On the intergeneric hybrids in cetaceans. Aquatic Mammals 11:101–108.

Tas'an and S. Leatherwood. 1984. Cetaceans live-captured for Jaya Ancol Oceanarium, Djakarta, 1974–1982. Reports of the International Whaling Commission 34:485–489.

Temte, J. L. 1993. The Marine Mammal Inventory Report: Independent verification of a captive marine mammal database. Marine Mammal Science 9:95–98.

Tobayama, T., and T. Kamiya. 1989. Observations on *Inia geoffrensis* and *Platanista gangetica* in captivity at Kamogawa Sea World, Japan. Pages 42–45 *in* W. F. Perrin, R. L. Brownell Jr., K. Zhou, and J. Liu (eds.), Biology and Conservation of the River Dolphins. Occasional Papers of the IUCN Species Survival Commission No. 3.

Townsend, C. H. 1914. At last—a school of porpoises. Zoological Society Bulletin 17 (2): 1081–1084.

Townsend, C. H. 1934. The fur seal of the Galapagos Islands. Zoologica 18 (2): 43–56.

Tyack, P. L. 1989. Let's have less public relations and more ecology. Oceanus 32 (1): 103–108.

Walker, W. A. 1975. Review of the live-capture fishery for small cetaceans taken in southern California waters for public display, 1966–73. Journal of the Fisheries Research Board of Canada 32:1197–1211.

Wells, R. S. 1989. Return to the wild: Completion of a 'dolphin sabbatical.' Whalewatcher 23 (4): 3–5.

Wells, R. S., and M. D. Scott. 1990. Estimating bottlenose dolphin population parameters from individual identification and capture-release techniques. Reports of the International Whaling Commission (Special Issue 12): 407–415.

Wilkinson, D., and G. A. J. Worthy. 1999. Marine mammal stranding networks. (This volume)

Wood, F. G., Jr. 1953. Underwater sound production and concurrent behavior of captive porpoises, *Tursiops truncatus* and *Stenella plagiodon*. Bulletin of Marine Science of the Gulf and Caribbean 3:120–133.

Wood, F. G. 1973. Marine Mammals and Man: The Navy's Porpoises and Sea Lions. Robert B. Luce, Washington, DC.

Wood, F. G. 1977. Birth of porpoises at Marineland, Florida, 1939 to 1969, and comments on problems involved in captive breeding of small Cetacea. Pages 47–60 *in* S. H. Ridgway and K. Benirschke (eds.), Breeding dolphins—present status, suggestions for the future. Report prepared for Marine Mammal Commission. (Available from National Technical Information Service, Springfield, VA. PB-273 673.)

Woodley, T. H., J. L. Hannah, and D. M. Lavigne. 1994. A comparison of survival rates for captive and free-ranging bottlenose dolphins (*Tursiops truncatus*), killer whales (*Orcinus orca*) and beluga whales (*Delphinapterus leucas*). International Marine Mammal Association, Guelph, Ontario. Draft Technical Report No. 93-01. 42 pp.

Woolfenden, J. 1979. The California sea otter: Saved or doomed? Boxwood Press, Pacific Grove, CA. 172 pp.

York, A. E. 1994. The population dynamics of northern sea lions, 1975–1985. Marine Mammal Science 10:38–51.

20

GARY K. MEFFE, WILLIAM F. PERRIN, AND PAUL K. DAYTON

Marine Mammal Conservation

Guiding Principles and Their Implementation

In the preceding chapters, you have read how humanity has adversely affected marine mammal species and populations. Some, like the North Atlantic population of gray whales (*Eschrichtius robustus*) and Steller's sea cow (*Hydrodamalis gigas*), have become extinct, and others, like the baiji (*Lipotes vexillifer*) and the vaquita (*Phocoena sinus*), are close behind. The causes are diverse and include direct hunting, incidental kill in fisheries, and habitat loss or degradation caused by development and pollution.

The same pattern, of course, exists for many other wild living resources, from fishes, reptiles, birds, and mammals to forests, grasslands, and coral reefs. No other species has approached mankind's capability for destruction, and none has so changed the earth's ecosystems, perturbed life's diversity, and altered evolutionary patterns. Ironically, human existence depends on a functioning natural world (Daily 1997), and this global ecological decline will eventually put our species in jeopardy. However, it is also true that no other species can examine itself, look at where it has been and what it has done, extrapolate into the future, and predict consequences of its actions. It is well within our ability to critically judge our actions and change course.

In this chapter, we offer a set of principles for the conservation of wild living resources, including marine mammals. These are modified and reorganized from the more detailed presentation by Mangel et al. (1996), which built on Holt and Talbot (1978). Because the problems facing marine mammals are not merely biological, solutions will require an understanding of human motivations and value systems and the recognition of what we do and do not know. The principles advocated here therefore require the application and integration of biological, ecological, economic, sociological, political, and institutional knowledge.

An ideal relationship between humans and nature would safeguard the viability of all biota and the ecosystems of which they are a part and on which they depend, while allowing human benefit, for present and future generations, through various consumptive and nonconsumptive uses. The challenge is to determine an appropriate balance between resource and ecosystem use on one hand and the health and quality of human life on the other. But it must be remembered that human health and prosperity ultimately depend on healthy, functioning, and diverse ecosystems (Daily 1997).

It is crucial to understand that the principles described here (summarized in Table 20-1) are not a "recipe" listing exactly what needs to be done. Rather, they are meant to initiate a comprehensive discussion of key questions and ideas. Knowledge and institutions are imperfect, so changes in principles and ways to implement them will be needed over

Table 20-1. Summary of the Principles Discussed in This Chapter

Principle I	Maintenance of healthy populations of wild marine mammals in perpetuity is inconsistent with ever-growing human consumption of marine resources.
Principle II	Regulation of the use of marine mammals must be based on an understanding of the structure and dynamics of the ecosystems of which they are a part.
Principle III	The human species, with all its activities, needs, aspirations, and diverse values, affects every marine ecosystem, and this fact must be addressed and accommodated in the management of any living marine resource. All stakeholders must be included in the process of determining optimal management strategies.
Principle IV	Assessment of the possible ecological, economic, and social effects of using marine mammals as resources should precede both proposed use and proposed restriction of ongoing use.
Principle V	Conservation requires communication and education that are interactive, reciprocal, and continuous.

time. In conservation, there are few self-evident and unvarying laws to guide us; uncertainties, complexities, and idiosyncracies abound at the interface of the human and natural worlds that preclude obvious and easy answers to conservation dilemmas. Individual solutions require creativity, perseverance, and dedication, and those solutions must be revisited and revised as more is learned.

The Principles

Principle I. Maintenance of healthy populations of wild marine mammals in perpetuity is inconsistent with ever-growing human consumption of marine resources.

Infinite growth in a finite system, while maintaining all the natural features of that system, is impossible. The human population cannot continue to expand in size and resource consumption without eventually overwhelming its natural resource base, whether marine mammals, other marine species, or natural resources in general (Fig. 20-1). Thus, the most basic long-term aspect of any conservation effort must be to control human population growth, per capita resource demand, and waste production. This principle is of prime importance because of the current global focus on "sustainable development" (Ludwig et al. 1993). Two standard-setting major reports, the Brundtland Commission's *Our Common Future* (World Commission on Environment and Development 1987) and its successor, *Caring for the Earth: A Strategy for Sustainable Living* (IUCN/UNEP/WWF 1991), have misconstrued the relationships among human population growth, resource consumption, and environmental deterioration. Both reports call for continued economic expansion in developed countries to boost the economic fortunes of less-developed countries; in fact, they advocate expanding global economic activities to 5 to 10 times current levels. However, they fail to examine what happens after this economic expansion. Is it followed by more expansion, ad infinitum? That would seem to be impossible, or at least terribly destructive, and in no sense sustainable. Or will it lead to cessation of growth and a leveling off at a higher plateau? If so, why not level off sooner, while natural resources are more abundant and less damaged, rather than put off the difficult work for future generations?

When humans use resources in ways that allow natural processes to replace what has been used, sustainability is achieved. That is, living off nature's "interest" rather than its "capital" is key to any concept of true sustainability and constitutes good resource management (Daly 1991). This approach, combined with a stable human population and a reduction in our demand on resources, seems essential for conservation.

Principle II. Regulation of the use of marine mammals must be based on an understanding of the structure and dynamics of the ecosystems of which they are a part.

As a general rule, neither the resource nor other components of the ecosystem should be perturbed beyond natural boundaries of variation. Biodiversity should be maintained at genetic, species, population, and ecosystem levels. Marine mammal management must be based on an understanding of the structure and dynamics of the natural system and the constraints presented by that system and by natural

Figure 20-1. (*facing*) Historic world population growth (*above*) and projected population growth (*below*) assuming various fertility scenarios. The medium-fertility scenario assumes that total fertility rates will ultimately stabilize by 2055 at replacement levels (2.1 children per woman). The high-fertility rates will converge by 2050 to between 2.50 and 2.60 children per woman, and the low-fertility scenario assumes that total fertility rates will eventually stabilize at levels between 1.35 and 1.60 children per woman. (Source: Population Reference Bureau and United Nations)

World Population Growth, 1750 - 1993

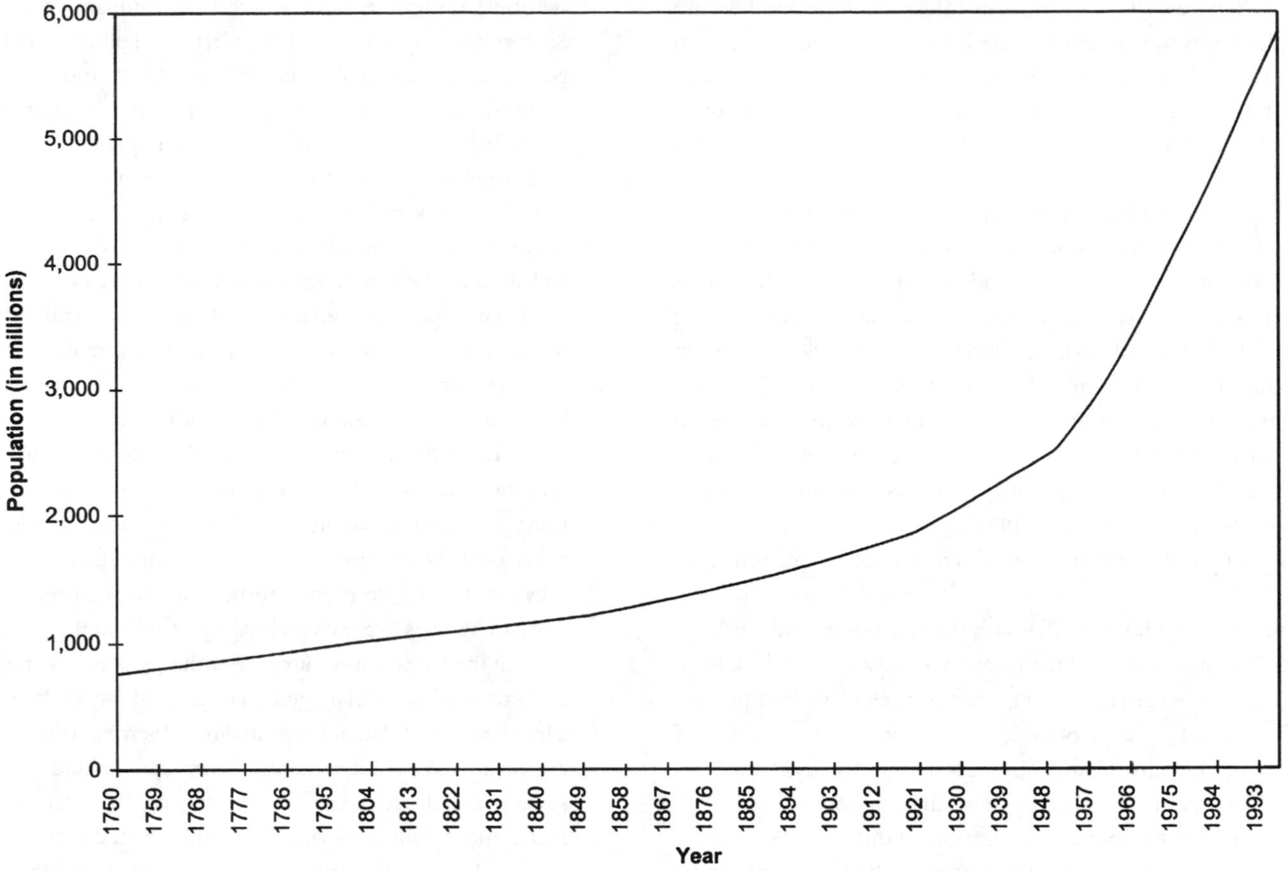

Projected World Population Levels by Fertility Rates

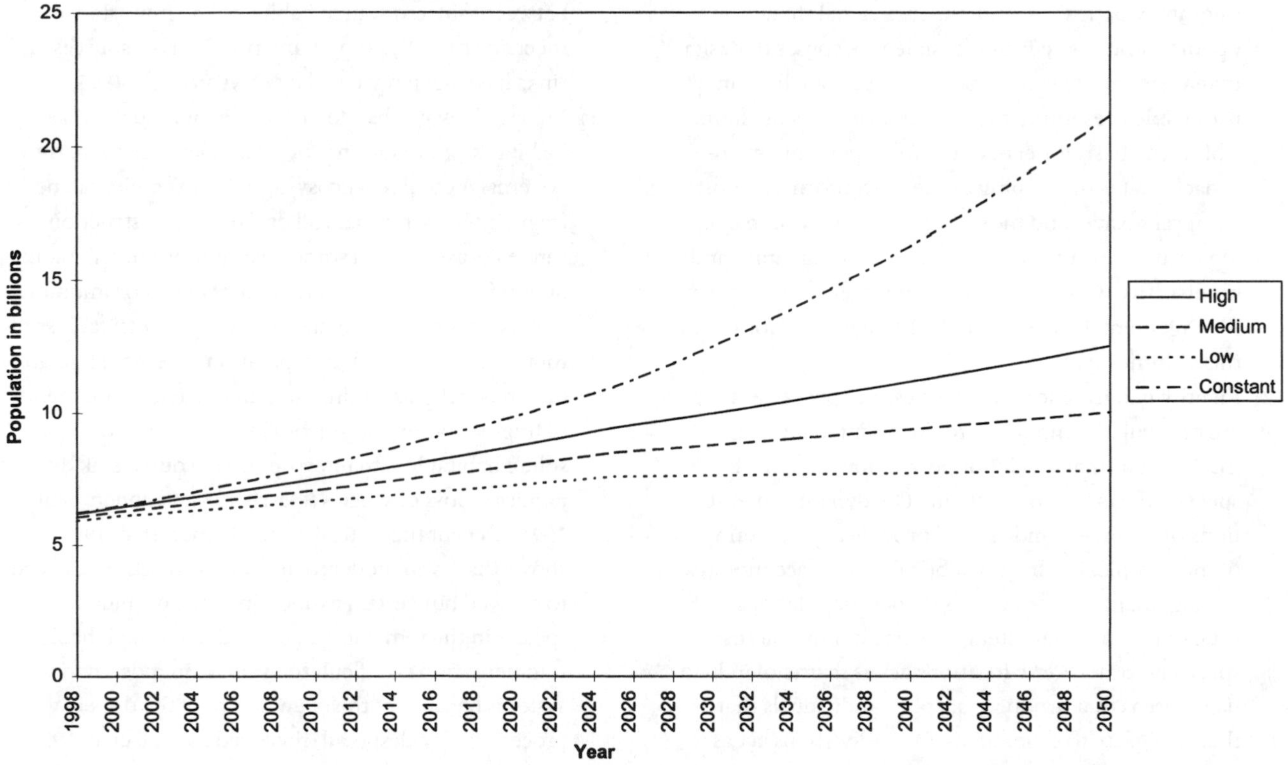

laws; this understanding needs to be conveyed to policy makers so that they can make informed decisions. Because the limits to resource use are based on natural, not human law, and because exceeding those limits can have catastrophic effects on both the ecological and the economic systems (Holling and Meffe 1996), they must be identified clearly.

All forms of life modify their environment (White 1967). Civilization as we know it could not have evolved without transforming ecosystems, and even the earliest civilizations caused considerable environmental degradation (Hong et al. 1994) and mass extinctions (Steadman 1995). However, the destructive capabilities of modern technology are greater than anything in history. This dictates that we explicitly be aware of technology's effects on natural systems and of the potential reduction or loss of biodiversity at all levels (Hughes and Noss 1992).

The following courses of action address this principle.

(1) Manage human effects on the ecosystem, and work to preserve all of the essential ecosystem features. Resource use should be guided by the goals of maintaining a full range of options for future generations and of minimizing changes in the structure and dynamics of populations and ecosystems that cannot be reversed within one human generation (about 20 to 25 years).

The more that is known about the critical features of a given ecosystem—such as nutritional dynamics, life history parameters of interacting species, needs for migratory pathways, and major external threats and opportunities—the more feasible it becomes to design management measures that accommodate human uses while preserving the integrity of the ecosystem. This is the basis for ecosystem management, an approach that is developing as the best-informed, most comprehensive, and most democratic way of managing natural resources for the benefit of humanity and biodiversity (Grumbine 1994, Interagency Ecosystem Management Task Force 1995; Mangel and Hofman, this volume).

(2) Identify geographic areas, species, and processes that are particularly important to the maintenance of a marine mammal species or population, and make special efforts to protect them. The dynamic interactions of "sources" and "sinks" provide a good example of the complexity that must be taken into account in management. Contributions of local populations to total population persistence are not uniform across space and time. Some locations act as *sources* of individuals—areas that produce "surplus" individuals that then emigrate to other areas. Other locations act as *sinks* that cannot maintain themselves indefinitely without immigrants from source areas (Pulliam 1988). Such systems are called *metapopulations*—collections of populations connected by periodic or regular movements of individuals. Metapopulations typically exist across habitat patches that are of uneven quality.

Examples of species that depend on the protection of source areas include marine turtles (Fig. 20-2), birds, gray whales, salmon, abalone, and sea urchins, as well as almost all encrusting invertebrates such as bryozoans, sponges, tunicates, and cnidarians. Thus, the concepts of sources and sinks and metapopulations often are central to understanding and maintaining the health of an ecosystem and the mammals therein.

Because most marine mammals ultimately depend on fishes and invertebrates with pelagic larvae, questions of sources, sinks, and distribution of forage species are critical. An important feature of marine sinks is that they are isolated from one another, yet the persistence of many species depends on healthy "seed" populations in the larval source areas. For this reason, marine systems need to be managed on a regional rather than a local basis, but data for regional management often are lacking. We need to identify larval sources and sinks and evaluate the processes affecting dispersal and recruitment. One important problem for species used for food by coastal marine mammals, such as abalone and sea urchins in the case of sea otters, is that complex coastal currents massively dilute larvae transported between isolated source habitats. The importance, mechanisms, physiology, and problems of sources and sinks have been reviewed by Dayton et al. (1995).

(3) Manage in ways that do not fragment natural areas. Habitat fragmentation is of great relevance to marine systems. A coral reef ecosystem, for example, can be fragmented by mechanical or chemical destruction, as can sea grass beds (in some areas important habitat for dugongs or manatees) and other benthic communities. Habitat fragmentation has two components: (a) loss of total habitat area and (b) separation of remaining habitat into small, discontinuous parcels. The consequences of fragmentation range from loss of gene flow to absolute habitat loss to interruption of source-sink dynamics to loss of species (Harris 1984, Saunders et al. 1991). Recent theoretical work (Tilman et al. 1994) shows that even moderate habitat destruction can lead to delayed but certain extinction of the dominant species in the remaining habitat. Even though habitat fragmentation is difficult to evaluate in most marine systems because of the open nature of the dispersal process, it is widespread (reviewed by Hall et al. 1994

Figure 20-2. This nesting beach provides a protected source location for a metapopulation of olive ridley sea turtles (*Lepidochelys olivacea*). (Photograph by Peter C. H. Pritchard, courtesy of Center for Marine Conservation)

and Dayton 1994 for hard-bottom and soft-bottom benthic species, respectively), and its avoidance should be emphasized in resource management. Obligatory bay and estuarine marine mammals, such as populations of Irrawaddy dolphins (*Orcaella brevirostris*) and hump-backed dolphins (*Sousa* spp.), are examples of potential victims of habitat fragmentation.

(4) Maintain or mimic natural processes at scales appropriate to the natural system. This means defining temporal and spatial scales in accordance with natural disturbances (e.g., hurricanes, tidal fluxes, influx of freshwater from floods, disease), pertinent biological processes (e.g., foraging and reproduction), and dispersal characteristics and capabilities of the relevant populations. All populations have evolved in a milieu of natural disturbances and natural variation, and resilience is determined by adaptation to these processes (Holling 1973, Wiens and Milne 1989). Management needs to take such evolutionary adaptations into account, especially with regard to dependency on disturbances (Starfield et al. 1993). Long-term fieldwork is needed to differentiate between baseline variation and rare catastrophes, which can be confused by short-term observation (Trivelpiece et al. 1990, Young and Isbell 1994).

The life history patterns of species illustrate the importance of structuring exploitation to mimic natural processes. For example, the survival of long-lived species with low growth rates, delayed maturation, and small clutch size depends on high adult survivorship and, usually, multiple reproductive episodes (Congdon et al. 1993). Marine mammals, sea turtles, sharks, and some marine birds have these characteristics and are therefore especially vulnerable to harvest or bycatch mortality. They are not adapted to compensate for high adult mortality. Prolonged excessive harvest or bycatch will inevitably reduce such species to small populations and may eliminate them entirely. Artificial efforts to offset the effects of excessive mortality, such as hatchery rearing or "headstart" programs designed to increase recruitment rates, address only the symptoms and not the underlying causes of declines and will not solve the problem (Frazier 1992, Meffe 1992). What is needed is precautionary management aimed at the cause of population decline, which is often the high take of adults.

Mass mortality caused by disease may be important to the long-term population dynamics of marine mammals, even though it may occur only sporadically and on a time scale not readily apparent from short-term observation (Harwood 1989, Harwood and Hall 1990; Geraci et al., this volume). Repeated catastrophic die-offs can be considered part of environmental stochasticity and can result in a lower population growth rate than predicted by mean survival and reproductive rates estimated from data collected in more "normal" times. Thus, the time scale for modeling assessment and management must be large enough to incorporate the effects of these rare but important events; a time scale that is too short may result in overestimating productivity, overexploitation, and eventual population crash.

(5) Avoid disruption of food webs. The food web is one of the great structuring features of natural communities (Pimm 1991). One of the most interesting differences between marine planktonic and terrestrial systems is that pelagic food webs are influenced only by the relative sizes of the food particles and hence are relatively unstructured taxonomically. Most important, the relatively small reproductive products may constitute a particularly important part of pelagic food webs (Isaacs 1976). For example, copepods are important predators on fish larvae, and those fish larvae that survive and develop become important predators on copepods. Many small plankters such as copepods, euphausiids, chaetognaths, hundreds of species of jellyfish, siphonophores, and salps are important predators of the larvae of even large carnivores such as tuna. Indeed, pollock in the Bering Sea are their own most important predators. For these and other reasons, traditional food web analysis has proven meaningless in biological oceanography.

Indirect or cascading influences also may be important. One example of a major shift resulting from the removal of top predators is in the Southern Ocean where the krill-based ecosystem seems to have responded in many ways to the removal of the krill-eating great whales by allowing expansion of populations of seals, penguins, and perhaps smaller whales that also eat krill (see Kimball, this volume). Cascading effects are also evident in the coastal kelp forests of western North America (Fig. 20-3): sea otters consume sea urchins, which in turn control the growth of the kelp forests in some areas (Estes and Palmisano 1974). Also, the introduction of exotic species into a food web can have destructive cascading effects (Carlton and Geller 1993).

(6) Assess and manage marine mammals on a population-by-population basis. Marine mammals may exist in many geographic stocks. Some of these have been identified and described, but many more are likely to be discovered. For example, wherever data have been adequate to allow close examination of stock identity for a small cetacean, geographic stocks have been found to exist (Perrin and Brownell 1994). Genetic investigation may reveal that what were thought to be populations within a species are actually separate species (e.g., Rosel et al. 1994 for *Delphinus* spp.). To ensure the survival of stocks and the genetic diversity that they represent, they must be assessed and managed appropriately. If needed information is lacking, a precautionary strategy should be adopted, and provisional management units should be as small as possible given practical constraints (Wade and Angless 1997). This strategy has been adopted by the International Whaling Commission (IWC) as part of its revised management procedure (see Gambell, this volume).

An important and relevant issue is consideration of the statistical power of analyses that are designed to detect differences among geographic samples that should be managed separately. Negative results of comparisons among stocks can be due to a lack of true stock differences or a lack of adequate statistical power. Thus, a finding of "no difference" should not automatically be the basis for pooling population segments for management unless the analysis is sufficiently powerful to detect a statistical difference of the scale of concern (Taylor and Dizon 1996).

(7) Avoid significant genetic alteration of populations. Although we lack definite rules that relate genetic variation to persistence of populations (Lande and Barrowclough 1987, Burgmann et al. 1993), it is clear that reduction of genetic variation and/or genetic alteration of populations can reduce the ability of organisms to adapt to changing environmental conditions. The genetic impacts of commercial fisheries on fish stocks was considered by Law et al. (1993), who documented modifications of life history attributes of species and interpreted these as effects of fishing mortality. Because existing genetic variation helps make it possible for organisms to respond to natural and human-induced environmental change, there is great virtue—if not necessity—in maintaining that variation.

(8) Understand that biological processes are often nonlinear and subject to critical thresholds and synergisms; these must be identified, understood, and incorporated

A

B

Figure 20-3. A healthy kelp forest (*A*) and barren grounds (*B*) after being denuded by sea urchins. (Photographs courtesy of Eric Hanauer) into management programs. Nonlinearity and threshold effects are pervasive in biological systems. For example, a pathogen may suddenly become a plague once it reaches a rate of infection threshold; reproduction cannot occur until population densities pass a threshold high enough for individuals to find one another; and populations of a given species may only be viable above some critical threshold of patch (habitat) size, below which a refuge is ineffective. Such effects are all nonlinear—a small change in a variable may have a large effect—and can occur suddenly and unexpectedly (May and Oster 1976). If not anticipated, such nonlinearity can seriously undermine the effectiveness of management programs. Similarly, synergisms—interactive effects of different agents in which the total effect is greater than the sum of the individual effects—can have serious implications for conservation (Young 1994). For example, seals in the North Sea may have been weakened by pollution, which in turn allowed their decimation in 1988 by viral disease (Harwood and Hall 1990). The same may have happened with striped dolphins (*Stenella coeruleoalba*) in the Mediterranean in 1990 (Aguilar and Raga 1993).

Principle III. The human species, with all its activities, needs, aspirations, and diverse values, affects every marine ecosystem, and this fact must be addressed and accommodated in the management of any living marine resource. All stakeholders must be included in the process of determining optimal management strategies.

The values that marine mammals offer society are diverse. Along with the utilitarian value of direct consumption, there are indirect values such as aesthetic, scientific, and information values, the value of preserving options for future generations, and the value to the present generation of preserving a way of life. Management also should take into account the effects of decisions about marine mammal use in the market, including effects on ecological functions that have broad (but not easily measured) benefits for human society and that serve to maintain ecosystem integrity (Ehrlich and Mooney 1983). The true overall value of marine mammals includes all of these and is greater than their immediate market value. Thus, a broad range of ecosystem attributes needs to be included in any valuation process, ideally in an empirical and comprehensive manner in which trade-offs can be assessed (Knetsch 1990).

Effective marine mammal conservation requires understanding and taking account of the motives, interests, and values of all stakeholders, but not by simply averaging their positions. Aesthetic, ethical, and ecological values vary among stakeholders and can lead to conflict, particularly when policy makers fail to consider the motivations of stakeholders. Some stakeholders may be willing to accept a great range of risks to the resource, but others may not be willing to accept any risk. Furthermore, "acceptable risk" may vary over time and by location, and may depend on available alternatives. The most effective means for resolving such conflict is by ensuring full participation of relevant stakeholders in the decision-making process and conducting systematic assessments of all living resource values. It should be understood, however, that such inclusiveness and comprehensive assessments of values could initially increase the cost of negotiation and intensify conflict.

Human groups have three foci that are fundamental in understanding and developing policies for conservation (Kellert and Clark 1991). The *cultural focus* considers the basic assumptions regarding the values and motives for using wild living resources. The *sociostructural focus* emphasizes community authority, power, and property relations associated with the allocation and use of resources. The *institutional/regulatory focus* stresses the character of formal organizations charged with the responsibility for giving expression to and implementing policies. Historical failures in recognizing the importance of these foci are legion, and they have resulted in major conservation failures, deficiencies, and misallocations of biotic, financial, and other resources (Gunderson 1985). For example, conservation of marine mammals in Latin America is severely hampered by a mix of socioeconomic and political difficulties that limit scientific knowledge; this limitation feeds back into the sociological problems (Vidal 1993).

The following actions will help implement this principle.

(1) Wherever possible, create incentives by delegating property rights to the "lowest" relevant community or societal level consistent with the scale and use of the resource involved. Increased tenancy and property rights for wild living resources among local and community stakeholders can enhance incentives for their conservation (Berkes 1985, Bromley 1991), even in cases where such resources are part of the "commons" (Monbiot 1994). Giving management responsibility to local stakeholders, particularly at the community level, fosters accountability and increases personal and community motivation for conservation, particularly if a close connection exists between conservation actions and the benefits of these actions. In other words, give local people responsibility for a resource that they depend on, and they will take good care of it (Fig. 20-4). This point was made forcefully in the debate

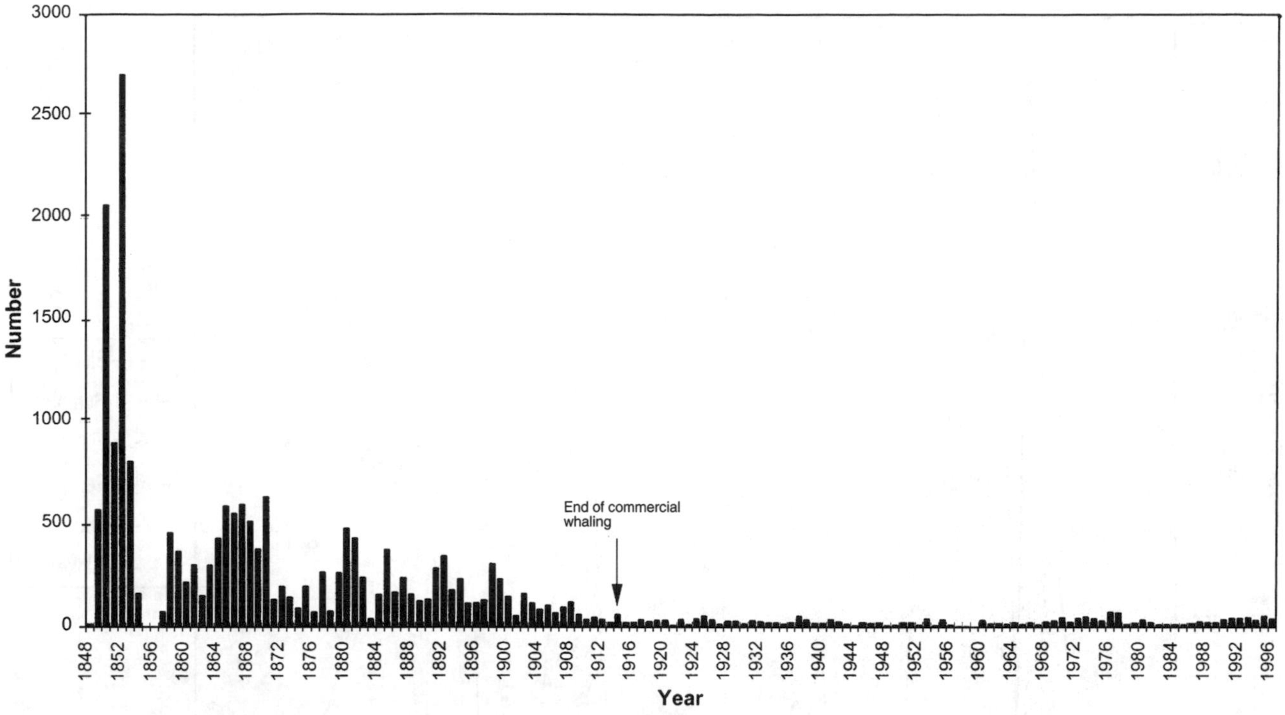

Figure 20-4. The historic rate of take of bowhead whales (*Balaena mysticetus*) in the western Arctic before and after the cessation of commercial whaling. (Courtesy of Jeff Breiwick, National Marine Fisheries Service)

surrounding bowhead whaling in Alaska and the western Canadian Arctic (Freeman et al. 1992). In many cases, there will be a direct local payoff to conservation through activities such as wildlife viewing; this strategy is being used in Uganda to conserve gorillas (Nowak 1995) and is widespread in marine systems through whale watching and similar activities.

In some cases, however, the wildlife will never have direct economic value, and the challenge is to ensure that those who can least afford it are not forced to pay for their conservation (Eltringham 1994). In these cases, it makes sense to shift responsibility to larger entities, such as national governments or the international community. For example, the cost of conservation of giant pandas (*Ailuropoda melanoleuca*) in China includes the establishment of new reserves, moving timber companies and their workers, and providing financial incentives to local residents to resettle (O'Brien et al. 1994). The Chinese government agreed to cover about 15% of the cost, with the remainder to be secured from outside sources. The continued existence of pandas should be of enough interest and value to the world community so that a worldwide campaign for support would be a reasonable part of the solution. Likewise, the conservation of marine mammals in some cases may be a responsibility whose cost should be borne by the global community, in particular by those developed countries that have benefitted economically from their existence.

Delegation of responsibility to the local community also can diminish resentment toward government officials, who are often viewed as having little stake in the preservation of traditional community values, institutions, or resources. Increasing local participation can additionally foster participation of stakeholders in the formulation of living resource conservation policy.

One difficulty in this approach is that the exploiting entities, such as corporations, may not be tied in their operations to a specific location and may deliberately "mine" a local resource and then seek out new resources in other locations (Fig. 20-5). An example is the early, successive overexploitation of whales in the North Atlantic, when privately owned fleets moved from the Barents Sea to Iceland to the Arctic as locally developed controls were instituted (Hjort 1933, Smith 1994). This type of situation requires management at an appropriate level above the local scale, in this case at the international level.

(2) Ensure that institutions and property rights are consistent with conservation, including questions of tenure and access. The "tragedy of the commons" (Hardin 1968) occurs when a relatively small number of users

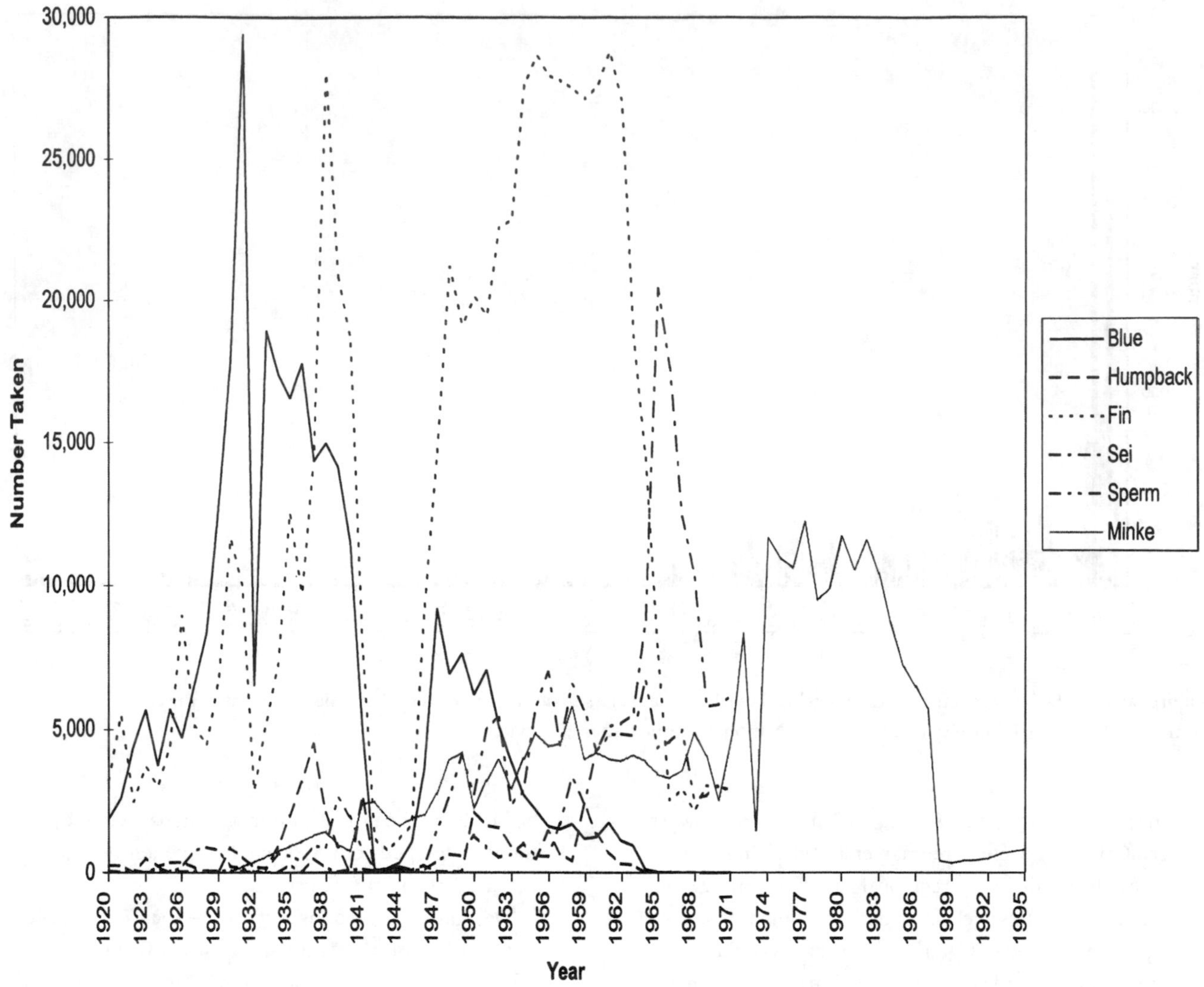

Figure 20-5. World catches of great whales in the Southern Ocean. As one species was exploited and depleted, whaling fleets moved on to the next. (Data as reported to the International Whaling Commission)

(for example, the whaling nations) compete to profit from a common resource (e.g., the whales of the Southern Ocean) while the cost (depletion of the resource because of overexploitation) is spread throughout society. Property rights and security of tenure, which are social institutions associated with the use of all wild living resources, are primary incentives for individual users with long-term interests. The lack of well-defined property rights (i.e., "open access"), which occurs in marine ecosystems, and the uncertainty of continued access are among the strongest disincentives to conservation. Property rights and institutions should be constructed that, as far as possible, achieve (a) internalization of costs that are now external to, and ignored by, markets for resources; (b) regulation of access to common property resources so that the resources will persist; and (c) security of tenure for the users of living resources, as long as they use the resources within socially and ecologically acceptable constraints.

User property rights come with associated user societal responsibilities and conservation constraints that must not be ignored. Users should pay for the right of access to public resources, such as marine mammals, to help assure responsible use and to help fund long-term conservation programs. Property rights and security of tenure will influence individuals to act in a conservative manner because it is advantageous for them to do so. Property rights are not, however, sufficient; we still require a management structure that incorporates a multitude of values and establishes a conservative system to protect the common resource.

(3) Design management strategies to minimize impacts

on people and communities whose livelihood depends directly on current use of a particular resource. In general, greater weight should be afforded to short-term socioeconomic considerations when developing management strategies for existing resource-use industries (e.g., commercial fisheries and whaling) than for new or developing industries for which there is little or no existing socioeconomic dependency. In the latter case, greater weight should be afforded to long-term biological considerations.

(4) Develop conflict resolution mechanisms to minimize strife among competing stakeholders. Three main paradigms describing resource use are the conservation paradigm (with the objective of conservation and maintenance of the resource), the rationalization paradigm (with the objective of economic performance and productivity), and the social paradigm (with the objective of community welfare and social equity) (Charles 1992). It is natural that users operating within different paradigms will come into conflicts for which different resolutions are advocated (Charles 1992). A clear understanding of the motivations and value systems of all parties from all three paradigms will help to find and develop common ground. For example, no parties want any whale species to go extinct. This does not serve the purpose of exploitation, aesthetic and moral concerns, or political goals. That is good common ground from which to begin to determine how to reach the objective of avoiding extinction and maintaining abundant populations. Defining the common ground to which all parties can agree is a critical first step in conflict resolution among competing interests.

(5) Ally science with policy making independently of the interests of marine mammal resource users. Biological and ecological data about marine mammals may sometimes be selectively interpreted to support the interests of particular stakeholders or subordinated to political interests; this is inappropriate use of science. The utility of science for policy development will be compromised if consensus is forced (Mangel et al. 1993) or if science is adjusted or compromised to match a preconceived notion. Better employment of scientific data can increase the capacity of policy makers to explore the full range of options, but this preferred policy-making process can be undermined when scientists are subordinated to political interests, made accountable to the resource managers, or paid by stakeholders to support their perspectives. By placing the scientific process in closer proximity to policy makers, independent of management and stakeholder interests, the value of scientific information can be considerably increased.

Potential conflicts in advice among "expert" sectors should be resolved insofar as possible before advice is offered to legislators, courts, or other authorities. Where expert views differ, the various assumptions, uncertainties, and risks should be clearly presented. Expert views also should be subject to broad-based, independent peer review (Meffe et al. 1998). For the reasons noted earlier, scientists should be careful to differentiate between scientific fact and value judgments regarding management practices or policies. Failure to do so can jeopardize the credibility of science and the scientist and allow decision makers to avoid being accountable for their decisions.

(6) Insofar as possible, agree on criteria and procedures to guide decision making on conservation measures at all levels to reduce the scope for influence by political or special interests. A decision that is reached by applying predetermined and well-reasoned rules is less susceptible to being overridden by special interests. Too often, authorized levels of resource use are a compromise between what is viewed by scientists as justifiable given the available data and what is demanded by the various interest groups. Limits on total takes are therefore set based on socioeconomic factors rather than scientific findings, often resulting in a decline of the resource. Methods to avoid this problem must be developed.

One possible method is to ensure that all stakeholders are aware of the uncertainties concerning the possible costs and benefits of resource use. In addition, stakeholders should have a common understanding of what constitutes evidence of unacceptable use-related effects and should agree beforehand on what will be done if evidence of such unacceptable effects becomes apparent. In fisheries, for example, it could be agreed that a 10% decline in catch per unit effort (or some other index or monitored variable) constitutes evidence of an unacceptable effect and that, if this is observed, it will automatically trigger a management response such as a 25% reduction in fishing effort. Establishment of predetermined decision rules can reduce the risk that short-term socioeconomic considerations will override long-term biological and ecological considerations; computer simulations can be used to help evaluate and select appropriate decision rules.

As with any management scheme, the status of the resource and related ecosystem components should be kept under continuing review, and the management plan should be revised if it does not work as expected.

An example of such a scheme is that used by the U.S. government for management of the incidental take of marine mammals in fisheries, which includes a threshold allowable take calculated from estimated population size, the potential for natural increase, and a precautionary safety factor, which when exceeded triggers take-reduction efforts (Wade 1998).

(7) Ensure that formal institutions responsible for policies and conservation programs have temporal and spatial perspectives consistent with the ecological character of the resource, as well as organizational structures that are (a) flexible and problem-oriented, (b) accountable, visible, and performance-oriented with clear, measurable, and explicit objectives, (c) team-oriented, participatory, and interdisciplinary, employing consensus decision making, and (d) capable of learning and corrective feedback (i.e., are adaptive). Institutions often lack spatial and temporal definitions of their mission congruent with that of stakeholders or consistent with ecological constraints of the resource (Kellert and Clark 1991). For example, the cumulative impact of many discrete actions often has ecosystem effects incompatible with a management focus on a single fiscal year or a single location. Failure can take a number of forms, including failures of integration or of specificity, failures of scale and priority, and failures of feedback. Many policy failures can be tied to incomplete specification of organizational goals, incentive and reward deficiencies, conflicting directives and organizational objectives, limited competence and training, conflicting interests and agendas, fragmented decision making and accountability, rigid and defensive communication structures, poor public involvement, and lack of high-quality information (Dowell and Wange 1986). Understanding the organizational behavior of regulatory institutions is thus a key to improving the effectiveness of conservation policy (Yaffee 1982, Clark and McCool 1985).

Resource management should be adaptive, not prescriptive (Gunderson et al. 1995). That is, management should not be based on an inflexible policy; both policy and management should change according to the best information at hand. Management then becomes a hypothesis to be tested—an experiment—rather than a prescribed course of action blindly followed. Consequently, managers must be willing and able to amend management as often and quickly as necessary, including the willingness to abandon management paradigms and to admit mistakes when evidence dictates. The management should be continually appraised according to biological, ecological, economic, and social targets. An important part of adaptive management is a strategy for learning about the systems of concern. Management policy and programs should be designed in part to help acquire useful information for adaptive change.

(8) Understand that science is only one part of marine mammal conservation and is limited to investigating and objectively describing certain kinds of phenomena and processes, and act accordingly. Science provides basic knowledge about the world and offers ways to gain additional knowledge and insight. What science can and cannot do needs to be clearly communicated to the public and decision makers. For example, science can be used to set the boundaries of activities consistent with conservation goals, including the uncertainty of these boundaries, but science cannot dictate where in the envelope society should operate. Similarly, science by itself is not capable of making judgments about aesthetics or ethics. Science can tell us about the likely outcome of a decision or action, but not which outcome we should value more highly. Scientists have their own values and belief systems, so complete objectivity is unattainable. Some value-laden decisions and interpretations (biases) may be "invisible" both to the scientists and to the public. Thus, care must be taken to avoid mixing the values of scientists with the knowledge of scientists. Trust and credibility must be maintained and enhanced (or, in some cases, reestablished). For science to be relevant, it must be germane to the contemporary issues of decision making. For science to become more policy-relevant, scientists must know how political processes work, they must know how to participate effectively in them (Clark 1993, Meffe and Viederman 1995), and they must be able to differentiate science and policy (factual knowledge and value judgments). This may necessitate a change in the way science is done (Huenneke 1995, Underwood 1995).

Principle IV. Assessment of the possible ecological, economic, and social effects of using marine mammals as resources should precede both proposed use and proposed restriction of ongoing use.

Use of natural resources was traditionally based on the beliefs that (a) "owners" of resources have the right to do whatever they want with them, (b) if a resource is not owned by someone, it can be used by anyone, and (c) use cannot be restricted unless some individual or entity with legal standing objects and can show that it, its property, or the public welfare is being affected adversely by the activity. These may have been reasonable tenets when resource use was low in comparison with resource availability and the resource users were part of the local community and routinely interacted with community members. Problems have arisen and become more serious as human populations, expectations of life style, per capita consumption rates, and technology for capturing, transporting, and marketing resources have grown and as users have become increasingly removed and alienated from local communities.

Consequently, we often have unregulated use of common property resources and management systems that require the public or the responsible agency to show that resource use is having an unacceptable effect before such use can be limited or regulated. This situation leads almost inevitably to (a) competition for access to resources, (b) faster development of resource-use industries than acquisition of knowledge concerning the resource and its ecosystem, (c) overcapitalization of resource industries, (d) overexploitation and depletion of resources, (e) damage to or waste of other components of the ecosystem, (f) loss of capital investment and related socioeconomic impacts because the long-term yield is far below the exploitation capacity that has developed, and (g) industrial management to protect capital investment and minimize short-term socioeconomic impacts, rather than to achieve resource protection and maintenance at a level providing long-term benefits. To avoid these, it is imperative that the possible effects of resource use be identified and considered in the planning or exploratory phase of resource development.

The intention of this principle is to make clear that the responsibility for demonstrating that use of a living resource will not be damaging rests with those who want to use it. The principle arises from the recognition that behaving in a risk-averse manner will avoid undesirable or unacceptable losses, achieve equity among user groups and between generations, and avoid overcapitalization and drastic increases in harvest rates. The following actions are necessary to implement this principle.

(1) Analyze how the resources and other ecosystem components might be affected by proposed use if the assumptions are not valid. Assessments of the possible effects of resource use should clearly identify (a) the data and assumptions on which they are based, (b) uncertainties concerning the reliability of the data or validity of the assumptions, (c) possible consequences of the planned actions if the assumptions or assessments are not valid, (d) possible measures that could be taken to reduce the risk of long-term or irreversible effects, and (e) plans for monitoring to ensure that the conclusions are valid (see next section). If parties cannot agree on what "assessment" means, then use should be delayed or curtailed to protect the resource and to minimize the tendency to use delaying tactics. In general, management plans should contain analyses of probable consequences, if the basis of the plan is in error, and they should provide contingencies that can be implemented in case of failure.

(2) Identify ecosystem variables that index effects, and make plans to monitor them adequately. Implementing this principle requires monitoring. In many cases it will not be possible to accurately predict the effects of various types and levels of marine mammal use on the targeted species or other ecosystem components. Thus, key variables should be identified and monitored in a consistent way to verify that use does not have unacceptable effects. It is generally very costly, if not impossible, to assess and monitor every system variable that could be affected by resource use. Consequently, a key task is to identify a representative subset of population and ecosystem variables and processes that are most likely to change in detectable ways in response to a given resource use and to design and carry out a program that will enable adverse effects to be detected before they reach harmful levels. Like management programs, monitoring programs should be periodically reviewed and modified as necessary to better meet the desired goals.

The plan for acquiring information during resource use should identify the data and assumptions on which the plan is based, the possible consequences of uncertainties concerning the validity of the assessment and the additional baseline studies, deliberate perturbation experiments, or monitoring programs proposed to be carried out to resolve the uncertainties. The plan should take into account the response times of the target, dependent, and associated species. Those doing the monitoring and analyzing the results should be independent of the potentially affected industries to ensure objectivity.

(3) Take a precautionary approach. When available information is insufficient to determine take levels that can be sustained without adversely affecting either the target populations or associated ecosystem components, the authorized take levels should be commensurate with the degree of uncertainty. Further, taking authorizations should be contingent on development and approval of a plan to acquire information that will ensure that resource use does not increase faster than knowledge of the size and productivity of the resource and its relationships with other ecosystem components.

It is generally appropriate to assume that uses of marine mammals will have unacceptable effects on both the target species and on other components of the ecosystem unless proven otherwise. The initial working hypothesis should be "take of marine mammals will have serious effects on their populations or their ecosystem," rather than the traditional "take of marine mammals will have no effect."

(4) Explicitly change the burden of proof from those responsible for conserving public resources to those who desire to exploit them, an approach in common with all other situations in which public resources are potentially threatened. An example of this is provided by the Commission and the Scientific Committee for the Conservation of Antarctic Marine Living Resources. In 1991 the Commission adopted a conservation measure requiring that members intending to develop new fisheries in the Convention Area notify the Commission at least three months in advance of its next meeting and provide information on the proposed fishery, including an assessment of its possible impacts on target, dependent, and associated species. In 1993 the Commission extended the provisions of this measure to include developing fisheries for which there is insufficient information to estimate potential yield and potential impacts on other species. The measure requires that a data collection plan be formulated and updated annually by the Scientific Committee. It also requires that each member active in the fishery or intending to authorize a vessel to enter the fishery prepare and submit an annual research and fishery operations plan by a specified date for review by the Scientific Committee and Commission. In addition, the measure requires that each vessel participating in an exploratory fishery carry a scientific observer to ensure that data are collected in accordance with data collection plans.

(5) Require those most likely to benefit directly from use of marine mammals to pay the costs of acquiring information to reduce uncertainty and investigate assumptions. An appropriate share of the cost of the programs for research, assessment, monitoring, and management should be borne by the primary beneficiaries of these programs. In some cases, this may be the general public; in others it may be particular individuals, corporations, or communities.

Incentives to support necessary research to reduce uncertainty can be offered to resource users and developers. For example, in the United States the allowable incidental take from a marine mammal population is determined in part by the lower end of the statistical confidence interval of an abundance estimate derived from surveys (Wade 1998). Thus, support of additional surveys by the user can result in a more precise abundance estimate (with a smaller confidence interval) and possibly a larger quota for incidental take. The same basic mechanism is included by the International Whaling Commission in its revised management procedure for regulating the kill of the large whales (see Gambell, this volume).

(6) Recognize the possible consequences of uncertainty and act accordingly; do not use uncertainty as an excuse for inaction. There are many different sources of uncertainty in ecological and economic systems. They include uncertainty (a) resulting from lack of information concerning the natural history, demography, and dynamics of the resource, (b) regarding possible second-order effects due to lack of information on numerical and functional relationships among related species and populations, (c) due to unpredictable, stochastic variation in both population and ecosystem parameters, (d) caused by basing decisions on best estimates when the variance is large (statistical uncertainty), and (e) caused by management that attempts to strike a balance between competing interests.

Because of the pervasive uncertainty about ecological and economic dynamics of marine systems, and the limits on our ability to control such systems, management decisions should include wide safety margins to minimize the risks of irreversible change or long-term adverse effects. Uncertainty should be addressed directly in the strategy for conserving living resources. Uncertainty should not be a cause for inaction, and biological uncertainty should not be allowed as an excuse to permit other factors to dominate decision making. More particularly, it should not be possible for private users of marine mammals to conduct what are, in effect, experiments on the behavior of ecosystems on which all society depends unless an informed society accepts and adequately ensures against the consequences.

If more were known about a particular ecosystem, the ability to make accurate predictions about responses of that system to perturbations would improve. However, the inherent complexity of ecosystems will preclude our ever gaining complete predictive knowledge of any system. Therefore, it must be recognized that uncertainty is a fundamental part of working with ecosystems. Before policy makers and the public at large can understand and accept uncertainty, scientists themselves must do so. Scientists must replace ostensible certitude about ecology with honest assessments of uncertainty. They must avoid presenting "facts" that lack a strong empirical basis, are subject to multiple interpretations, or have been contradicted outright. A number of technical methods for addressing uncertainty are available (Peterman 1990, Peterman and M'Gonigle 1992, Howson and Urbach 1993). These are the natural complements to classical statistics and need to be used more frequently.

(7) Invoke the full range of relevant disciplines at the earliest stage possible, and require comprehensive consultations. Virtually all marine mammal conservation issues have economic, biological, and social implications. Ignoring any of these in the planning stage may lead to later conflicts that will impair effective conservation.

The full breadth of relevant knowledge and skills should be involved in preparing legislation and in formulating and implementing policy, not only in prior assessment of the issues, but also in making decisions, resolving conflicts, and monitoring and evaluating execution. This often will involve breaking down longstanding and rigid institutional, professional, and personal barriers. A good example is the course taken by the International Whaling Commission in its ongoing assessment of whale stocks and whaling. In this it has employed behaviorists, veterinarians, statisticians, nutritionists, anthropologists, and specialists from numerous other disciplines to model and predict the ecological, economic, and social impacts of proposed whaling and its regulation (see Gambell, this volume).

It is possible to learn from traditional indigenous cultures if they have used resources in relatively nondestructive ways. There are examples of traditional uses that have not degraded the local ecosystem (Posey 1993). Thus, relevant indigenous expertise should be sought, evaluated, and, where appropriate, incorporated into conservation planning (see Fig. 20-4).

Principle V. Conservation requires communication and education that are interactive, reciprocal, and continuous.

Effective communication can greatly enhance the prospects of conservation by allowing stakeholders to understand the problems and the potential results of alternative courses of action. However, communications among scientists, the public, and decision makers are sometimes problematic or nonexistent. Interactive, open, and ongoing communication better serves all interests by bringing expectations into alignment. There is virtually unlimited opportunity for misunderstanding and failure of communication, so substantial effort is required to ensure its effectiveness. The following courses of action will help promote this principle.

(1) Ensure that communication is targeted to the proper audience and is based on mutual respect and sound information. Mutual respect requires clear, objective, and honest presentations with breadth and depth tailored to the target audience. Where differences of language and culture exist, it is important that all involved make an effort to overcome them. The same is true of those specialized in different disciplines. Practitioners have professional cultures, and without an appreciation of such cultural differences, communications will be more difficult and less productive.

A higher information content at the outset of communication, with clearly stated goals and objectives, will reduce misinterpretations. Scientific assessments should specify in ecological and socioeconomic terms the causes and effects of the conservation problem and the costs, benefits, and risks of possible alternative solutions. Where uncertainties exist, these should be clearly communicated, together with potential consequences, so as not to undermine the credibility and usefulness of science and scientists in the policy process (Bolin 1994). An iterative, two-way process is essential to identify misperceptions and the need for clarification. For example, the scientific process involves ongoing testing and self-correction, whereas decision makers must act decisively, and with assurance, within relatively short time frames. Similarly, the "burden of proof" for a scientist may differ considerably from that required by a court of law.

(2) Require internal and external review to verify objectivity and results. The credibility of communications will erode unless they are independently verified; therefore, each practitioner must be responsible for ensuring the validity of information communicated. Just as a scientist should submit to peer review, a journalist should check with different sources. Policy makers and managers should be responsible for ensuring that assessments are based on sound information and have been submitted to peer review (Meffe et al. 1998). The review process should extend to those well versed in socioeconomic and biophysical disciplines and familiar with the particular operational circumstances. Regular review deepens understanding of issues and uncertainties and of different professional cultures. It also highlights changes in scientific and technical understanding and illuminates the results of policies and decisions taken.

(3) Educate the public to inform their choices regarding conservation. Motivation of the various stakeholders ultimately determines the success of conservation efforts. Information should be provided to the public

to enhance their capacity to render informed and intelligent decisions consistent with conservation. Too often, at the stage when input is solicited by policy makers, it is too late to take the views of the public into account. Similarly, often little attention is given to educating the public about what to expect from management and from the resources themselves.

Educational programs at all levels should emphasize transdisciplinary problem definition and problem solving. Forums that encourage interaction and feedback are more likely to reveal unstated assumptions and values, clarify objectives, and highlight areas of uncertainty. Because backgrounds differ and people learn differently, the same information may need to be presented to various target audiences in different ways. Development of professional skills includes training in the appropriate use of specialized communications techniques and technologies. Models, when perceived as quantitative descriptions of current understanding, can be an especially effective form of communication. They can help create a common language and explore the consequences of the best understood information to communicate the likely outcomes of alternative actions and search for trade-offs. For example, models have been used to assess, in the absence of critical data, mobbing in Hawaiian monk seals (Starfield et al. 1995) and choice of management strategies in response to this behavior (Ralls and Starfield 1995).

(4) Develop institutions and procedures to facilitate transdisciplinary analysis and communication that inform decision makers. More attention must be paid to the skills necessary to facilitate transdisciplinary communication, which necessitates a basic understanding of how questions are approached in different disciplines. Managers and research institutions should define terms of reference and procedures for transdisciplinary studies that foster interaction and balanced products. The academic community should promote transdisciplinary problem solving among students and develop criteria for tenure and promotion that reward transdisciplinary work. Team-oriented approaches, which involve different specialists as well as those responsible for using and managing the resources, may be especially effective for specific problems in defined contexts.

Conclusions

The problems of conserving marine mammals are complex, difficult, and convoluted. Solutions will come not just from knowledge of the biological and ecological aspects, but from a broad understanding of a large range of human endeavors. Conservation, whether of marine mammals or any species or ecosystem, can best be achieved through an integration of expertise in such fields as economics, policy development, communication, political science, adaptive management, conflict resolution, law, human behavior, clarification of property rights issues, sociology, statistical uncertainty, philosophy, and ethics. These areas must then be melded with good biological and ecological knowledge, including honest assessment of what we do not know about ecosystems and species, the great uncertainties that underlie all of our endeavors. Above all, the challenges must be addressed while dealing with that overarching and most critical issue, the continued growth of the human population and our increase in use of the earth's resources.

There are no easy solutions to most marine mammal conservation problems, and expertise from many areas will be needed. Minds that can synthesize information from various disciplines, meld knowledge and ideas, and break down traditional disciplinary barriers will be needed to develop better ways of viewing problems and identifying solutions.

In closing, we observe that, because of the great uncertainties about biological, economic, and sociological aspects of marine mammal resources, three fundamental ideas may be good guidelines for human actions, including marine mammal conservation (from Meffe et al. 1997):

(1) Humility: Recognize and accept the limitations of human knowledge and the resulting limits to our capacity to manage the planet wisely and with confidence.
(2) Precaution: When in doubt (and that is certainly most of the time), think deeply, move with caution, and err on the side of conservation.
(3) Reversibility: Endeavor to not make changes that are irreversible.

These simple guidelines summarize, we think, a reasonable value system that can direct the actions needed for effective conservation of any resources. If the human species can learn humility, act cautiously, and not take actions that are irreversible, then our future, as well as that of marine mammals and the rest of the natural world, would seem to be much brighter. It remains to be seen whether *Homo sapiens* will adopt such a vision and live up to its moniker of "wise man."

Literature Cited

Aguilar, A., and J. A. Raga. 1993. The striped dolphin epizootic in the Mediterranean Sea. Ambio 22:524–528.

Berkes, F. 1985. Fishermen and the tragedy of the commons. Environmental Conservation 12:199–206.

Bolin, B. 1994. Science and policy making. Ambio 23:25–29.

Bromley, D. W. 1991. Environment and Economy: Property Rights and Public Policy. Blackwell, Cambridge, U.K.

Burgmann, M. A., S. Ferson, and H. R. Akakaya. 1993. Risk Assessment in Conservation Biology. Chapman and Hall, London.

Carlton, J. T., and J. B. Geller. 1993. Ecological roulette: The global transport of nonindigenous marine organisms. Science 261:78–82.

Charles, A. T. 1992. Fishery conflicts: A unified framework. Marine Policy 16 (5): 379–393.

Clark, J. N., and D. McCool. 1985. Staking out the Terrain. State University of New York Press, Albany, NY.

Clark, T. W. 1993. Creating and using knowledge for species and ecosystem conservation: Science, organizations, and policy. Perspectives in Biology and Medicine 36:497–525 + appendices.

Congdon, J. D., A. E. Dunham, and R. C. van Loben Sels. 1993. Delayed sexual maturity and demographics of Blanding's turtles (*Emydoidea blandingi*): Implications for conservation and management of long-lived organisms. Conservation Biology 7:826–833.

Daily, G. C. (ed.). 1997. Nature's Services: Societal Dependence on Natural Ecosystems. Island Press, Washington, DC.

Daly, H. 1991. Steady-State Economics, 2d ed. Island Press, Washington, DC.

Dayton, P. K. 1994. Community landscape: Scale and stability in hard bottom marine communities. Pages 289–332 *in* A. G. Hildrew, P. S. Giller, and D. Raffaelli (eds.), Aquatic Ecology: Scale, Pattern and Process. Blackwell Scientific, Oxford, U.K.

Dayton, P. K., S. F. Thrush, M. T. Agardy, and R. J. Hofman. 1995. Viewpoint: Environmental effects of marine fishing. Aquatic Conservation: Marine and Freshwater Ecosystems 5:205–232.

Dowell, R. V., and L. K. Wange. 1986. Process analysis and failure avoidance in fruit fly programs. Pages 43–65 *in* M. Mangel, J. R. Carey, and R. E. Plant (eds.), Pest Control: Operations and Systems Analysis in Fruit Fly Management. Springer-Verlag, New York, NY.

Ehrlich, P. R., and H. A. Mooney. 1983. Extinction, substitution, and ecosystem services. BioScience 33:248–254.

Eltringham, S. K. 1994. Can wildlife pay its way? Oryx 28:163–168.

Estes, J. A., and J. F. Palmisano. 1974. Sea otters: Their role in structuring nearshore communities. Science 185:1058–1060.

Frazier, N. B. 1992. Sea turtle conservation and halfway technology. Conservation Biology 6:179–184.

Freeman, M. M. R., E. E. Wein, and D. E. Keith. 1992. Recovering rights: Bowhead whales and Inuvialuit subsistence in the western Canadian Arctic. Studies on Whaling No. 2. Canadian Circumpolar Institute and Fisheries Joint Management Committee, Edmonton, Alberta, Canada. 155 pp.

Gambell, R. 1999. The International Whaling Commission and the contemporary whaling debate. (This volume)

Geraci, J. R., J. Harwood, and V. J. Lounsbury. 1999. Marine mammal die-offs: Causes, investigations, and issues. (This volume)

Grumbine, R. E. 1994. What is ecosystem management? Conservation Biology 8:27–38.

Gunderson, D. R. 1985. The great widow rockfish hunt of 1980–82. North American Journal of Fisheries Management 4:465–468.

Gunderson, L. H., C. S. Holling, and S. S. Light (eds.). 1995. Barriers and Bridges to the Renewal of Ecosystems and Institutions. Columbia University Press, New York, NY.

Hall, S. J., D. Raffaelli, and S. F. Thrush. 1994. Patchiness and disturbance in shallow water assemblages. Pages 333–377 *in* A. G. Hildrew, P. S. Giller, and D. Raffaelli (eds.), Aquatic Ecology: Scale, Pattern and Process. Blackwell Scientific, Oxford, U.K.

Hardin, G. 1968. The tragedy of the commons. Science 162:1243–1248.

Harris, L. D. 1984. The Fragmented Forest: Island Biogeography Theory and the Preservation of Biotic Diversity. University of Chicago Press, Chicago, IL.

Harwood, J. 1989. Lessons from the seal epidemic. New Scientist 121 (1652): 38–41.

Harwood, J., and A. J. Hall. 1990. Mass mortality in marine mammals: Its implications for population dynamics and genetics. Trends in Ecology and Evolution 5:254–257.

Hjort, J. 1933. Whales and whaling. Hvalradets Skrifter 7:7–29.

Holling, C. S. 1973. Resilience and stability of ecological systems. Annual Review of Ecology and Systematics 4:1–23.

Holling, C. S., and G. K. Meffe. 1996. Command and control and the pathology of natural resource management. Conservation Biology 10:328–337.

Holt, S. J., and L. M. Talbot. 1978. New principles for the conservation of wild living resources. Wildlife Monographs No. 59.

Hong, S., J.-P. Candelone, C. C. Patterson, and C. F. Boutron. 1994. Greenland ice evidence of hemispheric lead pollution two millennia ago by Greek and Roman civilizations. Science 265:1841–1843.

Howson, C., and P. Urbach. 1993. Scientific Reasoning: The Bayesian Approach. Open Court Publishing Company, La Salle, IL.

Huenneke, L. F. 1995. Involving academic scientists in conservation research: Perspectives of a plant ecologist. Ecological Applications 5:209–214.

Hughes, R. M,. and R. F. Noss. 1992. Biological diversity and biological integrity: Current concerns for lakes and streams. Fisheries 17:11–19.

Interagency Ecosystem Management Task Force. 1995. The Ecosystem Approach: Healthy Ecosystems *and* Sustainable Economies. Vol. 1—Overview. (Available from National Technical Information Service, Springfield, VA. PB95-265583.)

Isaacs, J. D. 1976. Reproductive products in marine food webs. Bulletin Southern California Academy of Sciences 75:220–223.

IUCN/UNEP/WWF. 1991. Caring for the Earth. A Strategy for Sustainable Living. Gland, Switzerland.

Kellert, S. R., and T. W. Clark. 1991. The theory and application of a wildlife policy framework. Pages 17–36 *in* W. R. Mangun (ed.), Public Policy Issues in Wildlife Management. Greenwood Press, New York, NY.

Kimball, L. A. 1999. The Antarctic Treaty system. (This volume)

Knetsch, J. L. 1990. Environmental policy implications of disparities between willingness to pay and compensation demanded measures of values. Journal of Environmental Economics and Management 18:227–237.

Lande, R., and G. F. Barrowclough. 1987. Effective population size, genetic variation, and their use in population management. Pages 87–123 *in* M. Soulé and K. Kohm (eds.), Minimum Viable Populations. Cambridge University Press, New York, NY.

Law, R., J. M. McGlade, and T. K. Stokes (eds.). 1993. The exploitation of evolving resources: Proceedings of an international conference held at Julich, Germany, September 3–5, 1991. Lecture Notes in Biomathematics 99: 264 pp.

Ludwig, D., R. Hilborn, and C. Walters. 1993. Uncertainty, resource exploitation, and conservation: Lessons from history. Science 260:17–36.

Mangel, M., and R. J. Hofman. 1999. Ecosystems: Patterns, processes, and paradigms. (This volume)

Mangel, M., R. J. Hofman, E. A. Norse, and J. R. Twiss Jr. 1993. Sustainability and ecological research. Ecological Applications 3:573–575.

Mangel, M., L. M. Talbot, G. K. Meffe, M. T. Agardy, D. L. Alverson, J. Barlow, D. B. Botkin, G. Budowski, T. Clark, J. Cooke, R. H. Crozier, P. K. Dayton, D. L. Elder, C. W. Fowler, S. Funtowicz, J. Giske, R. J. Hofman, S. J. Holt, S. R. Kellert, L. A. Kimball, D. Ludwig, K. Magnusson, B. S. Malayang III, C. Mann, E. A. Norse, S. P. Northridge, W. F. Perrin, C. Perrings, R. M. Peterman, G. B. Rabb, H. A. Regier, J. E. Reynolds III, K. Sherman, M. P. Sissenwine, T. D. Smith, A. Starfield, R. J. Taylor, M. F. Tillman, C. Toft, J. R. Twiss Jr., J. Wilen, and T. P. Young. 1996. Principles for the conservation of wild living resources. Ecological Applications 6:338–362.

May, R. M., and G. F. Oster. 1976. Bifurcations and dynamic complexity in simple ecological models. American Naturalist 110:573–599.

Meffe, G. K. 1992. Techno-arrogance and halfway technologies: Salmon hatcheries on the Pacific coast of North America. Conservation Biology 6:350–354.

Meffe, G. K., and S. Viederman. 1995. Combining science and policy in conservation biology. Wildlife Society Bulletin 23:327–332.

Meffe, G. K., C. R. Carroll, and Contributors. 1997. Principles of Conservation Biology, 2d ed. Sinauer Associates, Sunderland, MA.

Meffe, G. K., P. D. Boersma, D. D. Murphy, B. R. Noon, H. R. Pulliam, M. E. Soulé, and D. M. Waller. 1998. Independent scientific review in natural resource management. Conservation Biology 12:268–270.

Monbiot, G. 1994. The tragedy of enclosure. Scientific American (January): 159.

Nowak, R. 1995. Uganda enlists locals in the battle to save the gorillas. Science 267:1761–1762.

O'Brien, S. J., P. Wenshi, and L. Zhi. 1994. Pandas, people, and policy. Nature 369:179–180.

Perrin, W. F., and R. L. Brownell, Jr. 1994. A brief review of stock identity in small marine cetaceans in relation to assessment of driftnet mortality in the North Pacific. Reports of the International Whaling Commission (Special Issue 15): 393–401.

Peterman, R. M. 1990. Statistical power analysis can improve fisheries research and management. Canadian Journal of Fisheries and Aquatic Sciences 47:2–15.

Peterman, R. M., and M. M'Gonigle. 1992. Statistical power analysis and the precautionary principle. Marine Pollution Bulletin 24:231–234.

Pimm, S. L. 1991. The Balance of Nature? Ecological Issues in the Conservation of Species and Communities. University of Chicago Press, Chicago, IL.

Posey, D. A. 1993. Indigenous knowledge in the conservation and use of world forests. Pages 59–77 *in* K. Ramakrishna and G. M. Woodwell (eds.), World Forests for the Future: Their Use and Conservation. Yale University Press, New Haven, CT.

Pulliam, H. R. 1988. Sources, sinks, and population regulation. American Naturalist 132:652–661.

Ralls, K., and A. M. Starfield. 1995. Choosing a management strategy: Two structured decision-making methods for evaluating the predictions of stochastic simulation models. Conservation Biology 9:175–181.

Rosel, P. E., A. E. Dizon, and J. E. Heyning. 1994. Genetic analysis of sympatric morphotypes of common dolphins (genus *Delphinus*). Marine Biology 119:159–167.

Saunders, D. A., R. J. Hobbs, and C. R. Margules. 1991. Biological consequences of ecosystem fragmentation: A review. Conservation Biology 5:18–32.

Smith, T. D. 1994. Scaling Fisheries. Cambridge University Press, New York, NY.

Starfield, A. M., D. H. M. Cumming, R. D. Taylor, and M. S. Quadling. 1993. A frame-based paradigm for dynamic ecosystem models. AI Applications 7:1–13.

Starfield, A. M., J. D. Roth, and K. Ralls. 1995. "Mobbing" in Hawaiian monk seals (*Monachus schauinslandi*): The value of simulation modeling in the absence of apparently crucial data. Conservation Biology 9:166–174.

Steadman, D. W. 1995. Prehistoric extinctions of Pacific island birds: Biodiversity meets zoo-archeology. Science 267:1123–1131.

Taylor, B. L., and A. E. Dizon. 1996. The need to estimate power to link genetics and demography for conservation. Conservation Biology 10:661–664.

Tilman, D., R. M. May, C. L. Lehman, and M. A. Nowak. 1994. Habitat destruction and the extinction debt. Nature 371:65–66.

Trivelpiece, W. Z., D. G. Ainley, W. R. Fraser, and S. G. Trivelpiece. 1990. Skua survival. Nature 345:211.

Underwood, A. J. 1995. Ecological research and (research into) environmental management. Ecological Applications 5:232–247.

Vidal, O. 1993. Aquatic mammal conservation in Latin America: Problems and perspectives. Conservation Biology 7:788–795.

Wade, P. R. 1998. Calculating limits to the allowable human-caused mortality of cetaceans and pinnipeds. Marine Mammal Science 14:1–37.

Wade, P. R., and R. P. Angliss. 1997. Guidelines for Assessing Marine Mammal Stocks: Reports of the GAMMS Workshop April 3–5, 1996, Seattle, WA. U.S. Department of Commerce, NOAA Technical Memorandum NMFS-OPR-12. 93 pp.

White, L., Jr. 1967. The historical roots of our ecological crisis. Science 155:1203–1207.

Wiens, J. A., and B. T. Milne. 1989. Scaling of 'landscapes' in landscape ecology, or, landscape ecology from a beetle's perspective. Landscape Ecology 3:87–96.

World Commission on Environment and Development. 1987. Our Common Future. Oxford University Press, Oxford, U.K.

Yaffee, S. L. 1982. Prohibitive Policy. MIT Press, Cambridge, MA.

Young, T. P. 1994. Natural die-offs of large mammals: Implications for conservation. Conservation Biology 8:410–418.

Young, T. P., and L. A. Isbell. 1994. Minimum group size and other conservation lessons exemplified by a declining primate population. Biological Conservation 68:129–134.

Contributors

Donald C. Baur is a partner in the Washington, D.C., law firm of Perkins, Coie, practicing natural resources and environmental law counseling and litigation. Before entering private practice, he served in the Department of the Interior Solicitor's Office and as general counsel of the U.S. Marine Mammal Commission. He is the author of several law review articles on natural resources law and is currently editing a book on the Endangered Species Act for the American Bar Association. He is an adjunct professor at the Vermont Law School, where he teaches a course on marine biological diversity, and has taught a course in wildlife law at the Golden Gate Law School. He is a 1976 graduate of Trinity College and received his J.D. from the University of Pennsylvania School of Law in 1979.

Michael J. Bean has headed the Environmental Defense Fund's wildlife program since 1977. He is a member of the Science Advisory Board of The Nature Conservancy and director of the Pew Fellows Program in Marine Conservation. He has served on the Board on Environmental Studies and Toxicology of the National Research Council, National Academy of Sciences, and on the board of directors of the Environmental Law Institute. His book, *The Evolution of National Wildlife Law,* is generally regarded as the leading text on the subject of wildlife conservation law. He is a 1973 graduate of Yale Law School.

James M. Coe is deputy director of the Alaska Fisheries Science Center of the U.S. National Marine Fisheries Service in Seattle, Washington, and previously served as director of the Service's Marine Entanglement Research Program. Before that, he was research coordinator for the U.S. high seas driftnet fishery program and manager of dolphin mortality reduction research for the U.S. tuna purse seine fishery. His doctoral research is focused on emerging international policies for the management of fisheries bycatch and their practical implementation. He received a B.A. in zoology from the University of California, Santa Barbara, and a master's degree from the University of Washington, School of Marine Affairs.

Paul K. Dayton is a professor in benthic ecology at the Scripps Institution of Oceanography, La Jolla, California. With his students, he has studied marine bottom communities all over the Pacific from Alaska south to Argentina and Antarctica, as well as New Zealand and Australia. He is a recipient of the Mercer Award from the Ecological Society of America, a fellow of the American Association for the Advancement of Science, and a Pew Scholar in Conservation and the Environment. He received his B.S. degree in 1963 from the University of Arizona, Tucson, and his doctorate in 1970 from the University of Washington, Seattle.

Daryl P. Domning is professor of anatomy at Howard University, Washington, D.C., and a research associate at both the National Museum of Natural History, Smithsonian Institution, and the Natural History Museum of Los Angeles County, California. His research is currently focused on the evolution of sirenians in the West Atlantic–Caribbean and Mediterranean-Paratethyan regions. He has been a member of the IUCN Sirenia Specialist Group since 1984 and is founding editor of its newsletter, *Sirenews.* He has served for six years on the Committee of Scientific Advisors of the U.S. Marine Mammal Commission and has been a member of the state of Florida's Manatee Technical Advisory Council since its inception in 1981. He received his B.S. degree from Tulane University, and M.A. and Ph.D. degrees from the University of California at Berkeley.

Mark A. Fraker is a marine mammal biologist with 25 years experience in the Arctic and Pacific Northwest. He is currently president and senior wildlife biologist at TerraMar Environmental Research Ltd., Sidney, British Columbia, Canada. He has conducted research on the ecology of Arctic whales, their use by Native people, and the effects of offshore petroleum development. Recent work includes analyses of the interaction between steelhead trout and California sea lions at the Ballard Locks (Seattle) and of seal and sea lion predation on salmon farms in British Columbia. He previously served as adjunct professor at the University of Alaska, Anchorage.

Ray Gambell is the Secretary to the International Whaling Commission, based in Cambridge, England. From 1957 to 1963 he was engaged in fisheries research at the Marine Laboratory of the Department of Agriculture and Fisheries for Scotland in Aberdeen. From 1963 to 1976 he was actively engaged in studying the biology and life histories of the great whales, with special emphasis on age determination, reproduction, and population assessments of those species of commercial importance. His particular interests have focused on revising management policies for both commercial and aboriginal subsistence whaling and the development of more humane killing techniques. He received his B.Sc. and Ph.D. degrees in zoology from Reading University. He was appointed an Officer of the Order of the British Empire (OBE) by the Queen in the 1994 New Year's Honours for services to the biology and conservation of whales.

Joseph R. Geraci is currently senior director of biological programs at the National Aquarium in Baltimore, Baltimore, Maryland, and research professor in the University of Maryland School of Medicine, Comparative Medicine Program, Department of Pathology. He has been conducting research on marine mammal health for more than 30 years and has written more than 140 scientific publications, including five books. He holds a degree in veterinary medicine from the University of Pennsylvania and a doctorate in marine sciences from McGill University.

Michael L. Gosliner has served as general counsel for the U.S. Marine Mammal Commission since 1987. Before that, he was an attorney with the National Oceanic and Atmospheric Administration, specializing in marine mammal and endangered species issues. He received a B.A. in biology from the University of California at Berkeley and a J.D. from Hastings College of the Law, San Francisco. He has published various paper on issues related to wildlife law. His outside interests include natural history and photography. His fieldwork has resulted in the discovery of several species new to science, including two opisthobranch mollusks, which have been named for him.

John Harwood was director of Britain's Sea Mammal Research Unit from 1978 to 1996 and has been professor of biological sciences at the University of St. Andrews, Scotland, since 1996. He is a former fellow of St. Edmund's College, University of Cambridge, and has represented the United Kingdom in the activities of the International Council for the Exploration of the Sea and the International Whaling Commission for many years. He has coordinated a number of major international projects for the European Commission, including studies of the highly endangered Mediterranean monk seal and the bycatch of porpoises and dolphins in European fisheries. His research has primarily been concerned with the interaction between humans and larger vertebrates. He received his B.S. from the University of London and his Ph.D. from the University of Western Ontario, Canada.

Robert J. Hofman is scientific program director of the U.S. Marine Mammal Commission in Washington, D.C. He has organized and participated in workshops to determine possible means for resolving marine mammal–fisheries conflicts in the United States and elsewhere. He was the principal scientific advisor on the U.S. delegations involved in the negotiation of the Convention on the Conservation of Antarctic Marine Living Resources. He was the first U.S. representative on the Scientific Committee established by the Convention and in 1995 headed the U.S. delegation to the meeting of the Commission. He is the Marine Mammal Commission's representative on the interagency working group that recommends U.S. policy regarding fisheries and other matters in the Antarctic. He received B.S. and M.S. degrees from Indiana University of Pennsylvania and his Ph.D. from the University of Minnesota.

Steven K. Katona is president of the College of the Atlantic, Bar Harbor, Maine. He was a founding faculty member of the college and taught courses in marine biology, marine mammals, invertebrate zoology, animal behavior, and evolution before his appointment as president in 1993. Along with his students, he founded the college's marine mammal research group, Allied Whale, which pioneered development of the techniques for identifying individual humpback and fin whales photographically. He currently serves on the U.S. Marine Mammal Commission's Committee of Scientific Advisors, the Scientific Advisory Committee of the Society for Marine Mammalogy, the International Advisory Board of the Bermuda Underwater Exploration Institute, and the Advisory Commission of Acadia National Park. He received his B.A. in 1965 and Ph.D. in 1971 in biology from Harvard University.

Stephen R. Kellert is a professor at the Yale University School of Forestry and Environmental Studies. He has published nearly 100 scientific articles and five books. His recent books include *Kinship to Mastery: Biophilia in Human Development* (1997), *The Value of Life: Biological Diversity and Human Society* (1996), and *Ecology, Economics, Ethics: The Broken Circle* (1991). He has served on numerous professional boards and committees of the National Academy of Sciences and National Research Council.

Lee A. Kimball is an independent consultant on international treaty and institutional development based in Washington, D.C. Formerly she served as founding director of both the Council on Ocean Law and the Antarctica program of the International Institute for Environment and Development–North America, and as senior associate for institutions at the World Resources Institute. For 15 years she represented nongovernmental organizations in intergovernmental negotiations and on U.S. delegations, in particular regarding the Antarctic Treaty and the Law of the Sea Convention. Her 1996 study of international scientific and technical advisory mechanisms for environmental conventions was published by the American Society of International Law. She received a B.A. from Stanford University and her M.A. in international affairs from The Johns Hopkins School of Advanced International Studies.

Scott D. Kraus is director of research at the New England Aquarium in Boston, Massachusetts. He has been a visiting professor at the College of the Atlantic in Maine and has taught several years for the Massachusetts Bay Marine Studies Consortium. With Steven Katona, he published the original humpback whale catalog, and his early research focused on expanding the application of individual photo-identification studies into population biology. He has conducted a continuous research program on North Atlantic right whales since 1980, publishing numerous papers on many aspects of right whale biology and conservation. Kraus has recently started studies on reducing bycatch of small cetaceans in fishing gear using acoustic "pingers." His research is increasingly focused on conservation issues faced by endangered species and habitats, and the difficulties of identifying what it is that animals need to survive in an increasingly urban ocean. He received his B.A. from the College of the Atlantic, his M.S. in biology from the University of Massachusetts, and is currently completing a Ph.D. at the University of New Hampshire.

David W. Laist is the senior policy and program analyst on the staff of the U.S. Marine Mammal Commission. As a member of the Commission's staff since 1979, his principal responsibilities have involved evaluating research and management programs for marine mammal populations, particularly those listed as endangered or threatened, for protecting marine habitats of special importance to marine mammals, and for mitigating impacts of marine debris pollution. Formerly, as a staff member for the Center for Natural Areas and a private consultant in Washington, D.C., he worked on a variety of coastal management projects, including the design of a management system to expand the National Marine Sanctuaries Program. He received a B.A. from Hartwick College, Oneonta, New York, and a M.S. in marine ecology from Old Dominion University.

David M. Lavigne is executive director of the International Marine Mammal Association Inc., a not-for-profit organization concerned with the global conservation of marine mammals. From 1973 to 1996, he was a professor in the Department of Zoology, University of Guelph, Ontario, Canada, where he retains an adjunct professor position. He received his B.Sc. in zoology from the University of Western Ontario in 1968 and his M.Sc. in 1972 and Ph.D. in 1974 for work on vision in seals from the University of Guelph. Since 1975 the principal focus of his research has been the subject of pinniped bioenergetics. For this work, he earned a Dr Philos from the University of Oslo in 1988. The author of numerous publications on various aspects of marine mammal biology, he is also coauthor of *Harps & Hoods: Ice-Breeding Seals of the Northwest Atlantic* and coeditor of *Marine Mammals and Fisheries.*

Valerie J. Lounsbury is science resource manager at the National Aquarium in Baltimore, Baltimore, Maryland. She was previously affiliated with the Marine Mammal Laboratory of the Ontario Veterinary College, Department of Pathology, as a researcher, writer, and technical illustrator. She is coauthor and illustrator of *Marine Mammals Ashore: A Field Guide for Strandings.* She has a B.A. in biology from New College of the University of South Florida.

Marc Mangel is professor in the Department of Environmental Studies and Institute of Marine Sciences at the University of California Santa Cruz, part-time professor of population biology at the T. H. Huxley School of Environment, Earth Science and Engineering at the Imperial College of Science, Technology and Medicine, and coeditor of the journal *Behavioral Ecology.* Formerly he was professor of biological sciences at the University of California Davis and founding director of the Center for Population Biology there. He served for six years on the Committee of Scientific Advisors of the U.S. Marine Mammal Commission and has written *Decision and Control in Uncertain Resource Systems, Dynamic Modeling in Behavioral Ecology* (with Colin Clark), and *The Ecological Detective: Confronting Models with Data* (with Ray Hilborn). His research program is guided by interest in the ecological implications of life history variation. He received B.S. and M.S. degrees from the University of Illinois and his Ph.D. from the University of British Columbia.

Bruce R. Mate holds an endowed chair as a professor of fisheries and wildlife and oceanography at Oregon State University's Hatfield Marine Science Center, Newport, Oregon. He has twice served four-year terms on the Committee of Scientific Advisors of the U.S. Marine Mammal Commission, been an invited expert to the scientific meetings of the International Whaling Commission, and spent four years on the Scientific Committee of the Outer Continental Shelf Energy Program for the U.S. Department of the Interior. He received his Ph.D. in biology in 1973 from the University of Oregon, determining the migration habits of sea lions along the West Coast. He has been a pioneer in the development of satellite-monitored radio tags and has applied this tracking technology to manatees, several species of small cetaceans, and six species of endangered large whales to determine the migration routes between seasonally important reproduction and feeding areas.

James G. Mead is curator of mammals at the National Museum of Natural History, Smithsonian Institution. He joined the Smithsonian staff in 1972 after doctoral research at a Newfoundland, Canada, whaling station studying the functional anatomy and life history of cetaceans. To continue this work at the Smithsonian, he began to collect specimen material from stranded animals. These salvage efforts eventually led to the creation of a nationwide stranding network in the United States. His current research is focused on life history research, primarily with local species of bottlenose dolphins and beaked whales. He received his B.S. in biology and geology from Yale University in 1965, his M.A. in geology from the University of Texas, Austin, in 1968, and his Ph.D. in evolutionary biology from the University of Chicago in 1972.

Gary K. Meffe is an adjunct professor and conservation biologist in the Department of Wildlife Ecology and Conservation at the University of Florida. He previously served 12 years on the faculty of the University of Georgia's Savannah River Ecology Laboratory. His research interests include conservation biology, evolutionary and community ecology, and stream fish ecology. His many publications include lead authorship of a college textbook, *Principles of Conservation Biology* (1994, 1997), coauthor of *Biodiversity on Military Lands: A Handbook* (1996), and coeditor of *Ecology and Evolution of Livebearing Fishes* (1989). He currently serves as editor of the journal *Conservation Biology.* He earned his B.S. and M.S. degrees in zoology at Rutgers University and his doctorate at Arizona State University.

Simon P. Northridge is a research fellow at the Sea Mammal Research Unit, University of St. Andrews, Fife, Scotland, investigating interactions between fisheries and small cetaceans, primarily the bycatch of porpoises in gillnets. He is actively involved with collaborative studies with the U.K. fishing industry to determine means of reducing incidental take of cetaceans. His broader research interests include the impact of fisheries on the marine environment and the distributional ecology of marine mammals. He received his B.S. in zoology from Oxford University, his M.S. in biological computing from York University, and his doctorate on interactions between fisheries and marine mammals from Imperial College, University of London.

Kathryn J. O'Hara recently retired as director of the pollution program at the Center for Marine Conservation. For the past 11 years, most of her work was related to the issues of marine debris. She was responsible for directing marine debris education, research, and advocacy efforts, including coordinating national and international coastal cleanups. She served on numerous expert groups to address problems of ship-generated wastes, including serving as education chair of the U.S. Navy Ad Hoc Advisory Committee on Plastics, the National Research Council's Committee on Shipborne Wastes, and the Wider Caribbean Marine Debris Steering Committee coordinated by the Intergovernmental Oceanographic Commission of the United Nations. She is the author of *A Citizen's Guide to Plastics in the Ocean: More than a Litter Problem.* She received her B.A in zoology with a concentration in marine science from Duke University and her M.S. in marine science from the College of Charleston, South Carolina.

William F. Perrin is a senior scientist at the Southwest Fisheries Science Center of the U.S. National Marine Fisheries Service in La Jolla, California, adjunct professor at the Scripps Institution of Oceanography, research associate at the Smithsonian Institution and the Los Angeles County Museum, and editor of the journal *Marine Mammal Science.* He also serves on the Scientific Council of the Convention on Migratory Species of Wild Animals (the Bonn Convention), the International Whaling Commission Scientific Committee, and as an affiliated scientist at the Marine Laboratory of Silliman University in the Philippines. In the past he has been president of the Society for Marine Mammalogy, chairman of the Scientific Advisory Committee of the U.S. Marine Mammal Commission, chairman of the IWC small cetaceans sub-committee, and chairman of the IUCN Cetacean Specialist Group. He received his B.S. in biology from San Diego State University in 1966 and his Ph.D. in zoology from UCLA in 1972. His research has centered on the population biology (life history, systematics, and ecology) of cetaceans taken incidentally in the tuna purse-seine fishery in the eastern tropical Pacific and in other fisheries around the world. Recent interests include the systematics of the baleen whale group that includes the sei whale and Bryde's whales and taxonomic relationships among the porpoises. Currently he is working on problems of marine mammal and whale shark assessment and management in Southeast Asia jointly with scientists from the Philippines and Malaysia.

Timothy J. Ragen is a resource management specialist with the National Marine Fisheries Service in Juneau, Alaska. Previously he worked as a biologist and research analyst with the Marine Mammal Research Program of the Service's Honolulu Laboratory. Before joining the Program, he completed a National Research Council associateship at the National Marine Mammal Laboratory, Seattle, Washington, where he conducted modeling studies of the population dynamics of the northern fur seal. He received a B.S. degree from the University of Montana and an M.S. degree from Stanford University, and he completed his doctoral work at Scripps Institution of Oceanography, University of California, San Diego in 1990.

Randall R. Reeves became involved in marine mammal research and conservation during the mid-1970s when he did contract work on gray whales and harp seals for the U.S. Marine Mammal Commission, on Atlantic walruses for the National Fish and Wildlife Laboratory, and on right whales for the New England Aquarium. Since then, he has been involved in a wide range of field projects, encompassing river dolphins in Asia and South America; manatees in South America and West Africa; bowheads, narwhals, and white whales in the Arctic; and temperate-zone cetaceans in the North Atlantic. Currently, as chairman of the Cetacean Specialist Group of the World Conservation Union–IUCN Species Survival Commission, Reeves coordinates international efforts to conserve cetaceans, especially those living in riverine and coastal marine environments of Asia, South America, and Africa. His publications include field guides, species monographs, a children's book, and numerous articles in scientific journals and nontechnical magazines. He received his B.A. from the University of Nebraska, his M.P.A. from Princeton University, and his Ph.D. from McGill University.

John E. Reynolds III is professor of marine science and biology at Eckerd College, St. Petersburg, Florida, where he has taught marine mammalogy and comparative anatomy since 1980. His scientific research has primarily involved Florida manatees. He has served as chairman of the U.S. Marine Mammal Commission since 1991 and, before that, was a member of the Commission's Committee of Scientific Advisors. He received his B.A. in biology from Western Maryland College, and his M.S. and doctorate in biological oceanography from the University of Miami's Rosenstiel School of Marine and Atmospheric Science.

Victor B. Scheffer lives in Bellevue, Washington. After receiving a Ph.D. from the University of Washington, he joined the United States government in 1937 as a wildlife management biologist, specializing in studies of marine mammals, especially fur seals. He retired in 1969. On a National Science Foundation grant, he studied at Cambridge University in 1956–1957, where he wrote his first book, *Seals, Sea Lions, and Walruses* (1958). Eleven other books, most of them dealing with outdoor values and animal life histories, followed, including *The Year of the Whale* (1969), which helped spark the marine mammal conservation movement of the 1970s. He served as consultant to the National Oceanic and Atmospheric Administration in 1972–1973 and as the first chairman of the U.S. Marine Mammal Commission in 1973–1976. Between 1966 and 1972, he taught courses in vertebrate zoology and forest wildlife ecology at the University of Washington.

John R. Twiss Jr. has served as executive director of the U.S. Marine Mammal Commission since its establishment in 1974. Before that, he worked for the National Science Foundation in polar and oceanographic areas, including as National Science Foundation representative in charge of Antarctic field operations in the 1964–1965 field season, later as National Science Foundation representative leading research cruises of the USNS *Eltanin* in the Southern Ocean, and then in the International Decade of Ocean Exploration program. At the Marine Mammal Commission, his work necessarily covers the entire range of marine mammal issues. His outside interests focus on conservation and education. Among other things, he has served as chairman of the board of the Student Conservation Association (1986–1989 and 1997–present); on the strategic advisory council of the Yale School of Forestry and Environmental Studies; on the board of overseers and advisory council of the Leadership Decisions Institute; and on the board of Cape Eleuthera Island School. He received his B.A. from Yale in 1961.

Dean Wilkinson is the U.S. National Marine Mammal Stranding Coordinator and works for the Office of Protected Resources of the National Marine Fisheries Service. He also is executive secretary of the U.S. Working Group on Unusual Marine Mammal Mortality Events and chair of the Intentional Introductions Committee of the interagency Aquatic Nuisance Species Task Force. He is the author of the U.S. National Contingency Plan for Response to Unusual Marine Mammal Mortality Events. Mr. Wilkinson was the recipient of the U.S. Department of Commerce Bronze Medal for his work with the Government of Chile to develop a marine mammal conservation program. He received his B.A. degree from Augustana College in Rock Island, Illinois, and attended graduate school at The Johns Hopkins University, where he held a Woodrow Wilson Foundation fellowship.

Graham A. J. Worthy is an associate professor of marine mammalogy in the Department of Marine Biology and Wildlife and Fisheries Sciences at Texas A&M University, an adjunct associate professor at both the University of South Florida and the University of Central Florida, and the state director of the Texas Marine Mammal Stranding Network. He also serves on the Atlantic Scientific Research Group for the National Marine Fisheries Service. He is a charter member of the Society for Marine Mammalogy and a cofounder of the Comparative Nutrition Society. His research interests relate to the understanding of the physiological ecology of pinnipeds, cetaceans, and sirenians through the study of their energetics, growth, and nutrition. Under his direction, the Texas Marine Mammal Stranding Network has developed into one of the largest stranding networks in the country, and responds to all dolphin strandings along the Texas coast. He obtained his B.S., M.S., and Ph.D. degrees from the University of Guelph, Ontario, Canada.

Index

Page number citations followed by *t* refer to tables; those followed by *f* refer to figures